ENCYCLOPEDIA OF EXPLORATION
VOLUME II

Places, Technologies, and Cultural Trends

ENCYCLOPEDIA OF EXPLORATION
VOLUME II

Places, Technologies, and Cultural Trends

CARL WALDMAN
AND
JON CUNNINGHAM

Facts On File, Inc.

Encyclopedia of Exploration, Volume II:
Places, Technologies, and Cultural Trends

Facts On File, Inc.
132 West 31st Street
New York NY 10001

Library of Congress Cataloging-in-Publication Data

Waldman, Carl.
Encyclopedia of exploration / Carl Waldman and Alan Wexler.
p. cm.
Vol. 2 by Carl Waldman and Jon Cunningham.
Includes bibliographical references and indexes.
ISBN 0-8160-4678-6 (set)
ISBN 0-8160-4676-X (v. 1) — ISBN 0-8160-4677-8 (v. 2)
1. Discoveries in geography—Encyclopedias. 2. Explorers—Biography—
Encyclopedias. 3. Voyages and travels—Encyclopedias. I. Wexler, Alan.
II. Cunningham, Jon. III. Facts On File, Inc. IV. Title.
G80.W33 2004
910'.3—dc22   2004010625

Facts On File books are available at special discounts when purchased in bulk
quantities for businesses, associations, institutions, or sales promotions.
Please call our Special Sales Department in New York at
(212) 967-8800 or (800) 322-8755.

You can find Facts On File on the World Wide Web at
http://www.factsonfile.com

Text design by Erika K. Arroyo
Cover design by Cathy Rincon
Maps by Sholto Ainslie, Jeremy Eagle, Patricia Meschino, and Dale Williams

Printed in the United States of America

VB FOF 10 9 8 7 6 5 4 3 2 1

This book is printed on acid-free paper.

For Dylan Sikelianos . . . with his exploring mind
—Carl Waldman

For Frieda C. Hall, Eloise Cunningham,
Allan Cunningham, and Linda Cunningham . . . in appreciation
—Jon Cunningham

Note on Photos

Many of the illustrations and photographs used in this book are old, historical images. The quality of the prints is not always up to current standards, as in some cases the originals are from old or poor quality negatives or are damaged. The content of the illustrations, however, made their inclusion important despite problems in reproduction.

Contents

VOLUME II

List of Entries in Volume I

Pavie, Auguste-Jean-Marie
Pavy, Octave
Payer, Julius von
Peary, Robert Edwin
Peck, Annie Smith
Penha, Joseph de la
Pérez Hernández, Juan Josef
Péron, François
Perrin du Lac, François-Marie
Perrot, Nicolas
Petermann, August Heinrich
Pethahia of Regensburg
Pfeiffer, Ida Reyer
Philby, Harry St. John Bridger
Phillip, Arthur
Phipps, Constantine John
Piccard, Auguste
Piccard, Jacques Ernest-Jean
Pigafetta, Francesco Antonio
Pike, Zebulon Montgomery
Pilcher, Joshua
Pinto, Fernão Mendes
Pinzón, Arias Martín
Pinzón, Francisco Martín
Pinzón, Martín Alonso
Pinzón, Vicente Yáñez
Pires, Tomé
Pizarro, Francisco
Pizarro, Gonzalo
Pizarro, Hernando
Pliny the Elder
Polo, Maffeo
Polo, Marco
Polo, Niccolò
Ponce de León, Juan
Pond, Peter
Pope, John B.
Popham, George
Popov, Fyodot Alekseyev
Porte, François de la
Portolá, Gaspar de
Pottinger, Sir Henry
Powell, John Wesley
Poyarkov, Vasily Danilovich
Pribylov, Gavrilo Loginovich
Pring, Martin
Provost, Étienne
Przhevalsky, Nikolay Mikhailovich
Ptolemy
Pytheas
Quirós, Pedro Fernández de
Quoy, Jean-René-Constant
Radisson, Pierre-Esprit

Rae, John
Raleigh, Sir Walter
Rasmussen, Knud Johan Victor
Raynolds, William Franklin
Rebmann, Johann
Ribault, Jean
Ricci, Matteo
Rice, Alexander Hamilton
Richardson, James
Richardson, Sir John
Riche, Claude-Antoine-Gaspard
Richthofen, Ferdinand Paul
   Wilhelm von
Ride, Sally Kristen
Ritchie, Joseph
Rivera y Villalón, Pedro de
Robertson, James
Roberval, Jean-François de La
   Roque de
Robidoux, Antoine
Roe, Sir Thomas
Roerich, Nikolay Konstantinovich
Rogers, Robert
Roggeveen, Jakob
Rohlfs, Friedrich Gerhard
Rose, Edward
Ross, Alexander
Ross, Sir James Clark
Ross, Sir John
Rossel, Elisabeth-Paul-Edouard de
Russell, Osborne
Rut, John
Saavedra Cerón, Álvaro de
Sable, Jean Baptist Point
Sacajawea
Sadlier, George Foster
St. Denis, Louis Juchereau de
St. Vrain, Céran de Hault de
   Lassus de
Sargon
Saris, John
Sarmiento de Gamboa, Pedro
Sarychev, Gavriil Andreyevich
Schlagintweit, Adolf von
Schlagintweit, Hermann von
Schlagintweit, Robert von
Schmidt, Otto Y.
Schomburgk, Sir Robert Hermann
Schoolcraft, Henry Rowe
Schouten, Willem Cornelis
Schwatka, Frederick
Schweinfurth, Georg August
Scoresby, William, Jr.

Scoresby, William, Sr.
Scott, Robert Falcon
Scylax
Selkirk, Alexander
Semyonov, Pyotr Petrovich
Sequira, Diego López de
Serra, Junípero
Serrano, Francisco
Shackleton, Sir Ernest Henry
Sheldon, May French
Shelikov, Grigory Ivanovich
Shepard, Alan Bartlett, Jr.
Sherley, Sir Anthony
Shirase, Nobu
Silva Porto, Antonio Francisco da
Simpson, Sir George
Simpson, James Hervey
Simpson, Thomas
Sinclair, James
Singh, Kishen
Singh, Nain
Sitgreaves, Lorenzo
Smith, James
Smith, Jedediah Strong
Smith, John
Solander, Daniel Carl
Soleyman
Soto, Hernando de
Spalding, Henry Harmon
Sparrman, Anders
Speke, John Hanning
Spotswood, Alexander
Spruce, Richard
Squanto
Stadukhin, Mikhail
Stanhope, Hester Lucy
Stanley, David Sloan
Stanley, Sir Henry Morton
Stansbury, Howard
Stark, Freya Madeline
Stefansson, Vilhjalmur
Stein, Sir Marc Aurel
Steller, Georg Wilhelm
Stevens, Thomas
Strabo
Strzelecki, Sir Paul Edmund
Stuart, John McDouall
Stuart, Robert
Stuck, Hudson
Sturt, Charles
Sublette, William Lewis
Svarsson, Gardar
Sverdrup, Otto Neumann

List of Entries in Volume II

Preface

The term *exploration* comprises the concepts of traveling and seeking. *Discovery*, a term associated with exploration, refers to "finding." But the latter term has often been misused. One cannot "find" or "discover" a land that is already inhabited. But one can "discover" knowledge of that land and take it back to one's place of origin and pass on that knowledge. The history of exploration can therefore be characterized as the record of the diffusion of knowledge. The knowledge most relevant to exploration is geographic; how the world came to be mapped is thus central to chronicling exploration. In exploratory expeditions, information passes back and forth between continents and between cultures, affecting the realities both of the exploring and of the explored.

People have participated in exploration for a variety of reasons over the ages. Two basic human traits—curiosity and the desire for personal accomplishment—must be taken into account in all types of exploration. More specific motives include geographic and scientific inquiry, seeking a new homeland, conquest and/or colonization, commerce and profit, religious zeal, finding others who have gone missing, and searching for new literary or artistic themes. Those who explore come from diverse social and vocational backgrounds, among them, navigators, sailors, soldiers, officials, diplomats, colonists, missionaries, religious scholars, merchants, hunters, fur trappers, whalers, sealers, pirates, guides, interpreters, tribal leaders, cartographers, writers, painters, naturalists, geologists, historians, archaeologists, oceanographers, astronomers, aviators, astronauts, and mountain climbers. Some individuals contributed to exploration by promoting, organizing, and financing expeditions or by making technological breakthroughs, although they themselves may not have ventured far from their homelands.

Explorers lead fascinating, driven lives, and the stories of their expeditions are filled with adventure and danger. Many individuals have died in the pursuit of their dreams. Some have inflicted death, either directly or indirectly, on fellow explorers and especially on indigenous peoples. It can be said that explorers are at the head of the historical curve, the forerunners of good or bad. It also can be said that exploration is the starting point of many historical and cultural themes.

The explorers and the particular expeditions discussed in this work are only part of the story of exploration. Many more individuals have a role in the exploring and charting of the Earth and, in recent decades, outer space.

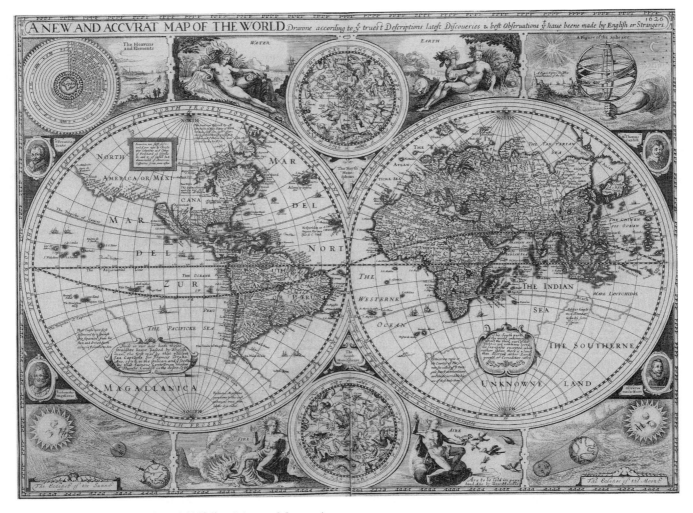

Map of the world by John Speed (1626) *(Library of Congress)*

The general topics examined and the terms defined offer some context to the field of exploration, but it is important to remember that the scope of the story of exploration includes the entire historical record, and its sphere of action encompasses the entire world and the solar system. So, in chronicling exploration, particular time periods, cultures, activities, and technologies are given great weight. But one should perceive exploration as a single window into humankind's larger journey through time.

Volume I of the *Encyclopedia of Exploration* presents biographical entries about explorers, organized alphabetically. Volume II, also organized alphabetically, presents various subjects related to exploration: types of exploration, activities relating to exploration, groupings of peoples known for exploration, historical periods, organizations, legends, places, routes, natural phenomena, cartographic terms, oceanographic equipment, navigational tools, and crafts used in transportation.

In the biographical entries of Volume I, expeditions are more likely to be described in detail than in Volume II's entries. At the beginning of each biographical entry can be found the following: alternate names and spellings of names, birth and death dates (when known), nationality (and, if different, the country for whom explorations were carried out), occupations, places of the world explored, and familial relationships to other explorers with entries. After an opening discussion of the individual's background, there follows a description of his or her career in exploration and, if applicable, voyages and routes. Each entry closes with a summary of the person's accomplishments and his or her broader relevance to the history of exploration.

Some of the entries in Volume II provide overviews of historical or geographic information; others are definitions of terms relating to exploration. Geographic terms include continents, regions, islands, capes, oceans, straits, mountain ranges, mountains, mountain passes, deserts, rivers, cities, and routes. In addition to the obvious choices for geographic entries on continents and oceans, which provide overviews, some places have been selected as entries because they generated many expeditions or are central to periods of exploratory history. It should be kept in mind that other such places without their own entries have fascinating stories of exploration attached to them; many such stories can be found in Volume I (see the cumulative index).

Cross-references, indicated by a term set in SMALL CAPITAL letters the first time it appears in an entry, are meant to guide a reader/researcher through the complex material in both volumes. The cross-references run across both volumes; the reader should remember to look for entries on people in Volume I and all other entries in Volume II. A reader should understand that for the sake of convenience, not all terms that are discussed in entries in Volume II are presented as cross-references. For example, the terms *Africa* and *Atlantic Ocean* are mentioned in passing throughout the book, yet their entries appear as "Africa, exploration of" or "Atlantic Ocean, exploration of the" and are not necessarily cross-referenced. It is unlikely that a reader will choose to look up Africa for a general discussion of its geography and exploration every time the term relates peripherally to an entry. But the reader should know that Volume II includes overview entries of every continent, as well as the Arctic region and the Atlantic, Pacific, and Indian Oceans. More-specific places that have their own entries, such as the Himalayas and the Mississippi River, are cross-referenced. Certain terms, such as *colonization,* are not cross-referenced since the heading might appear as "colonization and exploration." A glance at the appendices organized by categories or the List of Entries for Volume II will help clarify questions of organization. Each volume also lists all the entries in both volumes in the "List of Entries" in the front matter.

Appendices in Volume I include a list of explorers with entries organized by region explored (with some names listed more than once, plus a section on cartographers, geographers, and sponsors where relevant); a list of explorers with entries organized chronologically by birth date; a list of explorers with entries organized by sponsoring country, or, when no sponsoring nation can be cited, by nationality or native land; and a list of explorers with entries organized by most relevant occupation. Appendices in Volume II include a chronology based on the explorations of all the individuals in Volume I, a general bibliography, and the already mentioned list of the entries organized by categories. Each volume contains a general index of the material in that volume.

Maps are essential tools in studies of exploration. The photographs of period maps that accompany some of the entries in both volumes offer a glimpse of the evolving cartographic view of the world. Original maps in an appendix in Volume II serve to illustrate the subject matter. A bibliography, in which books are listed by geographic and other general groupings, is provided to encourage and facilitate additional study of the vast and fascinating subject matter.

Acknowledgments

The authors would like to thank Nicole Bowen, editor, and Laura Shauger, editorial assistant, for their vision, attention to detail, and patience, plus all the other talented people at Facts On File who helped with this project.

A to Z
Entries

Aconcagua

Aconcagua is a peak in the ANDES MOUNTAINS of western Argentina, near the border with Chile. At 22,834 feet above sea level, it is the highest mountain in South America and in the Western Hemisphere. Fourteen other peaks in the Andes are more than 20,000 feet above sea level and taller than Mount McKinley (see MCKINLEY, MOUNT), the highest peak in North America, at 20,320 feet.

In 1897, Italian mountaineer MATTHIAS ZURBRIGGEN first reached Aconcagua's snowcapped summit by the north face. His British companions, Edward Fitzgerald and Stuart Vines, had abandoned the climb because of altitude sickness. The Englishman EDWARD WHYMPER summitted Aconcagua soon afterward. Being the tallest peak in the Americas—taller than Ojos del Salado by 295 feet—Aconcagua has represented a special challenge in the history of MOUNTAIN CLIMBING.

aerial photography

Aerial photography involves taking photographs from aircraft or spacecraft. It is used in mapmaking; studying weather, wildlife, agriculture, urban areas, road systems, and pollution; and locating mineral resources and archaeological ruins. Yet another application is military surveillance and documenting events, such as disasters. The related term *aerial survey* refers to the study of Earth's surface using photographic or other images from aircraft. The term *photogrammetry* refers to the science of making measurements and maps from photographs.

Sometime in the early 20th century, this photographer, apparently hanging from a crane, attempted to obtain an aerial view. *(Library of Congress, Prints and Photographs Division [LC-USZ62-61731])*

Early aerial photography, starting in the mid-19th century, was conducted from a kite or a BALLOON. Along with advancements in aviation and SPACE EXPLORATION in the 20th century came those in aerial photography. Aerial photography, in conjunction with computers, is especially effective in the making of topographic maps and has allowed for the accurate mapping of most of Earth's surface. Aerial photography has also been used to map the surface of the Moon and other planets and to record geological data.

See also AVIATION AND EXPLORATION; GEOGRAPHY AND CARTOGRAPHY; MAPS AND CHARTS; PHOTOGRAPHY AND EXPLORATION; SURVEYING AND EXPLORATION.

Africa, exploration of

Africa, the second-largest continent after Asia, covers some 11,677,000 square miles, including its adjacent islands, and makes up almost one-quarter of the world's total land area. It is bounded by the Atlantic Ocean on the west and south; the Indian Ocean and RED SEA on the east; and the MEDITERRANEAN SEA on the north. It lies in both the Northern and Southern Hemispheres, with the EQUATOR running through it. The largest island is Madagascar off the southeast coast in the Indian Ocean.

The African coastline has few indentations, and the coastal plain is generally narrow except on the Mediterranean. The continent consists mostly of a rolling plateau with an average height of some 2,000 feet above sea level. Mountain ranges include the Atlas Mountains in the northwest, the Ruwenzori Mountains in the east, and the Drakensberg Mountains in the southwest. The High Veld, an arid plateau, covers much of South Africa. The Eastern Highlands, with an average height of more than 5,000 feet, are the highest portion of Africa; Mount Kilimanjaro (see KILIMANJARO, MOUNT), the continent's tallest peak, is part of them.

Major rivers include the NILE RIVER in the north, the CONGO RIVER (Zaire River) in equatorial Africa, the NIGER RIVER in the west, and the ZAMBEZI RIVER in the southwest. The largest lakes in eastern central Africa—Lakes Albert, George, Tanganyika, Rudolph, and Victoria—feed the Nile or the Congo. Lake Nyasa in the southeast has an outlet to the Zambezi. Lake Chad in northern central Africa has no outlet but, since it is fed by many streams, remains fresh.

Although mostly in the Tropics, Africa has a variety of climates. Arid regions include the SAHARA DESERT and the Kalahari Desert in the south. Open savannas flank the arid regions. In the western equatorial regions, where there is an abundance of rainfall, can be found dense jungle.

Africa's animal life can be separated into two zones: that in the north, including the Sahara Desert, and the sub-Saharan zone. The northern area has animals similar to those in Europe, such as deer, sheep, hare, and fox. It is south of the Sahara that the large African mammals are found, such as the elephant, rhinoceros, giraffe, zebra, lion, leopard, cheetah, hyena, baboon, and gorilla.

Some 3,000 ethnic groups have been identified in Africa, speaking more than 1,000 languages. The indigenous Negroid peoples were hunter-gatherers, often organized in villages or tribes. Some of these tribes developed into powerful kingdoms. The most powerful and wide-ranging African people in ancient times were the Egyptians, who farmed along the Nile Valley and delta. North of the Sahara, the aboriginal groups came to be replaced by Arabic peoples migrating from the east and Berbers, a non-Arabic people thought to be from the eastern Mediterranean region. In other parts of Africa many different peoples established powerful kingdoms, such as the kingdoms of Ghana in the fifth century, Mali in the 13th and 14th centuries, and Songhai in the 15th and 16th centuries, all in West Africa. In the 19th century, the Fulani were dominant in the western Sudan, and the Zulu in South Africa.

The exploration of North Africa's coastal areas, separated from Europe by the 36-mile-wide Strait of Gibraltar (see GIBRALTAR, STRAIT OF) in the northwest and actually linked to Asia by the Sinai Peninsula in the northeast, is part of the story of the entire Mediterranean region, with extensive contacts among ancient peoples. In the 15th century, during the EUROPEAN AGE OF EXPLORATION, other coastal areas became charted. Yet much of Africa's interior remained a mystery to other than indigenous peoples until the late 19th century, leading to Africa being known historically as the "Dark Continent."

Ancient Exploration and Migration

Africa holds a special place in the story of humankind since the earliest human life has been traced to there. Moreover, one of the first written languages was developed in North Africa in Egypt in about 6000 B.C., and the wheel was invented there 3,000 years later. HANNU, the first individual explorer known to history, from relief carvings with hieroglyphic text, was from Egypt. In about 2750 B.C., Hannu, sent by Pharaoh Sahure, journeyed 400 miles by way of the Nile River south to the land of PUNT, which extended beyond the southern end of the Red Sea. Even then, Punt was already a center of trade. Hannu arranged for a ship to be built there, then returned home to Egypt and to the king, who had sponsored his trip, bearing gold, silver, myrrh, and ebony (see EGYPTIAN EXPLORATION).

Another early journey of the ancient Egyptians dates to about 2270 B.C., when HERKHUF, a governor in the southern part of Egypt, traveled the Nile to explore central East Africa and trade for the luxury goods that Egypt could not produce itself. Seven centuries later, in about 1492 B.C., the Egyptian queen HATSHEPSUT commissioned a trading expedition to the land of Punt. The ancient Egyptians also traded with the Minoans of the island of Crete. Minoan pottery dating from about 2000 B.C. has been found in Egypt, indicating Minoan voyages along Africa's north coast (see MINOAN EXPLORATION). As for the ancient Greeks, it is known that, by the seventh century B.C., they had established an outpost in the Egyptian port city of Naucratis on the Nile's delta (see GREEK EXPLORATION). Over the next several centuries, the shifting course of the Nile and the ascendancy of the city of Alexandria led to the decline of Naucratis as both a colony and a trading post. There is some evidence to suggest the Greeks were familiar with areas farther west on the north coast of Africa as well. In the mythological *Odyssey,* for example, Homer refers to the "Lotus Eaters." Lotus grows in and is eaten on the Tripoli coast.

Other early voyages to Africa were undertaken by Phoenicians from the eastern Mediterranean, their homeland located roughly where Lebanon is today (see PHOENICIAN EXPLORATION). Known as wide-ranging mariners and traders, as well as colonizers, by the sixth century B.C., they controlled much of Africa's north shore. They also reportedly ventured much farther. In the writings of fifth-century Greek historian HERODOTUS appears an account of a journey commissioned in about 600 B.C. by Pharaoh NECHO II of Egypt. The expedition reportedly traveled down the Red Sea, around the African continent, through the Pillars of Hercules (the modern Strait of Gibraltar), and along the north coast until they arrived home. The crew went ashore to grow provisions, and the trip was said to have lasted three years. Not only does the length of the journey make sense but so do their observations on the relative position of the Sun. Furthermore, the winds and OCEAN CURRENTS would have been favorable for an east-to-west circumnavigation as described by Herodotus. Other ancient explorers reportedly had tried and failed to circumnavigate Africa in the opposite direction, from west to east. In about 485 B.C., a Persian nobleman named Sastapes attempted to atone for a crime by such a journey; his failure to do so resulted in his execution. In the latter part of the second century B.C., Greek EUDOXUS of Cyzicus disappeared during an attempt to sail around Africa from the west.

The fifth-century B.C. Carthaginian HANNO, from the city of Carthage, founded by the Phoenicians near present-day Tunis, was another ancient explorer of Africa. According to his account, as passed down in Greek translation, in about 470 B.C., he commanded 60 GALLEY ships carrying some 30,000 Carthaginians on a mission to establish cities along the West African coast. At present-day Mehdia, Morocco, Hanno founded the city of Thymiaterium. At Cape Cantin, he built a temple to Poseidon, Greek god of the sea. The Carthaginians encountered elephants farther down the coast, passed the Sahara Desert, and went on to establish another colony on what is probably the modern island of Herne. In all, Hanno founded seven cities and is thought to

have voyaged as far south as modern-day Sierra Leone (see CARTHAGINIAN EXPLORATION).

One of the earliest accounts of an expedition to Africa's interior comes from the Greek DIOGENES of the first century A.D. A merchant trading along the east shore of Africa, he claims to have been caught in a storm. Unable to control his direction for 25 days, he eventually managed to land ashore at what is now Dar es Salaam, Tanzania. Diogenes traveled from there into the interior, where he saw two great lakes (probably Lake Victoria and Lake Albert) and snow-covered mountains (probably the Ruwenzori Range), which the second-century PTOLEMY, from the North African city of Alexandria, referred to as the MOUNTAINS OF THE MOON.

The Romans had more extensive contacts with Africa than did the Greeks, in their case through conquest rather than commerce (see ROMAN EXPLORATION). At the conclusion of the three Punic Wars (which ended in 146 B.C. with the burning of Carthage), Rome assumed Carthage's dominance over its territories along much of the Mediterranean. They then consolidated their power by trading with and exacting tribute from conquered peoples. Many of the most significant forays by the Romans into Africa took place during the Augustan Age (48 B.C. to A.D. 68). In 31 B.C., Octavian defeated Marc Antony and Cleopatra and incorporated Egypt into the Roman Empire. In A.D. 29, Petronius led a military campaign to the upper Nile to quell tribal infighting and to assert control in Ethiopia. In A.D. 42, SUETONIUS PAULINUS crossed the Atlas Mountains on the northwest coast and explored the fringes of the Sahara. A Roman military expedition of A.D. 61–63 may have gone farther down the Nile than any other previous European trip did, returning with a variety of goods. At its peak in the second century A.D., the Roman Empire controlled the entire North African coast bordered by the Mediterranean, from Egypt to the land just beyond the Strait of Gibraltar, modern-day Morocco.

The first evidence of the movement of peoples in the equatorial regions of Africa dates to the first century A.D. In their drive to dominate the lower portion of the continent, the Bantu-speaking peoples pushed the Mbuti and the San cultures away from the Benue River Valley of modern-day Nigeria. This is the time period when villages developed into powerful political units, such as the kingdoms of Monomotapa and Kongo. Written records are scarce, and knowledge must be reconstructed from ethnographic studies and archaeological findings, but there is little doubt that these migrations and conquests helped shape the present-day ethnic composition and distribution on the African continent.

The Spread of Islam

The next great chapter in the exploration of Africa began with the establishment of Islam in A.D. 622 by the Prophet

Muhammad and continued into the 1300s (see MUSLIM EX-PLORATION). The breakup of the Roman Empire by the fifth century had left North Africa vulnerable to conquest. By A.D. 641, the Muslims had taken control of Egypt and begun their trek along the north coast. By the eighth century, they had invaded Morocco. Their zeal came partly from the promise of paradise after death (if death came in the service of Allah), but there is no doubt the missionaries also were spurred on by the prospect of trade. Although Arabs gained control of the lands around Ethiopia, the established Christian communities within that enclave resisted conversion and became isolated. The Arabs introduced camels (and methodical breeding methods) into the Sudan Desert, and they reinvigorated trading routes, increasing trade between Arabia, Egypt, and the Sudan. Islam also expanded into Turkey, Persia, India, and beyond while retaining its foothold in northern Africa.

Increased traffic by mariners along the African coast and the large number of caravans traversing the desert solidified the Arab hold on African trade. Africa had been a source of slaves through ancient times, and the Muslims joined in this trade. Other commodities that proved economically viable to the Arabs included gold and ivory. Salt was so highly valued that it was traded for gold. A source of gold was the western kingdom of Mali. In 1324, after the mansa (or ruler) of Mali, Mansa Musa, an Islamic convert, had made his pilgrimage to Mecca, he gave away so much of the precious metal he caused its value to decrease by 25 percent in Egypt. The Arabs and their fellow Muslims, the Moors of North Africa (who also, from 711 to 1492, held territory on the Iberian Peninsula), had a monopoly on the gold trade. Although they jealously guarded their routes, they faced increasing challenges from Europeans.

One of the great unifying forces of Islam is the obligation of the faithful to make a pilgrimage to the holy city of Mecca in what is now western Saudi Arabia at least once during their lifetime. This Islamic tenet thus broke down barriers of world travel and helped create a cosmopolitan culture. Two Arab travelers known to history, from the 10th century, are historian ABU AL-HASAN ALI AL-MASUDI, who visited Islamic cities in North Africa; and merchant and scholar ABU AL-QASIM IBN ALI AL-NASIBI IBN HAWQAL, who reportedly traveled across the Sahara Desert. ABU ABD ALLAH MUHAMMAD IBN BATTUTAH, active in the 14th century, is the most renowned of all Muslim travelers. Born in Tangier in 1304, by the time of his death in 1378, he may have been the most widely traveled person to that date, covering an estimated 75,000 miles, including all the regions where Islam was practiced. Traveling overland along Africa's north coast, Ibn Battutah made his pilgrimage to the Holy Land in 1325. After studying in Mecca for three years, he visited the port cities on the east coast of Africa. In

1352–53, he made an excursion to Mali, which was then at the height of its powers, and he wrote a detailed account of the trip, *Rihla,* published in 1357.

LEO AFRICANUS was another widely traveled Arab. In the early 16th century, as a diplomat in the service of the sultan of Morocco, he visited countries in North and central Africa. An English edition of his writings on Africa, now commonly known as *Description of Africa,* published in 1600, became the primary source for information on lands south of the Sahara in the Sudan and the city of TIMBUKTU.

Early Portuguese Expeditions

HENRY THE NAVIGATOR, prince of Portugal, was born in 1394, 17 years after King Fernando I had begun intensive efforts to enhance Portuguese trading enterprises. Among other achievements, that king had developed an innovative form of maritime insurance and had distributed free lumber for the production of any ships over 100 tons. Before he was 20, the young prince had helped capture the Moroccan city of Ceuta; by the time he was 26, Henry had been named Grand Master of the Order of Christ, a neo-Crusader group sponsored by the pope. His association with the Order of Christ aided two of Henry's goals: It gave him the opportunity to advance religious conversion (all Henry's ships bore sails with red crosses), and it provided him with funds to finance further explorations.

Henry established a school of navigation and geographic research at Sagres, and he set to work gathering information on the seas beyond his homeland (see NAVIGATION AND EXPLORATION). The school had strict policies on secrecy, and violators faced death. This interest in secrecy was born in nationalism; the Portuguese thought they needed to control their hard-won knowledge if they were to compete with other, more powerful European nations. Records of some expeditions were entirely destroyed by the Portuguese, and data on others remains known only to a small academic community to this day.

Prince Henry faced both physical barriers and psychological barriers in persuading his sailors to explore the unknown reaches of the west coast of Africa. To the medieval mind, Europe was a temperate land placed between the eternal cold of the north and the intense heat of the south, where the Sun came so close to Earth that the sea was at a continuous boil. These boiling waters of the middle were considered an impenetrable barrier to the lands of the Southern Hemisphere. In fact, the West African coast off the Sahara was dubbed the "Green Sea of Darkness" by the Arabs. The currents struck the shore in a manner very dangerous to ships, and the wind-borne sand of the desert often decreased visibility.

By the 14th century, the existence of the CANARY ISLANDS, 70 miles from Africa's northwest coast, was well known. Among the first accomplishments of Henry's mariners was the discovery in 1418 of the Madeira Islands to the northwest of the Canaries, much farther out to sea. The founding of his school and these early expeditions can be considered the start of the European age of exploration.

A major goal of the Portuguese of this period was to sail beyond Cape Bojador—the "Bulging Cape"—located on a particularly dangerous stretch of coast on what is now Western Sahara, and then known to Arabs as Abu Khatar, "the father of danger." Henry recruited an international crew of experienced seamen and sent them off. It took at least 14 attempts before the Portuguese navigator GIL EANNES finally succeeded in 1434. The fact that the "Green Sea of Darkness" could be navigated reinvigorated Prince Henry's naval academy, and Eannes was sent out again. This time he landed at a bay where he saw tracks of humans and camels. In 1435, AFONSO GONÇALVES BALDAYA traveled even farther, encountering native people, who injured one of his crew. Baldaya retreated, then continued to an area south of the TROPIC OF CANCER, to the north of Cape Blanco. In 1441, NUÑO TRISTÃO reached Cape Blanco.

In 1443, Prince Henry obtained special dispensations from the pope, including the exclusive right to sail past Cape Bojador. Determined to beat back the Muslims, bring Christianity to pagan tribes, and establish direct links with the gold trade, Henry sponsored even more ambitious maritime expeditions. Another dream of his was to locate PRESTER JOHN, a legendary Christian ruler whose name had endured for centuries as possibly sympathetic to European interests in Asia and Africa.

In 1444, Nuño Tristão reached the Senegal River Delta, the green part of Africa beyond the barren desert coastline. It was there that Muslim power ended and tribal cultures held sway. In 1444–45, DINÍS DIAS reached the westernmost point of Africa and named it Cape Verde. It was during this period that the Portuguese entered the institutionalized SLAVE TRADE. Slave ships would begin frequenting these coastal areas.

One of the first interior journeys of this period, in 1455, was made by the Venetian ALVISE DA CADAMOSTO. Prince Henry commissioned him to explore the trade routes that wound through Mauritania. In Mauritania, silver and copper were exchanged for slaves and gold from farther inland, and salt was traded for gold. When he sailed even farther south, to the mouth of the Gambia River, Cadamosto became one of the first Europeans to see the Southern Cross, a constellation not visible from the Northern Hemisphere. The next year, on a subsequent expedition, Cadamosto reached an island group directly to the west of Cape Verde, to which he gave the same name.

The last significant Portuguese journey under Prince Henry's sponsorship took place in 1458, when DIOGO GOMES traveled up the Gambia River. He met a king interested in Christianity, obtained some gold, and learned about gold mines in Sierra Leone. This trip resulted in an influx of Portuguese missionaries and brought new life to the hope of profitable commercial ventures in Africa.

By the time of Prince Henry's death in 1460, Portuguese explorers had reached as far south as Sierra Leone. The next Portuguese explorer of note was FERNÃO GOMES, who was granted exclusive trading rights along the coast of Guinea by King Alfonso in 1469. The contract was a privilege of unknown value, and it was up to Gomes to make it lucrative. But sailing south of the Gambia River below Cape Verde proved difficult. For five years, Gomes tried to explore the coastline south of Africa's eastern bulge. He encountered intense winds, tornadoes, and unpredictable fog, and his attempts to land were hampered by heavy surf and the shallow coastal waters of the continental shelf. Although Gomes succeeded in describing the south coast of Africa's bulge, his contract with the king was not renewed.

The Portuguese success in Africa led other European countries to challenge Portugal's monopoly there. The 1470s saw incursions into Africa by the English, the Flemish, and, most vexing of all to the Portuguese, the Spanish. In 1479, after losing a war with Spain, Portugal negotiated the Treaty of Alcacovas, which allowed it to retain its possessions in Africa. Portugal soon moved to assert control of its territories by building factory-fortresses, facilities where ships were repaired and resupplied and trade goods gathered from the African interior were stored for shipment back home. Among the most important of these were Elmina, located just east of Cape Three Points on the Gold Coast, and Gato, built in Benin. These ports soon became profitable centers where gold, ivory, pepper, and palm oil changed hands. These ports also were associated with such frightening diseases as malaria, and they inspired one of Europe's enduring nicknames for Africa: "the white man's grave."

The next significant travels by the Portuguese were credited to DIOGO CÃO, sponsored by King John I, in 1482 and 1485. A member of Prince Henry's retinue, Cão had studied at Henry's school at Sagres and was an experienced seaman by the time he was given command of these two expeditions. Sailing farther down the coast in the Southern Hemisphere than any before him, he came upon the mouth of the Congo River. He sent a small group of men up the river, where he hoped to make contact with Prester John and to acquire gold. Cão continued sailing southward while the men traveled inland. He found Africa to be larger than imagined and, after traveling 500 miles beyond the Congo, decided to backtrack. He returned to the river but could not find his men. Instead, he took several princes from the region back with him to Portugal, where they were well treated. On the follow-up trip in 1485, the African princes were returned home, and Cão recovered his men. He then traveled even farther down the coast, giving subsequent explorers an idea of the great distances involved in sailing around the continent.

Because of rumors of a Christian ruler in the interior, interest in the fabled Prester John was once again revived. Under the auspices of King John II, a delegation of two was formed to try to locate him. PERO DA COVILHÃ would travel first to the Arab lands, then to India, and finally back to Africa, while Afonso de Pavia, an Arabic speaker from the Canary Islands, would scout in Ethiopia. While traveling through Egypt, disguised as Muslims, they arrived in Suakin, Sudan's main port. Pavia disappeared there; Covilhã sailed on to India. Upon his return to Africa, Covilhã made his way to Ethiopia in 1493, where he was detained by a ruler—a Coptic Christian, but not the legendary figure Prester John. Twenty-seven years later, a Portuguese official reported seeing Covilhã there, apparently living comfortably.

Around the Cape of Good Hope

Even in the 1400s, it was still unclear to Europeans whether Africa was entirely surrounded by water. Earlier geographers had speculated the southern part of the continent might be connected to another large landmass, possibly the GREAT SOUTHERN CONTINENT, or Terra Australis. However, the dream of a sea route to the SPICE ISLANDS (the Moluccas) of the East, bypassing Arab merchants controlling the trade—a possibility envisioned by Henry the Navigator—remained extremely alluring.

In 1487, the experienced mariner BARTOLOMEU DIAS set out with three ships to find the southernmost point of Africa and possibly a route to India. By early January 1488, Dias and his crew found themselves in inhospitable southern waters. After being battered about, they eventually made land at Mossel Bay, an inlet of the Indian Ocean, then continued on to the Great Fish River. At that point, his men became restless and persuaded him to turn back. On the return trip, observing a cape and taking notice of the readings in his logbook, Dias realized he had rounded the southern tip of Africa. He set up a marker at the CAPE OF GOOD HOPE, claimed the land for Portugal, and returned to Lisbon in December 1488.

Instability between Portugal and the recently united lands of Aragon and Castile (Spain) delayed the next voyage by several years. In 1494, King John II of Portugal signed the Treaty of Tordesillas with Spain, securing (at least on paper) the rights for the sea lane to India. John died the following year and was succeeded by Manuel I. King Manuel I selected VASCO DA GAMA, a high-ranking naval officer and member of the royal staff, to establish ties with the rulers of the Orient. Da Gama decided the expedition needed larger vessels than those used by Dias if the men were to successfully round the tip and make the long journey.

The expedition of four ships set sail in July 1497. After the first leg of the journey, they spent a week in the Cape Verde Islands taking on fresh supplies and repairing damage to their ships. Next, to avoid the DOLDRUMS at the equator, the explorers cut a wide circular path southward, away from the coastline. In early November, they made landfall at Mossel Bay. The expedition had been on the open ocean for 96 days, a new record for Europeans. The ships then stayed closer to shore, meeting and exchanging small items with the native peoples. The winds and the weather made it slow going, and then SCURVY struck. The disease was not well understood at the time, and da Gama advised his men to cut out their sores with a knife. Many died during this part of the journey. In February 1498, they landed at Mozambique and took on much-needed fresh food. The Portuguese were now in Arab territory. They continued on to the port of Malindi in present-day Kenya, an active trading hub, where the visitors were well received and where they hired a Moor to guide them to India, their final destination. After waiting for the monsoon winds to become favorable, the fleet set out across the Indian Ocean and reached the west coast of India in May. Unfortunately for the Europeans, the experienced merchants in Calicut, the trading center on the Malabar Coast, were uninterested in the goods they had brought to trade. After trying unsuccessfully for three months to establish an outpost, da Gama and his entourage eventually gave up and set sail across the Indian Ocean in August.

The winds were not so favorable on this leg of the trip. Scurvy killed another 30 sailors, and it was only with luck that they made it back to Malindi. They then abandoned one of the ships, continued down the east coast of Africa, reaching the Cape of Good Hope in March 1499 and making it back to Portugal in September 1499. Da Gama and his remaining crew were warmly welcomed, not only because they had succeeded at reaching (and returning from) India, but also because they could offer a rough picture of Africa's east coast.

King Manuel I did not wait to take advantage of the route his country had been seeking for nearly a century. The next year, 1500, he sent out a fleet of 13 ships under the command of PEDRO ÁLVARS CABRAL. After traveling farther west than instructed (there is some debate about whether this detour was deliberate), Cabral reached the continent of South America, becoming the first European to land in Brazil, which he duly claimed for Portugal. In any case, Cabral continued on and came upon stormy weather at the Cape of Good Hope. Four ships were lost, including one with Bartolomeu Dias, who had sighted and identified the southernmost tip of Africa a dozen years earlier. Making several stops on the way, the remaining ships landed in Calicut, India. Again, the Portuguese were rebuffed in their efforts to trade with Arab merchants, and a post they established was attacked. In response, Cabral destroyed Arab trading vessels and bombarded Calicut. Farther south at the port of Cochin, he did manage to secure a cargo of spices before returning home to Portugal. Trade had been opened with the East, but so had warfare. The Portuguese then turned their attention to applying their naval power to establish their dominance in the Spice Islands and their interest in Africa waned.

The Growing Slave Trade

European exploration and colony building on the other side of the world fostered interest in the African slave trade. The Europeans looked to Africa for cheap labor for their newly established plantations and mines in the WEST INDIES and the Americas. Beginning in the 1560s, the English and French began to raid Portuguese slave ships; after Portugal was sufficiently weakened, other European countries established their own "legitimate" trading posts on the African coast. SIR JOHN HAWKINS, an Englishman, was one of the early innovators of the slave trade. In 1562, he took a shipload of slaves from Sierra Leone to the island of Hispaniola (present-day Haiti and the Dominican Republic), where he traded them for sugar and other goods. He then set sail for England, thus inaugurating the infamous triangular trade. In the last two decades of the 16th century, Queen Elizabeth I chartered a number of companies to do business on the African coast from the Mediterranean to Sierra Leone. The Dutch established their first outpost in 1612 in Guinea. Other European nations built trading centers in Africa throughout the 1600s, and the African slave trade continued for centuries.

The Challenge of the Interior

When it comes to understanding the subsequent exploration of interior Africa, it is instructive to recall the formidable barriers facing the Europeans. The vast Sahara Desert, spreading over 3.3 million square miles, covered almost all of northern Africa, extending 3,000 miles west to east and between 800 and 1,200 miles north to south. The temperature could vary by 80 degrees over a 12-hour period, and water was scarce. Travelers needed to know where the next oasis could be found, and they needed to know which foods and clothes were appropriate. Arab explorers, accustomed to a similar climate in the Middle East, had the advantage over Europeans. In addition, because Muslims in the Sahara were hostile to Europeans, European visitors were forced to disguise themselves as Muslims to travel in the region.

Africa's tropical regions imposed another set of hardships on Europeans. The heat and humidity demanded new approaches to dress and equipment, and the dense vegetation made clearing trails for exploratory expeditions (which typically included soldiers, native guides, porters, and pack animals) quite difficult. Most devastating of all, the African climate provided fertile breeding grounds for insects harboring diseases new to Europeans. These included yellow fever, encephalitis (sleeping sickness), and the dreaded malaria. It was not until the second half of the 19th century that Europeans learned to use quinine and mosquito netting to manage this often fatal disease. Moreover, the tsetse fly carried a protozoan that was destructive to the native livestock used to carry supplies, and frequently all the animals on an expedition would succumb to it (see DISEASE AND EXPLORATION).

The fact that much of Africa is located on a plateau did not make traveling any easier. While it is true the rivers wound their way from the highlands to the sea, they did not provide easy access to the continent's interior. As many explorers discovered, the rivers and their environs could be maddening barriers. The Falls, or Cataracts of Aswan, presented a challenge to would-be explorers of the Nile. The Nile also clogged with sudd (literally, "obstruction" in Arabic), large masses of rotting vegetation floating downstream. The Niger River proved just as confounding. Europeans were familiar with certain inland portions of that 2,600-mile river, but locating its outlet proved difficult. In fact, the Niger empties into a vast delta region, a swamp where it is nearly impossible to discern the direction of the current. The Congo River could be navigated from its mouth, but, after 100 miles, it formed a long stretch of falls known as the "Cauldron of Hell," where boats smashed on its rocks or were sucked into whirlpools. The Zambezi River was particularly uninviting at its mouth, where the pounding surf and swirling coastal waters created shifting sandbars. Upstream, explorers faced dangerous rapids and waterfalls.

Europeans also faced resistance from aboriginal peoples. Africans had been victimized by Arabs for millennia and were naturally suspicious of outsiders. The prejudices of Europeans, along with their guns and diseases (especially smallpox), confirmed native peoples' suspicions.

After the sea route to the Spice Islands was established in 1500, European exploration of Africa's interior slowed for more than 150 years. The exception to this was Catholic missionaries. In the early 1600s, the Spanish Jesuit PEDRO PÁEZ was active in Ethiopia and searched for the source of the Nile, while other Jesuits explored parts of present-day Zimbabwe and Angola.

Mysteries of Africa

During the 18th century, the concept of the "noble savage" came into vogue in Europe, and the British became fascinated with Africa, not for economic reasons, but out of intellectual curiosity. Much of the credit for this new enthusiasm belongs to JAMES BRUCE. A Scotsman who grew up in England, Bruce headed to Africa in 1768 with the goal of resolving the mystery of the source of the Nile. He and his assistant, Italian artist Luigi Balugani, traveled from Alexandria to Aswan, where the presence of hostile tribes caused them to head eastward across the desert to the Red

Sea. They then took a boat down the Red Sea to Ethiopia. The pair then resumed their inland trek to the Ethiopian capital of Gondar, where Bruce earned royal favor by instituting sanitary measures that helped stem an outbreak of smallpox at the palace. In late 1770, he left Gondar, moving northwestward until he came upon the Springs of Geesh emerging from underground streams. He mistakenly took this to be the source of the Nile and named it the Fountains of the Nile. In fact, he had located the source of the Blue Nile, a principal tributary of the Nile. Bruce returned home in 1774, where his findings were received skeptically. Nonetheless, he was elected a fellow of the ROYAL SOCIETY, England's oldest scientific organization, and his five-volume work, *Travels to Discover the Source of the Nile,* was praised.

In June 1788, nine members of an exclusive dining club in London founded the Association for Promoting the Discovery of the Interior Parts of Africa, which is better known as the AFRICAN ASSOCIATION. The leader of the organization, SIR JOSEPH BANKS, had excellent exploration credentials: He was then president of the Royal Society, and he had been a naturalist on JAMES COOK's first expedition. The questions that most interested members of the African Association concerned Timbuktu and the nearby Niger River. Timbuktu, the locus of trade for the kingdom of Mali, had been described in writings centuries earlier, but no European had ever seen it. The Niger captured the imagination because neither the source nor the outlet of that long river were known.

That year, 1788, the African Association soon dispatched two explorers. American JOHN LEDYARD was sent to travel westward from Cairo, and Englishman Simon Lucas was directed to begin his journey in Tripoli and head southward across the Sahara. Both trips relied on the spirit of the travelers, since the gentry of the African Association were parsimonious with their resources. Unfortunately, spirit could not make up for the lack of planning and modest size of these expeditions. Ledyard took ill and died in Cairo. Regional conflicts waging several hundred miles south of Tripoli forced Lucas into an early retreat. These initial failures mobilized the African Association to change its approach, and the group decided to avoid Muslim-controlled territory whenever possible.

The first expedition under their sponsorship to explore new territory was made by British army officer DANIEL HOUGHTON in 1790. Houghton began his journey at the mouth of the Gambia, which he took upstream for more than a hundred miles. He then crossed overland to the Senegal River. At this point, he was taken into the desert, robbed, and killed, but the reports that came back to his sponsors suggested he had penetrated the region farther than had any European before him. Information he had gathered on the Niger also helped subsequent explorers.

The Niger River and Timbuktu

MUNGO PARK, a Scottish surgeon, was the African Association's next recruit. The adventure-loving Park had acquired navigational skills on a trip to Sumatra while in the employ of the BRITISH EAST INDIA COMPANY. In May 1795, he began retracing Houghton's footsteps in search of the Niger. Despite resistance from Moors, who controlled this region, as well as local African tribes, he successfully traveled eastward and reached the Niger River at Segou in July 1795. He became the first European to see the Niger that far inland, which he described as "broad as the Thames at Westminster." He also noted that the Niger flowed eastward. Continuing in his mission to find Timbuktu, Park again followed the river into lands controlled by Moors. In August 1796, he was robbed of everything he had, including his clothes. In Silla, only 400 miles shy of his goal, but lacking supplies, Mungo Park turned back. After nearly a year, the explorer arrived at the mouth of the Gambia, where he boarded a vessel bound for America. In South Carolina, he secured passage on a ship to England, where he landed in December 1797.

Park had been gone for two and a half years and had been given up for dead, so his reappearance was greeted with delight by the British public. Two years later, his book, *Travels in the Interior Parts of Africa,* became a best-seller. Park married, had children, and opened a medical practice in Scotland. He also set to work developing a theory on the course of the Niger. Integrating his personal experiences and geographic knowledge with ideas from fellow Scotsman George Maxwell, Mungo surmised the Niger River first flows east for a distance, then turns south and then, farther on, turns southwest. Park's hypothesis was correct, although he would perish before proving it.

In an effort to test his theory, Park, with some help from the British government, put together a large expedition consisting of carpenters, soldiers, and sailors, many of whom were convicts who were to receive pardons upon the completion of the expedition. They were unable to induce any native people to accompany them as they made their way up the Gambia in March 1805. At the town of Kayee, they found and hired Issaco, an English-speaking guide who proved invaluable. Nonetheless, as they traveled east, the rainy season, disease, and an attack by the Moors took their toll. By the time the expedition made it to the Niger, only 10 of the original 40 men were still alive. Finally arriving in Segou, the group came into contact with unfriendly tribesmen, and Park's brother-in-law succumbed to illness. Issaco was sent back to the coast with the news in November 1805, and Park and the remaining members of his expedition set sail, never to be heard from again. In 1808, Issaco agreed to retrace their journey and attempt to learn what had become of the expedition. According to his reports, Park had suffered continual assaults along the course of the river but had managed to add 1,500 miles to the trek. His travels ended at the Bussa Rapids (now covered by Lake Kainji), where he and his group were overcome and killed by tribesmen. There was no physical evidence to support Issaco's accounts, but even if the final leg of the trip had been shorter, Park would still be counted one of the great pioneers in the history of African exploration.

British naval officer HUGH CLAPPERTON continued the European efforts to master the Niger River. As part of the Bornu Mission of 1821–25, sponsored by the British government, Clapperton, together with WALTER OUDNEY and DIXON DENHAM, pioneered the use of Tripoli as a staging area for African exploration. Although their primary objective was to study the Niger, the Bornu Mission covered a great deal of other territory. Traveling south and west across the Sahara, the expedition first investigated the Ahaggar Mountains. In February 1823, they made the European discovery of Lake Chad. The following year, on his way to the Niger, Clapperton reached the city of Sokoto, where slave traders prevented him from further exploration. He returned to England by traveling back through the Sahara, then mounted a second expedition later the same year, 1825. This time he made the approach from the Bight of Benin in the south. This new route led him to the Niger River at Bussa. He then explored inland, revisiting Sokoto, where he died from illness in 1827.

Clapperton had been accompanied on his last journey by RICHARD LEMON LANDER. Together with his brother John, Lander traveled to Bussa in 1830. They first traveled 100 miles up the Niger River and then began a dangerous CANOE trip down it. They followed the river to its outlet, a swampy delta with no discernible flow. Although Richard Lander was then held captive by native peoples of the delta until a large ransom was paid, he had determined the exact mouth of the Niger River. Four years later, Lander was attacked and killed on a trading mission up the Niger.

Meanwhile, in 1825, ALEXANDER GORDON LAING, a Scottish-born British army officer, was sent to make contact with the ancient city of Timbuktu. Laing followed Clapperton's route from Tripoli on the north coast of Africa and crossed the Sahara Desert. Attacked and severely wounded just outside Timbuktu, he pressed on, becoming the first European known to reach that city. After spending a month there, he headed home but was murdered en route, probably by Tuareg tribesmen. Although Laing had reached Timbuktu in 1826, reports of his visit did not reach Europe until two years after his death.

Its remote location and centuries of strong Muslim control had made Timbuktu more legendary than real to Europeans, and rumors of the city captured the European imagination. Frenchman RENÉ-AUGUSTE CAILLIÉ learned Arabic, studied Islam, and disguised himself as an Egyptian who had been held captive in France in order to make his way there in 1828. His ruse gave him safe passage through various lands, and he spent two weeks in Timbuktu before returning home, disappointed by the humble state of the city. His compatriots had difficulty accepting his accounts.

In 1830, the ROYAL GEOGRAPHICAL SOCIETY was founded in England by SIR JOHN BARROW and others. The next year, it merged with the African Association. The European exploration of Africa would continue, with much of the activity British-sponsored.

Southern Africa

Of all the lands of Africa, the countryside and climate most familiar to the European were those in South Africa. During the centuries that the major European powers had been preoccupied with trade, the southernmost region of Africa was viewed as a way station for the repair and resupply of ships. To do this effectively meant persuading farmers and craftspeople to establish settlements there, but the chartered companies who needed the way station were slow to invest. Finally, in 1657, with their colony on the verge of failure, the DUTCH EAST INDIA COMPANY worked out a plan allowing their settlers to own land in exchange for provisioning ships. These Dutch and French settlers came to be known as the Boers (literally "farmers" in Dutch). Once the Boers were permitted to own land, they enslaved the native Hottentots, claiming this was justified—even a divine right—according to their Calvinist religion. The Boers then proceeded to use native slave labor to create farms and establish cattle herds, and they developed their own subculture, including their own language, Afrikaans. In 1806, after the Napoleonic Wars, Britain assumed control of the Boer territory. Twenty-seven years later, in 1833, Britain outlawed slavery in its colonies. This, combined with the British move to physically circumscribe Boer lands, resulted in rebellion. Between 1835 and 1843, more than 10,000 Boers left the cape and headed northward in what came to be known as the Great Trek. During these years, the Boers defeated the Bantu-speaking Zulus in a series of battles, and they went on to establish more settlements.

Scotsman DAVID LIVINGSTONE arrived on the continent in 1841, a few years after these battles. A strict Presbyterian with some medical training, Livingstone came to Africa as a missionary. After arriving at the Kuruman mission on the southern border of the Kalahari Desert, Livingstone established his own outpost among the Kwena at Kolobengto to the northeast. Considerable tension existed between Livingstone and the Boers: He strongly disapproved of their slavery, and the Boers destroyed his house, threatened his friends, and pushed him north. By 1842, he had traveled farther north into the treacherous Kalahari region than any other European to date, and he had learned a great deal about local languages and customs.

Livingstone began his first true journeys of exploration in 1849, when he moved north across the Kalahari Desert in search of new territory to conduct his missionary activities and influence politics. That year, accompanied by British sportsman William Oswell, he made the European discovery of Lake Ngami. Two years later, this time accompanied by his wife, MARY MOFFAT LIVINGSTONE, daughter of the British missionaries to Africa, ROBERT MOFFAT and MARY MOFFAT, he made a second crossing of the Kalahari and reached a tributary of the upper Zambezi River. Livingstone received recognition and money from the British Royal Geographical Society for having reached Lake Ngami, and he began his lifelong association with that group.

In November 1853, Livingstone began the first known European crossing of the southern portion of Africa from west to east. Starting from Linyanti, the capital of the Makololo kingdom, he followed the Upper Zambezi north and then west to the port of Luanda on the Atlantic Ocean. The expedition traversed more than 1,500 miles of uncharted land over six months, but it was a very difficult trip, with food in short supply and fever plaguing the members of the party, including Livingstone. Livingstone was impressed, however, with the friendliness of many of the tribes he encountered. After a three-month rest in Luanda, he headed westward in fall 1854. A year later, he was back in Linyanti, again beset by fever. However, he pressed on, again heading west. In November 1855, on the Zambezi River, Livingstone made the European discovery of what he named Victoria Falls. He then crossed the Kafue and Luangwa tributaries and ended his journey near the mouth of the Quelimane River in May 1856. In December 1856, Livingstone returned to England, where he was lauded as the new hero of African exploration. Accounts of his travels were instant best-sellers, and his missionary zeal at public appearances inspired future explorers

In 1858, Livingstone and his family returned to Africa. Outfitted with a paddle-wheel steamer named the *Ma-Robert* (in honor of Livingstone's wife, mother of Robert), the well-equipped expedition, sponsored by the British government, began investigating the Zambezi River. They were halted at the Quebrabasa Rapids but continued their explorations on the Shire River, another Zambezi tributary. In 1859, accompanied by the naturalist John Kirk, Livingstone traveled overland and made the European discovery of Lake Nyasa (present-day Lake Malawi). The next goal was the exploration of the Ruvuma River, east of Lake Nyasa. In 1862, while on the Zambezi, his wife succumbed to tropical fever. With his basic work on the Zambezi completed, Livingstone again returned to England to rest.

Source of the Nile

Other explorers meanwhile had been continuing the search for the source of the Nile. The well-traveled Englishman SIR RICHARD FRANCIS BURTON and a former soldier in the British army, JOHN HANNING SPEKE, commissioned by the Royal Geographical Society, set about the task in 1856 with a new approach. Instead of following the river from its mouth, which had been done many times in the previous century, they used reports of lakes to the south to estimate the location of its source and then traveled inland from the east coast. After becoming the first Europeans to see Lake Tanganyika, the world's longest freshwater lake, and visiting Ujiji in spring 1858, they headed back to the coast. While Burton was recovering from illness in Tabora, Speke struck out on his own and made the European discovery of Lake Victoria, Africa's largest freshwater lake. Although he had little evidence, Speke declared this to be the source of the Nile. Burton and Speke had never been close, and their relationship rapidly deteriorated after Speke's claim, which Burton disputed. Speke returned to England before Burton, telling of his findings and igniting a controversy.

Speke's flimsy evidence necessitated another expedition. In 1860, Speke, accompanied by JAMES AUGUSTUS GRANT, retraced his path and returned to Lake Victoria. In July 1862, after traveling along the lake's shores, they discovered where the Nile left the lake and named it Ripon Falls. The men followed this outlet, the Victoria Nile, as far as Lake Kyoga, but left the river before seeing it connect with Lake Albert. This gap in information perpetuated the controversy. Speke did not live to be proven correct. On the eve of an 1864 debate over the Nile with his former partner Burton, he was killed in a hunting accident. It fell to the British couple SIR SAMUEL WHITE BAKER and FLORENCE BAKER to describe the river's course between the Victoria Nile and the Albert Nile, after they completed their own expedition in 1865.

While David Livingstone is most closely associated with the Zambezi River, his disciple, Anglo-American journalist SIR HENRY MORTON STANLEY, is linked to the Congo, as both explorer and developer. Livingstone's final years in Africa, from 1866 to 1873, involved a number of journeys around the lakes north of the Zambezi River. He was interested in describing their relationships with the major rivers, particularly the Nile. In April 1867, he reached Lake Tanganyika. Despite recurring bouts of illness, Livingstone continued exploring and came upon Lake Mweru in November 1867. In July 1868, he made the European discovery of Lake Bangweulu, a reservoir between the Chambezi and Lualaba Rivers, which form the Upper Congo. He next visited Ujiji, a center of the slave trade on the east shores of Lake Tanganyika, which reenergized his commitment to eradicate such trafficking. In November 1871, low on supplies and without European contact for more than three years, Livingstone was found in Ujiji by Stanley. Together the men explored Lake Tanganyika and determined it was not the source of the Nile. Stanley went back to England to write his adventures while Livingstone labored on. In May 1873, near Tabora on the Lualaba River, Livingstone died of dysentery. His African companions Susi and Chuma carried his body to the east coast, where it was returned to England and buried in Westminster Abbey.

That year, Englishman VERNEY LOVETT CAMERON was sent by the Royal Geographical Society to take supplies to the missing Livingstone and to do some exploring. While in Tabora in October, Cameron learned Livingstone had died five months earlier. Cameron arranged to have the late explorer's journals returned to England, and then he continued to investigate the regions containing the Nile and Congo watersheds. He learned that the Lukuga River was the outlet to Lake Tanganyika, and he helped define the separation between the two great rivers. His work on the Lualaba River, which converges with the Lukuga, helped set the stage for Stanley's later exploration of the Congo River. His mapping skills were excellent, and, in the course of his travels, he became the first European to make an east-to-west equatorial crossing of the African continent.

After Livingstone's death, Stanley returned to Africa in 1874 to complete work on his mentor's projects. He traveled to Lake Victoria, where he confirmed Speke's claim that it was indeed the source of the Nile, and then circumnavigated Lake Tanganyika, confirming that lake was not linked to the Nile. Stanley then headed west to follow the Congo River from its headwaters at the Lualaba River to its outlet in the Atlantic. This task was rife with dangers ranging from cannibalistic and hostile native peoples along the river's banks to a 200-mile stretch of rapids. But Stanley persevered. He named Livingstone Falls and arrived on the west coast of Africa in August 1877, more than two and a half years later.

Stanley went on to even more arduous adventures in the Congo region. In 1879, after England revealed it had little interest in the region, Stanley signed on with Belgium's King Leopold II to build a road. In the meantime, Italian-born Frenchman PIERRE-PAUL-FRANÇOIS-CAMILLE SAVORGNAN DE BRAZZA had convinced France that the area was worthy of attention, if for no other reason than to keep other countries from claiming too large a territory. Exploring from the north of the Congo River, he arrived at the north shore of Stanley Pool (now Malebo Pool) as Stanley was building a road up from the lower Congo to that same point, hacking his way through the jungle. The Frenchman's treaty with the local chief formed the basis for the colony of French Equatorial Africa. The lands where Leopold retained control, which became the Belgian Congo, experienced a period of ruthless enslavement, where nearly 1 million Africans were killed in Leopold's quest to harvest rubber.

Natural Science

A number of explorers made their contribution to African exploration through a focus on science (see NATURAL SCI-ENCE AND EXPLORATION). Swedes CARL PETER THUNBERG and ANDERS SPARRMAN, both students of renowned Swedish botanist Carl Linnaeus, conducted studies north of Cape Town in South Africa, in the early 1770s. Thunberg would become known as the "father of Cape Botany."

The Englishman SIR FRANCIS GALTON, a cousin of CHARLES ROBERT DARWIN, traveled in southwestern Africa along with amateur naturalist Karl Johan (Charles) Andersson, in 1850–52, to pursue studies in geography and wildlife. Galton's work *Narrative of an Explorer in Tropical South Africa* was widely read in Europe.

German GEORG AUGUST SCHWEINFURTH had a broad education in botany, zoology, and geology, and he became interested in other disciplines, such as anthropology, as his career progressed. Schweinfurth was also an artist who made drawings of plants and animals he encountered on his travels in the 1860s–70s. In his expedition of 1868–71, he explored the central tropical regions of the continent. He delineated the watersheds between the Nile and the Congo and made the European discovery of the Uele River (which feeds the Congo). Schweinfurth was the first to make contact with the Mubuti of the Congo, and he studied a number of other tribes as well. His two-volume book, *The Heart of Africa,* represented a significant leap forward in the European understanding of the diversity of life in Africa.

The travels of another German, OSKAR LENZ, a geologist, also added to the European knowledge of Africa. After three years in central Africa, he turned his attention to the Sahara Desert. In 1879, he traveled from Casablanca in Morocco, over the Grand Atlas Mountains and south through the Sahara to Timbuktu. In 1885, he made a two-year exploration of the Congo region, and he is noted as one of a handful, along with the Scottish geologist JOSEPH THOMSON, who traveled widely between 1879 and 1890, to visit both tropical and desert regions on the continent.

From Exploration to Colonization

In 1886–89, Hungarians LUDWIG VON HOEHNEL and SAMUEL TELEKI made the European discovery of Lake Rudolf, the Omo River, and Lake Stefanie in northern Kenya and southern Ethiopia, helping in the mapping of the "Dark Continent." By this time, Africa's major geographic mysteries had been solved, and the era of colonization had begun. From 1880 to 1912, the entire continent came under the domination of one European country or another. The French sought to build a railway across the Sahara, encountering fierce resistance from the nomadic peoples they tried to dominate. The British consolidated their control over South Africa by winning the South African War (1899–1902). Until the treaty ending World War I, Germany possessed Togoland, the Cameroons, German South-West Africa, and German East Africa. Italy held Libya, Eritrea, and Italian Somaliland. Many of the borders of these countries appear arbitrary, negotiated in Europe without consideration of geography or the ethnicity and history of the native peoples. Undoubtedly, the strategy of "divide and conquer" was employed to keep tribes from united action and to encourage in-fighting among subjugated groups. The refugee movements and political turmoil of today are the continuing legacy of colonial Africa. Although the last of the African colonies gained their political independence in the mid-1970s, the economic independence of most of the countries on the continent has yet to be achieved.

African Association (Association for Promoting the Discovery of the Interior Parts of Africa)

Due to the excitement generated by the explorations of the Scotsman JAMES BRUCE, and with the recent loss of their colonies in America, a number of Englishmen of high position founded the Association for Promoting the Discovery of the Interior Parts of Africa in London on June 9, 1788. It would become known simply as the African Association. The principal founder was SIR JOSEPH BANKS, a naturalist who had been the chief scientist on JAMES COOK's first expedition to the South Pacific Ocean in 1768–71 and was then president of the ROYAL SOCIETY, Great Britain's oldest and most prestigious scientific organization.

The immediate goals of the organization were the mapping of the NIGER RIVER and locating the city of TIMBUKTU in the kingdom of Mali, the supposed center of trade in West Africa. The British government, seeking opportunities for colonization as a result of British explorations, worked closely with the African Association. The first two expeditions dispatched to Africa—that of American JOHN LEDYARD and Englishman Simon Lucas—failed in their intended goals, with the death of Ledyard and Lucas being forced to turn back because of a regional conflict.

The first important expedition sponsored by the African Association was that of British army officer DANIEL HOUGHTON in 1790–91. He traveled on the Gambia, Senegal, and Niger Rivers and is credited with being the first to record that the Niger flowed from west to east. FRIEDRICH CONRAD HORNEMANN, a German who had long been fascinated with Africa, headed up another important trip for the association in 1798–1801. Leaving from Cairo, he was the first European in modern history to cross the SAHARA DESERT, and, based on accounts from his journals, found after his death in the field and later published, he was probably the first European to see Lake Chad in the northwestern corner of present-day Nigeria.

Perhaps the most famous explorer to work under the auspices of the African Association was MUNGO PARK, a Scottish surgeon. He made two trips sponsored by the group. The first, in 1795–97, started with ascending the Gambia. He fell into the hands of hostile Muslims but managed to escape, making his way to the Niger. Battling fever, he returned to the Gambia and made it back to England after 30 months, having been given up for dead. His subsequent book, *Travels in the Interior Districts of Africa* (1799), helped further interest in African exploration. His second journey, in 1805–06, was much more extensive and better financed, yet more tragic in its outcome. Taking the Gambia to the town of Kaiaf, then traveling overland to the Senegal, and on to the Niger at Bamako, the entourage took heavy losses from disease. After continuing on the Niger, Park was not heard from again. The best information indicates that his party was ambushed at Bussa, and that, in attempting escape, he drowned.

The travels of Swiss-born JOHANN LUDWIG BURCKHARDT on behalf of the African Association—on the NILE RIVER in Syria, Egypt, the Sudan, and Arabia in 1809–15—yielded much new information to Europeans, including the rediscovery of the city of Petra (Wadi Musa) in present-day Jordan.

Although resulting in many insights into the topography and human populations of Africa, the expeditions sponsored by the African Association were filled with bad luck and often the death of their leaders. In 1831, the African Association merged with the recently formed and more broadly defined ROYAL GEOGRAPHICAL SOCIETY, which went on to sponsor many expeditions to Africa as well as to other parts of the world.

See also AFRICA, EXPLORATION OF.

Age of Exploration   See EUROPEAN AGE OF EXPLORATION.

airship (dirigible)

An airship is a self-propelled and steerable BALLOON. Like a balloon, an airship uses lighter-than-air gases to create lift. The main body, the bag or envelope containing gas, is elongated, however, for aerodynamics. The engines plus propellers are suspended from the bag, as are the gondolas (cabins), carrying crew, passengers, and cargo. As in the case of a balloon, the ballast, usually sand or water, is released to increase lift; gas is released to decrease it. *Dirigible,* or *dirigible balloon,* the alternative term for an airship, is from the Latin *dirigere* for "to direct, to steer," in reference to the airship's directional capabilities, provided by one or more vertically hinged rudders. Horizontally hinged elevators give additional control for climbing or descending.

There are three basic types of airship construction: nonrigid, semi-rigid, and rigid. In the nonrigid class of airships, also known as *blimps,* the shape of the body is maintained by the pressure of the gas. In the semi-rigid class, referred by the general name *airship,* the shape of the body is also maintained by the gas, but in conjunction with a keel running the body's length. In the rigid class of airships, known as *zeppelins,* a rigid scaffolding-like frame maintains the body shape, with lift provided by individual gas cells. The earliest airships used the highly flammable hydrogen for their lighter-than-air gas; later ones used the safer helium.

A French engineer by the name of Henri Gifford constructed the first airship, drawing on balloon technology. It was a nonrigid type, with a cigar-shaped envelope and a single screw propeller driven by a steam engine. In 1852, he flew over Paris at about six miles per hour, though his craft could not be steered in a breeze. Two other Frenchmen, Charles Renard and Arthur Krebs, built a blimp that was steerable in light winds. In a flight in 1884, they proved that it could successfully return to its starting place. Airship technology developed rapidly over the next decades. A German, Count Ferdinand von Zeppelin, completed his first rigid airship in 1900. For a time afterward, zeppelins were used for commercial transportation in Germany.

Germany used rigid craft in World War I; France developed semi-rigid airships. All proved vulnerable to airplanes, however. Nonrigid airships proved the most useful because they could best hover over a location for aerial observation and were often used to patrol coasts. In 1919, after the war, a British-developed rigid airship made the first transatlantic crossing, from East Fortune, Scotland, by way of Newfoundland to Mineola, New York, on Long Island; it completed a transoceanic return flight to Pulham, England.

Airships have played a part in the history of polar exploration. After the war, an Italian, UMBERTO NOBILE, became an accomplished pilot and designer of airships. In 1926, in the *Norge,* a semi-rigid craft he had designed, he flew from the Norwegian islands of Spitsbergen (present-day Svalbard) over the NORTH POLE, to Teller, Alaska,

Umberto Nobile's airship *Norge* is tethered in its hangar in 1926. *(Library of Congress, Prints and Photographs Division [LC-USZ62-107120])*

where the ship was dismantled. The expedition had been organized by the Norwegian polar explorer ROALD ENGEL-BREGT GRAVNING AMUNDSEN and the American aviator LINCOLN ELLSWORTH, who had purchased the craft from the Italian government and hired Nobile as pilot on the expedition.

Nobile organized another flight two years later with plans to land at the North Pole. He designed another semirigid craft, the *Italia,* with polar conditions in mind. His crew consisted mostly of Italians with mountaineering experience in the Alps; three scientists went along for polar studies. Again departing from Spitsbergen, the *Italia* successfully circled the North Pole, but because of ice buildup on the craft, plans were abandoned to land there. The airship broke apart and was wrecked on the ice. Nobile and eight others in the gondola survived a crash landing; one of the crew later died before being rescued. Seven others perished, however, when the airship's bag drifted out of control. Amundsen, although not part of this expedition, died when his airplane crashed as he was on his way to Spitsbergen to join the search for survivors.

For a time, airships were used for commercial transatlantic crossings. But the frequency of crashes—including the 1937 disaster, in which the German-built *Hindenburg,* a rigid airship containing hydrogen gas, was enveloped in flame in Lakehurst, New Jersey, killing 36 of its 92 passengers—led to a decline in the use of airships following their heyday earlier in the 1930s. The nonrigid class, with helium as gas, became the norm. Some were used in World War II in the 1940s for observation purposes. Today blimps are used primarily for advertising as well as camerawork at sporting events. In 1997, the Zeppelin Company of Germany unveiled a new generation of airships, the first of the rigid class to fly since 1940.

See also AVIATION AND EXPLORATION.

alidade

The term *alidade* is derived from an Arabic phrase meaning "the revolving radius of a circle." First appearing in English in the 1400s, the term came to be applied to specific surveying and navigational instruments. One early device known as an alidade consisted of a surveying rule equipped with simple or telescopic sights; it was used to determine direction. An early navigational alidade was a straight bar with sights on both ends and a pivot in the middle; it was used to measure the angle of a celestial body in relation to the observer.

The term *alidade* is also applied to the central measuring component of other instruments. These include the ASTROLABE used in navigation; the plane table, a drawing board on a tripod, with a ruler for plotting the lines of a survey directly from observations; the theodolite, or transit, a telescope mounted on a tripod used in surveying; and a number of modern sighting tools.

An early astronomical alidade was described by PTOLEMY, a second-century Hellenized Egyptian living in Alexandria; it was referred to in some texts as "Ptolemy's ruler." During the Middle Ages, the Arabs used versions of the alidade in a variety of applications. In the early 17th century, telescopic sights were added to alidades.

See also NAVIGATION AND EXPLORATION; SURVEYING AND EXPLORATION.

Amazon River

The Amazon River is the longest river in South America and the second-longest in the world (after the NILE RIVER), extending some 4,000 miles across the continent. The Amazon drains 2.7 million square miles, from near the Pacific Ocean on the inter-Andean plateau to the Atlantic Ocean. It flows through Peru, eastward across Brazil, and enters the Atlantic at the EQUATOR, where it discharges roughly a fifth of all the freshwater that drains into the oceans. The river has hundreds of tributaries; of these, 17 are more than 1,000 miles long. The main headwaters of the Amazon, the Ucayali and Marañón Rivers, have their source in the snows of the high ANDES MOUNTAINS of Peru. During the wet season, the Amazon varies in width from five to 40 miles. Near the Atlantic, it opens into an estuary about 150 miles wide, scattered into many branches by islands formed from silt deposits. Often called the "Ocean River" because of its vastness, the Amazon is highly navigable, and large ships can reach Iquitos in northeastern Peru, 2,300 miles from the sea. Before the European conquest of South America, the Amazon had no single name; its different sections were known to native peoples by specific names. The name of the river is probably derived from the native word *amassona* for "boat destroyer," although others claim it was named by Europeans after the Amazons of Greek mythology.

Early Expeditions

VICENTE YÁÑEZ PINZÓN, a Spanish navigator, was the first European to visit the Amazon River Delta, in 1500. Pinzón accompanied CHRISTOPHER COLUMBUS on his first voyage to the Americas, as captain of the *Niña.* In November 1499, he set out on his own voyage with four ships. He landed in northeastern Brazil toward the end of January 1500, then sailed along the coast to the northwest. Pinzón ascended the river about 30 leagues, calling it the "Freshwater Sea," because of its size and amount of freshwater. Later reports by Pinzón's companions refer to the Amazon as the Río Marañón, a name later applied to one of its tributaries. Marañón is either a native word or perhaps is derived from the Spanish *maraña* for a "tangle." For explorers of the Amazon, the latter was appropriate, for the river's tangle of streams and islands is a challenge to the best navigators. Pinzón's landing in Brazil was long disputed because the Portuguese claimed discovery of Brazil with PEDRO ÁLVARS CABRAL's landing in April 1500.

The second exploration of the Amazon occurred almost a half-century later and from the other end of the river. GONZALO PIZARRO, the half brother of FRANCISCO PIZARRO, who took part in the Spanish conquest of Peru, was named governor of Quito in 1539, in what is now Ecuador. In 1541, Pizarro set out for an expedition into the forests to the east of the Andes in search of La Canela, the "Land of Cinnamon," which was reportedly rich in spices, and EL DORADO, a famed city of gold according to native stories. FRANCISCO DE ORELLANA, a Spanish explorer and relative of Pizarro, accompanied the expedition as second in command. When provisions ran out, Orellana and 50 to 60 companions broke off from the expedition with commands to search for food but did not return, as Orellana's ships were swept into the fast-flowing Napo River. Orellana and his men followed it into the Amazon. Along the way to the Atlantic, they encountered tribes whose women fought alongside the men (like the mythical Amazons, leading to one interpretation of the river's name). Orellana's expedition was the basis for the description of the Amazon River included in the Spanish cartographer DIEGO GUTIERREZ's 1562 map of South America, the first description of the continent's interior.

The Amazon River runs through wet and densely forested plain and to this day remains one of the most sparsely populated areas on Earth. Parts of the river system today still remain unexplored. For the Spanish settlers of Peru, the Amazon valley was a source of mystery and possessed the lure of hidden treasure, spurred on by native accounts and the reports of explorers such as Orellana. In 1558, the Spanish conquistador PEDRO DE URSÚA was commissioned by Marquis de Cunete, the Spanish viceroy in Peru, to find the fabled city of El Dorado in the forested Amazon basin of Peru. In command of 300 Spaniards and a number of native people and slaves, Ursúa left Lima in 1559, but due to delays he was unable to sail until October 1560. A mutiny erupted, led by LOPE DE AGUIRRE, and Ursúa was murdered. Aguirre led the men down the river and laid waste to several Indian villages along the way. The next year, the expedition became the second to cross South America from the Andes to the Caribbean.

Politics and Exploration

Politics played an important role, with and above the lure of treasure, in spurring on exploration. Budding empires such as Spain and Portugal attempted to spread their spheres of influence in South America, which promised to provide not only riches of spices and precious metals but also new outlets for trade and the simple commodity of free land—

the supply of which had been long lost in Europe. After Christopher Columbus landed in the Americas in 1492, Spain petitioned Pope Alexander VI for a monopoly on trade in the western Atlantic, which resulted in a line of demarcation to the west of which Spain was given trading rights, and to the east of which rights were granted to Portugal, Spain's chief rival. After the Treaty of Tordesillas, this longitudinal line was fixed at 370 leagues west of the AZORES.

The landing of Pedro Álvars Cabral in Brazil in 1500, in territory allowed to the Portuguese, seemed to give them rights to Brazil, while the headwaters of the Amazon were planted firmly in Spanish territory. In 1545, King Charles I of Spain sent Francisco de Orellana back to the Amazon to act as governor to assert Spanish control over the river and halt Portuguese expansion. But Orellana died while exploring the mouth of the river, and the expedition dissolved in failure. Meanwhile, among the Portuguese was a great effort to gain control of the Amazon, first by PEDRO DE TEIXEIRA. Originally part of an effort to expel British, Dutch, and French from encroaching on Portuguese territory in South America, Teixeira became, in 1618, the governor of the territory of Pará at the mouth of the Amazon. He made expeditions on the lower Amazon, mapping and aiming to remove French, Dutch, and British trading settlements for Portugal. In 1629, he commanded a major expedition up the Amazon with 120 Portuguese and 1,600 native people. After the expulsion of other European rivals, Portugal turned its attention to Spanish holdings in South America; the arrival of two Spanish friars from Peru in Pará raised concerns among the Portuguese that the Spanish had designs on the Amazon River. In 1637 Teixeira was sent by the new colonial governor, Jacome Raimundo Noronha, to explore and map the length of the Amazon and especially to scout locations for Portuguese fortification. Teixeira followed the reverse of Orellana's route, using one of the missionaries for a guide, and, in 1638, claimed for Portugal the Río Negro, one of the main northern tributaries of the Amazon with its source in the Colombian Andes. He sailed up the Napo in July 1638. After traveling to Quito on foot, he and his party became the first Europeans to reach that city from the east, and the first to sail up the Amazon.

Increasing Knowledge

The Spanish viceroy in Peru, perhaps unnerved by Teixeira's arrival, sent two Jesuits to accompany him on his return journey. Jesuit father CRISTÓBAL DE ACUÑA made surveys and kept a record of his voyage down the Amazon, and, in 1639, his account of the journey, *New Discovery of the Great River of the Amazons,* was printed, becoming the first published account of the river.

The Amazon was frequented by Portuguese slavers and by missionaries, but maps and descriptions of the river continued to be inaccurate and contained tantalizing blanks even a little more than a century later. Discoveries were often made by accident, as when Jesuit Father Roman in 1744 accompanied a group of Portuguese slavers through a passage called the Casiquiare Canal that connects the ORINOCO RIVER, another major South American river, to the Río Negro, a tributary of the Amazon, and which had been mentioned by Cristobal de Acuña but never verified. Roman's description was one of the many pieces of information reported by French explorer CHARLES-MARIE DE LA CONDAMINE to the French Academy of Sciences.

La Condamine first set out in 1734 for the equatorial region of South America as part of a French expedition to measure the difference of the curvature of the Earth at the equator and the polar region to determine the true shape of the Earth. When the project had been completed, La Condamine resolved to voyage down the Amazon to its mouth, obtaining maps of the Amazon from the Jesuits. He set out in 1743, traveling through the treacherous Andes to the Marañón River, one of the Amazon's tributaries, on which he set sail. The Marañón is a river extremely difficult to navigate, filled with dangerous reefs, dozens of arduous rapids, and high cataracts. Finally, La Condamine passed through the Pongo de Manseriche, a narrows three miles long. The Pongo de Manseriche is about 2,000 feet deep, surrounded on both sides by high precipices and narrowing to a width of as little as 100 feet. The Marañón squeezes through the pass rushing up to 12 miles an hour.

La Condamine made the first systematic scientific observations of the river, and the native peoples. He even applied his skills to resolving the boundary established between Spanish and Portuguese territory by the Treaty of Tordesillas, which almost 300 years later still remained disputed. On his return to France in 1745, he wrote an account of his explorations in South America, including a map of his journey along the Amazon, which was published in 1751.

Almost a half-century later, German naturalist and geographer ALEXANDER VON HUMBOLDT and French botanist Aimé Bonpland were given permission by the king of Spain, Charles IV, to explore Spain's possessions in the Americas. Humboldt had undertaken a geological survey of Spain's central plateau region, and, with his knowledge of geology, astronomy, and biology, he was well suited and driven to make a thorough investigation in South America. After some exploration along the coasts, Humboldt and Bonpland traveled into the Orinoco Basin, studying in detail the unique flora and fauna of the region as well as fixing the many geographic discrepancies of maps of the region. Humboldt crossed the Casiquiare Canal, which had been reported by La Condamine in a CANOE, proving finally that it connected the Orinoco and Río Negro, the only known connection between two major river systems. Throughout 1800, Humboldt explored this region, vastly increasing scientific knowledge of the lower Amazon Basin.

Inspired by Humboldt's account, as well as Englishman CHARLES ROBERT DARWIN's account of the voyage of the *Beagle,* two other British naturalists, ALFRED RUSSEL WALLACE and HENRY WALTER BATES, endeavored to collect insect specimens in the Amazon Basin. In 1848, they sailed to the mouth of the Amazon in Pará, Brazil. In 1852, Wallace sailed for England with his notes and specimens while Bates remained. Wallace's ship, however, caught fire and sank, along with his notes and specimens. Wallace himself was rescued after spending two weeks in an open boat on the sea. He published his account of his travels and research as *A Narrative of Travels on the Amazon and Río Negro* in 1853. Bates meanwhile had explored the Amazon 400 miles west from Manaus, the Amazon's juncture with the Río Negro. Afterward, he remained between Manaus and the mouth of the river at Pará, collecting specimens until 1855. In 1859, Bates returned to England and published *The Naturalist on the River Amazon* in 1863. In 10 years on the Amazon, Bates collected 14,000 insect specimens, including 8,000 newly discovered species. While Wallace's observations in the Amazon and southeast Asia led him to formulate a theory of natural selection independently of Darwin, which was published at the same time, Bates's collections lent strong support to the idea of natural selection.

Since then, the Amazon River and its basin have prompted much scientific exploration. However, many native tribes still live in relative isolation. The tropical rain forests house amazing biological diversity, with new species still to be discovered.

See also SOUTH AMERICA, EXPLORATION OF.

American Fur Company

Established in 1808 to take advantage of reports from the 1804–06 MERIWETHER LEWIS and WILLIAM CLARK expedition to rich beaver country west of the ROCKY MOUNTAINS, the American Fur Company and its various subsidiaries—the Pacific Fur Company, founded in 1810, and the South West Fur Company, founded in 1811—were an ambitious operation. The founder, JOHN JACOB ASTOR, born in Germany, had migrated to America from England. He had made his first profits in the FUR TRADE in 1784 by exporting furs from America to England. Over time, he perfected his business by brokering furs from Montreal and the Great Lakes region in America, but he was unhappy with the control his rivals—the HUDSON'S BAY COMPANY and the NORTH WEST COMPANY—had over prices.

The findings of Lewis and Clark inspired the plan of a chain of trading posts gathering furs from inland to the mouth of the COLUMBIA RIVER on the Pacific coast. Taking advantage of his contacts in Canton, Astor stood to reap handsome profits from the Chinese, who were especially fond of sea otter pelts. This venture was carried out by a new subsidiary, the Pacific Fur Company, with its immediate goal of establishing a trading post at the mouth of the Columbia River. To accomplish his mission, Astor outfitted two expeditions, one by sea and one overland. On September 8, 1810, Astor's ship, the *Tonquin,* set out from New York City, sailing around South America and arriving at the mouth of the Columbia in March of the following year. The captain, Jonathan Thorn, was a strict disciplinarian and did not get along with investors, who were members of the expedition. Upon arrival, a crew of builders under ROBERT STUART began construction of Fort Astoria while Captain Thorn commenced trading with the Nootka Indians. Relations deteriorated, however, when the quick-tempered captain slapped the face of an Indian chief at Nootka Sound, leading to the destruction of the vessel.

Meanwhile, the overland expedition had problems of its own. Led by businessman and the less-than-experienced woodsman WILSON PRICE HUNT, the group of 56, plus Indian guides, including Ioway MARIE DORION and her husband, PIERRE DORION, JR., had set out from St. Louis in spring 1811. They had intended to follow the trail of the Lewis and Clark Expedition, but fear of the unfriendly Blackfeet Indians caused them to take a less direct path. Upon reaching the Snake River, they sought to continue by CANOE and managed to trade with Indians for craft. After several days, however, the river proved unnavigable, and several members of the party drowned. The expedition split into groups and continued on foot. Those who survived reached Astoria in February 1812. Despite their hardships, they managed several important geographic discoveries, which included charting the Green River, Union Pass, and SOUTH PASS, a shortcut through the southern end of the Wind River Mountains.

Although the establishment of Fort Astoria resulted in the first permanent American settlement in the Pacific Northwest, the post did not fulfill Astor's ambitions. By June 1812, America was at war with England—in the War of 1812. Interference from the British navy and likely loss of their property led Astor's men to sell the outpost to the North West Company. A treaty with Britain in 1818 returned possession of Astoria to the American Fur Company, but, by that time, the Nor'westers (as the employees of the North West Company were known) were established in the area, and Astor's company was concentrating its efforts in the Great Lakes region.

With the help of a law barring foreigners from trading with American Indians, Astor consolidated his holdings. He bought out the assets of his partners in the South West Company. Then, pursuing the goal of monopoly power, he proceeded to buy out strong competitors and to crush weaker ones. Independent traders were also targeted.

The American Fur Company soon turned to the lucrative market in American bison (buffalo) hides harvested from the Great Plains. Through the formidable personality of KENNETH MCKENZIE at Fort Union in the 1830s, permission was secured from the formerly intractable Blackfeet to exploit the buffalo.

In 1834, Astor, having anticipated the turn of fashions in Europe, sold out his interests in the American Fur Company. The trade in beaver soon crashed, and the company was forced to scale back its operations. Astor went on to concentrate his efforts in real estate and became one of the richest men in the country.

See also COMMERCE AND EXPLORATION.

American Geographical Society (AGS)

The American Geographical Society (AGS), founded in 1851, is the oldest geographic society in the United States. Its headquarters are in New York City, and its archive is located at the University of Wisconsin in Milwaukee. Its members have included both professional geographers and nonprofessionals interested in the subject of geography. Unlike many other 19th-century organizations, such as the ROYAL GEOGRAPHICAL SOCIETY, it has been open to women as well as men from its inception.

AGS activities include scientific research relating to geography; the sponsoring of expeditions, lectures, and conferences; the awarding of honors to scholars and explorers; cartography; and magazine and book publishing. Present-day publications include *Focus,* a quarterly magazine for the general public; *Geographical Review,* a scholarly journal; *Ubique,* a semiannual newsletter; and a variety of books on geographic topics, among them *Around the World Program,* a book series on countries of the world with a companion guide for teachers. In the course of its history, the AGS has worked under contract with various branches of the U.S. federal government, academic institutions, and corporations.

An impetus for the founding of the AGS, in addition to the great interest in world exploration at the time, was the publicity surrounding the search for Englishman SIR JOHN FRANKLIN, who disappeared in the Canadian Arctic on an 1845 expedition, and the efforts of his wife, JANE FRANKLIN, to encourage rescue efforts. A number of scholars, businessmen, and statesmen created the organization to support exploration, support geographic research, and promote education. One early expedition that the AGS helped underwrite was an early exploration attempt of the NORTH POLE in 1860–61 by American ISAAC ISRAEL HAYES. In 1878–80, American physician and lawyer FREDERICK SCHWATKA, with AGS backing, led a team overland by sledge from HUDSON BAY to King William Island while searching for evidence of the Franklin expedition.

One of various explorers to receive a gold medal from the AGS was CHARLES CHAILLÉ-LONG in recognition of his contributions to geographic knowledge of Africa, such as determining in the 1870s that Lake Kioga was one of the principal sources of the White Nile, a branch of the NILE RIVER.

A number of famous 20th-century American explorers were associated with the AGS as well. ROBERT EDWIN PEARY, who led the first successful expedition to the North Pole in 1909, served as the society's president for a time. In 1951, MATTHEW ALEXANDER HENSON, who traveled to the North Pole with Peary, was honored at the AGS centennial banquet in 1951. LOUISE ARNER BOYD received AGS backing for her 1933 expedition to GREENLAND's east coast. The AGS was also an early promoter of AERIAL PHOTOGRAPHY in mapmaking, as applied in both the Arctic and Antarctic.

See also GEOGRAPHY AND CARTOGRAPHY.

Andes Mountains

The Andes Mountains are the second-highest mountain range in the world, after the HIMALAYAS. The range contains many of the highest peaks in the Western Hemisphere. The Andes probably received their name from the word meaning "high crest" in the Quechuan language of the Inca Indians. The Andes rise abruptly from the Pacific Ocean coast, thrust up by the collision between the Pacific Ocean and South American continental plates during the Cretaceous period, from 65 to 138 million years ago. The tectonic activity along this plate boundary continues to cause volcanic activity and earthquakes throughout the Andes and along the Pacific coast. The mountains run in a narrow band, generally about 200 miles wide, along the west coast of South America, from the Caribbean Sea in the north to the island of Tierra del Fuego in the south, a distance of about 4,500 miles. The Andes can be divided into three regions, generally referred to as northern, central, and southern.

The northern Andes, which rise in present-day Venezuela, Colombia, and Ecuador, are composed of three narrow ranges known as the Western, Central, and Eastern Cordilleras, so called by early Spanish explorers because of the resemblance of their long thin parallel ranges to ropes. The highest mountain of the northern ranges is Cristóbal Colón in Colombia, at a height of 18,947 feet. Many other peaks are higher than 15,000 feet.

The central Andes are made up of two Cordilleras, the range's broadest region, reaching a maximum width of 400 miles, and the highest region, with many peaks over 20,000 feet. The peaks of the central Andes include Pissis, at 22,241 feet; Huascarán, at 22,205 feet; Illampu, at 21,276 feet; Chimborazo, at 20,561 feet; and Cotopaxi, an active volcano at a height of 19,347 feet above sea level. Between the two ranges of the central Andes, in Bolivia and southern Peru, lies an elevated plain called the Altiplano. Rains falling on the Altiplano flow into Lake Titicaca at 12,500 feet, making it the highest navigable lake in the world, and a lake with no outlet to the ocean.

The Andes are generally smaller to the south. Close to the central Andes is ACONCAGUA, the highest mountain in the Western Hemisphere, at 22,834 feet, but, near the tip of South America the mountains rise to about 10,000 feet above sea level, and Cerro Yogan, the highest peak of Tierra del Fuego, an extension of the Andes, is 8,100 feet. Many of the highest peaks in the southern Andes are volcanic, and a good number of them are active.

Rain falling on the western slopes of the Andes runs into the Pacific Ocean. The heavy rains brought by the trade winds against the eastern slopes form the tributaries of the three major river systems in South America, the AMAZON RIVER, the ORINOCO RIVER, and the Río de la Plata.

The Andes, especially the plateau regions of the central Andes, were inhabited by native peoples for many hundreds of years before the rise of the Inca Empire in the 15th century. The first Inca emperor, Manco Capac, led an attack on the people living in a fertile valley some miles to the north of Lake Titicaca; the Inca settled there and made Cuzco their capital. The Inca spread throughout the Andes, and, in the 15th century, under the rule of Pachacuti Inca Yupanqui and his son, Topa Inca Yupanqui, the Inca Empire came to include an area of 350,000 square miles, with an extensive system of roads and rope bridges.

Early Expeditions

It is thought that the first European to reach the Andes overland was ALEJO GARCÍA, a Portuguese sailor who had been shipwrecked south of Rio de Janeiro, taking part in JUAN DÍAZ DE SOLÍS's 1515 expedition in search of a passage through South America. García and others who had been shipwrecked befriended the natives. García accompanied them, exploring the interior of the continent and reaching the Andes. He heard tales of the Inca Empire and even obtained several bars of silver for himself. The tales and silver came to the attention of Europeans, when a number of sailors were rescued by SEBASTIAN CABOT, an Italian sailing for England, and taken back to Europe in 1530.

The Spanish conquistador FRANCISCO PIZARRO, who had established himself in Panama, became partners with another Spaniard, DIEGO DE ALMAGRO, to find and conquer the Inca kingdom in the Andes. After taking an outlying Inca town, Pizarro sailed to Spain to seek support for a larger expedition. This support was granted to him, and, in 1531, he began his effort to conquer the Inca.

Pizarro led his forces over the Royal Inca Road, eastward through the Andes and the Piura Valley, entirely without Inca resistance. Finally, on November 15, 1532, the Spanish arrived in the deserted city of Cajamarca, where just out of town the Inca emperor Atahualpa encamped, with reportedly 50,000 men. The Spanish made a surprise attack on the Inca, charging with horses, which the Inca had never seen, and firing upon them with their cannon. The Spanish suffered few casualties, though they killed thousands of Inca, and took Atahualpa prisoner. Afterward, Pizarro marched through the Andes on the roads created by the Inca, capturing Cuzco, enslaving many of its inhabitants, and seizing its gold.

During their travels in the Andes, the Spaniards found amazing wealth in gold and other precious metals. The Andes Mountains are rich in precious metals and stones and had been mined by the native peoples for centuries. Attempting to obtain his release, Atahualpa offered to fill a room with gold, which Pizarro allowed him to do before killing him.

The Andes continued to be explored by the Spanish CONQUISTADORES searching for remnants of the Inca Empire and for other kingdoms with equivalent wealth. In 1534, SEBASTIÁN DE BENALCÁZAR set out to capture Quito, an Inca provincial capital in the north. Benalcázar gained the support of Canari Indians as he traveled and was met by the forces of Inca chief Ruminahui in present-day Ecuador, near its highest peak, Chimborazo, where he defeated them.

Diego de Almagro quarreled with Pizarro over their respective positions and power, and, in 1535, after appointment as governor of a new Peruvian province called New Toledo, to the south of Cuzco, he set out with 750 Spaniards and thousands of native allies. He embarked in the middle of winter, and his men suffered in the severe cold of the high Andes. After traveling through the central Andes, Almagro turned westward and reached the coastal Copiapo Valley, then followed the coastal plain of modern Chile into the Central Valley. Repeatedly attacked by native peoples and unable to find another civilization like the Inca, Almagro turned back.

The wet, eastern slopes of the Andes in the north were part of the area rumored to contain EL DORADO, and this story along with other tales of legendary wealth, such as a "Land of Cinnamon," inspired Spanish conquistadores to cross the eastern range of the Andes from Quito into present-day Colombia. These expeditions were headed by Sebastián de Benalcázar, out of Quito, in 1536; GONZALO PIZARRO, in 1541; and PEDRO DE URSÚA, who embarked from Lima, the Spanish capitol of Peru, in 1559. A German explorer, NIKOLAUS FEDERMANN, began his search for the land of El Dorado in Venezuela and Colombia. He became the first to cross the Andes from east to west in 1536.

Modern Exploration

The search for El Dorado died out for the most part in the 17th century, but Spaniards continued to scour the mountains for riches. The first modern scientific surveys of the Andes were made by Frenchman CHARLES-MARIE DE LA CONDAMINE in the first half of the 18th century. La Condamine was part of a French scientific expedition to measure the curvature of the earth at the EQUATOR. La Condamine traveled through the Andes inland to Quito from the South American coast, becoming the first European to see the process of rubber extracted from rubber trees. La Condamine spent several years around Quito making surveys and conducting work on the natural history of the region.

The next important modern explorer of the Andes was German naturalist ALEXANDER VON HUMBOLDT at the turn of the 19th century. Along with the French botanist Aimé Bonpland, he was granted permission by Spanish king Charles IV to explore Spanish possessions in the New World. Humboldt explored the effects of high altitude in the Andes, making observations on the boiling point of water, and, with Bonpland, attempted to climb Mount Chimborazo. The two reached to within 1,400 feet of the summit before having to turn back, establishing a height record for climbing of 19,000 feet not to be broken for 30 years. Humboldt crossed the Andes five times, as he explored the lands from Ecuador to Peru.

Much important exploration of the Andes was carried out in the first half of the 19th century as part of surveys, especially in the northern and central ranges. The southern Andes were explored in 1876 and 1877 by Argentinian Francisco Moreno. Moreno earned a doctorate in natural sciences at the University of Buenos Aires in 1854, before becoming a professor there, concentrating in anthropology. After many years teaching, he embarked on expeditions into areas south and west of Buenos Aires. In 1876, he explored the southern Andes and studied the Patagonian native peoples, visiting several lakes at high elevations and exploring Cerro Chaltel (Mount Fitzroy). He made another expedition to explore the Andes from 1882 to 1883.

With many of the world's highest peaks, the Andes are important in the history of MOUNTAIN CLIMBING. British mountaineer EDWARD WHYMPER summitted Chimborazo in 1880. Italian mountaineer MATTHIAS ZURBRIGGEN climbed Aconcagua in 1897. In 1906, a pioneering woman climber, ANNIE SMITH PECK, reached the top of Huascarán. Today, the range remains a big draw to climbers. The Andes also continue to supply valuable minerals and gems to miners. The mountains are also an area of activity for archaeologists. In 1911, American historian HIRAM BINGHAM located the Inca stronghold of Machu Picchu.

See also SOUTH AMERICA, EXPLORATION OF.

Anian, Strait of

The Strait of Anian is the name of a mythical waterway separating Asia and North America, extending from the northeast coast of North America to the west coast. Its name is derived from a reference in the writings of MARCO POLO, a

13th-century Italian traveler to the Far East. The search for the strait was, for a time, one and the same with the search for the NORTHWEST PASSAGE, although, as was discovered in the 19th century, a Northwest Passage does in fact exist in Arctic waters to the north of the North American continent. The hope of a more southerly waterway endured for centuries, not only for the advantages it would offer as a shortened trade route, but because a southerly route would make it accessible year-round in ice-free waters.

East and West Coasts

The search for the Strait of Anian occurred in several stages involving both the east and the west coasts of North America. Mariners of varying nations searched for a Northwest Passage along the northeast coast of North America, the first, in 1497, by Italian JOHN CABOT, sailing for England, in a voyage during which he made the European discovery of Newfoundland and Labrador. Portuguese GASPAR CÔRTE-REAL claimed to have found the outlet to the Strait of Anian in an undocumented voyage two years later. In his subsequent two voyages—in 1500 and 1501—he failed to back up his claim, which he perhaps fabricated to receive backing.

On the west coast, the Spanish carried out a number of expeditions in search of the outlet of such a strait. HERNÁN CORTÉS imagined the benefits of a water route, especially in terms of consolidating the Spanish hold over territories in Mexico. In 1535, he explored the California coast, but, in his haste, failed to recognize that Baja California was a peninsula and that California was not an island, as had been believed. The geography of the region was somewhat clarified by the 1539–40 explorations of FRANCISCO DE ULLOA, who ventured to the end of the Gulf of California (named by him the Sea of Cortés). There, he located the mouths of the Gila River and COLORADO RIVER. These discoveries left open the question of the Strait of Anian, however. In 1542, JUAN RODRIGUEZ CABRILLO explored as far as modern-day San Diego, becoming the first European to venture that far north.

In England, during the mid-1560s, a debate began concerning the relative merits of a Northwest Passage versus a NORTHEAST PASSAGE. The chief promoter of the former was SIR HUMPHREY GILBERT. He was a believer in the Strait of Anian, and, using the best knowledge available at the time, argued that it would start from the north coast of Labrador, and wind gradually to the southwest, where it would reach the Pacific Ocean about where Seattle, Washington, is today. After considerable effort, Gilbert managed to organize financing for an expedition to test his theory. His chief patron was Michael Lok. Their partnership led to the 1576 expedition of SIR MARTIN FROBISHER, which failed to locate any such passage. The English had a presence on the west coast as well at this time in the person

of SIR FRANCIS DRAKE. In addition to raiding Spanish ships and settlements, he searched for the strait, sailing as far north as Vancouver Island. Meanwhile, the Strait of Anian appeared on various maps of the period. On a 1584 map, Flemish cartographer ABRAHAM ORTELIUS placed Japan in the middle of the strait, equidistant from Asia and America.

Hardship and Fraud

The next chapter in the search for the Strait of Anian involved an outright fraud. Spaniard Lorenzo Ferrer Maldonado claimed to have sailed along the north coast of North America, through the Strait of Anian to the Pacific, and back to the Atlantic, all in summer 1588. The story was taken seriously at the time, especially by Michael Lok. In 1596, Lok's hope for finding the strait was again given new impetus when he met an elderly Greek who had taken the name JUAN DE FUCA while in the service of Spain. De Fuca claimed that, in 1592, he had explored an inlet on the northwest coast of North America, where he had sailed for 20 days to a region of icebergs. He believed it to be the Pacific outlet to the fabled strait. Lok's enthusiasm to raise funds for an expedition was great, but he was unable to convince his peers. De Fuca died before the trip could be arranged. A real strait to the south of Vancouver Island bears his name.

Inspired by de Fuca's story and anxious to complete the navigation of the reported strait, JENS ERIKSEN MUNK led a Danish expedition to the Arctic in 1619. His journey is notable more as a tale of the will to live than for discoveries made. With a crew of 63, he sailed into Hudson Strait. After an arduous journey through the ice of HUDSON BAY, the expedition landed on the west shore near present-day Churchill. In winter 1620, an outbreak of trichinosis from eating undercooked polar bear meat took hold, with horrific consequences detailed by Munk in his journals. SCURVY is also assumed to have taken its toll. Munk and two others were the only ones to survive the winter and, with the warm weather, ate new shoots of plants poking through the ice, regaining strength enough to sail back to Europe.

Another interesting tale in the search for the strait involved a rivalry between two English cities and their commercial interests. LUKE FOXE sailed for London and THOMAS JAMES headed Bristol's expedition. Both set out in May 1631, and both managed to reach Hudson Bay. Foxe had no desire to test his will against the winter and returned to England in the fall of the same year. James and crew spent a dreadful winter trapped in the ice, with scurvy becoming a major problem, yet he and his crew made it back to England in October 1632. They brought back with them the understanding that Hudson Bay was enclosed and not a gateway to the long-sought strait.

While expeditions were making little headway in the search for the strait, news came of an incredible voyage. It was another fraud, this time claimed on behalf of one Admiral Bartholomew de Fonte. The account of his voyage, *Memoirs for the Curious*, published in London in 1708, relates a 1640 trip in the Pacific from Peru to the north in search of a Northwest Passage. He claimed that, by navigating a maze of inland rivers in North America, he came upon a trading ship from Boston. Such was the art of the tale that it was accepted by no less than American statesman Benjamin Franklin.

End of the Myth
The man responsible for helping lay the myth to rest was Englishman SAMUEL HEARNE of the HUDSON'S BAY COMPANY. In 1770, with the help of Chipewyan Indian MATONABBEE, he worked his way northward, looking for gold and copper. By July 1771, he and his party had reached the Coppermine River, which they followed northward to its mouth in the Arctic Ocean. The return trip was arduous, and it took another year to make it back to Fort Prince of Wales. By cutting across the land and failing to find a waterway of sufficient size for oceangoing trading vessels, Hearne had determined the fallacy that was the Strait of Anian. Yet search for a passage would continue well into the 19th century in the Arctic waters to the north.

See also LEGENDS AND EXPLORATION.

animals and exploration
Animals have a special place in the history of exploration as a means of transportation, as economic incentive, as an area of study in natural science, and as sustenance.

The Horse and the Donkey
The horse, domesticated in Eurasia about 6,000 years ago, is part of the story of movement over all the continents. Some of its use was for the purpose of conquest. The Mongols, under GENGHIS KHAN and other leaders, became known as masterly cavalrymen as they swept throughout much of Asia (see MONGOL EXPLORATION). The Spanish CONQUISTADORES reintroduced the horse to the Americas—early species having been extinct since the end of the Pleistocene. By the end of the 18th century, the *sunka wakan,* or "mystery dog," as it was known to some Sioux (Dakota, Lakota, Nakota) bands, had altered the way of life of many Native Americans, especially in the American West, and would affect subsequent expeditions of nonnative peoples, who used horses for travel and at times did battle with mounted Plains Indians.

Donkeys, classified with horses in the family Equidae, played a major role as pack animals, especially the small variety known as the burro and especially in the American West. Mules, hybrids of jackasses (male donkeys) and mares (female horses), were also utilized.

The Dog
Another animal central to exploration was the dog, especially the breeds best suited to frigid lands, such as the Siberian husky, the Alaskan malamute, and the Eskimo dog. Ponies and dogs actually competed with one another on the final continent explored, Antarctica (see ANTARCTIC, EXPLORATION OF THE). For his attempt on the SOUTH POLE in 1910–12, the Englishman ROBERT FALCON SCOTT chose to use Manchurian ponies along with sled dogs and motorized sledges. His rival, the Norwegian ROALD ENGELBREGT GRAVNING AMUNDSEN, who had studied Inuit (Eskimo) travel methods, used only sled dogs and was willing to eat them if they gave out, not as a last resort, but as part of the plan. Amundsen won the race to the Pole. Until mechanized equipment became the norm, the sled dog made long-distance travel possible over the frozen deserts of the Arctic (see ARCTIC, EXPLORATION OF THE) and Antarctic.

Robert Falcon Scott took the sled dog Chris with him to the Antarctic in his expedition of 1910–12. *(Library of Congress, Prints and Photographs Division [LC-USZ62-101001])*

The Camel

The camel, especially the Arabian, or dromedary, camel, which has one hump, and the Bactrian camel, which has two humps, also played a small part in the annals of exploration, particularly in the Near East, North Africa, and central Asia among Arabs and other Muslims (see MUSLIM EXPLORATION), as well as Europeans in those regions, such as Englishman THOMAS EDWARD LAWRENCE (Lawrence of Arabia). Camels were also used on other continents. In 1857–58, American EDWARD FITZGERALD BEALE headed a U.S. wagon road-building project from western Texas to California, using camels as draft animals. Also, they were regularly used by Englishmen in the deserts of Australia, on such expeditions as those of ROBERT O'HARA BURKE and WILLIAM JOHN WILLS in 1860–61; PETER EGERTON WARBURTON in 1873; and ERNEST GILES in 1875–76.

Hunting

The pursuit of animals for meat and pelts led to travel to uncharted lands. An American, DANIEL BOONE, who traveled across the APPALACHIAN MOUNTAINS into what is now Kentucky, was a "longhunter" in search of deer, sale of the hides of which supplemented his income. The beaver helped shape North America beyond its own altering of waterways, because of all the expeditions for the purpose of the FUR TRADE. Its pelts became favored for felt in the making of hats with brims, a fashion style that began in Europe in the late 16th century and endured nearly to the mid-19th century. Other animals, such as muskrat, mink, marten, and fox, were also sought, bringing humans to their domain. Sea mammals—seals, sea otters, and whales—also spurred on many expeditions to extreme northern and southern waters (see WHALING AND SEALING). In the early 19th century, for example, a whaler father from England, WILLIAM SCORESBY, SR., and his scientist son WILLIAM SCORESBY, JR., explored the Arctic regions of GREENLAND and pioneered new methods of Arctic navigation.

Sealers—American NATHANIEL BROWN PALMER, Scot JAMES WEDDELL, and Englishman JOHN BISCOE—were among those men who first viewed the Antarctic continent in 1820s–1830s.

Natural Science

Animals also prompted exploration as subjects of natural science studies. Naturalists wrote about them and sketched and painted images of them (see NATURAL SCIENCE AND EXPLORATION). In the first half of the 19th century, for example, American JOHN JAMES AUDUBON undertook numerous expeditions in order to record images of North American wildlife. Other naturalists—such as Americans CARL ETHAN AKELEY, DELIA JULIA DENNING AKELEY, and MARY LEONORE KOBE AKELEY—collected specimens for museums in the early 20th century. Carl Akeley also helped found Africa's first wild game preserve, now known as the Virunga National Park, as a sanctuary for mountain gorillas and other animals.

Legendary Animals

Legendary animals also are part of the history of exploration. Sea serpents, supposedly giant snakelike creatures, and other sea monsters were part of the culture of early mariners, a believed threat of unknown waters for destroying wooden ships. Some of the reported stories served to scare off mariners from competing countries. KUPE, a 10th-century Polynesian, as legend has it, pursued the Squid King in the South Pacific Ocean, leading to the discovery and settlement of NEW ZEALAND and the resulting Maori descendants (see LEGENDS AND EXPLORATION).

Animals and Space Exploration

Animals were directly involved in the act of exploration as experimental passengers in early SPACE EXPLORATION. On November 3, 1957, the Union of Soviet Socialist Republics (USSR; Soviet Union) launched the SATELLITE Sputnik 2, carrying the first animal—a female dog named Laika—into space. Laika survived for several days, eventually dying from heat exhaustion due to high temperatures within the capsule. The Soviets continued launching dogs as part of the Sputnik program. The United States later launched monkeys to test the effects of zero-gravity conditions on life.

Antarctic, exploration of the

The Antarctic continent, or Antarctica, the world's fifth-largest continent, is centered on the SOUTH POLE, the southernmost place on Earth, and is largely contained within the ANTARCTIC CIRCLE, the point at which the Sun neither sets on the day of summer solstice, nor rises on the day of winter solstice. The southern limits of three oceans—the Atlantic, Pacific, and Indian Oceans—meet at Antarctica. The term *Antarctic*—for "opposite the Arctic," Earth's northernmost region—applies both to the surrounding waters and to the continent.

Up to 7 million square miles of the Antarctic Convergence, or the "Southern Ocean" (waters of all three oceans with lower temperatures and greater concentrations of salt), turns to PACK ICE in wintertime. An ice sheet—which, in certain areas, is as much as three miles thick—covers about 99 percent of the Antarctic continent. Ice accumulation and the force of gravity and pressure leads to glacial flows from higher elevations to lower. The flows, on reaching the sea, form floating ice shelves, which fringe about half of Antarctica's coastline, and parts of which sometimes break off into massive icebergs. The Antarctic continent is divided into two main regions: West Antarctica, which is the smaller region, contains the Antarctic Peninsula, Ellsworth Land, and

Marie Byrd Land; East Antarctica faces the Indian Ocean and contains Queen Maud Land, American Highland, Wilkes Land, and Victoria Land.

Antarctica was not always in its present location on the globe. Fossils of plants, insects, fish, and other animals date from the Triassic and Jurassic periods (during the Mesozoic era, the Age of Reptiles) and indicate that Antarctica broke away from the ancient landmass known as Gondwanaland (consisting of the present continents of South America, Africa, and Australia as well) about 65 million years ago. Antarctica is rich in mineral deposits and coal; these resources, however, have not been commercially exploited due to the difficulty of extracting them.

Antarctica is the coldest place on Earth, surrounded year-round by stormy seas and pack ice. In fact, parts of the coast are free of ice only several weeks at the end of summer. Average winter temperature is minus 70 degrees Fahrenheit. The lowest temperature ever recorded on the planet—minus 126.9 degrees Fahrenheit—was recorded in East Antarctica. In addition to extremely low temperatures, Antarctica's climate is characterized by rapid changeability, strong winds, and blizzards. There were no human inhabitants of Antarctica until modern times. Plant life on the continent is limited to moss, lichen, and only two kinds of flowering plants. Small insects live among the plants. Larger animals in the region, such as the emperor penguin and seals, spend only some of their time on land in Antarctica.

Early Exploration of Southern Waters

Antarctica was the last continent of Earth's seven continents to be explored and, without a native population, it can be said to have actually been "discovered." Long before humans first sighted Antarctica, Greek geographers of the fifth century B.C. hypothesized the existence of a frigid southern continent containing the southernmost place on earth, the South Pole. They later expanded this theory into the idea of the GREAT SOUTHERN CONTINENT, or Terra Australis, which was thought to occupy more temperate latitudes. It was not until the early 18th century, however, that physical evidence of Antarctica was indicated, when sealing and whaling voyages reached the edge of the pack ice surrounding the continent. In fact, the early story of the exploration of Antarctica is more about its margins—people seeing ice around it, touching on islands near it, seeing evidence that it exists, but not actually setting foot on the continent for many more years.

In the 18th century, several French expeditions to southern latitudes were undertaken in search of the fabled Great Southern Continent, including one in 1738–39 by JEAN-BAPTISTE-CHARLES BOUVET DE LOZIER, who discovered Bouvet Island. In 1772–73, YVES-JOSEPH DE KERGUÉLEN-TRÉMAREC led two expeditions to southern waters; in the course of the first, he located the Kerguelen Islands

in the southern Indian Ocean, close to the parallel of latitude referred to as the Antarctic Circle. The credit for determining Antarctica's boundaries falls to JAMES COOK, who circumnavigated the southern region of the globe on his second Pacific expedition of 1772–75. He attempted to sail as far south as possible but was blocked by pack ice on three different occasions. He did manage to cross the Antarctic Circle three times, however, reaching as far south as 71 degrees, 11 minutes. He also discovered the South Sandwich Islands. Somewhat ironically, Cook, the man who determined Antarctica's boundaries, never saw the land of the continent itself.

Early Sightings

Following Cook's probes, European interest in Antarctica languished for nearly 50 years. In 1819, inclement weather drove British sailor William Smith 480 miles southeast of CAPE HORN, where he discovered the South Shetland Islands. British naval officer EDWARD BRANSFIELD charted this island group, landing on King George Island. On January 30, 1820, farther to the south, he spotted snow-covered mountains on an expanse of land, which later explorers would chart as the northwest coast of the Antarctic Peninsula. The following November, American sealer NATHANIEL BROWN PALMER—who, for a time, was credited with the first sighting of the mainland before Bransfield's journey came to world attention—also sighted the Antarctic Peninsula.

Another early trip to the region was made by Baron FABIAN GOTTLIEB BENJAMIN VON BELLINGSHAUSEN, a German-born Russian naval officer in search of Terra Australis. He crossed the Antarctic Circle in early 1820. On January 28, he came within 20 miles of Princess Martha Coast of Greater (East) Antarctica and sighted the edge of the ice sheet (which some claim constitutes the first sighting of the continent). After backtracking to Australia, he made another foray south at 41 degrees east longitude, where threatening icebergs and blowing snow turned him back. In December 1820, he entered waters now known as the Bellingshausen Sea. He reached his farthest point south at 69 degrees on January 21, 1821, and discovered Peter I Island the following day. He also saw the peaks of the mountains on Alexander I Land, an island near the Antarctic Peninsula.

Another sealer, JAMES WEDDELL, was also seeking new hunting grounds in the Antarctic waters at this time. A Scot sailing for the English, he discovered the South Orkney Islands in 1822. In February 1823, benefiting from mild weather, Weddell was able to go beyond 74 degrees south latitude, but contrary winds forced him to return north shortly afterward. The southernmost point he reached in the Weddell Sea was not surpassed until the next century.

In the 1830s, the Enderby brothers, who had a business in whaling ships operating out of England since the

18th century, became interested in scientific exploration. Charles Enderby became a member of the ROYAL GEOGRAPHICAL SOCIETY in 1830, the year of its founding. Also that year, the society commissioned Englishman JOHN BISCOE to look for land south of the Indian Ocean. He achieved a latitude of 69 degrees south on January 28, 1831, off Queen Maud Land, but did not sight land until February 24, when he saw sheer ice cliffs, which he correctly guessed to be covering the land of the continent. He named the region Enderby Land after his employers. Biscoe carried out some of the first extensive mapping of Antarctica.

In 1837, JULES-SÉBASTIEN CÉSAR DUMONT D'URVILLE embarked on an exploration of the Antarctic for France and King Louis Philippe. The king suggested that Weddell's record of exploring farthest south should be bested. Dumont d'Urville's ships, the *Astrolabe* and the *Zélée,* were small and poorly equipped for polar exploration, but he managed to discover Joinville Island and to chart the channels and islands along Graham Land on the Antarctic Peninsula. After a rest and meetings with SIR JOHN FRANKLIN and John Biscoe in TASMANIA, he returned to the southern latitudes to look for the SOUTH MAGNETIC POLE, a location determined by terrestrial magnetism and in a different location from the South Pole. On January 20, 1840, Dumont d'Urville sighted ice cliffs on the shore, and, behind them, a mountain of snow and ice that rose thousands of feet into the sky. He named the new territory Adélie Land (also known as Adélie Coast), after his wife. He also determined that the South Magnetic Pole was nearby. An explorer with a strong scientific orientation, Dumont d'Urville painstakingly illustrated the 49-volume set of his explorations in the Pacific and Antarctica with drawings and maps, all of which added greatly to current knowledge of the regions. His was the first French expedition inside the Antarctic Circle as well as the last French one in the 19th century.

After much planning, the U.S. government launched the United States South Sea Surveying and Exploring Expedition in the 1830s. Naval officer CHARLES WILKES commanded the expedition of six ships, which left Norfolk, Virginia, in August 1838. After establishing a base camp at Cape Horn, he headed southward. Unfortunately, Wilkes's ships were ill-suited for their task. After surveying the Strait of Magellan (see MAGELLAN, STRAIT OF) on their return to Valparaíso, one of the ships and all her crew were lost. Later, in January 1840, another was badly damaged by pack ice off the Antarctic coast. That same month Wilkes navigated the icebergs of Piner's Bay and came within a half mile of the shore. Shortly thereafter, he encountered Dumont d'Urville's expedition, and controversy ensued as to who had seen the mainland first. It was later calculated that both had seen land on January 19. Wilkes went on to explore the edge of the Shackleton Ice Shelf. The expedition eventually circumnavigated the world, the first American expedition to do so.

Upon returning to the United States in 1842, Wilkes faced a court martial for endangering his men, but was cleared of all charges except for that of illegal punishment of some of his crew. Later explorers questioned the accuracy of Wilkes's maps upon finding an ocean where he had plotted land. Despite this controversy, Wilkes had accomplished much in biological, geological, and meteorological data collection.

SIR JAMES CLARK ROSS, who had made four journeys to the frigid waters of the north, ventured to the south in 1839. The British naval expedition's main interest was in the South Magnetic Pole. In contrast to other explorers at the time, Ross used ships that were well designed for navigating through pack ice: the *Erebus* and the *Terror.* On January 5, 1841, he entered the ice of the Ross Sea but was blocked from reaching the South Magnetic Pole by the sheet of ice that came to be called the Ross Ice Shelf. He mapped the region extensively, however, discovering Victoria Land, Mount Erebus, and Mount Terror at the base of the Transantarctic Mountain chain. He also set a new record for reaching the farthest point south, at 78 degrees, 4 minutes. The following year, he explored the Weddell Sea on the other side of West Antarctica and discovered the Ross Islands.

During the 1800s, numerous other ships made voyages to Antarctic waters, many of them for whaling purposes. In 1873, for example, EDUARD DALLMAN led a German whaling expedition to Antarctica, considered the first voyage that far south by that country.

On the Mainland

For all the trips that had been made to Antarctica, and the understanding that land existed under the ice, no known landing occurred until January 23, 1895. While on a commercial venture, Norwegian whaling captain CARSTEN EGEBERG BORCHGREVINK and members of his crew were the first to set foot on Victoria Land. On a subsequent expedition in 1899, sponsored by the British newspaperman GEORGE NEWNES, Borchgrevink took a ship called the *Southern Cross,* which had been specially retrofitted for polar exploration, and a crew of scientists to explore the land. Traveling on land by dog sled, they investigated the Newnes and Murray Glaciers. They then sailed to Mount Erebus and Mount Terror. They found the Ross Ice Shelf had retreated 30 miles since its discovery by Ross some 60 years prior. Borchgrevink and his crew suffered both physical and psychological hardships on the trip, including anemia, malnutrition, and depression. The creaking of the boat in pack ice also reportedly disturbed the crew. Perhaps the greatest accomplishment of Borchgrevink's exploratory expedition was proving that it was possible to spend the Southern Hemisphere's winter on Antarctica, thus setting the stage for a push inland to the South Pole.

The Belgians reached Antarctica in 1897. The leader of their expedition was ADRIEN-VICTOR-JOSEPH DE GERLACHE

This photograph of the midnight sun in the Antarctic was taken during Robert Falcon Scott's expedition of 1910–12. *(Library of Congress, Prints and Photographs Division [LC-USZ62-88392])*

DE GOMERY, aided by first mate ROALD ENGLEBREGT GRAVNING AMUNDSEN, a Norwegian. They explored the outer coast of the Antarctic Peninsula for three months until the *Belgica,* their ship, was trapped in pack ice. They drifted with the ice for over a year into the Bellingshausen Sea. The Belgians suffered from SCURVY but managed to catch several seals as sustenance. In spring 1899, they managed to free themselves of the ice by dynamiting a canal, and eventually returned to Belgium.

In the early 20th century, many nations launched expeditions to Antarctica. In 1901, ERICH DAGOBERT VON DRYGALSKI led a German expedition to the Indian Ocean coast of Antarctica, locating and naming Kaiser Wilhelm II Land and Mount Gauss. NILS OTTO NORDENSKJÖLD explored the South Shetland Islands, Graham Land, and Mount Haddington on Weddell Sea for Sweden. Between 1901 and 1904, ROBERT FALCON SCOTT explored Victoria Land and the Ross Ice Shelf, and he located Edward VII Land in the British National Antarctic Expedition, setting a southernmost record. Beginning in 1902, WILLIAM SPIERS BRUCE, on the Scottish National Antarctic Expedition, made the first

systematic oceanographic exploration of the Weddell Sea and charted Coats Land. And, between 1903 and 1905, JEAN-BAPTISTE-ÉTIENNE-AUGUSTE CHARCOT mapped the Antarctic Peninsula, Loubet Coast, and Adelaide Land for France. Several years later, Charcot surveyed the Palmer Archipelago and located the Fallières Coast.

To the South Pole

In the early 20th century, reaching the North Pole and the South Pole was considered to be the two greatest goals in exploration. SIR ERNEST HENRY SHACKLETON, who had been part of Scott's 1901 expedition, organized an expedition to the South Pole, the British Antarctic Expedition, which set out in July 1907. After locating the Beardmore Glacier and crossing the Polar Plateau, Shackleton missed claiming this prize by only 97 miles, turning back on January 9, 1909. On January 16, a second party, including the Australian scientist SIR DOUGLAS MAWSON, reached a point 190 miles inland from the west shore of the Ross Sea, where it was determined by COMPASS readings that they had reached the South Magnetic Pole.

That spring, on April 6, 1909, at the other side of the world, two Americans—ROBERT EDWIN PEARY and MATTHEW ALEXANDER HENSON—reached the North Pole (or within a couple of miles of it) by sledge from Cape Columbia on the north coast of Ellesmere Island. (Another American FREDERICK ALBERT COOK claimed he had reached the North Pole on April 21, the year before, but this claim is disputed.)

The British organized another attempt on the South Pole, to be led by Antarctic veteran Robert Falcon Scott, who departed England in June 1910. The plan was to set out from McMurdo Sound and follow the route pioneered by Shackleton (across the Beardmore Glacier and Polar Plateau), with preestablished food and fuel depots along the way. Motorized sledges, Manchurian ponies, and dog sleds were to provide transportation. In the interim, the Norwegian Roald Amundsen, who had intended to attempt to reach the North Pole, learned of Peary's success and decided to make an attempt on the South Pole instead. His approach, also supported by food and fuel depots, was to be launched from the Bay of Whales on the edge of the Ross Ice Shelf, 65 miles closer to the Pole, and across the Axel Heiberg Glacier. The Amundsen expedition, in contrast to Scott's expedition, made use of sledges pulled by dogs alone. Amundsen's party of five men, which set out on October 19, 1911, reached the South Pole on December 14. Scott's party, also of five, set out on November 1, 1911, and reached the Pole on January 17. To their great disappointment, upon reaching the Pole, Scott's party found a marker flag and other items left by the Norwegians. Tragically, Scott and his men—one of them physician and zoologist EDWARD ADRIAN WILSON, who had been with Scott on his earlier Antarctic expedition—all perished upon running out of supplies while trapped in a blizzard.

Others mounted expeditions during this period. Between 1910 and 1912, WILHELM FILCHNER led the Second German Antarctic Expedition, during which he located the Filchner Ice Shelf on the Weddell Sea and Luitpold Land. In 1911, Douglas Mawson led an Australian expedition to Antarctica which located George V Land. In 1912, NOBU SHIRASE led a Japanese expedition to Antarctica, which explored the Ross Ice Shelf and King Edward VII Land. And, beginning in 1914, Ernest Henry Shackleton led the British Imperial Trans-Antarctic Expedition in an attempt to make the first crossing of the Antarctic continent, from the Weddell Sea to the Ross Sea. After the expedition's boat was trapped in ice and sunk in the Weddell Sea, the crew managed to take refuge on Elephant Island. In a now-famous incident, Shackleton and five others made a hazardous open boat voyage to South Georgia Island, crossed the island overland to a whaling settlement on the other side, and eventually rescued the rest of the crew, remarkably with no loss of life.

Aerial Exploration

Much of the subsequent Antarctic exploration was by air. In 1929–30, American RICHARD EVELYN BYRD, who had recorded the first flight over the North Pole in 1926, repeated the accomplishment over the South Pole on November 29, 1929, during the First Byrd Antarctic Expedition. Other aviators who contributed to the aerial exploration of Antarctica were Australian Douglas Mawson, who undertook aerial surveys from 1929 to 1931, and American LINCOLN ELLSWORTH, who completed the first flight across the Antarctic continent in 1935.

Byrd's Antarctic career continued into the 1950s. In the Second Byrd Antarctic Expedition of 1933 to 1935, he became the first man to survive a winter alone in Antarctica. Between 1939 and 1941, during the early years of World War II, he established bases to counter German encroachments on territory claimed by Norway. From 1947 to 1948, after the war, Byrd carried out additional aerial reconnaissance for the United States, as part of Operation Highjump, a major fleet exercise; a total of 70,000 aerial-mapping photographs were taken by the fleet's aircraft.

International Cooperation

In 1956, Byrd served as senior adviser to the U.S. Navy's Operation Deep Freeze, conducted in preparation for the INTERNATIONAL GEOPHYSICAL YEAR (IGY) of 1957–58, with Antarctic geography a primary focus. One IGY undertaking was the Commonwealth Trans-Antarctic Expedition, headed by the Englishman SIR VIVIAN ERNEST FUCHS and the New Zealander SIR EDMUND PERCIVAL HILLARY. They accomplished the first successful crossing of Antarctica. The spirit of cooperation generated around IGY led to an Antarctic Treaty, declaring the continent a nonmilitary area to be used only for scientific study; the treaty was drafted in 1959 and has been in effect since 1961. Seven nations have active land claims—Argentina, Australia, Chile, France, Great Britain, NEW ZEALAND, and Norway. The treaty did not resolve these claims, but it did put a moratorium on future claims.

Under the treaty, Antarctic research has been ongoing, with 17 nations maintaining some 40 year-round bases with rotating staffs, on the continent. Today, Antarctica serves as a laboratory of sorts for geological, biological, and environmental research. The study of Antarctica's core samples provides information to scientists and geologists regarding the evolving world climate and the effects of pollution. In 1980, the discovery of the thinning of the ozone layer, the atmospheric gas that shields Earth from harmful ultraviolet radiation, by the British Antarctic Survey has helped make the world aware of the fragility of ecosystems and has led to a reduction in the production of chlorofluorocarbons (CFCs), pollutants linked to ozone depletion. In 1990, an international team with members

This engraving shows a scene from James Cook's expedition on January 9, 1773, just before the crossing of the Antarctic Circle. It appeared in the explorer's book *A Voyage towards the South Pole,* published in 1777. *(Library of Congress, Prints and Photographs Division [LC-USZ62-77398])*

from six countries, led by American Will Steger and Frenchman Jean-Louis Etienne, used dog sleds to complete the first unmechanized crossing of the Antarctic continent—a journey of about 4,000 miles. A central purpose of the expedition was scientific research, including the measurement of ground-level ozone levels and the pollutants concentrated in Antarctic mosses and lichens.

❖

Although most of Antarctica has now been visited, its harsh environment has preserved it as one of Earth's remaining vast wilderness areas. Despite the conveniences of modern technology, travel, and research there remains a challenge similar to that faced by early explorers.

Antarctic Circle
The Antarctic Circle is a parallel of latitude, a cartographic feature based on natural phenomena, situated at 66 degrees and 33 minutes south of the EQUATOR. The circle, as defined on Earth's surface at the southern end, marks the northern limit of the area in which the Sun does not rise on the summer solstice, on or about June 22, or does not set on the winter solstice, on or about December 22. The pe-

riod of continuous night or day increases from one day along the Antarctic Circle to six months at the SOUTH POLE. The equivalent cartographic feature at the opposite northern end of Earth is the ARCTIC CIRCLE.

The Antarctic Circle was not crossed until late in the history of exploration, despite numerous expeditions in search of the GREAT SOUTHERN CONTINENT. The first recorded crossing was made by Englishman JAMES COOK on January 17, 1773. The regions within the Antarctic Circle were uninhabited until the 20th century, when outposts for scientific research were built.

See also ANTARCTIC, EXPLORATION OF THE; GEOGRAPHY AND CARTOGRAPHY; LATITUDE AND LONGITUDE; MAPS AND CHARTS.

Apollo program (Project Apollo)
The modern concept of human landing on the Moon can be traced to early writers. One such dreamer was Lucian of Samosota, a Greek, who, in A.D. 160, wrote a story of flight to the Moon on artificial wings. Another was French science fiction writer Jules Verne. In 1865, he published *From the Earth to the Moon,* in which a three-man capsule is propelled into space by an aluminum cannon. An early scientist who

began to entertain the notion of space flight was Konstantin Eduardovich Tsiolkovsky (1857–1935), a Russian inventor who was intrigued by the idea of putting an artificial SATEL-LITE into orbit around Earth. He is credited with understanding that, in order to escape Earth's gravitational pull, a series of booster rockets would be necessary, each stage falling away after its fuel was spent. In the 20th century, many important advances in the ROCKET were made, including American physicist Robert Hutchings Goddard's liquid-fuel rocket of 1926 and the German V2, the direction of which could be controlled, developed during World War II. As the cold war between Russia and the United States came into being, so too did the "space race." The Union of Soviet Socialist Republics (USSR; Soviet Union) scored a major victory with the first successful launch of an artificial satellite in October 1957, when *Sputnik 1* was deployed. The United States launched its first satellite, *Explorer 1,* in January 1958. The following July, the United States established the NATIONAL AERONAUTICS AND SPACE ADMINIS-TRATION (NASA) for the purpose of research and to carry out programs in the areas of SPACE EXPLORATION. In April 1961, Russian YURI ALEKSEYEVICH GAGARIN became the first man in space, as part of the VOSTOK PROGRAM.

In 1961, President John F. Kennedy called for the United States to land a man on the Moon and return him safely to Earth before the end of the decade. NASA organized the Apollo program in that year; it would last until 1972. Meanwhile, NASA conducted a number of programs: the MERCURY PROGRAM of 1961–63, during which ALAN BARTLETT SHEPARD, JR., became the first American in space and JOHN HERSCHELL GLENN, JR., the first American to orbit the Earth; the GEMINI PROGRAM of 1964–66, which developed techniques for the trip to the Moon; and the unmanned Surveyor Program of 1966–68, which probed the lunar surface.

Among the complex problems to be solved were the acceptable range of acceleration speeds so ASTRONAUTS would not be crushed during liftoff, and the safe return through Earth's atmosphere, since friction created by air molecules would tend to incinerate a spacecraft.

Experiments and missions were carried out continuously by both the United States and Soviet Union. The Soviet Union had several firsts, but American technology slowly gained the advantage. The United States launched its own first successful Lunar Orbiter in August 1966, taking pictures of the Moon with the goal of charting appropriate landing sites for the manned mission. Through November 1968, 12 Lunar Orbiters and Surveyors were launched.

To propel the astronauts into orbit, a three-stage Saturn V rocket was used. The Apollo Spacecraft itself also consisted of three parts: the command module, the service module, and the lunar module. The total apparatus was 363 feet high and weighed 3,000 tons.

Once Moon orbit was achieved, the lunar module disconnected from the command module and service module, descending to the Moon's surface. After exploration, the ascent stage of the lunar module detached from the descent stage, re-docking with the command module. The service module was released just prior to reentry into Earth's atmosphere.

The loss of the three-person crew of *Apollo 1* by fire on the launching pad in 1967 did not lessen the resolve of the United States to be first in placing a human on the Moon. The goal was achieved on July 20, 1969, with the *Apollo 11* mission. NEIL ALDEN ARMSTRONG became the first human to walk on the Moon's surface, followed closely by Edwin "Buzz" Aldrin, Jr., while Michael Collins orbited the Moon in the command module.

There were a total of 17 missions that went under the Apollo name. Of the 12 manned missions, two went into Earth orbit (*Apollo 7* and *Apollo 9*); two went into lunar orbit (*Apollo 8* and *Apollo 10*); six landed on the Moon (*Apollo 11, Apollo 12, Apollo 14, Apollo 15, Apollo 16,* and *Apollo 17*), the final three making use of the Lunar Roving Vehicle (LRV) for wide-ranging exploration; one was lost during a test on the launch pad (*Apollo 1*); and one returned to Earth without having made its scheduled lunar landing (*Apollo 13*). Much scientific knowledge was gathered over the course of the Apollo missions, including information on seismic activities, magnetic fields, heat flows, and volcanic history. Close to 900 pounds of rocks and other physical samples were brought back to Earth, as well as 30,000 high-resolution photographs of the Moon from orbit and from the surface. The landing on the Moon and video footage of other Apollo missions has also created historic television moments.

Appalachian Mountains

The Appalachian Mountains, the second-largest mountain system in North America after the ROCKY MOUNTAINS, extend 1,500 miles from the St. Lawrence Valley in Quebec to the Gulf Coast plain in northern Alabama. The range's width varies from 100 to 300 miles. An old mountain range and much eroded, the greatest elevations are found along eastern parts, with plateau formations to the west. Peaks range in height from about 1,500 feet to 6,684 feet above sea level.

The Appalachians are discussed as three subdivisions: northern, central, and southern. The northern division extends from the Notre Dame and Shickshock Mountains of Quebec and includes the Highlands of Maine, the White Mountains of New Hampshire, and the Green Mountains of Vermont. The central division contains the Catskill Mountains of New York; the Blue Ridge Mountains of western Virginia, eastern West Virginia, western North Carolina, and northern Georgia; the Great Smoky Mountains of western North Carolina and eastern Tennessee; and the Allegheny Mountains of Pennsylvania, Maryland, Virginia, and West Virginia (to the west of the Blue Ridge). The southern division includes the Cumberland Plateau running along the southwestern border of Virginia and southeastern Kentucky, eastern Tennessee, northern Georgia, and northeastern Alabama; and the Cumberland Mountains, the high narrow mountains forming part of the Kentucky state line and separated from the Cumberland Plateau by the Cumberland River Valley. The Black Mountains, a spur of the Blue Ridge in western North Carolina, contain the highest peaks in the Appalachian chain; Mount Mitchell near Asheville, North Carolina, at 6,684 feet, is the tallest.

The Appalachians include a number of valley systems. The Hudson River Valley in New York is one of the largest valleys. The Great Valley extending southward from the Hudson River Valley comprises a number of smaller valleys in Pennsylvania, Maryland, Virginia, Tennessee, and Alabama. What is known as the Ridge-and-Valley Province, with long sharp ridges and narrow valleys, is bordered on the west by the Cumberland and Allegheny Mountains, on the north by the Alleghenies, and on the south by the Blue Ridge and Great Smoky Mountains.

The Appalachians are divided by both water gaps and wind gaps. Water gaps are valleys with rivers running through them; wind gaps are dry valleys. The CUMBERLAND GAP in the Cumberland Plateau is one of the most famous wind gaps because of its role as a natural pass for the westward movement of pioneers.

In terms of watershed, the Appalachians serve as the eastern Great Divide. Rivers on the eastern side empty into the Atlantic Ocean; those on the western side empty into the Gulf of Mexico. Among the largest are the Connecticut, Delaware, Hudson, James, Potomac, Rappahannock, Schuylkill, and Susquehanna Rivers, which flow eastward or southeastward; and the Allegany, Cumberland, Kanawha, Monongahela, and Tennessee Rivers, which flow westward.

The Appalachians presented an obstacle to western expansion. The earliest European explorers followed narrow Indian trails across them. In the north, rivers and the Great Lakes provided access to the west of the Appalachians. The first European crossing of the Appalachians was accomplished by the Spanish under HERNANDO DE SOTO during their meandering trek through the Southeast in 1539–43. After wintering near the Gulf of Mexico in northern Florida in 1539–40, the CONQUISTADORES headed northward through present-day Georgia and South Carolina into North Carolina. In May and June 1540, they crossed a section of the great range into what is now eastern Tennessee. Their exact route is unknown; they may have journeyed through the Great Smoky Mountains or south of them across the Blue Ridge. From there, they followed the Tennessee River southwestward, crossing through the northwest corner of Georgia into Alabama, and eventually reached the MISSISSIPPI RIVER far to the west.

17th Century

Europeans did not venture into the Appalachians again until the next century. In the far north, starting in 1603, the French established a presence in what is now eastern Canada under SAMUEL DE CHAMPLAIN and explored parts of the northern extent of the mountain chain. In 1615–16, ÉTIENNE BRÛLÉ, working for Champlain, explored the entire length of the Susquehanna River from present-day New York to Chesapeake Bay in Maryland and viewed other sections of the mountain system on his return to Montreal. Over the next decades, French Jesuit missionaries pushed into Indian lands in part of the Appalachian system, such as ISAAC JOGUES, among the Mohawk in the northern Catskills. The French, however, for the most part explored westward from their settlements along the St. Lawrence River to the western Great Lakes, then southward, thus bypassing the Appalachians. In the same period, some Dutch traders also ventured westward into the Catskills, but on a limited basis.

The English, who settled to the south along the Atlantic coast, where the Appalachians are the tallest, had no easy route westward. After the founding of Jamestown, Virginia, in 1607, it took many years for colonists to travel beyond the Piedmont Region between the coast and the mountains. An early expedition was headed by German-born physician JOHN LEDERER in 1669–70; he explored the Piedmont and Blue Ridge of Virginia and North Carolina on behalf of the Virginia colony. In the early 1670s, colonial military officer ABRAHAM WOOD sponsored a number of exploratory expeditions out of Fort Henry near present-day Petersburg, Virginia, to the Appalachian frontier of Virginia and North Carolina. In 1671, THOMAS BATTS and ROBERT FALLAM crossed the Blue Ridge and reached the Kanawha and New River Valleys of present-day West Virginia for him. Two years later, GABRIEL ARTHUR and JAMES NEEDHAM reached Tennessee. Over the next years, it was mostly traders to Indian tribes who traveled into the highlands.

18th Century

Travel into the Appalachians was rare until the 18th century. In 1716, ALEXANDER SPOTSWOOD, lieutenant governor of Virginia, headed an expedition through the James River gap in the Blue Ridge to the Shenandoah Valley of western Virginia. From 1713 until the 1740s, German-born CONRAD WEISER traveled throughout western New York and Pennsylvania as an interpreter, guide, and Indian agent. Traders and frontiersmen such as JAMES ADAIR, DANIEL BOONE, THOMAS CRESAP, GEORGE CROGHAN, JOHN FINLEY, CHRISTOPHER GIST, SIMON KENTON, JAMES ROBERTSON, and JAMES SMITH explored the Appalachian and trans-Appalachian country starting in the mid-17th century. Hunters sought game to the west of the mountains; with time, settlers sought lands.

As trails and passes were located, land grants were assigned. In the 1750s, Gist and Cresap developed an Indian trail from the Potomac in western Maryland through the Alleghenies to the Monongahela River in western Pennsylvania, which, soon afterward, during the French and Indian War of 1754–63, became known as Braddock's Road when widened to wagon width, after British general Edward Braddock (the first leg would become known as the National Road). In 1758, also during the French and Indian War, British general John Forbes built another road north of Braddock's Road, to advance on Fort Duquesne (present-day Pittsburgh) through the Alleghenies. A postwar extension joined the eastern end of the road with Philadelphia. In 1750, physician THOMAS WALKER led a surveying party through the Cumberland Gap of the Blue Ridge into what is now eastern Kentucky. In 1775, the Transylvania Land Company hired Daniel Boone and 30 others to open the Wilderness Road, from Fort Chiswell in the Shenandoah Valley through the Cumberland Gap, as a route to the Ohio Valley.

❖

These days the Appalachians are widely used for camping and hiking. Modern-day trails give a sense of exploration in prior centuries.

See also NORTH AMERICA, EXPLORATION OF.

Arab exploration   See MUSLIM EXPLORATION.

archaeology and exploration

Archaeology, a branch of anthropology involving the study of material remains of human cultures, is a form of exploration in its own right—exploration of the material past. In its search for physical evidence, archaeological studies provide the only source of information for the prehistoric period and supplement the written record for the historic period. Yet, since archaeology potentially looks at every part of the world ever inhabited or traveled by humans and since the discipline requires fieldwork, including surveys of possible sites and excavation of them, it has taken its practitioners to remote places, thereby contributing to world exploration in the broader sense. And, in some instances, archaeological discoveries resulted from exploration for other purposes.

The fields of archaeology include the following: prehistoric archaeology, archaeology of early and classical civilizations, historical archaeology, and underwater archaeology.

Studies are made of a variety of antiquities: human fossils; food remains; ruins of buildings; and artifacts such as tools, pottery, and jewelry. Some archaeologists use skills from other disciplines—chemistry, zoology, botany, geology, and geography—in specialized fields of archaeological studies. Paleoanthropology, the study of ancient human remains, uses archaeological methods. Archaeology began taking shape in the 18th century, became defined as a formal discipline in the 19th century, and was refined in the 20th century with more exacting methods of excavation and statistical sampling.

Most early archaeological studies were conducted in Europe, the Middle East, and the Americas. As early as the 15th century, excavations of Greek sculpture were carried out in Italy. Pioneers of classical archaeology include the German Johann Joachim Winckelmann, who, in the 18th century, laid the foundation for modern scientific archaeology with studies of the ancient Greeks and Romans, and the Italian Ennio Quirino Visconti, who studied Greek and Roman antiquities in the 18th century and into the 19th century. Heinrich Schliemann, the German who located the ruins of Troy in Turkey in the 19th century, and Sir Arthur Evans, the Englishman who uncovered the remains of an Aegean civilization of the Minoans in Crete in the early 20th century, captured the public's imagination with their discoveries. The finding in 1799 of the Rosetta Stone, an inscribed basalt slab giving the key to hieroglyphics of the ancient Egyptians, by troops accompanying Napoléon Bonaparte to North Africa, is considered the beginning of Egyptology, a branch of classical archaeology that centers its studies solely on ancient Egyptian culture.

Another important event in the shaping of archaeology is Danish archaeologist Christian Thomsen's classification in 1836 of three ages of human development in Europe, based on the principal materials used for tools: the Stone Age, the Bronze Age, and the Iron Age.

In the first part of the 19th century, there was a growing awareness of ancient American civilizations. In 1820, Caleb Atwater of Massachusetts published *Description of the Antiquities Discovered in the State of Ohio and Other Western States,* leading to increasing studies of earthworks and, over the next decades, an awareness of the Adena and Hopewell Indian mound-building cultures. In 1849, U.S. Army lieutenant JAMES HERVEY SIMPSON came upon Anasazi Indian ruins at Chaco Canyon in New Mexico and Canyon de Chelly in Arizona while on a military reconnaissance in New Mexico.

In 1911, American historian HIRAM BINGHAM located ruins of the great Inca civilization at Machu Picchu in Peru. The publication, in 1941 and 1943, of John Lloyd Stephens's accounts of his travels to Central America generated interest in the Maya and other pre-Columbian civilizations of the Americas and helped lead to growing archaeological activity.

Beginning in the late 19th century and early 20th century, British archaeologists, such as JAMES THEODORE BENT and GERTRUDE MARGARET BELL, carried out pioneering studies in the Middle East. In 1906–08, SIR MARC AUREL STEIN, an Anglo-Hungarian archaeologist, followed a stretch of the ancient SILK ROAD into western China and discovered the Caves of the Thousand Buddhas, a series of temples built into caves, at Tunhuang. The 1947 discovery of the Dead Sea Scrolls, fragments of the Hebrew Bible written by members of an early Christian sect, gave biblical archaeology new impetus.

The youngest branch of archaeology is underwater archaeology, in which shipwrecks and ruins of buildings lying beneath water are investigated. The development of specialized diving equipment, such as the SUBMERSIBLE, SUBMARINE, and the remotely operated vehicle (ROV), has made such studies possible.

Archaeology is now conducted around the world, with remarkable discoveries and new insights gained on a regular basis. Modern archaeologists, who travel widely and spend time in harsh landscapes on an endless quest, continue the spirit of world exploration.

See also EGYPTIAN EXPLORATION; GREEK EXPLORATION; MINOAN EXPLORATION; ROMAN EXPLORATION.

Arctic, exploration of the

The Arctic, unlike the Antarctic at the opposite end of the Earth, is a region and not a continent. It includes the northernmost of Earth's four oceans—the Arctic Ocean—as well as land areas, including the northern parts of three continents—North America, Europe, and Asia—and numerous islands. Most of the Arctic Ocean and many of the land areas are covered in ice year round, making it resemble the ice-covered landmass of Antarctica.

The term *Arctic,* derived from the Greek word *arktos* for "bear"—because the region is under the constellation known as the Bear—is applied variously. One definition is the area north of the ARCTIC CIRCLE, the parallel of latitude situated at 66 degrees 33 minutes, marking the point at which the Sun neither sets on the day of summer solstice nor rises on the day of winter solstice. Another broader definition is the area north of the summer isotherm, a shifting cartographic line where the average annual temperature is 32 degrees Fahrenheit or less and the mean temperature for the warmest summer month is 50 degrees Fahrenheit. The Arctic is also defined as the area north of the tree line, beyond which trees do not grow. (The tree line corresponds roughly to the summer isotherm.)

Arctic winters are long and severe, with few hours of daylight. Although there is little precipitation, gale-force winds stir up surface snow and create blizzard conditions and enormous drifts. Coastal regions generally have warmer temperatures and heavier precipitation than colder and drier inland regions.

The ancient continental shields—regions composed mostly of the igneous rock granite and the metamorphic rock gneiss—of North America, Europe, and Asia surround a large basin occupied by the Arctic Ocean, the smallest of the Earth's four oceans. The Arctic Ocean extends south from the NORTH POLE, the northernmost place on Earth, to the north coasts of the three continents. It opens to the Atlantic Ocean between northern Europe and eastern GREENLAND, with ICELAND in the middle; and between northern North America (and its islands) and western Greenland through the Davis Strait. It opens to the Pacific Ocean through the BERING STRAIT between northwestern North America and northeastern Asia. Among the larger rivers emptying into the Arctic Ocean are the Mackenzie and Coppermine Rivers in North America, and the Ob, Yenisey, and Lena Rivers in Asia. The total surface area of the Arctic Ocean is 5.4 million square miles. The following seas are part of the Arctic Ocean: Norwegian, Barents, Kara, Laptev, East Siberian, Chukchi, Beaufort, and Greenland. HUDSON BAY, linked to the Arctic Ocean via the Foxe Channel and the Atlantic Ocean via the Hudson Strait, can be considered an arm of either ocean. The deepest point in the Arctic Ocean is 17,880 feet, but the average depth is a relatively shallow 4,300 feet because of the shallow expanses on the continental shelves. Most of the Arctic Ocean is frozen all year, other than an area north of Scandinavia and northeast of Iceland. During the brief summer, the PACK ICE thaws and open water, containing some DRIFT ICE, appears along much of coastal Alaska, Canada, and SIBERIA.

The islands of the Arctic Ocean lie on the continental shelves extending from the continents. Greenland, to the northeast of North America, is the largest island in the region. Part of Greenland, as well as all of Iceland to its east, lies south of the Arctic Circle. The Canadian Arctic Archipelago—including Victoria Island, Ellesmere Island, Baffin Island, and the Queen Elizabeth Islands—extends north and east along the northern North American mainland. North of Scandinavia lies the archipelago of Svalbard (formerly known as Spitsbergen). North of Russia are Franz Josef Land, Novaya Zemlya, Severnaya Zemlya, the New Siberian Islands, and Wrangel Island.

The treeless coastal plains known as tundra extend throughout much of the Arctic. The subsoil remains frozen all year in a condition known as permafrost. As a result, surface water does not drain, creating numerous lakes, ponds, marshlands, and mud, along with fog. Little vegetation grows other than mosses, lichens, and scrub brush. Mountain ranges and low plateaus rise up from the plains especially in northern Alaska, the Yukon territory, and northeastern Siberia. Of the islands, Ellesmere Island, Baffin Island, Iceland, and Greenland consist predominantly of

Frederick Albert Cook took this photograph during his travels to Arctic regions in the late 19th or early 20th century. *(Library of Congress, Prints and Photographs Division [LC-USZ62-128023])*

highlands; Greenland in fact is a high plateau covered year round by an ice cap, except along its coasts.

Arctic fauna include many species of fish; aquatic mammals, such as the whale, walrus, and seal; and land mammals, such as moose, caribou, reindeer, musk ox, polar bear, wolf, fox, hare, and squirrel. In springtime, birds migrate to Arctic regions. Insects breed during the short summers, especially in marshlands.

Because of its harsh conditions, the Arctic has been sparsely populated over the centuries. Yet, long before the region came to be mapped, humans survived there for centuries. It is thought that the Arctic's earliest inhabitants, various peoples of Mongolic stock, migrated northward from central Asia and spread westward into Europe and eastward into North America. Major groups include the Sami (Lapps) and Komi (Zyrian) of Europe; the Samoyed (Nentsy) of western Russia; the Yakut, Tungus, Yukaghir, and Chukchi of eastern Russia; and the Inuit (Eskimo) and Aleut of North America.

Earliest Voyages to the Arctic

Greek scholar PYTHEAS of the fourth century B.C. was the first known European traveler to extreme northern latitudes. His account of his journey six days north of the British Isles, perhaps near or across the Arctic Circle, has not survived, but later geographers, such as Greek STRABO and Roman PLINY THE ELDER of the first century A.D., commented on his observations regarding ULTIMA THULE, supposedly the northernmost lands. Strabo was skeptical in regard to Pytheas's claims.

During the Middle Ages, Irish monks, such as SAINT BRENDAN, ventured out into the Atlantic on sea pilgrimages. Some of them established colonies on the uninhabited Iceland by A.D. 800. Yet, they were not known to have reached the Arctic Circle just to the north of Iceland.

The VIKINGS, accomplished navigators, explored northern waters and very likely crossed into the Arctic waters from their Scandinavian lands. Two early Norsemen known to have reached Iceland are NADDOD and GARDAR SVARSSON in the ninth century. The Norse presence drove away the Irish settlers. In the late 10th century, ERIC THE RED reached Greenland. Both Iceland and Greenland were colonized. His son LEIF ERICSSON is thought to have reached the Arctic regions of North America at the start of the 11th century. He came into contact with a people the Vikings referred to as *Skraelings,* who were very likely Inuit.

At about the same time, Norwegians and Russians reached the Arctic coast of northern Europe and established contacts for purposes of taxation and trade with indigenous peoples.

Passage to the Far East

Arctic exploration during what is known as the EUROPEAN AGE OF EXPLORATION, beginning in the 15th century, revolved primarily around the search for practical trade routes from Europe to the Far East. Some mariners sought an eastward route from the Atlantic to the Pacific north of Europe and Asia by way of the Arctic Ocean—a NORTHEAST PASSAGE. Others sought a westward route through the Americas—a NORTHWEST PASSAGE. All the great European powers of the time—Portugal, Spain, the Netherlands, England, and France—launched expeditions in search of one or both passages. With the geography of much of Europe and Asia well known, expeditions in search of the Northeast Passage traveled directly to northern latitudes. In the decades after the European discovery of the Americas in 1492 by CHRISTOPHER COLUMBUS—an Italian mariner sailing for Spain—many expeditions explored the coasts of both North and South America—exploring bays and rivers—before narrowing down the search for a Northwest Passage to the extreme north.

Early Portuguese Expeditions

Portuguese mariner GASPAR CÔRTE-REAL claimed to have made a voyage in 1499, in the course of which he explored the seas to the west of Greenland. He also claimed he had found the entrance to the Strait of Anian (see ANIAN, STRAIT OF), another name for the Northwest Passage. In 1500, he carried out a documented voyage into Davis Strait along the west coast of Greenland before being forced back by pack ice. On this journey he very likely crossed the Arctic Circle, becoming the first European to do so since the time of the Vikings. Côrte-Real's ship disappeared after heading southward.

Another Portuguese explorer, JOÃO FERNANDES, is thought to have led a Portuguese maritime expedition to North America, also in 1500 and also reaching Greenland. Other Portuguese for a time carried voyages to northeastern North America to reach the fishing grounds off Newfoundland but, having established an eastward water route to Asia around the tip of Africa and having established a foothold in the Americas in Brazil, carried out no more explorations to the Arctic. Spain, Portugal's chief competitor at the time, also concentrated its efforts to the south, fanning out from the Caribbean Sea.

Early British Expeditions

Italian JOHN CABOT, who made the earliest transatlantic voyages for England and reached northeastern North America, also neared Arctic waters. John Cabot possibly explored southwestern Greenland in his voyage of 1497, and one of his three sons, SEBASTIAN CABOT, possibly entered the Hudson Strait between the North American mainland and Baffin Island, and perhaps even reached eastern Hudson Bay, while in search of the Northwest Passage in 1509, although there is no documentation to determine how far west he actually reached.

Sebastian Cabot was the first governor of the London-based MUSCOVY COMPANY, the primary purpose of which was to locate the Northeast Passage. As such, he sponsored expeditions under HUGH WILLOUGHBY, RICHARD CHANCELLOR, and STEPHEN BOROUGH to the Arctic Ocean north of Europe in the 1550s, during which the two islands of Novaya Zemlya ("New Land" in Russian) north of Russia were reached. Willoughby also became the first Englishman to cross the Arctic Circle. The Muscovy Company continued to back other expeditions over the next years, among them a 1607 expedition headed by HENRY HUDSON. Hudson sailed westward to Greenland, exploring its east coast, then, returning east and north, he came upon Spitsbergen. On a second trip in 1608, he took the more conventional route—directly north and east—and explored Novaya Zemlya but was forced back by ice.

In the meantime, in the latter part of the 16th century, geographer SIR HUMPHREY GILBERT once again promoted the idea of a Northwest Passage. In 1576–78, SIR MARTIN FROBISHER headed three British expeditions to northern Canada, just south of the Arctic Circle, during which he made the European discovery of Frobisher Bay on southeastern Baffin Island. He also entered the Hudson Strait. In 1585–87, JOHN DAVIS also headed three expeditions to some of these same waters, exploring the strait named after him, reaching the northernmost latitude known attained until that time.

British expeditions to the region continued into the 17th century. In 1605–07, JAMES HALL, who had carried out three expeditions to western Greenland for Denmark and drafted charts of Greenland's west coast, also headed one for British merchants in 1612, during which he was killed by an Inuit for having kidnapped other Inuit on an earlier voyage. Henry Hudson sailed all the way through Hudson Strait and made what is considered the European discovery of Hudson Bay in 1610–11. Both are named for him. After wintering on James Bay, the southern extent of Hudson Bay, the crew mutinied; Hudson, his son, and some ailing crew members were set adrift in a small boat and were never seen again. SIR THOMAS BUTTON headed a follow-up expedition to the Hudson Bay in 1612–13, reaching the mouth of the Nelson River and exploring the coast of Southampton Island. WILLIAM BAFFIN, who had sailed with James Hall in 1612, and ROBERT BYLOT carried out two expeditions. The first, in 1615, took them to Hudson Bay's northwest coast and Foxe Basin, leading to a determination that Hudson Bay provided no navigable outlet for a Northwest Passage (although later explorers would search the region again). The second, in 1616, took them along the west coast of Greenland into Baffin Bay and along the northeastern Baffin Island (both were named for Baffin) as far north as Lancaster Sound between Baffin Island and Devon Island. They found the sound impassable because of ice conditions. Their northernmost record would endure for 200 years. (It would later be determined that Lancaster Sound was in fact the eastern entrance to a water route between the Atlantic and the Pacific.) In 1631, LUKE FOXE, and, in 1631–32, THOMAS JAMES, further explored Hudson Bay.

Danish Expeditions

Denmark launched its own expeditions to the Arctic regions in the early 17th century, sponsored by King Christian IV, known as the Danish Sailor King because of his efforts to make Denmark a maritime power. The Danish monarch hoped to reestablish contact with the Viking colonies after a lapse of two centuries. British mariner James Hall sailed for him in 1605 and again in 1606, reaching the west coast. No Scandinavian colonists were found, but the Danes had contact with the Inuit. An expedition the next year failed to reach Greenland. In 1619–20, Danish mariner JENS ERIKSEN MUNK sailed to Hudson Bay in search of the Northwest Passage and explored the Churchill River region.

Dutch Expeditions

Beginning in the late 16th century, the Dutch launched expeditions to the northern waters for purposes of trade and in the hope of navigating the Northeast Passage. The White Sea Trading Company, founded in 1565, backed a number of attempts. OLIVIER BRUNEL led two of them in 1584–85. Having reached the Ob River overland from Moscow, he hoped to reach its mouth by way of the Kara Sea. His passage was blocked by ice both times around Novaya Zemlya.

The Dutch launched many other expeditions to the region, three of them in the 1590s involving the navigator WILLEM BARENTS. Geographer JAN HUYGHEN VAN LINSCHOTEN, a principal backer, participated in the first two. The waters around Novaya Zemlya proved the westernmost limits of the Dutch expeditions of the period, although, during the first expedition in 1594, Linschoten's ship managed to pass along the southern end of Novaya Zemlya and enter the Kara Sea. On his third expedition in 1596–97, Barents headed north of Norway, charted Bear Island, and reached Spitsbergen, the first European to do so since the Vikings. He proceeded eastward and entered the Kara Sea north of Novaya Zemlya. After a difficult winter, Barents perished from SCURVY.

In 1609, after his earlier expeditions for the Muscovy Company, Englishman Henry Hudson, in the employ of the DUTCH EAST INDIA COMPANY, carried out another attempt to locate the Northeast Passage. He approached Novaya Zemlya once again, but, because of icy conditions, he headed westward across the Atlantic to the Americas and investigated the coast of Newfoundland and the Hudson River. As these expeditions seemed to prove the Kara Sea unnavigable, both the Dutch and the English turned their attention to the rich fishing and whaling grounds near Spitsbergen.

Russian Expeditions

In the mid-17th century, the Russians—especially Russian Cossacks—began exploring Arctic regions of Siberia overland from the west. In the 1640s–50s, MIKHAIL STADUKHIN, with a party of Cossacks, explored the Arctic coast of Siberia around the Kolyma River and on the Gulf of Anadyr. The earliest recorded sighting of the BERING STRAIT was by Cossacks led by SEMYON IVANOVICH DEZHNEV in 1648.

The following century, Czar Peter the Great sponsored a number of expeditions to northeastern Siberia and both the Arctic and Pacific Oceans, among them the First Kamchatka Expedition of 1725–30, under VITUS JONASSEN BERING, a Danish explorer in service to Russia, and Russian naval officer ALEKSEY ILYICH CHIRIKOV. Bering first charted the Bering Strait in 1728; the strait was subsequently named for him. Starting in 1733, Bering and Chirikov also led the Great Northern Expedition to the Arctic and Pacific coasts of Siberia, during which they explored the Gulf of Anadyr and the Chukchi Sea, crossed the Bering Strait, and, in 1741, made the European discovery of Alaska. Bering, along with 18 of his crew, perished from scurvy in the fall of that year. In 1742–43, SIMEON CHELYUSKIN, also part of the Great Northern Expedition, explored along the Arctic coast from the White Sea to the Leptev Sea, in the course of which he rounded Cape Chelyuskin, the northernmost point of Asia.

The Russians continued explorations of northern Siberia and the Arctic Ocean. In 1760–62, IVAN BAKHOV navigated from the Lena River eastward to the mouth of the Kolyma River. The next year, STEPAN ANDREYEV traveled overland from Fort Anadyr on the Bering Sea to the Arctic coast. While exploring the Bear Islands opposite the mouth of the Kolyma River, he sighted New Siberia Island, part of the island group known as the New Siberian Islands, thus making the European discovery of that group. In the Northeastern Secret Geographical and Astronomical Expedition of 1785–93, searching for the Northeast Passage, Englishman JOSEPH BILLINGS, along with ANTON BATAKOV and GAVRIIL ANDREYEVICH SARYCHEV, explored the Chukchi Peninsula and the Bering Strait.

The Fur Companies

The late 18th century saw renewed activity in the Arctic, especially by fur companies. The establishment of the HUD-

SON'S BAY COMPANY in 1670 to develop the FUR TRADE with Native Americans and the settlement of Hudson Bay led to a number of expeditions; among them were ones led by JAMES KNIGHT and HENRY KELSEY to the Marble Island region off the bay's northwest coast, in 1719–21. All members of Knight's expedition perished, leading to Kelsey's subsequent search expeditions. In 1741, CHRISTOPHER MIDDLETON explored Wager Bay and Repulse Bay on the west coast. And, in 1746–47, WILLIAM MOOR explored Chesterfield Inlet and reexplored Wager Bay.

In the 1760s–70s, SAMUEL HEARNE led a number of overland expeditions from the west coast of Hudson Bay for the Hudson's Bay Company. The company's charter included an obligation to search for the Northwest Passage as a shipping route to the Pacific Ocean. On his third expedition, with the help of Chipewyan Indian guide MATON-ABBEE, Hearne followed the Coppermine River northward, reaching its mouth on the Arctic Ocean in July 1771. On the return journey Hearne made the European discovery of the Great Slave Lake.

The NORTH WEST COMPANY, organized in 1779, also sponsored northern expeditions. In 1789, ALEXANDER MACKENZIE, a fur trader for the North West Company, explored from Great Slave Lake along the Mackenzie River, named after him, to its mouth on the Arctic Ocean.

Also in the late 18th and early 19th centuries, the RUSSIAN-AMERICAN COMPANY sent out expeditions, exploring coastal and interior Alaska.

Renewed British Efforts

Starting in the late 18th century and well into the 19th century, Britain began looking to the Arctic once again, in large part in the hope of navigating the Northwest Passage. The government continued to have a role as a sponsor. The ROYAL SOCIETY, a scientific organization founded in 1670, also played a part as did the Hudson's Bay Company.

The Royal Society was the principal backer of the first scientific attempt on the North Pole. In 1773, naval officer CONSTANTINE JOHN PHIPPS headed an expedition of two ships with reinforced hulls to resist ice. Although passage north was blocked by ice east of Greenland and the expedition fell far short of its goal, Phipps's writings on Arctic navigation proved useful to later explorers. A British whaler and his son, WILLIAM SCORESBY, SR., and WILLIAM SCORESBY, JR., reported to the Royal Society, at the time headed by SIR JOSEPH BANKS, about their findings relating to Arctic navigation and natural science during whaling expeditions in 1806–17.

Beginning in 1818, SIR JOHN BARROW, second secretary of the Admiralty and later one of the founders of the ROYAL GEOGRAPHICAL SOCIETY, organized a number of expeditions for the British government to the Arctic. Among those who sailed for him were SIR JOHN ROSS, DAVID BUCHAN,

SIR WILLIAM EDWARD PARRY, SIR JOHN FRANKLIN, SIR GEORGE BACK, and FREDERICK WILLIAM BEECHEY. In 1818, Ross explored Lancaster Sound in the Canadian Arctic, and Buchan led an attempt on the North Pole by a hoped-for seaward passage due north. Ross mistakenly concluded that the sound was enclosed by a mountain, and Buchan would be repelled by ice. In 1819–27, Parry led four Arctic expeditions, the first three to the Canadian Arctic. He passed through Barrow Strait and reached as far west as Melville Island; explored Hudson Bay and Foxe Basin and the Fury and Hecla Strait between the Melville Peninsula and Baffin Island; explored the Gulf of Boothia and Prince Regent Inlet; and set a northernmost record in an attempt to reach the North Pole by small flat-bottom boats and sledges from Spitsbergen. In 1819–22, Franklin headed a British naval overland expedition eastward along Canada's Arctic coast from the mouth of the Coppermine River, along Coronation Gulf, to Kent Peninsula. Beechey, in his 1825–28 expedition to the Pacific, reached Point Barrow on the north coast of Alaska. And in 1833–35, Back led an overland expedition north and east of the Great Slave Lake, locating what became known as the Back River and exploring the Arctic coastline.

John Ross and his nephew, SIR JAMES CLARK ROSS, headed a privately funded expedition in 1829–33, during which they explored the Boothia Peninsula and determined the location of the NORTH MAGNETIC POLE (the exact northern point of Earth's magnetic polarity). In 1837–39, THOMAS SIMPSON and PETER WARREN DEASE, in the employ of the Hudson's Bay Company, surveyed much of the Arctic coastline of Alaska and Canada.

In Search of Franklin

In 1845, the year of Barrow's retirement from the Admiralty, Sir John Franklin led another British naval expedition to the Canadian Arctic in an attempt to navigate the Northwest Passage from east to west. The *Erebus,* under Franklin's command, along with the *Terror,* under Lieutenant FRANCIS RAWDON MOIRA CROZIER, sailed from England on May 29, 1845; the ships were last seen by a Scottish whaling vessel on July 26, 1845, in upper Baffin Bay, west of Greenland, near the approach to Lancaster Sound. By 1847, without any word from or of the expedition, concern began to mount. Over the next decades, some 50 expeditions, involving approximately 2,000 men, were launched to solve the mystery of what happened to the Franklin expedition (see SEARCHES FOR MISSING EXPLORERS).

In 1847–49, SIR JOHN RICHARDSON, along with JOHN RAE of the Hudson's Bay Company, led a British land-based expedition that reached Canada's Arctic coastline by way of the Mackenzie River, then proceeded eastward to Dolphin and Union Strait. In 1849–50, Rae continued the search on his own, reaching Victoria Island. In 1848–49, Sir James

Clark Ross led a British naval expedition that traveled through Lancaster Sound as far as Barrow Strait and southward from Somerset Island into Peel Strait. In 1850–51, Sir John Ross returned to the Arctic on a privately funded expedition and wintered in Barrow Strait. In 1850–54, SIR ROBERT JOHN LE MESURIER MCCLURE led an expedition that entered Arctic waters from the west by way of the Bering Strait. While proceeding eastward, he located Prince of Wales Strait between Banks Island and Victoria Island; he also reached a point far enough west—Melville Island, which had previously been reached from the east—to prove that the Northwest Passage did in fact exist. At about the same time, in 1850–55, SIR RICHARD COLLINSON, also approaching from the west, explored the Arctic coasts of Alaska and Canada as far east as Victoria Island. Spending the winter of 1852–53 there, he retrieved some pieces of iron from Inuit that had probably come from one of Franklin's ships. Also during this period, in 1852–54, SIR EDWARD BELCHER headed an expedition from the east that navigated west of Lancaster Sound. SIR FRANCIS LEOPOLD MCCLINTOCK located Eglington Island and Prince Patrick Island at the edge of the Beaufort Sea.

Meanwhile, in 1848, Lady JANE FRANKLIN had offered a reward for the rescue of her husband or for information as to his fate. She later gained the support of American shipping magnate Henry Grinnell, who, in 1850–51, sent out an expedition under EDWIN JESSE DE HAVEN, a U.S. naval officer. While trapped in the pack ice north of Baffin Island and Lancaster Sound and drifting with it for some 1,000 miles, De Haven located Grinnell Land on northern Devon Island. Lady Franklin paid for a number of expeditions from her own funds as well. In 1853–55, ELISHA KENT KANE, another naval officer who had sailed with De Haven, led the second U.S. Grinnell expedition in search of John Franklin. On this voyage, expedition members explored Greenland's Humboldt Glacier and Ellesmere Island.

The expedition that located the first irrefutable proof of the missing Franklin expedition was headed by John Rae. In his expedition of 1853–54, during which he explored the Boothia Peninsula and located a strait (Rae Strait), thus proving that King William Island was not connected to the Canadian mainland, he interviewed an Inuit who told him of a story of Europeans marching southward from King William Island toward the estuary of the Back River and eventually perishing. Rae also found relics from the Franklin expedition. Yet, Rae also reported that evidence indicated expedition members had practiced cannibalism in their final days.

In 1857, Lady Franklin sponsored another expedition, headed by Francis McClintock. McClintock approached from the east and Baffin Bay. While in Arctic waters, he erected a monument on Beechey Island commemorating Franklin's Arctic exploits. He also circumnavigated King William Island, confirming that it was an island. On King William Island, a party under McClintock found a sledge and several skeletons. Another party led by Lieutenant W. R. Hopson crossed Simpson Strait to the Boothia Peninsula and found letters written by Franklin's men indicating that Franklin and other expedition members had died while the ship had been icebound and that the survivors under Lieutenant Crozier had perished while heading for Fort Resolution, a Hudson's Bay Company's post on the Back River. McClintock returned to England with his reports in 1859.

Other expeditions continued to search for more clues. In 1860–62, CHARLES FRANCIS HALL, backed by Henry Grinnell, explored Frobisher Bay, where he found evidence of Frobisher's expedition centuries before. On still another expedition funded by Grinnell in 1864–69, Hall sailed to King William Island and Boothia Peninsula, and, from Inuit in the region, he obtained relics of the Franklin expedition. He also located a skeleton. In 1878–80, FREDERICK SCHWATKA, sponsored by the AMERICAN GEOGRAPHICAL SOCIETY and a whaling company, traveled overland by sledge from Hudson Bay to King William Island, covering more than 3,000 miles. He, too, found artifacts and human remains from the Franklin expedition.

Many Nations

The search for John Franklin was international news and helped inspire Arctic exploration by a number of nations. The major goal now was to reach the North Pole. In 1860–61, during the period he helped underwrite voyages in search of Franklin, Henry Grinnell also sponsored an expedition under American ISAAC ISRAEL HAYES, which explored the Greenland ice cap and attempted to find an open polar sea north of Greenland and Ellesmere Island, Canada's northernmost point, in the hope of reaching the North Pole. In 1868, a Swedish expedition under geologist NILS ADOLF ERIK NORDENSKJÖLD set out from Spitsbergen for the Pole but was turned back by pack ice; he failed again in 1872–73. Meanwhile, in 1871, American Charles Francis Hall, again backed by Grinnell, reached as far as the Lincoln Sea from northern Ellesmere Island, setting a new northernmost record. In 1875–76, SIR GEORGE STRONG NARES sailed beyond northern Ellesmere Island in still another failed attempt but broke the northernmost record.

Germany became active in Arctic explorations with two expeditions to Greenland under KARL CHRISTIAN KOLDEWEY in 1868–70. German geographer AUGUST HEINRICH PETERMANN still promoted the idea of an "open polar sea." His ideas also helped inspire the Austro-Hungarian Arctic Expedition, under Austrian JULIUS VON PAYER and German-born KARL WEYPRECHT, which made the European discovery of Franz Josef Land, an archipelago north of Novaya Zemlya.

In 1878–79, Swedish geologist Adolf Nordenskjöld led the Vega Expedition, which made the first successful navigation of the long-sought Northeast Passage from Norway along Asia's Arctic coast to the Bering Strait. By returning to Europe by way of the Suez Canal in 1880, it also completed the first circumnavigation of Europe and Asia.

An American attempt at reaching the North Pole and making an east-to-west crossing of the Northeast Passage in 1879–81, headed by GEORGE WASHINGTON DE LONG, resulted in the eventual death of De Long and 12 expedition members after the ship had become trapped in ice north of Wrangel Island.

For the International Polar Year of 1882–83, a number of nations dedicated themselves to studying natural phenomena in Arctic regions of the world. Among the expeditions was the U.S. Army's Lady Franklin Bay Expedition headed by ADOLPHUS WASHINGTON GREELY in 1881–84, with the participation of OCTAVE PAVY. This expedition explored the northwest coast of Greenland and Ellesmere Island and set a new northernmost record. Relief vessels were unable to break through the ice of Smith Sound and reach Greely's base, however, and 17 members of the expedition perished from cold and starvation. In 1886–1900, another American explorer, ROBERT EDWIN PEARY, carried out five expeditions to the same regions. It was in 1900 that Peary, on reaching Greenland's northernmost point, Cape Morris Jesup, demonstrated conclusively that it was an island and not a land mass extending to the North Pole. In 1888, Norwegian FRIDTJOF NANSEN made a crossing of southern Greenland. In 1893–96, he headed a Norwegian expedition that attempted to approach the North Pole by purposely having a ship become icebound and drift northward from the New Siberian Islands, then continuing by kayak and sledge. The expedition failed to reach the Pole but set a new northernmost record. A British expedition under FREDERICK GEORGE JACKSON rescued Nansen on Franz Josef Land. In 1892–94, Estonian geologist EDUARD VON TOLL led a Russian expedition to the Siberian Arctic by way of Cape Chelyuskin and explored the deltas of the Yana, Indigirka, and Kolyma Rivers. In 1897, Swede SALOMON AUGUST ANDRÉE tried to reach the Pole from Spitsbergen by air, in a BALLOON, perishing in the attempt. In 1898–1902, Norwegian OTTO SVERDRUP, after exploring the west coast of Ellesmere Island, reached the Sverdrup Islands, which are named after him. At the turn of the last century, in 1899–1900, LUIGI AMEDEO DI SAVOIA D'ABRUZZI led an Italian expedition that attempted to reach the Pole from Franz Josef Land; it failed to do so but set a new northernmost record.

Denmark sent out a number of expeditions to Greenland, to which it had a territorial claim. In 1902–04, LUDWIG MYLIUS-ERICHSEN, accompanied by Danish-Inuit ethnologist KNUD JOHAN VICTOR RASMUSSEN, explored the northwest coast. In 1906–07, Mylius-Erichsen explored the northeast coast, locating the peninsula known as the Northeast Foreland, losing his life to the extreme conditions. Rasmussen continued his studies in the Arctic into the 1920s.

It was a Norwegian who made the first successful navigation of the Northwest Passage—ROALD ENGELBREGT GRAVNING AMUNDSEN. Departing Norway in June 1903, he sailed past Greenland to Baffin Bay and Lancaster Sound, then down Peel Strait into Franklin Strait. The expedition wintered at a bay on the south coast of King William Island, and he and his crew made measurements in the area until August 1905. In making the passage, he then proceeded through Rae Strait, staying close to the shore in Queen Maud Gulf, through Dease Strait and Coronation Gulf, into what came to be known as Amundsen Gulf. On September 2, the group became trapped in ice near King Point. In July 1906, when the ship was finally freed from the ice, the expedition continued along the northern Canadian border, around Alaska and into the Bering Strait.

The North Pole Attained

Robert Peary's expeditions to Greenland helped prepare him for an assault on the North Pole and convinced him the best route was from northern Ellesmere Island. In 1902, he made an unsuccessful attempt to reach the North Pole by way of Robeson Channel, the northernmost stretch of water between Greenland and Ellesmere Island; and, then again, in 1905–06, from Cape Columbia on Ellesmere Island's north coast. On both expeditions, he set northernmost records.

In July 1808, Robert Peary departed New York for a third attempt, again from Cape Columbia. Peary, his assistant, MATTHEW ALEXANDER HENSON, and four Inuit departed the next spring, on March 1, and, after a month-long trek across the frozen sea with sledges and dogs, reached the North Pole on April 6, 1909. In the meantime, another American, FREDERICK ALBERT COOK, claimed to have reached the North Pole by the Ellesmere Island route on April 21, 1908. The controversy on who actually had been first to the Pole lasted for some time. Peary, with more geographic data to support his claim, received official recognition from the U.S. Congress in 1911. (He may have in fact missed the exact geographic North Pole by a couple of miles; it is now thought that Cook never even came close.)

Ongoing Explorations

Although the Northeast Passage, Northwest Passage, and North Pole had all been conquered, much of the Arctic still remained unexplored. Arctic exploration continued to be an international effort, although nations with Arctic lands became especially active. In 1904–11, Quebecois mariner JOSEPH ELZÉAR BERNIER maintained that any country adjacent to the Arctic had rights to any islands within a triangle from the north shore of its mainland to its apex at the North Pole and led a number of expeditions to chart northern islands and assert Canadian sovereignty. In 1913–18, Canadian-born anthropologist VILHJALMUR STEFANSSON, of Icelandic ancestry, led an expedition to the Beaufort Sea and located uncharted islands in the Canadian Arctic Archipelago north of Prince Patrick Island. In 1908, Russian mariner and fur trader NIKIFOR ALEKSEYEVICH BEGICHEV determined that Bolshoy Begichev in central Siberia is an island and not part of a peninsula.

A new phase of Arctic exploration began in the 1920s, as a result of progress in aviation (see AVIATION AND EXPLORATION). American RICHARD EVELYN BYRD, after making a series of flights over the Greenland ice cap in 1924–25, carried out the first flight over the North Pole in 1926. Several days later, Norwegian Roald Amundsen, American LINCOLN ELLSWORTH, and Italian UMBERTO NOBILE flew over the Pole in an AIRSHIP. In 1928, eight men died in the course of Nobile's abortive attempt to land at the Pole by airship. Roald Amundsen died on his rescue flight. In 1930, HENRY GEORGE WATKINS led a British expedition that made use of aircraft as well as watercraft to survey the coasts of Greenland. American Arctic explorer LOUISE ARNER BOYD made the first flight by a woman over the North Pole in 1955.

In 1931, Australian SIR GEORGE HUBERT WILKINS attempted unsuccessfully to reach the North Pole from Spitsbergen by SUBMARINE. The U.S. atomic submarine *Nautilus* under Commander William R. Anderson did so in 1958.

Various nations also began establishing permanent scientific bases in Arctic regions. For example, in 1929–30, ALFRED LOTHAR WEGENER of Germany established the first permanent weather stations on the interior of the Greenland ice cap, and, in 1937, OTTO Y. SCHMIDT of the Union of Soviet Socialist Republics (USSR; Soviet Union) set up the first manned scientific post near the North Pole. During the INTERNATIONAL GEOPHYSICAL YEAR of 1957–58, different nations established more than 300 Arctic observation stations, some of them on ice floes. Most of the Arctic has now been surveyed by AERIAL PHOTOGRAPHY and remote sensing by aircraft and artificial SATELLITE.

❖

The exploration of the Arctic, with its harsh climate and ice-choked waters, has been one of the great challenges humankind has faced, with many lives lost. Some remote regions have now been settled, many of them for the development of mining and fishing. Animal husbandry is practiced in some northern lands, especially reindeer herding. Roads provide access to some communities; others are reached only by air. Icebreakers now keep many of the waterways open. The Arctic is also a valuable laboratory for scientists studying Earth's history and monitoring pollution.

Arctic Circle

The Arctic Circle is a parallel of latitude, a cartographic feature based on natural phenomena, situated at 66 degrees and 33 minutes north of the EQUATOR. The location of the Arctic Circle is determined by the fact that Earth is tilted on its axis by 23 degrees and 27 minutes as it revolves around the Sun. Above the Arctic Circle the Earth's relationship to the Sun is different than it is for the rest of the Northern Hemisphere, with a 24-hour period each year when the Sun does not set and a 24-hour period of continuous darkness.

From December 22 to June 22, the amount of daylight within the Arctic Circle is on the increase. On or about June 22, the summer solstice, the entire region experiences 24 hours of daylight, as Earth is tilted toward the Sun for a complete revolution. From June 22 until December 22, the amount of daylight is decreasing, and, on or about December 22, the winter solstice, the area is in darkness for 24 hours, while the region is in Earth's shadow. The situation is more extreme at the NORTH POLE, which sees the sun continuously from March 20 until September 23, with no sunlight from September 23 to March 20. These effects are mitigated by the transmission of light through the atmosphere, and the fact that the North Pole is a single point, and the land surrounding it has less extreme conditions.

The annual pattern of daylight has led to the region of Scandinavia north of the Arctic Circle being dubbed "the land of the midnight sun." Such a name tells only half the story, for there is the equal period of time when the sun is not to be seen. While these solar relationships are taking place in the north, the reverse take place in the ANTARCTIC CIRCLE, with the same net amount of sunlight in the annual cycle.

It is believed that the first European who is thought to have traveled near or north of the Arctic Circle and recorded the event was 4th century B.C. Greek PYTHEAS, during his search for ULTIMA THULE. Pytheas was an astronomer as well as an explorer and remarked on the extended length of days in the region. During the EUROPEAN AGE OF EXPLORATION, the first explorer to venture near the Arctic Circle—and perhaps beyond it—was Portuguese GASPAR CÔRTE-REAL, who, in 1500, explored the west coast of GREENLAND. In 1553–54, SIR HUGH WILLOUGHBY commanded the first English expedition to cross it. The question of the Arctic Circle as a barrier to be crossed by humanity is not important, since the lands within its border were well populated: by the Sami (Laplanders) in Scandinavia; the Samoyed, the Yakut, and the Tungus in SIBERIA; and the Inuit (Eskimo) in North America. It did take time, however, for the rest of the world to be aware of these communities.

See also ARCTIC, EXPLORATION OF THE; GEOGRAPHY AND CARTOGRAPHY; LATITUDE AND LONGITUDE; MAPS AND CHARTS.

Asia, exploration of

Asia, Earth's largest continent, with its outlying islands included, covers some 17,139,000 square miles, almost one-third of the planet's total land area. It is situated in the Eastern Hemisphere and almost entirely in the Northern Hemisphere.

The western limits of Asia are not readily defined since it is not entirely surrounded by water, being the eastern four-fifths of the landmass Eurasia (see EUROPE, EXPLORATION OF). To its north is the Arctic Ocean (the chief subdivisions being the Kara Sea, Laptev Sea, and East Siberian Sea); to its east, the BERING STRAIT and Pacific Ocean (the chief subdivisions being the Bering Sea, Sea of Okhotsk, Sea of Japan, Yellow Sea, East China Sea, and South China Sea); to its south, the Indian Ocean (the chief subdivisions being the Bay of Bengal, Arabian Sea, Persian Gulf, and Gulf of Aden); and to its southwest, the MEDITERRANEAN SEA and the RED SEA (an arm of the Indian Ocean). In the west, in order to distinguish Asia from Europe, most geographers use an imaginary line running from the northern extent of the Ural Mountains on the Kara Sea, then south along the Ural River to the Caspian Sea, then west along the Caucasus Mountains to the Black Sea, then along the Bosporus Strait (linking the Black Sea and the Sea of Marmara, both forming an arm of the Mediterranean), and the Dardanelles (a strait linking the Sea of Marmara with the Aegean Sea, also part of the Mediterranean). The Isthmus of Suez (including the human-made Suez Canal) separates Asia from Africa. The most northerly point of Asia's continental mainland is Cape Chelyuskin; most southerly, the southern end of the Malay Peninsula; most westerly, Cape Baba in northwestern Turkey; and most easterly, Cape Dezhnyov.

This vast region has varied topography, consisting of plains, plateaus, and mountains. On the Asian mainland are found both the lowest and highest points on Earth's surface: the shore of the Dead Sea, at 1,340 feet below sea level, and Mount Everest (see EVEREST, MOUNT), at 29,035 feet above sea level, part of the HIMALAYAS. Extending from Arctic to equatorial regions, Asia also has a wide variety of climates—from tundra to tropical—and a variety of vegetation and animal life.

Animals found on other continents have adapted to the varying climatic and vegetation zones of Asia, such as reindeer, deer, antelope, gazelles, tigers, elephants, rhinoceroses, wolves, hyenas, monkeys, sables, foxes, marmots, hares, peacocks, and crocodiles. Some animals unique to Asia are the orangutan, the second-largest of the apes after gorillas, found on the islands of Borneo and Sumatra; the giant panda, a type of bear, in southwestern China; the snow leopard, on the plateaus and mountains of central Asia; and the Komodo dragon, the world's largest lizard, in Indonesia.

The exact derivation of the name *Asia* is not known. The Greek form may be derived from the Assyrian word *asu,* meaning "east" or "sunset," or from a local name for the plains of Ephesus in western Anatolia (Asia Minor), eventually meaning all the lands to the east.

Realms of Asia

Because of its vast size, geographers and historians discuss Asia as comprising various realms, such as East Asia, central Asia, Southeast Asia, South Asia, and Southwest Asia. Other terms that appear in the historical record are *Near East,* originally used for the area occupied by the Ottoman Empire of the Turks, then applied to any parts of Southwest Asia situated close to Europe, from the Mediterranean Sea to the Persian Gulf and even beyond in South Asia, including Afghanistan and Pakistan (and sometimes Egypt, Libya, and other Arabic nations of North Africa, as well as the Sudan); the *Middle East,* originally used for the area extending from the Persian Gulf to India and other countries of the Indian subcontinent, then, in the 20th century, used synonymously with the *Near East;* and the *Far East,* or the *Orient,* generally used for those East Asia and Southeast Asia nations facing the Pacific Ocean (and sometimes for the *Indian subcontinent* as well).

Southwest Asia, or the Middle East (or Near East), consists primarily of arid lands, much of it desert. The most fertile land is situated around the Tigris and Euphrates river valleys in present-day Iraq, part of a region once referred to as the Fertile Crescent. The Anatolian Peninsula, the Asian part of modern-day Turkey, has been referred to as Asia Minor. Other modern-day nations in western Asia are Iraq, Iran (formerly Persia), Syria, Lebanon, Israel, Jordan, Armenia, Azerbaijan, Georgia, and the eastern part of Turkey. Saudi Arabia and a number of smaller countries are situated on the Arabian Peninsula, in the south of which is the desert known as the Rub' al-Khali, or EMPTY QUARTER. Farther to the west in South Asia lie the more mountainous countries of Afghanistan and Pakistan.

The nations of Kazakhstan, Kyrgyzstan, Tajikistan, Turkmenistan, and Uzbekistan (comprising a region once referred to as Turkistan), lying north of Afghanistan, were once part of the Union of Soviet Socialist Republics (USSR; Soviet Union). These, like central Russia, central China, Mongolia, Tibet, Nepal, and Bhutan are often referred to as part of central Asia.

To the east of Afghanistan sits the high Tibetan Plateau (Qing Zang Gaoyuan) of western China. The Himalayas stretch along the southern side, while the Tian Shan mountains extend on the north from the Pamir range of Tajikistan to the border between western China and Mongolia. To the north and east are great deserts, the Takla Makan and the GOBI DESERT. To the northwest are the steppes of central Asia. In northernmost Asia, stretching from the Ural Mountains to the Pacific Ocean, is found the generally flat region of some 5 million square miles known as

SIBERIA, mostly in Russia with a small part in northern Kazakhstan.

To the south of the Himalayas is the Indian subcontinent, with the present-day nations of India, Bangladesh, and Pakistan (Pakistan sometimes is grouped as part of the Middle East). The GANGES RIVER and INDUS RIVER traverse parts of it. The southern part of the subcontinent includes the Deccan Plateau. The island of Sri Lanka (CEYLON) lies in the Indian Ocean to the southeast, and the Maldives, to the southwest.

Crossing from central Asia to the Indian subcontinent is made difficult by the Himalayas and other mountain ranges. The main passes are located in the mountains of northern Pakistan, the most famous of these being the KHYBER PASS through the Safed Koh mountain range, extending from the Hindu Kush range, which connects to Kabul in Afghanistan.

East Asia includes eastern Russia (known as Far East Russia), North Korea, South Korea, eastern China, Japan, and Singapore. Southeast Asia includes Vietnam, Laos, Cambodia, Thailand, and Myanmar, as well as the islands of the Malay Archipelago (historically referred to as the EAST INDIES). The eastern rim of the continent of Asia has a number of plateaus dissected by the YANGTZE RIVER (Chang) and YELLOW RIVER (Huanghe).

Early Contacts between East and West

Before written records, the earliest hints of exploration of Asia come from the myths and folklore of the Babylonians, Egyptians, and Greeks. Recent archaeological finds support the conclusion that many of these stories are mythological versions of early voyages undertaken for conquest and to establish trade routes. The voyage of Jason and the Argonauts to find the Golden Fleece has been represented as the story of initial Greek journeys through the dangerous Bosporus Strait to establish trade with Black Sea ports. This theory is buttressed by the discovery of ancient Greek shipwrecks along the mythical route. The story of the Trojan War may represent an early Greek attempt to gain full control of this trade route through the Bosporus. The Babylonian epic of Gilgamesh contains an account of early Sumerian voyages similar to Akkadian voyages in the historical accounts of the region.

Civilization grew and flourished in the fertile regions of the Middle East in the third millennium B.C. Rulers began to dispatch explorers on diplomatic and military missions with the goals of expanding territory, developing commerce, and enhancing their own prestige. In about 2450 B.C., Egyptian HANNU, the first explorer of record, navigated the Red Sea along the coast of the Arabian Peninsula (see EGYPTIAN EXPLORATION). The next known exploratory efforts date to 2340 B.C., when SARGON of Akkad, who had consolidated his rule over Mesopotamia, sent out missions establishing trade contacts throughout Arabia and as far east as the Indus River. Along the fertile banks of the Indus, the Harrapa culture, the earliest known settled civilization to rise in Asia was flourishing. Harrapa people built cities, with populations of up to 40,000, and dug complex irrigation channels for their agriculture. In addition to Mesopotamia, the Harrapa civilization had trade contacts with lands to the west as far as the southeastern border of Afghanistan.

The greatest extent of the Akkadian Empire lasted only 40 years before it contracted under political pressure and finally collapsed, splitting into smaller states including Babylonia and Assyria. The Hittites who were living in Anatolia gradually expanded their power, most famously through the use of the chariot in warfare. By the 14th century B.C., they had conquered much of the area in modern Turkey and in the northern regions of Mesopotamia. They later developed extensive trade relations with the Greeks, one of the earliest historical instances of the exchange of ideas between East and West. This transfer process continued over the centuries through both trade and military incursions.

The Harrapa civilization disappeared sometime about 1800 B.C. In about 1500 B.C., a group of nomads called Aryans, who were living in central Asia, migrated southward through Afghanistan into northern India and settled in the northern Indus Valley as well as the northwestern part of the Gangetic Plain. By 800 B.C., the Aryans ruled most of northern India. They spread westward to the Iranian plateau, an area almost completely surrounded by high mountains and deficient in navigable rivers. The most significant of these tribes were the Medes in the northwest and the Persians in the south. The Assyrian Empire expanded to the west by the ninth century B.C. and came to include the entire Fertile Crescent region; it flourished until 612 B.C., when the Medes (with the help of the Babylonians) conquered the Assyrian capital of Ninevah. Then, in 550 B.C., Persian Cyrus the Great overthrew the Medes and established the Persian Empire. The Persians spread their conquests eastward, through the mountain passes of Afghanistan into the Indus Valley.

During the sixth century B.C., Greek society, although centered in Greece, was fragmented into small city-states throughout the Mediterranean region and into the Middle East. Among the Greeks were many capable and memorable seafarers (see GREEK EXPLORATION). Many Greek people lived in colonies on the coast of Anatolia. The expanding Persian Empire eased the difficulties of traveling and brought together merchants and mariners from all over the world. In about 548 B.C., Egyptian COSMAS INDICOPLEUSTES, having become a Christian, wrote an account known as *Topographia Christiana* (Christian Topography), based in part on his travels as a merchant to India and Ceylon. In about 520–494 B.C., Greek HECATAEUS OF MILETUS traveled in Asia Minor and Egypt. He later wrote what is considered the earliest systematic description of the known world, *Tour Round the World.*

The Persians, seeking further economic and military success, hired expert mariners—especially from among the Greeks—to explore the uncharted regions of their empire. In 510 B.C., Persian emperor Darius I sent Greek mariner SCYLAX to determine the course of the Indus River. Greek historian HERODOTUS of the fifth century B.C. reports that Scylax followed the Indus to the Arabian Sea, explored the coasts of present-day southwestern Pakistan and Iran, and then the Gulf of Aden and the Red Sea, finally returning to Persia in 507 B.C. Like many travelers in the mountainous regions of the east and the Arabian coasts, Scylax came back with fantastic descriptions of natives, describing people with giant ears or only one eye.

In the late fifth century B.C., Greek physician CTESIAS OF CNIDUS served as court doctor to Darius II of Persia. During that time, he traveled throughout the Persian Empire and India. Ctesias aimed to discredit much of what Herodotus had reported about the lands of the east. In Herodotus's account, the lands beyond the Indus River were unpopulated, the home of giant animals and birds. By this time, however, Aryans in the Gangetic Plain had established powerful kingdoms, the westernmost of which had common interactions with the Persians. Ctesius may have visited as Far East as the Ganges, or relied on reports from the Aryans. Ctesius's account was no less fantastic than that of Herodotus, detailing men with giant feet and others with doglike faces, as well as huge worms in the Ganges that devoured camels and oxen.

Knowledge of this territory was crucial for the maintenance and expansion of the Persian Empire. It was also essential to Macedonian king ALEXANDER THE GREAT. In 334 B.C., he had consolidated his rule over the Greek city-states. Inspired by the writings of Herodotus and other accounts of the East, he made a military assault on the Persian Empire. Alexander advanced onto the Anatolian plateau, conquering all of Asia Minor. He then moved southward and conquered peoples of present-day Lebanon and Israel and, after crossing into Africa, he gained control of Egypt as well. In 331 B.C., Alexander crossed into present-day Syria and pushed on to the Tigris and Euphrates Rivers and defeated Darius III. He continued eastward through present-day Iran and Afghanistan in pursuit of Persian forces. In 329 B.C., he crossed the Hindu Kush into present-day Pakistan and headed northwestward into present-day Uzbekistan. The region at the time was known as Bactria, part of the Persian Empire. Alexander eventually recrossed the Hindu Kush, proceeding to India in 327 B.C.

Earlier, in 329 B.C., Greek NEARCHUS had traveled through Bactria to provide reinforcements for Alexander's campaign. By 325 B.C., Alexander's army had halted in India, unable or unwilling to cross the Jhelum River.

Alexander decided to return to the west but put together a voyage of exploration under Nearchus, consisting of 5,000 men and 150 ships. Alexander hoped that such an expedition would find a route to connect the eastern and western portions of his empire. Nearchus reached the Indus delta and then continued westward along the coast of present-day Pakistan. His ships sailed into the Gulf of Oman and into the Persian Gulf along the coast of present-day Iran. Nearchus reported meeting primitive people he called "hairy men," who used their long fingernails as tools, and other people who lived entirely on fish, building their dwellings from whalebones. The expedition also encountered whales, creatures hitherto unknown to Mediterranean sailors. At the head of the Persian Gulf, Nearchus sailed up the Euphrates to the Tigris, where he rejoined Alexander. Nearchus went on to plan additional voyages around the Arabian Peninsula and even Africa. Alexander's death in Persia in 323 B.C. and the subsequent breakup of the empire put a stop to such ambitious plans of exploration.

By this time, the ancient kingdom in India known as Magadha had expanded, absorbing neighboring kingdoms until it was the most powerful kingdom east of the Indus. In about 321 B.C., Chandragupta Maurya became king of Magadha, establishing the Mauryan dynasty. In 305 B.C., Chandragupta extended his control up to the border of Afghanistan, destroying one of the Hellenistic kingdoms that remained after the collapse of Alexander's empire. The ruler of another Hellenistic kingdom sent a Greek diplomat, MEGASTHENES of Ionia, in about 302 B.C., as ambassador to the Mauryan Empire. Megasthenes traveled throughout northern India, making observations of Hindu culture and the natural history of the region. He was the first Westerner to make accurate observations of the Ganges River and to correctly surmise its source. The Mauryan dynasty extended its control to nearly the entire Indian subcontinent in the third century B.C., except the tip and the lands beyond the Brahmaputra River.

Meanwhile, in the mid-third century B.C., the Greeks established a kingdom in Bactria. By about 150 B.C., this kingdom had encroached on Mauryan territory, expanding to meet the Ganges River in the east. An early Greek visitor to India was EUDOXUS of Cyzicus, who, in about 120 B.C., made one of the earliest known sea voyages from Egypt to India and established coastal trade links.

The Roman Empire, centered in Rome in what is now Italy, became a power in the Middle East during the second century B.C. (see ROMAN EXPLORATION). The Romans conquered territory along the eastern Mediterranean coast to the borders of Persia by 62 B.C. After conquering Egypt, they turned their attention to the southern end of the Arabian Peninsula (present-day Yemen), to an area they dubbed Arabia Felix ("Happy Arabia") because of its wealth. Arabia Felix had been well known to Egyptians as a principal source of incense and spices, precious commodities valued along-side gold. The incense was taken from the sap of frankin-cense and myrrh trees, and the spices, such as cinnamon, were imported over sea from India. (The wealth of the king-doms in Arabia Felix is thought to have inspired the first recorded Egyptian voyager, Hannu.)

In about 25 B.C., a Roman officer in Egypt, GAIUS AELIUS GALLUS, began an expedition in an effort to con-quer this region and establish Roman control of the SPICE TRADE. Gallus continued his expedition to the east bank of the Red Sea and then proceeded overland to the Sabaean city of Marib. Unable to subjugate the Sabaeans, Gallus returned to Roman Egypt, with new geographic knowledge. In A.D. 18, Greek geographer STRABO published his work *Geogra-phy* in Rome, based on his own travels in Europe, Africa, and Asia as well as on the work of earlier writers. In A.D. 45, HIPPALUS, a Greek in service to Roman-ruled Egypt, navigated a practical route out of sight of land from the mouth of the Red Sea to India.

The Chinese Empire

The first archaeological evidence for a kingdom among the Chinese is that of the Chang (Shang) dynasty, which arose in about 1570 B.C. In control of the central part of China, the Chang dynasty consisted of a number of smaller states. One of them, Chou, revolted in about 1045 B.C., and the Chang dynasty collapsed. The subsequent Chou (Zhou) dynastic period was marked by contention between the states, with interstate warfare leading to the downfall and annexation of certain states. By the third century B.C., there were only seven states in China. The state of Ch'in conquered the rest of the Chou states and began the Ch'in (Qin) dynasty, from which the name *China* is thought to be derived. Although a short-lived empire, it had a tremendous impact on Chinese civilization. A unified system of weights and measurements and a system of writing were introduced throughout the em-pire. A revolt in the state of Han led, after a brief interreg-num, to the Han dynasty, which lasted more than 400 years, from about 206 B.C. to A.D. 220, during the period the Roman Empire became dominant in the West.

The extension of the Han dynasty through China made travel easier and safer (see CHINESE EXPLORATION). In ad-dition, there became a need for communication through-out all of eastern Asia for military and trading alliances. In 128 B.C., CHANG CH'IEN, an officer in service to the em-peror Wu Ti, was sent westward on a diplomatic mission to the Yue-chi (also known as the Scythians), a nomadic people living in present-day Afghanistan. Chang was captured by the Hsiung-nu (Xiongnu, known in the West as the Huns) but escaped 10 years later. In about 118 B.C., Chang re-sumed his westward journey and finally arrived at Bactria in northern Afghanistan. There, he heard reports of civiliza-tions farther to the west, including Persia, Mesopotamia,

and Rome. He also discovered Chinese bamboo and cloth there, which had been shipped over the SPICE ROUTE, through India, a land of which the Chinese reportedly had no contacts. For some time, the southern end of India had been an important link in the spice trade, with mariners bringing spices and other goods from China, Southeast Asia, and the SPICE ISLANDS (the Moluccas), while overland cara-vans traveled up the west coast of India and through the Khyber and other passes into Afghanistan. Arab seafarers from the kingdoms of southern Arabia sailed through the Arabian Sea, then bringing Chinese and Indian goods to Alexandria in Egypt and throughout the Mediterranean world. Chang Ch'ien took reports of his findings back to the Han emperor. In 115 B.C., he was again sent out to make an alliance with nomads in western China. Although un-successful in this mission, he in turn sent envoys laden with silks and gold from there to Persia and to the eastern Roman provinces. This initial opening of trade links between China and the Hellenized lands of the eastern Mediterranean marked the birth of the trade route known as the SILK ROAD.

KAN YING was another early Chinese explorer, sent out in A.D. 97 on a diplomatic mission to meet with the Romans regarding threats to travel along the Silk Road from central Asian peoples. It is not certain how far east he reached, but his was one of the few voyages made by Chinese through central Asia. For much of Chinese history, the Chinese em-perors discouraged travel outside of the empire, relying on nomadic peoples in central Asia and the Persians and others to carry their trade to the West.

What might be considered as early travel writing was recorded by WEN-CHI, a Chinese woman born into a noble family of the Han dynasty in the late second century A.D. As a child of about 12, she was abducted by the Hsiung-nu (Huns) and lived as a nomad on the Mongolian steppes. She wrote about her experiences in *Eighteen Songs of a Nomad Flute*.

The Han empire collapsed into smaller states in A.D. 220. Many of these, especially those in the south, prospered, but the disunity hindered any kind of travel. During this turbulent time, however, Buddhism, which had its origin around the Ganges River in India, slowly grew in influence. Arising as a monastic offshoot of the ancient Hindu reli-gion in the northeastern Gangetic Plain, Buddhism is iden-tified with Siddhartha Gautama, called the Buddha, the son of an Aryan king, generally agreed to have been born in 563 B.C. Buddhism made its greatest gains in India when Ashoka, the king of the Mauryan Empire, after a bloody campaign in 261 B.C., renounced warfare and adopted the religion. Ashoka sent missionaries throughout his kingdom and beyond, even into central Asia.

By the fourth century A.D., Buddhism had taken root in China. But there were many doctrinal disputes among the Chinese Buddhists because of a lack of religious texts. In

A.D. 399, Buddhist monk and scholar FA-HSIEN set out to reach India and obtain Buddhist texts in Sanskrit, which he planned to translate. He traveled with three other monks westward through China and along the Silk Road. He crossed the Takla Makan desert and over the Pamir plateau and into Afghanistan. From there, he followed the Kabul River to the upper Indus Valley, before setting off eastward across the Gangetic Plain. Fa-hsien spent three years copying Buddhist documents and visited many important Buddhist shrines. He also spent two years on Ceylon, which had been among the first lands converted by Ashoka's zeal. He began his homeward journey in about 413 by sea, through the islands of Southeast Asia. Upon his return, he translated the texts he had copied and wrote an account of his journey.

The reunification of China occurred in 581, under the Sui dynasty, during which Buddhist philosophy, rather than the traditional philosophies of Confucianism and Taoism (Daoism) from earlier dynasties, was promoted. The Sui dynasty was short lived and was followed by the T'ang (Tang) dynasty, which lasted hundreds of years, from about 618 to 907.

New political stability and a new religious philosophy inspired new journeys. Buddhist monk HSÜAN-TSANG made his own attempt to resolve further doctrinal problems, convinced of the feasibility of a trip to India by Chang Ch'ien's and Fa-hsien's earlier journeys. But travel outside the empire was forbidden. In 629, Hsüan-tsang embarked in secret from Lanchow, at the western extent of China's Great Wall. He crossed the Gobi Desert, entered the Sinkiang province, crossed the Tian Shan mountains, traveled through the Kirghiz region of central Asia and the lands southeast of the Aral Sea, then crossed the Hindu Kush into Afghanistan. He remained there for two years at a Buddhist monastery. Hsüan-tsang then reached India through the Khyber Pass and crossed plains in the north to the upper Ganges River Valley. He followed the valley until he reached the Nalanda, a Buddhist University in Baragaon. He studied there for five years, collecting Buddhist texts and relics. Hsuan Tsang later followed the Ganges to its mouth. He was deterred from setting out by sea to Ceylon due to political instability, so he then traveled inland to the Deccan Plateau. He followed the Indus River Valley, then joined a trade caravan. When he finally returned to China in 645, though he had defied the emperor's orders, he was warmly welcomed, all recognizing his achievement. His travels in India had been the most extensive in Chinese history.

Another early Chinese traveler to India was I-CHING, in an effort to obtain and translate accurate Buddhist texts to answer lingering metaphysical problems. In 671, he sailed southward along Asia's coast, from Canton to Sumatra, then to eastern India. He ended up spending almost two-and-a-half decades in India and the East Indies.

In the meantime, the West was in a state of collapse. The Roman Empire had converted to Christianity and was split into two realms, the western part weakened by barbarian invasions, and the eastern part threatened by the Persians and the Turks. While the West decayed into feudalism, and travel became extremely dangerous, if not impossible, the T'ang empire was flourishing. Its two main cities, the capital Chang'an and Louyang, grew to be metropolises, while states in central Asia paid the T'ang empire tribute, and travelers, merchants, and envoys visited from Japan, Korea, and Tibet. The T'ang dynasty was cosmopolitan and had an unparalleled influence throughout the East.

The first European explorer of record who claimed to have reached China—its western frontier—was Rabbi BENJAMIN OF TUDELA, a Spaniard who, in the second half of the 12th century, reached central Asia via Persia. He later visited India and Ceylon.

In the first half of the 15th century, during the Ming dynasty, Admiral CHENG HO led seven Chinese maritime expeditions composed of a JUNK fleet, sailing from China to the Indian Ocean, the Persian Gulf, and the Red Sea, reaching East Africa. His voyages opened up Chinese trade with foreign peoples.

Early Christian Influence in Asia

During his reign of A.D. 98–117, Roman emperor Trajan annexed parts of the Middle East including Assyria and Mesopotamia. Yet Hadrian, who succeeded Trajan in 117, released the eastern conquests. Hadrian also ordered the construction of Hadrian's Wall around the boundaries of the empire. This was also the era that Christianity began its expansion from Jerusalem throughout the Roman Empire. In 330, Roman emperor Constantine I (Constantine the Great) recognized Christianity as the official religion and established a new capital, Constantinople (present-day Istanbul, Turkey). In 395, the Roman Empire was divided into the Western Roman Empire and the Eastern Roman Empire (also known as the Byzantine Empire), the latter influential in the Middle East for centuries.

Adherents of the Christian religion undertook pilgrimages to the Holy Land to fulfill vows. One of the earliest pilgrimages on record dates to 217, when Bishop Alexander traveled from Cappadocia to Jerusalem. The tone of the account of that voyage suggests such pilgrimages were common before then. After Constantine's conversion to Christianity, and especially after his mother, St. Helena, took a trip to the Holy Land and, according to legend, recovered what was claimed to be the true cross of Jesus's crucifixion, pilgrimages to visit holy sites and to recover holy relics grew even more popular.

The most detailed early description of the Holy Land comes from sixth-century Scottish abbot Adamnan, who wrote a detailed account of the journey of Frankish pilgrim ARCULF. His three-volume geography, *De Locis Sanctis* (Concerning Sacred Places), described various biblical sites, including the Dead Sea, Jordan River, and such cities as Jerusalem, Bethlehem, and Damascus. The work was presented to Aldfrith, the king of Northumbria (in Britain), in 698.

Islamic Expansion

Islam was founded on the Arabian Peninsula by the Prophet Muhammad in A.D. 622. By the time of his death in 632, the entire Arabian peninsula had been united under Islam. Armies of Arab Muslims soon crushed Persia, already weakened by its long conflict with the Eastern Roman Empire, and expanded into neighboring regions, including Jerusalem. By the next century, the Islamic Empire expanded eastward to the edge of the Chinese Empire in central Asia and westward through North Africa. And Islamic learning and trade flourished, with discoveries in mathematics, science, and navigation (see MUSLIM EXPLORATION).

In 711, Mohammed bin Qasim, entering the Indian subcontinent from Afghanistan, much as Alexander had done, conquered Sind, the area of modern-day Pakistan around the Indus River. The Muslims did not press on beyond Pakistan by land at that time. In 758, Muslim seafarers, who were routinely sailing all through the Indian Ocean, ransacked the port of Canton, which led to the closing of the city for 50 years. In 850, Arab trader SOLEYMAN sailed from the Persian Gulf to India, then embarked by Chinese junk through the Bay of Bengal to the Chinese port Khanfu in present-day Canton. Soleyman's extensive observations of India and China were later recorded along with descriptions of other lands in a document known as the *Sequence of Historical Events*.

Muslim rule extended even farther eastward in later centuries. Afghan sultan Mahmud of Ghazni conquered the region of Punjab in India in the early 11th century and made Lahore his capital. Between 1175 and 1186, Turkish Muhammad of Ghur conquered the regions of Sind and Punjab. He was assassinated in 1206. That year, his general, Qutubuddin Aybak, established the Delhi Sultanate, an independent Muslim kingdom in India, which endured until 1526. The sultanate included most of Punjab and Sind during this period.

The emphasis on acts of devotion and on Islamic studies, along with the duty of every Muslim to make at least one pilgrimage to the holy cities of Medina and Mecca, inspired a new emphasis on travel. In 914–34, Arab historian ABU AL-HASAN ALI AL-MASUDI visited every country in the Islamic world, which by then included most of North Africa. In 943–73, ABU AL-QASIM IBN ALI AL-NASIBI IBN HAWQAL made his own similar journeys. In 1017, Arab scholar ABU AR-RAYHAN MUHAMMAD IBN AHMAD AL-BIRUNI traveled to India for the first time. Among his many works was the book *India*. In 1182–1217, ABU AL-HASAN MUHAMMAD

IBN JUBAYR, a Muslim official and scholar, made four pilgrimages from Moorish Spain to Arabia.

In 1325, ABU ABD ALLAH MUHAMMAD IBN BATTUTAH, a Muslim born in Morocco, began his travels throughout the Islamic world, including a pilgrimage to Mecca, where he settled for a time in order study Islamic law. He eventually traveled eastward, reaching Delhi in India, where he served Islamic sultan Mohammed Tuglaq for seven years. He was then assigned as the sultan's ambassador to the Mongol emperor of China but, on his way to China, was robbed of the gifts he had been given for the emperor. After staying in the Maldives for two years, he returned to India, then sailed to the Malay Peninsula and the island of Sumatra, before reaching China. In 1346, he set out for home, returning to Tangier in 1350. He later traveled southward in Africa. Ibn Battutah's writings about his extensive travels provide vivid details of the lands that Europe would "discover" more than a century later.

In the mid-11th century, as the Turks began to take control of the lands controlled by the Arabs, the conquerors themselves converted to Islam. The Turks were more zealous in some ways than their predecessors: They halted Christian pilgrimages to Jerusalem and began new assaults on Constantinople. Byzantine leader Alexius I Comnenus appealed to the West for help defending against them. In 1095, Pope Urban II gave a speech encouraging aid to Byzantium against Islamic attackers. This instigated what became the first of the European CRUSADES to the Middle East. European nobles mustered armies and advanced beyond Constantinople. They captured Jerusalem and established what were known as Crusader states, Christian nations in Palestine. Crusaders carried home both goods and ideas from the East and helped spur on interest in more trade. Europeans maintained a presence in the Middle East for about 200 years—in the course of which a number of other Crusades were launched—until the region was ultimately retaken by Ottoman Turks. The Turks went on to capture Constantinople in 1453, which resulted in the breakup of the Eastern Roman Empire.

Mongol and European Contacts

In 1206, GENGHIS KHAN consolidated his rule over the nomadic Mongols (see MONGOL EXPLORATION). With his establishment of a capital at Karakorum in the northern Gobi Desert, he began to threaten the domination of the Turks, and embarked on a path that would spur unprecedented contact between the East and West. His armies overran the Ch'in empire of northern China in 1215 and pushed west and south. Like Alexander the Great, Genghis Khan sought geographic information to aid in subjugation of the peoples of Asia. In 1219, CH'ANG-CH'UN, a Chinese Daoist priest and scholar, carried out a mission of reconnaissance for the khan through central Asia. By the time of his death in 1241,

Genghis Khan had established the largest empire ever to exist in human history, from the Caspian Sea in the west to the Pacific coast of China. In fact, the Mongol armies had reached as far west as Hungary.

In 1245, Pope Innocent IV summoned GIOVANNI DEL CARPINI, an Italian born in Perugia and one of the first Franciscans, to undertake a diplomatic mission to Genghis Khan to see if the Mongols might be persuaded to assist the Europeans against the Islamic Turks. Carpini and an interpreter traveled through eastern Europe, across Ukraine, to the Volga River, where they encountered a Mongol party. They were granted safe passage and hardy Tartar horses and crossed the steppes of central Asia, reaching Karakorum in 1246. The new khan, Kuyuk, was no more ill-disposed to the Islamic Turks than he was to Christians, and Carpini left without any alliance or even promise of peace. In 1253, King Louis IX of France sent Flemish WILLIAM OF RUBROUCK on a diplomatic mission to the Mongols at Karakorum. He met with the khan Mangu but achieved no lasting political settlement. Both Carpini and Rubrouck wrote accounts of their journeys, some of the first European reports of the Orient.

The Mongol Empire, although now fragmented after Genghis's death, maintained considerably powerful kingdoms called khanates. After these diplomatic missions from the west to the east, the next travelers were mercantile. MAFFEO POLO and his brother NICCOLÒ POLO were minor noblemen and merchants in Venice. The Polo brothers traded in jewels and precious stones out of Constantinople. In 1260, Maffeo and Niccolò sought a better price for their jewels, traveling to the court of Barka Khan near the mouth of the Volga River. As they prepared to return across the Crimea to the Black Sea, a war between Barka Khan and the khan of Persia erupted, and the Polos were forced to travel eastward in 1263, to Bukhara in present-day Uzbekistan. Bukhara was an important outpost along a main caravan route, and the Polos remained there, unable to travel west until 1266. Then, they encountered a group of Tartar envoys on their way to the court of Kublai Khan, one of the inheritors of the empire of Genghis Khan, who ruled China from Cambaluc (near present-day Beijing). The Polos traveled with the Tartars along the Silk Road. Kublai Khan welcomed the Polos, the first Europeans he had encountered, and expressed interest in Western culture. He hoped to have Western missionaries convert the Mongols, who were without a strong faith, to Christianity, which he thought would have a civilizing and unifying effect on them. After a year, the Polos were allowed to return home, and with the aid of a passport—a large slab of gold—they traveled westward through China.

The Polo brothers returned to Venice in 1269, remaining for only two years before they embarked again, eager to reestablish ties with the Mongol emperor. Niccolò's 17-year-old son, MARCO POLO, accompanied them as they sailed from Venice to Acre on the east coast of the Mediterranean. Niccolò, Maffeo, and young Marco crossed Mesopotamia through Persia to Hormuz, a port on the Persian Gulf coast, where they hoped to find oversea passage to Cambaluc. They could find no boats on which they were willing to embark, however, and set off overland in 1272. The three crossed southern Persia into Afghanistan, where Marco fell ill. Maffeo and Niccolò remained with Marco for a year in the mountains until he recovered, before following the Oxus River, onto the Pamir plateau. They reached Lop Nor, an important trading city on the far western edge of China, and joined a caravan into Mongolia, where, after three years of travel, they reached the court of Kublai Khan.

The khan was so impressed with Marco, just 21 years old at the time, that he appointed him to a diplomatic post. As part of his official duties, Marco traveled throughout China and Southeast Asia. He visited the Chinese provinces along the Yellow River, Yangtze River, and upper Mekong River. He visited the interior of what is now Myanmar, Thailand, and Vietnam. He also sailed to the islands of Indonesia. In 1292, anxious about their fortunes because of Kublai Khan's advanced years, Marco, Maffeo, and Niccolò sought a way to return to Italy. An opportunity presented itself to escort to Persia a Mongolian princess who was betrothed to the khan of Persia. The three Polos and the princess traveled by sea, the land route being blocked by warfare. They arrived safely back at Hormuz in 1294. Marco Polo's account of the East, known in short as *The Travels of Marco Polo,* became one of the most influential works in European exploration.

Kublai Khan's tentative approval of Christianity and curiosity about the West led to further exploration in the East, this time by Franciscans, dedicated Roman Catholic missionaries. JOHN OF MONTECORVINO was a Franciscan friar from Italy. After serving as an emissary to the pope for the Byzantine emperor in the 1270s, Pope Nicholas IV assigned John to be his representative in the Persian capital at Tabriz. After two years, John sailed by way of the Arabian Sea to the southern tip of India. After founding the first Catholic missions there, he embarked into the South China Sea, following it into the Yellow Sea to Cambaluc, where he met Kublai Khan in 1294. He continued his missionary work in China under the khan's approval, establishing a cathedral and a church school in the Chinese capital, and China's first permanent Christian settlements. In 1307, he became Cambaluc's first archbishop and was named patriarch of the Orient. He reported on his experiences in letters to the Vatican.

In 1280, RABBAN BAR SAUMA, a China-born Christian descendant of Turks who had been aligned with the Mongols, set out on a pilgrimage to Jerusalem. He and a companion followed the Silk Road below the Takla Makan desert and arrived in Mongol-held territories in Persia two years later. Reports of danger along the route kept Bar Sauma from reaching Jerusalem, but he went on to be appointed to a delegation representing Mongol interests in the West and visited Constantinople and other European cities.

In about 1318, Franciscan missionary ODORIC OF PORDENONE set out overland across Asia Minor and Persia to the port of Hormuz at the mouth of the Persian Gulf. From there, he sailed to India, where he collected the bones of recently martyred Christians. After visiting islands in the Indian Ocean, he sailed to the Chinese port of Hangchow in about 1322. He proceeded along the Great Canal, inland to Cambaluc, where he met and stayed with John of Montecorvino. Odoric interred the bones of the martyrs there, remaining about six years before returning overland to Europe, traveling north from the Great Wall into Mongolia, then south and west. His route took him along the northern slopes of the Himalayas and into Tibet. He later wrote an account of his travels in the Far East, detailing the spice trade in India and Sumatra, as well as the size and marvels of Chinese cities such as Hangchow and Zaiton. His travels provided Europeans with important geographic information, which Spanish geographer ABRAHAM CRESQUES incorporated into his *Catalan Atlas* of 1375.

Another early overland traveler to the Far East was Italian missionary GIOVANNI DE MARIGNOLLI, who traveled to China, India, and Indonesia in 1339–53. Early the next century, in 1403–06, RUY GONZALEZ DE CLAVIJO headed a diplomatic mission for Spain to meet with Mongol emperor Tamerlane in his capital of Samarkand in present-day Uzbekistan in central Asia.

In about 1419, after the Mongols had been expelled from China, NICCOLÒ DI CONTI, a Venetian merchant, traveled to Damascus. He remained there for several years learning Arabic, then traveled to Baghdad and Hormuz at the southern end of the Persian Gulf. Conti learned Persian and studied the peoples living on the Persian coast before continuing his journey eastward. After traveling through India and Southeast Asia, Conti returned by boat to the Arabian Peninsula. He landed in Aden, then traveled up the Red Sea coast to the port city of Jidda in 1444.

Reports of the travels of diplomats, merchants, and missionaries continued building the growing interest in the Far East among Europeans during the RENAISSANCE.

Growing Contacts between East and West

Through much of the 15th century, the first part of the EUROPEAN AGE OF EXPLORATION, the Portuguese, under the influence of HENRY THE NAVIGATOR, prince of Portugal, sought a sea route around Africa. In 1492, Italian mariner CHRISTOPHER COLUMBUS proposed to the king and queen of recently united Spain to sail westward to reach the Orient, a route many thought far too long. Columbus, while wrong about the distance around the globe to Asia, reached the Americas in 1492 and obtained for Spain trading rights in the Atlantic Ocean. Soon afterward, in 1497–99, Portuguese mariner VASCO DA GAMA sailed around Africa's CAPE OF GOOD HOPE into the Indian Ocean and reached India, gaining access by sea to the lucrative Asian trade.

Their voyages led to a period of extensive maritime activity between Europe and India and the East Indies. In 1503–09, Portuguese admiral FRANCISCO DE ALMEIDA led a number of naval expeditions to the southwest coast of India, where he established Portuguese trade dominance. His son LOURENÇO DE ALMEIDA explored Ceylon and the Maldives.

The islands of the Malay Archipelago and the city of Malacca on the Malay Peninsula occupied an important point in the routes in trade from China, Japan, and the Malay Peninsula to India and countries bordering the Arabian Sea. Some of the islands—such as the Spice Islands—were themselves an important source of spices. The first known European visitor to the Spice Islands is thought to have been an Italian, LUDOVICO DI VARTHEMA, in 1505. He reported finding pepper, mace, cloves, and nutmeg. By this time, people on many of the larger islands had converted to Islam, although they preserved their native cultures on smaller islands.

In 1509, a fleet of Portuguese ships commanded by DIEGO LÓPEZ DE SEQUIRA arrived off the coast of Sumatra. FERDINAND MAGELLAN and FRANCISCO SERRANO sailed under the command of de Sequira. The Portuguese made an unsuccessful attempt to conquer the important port city of Malacca on the southern end of the Malay peninsula. In 1511, AFONSO DE ALBUQUERQUE and Serrano managed to occupy Malacca. An expedition was soon sent out under Antonio de Abreu to find a route to the Spice Islands. While unsuccessful in that purpose Abreu explored the islands of Java, Madura, and Sumbawa. When another Portuguese fleet arrived in 1514, Portuguese control of the region was solidified. In Malacca, the Portuguese encountered Chinese ships, and, that year, Portuguese traders reached Canton on the mainland. Although not permitted to land, they made a heavy profit trading their goods. In 1517, Portuguese envoy TOMÉ PIRES traveled by ship from India to China. He is thought to have stayed in China for about 20 years. The Portuguese also conquered the Persian Gulf port of Hormuz in 1514.

The English meanwhile hoped to develop trading contacts with Persia. ANTHONY JENKINSON, a merchant and member of the MUSCOVY COMPANY, traveled from Russia to Persia in 1562–63. Another English merchant, SIR ANTHONY SHERLEY, traveled to Persia in 1598. Sherley managed to obtain some trade concessions for English merchants and then became employed by Persian shah Abbas the Great. After serving as an ambassador to Moscow and other countries for the shah, Sherley attempted to garner support for a Persian expedition against the powerful Turks. Later, under the aegis of the Holy Roman Emperor Rudolf II, Sherley unsuccessfully agitated the Arabs to rise against the Turks.

Ferdinand Magellan had returned to Portugal from the East in 1512. He fell out of favor with the Portuguese king despite his military service. When he conceived of a plan to reach the Far East and the Spice Islands by sailing westward, as Christopher Columbus had hoped to do, he sought out support from Charles I of Spain. He proposed that the Spice Islands actually lay in the region allotted to Spanish trade by the 1494 Treaty of Tordesillas, which under the authority of the pope had established spheres of influence to adjudicate rival claims of the Portuguese and the Spanish. Magellan departed Portugal in 1519 with an expedition of five ships. After sailing southward along the coast of South America, he managed to navigate through a strait—which became the Strait of Magellan (see MAGELLAN, STRAIT OF). Setting out westward, he expected to sight the Spice Islands after a short time. However, it was not until after more than three months sailing that the expedition sighted land. After landing for a short time on the island of Guam, Magellan sailed 10 more days, reaching the Philippines and claiming the islands for Spain. Magellan was killed by natives in the Philippines on April 27, 1521. Two of the ships finally reached the Spice Islands; one of them under Spaniard JUAN SEBASTIÁN DEL CANO subsequently completed the first CIRCUMNAVIGATION OF THE WORLD.

The Spanish route westward broke the Portuguese monopoly on trade with the Far East. Spain sent reinforcements to claim the Spice Islands and to solidify its possession of the Philippines in 1525 and 1528. But, in 1529, Spain relinquished its claim to the Spice Islands to Portugal for a payment of 350,000 gold ducats. The Spanish retained their control of the Philippines despite a longitudinal boundary line that was fixed in the treaty.

At this time, although foreign merchants were not allowed in China, missionaries were given free access. Italian missionary MATTEO RICCI joined the annual fleet of merchant vessels departing from Portugal and bound for India around the Cape of Good Hope, reaching Goa on the west coast of India in late 1578. He engaged in theological studies there for four years. Ricci eventually sailed to the Portuguese island of Macao, where he studied Chinese for a short time. He then sailed to Canton, where he was given permission to establish a Christian mission. With another Jesuit, Father Michele Ruggieri, Ricci remained there for seven years, studying Chinese, and introduced into China Western scientific and geographic knowledge. In 1591, the two Jesuits were eventually driven away by townspeople suspicious of their motives. They traveled northward to the capital at Peking (Beijing) and

met with the Chinese emperor Wan-Li in 1601. Ricci became the court astronomer and mathematician, was granted a mission in Peking, and was allowed to move freely throughout China.

It still was unknown among Europeans whether the land that Marco Polo had called Cathay and reached overland was the same as the lands visited by the Portuguese. In 1603, BENTO DE GÓES, a Portuguese Jesuit at a mission in north-central India, set out to cross Asia overland and attempted to reach Matteo Ricci in Peking, in an attempt to prove that Cathay and China were one and the same. Góes traveled into Afghanistan, passing through Kabul before crossing the Hindu Kush. By 1605, he had reached the western edge of the Takla Makan desert. He joined a trade caravan heading eastward crossing the entire width of northern China in a single year. He reached Suchow, some 200 miles inland from the Yellow Sea, where he was stopped by Chinese authorities. He sent a message to Ricci in Peking, but it was not until April 1607 that he received a reply. He died several days later, after finally having solved an age-old geographic mystery, proving that Cathay and China were indeed the same.

In the East Indies, the English and the Dutch began to encroach on the Spanish and Portuguese spice trade. During the first English circumnavigation of the world, SIR FRANCIS DRAKE, after crossing the Atlantic and Pacific Oceans, arrived in the Spice Islands in 1579. By concluding a trade agreement with the sultan of the Spice Islands, Drake challenged the Spanish and Portuguese monopoly on the East Indies trade.

The first Englishman known to have reached India, the Jesuit missionary THOMAS STEVENS, traveled there on a Portuguese ship and settled at Goa. In 1583, he helped gain the release of RALPH FITCH and JOHN NEWBERRY, part of an English trade and diplomatic expedition to the Mogul (Mughal) Empire, which had been founded by Babur, a central Asian Turk—a Muslim descendant of both Tamerlane and Genghis Khan—in 1526 (and lasted into the 19th century). In the second half of the 16th century, under Akbar, Babur's grandson, the empire was at its height, extending in northern India from Afghanistan to the Bay of Bengal.

In 1600, to develop trade in the region, the BRITISH EAST INDIA COMPANY was founded. In 1601–03, SIR JAMES LANCASTER conducted the company's first maritime trading voyage. Other British East India Company voyages would follow in the ensuing years, including those of JOHN JOURDAIN in 1608–12, CHRISTOPHER NEWPORT in 1613–17, and THOMAS ROE in 1615–19.

In the meantime, the Dutch became active in the East Indies trade. In 1595–97, the brothers CORNELIUS HOUTMAN and FREDERIK HOUTMAN led the first Dutch trade expedition to the East Indies. The DUTCH EAST INDIA COMPANY was chartered in 1602 to follow up on trade agreements in the region. In 1641, the Dutch captured the important port city of Malacca.

The French, also interested in the region, founded the FRENCH EAST INDIA COMPANY in 1664. Most of its trading activity was carried out from coastal ports in India and from the island of Bourbon (present-day Réunion) in the Indian Ocean.

European colonial powers remained constantly at odds as the power of each expanded, until the Napoleonic Wars in the early 19th century, after which the islands of the Far East were carved up into spheres of influence.

Early European Travel to Japan

In about 1537, Portuguese FERNÃO MENDES PINTO, while traveling with one of Vasco da Gama's sons to India, was captured and sold into slavery by Turks. He escaped in Malaya, and, in 1541, he arrived in Peking with a European trading expedition, entering into diplomatic service with the Chinese government. He accompanied the Chinese to Vietnam and the Mekong Delta, and, sailing across the South China Sea, he became the first known European to reach Japan in 1542. On his return to Portugal in 1558, he wrote an account of his travels, *Periginacoes* ("Peregrinations" or "Wanderings"), which was not published until 1614, 30 years after his death. His stories, many of them too fanciful to be believed, earned him the title "Prince of Lies."

Spanish missionary FRANCIS XAVIER traveled as a missionary to India in 1541, sailing around the Cape of Good Hope with the Portuguese. After spending time in the Portuguese-held Goa, Xavier continued eastward, sailing to the Malay Peninsula and the Spice Islands. In 1549, he embarked on a missionary expedition to Japan and became one of the first Europeans to visit there. He met Fernão Pinto in Kagoshima on Japan's southernmost island, Kyushu.

In 1600, WILLIAM ADAMS, an Englishman in the employ of the Dutch, reached Japan for the purpose of trade. Forced to spend the rest of his life in Japan by the military ruler of Japan, he acted as a consultant on shipbuilding and navigation. He also negotiated with Englishman JOHN SARIS in 1613, granting trading privileges in Japan for the British East India Company.

European Circumnavigators and Scientists in Far Eastern Waters

Ferdinand Magellan and Sir Francis Drake are considered the first circumnavigators of the world with their 16th-century voyages from the Atlantic to the Pacific. OLIVER VAN NOORT, following a similar route taking him through the East Indies, completed the first Dutch voyage around the world at the start of the 17th century. In the 18th century, a number of other British ships made the long journey. ROBERT GRAY carried out the first American voyage

around the world in 1787–90, while on a trading expedition from Boston around South America to British Columbia and then to China and around Africa back to Boston. And, in 1767–69, LOUIS-ANTOINE DE BOUGAINVILLE headed the first French expedition to circle the world, during which he searched for the mythical GREAT SOUTHERN CONTINENT.

In the late 18th and 19th centuries, such long voyages became commonplace—following routes around the world, or to the Pacific, then back over the same waters. They were often undertaken for scientific purposes, with surveyors, cartographers, and naturalists aboard, leading to new geographic information about Far Eastern coastlines. The search for the eastern outlet of a NORTHEAST PASSAGE through Arctic waters north of Europe and Asia, as conducted by Englishman JAMES COOK in his final voyage of 1776–80, also took expeditions to the Asian side of the North Pacific and through the Bering Strait. In 1793–95, Frenchman THOMAS-NICOLAS BAUDIN headed a scientific expedition to China, the East Indies, and India for the Museum of Natural History in Paris, retracing his route on the way back to Europe. In the course of the first Russian circumnavigation of the world, in 1803–06, ADAM IVAN RITTER VON KRUSENSTERN and YURY FYODOROVICH LISIANSKY surveyed parts of Asia's North Pacific coast. In 1825–28, FREDERICK WILLIAM BEECHEY headed a British expedition to the Pacific, during which he explored the Bering Strait, proving beyond any doubt that Asia and North America were not connected by land.

Growing British Activity in the East

The British East India Company became a political as well as an economic force in Asia and directed colonial activity. In the second half of the 18th century, the British government came to play a more direct role in Asian affairs. The Regulating Act of 1773 made the appointment of the governor of the region of Bengal subject to British government approval. The East India Act of 1784 set up a board of control to handle political, military, and financial matters.

The British East India Company's monopoly in Indian trade was taken away by acts of Parliament in 1813 and 1833. The Indian Mutiny (also known as the Sepoy Rebellion) of 1857, in which native soldiers (sepoys) in the Bengal army revolted against the British, led to assumption of full political control over India by the British Crown the next year.

The Turks and Persians maintained both overland control of trade from the East and control of various sea routes from their homelands to India. Until the late 18th century, when European influence in the East, especially that of the British in India, was rekindled, very little European exploration of these regions occurred. That which did occur was undertaken by colonial powers in order to understand and secure their holdings. The British worried that Napoléon and the French, supported by the Persians and the Russians, would attack India. This concern led them to send SIR HENRY POTTINGER, a British army officer, and CHARLES CHRISTIE, a military surveyor, to explore the interior of present-day Pakistan and Afghanistan and across Persia in 1810. The men developed an accurate understanding of the geography of the region, essential to the British defense of India. Some years later, in 1832, Englishman SIR ALEXANDER BURNES, posing as a native Afghan, explored Afghanistan in more detail. He also traveled into Persia to the Persian Gulf.

In 1802, the British organized the Great Trigonometrical Survey to map the Indian subcontinent and the mountain country to the north. SIR GEORGE EVEREST, after whom Mount Everest was named, played a part, as did native explorers working for the British later in the century. These native explorers were known as the PUNDITS and included NAIN SINGH, KISHEN SINGH, and KINTUP.

Meanwhile, in China at the end of the 18th century, the only port open to foreign traders was Canton. It served as a hub for trade silk, tea, and opium. The British sent emissaries in 1793 and 1816, but both times were unable to obtain the trading concessions they desired. Conditions under which the British traded continued to decline, the principal concern of the Chinese being the spread of opium by British merchants to much of the population. In 1839, after negotiations, the British turned over all the opium then in traders' hands. Yet, opium played a key position in British trading strategy, and, using the excuse that further Chinese demands were untenable, Great Britain went to war with China in the First Opium War of 1839–42, which was settled when the Chinese agreed to pay a large indemnity, and more important, to open four new ports for foreign trade. In 1856, the British again went to war with China—the Second Opium War—this time giving aid to a Chinese aspirant to the throne who had been converted to Christianity. In 1860, the British marched into Peking. The Chinese paid another indemnity, the import of opium was legalized, freedom was granted to preach Christianity, and the interior of China was opened to European travelers.

In 1872–73, Englishman NEY ELIAS, who worked as a civil servant in a foreign office in China took advantage of the new travel freedom and journeyed from China across the Gobi Desert, Altai Mountains, and Siberia to Europe. In 1885–86, he became the first Englishman to cross the Pamir range.

Russian Exploration Eastward and Southward

The exploration of Siberia followed a different course of history than that of the rest of central Asia and the Far East since most of it was carried out by Russians and Russian Cossacks traveling overland from the west. The Cossack YERMAK commanded a military campaign across the Urals in 1581–82, on behalf of Russian czar Ivan IV Vasilyevich, or Ivan the Terrible, and initiated Russian expansion into Siberia (see COSSACK EXPLORATION).

In 1631–33, PYOTR BEKETOV established Russian dominion to the Yenisey, Lena, Aldan, and Amur Rivers of central Siberia, and, in 1652–60, he expanded Russian interests into southeastern Siberia, south of Lake Baikal. Not long afterward, in 1643–48, VASILY DANILOVICH POYARKO led a military expedition to explore the Amur River, which fed the Sea of Okhotsk, and other rivers of southeastern Siberia.

Meanwhile, in 1641–44, MIKHAIL STADUKHIN explored the Arctic coast of eastern Siberia, reaching the mouth of the Kolyma River. In 1648, SEMYON IVANOVICH DEZHNEV led an expedition in small boats from the mouth of the Kolyma River eastward along the Arctic coast of Siberia and succeeded in rounding the Chukchi Peninsula of northeastern Siberia and making the earliest recorded sighting of the Bering Strait. In 1695–96, LUKA MOROZKO and VLADIMIR VASILYEVICH ATLASOV led expeditions onto the Kamchatka Peninsula.

In 1713–14, fur trader SEMYON ANABARA explored the Shantar Islands in the Sea of Okhotsk. In 1726–33, EMELYAN BASOV led a series of expeditions along Siberia's Lena River in search of a seaward route to the Pacific Ocean.

In 1719–27, German naturalist DANIEL GOTTLIEB MESSERSCHMIDT headed a scientific expedition to central Siberia—from the Lena and Yenisey Rivers in the north to Lake Baikal and the Amur River in the south—on behalf of Russian czar Peter I (Peter the Great). He reported on the geography, peoples, and wildlife of the region.

Starting in 1725, VITUS JONASSEN BERING, a Danish mariner in service to Russia, headed the First Kamchatka Expedition to the Pacific coast of Siberia for Czar Peter. Part of his mission was to determine if there were lands connecting northern Asia and North America. His explorations of the Bering Strait proved tentatively that there was not until conclusive proof in the early 19th century. In 1733–40, Bering and Russian ALEKSEY ILYICH CHIRIKOV commanded the Great Northern Expedition (including the Second Kamchatka Expedition) for the Russian navy to the Arctic and Pacific coasts of Siberia, the Kuril Islands, and inland areas of eastern Siberia; Germans JOHANN GEORG GMELIN and GEORG WILHELM STELLER and Russian STEPAN KRASHENINNIKOV served as naturalists. In 1741, the expedition made the European discovery of Alaska. Russians soon expanded the FUR TRADE from Siberia to North America.

Russians also explored southward to the Caspian Sea, bordered by present-day Russia, Kazakhstan, Azerbaijan, Turkmenistan, and Iran. In 1715–17, ALEKSANDR BEKOVICH-CHERKASSKY and, in 1819–26, GRIGORY GAVRILOVICH BASARGIN led military expeditions to the Caspian Sea, which helped determine the geography and watershed of the world's largest landlocked body of water (which loses more of its water to evaporation than it receives from rivers, such as the Ural and Volga).

Arctic Asia and the Northeast Passage

The search for the Northeast Passage led to the exploration of Arctic Asia. The earliest voyages in the mid-16th century —many of them sponsored by the London-based Muscovy Company—failed to navigate beyond the island group known as Novaya Zemlya because of icy conditions, thus in effect only exploring the European Arctic. In 1594, geographer JAN HUYGHEN VAN LINSCHOTEN, in one of two ships of a Dutch expedition with WILLEM BARENTS managed to pass along the southern end of the Novaya Zemlya into the Kara Sea, the start of the Asian Arctic. In 1596, Barents himself rounded Novaya Zemlya's northern end.

Russians also explored the Arctic coastline of Siberia from both land and sea. In the 1640s, MIKHAIL STADUKHIN explored the Arctic coast of Siberia around the Kolyma River. And, in the 18th century, Vitus Bering, the Dane exploring for Russia, explored Arctic regions as part of the Great Northern Expedition. Other nations sent expeditions in search of the eastern outlet of the Northeast Passage, such as the British expedition under James Cook in 1776–80.

On a voyage in 1878–79, a Swede, NILS ADOLF ERIK NORDENSKJÖLD, backed by Sweden and Norway, attempted the Northeast Passage using a combination steamship-sailing ship. In August 1878, his expedition sailed past the northernmost point of the Asian Continent at Cape Chelyuskin and, the next month, reached North Cape, where it was icebound through the winter. With the melting of the ice, the expedition continued westward, and, in July 1879, entered the Bering Strait, having completed the passage. It later visited Japan and Ceylon before making use of the Suez Canal to return to Sweden in 1880.

The Mystery of Tibet

Tibet is one of the most isolated regions in the world, surrounded by the Himalayas, with the Karakoram range on the west, and the Kunlun range on the north. Referred to as the "Roof of the World," it is the highest region in the world, with an average elevation of 16,000 feet. Moreover, for much of its history the last two centuries, it has been under Chinese control and forbidden to foreign travel. Its capital, LHASA, became known as the "Forbidden City."

The first known European to reach Tibet was Italian missionary ODORIC OF PORDENONE, along the northern edge of the Himalayas, on his return trip from China in the 1320s. He may have reached Lhasa, but documentation is inadequate. The next European visitors to the region, three centuries later, were also missionaries. In 1624–25, Portuguese (or Spanish) Jesuit ANTONIO DE ANDRADE traveled twice across the Himalayas from northern India into Tibet,

where he founded a mission at the Tibetan town of Tsaparang. Soon afterward, in 1626, Portuguese Jesuits JOÃO CABRAL and ESTEVÃO CACELLA also reached Tibet from India and founded a mission at Shigatse. In 1631–35, Portuguese (or Spanish) Jesuit FRANCISCO DE AZEVADO, continued the work Andrade had begun at Tsaparang. Three decades later, in 1661–62, German Jesuit JOHANN GRUEBER and Flemish Jesuit ALBERT D'ORVILLE traveled from Peking across western China to Tibet, becoming the first Europeans known to visit Lhasa for certain; they stayed only a month before proceeding to India. The next century, in 1716, Italian Jesuit IPPOLITO DESIDERI and Portuguese Jesuit Emmanuel Freye reached Lhasa. Desideri remained there five years, studying the Tibetan language.

The next visits by Europeans were diplomatic in nature, by GEORGE BOGLE in 1774 and by SAMUEL TURNER in 1783, both Englishmen in the employ of the British East India Company. The British attempt to establish trade contacts with Tibet and counter the Chinese claim to the region proved largely unsuccessful, as a result of a failed Nepalese invasion of Tibet in the 1790s, encouraged by the British.

European visits to Tibet were also uncommon in the 19th century. In 1811–12, the Englishman THOMAS MANNING was turned down by the British East India Company for a proposed visit to Tibet but traveled there anyway in Asian disguise, reaching Lhasa in 1811 and managing an audience with the seven-year-old Dalai Lama, the spiritual leader of Tibetan Buddhism. In 1812, Englishmen HYDER JUNG HEARSEY and WILLIAM MOORCROFT, in seeking to locate the source of the Ganges River, managed to cross into Tibet, disguised as wandering holy men, and to explore part of the Himalayas.

In 1845–46, French Lazarist missionaries ÉVARISTE-RÉGIS HUC and Joseph Gabet, disguised as Tibetan monks, managed to enter Tibet from China and reach Lhasa, but they were forced to leave by the Chinese ambassador after two months. In the 1850s, German brothers ROBERT VON SCHLAGINTWEIT, ADOLF VON SCHLAGINTWEIT, and HERMANN VON SCHLAGINTWEIT carried out explorations of the Himalayas in India and Tibet. In the second half of the 19th century, the pundits, in their surveying work for the British, traveled inside Tibet in disguise, hiding their measuring tools.

In 1879, a Russian explorer of much of central Asia, NIKOLAY MIKHAILOVICH PRZHEVALSKY, crossed Sinkiang and entered Tibet from the north, reaching within 125 miles of Lhasa before being forced to turn back by Tibetan officials. ANNIE ROYLE TAYLOR, a British missionary in the China Inland Mission and a member of the ROYAL GEOGRAPHICAL SOCIETY, in the course of her travels in central Asia, became the first European woman to enter Tibet in 1892, crossing the border from China. She, too, failed to reach Lhasa, sent back north by officials. She tried again two years later from India but reached only as far as the Tibetan border city of Yatung. Swedish explorer SVEN ANDERS HEDIN, who traveled throughout Asia, entered Tibet on two different occasions in the late 19th and early 20th centuries, carrying out geographic studies. But he, too, was refused entrance into Lhasa.

In the early 20th century, in 1900, a young Russian student, GOMBOZHAB TSYBIKOV, entered Lhasa disguised as a Buddhist. He remained there a year and visited a number of monasteries. He was soon followed by another Russian, Agran Dorjien. Dorjien became the Dalai Lama's teacher and political adviser. The British, competing with the Russians for economic control of central Asia, sent a military expedition into Tibet under SIR FRANCIS EDWARD YOUNGHUSBAND in 1904, which led to the Treaty of Lhasa with the Tibetans. In 1910, Chinese troops occupied Lhasa, although Tibet again became independent after the Chinese revolution of 1911–12.

Frenchwoman ALEXANDRA DAVID-NÉEL, a student of eastern philosophy and frequent traveler in India and China, moved to India in 1912, and, from there, made several trips into Tibet, never reaching Lhasa. In Japan, she met Ekai Kawaguchi, a Japanese philosopher and monk who had managed to spend 18 months in Lhasa disguised as a Chinese Buddhist monk. In 1924, after more than three years traveling through China and Mongolia, David-Néel, disguised as a beggar at Kawaguchi's side, finally reached Lhasa, becoming the first European woman to do so. She remained there two months, visiting all the holy sites.

In 1951, Tibet again lost its independence with the invasion of Communist China. Travel there has continued to be restricted.

19th-Century French Explorers of Southeast Asia

In 1861, the French navy conquered Cochin China, the area that is now southern Vietnam in Southeast Asia. MARIE-JOSEPH-FRANÇOIS GARNIER accompanied the expedition and was named governor of Saigon (present-day Ho Chi Minh City). Garnier later obtained support from the French government to explore the Mekong River, hoping to find an easy trade route into Southeast China. ERNEST-MARC-LOUIS DE GONZAGUE DOUDART DE LAGRÉE, a French officer who had served as the French ambassador to the king of Cambodia, was appointed to lead the expedition. The expedition of 1866–68 determined that because of rapids and falls along the Mekong it would never make a practical waterway. Doudart de Lagrée later died from illnesses contracted on the expedition. Garnier, for his part, explored the Angkor ruins and the upper Red and Yangtze Rivers.

Another early French explorer in the region was the trader JEAN DUPUIS. In 1871–73, he traveled down the Red River from Yunnan to the northeast coast of Vietnam in search of a practical trade route. His arrest by Vietnamese officials led to French intervention. In 1891–95, AUGUSTE-JEAN-MARIE PAVIE headed the Pavie Mission with the assigned task of surveying Indochina (present-day Cambodia, Thailand, Laos, and Vietnam). The French would maintain a colonial presence in Southeast Asia through much of the 20th century.

19th- and 20th-Century European Explorers of the Middle East

Beginning in the early 19th century, increasing numbers of Europeans traveled to Arabia and other parts of the Middle East for a variety of purposes. After studying Arabic and the culture and history of the Middle East in Germany, Swiss-born JOHANN LUDWIG BURCKHARDT obtained a commission from England's AFRICAN ASSOCIATION to explore in Africa. In 1809, he traveled to Aleppo in present-day Syria to prepare for the journey. He visited ancient Palmyra and lived with the Bedouin for two years, perfecting his Arabic and arranging to travel across the Sahara with a group of Muslims returning to their homelands after a pilgrimage. In June 1812, he headed southward through the valley of the Jordan River. Along the way, he explored the ancient city of Petra, which had not been seen by Europeans since the Crusades. Unable to obtain caravan passage in Cairo, Burckhardt explored northeastern Africa then crossed back into Arabia via the Red Sea. In 1814, he made a pilgrimage to Mecca and Medina to improve his credentials as a Muslim. On his way back to Cairo, he explored the Sinai Peninsula. In 1817, Burckhardt died of dysentery before he was able to find a caravan to take him south in Africa. His writings were published by the African Association, however, and influenced later European travelers to the region.

A diplomatic mission resulted in the first European east-west crossing of Arabia. In 1819, GEORGE FOSTER SADLIER, a British army officer in India, was sent to negotiate with Ibrahim Pasha, a Turk engaged in consolidating Turkish power over Arabia. Sadlier landed at Qatif, north of Bahrain on the Persian Gulf coast of Arabia, and headed inland to meet with Pasha. In the course of the expedition, he learned Pasha had moved on to Medina. Sadlier continued on across the desert to Medina, and finally met with the leader. Afterward, he continued to the Red Sea coast and returned to India.

The British East India Company, interested in improving travel across the Arabian sea route from Suez to Bombay in India, sought to establish coaling stations on the south coast of the Arabian Peninsula. To that end, in 1834, it sent British officer JAMES WELLSTED to survey the region. Wellsted, landing in what is now Yemen and Oman, undertook excursions into the interior. He made archaeological studies of ancient ruins and became the first European to glimpse the vast interior desert, the Rub' al-Khali (or the Empty Quarter).

British officer, adventurer, and linguist SIR RICHARD FRANCIS BURTON, who would go on to become renowned for his explorations in Africa, also explored in Arabia. In 1842–49, he had spent time in the Sind region of Pakistan as interpreter for his regiment. Intrigued by his encounters with Muslims and bolstered by his growing knowledge of Islam and Arabic, Burton planned his own journey into Arabia. He proposed to undertake a pilgrimage to Muslim holy cities, then continue southwestward to the Empty Quarter, which had been spotted by Wellsted but remained completely unexplored by Europeans. In 1853, he sailed to Suez. Disguised as an Afghan physician, he joined up with a caravan of pilgrims. He reached Mecca in early 1854 and Medina shortly thereafter. After becoming sick, he was forced to abandon his plans and return by steamer to Cairo. His account of his pilgrimage was immensely popular in England.

Hoping to expand French power in the Arabian Peninsula, Napoléon III sponsored a missionary expedition into Arabia by WILLIAM GIFFORD PALGRAVE, a London-born Christian missionary. Palgrave's expedition was also backed by various business interests seeking to increase imports of cotton and pureblood Arabian horse breeding stock. Palgrave left Europe for the Middle East in June 1861. After arriving on the Arabian Peninsula in present-day Jordan, he disguised himself as a Syrian doctor. He then traveled for 13 months over 1,500 miles, heading east over the Nafud desert and finally arriving on the Persian Gulf coast at Qatif, completing the first west-to-east European crossing of Arabia.

In 1893, SIR PERCY MOLESWORTH SYKES traveled to Persia. Sykes, a British diplomat and surveyor, sailed across the Caspian Sea to Asterabad in northeastern Persia. From there he followed the Atrek River eastward to Meshed. He made a north-south crossing of the great central desert in Persia, the Dashi-e-Lut. In 1894, Sykes explored the southern province of Baluchistan and became the first European to climb the extinct volcano Kuh-i-Taftan. He traveled extensively through central Persia as diplomatic counsel from 1894 to 1896. As a participant in a government survey, he explored southeastern Persia on the border of present-day Pakistan. He made visits to Persian Gulf ports and visited the Arabian Peninsula. In 1898, he took part in a surveying expedition, looking for a suitable route to connect a telegraph wire from Kerman (in the interior) to Bandar Abbas (on the Persian Gulf). In 1906, he returned to northeastern Persia as the British consul at Meshed. During World War I, he took part in British survey expeditions throughout southwestern Asia and organized a Persian military unit in support of British forces.

Englishman THOMAS EDWARD LAWRENCE (Lawrence of Arabia) began his travels in Arabia with a walking tour of Syria in 1910. The next year, he took part in an archaeological dig with the British Museum in Mesopotamia and,

two years later, spent a year digging in the northern part of the Sinai Peninsula. Having learned to speak colloquial Arabic and having become acquainted with day-to-day Bedouin life, he joined the British army's intelligence department at Cairo at the outbreak of World War I in 1914. He spent some time assessing the potential for an Arab uprising against the Turks in Arabia, who were aligned with Germany and the Axis powers. In 1915, Lawrence met with the Arab leaders Hussein Ibn Ali and his son Faisal Ibn Hussein. He helped these leaders raise an Arab army, then commanded a force that attacked Turkish rail lines in the Hejaz region of northeastern Arabia. Lawrence made many geological observations and determined the longitudinal locations of important landmarks. After the war, he worked on Arab affairs. Eventually his disappointment with the replacement of Turkish colonial rule by British and French colonial rule drove him to retire from public life. In 1929, he proposed that the Royal Air Force explore the Empty Quarter by AIRSHIP, but that plan was never put into action.

HARRY ST. JOHN BRIDGER PHILBY, a British officer in Baghdad at the outbreak of World War I, who had studied Persian and Arabic, was also involved in supporting the Arab rebellion. In 1917, he traveled to the Arabian Peninsula to meet with local Arab ruler Ibn-Saud to generate support. He ventured on to the ancient ruins at Dariyan, then followed the Muslim pilgrim route toward Mecca, arriving on the Red Sea coast at Jidda. Philby's journey completed the first east-to-west crossing of Arabia by a European in almost a century. He continued to travel through Arabia, exploring the southern provinces of the Nejd region as far as the boundaries of the Empty Quarter. He explored Arabia in the following years and resigned from the British Diplomatic Corps in 1924 in order to become an agent for mining and oil interests in the area.

Another Englishman, BERTRAM SYDNEY THOMAS, was the first known European to cross the Rub' al-Khali. First a British political officer in the Persian Gulf region, Thomas later entered service for the government of Oman as a minister of the Sultan of Muscat. In 1927, he landed at Ras al Hadd on the southeastern tip of the Arabian Peninsula and began making preliminary journeys northward in preparation for his expedition. Accompanied by a party of Bedouin, Thomas and his party headed northward from Salalah in October 1930. In early January 1931, the expedition reached the waterhole at Shana, roughly halfway through the desert. Several weeks later, it arrived at Doha on the Persian Gulf coast of Qatar, Thomas thus becoming the first European to cross the Rub' al-Khali.

About a year later, in January 1932, Harry Philby made his own expedition into the Empty Quarter. In March 1932, he arrived at the mouth of the Wadi Dawasir, near the Arabian oasis settlement at Sulaiyil. Philby's east-to-west expedition is regarded as a more accurate and thorough investigation of the region than that of Thomas.

WILFRED PATRICK THESIGER, who served with the British in North Africa and Syria during World War II, was also known for his photography. After the war, he journeyed to the Arabian Peninsula to investigate locust control measures. Perhaps inspired by his contact with the Bedouin, Thesiger also traveled to Arabia. In 1946, he embarked on his first expedition into the Empty Quarter. With native guides, he traveled in a giant circle, beginning and ending at Salahah in present-day Oman on the Arabian Sea. Thesiger made a second journey across the Rub' al-Khali in 1947–48, again with native guides, traveling from Al Mukalla in present-day Yemen on the Gulf of Aden to the Persian Gulf in present-day United Arab Emirates.

Scholarly Pursuits in the 19th and 20th Centuries

Some expeditions by Europeans in Asia advanced knowledge of the land, its peoples, and wildlife. Among the Europeans who traveled there were renowned 19th-century naturalists (see NATURAL SCIENCE AND EXPLORATION). In 1829, late in his career, German ALEXANDER VON HUMBOLDT traveled across Siberia to the Yenisey River and the Chinese frontier on a mineralogical research expedition for the Russian government. In 1847–51, British botanist SIR JOSEPH DALTON HOOKER, who had conducted studies around the world, studied the plant life of Nepal and Bengal, then of the Middle East in 1860. In 1854, ALFRED RUSSEL WALLACE, a British naturalist, after studies in South America, embarked on an expedition to the Malay Archipelago in the Far East. Over the next eight years he traveled more than 14,000 miles through the Malay Archipelago, exploring Timor and the Moluccas and all the way to Malacca on the tip of the Malay Peninsula. He collected more than 127,000 specimens and, from his observations, postulated a boundary line separating Asian and Australian types of animals. He also developed a theory of evolution by natural selection, which spurred CHARLES ROBERT DARWIN to publish his own theory. The two theories were published jointly in 1858, while Wallace was still in Asia.

In 1854–57, German brothers Robert, Adolf, and Hermann von Schlagintweit carried out studies in geology and terrestrial magnetism studies in India, Tibet, and western China. Another German, geologist FERDINAND PAUL WILHELM VON RICHTHOFEN, conducted studies in China—in the eastern, central, and southern regions—in 1868–72.

In 1857–58, Russian geographer and astronomer PYOTR PETROVICH SEMYONOV made the first European crossing of the Tien Shan mountains between Russia and China and explored the Dzungaria region and the Altai Mountains of China. Russian ALEKSEY PAVLOVICH FEDCHENKO, who specialized in anthropology and zoology, and

his Russian botanist wife, OLGA FEDCHENKO, led a series of scientific expeditions into the Pamir region in 1868–71. Another Russian, Nikolay Mikhailovich Przhevalksy, made four scientific expeditions to central Asia in 1870–85, reporting on geography and wildlife.

Europeans carried out linguistic, anthropological, and archaeological studies as well (see ARCHAEOLOGY AND EXPLORATION). In 1833, Sir Henry Rawlinson, a British officer in service to the British East India Company, was sent to Persia where he remained until 1839, attempting to reorganize the Persian Army. While there, he began copying ancient inscriptions—a decree of the Persian emperor Darius I—that had been carved into a cliff face at Behistun. These were written in cuneiform, the written language of the ancient Sumerians, later utilized by the Akkadians as well. Although Rawlinson was honored by the Royal Geographical Society for his exploration in Persia, he is best known for the first decipherment of cuneiform inscriptions, which brought to life the history and culture of the ancient civilizations in Mesopotamia.

In 1860, while conducting studies in Southeast Asia, French naturalist HENRI MOUHOT located the ruins of an ancient Hindu temple complex—Angkor Wat—built by the Khmers at Angkor in Cambodia. In 1861–64, Hungarian linguist ARMIN VAMBÉRY traveled in Armenia, Persia, Uzbekistan, and Turkestan, managing to visit the cities of Bukhara and Samarkand, forbidden to non-Muslims. In 1876, Englishman CHARLES MONTAGU DOUGHTY visited the ruins of the ancient city Petra in Arabia, examining inscriptions there, as well as at Mada' in Salih and on an ancient wall at Tayma, where he discovered an inscription corresponding to the biblical tale of Job.

A student of Richthofen, Swedish explorer Sven Anders Hedin, while mapping much of central Asia during the late 19th and early 20th centuries, made archaeological findings along the Silk Road. In 1906–08, Hungarian archaeologist SIR MARC AUREL STEIN followed the Silk Road into western China and located the Caves of the Thousand Buddhas at Tunhuang. Among his other travels was an expedition retracing the route followed by Alexander the Great's army on its return from the Indus Valley to Persia.

Russian painter NICHOLAS KONSTANTINOVICH ROERICH and his wife, writer Elena Blavatsky, carried out studies in both natural science and anthropology, after founding the Urusvati Himalayan Research Institute in northern India in 1928. His some 500 paintings also serve as a record of Asian geography and life.

European Women in Asia

Many European women traveled in Asia in the 18th and 19th centuries, especially in the Middle East, in search of adventure or for intellectual and spiritual pursuits. In 1810, Englishwoman Lady HESTER LUCY STANHOPE made a pilgrimage to Jerusalem. After traveling in the region disguised in native male attire, she crossed the Syrian Desert to the ruins of the ancient city of Palmyra in 1813. She first lived among a band of Bedouin before building herself a large fortress atop Mount Lebanon, where she practiced a unique system of religion, combining elements of local Christian and Muslim sects, until her death in 1839.

British couple ANNE ISABELLA BLUNT and WILFRED SCAWEN BLUNT traveled in the Arabian Peninsula as undisguised Christians. Wilfred Blunt was first a diplomat and then a poet and anti-imperialist activist; his wife, Lady Anne, was the granddaughter of Lord Byron and an accomplished artist. A breeder of Arabian horses, Blunt traveled deep into the Arabian Peninsula with his wife to purchase purebred stock in 1878. The two continued from Arabia into present-day Iraq, starting from Iskenderun on the southeast coast of Turkey. After following the Euphrates River down to Baghdad, the Blunts followed the Tigris River northward. Befriending an Arab sheik in Damascus, they reentered Arabia, studying the Bedouin in the Nefud region. Outspoken against European colonialism, the Blunts were well received by local peoples. Lady Blunt wrote about her experiences as the first European woman to travel undisguised in Arabia.

Other European women traveled to Asia and shared their experiences with the public through their writings, as the Chinese woman Wen-Chi had done centuries before. Among these was Austrian IDA REYER PFEIFFER, who traveled around the world twice in the mid-19th century, including overland in parts of Asia, and wrote about the lands she visited in two books, *A Woman's Journey Round the World* (1852) and *A Woman's Second Journey Round the World* (1856). Also in the mid-19th century, Englishwoman LUCY ATKINSON and her husband, painter THOMAS WITTLAM ATKINSON, traveled in Siberia, Mongolia, and central Asia. Later 19th-century travel writers were Englishwomen ELIZABETH SARAH MAZUCHELLI and ISABELLA LUCY BIRD BISHOP. Mazuchelli traveled throughout the eastern Himalayas with her husband, Anglican clergyman Francis Mazuchelli. Bishop traveled throughout much of Asia, including Japan, China, the Malay Peninsula, India, the Middle East, and Korea. And Englishwoman Annie Royle Taylor and Frenchwoman Alexandra David-Néel wrote about their experiences in Tibet. American FANNY BULLOCK WORKMAN, after traveling throughout Europe and North Africa and mountaineering in the Alps, toured India, Burma, and Java by bicycle and countries of the Far East. She also climbed in the Himalayas and other mountain ranges in central Asia. With her husband, she wrote a number of books about her travels, including *In the Ice World of the Himalaya* (1900).

After mountaineering expeditions in Europe, Englishwoman GERTRUDE MARGARET BELL began to study the ancient heritage of Persia. In the late 19th century, Bell traveled extensively there, becoming fluent in Persian. In 1900, she made a trip through present-day Israel, Turkey, Syria, and Iraq. By that time fluent in Arabic, she joined a native trade caravan in Damascus in 1913, intending to travel to Riyadh in present-day Saudi Arabia. Muslim opposition forced her back at Ha'il, and she returned to Damascus through Palmyra. Bell made archaeological excavations throughout the Middle East. She worked for British intelligence during World War I and was instrumental in organizing the modern nation of Iraq.

Russian botanist Olga Fedchenko continued her studies in central Asia in the late 19th and early 20th centuries after the death of her husband, Aleksey Pavlovich Fedchenko. She traveled in the Pamir region, along the Caspian Sea, in the Caucasus Mountains, and in the Ural Mountains.

FREYA MADELINE STARK, an Englishwoman born in France, worked on a newspaper in Iraq. She visited Turkey, Syria, Persia, Kuwait, and Arabia. In 1935, she explored the fertile valley of the Wadi Hadramawt in present-day Yemen, inland from the Gulf of Aden. In 1937, she participated in the first archaeological excavations in Yemen, excavating the Moon Temple of Hureidha. Later in life, Stark traveled to central Asia and the Far East. She was a photographer as well as an author.

Climbing the Himalayas

The Himalayas, with nine of the world's 10 tallest peaks, have attracted mountain climbers from around the world. In 1909, Italian LUIGI AMEDEO DI SAVOIA D'ABRUZZI attempted to climb K2 (formerly known as Mount Godwin-Austen), the world's second highest peak at 28,250 feet, in the Karakoram range of the western Himalayas. Fanny Bullock Workman, for a time, held the altitude record for a woman, which helped set in the Himalayas with the help of Italian mountaineer MATTHIAS ZURBRIGGEN.

Mount Everest, the tallest peak in the world, is considered the greatest prize in MOUNTAIN CLIMBING. In the 1820s, the British, with assistance from Nepalese SHERPAS as guides and porters, made several unsuccessful attempts to reach the summit. During an attempt in 1924, GEORGE HERBERT LEIGH MALLORY and Andrew "Sandy" Irvine lost their lives. Nepalese TENZING NORGAY and Englishman SIR EDMUND PERCIVAL HILLARY summitted Mount Everest on May 29, 1953.

❖

In 2000, the continent of Asia had an estimated 3.73 billion inhabitants, three-fifths of the world's population. Many of the themes of ancient times—numerous cross-cultural contacts and political turmoil—still hold true in Asia. Economic development has led to accelerating change. Outside nations, such as the United States and Great Britain, still play a part in Asian affairs.

Association for Promoting the Discovery of the Interior Parts of Africa   See AFRICAN ASSOCIATION.

astrolabe

The astrolabe is an obsolete tool used for measuring the angle of a celestial body above the horizon. With this measurement, along with knowledge of the day of the year and a table of figures, latitude as well as time of day can be determined.

The astrolabe consists of a disk with graduated markings, a sighting arm that pivots from the center of the disk—an ALIDADE—and a plumb line. By adjusting the sighting arm to view a celestial body and taking a measurement in relation to the plumb line, an angular measurement may be recorded. A table or tables, specific to the celestial body itself, having been compiled from previous measurements throughout the year, yields information on latitude and time of day based on the angular measurement (see EPHEMERIS). For navigation at sea, the astrolabe was modified to improve accuracy. The mariner's astrolabe was made of heavy metal and had a ring on top for a person's thumb or finger so the device could be suspended to keep it plumb. Still, with the constant motion of a ship at sea, multiple readings would be needed for a useful measurement. Properly used, the mariner's astrolabe was accurate to within half a degree. Astrolabes were made in varying sizes and were often ornate, with maps of stars, signs of the zodiac, and other artistic embellishments imprinted on the disk.

The invention of the astrolabe is credited either to Apolonius of Perga, a Greek mathematician of the third century B.C., or to HIPPARCHUS, a Greek astronomer of the second century B.C. It may, however, predate them. Arab Muslims (see MUSLIM EXPLORATION) reinvented or rediscovered the device in about A.D. 700, but used it mostly in the desert where it could be stabilized. Europeans used the device, along with the more recently designed CROSS-STAFF, during the EUROPEAN AGE OF EXPLORATION in the 15th century. In 1484, German cartographer MARTIN BEHAIM was knighted by the king of Portugal for having developed an improved version of the astrolabe. The device remained important until the invention of the SEXTANT in the 1730s.

See also LATITUDE AND LONGITUDE; NAVIGATION AND EXPLORATION.

astronauts   (cosmonauts)

The term *astronaut* refers to a crew member on piloted spaceflights. Derived from the Greek words *astron* for "star" and *nautes* for "mariner," the term is used in the United States and other English-speaking countries. The equivalent Russian term is *cosmonaut,* which has the Greek root word *kosmos* for "world." The French use the term *spationaut.* The term *astronautics* refers to the science and technology of spaceflight.

Although the International Astronomical Federation defines space travel as beginning 62 miles above earth, the U.S. Defense Department applies the rating of pilot-astronaut to those pilots who fly higher than 50 miles. The U.S. agency, the NATIONAL AERONAUTICS AND SPACE ADMINISTRATION (NASA), uses the term *nonastronaut* for payload specialists launched into space—as for the SPACE SHUTTLE program—typically scientists conducting experiments, but also physicians, politicians, journalists, and teachers with assigned tasks. In preparation for missions, they receive much of the same training as astronauts.

The earliest human involvement in the conquest of space took place from Earth. But humans in space can adapt to changing situations, repair technology, and perform more experiments than computerized machines, such as spacewalks. Moreover, in addition to demonstrating how humans can function in space, studies of the effects of space on astronauts have led to new medical knowledge relevant to all humans. During the earliest piloted space missions, the spacecraft was completely or mostly controlled from Earth, but the role of astronauts has increased as missions have become more complex. Politicians who have pressed for space programs, scientists and engineers who helped develop the technology, and technicians who have monitored equipment all played and continue to play a part in SPACE EXPLORATION. Yet it is the astronauts and cosmonauts who have put a face on the shared endeavor and are perceived as modern explorers.

The first human in space and to orbit Earth was Russian cosmonaut YURI ALEKSEYEVICH GAGARIN in 1961, as part of the VOSTOK PROGRAM of the former Union of Soviet Socialist Republics (USSR; Soviet Union). The first woman in space, Russian VALENTINA VLADIMIROVNA TERESHKOVA, in 1963, also was a Vostok cosmonaut for the Soviet Union. The United States meanwhile organized the MERCURY PROGRAM to develop its manned spaceflight. In 1961, American ALAN BARTLETT SHEPARD, JR., accomplished the first U.S. suborbital spaceflights. The first American to orbit Earth was JOHN HERSCHELL GLENN, JR., in 1962. Years later, in 1977, he became the oldest man in space on a space shuttle. The first human to walk in space was the cosmonaut ALEXEI ARKHIPOVICH LEONOV, in 1965, as part of the VOSKHOD PROGRAM. That same year, EDWARD HIGGINS WHITE, II, became the first American to walk in space, as part of the GEMINI PROGRAM. As part of the APOLLO PROGRAM, American NEIL ALDEN ARMSTRONG became the first human to walk on the Moon in 1969. Edwin "Buzz" Aldrin, Jr., also walked on the Moon during this mission, while Michael Allen Collins orbited it. In 1983, astronaut SALLY KRISTEN RIDE became the first American woman in space on a space shuttle. But these names and events only represent the milestones. Many others have participated in space exploration, and some have given their lives. In 1967, three astronauts died in a fire during a prelaunch checkout of their Apollo spacecraft. In 1971, four cosmonauts died in two SOYUZ PROGRAM missions. In 1986, seven astronauts and nonastronauts perished during the launch of the *Challenger* space shuttle. And another seven crew members died in February 2003 when the *Columbia* space shuttle broke up on reentry.

The first U.S. astronauts were all male and selected from military test pilots, seven in 1959. The first astronauts had to be younger than 40, no taller than 5 feet 11 inches, and physically fit. They also had to have a Bachelor of Science degree in engineering, to have graduated from a test-pilot school as a qualified jet pilot, and have a minimum of 1,500 hours of flying time. In 1965, NASA established a new category, the scientist-astronaut who was required to have a doctorate in medicine, engineering, or science. Women also came to be included as astronaut candidates. The roles of pilots and of mission specialists now have separate requirements. In addition to rigorous physical training equal to that of top athletes, astronaut and cosmonaut training includes studies in physics, astronomy, meteorology, computer science, and guidance and navigation. Every aspect of the mission, from liftoff to recovery, is covered; space conditions, such as restrictive spacesuits, cramped quarters, and weightlessness, are simulated; and responses to possible malfunctions and difficulties are practiced.

The Soviet Union also chose its first cosmonauts from the air force, choosing 21 men in 1960. The first cosmonauts had to be younger than 30, no taller than 5 feet 7 inches, and physically fit. They also had to be military officers who had graduated from the Soviet air force. With time, age and fitness requirements were relaxed, but education requirements were stiffened. The Soviet Union chose its first female cosmonauts in 1962 and first civilian cosmonauts in 1963. The Soviet Space Agency has evolved into the much smaller Russian Space Agency.

Other countries have contributed to the pool of astronauts and cosmonauts and payload specialists for U.S. and Soviet/Russian spaceflights. In the 1970s, the Soviet Union trained individuals from other countries as cosmonauts. In the 1980s, European scientists first flew aboard the space shuttle as part of the Spacelab SPACE STATION program. Canada, France, Germany, Italy, and Japan all have developed astronaut programs. In 1991, the EUROPEAN SPACE AGENCY created a pool of astronauts, mostly scientists, from 11 member nations and Canada.

Atlantic Ocean, exploration of the

The Atlantic Ocean is the second-largest of Earth's four oceans, after the Pacific, covering more than 32 million square miles. If adjoining seas are included—the North Sea, Baltic Sea, MEDITERRANEAN SEA, Black Sea, Gulf of Mexico-Caribbean Sea, and HUDSON BAY—the total area is more than 35 million square miles. (Hudson Bay, linked to the Atlantic Ocean via the Hudson Strait and to the Arctic Ocean via the Foxe Channel, is discussed as an arm of both oceans.) The Atlantic has an average depth of about 12,000 feet. Forming an S shape, it is bounded by North America and South America on the west and Europe and Africa on the east. It extends in the north to the Arctic Ocean and in the south to the Antarctic continent, the Weddell Sea being a part of it. (Sometimes the waters surrounding the Antarctic Ocean—the southern limits of the Atlantic, Pacific, and Indian Oceans—are referred to as the Southern Ocean.) It is connected with the Arctic Ocean by the Greenland Sea and Smith Sound; and with the Pacific Ocean by Drake Passage, the Strait of Magellan (see MAGELLAN, STRAIT OF), and, in modern times, the Panama Canal. The Atlantic and Indian Oceans merge in the expanse between the tip of Africa and Antarctica. In modern times, the Suez Canal provides a water route between the Mediterranean Sea and the RED SEA, a branch of the Indian Ocean. The name *Atlantic* is derived from Atlas, a deity from Greek mythology who supposedly bore the heavens and Earth on his shoulders.

The portion north of the EQUATOR is known as the North Atlantic; the portion south of the equator, the South Atlantic. Each has distinct OCEAN CURRENTS. The North Atlantic generally has currents flowing clockwise, one of them known as the GULF STREAM; South Atlantic currents generally flow counterclockwise.

The Atlantic has relatively few islands, many of them in the Caribbean Sea (see WEST INDIES). Many of the world's largest rivers drain into the Atlantic, including the AMAZON RIVER and ORINOCO RIVER of South America; the MISSISSIPPI RIVER and St. Lawrence River of North America; and the CONGO RIVER (Zaire River), NIGER RIVER, and NILE RIVER (which drains into the Mediterranean) of Africa. The Atlantic has the highest salinity of the world's oceans, in large part as a result of the salty undercurrent from the Mediterranean. The Atlantic Ocean also offers some of the world's most productive fishing grounds, in particular off northeastern North America, the British Isles, and ICELAND.

The Ancients and the Atlantic

The oceans served as the highways of world exploration between continents and islands. Yet, understanding them and charting them is a story unto itself. People living along the Atlantic coasts of Europe, Africa, and the Americas knew of the great body of water from one perspective, but they were not known to have navigated the waters in primitive craft any great distance from the shorelines. What becomes noteworthy regarding ancient times is extended journeys. The Mediterranean Sea, an arm of the Atlantic, was navigated by ancient peoples long before it is known they ventured into the Atlantic. Yet, some of those same ancient peoples are known as the first navigators of the Atlantic, by GALLEY ship. The writings of fifth-century B.C. Greek historian HERODOTUS indicate that, sailing for the Egyptian pharaoh NECHO II in about 600–597 B.C., Phoenicians followed the Red Sea southward from the Gulf of 'Aqaba to the Indian Ocean and possibly rounded Africa, returning to the Mediterranean by way of the Atlantic and Strait of Gibraltar (see GIBRALTAR, STRAIT OF). It is also possible that the Phoenicians, or even the Minoans of the island of Crete before them, ventured westward through the Strait of Gibraltar long before the historical record indicates. It is in fact recorded by Greek and Roman writers that Carthaginians— HANNO and HIMILCO of Phoenician descent—passed through the Strait of Gibraltar into the Atlantic in the fifth century B.C. and explored along parts of the coasts of Africa and Europe respectively and established trade routes. The Carthaginians may have even reached the AZORES, an island group 900 miles west of Portugal. The Greeks were among the early mariners to explore Atlantic waters. In a fourth-century B.C. voyage, probably to establish trading contacts, a scholar PYTHEAS traveled from the Mediterranean into the North Atlantic and may have even reached the ARCTIC CIRCLE. The Romans, who rose to power in the Mediterranean region after the Greeks, also dispatched ships into the Atlantic, at first for purposes of conquest. In the first century B.C., GAIUS JULIUS CAESAR led a Roman military expedition to the British Isles, as did SUETONIUS PAULINUS and GNAEUS JULIUS AGRICOLA in the first century A.D. (see CARTHAGINIAN EXPLORATION; GREEK EXPLORATION; MINOAN EXPLORATION; PHOENICIAN EXPLORATION; ROMAN EXPLORATION).

Northern European peoples are also part of the story of the Atlantic navigation. According to legend, in the sixth century A.D., Irish monk SAINT BRENDAN sailed westward from Ireland into the Atlantic in a type of small craft known as a CURRAGH, reaching ST. BRENDAN'S ISLE, which has been theorized as a number of different islands in the North Atlantic, among them Iceland, the Azores, the CANARY ISLANDS, and even the Bahamas off North America. It is thought that there were Irish colonies in Iceland by the early seventh century. The Vikings also explored Atlantic waters throughout northern Europe (see VIKING EXPLORATION). By the ninth century, two different Norse mariners, NADDOD and GARDAR SVARSSON, had reached Iceland. By the late 10th century, ERIC THE RED had reached GREENLAND. And, by the early 11th century, LEIF ERICSSON had reached northeastern North America.

European and African Waters

The sources describing early Atlantic voyages are vague. Much concerning another voyage of the late Middle Ages— that of Italian UGOLINO VIVALDI at the end of the 13th century—is also uncertain. He hoped to reach India by way of the Atlantic, but it is not known whether he hoped to circumnavigate Africa or travel westward across open waters. It is known that he disappeared near the Canary Islands. That island group, only 70 miles off the coast of Africa, was definitely known to mariners as early as the first century B.C., as reported by Roman historian PLINY THE ELDER. The recorded exploration of the Azores, 900 miles west of Portugal, dates from the 14th century, when seafarers from Genoa in Italy and the Spanish Island of Majorca ventured into the Atlantic.

In the 15th century, with the many maritime voyages sponsored by HENRY THE NAVIGATOR, prince of Portugal— the start of what has become known as the EUROPEAN AGE OF EXPLORATION—the Azores came to be thoroughly charted by GONÇALO VELHO CABRAL. Both the Canaries and Azores became important stopover points for European voyages in the Atlantic over the next centuries.

Prince Henry also sent out voyages of exploration along the African coast in the type of ship designed by his shipbuilders, the CARAVEL. Soon after his death in 1460, his mariners reached Cape Palmas, where the African coast turns eastward. By the end of the century, with the Portuguese voyages of BARTOLOMEU DIAS and VASCO DA GAMA, the extent of Africa was known to Europeans.

Transatlantic Voyages

Spain also began sponsoring Atlantic expeditions at this time. By the 1480s, Italian mariner CHRISTOPHER COLUMBUS had conceived of a plan to sail westward across the Atlantic to the Orient. Portugal turned down his request for backing, but King Ferdinand II and Queen Isabella I of Spain provided support. In August 1492, Columbus set sail, reaching the West Indies in October. Columbus carried out three more transatlantic voyages; in the course of the third, he reached the coast of South America. Other Spanish expeditions, many of them led by men who had originally sailed with Columbus, explored waters of the Caribbean Sea and the Gulf of Mexico, which came to be known as the SPANISH MAIN.

Other European nations began sponsoring transatlantic voyages, and Atlantic crossings along both northern and southern sea-lanes became commonplace over the next decades. In 1497, Italian mariner JOHN CABOT, sailing for England, reached Newfoundland and the east coast of Labrador in northeastern North America. In 1501, Portuguese GASPAR CÔRTE-REAL, after reaching the west coast of Greenland the year before, made the second documented voyage to North America, exploring coastal Labrador and Newfoundland in the hope of finding the NORTHWEST PASSAGE to the Pacific Ocean. In 1524, Italian mariner GIOVANNI DA VERRAZANO, exploring for France, while also seeking the Northwest Passage, explored North America's east coast from South Carolina to Newfoundland. Meanwhile, in 1513, Spaniard VASCO NÚÑEZ DE BALBOA became the first

European to see the Pacific from the west coast of the Americas, and, in the course of the first CIRCUMNAVIGATION OF THE WORLD in 1519–22, headed by Portuguese mariner FERDINAND MAGELLAN sailing for Spain, the extent of South America was determined.

The North Atlantic came to be well charted in the 16th century. The continuing search for the Northwest Passage took mariners, such as SIR MARTIN FROBISHER and JOHN DAVIS, both sailing for England, to its northern extent at the Arctic Circle in the 1570s and 1580s. (Davis also probably was the first European to reach the Falkland Islands off South America in an expedition in the early 1590s.) Early in the 17th century, in 1610–11, HENRY HUDSON, also sailing for England, explored the Hudson Bay, an arm of the Atlantic.

Southern Latitudes

Much of the South Atlantic was still unknown, however. The search for the GREAT SOUTHERN CONTINENT, also known as Terra Australis—a continent theorized by the ancients to exist in the Southern Hemisphere balancing out landmasses of the Northern Hemisphere—took expeditions mostly to the South Pacific, but also to the South Atlantic far from the coasts of Africa and South America. In 1739, Frenchman JEAN-BAPTISTE-CHARLES BOUVET DE LOZIER came upon Bouvet Island in the South Atlantic Ocean near the ANTARCTIC CIRCLE while looking for Terra Australis. The 1772–75 expedition of Englishman JAMES COOK, during which he circumnavigated Antarctica, proved that the fabled land did not exist in southern waters. While encircling Antarctica, he crossed the Antarctic Circle three times. He also charted South Georgia Island and the South Sandwich Islands east of South America.

An English mariner by the name of William Smith first reached the South Shetland Islands between CAPE HORN at the tip of South America and the Antarctic Peninsula. Early sightings of the Antarctic mainland were made by British naval officer EDWARD BRANSFIELD and American sealer NATHANIEL BROWN PALMER in 1820—on the Antarctic Peninsula near where the Atlantic and Pacific waters meet. That same year, German-born Russian naval officer FABIAN GOTTLIEB BENJAMIN VON BELLINGSHAUSEN sighted the edge of the Antarctic ice sheet from Atlantic waters. In 1821–23, Scottish sealer JAMES WEDDELL located the South Orkney Islands and reached the Weddell Sea east of the Antarctic Peninsula. The southernmost point he reached in the South Atlantic was not surpassed until the next century.

Oceanography

The study of the world's oceans—oceanography, a branch of geography—is a part of the saga of world exploration. By the mid-19th century, the discipline had evolved from the largely speculative to the scientific. The British voyage of the *Chal-lenger* under SIR GEORGE STRONG NARES and SIR CHARLES WYVILLE THOMSON in 1872–76, the first of such oceanographic voyages, brought back a great deal of information, including the observation that the Atlantic was generally shallower than the Pacific, and led to other such research voyages, including that of the *Challenger II* in 1948. During the INTERNATIONAL GEOPHYSICAL YEAR (IGY) of 1957–58, 37 nations contributed the use of 80 ships to study the world's oceans (see OCEANOGRAPHY AND EXPLORATION).

❖

The Atlantic Ocean holds a special place in the history of exploration because ancient expeditions into it and early crossings of it changed humankind's view of the world. It became the link between what was defined as the New World and the Old World.

Atlantis

Atlantis is the name of a mythical island or continent, believed to have been sunk beneath the ocean by an earthquake. An account of Atlantis was written by Greek philosopher Plato in about 350 B.C. in his dialogues *Timaeus* and the *Critias*. The name Atlantis is derived from "Island of Atlas," Atlas being the Titan condemned to hold the sky on his shoulders after defeat by the Olympian gods. Athenian statesman Solon, an ancestor of Plato, reportedly heard the story from an Egyptian priest and named the land. Plato may have also drawn on Greek folktales.

According to Plato, Atlantis existed in the 10th millennium B.C. He described it as a large island in the Western Ocean, a body of water beyond the known world, west of the Pillars of Hercules (see GIBRALTAR, STRAIT OF). With powerful kings, the Atlanteans supposedly extended their domain deep into Europe and Africa and amassed great wealth. They succumbed to greed, however, and attempted to enlarge their empire to the east. When their armies reached Athens, they met with defeat. The Athenians then liberated Atlantis. In a night of divine judgment, however, storms and earthquakes caused Atlantis to be swallowed up by the sea. The occupying Athenians were also drowned, leaving only a remnant from which Greek civilization was to be rebuilt.

Atlantis is sometimes associated with the island of Crete to the southeast of the Greek mainland in the MEDITERRANEAN SEA and the Minoans. Minoan civilization had been the center of culture and military power from about 3000 to 1000 B.C., before the ascension of the Greeks, and an earthquake or earthquakes may have contributed to its decline. Plato may have heard stories of this earlier civilization, and used an account of it to demonstrate the superiority of a republican form of government over a monarchy.

Situs Insulæ Atlantidis, à mari olim Obforptæ ex mente Ægyptiorum et Platonis defcriptio.

Africa.

Oceanus

Hifpania.

Infula Atlantis.

Atlanticus.

America.

This map, showing the hypothetical continent of Atlantis, appeared in Athansius Kircher's 1665 book, *Mundus Subterraneus. (Library of Congress, Prints and Photographs Division [LC-USZ62-76292])*

Proclus, a philosopher who was a follower of Plato, appeared to believe in the literal existence of Atlantis. He wrote in the fifth century A.D. of three great islands and seven lesser islands, which could arguably be the Greater and Lesser Antilles of the Caribbean Sea. His writings may be evidence of knowledge of this area by ancient seafarers. Another ancient writer who wrote about Atlantis was Roman PLINY THE ELDER of the first century A.D.

The story of Atlantis has parallels to the story of the Garden of Eden, a utopia gone wrong. Sir Francis Bacon, the English philosopher of the 16th and 17th centuries, wrote *The New Atlantis,* in which he uses the name of the mythical land for an ideal state founded on scientific principles.

The legend of Atlantis has continued to resonate with the human imagination, and societies still exist committed to proving its existence. In addition to Crete, Thera (Thíra) in the Aegean Sea, which is thought to have experienced a massive volcanic eruption in about 1640 B.C., has been cited as the origin of the legend. Other theories associate Atlantis with the CANARY ISLANDS, the Scandinavian Peninsula, and the Americas.

See also GREEK EXPLORATION; LEGENDS AND EXPLORATION; MINOAN EXPLORATION.

Australia, exploration of

The continent of Australia is located southeast of Asia, entirely in the Southern Hemisphere, between the Indian Ocean and Pacific Ocean. It is almost 3 million square miles, the smallest landmass classified as a continent. It is also one of the flattest landmasses, with an average elevation of about 1,000 feet descending to coastal plains. The GREAT DIVIDING RANGE, running north to south in the east, separates an eastern coastal plain from a series of low plateaus to the west. The most fertile regions are along the east and southeast coasts. Much of Australia's interior—or outback—is arid and sandy, but the river systems flowing from the highlands create some swamplands as well. The north's climate is tropical, and the south's temperate. The flora and fauna of Australia evolved in relative isolation over the course of thousands of years, giving rise to such unique animals as the kangaroo, the platypus, and the emu. Australia was the last inhabited continent explored by Europeans.

The Aborigines

Australian native peoples are known as Aborigines, a term that has its origin in Latin meaning "from the beginning." As long as 40,000 years ago, the ancestors of the Australian Aborigines traveled from the island of Java to Australia, perhaps by a LAND BRIDGE. They were equipped with small boats, they could swim, and they were nomads, wandering from place to place in search of food and water. Historians are uncertain if their migration was precipitated by a traumatic event, by curiosity, or by a gradual change in conditions.

The Aborigines lived in isolation on Australia, and their culture changed little. They took shelter where they could find it. They gathered or hunted food and did not cultivate crops or raise animals. They made tools of wood and stone. Their most famous tool was the boomerang, a curved piece of wood crafted to return to its thrower if it missed its target. Aboriginal clothing was minimal to nonexistent. Yet, their culture was complex. Europeans discovered more than 500 distinct Aboriginal languages. Their animist religion had a strong connection to the world of dreams, and their cave paintings demonstrated abstraction.

Ancient Exploration

Some artifacts suggest Australia had received foreign visitors before its indisputable discovery by Europeans in the 16th century. In 1909, a coin from the second-century B.C. era of Egyptian pharaoh Ptolemy was discovered near Cairns on the continent's northeast coast. In 1879, a statuette of a Daoist god believed to date from seventh-century-China was found in northern Australia. In 1948, a fragment of china from the 15th-century Chinese Ming dynasty was discovered on the ocean floor in the Gulf of Carpentaria. These finds—and the proximity of Australia's north coast to New Guinea and other islands—suggest that the ancient Chinese (see CHINESE EXPLORATION), who explored and traded in that area, traveled to Australia after the aboriginal migrations and before the modern European trade took hold.

Portuguese Exploration

There is some confusion about precisely when Europeans discovered Australia. Since the time of the ancient Greeks (see GREEK EXPLORATION), Westerners had believed that a GREAT SOUTHERN CONTINENT balanced the rotation of the earth. Terra Australis (Latin for southern land) was envisioned as a lush land, rich in resources and densely populated, and it fired the European imagination for centuries. But it was participants in the SPICE TRADE who made the first European sightings of a continent in the Southern Hemisphere. The Portuguese, who had established an eastward maritime route around Africa to the SPICE ISLANDS (the Moluccas of present-day Indonesia), controlled shipping from the Malay Archipelago, and they were probably the first to see the coast of Australia. Between 1510 and 1530, the Portuguese explored the region to see what goods of value could be found in their colonial domain. They were highly secretive, with severe penalties for anyone who revealed the charts of their profitable routes. The best evidence of a Portuguese discovery of Australia comes from the Dieppe Maps, a collection of French-made maps, the earliest dating from 1541, which accurately describe a portion of Australia's north coast and which feature many Portuguese names.

Dutch Exploration

The European credited for the earliest definitive sighting of Australia is Dutchman WILLEM JANSZ. In 1605, he sailed for the DUTCH EAST INDIA COMPANY with two goals: to look for gold in New Guinea and to search for Terra Australis. After exploring the south coast of New Guinea and discovering it dry and uninviting, Jansz turned southward. He entered the Torres Strait, came upon Cape York Peninsula in Australia's northeastern corner. He followed the shoreline for some 150 miles, not convinced the landmass was distinct from New Guinea. Jansz and his crew eventually landed, and several sailors were killed by Aborigines. Jansz claimed the territory for his country and named it New Holland. (Soon afterward, LUIS VÁEZ DE TORRES, sailing for Spain, charted the strait, now known as Torres Strait, separating New Guinea from Australia.)

The Dutch were soon making regular visits to the various shores of Australia, particularly once they mastered the "Roaring Forties," the strong and constant winds which blow between 40 and 50 degrees latitude. In 1616, DIRK HARTOG located Dirk Hartog's Island and reached the west coast of the mainland. (The pewter plate he left behind to claim the island was retrieved in 1801 by French naval officer LOUIS-CLAUDE DE SAULCES DE FREYCINET and is presently on display in the States Museum in Amsterdam.) In 1619, FREDERICK HOUTMAN also sighted the west coast, and a Dutchman named Edel landed near Perth in southwest Australia. Three years later, in 1622, another Dutch expedition continued the coastline exploration even farther southward. After being blown off course in 1623, Jan Carstensz saw the coast of Arnhem Land, which he named after his ship. In 1627, FRANÇOIS THYSSEN located the south coast, also by accident. He followed it for some 1,000 miles, but saw only desert lands, and turned back to the west just before vegetation increased to the southeast.

The first Europeans to make their home in Australia did so involuntarily. In June 1629, the Dutch East India ship the *Batavia* was wrecked on the rocky islets of the Houtman Abrolhos off the west coast. Captain François Pelsaert moved as many of the passengers and crew as he could to two islands, then sailed for help in a small boat. While he was away, seaman Jerome Cornelis attempted to seize control. Several battles ensued between the people on the two islands, with much loss of life. When Pelsaert returned with help, the mutineers were interrogated, leading to executions. Two men, whose lives were spared, were put ashore on the mainland, never to be seen again.

Dutch navigator ABEL JANSZOON TASMAN opened the next chapter in the exploration of Australia and its related territories. In 1642, he was sent by the Dutch East India Company to find Terra Australis. He took a more southerly course than was usual, but soon found himself directed by the winds to a latitude of 42 degrees. On November 24, 1642, he sighted the shores of what he named Van Diemen's Land, after the governor-general of the Dutch East Indies. (It was later renamed TASMANIA by the English in honor of Tasman.) On the same journey, Tasman made the European discovery of NEW ZEALAND.

In 1644, Tasman returned to southern waters to explore the coasts of New Guinea and Australia. After sailing through the Moluccas and past New Guinea, he came to the western side of Cape York Peninsula and explored the Gulf of Carpentaria. He proceeded westward along the north coast, traveling as far as the Northwest Cape, establishing the continuity of the coastline and proving that Australia and New Guinea were distinct places. His findings were of great importance to geographers, but the desolate nature of the land he described did not inspire Dutch commerce.

English and French Coastal Exploration

The first known Englishman to set foot on Australia was WILLIAM DAMPIER. His first landing was by chance. In 1688, his ship of PRIVATEERS was forced to the barren north shore by a typhoon. The crew went ashore and spent five weeks investigating the land and its people. Dampier's account, published in 1697 as *A New Voyage Round the World,* was read by King William III, who commissioned Dampier to make a second journey to New Holland, this time supported by the Royal Navy. On July 31, 1699, Dampier and his crew of the *Roebuck* sighted Dirk Hartog's Island. The expedition sailed some 900 miles northward along the west coast, looking for river outlets along the way. Both water and food were in short supply, and his men suffered from SCURVY. The sailors also had unfriendly encounters with the Aborigines. On the return voyage, the ship fell apart at Ascension Island, forcing a return to England in a British naval vessel. Dampier reported that Australia was a collection of large islands separated by straits. His information about the dry climate and poor soil discouraged further British exploration for some time to come.

Many questions remained about the coastal outline of Australia. When the French and British returned in search of new colonial territories in the last decades of the 18th century, the best land on the east shores had not yet been reached.

In 1768, LOUIS-ANTOINE DE BOUGAINVILLE, exploring the Pacific for France, saw the endless breakers of the Great Barrier Reef off the east shore of Australia. Recognizing the danger, he proceeded to the calmer waters of New Guinea.

That same year, the British ROYAL SOCIETY prepared a voyage to Tahiti under the command of JAMES COOK. He was charged with studying the transit of Venus, information which permitted scientists to measure the distance between Earth and the Sun. After making his astronomical observations, Cook unsealed his orders for the remainder of the expedition and learned he was to search for Terra Australis. He sailed in the southern latitudes and first came upon New Zealand before reaching Cape Howe on the southeast coast of Australia. He then proceeded northward, charting the coastline and taking note of accessible harbors. When he came to the Great Barrier Reef, he attempted to navigate its shoals, a decision with nearly disastrous consequences. After safely passing through nearly 1,000 miles of the reef, the *Endeavour* (Cook's ship) ran aground on sharp coral in four feet of water. Although Cook jettisoned 50 tons of ballast, cannon, and supplies, the ship would not move and began to leak badly. Eventually, the crew managed to beach the *Endeavour* and, over a six-week period, made repairs to it. Continuing northward, Cook again hugged the shore, rounding Cape York Peninsula before heading northwest to England. During the three-year expedition, Cook's scientific staff, including SIR JOSEPH BANKS, collected much information and many specimens. In his report he foresaw better prospects for settlement than had earlier explorers. He also reported favorably about the way of life and friendliness of Aborigines.

A French expedition embarking in 1785 under JEAN-FRANÇOIS DE GALAUP, comte de La Pérouse, to the Pacific Ocean, one of its assignments to chart the north coast of Australia, went missing in 1788 on leaving Botany Bay on Australia's west coast. A 1791–94 expedition under ANTOINE-RAYMOND-JOSEPH DE BRUNI, chevalier d'Entrecasteaux, while searching for de Galaup, explored the coast of Van Diemen's Land and the Great Australian Bight along the south coast.

Colonization

The loss of its colonies in America, along with an ever-growing population of convicts, inspired Great Britain to turn its attention to Australia for development and as a disposal site for its unwanted subjects. In 1788, Captain ARTHUR PHILLIP arrived at Botany Bay with more than 1,000 British settlers. Finding the anchorage unsuitable and the land uninviting, he sailed northward to Port Jackson and founded Australia's first permanent settlement at the location of present-day Sydney. Life was difficult for the nearly 800 convicts, 200 soldiers, and handful of wives and children who made up the colony. The lack of rain and poor soil meant poor farming conditions, and the settlers suffered from persistent scurvy. As a result, during the first years of the New South Wales colony's existence, the British settlers mounted few exploratory expeditions.

Continuing Coastal Exploration

The seemingly insurmountable barrier of the BLUE MOUNTAINS, part of the Great Dividing Range flanking Sydney, discouraged overland expeditions, but some exploration of the coastline continued. In 1795, GEORGE BASS, a young surgeon, and naval officer MATTHEW FLINDERS sailed the eight-foot boat *Tom Thumb* south to Botany Bay and Georges River. The following year, Governor John Hunte gave them a slightly larger boat—which they also named *Tom Thumb*—and they traveled on it to Port Hacking. The shores of Van Diemen's Land were not known fully, and, in 1798, Bass and Flinders carried out another expedition, circumnavigating that island and discovering the Bass Strait, which separates Van Diemen's Land from the mainland, cutting the travel time for ships from the south by a week.

In 1801, Flinders was commissioned by the British Admiralty to make a detailed survey of the uncharted coastline of the continent. He began his expedition on the south coast and slowly proceeded westward from Cape Leeuwin to King George Sound. It was still not known if Australia consisted of one large landmass or smaller islands separated by ocean. Flinders was also on the lookout for rivers draining the land west of the Great Dividing Range. In spring 1802, he entered Spencer Gulf and, for a time, mistakenly thought he had found a gap between islands. In early April, he encountered a French ship sailing from the opposite direction and joined the captain, THOMAS-NICOLAS BAUDIN, on board for dinner. The two men exchanged findings, and Flinders went on to make a complete circumnavigation of Australia. The map he produced had only a small stretch of coastline left blank to the south of Cape York Peninsula, where the reef kept him from shore. In later years, 1826–29, a French expedition under JULES-SÉBASTIEN-CÉSAR DUMONT D'URVILLE surveyed the entire south coast.

Beyond the Great Dividing Range

The crossing of the Blue Mountains was spurred on by a desperate need for more grazing lands. An 1810 drought in Sydney increased pressure on the settlers. Three years later, with the drought still on, farmer and landowner GREGORY BLAXLAND sought help from Governor Lachlan Macquarie. Together with William Lawson and WILLIAM CHARLES WENTWORTH, Blaxland headed into the Blue Mountains with the strategy of keeping to the ridge tops instead of going up and down the mountains as previous explorers had done. This approach worked, and they eventually reached a peak affording a view of grasslands to the west ideal for pasture. Governor Macquarie quickly followed up on Blaxland's

work by sending surveyor George Evans to the region and, in 1815, Evans located the Lachlan River. That same year, Macquarie had a road built through the mountains to an area he named Bathurst, after the British Secretary for the colonies. In 1817, surveyor general JOHN JOSEPH WILLIAM OLESWORTH OXLEY began his own investigations into Australia's interior, intending to travel on the Lachlan River. When swampland halted his party, he headed northwestward along the Macquarie River, only to be confronted again by swamp. Turning eastward, he then located the Liverpool Plains.

British botanist ALLAN CUNNINGHAM sought not only grazing lands for sheep and cattle, but also routes for moving livestock to market. In 1823, Cunningham made the European discovery of Pandora's Pass, between the Liverpool Plains and the Hunter River Valley, north of Sydney. Cunningham's most celebrated accomplishment was the European discovery of the agricultural tablelands, which became known as the Darling Downs in 1827. New lands were settled almost as quickly as they were located, as people migrated from Great Britain and as the European market for fine wool expanded.

In 1828, HAMILTON HUME and WILLIAM HOVELL traveled through the Great Dividing Range to explore the land ranging from beyond the mountains to the south coast. The trip was marred by fighting between Hume, who was experienced in the bush, and Hovell, who was accustomed to giving orders. Mosquitoes, ticks, and leeches added to their discomfort. Nonetheless, while on a southwestern course, Hume and Howell made the European discovery of the Murrumbidgee and Murray Rivers and eventually reached the coast at Geelong, the site of present-day Melbourne.

The desire for new land continued. Ralph Darling, new governor of the New South Wales colony, turned his attention to the rivers and swampland Oxley had reached earlier. In 1828, Darling charged CHARLES STURT with seeking the secret to the drainage of the Lachlan and Macquarie Rivers. Once again, the swamplands were difficult to cross. At times, Aborigines attempted to halt the Europeans' progress by torching the reeds in front of them. In February 1829, Sturt and his group, which included Hamilton Hume, came to the broad, slow, salty Murrumbidgee River. The following November, Sturt returned and followed the Murrumbidgee to its junction with the Murray. The expedition traveled another 400 miles along the Murray before reaching Lake Alexandrina, the river's outlet. By this time, the challenging climate and insects had taken their toll. Provisions were scarce. Exhaustion set in, and crossing the mountains was beyond the explorers' strength. Sturt decided they should return the way they had come. Fighting the current proved difficult, but, by April 1830, the group had come close enough to the settlement of Wantabadgery to send for relief. The explorers were rescued the same day they consumed the last of their food. The major accomplishment of the expedition was discovering fertile land in the Murray River Valley, and, within a few years, that region was settled.

River Systems

Perhaps the most determined—and eventually, most successful—explorer of Australia's rivers was SIR THOMAS LIVINGSTONE MITCHELL. In 1831, Mitchell and a crew of 15 convicts headed northward from the Liverpool Plains to explore new territory. The expedition located the MacIntyre River, one of the tributaries of the Upper Darling. On the return trip, however, supplies ran low, and several men were killed by Aborigines. In 1835, Mitchell explored the lowlands northwest of Bathurst. He followed the Bogan River for 100 miles and then turned westward, traveling overland to the Darling River. Mitchell's group remained on the Darling River for some 150 miles until it joined with the Murray. The expedition had several hostile encounters with Aborigines, killing several of them.

Europeans had yet to understand the relationship of the various rivers. In 1836, Mitchell set off from the upper reaches of the Lachlan River, followed the Lachlan to where it joined the Murrumbidgee, then proceeded along the Murrumbidgee to its junction with the Murray. Mitchell's historic journey debunked many misconceptions and established the connections between the Murray and its tributaries, Australia's only major river system.

Looking Westward

Once the various tracts of grassland had been found in New South Wales, and trails between them and the Adelaide and Melbourne settlements were established, officials began to look westward. British army officers SIR GEORGE GREY (then a captain) and Lieutenant Lushington made the first journey in this next phase in Australian exploration. In 1837, they left Brunswick Bay, intending to travel overland to Perth (a journey of some 1,200 miles). They explored the Prince Regent River and the King Leopold Range. In a mountain cave east of the Glenelg River, they made their most famous discovery—a series of colorful paintings of 10-foot-high people, aboriginal works now known as the Wondjina figures. After four months, because of intense heat and dwindling supplies, Grey and Lushington returned to their starting point. The following year, they departed from Perth and explored the Swan River.

Sheep rancher EDWARD JOHN EYRE carried on the exploration of the interior of the continent. His first trip, in 1839, took him to Lake Torrens, a salt lake north of Adelaide. The next year, he traveled beyond that lake and made the European discovery of the largest lake in Australia, a body of water that would later be named Lake Eyre. In late February 1841, together with his assistant John Baxter, three Aboriginal guides, and nine horses, Eyre began a westward

journey from Fowler's Bay across the Nullarbor Plain. The expedition suffered in the blowing sand. Water was in short supply. At the end of April, two of the Aborigines killed Baxter and made off with some of the expedition's provisions. Eyre and Wylie, his remaining companion, continued their trek. Just over a week later, they reached land where water was plentiful and kangaroos could be found. In early July, more than four months after they had begun, the two men arrived in what is now Albany, completing the first east-to-west crossing of southern Australia.

Eyre's discovery of the lakes north of Adelaide inspired Charles Sturt to search for an inland sea on a south-to-north crossing of the continent. Sturt's belief in such a sea influenced him to take a boat with him when he left Adelaide in August 1844. He and his crew of 16, including JOHN MCDOUALL STUART, followed first the Murray and then the Darling River before heading northward. Drought conditions forced the party to spend six months at Depot Glen, where there was a waterhole. The punishing heat undermined the men's health and spirits. After a rain, the group finally pushed on to the northwest for another 450 miles until conditions again deteriorated. After retreating and setting up camp, Sturt and Stuart once more attempted to reach the center of the continent. This time they were stymied by the difficult terrain of the Simpson Desert. The party turned back and, suffering from scurvy, reached Adelaide in January 1846. Sturt himself had come close to total blindness and never fully recovered.

In order to connect New South Wales with the shipping lane to India, the settlers needed to find a land route to Port Essington in northwestern Australia. Two explorers competed for the glory of first mapping this route: Sir Thomas Livingstone Mitchell, who had previously explored the Darling and Murray Rivers, and FRIEDRICH WILHELM LUDWIG LEICHHARDT, who, in 1843, had walked 500 miles along the east coast from the Sydney area to Moreton Bay. Leichhardt had intended to join Mitchell's party, but that expedition was delayed by problems with government funds. In August 1844, Leichhardt got the jump on his rival by sailing first to Moreton Bay, then proceeding northward through the Great Dividing Range. Leichhardt had not planned wisely, and his party ran low on food. At Cape York Peninsula, after much difficulty and demonstrating more courage than sense, his expedition pressed on to the west. In the end, he and his party succeeded in being the first to reach Port Essington. On their return to Sydney, they were greeted as heroes and Leichhardt was given a large cash award. In 1848, Leichhardt set out from McPherson Station with seven others on an expedition to cross Australia from east to west but was never heard from again, prompting a number of searches over the next decades.

Mitchell, who had learned of Liechhardt's triumph after commencing his own journey, decided upon a different route through the Great Dividing Range. Exploring previously uncharted territory, he located the Barcoo River and fertile grazing lands in the interior of Queensland.

EDMUND KENNEDY, who had been a member of Mitchell's expedition, led an expedition back to the Barcoo in 1847. He studied that intermittent river before heading northward with the goal of reaching Cape York at the Torres Strait. Once again, scarce food and hostile Aborigines made for a difficult journey. In fact, Kennedy was killed by Aborigines after he broke away from his group on the expedition's final leg. Of the 13 original explorers, only three survived. Cape York Peninsula was not fully explored until 1865, when Frank and Alexander Jardine forged through the territory.

Exploring from the West

SIR AUGUSTUS CHARLES GREGORY, an employee of the Western Australia Survey Department, opened new lands for sheep and cattle grazing on the west coast. In 1846, accompanied by his brother FRANCIS THOMAS GREGORY, Augustus Gregory attempted unsuccessfully a west-to-east crossing from Perth. On this trip he found coal in the Irwin River Valley and located pasturelands in the Champion Bay region. In 1848, traveling eastward from Shark Bay, he discovered mineral deposits and more grasslands in the Murchison Basin. In 1855, Augustus Gregory explored northern Australia from Pierce Point in Arnhem Land. He had two goals: to search for remains of Leichhardt's ill-fated 1848 expedition and to find additional grazing lands. This lengthy journey over varied terrain yielded the European discovery of Sturt's Creek and Gregory Lake and an exploration of the northern border of the Great Sandy Desert. Gregory then proceeded eastward and crossed the rivers that empty into the Gulf of Carpentaria. On the last section of his journey, he traversed the Great Dividing Range and the Belyando River before finally reaching Australia's Pacific coast near the modern-day city of Rockhampton, thus completing the first west-to-east crossing of northern Australia.

Gregory conducted another noteworthy expedition in 1858, during which he explored central Australia along the Barcoo River, Cooper's Creek, and Flinders Range. In addition to discovering more useful land, this trip also discredited the myth of a great horseshoe lake, which made the center of Australia impassable. Gregory's findings were confirmed by PETER EGERTON WARBURTON's travels in 1857–58. Warburton mapped the lakes north of Adelaide and found much open country.

In the meantime, in April 1851, the discovery of gold at Summer Hill Creek in New South Wales led to an accelerated settlement of that region. Other gold strikes occurred in Victoria and Queensland, leading to additional migrations of people from coastal settlements.

South-to-North Crossing

The government of South Australia, intent on establishing a telegraph line, offered a £2,000 prize to the first person to make a south-to-north crossing. Two teams vied for the honor: the Great Northern Exploration Expedition, commissioned by officials in Victoria and led by ROBERT O'HARA BURKE and WILLIAM JOHN WILLS, and a private expedition led by John McDouall Stuart, who headed out first from his sheep ranch north of Adelaide. In August 1860, Burke and Wills left Melbourne with the most well-equipped group Australian exploration had ever seen. Unfortunately, the two lacked experience, and their journey was plagued with trouble from the start. When they reached Menindee in late September, squabbling broke out, and party leader Burke decided to press on before the rear guard arrived with additional supplies. He took seven men with him and they arrived at Cooper's Creek on November 11. After establishing a base camp there, Burke, Wills, and surveyor assistant John King made a dash for the north coast on December 16. They arrived near the Gulf of Carpentaria on February 9, 1861, but swampland prevented them from actually sighting it. On April 21, when Burke, Wills, and King returned to Cooper's Creek with very little food left, they discovered that the camp had been recently abandoned. The situation went from bad to worse: They headed southward, only to circle back to camp a month later; once again, they had narrowly missed a relief party. Burke and King went on for help, leaving Wills behind. He died of starvation. Burke also soon died, but King was given food by Aborigines. He was reached in September by Alfred William Howitt. The four expeditions sent out to rescue Burke and Wills were responsible for many of the discoveries made along the route.

The trail that became the route for the Central Overland Telegraph Line was blazed by John McDouall Stuart, although it took that experienced explorer four tries. On his first attempt in 1859, he explored west of Lake Eyre and made the European discovery of the Neales River. On his second attempt, the next year, he made the European discovery of the Macdonnell Ranges, north of the Great Victoria Desert, and he also reached the geographic center of the continent. He turned back at Attack Creek because of the harshness of the land and a lack of food and water. In late November 1860, Stuart embarked on his third attempt to cross the continent. By the following summer, he had pressed farther north to Newcastle Waters, but the scrub was too brutal to penetrate, and he turned back, less than 300 miles from the north shore. He began his fourth effort in October 1861. This time, he succeeded in finding a route through the scrublands, and he also found relief when he reached the Roper River. His journey ended at Van Diemen Gulf in July 1862. The government of South Australia paid him the £2,000 prize and also awarded him a land grant. But his years in punishing conditions and his bouts of scurvy had left him partially paralyzed and blind. In 1864, he returned to England, where he died two years later at age 51. The telegraph line that followed his trail took another 10 years to build.

The Western Deserts

The explorers who investigated the center of the continent found useful ranch lands, but they also found great and uninhabitable deserts, which presented a final frontier. JOHN FORREST and his brother ALEXANDER FORREST took up the challenge of exploring the western deserts. In 1869, John Forrest trekked eastward from Perth to look for evidence of the last Leichhardt expedition, which had vanished 20 years earlier. This trip led him to the periphery of the Great Victoria Desert. In 1871, Alexander Forrest explored the Swan River, from which he made a loop through the southwestern portion of the Great Victoria Desert.

The Forrest brothers, exploring from the west, soon had a rival in ERNEST GILES, who made his approach from the east. In 1872, Giles made his first westward trip from Charlotte Waters to Lake Amadeus, south of the MacDonnell Ranges, where the desert country forced him back. In 1873, Giles attempted another crossing and came upon the Gibson Desert, which he named for his assistant who perished within its limits. John and Alexander Forrest mounted another expedition in 1874, which succeeded in crossing the southern portion of the Gibson Desert. After proceeding to Lake Eyre and south to Adelaide, they became the first Europeans to make a west-to-east crossing of the western half of the continent. But Giles was not to be outdone, and, in 1875, using camels, he made a daring east-to-west crossing of the Great Victoria Desert from Adelaide to Perth.

Another explorer of Australia's final frontier was WILLIAM CHRISTIE GOSSE. Gosse explored central Australia in 1873 and reached the giant sandstone formation known as Ayer's Rock.

The last region of Australia to be reached by Europeans was the Kimberley Plateau and its mountains, first traversed by Alexander Forrest in 1879. Shortly thereafter, gold was discovered in Western Australia, and adventurers quickly learned techniques for traveling and surviving in the desert.

There was still much work yet to be done in surveying the continent, but, by the late 19th century, the usable grazing lands had been mapped. In 1896, two south-to-north crossings of the western deserts were made independently by Lawrence Wells and David Carnegie. The Simpson Desert, which had been declared too dangerous to cross, was finally conquered in 1936 by C. T. Madigan. He waited seven years to travel, until heavy rains brought the desert to life and provided food for his camels. Today, there are still vast expanses of unpopulated desert in Australia. Every year, motorists who run out of gas and leave their vehicles lose their lives in the heat.

❖

The Australian continent is unique in that it is home to just one nation, the Commonwealth of Australia, which includes the island of Tasmania. Established in 1901, Australia is a self-governing member of the Commonwealth of Nations. The sixth-largest nation in the world, it consists of six states—New South Wales, Queensland, South Australia, Tasmania, Victoria, and Western Australia—and two territories—the Australian Capital Territory and the Northern Territory. Australia also has a number of island dependencies.

aviation and exploration

The term *aviation* applies to the science and operation of heavier-than-air craft, such as gliders, airplanes, and helicopters. Lighter-than-air craft, such as the BALLOON or AIRSHIP (dirigible), are generally classified separately. Both types of aircraft—heavier-than-air and lighter-than-air—have been used in aerial exploration. Lighter-than-air craft offered a new means of viewing unknown areas of Earth, starting in the 19th century. Airplanes revolutionized exploration and cartography in the 20th century, especially in conjunction with AERIAL PHOTOGRAPHY. Spacecraft, such as the SPACE SHUTTLE, that have been developed using techniques of aviation have made SPACE EXPLORATION possible as well. The science and practice of all types of flight are classified under the general term *aeronautics*.

The Dream of Flight

The concept of human flight is part of the mythology of many ancient peoples. Its practical application can be traced back to at least the fifth century and the first known experiments with kites, a rudimentary airfoil. In the 13th century, English monk Roger Bacon theorized about the properties of air, which he believed could support a craft as water does boats. Another early visionary who explored the concept of human flight was Italian artist and inventor Leonardo da Vinci, who, in the 16th century, studied the flight of birds and drafted designs of various types of human-bearing craft involving the use of muscular power.

First Human Flight

Theories and designs of heavier-than-air craft were put into effect in the 19th century. British inventor Sir George Cayley is considered the founder of aerodynamics, the science of air flow. Many other scientists and engineers of different nationalities experimented with models of aircraft and muscle-powered craft. German inventor and aeronautical engineer Otto Lilienthal made some 2,000 glider flights, starting in 1891, before crashing to his death in 1896. On December 17, 1903, American Orville Wright flew the first airplane, that is a heavier-than-air craft under power and control, off the beach near Kitty Hawk, North Carolina, in a flight that lasted 12 seconds. He flew a second time that day. His brother, Wilbur Wright, also made two flights that day, including one lasting 59 seconds and carrying him 852 feet. With more practical designs and more powerful engines, subsequent airplanes managed to stay aloft for more than just short distances. On July 25, 1909, Frenchman Louis Blériot flew from France to England.

Early Challenges

Aviation research and development accelerated during World War I (1914–18), and airplanes played a role in surveillance and in attacking targets. After the war, on June 14–15, 1919, British aviators John William Alcock and Arthur Whitten Brown made the first nonstop transatlantic flight, from St. John's, Newfoundland, to Clifden, Ireland. On May 20–21, 1927, American aviator Charles A. Lindbergh made the first nonstop solo crossing of the Atlantic Ocean, from New York City to Paris. In May 1928, exactly one year after the Lindbergh flight, American aviator Amelia Earhart became the first woman to fly solo across the Atlantic Ocean. In 1937, she disappeared while attempting a flight around the world. In the mid-1920s, airmail service was initiated. The transportation of passengers began in 1937.

Aerial Exploration

While many flew to test the capabilities of aircraft and to set distance records, or for commercial purposes, others saw the potential of aircraft in the exploration of remote parts of the Earth, especially the Arctic and Antarctic regions. In 1924–25, American RICHARD EVELYN BYRD, with pilot Floyd Bennett, made a series of flights over the GREENLAND ice cap. In 1925, Norwegian ROALD ENGELBREGT GRAVNING AMUNDSEN and American LINCOLN ELLSWORTH failed in an attempt to fly over the NORTH POLE in two seaplanes. The next year, on May 12, accompanied by Italian UMBERTO NOBILE, they managed to do so in an airship. However, Byrd, again with Bennett piloting, had passed over the Pole three days earlier in an airplane (if his calculations were correct). Other of Byrd's accomplishments include the first flight over the SOUTH POLE in 1929–30, and a general aerial reconnaissance of Antarctica in 1947–48.

Australian photographer and aviator SIR GEORGE HUBERT WILKINS also contributed to polar aerial exploration. In 1928, he made an airplane flight over the Arctic from North America to Europe, and, in 1933–34, he joined Lincoln Ellsworth in flights over Antarctica. In 1929–31, Australian SIR DOUGLAS MAWSON conducted aerial surveys of Antarctica. In 1930, HENRY GEORGE WATKINS (Gino Watkins) led a British expedition, which made use of aircraft as well as watercraft to survey the coasts of Greenland.

American Arctic explorer LOUISE ARNER BOYD made the first flight by a woman over the North Pole in 1955.

Yet, it was not just the polar regions that were explored and mapped from the air. In 1924–25, American ALEXANDER HAMILTON RICE made the first use of aircraft to explore South America. The world's tallest waterfall, Angel Falls, located in the rain forest of southeastern Venezuela, was first mapped in 1935 by American aviator and adventurer James C. Angel. Flights have also been used to increase knowledge of mountains and mountain ranges, such as Mount Everest (see EVEREST, MOUNT) in the HIMALAYAS in 1933. Aerial photography has been central to aerial exploration and modern cartography.

Azores

The Azores are a group of nine (main) islands about 900 miles to the west of Portugal in the Atlantic Ocean. Along with the CANARY ISLANDS and the Madeira Islands to their southeast, their presence encouraged early maritime explorations. In ancient times, sailing out of the sight of land in unknown waters was a new and frightful undertaking. The discovery and mapping of the Azores coevolved with basic techniques of navigation and led to determining the wind systems of the Atlantic.

The earliest knowledge of the Azores is highly speculative. In an account of Carthaginian HIMILCO's journey in about 480 B.C., there is mention of islands that could be the Azores. Some have postulated that the seafaring Irish clerics of the fifth and sixth centuries A.D., such as SAINT BRENDAN, visited the Azores.

The recorded exploration of the Azores dates from the 14th century, when seafarers from Genoa in Italy and the Spanish island of Majorca ventured into the Atlantic. The sailors who made these trips remain nameless for the most part, yet their findings have been passed down through maps that have been reliably dated. After the Canary and Madeira Islands off the northwest coast of Africa were located in the 1330s, travels in the area expanded greatly. Portugal and Spain joined in the exploration of the region. The earliest map showing one island from the group dates from 1351, while maps from the 1380s show greater knowledge, omitting only the two westernmost islands.

Portugal, the closest European nation, came to show the greatest interest in the Azores. When HENRY THE NAVIGATOR, prince of Portugal, was beginning to encourage the exploration of the African coastline, he sent GONÇALO VELHO CABRAL westward to chart the Azores. Cabral's first journey of 1431 ended 25 miles short of the island group at the Formigas Rocks. In 1432, he was sent out again and located Santa Maria. He charted the rest of the islands on subsequent trips. These journeys entailed some of the earliest European applications of the magnetic COMPASS for ocean navigation. The Azores were named Ilhas dos Acores, or Isles of Hawks, by Prince Henry. Cabral was made master of the islands, which he began to colonize with people from Portugal and Belgium in 1445. In 1486 a Flemish community was organized on the island Fayal by German cartographer MARTIN BEHAIM, in service to Portugal. In subsequent years, during the continuing EUROPEAN AGE OF EXPLORATION, the Azores served as a convenient stopover point for transatlantic voyages.

See also ATLANTIC OCEAN, EXPLORATION OF THE.

B

---

backstaff   See CROSS-STAFF; QUADRANT.

balloon

A balloon is an aircraft that consists of one or more large spherical, fabric bags, containing air heated by a small gas burner or a lighter-than-air gas to provide lift. Some balloons have gondolas suspended below the bag to carry people; other balloons carry scientific equipment. Hydrogen or helium serve as the lighter-than-air gases. Altitude is gained by discarding ballast, typically bags of sand, or lost by releasing some of the hot air or gas. Unlike an AIRSHIP (also known as a dirigible or dirigible balloon), a balloon has no propulsion system or steering mechanism. A "captive balloon" is fastened to a mooring cable to prevent free flight, as opposed to a "free balloon." The term *aviation* is generally not used in reference to balloons, but to heavier-than-air craft, such as airplanes.

A number of men began experimenting with balloons in the late 18th century, many of them Frenchmen who conducted their first ascents in 1783. Two brothers, Jacques Étienne Montgolfier and Joseph Michel Montgolfier, papermakers from the village of Annonay, sent up a linen balloon lined with paper and filled with heated air to 6,000 feet; Jean-François Pilatre de Rozier and Marquis d'Arlandes made the first ascents by humans in Montgolfier hot-air balloons, first in a captive balloon and later in a free balloon; and Jacques Alexandre César Charles, a physicist and chemist, used hydrogen instead of hot air to travel with as-

sociates 27 miles in a two-hour flight. The next year, aeronaut Jean Pierre Blanchard, with John Jeffries, an American physician, successfully crossed the English Channel from Dover to Calais, the first sea voyage. Also in 1784, James Tytler, a Scottish writer, made the first balloon ascent in England. In 1793, Blanchard made the first ascent in America at Philadelphia.

Balloon technology kept improving, and ballooning was undertaken for practical purposes. In 1804, physicist Joseph Louis Gay-Lussac ascended on a number of occasions to study magnetic forces and to observe the air composition and temperature at varying altitudes. Also in the 19th century, photographers first took pictures with cameras suspended in balloons, the beginnings of AERIAL PHOTOGRAPHY. Balloons, especially captive balloons, were used in warfare for observation, starting in the American Civil War of 1861–65, and, in the 20th century, were also used as obstacles against low-flying aircraft.

In 1893, Swedish engineer SALOMON AUGUST ANDRÉE began developing ballooning for the purpose of polar exploration. He developed a steering mechanism that enabled him to follow a course not entirely limited by wind direction. In 1897, accompanied by Nils Strindberg and Knut Fraenkel, he attempted to reach the NORTH POLE in a balloon, the *Ornen* (the Eagle), with hydrogen providing lift. When the steering device failed on takeoff, the balloon drifted uncontrollably. Ice buildup eventually forced it down after about 400 miles, far from the Pole. Andrée and his companions, after a three-month trek across the

Published in 1884, these illustrations celebrated the first centenary of ballooning. *(Library of Congress, Prints and Photographs Division [LC-USZ62-12734])*

ice, perished, their bodies not being found for another 33 years.

Swiss physicist AUGUSTE PICCARD pioneered the use of the airtight gondola for high-altitude ascents. In 1931, he and Paul Kipler, using hydrogen for lift, set a new world balloon record of 51,793 feet, becoming the first humans to penetrate the stratosphere. In 1932, Piccard reached 55,577 feet. His twin brother, Jean-Félix Piccard, ascended with his wife to an altitude of 57,564 feet in 1934. Manned balloons have since reached an altitude of 100,000 feet; unmanned balloons have reached as high as 140,000 feet.

In 1978, Americans Ben Abruzzo, Maxie Anderson, and Larry Newman accomplished the first successful transatlantic balloon flight, from Presque Isle, Maine, to Miserey, France, also setting a distance record of 3,000 miles and an endurance record of 137 hours 6 minutes, using helium. The first nonstop circumnavigation of the earth by balloon, from Switzerland to Egypt, was achieved in 1999 by Bertrand Piccard, Auguste Piccard's grandson, and Brian Jones, a British pilot, in a hybrid gas and hot-air balloon.

Most scientific ballooning now involves unmanned ascents, for meteorological purposes. Manned sport ballooning has enjoyed a resurgence in recent years. In Europe, hydrogen is favored for buoyancy; in the United States, hot-air ballooning is more common.

See also AVIATION AND EXPLORATION.

balsa raft   See RAFT.

Barbary Coast

The term *Barbary Coast* was once used to describe the coastal areas of northwestern Africa, from Ceuta at the Strait of Gibraltar (see GIBRALTAR, STRAIT OF) to Egypt. What became known as the Barbary states—independent states controlled by Muslims (see MUSLIM EXPLORATION) —were Morocco, Algeria, Tunisia, and Tripolis, also known as Tripolitania (Oea, a city in Tripolis, also became known as Tripoli, the name of a specific city in present-day Libya). Barbary was named for Khayr ad-Din Barbarossa, a Turkish pirate. In 1518, Barbarossa captured the port city of Algiers from Spain and turned it over to Turkish control. He regularly plundered the shores of Greece, Spain, and

Italy. In 1533–44, he was appointed an admiral in the Turkish navy.

In 1541, when Charles I of Spain (Holy Roman Emperor Charles V) failed in his final attempt to rout the Turks from North Africa, the era of the Barbary pirates, or corsairs, had begun (see PRIVATEERS). They would sail from their protected harbors into the Atlantic Ocean and take gold, silver, slaves, and other plunder from the Spanish treasure ships—mostly of the GALLEON type—as well as goods from European ships trading in the MEDITERRANEAN SEA. Their thievery was so costly that most countries found it less expensive to pay them tribute than to suffer a complete loss of their cargoes. The tribute and the goods of the pirate industry became the basis of the economy in North Africa.

After the British and the French enlarged their navies, they occasionally engaged the centers of piracy with blockades and bombardments. These tactics proved ineffective. In 1800, the tribute system between the Barbary states and the United States broke down, and the United States entered into a war with them. The United States eventually triumphed and, after 1815, no longer paid tribute. In 1830, France successfully completed a three-year blockade of Algiers and began the domination of Algeria. In 1835, Turkey asserted control of Tripolitania and, because of international pressure, ended pirate activities. At the same time, France, England, and Austria clamped down on Morocco's support of corsairs. Thus ended the larcenous careers of the Barbary pirates.

The name *Barbary Coast* also has been used to refer to the old waterfront neighborhood of San Francisco, known for its saloons, brothels, and gambling dens; it was destroyed in the earthquake of 1906.

bathyscaph

The bathyscaph (also spelled *bathyscaphe*) was the first successful deepwater diving vessel, an early SUBMERSIBLE with its own pressurized oxygen supply and not tethered to a ship on the water's surface. The name is derived from Greek and means "deep boat." The fourth-generation bathyscaph, *Trieste II,* was the first manned vehicle to explore the MARIANAS TRENCH, the deepest place in the ocean, nearly seven miles down.

In 1947, the bathyscaph was invented by Swiss physicist and high-altitude balloonist AUGUSTE PICCARD, improving on the design of the BATHYSPHERE, designed by Americans CHARLES WILLIAM BEEBE and Otis Barton. Piccard's first bathyscaph was named the *FNRS-2*, after the Fonds National de la Recherche Scientifique, the Belgian National Scientific Fund, which sponsored the project (the first *FNRS* was a BALLOON). The *FNRS-2* was an unmanned vessel with a limited mission. It was designed simply to descend to a great depth (4,500 feet), to unballast via a timed opera-

tion, then resurface. This it accomplished successfully in November 1948, validating Piccard's engineering and testing the strength of materials used. The *FNRS-2* was bought by the French navy, which reconstructed it for additional projects and rechristened it the *FNRS-3.*

After his work on the *FNRS-2*, Auguste Piccard designed a manned vehicle for much deeper diving. His son, JACQUES ERNEST-JEAN PICCARD, oversaw the construction of this bathyscaph, which would come to be named *Trieste,* after the town in Italy where it was assembled. The *Trieste* had the primary design consideration of being able to resist the enormous water pressure that occurs at great depths. To accomplish this with maximum efficiency and minimum weight, only the capsule that the operators occupied would be required to withstand the force. The manned capsule was made in the shape of a sphere as had been earlier submersibles, since this shape causes pressure to be distributed evenly on its surface. Holes were drilled into the sphere for Plexiglas windows and wires used to control the vessel. The rest of the craft was designed to be open to the ocean; in other words, it would not be required to resist water pressure. Such was the case with the gasoline flotation tanks and the holds for iron shot, which served as ballast. The ship could be maneuvered at approximately one knot per hour via small propellers driven by electric motors.

The mechanisms for controlled submersion and resurfacing were unique and ingenious. For buoyancy previous to diving, a combination of gasoline and air was used. When diving, the air tanks were flooded with seawater, and gasoline was discharged in limited quantities. The process of drifting to the ocean floor is an intrinsically unstable operation, and so the careful release of gasoline, which is lighter than seawater, was a revolutionary aspect in the design of the bathyscaph. Resurfacing was accomplished through the jettisoning of ballast in the form of iron shot, about the size of BBs. There were two compartments where the shot was kept, both in a funnel-type arrangement. The release of shot was controlled by an electromagnet at the funnel's neck. While the magnet was charged, the shot was held in place like a plug. This design had a built-in safety feature, in that, if power failed to the magnets, the shot would be dumped automatically and the vessel would return to the surface.

The first test dive of the *Trieste* took place on August 11, 1953, at the Harbor of Castellammare and was manned by both Piccards, father and son. The first deep-water dive took place two weeks later off the Island of Capri to a depth of 3,540 feet. On September 30 of that year, they reached a depth of 10,300 feet south of Ponza Island. The *Trieste* performed exceptionally well, with only minor problems. The holes in the sphere where wires ran to the rest of the vessel leaked slightly, but these leaks corrected themselves with increased depth. The Plexiglas portholes for viewing never let so much as a drop of water into the capsule. In 1954, the bathyscaph accomplished a descent to a depth of 13,125 feet.

After 22 dives, the U.S. Navy eventually purchased the craft and contracted Jacques Piccard as adviser and pilot. More dives were conducted in the MEDITERRANEAN SEA in 1957–58, after which the *Trieste* was brought to San Diego Harbor for exploration in the Pacific Ocean.

In 1958, the navy undertook Project Nekton, with the goal of reaching the greatest depth in the ocean. This involved the retrofitting of the *Trieste.* Designed for a depth of 10 miles, the *Trieste II,* as it was renamed, weighed 13 tons. It had a thicker personnel capsule and larger flotation tank. The new sphere was five inches thick, except around the portholes, where it was seven inches thick. The gasoline float was increased from a capacity of 28,000 gallons to 34,200 gallons. The first test dive for Project Nekton took place November 4, 1959, off Guam. On January 8, 1960, the *Trieste* attained a new record of 23,000 feet at a location called Nero Deep.

The attempt at Challenger Deep, the name given to the deepest place in the Marianas Trench, was made on January 23, 1960, by Jacques Piccard and navy lieutenant Don Walsh. Despite instruments damaged from the tow to the location, Piccard made the decision to go ahead with the dive. Timing was important because of limited oxygen for the dive and for retrieval of the crew. Poor weather delayed the trip by one hour. At eight in the morning, Piccard and Walsh began their descent. They encountered several thermoclines, places where one layer of water meets another of differing density, causing the ship to be repelled. These were penetrated, and, by 1:06 P.M., they had settled to the bottom at 35,800 feet. They had navigated the narrow chasm that formed the trench and found the bottom, a brown mud consisting largely of the remains of diatoms, a type of algae. A lone flatfish was sighted, proving that chordates (animals with a spinal chord) were able to survive in such an environment.

Although there is a curiosity and motivation regarding exploration of the most extremes depths of the globe, most of the ocean presents more moderate depths. For this reason, and because of the limited tasks that the bathyscaph was able to perform, it has been replaced by the SUBMARINE, which is designed for a wide variety of applications.

See also OCEANOGRAPHY AND EXPLORATION.

bathysphere

The bathysphere is a container constructed of steel, designed for deep-sea observation and study, at depths not able to be reached by a DIVING BELL. In 1926, American CHARLES WILLIAM BEEBE made the claim of having designed a craft that could descend one mile below the ocean's surface, a SUBMERSIBLE with its own pressurized oxygen supply.

Beebe was a zoologist and bird expert who had bought a copper diving helmet and accompanying apparatus prior to a trip to the Galapagos Islands to study fish (see DIVING SUIT). The helmet worked well and inspired him to design a craft to hold humans. He and the engineer Otis Barton decided on the shape of a sphere rather than a cylinder, which had been Beebe's original idea. A sphere would be able to resist water pressure evenly, whereas any other shape would have weak points. Their vessel weighed 5,400 pounds and measured four feet nine inches in diameter. It was tethered by a steel cable to a winch aboard a ship, but had its own supply of oxygen in tanks inside the sphere.

The bathysphere's first dives were conducted in 1930 off the coast of Bermuda. Beebe and Barton encountered problems that needed fixing, but, by 1932, they were confident enough to make a live radio broadcast as they attempted their deepest dive ever, which exceeded 2,000 feet. On a subsequent dive, they reached the limit of their length of steel cable, 3,028 feet, five times deeper than ever before accomplished. Barton continued to work with the invention and to make underwater films. In 1949, Barton attained a depth of 4,500 feet, the ultimate depth for the bathysphere. A more advanced type of bathysphere was the BATHYSCAPH, designed by Swiss AUGUSTE PICCARD and first used in 1947.

See also OCEANOGRAPHY AND EXPLORATION.

Bering Strait

The Bering Strait is the waterway between the northeastern end of the continent of Asia, that part of Russia known as SIBERIA, and the northwestern end of the continent of North America, present-day Alaska. It is located at a latitude of 65 degrees and 30 minutes north and a longitude of 169 degrees west. The strait connects the Bering Sea, a northern arm of the Pacific Ocean, with the Arctic Ocean. The narrowest part of the strait—51 miles wide—is between Cape Dezhnev in Russia and Cape Prince of Wales in Alaska. The Diomede Islands lie between the capes. Part of the strait is normally frozen over from October to June.

The Bering Strait forms the western outlet of the NORTHWEST PASSAGE and the eastern outlet of the NORTHEAST PASSAGE, water routes sought by European nations for centuries. There were reports of such a strait—the western outlet of the fabled Strait of Anian (see ANIAN, STRAIT OF)—in the mid-16th century, with representations of it on early maps. The earliest recorded sighting of the strait was by a party of Cossacks under SEMYON IVANOVICH DEZHNEV in 1648; they are thought to have passed through it as well. VITUS JONASSEN BERING, a Danish explorer in service to Russia, first charted the strait in 1728; the strait was subsequently named for him. It was further explored by Englishmen JAMES COOK in 1778 and FREDERICK WILLIAM BEECHEY in 1826.

It is theorized that at times during Earth's last ice age in the millennia before 8000 B.C., when more of Earth's water was frozen in glaciers and now-submerged land was exposed, there was a LAND BRIDGE where the Bering Strait is today. Archaeological evidence indicates that Paleo-Indians, tracking big game, migrated to the Americas across the Bering Strait land bridge and are ancestral to the Native American population.

See also ARCTIC, EXPLORATION OF THE; PACIFIC OCEAN, EXPLORATION OF THE.

Blanc, Mont

Mont Blanc is a mountain in the Alps of Europe, located in southwestern France in the Haute-Savoie Department, formerly the Duchy of Savoy. The name is also applied to the massif or range of which the mountain is a part, along the border between France and Italy. The French *Mont Blanc,* or Italian *Monte Bianco,* translates as "white mountain." At 15,771 feet above sea level, Mont Blanc is the highest mountain in the Alpine system. From the summit to about 8,000 feet high, an ice cap, 75 feet thick, covers the mountain. The Mont Blanc massif is considered part of the Savoy Alps of the Western Alps (the Western and Eastern Alps being delineated by a furrow that leads from the Rhine Valley in northern Switzerland to Lake Como in northern Italy).

Mont Blanc is important in the history of exploration since concerted attempts to climb it laid the foundations of modern MOUNTAIN CLIMBING, from 1760, when Swiss naturalist Horace Bénédict de Saussure offered a reward to reach the top, until 1786 when Savoy natives JACQUES BALMAT and Michel Paccard did so.

Blue Mountains

The Blue Mountains of Australia are a collection of high sandstone mountains, 40 miles to the west of Sydney. Named for a blue haze produced by the oils of abundant eucalyptus trees, they are part of the GREAT DIVIDING RANGE, a continuous chain of mountains forming a crescent along the eastern edge of the continent. They rise up more than 3,000 feet above the lowlands. On the eastern side, canyons and ravines end in dead ends, some in the form of waterfalls cascading from high above. Past the easternmost wall of ridges, there is a succession of peaks and valleys, covered with scrub brush. The Blue Mountains present a formidable barrier and hemmed in the settlement of Sydney for 25 years before explorers were able find routes through them to usable land in the interior.

The first explorers of the Blue Mountains were escaped convicts and their pursuers. Legend held that non-Aborigine communities lay beyond the mountains in lands with bountiful food sources. Another myth held that it was but a short distance to China over the mountains. To debunk this latter myth, New South Wales colony governor John Hunter (the second governor after ARTHUR PHILLIP) sent out a party of convicts and soldiers under John Wilson, an ex-convict who had become an experienced bushman, in January 1798. Many of the expedition members were quickly discouraged and returned to base, but Wilson and his guides pushed on and came upon a large but slow river, probably the Lachlan. Ensign Barrallier led another early expedition in 1802. A skilled surveyor, he made a map of his route into the mountains. Yet, since he failed to locate suitable land for development, his accomplishments were disregarded.

In 1813, after a drought of nearly three years, the settlers' need for farm and grazing lands became acute. GREGORY BLAXLAND, a farmer, became determined to cross the mountains in search of arable land. On May 11, 1813, he left South Creek with a fellow farmer, WILLIAM CHARLES WENTWORTH; surveyor William Lawson; an Aboriginal guide named James Burnes; and several convict servants. They decided on a novel strategy. Instead of setting a straight course up and down the mountains, they followed the high ridges. On May 28, they came to Mount York, from which they could see pastureland dotted with trees. Blaxland estimated that these lands would be sufficient to absorb settlers for the next 30 years.

With these encouraging findings, Lachlan Macquarie, now governor, commissioned surveyor George William Evans to investigate later in 1813. Evans proceeded to Mount Blaxland, from where he proceeded to the Fish River, past the Great Dividing Range. He followed the Fish River to the Campbell River, which joins the Macquarie River, named after Governor Macquarie. Evans's explorations inspired Macquarie to build a road to the fertile new lands. It was built in only six months and enabled the town of Bathurst to be established in the Blue Mountains' western foothills. With Bathurst as a staging area, Surveyor General JOHN JOSEPH WILLIAM MOLESWORTH OXLEY charted the Lachlan River in 1817 and the Macquarie River in 1818.

Although developed, especially for vacation use, the Blue Mountains include a number of designated wilderness areas.

See also AUSTRALIA, EXPLORATION OF.

British East India Company
(East India Company)

The British East India Company (known in Great Britain simply as the East India Company), founded in 1600 and active until 1874, was the largest and longest-lasting of the joint-stock East India Companies of various nations, formed to conduct trade between Europe and the East. With a charter from the British Crown, the British East India

Company enjoyed monopoly privileges in the Eastern Hemisphere. It also came to act as the government of India, prosecuting crime, dispensing punishment, and seizing land. Members of the British government encouraged these activities because of their many benefits: a favorable balance of trade, cash payments, loans to finance warfare, and aid in the conquest of the Indian subcontinent.

Early Conflicts

Queen Elizabeth I granted the charter under the title "The Governor and Company of Merchants of London Trading into the East Indies" in 1600, with a monopoly on trade in the region (see EAST INDIES). A governor and 24 directors chosen from its stockholders managed the company. Merchants RALPH FITCH and JOHN NEWBERRY had established the original diplomatic contacts between England and India in the 1580s. After the founding of the company, the queen sent her envoy, John Mildenhall, to India to negotiate trading privileges, but he was rebuffed by the Mogul (Mughal) ruler, who had a prior trade relationship with the Portuguese. In the meantime, a fleet of three ships, laden with goods to trade, was sent to the ports of Achin on Sumatra and Bantam on Java. The fleet returned in 1603, carrying a cargo of pepper and other spices. That same year, the English fought the Portuguese at the port of Surat in northwestern India and gained the right to trade there as well. In 1610–11, it established its first factories—that is, trading posts—in India in the Indian provinces of Madras and Bombay.

At that time, trade in India, Malaysia, Indonesia, and the SPICE ISLANDS (the Moluccas) was dominated by the Portuguese. The Portuguese did not have sufficient military power to keep out challengers, however, and the Dutch, French, and English were all active in the region, forming alliances with native kings at various trading centers. In 1612, Thomas Best was sent with letters from English king James I, asking the ruler of India to cooperate with England against Portugal. In a legendary naval battle, Best, with two small ships, outmaneuvered a Portuguese fleet of 29. In 1615, the British government sent another emissary to firm up relations between India and England. SIR THOMAS ROE arrived in Surat in September of that year, and, from there, made a difficult overland journey to Ajmer, where the Mogul capital was located at the time. Roe spent three years at the court of King Jahangir; his diplomatic efforts set the stage for future advances in English-Indian trade.

With its long tradition of trade with the Middle East, India had developed a wide variety of finished products to export and expected to receive high-quality products in exchange. England exported velvets, satins, fine tableware, saddles, spyglasses, and enamel work, among other fine goods. In return, India traded silks (both raw and finished), diamonds, medicines, and brass and bronze work. India used some of these items, in particular the silk cloth, to barter for spices with nations farther to the east.

In 1620, the Raja of Golconda agreed to allow the East India Company to build an outpost near the Dutch settlement of Pulicat on the Coromandel Coast. Originally called Fort St. George, this became the bustling city of Madras and a major hub of activity for the East India Company. As profits began to swell for the company, discontent grew among merchants who were shut out of the Indian trade, and they petitioned Parliament for their fair share. In 1623, to strengthen the East India Company's position, King James granted it the power of law enforcement on both land and sea. Conflict with the Dutch came to a head that same year with the Amboina Massacre. The British and the Dutch had shared trading rights with the tiny island of Amboina, just off the coast of New Guinea. To consolidate their hold on the Spice Islands, the Dutch fabricated charges of conspiracy against the English stationed there, convicting and executing 10 of them, along with nine Japanese. Henceforth, the British concentrated on its trade with India.

With the ascension of Charles I to the throne, the British East India Company encountered more difficulties. The new king was sympathetic to those merchants who made trips to India and back without official sanction. In 1635, Charles went so far as to create his own company to challenge the exclusive privileges of the older concern. His venture was a disaster, however, and the East India Company responded by continuing to refine its operations. Skirmishes with the Dutch remained a vexing problem for the company until the 1654 English peace treaty with Holland. The company was also sustaining increasing losses from piracy. It was widely understood that complicity between pirates and local sultans enabled this thievery to exist, and, in 1657, Oliver Cromwell, the Puritan leader who ruled England in 1653–58 under the title of Lord Protector, restored trading powers to the company that Charles had eroded. In 1661, a completely rewritten charter expanded the trading company's rights even further.

Issues at Home

As the company entered the latter half of the 17th century, trouble in the Pacific diminished and dissent at home increased. The silk weavers of London complained that their position was being undercut by the importation of finished cloth, and British merchants continued to voice their arguments against monopoly protections. Events came to a head in 1694, when it was revealed that the East India Company had paid £80,000 for "secret services," including the renewal of their charter with favorable terms. In 1698, Parliament authorized the establishment of a new trading company, and this event brought chaos to the India trade. The businessmen of both concerns suffered, and, in 1702, the two companies were merged into the "United Company of Merchants of England trading to the East Indies" but still were popularly known as the East India Company. At the time of its final consolidation, the new company lent £1,200,000 to the British government in 1708, and, as a result, for a time, disagreements were quieted.

The 18th century saw the rise of the importance of tea for the East India Company. Introduced by the Dutch in Europe the previous century, tea had become an essential commodity in many British households. Great Britain had gone so far as to pass a law in 1745 requiring the company either to supply tea at reasonable prices or to face sanctions.

Great Britain was at war with France during much of the 18th century, and the conflict extended to the Far East. In mid-century, Robert Clive led British forces on victories over the French and Dutch. In 1761, the British gained control of the French trading port of Pondicherry, thus circumscribing the ambitions of the FRENCH EAST INDIA COMPANY in India. The 1763 Treaty of Paris gave some trading privileges back to the French, but the British would no longer be defied by other European powers in India.

In the waning years of the 18th century, with outside conflict quashed, the power and profits of the British East India Company increased steadily. Seeing their enormous trading profits disappearing into private hands, the British government levied an annual payment of £400,000 on the company and limited its dividends to 12.5 percent.

The incident that motivated the British government to begin to assert legal control in India came to be known as the Tanjore question. The raja of Tanjore had been deposed by his rival, the nabob of Arcot, Muhammad Ali. Without the consent of his superiors, the president of Madras was complicit in this coup. The raja was subsequently reinstated, but, in the meantime, the nabob had mortgaged the assets of Tanjore, leading to financial repercussions in England.

The Regulating Act of 1773 made the appointment of the governor of Bengal subject to British government approval. The first to hold the post was Warren Hastings, who had a great influence in the future organization of the country. The East India Act of 1784 made the British government even more responsible for activities in India by setting up a board of control to handle political, military, and financial matters. The East India Company's monopoly in Indian trade was taken away by acts of Parliament in 1813 and 1833. The Indian Mutiny (also known as the Sepoy Rebellion) of 1857, in which native soldiers (sepoys) in the Bengal army revolted against the British, led to assumption of full political control over India by the British Crown under the terms of the Act for the Better Government of India the next year. The assets of the company were finally dispersed in 1874 with the East India Stock Dividend Redemption Act.

❖

The activities of the British East India Company contributed to the spread of geographic knowledge about Asia to Europeans. It also actively promoted the exploration of lands. The Great Trigonometrical Survey of India, headed for a time by British officer and surveyor SIR GEORGE EVEREST, was initiated by the British East India Company.

See also COMMERCE AND EXPLORATION.

bullboat   See CORACLE.

bulrush boat   See CANOE.

C

Canary Islands

The Canary Islands are a group of seven volcanic islands 70 miles off the coast of Africa in the Atlantic Ocean near the border of present-day Morocco and Western Sahara, about 600 miles to the southwest of the Iberian Peninsula. They mark the beginning of the Canary Current, part of the circular system of currents in the Northern Hemisphere that are generated by the northeast TRADE WINDS.

The record of the discovery of the Canaries predates the EUROPEAN AGE OF EXPLORATION of the 15th through the 17th centuries; consequently, the islands served as a point of reference in the unknown seas to the west of Africa, along with the Madeira Islands, and later the AZORES. These islands became a testing ground as explorers learned to navigate the open seas. The Canaries also became a way station for longer voyages.

PLINY THE ELDER, a Roman historian, demonstrated definite knowledge of the Canary Islands in 40 B.C., and subsequent writers, such as Plutarch, referred to the "Fortunate Islands," probably the Canaries, although they were possibly confused with the Madeiras and Azores. In the early first century A.D., King Juba of Morocco sent explorers to the islands. They brought back a detailed record of their flora and fauna. It was also noted that there were signs of previous human habitation, although no living people were found at the time. It has been theorized that Irish monk SAINT BRENDAN reached the Canaries in the sixth century.

In the late Middle Ages, merchant ships began to pass routinely beyond the Strait of Gibraltar (see GIBRALTAR, STRAIT OF)—from the MEDITERRANEAN SEA into the Atlantic Ocean—and the Canary Islands were rediscovered. Arab Muslims reached the Canaries in the 12th century. There were a number of voyages in the early 14th century, including one by French mariners in 1334 and one, about the same time, by an Italian, Lanzarotto Malocello, who gave his name to the Island Lanzarote; a map indicating his findings dates to 1339. In *Teseida,* published in about 1341, Italian storyteller Giovanni Boccaccio relates trips by Spanish, Italian, and Portuguese seamen. Some of the visitors attempted to seize power but failed to maintain control for long. In the second half of the century, the islands were regularly visited by Franciscan missionaries, yet attacks on them by the inhabitants halted missionizing attempts for a time.

The peoples who lived on the Canary Islands at the time of the European rediscovery were the Guanches. Like the Berbers of North Africa, they were an ethnically mixed population of varying height, hair, and skin color. Their exact place of origin is unknown; cultural and linguistic evidence traces their origins to the Middle East. Through isolation over time, the society of the Guanches had come to a state that the Europeans deemed as savage. Their extermination was carried out by 1496.

In the early 15th century, the Canaries became the object of closer scrutiny, as various European nations sought exploitable resources. In 1402, the Gadifer de la Salle and Jean de Béthencourt, both Normans, explored the islands in search of gold. No gold was found, but Béthencourt made himself king with the backing of Spain. From 1427 until mid-century, Portugal was most active in exploring the Canaries. They also used them to aid in sailing westward, which led to the charting of the Azores. In 1479, after a war between Spain and Portugal, the Treaty of Alcacovas established Spanish dominion over the islands. Portugal managed to keep its possessions on the coast of West Africa, the more profitable side of the bargain.

As Europe entered the era of transoceanic travel, the Canary Islands became an important point of launch for numerous voyages of exploration. In 1492, an Italian, CHRISTOPHER COLUMBUS, exploring for Spain, made a stop at the islands to resupply his ships and to make repairs. Since they are located at a latitude where the weather is pleasing, it was his intention to sail due westward from the Canaries to Asia. Another voyage of note that gained assistance from the islands was Portuguese FERDINAND MAGELLAN's first CIRCUMNAVIGATION OF THE WORLD, also for Spain, which was begun in 1519.

See also ATLANTIC OCEAN, EXPLORATION OF THE; MUSLIM EXPLORATION.

canoe

A canoe is a type of small, light boat, with a watertight hull shaped for speed and navigability, typically propelled by at least one paddle. Predating the historical record, it evolved from the RAFT, which does not have a watertight hull or a streamlined shape. The canoe has many variations around the world. The term *canoe,* from an Arawak (Taino) Indian word, is most often applied to narrow boats with identically shaped bows and sterns and curved sides and that are propelled by a paddle. But, the term encompasses boats with varying shapes as well, some of them with sails. In the broader classification of the term can be included such craft as the kayak, umiak, baidarka, CORACLE (bullboat), OUTRIGGER, and reed-bundle boat.

Canoes are made from a variety of materials, depending upon what is available in the local environment. In the South Pacific islands and the Americas, where wood is plentiful, the craft began as the simple dugout canoe (also called "dugouts"), fashioned from a log with the inner core hollowed out. On the west coast of North America, where cedar trees grow very large, early Native American dugouts were sometimes 100 feet long and were propelled by numerous paddlers. The Haida and Tlingit Indians would fell a tree near the ocean's shore, where they would build seaworthy vessels for use along the coast. The PIROGUE, used in the 19th-century FUR TRADE in North America, was a dugout.

Also in North America, light birch-bark canoes of varying designs were developed among Algonquian-speaking

Shown here, in a photograph from about 1900, is a Native American dugout canoe on the Columbia River. *(Library of Congress, Prints and Photographs Division [LC-USZ62-101283])*

peoples and other tribes. Pieces of birch bark were stretched over a framework of saplings, then sewn together with root fibers and sealed with pitch or tar. These remarkably light canoes were practical for portages, that is, the carrying of the craft between waterways. The Iroquois (Haudenosaunee) Indians used elm bark as a covering.

For the kayak, Inuit (Eskimo) traditionally covered a frame of bone (often whalebone) or driftwood with sea mammal skins; the deck was also covered, except for a cockpit; the paddler typically used a double paddle. The umiak is a larger, open variation. The Aleut variation of the kayak is known as the baidarka. Another hide boat found in North America among some tribes of the northern plains is the bullboat, made from buffalo hides stretched over a circular frame. The similarly made coracle of parts of Europe and Asia were also round or oval in shape.

Pacific Islanders invented the double canoe—two canoes placed parallel and lashed together with rods. This made the resulting boat more stable and was related to the OUTRIGGER, which had a float parallel to the main body of the craft, also for stability. Sails were typically added. In the shape of a crab claw, they were woven from palm fronds and other fibrous material. The Englishman JAMES COOK observed double canoes with crab-claw sails in Hawaii. There is evidence that the peoples of the Pacific islands conducted much interisland travel with these highly evolved craft.

Another variation is what is known as the reed-bundle canoe or reed-bundle boat, made from plants of the sedge family. Those found in Africa on the NILE RIVER and made from papyrus are also called papyrus boats; those on lakes in the ANDES MOUNTAINS of South America and made from tule, a type of bulrush, are known as bulrush boats. To make these craft, reeds are tied together into bundles; the bundles are then stacked on one another. The reed bundles become waterlogged after use, but dry out in the sun. Reed boats have two main variations in their appearance. Some are double-ended, with two raised ends like a typical canoe, while others have a single raised prow and a broad stern, like a modern rowboat. Reed canoes were probably first propelled with poles, then later with paddles or oars. Sails were also sometimes used.

Canoes, in general, are used for navigating the lakes and rivers in the interior of continents or along coastlines rather than for transoceanic voyages. They played a part in countless expeditions—especially in Africa, South America, and North America. In North America, they were central to the FUR TRADE, used by Indians and non-Indians alike.

Modern canoes are made from molded plastic or fiberglass, aluminum and magnesium alloys, rubber, canvas, and other materials as well as wood. The catamaran, a refinement of the double canoe, is one of the fastest small sailboats.

See also SHIPBUILDING AND EXPLORATION.

Cape Horn

Cape Horn is the southernmost point of land off the coast of South America. Its importance in the history of exploration is that it marked the gateway between the Atlantic Ocean and Pacific Ocean in the west, similar to the CAPE OF GOOD HOPE at the southern end of Africa between the Atlantic Ocean and the Indian Ocean. The European discovery of Cape Horn took place in three stages. The first to cross from the Atlantic into the Pacific was Portuguese FERDINAND MAGELLAN, in service to Spain, in 1520. The passageway he used, which came to be known as the Strait of Magellan (see MAGELLAN, STRAIT OF), was actually north of Cape Horn, between the main continent and a large island. Magellan observed fires burning on this island, maintained by the Native Americans, and named it Tierra del Fuego, meaning "Land of Fire." There had been speculation for centuries that the South American continent was connected to a southern landmass referred to as the GREAT SOUTHERN CONTINENT, or Terra Australis, with Atlantic and Pacific waters separated. Magellan's passage from the Atlantic to the Pacific solved a crucial question of the geography of the region.

The second stage of discovery took place much later and by chance. In 1578, after he had sailed through the Strait of Magellan, Englishman SIR FRANCIS DRAKE was blown south and east by strong westerly winds and found open sea. After returning to his intended course, he found time to check his logbooks and chart his location. It was then he realized that he had found a whole new expanse of ocean. The sea between Cape Horn and Antarctica is now known as Drake Passage.

The final stage of finding and describing Cape Horn did not come until 1616. It was then that Dutch merchant JAKOB LE MAIRE and mariner WILLEM CORNELIS SCHOUTEN found South America's southernmost point of land. They named it Cape Horn, not because the area resembled a horn, but after their home port of Hoorn in the Netherlands.

There is some confusion concerning the place names of Cape Horn and Tierra del Fuego. The area referred to by these names contains many islands. The largest, originally named Tierra del Fuego, is now called Isla Grande de Tierra del Fuego, part of the Tierra del Fuego Archipelago. The island occupying the most southern latitude—known as Horn Island—is about 45 miles from the largest island. The southernmost point on Horn Island is Cape Horn.

Cape Horn/Tierra del Fuego has the distinction of being the most southerly location of regular human habitation. The latitude where it is located (56 degrees) is mirrored in the north by the coast of Labrador. With the winds that circulate, unimpeded by land, and the frigid currents from Antarctica, the region has some of the worst weather on the planet.

See also SOUTH AMERICA, EXPLORATION OF.

Cape of Good Hope

The Cape of Good Hope is a formation of land along the south coast of Africa. Rounding it by ship has come to represent the transition from the Atlantic Ocean to the Indian Ocean in the east, as CAPE HORN at the southern end of South America does so between the Atlantic Ocean and Pacific Ocean in the west.

There is some confusion as to the identity of the first nonnative peoples to round the Cape of Good Hope. A fifth-century B.C. Greek historian, HERODOTUS, made the claim of an expedition by the Phoenicians, sponsored by NECHO II of Egypt, in about 600–597 B.C. A 15th-century cartographer, Fra Mauro, gave credit to the Chinese for accomplishing the feat in 1420.

The first European known to have sailed around the southern extent of Africa is Portuguese BARTOLOMEU DIAS. Hoping to find a sea-lane around Africa to the SPICE ISLANDS (Moluccas) in the Indian Ocean, he embarked on his voyage in 1487. After encountering unfavorable winds along Africa's south coast, he sailed southward and, when the winds shifted, continued eastward. He made landfall at Mossel Bay. By checking his navigational measurements, he realized that he had passed the southern tip of the continent. He continued up the coast as far as the Great Fish River. On the return trip to Portugal, in the summer of 1488, he set up a *PADRÃO* (pillar) at the place that is now known as the Cape of Good Hope. Sources vary as to whether he gave it that name, or named it Cabo Tormentoso, for "Cape of Storms," after the weather he encountered there, and that King John II of Portugal renamed it Cabo da Bõa Esperança, or "Cape of Good Hope." In 1497, VASCO DA GAMA, also sailing for Portugal, rounded the Cape of Good Hope and continued on to India, establishing a new trade route between Europe and Asia. From that time, such journeys became routine.

The Cape of Good Hope is referred to in general usage as the southern tip of Africa. Yet, the southernmost point on the African continent is actually located at Cape Agulhas, 34 degrees and 52 minutes south latitude, some 40 miles southeast of the Cape of Good Hope. Moreover, on the projection of land referred to as the Cape of Good Hope, there are actually two points equally to the south, about a mile apart with a stretch of water between them.

Although the Cape of Good Hope is located in the most temperate zone of the African continent, it is not easy to navigate its waters. The winds in the region circulate fiercely from the west, much like the winds around Cape Horn, and the weather is unpredictable and the seas often rough. The surrounding land is inhospitable. It was not until the mid-16th century that settlements were established to reprovision ships sailing past on their way to other destinations. The modern city of Cape Town, South Africa, is situated to the north of the Cape of Good Hope.

See also AFRICA, EXPLORATION OF; CHINESE EXPLORATION.

caravel

The term *caravel,* originally derived from *karabos* for a kind of light boat, has been applied in a variety of spellings to small boats from different countries. In the history of exploration, it has come to be used for European boats extensively used in the 15th and 16th centuries.

Caravels were light and maneuverable ships with two or, more commonly, three masts. They typically had a LATEEN RIG, but their front two masts could be square-rigged to take advantage of the prevailing winds in open seas. They were most often carvel-built, a type of construction in which planks are shaped to be flush edge to edge, with caulked seams, rather than overlapping planks as in clinker-built technology. This design feature reduced friction between hull and water. Caravels had flat sterns and center rudders like other European ships. Their sizes varied, the smallest about 60 tons and the largest exceeding 200 tons.

The caravel was developed by the shipbuilders of HENRY THE NAVIGATOR, prince of Portugal. It combined elements of the European ships of the day, such as the COG and the ROUNDSHIP, with those of the Arab DHOW. Other European ships, although sturdy, were clumsy in navigating shorelines and ports. Dhows had maneuverability, yet were vulnerable in high seas. The caravel's hull could resist the pounding of waves; its shallow draught allowed for coastal navigation; and its triangular sails could take advantage of a variety of winds. While the caravel was easy to control and dependable in rough weather, it was not the most comfortable of ships. Crews slept on deck or with the supplies in the hold. Captains had small cabins on the rear deck. Lack of space also made the caravel less suitable for trading voyages.

The invention of the caravel proved a great help to the Portuguese in the 15th-century exploration of the African coast. Italian CHRISTOPHER COLUMBUS, exploring for Spain, used two caravels, the *Niña* and the *Pinta,* for his first transatlantic journey. In the 16th century, Spanish explorers VASCO NÚÑEZ DE BALBOA and HERNANDO PIZARRO built caravels in the Americas to sail the Pacific Ocean. The Monument of the Discoveries in the Portuguese city of Lisbon contains a parade of explorers on an artistic representation of a caravel.

See also SHIPBUILDING AND EXPLORATION.

carrack

The *carrack,* as it was called in northern Europe, or *nao* as it was known in Spain and Portugal, was a large oceangoing ship, descended from the COG of the Middle Ages. It evolved from ships that were clinker-built, a design feature

The 42-foot *Niña II* is a replica of one of Christopher Columbus's caravels that crossed the Atlantic Ocean in 1492. *(Library of Congress, Prints and Photographs Division [LC-USZ62-99661])*

Roman soldiers scale the walls of Carthage in 146 B.C., as shown in a 1539 engraving by George Pencz. *(Library of Congress, Prints and Photographs Division [LC-USZ62-88804])*

utilizing overlapping planks, to those that were carvel-built, with flush planks. As its size increased, it came to accommodate three or more masts. The foremasts were typically square-rigged, while the mizzenmast (rear mast) had a LATEEN RIG. Because of its size and square mainsails, the carrack was at its best on the open seas running with the wind.

A distinctive characteristic of the carrack was its high decks at bow and stern, on which structures known as castles were constructed. They provided quarters for the captain, offered points of observation, strengthened the ship against wind and wave, and gave shelter and comfort to officers and crew.

Carracks were merchant vessels, designed to maximize cargo capacity (see MERCHANT SHIP). Their roomy holds made them attractive for long voyages of exploration as well. They ranged from about 80 tons to more than 1,000 tons displacement.

The carrack ascended in importance over the smaller CARAVEL during the EUROPEAN AGE OF EXPLORATION. With the increasing number of transoceanic voyages of exploration and trade, the storage capacity of the carrack became a crucial factor, as did its durability in stormy seas in a range of latitudes. The carrack was the prototype for the massive GALLEON.

See also SHIPBUILDING AND EXPLORATION.

Carthaginian exploration

Carthaginians were inhabitants of the ancient city of Carthage, situated on a peninsula in the Bay of Tunis in what is now Tunisia on the north coast of Africa. Legend holds that a queen by the name of Dido founded the city, but it is thought to have been established by Phoenicians from Tyre (Sur) as a trading post in the late ninth century B.C. The city had two harbors, connected by a canal; a walled fortress overlooked the harbors from a hill. The name *Carthage* is from the Latin *Carthago* or *Cartago,* derived from a Phoenician word for "new city."

The colony of Carthage evolved into a city-state under an aristocracy of nobles and wealthy merchants. Through conquest and trade, it came to be influential throughout the MEDITERRANEAN SEA region and competed first with the Greeks, then the Romans. By the sixth century B.C., Carthaginians had subjugated the Libyan tribes and earlier Phoenician colonies and controlled the coast of North Africa from the western extent of Egypt to the Atlantic Ocean, as well as various islands. The Carthaginians failed in their attempt to conquer all the Greek city-states in Sicily, however.

Rome challenged Carthage's control of the western Mediterranean in the third century B.C., in a series of three wars known as the Punic Wars, after the Roman name for the Phoenicians, *Poeni.* In the First Punic War (264–241

B.C.), Rome sought to gain control of Carthaginian trading posts in Corsica, Sardinia, and Sicily. The Carthaginian general Hamilcar Barca was forced to make peace with the Romans after a naval defeat by the Roman consul Gaius Lutatius Catullus and to give up holdings in Sicily. Deprived of revenue, the Carthaginians developed their trading interests on the southern Iberian Peninsula, which they had inherited in the fifth century B.C. from their kinspeople the Phoenicians after the collapse of the Phoenician cities of Tyre and Sidon in the eastern Mediterranean. In 237–228, the Carthaginians, under Hamilcar Barca, campaigned in southern Spain against indigenous Iberians and Celtiberians (Celtic tribes who had settled among the Iberians). In 227, Cathage founded the city of Cathargo Nova (present-day Cartagena) on the southeast coast. It served as the major Carthaginian supply base on the Iberian Peninsula for northward expansion through Roman contacts. Rome and Carthage negotiated a treaty in 226 in which Carthaginian influence extended as far as the Ebro River, with Roman interests to the north of the river. One exception was the seaport of the Roman-allied Saguntum (modern-day Sagunto), 100 miles south of the Ebro.

In 219, the Carthaginian general Hannibal laid siege to and captured Saguntum. In 218, the Roman senate declared Spain a Roman province, marking the official start of the Second Punic War (218–201). Two Roman legions sent to engage Hannibal's forces failed to intercept the Carthaginians, who in a remarkable journey with a full baggage train and elephants, proceeded to cross the Pyrenees, march along the Mediterranean's north coast, and cross the Alps into Italy. The struggle continued on two fronts, with the Romans in Spain tying up the Carthaginian forces that might have reinforced Hannibal's force in Italy. Hannibal had early successes, such as the Battle of Cannae in 216, one of the worst defeats in Roman history, but Rome itself held against his forces. Roman victories elsewhere, such as at Cathargo Nova in 209, led to Hannibal's recall to Africa in 203. In 202, Publius Cornelius Scipio defeated Hannibal at Zama in North Africa, after which he was known as Scipio Africanus. With the end of the Second Punic War, in 201, the Carthaginians gave up any claim to lands on the Iberian Peninsula.

The Third Punic War (149–146) evolved out of the ambitions of Rome's growing mercantile community and designs on Carthaginian commercial enterprises, which led to military action and treaty violations. In 146 B.C., Roman legions under Scipio Aemilianus Africanus Numantinus, the adopted grandson of Scipio Africanus, captured and sacked Carthage.

A new city, also named Carthage and founded by the Romans in 29 B.C., became an important center of Roman administration. In A.D. 439–533, Carthage was the capital of the Vandals, a Germanic tribe, who overran Rome in 455.

In 533, it became part of the Byzantine Empire. It was again sacked, this time in 698. But the site continued to be inhabited and is presently a suburb of Tunis.

Carthage, although originally a Phoenician colony, was a melting pot, and the role of Carthaginians in the history of exploration is typically discussed on its own as distinct from that of the Phoenicians. Their most famous exploratory expeditions took place in the fifth century B.C., by which time Carthage was a maritime power. In about 470 B.C., statesman and admiral HANNO led as many as 60 GALLEY ships from Carthage westward along Africa's north coast, through the Strait of Gibraltar (see GIBRALTAR, STRAIT OF) into open Atlantic waters, then southward along Africa's west coast, establishing colonies along the way. He founded one settlement at the mouth of the Senegal River and perhaps explored as far as Cape Verde and the Gambia River, or even beyond to the Gulf of Guinea. In about 450 B.C., another Carthaginian, HIMILCO, perhaps Hanno's brother, also explored Atlantic coastal areas, including the Iberian Peninsula and northward along what is now France's coast and possibly as far north as the British Isles, considered the first such voyage beyond dispute. He may have explored the AZORES as well. In any case, it is known that Carthaginians came to maintain a trade monopoly in the Atlantic Ocean beyond the Strait of Gibraltar and continued the Phoenician tradition of maritime commerce and the resulting exploration and colonization.

See also GREEK EXPLORATION; PHOENICIAN EXPLORATION; ROMAN EXPLORATION.

cartography   See GEOGRAPHY AND CARTOGRAPHY.

Cathay Company

The Cathay Company, or Company of Cathay, was a short-lived venture established for the purpose of mining gold from the shores of Frobisher Bay on Baffin Island in the North Atlantic Ocean, part of what is now northern Canada. The beginnings of the Cathay Company stem from the English expedition by SIR MARTIN FROBISHER in search of the NORTHWEST PASSAGE that set out in spring 1576, in which he secured of a small quantity of ore that he believed contained gold. He arrived back in England that October. His rock was initially analyzed by two scientists, who reported it to be nothing more than worthless pyrites, or FOOL'S GOLD, but an Italian alchemist by the name of Aquello claimed he had found a speck of gold in the samples.

With this meager evidence, Michael Lok, who had been involved with a joint-stock company known as the MUSCOVY COMPANY, and other investors formed the Cathay Company to extract the riches from this newly visited land (Cathay was the medieval name for China). Queen Elizabeth I also invested and, by refusing a royal charter and appointing a royal commission to oversee additional voyages, kept greater control. A contingent of three ships was funded, which sailed in spring 1577. On this trip they mined about 200 tons of the ore, which was then analyzed by a pair of German chemists who found that it contained some quantities of gold and silver. The calculation was made that a profit of five pounds per ton could be made from the retrieval of the ore, and a much larger expedition was planned.

In spring 1578, without waiting for the conclusive results of the smelting of the initial shipment of ore, Frobisher left Harwich with 15 ships and a staff of professional miners. Their trip was fraught with difficulties. Frobisher still had an interest in finding the Northwest Passage, but the onset of winter compelled him to return to England with his cargo, which had been laboriously acquired while he had been exploring.

Frobisher arrived back in England with 1,350 tons of ore. Upon his arrival it was learned that the previous shipment had proved worthless, and all that was to be done was to dump the new load. The Cathay Company had lost £20,000 of investors' money. Without a royal charter as legal protection, Michael Lok became the principal target for lawsuits and ended up in debtor's prison. Martin Frobisher, however, remained a favorite of Queen Elizabeth I, who subsequently knighted him for his efforts against the Spanish Armada in 1588. He died from a wound received while fighting against the French in 1594.

See also COMMERCE AND EXPLORATION.

caving   See SPELEOLOGY.

Central America, exploration of

Central America is the narrow stretch of land, in effect a LAND BRIDGE—some 201,300 square miles—connecting North America to South America and separating the Caribbean Sea from the Pacific Ocean. It extends from the southern boundary of Mexico to northwestern Colombia at the northern extent of South America and includes the nations of Guatemala, Belize, El Salvador, Honduras, Nicaragua, Costa Rica, and Panama. (Based on varying rock formations, Central America is sometimes defined as beginning at the Isthmus of Tehuantepec in southern Mexico, extending to the Atrato River Valley in Colombia.) Geographers consider Central America to be part of North America (see NORTH AMERICA, EXPLORATION OF). The history of its exploration and colonizing is more closely tied to that of South America, however (see SOUTH AMERICA, EXPLORATION OF). The term *Middle America* refers to Mexico and Central America, and sometimes the WEST INDIES as well.

Much of Central America is mountainous. The forested highlands in the north are part of the mountain system of western North America; those in the south are an extension of South America's ANDES MOUNTAINS. Active volcanoes can be found between those two ranges. Tajumulco, a volcano in Guatemala, is Central America's highest peak, at 13,846 feet above sea level. Earthquakes are common in Central America. The Nicaragua Depression is centrally situated; the region's two largest lakes, Lake Nicaragua and Lake Managua, can be found there. Numerous rivers and streams flow down from the mountains, the longest rivers draining into the Caribbean, and mostly smaller streams draining into the Pacific. The coastal plain on the Caribbean side is generally broader than on the Pacific side. Central America's climate is tropical, except in higher altitudes. The Pacific coast and western mountain slopes receive about half the rainfall of the rain forest of the Caribbean side because of conditions of cold stable air created by the cold California Current as opposed to relatively warm ocean waters to the east. The land bridge of Central America connects two previously isolated ecosystems and has flora and fauna typical of both.

Native Peoples

In pre-Columbian times, Central America was a densely populated area. Native peoples of a variety of different language families, with infusions from both the north and the south, lived in autonomous bands united politically and religiously under chieftains. For subsistence, they farmed as well as hunted and fished, living a life similar to peoples of the West Indies. The Maya developed the most complex civilization in the region with autonomous city-states, located around ceremonial centers, situated on the Yucatán Peninsula in present-day Mexico, as well as in present-day Belize, Guatemala, and western Honduras and El Salvador. Its civilization consolidated before A.D. 300 and flourished from A.D. 300 to 900, a cultural phase sometimes referred to as the Classic period and involving the Lowland Maya of Belize, central Guatemala, and southeastern Mexico. The Highland Maya of southern Guatemala flourished in post-Classic times, as did the Maya to the north on the Yucatán Peninsula, who experienced a new flowering of culture after invasion by the Toltec from the west after about 1000. More than 100 Maya sites are known, consisting of magnificent stone structures: temple pyramids, astronomical observatories, palaces, monasteries, baths, plazas, bridges, aqueducts, reservoirs, and ball-courts.

Conquistadores

The first Europeans to reach Central America were Spanish, part of an expedition under RODRIGO DE BASTIDAS in 1501. He explored South America's northeast coast along present-day Venezuela and Colombia and reached the

Gulf of Darién, the eastern extent of Panama. Italian mariner CHRISTOPHER COLUMBUS more thoroughly explored the Central American coastline the next year from the other direction, during his fourth voyage to the Americas for Spain. He first reached the Islas de la Bahía (Bay Islands) in the Gulf of Honduras. He landed near present-day Trujillo, Honduras, where he encountered Maya from the Yucatán. He explored southward along the coast of Nicaragua, Costa Rica, and the Isthmus of Panama, making contact with other indigenous peoples at various landfalls.

In 1508, DIEGO DE NICUESA was granted a license by the Spanish king to found a colony west of the Gulf of Urabá (with ALONSO DE OJEDA granted the rights to a colony east of the gulf in Colombia). The next year, Nicuesa launched an expedition from Hispaniola (present-day Haiti and the Dominican Republic). He was unable to reach his proposed site at the mouth of the Darién River and landed at Nombre de Dios to the west. In the meantime, VASCO NÚÑEZ DE BALBOA, who had been part of Bastidas's expedition, founded a colony at Santa María la Antigua del Darién, the original site. Nicuesa eventually traveled there to claim his governorship, but Balboa and his followers refused to cede power and sent Nicuesa and 17 others out to sea in an unworthy vessel, never to be heard from again. In 1513, Balboa set out to the west with an expedition of nearly 200 Spaniards and 1,000 natives and slaves. Crossing through the rugged mountains and thick jungle of the Isthmus of Panama, the expedition came to a hill that seemed to offer an unobstructed view to the south and west. Balboa and his dog ascended the hill, and he became the first European to sight the Pacific Ocean on September 25. Four days later, Balboa and his men reached the shore of the Pacific Ocean.

In 1514, PEDRO ARIAS DE ÁVILA traveled to Darién to assume governorship of the colony. In 1519, the same year he had Balboa executed, he founded Panama City on the Pacific coast, making it the colony's principal settlement. (Since Nombre de Dios and Darién were abandoned for part of their history, Panama City is considered the oldest permanent European settlement on the mainland of the Americas.) Arias de Ávila sponsored expeditions to surrounding regions. Among them were those of FRANCISCO PIZARRO and DIEGO DE ALMAGRO along the west coast of South America.

In the meantime, in 1522, ANDRÉS NIÑO led the seaward part of an expedition northward—with Gil González de Ávila leading an overland contingent. Niño, with four ships constructed on the Bay of San Miguel in the Pacific, explored along the Pacific coast of Panama, Costa Rica, Nicaragua, and Honduras as far north as Mexico. On rejoining González de Ávila, he helped him fight off an attack by Indians, then explored coastal regions of Costa Rica and

Honduras as well as interior parts of Nicaragua, including Lake Nicaragua. Soon afterward, in 1522–24, the region they had explored was colonized by FRANCISCO FERNÁNDEZ DE CÓRDOBA, under the command of Pedro Arias de Ávila. He founded León near Lake Managua and Granada on Lake Nicaragua. Fernández renounced his allegiance to Arias de Ávila and tried to establish his own colonial domain. Arias de Ávila, who had recently been replaced as governor in Panama, led forces against him and installed himself as governor of the region, maintaining control until his death in 1521.

Other CONQUISTADORES invaded Central America from the north. In 1523–26, PEDRO DE ALVARADO, who had fought under HERNÁN CORTÉS against the Aztec in Mexico, led an expedition southeastward to Guatemala and El Salvador and established Spanish dominion over that region. The European conquest of Central America, as that of other parts of the Americas, was aided by the rapid spread of European diseases, including smallpox, dysentery and influenza (see DISEASE AND EXPLORATION). Those who survived disease and warfare were forced into serfdom as farmers.

Modern Nations and Peoples

The opening of the Panama Canal across the Isthmus of Panama in 1914 provided a practical passage between the Atlantic and Pacific Oceans. Central American nations achieved independence from Spain in the 19th century, although Panama was considered part of Colombia until the early 20th century. Belize was the exception, colonized in 1638 by English logwood cutters out of Jamaica, as well as by Spanish settler. The British defeated the Spanish in 1798. Formerly known as British Honduras, Belize achieved independence in 1981.

The present inhabitants of Central America are an ethnic mix, including European, especially Spanish; Native American; mestizo (people of mixed heritage, chiefly of Spanish and Native American ancestry); African; and mulatto (people of mixed European and African backgrounds). Agriculture is still central to the various economies, although they are becoming increasingly diversified.

Ceylon (Sri Lanka)

Ceylon (or Sri Lanka, as it has been known since 1972), is an island nation of 25,332 square miles just to the east of the southern tip of India. The climate is subtropical and humid, especially during the monsoon season. The island exports a variety of agricultural products, such as tea, rubber, and coconut. A number of spices are grown there as well, including cinnamon, pepper, cloves, nutmeg, and cardamom. Ceylon has also been the source of numerous precious stones and minerals over the centuries. The fertility of its soil and its abundance of natural resources led to Ceylon acquiring the label "Pearl of the Orient."

The earliest known inhabitants of Ceylon descended from the Veddas, an aboriginal group of which several thousand still exist. Today they make their home in the isolated mountainous regions. The Veddas were conquered in the sixth century B.C. by the Sinhalese of northern India. The introduction of Buddhism in the third century B.C. led to a cultural renaissance in Ceylon, and the island became a center for the religion. With its proximity to the mainland, Ceylon has been vulnerable to invasion from India, and Hindu Tamils have made regular incursions since the 12th century, a conflict which continues to this day. The population of Ceylon is about two-thirds Sinhalese and one-third Tamil.

Trade between Ceylon and the Coromandel coast (the east coast) of India took place for many centuries. A favorite commodity of India was the betel nut, which grew in large quantities and helped make the island prosperous. In the 12th and 13th centuries, Arab Muslims established a strong presence on the island as they developed the SPICE TRADE. Ceylon was particularly important as the source of cinnamon, found there exclusively at the time.

Ceylon was important not only for spices but also because of its strategic location. Situated in the center of the shipping lanes of the Indian Ocean, the island offered many advantages to those who could maintain forces at her ports. The first Europeans to come were the Portuguese in 1505. Because of rivalry from Arabs, they made a pact with the reluctant Sinhalese ruler to provide military protection in exchange for cinnamon. In 1557, King Dharmapala converted to Christianity and fell further under the control of the Portuguese. This sparked rebellion among the Sinhalese, who were led most effectively by Raja Sinha. Sinha laid siege to the port city of Columbo for six years, until he was eventually defeated by Portuguese naval power. In 1597, Dharmapala died and his crown was surrendered to Portugal. This inspired another uprising, led by Wimala Dharma Suriya.

The Portuguese did not only have to contend with rebellion from the inhabitants of the land. The Dutch, who had grown in their sea power, began casting a jealous eye toward Ceylon and first arrived in 1602 in an expedition headed by Jons Van Spillbergen. Hoping to replace the Portuguese, who were hated, a Dutchman by the name of Sebald de Weert made friendly contact with Wimala Dharma Suriya at the port of Batticaloa the next year. His agreement to aid the people of Ceylon in expelling the Portuguese in exchange for cinnamon turned violent, however. He butchered several cows to feed his crew, in defiance of the taboo against killing these animals, and Wimala had him killed. The Portuguese continued their profitable trade. In 1614, from their base in Goa, they managed to monopolize the cinnamon trade. The tide turned again, though, in 1628 with the ascension of Raja Sinha II to the throne. He formed

an alliance with the Dutch in 1636, who proceeded to move on the most important ports. In 1639, the port of Trincomalee was handed over to them. With help from native allies, they captured the ports of Negombo and Galle in 1640. The most difficult prize was Columbo, which fell to them in 1656.

The Dutch controlled Ceylon and its lucrative spice trade through the DUTCH EAST INDIA COMPANY until 1795, when the British took over their possessions. The British established plantations to grow tea, rubber, and coffee. They also brought unity to the government of the island and established schools. During World War I (1914–18), there arose a movement for independence among the island's inhabitants, which was finally achieved on February 4, 1948.

See also ASIA, EXPLORATION OF; MUSLIM EXPLORATION.

chart See GEOGRAPHY AND CARTOGRAPHY; MAPS AND CHARTS.

Chinese exploration

The political center of China throughout its history has been the basins of the YELLOW RIVER (Huanghe) and YANGTZE RIVER (Chang). From this agricultural region, a uniform culture spread to the south and west, throughout much of eastern Asia, consisting of various peoples with diverse languages. The name *China,* applied by foreigners, is thought to be a corruption of Ch'in (Q'in or Qin), the name of a dynasty in the third century B.C.; the modern Chinese refer to their nation as Zhongguo, for "Middle Kingdom" or "Central Country."

The history of China is traced through a secession of dynasties. Little is known of the most ancient of them, information being semilegendary—relating to the culture hero Huang Ti—with some archaeological evidence confirming emerging Bronze Age civilizations. Evidence of the use of writing and the historical record begins with the Chang (Shang) dynasty, from about 1570 to 1045 B.C. During the subsequent Chou (Zhou) dynasty, from about 1045 to 256 B.C., the use of iron and the activities of merchants are documented. The Chou dynasty also saw the flowering of Chinese literature and philosophy. Confucius and Lao Tzu (Laozi) developed philosophies that would influence the Chinese for generations to follow, known as Confucianism and Taoism (Daoism). During the later Ch'in (Qin) dynasty, from about 221 to 206 B.C., a centralized government was organized and the Great Wall, a fortification protecting China from northern invaders, was started. The subsequent Han dynasty, from about 206 B.C. to A.D. 220, was an expansionist period, with foreign trade flourishing and Chinese power and influence in the East rivaling that of the

Romans in the West. Buddhism was introduced into China during the Han dynasty.

A pattern in the long procession of these early and later dynasties was a period of outward expansion from the heart of the country and then an eventual period of withdrawing because of internal corruption and stagnation or military pressure, as from the militaristic Hsiung-nu (Xiongnu; Huns) from the north. Native dynasties were at times supplanted by outsiders. The Mongols, starting under GENGHIS KHAN, ruled China in the 13th and 14th centuries A.D. (see MONGOL EXPLORATION).

China, especially during the periods of expansion, has a rich history of travelers who ventured across and beyond China's varied terrain. In about 138–109 B.C., during the Han dynasty mentioned above, CHANG CH'IEN undertook two Chinese diplomatic missions to western lands. His travels took him to the Altai Mountains of central Asia and Afghanistan and to Sinkiang in western China. On two different occasions, he was captured and held by the Hsiung-nu. In A.D. 97, also during the Han Dynasty, another diplomat, KAN YING, was sent on a mission to Rome in an effort to secure the SILK ROAD for Chinese interests. He reached the Middle East, not Rome, yet probably had contact with Europeans. In about A.D. 190, a Chinese woman, WEN-CHI, was abducted by the Hsiung-nu and lived as a nomad on the Mongolian steppes. She later wrote *Eighteen Songs of a Nomad Flute* about her experiences.

In later years, a number of Buddhist monks traveled south from China to India, to see the founding place of Buddhism along with its sacred sites. One such pilgrim was FA-HSIEN, who, in A.D. 399–414, during the T'sin (Jin) dynasty of 265–420, a period of fragmented political control, headed west and south across China, crossing the Takla Makan Desert, Pamir Plateau, and HIMALAYAS into Afghanistan and northern India. From there, he sailed to CEYLON (present-day Sri Lanka).

In 629–645, during the more centralized T'ang (Tang) dynasty of 618–907 (which followed the Sui Dynasty of 581–618, a period of reunification), HSÜAN-TSANG explored much of central Asia and the Indian subcontinent. I-CHING also traveled to India during the T'ang dynasty, in 671–695. He traveled by sea, however, in the type of boat known as a JUNK. His writings include information on the islands of the EAST INDIES and the Malay Peninsula.

Centuries later, in 1221–22, another Chinese scholar embarked on a different kind of mission: CH'ANG-CH'UN traveled from China to Afghanistan to report about the lands and peoples of central Asia to Genghis Khan, then camped in Afghanistan. During the rule of Genghis's grandson Kublai Khan, founder of the Yuan dynasty of 1279–1368, Italian merchant MARCO POLO visited China and, in 1275–92, served as a diplomat to the Mongol emperor, traveling throughout the Mongol Empire, exploring

China, Tibet, Southeast Asia, Indonesia, Mongolia, and possibly SIBERIA. (Reports of contacts between Chinese and Romans date from 100 B.C. The first European who claimed to have reached China—its western part—was the Spanish rabbi BENJAMIN OF TUDELA in the 12th century.)

The geographic information gathered in the course of these travels and those of other diplomats, merchants, and scholars was recorded by cartographers. In 1311–20, CHU SSU-PEN, during the Yuan dynasty, produced a world map with accurate information on China and surrounding lands, including the continent of Africa.

Perhaps the most famous Chinese explorer of all was CHENG HO, who, in 1405–34, during the Ming dynasty of 1368–1644, carried out seven Chinese maritime expeditions, exploring the Indian Ocean, the Persian Gulf, and the RED SEA, as well as coastal East Africa. By the early 16th century, contacts between East and West, especially by sea, became a more routine occurrence.

chronometer

The term *chronometer* has been applied to a variety of instruments that keep relatively accurate time. The motivation to invent a dependable chronometer had its origins in a need to determine longitude for purposes of navigation.

Since longitude is an angular measurement between a fixed location (the meridian) and a variable location on Earth, and since Earth rotates every 24 hours through the entire 360 degree range of longitude, a time difference of one hour between the fixed and variable location is equivalent to 15 degrees of longitude (360 divided by 24). The time of a chronometer is set to that of a fixed location; the time at the location to be measured is calculated (typically using the Sun for such a calculation); the two times are then compared for a reading of longitude. Of course the accuracy of a longitude measurement would be dependent on the accuracy of the chronometer set to the time at the fixed location.

Sailors had used numerous means over the centuries to keep time. Water clocks (clepsydra) were especially vulnerable to the motion of a ship at sea, and, while the hourglass was less so, both required constant human supervision. The first spring-driven clocks of the 16th century were an obvious improvement, yet variations in temperature and humidity compromised their readings.

The first accurate chronometer was invented by John Harrison, a carpenter in Yorkshire, England. In 1735, he completed his first model, then refined it over the next years. The breakthrough he made was the use of several different metals to compensate for changes in temperature. The first extended voyage using his mechanism was made by Englishman JAMES COOK in 1772, who used a duplicate of Harrison's fourth version, completed in 1760.

The Washington Meridian Conference, held in 1884, established Greenwich, England, as the location of the PRIME MERIDIAN, the reference point from which angles of longitude were to be measured. Previously, most countries favored their own capital city as the reference point for navigators. Advances in chronometers have also been made since the 18th century. Inexpensive devices that keep time using the vibration of a quartz crystal are highly reliable.

See also LATITUDE AND LONGITUDE; NAVIGATION AND EXPLORATION.

Cibola (Seven Cities of Antillia, Seven Cities of Cibola)

The legend of the Seven Cities of Cibola originated in Europe in about 1150 as the Seven Cities of Antillia (also Antilia or Antilla). According to the legend, during the eighth century when the Moors were invading Spain, there were seven Portuguese bishops who fled their oppressors, sailing to the west with their parishioners. On encountering new lands, they established seven cities, each of which became fabulously wealthy.

The discovery of American Indian civilizations with precious metals by the Spanish CONQUISTADORES furthered the legend. In 1519–21, HERNÁN CORTÉS conquered the Aztec and appropriated their gold and other wealth; in 1531–32, FRANCISCO PIZARRO did the same among the Inca. Neither of these peoples' homelands or cities fit the description of Antillia, but the possibility of finding the proof for the Antillia legend grew in the Spanish imagination. The name *Cibola,* originally referring to the land of the Zuni Indians, came to be associated with Antillia; the legend evolved into the "Seven Cities of Cibola," where the streets were supposedly paved with gold and houses were set with precious stones.

The first reports of Cibola came from Spaniard ÁLVAR NÚÑEZ CABEZA DE VACA during his wanderings in North America starting in 1528. After being stranded in Texas during a voyage of exploration, he made his way westward through the American Southwest. In the course of his travels, he came in contact with Native Americans who told him of settlements in the region with great wealth. Cabeza de Vaca reported these rumors to ANTONIO DE MENDOZA, the viceroy of New Spain, upon his arrival in Mexico City in 1536.

Mendoza sent a small reconnaissance expedition to investigate these reports. In spring 1539, Friar MARCOS DE NIZA and the North African ESTEVANICO (who had accompanied Cabeza de Vaca on his previous trek) made their way to the north in search of the Seven Cities of Cibola. At one point, Niza sent Estevanico ahead, with instructions to send him back a cross, the size of which would indicate the wealth to be found in the city. Estevanico reached a Zuni Indian pueblo, probably Hawikuh, and, possibly because of the turquoise he saw there (assuming such turquoise was indicative of great wealth), sent back a large cross. Estevanico was killed by the Zuni before reuniting with Niza. Niza approached himself and, from a distance, saw Hawikuh. It is thought that its glistening in the Sun with decorative stones led Niza to make an overly optimistic assessment of the prospects for plunder.

In early 1540, FRANCISCO VÁSQUEZ DE CORONADO set out from Mexico with a formidable army and entourage to conquer the newly discovered kingdom. On July 7, they reached Hawikuh and overcame the inhabitants with little difficulty. There were no gold, silver, or precious stones to speak of, yet Coronado maintained his hope that other locations would prove more profitable. To this end, he sent out PEDRO DE TOVAR with the missionary JUAN DE PADILLA—an advocate of the Antillia legend of the seven bishops. Heading northwestward, Friar Padilla encountered the Hopi Indians, the homeland of which indicated no great riches. Another excursion was made by GARCÍA LÓPEZ DE CÁRDENAS, who reached the Grand Canyon. HERNANDO DE ALVARADO, while scouting to the east for Coronado, met two captive Plains Indians, the TURK and Ysopete, at the Cicuye Pueblo (Pecos Pueblo) on the Pecos River. The Turk spoke of QUIVIRA, a wealthy Indian land to the northeast, which prompted Coronado's subsequent explorations of the southern plains. Yet, again, no wealthy cities were found.

Such legends persisted among the Spanish explorers of North America. Similar legends in South America, that of EL DORADO and LOS CÉSARES, spurred on explorations of that continent. As the lands of more and more native peoples were reached without ever producing wealth comparable to that of the Aztec and Inca civilizations, the legends faded.

See also LEGENDS AND EXPLORATION; TREASURE AND EXPLORATION.

City of los Césares   See LOS CÉSARES.

Cipangu (Cipango)

The name *Cipangu,* also spelled *Cipango,* refers to an island east of Asia described by Venetian merchant MARCO POLO in his work *The Book of Ser Marco Polo, the Venetian, Concerning the Kingdoms and Marvels of the East* (which came to be known as the *The Travels of Marco Polo* and various other titles), published at the end of the 13th century after his return from extensive travels in the Far East over two decades.

Marco Polo described Cipangu as an island containing palaces with roofs of gold and streets paved in marble, one of more than 7,000 islands in an archipelago in the Sea of China, off the Pacific coast of Asia. Later explorers studied the work as a source of geographic information. In the 1490s, Italians CHRISTOPHER COLUMBUS, who sailed for Spain, and JOHN CABOT, who sailed for England, hoped to reach Cathay (the name for China at the time) and Cipangu by way of the Atlantic Ocean. They believed the island a major source of spices. Columbus calculated that Cipangu must be about 1,500 miles off Asia. On reaching the WEST INDIES in the Americas in 1492, believing the islands to be off the Asian mainland, Columbus associated them with Cipangu. Cabot, after reaching North America in an expedition in 1497, raised money for a second voyage the next year, promoting Cipangu as the goal for the sake of the SPICE TRADE. The outcome of that expedition is uncertain: Some reports describe it as lost at sea off North America; others maintain Cabot returned to Europe after exploring northeastern North America as far south as Chesapeake Bay, dying soon afterward.

The fabled island of Cipangu has been most often associated with Japan, which contains the largest islands east of China. Japan has three main islands and more than 3,000 smaller islands. At the closest point to Asia, off present-day South Korea, Japan is only 120 miles distant from the mainland. The widest point of the Sea of Japan between Asia and Japan is just over 600 miles. It is not known what Marco Polo meant by the Sea of China. What is now known as the China Sea (which includes the East China Sea and the South China Sea) extends from southern Japan to the southern end of the Malay Peninsula. There are many islands east of Asia in this region, including those of the EAST INDIES and OCEANIA. In the East Indies are the Moluccas, now part of the Republic of Indonesia, which were once known as the SPICE ISLANDS because of the number of spices produced there. In his account, Marco Polo's geographic descriptions are at best inexact, leaving much room for speculation.

See also LEGENDS AND EXPLORATION.

circumnavigation of the world

It is not known when humans first dreamed of circling the world. The ancient Greeks made the case that the Earth was a sphere as early as the fifth century B.C. (see GREEK EXPLORATION). The first known GLOBE, a spherical representation of the Earth, dates from the second century B.C. in Greece. In the second century A.D., hellenized Egyptian PTOLEMY presented his ideas on a curved Earth in his influential work *Geographia*. Yet, although various scholars and mariners, especially among the Muslims (see MUSLIM EXPLORATION), maintained the idea of a curved Earth in the Middle Ages, it did not become a fully accepted concept among Europeans until a route was established south and east around Africa in the 15th century during the RENAISSANCE. Believing in the Earth's curvature, European mariners, such as Ital-

ian mariner CHRISTOPHER COLUMBUS, promoted the idea of reaching the Orient westward from Europe rather than the earlier established eastward route. Columbus, in his expeditions for Spain in the late 15th century, of course never did reach the Orient, making the European discovery of the Americas instead. But a Spanish expedition under Portuguese mariner Fernão de Magalhães, known in Spain as FERDINAND MAGELLAN, did so some years later, and, continuing westward, completed the first circumnavigation of the world.

The First Circumnavigator

After Columbus's voyages, a water route beyond the Americas remained illusive with all inland waterways proving to be bays or rivers, and not the hoped-for NORTHWEST PASSAGE or Strait of Anian (see ANIAN, STRAIT OF) to the Pacific Ocean. Magellan, who had participated in Portuguese expeditions to India and the EAST INDIES early in his career, sought to enter the SPICE TRADE with an expedition to the SPICE ISLANDS (Moluccas). On falling out of favor with Portuguese king Manuel I and failing to receive backing for an expedition, he renounced his Portuguese citizenship and moved to Spain in 1517. Knowing that Portugal controlled the route around Africa to the Far East and that the coast of South America appeared to curve southwestward, he sought support from Spanish king Charles I (Holy Roman Emperor Charles V) for an expedition westward around South America. Magellan reportedly used a copy of the globe designed in 1492 by German cartographer MARTIN BEHAIM to present his case. Magellan received backing, and an expedition of five ships was launched from Sanlúcar de Barrameda, south of Seville, on September 20, 1519.

After crossing the Atlantic, Magellan and his men explored the coasts of present-day Brazil, Uruguay, and Argentina. After the destruction of one ship, the remaining four continued around South America, attempting the passage through what came to be known as the Strait of Magellan (see MAGELLAN, STRAIT OF), north of CAPE HORN. The crew of one ship mutinied and turned back. The remaining three continued westward and, in November 1520, reached the Pacific Ocean, which Magellan named for its apparent calmness. He and his men sailed along the west coast of South America for a time, then, without any awareness of the vastness of the Pacific, began the westward crossing of that ocean as well. After being out of sight of land for more than three months, and with SCURVY affecting a number of the crew, the expedition finally made landfall in the Mariana Islands, part of Micronesia (see OCEANIA), in March 1521. Magellan and his men went on to make the European discovery of the Philippines. There, on April 27, Magellan was fatally wounded in a skirmish with native peoples on the island. The first two commanders to replace him were also killed by natives, and command of

Sechster Theil,

Kurtze / Warhafftige

Relation vnnd Beschreibung der Wun-
der barsten vier Schiffahrten/ so jemals ver-
richt worden. Als nemlich :

Ferdinandi Magellani Portugalesers/mit Sebastiano de Cano.
Francisci Draconis Engelländers.
Thomæ Candisch Engelländers.
Oliuarii von Noort, Niderländers.

So alle vier vmb den gantzen Erdtkreiß gesegelt / auß vnterschiede-
nen Authoribus vnd Sprachen zusammen getragen/ vnd mit nöhti-
gen LandtCharten/feinen Figurn vnd nützlichen Erklärungen gezie-
ret/ vnd verfertiget. Durch

LEVINUM HULSIUM.

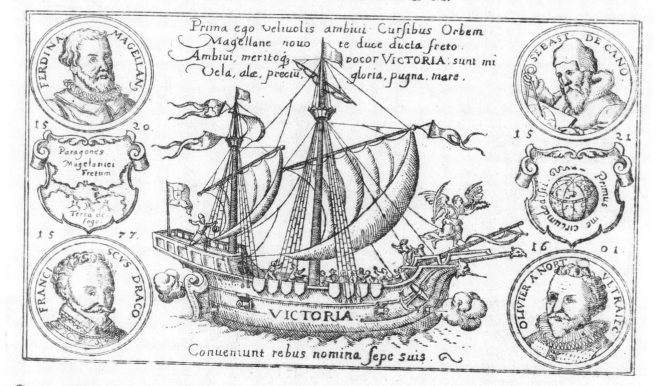

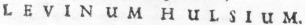

Prima ego veliuolis ambiui Cursibus Orbem
Magellane nouo te duce ducta freto.
Ambiui, meritoq, vocor VICTORIA: sunt mi
Vela, alæ, preciu, gloria, pugna, mare.

VICTORIA

Conueniunt rebus nomina sepe suis.

FERDINAND MAGELLAN · 1520
Paragones Magelanici Fretum · Terra de fogo · 1577
FRANCISCVS DRACO
SEBAST. DE CANO · 1521
Primus me circum. Mea dexti... · 1601
OLIVIER A NORT · VLTRAIEC · 1601

Getruckt zu Franckfurt / bey Hartmanno Palthenio / in Ver-
legung der Hulsischen / Im Jahr/ 1626.

This title page of a 1626 book includes the images and Latinized names of circumnavigators. *(Library of Congress, Prints and Photographs Division [LC-USZ62-84951])*

the expedition eventually fell to JUAN SEBASTIÁN DEL CANO, a Spaniard of Basque ancestry. After burning one of the ships because of crew shortages due to death and desertion, the two remaining ships proceeded westward, finally reaching the intended destination, the Spice Islands, in November 1521. The Spanish obtained a cargo of cloves and set sail in January 1522. One under del Cano continued westward into the Indian Ocean. The other, not considered seaworthy enough to make the passage around Africa, turned back eastward in the hope of reaching a Spanish port in present-day Panama in Central America. Del Cano's ship, the *Victoria,* successfully crossed the Indian Ocean, journeyed around the CAPE OF GOOD HOPE back into the Atlantic Ocean, not making a landfall until reaching the Portuguese-held Cape Verde Islands off the coast of West Africa. After detention for a time by the Portuguese, the *Victoria,* carrying 18 survivors, reached Sanlúcar de Barrameda on September 6, 1522.

Although Magellan himself did not complete the voyage, as its initiator, he is honored as the first circumnavigator of the world. That he had traveled from Europe around Africa to the East Indies and back on earlier expeditions in addition to organizing the historic westward voyage means that he, too, in effect traveled around the world. FRANCESCO ANTONIO PIGAFETTA, Magellan's private secretary, kept a record of the westward circumnavigation, published as *Primo Viaggio Intorno al Mondo* (First journey around the terrestrial globe).

Other 16th-Century Circumnavigators

The second circumnavigation of the world occurred nearly a half-century later, led by Englishman SIR FRANCIS DRAKE. Its purpose was to locate the GREAT SOUTHERN CONTINENT, or Terra Australis, believed to exist in southern waters, as well as a water route through the Americas. Drake also had a secret military commission from Queen Elizabeth I to conduct raids against Spanish colonies and ships along the Pacific coast of the Americas. Drake set sail from Plymouth, England, on December 13, 1577, with five ships and 166 men. Unlike Magellan, Drake passed south of Cape Horn in what became known as Drake Passage and headed along the west coast of South America. By then, two of the ships had been abandoned, one had sunk, and one had turned back, leaving only Drake's flagship, originally called the *Pelican,* now known as the *Golden Hind.* After managing to capture a Spanish treasure ship off Callao, Peru, Drake proceeded along the coast of North America, seeking the western outlet of the Northwest Passage as far north as Vancouver Island near the present United States–Canada border. In July 1578, almost a year after entering the Pacific Ocean, Drake headed westward across the Pacific. In the Philippines, he again made successful attacks on Spanish ships. It is not known whether Drake purposely continued westward or intended to return to England by the route he had come

and was forced westward by the pursuit of Spanish ships. In any case, he headed for and reached the Spice Islands in October 1579, where he traded for spices, then sailed across the Indian Ocean and around the Cape of Good Hope into the Atlantic. The *Golden Hind* returned triumphantly with a cargo of Spanish treasure and spice to England on September 26, 1580, whereupon Drake was knighted by his queen. Francis Fletcher, the chaplain on the expedition, wrote an account of the expedition in *The World Encompass'd.*

The first expedition with the express purpose of circumnavigating the world was by another Englishman, navigator Thomas Cavendish, who sought to retrace Drake's exploits. He did so in 1586–88, although his passage around South America was by way of the Strait of Magellan. Afterward, he plundered Spanish settlements and ships as far north as California, then continued westward by way of the Philippines, East Indies, and Cape of Good Hope. His second attempt at a circumnavigation led to his death at sea in 1592.

The Dutch, another maritime power of the EUROPEAN AGE OF EXPLORATION, launched a commercial venture around the world soon afterward. In September 1598, two fleets under OLIVER VAN NOORT departed Rotterdam and followed the routes traveled by earlier circumnavigators. Noort's return to the Netherlands in August 1601, despite a perilous journey, was the first Dutch circumnavigation of the world.

17th-Century Circumnavigators

Sailing around the world was still a rare accomplishment in the 17th century. Englishman WILLIAM DAMPIER did so while conducting privateering raids and explorations in 1683–91 (see PRIVATEERS). His book *A New Voyage Round the World* helped him gain sponsorship for a 1699 expedition to the Pacific, during which he and crew members became the first Englishmen to land on Australia, before returning to England in 1701.

18th-Century Circumnavigators

The British continued to use the route established in earlier centuries in their actions against Spain. In 1740–44, GEORGE ANSON commanded a military fleet in a voyage around the world. Some of the ships were lost in stormy weather off Cape Horn, and many of his men were lost to scurvy, but Anson managed to explore islands along the coast of Chile and raid Spanish ships off Peru and the Philippines. JOHN BYRON, who was part of Anson's expedition and was shipwrecked off Patagonia and imprisoned by Indians who turned him over to Spanish authorities, headed a subsequent naval expedition in search of the Great Southern Continent, circumnavigating the world in 1764–66, during which he made the British claim to the Falkland Islands in the South Atlantic and explored South Pacific island groups.

Meanwhile, JAKOB ROGGEVEEN completed a voyage around the world in 1721–22. He also set out westward from the Netherlands in search of the Great Southern Continent on an expedition sponsored by the DUTCH WEST INDIA COMPANY. His ships were confiscated by officials of the DUTCH EAST INDIA COMPANY in the Dutch port of Batavia (present-day Jakarta, Indonesia) for trespassing, and he was sent home via the Indian Ocean and the Cape of Good Hope.

In 1766–69, LOUIS-ANTOINE DE BOUGAINVILLE commanded the first French expedition around the world. The purpose of the government-sponsored scientific expedition was to locate the Great Southern Continent as well as chart islands in the Pacific. In the western Pacific, Bougainville explored the Solomons and other island groups. His account of the expedition was published as *A Voyage Around the World.*

About the same time, in 1766–68, a British expedition under SAMUEL WALLIS and PHILIP CARTERET, again searching for the Great Southern Continent, sailed around the world, in the course of which Wallis made the European discovery of Tahiti, and Carteret located Pitcairn Island. In his first Pacific expedition of 1768–71, Englishman JAMES COOK returned home by way of a westward route, thus encircling the globe. It was also Cook who ended speculation about the existence of a Great Southern Continent. In the course of his second voyage, in 1772–75, he made a circumnavigation of Antarctica—traveling from the Atlantic into the Indian Ocean, then into the Pacific and back into the Atlantic—demonstrating that no other continent existed in southern waters. In doing so, he again circumnavigated the globe, albeit by a shortened route in southern latitudes. In 1791–95, another British expedition, headed by GEORGE VANCOUVER, with the participation of WILLIAM ROBERT BROUGHTON, made an eastward circumnavigation of the world. He traveled around the Cape of Good Hope to Australia, then to NEW ZEALAND, the HAWAIIAN ISLANDS, and the Pacific coast of North America. Charting the Gulf of Alaska to southern California, Vancouver proved that no outlet to the Northwest Passage existed in that region. He returned to the Atlantic by way of Cape Horn. His account was published as *A Voyage of Discovery to the North Pacific and Round the World.*

The first circumnavigation of the world by a U.S. flagship occurred in 1787–90, when ROBERT GRAY, an American captain on a trading expedition, sailed from Boston to British Columbia and then to China and back to Boston.

19th-Century Circumnavigators

The first official U.S. circumnavigation did not take place until 1838–42. Headed by CHARLES WILKES, with the participation of GEORGE FOSTER EMMONS, the United States South Sea Surveying and Exploring Expedition explored coastal regions of South America, Antarctica, Pacific Ocean island groups, and North America's Pacific Northwest.

Earlier in the 19th century, in 1803–06, ADAM IVAN RITTER VON KRUSENSTERN and YURY FYODOROVICH LISIANSKY completed the first Russian circumnavigation of the world. Sailing from Kronstadt in the Baltic Sea, the expedition took the westward route, as related in Krusenstern's account *Voyage Around the World in the Years 1803, 1804, 1805, and 1806.* OTTO VON KOTZEBUE, who participated on this voyage as a 15-year-old, led a Russian expedition of his own in 1815–18, in which he searched for outlets of the NORTHEAST PASSAGE and Northwest Passage off Asia and North America in the North Pacific. Other Russian expeditions around the world soon followed, headed by MIKHAIL PETROVICH LAZAREV in 1813–16 and 1822–25; VASILY MIKHAILOVICH GOLOVNIN in 1817–19; and FYODOR PETROVICH LITKE in 1826–29. In 1819–21, German-born FABIAN GOTTLIEB BENJAMIN VON BELLINGSHAUSEN, who had sailed around the world with Krusenstern, circumnavigated Antarctica for Russia.

The French also carried out a number of expeditions circumnavigating the world in the first half of the 19th century, for both military and scientific purposes: LOUIS-CLAUDE DE SAULCES FREYCINET in 1817–20, LOUIS-ISADORE DUPERREY in 1822–25, HYACINTHE-YVES-PHILIPPE POTENTIEN DE BOUGAINVILLE in 1824–26, and ABEL-AUBERT DUPETIT-THOUARS in 1836–39. All these French explorers wrote about their journeys.

By Sea, Land, and Air

By the mid-19th century, such maritime voyages were commonplace, and the fact that they circumnavigated the globe was not the primary goal. Another kind of voyage, some of it by land, gained attention at this period of history. In 1847–48 Austrian travel writer IDA REYER PFEIFFER accomplished a westward journey around the world, most of it by sea, but some by land. She wrote about her experiences in *A Woman's Journey Round the World.* In another work, *A Woman's Second Journey Round the World, from London to the Cape of Good Hope, Borneo, Java, Sumatra, Celebes, Ceram, the Moluccas etc., California, Panama, Ecuador, and the United States,* she wrote about her world travels of 1851–55.

There have been other firsts relating to the circumnavigation of the world in the 20th century. From April 6 to September 28, 1924, four American aviators in two Liberty-engined Douglas Cruiser airplanes flew around the world; Seattle, Washington, was the point of departure and arrival. In 1964, American Jerrie Mock became the first woman to pilot a plane, a Cessna 180, around the world. (American Amelia Earhart's attempt in 1937 ended in her disappearance.) In 1967, Sir Francis Charles Chichester, a British aviator and yachtsman, completed the first solo maritime journey around the world in his yacht *Gipsy Moth*

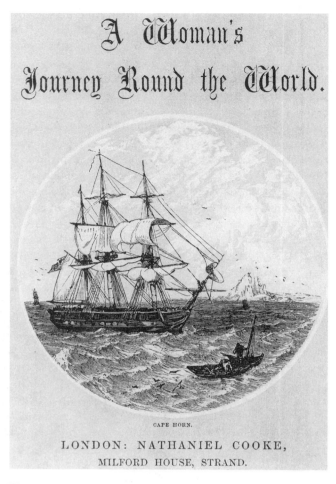

A Woman's
Journey Round the World.

CAPE HORN.

LONDON: NATHANIEL COOKE,
MILFORD HOUSE, STRAND.

This title page of an 1854 book by Ida Pfeiffer about her trip around the world shows Cape Horn. *(Library of Congress, Prints and Photographs Division (LC-USZ62-108115])*

IV; in 1999, Bertrand Piccard, AUGUSTE PICCARD's grandson, and Brian Jones, a British pilot, completed the first nonstop circumnavigation of the earth by BALLOON in the *Breitling Orbiter 3* after many other unsuccessful attempts by other aviators.

cog (coque, kogge)

The cog (or coque or kogge) was a ship developed along the north coast of Europe in about 1200 for the purpose of trade. It was stout in its shape, like the ROUNDSHIP, in order to hold a maximum amount of cargo. It had elevated decks at the bow and stern—the forecastle and the sterncastle. In its standard form, it had a single mast holding a single square sail. Wind power was supplemented by a modest number of oars. The original form of the cog was double-ended with a side rudder, like the LONGSHIP of the VIKINGS, from which it was descended. Also, like the longship, it was clinker-built, meaning that the planks forming its hull over-lapped, with caulking added to make a watertight seal. The cog was of modest size in comparison with the largest ships of the day. Its length was probably no more than 80 feet, and its width (beam), no more than 30 feet. This was due to a combination of the bulky shape of the vessel and the limitations imposed by the clinker construction.

A number of embellishments of the cog and roundship as they coevolved would become important features in later vessels. Just as in the roundship, the side rudder of the cog was replaced by a center-mounted rudder for better control. Primarily a trading ship without great agility, the cog was not practical in warfare. Yet, with its high hull and sturdy construction, it could withstand attacks from smaller, lower, more maneuverable boats. The castles at bow and stern could be used as platforms for fighting, as well as shelter.

The dependability of the cog helped make trading profitable for the HANSEATIC LEAGUE, an association of commercial interests rising from Germany and active especially in the region of the Baltic Sea. When Hanseatic League merchants traveled to the MEDITERRANEAN SEA, the efficiency of their ships was recognized by the merchants of the region, and cogs came into wide use there as well. The hulk—a ship reportedly developed in the Mediterranean—may have been in fact a version of the cog.

During its period of common use, from 1200 to 1450, the cog offered shipbuilders the opportunity to experiment with numerous features of design and construction. These included the keel, the hull, the rigging, and the previously mentioned castles and rudder. The lessons learned with the cog and the roundship gave shipbuilders the knowledge necessary to shape seaworthy ships with larger storage capacity and maneuverability in a variety of conditions, such as the CARRACK and the CARAVEL, used in transoceanic voyages of exploration.

See also SHIPBUILDING AND EXPLORATION.

colonization and exploration

The term *colonization* refers to the act of establishing a colony, that is, a group of people settling in a new region and forming a community fully or partly subject to their original homeland. In some instances, colonization evolves slowly through the actions of individuals or small groups of people and evolves over a long period of time. In other instances, colonizing expeditions are sponsored by the mother country—or an agency, typically a commercial entity working in conjunction with the government—with an organized plan of settlement. Conquest is often the first stage of colonization, yet not necessarily on a large scale (see CONQUEST AND EXPLORATION).

In addition to domination, *colonization* implies exploitation, with countries developing and controlling provinces to promote their own economic, political, military, cultural, and religious interests, typically over indigenous peoples but also in competition with other nations. The related terms *colonialism* and *imperialism* imply a philosophy and policy of colonization by the parent nation. *Colonialism* is sometimes used to indicate a policy of strictly regulated political and economic control, and *imperialism,* to indicate a less formal policy, although some scholars associate imperialism with the economic expansion of capitalist states, or for European expansion after 1870. Treaties and alliances were often shaped—sometimes against the will of local inhabitants—to "legalize" whatever the relationship between colonizer and the colonized.

The two main types of colonies are those of settlement and those of exploitation. The concept of migration is implicit in colonies of settlement, with people making new homes and starting new lives (see MIGRATION AND EXPLORATION). Typically native peoples were excluded from such colonies (see NATIVE PEOPLES AND EXPLORATION). In colonies of exploitation, sometimes also called dependencies, the primary purpose of maintaining the colony was economic, with citizens of the parent nation traveling there as administrators and/or military officers along with merchants, workers, and very likely missionaries (see COMMERCE AND EXPLORATION). In these colonies, native peoples typically were considered a labor resource, either through hiring or by force. Sometimes a newly established colony had been part of a preexisting empire—either the controlling nation or the subject people—with a new nation seizing control. Sometimes one political or ethnic group of a region came to exert control over another group or other groups in that same region, sometimes referred to as an "internal colony." And, elements of all the above colonial variations might exist to some degree in a sphere of influence as held by one nation over another region rather than as a defined colony. A people might be forced to pay tribute or taxes to another people, for example.

Colonization and exploration are related in a number of ways: Colonization served as an incentive to exploratory expeditions to uncharted lands, with governmental and commercial sponsors devising plans to develop new regions; as a result of explorations, with emigrants deciding to travel to distant lands based on the reports of explorers; or as a natural outgrowth of the establishment of colonies, with colonists themselves traveling beyond original settlements.

Ancient Colonizers

Most of the ancient peoples of the MEDITERRANEAN SEA discussed in this book as especially important to the history of exploration in opening up contacts with regions beyond their homeland—Egyptians, Phoenicians, Greeks, and Romans—founded colonies (See EGYPTIAN EXPLORATION; GREEK EXPLORATION; PHOENICIAN EXPLORATION; ROMAN EXPLORATION). That they were either merchants who established commercial centers far from home or empire builders seizing territory relates to both exploration and to colonization.

From their homeland along the NILE RIVER, the Egyptians pushed into other parts of Africa, and, during the 18th century B.C., under the pharaoh Thutmose III, conquered territory in Asia as far east as the Euphrates River, including some Phoenician cities and all of what is now Syria. They themselves were colonized for parts of their history, by Libyans, Nubians, Assyrians, Persians, Greeks, and Romans.

Spreading out from present-day Lebanon, the Phoenicians founded trading posts throughout the Mediterranean area and came to control surrounding regions politically. One such center was Carthage in North Africa, founded in the late ninth century B.C.; the Carthaginians also established dominion over other regions.

The Greeks came to control most of the islands in the eastern Mediterranean and also founded settlements in coastal regions of present-day Italy and France, the Iberian Peninsula, parts of Asia Minor and other coastal regions of the Black Sea, and present-day coastal Libya in North Africa. By 500 B.C., they had some 700 settlements under their control. Macedonian ruler ALEXANDER THE GREAT of the fourth century B.C. united the Greek city-states under him and led Greco-Macedonian forces beyond the Mediterranean into Asia as far as India. In the course of his short reign, he founded more than 70 cities in foreign lands.

By A.D. 117, at its greatest extent, the Roman Empire included territory from Italy eastward to Constantinople (present-day Istanbul, in Turkey) and Palestine, southward to North Africa, and northward to Gaul (France) and Britain. At their military posts in foreign lands, the Romans devised a system of colonization in which Roman women were sent along to grow crops and for handiwork and to bear children, so that the post would be self-sufficient and grow.

In addition to these Mediterranean peoples, the ancient Chinese were known as both explorers and colonizers, ever seeking to expand their interests beyond the heart of their territory, the YELLOW RIVER (Huanghe) in eastern Asia. The period of the Han dynasty, from about 206 B.C. to A.D. 220, was an expansionist period, with foreign trade flourishing and Chinese power and influence in the East rivaling that of the Romans in the West.

Medieval Colonizers

The creation of the new religion, Islam, on the Arabian Peninsula in the 620s–630s led to the ascendancy of Arab Muslims in the region. Over the next years, Muslim forces conquered much of the Near East, parts of central Asia, and all of North Africa (see MUSLIM EXPLORATION). In 711, they invaded the Iberian Peninsula, where the Moors—a

Muslim people out of North Africa—maintained a colonial presence until 1492. Travel throughout Muslim lands and beyond became commonplace. For example, the most famous Arab traveler, ABU ABD ALLAH MUHAMMAD IBN BATTUTAH, traveled throughout Egypt, Arabia, central Asia, North Africa, and Spain in the 15th century.

From about 800 to 1100, the Vikings out of Scandinavia were active in Europe as traders, raiders, and settlers (see VIKING EXPLORATION). They came to have settlements in the British Isles and neighboring islands in the North Atlantic, western and eastern Europe, ICELAND, GREENLAND, and northeastern North America. The successful large-scale colonizing expedition of ERIC THE RED to Greenland in 985 or 987 led to explorations farther westward to northeastern North America by his son, LEIF ERICSSON, and eventual attempts at colonies in what is referred to in Viking texts as VINLAND, thought to be in Newfoundland. Later descendants of the Vikings—generally referred to in texts as Normans—also established colonies, such as Roger I, who captured Sicily from the Arabs in 1061–91.

In the case of both the Muslims and Vikings, the colonies were not politically regulated by rulers in the original homelands but came to be ruled locally yet maintaining cultural and commercial ties.

With the CRUSADES—the series of religion-inspired incursions into the Near East of the late 11th century to the late 13th century—to counter the expansion of the Seljuk Turks (Muslim people in the Near East), Europeans from a number of different nations established colonies. Yet, they did so without necessarily a political center at home—rather a religious one, the seat of the Catholic Church in Rome. During those centuries the Venetians and Genoese established commercial colonies along trade routes to the East and regulated them for the task at hand—the free flow of goods.

It was the rise of the Mongols, who created a vast empire throughout most of Asia and into eastern Europe in the 13th century under GENGHIS KHAN—with numerous ethnic groups as tribute peoples—that enabled new trade contacts between East and West (see MONGOL EXPLORATION). Merchants, such as Venetian MARCO POLO in the 1270s, could travel the SILK ROAD, parts of which had been controlled by Muslims in earlier centuries.

The European Age of Exploration

Starting in the 15th century, at the beginning of what is referred to as the EUROPEAN AGE OF EXPLORATION, a number of European nations developed oceangoing ships and began seeking new trade routes to the East. There resulted from their wide-ranging maritime voyages a new understanding of world geography, including the extent of Africa and the existence of the Americas between Europe and Asia. Numerous colonies were founded in the years to come, many as

trading posts but others evolving into or founded as permanent settlements: by the Portuguese in Africa, Asia, and South America in the 15th century and 16th century; by the Spanish in South America, Central America, and North America in the 16th century; and by the Spanish, English, French, and Dutch in North America in the 17th century (after some failed attempts by the French and English in the 16th century, including what is known as the LOST COLONY). In fact, much of the exploratory activity of this period of history directly relates to the claiming of territory and the founding of colonies—from Italian CHRISTOPHER COLUMBUS's founding of Santo Domingo on Hispaniola in the present-day Dominican Republic in the WEST INDIES in 1496, the oldest permanent settlement in the Americas, to the founding of Plymouth colony by the PILGRIMS in present-day Massachusetts in 1620.

The various European powers enacted laws to manage their foreign holdings. The Spanish in particular developed a complex system of governance relating to the CONQUISTADORES and the native population in the early 15th century. A royal decree known as the *requerimiento* was read by conquistadores to Indian tribes informing them of their duty to the Catholic Church and the Spanish Crown and their right to freedom if they submitted, along with the threat of war and enslavement if they did not. To achieve anything resembling freedom, however, the Indians had to prove themselves "civilized" in terms of religion, language, shelter, and dress. Because of reports by missionaries of the widespread abuses of the system (even if Indians managed to work out a translation of the decree and reacted peacefully, they were still often brutalized and taken as slaves for personal use or profit), the pope and the Crown further structured Indian policy. In 1512, the Laws of Burgos established the *encomienda* system, which required male Indians to work nine months out of each year in return for entry into Spanish society. In 1542, the *repartimiento* replaced the *encomienda;* this was a system of land grants, giving the grantee the right to exploit the native population with an annual levy for labor and produce. These various laws enabled the creation of a *hacienda*—a large estate typically used for farming and ranching.

The Colonial Age

Out of the exploration and colonization of the 15th and 16th centuries there developed the trade empires of the major European powers—Portugal, Spain, the Netherlands, England, and France—and the beginning of modern colonialism. The overseas colonies served as a source of raw materials and as markets for manufactured goods, leading to the rapid growth of maritime traffic between parent companies and their colonies. In the late 16th and early 17th centuries, chartered companies, such as the BRITISH EAST INDIA COMPANY, DUTCH EAST INDIA COMPANY, and FRENCH EAST INDIA

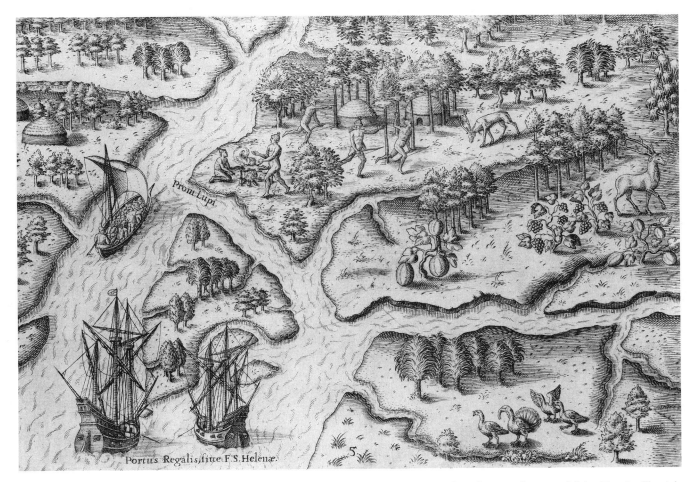

Jacques Le Moyne depicted the French arrival at Port Royal in South Carolina in 1562 in this map. It was published by the Flemish engraver Théodore de Bry in 1591. *(Library of Congress, Prints and Photographs Division [LC-USZ62-380])*

COMPANY, working in conjunction with governments, became a primary instrument of colonization. Through them, the English and Dutch came to dominate the trade of the EAST INDIES, wresting control of it away from the Portuguese and founding numerous colonies. The French also came to establish a colonial presence there.

Economic growth was promoted by the policy of mercantilism, a trade policy of state intervention in economic matters, especially to maximize exports and increase a nation's store of gold and silver. Thus, in a mercantile system, colonial possessions did not compete economically with the controlling countries but were regulated in order to provide wealth to them.

Great Britain grew into the largest colonial power through naval power. In the mid-18th century, the British had gained control of the Indian subcontinent, most of which had been part of the Mogul (Mughal) Empire, centered in northern India. Soon afterward, however, it lost control of many of its colonies in North America during the American Revolution of 1775–83, prompted in part because of legislation known as the mercantilist Navigation Acts, passed in 1651, which restricted shipping to and from colonies to British companies, ships, and crews.

Yet, Great Britain continued to establish colonies in other parts of the world, such as Australia. The first permanent British settlement there, a penal colony for prisoners from the British Isles, was founded in 1788 under ARTHUR PHILLIP. Over the next decades, the growth of Australia as a colony led to expeditions. About the same time, European interests began moving inland from Africa's coastal regions and settling new lands. In 1752, for example, AUGUST BEUTLER led a group of Dutch colonists from the Cape Town colony into the Transkei region. Colonial ambitions in Africa led to numerous expeditions well into the 18th century, and the continent would come to be carved up among European nations. In what is called the "Scramble for Africa," European nations partitioned Africa at the Berlin West Africa Conference (1884–85).

The colonial, or imperial, age lasted until the mid-20th century. National liberation movements arose especially after World War II of 1941–45, when subject peoples demanded self-determination and were granted or won independence from the imperial powers through negotiations and violence. Remnants of the centuries of colonization still exist, but as self-governing dependencies.

❖

Many explorers who had expeditions financed to further colonization and/or helped bring about colonization themselves did not regard themselves as colonizers. Some responded to exploration as a calling unto itself, or traveled to foreign lands for other ideals, such as missionaries who sought to protect native peoples from the effects of colonization even as they converted them and thus facilitated additional settlement by outsiders. Yet colonization has been a historical current since ancient times and, as such, has to be studied at the very least as context to exploration in general.

Colorado River

At 1,450 miles long, the Colorado River is the longest river west of the ROCKY MOUNTAINS in North America, and one of the major rivers of the United States. Originating just west of the Continental Divide in the Rockies of northern Colorado, it follows a southwesterly course across Colorado and southeastern Utah. After the Green River, its chief tributary, joins the Colorado in southeast Utah, the river then flows westward through the Grand Canyon, and then southward, where it functions as the lower section of the border between Arizona and Nevada and the entire border between Arizona and California. It then flows approximately 90 miles across northwestern Mexico, where the border lies between the states of Sonora and Baja California, and empties into the Gulf of California.

In addition to the Green River, the Colorado River receives a number of other sizable tributaries, including the Gunnison, Yampa, Dolores, San Juan, Virgin, Little Colorado, Salt, and Gila Rivers. The entire system drains about 245,000 square miles in seven states (Colorado, Wyoming, Utah, New Mexico, Nevada, Arizona, and California) and an additional 2,000 square miles in Mexico.

The Colorado's powerful current has carved a series of deep canyons and gorges through its first 1,000 miles. The best known example is the Grand Canyon, where the river cut through consecutive layers of rock and gradually enlarged and deepened its own course. The effects of the current, in combination with the wind and weather, created a canyon 277 miles long, 18 miles wide, and up to a mile deep. Its course there is marked by a series of rapids and waterfalls. The large amounts of sediment carried by the Colorado have created an extensive delta in Mexico. Along its lower course, because of the great amount of sediment, the water seems reddish in color, leading to the name given by the Spanish, *colorado* for "reddish."

Spanish Exploration

It is thought that the first European to see the Colorado was Spaniard FRANCISCO DE ULLOA in 1539–40. He headed an expedition sent out from Mexico by HERNÁN CORTÉS, which explored the Pacific coast of Mexico, the Gulf of California, and the mouth of the Colorado. Using one of his ship's boats, he traveled far enough north to see mountain peaks in the distance, situated in present-day California. In 1540, a Spanish overland expedition under FRANCISCO VÁSQUEZ DE CORONADO out of Mexico entered what is now the American Southwest and set up headquarters at the Zuni Indian pueblo of Hawikuh in present-day western New Mexico. One of his lieutenants, PEDRO DE TOVAR, exploring to the northwest, reached the Hopi pueblo of Awatovi in present-day northeastern Arizona. There he learned of a great river to the west. Based on this information, Coronado sent out another expedition under GARCÍA LÓPEZ DE CÁRDENAS, who with his contingent became the first known Europeans to see the Grand Canyon. Meanwhile, HERNANDO DE ALARCÓN, with the seaward portion of Vásquez de Coronado's expedition, sailed northward with supplies. After exploring the Gulf of California, he traveled a good distance up the Colorado—about 200 miles to the vicinity of its confluence with the Gila River, near present-day Yuma, Arizona, where he left a marker. MELCHIO DÍAZ, another one of Vásquez de Coronado's lieutenants, later found the marker.

In 1582–83, a Spanish merchant by the name of ANTONIO ESTEVAN DE ESPEJO financed his own expedition to western New Mexico and eastern Arizona in search of missing missionaries, during which he reached the Little Colorado River in Arizona. Two decades later, in 1604–05, JUAN DE OÑATE, who had founded the first permanent Spanish settlement in New Mexico in 1698, explored westward and explored the lower Colorado, reaching the Gulf of California. The man who charted much of the region of the lower Colorado, as well as the Gila River, was Italian Jesuit missionary EUSEBIO FRANCISCO KINO, trained in astronomy and mathematics, who led some 50 exploratory expeditions in northern Mexico and southern Arizona out of a mission in what is now Sonora, Mexico, in the late 17th and early 18th centuries. He dispelled the myth once and for all that that the California Peninsula was an island. Later in the 18th century, in 1774–76, JUAN BAUTISTA DE ANZA followed the Gila River to the lower Colorado on two expeditions to California. Franciscan missionary FRANCISCO TOMAS HERMENEGILDO GARCÉS accompanied him on the first expedition and part way on the second. In 1776, Garcés, seeking native converts, reached the Grand Canyon. In 1776–77, Franciscan missionaries FRANCISCO ATANASIO

DOMÍNGUEZ and FRANCISCO SILVESTRE VÉLEZ DE ESCALANTE, in an unsuccessful effort to create a route between the Spanish settlements of Santa Fe, New Mexico, and Monterey, California, explored parts of the Colorado itself, as well as the Dolores River in western Colorado and the Green River in Utah.

U.S. Exploration

In the mid-19th century, after the United States assumed control of the Southwest from Mexico with the Mexican Cession of 1848, following the U.S.-Mexican War, U.S. Army Corps of Topographical Engineers launched a number of surveying expeditions to the West, among them one under JOSEPH CHRISTMAS IVES in 1857 to determine the navigable limits of the Colorado. Geologist JOHN STRONG NEWBERRY was part of this expedition as was Mojave Indian IRATEBA as a guide. From the river's mouth, Ives and his party reached as far north as the Black Canyon along the border between Arizona and Nevada. In another military expedition, in 1859, JOHN N. MACOMB, also of the Corps of Topographical Engineers, again joined by Newberry, located the junction of the Grand and Green Rivers in eastern Utah, which they determined as the source of the Colorado. The Grand River is now considered part of the Colorado, and its name has been dropped. Grand Lake far to the northeast in northern Colorado is now considered the Colorado River's source.

In 1869, geologist JOHN WESLEY POWELL made the first detailed scientific exploration of the Colorado River, the Green River, and surrounding territory. During that expedition, Powell and his party navigated through the Grand Canyon in wooden boats. In 1871, Powell embarked on another descent of the Colorado. He wrote a report of his journey for the government in which he suggested that the land could support only a limited amount of irrigated agriculture.

The Colorado River and its tributaries are the primary source of water for much of the American West, especially the Southwest, and a part of northern Mexico as well. About two-thirds of the system's water is used for irrigation; much of the rest of it supplies urban areas. Numerous dams have been built along the system, which serve to generate hydroelectric power, store water, and control floods. Along the border of Arizona and Nevada, where the Colorado runs through Black Canyon, the construction of Hoover Dam has created the reservoir known as Lake Mead. The lakes formed by dams also provide recreational activities, as do sections of the rivers for fishing and whitewater rafting. Yet population increases in the vast Colorado River region have already begun to strain the water supply.

See also NORTH AMERICA, EXPLORATION OF.

Columbia River

About a third of the course of the Columbia River, one of the longest rivers in western North America, is in Canada, the rest in the United States. From its source at Columbia Lake in southeastern British Columbia, it travels 1,214 miles before it empties into the Pacific Ocean at Astoria, Oregon. In British Columbia, the river flows northwesterly for about 200 miles between the ROCKY MOUNTAINS to its east and the Selkirk Mountains to its west. This section is also known as the Rocky Mountain Trench. After flowing along the northern edge of the Selkirk Mountains, it turns southward and widens into the Upper and Lower Arrow Lakes. It is joined by the Kootenai (spelled Kootenay in Canada) and Pend d'Oreille Rivers. Continuing southward, it flows into the state of Washington in the United States.

The Columbia continues its southerly course across Washington for about 100 miles until its juncture with the Spokane River. From there, it curves westward in an arc known as the Big Bend, then follows a generally southerly route until its juncture with the Snake River, at which point it turns westward again and forms the border between the states of Washington and Oregon. It crosses the Cascade Range through the Columbia River Gorge. Along its route, it passes through several canyons and deep valleys of both the Cascades and the Coastal Range as well. Numerous rivers feed the lower Columbia, among them the Deschutes and Willamette flowing from the south, and the Cowlitz from the north. The lower Columbia angles to the northwest on its final stretch and eventually opens up to a broad estuary and Gray's Bay, 20 miles from open ocean, the Pacific. Including its tributaries, the Columbia River drains nearly 260,000 square miles.

The upland country between the Rockies and the Cascades is known as the Columbia Plateau after the river. Native Americans of this region, who depended on the Columbia and its tributaries for sustenance—especially for the salmon spawning runs upriver—are sometimes grouped together as Plateau Indians.

From the Sea

Early explorations along the Pacific coast of North America were motivated in large part by the hope of finding the outlet to the NORTHWEST PASSAGE. Spanish naval officer BRUNO HECETA was the first European to discern the Columbia River from the sea. While exploring the Pacific coast in August 1775, he entered a bay, where he noticed strong currents, making him believe a river fed it. He named the river Río San Roque. The currents drove his ship out to sea before he could explore upriver, and he returned to Mexico.

In April 1792, an American sea captain named ROBERT GRAY, who had earlier completed the first CIRCUMNAVIGATION OF THE WORLD by a U.S. flagship, the *Columbia*, was off the Pacific Northwest coast on a second trading expedition out of Boston. His goal, as in the earlier expedition, was to exchange trade goods for furs from Indian tribes, then sail to China and barter the furs for tea. While sailing southward along the coastline, he located a point where the current and waves seemed to indicate a river emptying into the Pacific, which he thought might be the large river reported by Indians—the Oregon, as it was known (a Native American word, the derivation of which is unknown). A sandbar made passage dangerous. After exploring to the north—during which time he met up with a British ship and conferred with its captain, GEORGE VANCOUVER—he returned south and crossed a sandbar into what was known as Deception Bay, now known as Gray's Bay. After trading with Indians along the bay, he entered the river—which he renamed the Columbia after his ship—sailing about 36 miles into it. The United States made a claim to the region based on his findings. England also claimed the region. Later that year, British naval officer WILLIAM ROBERT BROUGHTON, sailing a second ship under Vancouver's overall command, navigated 119 miles upriver and made the first accurate charts of the area over a period of three weeks.

Lewis and Clark

The Columbia River also was an important route of transportation for the Lewis and Clark Expedition of 1804–06, sent out by U.S. President Thomas Jefferson, which departed St. Louis on May 14, 1804. One of Jefferson's hopes was that the expedition would find a water route all the way to the Pacific. While MERIWETHER LEWIS and WILLIAM CLARK and their Corps of Discovery were forced to travel much of the way overland, after crossing the Rockies and the Continental Divide, they reached the Clearwater River, and, under the guidance of Nez Perce Indians, they carved dugout CANOEs. The Clearwater took them to the Snake River, which took them to the Columbia on October 16, 1805. They continued by canoe, navigating through rapids and around waterfalls. On November 7, the explorers reached the mouth of the Columbia in Gray's Bay on the Pacific. They built Fort Clatsop on the south shore, where they spent the winter, exploring the region and setting out back eastward on March 23, 1806, arriving in St. Louis on September 23.

Trade and Settlement

In 1810, JOHN JACOB ASTOR of the AMERICAN FUR COMPANY, and its subsidiary the Pacific Fur Company, sponsored a maritime expedition to the mouth of the Columbia, where the settlement of Astoria was built the next year, also on the south shore. An overland party, known as the Astorians, under WILSON PRICE HUNT, departed St. Louis soon afterward in 1811, traveling the Columbia on the last leg, arriving at Astoria early in 1812. In 1810–11, DAVID THOMPSON, a British-born fur trader of the NORTH WEST COMPANY, who had already mapped large areas of Canada,

became the first known non-Indian to follow the Columbia River from its source to its mouth and visited Astoria. In 1813, during the War of 1812, the Astorians sold the post to the North West Company rather than make a stand against a British warship.

Following the war, by the terms of the Treaty of Ghent —based on the activities in the region of Robert Gray, Lewis and Clark, and Astor—the British returned Astoria to American possession. In 1818, the United States and Great Britain signed a treaty, agreeing that for 10 years their subjects and citizens of both nations could jointly occupy the Oregon Country (which comprised much of the Pacific Northwest at the time, from the Continental Divide to the Pacific Ocean and from the present border between California and Oregon to Russian Alaska).

Other traders worked the region over the next years. In the 1820s–30s, JOHN MCLOUGHLIN of the HUDSON'S BAY COMPANY was based at Fort Vancouver (present-day Vancouver, Washington, opposite Portland, Oregon) on the Columbia for operations throughout the Pacific Northwest, including expeditions under PETER SKENE OGDEN and JOHN WORK. In 1827, American traders JEDEDIAH STRONG SMITH and JOSHUA PILCHER visited the post. In the 1830s, Boston merchant NATHANIEL JARVIS WYETH led two fur-trading expeditions to the region; Methodist missionary Jason Lee, who later founded schools in Oregon, accompanied him on the first. The establishment of the Oregon Trail brought more settlers to the Columbia River region, including Presbyterian missionaries MARCUS WHITMAN and HENRY HARMON SPALDING. In 1843, Kentucky-born JESSE APPLEGATE helped lead a wagon train with about 1,000 emigrants, known as the "Great Migration of 1843." Many of them settled in the Willamette Valley.

❖

In 1846, Britain ceded Oregon Country to the United States, paving the way for the establishment, over the years, of the present international, state, and provincial boundaries of Columbia River country.

See also NORTH AMERICA, EXPLORATION OF.

commerce and exploration

The term *commerce* refers to the exchange of goods or services between peoples. It is used interchangeably with the term *trade*, although the former in some usage indicates the exchange of goods on a large scale, such as commercial dealings between nations, as well as traffic in goods that have to be transported over a distance.

The theme of commerce runs through the history of exploration. A desire for commerce helped spur on voyages to distant lands, and new forms of commerce resulted from voyages. Exploration was often a moneymaking endeavor.

Many SPONSORS OF EXPLORATION, whether merchants or rulers of nations, hoped to profit from their investments in expeditions, as did the explorers themselves.

Ancient Peoples and Commerce

The ancient peoples most studied with regard to exploration were in many cases known as merchants, in particular the Minoans, Phoenicians, and Greeks, who developed markets along the coasts of the MEDITERRANEAN SEA and beyond through maritime exploration (see GREEK EXPLORATION; MINOAN EXPLORATION; PHOENICIAN EXPLORATION). Yet commerce is a part of the story of some of the other ancients, such as the Egyptians (see EGYPTIAN EXPLORATION). When Queen HATSHEPSUT sent out an expedition to the southern land of PUNT by way of the RED SEA in about 1492 B.C., it was in the hope of locating sources of goods, such as gold and spices.

The Egyptians also hired proven mariners—the Phoenicians and Greeks—to seek out sources of goods on their behalf, as did the Romans (see ROMAN EXPLORATION). A Greek, HIPPALUS, for example, sailed to India in the first century A.D. on behalf of Egypt, then under Roman domination.

The Chinese also sent out expeditions for purposes relating to commerce (see CHINESE EXPLORATION). That which first established what became known as the SILK ROAD, the route over which silk was transported from the Far East to Europe, was carried out by the diplomat CHANG CH'IEN in 115 B.C., during which his envoys made trade arrangements with peoples of the eastern Mediterranean. In A.D. 97, another diplomat, KAN YING, was sent on a mission to Rome in an effort to secure the Silk Road. And the seven journeys of the admiral CHENG HO in the early 15th century, although they may have been initiated for political and military purposes, had the effect of opening up coastal regions of the Indian Ocean to Chinese trade.

Medieval Commerce

After the breakup of the Roman Empire in the fifth century A.D., new trade relations developed between Europe, Africa, and Asia in the Middle Ages. A people who became active in trade during this period were the Arabs, who traveled the Indian Ocean between the Near East, East Africa, and Southeast Asia. After the rise of Islam in the seventh century A.D., Arab Muslims ranged even farther for purpose of trade. In many instances, they acted as middlemen between Asian and European interests. Much of the commercial activity surrounded the SPICE TRADE, with the West's demand for spices that were produced in the East. Arabs also controlled the African SLAVE TRADE, capturing or trading for slaves and selling them in European and Asian markets. Salt was another valued commodity produced in Africa. A 10th-century merchant ABU AL-QASIM IBN ALI AL-NASIBI IBN HAWQAL wrote about the trade routes of the SAHARA DESERT. Another Arab merchant, ABU ALI AHMAD IBN RUSTA, wrote about his travels in Europe.

Commerce between Asia and Europe slowed down in the mid-11th century, however, when the Turks, who also came to adopt the Islamic religion, conquered many Arab lands and threatened Constantinople (present-day Istanbul), the seat of the Eastern Roman Empire (Byzantine Empire). The resulting CRUSADES—military actions by Europeans against the Muslims of the Near East from the late 11th century to the late 13th century—thus had a commercial purpose of reopening trade routes as well as the religious one of spreading Christianity. The Crusades in turn had the effect of sparking new commerce because returning Crusaders had a new interest in Eastern goods.

During the Crusades, Italian port cities took on a central role in East-West commerce. Venice and Genoa, port cities in northern Italy, became primary launching points for trade. It was from Venice that Venetian merchants NICCOLÒ POLO, his brother MAFFEO POLO, and Niccolò's son MARCO POLO set out for the East in the late 13th century, in order to develop trade contacts with the Mongols, who then controlled China and much of central Asia. Marco Polo's writings about his extensive travels led to even greater interests in Eastern products.

In the meantime, trade with foreign interests had become safer because merchants began to form associations for the protection of travelers abroad. The HANSEATIC LEAGUE, a commercial union of German cities and towns and their merchants, was active by the mid-12th century. The Baltic Sea became a hub of trade to other parts of Europe and the eastern Mediterranean. Europe was known as a source of raw materials, such as tar, timber, tin, furs, and wool; some manufactured goods, such as woolen garments and linens; and prepared foods, such as salted fish, wine, oil, and fruit. Asia was known as a source of luxury items, especially spices, tea, textiles, and jewelry.

Commerce during the European Age of Exploration

Because of Muslim domination of overland trade routes and the expense of overland expeditions, European powers hoped to develop water routes. The fall of Constantinople to the Turks in 1453 made it even more economically imperative that European nations bypass Muslim strongholds. HENRY THE NAVIGATOR, prince of Portugal, had earlier begun the process of a maritime solution when he had founded a naval depot, an observatory, and a school of navigation at Sagres near Cape St. Vincent in Portugal, and had assembled together astronomers, mapmakers, and mariners. One of his main goals was to make a seaworthy vessel, combining sturdiness and maneuverability, the result of which was the CARAVEL (see SHIPBUILDING AND EXPLORATION).

Navigational instruments were also refined (see NAVIGA-TION AND EXPLORATION). Before long, Henry was sponsoring expeditions along the coast of Africa, and, by the turn of the century, the Portuguese were sailing in the Indian Ocean. In 1498, VASCO DA GAMA reached India, where he traded a load of European goods for a cargo of pepper.

In the meantime, in 1492, Italian mariner CHRISTOPHER COLUMBUS, funded by and sailing for Spain, had reached the Americas by making a westward crossing of the Atlantic Ocean. Although he was disappointed in his hope of finding spices and gold, his four voyages back and forth between Europe and the Americas started the process of creating a desire for new products, such as tobacco, unknown in the rest of the world at the time, and creating new markets and trade relationships.

Subsequent Spanish expeditions—in particular those of HERNÁN CORTÉS among the Aztec Indians of Mexico in the 1520s and FRANCISCO PIZARRO among the Inca Indians of Peru in the 1530s—revolutionized the economy of Europe in that they led to an infusion of great amounts of plundered gold to Spain and prompted other expeditions for the purpose of colonization (see TREASURE AND EXPLORATION). The mining of silver by American Indians for the Spanish also contributed to the Spanish economic ascendancy. There was a demand for the commodity of precious metals in Asia as well as in Europe. In addition to the Portuguese and Spanish, the English, French, and Dutch began sailing the Atlantic for the Americas, with investors hoping for a return from these ventures in the form of wealth appropriated from native peoples or in the FUR TRADE.

Out of the explorations along the African coast and the colonization of the Americas, there also expanded the commerce in human lives. In 1562–63, Englishman SIR JOHN HAWKINS completed the first voyage in what became known as the "triangular trade" between Europe, Africa, and the Americas. European ships would transport manufactured goods to Africa's west coast, where they would be bartered for slaves. The slaves would then be taken to the North and South American colonies, where they would be exchanged for mostly agricultural goods, especially cotton, tobacco, sugar, and molasses, as well as rum, which would then be transported back to Europe.

The Merchant Companies

Starting in the 15th century, many exploratory expeditions were launched by merchants, organized in syndicates and legal partnerships. For example, a number of merchants of Bristol in England, who had been active in commerce since the Middle Ages, organized a syndicate to back the expedition of Italian mariner JOHN CABOT—who had earlier participated in the spice trade in the Mediterranean—across the Atlantic in 1497, in the hope of reaching the spice markets of the Far East. Cabot headed a second such expedition the next year, again with Bristol backing, and searched for a

water route through North America from the Atlantic Ocean to the Pacific Ocean—the NORTHWEST PASSAGE.

In the 16th century, a number of merchant companies were formed to back expeditions, often with shareholders. These companies would purchase their own ships and hire captains and crews to man them. Governments went into the business of chartering these privately owned and managed companies and sometimes investing in particular expeditions. The royal charters granted the merchant companies a monopoly over trade with certain regions.

One of the earliest of the merchant companies was the London-based MUSCOVY COMPANY, founded in 1551, with SEBASTIAN CABOT, John Cabot's son, as the first director, which became involved in the search for a route eastward north of Europe, the NORTHEAST PASSAGE. Although it was unsuccessful in that purpose, with expeditions encountering ice conditions time and again, the Muscovy Company's activities led to the charting of northern coastal regions and islands and opened up new markets in Russia.

The CATHAY COMPANY was a short-lived company, created in the winter of 1576–77 as result of an expedition headed by SIR MARTIN FROBISHER that had been launched the prior spring to find the Northwest Passage. On southeastern Baffin Island off the North American mainland near the ARCTIC CIRCLE, Frobisher had discovered what he believed to be gold, but which turned out to be FOOL'S GOLD, or pyrite, a worthless mineral.

The LEVANT COMPANY, which was granted a royal charter in 1581, then reorganized in 1607 as a joint-stock company, was created to develop trade between the British Isles and the countries of the LEVANT, the eastern Mediterranean, in order to circumvent the Venetians, who had had a monopoly on the traffic between Europe and that region.

At the beginning of the 17th century, both the English, in 1600, and the Dutch, in 1602, founded an East India Company—differentiated now as the BRITISH EAST INDIA COMPANY and DUTCH EAST INDIA COMPANY—to develop trade with India and the SPICE ISLANDS (the Moluccas), as well as other islands in the EAST INDIES and other lands in the Far East. In 1621, the Dutch founded the DUTCH WEST INDIA COMPANY for trade in the Americas. The French set about developing the Asian trade with the founding of the FRENCH EAST INDIA COMPANY later in the century, in 1664.

Among the other companies formed to develop foreign trade in the 17th century was the COMPANY OF MERCHANTS OF LONDON DISCOVERERS OF THE NORTHWEST PASSAGE in 1612, which sponsored a number of unsuccessful expeditions to find the passage, and the HUDSON'S BAY COMPANY in 1670, organized to develop the fur trade around North America's HUDSON BAY.

The VIRGINIA COMPANY is a name used for both the Virginia Company of London and the Virginia Company of Plymouth. They were granted royal charters at the same time in 1606, leading to the founding of Jamestown in present-day Virginia in 1607 by CHRISTOPHER NEWPORT and JOHN SMITH and the founding of Plymouth Colony by the PILGRIMS in present-day Massachusetts. Although the purpose of these companies was to colonize North America, it was hoped that discoveries of precious metals or the development of new agricultural products would make the ventures profitable. At Jamestown, the colonists grew tobacco, which was shipped back to Europe and other parts of the world over the years. The Pilgrims participated in the fur trade with Indians.

In addition to supplying raw materials, the establishment and subsequent growth of colonies—in Africa and Australia as well as the Americas—also meant the creation of new markets for manufactured goods (see COLONIZATION AND EXPLORATION).

The North American Fur Trade

The fur trade led to the early exploration of North America more than any other activity. Much of it was in the direct form of trade with Native Americans, but non-Indians also came to hunt and trap animals for their furs. Some of the most famous names in the history of North American exploration were fur traders. French fur traders included JACQUES CARTIER, who explored along the St. Lawrence River in the early to mid-16th century; SAMUEL DE CHAMPLAIN, who explored parts of the Northeast in the early 17th century; RENÉ-ROBERT CAVELIER DE LA SALLE, who explored along the Great Lakes and MISSISSIPPI RIVER; and MÉDARD CHOUART DES GROSEILLIERS and PIERRE-ESPRIT RADISSON, involved with the founding of the already mentioned Hudson's Bay Company in 1670 to develop the fur trade in the Hudson Bay region. French-Canadian fur traders included LOUIS-JOSEPH GAULTIER DE LA VÉRENDRYE and his brother François, and PIERRE-ANTOINE MALLET and his brother Paul, among the first non-Indians to reach the Great Plains in the 1730s–1740s.

Fur traders of English and Scottish ancestry for the Hudson's Bay Company included HENRY KELSEY, who explored the Canadian plains in 1690–92; ANTHONY HENDAY, who traveled even farther west on the Canadian plains in 1754–55; SAMUEL HEARNE, who reached the Arctic Ocean in 1770–72; and DAVID THOMPSON, who explored the ROCKY MOUNTAINS in 1793. Thompson went on to chart COLUMBIA RIVER country for the NORTH WEST COMPANY, first organized in 1779, which was responsible for many expeditions in the Canadian and American West. SIR ALEXANDER MACKENZIE, the first known non-Indian to travel across North America north of the Rio Grande in the 1780s–1790s, was also a trader for the North West Company.

American entrepreneurs also became the first non-Indians to travel widely in the American West. In the years after the expedition under MERIWETHER LEWIS and WILLIAM CLARK from St. Louis to the Pacific Ocean and back in 1804–06, a number of traders developed the MISSOURI RIVER and Rocky Mountain fur trade. JOHN JACOB ASTOR founded the AMERICAN FUR COMPANY in 1808; MANUEL LISA and a number of partners founded the ST. LOUIS FUR COMPANY in 1809; and WILLIAM HENRY ASHLEY and ANDREW HENRY founded the ROCKY MOUNTAIN FUR COMPANY in 1822. Many of the men who worked in Ashley's fur brigades as trappers—such as JEDEDIAH STRONG SMITH and THOMAS FITZPATRICK—became known as MOUNTAIN MEN and had much to do with pioneering the routes in the American West, all the way to California.

Other traders worked the region to the south. In 1822, WILLIAM BECKNELL pioneered a wagon route from present-day Missouri via the Cimarron Cutoff of the Santa Fe Trail to Santa Fe, New Mexico. In 1833, CHARLES BENT and WILLIAM BENT established Bent's Fort as a trade center on the Arkansas River in what is now southeastern Colorado.

In the meantime, traders for the RUSSIAN-AMERICAN COMPANY, founded in 1799 and headed by ALEKSANDR ANDREYEVICH BARANOV, explored parts of Alaska.

❖

The activities mentioned above are some of the obvious connections between commerce and exploration. Yet, the profit motive has played a part in exploration in other, less apparent ways. For example, those creating the technologies surrounding exploration, such as shipbuilders and the makers of navigational equipment, expanded their commercial activities because of it. Writings about exploration and travel have been a solid area of publishing over the centuries. Images from expeditions—paintings and photographs—have also been marketed. Mapmaking firms grew with new geographic findings. The findings of natural scientists who traveled into wilderness areas led to new medicines that could be sold worldwide. Churches sponsoring missionaries in distant lands increased their followings and their coffers. In recent times, the exploration of the ocean depths and space has also led to the development of new technologies.

Company of Merchant Adventurers See
MUSCOVY COMPANY.

Company of Merchants of London Discoverers of the Northwest Passage (Company of Merchants of London, Discoverers of the North-West Passage; North-West Company; Northwest Company)

The Company of Merchants of London Discoverers of the Northwest Passage, a joint-stock company, was given a royal charter in England in 1612. Its name also appears as the

Company of the Merchants of London, Discoverers of the North-West Passage, or simply the North-West Company, also spelled as Northwest Company (but not to be confused with the NORTH WEST COMPANY, founded in Canada for the FUR TRADE).

Investors, some of whom had been part of the MUSCOVY COMPANY, formed the company because they believed HENRY HUDSON's expedition of 1610–11 had located the hoped-for NORTHWEST PASSAGE from the Atlantic Ocean to the Pacific Ocean, based on information brought back by ROBERT BYLOT after a mutiny and Hudson's death. Such a water route would give access to the commerce of the Orient. Bylot became a member of the company as did the reputable geographer RICHARD HAKLUYT.

The company sponsored subsequent expeditions under SIR THOMAS BUTTON in 1612–13, William Gibbons in 1614, and WILLIAM BAFFIN in 1615 and 1616. Bylot participated in all four voyages. The failure to locate a western outlet from HUDSON BAY caused the eventual disbanding of the company.

See also COMMERCE AND EXPLORATION.

compass

The compass is an instrument to determine direction, taking advantage of the Earth's magnetic polarity. It consists of a small bar magnet—a magnetized needle—allowed to spin freely so as to point in the direction of magnetic north. A disc under the needle or around the edge of the device displays markings for north, south, east, and west. When the marking for north is aligned with the needle, a direction may be read.

In addition to revolutionizing navigation, the magnetic compass—variations of which came to be known as the mariner's compass—made surveying and cartography more accurate, being the first tool used to make charts from direct observation. While drawing a coastline, a mapmaker could take multiple readings from a compass to determine its direction. This did not represent ultimate accuracy, but it was an improvement over freehand methods.

The origins of the compass are lost to history. It probably was by accident that the Chinese, sometime before A.D. 1040, discovered that an iron needle rubbed on a lodestone (a variety of magnetite with natural magnetism), if allowed to float freely on water on a piece of straw, would always point to the same direction (the Chinese aligned their compasses to the south). The Chinese themselves did not use the compass for navigation but for feng shui, a practice that assigns spiritual properties to the four different directions; compasses were used to align buildings in the most propitious direction. The Chinese may have introduced the compass to Arabs and other Muslims, who made use of it before Europeans.

One of the earliest accounts of European contact with the compass comes from Petrus Peregrinus de Maricourt, a French Crusader, who wrote of it in the mid-13th century. For the ancient seafarer it was more important to understand the winds than to make abstract calculations, so early mariner's compasses were marked with the 12 primary winds instead of the four directions. It was in Amalfi, Italy, between 1295 and 1302, that the compass as we know it was developed. Yet, when first introduced, its functioning was so mysterious that many Europeans thought it a work of the devil or of evil spirits, and captains sometimes had to keep the presence of a compass on board ships secret from crews.

As use of the compass became more advanced, navigators came to understand the difference between true north and magnetic north, and to recognize regional variations in Earth's magnetic field. A variation on the compass, the GYROCOMPASS, an electronic device using a gyroscope, can determine true north as opposed to magnetic north. Compasses are sometimes mounted in other instruments, such as the transit used in surveying.

See also CHINESE EXPLORATION; GEOGRAPHY AND CARTOGRAPHY; MUSLIM EXPLORATION; NAVIGATION AND EXPLORATION; NORTH MAGNETIC POLE; SOUTH MAGNETIC POLE; SURVEYING AND EXPLORATION.

Congo River (Zaire River)

With a length of 2,720 miles, the Congo River, also known as the Zaire River, a modification of the local word *mzadi*, which means "great water," is the second-longest river in Africa, after the NILE RIVER. (The name of the river was changed from Congo to Zaire in 1971 at the same time the nation known as the Congo became Zaire. In 1997, when the nation of Zaire became the Democratic Republic of the Congo, the Congo name once again was applied to the river.) Its major tributary, the Lualaba, is considered the Upper Congo. Together, the Congo and the Lualaba Rivers drain 1,425,000 square miles of land in central Africa, largely in the country of the Democratic Republic of the Congo, but also including parts of the Republic of the Congo, Cameroon, Burundi, Tanzania, Zambia, and Angola. The river is navigable for 1,000 miles along its center, where it has a width of between four and 10 miles. With its tributaries included, this section forms a navigable system of 8,000 miles. The river is unusual in that it crosses the EQUATOR twice, which led to some confusion over its course, since early geographers thought this impossible. The Congo discharges 1.5 million cubic feet of water per second into the Atlantic Ocean. This massive outflow helped create speculation that the Congo was connected to the NIGER RIVER. It was also theorized for a time that the Congo was part of the Nile River or the ZAMBEZI RIVER. The Congo's relative navigability and size played an important part in early European contact with the interior of Africa and subsequent African exploration. The former name of the river, the *Congo,* is also applied to the region in general.

Portuguese Exploration

DIOGO CÃO made the European discovery of the Congo (Zaire) River in 1482. He sailed for King John II of Portugal, who sought a water route around Africa for the SPICE TRADE of the EAST INDIES. When Cão came upon the mouth of the river, he placed a PADRÃO, a limestone pillar, to claim the land for his sovereign. (For a time, the Congo River would be known to Europeans as the Rio de Padrão or "Pillar River.") The native peoples were friendly and participated in simple trade. Cão learned that upriver there existed a center of power, the kingdom of the Kongo, ruled by Mani Kongo from his city of Mbanza. Cão had been instructed to search for a legendary Christian king PRESTER JOHN, sought by Europeans for centuries, and the Kongo offered a starting point. Cão deployed four Africans among the crew, who had been educated for just such a mission, then continued on his primary task of exploring the African coast. After traveling some 500 miles to the south, Cão headed back northward, stopping at the river on the return trip. Failing to meet up with his emissaries, he continued on to Portugal with four local potentates as hostages. In 1485, Cão made a second journey to the Congo. Since he returned the four African princes to their homeland, the native peoples once again greeted him with hospitality. On this expedition Cão sailed upriver in his CARAVEL. He made it 100 miles inland, where he was prevented from further exploration by the last of the Livingstone Falls, also known as "The Cauldron of Hell." A delegation was dispatched to Mbanza, bearing gifts from King John along with a request for representatives of the kingdom to visit Portugal.

The next record of Portuguese contact with the kingdom of the Kongo at Mbanza comes from the 1491 expedition of Gonçalo de Sousa. He was dispatched with three ships and a complement of soldiers, builders, and farmers to establish a settlement and trading post in the region. The result of this undertaking was disastrous, with many, including de Sousa, dying of disease. The survivors straggled into Mbanza under the command of Gonçalo de Sousa's nephew, Rui de Sousa. The Mani Kongo along with a large throng of fascinated people welcomed them. The king very quickly embraced Christianity, although he may have done so to form a political alliance with the Portuguese against his enemies rather than through sincere religious devotion. Whatever his motivation, a church was constructed, and the king was baptized as were the members of his court. Not all the local population were willing to go along with the new order, however, and conflicts later arose.

The kingdom of the Kongo was perhaps the largest highly developed civilization in Africa at the time, eclipsing Mali, which had gone into decline. The political structure of the Kongo was advanced, with a system of local rulers, governors, and the king, who was able to obtain cooperation among the various tribes in the realm. There were several types of cloth produced by these peoples; it was of such a high quality that the Portuguese mistook it for satin and taffeta of European origin. Native artisans were able to smelt iron thus enabling them to fashion weapons, tools, and musical instruments. They used copper for jewelry, statuettes, and other ornaments. Although the concept of a "cash crop" had not been formulated, the agricultural system was advanced. Trade was a local affair and not an industry carried out with surplus goods.

The prehistory of the peoples of the Congo Basin is intertwined with the Bantu migrations, which probably began early in the first century A.D. The Bantu came from the Upper Nile Valley, where they grew sorghum and millet using a form of slash-and-burn agriculture. As a result of their successes, there came rapid population growth. The combination of increased population and decreased fertility of their lands created pressure to seek new homelands. Over the course of centuries, the Bantu migrated to the south, interbreeding with and displacing other tribes. They found new sources of food, such as the banana and the yam, which had been transplanted from the Pacific Islands to Africa's east coast. Bantu power was consolidated in about A.D. 1000 through new techniques in warfare, which helped them stay in power. Over time, a mythology developed concerning the origins of the Bantu people.

The death of the christianized Mani Kongo resulted in a war of succession between two of his sons, one pagan and the other Christian. The Christian son, Affonso (his Portuguese name), proved victorious. Innocent of the potential motives of Portugal, he encouraged their missionaries, soldiers, and traders. The Portuguese goods were so irresistible that the people of his kingdom were willing to trade slaves for them.

From 1511, there survives a letter Affonso wrote to King Manuel of Portugal appealing for help in curbing the abuses of the slave traders on the island of São Tomé. His appeals were ignored, and the situation in Mbanza and the entire kingdom degenerated rapidly under the pressures of the SLAVE TRADE. With little oversight from the Portuguese, the soldiers of fortune and profiteers plundered the Kongolese culture. Even the priests who had come to "civilize" these people sought profits through the commerce in human life. Affonso continued to trust his Christian brethren overseas. He asked for ships to wage his campaigns against neighboring tribes, and, when these were not forthcoming, he asked for shipbuilders. Assistance was withheld, however, and, when Affonso died in 1542, his country was in turmoil.

Various Nations

The latter half of the 16th century saw increased conflict in the region of the Congo Basin. The Portuguese installed puppet governments, and a fierce tribe called the Yakas staged raids against them. The factional violence of other European peoples active in the region—British, French, and Dutch—also increased. The Dutch conquered the Congo region for a short time. In 1641, they took the port of Mpinda at the mouth of the river. The reigning Mani Kongo at the time sought to drive a wedge between the Protestant Dutch and the Catholic Portuguese. This Dutch possession was fleeting, however, and the Congo reverted back to Portugal in 1648. As Europeans capitalized on the slave trade for the colonies in the Americas, they relied on native peoples to provide captives, trading for the most part in coastal ports, and the interior regions of the river remained largely a mystery to them for almost three centuries.

England became interested in Africa from a scientific point of view during the Age of Enlightenment. The idea of the "noble savage" caught on, and government-sponsored expeditions to the continent were mounted. James Kingston Tuckey headed the first of these to the Congo in 1816. Tuckey's was one of two expeditions to trace the course of the Niger River. His instructions were to investigate the tributaries he found as he sailed up the Congo River to the Niger. His expedition was beset by malaria and dysentery. Tuckey was able to map 150 uncharted miles of the river before he died in the effort. Fewer than half of his men made their way back to England.

In 1868, after studying the sources of the White Nile in the southern Sudan, German naturalist GEORG AUGUST SCHWEINFURTH made his way to the Congo Basin. He made the European discovery of the Uele River, part of the Congo system. His drawings of wildlife along with his scientific observations added much to the early understanding of the region. He was the first European to come in contact with Mubuti, who dwelt in the forests to the north of the river.

The expeditions of DAVID LIVINGSTONE and HENRY MORTON STANLEY finally led to the charting of the entire river. In 1871, with sponsorship from his newspaper, the *New York Herald,* Stanley went to Africa in search of Dr. David Livingstone, who had been incommunicado for some time. Livingstone was investigating possible connections of the Nile and the Congo Rivers to lakes in modern-day Tanzania. When Livingstone died in May 1873, Stanley took up the work that his mentor had failed to complete. Among the goals on his subsequent 1874 expedition was to find the Congo River's source, then follow the river all the way to the Atlantic Ocean. In 1876, after successfully circumnavi-gating Lakes Victoria and Tanganyika, he turned his attention to the Congo River.

Stanley had a rival in his exploration of the Congo. VERNEY LOVETT CAMERON, a British naval officer, had been sent by the ROYAL GEOGRAPHICAL SOCIETY to relieve Livingstone. In 1873, Cameron began his journey from Bangamoyo in Tanzania. By the time Cameron had retraced Livingstone's route, Livingstone had already died. Rather than head home, Cameron struck out to the west to make new discoveries. After exploring and mapping Lake Tanganyika in 1874, he reached Nyangwe, a center of the slave trade on the Lualaba River. Cameron guessed that the Lualaba was a Congo River tributary, so following its flow downstream by CANOE would have been a productive plan. Yet, the people of Nyangwe were hostile and would not sell him the necessary boats. When he realized the futility of the plan, Cameron accepted the offer of the half-Arab, half-black slave trader Tippoo Tib to join his caravan on its way to the west coast. The expedition left Nyangwe in August 1874 and arrived at the Angola coast more than a year later. Cameron had beaten out Stanley in being the first European to make an east-to-west crossing of the southern part of the continent, but since he had been compelled to travel overland, the Congo River remained largely unexplored.

In 1876, Stanley also landed in Nyangwe, but knowing where Cameron had failed, he did not depend on the city's inhabitants for canoes. Instead, it was Stanley's strategy to follow the Lualaba by land until he came to a place where he could obtain transport. Since the plan was still quite hazardous because of the warring tribes along the route, Stanley convinced the same Tippoo Tib to provide the services of his small army. On November 5, 1876, the group set off from Nyangwe on this untested path. Making headway was very difficult as they hacked their way through the jungle. Many died from disease. On Christmas Day, Stanley and Tippoo Tib spent their last day together. They had only progressed 200 miles along the river but, by this time, Stanley had acquired more than 20 canoes, mostly by theft. Stanley and his men traveled down the river and, on January 4, 1877, came to Stanley Falls. These cataracts took them three weeks to portage. Although the next 1,000-mile stretch of river was easy to navigate, passage was fraught with danger because the banks of the river were lined with warriors. Stanley fought 24 battles with tribes along the river and many more brief skirmishes. In the village of Rubunga, he had a short rest but was soon ambushed. On the Bateke Plateau the river once again turned difficult, but the tribes of the region were more hospitable. In March, Stanley reached a 200-mile stretch of cataracts, which would end at Livingstone Falls and "The Cauldron of Hell." Bypassing the rapids was extremely difficult, and, in doing so, Frank Pocock, the last of Stanley's European companions, was killed. On August 1, 1877, Stanley and his guides came to the furthest point that Captain Tuckey had reached approaching from the opposite direction 60 years earlier. Stanley soon straggled back into the settlement of Boma, where he was treated grandly by Portuguese inhabitants. After a journey of more than 7,000 miles, he had proven the Nile's independence of the Congo River as well as the Lualaba's connection, and had followed the great river to its outlet.

Stanley had witnessed many of the horrors of the slave trade while on his travels. Livingstone had worked on replacing it with a more benign commerce. Indeed, by the late 19th century, the eradication of slavery was a cause in England at the time. It was understandable then that Stanley felt some frustration when, returning to England in 1878, his plans to develop the Congo fell on deaf ears. King Leopold II of Belgium saw the region's potential for profit, however. In 1876, he had sponsored a conference concerning the region, portraying himself as having only the highest humanitarian motives. He actually hoped to create his own African country. For assistance in this endeavor, he hired Stanley.

Possession of the Congo was not to go uncontested. The colonial scramble for Africa was beginning. France, which was wary of King Leopold, sponsored an expedition by PIERRE-PAUL-FRANÇOIS-CAMILLE SAVORGNON DE BRAZZA, a 26-year-old naval officer. Exploring along the Ogowe River to the north of the Congo, de Brazza came near its source, then set out across the land to find the larger river. In early 1878, de Brazza made it to the Bateke Plateau. He then reached the Alima River, which turned out to be a Congo River tributary. Using these rivers, he returned to the coast.

By the end of 1878, Stanley was planning his expedition for Leopold, and de Brazza was organizing on behalf of France. In August 1879, Stanley arrived at the Congo River with his crew and supplies, with the intention of building a road past Livingstone Falls. De Brazza followed the same route as on his previous journey, but now with the goal of reaching Stanley Pool above the rapids. In September 1880, de Brazza arrived in the village of Mbe (which would become Brazzaville) on the banks of the Congo and negotiated a treaty with the tribal leader Makoko. While he was there, he encountered Stanley.

From 1879 to 1884, Stanley worked for Leopold and established the Congo Free State. Leopold became the personal sovereign of the land. In 1891–92, he issued a number of decrees, which allowed him to extract the wealth of the country. The carnage that followed stands as one of the darkest periods of colonial history. Mercenaries were recruited to compel the population to harvest latex from rubber trees. Those who failed to meet their quota were enslaved on plantations or had their right hands cut off. In fact, hands became a form of currency the soldiers used for payment from the king. Leopold became extraordinarily rich, buying mansions throughout Europe and living in lux-

ury. There were investigations into his abuses, and, in 1908, he was forced to turn control of the Congo over to Belgium.

It is worth noting that Stanley made another journey through the Congo region in 1887–89 on a mission to rescue German official MEHMED EMIN PASHA. Another explorer of the Congo region who bears mentioning is OSKAR LENZ, a German geologist who, in the 1870s–80s, explored both the Saharan and sub-Saharan regions of the continent.

❖

Today, the Congo region produces copper, palm oil, cotton, sugar, and coffee. There is steamer traffic between Kinshasa and Kisangani, the main river ports, and interest in the hydroelectric potential of the river has been increasing.

conquest and exploration

Since prehistory humans have been creating and expanding territory and political power through conquest, and one people conquering another people is part of the history of exploration. Sometimes expeditions were launched with conquest in mind; in other cases, military expeditions were primarily exploratory, but were the only safe ways to travel because of possible armed responses or banditry, and often preceded the travels of others. Conquest thus helped expand geographic knowledge and led to opening routes and enabling further travels. The aftermath of conquest was often colonization, although colonization sometimes occurred in lands where no military action was necessary (see COLONIZATION AND EXPLORATION). The imperatives of conquest were not just territorial and political, but also sometimes economic (see COMMERCE AND EXPLORATION) and sometimes religious (see RELIGION AND EXPLORATION).

Much of history is about empire building, and, in order to understand the context of all exploration, one has to understand the ebb and flow of civilizations and their evolving territorial holdings. Yet, some peoples and certain individuals are especially studied as explorers because their military efforts took them to lands not yet mapped and led to a dramatic increase in geographic knowledge.

Because exploration on all the continents except Antarctica involved travel through native lands, native peoples have been butchered and enslaved, and their homes and lands have been laid to waste (see NATIVE PEOPLES AND EXPLORATION). The spread of diseases against which indigenous peoples had little resistance proved more deadly than military action in the history of conquest (see DISEASE AND EXPLORATION). Many of the outbreaks of violence between explorers and aboriginal peoples were on a small scale and did not involve armies or navies. Yet, they too can be viewed as a form of conquest in that lands were appropriated and peoples displaced. The SLAVE TRADE, since it involved the commerce in human life, can also be viewed as another form of conquest associated with exploration.

Alexander the Great

One historical figure recognized as an explorer as well as a conqueror is ALEXANDER THE GREAT, or Alexander III, of Macedonia. He succeeded his father, Phillip II, to the throne at the age of 20, whereupon he outmaneuvered his rivals and consolidated his power over the Greeks. In 334 B.C., he embarked upon his Persian expedition, conquering much of Asia Minor. In 332 B.C., his Greco-Macedonian forces defeated the Phoenicians at Tyre on the eastern MEDITER-RANEAN SEA and subjugated the Egyptians. That same year, he founded the city of Alexandria in North Africa. In the next years, he pushed eastward into Asia, reaching as far as India by 327 B.C., eventually crossing the INDUS RIVER. His troops had traversed much of the Middle East and Central Asia, overcoming resisting peoples and founding new cities. His purpose was to expand his empire, but, in doing so, he sought knowledge of conquered lands. Surveyors traveled with his troops, recording information as they went, as did scientists, who sent specimens of flora and fauna back to Greece. He also sent out exploratory expeditions to neighboring regions, such as that under NEARCHUS in 325–324 B.C., which explored along the coasts of Pakistan and Iran from the Indus Delta to the head of the Persian Gulf.

Genghis Khan

Another conqueror/explorer was GENGHIS KHAN of the Mongols (see MONGOL EXPLORATION). After uniting the Mongol tribes and defeating the Chinese, he pushed westward and southward bringing much of central Asia, including southern Russia, and the Near East under Mongol domination. He sought geographic information as well as cultural and sent out emissaries on exploratory expeditions to learn about geography and peoples. Among them was the Taoist sage CH'ANG-CH'UN in 1221, who traveled from eastern China through central Asia to Afghanistan. His conquests had the added effect of breaking the monopoly held on the SILK ROAD through Asia held at the time by Muslims and started a period of contact between East and West by diplomats and merchants, including Venetian merchant MARCO POLO, who reached the court of Genghis's grandson Kublai Khan in 1275.

Roman Generals

The Romans, in the expansion of their empire, provided geographic knowledge that came to be disseminated through the writings of geographers (see ROMAN EXPLORATION). One Roman geographer, PLINY THE ELDER, had even served as a Roman cavalry officer in both Europe and Africa, before writing *Historia Naturalis,* published in A.D.

77. Another geographer, PTOLEMY, a hellenized Egyptian living in Alexandria while it was under Roman rule, published *Geographia,* a description of world geography, in A.D. 127–147, drawing on information brought back from expeditions of conquest.

Roman generals whose expeditions are discussed as part of the history of exploration include GAIUS JULIUS CAESAR, who, in 58 B.C., led troops into Gaul (present-day France) and, in 55–54 B.C., to Britain; GAIUS AELIUS GALLUS, who, in 25 B.C., invaded the Arabian Peninsula; SUETONIUS PAULINUS, who, in A.D. 42, led a military expedition from the coast of North Africa southward across the Atlas Mountains to the northern edge of the SAHARA DESERT; JULIUS MATERNUS, who, in A.D. 50, led troops across the Sahara, possibly reaching Lake Chad; and GNAEUS JULIUS AGRICOLA, who, in A.D. 80, led a military exploration into Scotland.

Vikings

The Scandinavian peoples known as Vikings or Norsemen—Danes, Norwegians, and Swedes of the Middle Ages—traveled widely and were known as raiders by the people of Europe because of their numerous attacks (see VIKING EXPLORATION). In the ninth, 10th, and 11th centuries, they spread southward and carried out raids on other Europeans, especially those in coastal areas in western Europe, but also inland in eastern Europe. They also traveled to ICELAND, GREENLAND, and northeastern North America. They did not have organized armies and generals but were leaders of small groups of warriors. Warfare was carried out and plunder taken for individual prestige, but it also enabled settlement in new homelands. Many of those Viking explorers traveled beyond Europe—ERIC THE RED in Greenland or his son, LEIF ERICSSON, in VINLAND in North America—and are known primarily as colonizers rather than as conquerors.

Conquistadores

Much of the Spanish exploration of the Americas involved individuals known as CONQUISTADORES, the Spanish word for "conqueror." The name is applied to them because of their actions against native peoples—for their territory, wealth, or labor. The two most famous conquistadores are HERNÁN CORTÉS, who conquered the Aztec Indians in Mexico in the 1520s, and FRANCISCO PIZARRO, who conquered the Inca Indians in Ecuador and Peru in the 1530s.

The Great Navies

Exploration, conquest, colonization, and commerce throughout history have been dominated by those peoples with the best ships (see SHIPBUILDING AND EXPLORATION). The LONGSHIP of the Vikings gave them an advantage in medieval Europe, as the JUNK gave the Chinese an advantage in the Far East in the 15th century, and as the CARAVEL, CARRACK, and GALLEON facilitated the exploration and empire building of the Portuguese, Spanish, English, and Dutch during the EUROPEAN AGE OF EXPLORATION, from the 15th into the 17th century, and afterward. Warships enabled conquest and merchant ships enabled the building and maintaining of trade empires.

Rival Powers

Military actions were carried out against other colonial powers as well as against native peoples. For example, PRIVATEERS—such as Englishman SIR FRANCIS DRAKE, commissioned by England in the 16th century to raid Spanish ships and ports in the Americas while undertaking explorations—relate to the subject of conquest. And, on a larger scale, the history of exploration over the centuries has played out against a backdrop of competition of rival nations, with warfare often resulting from lands explored and colonized far from home, such as in the French and Indian Wars of the 17th and 18th centuries in North America.

❖

Not all expeditions by organized militaries were for the purpose of conquest. For example, the navies of many nations sponsored or played a part in expeditions strictly exploratory in nature, such as the first French CIRCUMNAVIGATION OF THE WORLD under the naval officer LOUIS-ANTOINE DE BOUGAINVILLE in the 1760s. And armies had surveying units, such as the U.S. Army's Corps of Topographical Engineers, which helped map the American West, and the British army's Bengal Engineers, who directed the work of the PUNDITS—native Indian explorers—in the Great Trigonometrical Survey of India, both in the 19th century.

conquistadores (conquistadors)

The term *conquistador* (plural form, *conquistadores* or *conquistadors*) is Spanish for "conqueror," from the Spanish verb *conquistar*, "to conquer." It has come to be applied historically to any one of the Spanish conquerors of the Americas, especially of Mexico and Peru in the 16th century. It refers both to the leaders and to the men who served under them. Because of association with brutality toward native peoples, as well as against Spanish rivals, the term has also come to be used in reference to any ruthless adventurer.

Some of the conquistadores had served against the Moors—Muslims (see MUSLIM EXPLORATION) out of North Africa who had invaded the Iberian Peninsula in A.D. 711 and occupied parts of it until final defeat in 1492 —or in other European campaigns. Many came from the Estremadura region of the kingdom of Castile and had originally served under Spanish monarchs Ferdinand II

and Isabella I, who helped unify Spain and sponsored the 1492 voyage to the Americas by Italian mariner CHRISTOPHER COLUMBUS. Many of the most famous conquistadores were active in the Americas during the reign of Charles I (Holy Roman Emperor Charles V). Many of the men filling out the ranks were not professional soldiers, however.

There was no standing Spanish army or navy in the Americas. The exploratory expeditions and military actions were often planned by and paid for by the conquistadores themselves. Or the conquistadores sought backing from commercial companies who might provide ships, horses, weapons, and clothing against possible profits from plunder. The leader and main investor typically held the title of "captain" and was often a man of high position, such as an appointed government official or nobleman (*hidalgo*) or any *encomendero,* that is someone holding an *encomienda,* a royal land grant. Participants came from a variety of backgrounds and social classes. Freed slaves sometimes joined the force. Priests often traveled with the expedition so that the Catholic Church was also represented (see RELIGION AND EXPLORATION). The conquistadores were armed with swords, lances, crossbows, and at least a few small cannons. They wore armor that could repel native arrows. They utilized horses in battle when the landscape permitted. They often sought the support of native peoples against rival peoples. They also regularly used the strategy of capturing an indigenous leader and holding him hostage in order to pacify his followers. The attainment of gold and silver from native peoples became the primary objective and, when successful, led to royal approval and the granting of huge tracts of land (see TREASURE AND EXPLORATION).

Hernán Cortés

HERNÁN CORTÉS is one of the most famous conquistadores. His father, a noble of modest means, served in the military. The young Cortés had studied law before entering the army himself. He served in campaigns in Italy before traveling to the Americas in 1504, becoming a minor official in the WEST INDIES. He served in the conquest of Cuba under conquistador DIEGO VELÁSQUEZ, a veteran of Moorish campaigns, in 1511. Seven years later, Cortés received a commission from Velásquez for an expedition to the Yucatán Peninsula. Following a dispute, Velásquez dismissed Cortés, but Cortés proceeded on the expedition anyway. Velásquez sent professional soldier PÁNFILO DE NÁRVAEZ—cited as one of the cruelest of conquistadores by Spanish missionary Bartolomé de las Casas, based on his actions against the Arawak (Taino) Indians of Cuba—to arrest Cortés, but Cortés defeated Nárvaez on the Mexican mainland. Nárvaez was imprisoned, and most of his men joined Cortés in the conquest of the Aztec, which he accomplished in 1521. In the course of his conquest, he took Aztec ruler Montezuma hostage. The great riches obtained from the Aztec and shipped to Spain led to Cortés's being named Captain General of New Spain (the original Spanish name for Mexico). BERNAL DÍAZ DEL CASTILLO, who served under Cortés, went on to write an account of the conquest of the Aztec, entitled *Crónica de la conquista de Nueva España (The True History of the Conquest of New Spain),* which is an essential source of information about conquistadores.

Francisco Pizarro

Another famous conquistador, FRANCISCO PIZARRO, was born out of wedlock and raised outside his father's aristocratic family, and he may have served in the military under his father in Italy. In 1502, he traveled to the West Indies in the service of Nicolas de Ovando, the appointed governor of Hispaniola (present-day Haiti and the Dominican Republic) after Christopher Columbus. In 1509, Pizarro later traveled to the South American mainland as part of ALONZO DE OJEDA's expedition to what is now Colombia and was left in charge of a colony at San Sebastián. He moved the colony to present-day Panama, where he participated in explorations of the region as the lieutenant under VASCO NÚÑEZ DE BALBOA. In 1519, Pizarro arrested Núñez de Balboa on behalf of Panama's governor, PEDRO ARIAS DE ÁVILA. Pizarro eventually was appointed mayor of Panama City and received grants of land. Reports of a wealthy Indian civilization to the south led to Pizarro's expeditions to present-day Ecuador and Peru and the conquest of the Inca in the 1530s. In the course of his actions, he held Inca leader Atahualpa captive as part of his strategy.

De Soto and Coronado

Two famous conquistadores in North America were HERNANDO DE SOTO, who had served under Pizarro and traveled through much of the American southeast in 1540–42, and FRANCISCO VÁSQUEZ DE CORONADO, who explored much of the American Southwest and southern plains, also in 1540–42. They too sought wealthy Indian civilizations and, although they failed to locate great riches as Cortés and Pizarro did among the Aztec and Inca, their expeditions led to Spanish colonization and development of native lands.

Lope de Aguirre

One of the most brutal of all the conquistadores was LOPE DE AGUIRRE, who turned his violence against fellow Spaniards as well as against indigenous peoples. He had first worked in the Americas as a horse trainer but later served as a soldier under other conquistadores. In 1560, while part of an expedition on the AMAZON RIVER in search of the fabled wealthy kingdom of EL DORADO, he led a mutiny against PEDRO DE URSÚA and had him killed along with his mistress Doña Inez de Atiensa. The expedition went on to lay waste to native villages. Aguirre later killed his own daughter rather than have her be captured by rival Spanish forces.

❖

It was not just the weaponry of the Spaniards and political rivalries of indigenous peoples themselves that enabled relatively small Spanish forces to defeat Native Americans. The Spaniards were helped in their conquest by the destructive force of European diseases, especially smallpox, against which native peoples had no resistance (see DISEASE AND EXPLORATION).

coracle

A coracle is a small, round or oval boat, typically made with a frame of wood—typically wicker—covered with either animal hide or canvas. It is designed to carry a single person and a small amount of cargo. The use of the coracle certainly predates the historical record. One of the earliest existing models of a boat is a clay sculpture—in the shape of a coracle—from the fourth millennium B.C., found in Eridu in Mesopotamia. Later versions of round boats appear in relief carvings from Assyria.

The coracle has had a long history in the British Isles as well. It was used for fishing, as well as interisland transportation and trading trips. The coracle is thought to be the prototype of the larger CURRAGH, which SAINT BRENDAN used to travel the Atlantic Ocean to the north and west of Ireland. The coracle continues to be used today in England and Ireland for fishing and river travel.

The Arikara, Hidatsa, and Mandan Indians of the upper MISSOURI RIVER shaped similar circular craft out of buffalo hide stretched over a willow frame and sealed with animal fat and ashes. Their version is known as the bullboat.

See also SHIPBUILDING AND EXPLORATION.

cosmonauts See ASTRONAUTS.

Cossack exploration

The Cossacks are a peasant people of mixed descent, who have inhabited, over the course of their history, parts of the Russian czarist empire, the Union of Soviet Socialist Republics (USSR, Soviet Union), and presently Russia and other former Soviet republics. The name is associated with those peoples inhabiting steppe country, extending from the region north of the Black Sea and the Caucasus Mountains eastward to the Altai Mountains in SIBERIA. Some Cossacks were descended from Ukrainians and Poles in addition to

Russians; many Cossack ancestors were runaway serfs. They became known for military prowess and horsemanship. The name *Cossack* is derived from the Turkish word *kazak,* for "free person."

The formation of Cossacks is traced back to the 14th and 15th centuries. By the early 16th century, Cossack villages were situated along the Dnieper River and eventually the Don and Ural Rivers as well. The villagers, who owned land in common, were governed by assemblies, presided over by elected elders with one elder overseeing several communities, especially in times of war. Starting in the 16th century, the Russian czarist government extended its control to frontier regions and subjugated the Cossacks, who had earlier helped conquer the Tartars (peoples of Turkic origin who had invaded parts of Asia and Europe under the Mongols in the 13th century). The Cossacks came to be organized for the most part as cavalry units and carried out numerous expeditions into Siberia. By the late 18th century, following their participation in failed peasant revolts against czarist rule, the Cossacks had lost most of their political autonomy, yet they had become a privileged military class. In the 19th and early 20th centuries, they were used by the czarist government to quell uprisings but refused to do so in the Bolshevik Revolution of 1917. In the subsequent civil war of 1918–20, they opposed the Red Army. Under the Soviet system, the Cossacks lost their special status in the military. They also lost much of their wealth and were forced to relocate and farm collectively. In World War II (1941–45), a number of Cossack cavalry divisions were formed to fight the invading Germans. Since the dissolution of the Soviet Union, they have experienced a cultural revival as well as newfound unity and influence.

Because of their location on the edge of the frontier, their mobility, and their skill in warfare, the Cossacks played a significant role in the history of Russian exploration. It was YERMAK (also known as Yermak Timofeyevich or Yermak Timofeiev), who, in 1581–82, led a force across the Ural Mountains and conquered the Tartars at Sibir (from which the name *Siberia* is derived). His activity marked the beginning of Russian expansion eastward. By 1610, Russian fur traders had reached the Yenisey River, and, by 1638, the Sea of Okhotsk, opening up on the Pacific Ocean. But it was often Cossack forces that gained control of a region and established permanent settlements, which led to further exploration.

In 1631–33, PYOTR BEKETOV established Russian dominion to the Yenisey, Lena, Aldan, and Amur Rivers of central Siberia, and, in 1652–60, he expanded Russian interests into southeastern Siberia, south of Lake Baikal. In 1643–48, VASILY DANILOVICH POYARKOV led a military expedition and explored the Amur River, feeding the Sea of Okhotsk, and other rivers of southeastern Siberia.

Meanwhile, in 1641–44, MIKHAIL STADUKHIN explored the Arctic coast of eastern Siberia, reaching the mouth of the Kolyma River. In 1648, SEMYON IVANOVICH DEZHNEV led an expedition of Cossacks in small boats from the mouth of the Kolyma River eastward along the Arctic coast of Siberia and succeeded in rounding the Chukchi Peninsula of northeastern Siberia and entering the BERING STRAIT. In 1695–96, LUKA MOROZKO and VLADIMIR VASILYEVICH ATLASOV led expeditions onto the Kamchatka Peninsula.

Cossack activity eastward continued in the 18th century. In 1713–14, fur trader SEMYON ANABARA explored the Shantar Islands in the Sea of Okhotsk. In 1726–33, EMELYAN BASOV led a series of expeditions along Siberia's Lena River in search of a seaward route to the Pacific Ocean.

The exploration of Siberia was carried out by non-Cossacks as well, but the Cossack role as pioneers, soldiers, and fur traders pushing eastward was critical to the region's history.

See also MONGOL EXPLORATION.

coureur de bois

The French term *coureur de bois,* which translates into English as "runner of the woods," was originally applied to unlicensed entrepreneurs, mostly in the FUR TRADE in northeastern North America during the 17th century. In order to control trade with Native Americans, the colonial government of New France issued a limited number of licenses. As a result, many men defied the regulations and went into business on their own as trappers or traders in the wilderness. Their number is not known, but it has been estimated that one-third of adult able-bodied men in New France by the end of the century were coureurs de bois, leaving many of the eastern settlements deprived of male support. Efforts by royal representatives and the Roman Catholic Church failed to curtail them, and they played an intrinsic part in the history of the fur trade and in the exploration of North America, much like the later MOUNTAIN MEN, who worked the ROCKY MOUNTAINS in the 19th century.

The French term VOYAGEURS, for "travelers," was applied to those men who worked for licensed traders and who traveled by CANOE Indian-style—paddling and portaging—on trade routes. Many voyageurs went into business for themselves—thus becoming coureurs de bois—or in conjunction with other unlicensed traders. The coureurs de bois adopted many Indian customs. Some settled among and intermarried with Indians. Their descendants—typically of French and Cree ancestry as well as Scottish and other tribal ancestry, such as Chippewa (Ojibway) and Assiniboine—became known as Métis, or "mixed-blood." The trade in liquor and firearms developed by some coureurs de bois led to outbreaks of violence between non-Indians and some native peoples, however.

The coureurs de bois were wide-ranging. Much of their activity was in the region of the western Great Lakes, but some ventured down the MISSISSIPPI RIVER into French Louisiana and farther westward onto the Canadian and American plains. Frenchmen MÉDARD CHOUART DES GROSEILLIERS and his brother-in-law PIERRE-ESPRIT RADISSON, who developed the fur trade around Green Bay in the 1650s and explored much of the country around Lake Michigan and Lake Superior, were coureurs de bois. On their return to Montreal in 1660, their furs were confiscated for unlicensed trading, leading to their work for the English and the founding of the HUDSON'S BAY COMPANY in 1670. The large fur-trading companies dominated the western fur trade in subsequent years.

cross-staff (balestila, Jack's staff, Jacob's staff)

The cross-staff, also known as Jacob's staff, Jack's staff, or balestila, like the earlier invented ASTROLABE, is an obsolete navigational instrument used for measuring the angle of a celestial body above the horizon. With this measurement, along with information about the celestial body based on earlier measurements, the user can determine latitude and time of day. The device was probably invented in one of the Low Countries (the region of present-day Belgium, Luxembourg, and the Netherlands) and probably in the early 15th century.

A cross-staff consists of two pieces of wood, the staff about three feet long with a sliding crossbar attached to it. On the staff is mounted a sight, and on each end of the crossbar, a hole. To measure the altitude of the celestial body, a navigator looks along the staff with the crossbar aligned vertically, then slides the crossbar to the point at which the celestial body appears through the upper hole and the horizon through the lower. The intersection of the crossbar and a scale written on the staff indicates altitude. A reading of the NORTH STAR, for example, would gauge its height in the sky; the lower it is, the farther south a ship was.

The cross-staff came into favor over the astrolabe with some mariners in the 15th century. CHRISTOPHER COLUMBUS, the Italian navigating for Spain, possibly carried as navigating equipment a magnetic COMPASS, a primitive triangular QUADRANT, an astrolabe, and perhaps one cross-staff. He also had a table of figures to give meaning to the readings from these early navigational tools (see EPHEMERIS).

English navigator JOHN DAVIS modified the design of the cross-staff in the late 16th century by adding a reflector so that the user would not have to look directly into the Sun but could take readings with his back to it. This became known as the backstaff, the antecedent of a type of quadrant known as the Davis Quadrant. The SEXTANT, invented in the 1730s, became the favored tool of celestial navigation, but people went on making cross-staffs until the end of the century.

See also LATITUDE AND LONGITUDE; NAVIGATION AND EXPLORATION.

Crusades

The Crusades were any of the military expeditions undertaken by European Christian powers, from the late 11th century through the late 13th century, to recover the Holy Land in the Near East from the Muslims. The first Crusades are relevant to the history of exploration since they marked the first attempt at expansionism and colonialism by Christian nations beyond Europe. They also led to increased contacts among differing cultures and growing geographic awareness.

Background

Palestine, the historic region on the east coast of the MEDITERRANEAN SEA (presently controlled by Israel), was at the center of trade routes linking three continents—Asia, Europe, and Africa. Adherents of the Jewish, Christian, and Islamic religions consider it a Holy Land; the city of Jerusalem in particular has sacred sites central to the belief systems of all three religions. In addition to the ancient local peoples—such as the Canaanites (related to the Phoenicians), Philistines, and Israelites—Palestine had been occupied at times by Hittites, Egyptians, Assyrians, Babylonians, Persians, Greeks, and Romans. It fell to the Arab Muslims in A.D. 638. Yet the region remained relatively open—a center of commerce and religious and intellectual activity until the late 11th century when the Seljuk Turks became the dominant Islamic people in Asia Minor (the Anatolian Peninsula) and took control of Jerusalem. Their harassment of Christian pilgrims to Jerusalem and their aggressive stance toward Constantinople (present-day Istanbul), the seat of the Eastern Roman Empire (Byzantine Empire), became a concern to Christian leaders. Alexius I Comnenus, the Byzantine emperor, appealed to the West for help defending against invaders. Soon afterward, in 1095, Pope Urban II gave a speech at the Council of Clermont in France encouraging aid to Byzantium against the Islamic threat.

Wandering preachers, such as Peter the Hermit (Peter of Amiens), helped spread the message of a "holy war." Some of those who would become involved over the next years did so for the sake of territorial and economic interests in addition to religious ideals. The prosperity and growing populations in Europe at that time prompted a looking outward to distant lands with curiosity, ambition, and dreams of adventure: Religious leaders wanted to make inroads into Muslim lands and unite the Latin and Orthodox branches of Catholicism; nobles saw the potential for territorial expansion; merchants recognized trade possibilities; knights saw the opportunity of using their skill in battle; and peasants saw the opportunity for a new life in *Outremer,* a French term for "beyond the seas." In any case, for varying reasons, the call to conquest was heard by people of many different social backgrounds and callings over the subsequent centuries.

Different numbering systems have been applied to the numerous Crusades. In addition to the nine Crusades sanctioned by the Catholic Church, there are a number of other endeavors, some of them with names, such as the "Peasants' Crusade" and the "Children's Crusade."

Peasants' Crusade

In the so-called Peasants' Crusade of 1095–96, not an officially sanctioned endeavor, several thousand French and German peasants gathered and headed to Jerusalem by way of Constantinople. Peter the Hermit was one of several leaders. On the way, some of them sacked Belgrade; others attacked Jewish communities. Soon after their arrival in Constantinople, Alexius I provided them with boats to Jerusalem, where they were easily defeated by the Turks. Some managed to escape, returning to Europe; others, such as Peter the Hermit, joined the gathering Crusader forces.

First Crusade

What is known as the First Crusade consisted of organized armies under a number of nobles. Other people joined them en route or traveled to port towns, then sailed to Constantinople on their own to meet up with the Crusaders, creating a force of an estimated 25,000 to 30,000 in late 1096 and early 1097. The majority were Franks, descended from those peoples united in France under Charlemagne in the eighth and ninth centuries. From Constantinople, the Crusaders crossed to Asia Minor and traveled southward overland through Muslim states and principalities in present-day Turkey, Syria, Lebanon, and Israel. Major victories in the First Crusade included the capture of Nicea (present-day Iznik, Turkey) in 1097; the capture of Antioch (a site in present-day Turkey) in 1098; and, in a bloody massacre in which the Crusaders massacred most of the Arab and Jewish inhabitants, the capture of Jerusalem in 1099. Godfrey of Bouillon became the first ruler—known as defender of the Holy Sepulcher—of the Latin Kingdom of Jerusalem. Other Crusader states founded at this time were the County of Edessa (in northern Syria and southern Turkey); the Principality of Antioch (in Syria); and the County of Tripoli (in Lebanon). Some Crusaders thus maintained a presence in the region, in particular members of the military orders, the Knights Hospitalers and the Knights Templars; others returned home.

Second, Third, and Fourth Crusades

The later Crusades were intended to offer support to the Crusader states and expand Christian-held territory. After the fall of Edessa to the Turks in 1144, Bernard of Clair-

vaux called for another crusade. In the Second Crusade of 1147–49, armies under Holy Roman Emperor Conrad III and then king of France Louis VII failed to take Damascus in Syria.

The Third Crusade was declared in 1187 by Pope Gregory VIII and was carried out in 1189–92. Leaders included King Richard I Lionheart of England, King Philip II Augustus of France, and Holy Roman Emperor Frederick I Barbarossa. In battle with Muslim forces under the renowned commander Saladin, a Kurd serving as vizier of Egypt, the Crusaders managed to fight to a truce. They retained Acre (Akko) in Syria and Jaffa, 35 miles northwest of Jerusalem in Palestine, and a narrow strip of coast and the right of free access to Jerusalem. Meanwhile, Tripoli and Antioch were controlled by Christians.

A number of expeditions to the Holy Land in subsequent years are not all listed as major Crusades. That known as the Fourth Crusade, in 1202–04, never reached the Holy Land. Its Frankish leaders joined the Venetians in retaking Zara (Zadar) on the Adriatic coast of present-day Croatia, then part of the Kingdom of Hungary. The Franks then joined in a dynastic struggle for Constantinople itself. After seizing and looting the city, they deposed the Byzantine leaders and established the Latin Empire of Constantinople, with Venice now controlling the sea route between the two cities. Even though Pope Innocent III condemned their acts of violence against fellow Christians, the Fourth Crusade led to increased distancing between the Roman Catholic and Greek Orthodox churches.

Children's Crusade

In the so-called Children's Crusade of 1212, a visionary French shepherd teenager, Stephen of Cloyes, inspired other children to try to liberate the Holy Land, a cause that their elders had betrayed in the Fourth Crusade. A group traveled to Paris to seek the support of French king Philip II. On his refusal to help, some of the youth returned to their homes, but others remained devoted to the cause. A youth from Cologne named Nicholas similarly inspired German children. Some of them reached Italy and others, Marseilles. It is thought that some of the youth perished from hunger and disease, and that others set out from Marseilles and other ports by ship, only to be sold into slavery by the crews.

Final Crusades

Soon afterward, in 1217–21, the Fifth Crusade, the final one sponsored by the papacy, was launched against Muslim forces in Egypt. Christian forces captured Damietta (Dumyāt), at the mouth of the NILE RIVER, but evacuated it two years later after failing to capture Cairo.

In the Sixth Crusade of 1228–29, Holy Roman Emperor Frederick II moved on Jerusalem with the support of the Teutonic Knights, a military order, and, through negotiations, reached a truce with Muslim leaders granting the

Franks control of Jerusalem, except for Islamic holy places. Feuding between the Knights Hospitalers and Knights Templars led to a weakening of the Crusader states, and the Turks retook Jerusalem in 1244.

In the Seventh Crusade of 1248–50, King Louis IX of France attacked Cairo but was captured. Freed by ransom, he stayed in the Near East to rebuild Jaffa and Acre. After his return to France, Jaffa and Antioch fell to Muslim forces. Louis organized the Eighth Crusade of 1270, but he died in northern Africa after invading Tunis. Prince Edward (later King Edward I of England) launched the Ninth Crusade of 1271–72, reaching Acre, where he negotiated an 11-year truce. Yet, in 1271, Tripoli fell to the Muslims. And in 1291, so did Acre, the last Christian stronghold in the Near East. In the meantime, the Byzantines retook Constantinople in 1261, ending the Latin Empire of Constantinople as well.

Economic Outcome

The Crusades had no lasting territorial effect after the fall of the Crusader states to the Muslims. Yet, they did have a lasting economic effect. During the Crusades, Italy became the primary route for travel from Europe to the Near East and North Africa. As a result, Italian cities prospered, and Italian merchants replaced Byzantines and Muslims as the dominant traders in the Mediterranean. Italian port cities remained the commercial center of activity in the region—and the link between East and West—for years to come. And a growing number of Italian merchants, such as MARCO POLO, would travel from Europe to the Far East in the late 13th and 14th centuries. Italian commercial power and expanding worldview helped bring about the start of the period of history known as the RENAISSANCE. Italian control of trade routes helped set the stage for the EUROPEAN AGE OF EXPLORATION, starting in the 15th century, when other European nations began seeking Atlantic Ocean and Pacific Ocean routes to the Far East.

❖

In the years after the Crusades to the Holy Land, other military expeditions against non-Christians were promoted as "Crusades," such as in eastern Europe. Some of the Crusader military orders even participated. But the term, used historically—and certainly in the context of world exploration—generally refers to the expeditions mentioned above.

See also RELIGION AND EXPLORATION

Cumberland Gap

The Cumberland Gap is a pass through the Cumberland Mountains, a range of the APPALACHIAN MOUNTAINS, in northeastern Tennessee near its juncture with Virginia and Kentucky. The walls flanking it are more than 500 feet high; its altitude is 1,640 feet; along some stretches it is only wide enough for a small road. Formed naturally, the Cumberland Gap is a wind gap—that is, a dry valley—one of the gaps that separate the Blue Ridge Mountains into smaller sections.

In 1750, Virginia-born THOMAS WALKER, a physician appointed chief agent of the Loyal Land Company, led a surveying party westward from Staunton, Virginia, and crossed the Blue Ridge into the Holston River Valley, then over Powell's Mountain into Powell's Valley. It was there he located the mountain pass that he named the Cumberland Gap after the Duke of Cumberland, a British general.

In 1769, DANIEL BOONE, sponsored by the Transylvania Company, who hoped to develop lands to the west, traveled through the Cumberland Gap with JOHN FINLEY and a number of other frontiersmen on a hunting expedition to Kentucky, which lasted until 1771. In 1773, Boone led a colonizing expedition into the pass but was turned back by Indians. In 1775, the Transylvania Company hired Boone to establish a road from Fort Chiswells in the Shenandoah Valley through the Cumberland Gap into Kentucky; Boone and a party of about 30 axmen cleared and marked the route. This became known as the Wilderness Road or Boone's Trace. Most of the early immigrants to Tennessee and Kentucky journeyed over this road.

curragh (curach, currach, skin-boat)

The curragh (also *currach* or *curach*) is a type of boat constructed from oiled animal hides covering a light wooden frame. It is also called a skin-boat. Pointed at both ends, it resembles a large CANOE. Although normally propelled by oars, it can be rigged with a sail. The curragh, used especially in waters off Ireland, is thought to have evolved from the British CORACLE.

Used for ocean fishing to this day in Ireland, the curragh is a vessel more seaworthy than its appearance would indicate. The experienced sailor is able to handle rough seas in this vessel due to its maneuverability and stability, thus making transoceanic voyages possible, although perilous.

Curraghs were in common use in the fourth century A.D. They were larger than today's versions and could carry 70 persons or more. It would have been in one of these curraghs that Irish monk SAINT BRENDAN and other monks traveled westward into the Atlantic Ocean in the sixth century A.D.

See also SHIPBUILDING AND EXPLORATION.

D

Davis Quadrant   See QUADRANT.

dead reckoning

The navigation term *dead reckoning* refers to the act of determining the position of a watercraft or aircraft from the following data: a known starting point; records of the courses sailed or flown; distance made (which may or may not be estimated from velocity); and the drift (the velocity of the current, either known or estimated). By definition, dead reckoning does not include celestial observations. Yet the principles of dead reckoning are part of virtually every navigation system.

There is a mistaken belief that *dead* in the term *dead reckoning* derives from the word *deductive* rather than from *dead* having the meaning of "directly" or "exactly," as in "dead ahead" or "dead center." Yet it can be said that information "deduced" from dead reckoning often is combined with information determined from fixing a position through celestial navigation in order to more accurately ascertain the position of a craft. Celestial navigation names the process of using observed positions of heavenly bodies to determine the position of a craft. It is more useful with north-south latitudinal mapping because the elevation of the NORTH STAR is always equal to the observer's latitude (given an average error of less than half a degree, or 35 miles); thus, a navigator may determine the craft's north-south position by the apparent height of the North Star. Dead reckoning, however, requires precise calculations.

In order to navigate by dead reckoning, early mariners used a COMPASS to determine the ship's direction. They then measured speed with a chip long—a wooden float attached to a long rope with knots in it. As the float entered the water, they overturned a sandglass, and they then counted the number of knots the rope pulled off a reel behind the ship during the time in which the sand passed from the top to the bottom of the glass. (The term *knot,* or one nautical mile per hour, originated with the chip log: if the first knot appeared as the sand ran out, speed was determined to be one nautical mile per hour, or one knot.) Time, distance, and direction were measured each time the ship tacked because of wind direction. A TRAVERSE BOARD was used to keep track of the zigzag course. Dead reckoning took other information into account, such as wave patterns and directions, floating debris, cloud formations, and birds.

Careful and consistent record keeping can result in an accuracy rate of 90 percent for dead reckoning. Although it is not considered especially useful over large distances, an Italian mariner of the late 15th century, CHRISTOPHER COLUMBUS, is believed to have used dead reckoning throughout his travels.

Dead reckoning contrasts not only with celestial navigation but also with pilotage (navigation by visible landmarks or by radar). Navigating by such modern pilotage methods as the SATELLITE-based Global Positioning System is highly precise, but dead reckoning navigation remains a useful low-technology fallback.

See also NAVIGATION AND EXPLORATION.

dhow (baggala, boom, sambuk)

Dhow is a traditional term, used by Europeans, referring to a ship of Arab design with a LATEEN RIG. In places where the dhow is still in use, it is called variously the *sambuk,* the *baggala,* and the *boom,* each distinguished by the shape of its hull.

The dhow is constructed with planking set edge to edge. In the past, the planks were held together with cordage; in modern practice, nails are used. The bow has a long overhang, and the poop is raised. Sails were originally made of palm or date leaves; cotton was later introduced. The lateen rig allowed the boats to point up close to the wind and move at a relatively fast pace. Dhows are typically single-masted, but larger versions might have three or more masts with sails shaped to maximize use of the wind.

The earliest dhows were used for local fishing, transportation, and trade. Records exist of their movement between the RED SEA and India as early as the first century B.C. As Arab trade grew in the Middle Ages, larger and larger dhows could be found from the Middle East to East Africa and China. According to accounts from the ninth century A.D., the dhow grew to a size capable of transporting 800 people. Modern versions of the dhow range from a small handful of crew and passengers to a maximum of about 200.

See also SHIPBUILDING AND EXPLORATION.

William Henry Jackson took this photograph of an Arab dhow in 1894. *(Library of Congress, Prints and Photographs Division [LC-D4271-146])*

dirigible   See AIRSHIP.

disease and exploration

Disease has been a significant factor in the history of exploration; it has both impeded the efforts of explorers and been spread by them. Diseases suffered by explorers at sea or in the field slowed and sometimes halted their journeys. The meeting of hitherto isolated groups of humans engendered and intensified disease. And, in the case of the epidemic known as the Black Death, it created economic conditions that affected the course of exploration.

The Black Death

Expansion of human groups into new lands goes hand in hand with the expansion of diseases; explorers carry their diseases with them and suffer diseases in the lands they explore or conquer. One of the most devastating pandemics in European history probably resulted from this process of contacts between peoples of distant lands, that of the bacterial infection resulting in the bubonic plague or the Black Death, known at the time as the "Pestilence" or "Great Mortality." The bubonic plague was carried by a number of mammals, especially rats, and passed to humans by fleas. It is thought to have originated in China and spread as a result of expansion by the Mongols in the 13th century (see MONGOL EXPLORATION), when trade routes were opened between East and West. The first known European outbreak occurred in southern Russia. Then, probably first in 1347, Italian merchant ships from the Black Sea carried it to the Mediterranean region. It spread widely throughout Europe until 1351, with recurrences well into the 18th century. The plague devastated Europe's population; it is estimated that a quarter to a third perished. Cities were particularly hard hit because of the concentration of people. In Italy, for example, almost two-thirds of the population of Venice died, and three-quarters of that of Florence.

Ecclesiastics, whose vocation to go among the sick giving comfort and last rites, were at great risk of infection; university scholars were also decimated. For a time, living standards for the survivors rose considerably as they benefited from the economic wealth built up for a population that had been cut by a third. Laborers leaving the land, which was growing increasingly unproductive because of a long-term climate change called the Little Ice Age, moved to the cities where, because of work shortages, wages rose. Food prices fell, even with the crop losses, because of low population levels. Many laborers were thus able to accumulate some wealth and enter the middle class. With more capital available to invest in ships and trading ventures, the economic importance of trade increased, while at the same time the decrease in the value of much agricultural land diminished the wealth of the landed nobility. The laboring and merchant classes to some extent began to fill the political vacuum once dominated by clerics and nobles.

Despite these gains, the recurrence of the plague for centuries caused continuing economic and social instability, and population levels did not begin to recover until the 18th century. The plague originally slowed down the development of foreign trade and exploration. However, the new opportunities that had opened up in an economic, social, and political fabric, which had existed for centuries, resulted, by the 15th century, in an energized European society. Ironically, this energy helped lead to European expansion, which was to cause the spread of European diseases to the Americas.

European Diseases in the Americas

Native Americans of every region suffered decimating outbreaks of European diseases. Loss of life ranged from 25 to 50 percent and caused the near extinction of some peoples. They suffered far more even from diseases such as measles, which in Europe were seldom fatal. It has been theorized that the difference was caused by the greater number of domesticated animals, the progenitors of many diseases in humans, in Eurasia than in the Americas, in combination with continental isolation and lack of the necessary antibodies to fight off infection.

Smallpox was the most destructive of the European diseases. It aided HERNÁN CORTÉS in his conquest of the Aztec Indians in present-day Mexico in the 1520s. When FRANCISCO PIZARRO arrived in the Inca city of Tumbes in present-day Ecuador in 1530, only 11 years after Cortés had arrived in Mexico, he saw that smallpox had been there before him. It had killed Emperor Huayna Capac along with his heir apparent, leading to a bitter civil war between adherents of two of his sons for possession of the empire. It was this conflict, decimating the population and crippling the Inca armies, along with smallpox, that primarily enabled Pizarro to conquer the Inca with an army of 180 men. The Mandan of the upper MISSOURI RIVER in North America are said to have declined from 1,600 to 131 during the smallpox epidemic of 1837. Smallpox ravaged neighboring people in repeated outbreaks; from 1837 to 1870, at least four different epidemics struck other Plains Indians of North America.

Other diseases of Europe, such as dysentery, measles, scarlet fever, typhoid, typhus, influenza, tuberculosis, cholera, diphtheria, chicken pox, and venereal infections, swept through the Americas with incredible speed, far in the vanguard of Europeans themselves. It is possible that the great Temple Mound Culture of the Mississippi Valley and Southeast died out as a result of a pandemic that started with the contact of a few Indians with the earliest European explorers of the late 15th or early 16th century. Settlers in New England, as they moved through the forests prospecting for land, often found signs of wholesale depopulation in numerous deserted villages and ceremonial sites, prepared fields, and even stored food.

European Diseases in Other Lands

The pattern of indigenous peoples succumbing to European illnesses continued with the exploration and colonization of Australia and NEW ZEALAND. Illnesses such as smallpox, venereal disease, measles, and influenza—some of which were not life-threatening to the British—devastated the Aborigines in Australia. The Maori population of New Zealand declined rapidly, from about 120,000 in 1769 to 42,000 in 1896, as a result of European diseases, such as influenza, measles, and whooping cough.

From America Back to Europe

Contacts among Europeans and Native Americans led to new forms of disease being carried back to Europe, in particular syphilis. Based on evidence from skeletons, it had been known in Europe from prehistory. Yet it appeared in a far more virulent form immediately after the European discovery of the Americas. An outbreak occurred in Barcelona in 1493 soon after the celebrations of Columbus's return and quickly became an epidemic throughout Europe, differing from the hitherto common form of syphilis in rapidly causing mortality. The most probable theory for this occurrence is that it resulted from sexual relations between Native Americans and the European explorers. Perhaps the syphilis bacterium assumed a new form as a result of its success among the native peoples with their lack of resistance.

Cholera was a severe infectious disease endemic in India and some other tropical countries. Characterized in severe cases by violent diarrhea, vomiting, thirst, muscle cramps, and sometimes circulatory collapse leading to death, cholera caused severe epidemics in Europe in the late 18th century as a result of British colonization of India, and later in the Americas. The horror of cholera lay in the speed with which death often followed its first onset, sometimes within hours.

Diseases among Explorers

SCURVY was a scourge of explorers for centuries and is a recurring theme in the saga of world exploration. This deficiency disease results from the failure to supply the body with the required amount of vitamin C. A weakening of the capillaries results in hemorrhaging, leading to a multitude of symptoms and eventually death. Scurvy is thought to have caused more loss of life during the EUROPEAN AGE OF EXPLORATION than shipwrecks. It took its toll on numerous crews on open-sea voyages. Even after it came to be understood in the 18th century, it caused death on expeditions when food supplies ran low.

Malaria, a debilitating infectious disease caused by single-celled parasites, characterized by chills, shaking, and periodic bouts of intense fever, which had been known in Europe from Roman times, reached the Americas soon after the first European explorers arrived. It affected native peoples and colonists alike, such as the first settlers of Jamestown in Virginia. Spanish Jesuits in South America discovered a treatment for malaria in cinchona bark, the ingredient of quinine, which they brought back to Europe in 1638. Nevertheless, it continued to be a problem for centuries. Englishman SIR GEORGE EVEREST, for example, who, in the early 19th century, laid the groundwork for topographic mapping of northern India and the HIMALAYAS (and for whom Mount Everest [see EVEREST, MOUNT] is named), was hampered in his work by malaria. Englishmen SIR RICHARD FRANCIS BURTON and JOHN HANNING SPEKE had bouts of malaria and other ailments in Africa in the 1850s. Scottish missionary DAVID LIVINGSTONE died in Africa in 1873 from dysentery, an acute or chronic disease of the large intestine of humans, characterized by severe diarrhea and abdominal cramps.

Dysentery was common on ships, especially slavers, where unsanitary conditions prevailed. Many Africans transported to the Americas for the SLAVE TRADE died in transit, chiefly because of dysentery. It has been theorized that a large proportion of Africans who survived their horrific journey had a genetic condition called "salt-sensitivity," perhaps the result of ancestors who survived droughts in Africa, which made them able to withstand the loss of salts accompanying the diarrhea of dysentery. Two-thirds of the English population of Jamestown was wiped out by dysentery. SIR FRANCIS DRAKE and SIR JOHN HAWKINS, 16th-century English maritime explorers, suffered from dysentery and also malaria. JOHANN LUDWIG BURCKHARDT, a 19th-century Swiss explorer in the Middle East, died in Cairo of dysentery.

Yellow fever, a noncontagious, infectious disease caused by a virus, and characterized in severe cases by high fever and jaundice, originated in Africa and came to the Americas and Europe via the slave trade. It delayed the exploration and colonization of Africa by Europeans until the latter part of the 19th century, when it was realized that it spread by mosquito bites; thereafter improved methods of sanitation, including draining of swamps and quarantine of ships, helped to bring it under control.

❖

In global terms, the increasing contact between population groups resulted in a more uniform level of contact and exchange of diseases and immunity. Moreover, knowledge and treatment of the diseases that attacked explorers in the field, both infectious and dietary, grew with time. Great plagues like the Black Death became less common by the end of the 18th century, although pandemic diseases still have the ability to decimate populations.

diving bell

A diving bell is a device used to supply air to and convey a diver or group of divers to a desired location. The evolution of this device charts humankind's problems of exploring the ocean's depths, namely regarding air supply and water pressure. The technical challenges of these factors and how slowly they were solved demonstrates humankind's coming to terms with the physical world.

Mention of such a device is found in Greek philosopher Aristotle's *Problematum* from about 360 B.C. In this work, he describes a "kettle," which is lowered into the sea to supply air to sponge divers. The detail he furnishes makes clear that the device was a workable model of the diving bell. The only other indication of such a contraption in ancient history comes from ALEXANDER THE GREAT's attack on Tyre in 322 B.C., as reported in medieval texts about his campaigns. The Phoenicians had placed obstacles in the water to defend the port city in the eastern MEDITERRANEAN SEA. Alexander ordered them removed so the campaign could commence. To observe the progress of the work, he was reportedly lowered into the sea in some sort of device. From an Arab historian in the seventh century A.D., there exists a detailed description of this device as a wooden box sealed with wax, having glass windows, and weighted with stone. It was tied to a cable and attached to a pole placed between two ships, then lowered and raised according to a message given by a signal rope controlled by the occupants of the box. A 13th-century illustration depicts the same incident with Alexander using a giant glass jar. The actual truth of the matter will never be known of course, but these varied conceptions of the diving bell give some sense of the longstanding interest in the device.

The next record of a diving bell–like invention is from 1531. Italian physicist Guglielmo de Lorena constructed a large barrel that could be used to walk along the bottom of a body of water. It was assisted by people with ropes on the surface and could provide enough air to maintain the diver underwater for about an hour. The motivation for this invention was the exploration of Lake Nemi, which was thought to have the remains of ships and treasure belonging to Roman emperor Caligula. A diver using Lorena's creation was successful in locating these ships where others had failed. A short time later, a larger diving bell was produced by a pair of Greek inventors. In 1538, they demonstrated it to Charles I of Spain (Holy Roman Emperor Charles V) and a large crowd of spectators in Toledo. Their bell carried both inventors to the bottom of the river and back with a burning candle remaining lit.

The sensation caused by the demonstration in Toledo gave rise to interest in such devices throughout Europe. A number of people made versions, and their use in salvaging treasure became more widespread. In 1616, a German named Franz Kessler tested a model that was unencumbered by ropes. He sunk to the bottom with weights and resurfaced by detaching them. Yet the task proved too cumbersome for his design to gain widespread use.

A breakthrough in the design of the diving bell was made by French physicist Denis Papin in 1689. He thought to supply his apparatus with fresh air from the surface pumped through a tube. The diver would not be limited by the quantity of air in the bell or the compression of air that took place as the bell descended. At a depth of 33 feet, the weight of water is twice that of the weight of atmospheric pressure. Since gas is compressible, this causes the air inside the bell to be reduced by half in volume. This holds true for each additional 33 feet of descent. As a result, in practical operation, the volume of air a diver has access to becomes significantly reduced. The theory of Dr. Papin's device was sound, but he was limited by the power of the pumps of the day, which were unable to generate a pressure of more than three atmospheres, and his diving bell did not break records for depth beyond 70 feet. Still, his contribution was important.

Edmund Halley, an English astronomer and mathematician and a contemporary of Papin, was responsible for another advance in the diving bell. He used lead casks filled with air and regulated by the diver with a valve. This solution to the problem of air supply proved practical and was in use until 1788, when stronger pumps were invented, thus reviving the ideas of Papin.

John Smeaton, an English engineer who invented a pump powerful enough to supply a Papin-type bell, is also responsible for the last great chapter in the history of the diving bell. His device, known as a caisson, was considerably larger than anything that had come before. Designed for underwater construction and capable of holding 12 men, the caisson ushered in a new era in underwater exploration, salvage, and construction. It also revealed new problems caused by working at great depths. Divers using the caissons would be subject to a mysterious cause of death, which was only later diagnosed as the bends, a painful release of nitrogen gas into the bloodstream. This problem was initially solved by slowing the time of ascent to the surface.

The diving bell had limited use in direct exploration. The scientific discoveries to which it contributed were tangential to its practical uses, such as salvaging operations, due to the capital-intensive nature of its operation. With a boat, its crew, and experienced divers required, it was expensive to use. It could also be dangerous. Because of invisible currents and numerous underwater entanglements, there were still many ways for divers to lose their lives.

Diving bell technology, with an attached supply of air, led to that of the SUBMERSIBLE, such as the BATHYSPHERE, BATHYSCAPH, and the SUBMARINE, which maintain surface air pressure inside while descending deep into the ocean, allowing for extensive exploration. Remotely operated vehicles (ROVs) are now also utilized. Yet diving bells, of improved design and material and with better lighting, heating, and communication systems than earlier models, are still in use, especially in construction, such as on submerged portions of bridges, piers, and jetties, and in transporting divers to underwater work stations. As the diving bell has evolved so has the DIVING SUIT.

See also OCEANOGRAPHY AND EXPLORATION.

diving suit

A diving suit, equipment for underwater diving, is a waterproof outfit, including a helmet and breathing apparatus allowing air to be supplied from the surface pumped though a tube. Early references to diving are found in writings of the ancient Greeks and Romans. In the *Iliad*, the epic poem probably of the eighth century B.C. and attributed to the Greek poet Homer, divers are described as playing a part in the Trojan Wars. Ancient divers used stones as weight and ropes as guides. The invention of the diving suit and other diving gear enabled divers to spend more time underwater for a variety of tasks: gathering sponges, coral, and pearls; examining and repairing the underwater parts of ships; working on underwater supports for structures such as bridges and docks; salvaging sunken ships and their contents; military operations, in particular reconnaissance and sabotage; and scientific studies.

The development of the diving suit paralleled that of the DIVING BELL, as inventors sought means to supply air below the surface. Various attempts were made at watertight suits in the 17th century with piped air. In 1819, German inventor Augustus Siebe developed the first efficient diving suit, consisting of a copper helmet attached to a watertight canvas and leather jacket with weights attached around the chest. A surface pump pushed air to the diver through hoses attached to the helmet. The pressure of the pumped air kept the water level below the diver's chin, and the air could escape through vents at the bottom of the jacket. The fact that a diver had to remain vertical to prevent water from entering the vents led to refinements—a full closed suit with valves that let air exit without letting water enter. The suit proved more practical than the diving bell in that divers could walk along the bottom and could look in all directions rather than just through fixed windows.

Siebe's basic design for helmet diving suits has endured to this day. Improvements include the use of rubber for the suit. Leaded boots keep the diver on the bottom and leaded weights around the chest help to maintain equilibrium. Additional valves help regulate buoyancy. The attached lifeline to the surface in addition to the air pipe also includes a line of communication. Armored steel suits are also used for deeper dives along with a special mixture of gases added to oxygen to help prevent decompression sickness on surfacing.

A deep-sea sponge diver climbs back into a boat in his diving suit, as shown in this 1940s photograph. *(Library of Congress, Prints and Photographs Division [LC-USW3-043126-C])*

Helmet diving, despite modern improvements, restricts lateral movement because of the necessary connection to the surface, and inventors sought an alternative, leading to the development of the scuba (for "self-contained underwater breathing apparatus"), in which the diver carried an air supply. In 1865, French inventors Bénoit Rouquayrol and Auguste Denayrouze developed a combined system. In addition to surface-supported hoses, it included cylinders worn by the diver containing compressed air. Yet a helmet and suit were still required, and the cylinders functioned poorly. Modern scuba diving began with the invention of the Aqua-Lung (or aqualung) by Frenchmen JACQUES-YVES COUSTEAU and Émil Gagnon, first successfully used in 1943, consisting of a cylinder of compressed air connected through a pressure-regulating valve to a face mask. Scuba divers, although they have reached depths of about 300 feet, usually do not descend below 130 feet because of the effects of nitrogen narcosis (popularly known as "raptures of the deep"), caused by the narcotic effects of nitrogen in the air at high pressure. The condition is marked by a loss of judg-

ment that often causes the diver to discard equipment or engage in other dangerously foolish behavior. Helmet divers can avoid nitrogen narcosis until a depth of about 200 feet.

Scuba diving, which replaced helmet diving in many practical applications much as the SUBMERSIBLE replaced the diving bell, also has become a recreational activity. A recent invention granting even greater freedom to the scuba diver is the rebreather, a device that recycles air exhaled by the diver. Moreover, the rebreather does not emit noisy bubbles the way open-circuit scuba does, enabling a greater interaction with marine life.

See also OCEANOGRAPHY AND EXPLORATION.

doldrums

The term *doldrums* refers to ocean regions slightly north of the EQUATOR where there is no regular system of cross-oceanic winds. These regions are also known as the "equatorial belt of calms." Because of the relative intensity of the sunlight in the doldrums, a continuous updraft of air is created. Evaporation occurs simultaneously, and the air is especially humid, leading to squalls. Since the doldrums are an area of low pressure, weather systems from the Northern Hemisphere and Southern Hemisphere are able to converge, and hurricanes form with regularity.

For centuries, fear of the doldrums gripped the crews of sailing ships that might drift for days, weeks, and even months. Among the earliest observations of the phenomenon of the doldrums came from Portuguese expeditions along the west coast of Africa, such as those sponsored by HENRY THE NAVIGATOR, prince of Portugal, in the 15th century. His expeditions experienced the doldrums at about the latitude of Cape Verde.

One example of a voyage affected by the doldrums was the first CIRCUMNAVIGATION OF THE WORLD headed by Portuguese FERDINAND MAGELLAN, exploring for Spain, in 1519–22. While crossing the Atlantic Ocean westward, the expedition's progress was slowed significantly. On the second leg of the voyage in the Pacific Ocean, his ships drifted for 96 days.

drift ice (drifting ice)

The term *drift ice*, or *drifting ice*, refers to any floating and moving ice in a body of water. It is generally used, however, as distinct from an extensive, fixed ice field, or to the annually created PACK ICE, which also drifts but at much slower rates.

Different names are applied to different kinds of drift ice. Relatively small fragments of ice, less than seven feet in diameter, typically found near pack ice, are known as *brash ice*, or *brash*. The term *growler* is applied to larger pieces of ice floating low in the water that make a growling noise when waves wash over them. *Bergy bits* refers to pieces of ice between seven and 16 feet in diameter. *Pan* refers to a fragment of the uniformly chunk of flat ice at the surface of water. *Ice floe,* or *floe,* refers to a relatively flat and low expanse of ice detached from an ice field. *Iceberg,* or *berg,* refers to a larger mass, tabular, rounded, or irregular in shape, which has calved, or broken off, from an ice shelf (a huge slab of permanent ice that floats on water near the edges of Arctic and Antarctic landmasses) or from the face of a glacier (a formation of ice on land where snowfall exceeds melting and the resulting mass moves downward from above the snowline under the force of gravity and pressure). Thousands of icebergs are calved each year. They can be huge; the largest one on record, sighted in the Ross Sea off Antarctica in 1956, was 208 miles long and 60 miles wide. Only a small percentage of these various kinds of drift ice are underwater, about one-fifth.

Drift ice occurs in the relatively short summer thaws in Arctic and Antarctic waters. When the water freezes over again in wintertime, drift ice from the previous season or seasons becomes trapped in it, giving the pack ice irregular shapes. Some drift ice travels great distances before melting. Icebergs last on average about four years. Arctic icebergs, many of them from GREENLAND, have been sighted as far south as 30 degrees latitude north; Antarctic icebergs have been sighted as far north as 27 degrees latitude south.

Because of the range of icebergs, they have proven a hazard to navigators over the centuries. Between 1870 and 1890, for instance, more than 50 ships collided with icebergs, 14 of them sinking. After the sinking of the British ocean liner *Titanic* in 1912 due to a collision with an iceberg, an International Ice Patrol, consisting of ships and aircraft from a number of countries, have monitored northern waters. Yet drift ice, like pack ice, can offer refuge to stranded explorers. For instance, during the British expedition to Antarctic in 1914–17 led by SIR ERNEST HENRY SHACKLETON, his men survived part of the time on ice floes after their ship was crushed in the pack ice. And, starting in

This photograph of drift ice at the edge of the Ross Ice Shelf in the Antarctic was taken during Richard E. Byrd's 1947 expedition. *(Library of Congress, Prints and Photographs Division [LC-USZ62-101004])*

the 20th century, scientific stations have been located temporarily on ice floes and icebergs.

drift voyage

The term *drift voyage* refers to a transoceanic journey between continents by primitive boat or RAFT, propelled by OCEAN CURRENTS. With the extensive sea travel carried out over the centuries along coastlines for fishing and trading—plus the westward current in the South Atlantic Ocean, the westward current north of the EQUATOR in the Pacific Ocean, and the eastward current in the North Pacific—it is theorized that some unintentional drift voyages occurred, or perhaps even intentional ones. Norwegian anthropologist THOR HEYERDAHL, in his *Kon-Tiki* voyage across the Pacific from Peru to the Tuamotu Islands in 1947, and his *Ra* voyage across the Atlantic from Morocco to Barbados in 1970, demonstrated that small wooden or reed crafts could make such ocean crossings.

Scholars have used cultural similarities of artifacts on different continents to make the case for prehistoric drift voyages—from Europe, Africa, and Asia to the Americas. Yet there is no conclusive archaeological evidence of such early transoceanic contacts. Some ancient transoceanic voyages, such as the legendary sixth-century voyage of SAINT BRENDAN and the archaeologically proven 11th-century journeys of the Vikings (see VIKING EXPLORATION), are not considered drift voyages because the mariners controlled their courses.

The term *drift voyage* has also been applied to the motion of ships in the Arctic and Antarctic while trapped in PACK ICE.

Dutch East India Company

The Dutch East India Company, one of the various European East India Companies, chartered in 1602, was the premier joint-stock trading company of the Netherlands during the 17th and 18th centuries. The company routed the Portuguese from their possessions in the SPICE ISLANDS (the Moluccas) and, with monopoly protection from the Dutch government, made enormous profits in the SPICE TRADE and other commerce. In search of even greater riches, the company sponsored explorations throughout the Pacific Ocean.

What is now the Netherlands had been inherited by Charles I, who became king of Spain in 1516 and Holy Roman Emperor in 1519. Over the years, the Dutch had gained more autonomy from Spain, and Charles's son King Phillip II had continued to try to assert control over the region. Holland, which had been a territory of Spain, declared its independence in 1581. In 1588, the Spanish Armada was defeated by the English. The Dutch, who had

a tradition of seamanship, worked hard to build a fleet of ships to strengthen their position of independence. The greatest navies soon belonged to the British and the Dutch. The Dutch East India Company was formed in 1602 to reap profits from the Indian Ocean and Pacific trade. It was also allowed to engage the Spanish and Portuguese on the high seas and at their trading posts. In 1594, Phillip had closed the Portuguese port of Lisbon, part of his domain, to Dutch merchant vessels. This had acted as an incentive to the Dutch to develop other markets. They had sent a trading mission to the EAST INDIES the following year under CORNELIUS HOUTMAN. Houtman had succeeded in forming relations at Bantam, Bali, and Sumatra.

Competing Nations

The East Indian trade became very competitive very quickly, and with various European companies bringing about a lowering of prices, the various Dutch interests decided to merge. In 1602, the General United East India Company was granted a charter by the government of the Netherlands, which gave broad powers, including the exclusive right to trade between the CAPE OF GOOD HOPE and the Strait of Magellan (see MAGELLAN, STRAIT OF), the right to make war on other European countries, to form alliances with the princes of the east, and to perform various administrative and judicial functions. The government reserved the right to revoke privileges if necessary and to share in the profits.

The Dutch were aided in their trading endeavors by extensive experience as merchants and bankers, and they had become accomplished shipbuilders and mariners. They also had goods that could be exchanged for the spices and textiles of the East. These goods included high-ticket items such as porcelain, velvets, and marble work, along with more mundane items such as soaps, oils, and cured herring. Convoys were sent from the Netherlands three times a year, accompanied by heavily armed naval ships.

The ascendancy of the Dutch in the Spice Islands, and in Malaysia, Sumatra, and Java to the west, did not come without military action. The Portuguese had spread themselves thin militarily in the East Indies. In 1615, the Dutch drove the Portuguese from Amboina. In 1619, Jan Pieterszoon Coen conquered Jacatra and founded the city of Batavia in Java (present-day Jakarta, Indonesia) as the headquarters of the company. From Batavia, the Dutch East India Company conducted business throughout the East Indies to parts of China, Japan, India, and Iran in Asia, as well as the Cape of Good Hope in Africa, where they founded the first European settlement in South Africa. In the 1650s–1660s, the Dutch captured Malacca, CEYLON (present-day Sri Lanka), and Celebes. (In the meantime, in 1648, the Dutch had achieved independence from

Spain, as the United Provinces.) The English and the BRITISH EAST INDIA COMPANY also were making inroads in the region. It was eventually resolved that the Dutch would control the Spice Islands, and the English would dominate India. Despite the expenses of waging war, the Dutch East India Company's stock rose to six times its original capitalization and paid annual dividends of between 12 and 75 percent.

Exploratory Expeditions

The Dutch East India Company had launched exploratory expeditions from its inception. In 1605, WILLEM JANSZ, sailing for the company, had made the first recorded sighting of Australia by a European. Having become established in the East Indies, the company launched a number of expeditions to locate the GREAT SOUTHERN CONTINENT, the fabled Terra Australis. In 1642, ABEL JANSZOON TASMAN sailed from Batavia to the South Pacific and made the European discovery of an island south of Australia, naming it Van Diemen's Land, after the governor general of the Dutch East Indies (it has since been renamed TASMANIA). Later that year, Tasman made the European discovery of NEW ZEALAND, Fiji, and other islands. Another important explorer in the employ of the Dutch East India Company was JAKOB ROGGEVEEN, who made the European discovery of Easter Island in 1722.

18th Century

In the 18th century, Dutch strength in the East Indies began to decline. The English had solidified their position in world trade by putting more efforts into colonization. The French and the FRENCH EAST INDIA COMPANY had also developed trade in the region. Rampant corruption overtook the Dutch East India Company, and, by 1724, it was unable to pay dividends to investors and survived by taxing the native population. The British successfully attacked Dutch possessions in the Far East in 1780. As of 1795, the French were in control of the United Provinces—known as the Batavian Republic (until 1806 when the Kingdom of Holland was established)—and dissolved the Dutch East India Company in 1798.

See also COMMERCE AND EXPLORATION.

Dutch West India Company (West India Company)

The Dutch West India Company, or the West India Company, a joint-stock trading and colonizing company, was chartered by the States-General of the Dutch republic in 1621 to develop new commercial interests in the Americas and Africa. It began its commercial activity two years later. The DUTCH EAST INDIA COMPANY had been active in Asia since 1602.

By the terms of the charter, the company regulated all Dutch trade along the African coast from the TROPIC OF CANCER to the CAPE OF GOOD HOPE and along the American coast from Newfoundland to the Strait of Magellan (see MAGELLAN, STRAIT OF). Within these regions, the company had administrative and judicial independence, but it needed approval from the States-General for declarations of war.

North America

In North America, following the explorations of the Englishman HENRY HUDSON in New York Bay and the Hudson River, Dutch fur traders (*swanneken*) had begun to trade for fur with Native Americans of the region. The United New Netherland Company held a charter to develop the region in 1614–17, then lost it, leading to a period of activity by independent traders from 1617 to 1624. The next years, the Dutch West India Company occupied Fort Orange on the site of Albany, Fort Nassau on the Delaware River, Fort Good Hope on the site of Hartford on the Connecticut River, and Fort Amsterdam on the southern tip of Manhattan Island. The region taking in all of Manhattan Island became known as New Amsterdam.

During the early years of Dutch colonization, traders negotiated with Native Americans for small tracts of land to build isolated trading posts and village sites. Starting in the 1630s, with the depletion of fur resources in coastal areas and the threat of British expansion out of New England, the Dutch embarked on a course of agricultural colonization requiring more lands. The patroon system was devised to expedite development. Like seigneurs in New France and proprietors in the British colonies, patroons were colonial landlords who collected rent from tenant farmers. In return for purchasing available tracts of land from American Indians and settling at least 50 Europeans on each, patroons received deeded title from the Dutch West India Company. During this period, the company lost its trade monopoly. Independent traders, whose activity on the frontier was more difficult to regulate, began taking greater advantage of native peoples, leading to violence, with repeated outbreaks until England wrested control of New Netherland from the Dutch in 1664.

South America

The Dutch West India Company, in competition with Spanish and Portuguese interests, hoped to develop regions of northern and eastern South America. In 1623, the company established a presence in east Brazil—in Bahia and Pernambuco—but, by 1661, had been driven out from the last of its posts. It also was active in Suriname (also called Surinam, Dutch Guiana, Netherlands Guiana) starting in the 1620s, and in the Netherlands Antilles, part of the WEST INDIES, starting in the 1630s. The Dutch maintained colonies in this part of the world for centuries.

E

East India Company   See BRITISH EAST INDIA
COMPANY; DUTCH EAST INDIA COMPANY; FRENCH EAST
INDIA COMPANY.

East Indies

The term *East Indies* has changed in meaning over the centuries. During the EUROPEAN AGE OF EXPLORATION, starting in the 15th century, the phrase had its broadest
meaning, referring to the lands from coastal India, CEYLON
(Sri Lanka), the Malay Peninsula, and other coastal regions
of Southeast Asia, plus all the islands in the region as far
east as New Guinea and as far north as the Philippines. It
later came to be used specifically for the islands of the Malay
Archipelago, the largest island group in the world at 1.1 million square miles—that is, the Sunda Islands, which include
Sumatra, Java, Sulawesi (Celebes), Borneo, Bali, and Timor;
the Moluccas (once known as the SPICE ISLANDS); New
Guinea; the Philippine Islands (including Mindanao and
Luzon); plus thousands of smaller islands. The term *Indonesia* has also been used historically as synonymous with *East
Indies*. Nowadays, the term *East Indies* is most often used to
mean specifically the islands of the nation known as the Republic of Indonesia. Geographically speaking, the East Indies form a natural barrier between the Indian Ocean and
the Pacific Ocean. Most of the larger islands have central
volcanic mountains with surrounding coastal plains. The climate is tropical.

As home to the Harrapa civilization along the INDUS
RIVER, India gave rise to one of the earliest organized societies on Earth, starting in about 2500 B.C. The islands to the
southeast were settled many millennia before then. As the
source of spices and other unique goods, the region was a
draw for merchants from China and Arabia long before the
Christian era. In about the first century A.D., the movement of Hindu and Buddhist monks from India into the
East Indies had a profound cultural impact on the region.
The Chinese developed commerce in the region, especially
in the early 15th century. The Arab Muslims, who had always traded there, made their most successful efforts at religious conversion in the 15th century, with the result that
the majority of Indonesians are Muslim. The peoples
who live in Indonesia are of two basic groups—the Malayan
and the Papuan. There are many subgroups and people of
mixed ancestry.

Of the historical journeys to the East Indies from other
places, one of the earliest is that of Italian MARCO POLO,
who visited the islands of Indonesia in the course of his
1275–92 adventure. Chinese CHENG HO traveled among
the islands during his "Seven Voyages" and mapped coastlines from China to the Red Sea and Africa between 1405
and 1433. Portuguese VASCO DA GAMA made the first contact with the East Indies from Europe by sea when he arrived
in the Indian port of Calicut in 1498. In subsequent years,
ships of numerous other European nations—the Netherlands, England, Spain, and France—developed commerce

with the peoples of the East Indies, especially the SPICE TRADE. Trading companies—such as the DUTCH EAST INDIA COMPANY, BRITISH EAST INDIA COMPANY, and FRENCH EAST INDIA COMPANY—became economically and politically important in the region. The Moluccas, central to trade, even became known as the Spice Islands. The islands of the East Indies also served as a convenient stopover point for European ships sailing on a CIRCUMNAVIGATION OF THE WORLD.

See also SPICE ROUTE; SPICE TRADE.

Egyptian exploration
(ancient Egyptian exploration)

Ancient Egypt was a civilization that flourished along the valley and delta of the NILE RIVER in northeastern Africa for more than three millennia, from before 3300 B.C. until 30 B.C. Many of the themes associated with ancient Egyptians are familiar: the great pyramids and their burial chambers; sphinxes and other statues combining human and animal forms; large temple complexes; and hieroglyphics. Their place in the history of exploration is not so widely known, however.

Egyptian history is divided into periods for purposes of study. In prehistoric times, the people who became the ancient Egyptians migrated from western Asia to the Nile and settled among indigenous Africans. By about 3500 B.C., in predynastic Egypt, two kingdoms competed with each other, referred to as Lower Egypt of the Nile's northern delta area, and Upper Egypt to the south. Their unification in about 3000 B.C. led to a succession of 30 dynasties of native pharaohs (or monarchs) and an expanding empire.

For purposes of study, the dynasties are grouped into the Old Kingdom (or Old Empire), the First Intermediate Period, the Middle Kingdom (or Middle Empire), the Second Intermediate Period, the New Kingdom (or New Empire), the Third Intermediate Period, and the Late Period. In the Second Intermediate Period, the Hyksos, a Semitic people from Syria, ruled Egypt; and, in the last two stages, after a long-term war with the Hittites of Asia Minor, which weakened the Egyptian Empire despite a treaty in about 1290 B.C., other peoples held power for a time—the Libyans, Nubians, Assyrians, and Persians—but native leaders did manage to come to power once again. The conquest of the region by Macedonian ALEXANDER THE GREAT in 332 B.C. led to a hellenized culture in Egypt (that is, a culture influenced by the Greeks). A succession of Greek rulers known as the Ptolemies—Ptolemy I to Ptolemy XIV—ruled through 30 B.C., when the Romans annexed the region.

In the course of their history, the Egyptians developed their maritime skills on the Nile River and eventually ventured into the MEDITERRANEAN SEA and the RED SEA as well, although their GALLEY ships were not as seaworthy as those of other ancient exploring peoples in the region, and

they did not apparently venture as far west as did the Minoans and Phoenicians. The Egyptians sought raw materials and products from ancient kingdoms to the east into Asia and to the south and west into Africa, such as lumber, precious metals, and spices, as well as slaves and exotic animals. They also engaged in conquest and, under Thutmose III during the 18th dynasty (during the New Kingdom) in the mid-15th century B.C., controlled territory eastward into Asia as far as the Euphrates River, including some Phoenician cities and all of what is now Syria.

The earliest recorded sea voyage (although there had no doubt been countless beforehand) involves the Egyptians of the Old Kingdom. In about 2780 B.C., according to their picture writing known as hieroglyphics, Snefru, the first pharaoh of the fourth dynasty (during the Old Kingdom), sent a trading expedition—probably across the eastern Mediterranean to the Phoenician city of Byblos near present-day Beirut, Lebanon—to trade for cedar logs. Moreover, the earliest actual explorer on record was an Egyptian, HANNU, who in about 2450 B.C., during the fifth dynasty (during the Old Kingdom), journeyed southward for the pharaoh Sahure via the Nile to the land of PUNT—the exact location of which is unknown—for precious metals and spices. Another early explorer was HERKUF, an Egyptian governor of a southern province, who, in about 2270 B.C., during the sixth dynasty (of the Old Kingdom), led a trading expedition for the pharaoh Mernera from the upper Nile River southward to the interior of central East Africa. In about 1492 B.C., during the 18th dynasty (during the New Kingdom), Egyptian queen HATSHEPSUT (Thutmose III's stepmother), who had assumed the power of pharaoh after the death of her husband, sent a trading expedition under her lieutenant Nehsi down the Red Sea to what is again identified as the land of Punt. And, in about 600–597 B.C., during the 26th dynasty (during the Late Period), the pharaoh NECHO II commissioned a Phoenician maritime expedition into the Red Sea and Indian Ocean, which perhaps circumnavigated Africa.

During the reign of the Ptolemies, there were other expeditions as well that helped unite the ancient world. In 120–115 B.C., EUDOXUS, a Greek navigator in service to Egypt, made two trips across the Arabian Sea to India. On the second journey, he made a landing on the coast of East Africa. Eudoxus also attempted a circumnavigation of Africa. And, in A.D. 45, HIPPALUS, another Greek in service in Egypt, located a more direct route from across the Arabian Sea out of sight of land to India.

See also GREEK EXPLORATION; MINOAN EXPLORATION; PHOENICIAN EXPLORATION; ROMAN EXPLORATION.

El Dorado

El Dorado means "the gilded man" in Spanish and refers to a legendary place of great wealth in South America. The term *El Dorado* is credited to Spaniard SEBASTIÁN DE BE-NALCÁZAR, who, in 1535, reportedly heard tales of the land from a captured Native American of present-day Colombia. The idea of the land predated de Benalcázar's information by several years, however. Germans, who had settled the coastal region that is now Venezuela, had also heard from the inhabitants of lands or cities of treasure.

The earlier explorations of Spaniard ALEJO GARCÍA were driven by the stories of a "White King," who possessed a large quantity of silver. Traveling through the mountains of Colombia to the site of present-day Bogotá, with a contingent of Indian conscripts sometime between 1522 and 1526, he managed to secure a small quantity of silver—from an unknown people—spurring on Italian SEBASTIAN CABOT in his 1526–30 explorations of the Río de la Plata and its drainage for England, as did a similar legend of a city in the south known as LOS CÉSARES. Spaniard DIEGO DE ORDAZ, who explored the ORINOCO RIVER, heard stories of a people, the "Guiana," who lived in a fabulously wealthy land, supposedly with a capital city called Manoa, paved with gold and which glittered with jewels.

The riches of the Inca Indians, which probably formed the basis of these stories, would elude the Spanish for seven more years. The origin of the El Dorado myth is thought to have come from an annual ceremony of the Chibcha Indians—living on the upper Magdalena River near present-day Bogotá—who reportedly applied their king with a resin, then sprinkled him with gold dust. He floated out on a lake, where the gold was washed off while people threw offerings of emeralds and other precious items around him. As this story became embellished and fictionalized, people claimed this ceremony took place weekly, and then daily. In actuality the practice had died out long before Europeans arrived in the area.

In the North

An early official search for El Dorado was conducted by AMBROSIUS ALFINGER in 1531–33. The German head of a colonizing expedition to Venezuela for Charles I, king of Spain (Holy Roman Emperor Charles V), he explored the lowlands surrounding the Magdalena River in northern Colombia. He died in 1533, but the search was taken up by his fellow countrymen. GEORG HOHERMUTH VON SPEYER traveled through the same area and farther southward to the plains of Colombia and Venezuela in 1535–38. The German with the most extensive journeys in the area, from 1530 to 1539, was NIKOLAUS FEDERMANN. Spanish conquistador GONZALO JIMÉNEZ DE QUESADA, also seeking El Dorado, explored the region in 1536, which led to some disagreements over boundaries between the Spanish, Federmann, and his sponsor, the Welser family.

The explorations continued, conducted mainly by the Spanish. FRANCISCO PIZARRO had had great success with the subjugation of the Inca Empire in the 1530s, and this naturally whetted Spain's appetite for gold and precious stones. The brother of Jiménez de Quesada, Hernán Pérez de Quesada, traveled in the plains of the Orinoco River in Venezuela in 1541. Years later, in 1569–72, Jiménez de Quesada himself led a second expedition in search of El Dorado in eastern Colombia as far as the confluence of the Orinoco and Guaviare Rivers.

South and East

Without results in the north, the search area was expanded. ALVAR NÚÑEZ CABEZA DE VACA, another Spanish military officer, explored the regions of the upper Paraguay River with 400 soldiers in 1543–44. His efforts were impeded by thick jungle. In 1541, GONZALO PIZARRO, brother of Francisco Pizarro, set out eastward from present-day Quito to find the land of cinnamon, which was also purported to have a wealth of gold. It was on this journey that his lieutenant, FRANCISCO ORELLANA, separated from the expedition with a group of men and traveled down the AMAZON RIVER to its mouth. Along the way, he heard tales of a land with great riches to the north. The 1560 expedition of PEDRO DE URSÚA was inspired by such reports, which resulted in the exploration of the Huallaga, Marañón, and Ucayali Rivers. This was the expedition on which Ursúa was murdered by LOPE DE AGUIRRE and his coconspirators. The quest for El Dorado was also conducted in the region of Guiana, east of Venezuela. DIEGO DE ORDAZ had heard rumors of great wealth in the region in 1532. Decades later, in 1584, ANTONIO DE BERRÍO traveled on the Orinoco looking for El Dorado and, failing to find it, moved across to Guiana and other places to the east.

The last great chapter in the search for El Dorado involved Englishman SIR WALTER RALEIGH in 1595. In his zeal for treasure and with his country in competition with Spain, he led a royal expedition of five ships to find the elusive land. Landing in Trinidad, he attacked the Spanish settlement there and interrogated Antonio de Berrío concerning what he knew of El Dorado. Raleigh proceeded to the mainland, where he, too, explored the Orinoco River and Guiana. After his return to England, he became involved in political intrigues, which resulted in a death sentence. In a desperate attempt to save his life, he proposed a second expedition to find El Dorado, which was undertaken in 1617. In Trinidad, Raleigh became sick with fever while his son ventured into Spanish territory. He and his men engaged the Spanish army at San Thomé, where Raleigh's son was killed. Consistent with his previous sentence, for disobeying orders not to attack the Spanish, and for failure to find El Dorado, Raleigh was executed soon after his return to England.

An Enduring Legacy

The stories that grew around the legend of El Dorado have had an enduring character. British poet John Milton made reference to it in *Paradise Lost,* French writer Voltaire used the concept in *Candide,* and American writer Edgar Allan Poe made it the subject of a poem. To this day, the phrase is synonymous with a place of luxury and ease. The lure of El Dorado for Europeans was based in reality, given the treasures of the Inca Empire. It is likely that the indigenous peoples who told the wondrous tales of the golden kingdom were anxious to have their foreign conquerors move along to other territories. Yet evidence indicates that the myth of El Dorado was believed to some degree by these peoples, who traded precious objects made with gold and jewels from region to region.

See also LEGENDS AND EXPLORATION; TREASURE AND EXPLORATION.

Empty Quarter (Rub' al-Khali, Arabian Desert, Great Sandy Desert)

The Empty Quarter (Rub' al-Khali in Arabic), also called the Arabian Desert and the Great Sandy Desert, is one of the largest sand deserts in the world. It occupies the southern regions of the interior of the Arabian Peninsula, stretching over an area of about 225,000 square miles. The desert accounts for about one-quarter of the land area of present-day Saudi Arabia, from highlands in Nejd to the north to the plateaus of Hadhramaut in the south. Its western edge rises to an altitude of more than 660 feet and slopes nearly to sea level in the east. The Rub' al-Khali receives hardly any precipitation, making it one of the driest places on Earth. During the summer, daytime temperatures regularly exceed 100 degrees Fahrenheit; during the winter, they fall into the 50s. Today, the Rub' al-Khali is a major source of oil deposits, including the world's largest oil field. Yet the vast desert remained largely unknown and untraversed by Westerners until the mid-20th century.

Ancient Exploration

As early as about 2450 B.C., Egyptian explorer HANNU sailed in the RED SEA along the Arabian coast, looking to improve trade with the kingdoms to the south in the land of PUNT. His exact place of landing is not known, but it is assumed that he visited lands of the Arabian Peninsula, possibly including the fringes of the Empty Quarter.

The Romans (see ROMAN EXPLORATION) perceived Arabia as three geographic parts: Arabia Petrea (or "Stone Arabia") to the west, including Egypt; Arabia Felix (or "Happy Arabia") to the south; and Arabia Deserta ("Desert Arabia"), the vast desert region of the Arabian Peninsula, including the Empty Quarter. On gaining control of Arabia Petrea in the first century B.C., they turned their attention to Arabia Felix, a cluster of prosperous kingdoms situated at the far southern extreme of the peninsula at the edges of Arabia Deserta. These kingdoms were intermediaries in the important and lucrative SPICE TRADE between India and Egypt. In addition, the highly valued incenses frankincense and myrrh were obtained from trees growing in remote desert mountains.

In about 25 B.C., GAIUS AELIUS GALLUS, a Roman officer in Egypt, set off with an expedition into the southern kingdom of Saba and its principal city, Marib. Saba was one of the primary kingdoms involved with trade in incense and spices. Gallus hoped to conquer the Sabaeans and open direct trade contacts with India and the rest of the Orient. He returned to Egypt unsuccessful, but with a wealth of geographic knowledge about the areas south and east of the Red Sea. For nearly the next two millennia, the interior region of the peninsula and the overland trade routes that brought incense and spices from Arabia Felix remained unexplored and unknown to outsiders.

The desert regions of Arabia, including the Empty Quarter, have been inhabited since ancient times by nomadic people called Aribi by the Akkadians. Probably in the 10th century, these nomads domesticated the camel, which allowed them to cover the long desert stretches between oases. The desert regions are known to Arabs as el-Badieh ("Great Wilderness" in Arabic), and the nomadic inhabitants as Bedouin. Traversed with impunity by the Bedouin, the Rub' al-Khali remained mysterious even to other inhabitants of the Arabian Peninsula. With the rise of Islam in the sixth century A.D., the Rub' al-Khali was known as the location of mythical cities destroyed by fire from heaven or buried in sands for excess and sin (see MUSLIM EXPLORATION).

19th Century

As European power and influence grew, travel into Arabia for various reasons increased. Some went fulfilling quests for knowledge, both geographic and cultural, such as JOHANN LUDWIG BURCKHARDT of Switzerland, who lived with the Bedouin and took a pilgrimage to the Islamic holy cities of Mecca and Medina in present-day Saudi Arabia as a Muslim in 1814–15. Eventually, with military and political influence in the Orient growing, countries such as Great Britain sent diplomatic missions tracking across largely uncrossed territory to meet with native leaders.

GEORGE FOSTER SADLIER, a British army officer in India, was sent in 1819 on a diplomatic mission to Ibrahim Pasha, a Turk who was engaged in consolidating Turkish power over Arabia. Sadlier landed at Qatif on the Persian Gulf coast of present-day Saudi Arabia, then headed inland. By the time he had crossed much of the Arabian Peninsula, he learned that Pasha had moved on to Medina. Sadlier continued on to that city. From there, he headed to the Red Sea port of Yenbo, north of Jidda, becoming the first European to cross the Arabian Peninsula, although to the north of the Empty Quarter.

A Bedouin caravan travels the desert country of Arabia in this late 19th- or early 20th-century photograph. *(Library of Congress, Prints and Photographs Division [LC-USZ62-76262])*

The BRITISH EAST INDIA COMPANY, interested in improving travel across the Arabian sea route from the Isthmus of Suez to Bombay, India, sought to establish coaling stations on the south coast of the Arabian Peninsula and, in 1834, sent British army officer JAMES WELLSTED to survey the region. Wellsted undertook excursions into the interior from present-day Yemen and Oman and became the first European to glimpse the vast interior of the Empty Quarter.

WILLIAM GIFFORD PALGRAVE, an Englishman who had done missionary work in India and Lebanon, conceived a plan to make a missionary expedition into the heart of the Arabian Peninsula. Hoping to expand French power over the region, which would become vitally important with the building of the Suez Canal, Napoléon III of France supported Palgrave's expedition, as did various business interests looking to increase imports of cotton and pure-blood Arabian horse-breeding stock. Palgrave left Europe for the Near East in the summer of 1861. Arriving in present-day Jordan, he traveled eastward over some 1,500 miles into present-day Saudi Arabia. Crossing the Nafud Desert, he reached the Persian Gulf coast at Qatif, becoming the first European to cross Arabia from west to east.

Despite these northern crossings of the Arabian Peninsula, the Empty Quarter to the south remained for Europeans what SIR RICHARD FRANCIS BURTON called a "huge white blot on our maps." A British officer and adventurer

and a talented linguist, Burton obtained a year's leave of absence in 1853. He proposed to undertake a journey to the Muslim holy cities of Medina and Mecca, then continue into the southwest to explore the Empty Quarter. Disguised as an Afghan physician, Burton traveled with Muslim pilgrims to the Islamic holy sites. Before he could embark into the Empty Quarter, however, he was struck ill and had to return by steamer to Egypt.

20th Century

HARRY ST. JOHN BRIDGER PHILBY, more than a half-century later in 1914, was a British officer sent from India to Baghdad at the outbreak of World War I. He journeyed for the first time through Arabia in 1917 to meet with Ibn-Saud to generate support for an Arab rebellion against the Turks. He ventured on to explore ancient ruins at Dariyan, then followed the Muslim pilgrim route toward Mecca, arriving on the coast of the Red Sea at Jidda. With that, Philby completed the first east-to-west crossing of Arabia by a European in almost a century. Philby continued to travel through Saudi Arabia, exploring the southern provinces of the Nejd region as far as the boundaries of the Empty Quarter. He continued to explore Arabia in the following years, resigning from the British diplomatic corps in 1924 to become an agent for mining and oil interests in the area. Philby became a political adviser to Ibn Saud, pressing for permission to lead an expedition into the Empty Quarter. He received approval in 1931 to search for the ruins of the legendary city of Wabar, which according to Muslim tradition was destroyed by God for its wickedness. However, another Englishman, BERTRAM SYDNEY THOMAS, would become the first European to cross the Empty Quarter.

Thomas, first a British political officer in the Persian Gulf region, later entered service for the government of Oman as a minister of the Sultan of Muscat. In the mid-1920s, he journeyed by camel to and along the east coast of Oman from Muscat. In 1927, he landed at Ras al Hadd on the southeastern tip of the Arabian Peninsula and began making preliminary journeys northward to prepare to cross the Empty Quarter. Accompanied by Sheikh Salih Bin Yakut and a party of Rashidi Bedouin, Thomas headed northward from Salalah in October 1930. In early January 1931, the expedition reached the water hole at Shana, roughly halfway through the forbidding desert. Several weeks later, they arrived at Doha on the Persian Gulf coast of Qatar, completing the crossing.

About a year later, in January 1932, Harry St. John Philby set out from the wells at Dulaiqiya, west of Qatar near Hofuf in Saudi Arabia, to travel southward into the Empty Quarter. His expedition located several large craters near a site in the middle of the wastes known as Al-Hadida. At the craters, he discovered quantities of iron, which he later determined were fragments of a giant meteor. Some Muslim authorities judged them to be remnants of the fabled Wabar. From this site, Philby headed westward over the sands. In March, he arrived at the mouth of the Wadi Dawasir, near the Arabian oasis settlement at Sulaiyil, completing the crossing. Philby's expedition, while not the first to cross the Empty Quarter, is regarded as the most thorough scientific exploration of the region up to that time. Spending more time in the desert, he brought back many samples of the scarce plant and animal life of the region and made accurate meteorological and geological observations.

WILFRED PATRICK THESIGER, another Englishman, worked as a British civil servant in the Sudan in the 1930s. During World War II, he served in North Africa and Syria. After the war, he journeyed to the Arabian Peninsula to investigate locust control measures. Inspired perhaps by his contact with the Bedouin, Thesiger made subsequent trips in Arabia, taking pictures and writing. In 1946, he embarked on his first expedition into the Empty Quarter. With Rashid native guides, Thesiger made a giant circle from Salahah in Oman on the Arabian Sea. He made a second journey across the Empty Quarter in 1947–48, also with Rashid tribespeople, from Al Mukalla in Yemen on the Gulf of Aden to the Persian Gulf in United Arab Emirates. His first book, *Arabian Sands,* was hailed and continues to remain as haunting and accurate a portrait of the peoples and lands of the Arabian Desert as the photographs he took.

Thesiger's two journeys were the last European expeditions to use camels and Bedouin guides.

❖

With improved technology and the discovery of oil in the Empty Quarter, the area was mapped by SATELLITE and explored thoroughly in the latter half of the 20th century.

See also ASIA, EXPLORATION OF.

ephemeris

The word *ephemeris* (plural form, *ephemerides*) is both Greek and Latin for "diary." The Greek root word from which *ephemeris* derives, *ephemeros,* means "daily." For a time, the English term *ephemeris* was used to refer to a diary, or, more generally, to that which exists only for a day or a short time, the concept associated with the adjective *ephemeral.* But the term came to be used specifically for a list of tables, or for a compilation of such tables in an almanac or publication relating to astronomical data. The information in an ephemeris might include the position of celestial bodies—the Sun, Moon, planets, stars, comets, and asteroids—for each day of the year, or for other regular intervals, along with related facts, such as time of sunrise, sunset, moonrise, and moonset. As such, an ephemeris is a tool of astronomy and navigation.

Ephemerides have been standardized and published in different countries. The oldest such publication is the *Connaissance de Temps* of France, first published in 1679. In England, the British Royal Observatory at Greenwich began publishing the *Nautical Almanac and Astronomical Ephemeris* (or the *Nautical Almanac*) in 1767. Its original purpose was to provide astronomical data necessary to determine longitude at sea. In 1852, the U.S. Naval Observatory began publishing *American Ephemeris and Nautical Almanac,* adjusted for the meridian at Washington, D.C., rather than the PRIME MERIDIAN at Greenwich.

The term *ephemeris time* (ET), formerly applied to astronomical time, is defined by orbital motions of celestial bodies to correct inaccuracies caused by the fact that Earth does not rotate at uniform speed, making the solar day an imprecise unit of time. Ephemeris time is now known as dynamical time, from terrestrial dynamical time (TDT or TT) or barycentric dynamical time (TDB), two different systems of measurement.

See also LATITUDE AND LONGITUDE; NAVIGATION AND EXPLORATION.

equator

Equator is a geographic and cartographic term for an imaginary east-west circle on Earth's surface, everywhere equidistant from the NORTH POLE and the SOUTH POLE, and dividing Earth into regions defined as the Northern Hemisphere and the Southern Hemisphere. The largest of all such imaginary east-west lines, it is that from which terrestrial latitudes are measured and is thus considered the prime parallel or zero latitude. The equator, as it appears on a map or a GLOBE, intersects northern South America, central Africa, Indonesia, and stretches of the Pacific, Atlantic, and Indian Oceans.

Celestial equator (also *equinoctial circle* or *equinoctial line*) is an astronomical term for the circle on the celestial sphere, lying midway between the celestial poles in the same plane as the geographic equator. (*The celestial sphere* is the imaginary sphere of infinite radius used for defining the positions of celestial bodies, with Earth considered the center of the sphere.) When the Sun's path intersects the celestial equator, twice a year, on March 21, the vernal equinox, and September 23, the autumnal equinox, day and night are of equal length. The equatorial coordinate system is the most commonly used astronomical coordinate system for indicating the positions of celestial bodies, thus relating to navigation.

The equator, the TROPIC OF CANCER, the northern limit of the Sun's apparent annual path across the sky, and the TROPIC OF CAPRICORN, the southern limit of the Sun's apparent path, were the first three reference lines on maps. Ancient cartographers had conceived of this system, based on the Sun's motion, some time before the third century B.C. Greek astronomer and geographer ERATOSTHENES used it to help determine Earth's circumference and tilt with a high degree of accuracy.

See also GEOGRAPHY AND CARTOGRAPHY; LATITUDE AND LONGITUDE; MAPS AND CHARTS; NAVIGATION AND EXPLORATION.

Europe, exploration of

At about 4 million square miles, Europe, including adjacent islands, is the sixth largest continent. It is actually the western fifth of Eurasia, the western fifth of a vast landmass (see ASIA, EXPLORATION OF). To distinguish Europe from Asia, most geographers use an imaginary line running from the northern extent of the Ural Mountains on the Kara Sea, then south along the Ural River to the Caspian Sea, then west along the Caucasus Mountains to the Black Sea, then along the Bosporus Strait (linking the Black Sea and the Sea of Marmara, both forming an arm of the MEDITERRANEAN SEA), and the Dardanelles (a strait linking the Sea of Marmara with the Aegean Sea, also part of the Mediterranean). The Mediterranean Sea and the Strait of Gibraltar (see GIBRALTAR, STRAIT OF) separate Europe from Africa.

To the west of Europe is the Atlantic Ocean (with the North Sea and Baltic Sea as subdivisions) and to the north is the Arctic Ocean (with the Norwegian Sea, Barents Sea, and White Sea as subdivisions). The British Isles are part of Europe. Mediterranean islands include the Balearics, Corsica, Sardinia, Sicily, Crete, Malta, and Cyprus (which is actually closer to Asia). The archipelago of Novaya Zemlya and the Faeroe Islands are also defined as part of Europe, as are ICELAND, about 600 miles west of northern Europe in the North Atlantic, and the archipelago of Svalbard (Spitsbergen), about 400 miles north in the Arctic Ocean. The AZORES, about 900 miles west of southern Europe in the Atlantic, although politically tied to Europe, are typically discussed as a separate entity.

Much of Europe, which can be viewed as a large peninsula of Eurasia itself, consists of peninsulas, the largest being the Scandinavian, Iberian, Italian, Balkan, Kola, and Jutland Peninsulas. The northernmost point of the European mainland is Cape Nordkinn (North Cape) in Norway; the southernmost is Punta de Tarifa in southern Spain near the Strait of Gibraltar; the westernmost is Cabo da Roca in Portugal; and the easternmost is the Ural Mountains in Russia.

A west-east mountain chain—the Alpine—traverses Europe; the Pyrenees, the Alps, the Carpathians, the Balkans, and the Caucasus are all part of it. The highest point in Europe is Mount Elbrus in the Caucasus, at 18,481 feet above sea level. The lowest point is located along the Caspian Sea's north shore, at 92 feet below sea level. Between the mountainous Scandinavian Peninsula in the north and the Alpine chain in the south, and extending from the Atlantic Ocean to the Urals, lies the Great European Plain. The Central European Uplands, consisting of a number of ranges, break up the plain. In the east is some steppe country. The largest rivers in Europe, from west to east are the Tagus, Garonne, Loire, Rhône, Rhine, Elbe, Oder, Vistula, Danube, Dnieper, Don, and Volga.

The prevailing westerly winds from the Atlantic Ocean that pass over the North Atlantic Drift lead to a moderating effect and significant rainfall, especially in the west, with cooler and drier weather to the east. Part of the continent lies above the ARCTIC CIRCLE. Mediterranean regions have hot and dry summers and rainfall generally only in winter. Most of Europe, except the tundra regions in the extreme north and the grasslands of the Great European Plain, was originally forested.

Large mammals including bears, wolves, bison, boars, deer, and elk were native to Europe, along with the smaller mammals still found there. Europe has a wide variety of birds, among them the eagle, falcon, finch, nightingale, owl, pigeon, and sparrow. European waters have a wide variety of fish, such as cod, mackerel, herring, and tuna; sturgeon are found in the Black Sea and Caspian Sea.

Europe is commonly discussed as seven geographic regions: Scandinavia (present-day Denmark, Finland, Norway, Sweden, and Iceland); the British Isles (present-day United Kingdom and Ireland); western Europe (present-day

Belgium, France, Luxembourg, Monaco, and the Netherlands); southern Europe (present-day Andorra, Italy, Malta, Portugal, San Marino, Spain, and Vatican City); central Europe (present-day Austria, the Czech Republic, Germany, Hungary, Liechtenstein, Poland, Slovakia, and Switzerland); southeastern Europe (present-day Albania, Bosnia and Hercegovina, Bulgaria, Croatia, Greece, Macedonia, Romania, Slovenia, Yugoslavia, and the western part of Turkey); and eastern Europe (present-day Belarus, Estonia, Latvia, Lithuania, Moldova, Ukraine, and the western part of Russia). An eighth region, Transcaucasia (Armenia, Azerbaijan, and Georgia), is sometimes included as part of Europe (and sometimes as part of Asia).

The etymology of the name *Europe* has been variously explained. Europa is a figure of Greek mythology, seduced by Zeus in Phoenicia and taken to Crete where she gave birth to Minos, the supposed ancestor of the Minoans. The name has also been associated with the Phoenician word *Ereb*, "sunset" or "west" in contrast to the word *Asia*, possibly meaning "sunrise" or "east." The Hellenes—people of ancient Greece—used *Europe* to describe their lands west of the Aegean Sea. In its root form, *Europe* might simply have meant "mainland."

The Flow of Peoples

Because so much of world exploration, as the saga is generally presented, involves the travels of Europeans and their descendants to and on other continents, far fewer of those individuals defined as "explorers" in this and other works are known for exploration of Europe than of elsewhere. One has to expand the definition of "exploration" to include migration to tell the entire story of how Europe was "discovered" by outsiders (see MIGRATION AND EXPLORATION). Since there are no written records regarding many of these migrations, and geographic knowledge was not necessarily disseminated as a result of them, these movements of peoples are not exploration in the strict sense—that of mapping the world. But to understand how Europe came to be perceived as a geographic entity distinct from the rest of Eurasia, it is necessary to touch upon the flow of at least some of the larger groupings on the continent in prehistoric as well as historic times.

Early Migrations and Civilizations

By the sixth millennium B.C., farming was established in Europe; Neolithic (New Stone Age) cultures were replacing earlier Paleolithic (Old Stone Age) hunting and gathering cultures. It is thought that it was peoples from western Asia who brought agricultural knowledge with them to the new lands. By about 2200 B.C., during the Bronze Age, Indo-European-speaking peoples arrived in the Balkans—probably originally from the Black Sea region of eastern Europe or western Asia—and spread from there to the rest of Europe, displacing or merging with native descendants of earlier Neolithic peoples.

Three highly developed Bronze Age cultures emerged in the region, known collectively as Aegean: the Mycenaean culture on the mainland; the Cycladic culture on the Cyclades island group; and the Minoan culture on the island of Crete. Based on the dispersion of artifacts, archaeologists have determined that the Minoans, who flourished from about 3000 to 1000 B.C., were active mariners and traders throughout much of the Mediterranean region, reaching as far west as the east coast of present-day Spain (see MINOAN EXPLORATION). They also had contacts with ancient Egyptians of North Africa, who became knowledgeable about Mediterranean navigation as well, although more along the African and Asian coasts than European coasts.

About the same time Indo-Europeans were spreading westward, in about 2340–2305 B.C., SARGON, the ruler of Akkad in Mesopotamia, established trade contacts with peoples of both the east and west, including of the eastern Mediterranean Sea; he may have even launched naval campaigns in the Mediterranean, which, if true, would make his men among the earliest known Asian visitors in European waters and along European shores.

Another ancient people who are regarded as explorers of the Mediterranean region are the Phoenicians of present-day Lebanon in Asia, who, by the mid-13th century B.C., had begun displacing the Minoans as the most wide-ranging Mediterranean maritime traders (see PHOENICIAN EXPLORATION). They established a number of trading centers far from their home in coastal Europe—present-day Italy, France, and Spain—as well as in North Africa. They also developed an alphabet and a standardized system of weights and measures.

By the early Iron Age, beginning about 1000 B.C., the European population was growing, with Indo-European and other peoples migrating to new homelands along major river routes. Among the peoples who would move about Europe over the ages were Indo-Europeans speaking Baltic, Celtic, Germanic, Hellenic, Illyrian, Italic, Phrygian, and Slavic languages, as well as non-Indo-European-speaking Bulgaric, Caucasic, Finnic, Mongolic, Ugric, and Turkic peoples. Some of them migrated there from the Asian steppes. Other groups, such as the Basques and Etruscans, spoke languages not seemingly related to any of the above.

Carthaginian Explorers

Among the outposts founded by the Phoenicians was Carthage in present-day Tunisia in North Africa, probably in the late ninth century B.C. It became a thriving city over the next centuries. Its people are discussed historically as Carthaginians, even though most were presumably of Phoenician ancestry. Two generals out of Carthage are the first individuals of record to have crossed through the Strait of Gibraltar into the Atlantic Ocean (see CARTHAGINIAN EXPLORATION). In about 470 B.C., HANNO headed an expedition from the strait southward along Africa's west coast; and, in about 450 B.C., HIMILCO headed an expedition northward along Europe's coast. It is not known how far north Himilco reached in his journey of four months—possibly only the northern extent of the Iberian Peninsula, but even possibly the British Isles. Other ancient mariners venturing out of the Mediterranean—accounts of whom did not survive—may have explored Europe's Atlantic coast even earlier.

The Hellenistic Period

Over the centuries, starting sometime after 2200 B.C., various peoples speaking related Greek (or Hellenic) dialects reached the Balkan Peninsula from the north and competed with indigenous peoples. One group, the Achaeans, are thought to have been ancestral to the Mycenaeans who replaced the Minoans as dominant in the region. Other Greek-speaking peoples followed, sometimes classified as Aeolians, Dorians, and Ionians. Their descendants came to be known collectively as Hellenes or Greeks. The Mycenean civilization broke up after 1200 B.C. From about 1000 to 750 B.C., after the Mycenenean collapse, the region suffered what is sometimes referred to as the Greek Dark Age. During what is known as the Archaic Age, from about 750 to 480 B.C., independent city-states formed and eventually united against the threat from Persia (present-day Iran). The period from about 480 to 323 B.C., in which Greek influence spread throughout the region, is known as the Greek Classical Age. Like the Minoans and Phoenicians, the Greeks developed a trade network throughout the Mediterranean and into the Black Sea as well, founding hundreds of coastal settlements (see GREEK EXPLORATION). Having adopted the Phoenician alphabet, they too spread a uniform culture.

During both the Archaic and Classical Periods, a number of individual Greeks began gathering geographic information. In the early fifth century, in the 490s B.C., an Ionian Greek HECATEUS OF MILETUS published an account of his travels known as *Tour Round the World,* in which he described his travels throughout the Mediterranean region. It was used as a source by Greek historian HERODOTUS, who, later in the fifth century B.C., also traveled extensively to parts of Europe, Asia, and Africa and published a work known as *History.*

A people living to the north of Greece, the Macedonians, rose to power in the mid-fourth century B.C. under Phillip II and his son ALEXANDER THE GREAT. Although not Greek-speaking, the Macedonian rulers came to think of themselves as part of the Greek tradition and furthered Greek culture through Alexander's conquests in North Africa and Asia. During this period, in about 325 B.C.,

Greek scholar PYTHEAS headed a maritime expedition through the Strait of Gibraltar and northward along Europe's Atlantic coast, reaching the British Isles and exploring parts of the North Sea and Baltic Sea.

The Roman Period

A number of different Indo-European peoples meanwhile had occupied the Italian Peninsula, among them the Italics and Villanovans. One of the Italic group—the Latins—founded Rome on the Tiber River in the eighth century B.C. They absorbed cultural elements from the Greek colonies to the south, including their alphabet, which they altered to fit their Latin language. In its early stages, until the end of the sixth century B.C., Rome was occupied by the Etruscans out of the north. In the fourth century B.C., they defended their city against invading Gauls, a subgroup of the Celts who had settled in France. By the second century B.C., the Romans had conquered the Carthaginians, Macedonians, and Greeks and had become the dominant power in the Mediterranean, eventually expanding their empire into northern Africa, southwestern Asia, and northern Europe. In the late second century B.C., the Romans defeated the Teutons and Cimbi, Germanic peoples from the Jutland Peninsula who had migrated southward.

A number of Roman generals are discussed as explorers because of their expeditions to unmapped regions of Europe (see ROMAN EXPLORATION). In the first century B.C., GAIUS JULIUS CAESAR invaded Gaul (present-day France) and Britain. His reports, along with those of other military leaders, helped Greek geographer STRABO publish *Geography,* a description of lands of the Roman Empire, in A.D. 18. In the decades to come, other Roman military leaders, such as SUETONIUS PAULINUS and GNAEUS JULIUS AGRICOLA, further explored the British Isles.

At the end of the fourth century A.D., the Roman Empire was divided into the Western Roman Empire and the Eastern Roman Empire (or Byzantine Empire), with its capital at Constantinople (present-day Istanbul). The Western Roman Empire gradually broke up by the fifth century because of economic decline, internal political unrest, and the continuing pressure of the Huns as well as Germanic peoples from the north. The Franks came to control much of Gaul, with the Alemanni in Switzerland their subjects; the Ostrogoths controlled most of Italy; the Visigoths had reached Spain; the Angles, Frisians, Jutes, and Saxons had invaded the British Isles; and the Vandals had occupied the Roman provinces of North Africa. These peoples came to adopt many Roman customs. In the sixth century, many of these lands were retaken by the Byzantine emperor Justinian. Yet other waves of peoples would come to power for a time, such as the Lombards, a Germanic people in Italy; and the Avars, a Mongolian-Turkic people, and the Slavs in the Balkans.

Muslims in Europe

Muslims, the followers of Islam, a religion founded by the Prophet Muhammad (or Mohammed) on the Arabian Peninsula in the seventh century A.D., played a part in the exploration of Europe as migrating peoples and as individual travelers, many of them Arabs but not all (see MUSLIM EXPLORATION). Moving westward from Asia, Muslims conquered peoples of North Africa, including the Berbers, and from there, in 711, crossed the Strait of Gibraltar in an invasion of Spain, eventually gaining control of most of the Iberian Peninsula and even land across the Pyrenees in southern France. Those Muslims occupying parts of Europe were a mixture of Arab and Berber peoples, known as Moors. The Moors, although unable to push farther into Europe because of a Frankish kingdom united under Charlemagne, who defeated them in northern Spain in 778, maintained a presence on the Iberian Peninsula until 1492.

The Muslim world, although not a political entity like the Roman Empire, manifested religious and cultural unity, and, over the centuries of the late Middle Ages and early RENAISSANCE, individuals traveled widely for religious, commercial, and scientific reasons. Among those who visited parts of Europe and helped disseminate geographic and cultural information concerning it were merchant ABU ALI AHMAD IBN RUSTA, historian ABU AL-HASAN ALI IBN AL-HUSAYN AL-MASUDI, religious scholar AHMAD IBN FADLAN, and merchant and geographer ABU AL-QASIM IBN ALI AL-NASIBI IBN-HAWQAL in the 10th century; cartographer ABU ABD ALLAH MUHAMMAD ASH-SHARIF AL-IDRISI and official and religious scholar ABU AL-HASAN MUHAMMAD IBN JUBAYR in the 12th century; and religious scholar and geographer ABU ABD ALLAH MUHAMMAD IBN BATTUTAH in the 14th century.

Most of the Turkish population also converted to Islam. The Ottoman Turks became the dominant people in the Middle East and captured Constantinople in 1453, bringing the Eastern Roman Empire to an end. The Ottoman Empire, although weakening over time, endured until 1923, when the republic of Turkey was established.

Vikings out of the North

The Vikings, or Norsemen, of Scandinavia traveled widely as traders, raiders, and settlers from about 800 to 1100 (see VIKING EXPLORATION). Some groups settled the east coast of the Baltic Sea and, from there, traveled inland into eastern Europe as early as the eighth century. Some groups followed the Neva River, which took them to Lake Ladoga. Some eventually reached the south-flowing Dnieper River, along which they had access to the Black Sea and Constantinople, which they raided in 860, and into the Mediterranean. Vikings also followed the Volga River to the Caspian Sea. The Vikings invaded coastal settlements in the British Isles by the end of the eighth century and established a number of settlements. They also came to control surrounding islands, such as the Hebrides, Orkneys, Shetlands, and Faeroes. In the early ninth century, Vikings also gained control of parts of coastal France and traveled up rivers on raids. A group attacked Paris in 845. Those Vikings who settled in the region became known as Normans, a derivation of "Northmen," and the region they controlled became known as Normandy.

Vikings from these settlements launched expeditions to the south. In 858, one expedition passed through the Strait of Gibraltar into the Mediterranean. Normans came to expand their holdings; in the second half of the 11th century, William I the Conqueror invaded England, and Roger I, Sicily.

The Vikings reached Iceland in the ninth century. The Irish had already settled the island by 800 and possibly earlier. According to one Norse saga, in about 860, NADDOD, a Norwegian Viking, was blown off course while traveling from Norway to the Faeroes and reached the east coast of Iceland. Another Norse saga holds that, about the same time, GARDAR SVARSSON circumnavigated Iceland and built the first Viking house on its north coast.

From Iceland, the Vikings ventured even farther to the west. Norwegian Viking ERIC THE RED is considered the European discover of GREENLAND (geographically defined as part of North America) in about A.D. 982. His son LEIF ERICSSON and other Viking explorers reached VINLAND on the North American mainland soon afterward.

Mongol Inroads

During the Middle Ages, in the 13th and 14th centuries, the Mongols, a people out of eastern Asia, in the expansion of their vast empire, penetrated as far west as Germany and Hungary, leading to a growing knowledge of European geography among Asian peoples (see MONGOL EXPLORATION). A number of European nations established diplomatic relations with the Mongols, and east-west travel increased along the SILK ROAD.

In 1280, soon after Venetian merchants MAFFEO POLO, NICCOLÒ POLO, and MARCO POLO arrived in China, a Turk by the name of RABBAN BAR SAUMA, raised as a Nestorian Christian, traveled throughout the Middle East and Europe. (The Nestorians were a sect of Eastern Christians who followed the teachings of Nestorius, patriarch of Constantinople, condemned as a heretic in 431 for believing in two distinct natures, God as a divine being and Jesus as a man.) He visited Armenia and Georgia as well as Constantinople and a number of cities in Italy and France as part of a Mongol delegation.

Arctic Europe

During what is known as the EUROPEAN AGE OF EXPLORATION, from the 15th century into the 17th century, when

European nations developed water routes around the world, Arctic Europe came to be explored in the course of the search for the NORTHEAST PASSAGE—a sea route between the Atlantic Ocean and Pacific Ocean, from along the north coast of Norway to the eastern edge of SIBERIA at the BERING STRAIT (see ARCTIC, EXPLORATION OF THE). Many of the important expeditions to northern waters in the 16th century were those sponsored by the London-based MUSCOVY COMPANY, in the hope of establishing trading contacts with the Far East.

In 1553–54, HUGH WILLOUGHBY, RICHARD CHANCELLOR, and STEPHEN BOROUGH headed an expedition that rounded Cape Nordkinn and entered the White Sea. Chancellor and Borough traveled overland to Moscow; Willoughby, continuing westward, sighted the archipelago of Novaya Zemlya. In 1556–57, Willoughby led another expedition, which sailed even farther east, reaching the entrance to the Kara Sea south of Novaya Zemlya. In 1557–64, another representative of the Muscovy Company, ANTHONY JENKINSON, undertook two expeditions to Russia, using the White Sea route, from where he continued overland, exploring parts of eastern Europe and central Asia. In 1584–85, Dutch mariner OLIVIER BRUNEL headed two expeditions in search of the Northeast Passage, also reaching Novaya Zemlya. Later expeditions would sail past Novaya Zemlya, reaching Arctic Asia.

In 1607, during a Muscovy Company expedition to find the NORTHWEST PASSAGE, Englishman HENRY HUDSON, after sailing westward and exploring Greenland's east coast, returned east and north, and came upon Svalbard, or Spitsbergen, the archipelago in the Arctic waters north of Norway.

The Northeast Passage would not be navigated in its entirety for three centuries. In 1878–79, Swede NILS ADOLF ERIK NORDENSKJÖLD, with the backing of both Sweden and Norway, crossed from the Atlantic to the Pacific through Arctic waters.

Travel Writing and Natural Science

The tradition of traveling and writing about it—as both ancient Greeks and medieval Muslims had done—continued in later centuries and is part of the story of the exploration of Europe. In the mid-17th century, a Turkish writer by the name of ÇELEBI EVLIYA traveled throughout the Ottoman Empire, including lands in eastern Europe and the Balkans as well as in western Asia and northern Africa. He described geography and customs of diverse peoples in a 10-volume work known as *Seyahatname* (Travel Book). Another early travel writer was Englishwoman CELIA FIENNES, who, in the late 17th and early 18th centuries, traveled throughout England, writing about her experiences in a journal, which was published as *Through England on a Side-Saddle*.

Other individuals traveled in parts of Europe to advance scientific knowledge. Among these were the 19th-century Scotsman EDWARD FORBES, who studied the fauna and flora of the waters around the British Isles and in the Mediterranean, and 19th-century Russian PETER KROPOTKIN, who studied the geography, wildlife, and native culture of northern Finland in addition to parts of Asia.

Mountain Climbing in Europe

MOUNTAIN CLIMBING came of age in the Alps in southern central Europe, where many modern techniques developed. In the late 18th century, Frenchmen JACQUES BALMAT and Michel Paccard made the first ascent of Mont Blanc (see BLANC, MONT), the highest peak in the Alps, and the second-highest in Europe, at 15,771 feet. Englishman EDWARD WHYMPER climbed the Matterhorn in 1865, the last high alpine peak to be conquered. Later renowned climbers undertook climbs in the Alps in the late 19th and early 20th centuries, among them Italian MATTHIAS ZURBRIGGEN, who became a guide in expeditions around the world, and American ANNIE SMITH PECK, one of the women pioneers of mountaineering.

Because of their geographic remoteness as well as political isolation, the other high ranges in Europe—the Caucasus and Urals—are not central to the early history of mountain climbing as an international activity. In the 20th century, the Urals became a training ground for climbers of the Union of Soviet Socialist Republics (USSR; Soviet Union). And, in more recent times, the high peaks in both ranges have served as challenges to climbers.

❖

With the flow of so many diverse peoples to and in Europe, the continent has been a melting pot over the centuries, and its political map has been redrawn time and again. Peoples from other continents—in particular Africa and Asia—continue to migrate there. Europe presently has the second-highest overall population density of the continents, after Asia. Peoples of many nations with varying languages and traditions live in close proximity to one another. The founding of the European Union in 1993, a confederation of 15 nations formerly known as the European Economic Community, most of which now use the same euro currency, has led to greater economic unity.

European age of exploration

Starting in the 15th century and into the 17th century, various European nations launched many important maritime voyages, among the most famous in history, which led to a new understanding of world geography. These explorations are associated with the RENAISSANCE, the cultural phase between medieval and modern times in Europe. Many texts on the subject of exploration speak of an "Age of Discovery" in reference to this period of great activity. The concept of "discovery" as it relates to exploration is problematic, however, in that it marginalizes the historic role of indigenous peoples. The Renaissance was indeed a time of intellectual discovery—in geography as well as other cultural pursuits—but it is misleading when applied to Europeans visiting already inhabited lands. Other texts cite an "Age of Exploration." Yet this phrase ignores the periods of great exploring activity among other cultures. One might, for example, be referring to a Muslim age of exploration, from the ninth to the 14th century, when Muslims from a number of different nations ventured beyond the lands along the MEDITERRANEAN SEA into other parts of Europe, Africa, and Asia (see MUSLIM EXPLORATION). Or one might be referring to a Chinese age of exploration, such as during the Han dynasty, from about 206 B.C. to A.D. 220, an expansionist time with new contacts established by the ancient Chinese in distant lands, or during the Ming dynasty of 1368–1644, when their mariners explored coastal East Africa (see CHINESE EXPLORATION).

Other texts speak of a "European Age of Exploration." This is the most accurate phrase in that it distinguishes itself from the cultural contributions of other peoples, making it the least Eurocentric in implication. There were other great periods of exploration among European civilizations, in particular the ancient Greeks and Romans (see GREEK EXPLORATION; ROMAN EXPLORATION). But they were specific to these peoples and their patterns of expansion and might better be called the "Greek Age of Exploration" and the "Roman Age of Exploration." The European age of exploration was just that. It involved many European nations—Portugal, Spain, Holland, England, and France—and many individuals of different nations, often sailing for countries other than their place of birth. And it was a momentous time in Europe, where it led to an understanding of the true extent of the Earth and extensive contacts among peoples of the Eastern and Western Hemispheres.

Foundations

Many developments led up to and contributed to the European Age of Exploration. First, there was a movement away from feudalism, the system based on obligation, toward the centralized nation-state. Exploration thus became a national purpose. The related decline of seignorialism, the system of political, economic, and social relations between seigneurs, or lords, and their dependent farm laborers, also was in decline as merchant capitalism took hold. There were new incentives to obtain products and expand markets.

Since the time of the CRUSADES of the late 11th to late 13th centuries, Italians controlled trade routes in the eastern Mediterranean Sea and trade with the Far East, leading other European nations to seek out new routes. These early stirrings of European expansion in the 13th and early 14th centuries came to an end when the "Black Death," the bubonic plague, arrived in Europe in the mid-14th century, probably brought by Italian merchant ships from the Black Sea (see DISEASE AND EXPLORATION). The economic and social dislocation caused by the loss of as much as a third of Europe's population, many of them city dwellers, ecclesiastics, intellectuals, and merchants, who had been in the forefront of commercial and political efforts outside of Europe, made such ventures far more difficult to mount. As living conditions for survivors of the plague rose as a result of rising wages and falling food prices, the need and desire for expansion beyond Europe diminished. During this hiatus, however, the seeds of future expansion were being sowed; many of the laborers attracted to the depopulated cities were able to save enough money to enter the middle class and to invest in overseas trading ventures; they also created a market for spices and other foreign goods. At the same time the decrease in the value of much agricultural land caused by a dramatic climate change called the "Little Ice Age," which began after 1300, steadily diminished the wealth of the landed nobility. The laboring and merchant classes to some extent began to fill the political vacuum once dominated by clerics and nobles.

The growing Muslim power in the Near East, culminating in the fall of Constantinople (present-day Istanbul) to the Ottoman Turks in 1453—which, in effect, was the end of the East Roman Empire (or Byzantine Empire) centered there—along with the earlier breakup of the empire of the Mongols to the east, meant that established overland trade routes to the Orient, critical to the SPICE TRADE, were no longer secure, and a sea route to Asia became a necessity for merchants. Moreover, the economic system of mercantilism or bullionism, in which a nation's wealth and power are determined by its quantities of gold and silver, became dominant. Europeans hoped to divert the Muslim trade in African gold and ivory to their homelands, or to find new sources of gold. New sources of furs were also sought. And there was a new crusading spirit among the Christian nations of Europe—as there had been during the Crusades to the Mediterranean region in previous centuries—to conquer Muslim-held territory and spread the Christian doctrine. The Reformation and resulting establishment of Protestant churches, with governments eventually adopting official religions, led to growing competition to convert native populations.

The fall of Constantinople to the Ottoman Turks had intellectual ramifications as well, some of which are also discussed as leading up to and defining the encompassing concept of the Renaissance. It had the effect of driving Byzantine scholars to western Europe and leading to greater awareness of Greek and Roman classical studies such as that of hellenized Egyptian PTOLEMY of the second century A.D., as well as of Muslim studies and technologies. The Spanish reconquest of territory controlled by the Moors in the course of the 15th century also made scholarly texts available to Europeans. The development of printing by the German goldsmith and printer Johannes Gutenberg about the same time also contributed to the dissemination of knowledge. Shipbuilding was being revolutionized, with the development of the CARAVEL, which combined the sturdiness and roominess of European ships with the maneuverability of Arab vessels (see SHIPBUILDING AND EXPLORATION). Methods of navigation became more modernized with the growing use of the ASTROLABE, which the ancient Greeks had invented and Arab Muslims had used, as well as the recently invented CROSS-STAFF (see NAVIGATION AND EXPLORATION).

Along the West Coast of Africa

The date 1492, when CHRISTOPHER COLUMBUS first reached the Americas, is sometimes cited as the start of the European age of exploration. Yet it can be more accurately said that the Portuguese initiated this cultural period, and that HENRY THE NAVIGATOR, prince of Portugal, more than any other individual, inspired it. In 1416, he decided to make his home at Sagres near Cape St. Vincent, the southwesternmost point in Portugal, and there founded a naval depot. He also soon founded an observatory and a school of navigation, bringing together astronomers, mapmakers, and mariners. Among the projects was developing the caravel and studying navigational equipment. One of the scholars was MARTIN BEHAIM, who would contribute to technology, working on the astrolabe and cartography, and making the oldest extant GLOBE.

In 1418 and 1419, Henry, who would become known as "the Navigator," even though he never made a voyage of exploration himself, sent out his first two expeditions, which explored the Atlantic islands of Porto Santo and Madeira. Many more expeditions would follow, reaching farther and farther southward along the Atlantic coast of Africa. The AZORES, about 900 miles out to sea, were located and colonized by GONÇALO VELHO CABRAL in the early 1430s. GIL EANNES's rounding of Cape Bojador (the "Bulging Cape," which, as far as Europeans knew, was the southernmost limit of the African coast) in 1434, dispelled many superstitions and misconceptions about sailing into southern waters. Two years later, AFONSO GONÇALVES BALDAYA reached the TROPIC OF CANCER. In 1444–45, DINÍS DIAS reached Cape Verde, Africa's westernmost point. The Portuguese soon established a presence along the African coast and began developing the SLAVE TRADE. In 1455, Italian ALVISE DA CADAMOSTO, sailing for Portugal, became the first known European to observe the constellation known as the Southern Cross. The next year, he reached an island group directly to the west of Cape Verde, which was called by the same name—the Cape Verde Islands. Soon after Henry's death in

1460, his mariners reached Cape Palmas, where the African coast turns eastward.

John II, who became king of Portugal in 1481, sponsored a new round of expeditions southward. In 1482–84, DIOGO CÃO headed an expedition in which he reached the CONGO RIVER (Zaire River). In a subsequent expedition of 1485–86, he traveled as far southward as present-day Namibia, almost reaching the TROPIC OF CAPRICORN. In 1487–88, BARTOLOMEU DIAS finally determined the southern extent of Africa, sailing around the tip of the continent and locating the CAPE OF GOOD HOPE.

Early Transoceanic Voyages

By the 1480s, Italian mariner and map dealer Christopher Columbus had devised a plan to sail westward across the Atlantic Ocean to the Orient. He presented the idea to King John, whose geographers proclaimed it unfeasible. King Ferdinand II and Queen Isabella I of Spain, however, were eventually convinced to give backing to such an expedition, and, in August 1492, Columbus set sail, reaching the Americas the following October. Between 1493 and 1502, Columbus led three more transatlantic expeditions, insisting until his death in 1506 that he had reached Asia. Others, some of whom had sailed with Columbus, also explored the Americas for Spain in the late 15th century and early 16th century, with most of their activity in the Caribbean Sea. These included AMERIGO VESPUCCI (an Italian), VICENTE YÁÑEZ PINZÓN, FRANCISCO MARTÍN PINZÓN, ARIAS MARTÍN PINZÓN, PÁNFILO DE NARVÁEZ, ALONSO DE OJEDA, JUAN DE LA COSA, and RODRIGO DE BASTIDAS. Spain was now fully engaged in world exploration as well as colonization. In 1493, Pope Alexander VI established a Line of Demarcation, defining the spheres of Spanish and Portuguese claims in the Americas; it was modified the next year in the Treaty of Tordesillas. It ran due north and south about 1,110 miles west of the Cape Verde Islands. All lands lying east of this line were to belong to Portugal, which verified their claim on Brazil; all those to the west were considered Spanish possessions.

England also soon dispatched ships, which reached the Americas. Italian mariner JOHN CABOT, who had unsuccessfully sought backing from Spain for an Atlantic crossing in the 1480s, presented his plan to King Henry VII of England, who, in defiance of the Line of Demarcation, offered his support. In 1497, Cabot reached Newfoundland and the east coast of Labrador in northeastern North America, the first documented European voyage to North America since the Vikings crossed the North Atlantic centuries before (Amerigo Vespucci may have explored northward from the WEST INDIES that same year). On a second expedition in 1498, Cabot may have traveled southward along the coast as far as the Chesapeake Bay before being lost at sea.

Meanwhile, the Portuguese had continued seeking a water route to the Orient. In 1497–98, VASCO DA GAMA proved the practicality of an eastward route by rounding the Cape of Good Hope, entering the Indian Ocean and reaching India. Other voyages along this route would soon follow, establishing a Portuguese presence along coastal East Africa as well as in the EAST INDIES. Moreover, the international spice trade now became a maritime enterprise. And, in 1501, Portuguese GASPAR CÔRTE-REAL, after reaching the west coast of GREENLAND the year before, made the second documented voyage to North America, exploring coastal Labrador and Newfoundland in the hope of finding a NORTHWEST PASSAGE to the Pacific Ocean.

It was an exciting time in Europe, with ships setting on new quests and others returning with information of exotic lands, along with proof of landings in the form of people, wildlife, and plants. And cartographers culled information from the returning mariners to create new representations of the world. In 1507, German MARTIN WALDSEEMÜLLER published the first world map depicting South America as a distinct continent; he chose the name America after a Latinized version of Vespucci's first name, based on the Italian mariner's accounts of his voyages.

In the meantime, Spanish colonization of the Americas was under way, leading to more sea traffic and more explorations. In 1513, JUAN PONCE DE LEÓN, who had been the governor of Puerto Rico, explored northward to Florida, and VASCO NÚÑEZ DE BALBOA, who had founded Santa María de la Antigua del Daríen on the Isthmus of Panama, the first permanent European settlement on the mainland of the Americas, became the first European to see the Pacific Ocean from the west coast of the Americas.

Another defining moment in European consciousness and in world history—similar in impact to Columbus's and Vasco da Gama's expeditions—was the first CIRCUMNAVIGATION OF THE WORLD completed in 1522 by one of a fleet of five ships that had set out three years earlier under FERDINAND MAGELLAN, a Portuguese mariner sailing for Spain.

The French soon began pursuing maritime exploration. In 1524, Italian mariner GIOVANNI DA VERRAZANO, while looking for a Northwest Passage to the Orient, explored North America's east coast from present-day South Carolina to Newfoundland. In the 1530s–40s, JACQUES CARTIER, also seeking a Northwest Passage, explored the St. Lawrence River system and surrounding areas in what is now eastern Canada.

Inland Expeditions

More and more inland expeditions were launched as well in the first half of the 16th century, especially by Spain in the Americas. In 1519–20, HERNÁN CORTÉS explored parts of what is now Mexico for Spain and conquered the Aztec Indians. In 1531–33, FRANCISCO PIZARRO led a Spanish expedition to Ecuador and Peru and conquered the Inca. The resulting riches obtained, along with the development of mining, made Spain the richest nation for years to come and helped create the Spanish Empire, the largest empire since the fall of the Roman Empire centuries earlier. In 1540–41, FRANCISCO DE ORELLANA traveled down South America's AMAZON RIVER, from the Napo River to the Atlantic coast. Also in the early 1540s, HERNANDO DE SOTO led the first extensive expedition in the American Southeast, and FRANCISCO VÁSQUEZ DE CORONADO explored much of the American Southwest and southern plains. Some of these expeditions were spurred on by legends of wealthy lands, such as EL DORADO in South America and the Seven Cities of CIBOLA in North America (see TREASURE AND EXPLORATION).

European and Canadian Arctic

Private companies, typically with government support, were formed to develop trading and colonization. The express purpose of one of these, the MUSCOVY COMPANY, founded in 1551, was to locate a NORTHEAST PASSAGE, a shorter eastward water route to Asia than around Africa. The first expedition outfitted by the company was that of SIR HUGH WILLOUGHBY; in 1553–54, it explored the waters of the European Arctic.

The Dutch also became active in maritime exploration. In 1584–85, OLIVIER BRUNEL made two voyages in search of the Northeast Passage, reaching Novaya Zemlya. In 1596–97, WILLEM BARENTS, also searching for the Northeast Passage, reached Bear Island and Spitsbergen (present-day Svalbard).

Continuing expeditions by the English led to new European knowledge of the Canadian Arctic. In 1576–78, MARTIN FROBISHER led three expeditions to the Arctic in search of the Northwest Passage, locating Frobisher Bay on southeastern Baffin Island. In 1585–87, JOHN DAVIS, who designed the Davis Quadrant, also led three English expeditions to the Arctic seeking the Northwest Passage and locating the eastern entrance of Hudson Strait.

Pacific Coast of the Americas

Another region reached by Europeans in the 16th century was the Pacific coast of the Americas, the European exploration of which had started with Magellan's journey around the world. In 1542–43, JUAN RODRÍGUEZ CABRILLO and BARTOLOMÉ FERRELO reached the present Oregon-California border of North America. SIR FRANCIS DRAKE, during the first English circumnavigation of world in 1577–80, reached as far north as Vancouver Island in present-day Canada.

West and South Pacific

This period of activity saw the increasing exploration of the West and South Pacific as well. In 1564–65, MIGUEL LÓPEZ DE LEGAZPI founded the first permanent Spanish settlement in the Philippines. In an expedition of 1567–69, ALVARO DE

MENDAÑA and PEDRO SARMIENTO DE GAMBOA made the European discovery of the Solomon Islands.

Cartography

As exploration flourished in the latter part of the 16th century, so did cartography. Spanish cartographer DIEGO GUTIERREZ produced the first map detailing the inland river systems of South America. Flemish cartographers GERARDUS MERCATOR and ABRAHAM ORTELIUS produced world atlases. Englishmen SIR HUMPHREY GILBERT and RICHARD HAKLUYT wrote about geography, and MARTIN LLEWELLYN published the first English atlas of the Far East.

17th Century

It is even harder to fix a date for the end of the European age of exploration than for the beginning. The end of the 16th century is sometimes given, probably because of convenience. But perhaps the subsequent half-century mark, 1650, is a better date. There had been a belief in a GREAT SOUTHERN CONTINENT, known in Latin as Terra Australis, since the time of the ancient Greeks. The existence of Terra Australis proved to be a fable. Yet Dutch mariners in the first half of the 17th century did make the European discovery of Australia in the Southern Hemisphere and chart many of its coastlines. Early coastal explorations were carried out by Dutch mariners, including WILLIAM JANSZ in 1605, DIRK HARTOG in 1616, FREDERICK HOUTMAN in 1619, FRANÇOIS THYSSEN in 1627, and ABEL JANSZOON TASMAN in 1644. The Dutch were active in North America as well in the early 17th century. Englishman HENRY HUDSON, sailing for the Netherlands in 1609, explored New York Bay and the Hudson River in search of the Northwest Passage. In

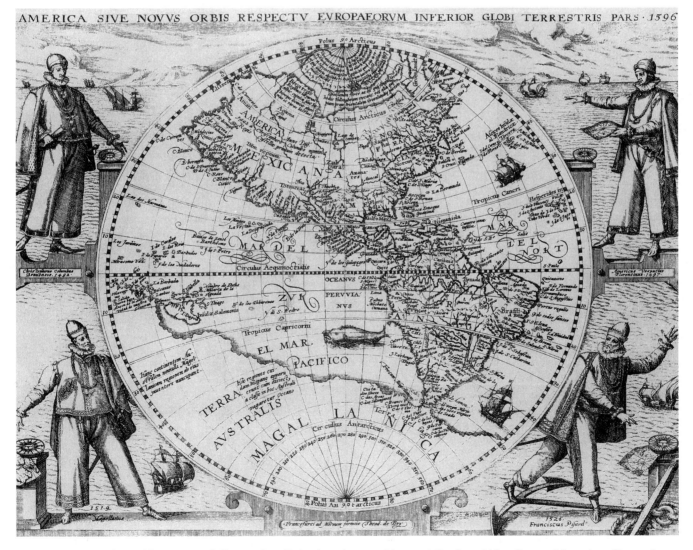

The Americas are flanked by images of Christopher Columbus, Amerigo Vespucci, Ferdinand Magellan, and Francisco Pizarro in this replica of a 1596 map. *(Library of Congress, Prints and Photographs Division [LC-USZ62-89908])*

1610–11, on an expedition for his native country of England, he made the European discovery of HUDSON BAY.

It was Hudson's expedition to the Hudson River region that led to a Dutch claim and the eventual founding of New Netherland. By that time, SAMUEL DE CHAMPLAIN was already colonizing New France in present-day Quebec. In 1607, the English under JOHN SMITH had founded the colony of Jamestown in Virginia; in 1620, the PILGRIMS, among them EDWARD WINSLOW, founded the Plymouth colony in Massachusetts. There had been earlier attempts at colonies in the 16th century by both French interests under JEAN RIBAULT in present-day South Carolina and British interests sponsored by SIR WALTER RALEIGH in present-day North Carolina, but they had failed. By the mid-17th century, however, all the European nations that had sent maritime expeditions around the world were developing colonies. The slave trade was well under way as well. Millions of Africans would be transported across the Atlantic to the Americas.

A Continuum of Exploration

Perhaps a way to think of the subsequent European period of exploratory activity is an age of European COLONIZATION AND EXPLORATION. Many of the ensuing important European expeditions around the world were land based; parts of Asia, the Americas, Africa, and Australia would not be charted until the 19th century. Yet European mariners continued to contribute to world knowledge as well. In the 18th century, another European country, Russia, launched maritime expeditions. One of them, in 1740–41, under Danish mariner VITUS JONASSEN BERING would lead to a Russian claim on and a colonial presence in Alaska. A good number of the expeditions sent out by the British later in the 18th century—such as those headed by England's JAMES COOK—were scientific in nature, many of them to the Pacific Ocean and part of the mission to find the Great Southern Continent. In the course of his voyage of 1772–75, Cook made a circumnavigation of Antarctica, demonstrating that no other continent existed in southern waters. Cook did not sight Antarctica himself. The discovery of the last known continent on Earth occurred in the early 19th century, the first sightings in 1820–21, by British naval officer EDWARD BRANSFIELD, American sealer NATHANIEL BROWN PALMER, and Russian naval officer FABIAN GOTTLIEB BENJAMIN VON BELLINGSHAUSEN. Arctic regions also were further charted in maritime expeditions of the 19th century.

❖

The European age of exploration changed the world in terms of geographic knowledge, commerce, and colonization. It led to the diffusion of technologies and agricultural products as peoples of different continents learned from one another. It resulted in the development of European empires and the exploitation of native peoples and their resulting depopulation and cultural dispossession from disease, warfare, and slavery.

See also COMMERCE AND EXPLORATION; CONQUEST AND EXPLORATION; GEOGRAPHY AND CARTOGRAPHY; LEGENDS AND EXPLORATION; NATIVE PEOPLES AND EXPLORATION; RELIGION AND EXPLORATION.

European Space Agency (ESA)

The European Space Agency (ESA) is an organization of European nations dedicated to the development of space research and technology for peaceful purposes. ESA was formed in 1975 from the merger of the European Space Research Organization (active since 1962) and the European Launcher Development Organization (active since 1964) and presently has 15 members: Austria, Belgium, Denmark, Finland, France, Germany, Ireland, Italy, the Netherlands, Norway, Portugal, Spain, Sweden, Switzerland, and the United Kingdom. Canada participates as an observer. ESA promotes programs for launchers, science, telecommunications, Earth observation, and piloted spaceflight. Member nations are obliged to invite ESA's participation in any space project. And a nation's financial contribution is determined by the extent of involvement in various projects.

ESA headquarters are in Paris, France. The European Astronaut Center, located in Cologne, Germany, is responsible for the selection and training of ASTRONAUTS. The European Space Research and Technology Center, in Noordwijk, the Netherlands, conducts research and directs artificial SATELLITE projects. The European Space Operations Center, in Darmstadt, Germany, controls, monitors, and retrieves data from satellites. The European Space Research Institute, in Frascati, Italy, documents information and manages data obtained from remote sensing satellites. There is also a meteorological office in Toulon, France. Launching facilities are found in Norway, Sweden, and French Guiana, and tracking stations are located in Belgium, Germany, Italy, and Spain.

ESA has contributed greatly to SPACE EXPLORATION since its founding. The Ariane ROCKET, developed in the 1970s–80s, has been a mainstay in satellite launching. Arianespace, a division of ESA, is the first commercial space transportation company and launches a large portion of commercial satellites. ESA developed *Spacelab,* a module for scientific and medical studies, which first flew on the SPACE SHUTTLE in 1983. ESA ASTRONAUTS (the French call them *spationauts*) spent time on the *Mir* SPACE STATION of the Union of Soviet Socialist Republics (USSR; Soviet Union), since its first module was put into orbit in 1986. In 1986, ESA launched the *Giotto* SPACE PROBE, which studied Halley's Comet, and, in 1990, participated with the United States in the *Ulysses* probe, which flew over the poles of the

Sun. In 1995, ESA placed the Solar and Heliospheric Observatory and Infrared Space Observatory into orbit. The joint U.S.-ESA space probe *Cassini,* launched in 1997, is intended to explore Saturn, its rings, and some of its moons on arrival in 2004. The probe *Mars Express,* launched in 2003, will study the planet Mars into 2005. ESA is also involved in the ongoing construction of the International Space Station.

ESA has proven itself as a model of international cooperation while furthering knowledge of space and creating a successful commercial venture in the launching of satellites. It has also helped promote the idea of developing space programs around the world.

Everest, Mount

Mount Everest is a mountain peak in the central HIMALAYAS of Asia, located on the border between Nepal and the Tibet region of China. According to a survey by SATELLITE, Mount Everest's summit is 29,035 feet above sea level. (An earlier survey by the Indian government had determined 29,028 feet.) The Tibetans call the peak *Chomo-Lungma,* for "mother goddess of the land"; the Chinese (see CHINESE EXPLORATION), who claim it as part of China, use *Qomolangma Feng,* for "sacred mother of waters." The English name, *Everest,* was given in 1856 by Englishman Andrew Waugh in honor of fellow Englishman SIR GEORGE EVEREST, under whom he had worked as a surveyor in India. As the highest elevation in the world, summiting Mount Everest came to symbolize a long sought-after goal in the history of world exploration and the ultimate challenge in MOUNTAIN CLIMBING.

The British, with assistance from Nepalese SHERPAS, made pioneering attempts on Mount Everest in the 1820s. In a climb via the north side in 1924, GEORGE HERBERT LEIGH MALLORY and Andrew "Sandy" Irvine lost their lives. Attempts continued the following years, falling short. In 1933, two British airplanes flew over the peak for the first time.

The summit was finally reached by Nepalese TENZING NORGAY and Englishman SIR EDMUND PERCIVAL HILLARY via the southeast side on May 29, 1953. Four Swiss mountain climbers repeated the achievement three years later. In 1963, an American team completed an ascent via the west; in 1975, a British team did so via the southwest; and, in 1980, a Japanese team did so via the north.

More than 600 climbers of many nations have now climbed Mount Everest. Nearly a third of that number have lost their lives on the mountain. As recently as 1996, eight climbers died in a blizzard on the descent after having reached the top. Many bodies have remained on the mountain. Mallory's remains were not located until 1999.

F

fool's gold (pyrite, iron pyrite)

Fool's gold, a mineral composed of iron sulfide, FeS_2, is known by the technical name pyrite, or iron pyrites. Brassy yellow in color with a metallic luster, it often occurs in cube-shaped crystals. Its resemblance to gold led to its playing a part in the history of exploration.

In 1542, JACQUES CARTIER, exploring northeastern North America for France, in his search for the mythical Native American land of SAGUENAY, found what he believed to be gold and precious stones near the St. Lawrence River of present-day Canada. When tested in France, the minerals turned out to be pyrite and quartz.

In 1576, SIR MARTIN FROBISHER, exploring for England, brought a sample of pyrite back from Baffin Island in Frobisher Bay in what is now northern Canada, believing it to be gold. His rock was initially analyzed by two scientists, who reported it to be nothing more than worthless pyrite, but an Italian alchemist by the name of Aquello claimed he had found a speck of gold in the samples.

The CATHAY COMPANY was founded to develop mining interests, with London merchant Michael Lok a principal investor. Frobisher carried out two other expeditions, with mining operations the financial incentive, in 1577 and 1578, and returned with some 200 tons and 1,350 tons of ore respectively, which yielded nothing of value to the investors.

Fountain of Youth

The first known mention of a Fountain of Youth, the water of which would supposedly give the drinker eternal youth, relates to the legend of PRESTER JOHN, a fabled Christian monarch who was believed to rule territory in either Asia or Africa in the 12th century or afterward. Yet, the search for such a fountain is most associated with the explorations of the Spanish conquistador, JUAN PONCE DE LEÓN, as reported by Spanish historians Gonzalo Fernández de Oviedo and Antonio de Herrera.

By 1509, Ponce de León had been given the right by King Ferdinand of Spain to subjugate the native population of Puerto Rico and to take four-fifths of the spoils for himself, turning over the remaining fifth to the king. He had quelled Native American resistance and, over the next three years, ruled Puerto Rico as its governor, becoming wealthy from gold on the island. From the Carib Indians, Ponce de León heard reports of a land to the north, known as "Bimini" or "Boyuca," where there was supposedly gold in abundance and where a spring gushed with a magic water that gave perpetual youth to those who drank it or bathed in it. On losing his position as governor for political reasons in 1512, he was granted, as partial compensation, the commission to search for Bimini and colonize it.

In March 1513, Ponce de León left Puerto Rico in search of his new territory and the so-called Fountain of Youth. He sailed among the islands of the Bahamas and briefly explored the coastlines. On April 2, he landed on the coast of Florida, near present-day St. Augustine. The next day was Easter, and he named his discovery *Pascua Florida,* after the Spanish tradition of celebrating Easter with flowers. Ponce de León believed this new land to be an island and spent seven weeks exploring its coast. He was frustrated in his search for gold and the restorative waters by Indian resistance. In September, after resupplying his ships in Puerto Rico, Ponce de León returned to the Bahamas, where he spent six weeks looking for the fabled fountain without results.

The search for the Fountain of Youth was delayed while Ponce de León fulfilled military obligations for the king. In 1521, at his own expense, he departed for the west coast of Florida with two ships and 200 men and landed near modern-day Tampa. It was his intention to establish a base from which to bring the land under control and to find the mythical fountain. Once again, the Indians were not welcoming, and they killed many of his party and wounded Ponce de León himself. The expedition sailed back to Cuba, where he died at age 61.

The legend of the Fountain of Youth faded with time. Two of the islands of the Bahamas became known as the Bimini Islands after the fabled land.

See also LEGENDS AND EXPLORATION.

French East India Company

In 1664, Jean-Baptiste Colbert, a statesman in the employ of French king Louis XIV, organized a joint-stock company, known as the French East India Company. The following year, the company established a base of operations on the island of Bourbon (present-day Réunion) in the Indian Ocean, which had been settled by France earlier in the century. In 1675, the company began trading at the port of Surat in northwestern India; the following year, at Pondicherry on the Coromandal coast of India. The latter became the company's most important port.

The company was profitable, trading from the EAST INDIES to Iran and China, but suffered from the extravagances of the French king. Drawing against the company's holdings, Louis XIV not only lavished his court with luxuries, he also engaged his nation in expensive wars. In 1719, facing bankruptcy, the French East India Company merged with several other French trading companies active in North America and Africa, including the Mississippi Company. The new concern was known as the *Compagnie des Indes.* Scottish financier John Law formulated a plan for the colonization and commercial exploitation of the Mississippi Valley and other French holdings in the Louisiana, known as the Mississippi Scheme. The company was heavily promoted, leading to a great inflation in its stock, and many French migrated to Louisiana. In October 1720, however, due to overexpansion of its activities and the lack of assets, the company's stock crashed. Law fled from France.

The French East India Company regained its independent status in 1723. It suffered continuing losses. In 1730, it gave up participation in the transatlantic SLAVE TRADE. The next year it ceased all trade activities in Louisiana. And in 1736, it ceased the coffee trade in other parts of the Americas. The company henceforth concentrated its efforts on promoting trade with India. It established sugar plantations on Île de France (present-day Mauritius) and imported slaves to work the plantations. The company prospered for a time under the leadership of the governors in India, including Benoît Dumas, who oversaw its interests in 1735–41, and Joseph François Dupleix, who came into increased competition with the BRITISH EAST INDIA COMPANY in 1742–54. In 1751, British military leader Robert Clive captured Arcot in southern India. In 1761, other British forces captured France's premier port, Pondicherry. As a result, the French East India Company went into a rapid decline. By 1769, the company had ceased operations and had turned its possessions over to the French government.

See also COMMERCE AND EXPLORATION.

fur trade

The fur trade, the commerce in animal skins and pelts, has played a significant part in world exploration and development. Trade in furs has taken place since ancient times in all hemispheres and among various peoples. Yet it is most directly tied in with the history of exploration in the Northern Hemisphere, especially in northern parts of North America and in SIBERIA in eastern Asia. Europeans of all the colonial powers, especially in the 16th through 18th centuries—the French, Dutch, English, Russians, and, to a lesser extent, the Spanish—bartered trade goods, such as iron tools and utensils, cloth, glass beads, firearms, and alcoholic beverages, with indigenous peoples in order to fulfill a demand for furs in Europe, especially beaver pelts for felt for the making of hats with brims, a fashion style that first caught on in the 1580s. But the pelts of other animals, such as muskrat, mink, marten, fox, sea otter, and seal, were also sought. After the founding of the United States, Euro-Americans continued working the fur trade. Some became hunters and trappers themselves. And some native peoples acted as middlemen between other tribes and the European or Euro-American traders. The fur trade involved the capture of fur-bearing animals through hunting and trapping, skinning them, then transporting the skins for processing into fur clothing and felt.

French Trade

In early colonial times, the French most thoroughly exploited the fur trade. Whereas mining and the raising of livestock had a greater economic bearing on the development of Spanish colonies, and farming dominated the economy and land use of the English colonies, commerce in furs determined French expansion. The French and Indian fur trade began with JACQUES CARTIER in 1534 along the St. Lawrence River. His original intent had been to find a NORTHWEST PASSAGE from the Atlantic Ocean to the Pacific Ocean and gain maritime access to the Orient, but he found instead an untapped source of furs among Native Americans, who were eager to trade for European goods. SAMUEL DE CHAMPLAIN began colonizing New France in 1604, with trade with Native Americans central to the colony's economy. Over the next years, Champlain explored the northern woods and established trade agreements with various tribes to deliver their pelts to French trading posts. Port Royal in Acadia (now Annapolis Royal, Nova Scotia), Quebec City, and Montreal all became thriving centers of commerce.

Eastern Algonquian-speaking tribes, such as the Cree, Algonkin, Montagnais, Naskapi, Abenaki, and Micmac, were all involved in the French fur trade. Yet the Iroquoian-speaking Huron (Wyandot) became the foremost suppliers. From the years 1616 to 1649, the Huron, in conjunction with the Algonquian Ottawa and Nipissing, developed a trading empire among Native Americans from the Great Lakes to the HUDSON BAY to the St. Lawrence. Each of the three main trading partners had its own river and portage route for travel by CANOE, plus a yearly schedule, linking them up with each other and other tribes as well. Acting as middlemen, the Huron traded agricultural products to other tribes for pelts, which they then carried to the French in Quebec city or Montreal, to trade for European wares. In their flotillas of canoes, now laden with goods, they then completed the trade circle, returning to other peoples to exchange some of the European trade goods for still more furs.

This complex trade relationship lasted until the mid-17th century, ending with the military and economic expansion from the south by the five Iroquois (Haudenosaunee) nations—Mohawk, Oneida, Onondaga, Cayuga, and Seneca—who at the time were trading partners of the Dutch working out of Fort Orange (present-day Albany) in New Netherland. The Dutch also carried out some trade for furs with the Algonquian-speaking Lenni Lenape (Delaware) and Wappinger Indians out of New Amsterdam in present-day New York City. In the meantime, many Frenchmen, some of them sponsored by de Champlain and others by the Catholic Church, were venturing along lakes and rivers into the wilderness in search of new sources for furs. Many more would follow. The men who earned a livelihood by paddling large canoes into the wilderness in quest of furs for licensed traders came to be known as VOYAGEURS; the independent, unlicensed entrepreneurs who defied regulations, many of them living among the native population, became known as COUREURS DE BOIS. Both voyageurs and coureurs de bois would propagate a group of people associated for years with the fur trade—the Métis—mixed-bloods of predominantly French and native descent, or of Scottish and native descent, especially Cree, Chippewa, and Assiniboine.

The fur market varied in profitability, one crash occurring in 1696. Yet the French fur trade expanded into new regions. Under royal management, New France extended its territory from the Great Lakes across the MISSISSIPPI RIVER into the Louisiana Territory. PIERRE-ANTOINE MALLET and his brother Paul as well as PIERRE GAULTIER DE VARENNES DE LA VÉRENDRYE helped open the trans-Mississippi region in the first half of the 18th century. French traders also expanded their markets in the south, from settlements along the Gulf Coast northwestward along the Mississippi and Red Rivers—parts of present-day Louisiana and Texas. New Orleans, founded in 1718, became a bustling center of commerce. And during the 18th century, the French established a special trade relationship with the Taovaya in the Southwest, the French name for both Wichita and Caddo Indians, who acted as middlemen for them as the Huron had done for the French the century before.

British Trade

England, after the takeover of New Netherland from the Dutch in 1664, inherited a trade relationship with the Iroquois. They also developed trade relations with tribes in the fur-rich untapped Hudson Bay region. Claim to the area was based on the voyage of HENRY HUDSON in 1610. The fur-trading expedition of MÉDARD CHOUART DES GROSEILLIERS and his brother-in-law PIERRE-ESPRIT RADISSON to the region in 1668–69 led to the founding of the HUDSON'S BAY COMPANY in 1670. The English, rather than sending traders inland to collect furs as the French did, established trading posts for barter with the Indians—especially the Cree and Chipewayan—at the mouths of the large rivers that drained into the bay. Ships could come and go in the summertime when the northern waters were free of ice. At this time, England did not know the extent of Rupert's Land, as its northern holdings were called, after Prince Rupert, the Hudson's Bay Company's chief backer and first governor. The French also claimed the Hudson Bay region and sent out various military expeditions against British posts, with some successes, and continued to play a dominant role in the fur trade until England's ultimate victory in the French and Indian Wars and the Treaty of Paris in 1763.

Starting in the 1780s, the Hudson's Bay Company also encountered fierce competition from the NORTH WEST COMPANY, founded by Scottish interests in Montreal. The rivalry spurred a period of extensive exploration in which new Indian contacts were established, especially among the tribes of the Canadian West. A "Nor'wester," SIR ALEXANDER

MACKENZIE, became the first non-Indian to cross the North American continent north of Mexico in the early 1790s. DAVID THOMPSON, who worked for both companies at different times in his career, mapped much of the Canadian West in the late 18th and early 19th centuries. The two companies merged in 1821 under the name of the older company, and the Hudson's Bay Company thrived in the fur trade for years to come.

Russian Trade

During the period of conflict between France and Great Britain, Russia also began developing its fur trade. Russia had been a world source of furs for centuries, especially luxury furs. With fur-bearing animals depleted in western parts, the *promyshlenniki*—Russian fur traders and hunters— pushed eastward into Siberia. Early traders, such as YEROFEY PAVLOVICH KHABAROV, who explored the Amur River in southeastern Siberia in the mid-17th century, conducted some trade in the region. In the mid-18th century, EMELYAN BASOV, one of the Cossacks who explored eastern Russia, developed the fur trade as far as the Kamchatka Peninsula.

In the years after Danish VITUS JONASSEN BERING's and Russian ALEKSEY ILYICH CHIRIKOV's voyage of exploration to Alaska on behalf of Russia in 1741, the *promyshlenniki* extended operations to North America, reaching the Aleutian Islands and the Alaskan mainland, where the sea otter was plentiful. In the early years, the traders formed ad hoc companies, with no rules governing their operations or their exploitative treatment of the Aleut, the native peoples on the Aleutian Islands, and the Inuit (Eskimo), on the mainland. The typical early Russian method of acquiring furs was to enter a native village, take hostages either by means of violence or with the threat of violence, pass out traps to the men, then demand furs in exchange for the lives of the women and children. If the men failed to deliver furs, hostages would be executed. Then, when the furs were collected, the Russians would depart until the next season.

By the 1780s, British and American traders also worked the Pacific coast, especially in Nootka Sound in present-day British Columbia. But they also extended their activity to Alaska in the north and in California in the south. Ships would sail from Boston around South America to fur country, then transport the sea otter skins to China, where there was a great demand.

To protect their territorial claims and economic interest, the Russians, under the impetus of GRIGORY IVANOVICH SHELIKOV, and his employer, Ivana L. Golikiv, who had set up a base at Okhotsk in Siberia, began establishing permanent colonies, the first at Three Saints on Kodiak Island in 1784. Because of Shelikov's efforts and those of ALEKSANDR ANDREEVICH BARANOV, in his employ, in 1799, the RUSSIAN-AMERICAN COMPANY was chartered, with a monopoly in all Russian territory in North America. By 1812, that territory extended to northern California, where Fort Ross was founded near Bodega Bay.

American Trade

During colonial times, U.S. interests participated only minimally in the fur trade. The deerskin trade flourished in the Southeast, however. In 1808, JOHN JACOB ASTOR founded the AMERICAN FUR COMPANY, having various subsidiaries to follow, such as the Pacific Fur Company, with a trading post at Astoria, Oregon, and the South West Company, operating near the Great Lakes. The next year, a group in St. Louis on the Mississippi River founded the ST. LOUIS MISSOURI FUR COMPANY. Among the partners were JEAN PIERRE CHOUTEAU, his son AUGUSTE PIERRE CHOUTEAU, MANUEL LISA, WILLIAM CLARK, ANTOINE PIERRE MENARD, and ANDREW HENRY.

Both enterprises sponsored numerous expeditions into the western wilderness. In 1816, the American Congress enacted a law excluding British traders from the United States. Another American entrepreneur, WILLIAM HENRY ASHLEY, became a powerful force in the fur trade with his ROCKY MOUNTAIN FUR COMPANY, founded by him and Andrew Henry in 1822. Many of the men who worked for and traded with him came to be known as the MOUNTAIN MEN. Among the most famous of them were THOMAS FITZPATRICK, JEDEDIAH STRONG SMITH, and WILLIAM LEWIS SUBLETTE. In the 1820s–1830s, they traveled the Native American trails and passes of the West as hunters, trappers, and traders, and like the voyageurs and the coureurs de bois of French Canada, they learned wilderness survival skills from Native Americans.

During these same years, the U.S. government also played a part in the fur trade, through a system of federal trading houses, called the "factory system." From 1790 to 1799, the U.S. Congress passed four Trade and Intercourse Acts pertaining to Indian affairs and commerce. Among other regulations, the acts provided for the appointment of Indian agents and licensing of federal traders, who could barter with the Indians for furs. In 1802, a follow-up Trade and Intercourse Act codified the four earlier ones. And, in 1806, an Office of Indian Trade was created within the War Department to administer the federal trading houses. The "factory system" was abolished in 1822, at which time provisions were made for the licensing of independent traders, who were better able to operate in the wilderness.

❖

The international fur market experienced a decline starting in the late 1830s, partly because the beaver hat went out of style in favor of the silk hat. Other factors contributed to the end of the centuries-long fur boom: the depletion of fur-bearing animals and the advance of farming settlements. As for the mountain men and other counterparts, many of

A trapper poses for a photograph in his canoe with his dogs and hides sometime in the early 20th century. *(Library of Congress, Prints and Photographs Division [LC-USZ62-130283])*

them stayed active in the American West long after the fur decline, as soldiers, scouts, and guides. In 1867, Russia gave up its North American venture and sold Alaska to the United States, and in 1869, the Hudson's Bay Company sold off its vast territorial holdings to the Canadian government. Yet the fur trade had made its mark in the history of exploration; the traders had pioneered routes, mapped vast regions, and opened up vast areas to non-Indian settlement and other types of commercial development. Nowadays, the fur trade is still carried out in the far north, mostly by indigenous peoples.

See also COMMERCE AND EXPLORATION; NATIVE PEOPLES AND EXPLORATION.

G

galleon

The term *galleon* refers to a large ship with three to four decks and three square-rigged masts, except typically for the third (mizzen) mast, which had a triangular sail to help control direction. It was developed by the Spanish from the smaller CARRACK starting in the 15th century, with refinements throughout much of the 16th century. While the carrack started at around 80 tons, the galleon ranged from 500 to 1,400 tons displacement.

The galleon, too large for exploring uncharted coastlines, was designed for carrying cargo and for warfare. The Spanish used it to haul treasure and other resources from the Americas, taken from the Aztec and Inca Indians (see TREASURE AND EXPLORATION). They also used it to defend against fighting ships of other nations, notably the English. The size of the galleon not only made it harder to sink, but also allowed it to carry more guns, which were located in batteries on its broadsides.

As the flow of goods from their principalities increased, the Spanish devised a convoy system where 10 or more ships sailed together, guarded by galleons. In order to counter these measures, the English created smaller and faster fighting vessels, able to dodge the galleon's formidable firepower.

See also SHIPBUILDING AND EXPLORATION.

galley

The term *galley* or *galley ship* refers to a variety of vessels that were powered mainly by oar. The term is primarily associated with the vessels of ancient civilizations surrounding the MEDITERRANEAN SEA. The ancient Egyptians used galleys for transportation and trade on the NILE RIVER, RED SEA, and Mediterranean. By 1500 B.C., Egyptian ships were as large as 130 feet long and 16 feet wide. The Minoans also used galleys. Other ancient mariners, the Phoenicians, invented an early form of the galley, constructing it from cedar planks and using caulk to seal the seams. If the Phoenicians did make the journey around Africa in about 600 B.C., as fifth-century B.C. Greek historian HERODOTUS recorded, it would have been a galley that they used. Other Mediterranean peoples, the Greeks and the Romans, built later versions of the galley.

It is believed that most ships were constructed hull-first. Planks were fashioned and held together end to end with dovetail joints. On the edges, holes were drilled, and dowels of a hardwood were used to connect the planks along their length. The preferred woods for the planks were cedar, cypress, and pine. The ribs, which were inserted later, were made of a hardwood such as oak. Caulking was also necessary and was accomplished with a variety of fibrous materials and additives such as pitch and lime. Later shipbuilders began making the frame of their vessels first, then attaching the planking. Metal nails were used to hold the hull and frame together, copper being favored for its resistance to rust. In addition to caulking, a sheath of lead might also be added to prevent leaking and add to a ship's durability.

Galleys came to be as long as 150 feet with 50 oars, typically one man to an oar. Designers learned to build the

The *Grande Hermine*, a 16th-century French galleon, is flanked by cameos of Jacques Cartier and Francis I, king of France. (*Library of Congress, Prints and Photographs Division [LC-USZ62-105525]*)

ships seven to eight times as long as they were wide for maximum speed. The oarsmen, often slaves, prisoners of war, or convicts, sat on benches to which they were chained. There would be decks built on either end of the ship for officers and passengers. Cargo and supplies would be stored in containers at the open center of the boat. Some galleys had sails, but typically more for decoration than for taking advantage of wind power.

As galleys advanced in design and size, more levels were added. The bireme was a version with two levels of oarsmen; the trireme had three levels. A galley containing five levels of oarsmen, was first recorded as being produced in the Italian city of Syracuse in 398 B.C., and galleys with as many as six levels of rowers have been recorded.

The galley was not suited for long trading voyages on the open ocean. To provision a crew that expended as much energy as the required number of oarsmen would not have been economical. The standard practice was to pull the ship on to shore at the end of the day and make camp. Cooking was done on the beach, not in the ship.

The galley was the primary warship of ancient civilization. The Greeks introduced the ram—a sharp projection on the front of a ship—for the purpose of ramming into and sinking an enemy vessel. The Romans made hooks to pull

enemy vessels to theirs and used planks as bridges to board them. After A.D. 395, when the Roman Empire was divided into the Western Roman Empire and the Eastern Roman Empire (the Byzantine Empire), the Byzantine navy came to use a type of fast galley, known as the dromon, or racer, with one or more banks of oarsmen to accompany and protect the larger cargo galleys.

At the beginning of the 14th century, the development of the galley reached its pinnacle. The *galea grossa,* designed and built for the needs of the traders of Venice, could be as large as 250 tons and complemented rowing with sail power. These ships, launched from the great cities of the eastern Mediterranean, through the Strait of Gibraltar (see GIBRALTAR, STRAIT OF) and north to England, were active into the 17th century. Yet, after Portugal established a trade route around Africa in the 16th century, and sail power was made more efficient, use of galleys dropped off. The design of boats in northern Europe during the Middle Ages came to rely predominantly on wind power, but in order to survive the unpredictable winds, they too would have a bank of oars. By the 15th century, most oceangoing ships were too heavy to row.

The LONGSHIP of the Vikings is a type of galley. In modern usage the term *galley* refers to the kitchen of a ship.

See also EGYPTIAN EXPLORATION; GREEK EXPLORATION; PHOENICIAN EXPLORATION; MINOAN EXPLORATION; ROMAN EXPLORATION; SHIPBUILDING AND EXPLORATION.

Ganges River

The Ganges, the most important river of the Indian subcontinent, flows 1,560 miles from the HIMALAYAS in northern India, over the area called the Gangetic Plain, through Bangladesh to the Indian Ocean. Formed by the confluence of the Bhagirathi and the Alaknanda Rivers, the Ganges River's annual discharge is rivaled only by the AMAZON RIVER in South America and the CONGO RIVER (Zaire River) in Africa. The Bhagirathi River, originating in an ice cave of the Gangotri at a height of 13,000 feet, is considered the source of the Ganges, later met by the Alaknanda River, fed by melting snow and glaciers. The Yamuna River is a main tributary. The Ganges changes names as it passes through India and Bangladesh. The main course of the river flows south and is joined by the Brahmaputra River and then by the Meghna River (the name by which it is known thereafter), as well as numerous other tributaries, before entering the Bay of Bengal. The delta region is referred to as the Ganges Delta or the Ganges-Brahmaputra Delta.

Of significant religious importance to the Hindu population, which composes a majority of India, the river is named after the Hindu goddess Ganga, daughter of Meru, the mountain god Himalaya. Hindus consider drinking from and bathing in the waters of the Ganges a sacred act, and the ashes of deceased persons are scattered in the river. Along the river and in the mountains by its headwaters are many holy sites visited by Hindu pilgrims, for the Lord Vishnu is said to have bathed there. The Ganges, with its snow-fed waters, is economically significant in addition, providing irrigation waters and fertilizing important food-crops including rice, sugarcane, lentils, oil seeds, potato, and wheat.

Ancient Contacts

After the early Indus Valley civilization disappeared from India, replaced by Aryan tribes migrating from central Asia, the Gangetic Plain became a center of civilization. Starting in the sixth century B.C., the kingdom of Magadha grew in power and was later called the Mauryan Empire as it expanded into central India. By this time, the Persian Empire to the west had conquered as far east as the INDUS RIVER. In the fourth century B.C., Greek historian HERODOTUS wrote his account of the wars between the Greeks (see GREEK EXPLORATION) and the Persians, using his own travels, reports from traders, and earlier accounts to describe the geography of the known world. In Herodotus's account, the lands east of the Indus River were unpopulated and the home of giant birds and other fantastic animals.

From 420 to 400 B.C., a Greek by the name of CTESIUS OF CNIDUS, in service as court physician to Darius II, emperor of Persia, traveled through Persia and east into India. Ctesius was the first Westerner to report about the Ganges River, and he discredited Herodotus's descriptions of the lands east of the Indus. Ctesius reported things no less fantastic than Herodotus, telling of men with giant feet, or dog-like faces, as well as huge worms in the Ganges that devoured camels and oxen. The latter, however, could be a description of the crocodiles that inhabit the river.

In 334 B.C., after ALEXANDER THE GREAT of Macedonia consolidated his rule over the Greek city-states, inspired by the writings of Herodotus and other accounts of the East, he made a military assault on the Persian Empire. Alexander advanced onto the Anatolian plateau, the Asian part of modern-day Turkey, conquering all of Asia Minor. After consolidating power over the countries on the Mediterranean coast as far west as Egypt, Alexander defeated Darius III of Persia, continued east through Afghanistan, and finally crossed the Hindu Kush range into India. Alexander's goal was to conquer India as far as the Ganges River, but his soldiers mutinied, fearing the strength of the Mauryan kings.

Alexander's empire collapsed into smaller kingdoms after his death in 323 B.C., while the Mauryan Empire continued to flourish around the Ganges. The ruler of a kingdom in ancient Syria sent a Greek diplomat, MEGASTHENES of Ionia, in about 302 B.C., as ambassador to the Mauryan Empire. Megasthenes traveled throughout northern India, making observations of Hindu culture and the natural history of the region. He was the first Westerner to make accurate observations of the Ganges River and to surmise its source correctly. Somewhat later in the middle of the third century B.C., a Hellenistic kingdom was established in Bactria, covering modern-day Afghanistan, Uzbekistan, and Tajikistan, and which, by about 150 B.C., had expanded to meet the Ganges River in the east. This kingdom collapsed under internal and external pressure. By that time, however, the Ganges had ceased to be a place shrouded in mystery for the Western world.

Chinese Buddhists

Contact between India and the lands to its east, including the flourishing Chinese Empire, was made extremely difficult by the high mountains and rugged terrain separating the two regions. But Buddhism, an offshoot of the ancient Hindu religion, spread slowly from the Ganges River Valley to the north and east. In the late fourth century A.D., a Buddhist monk called FA-HSIEN traveled into northern India by way of Afghanistan to retrieve ancient Buddhist texts and to visit Buddhist shrines. It was a long and arduous journey through deserts and high mountains, and Fa-hsien returned without seeing the Ganges. In the seventh century, another Chinese Buddhist monk, HSÜAN-TSANG, conscious of the continued need for Buddhist texts from India to solve disputes and fill in gaps in religious knowledge, made his own journey into India. Hsüan-tsang eventually reached the valley of the Ganges, followed the river, and reached the Buddhist university in Baragaon.

Another famous Chinese pilgrim, I-CHING, inspired by the journeys of Hsüan-tsang, made his own trip to the Ganges River and the Buddhist holy sites there in A.D. 671. He traveled overland initially, but because of political turmoil in Tibet and the presence of Muslims (see MUSLIM EXPLORATION) in Afghanistan, I-ching boarded a Persian ship. He sailed to the mouth of the Ganges, then trekked overland, visiting holy sites before finally settling to study in Magadha, the ancient birthplace of Buddhism.

Charting the River

Although there had been parties of exploration sent by Indian rulers during periods of stability during the turmoil following the invasion of Islamic Turks in the 11th century, the river remained uncharted. In 1624–25, ANTONIO DE ANDRADE, a Jesuit missionary (either Portuguese or Spanish), who traveled from northern India across the Himalayas into Tibet, reported finding waters feeding the Ganges. Yet it was not until the British gained control of the Indian subcontinent in the 18th century that systematic exploration of the river was made. A British survey team, inspired by the tradition of expanding scientific knowledge of the Age of Enlightenment, as well as more practical political and tactical considerations, determined that the Bhagirathi River issuing from the foothills of the Himalayas was indeed the source of the Ganges, confirming the deduction of Megasthenes more than 2,000 years prior.

See also ASIA, EXPLORATION OF.

Gemini program (Project Gemini)

The Gemini program was one of a series of programs carried out by the United States for the purpose of SPACE EXPLORATION. Following the creation of the APOLLO PROGRAM in 1961 for the purpose of placing humans on the Moon, the NATIONAL AERONAUTICS AND SPACE ADMINISTRATION (NASA) instituted a number of programs to help accomplish such an undertaking: the manned MERCURY PROGRAM of 1961–63 to launch the first Americans into space; the manned Gemini program of 1964–66 to help develop the necessary techniques for a lunar mission; and the unmanned Surveyor program of 1966–68 to probe the lunar surface. The Gemini program competed with the VOSKHOD PROGRAM of the Union of Soviet Socialist Republics (USSR; Soviet Union).

Gemini missions were designed to keep two ASTRONAUTS in space for extended periods of time, perfect rendezvous and docking techniques, conduct experiments on equipment and human adaptation to conditions in space, and make accurate landings. All the missions were launched from Cape Canaveral (now Cape Kennedy), Florida, with a Titan II intercontinental ballistic missile (ICBM) as the propelling ROCKET. The Mission Control Center (MCC) was based in Houston, Texas.

The Gemini spacecraft had two modules: the adaptor module for orbital and docking operations, and the reentry module to return to Earth. Gemini spacecraft were controlled by the pilot, unlike those of the Mercury program. Landings were by parachute into the Atlantic Ocean or Pacific Ocean.

Twelve Gemini flights were conducted, the final 10 piloted. The most famous of these was *Gemini 4* in June 1965, during which EDWARD HIGGINS WHITE II became the first American to participate in extravehicular activity (EVA), more popularly known as "walking in space." (ALEXEI ARKHIPOVICH LEONOV was the first human to walk in space, for the Soviet Union, in March of that same year on *Voshkod 2*.) *Gemini 4* set a record of four days in space; *Gemini 5*, seven days; and *Gemini 7*, 14 days. *Gemini 6* and *7* were in orbit at the same time and accomplished a rendezvous of within a few feet. A variety of rendezvous and dockings, with differing target vehicles, were accomplished from *Gemini 6* on. In the entire Gemini program, astronauts logged about 2,000 hours in space and about 12 hours in EVA.

geography and cartography

Geography is the science of Earth's surface form. The first-known use of the term, literally meaning "earth description," is by third-century B.C. Greek scholar ERATOSTHENES. Geographic studies encompass both physical and cultural features, that is, both the natural environment and the human environment.

The two broad classifications of geography are physical geography—including geomorphology, climatology, biogeography, soils geography, HYDROGRAPHY, and oceanography (see OCEANOGRAPHY AND EXPLORATION); and cultural geography, also called human geography (and formerly anthropogeography)—including historical geography, political geography, military geography, economic geography, ethnography, historical geography, urban geography, demography, and linguistic geography. Geography is thus an integrating discipline, bridging earth sciences and social sciences. There are two general approaches to geographic studies: "systematic geography," focusing on an individual feature; and "regional geography," focusing on relationships among differing features or regions.

Geographic studies necessitate the collection of data through a variety of means in the field, such as surveys, photography, or geological investigations; through a quantitative study of collected data using mathematical and statistical analysis; or by studying historical sources (see PHOTOGRAPHY AND EXPLORATION; SURVEYING AND EXPLORATION). The results of such studies can be presented in various ways, the most practical being a combination of words and images in maps and charts. (Those two terms—*map* and *chart*—have been used interchangeably for any representation of the surface of Earth or of the heavens; yet the latter term, when used with regard to exploration, most often refers to a navigator's map relating to the marine environment or an aviator's chart for flying—see MAPS AND CHARTS.) Cartography is the art and science of making maps and charts. The history of the gaining of geographic information and representing that information cartographi-cally by geographers/cartographers is parallel to the history of exploration.

Ancient European Geographers

The first geographers were those ancient travelers or scribes who recorded information about lands. The earliest existing maps, clay tablets inscribed by Akkadians of ancient Mesopotamia—showing settlements, cultivated plots of lands, streams, and hills—dates to about 2300 B.C., at the time of the ruler SARGON. Other early maps of the region, dating as far back as 2000 B.C., show plans of properties for the purpose of taxation. Another Mesopotamian people, the Babylonians, carved what is considered the earliest extant world map—a clay tablet from the sixth century B.C.—on which the city of Babylon is depicted, flanked by Assyria to the east and Chaldea to the southwest, and surrounded by oceans and what are thought to be islands.

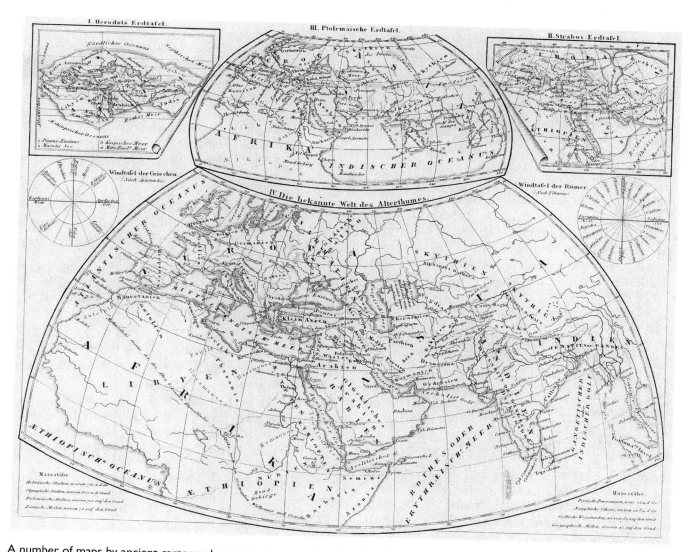

A number of maps by ancient cartographers were re-created in the 1851 *Iconographic Encyclopaedia of Science, Literature, and Art* by Johann G. Heck. *(Library of Congress, Prints and Photographs Division [LC-USZ62-115363])*

Early mariners, such as Minoans, Egyptians, Phoenicians, and Greeks, who traveled throughout the MEDITERRANEAN SEA, especially for purposes of trade, helped spread and record geographic information. Most of the sea's shorelines were known to the various seagoing peoples by about 1400 B.C., and, in ensuing centuries, ancient mariners explored other waterways. An extant Egyptian map drawn on papyrus, which shows Nubian gold mines between the NILE RIVER and RED SEA, dates to 1300 B.C. By at least the sixth century B.C., Egyptians and Phoenicians were venturing along the Red Sea and into the Indian Ocean (see EGYPTIAN EXPLORATION; PHOENICIAN EXPLORATION). By the fifth century B.C., the Carthaginians—predominantly of Phoenician ancestry—had also navigated past the Strait of Gibraltar (see GIBRALTAR, STRAIT OF) and explored the Atlantic coastlines of Europe and Africa (see CARTHAGINIAN EXPLORATION).

The ancient Greeks made geography a scientific and philosophical study. In the sixth century B.C., Greek philosopher Anaximander drafted the first known map to represent a concept of the world, with the Aegean Sea off Greece represented as the center, encircled by Mediterranean lands and oceans. A form of ancient geographic text thought to have originated about the same time and associated with Greek mariners was the PERIPLUS, an account of a sea voyage, describing landmarks and waterways. Also in the sixth century B.C., HECATAEUS OF MILETUS published a work called *Periegesis* (Tour Around the World) about his travels in Asia Minor and Egypt. In the fifth century B.C., another Greek historian, HERODOTUS, chronicled the history and geography of the Mediterranean world, drawing on the writings of Hecataeus and other ancient travelers. In the fourth century B.C., a scholar, PYTHEAS, also an accomplished navigator, traveled along the Atlantic coast of Europe and perhaps even reached the ARCTIC CIRCLE.

The Greeks also first made the case that Earth was round, as put forth, in the fifth century B.C., by a philosopher, Parmenides. In the fourth century B.C., Greek philosopher Aristotle recognized that all matter tends to fall toward a common center; that, in traveling from north to south, new constellations become visible while others disappear; and that, during an eclipse, Earth casts a circular shadow on the Moon. A scholar, Eratosthenes, who served as head of the library at Alexandria in North Africa in the third century B.C., is cited as the first systematic geographer. He drew a map of the known world, representing parts of Europe, Asia, and Africa, which was the first to use grid lines, an early version of lines of LATITUDE AND LONGITUDE. He also first accurately calculated the circumference of Earth. A second-century B.C. astronomer and mathematician, HIPPARCHUS, further developed the concept, making the east-west lines parallel and the north-south lines at right angles to them. A

Greek geographer, Crates of Mallus, made the first known GLOBE in the second century B.C.

With the rise to power of the Romans and the expansion of the Roman Empire around and beyond the Mediterranean region, geographic knowledge became even more organized—for military and trade purposes. Early in the first century A.D., Greek STRABO published the 17-volume *Geography* in Rome, summarizing his own travels and accounts of others' travels. Later in the century, PLINY THE ELDER, a Roman, published *Historia Naturalis* with geographic accounts of Europe, Asia, and Africa. The last greatest classical geographer—as well as mathematician and astronomer—was hellenized Egyptian PTOLEMY of the second century A.D. Like Eratosthenes, he worked out of Alexandria. His eight-volume work, *Geographia*, or *Introduction to the History of the Earth*, summarized the geographic and cartographic knowledge of his time—including a compilation of 8,000 places and their coordinates of latitude and longitude. The work influenced Western thought for centuries.

Other Cultures

It is a mistake to ignore the geographic accomplishments of other peoples around the world, such as the Chinese, with regard to geography and cartography (see CHINESE EXPLORATION). Mention is made of the use of maps in ancient China as far back as the seventh century B.C. The earliest extant Chinese maps—drawn on silk—date to the second century B.C., showing highly developed cartographic techniques including representations of topography. The ancient Marshall Islanders (see OCEANIA) made charts from cane sticks lashed together to indicate wind and wave patterns, with shells and corals attached to depict islands. The Polynesians used palm sticks for similar charts. By the time the Spanish arrived in Central and South America in the 16th century, the Inca, Maya, and Aztec Indians were also making maps on calico and other materials. Some Native North Americans drew maps on rawhide. The Inuit of Arctic North America carved coastal maps in ivory.

The Middle Ages

After the collapse of the Roman Empire, among Europeans of the Middle Ages, the Vikings were the most active voyagers (see VIKING EXPLORATION). They were also geographers in that they passed on their geographic discoveries, such as voyages to North America, in written accounts. (The VINLAND MAP, visually depicting these voyages, turned out to be a forgery.)

Most European mapmaking of the medieval period was carried out by Christian monks—such as sixth-century Egyptian-born COSMAS INDICOPLEUSTES and eighth-century Spaniard BEATUS OF VALCAVADO—whose religious beliefs affected content as much as did accurate geographic knowledge. On early world maps, from about the fourth to the 14th century—known by the Latin term *MAPPA MUNDI* —there is no attempt to represent true scale or latitude and longitude. The PORTOLAN CHART—a navigational chart similar to the periplus of the ancient Greeks—containing accurate geographic information, although without latitude and longitude, was common by at least the beginning of the 14th century.

The greatest geographers and cartographers of the Middle Ages were the Arab Muslims, who maintained the cartographic principles of Ptolemy and the Greeks (see MUSLIM EXPLORATION). In the 11th century, scholar ABU AR-RAYHAN MUHAMMAD IBN AHMAD AL-BIRUNI made observations on Earth's circumference and latitude and longitude. In the 12th century, ABU ABD ALLAH MUHAMMAD ASH-SHARIF AL-IDRISI produced an influential work, *The Book of Roger,* which contained 70 accurate maps making use of a grid system, as well as accounts of his and others' travels in Europe, North Africa, and the Middle East. In the 13th century, SHIHAB AL-DIN ABU ABD ALLAH YAQUT AL-RUMI, a Greek-born Muslim, published a gazetteer-type geographic study. And, in the 14th century, ABU ABD ALLAH MUHAMMAD IBN BATTUTAH traveled more than any other known individual to date, as far as the edge of SIBERIA in Central Asia and across the SAHARA DESERT in Africa, and wrote detailed descriptions of the lands he visited. In the meantime, the Chinese recorded information on distant lands. In 1311–20, cartographer CHU SSU-PEN produced a world map with accurate information on Africa.

By the late Middle Ages, Europeans were again looking eastward. The CRUSADES of the late 11th century to the late 13th century took them to the Near East. Also in the 13th and 14th centuries, a number of diplomats, missionaries, and merchants, such as Venetian merchant MARCO POLO in the 1270s–90s, traveled to regions of the Far East as well. Marco Polo wrote descriptions of places he had visited. Much of this information was incorporated by Spaniard ABRAHAM CRESQUES in his *Catalan Atlas* of 1375, a world map based on geographic information obtained from Marco Polo and other travelers.

The European Age of Exploration

The 14th century is cited as the beginning of the RENAISSANCE in Europe, a time of an expanding worldview, and the 15th century as the start of the EUROPEAN AGE OF EXPLORATION, initiated by the Portuguese voyages of exploration along the west coast of Africa. In 1492, the same year that CHRISTOPHER COLUMBUS made the post-Viking European discovery of the Americas, German cartographer MARTIN BEHAIM, working for the Portuguese, developed a globe of the world depicting islands in the Atlantic Ocean.

The 16th century experienced a burst of cartographic creativity in Europe, as mapmakers recorded the abundance of new geographic information from the voyages of exploration

to the Americas and beyond. The rediscovery and translation into Latin of Ptolemy's *Geographia* in about 1410 helped set the stage. The development of printing via German Johannes Gutenberg's invention of the movable type printing press, as well as advances in engraving in the mid-15th century, made cartography more practical. (The earliest European printed maps were made from woodcuts.) The printing press also made books on geography available to the general public. And the extent of the Earth came to be understood finally with the first CIRCUMNAVIGATION OF THE WORLD for Spain under FERDINAND MAGELLAN in 1519–22.

Among the many cartographic breakthroughs were the first world map depicting the Americas and showing a coastline from present-day Newfoundland to Argentina by German MARTIN WALDSEEMÜLLER in 1507. Spanish cartographers active in mid-century, such as GONZALO FERNÁNDÉZ DE OVIEDO Y VALDEZ and DIEGO GUTIÉRREZ, depicted explorations in the Caribbean and South America. In 1569, Flemish cartographer GERARDUS MERCATOR created the first map accurately depicting latitude and longitude through his mapmaking techniques known as the MERCATOR PROJECTION, one method of representing

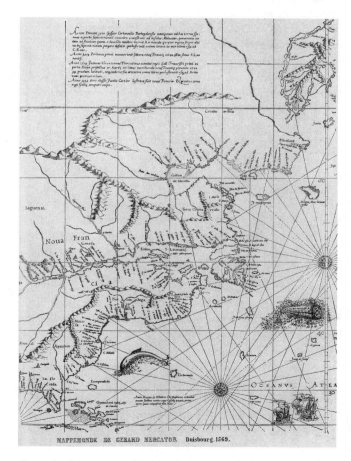

Gerardus Mercator published this world map in 1569. *(Library of Congress, Prints and Photographs Division [LC-USZ62-92883])*

Earth's curve on a flat surface. Because of its accuracy, this cartographic technique revolutionized navigation (see NAVIGATION AND EXPLORATION). The next year, another Flemish cartographer, a friend and associate of Mercator, ABRAHAM ORTELIUS, produced a world atlas. In his annual editions through the end of the century, he stayed abreast of new geographic discoveries.

A number of Englishmen also contributed to the field of geography and cartography during this period. In 1576, SIR HUMPHREY GILBERT published a work furthering the idea of a NORTHWEST PASSAGE across North America. Although some of his ideas were based on fable, the work contributed to the continuing European fascination with world geography. In the 1580s, RICHARD HAKLUYT published three influential books on exploration and geography, including *The Principal Navigations, Voyages, and Discoveries of the English Nation.* In 1598, MARTIN LLEWELLYN published the first English atlas to show sea routes to the Far East.

An Organized Field of Study

Geography and cartography became more organized as a field of study in the 17th and 18th centuries. In 1625, Nathaniel Carpenter advanced geographic methodology by emphasizing spatial relationships among Earth's physical features. In 1634, Dutch cartographer WILLEM JANSZOON BLAEU published a comprehensive atlas detailing world explorations up to that time, carrying on the tradition established by Ortelius. A German geographer by the name of Bernhardus Varenius became influential in theoretical geography. He defined three branches of the science in his work *Geographia generalis,* published in 1650: one studying the form and dimension of Earth; another studying variables depending upon the position of Earth, such as climate, seasons, and tides; and a third studying relationships of different regions.

Yet many erroneous geographic concepts persisted, such as that of a GREAT SOUTHERN CONTINENT, the legendary Terra Australis, first conceived in ancient times and still promoted in the mid-18th century by French scholar CHARLES DE BROSSES. English mariner JAMES COOK, who brought an appreciation of the sciences to his seamanship and explorations, finally put that particular notion to rest in his voyage of 1776–80 by circumnavigating Antarctica. By the late 18th century, science was typically an official adjunct to exploration. Many maritime expeditions of that period and the early 19th century, like those of Cook and that of Frenchman ANTOINE-RAYMOND-JOSEPH DE BRUNI, chevalier d'Entrecasteaux, in the 1790s to the South Pacific Ocean, included naturalists and geographers (see NATURAL SCIENCE AND EXPLORATION). Mapping new regions became the incentive for many overland expeditions, such as those of British fur trader and cartographer DAVID THOMPSON, starting in the 1780s, in western Canada.

Modern Geography

German naturalist ALEXANDER VON HUMBOLDT, who traveled widely, especially at the turn of the 19th century, is sometimes cited as the "father of modern geography." His great contribution was the classification and comparative description of geographic features observed in the field, the approach known as systematic geography, as put forth in his five-volume work *Kosmos,* published in 1845–62.

Another German, Carl Ritter, promoted the comparative study of particular areas, the approach known as regional geography, as presented in his 19-volume work *Geography and Its Relation to Nature and the History of Man,* published in 1822–59. The German geographer, Friedrich Ratzel, helped develop the field of cultural geography—the study of the distribution of people and their cultures in particular regions of Earth—in his work *Anthropogeographie,* published in 1882.

Many other geographers of the 19th and 20th centuries helped shape the discipline as it has come to be practiced today. And a number of geographic societies founded in the 19th century—such as England's ROYAL GEOGRAPHICAL SOCIETY; the United States's AMERICAN GEOGRAPHICAL SOCIETY and National Geographic Society; and France's Société de Géographie—helped further interest in the field and promote the gathering of information through the sponsorship of expeditions.

Expanding Technologies

Modern technology has revolutionized geographic studies and cartographic representations. Photography, including infrared photography and AERIAL PHOTOGRAPHY, some of it by SATELLITE, along with specialized sensors, such as multispectral scanners, has aided in the recording of geographic information and computers in the quantitative analysis of it. Computers are also used in mapping. The Geographic Information System (GIS), a computer system introduced in the 1960s, processes huge amounts of data and can create two- or three-dimensional images of an area. The vast majority of Earth's surface has now been accurately mapped.

Many different processes are utilized in modern mapmaking, among them photoengraving, wax engraving, lithography, or modeling in clay, plaster of paris, or plastic.

Gibraltar, Strait of (Bab al-Zakak, Gaditan Strait, the Straits, Straits of Gibraltar)

The Strait of Gibraltar (or the Straits of Gibraltar, or simply the Straits) is a narrow passage connecting the MEDITERRANEAN SEA to the east with the Atlantic Ocean to the west, situated between Europe to the north and Africa to the south. About 30 miles long and eight to 24 miles wide, the strait has a continuous current flowing easterly from the Atlantic, and a westerly undercurrent carrying salty outflow from the Mediterranean. The term *Gibraltar* is derived from the Arabic *jebel* for mountain and *Tariq,* the name of a Moorish general who invaded Spain in 711. Another name is Gaditan Strait from the Latin *Fretum Gaditanum.* The Arab name is Bab al-Zakak.

The eastern entrance to the Strait of Gibraltar is flanked by two promontories, known since ancient times as the Pillars of Hercules (or the Gates of Hercules). The European promontory, the Rock of Gibraltar (also Calpe, a name given by the Romans), a limestone formation, is situated on a British-ruled peninsula connected to the Iberian Peninsula and Spain; the town of Gibraltar lies at the peninsula's northwestern end. The African promontory, known as Jebel Musa (also Abyla), lies to the west of Ceuta, a Spanish town surrounded by the nation of Morocco. A Greek myth holds that Hercules, the son of the god Zeus, wrenched apart a mountain range to join the seas; another is that he left the pillars there during his travels.

The narrow strait served as a barrier to ancient peoples navigating the Mediterranean. It is not known which mariners of the ancient world first ventured through it into the Atlantic. Artifacts crafted by Minoans from the island of Crete in the eastern Mediterranean have been found as far west as the Balearic Islands off the east coast of Spain. The Phoenicians from the Mediterranean east coast also traveled the entire sea in their GALLEY ships. The writings of the fifth-century B.C. Greek historian HERODOTUS indicate that, sailing for the pharaoh NECHO II in about 600–597 B.C., Phoenicians followed the RED SEA southward from the

This late 19th-century photograph shows the Rock of Gibraltar, which flanks the Strait of Gibraltar from the European side. *(Library of Congress [LC-USZ62-91741])*

Gulf of Aqaba to the Indian Ocean and possibly circumnavigated Africa, returning to the Mediterranean by way of the Atlantic and Strait of Gibraltar. It is known from other Greek and Roman writings that, in the fifth century B.C., Carthaginians—Phoenicians from the city of Carthage in North Africa, in particular HANNO and HIMILCO—navigated past the Strait of Gibraltar and explored the Atlantic coastlines of Europe and Africa. The Carthaginians, in order to control trade with Atlantic coastal regions, guarded the strait and promoted the idea of sea monsters and other hazards beyond. The Greeks eventually managed to pass through it, the mariner and scholar PYTHEAS for one, in the fourth century B.C. It came to offer a regular route for trading ships between lands of the Mediterranean and of the Atlantic coasts of Europe and Africa.

See also CARTHAGINIAN EXPLORATION; GREEK EXPLORATION; MINOAN EXPLORATION; PHOENICIAN EXPLORATION; ROMAN EXPLORATION.

globe

The term *globe* refers to a round body. It also is applied to a spherical map, or model, of Earth or the heavens. A model of Earth, known as a terrestrial globe, represents Earth without the typical distortion of flat maps. A model of the heavens, known as a celestial globe, is a representation of the nighttime sky as seen from Earth. Both types of globes, like flat maps, are tools of navigation.

Globes have been made from wood, metal, plaster, or papier-mâché. The cartographic information is engraved and sometimes drawn on the sphere, or on printed parchment or paper sections with the information—known as gores—glued over it. For modern globes, plastics are also sometimes used. Some terrestrial globes show relief features of Earth. Globes are often attached to a rod running from the NORTH POLE to the SOUTH POLE, which represents the axis around which the Earth rotates, and are tilted at an angle of about 23.5 degrees, indicating the tilt of Earth away from the axis of the Sun.

The primary advantage of a globe is accuracy regarding the shape and curvature of Earth (although most do not show the flattening of Earth at the Poles or the bulge below the EQUATOR). Globes have the added advantage over flat maps of representing long routes, such as by air or sea, as well as natural events that follow the curvature of Earth, such as earthquake shocks and tidal waves. The disadvantages of globes for navigators are their bulkiness and their limitation in showing detail for portions of the Earth.

The ancient Greeks first scientifically made the case that Earth was a sphere. In the fifth century B.C., Greek philosopher Parmenides hypothesized that Earth was round. In the fourth century B.C., Greek philosopher Aristotle recognized that all matter tends to fall toward a common center; that, in traveling from north to south, new constellations become visible while others disappear; and that, during an eclipse, Earth casts a circular shadow on the Moon. The first known globe dates from about 150 B.C., reported to have been constructed by Greek geographer Crates of Mallus. In the second-century A.D., Greek-Egyptian PTOLEMY wrote about the accuracy of globes as well as their limitation in scale. Yet, the view that Earth was flat persisted among many peoples for centuries to come. In 1230, an English mathematician and astronomer, JOHN HOLYWOOD, published *Treatise on the Sphere,* presenting the idea that Earth might be spherical. It was not until the 14th century and the RENAISSANCE, however, that geographic theories of the ancient Greeks and the Muslims became widely known in Europe and changed long-held views. In any case, by the 15th century, European scholars generally accepted the notion of Earth's roundness.

The oldest extant globe was made in 1492 by German cartographer MARTIN BEHAIM—Behaim's *Erdapfel,* or "earth apple," as it was called. Behaim used a plaster mix over a spherical mold and pasted strips of parchment to the surface; he then mounted it on a wooden tripod. The 15th–16th-century Italian artist and scientist Leonardo da Vinci also made globes. GERARDUS MERCATOR, famous for the MERCATOR PROJECTION, a type of mapmaking with a practical depiction of LATITUDE AND LONGITUDE, constructed a world globe in 1541 and, 10 years later, a celestial globe. The earliest known English globes were made by Emery Molyneux in 1592, much of the geographic information for them provided by English mariner JOHN DAVIS.

See also GEOGRAPHY AND CARTOGRAPHY; GREEK EXPLORATION; MAPS AND CHARTS; MUSLIM EXPLORATION; NAVIGATION AND EXPLORATION.

gnomon

A gnomon is any device used to tell time by the shadow it casts. The term is also applied to the specific part of a sundial that casts the shadow. Gnomons have been made in a variety of forms throughout the ages. The gnomon was possibly the first scientific instrument and one of the earliest devices—along with the sounding pole for measuring water depth—used for the purpose of navigation. From the length of a shadow cast, an approximation of latitude could be made. Gnomons were produced as portable objects, and there is mention of them being taken along on ancient sea voyages. Early mariners would have taken them ashore to determine relative location.

Poles and large stones have been used as gnomons. The ancient Egyptians told time by the shadows cast by pyramids and obelisks. Some gnomons had notches in their side to provide readings. In the Middle Ages, the Vikings made use of a type of sundial known as a sun-measuring disk, or shadow board, which floated in a tub of water to level it. The gnomon—in this case, an adjustable center pin—could be raised or lowered based on the height of the sun at different times of the year. The shadows cast on concentric circles on the disk on which were marked directional points would help determine latitude.

See also LATITUDE AND LONGITUDE; NAVIGATION AND EXPLORATION.

Gobi Desert

The Gobi Desert, located in present-day Mongolia and northern China, with an area of about 500,000 square miles, is one of the largest deserts in the world. Shaped like a crescent and extending about 1,000 miles from east to west and 600 miles from north to south, it sits on a plateau from 3,000 to 5,000 feet above sea level and is mostly surrounded by steppe land and high mountains. These include the Da Hinggan Ling to the east, the Altun Shan and Nan Shan to the south, and the Altai, Hangayn Nuruu, and Yablonovy to the north. The far western region of the Gobi, from the foot of the Pamir Plateau, through the Tarim River basin to Lop Nor, the dried-up bed of an immense salt lake, is often considered separately and called the Takla Makan.

The name *Gobi* is Mongolian for "waterless place," while the Chinese refer to the desert as Yintai Shamo, meaning "sand desert," and Han-hai for "dry sea." Only the southwestern quarter of the desert, however, is entirely without water; the remainder is covered with sparse vegetation, mostly grass, shrubs, and thorns. Most of the Gobi is covered with a shallow layer of gravel; only a small percentage consists of sand dunes.

Nomadic peoples inhabit the Gobi, their flocks surviving on what vegetation there is. Frequent high winds lead to dangerous sandstorms. Violent late-summer thunderstorms create large shallow lakes, but the only reliable sources of water for inhabitants of the plateau are wells and springs. The temperature in the Gobi varies from the extremes of minus 40 degrees Fahrenheit in the short winter to 113 degrees in the summer.

Mongols and Chinese in the Gobi

The Mongols, who inhabited the Gobi Desert and surrounding steppe country, were a nomadic people who hunted and maintained herds of horses and sheep and lived in tents (see MONGOL EXPLORATION). They were divided into warring tribal groups until GENGHIS KHAN united them in the early 13th century. He founded his capital—Karakorum—in the northern Gobi.

The main east-west trade route, called the SILK ROAD, ran along a narrow band called the Hexi Corridor, skirting the southern edge of the Gobi Desert. But the desert itself contained several important caravan trails, carrying goods from Partizansk in Russia to Hami in China, and from Zhangjikou in China to Ulaanbaatar, a major city of Mongolia. The Gobi proved a dangerous place for Chinese traveling westward (see CHINESE EXPLORATION). HSÜAN-TSANG, a Chinese Buddhist monk hoping to reach India to obtain original Buddhist texts and visit holy sites, denied passage by the T'ang emperor, set out in secret, in about A.D. 629, from the western end of the Great Wall of China, and entered the Gobi. Abandoned by his guide, Hsüan-tsang wandered through the desert strewn with the bleached bones of animals. He was saved when his horse, smelling water, carried him to an oasis. From there, nomadic tribesmen escorted him out of the Gobi, and he resumed his travel to the west.

Europeans in the Gobi

The earliest European reports of the Gobi Desert come from the travels of MARCO POLO. Polo, a native of Venice, was the son of NICCOLÒ POLO, a merchant who along with Marco's uncle MAFFEO POLO had traveled across Asia to the court of the Great Khan in the East. In 1271, at age 17, Marco accompanied his father and uncle on their second journey to the East. After failing to find acceptable passage by sea, the Polos decided to travel overland. They traveled through Afghanistan, along the edge of the Takla Makan desert, to the city at Lop Nor on the edge of the Gobi. They joined a camel caravan crossing the desert and were met in Inner Mongolia by a representative of Kublai Khan. After 24 years in service to the kahn, the Polos returned to Venice. Marco Polo recorded his voyages, which were met with intense skepticism.

There was relatively little western travel through the Gobi Desert, and, when there was, it followed the pattern of the Polos, staying on traditional caravan trails. As a result, the desert remained mostly uncharted through the 19th century, despite visits by a number of Europeans of varying nationalities. A French Jesuit priest named Jean François Gerbillon traveled across the desert in the 1680s. The first significant exploration of the Gobi was undertaken by NIKOLAY MIKHAILOVICH PRZHEVALSKY, a Russian Cossack and career military officer. Przhevalsky volunteered in 1867 for service along the Russia-China border, writing a report about the region's natural history and the culture of its native peoples. Afterward, he formulated a plan for exploring the interior of Mongolia and China, which was sponsored by the Russian Imperial Geographic Society. In 1870, Przhevalsky and two Russian companions obtained camels and crossed the Gobi Desert to Peking (Beijing) in China. Przhevalsky later explored the Takla Makan desert, and became the first European to visit Lop Nor since Marco Polo.

In 1872–73, Englishman NEY ELIAS traveled from China across the Gobi Desert, the Altai Mountains, SIBERIA, and the Ural Mountains into Europe; he later led a number of other exploratory expeditions to central Asia. In 1923, during one of his many expeditions to central Asia, Swede SVEN ANDERS HEDIN headed a scientific survey of the Gobi. American paleontologist Roy Chapman Andrews carried out a scientific expedition to the Gobi on behalf of the American Museum of Natural History that year and four others over the next years until the Chinese Civil War ended his travels in 1930. In addition to expanding geological understanding of the Gobi, he found there the first fossilized dinosaur eggs.

❖

A highway now crosses the Gobi Desert. A railroad, the Trans-Mongolian, links the city of Ulan Bator, Mongolia, with Jining, China.

gold rush   See TREASURE AND EXPLORATION.

Gonneville's Land

In 1504, a French seafarer named Binot Palmière de Gonneville (also cited as Palmier, Paulmier, or Paulmyer de Gonneville) returned to his hometown, the seaport of Honfleur in northwestern France, and claimed that, in the course of a voyage to the Americas the year before, his ship the *Espoir* had been driven off course into the southern Atlantic Ocean by a storm, and that he and his men had located a land where the inhabitants lived in peace and contentment and with plentiful resources. Gonneville and his crew claimed to have stayed there six months. As evidence of this paradise—an Eden, as he described it—he displayed furs and feathers from unknown species as well as exotic pigments. He had also brought 24 "savages" back to Europe, one of them the son of a ruler, named Essomeric.

Gonneville's Eden became known as Gonneville's Land, and the story of it endured for centuries. At the time, many Europeans were convinced of the existence of a GREAT SOUTHERN CONTINENT, or Terra Australis, and Gonneville's Land became associated with it. More than two centuries later, maps showed a "Terre de Gonneville" in the South Atlantic as part of Terra Australis. In 1738–39, JEAN-BAPTISTE-CHARLES BOUVET DE LOZIER carried out an expedition in search of the fabled continent, locating what became known as Bouvet Island in the South Atlantic in the process. Moreover, noted French scholar CHARLES DE BROSSES, in his work *Histoire de la navigation aux terres australes* (History of Navigation to Southern Lands), published in 1756, cited Gonneville's 16th-century expedition as one of several voyages indicating the existence of Terra Australis.

Given that Gonneville's return to France is documented, and that Essomeric was known to be baptized and to have started a family in Normandy, the fact of

Gonneville's expedition is not disputed. It is likely that Gonneville's Land was actually somewhere in South America, probably Brazil. That would make Essomeric and the other visitors the earliest Native Americans to visit France.

Great Dividing Range

The Great Dividing Range, or Great Divide, is a mountain chain along the eastern edge of Australia, from Cape York Peninsula in the north to TASMANIA, an island off the southeast coast, in the south. The range as a whole is also called the Eastern Highlands. Sections of the range are known by various names, including Atherton Plateau, Australian Alps, BLUE MOUNTAINS, Clarke Range, Drummond Range, Expedition Range, Grampians, Gregory Range, McPherson Range, New England Range, Snowy Mountains, and Warrumbungle Range. The mountains not only divide the fertile east coast from the grasslands to the west, but also separate the rivers that flow into the Pacific Ocean from those that enter the Indian Ocean. The daunting terrain of the Blue Mountains kept early colonists from venturing very far from their coastal settlement at Sydney for several decades. Other parts of the Great Dividing Range proved just as difficult. Some plateau regions became productive grazing lands, however. Mount Kosciusko, Australia's highest peak at 7,310 feet above sea level, is located in the Australian Alps.

Early Expeditions

After GREGORY BLAXLAND, WILLIAM CHARLES WENTWORTH, and William Lawson succeeded in penetrating the Blue Mountains to Mount York in 1813, the exploration of the Great Dividing Range began in earnest. The energetic governor of New South Wales, Lachlan Macquarie, sent George William Evans to survey the new territory later that year. He came across lands that could be developed for grazing. By order of the governor, a road was quickly built using the supply of convict labor. The laborers, many of whom were sent to Australia for petty offenses, earned their freedom for their efforts. Bathurst, a new settlement, became a launching point for many subsequent expeditions.

Hopes for the discovery of more productive lands were high, but finding usable routes for transportation were also a priority. In 1817, Macquarie sent JOHN JOSEPH WILLIAM MOLESWORTH OXLEY from Bathurst to follow the course of the Lachlan River. He was accompanied by Evans and botanist ALLAN CUNNINGHAM, who would go on to make significant discoveries of his own. Oxley was stopped when the Lachlan became marshland, but he then circled around to the Macquarie River and explored new territory in the range. His expedition the following year was more successful, but more difficult. In April 1818, he led a party to the upper Macquarie River, also hoping to find it a useful means of transportation. They encountered heavy rains, and much

of his party stayed behind. Making his way downstream via boat, he came upon thick reeds towering seven feet above the waterline. After slogging through this second stretch of marshland and crossing mountains, which he called the Arbuthnot Range, Oxley came upon the Liverpool Plains, another region ideal for grazing. The problem of transportation had yet to be solved, however. Oxley and company headed east through the mountains, touching the southern border of the New England Range and reaching the east coast at Port Macquarie.

There were finally some results in finding transportation for people and their livestock in 1823. In June of that year, Allan Cunningham started out from the Hunter River Valley to the north of Sydney on an arduous journey of 500 miles. His efforts were rewarded with the European discovery of Pandora's Pass in the Liverpool Range, connecting Bathurst with the Liverpool Plains. The migration of farmers to the mountains took on new dimensions.

The expedition in 1824 of HAMILTON HUME and WILLIAM HILTON HOVELL led to the European discovery of the Australian Alps. From the Lake George region to the south of Bathurst, they trekked along the western side of the Great Dividing Range, first crossing the Murrumbidgee River. Heading on a southwest course, they encountered the beginnings of the Murray River, then crossed the Ovens and Goulburn Rivers as well. They located more farmland before crossing the Alps on their way to Port Phillip Bay at the location of present-day Melbourne, a suitable place for settlement. But Hovell misidentified the geographic coordinates of that site as Western Bay, where the soil is poor. A contingent of colonists who attempted to settle Western Bay by mistake were compelled to abandon the spot, delaying the settlement of what would become the state of Victoria for a number of years.

In 1827, Allan Cunningham carried out his most important expedition farther to the north in the Great Dividing Range than had been attempted before. He set out in May of that year with a guide named Macintyre, six men, and 11 horses across the Liverpool Range. He skirted the western border of the New England Range and located several rivers along his path—the Naomi, Gwydir, Dumaresq, and Macintyre. On June 8, he encountered a vast expanse of grassland from a hill near the Macintyre. He named it Darling Downs after the governor of New South Wales, Sir Ralph Darling. Darling Downs would prove to be the best farmland in the state of Queensland. The following year, he found a route from the Downs to the Pacific coast through the mountains, known as Cunningham's Gap, which made development of the region practical.

Post-Settlement

As the country was preoccupied with the settlement of the new grazing lands, interest in new explorations waned for a period. In 1840, Polish geographer SIR PAUL EDMUND DE STRZELECKI explored the Australian Alps and climbed the tallest peak in the Great Dividing Range and all of Australia, naming it Mount Kosciusko, after Polish national hero and military leader Tadeusz Kościuszko. The next great explorer of the Great Dividing Range was Prussian naturalist FRIEDRICH WILHELM LUDWIG LEICHHARDT. After traveling by foot along Australia's east coast from Sydney to Moreton Bay in 1843, he found private sponsorship for a larger expedition north through the mountains, much to the consternation of SIR THOMAS LIVINGSTONE MITCHELL, who had intended to lead a party along the same route. In October 1444, Leichhardt led his 10 men—among them two Aborigine guides—from Darling Downs through the mountains to the north, always keeping within 10 miles of a supply of water. The journey was beset with problems, as pack animals escaped and food was consumed at too rapid a rate, but Leichhardt did not lack for courage. On June 25, 1445, the party succeeded in crossing the range to the north and came upon the Mitchell River, where they were attacked by Aborigines. John Gilbert, an ornithologist in the group, was killed; others were injured. On Leichhardt's insistence, the expedition continued westward, arriving at Port Essington, the site of present-day Darwin, on December 17. Leichhardt was given a hero's welcome and received a large cash prize. He would later disappear on his attempt to cross Australia from east to west in 1848, generating one of the great unsolved mysteries of Australian exploration.

Sir Thomas Mitchell organized his own expedition through the Great Dividing Range in 1845. With a large contingent of 28 men, plus 250 sheep, horses, and oxen, he left the interior near Bourke in December. A messenger soon informed him of the successful conclusion of the Leichhardt expedition, but Mitchell continued on his own route. As he and his group curved to the northeast, they explored new territory. Heading westward, they traversed the Chesterton Range and Warrego Range, then came to the start of the Grey Range. Mitchell's quest for new land was satisfied when he reached the productive grazing lands of the Maranoa region.

The exploration of the Great Dividing Range was largely motivated by a need for new pasture to support the herding industry. England had become a lucrative market for the fine wool that Australia produced, and migrations from the British Isles increased as the passage became less expensive. Newly explored lands were settled at a rapid rate.

❖

In the 20th century, some mountain areas themselves have been settled. The Australian Alps are now known for their skiing resorts.

See also AUSTRALIA, EXPLORATION OF.

Great Southern Continent (Terra Australis, Terra Australis Incognita)

The Great Southern Continent, also known as Terra Australis (Latin for "southern land") or Terra Australis Incognita ("unknown southern land"), was an imaginary land thought to exist in the Southern Hemisphere. The first to conceive of its existence were the ancient Greeks (see GREEK EXPLORATION), who had realized that the Earth was a sphere and devised a geographic theory based on balance and symmetry, including a southern region to mirror the lands of the known world. They maintained that the south must contain a similar ratio of land to sea as the north and must be located in similar temperate zones, thus capable of producing a similar abundance of flora and fauna. In the second century A.D., hellenized Egyptian geographer PTOLEMY proposed that such a continent connected the southern tips of Africa and Asia, which would make the Indian Ocean an inland sea.

An Enduring Legend

The concept of Terra Australis proved to be enduring. The publication in Latin of Ptolemy's writings in about 1410 gave new impetus to it among Europeans. Terra Australis was depicted in numerous ways by the mapmakers of the 15th century and afterward during the EUROPEAN AGE OF EXPLORATION. It was sometimes presented as rather featureless, used to fill space where lands were unknown; or it was presented with rivers and detailed coastlines, offering cartographers a chance to exercise their imagination, as in a map by Flemish ABRAHAM ORTELIUS in 1570, part of the first atlas of modern design. In some instances, the fabled continent was drafted as occupying the entire southernmost portion of the world and contiguous with the southern portions of Africa and South America.

Aside from the ancient idea of balance, there were two other reasons why the belief in Terra Australis persisted in the European mind. One was the failure to grasp the size of the Pacific Ocean. Although astronomical measurements had determined the size of Earth, the integration of this knowledge with knowledge of explored lands was slow to be realized, largely due to the lack of a dependable way to measure longitude (see LATITUDE AND LONGITUDE). Indeed, many earlier geographic discoveries in the Pacific had to be rediscovered during the 17th and 18th centuries since their locations were poorly understood. The other reason Europeans believed in Terra Australis's existence was simply wishful thinking. Terra Australis might yield untold riches to a nation laying claim to it. The dream of such a prize spurred on many expeditions to the South Pacific. One French mariner who perhaps reached southern waters while driven off course in a storm—Binot Palmière de Gonneville—reported locating a paradise in 1504. Although he probably landed in South America, perhaps Brazil, his reported Eden became known as GONNEVILLE'S LAND and helped drive the myth of an unknown southern continent.

16th Century

The scientific search for Terra Australis began with the first CIRCUMNAVIGATION OF THE WORLD by FERDINAND MAGELLAN, a Portuguese mariner sailing for Spain, in 1519–22. Having traveled through the Strait of Magellan (see MAGELLAN, STRAIT OF) between the continent of South America and Tierra del Fuego, Magellan disproved the notion that Terra Australis was connected to the greater landmass, and, although he believed Tierra del Fuego to be an island, he did not have enough data to convince the mapmakers of the day. The theories of Magellan would not be confirmed until Englishman SIR FRANCIS DRAKE's journey in 1577–80, when he rounded the southern tip of CAPE HORN and navigated through Drake's Passage.

In 1567, ÁLVARO DE MENDAÑA and PEDRO SARMIENTO DE GAMBOA were sent by Spain to discover and claim the Great Southern Continent for their homeland. They found the Solomon Islands of Melanesia in the West Pacific, which they believed to foreshadow the continent itself. On a second journey of colonization in 1595, de Mendaña sailed with four ships. He came upon the Marquesas Islands of Polynesia, but the natives were not welcoming, and he pressed on. De Mendaña died at sea, and his wife, nicknamed "the Governess," succeeded to command and steered the expedition to the Philippines.

17th Century

The Spanish continued to be interested in Terra Australis. In 1605, PEDRO FERNÁNDEZ DE QUIRÓS, a Portuguese mariner sailing for Spain, was outfitted with three ships and sailed westward into the Pacific from Lima on the coast of Peru. He had accompanied de Mendaña on his journey a decade earlier and had persisted in his faith of finding the fabled land. His travels were marked by a lack of leadership, and although he came upon several previously unknown islands, his contributions were overshadowed by those of LUIS VÁEZ DE TORRES, who captained one of the ships in the Spanish fleet. He had been separated from Fernández de Quirós, and, continuing to follow the orders he had received in Peru, sailed on a northwestward course. Following the south coast of New Guinea, he passed through the Torres Strait without seeing the southern tip of modern-day Australia. He had demonstrated, however, that New Guinea was an island, and that, if Terra Australis did exist, its size was smaller than expected.

Unknown to Váez de Torres, the continent he had barely missed had been located some months earlier by a Dutchman. While exploring the same region, WILLEM JANSZ sighted Australia's Cape York Peninsula. Having missed the gap, which would become known as Torres Strait, he believed Australia to be a southern extension of New Guinea, which he named New Holland nonetheless. The Dutch had extended their claims in the region but were slow to capitalize on their findings. The waters along the west coast of Australia were hazardous, and the prospect of profitable activity seemed remote. Consequently, Europeans failed to appreciate the size of the new land (which, although it was almost 3 million square miles, was significantly smaller than the theorized Terra Australis).

FREDERIK HOUTMAN explored the coast near the present-day city of Perth in 1619. In 1629, a ship sailing for the DUTCH EAST INDIA COMPANY, the *Batavia,* was wrecked on the west coast of Australia, and archaeological evidence shows that survivors had made a settlement there, the first of its kind.

The next major journey of exploration in search of the Great Southern Continent was also sponsored by the Dutch East India Company and was headed by ABEL JANSZOON TASMAN in 1642. Sailing from west to east, he came upon Van Diemen's Land (present-day TASMANIA), the large island to the south of Australia. Continuing westward, he also made the European discovery of NEW ZEALAND. Next, he explored the Fiji Islands.

As the century progressed, the English began their explorations in the South Pacific. Initially motivated at the prospect of raiding Dutch and Spanish vessels in the region, WILLIAM DAMPIER became the first Englishman to set foot on New Holland during his CIRCUMNAVIGATION OF THE WORLD in 1679–91. Sir Francis Drake was also active in the region at the time.

18th Century

The failure to find a "Great Southland" that fit the expectations of the European imagination did not stop expeditions from being sponsored. In an expedition financed by the DUTCH WEST INDIA COMPANY, JAKOB ROGGEVEEN sailed from Europe in 1721 to continue the quest. His efforts were rewarded with the European discovery of Easter Island and Samoa in the Pacific. His findings eliminated a number of theories about the location and size of Terra Australis, and, after his travels, the Dutch committed considerably fewer resources to the finding of such a land. In 1739, Frenchman JEAN-BAPTISTE-CHARLES BOUVET DE LOZIER made the European discovery of Bouvet Island in the South Atlantic Ocean near the ANTARCTIC CIRCLE while looking for the fabled southern landmass.

In the latter half of the 18th century, England and France began to take the lead in Pacific exploration. With improved techniques in navigation, a mania for natural science, and a growing hunger for land, these two countries transplanted their historic rivalry to the uncharted regions in the south. French scholar CHARLES DE BROSSES, who published *Histoire de la navigation aux terres australes* (History of Navigation to Southern Lands), continued to promote the equilibrium theory of land in the Southern Hemisphere to counterbalance the Northern Hemisphere.

The 1764–66 expedition of JOHN BYRON is called by some the first scientific voyage of exploration. After claiming the Falkland Islands for Great Britain, he traveled extensively in the South Pacific. In 1766–69, Frenchman LOUIS-ANTOINE DE BOUGAINVILLE, a soldier with an analytical mind, explored the region. He sought Terra Australis along the east coast of New Holland and among the New Hebrides Islands, of which he made the European discovery. Although he did not find Terra Australis, his expedition collected a wealth of plant and animal specimens, giving support to the practice of scientific exploration.

Also in 1766, SAMUEL WALLIS and PHILLIP CARTERET were sent by England to find the Great Southern Continent. In April 1767, they were separated by bad weather. Wallis went on to make the European discovery of Tahiti, where the natives proved to be exceptionally hospitable, while Carteret came upon Pitcairn Island. Carteret also filled in the map with the Santa Cruz Islands, rediscovered since Fernández de Quirós's voyage for Spain, and helped define the geography of the Solomon Islands. In 1772–73, Frenchman YVES-JOSEPH DE KERGUÉLEN-TRÉMAREC continued the search on behalf of France and came upon an archipelago in the southern reaches of the Indian Ocean, which he believed to be the coast of Terra Australis and which he called "La France Australe"; they later became known as the Kerguelen Islands.

James Cook

The man who finally laid to rest the idea of the Great Southern Continent was Englishman JAMES COOK. Cook had acquired superior skills as a surveyor and mapmaker while serving in the Royal Navy during the Seven Years War in Canada. He was meticulous and innovative in his work, producing accurate charts. He also had the advantage of a CHRONOMETER on his second journey, a tool necessary for the accurate determination of longitude. His was one of the first voyages to test the instrument. The purpose of Cook's first journey to the South Pacific in 1768 was ostensibly to time the transit of Venus across the Sun as a means to learning the distance between Earth and the Sun. After this task was accomplished, he opened a letter with additional orders, which sent him on a search for Terra Australis. At this stage of his expedition, he sailed as far south as 40 degrees south latitude, beyond where the continent was thought to exist. He then sailed around the two islands that make up New Zealand, making a high-quality map of it in the process. Next he charted much of the east coast of New Holland. Cook's next expedition in 1772–75 compelled Europe to abandon the dream of the fabled land. His instructions were to circumnavigate the southern polar region as closely as possible. The trip was not easy, with the bitter cold freezing the rigging of his vessels, dense fog, and dangerous PACK ICE. Nonetheless, he succeeded in his mission. He is given credit for being the first to cross the ANTARCTIC CIRCLE, which he did three times. The southernmost latitude he attained was 71 degrees. He did not sight the mainland of Antarctica on this trip, however, since his ship was blocked by ice.

❖

There was still important knowledge to be gained of southern waters. Since New Holland had not yet been circumnavigated, most assumed it to be a collection of islands rather than a single continent. MATTHEW FLINDERS accomplished its circumnavigation in 1802–03. He is also responsible for lobbying heavily to rename the continent Australia (see AUSTRALIA, EXPLORATION OF). Early sightings of the land that came to be known as Antarctica were made by Englishman EDWARD BRANSFIELD, American NATHANIEL BROWN PALMER, and Russian FABIAN GOTTLIEB BENJAMIN VON BELLINGSHAUSEN, all in 1820. It would take some years to grasp the extent of the Antarctic continent (see ANTARCTIC, EXPLORATION OF THE).

In the course of the search for the Great Southern Continent, two new continents were brought to the world's attention. One of them, Australia, came to bear a name derived from *Terra Australis*.

Great Victoria Desert

The Great Victoria Desert is the vast, arid region located in southwestern Australia to the north of the Nullarbor Plain, which separates it from the Great Australian Bight, an inlet of the Indian Ocean. Some 450 miles long from east to west and with an average altitude of 500 to 1,000 feet, it consists mostly of hilly sand country with some salt lakes and grasslands. It was the last region of Australia to be explored, with the exception of the smaller Simpson Desert in the center of the continent.

This barren area was originally visited by various groups of Aborigines. By the time Europeans turned their attention to it, most of the good grazing land in Australia had been charted. There was a sense among geographers that little of value would be found in the extensive tracts of sand. Still, with the lure of the unknown beckoning, a minor rivalry began among a handful of explorers in the early 1870s. JOHN FORREST had led an expedition in 1869 from Perth on a search for the remains of the FRIEDRICH WILHELM LUDWIG LEICHHARDT expedition, which had vanished 20 years before. On this trip he had gone as far east as Mount Weld on the western edge of the desert, finding some new grasslands suitable for grazing.

On an unsuccessful attempt to make an east-to-west crossing of the continent, WILLIAM CHRISTIE GOSSE traveled deeper into the desert in 1873. He passed through the end of its northern region, below the Musgrave Ranges to the north. It was on this journey that he came upon Ayer's Rock, one of Australia's most distinctive geological features, a block of sandstone rising 2,845 feet above the surrounding flatlands.

In 1874, John Forrest returned to the western desert regions with his brother ALEXANDER FORREST, hoping to make the first west-to-east crossing of Australia. Traveling across the southern portion of the Gibson Desert, he succeeded in reaching the Peake telegraph station after five and a half months. His success led ERNEST GILES to form his own plan of exploration.

On a journey in 1872–73, Giles had attempted to cross the Great Victoria and the Gibson Deserts, but had failed to do so, losing his companion, Alfred Gibson, in the process, for which he named the region. Giles had gained valuable experience on this trip, however, and proved the worth of camels for traveling through the brutal conditions of the desert. In May 1875, he left Port Augusta with Henry Tietkins, an Afghani camel driver named Saleh, and 24 camels. The land they crossed in the southern portion of the desert was desolate. Relief was found midway through the trip when they crossed a northern projection of the Nullarbor Plain and were able to replenish their water supplies. In November, after traveling 2,500 miles, the party reached Perth, having made the first successful east-to-west crossing of Australia.

Ernest Giles named the region the Great Victoria Desert after Queen Victoria of Great Britain. A subsequent explorer to help map it, David Lindsay, took a different diagonal route in 1891. The Great Victoria Desert became part of the states of South Australia and Western Australia.

Greek exploration (ancient Greek exploration)

The geographic region referred to as ancient Greece was centered on the Balkan Peninsula and the Peloponnesus, a large peninsula connected to the southern end of the Balkan Peninsula, and on Crete and other nearby islands in the western MEDITERRANEAN SEA. But ancient Greeks, or Hellenes, as they called themselves, came to inhabit much of the northern Mediterranean and Black Sea coastal regions, during the first millennium B.C. Greek civilization has been called the cradle of Western civilization because of achievements in science, mathematics, philosophy, literature, and art, as well as the introduction of the political system of democracy. The Greeks also played a significant role in the history of exploration.

Pre-Hellenic Greece is referred to as Aegean civilization, with three highly developed Bronze Age cultures—Minoan, Mycenaean, and Cycladic. The Minoan culture thrived on the island of Crete; the Mycenaean culture on the mainland; and the Cycladic culture on the Cyclades island group. The Minoans, as wide-ranging traders, were some of the earliest explorers of the Mediterranean until their decline toward the end of the second millennium, at which time the rival Phoenicians of present-day Lebanon became the most active mariners.

Beginning about 1400 B.C., various peoples speaking related Greek dialects reached the Greek peninsula from the north—Achaeans, Aolians, Ionians, and Dorians. From about 1000 to 750 B.C., after the Mycenaean collapse, the region was in a political vacuum with warfare and poverty rampant—the Greek Dark Age, as it is sometimes called. During what is known as the Archaic Age, from about 750 to 480 B.C., independent city-states formed and eventually united against the threat from Persia (present-day Iran). The Persian Wars began in 512 B.C., when the revolt of Greek colonies in Asia Minor against their Persian landlords led to an unsuccessful Persian invasion of Greece—with Greek victories at Marathon, Salamis, and Plataea—and lasted until 449 B.C.

During the Classical Age, from about 480 to 323 B.C., Greek civilization reached its pinnacle. From 480 to 359 B.C., Athens was the most powerful city-state and led an alliance of almost 150 city-states in the creation of the Athenian empire surrounding the Aegean Sea. The Peloponnesian War between Athens and the city-state of Sparta, situated to its south in Peloponnesus, in 431–404 B.C., led to the decline of Athens. The Macedonians, a people living to the north of Greece, became a dominant military power first under Phillip II and then under his son, ALEXANDER THE GREAT, leading to their supremacy from 359 to 323 B.C. Although not Greek-speaking, the Macedonian rulers came to think of themselves as part of the Greek tradition and furthered Greek culture through conquest of the Egyptians of northern Africa and eastward into Asia as far as India. After Alexander's death, his generals ruled in what is referred to as the Hellenistic period, which lasted until 31 B.C. and the ascendancy of the Romans.

The Minoan mastery of navigation was passed to the Greeks, who carried out the tradition of trade throughout the Mediterranean region and into the Black Sea, which is connected to the Aegean Sea by the Bosporus, the Sea of Marmara, and the Dardanelles. By about 500 B.C., the Greeks had colonized parts of Asia Minor, Mediterranean coastal regions of present-day Italy and France, the Iberian Peninsula, and even the present-day coastal Libya in northern Africa. They came to have some 700 settlements, some of which evolved into independent city-states. Transported items in the complex trading network of the Mediterranean and Black Sea regions included silver, copper, tin, amber, obsidian, ivory, timber, dyes, grains, salt, fish, wine, olive oil, pottery, and glass. The Greeks also may have ventured into the Atlantic Ocean as early as the sixth century B.C. Their commercial activity contributed to the diffusion of cultural traits and geographic knowledge. The Greek invention of the ASTROLABE in the third or second century B.C. helped further maritime exploration.

The names of certain Greek individuals have endured in the historical record as explorers, historians, and cartographers, in some cases in the employ of other peoples. In about 520–494 B.C., historian HECATAEUS OF MILETUS ascended the NILE RIVER. In 510–507 B.C., mariner SCYLAX descended the INDUS RIVER for Persian emperor Darius I and sailed from the Arabian Sea to the RED SEA. In about 440–420 B.C., historian HERODOTUS traveled throughout eastern Mediterranean Sea and Black Sea lands and chronicled much about ancient history and exploration. He also traveled up the Nile. In about 420–400 B.C., physician and writer CTESIAS OF CNIDUS traveled in Persia and India.

One great journey was actually a military retreat. In 401 B.C., soldier and historian XENOPHON led Greek mercenaries on a great retreat from Persia through present-day Iraq, Turkey, Armenia, and Georgia to Greece. Macedonian Alexander the Great's remarkable trek into Africa and Asia in 334–323 B.C., exploration by conquest, brought new awareness of Asia to European cultures. NEARCHUS, a Greek serving under Alexander, explored the coasts of Pakistan and Iran from the Indus Delta to the head of the Persian Gulf in 325–324 B.C. MEGASTHENES, a Greek diplomat, traveled from Syria to northern India in 300–290 B.C., reaching the GANGES RIVER.

In the meantime, the maritime expedition of PYTHEAS in about 325 B.C. along the coasts of Spain, France, and Britain as far as the Baltic Sea brought knowledge of northern Europe to the Mediterranean peoples. The water route between Africa and India was explored in 120–115 B.C. by EUDOXUS, a Greek navigator in service to Egypt, who made two trips across the Arabian Sea to India. On the second, he landed on the coast of East Africa; he later unsuccessfully tried to circumnavigate Africa. In A.D. 45, HIPPALUS, another Greek in service of Egypt, at that time under Roman domination, navigated a direct sea route across the Arabian Sea from Africa to India. And, in A.D. 50, DIOGENES, a Greek merchant, explored inland on Africa's east coast, possibly as far as Lake Victoria and Lake Albert.

Some of the knowledge of these ancient travels was recorded by ERATOSTHENES, a Greek scholar heading the library at Alexandria in northern Africa. In 240–195 B.C., he wrote what is considered the first systematic treatise of geography. STRABO, another Greek scholar, published an important work on geography in Rome in about A.D. 18. The *Periplus of the Erythraean Sea*, written in about A.D. 100 by an anonymous Greek trader who lived in Egypt, provided information about East Africa, including commercial activities in the region (see PERIPLUS). PTOLEMY, a hellenized Egyptian, published a description of world geography in A.D. 127–147.

See also EGYPTIAN EXPLORATION; GEOGRAPHY AND CARTOGRAPHY; MINOAN EXPLORATION; NAVIGATION AND EXPLORATION; PHOENICIAN EXPLORATION; ROMAN EXPLORATION.

Greenland

At about 840,000 square miles, Greenland is the largest island in the world. From northernmost Cape Morris Jesup to southernmost Cape Farewell, it is about 1,650 miles long; its widest point from east to west is about 800 miles. The coastline, deeply indented with fjords, runs an estimated 27,000 miles. Most of Greenland lies north of the ARCTIC CIRCLE. The Arctic Ocean lies to the north; the Greenland Sea to the east; the Nares Strait to the northwest, separating it from Ellesmere Island; the Denmark Strait to the southeast, separating it from ICELAND; the Davis Strait and Baffin Bay to the west, separating it from Baffin Island; and the Atlantic Ocean to the south. Disko Island in Davis Strait is the largest of the many offshore islands. The Danish name is Grønland; the name in Greenlandic (Inuit, with some Danish words) is Kalaallit Nunaat.

More than three-quarters of Greenland, a high plateau, is covered with an ice cap, the maximum thickness of which is 14,000 feet. Coastal regions and islands are mainly ice free, although some smaller ice caps and glaciers can be found locally near the coasts. The east and west coasts are flanked by mountain chains; Mount Gunnbjørn in southeastern Greenland, at 12,139 feet above sea level, is the highest peak. Greenland produces many of the world's icebergs and ice floes, with ice moving outward from the island's center and calving on reaching the sea (see DRIFT ICE), making the Davis Strait to the west and the Greenland Sea to the east especially hazardous to navigation. The south coast has the warmest climate, moderated by the North Atlantic Drift, a continuation of the GULF STREAM. Vegetation, like much of the Canadian Arctic to the west, consists mostly of mosses, lichens, grasses, and sedges. Some dwarf trees can be found in the south. Greenland also has similar fauna to that of the Canadian Arctic, such as reindeer, musk ox, polar bear, wolf, fox, and hare.

Greenland's indigenous peoples are ancestrally related to the Inuit (Eskimo) of Canada and Alaska and are grouped together as Greenland Inuit. A number of bands traditionally lived along the west coast, including a group north of Cape York on the Hayes Peninsula known by non-natives as Polar Eskimo; a band known as the Anmagssalik (now also the name of a town) traditionally lived along the east coast.

The Vikings

ERIC THE RED is considered the European "discoverer" of Greenland. The account of his journey there in about A.D.

982 is preserved in the literature of the Vikings known as *Eiríks saga*, or the *Saga of Eric the Red*. He may not have been the first Viking to reach or see Greenland since a mariner by the name of Bjarni Gunnbjörn supposedly reported lands to the west of Iceland. Eric the Red established a settlement at an inlet he called Ericsfjord, where present-day Julianehaab is located. From Greenland other Vikings—such as his son, LEIF ERICSSON—explored farther westward, eventually reaching the North American mainland in about 1000. The Norse settlement endured until the early 15th century, when the outbreak of the bubonic plague cut off communication with Scandinavia.

Early Arctic Expeditions

The history of further exploration of Greenland is tied in with that of Arctic Canada. Many European ships navigating the Davis Strait in search of the NORTHWEST PASSAGE explored Greenland's west coast as well as Baffin Island's east coast. Italian mariner JOHN CABOT possibly explored southwestern Greenland in his voyage for England in 1497. In his voyage of 1500, Portuguese mariner GASPAR CÔRTE-REAL is known to have sailed along the west coast of Greenland before being turned back by PACK ICE. In 1576,

Englishman SIR MARTIN FROBISHER stopped at southern Greenland and claimed the region for England—the first confirmed stopover since the Vikings—calling the land "West England," although the claim was not maintained. Davis Strait is named after Englishman JOHN DAVIS, who carried out three expeditions to the waters west of Greenland in the 1580s. Englishman HENRY HUDSON navigated along Greenland's east coast for London's MUSCOVY COMPANY in 1607. Englishman JAMES HALL carried out three expeditions to western Greenland for Denmark in 1605–07, hoping to locate Scandinavian colonists, and made a number of landings and drafted charts of the region. Contact was made with Inuit, but not colonists. In 1612, Hall also headed an expedition to the region for England. In 1616, Englishmen WILLIAM BAFFIN and ROBERT BYLOT explored along Greenland's west coast, reaching Baffin Bay.

In 1721, a Norwegian missionary named HANS EGEDE gained Danish support for a colony to Greenland. It was still hoped that descendants of Viking settlers would be found there. Egede, who landed at present-day Nuuk (formerly known as Godthaab), failed to find Scandinavian survivors there but founded the first permanent European settlement

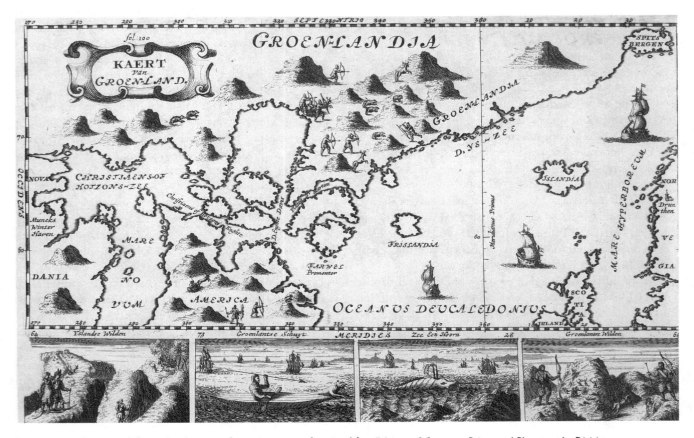

Below an early map of Greenland appear four vignettes of native life. *(Library of Congress, Prints and Photographs Division [LC-USZ62-77699])*

and preached to the Inuit until 1736. A number of trading posts were soon established. Denmark increased the population by deporting undesirable subjects there, much as Great Britain shipped convicts to Australia.

Mapping Greenland

As of 1800, much of Greenland had yet to be mapped. In 1806–13, a German mineralogist named Karl Ludwig Giesecke studied the southeast coast by umiak, a type of Inuit boat (see CANOE). In 1822, Englishman WILLIAM SCORESBY, JR., explored the east coast in the region of Scoresby Land and Scoresby Sound. Many other explorers of varying nations contributed to growing knowledge of the huge island over the years. In 1853–55, American ELISHA KENT KANE, while leading an expedition in search of SIR JOHN FRANKLIN, explored Greenland's Humboldt Gla-cier on the northwest coast, one of the largest glaciers in the world. In 1869–70, German KARL CHRISTIAN KOLDEWEY and Austrian JULIUS VON PAYER explored the east coast.

The Danish Committee for the Geographical and Geological Investigation of Greenland was founded in 1876, leading to a methodical program of research. In 1902–04, Danish LUDWIG MYLIUS-ERICHSEN, accompanied by Danish-Inuit ethnologist KNUD JOHAN VICTOR RASMUSSEN, explored the northwest coast. In 1906–07, Mylius-Erichsen explored the northeast coast, locating the peninsula known as the Northeast Foreland. Rasmussen, who continued his studies of the Inuit people into the 1920s, founded the settlement of Thule, named after the legendary land of ULTIMA THULE, on North Star Bay in the northwest, in 1910. In 1900, American ROBERT EDWIN PEARY reached Greenland's northernmost point—Cape Morris Jesup—and demonstrated conclusively that Greenland was an island and not a landmass extending to the NORTH POLE. American LOUISE ARNER BOYD contributed to the growing geographic and scientific knowledge of Greenland with her studies along the east coast in 1931 and 1933.

Into the Interior

In the meantime, expeditions had begun to venture into Greenland's interior. During his attempt to reach the North Pole in 1860–61, American ISAAC ISRAEL HAYES undertook an inland voyage from the northwest coast and measured the Greenland ice cap at a point where it was some 5,000 feet thick. In 1888, Norwegian FRIDTJOF NANSEN and five others, among them OTTO NEUMANN SVERDRUP, made an east-to-west crossing of southern Greenland on snowshoes and skis, reaching a maximum altitude of 9,000 feet on the ice cap. Rasmussen made a west-to-east crossing in 1912. In 1924–25, American aviator RICHARD EVELYN BYRD carried out the first flights over the Greenland ice cap and charted some 30,000 square miles of territory. In 1929–30, the

German Greenland Expedition under German geologist ALFRED LOTHAR WEGENER established the first permanent weather stations on the ice cap. And in 1930–31, Englishman AUGUSTINE COURTAULD spent the winter alone at about the geographic center of the ice cap, collecting meteorological data, as part of the British Arctic Air Route Expedition of 1930–32 under HENRY GEORGE WATKINS (Gino Watkins). The University of Michigan sponsored a similar American expedition simultaneously. After World War II, scientific expeditions were carried out on a larger scale.

❖

Denmark made Greenland a crown colony in 1924. In a 1979 referendum, Greenlanders voted for home rule, and the island, although still considered part of Denmark, is presently self-governed. The capital and largest city is Nuuk.

See also ARCTIC, EXPLORATION OF THE.

Gulf Stream

The Gulf Stream is one of many OCEAN CURRENTS. A warm water current in the Atlantic Ocean, it greatly affects the climate of North America and Europe and has played an important role in routes used by ships. It is created by easterly winds putting pressure on the Atlantic Ocean, a pressure built up in the Gulf of Mexico. Warming caused by proximity to the EQUATOR also contributes to higher pressure. The water seeks an outlet and forms a northward flowing current, past Florida and along the east coast of North America. At Cape Hatteras, as it runs into the southern branch of the cold Labrador Current, the current takes an eastward course. Farther east it splits into two branches, one passing western GREENLAND, the other passing western ICELAND. The current then continues north to Scandinavia and England, circling around to Spain and Portugal, where it cools down and dissipates. The Gulf Stream has been called "the great river within the ocean."

The Gulf Stream may be observed as it crosses the Atlantic. Its water is a dark gray-blue whereas other water surrounding it is gray-green. This results from the relative lack of minerals and plankton. For great stretches, the Gulf Stream is about 100 miles wide and a mile deep. As it leaves the Gulf of Mexico, its temperature is 80 degrees. The average speed of the Gulf Stream is four knots, which decreases as it branches and widens. It makes the climate milder along its course and creates the unique patterns of rainfall in eastern North America.

Italian mariner CHRISTOPHER COLUMBUS, exploring for Spain, was one of the first Europeans to use the Gulf Stream in navigation. The winds and other ocean currents that propelled him to the Caribbean Sea in 1492 presented an obstacle for his return trip to Spain the next year. Rather than sail back into them, he headed northward and rode the Gulf Stream. In 1513, Spanish conquistador JUAN PONCE DE LEÓN explored the regions where the current originates. In the northeast, the Gulf Stream worked against sailing ships traveling westward from Europe to the northern reaches of North America, delaying extensive exploration of those regions, even as it aided them on their return Atlantic crossings. Whaling captains in colonial New England knew of the Gulf Stream as an area of no whales.

See also ATLANTIC OCEAN, EXPLORATION OF THE.

gyrocompass (gyroscopic compass, gyrostatic compass)

A gyrocompass—or gyroscopic COMPASS or gyrostatic compass—is an electronic device used to determine true north as opposed to magnetic north. The device, if properly maintained, is highly accurate and has a variety of applications aboard a modern ship, such as providing a reference for the interpretation of celestial observations and directing automatic steering mechanisms.

The basic gyroscope is a balanced mass, usually a disk, which is able to spin in any direction about its axis. Once the rotational element is set in motion, its spin axis maintains its direction. This principle is called gyroscopic inertia. In the gyrocompass the axis of the gyroscope is set to run parallel with Earth's north-south axis, or meridian.

The modern version of the gyroscope was developed by French physicist Jean-Bernard-Léon Foucault by 1852. Its uses were multiplied when electric motors were added. The gyrocompass was invented in the early 20th century by American and European scientists and subsequently refined. SUBMARINE navigation benefits from the gyrocompass because of its immunity from the magnetic effects of the steel hull. The gyrocompass is a key component of navigation in modern commercial ships.

See also NAVIGATION AND EXPLORATION.

H

Hadley's Quadrant See QUADRANT; SEXTANT.

Hakluyt Society

The Hakluyt Society is a London-based charity organization, founded in 1846, dedicated to the advancement of knowledge and education regarding world history, especially from the point of view of world exploration, geography, and navigation. It is named after RICHARD HAKLUYT, the 16th–17th-century English geographer, who, through his writings, helped chronicle important expeditions and spread geographic knowledge to a wide public.

The Hakluyt Society's main activity, still vital today, has been publishing primary sources on exploration in English, including the writings of explorers of many different nationalities, such as Russian FABIAN GOTTLIEB BENJAMIN VON BELLINGSHAUSEN, Englishman JAMES COOK, Russian Cossack SEMYON IVANOVICH DEZHNEV, Englishman SIR FRANCIS DRAKE, Portuguese VASCO DA GAMA, Arab ABU ABD ALLAH MUHAMMAD IBN BATTUTAH, Frenchman JEAN-FRANÇOIS DE GALAUP, comte de La Pérouse, German FRIEDRICH WILHELM LUDWIG LEICHHARDT, and many more. The society's published works—about 200 editions, in about 350 volumes—relate to travels on or around all the continents and oceans and cover the last 2,000 years.

Hanseatic League

The Hanseatic League was a commercial union of German cities and towns and their merchants during the Middle Ages and the RENAISSANCE. The league was the most successful trade association of its time. It grew out of smaller unions of merchants conducting business in foreign lands, known as Hansas. The date of inception is unknown, but it was active by the mid-12th century, created by merchants to establish favorable trade conditions. By the 13th century, the Hanseatic League had evolved into an alliance of cities and towns, which came to number, by the 15th century, as many as 180. Its legislative assembly was known as the Hansetag.

Sharing resources and developing new markets together, league members were able to generate greater profits. Moreover, without a strong centralized government to offer merchants protection from attacks on land and at sea, they had to defend themselves, which was facilitated by banding together. The city of Lübeck in northern Germany was the first permanent Hanseatic trading center. Activity of the Hanseatic League extended throughout Germany, northward to Scandinavia via the Baltic Sea, and eastward to Russia. Members controlled the trade in copper and iron from Sweden, fur from Russia, and, most important, herring and cod caught in the region. But they conducted trade with interests in western Europe as well, including the British Isles. Members of the Hanseatic League even founded franchises in foreign lands.

The COG, a small dependable ship dating from about 1200, enabled extensive trade by sea, even as far as the MEDITERRANEAN SEA. All the commercial activity increased geographic knowledge among league members, created regular routes of travel, and helped unite distant lands.

The Hanseatic League declined in effectiveness by the mid-17th century, largely because of growing English and Dutch power and political strife and warfare in Germany. The Hansetag met for the final time in 1669, with only six municipalities represented.

See also COMMERCE AND EXPLORATION.

Hawaiian Islands (Hawai'i)

The Hawaiian Islands are a group of eight major islands and a number of small islands in the Pacific Ocean, between 19 and 22 degrees north latitude and 155 and 161 degrees west longitude. The islands are of volcanic origin. The largest of them is Hawaii, while the most developed and populous is Oahu. The other primary islands are Kahoolawe, Kauai, Lanai, Maui, Molokai, and Niihau.

The peoples who lived on the Hawaiian Islands prior to the arrival of Europeans were of Polynesian ancestry. Although darker-skinned than Polynesians to the south in the other parts of OCEANIA, they spoke the same basic language, had many religious and cultural traits in common, and used a similar type of boat, the OUTRIGGER. The best estimate of the time of their migration is about A.D. 750.

Although it was later claimed in Italy that the Hawaiian Islands were visited in 1555 by Italian Juan Gaetano, who had been a chronicler on the 1542 voyage of Ruy López de Villalobos to the SPICE ISLANDS (the Moluccas), the story remains unconfirmed. As a result, the credit for the European discovery of the island group goes to Englishman JAMES COOK. On his third Pacific expedition, after sailing in the South Pacific he was headed northward to find the western outlet of the NORTHWEST PASSAGE. On January 18, 1778, he came upon the western half of the islands, which he named the Sandwich Islands, after the Earl of Sandwich. The inhabitants proved friendly. It was Cook who noticed the similarity in their language with that of other Polynesians and thus defined the wide boundaries that constitute Polynesia. He and his crew stayed for 12 days before continuing northward.

After his explorations to the north, Cook returned to the islands in January 1779. On this second stopover he discovered Maui and the largest island, Hawaii. His reception on these other islands was hospitable, but, on the expedition's departure in February, the chiefs made no secret that they were glad to see him go. When his ship, the *Resolution*, suffered a damaged foremast, and he returned a week later, relations deteriorated. One of his auxiliary boats was stolen and the next day Cook went ashore with 10 marines to take a chief hostage until the boat was returned. A melee broke out after Cook fired his gun, and Cook, along with four marines and several native people, was killed. His dismembered body was returned to the crew by the tribespeople, and CHARLES CLERKE assumed command of the expedition.

The island of Maui was visited for one day by Frenchman JEAN-FRANÇOIS DE GALAUP, comte de La Pérouse, in May 1786, as part of his scientific exploration of the Pacific. GEORGE VANCOUVER, who had been a member of Cook's second and third Pacific voyages, returned to the islands on his 1791–95 voyage and charted their location. He also made the first accurate map of the islands.

At the time of Cook's discovery, the tribes of the islands were engaged in warfare. During Vancouver's visit, king Kamehameha I acknowledged rights of the British to settle in the territory. In 1810, the islands were unified, and Kamehameha became the sovereign. Agriculture was developed, and the islands became an important reprovisioning station for whaling fleets. British, French, and American interests were established, and, by the 1830s, a thriving sugar industry was in operation. In 1893, with the instigation of the American population and with the help of the American companies on the island, Queen Liluokalani was deposed. The U.S. minister to Hawaii, John L. Stevens, set up a provisional government, which sought annexation of the islands. President Grover Cleveland refused, due to the nature of the change in government, but his policy was reversed under William McKinley, who annexed the territory in 1898. Hawaii became the 50th state of the United States on August 21, 1959.

See also POLYNESIAN EXPLORATION; PACIFIC OCEAN, EXPLORATION OF THE.

Himalayas

The Himalayas are the highest mountain range in the world. Located in a strip between 200 and 250 miles wide on average, they separate the Indian subcontinent from Tibet and China and the rest of central Asia to the north. The Himalayas form a broad arc of 1,600 miles from the INDUS RIVER in the northwest to the Brahmaputra River on the east and are buttressed on the west by the Hindu Kush mountain range, and on the east by the Assam range, rising up from India's flat Gangetic plain. The mountain range leads into the high Tibetan plateau. The Himalayas, whose name means "abode of snow" in Sanskrit, are one of the world's geologically young mountain ranges, which contains nine of the world's 10 highest peaks, including Mount Everest (see EVEREST, MOUNT), K-2, and Mount Kanchenjunga. They developed between 30 and 50 million years ago, as the Indian tectonic plate collided with Asia. There continues to be tectonic activity as the mountains are slowly uplifted, with earthquakes that strike eastern Pakistan and northern India.

Composed of a series of parallel ridges, the Himalayas can be divided into three main regions: Great Himalayas, Middle (or Inner or Lesser) Himalayas, and Outer (or Sub-Himalayas). The Great Himalayas are a snowy range containing the highest peaks, the average height exceeding

20,000 feet. This region runs in a narrow band of about 15 miles the length of the Himalayas, projecting erratically into the Middle Himalayas to the south. The Middle Himalayas, roughly 50 miles wide, are composed of peaks of a regular height of about 6,000 to 10,000 feet. The Outer Himalayas (including the Siwalik range), averaging about 3,000 to 4,000 feet, slope gently into the northern plains of India and Pakistan, beginning at a width of 30 miles in the west, and narrowing to nothing in East India.

The Great and Middle Himalayas are also divided, along with the other mountains around the Tibetan plateau, into a series of mountain chains: the Kunlun, which forms the northern edge of the Tibetan Plateau; the Trans-Himalayan chain of Muztagh, also called Karakoram, which ends at the source of the Indus River; the Ladakh chain, broken into two parts by the Indus River; the Zaskar chain, containing the majority of snowy peaks; and the Middle Himalayan Nag Tibba, Dhaola Dhār, Pir Panjal, and Mahabharat ranges.

The Great Himalayas are mostly snow covered and harsh, containing a few high valleys, where the scattered inhabitants, largely Tibetan Buddhists, remain isolated. Travel is extremely difficult and often impossible. The hidden valleys have inspired countless tales of lost paradises, such as Shangri-La, a mythical land of well-being and long life.

The peaks in the Himalayas, as the tallest in the world, are significant in the history of MOUNTAIN CLIMBING. Inhabitants of the Himalayan regions of Nepal and Sikkim called SHERPAS, familiar with the terrain and skilled in mountaineering, are often called upon as mountain guides and climbers. The Middle Himalayas contain fertile valleys and high forested mountains and are modestly populated, along with the Outer Himalayas, with Hindus of Indian ancestry. Travel in the Middle Himalayas is made difficult by frequent gorges and jagged mountains.

Mapping the Himalayas

The first systematic attempt to map the Himalayas was made in 1590 at the command of Akbar, a Mogul (Mughal) emperor of India. In what had been an Islamic state, while expanding his empire, Akbar allowed freedom of religion and accepted Hindus, Buddhists, and even Christian missionaries at his court. In 1590, he sent an expedition into the mountains to the north.

It was not until the British controlled India in the 19th century that the peaks of the Himalayas were mapped and their heights obtained with great accuracy. In 1806, a British officer, Colonel William Lambton, began what would be called the Great Trigonometrical Survey, sponsored at first by the BRITISH EAST INDIA COMPANY, then headed by the British government. He planned to survey a one-degree swath of India along a straight meridian line from the base of the subcontinent through the Himalayas. Lambton

worked until his death in 1823, succeeded in his job by SIR GEORGE EVEREST. In 1841, the peak now known as Mount Everest was recorded. Everest was succeeded as Surveyor General of India by Andrew Waugh, who helped complete much of the later work on the Great Trigonometrical Survey, measured the heights of the highest peaks in the Himalayas, and named Mount Everest for his predecessor. The PUNDITS, trained Indian emissaries for the British government, carried on the survey in the work in the second half of the century. Meanwhile, in 1854–57, German brothers ADOLF VON SCHLAGINTWEIT, HERMANN VON SCHLAGINTWEIT, and ROBERT VON SCHLAGINTWEIT explored and surveyed the Himalayas and adjoining ranges for the British East India Company.

Mountain Climbers

In the late 19th and early 20th centuries, the challenge of the Himalayan peaks drew more and more climbers. American FANNY BULLOCK WORKMAN made a number of climbs; Swiss mountain climber MATTHIAS ZURBRIGGEN served as her guide on some of them. In 1909, LUIGI AMEDEO DI SAVOIA D'ABRUZZI attempted to climb K2; he did not reach the summit but set an altitude record to that date. British climber GEORGE HERBERT LEIGH MALLORY lost his life in 1924 during an attempt on Mount Everest.

By mid-century, May 1953, Nepalese TENZING NORGAY and Englishman SIR EDMUND PERCIVAL HILLARY reached the highest point of the world, the top of Mount Everest. Since that time, the Himalayas have continued to be a focus of international mountain climbing.

❖

In addition to mountain climbers and visitors to Tibet and its city of LHASA, the Himalayas have also attracted painters, such as 20th-century Russian painter NICHOLAS KONSTANTINOVICH ROERICH. Travel through the Himalayas is still difficult, accomplished for the most part by pack animal.

See also ASIA, EXPLORATION OF.

Hudson Bay

Hudson Bay, along with James Bay at its southern end, is an inland sea of North America. Linked to the Atlantic Ocean via Hudson Strait and to the Arctic Ocean via the Foxe Channel, it can be considered an arm of either one. Just south of the ARCTIC CIRCLE, it borders, from east to west, Quebec, Ontario, Manitoba, and Nunavut Territory in Canada. Baffin Island, part of Nunavut, lies to the north. Hudson Bay has an area of some 475,000 square miles, at about 850 miles long and 650 miles wide. The bay's average depth is about 330 feet; its maximum depth, about 2,846 feet. The 15,700-square-mile Southampton Island in the northwestern corner is the largest island. Other large islands lie off the east coast: Coats Island, Mansel Island, and the Belcher Islands. Akimiski Island is situated in James Bay. Lands to the west of Hudson Bay are generally barren and rocky; to the east are found mostly low-lying marshlands. Many rivers—among them the Rupert, Nottaway, Albany, Nelson, and Churchill—drain into the bay. The bay is covered by ice from October to mid-July, but open to navigation from mid-July to October.

Hudson Bay played an important role in the history of exploration in two ways: first, as the hoped-for eastern entrance to the NORTHWEST PASSAGE across North America from the Atlantic to the Pacific Ocean; and, second, as the base of operations for the HUDSON'S BAY COMPANY and the development of the FUR TRADE throughout much of North America.

Northwest Passage

Native peoples, partners in the fur trade—in particular the Inuit (Eskimo), Cree Indians, and Chipewyan Indians— knew of Hudson Bay since ancient times. It is possible that Englishman SEBASTIAN CABOT entered the Hudson Strait between the North American mainland and Baffin Island and perhaps even reached eastern Hudson Bay, while in search of the Northwest Passage in 1509, not long after the European discovery of the Americas, although there is no definite documentation. Englishman HENRY HUDSON is given credit for being the first European to navigate through the strait in 1610. He lost his life there the next year, after wintering at James Bay; his crew mutinied because he was supposedly hoarding scarce supplies of food and set him adrift with his son and ailing crew members in a small boat. Yet England's claim to the region was based on his voyage, and both the strait and bay were named for him.

In the years after Hudson's voyage, numerous expeditions explored Hudson Bay for England in the continuing search for the Northwest Passage. SIR THOMAS BUTTON reached the mouth of the Nelson River and explored the coast of Southampton Island in 1612–13; WILLIAM BAFFIN and ROBERT BYLOT explored the bay's northwest coast and Foxe Basin in 1615; LUKE FOXE explored western and northern parts of the bay, including Foxe Channel in 1631; and THOMAS JAMES thoroughly explored James Bay in 1631–32. JENS ERIKSEN MUNK, meanwhile, explored Hudson Bay for Denmark, reaching the Churchill River region on the southwest coast in 1619–20.

Fur Trade

Later in the 17th century, in 1668–69, Frenchman MÉDARD CHOUART DES GROSEILLIERS, backed by an English group of merchants, sailed from England to Hudson Bay and founded Charles Fort (Rupert House) on the Rupert River on its east side, from where he traded with Cree Indians for furs. In 1670, after his return to England with his cargo, the Hudson's Bay Company was granted a royal charter and a trade monopoly over all the lands whose rivers drain into the bay. Later in 1670, PIERRE-ESPRIT RADISSON, Sieur des Groseilliers's brother-in-law, led a second trading expedition there and founded a post at the mouth of the Nelson River on the bay's west coast. In 1671–72, French missionary CHARLES ALBANEL, who had traveled with Groseilliers and Radisson on an earlier expedition to the western Great Lakes, traveled overland from the St. Lawrence River to the mouth of the Rupert River on James Bay.

Over the next decades the Hudson's Bay Company sponsored a number of expeditions in the continuing search for the Northwest Passage. In 1719, an expedition under JAMES KNIGHT explored the Marble Island region off the bay's northwest coast. HENRY KELSEY led three other expeditions from York Factory on the Nelson River to the same region in 1719–21. Later expeditions along the west coast included that of CHRISTOPHER MIDDLETON in 1741, during which he explored Wager Bay and Repulse Bay, and that of WILLIAM MOOR, in 1746–47, during which he explored Chesterfield Inlet and more of Wager Bay. The Hudson's Bay Company next turned its attention to overland expeditions west and north, such as those of SAMUEL HEARNE in the 1760s–70s.

Political Claims

During many of these years England and France struggled for possession of Hudson Bay as it did for other Canadian lands. In 1713, France ceded its claim by the Peace of Utrecht. In 1763, in the Treaty of Paris following the French and Indian War, it ceded all its claims to lands in North America. Yet, in 1782, during the American Revolution, French naval officer JEAN-FRANÇOIS DE GALAUP, comte de La Pérouse, who went on to explore the Pacific Ocean, commanded a small French fleet that destroyed a number of British trading posts, including Fort Prince of Wales, where he captured Samuel Hearne. Hearne was later released.

See also ARCTIC, EXPLORATION OF THE; NORTH AMERICA, EXPLORATION OF.

Hudson's Bay Company (HBC)

The Hudson's Bay Company was one of two great fur-trading corporations that helped open the West of what is now Canada and northern parts of the United States. It was granted a charter by the English government in 1670, Charles II conferring on his cousin Prince Rupert, count Palatine of the Rhine, and 17 other noblemen a FUR TRADE monopoly as well as near sovereign rights to the region drained by rivers flowing into HUDSON BAY. The vastness of the territory was unknown at the time, but Rupert's Land, as it came to be known, included almost half of present-day

Canada—what is now all of Manitoba, plus large parts of Alberta, Saskatchewan, Ontario, Quebec, Nunavut, and the southeast corner of the Northwest Territories. Moreover, northern portions of present-day North Dakota and Minnesota were also eventually claimed. The Hudson's Bay Company (HBC) is still in existence, but only as a department store retailer.

Groseillers and Radisson

The impetus for starting the Hudson's Bay Company came from two French COUREURS DE BOIS, or independent fur traders, MÉDARD CHOUART DES GROSEILLIERS and his brother-in-law PIERRE-ESPRIT RADISSON. After being arrested for unlicensed trading and having a load of furs confiscated by French authorities in Montreal, the two elicited backing from merchants in London. In 1668–69, on separate ships, they sailed from England to Hudson Bay as part of a fur-trading expedition. Radisson's ship was damaged off Ireland and returned to England. Sieur des Groseilliers reached Hudson Bay and founded Charles Fort (Rupert House) on the Rupert River on its east side. He successfully traded with Cree Indians for furs. Although that expedition failed to earn a profit because of the damage to Radisson's ship, it proved the feasibility of sailing into Hudson Bay, wintering there, and returning with a cargo of furs, and led to the royal charter for the company and a subsequent expedition by Radisson in 1670. The Gentlemen Adventurers, as the partners were called, also hoped to locate mineral wealth. Still another motivation for investing in such a company was discovering a NORTHWEST PASSAGE from the Atlantic Ocean to the Pacific Ocean for access to the Far East, a goal that was included in the company's charter.

The Hudson's Bay Company slowly expanded its operations into the 18th century. Posts were established at the Nelson, Albany, Moose, Severn, Eastmain, and Churchill Rivers. A number of exploratory expeditions by Englishmen were sponsored. In 1690–92, HENRY KELSEY explored the Assiniboine and Saskatchewan Rivers, reaching the Canadian prairies and plains. In 1719–21, JAMES KNIGHT explored northwestern Hudson Bay in search of the Northwest Passage; after being shipwrecked on Marble Island, Knight and his entire crew perished; Kelsey led a number of expeditions to the region to search for him. In 1754–55, ANTHONY HENDAY explored the Canadian plains within 40 miles of the ROCKY MOUNTAINS. In the 1760s–70s, SAMUEL HEARNE explored inland from southwestern Hudson Bay on three expeditions. He also established the company's first inland trading fort, Cumberland House on the Saskatchewan River. In 1770–72, with the help of Chipewyan Indian guide MATONABBEE, Hearne reached the Arctic Ocean and made the European discovery of the Great Slave Lake. In 1772–75, MATTHEW COCKING explored from southern Hudson Bay to western Saskatchewan.

During many of these years, France and England vied for control of the region as they did for other parts of North America. The Peace of Utrecht, 1713–14, a series of treaties resolving conflicts in Europe, brought some stability to the fur trade, as did the Treaty of Paris in 1763, which ended the French and Indian Wars and gave England control over formerly French-held territory in North America. Yet, during the American Revolution in 1775–83, French forces were again active in the Hudson Bay area.

Competition with the North West Company

The Hudson's Bay Company faced growing competition in the fur trade in the latter part of the 18th century. Scottish interests organized the NORTH WEST COMPANY in the 1780s, and, taking advantage of French expertise in the field, its traders became active over a greater expanse of territory than the Hudson's Bay Company traders. In the 1780s–90s, DAVID THOMPSON, a skilled geographer and cartographer of Welsh ancestry, journeyed westward as far as present-day Calgary, Alberta, explored up the Saskatchewan River into the Rocky Mountains, and pioneered a route from Hudson Bay to Lake Athabasca. Without the backing he desired for further surveys, however, he joined the Nor'westers (as the employees of the North West Company were known) in 1797. The AMERICAN FUR COMPANY, founded in 1808 by JOHN JACOB ASTOR, also proved a formidable competitor to the south. As a result, the Hudson's Bay Company began sending traders farther inland to locate new sources of furs.

After 1808, Thomas Douglas, earl of Selkirk, gained influence within the Hudson's Bay Company, and started a new policy of settling Scottish and Irish farmers on company lands. The founding of the Red River Settlement along the Red River in present-day Manitoba led to violence in 1816 between the colonists and the Métis, the mixed-blood descendants of Native Americans and French and Scottish traders, backed by Nor'westers. That conflict and others led to an amalgamation of the two companies in 1821. Although the North West Company was the more active of the two in the fur trade at that time, the older Hudson's Bay Company controlled many of the favored westward routes, and the name of the latter company was retained. Control of additional lands—all the way to the Pacific and Arctic Oceans—were under the control of the new monopoly. In 1838, the company's license for sole trading rights was renewed for 21 years.

After the Merger

After 1821, Hudson's Bay Company representatives sponsored explorations of a vast region. In the 1820s–30s, JOHN McLOUGHLIN, based on the COLUMBIA RIVER and in charge of operations in the Pacific Northwest, a region subject to joint Canadian and American occupancy at the time, directed traders, such as PETER SKENE OGDEN and JOHN

This advertisement for the Hudson's Bay Company appeared in *The Klondike Official Guide*, published by the Department of Interior of Canada in 1898. *(Library of Congress, Prints and Photographs Division [LC-USZ62-104304])*

WORK, in trading expeditions throughout the region, even as far south as Great Basin in what is now Utah. They thus competed with American MOUNTAIN MEN then working the West. In 1824, ALEXANDER ROSS explored the Snake River from present-day Montana to the mouth of Boise River in present-day Idaho. In the 1830s–40s, SIR GEORGE SIMPSON, head of the vast northern department, sponsored his cousin THOMAS SIMPSON along with PETER WARREN DEASE in surveys of Alaska's and Canada's Arctic coastline; he also sponsored JOHN RAE in a survey of the territory north of Fury and Hecla Strait in the eastern Canadian Arctic. In 1840, ROBERT CAMPBELL located the source of the Pelly River in the Yukon Territory. And, in 1841, JAMES

SINCLAIR, leading emigrants westward from the Red River Settlement to the Oregon Country for the company, pioneered a wagon route through the Canadian Rockies.

In 1859, with the expiration of the current license, the Hudson's Bay Company lost its trading monopoly throughout Rupert's Land. After the British North America Act of 1867 and the confederation of the colonies of Nova Scotia, New Brunswick, Quebec, and Ontario into provinces of the Dominion of Canada, property rights were also reevaluated. In 1869, the Dominion of Canada acquired Rupert's Land. The next year, the Red River area became a new province, Manitoba; the rest of Rupert's Land became the Northwest Territories, the southern portions of which became the provinces of Alberta and Saskatchewan. The Hudson's Bay Company retained some lands and its posts.

The Modern Company
In the 20th century, the Hudson's Bay Company diversified into manufacturing and retail, developing a chain of Canadian department stores. During World War I (1914–18), it operated a steamship line, transporting food and munitions for the war effort. In 1930, the company was forced to split up and divest, with Canadian retail interests becoming incorporated as a separate organization, and London interests remaining active in the international fur trade. Many of the remaining lands were eventually sold off. During World War II (1941–45), the Hudson's Bay Company again provided resources in the war effort, including supply vessels for patrols. In 1970, company headquarters were transferred from London to Winnipeg, Manitoba. The Bay, Zellers, Home Outfitters, and hbc.com are the current company divisions.

See also COMMERCE AND EXPLORATION.

hydrography
Hydrography, a branch of geography, is the study of bodies of water and the land that surrounds them. The main purpose of the hydrographer is to survey, chart, and sound bodies of water so that navigation may be conducted with the greatest degree of safety. To this end, the findings of hydrographic surveys are published for those who have practical need of them. Sometimes a distinction is made between hydrography as the study of surface water sources and supplies, and hydrology, the study of underground sources.

In modern practical use, hydrography has come to include the observation of magnetic variations, currents, tides, waves, and weather conditions, although such subjects—at least regarding the world's oceans—are generally considered as part of the discipline of oceanography. Hydrography begins with very precise measurements of locations. These reference points are called origins. From these points, other features are located.

Hydrography became organized as a field of study in England during the reign of Queen Elizabeth I in the second half of the 16th century. An 18th-century Englishman, JAMES COOK, was a noted hydrographer.

See also GEOGRAPHY AND CARTOGRAPHY; OCEANOGRAPHY AND EXPLORATION; SURVEYING AND EXPLORATION.

hypsometer

A hypsometer is a device used to measure the altitude of a location (hypsometry being the measurement of elevation relative to sea level). One of the earliest methods for determining altitude relied on the variation of the boiling point of water with altitude. Since there is less atmospheric pressure the higher one travels, the temperature at which water boils is proportionally lower. A hypsometer measures the deviation in boiling point from water at sea level (212 degrees Fahrenheit). It consists of a cylindrical vessel in which water or another liquid is boiled; in the outer partitions of a jacketed column, steam circulates, while in the central one a thermometer gives a reading of the steam's temperature without immersion in the boiling water.

Although comparing boiling times had been used to measure elevation for years, a practical hypsometer was not designed until 1845. Its inventor was French chemist and physicist Henri-Victor Regnault, who was at that time a professor at the Collège de France.

In addition to the obvious applications in mapping the contours of mountainous regions, the hypsometer was important to early explorers who sought to understand river systems. By comparing the location and elevation of an unknown river with that which was known about another river in question, a person could trace drainage patterns and thus determine the relationships between a river and its tributaries.

See also GEOGRAPHY AND CARTOGRAPHY.

I

iceberg   See DRIFT ICE.

Iceland

Iceland, or Ísland in the Icelandic language, is an island in the North Atlantic Ocean, just south of the ARCTIC CIRCLE, about 180 miles east of GREENLAND across the Denmark Strait, and about 600 miles west of Norway across the Norwegian Sea. Along with tiny neighboring islands, it constitutes the Republic of Iceland, considered the westernmost nation of Europe.

The island of Iceland is about 300 miles from east to west and about 190 miles from north to south. The coastline, with deep fjords, especially in the north and west, is about 3,730 miles long. The total land area including islands is about 39,800 square miles. Iceland consists of a plateau, averaging about 2,000 feet in height. Some 200 volcanoes, many of them still active, such as Mount Hekla, rise up from the tablelands. Because of the warming effect of the North Atlantic Drift—a continuation of the GULF STREAM— southern and western regions have a milder climate. About one-fourth of the island is habitable, with most settlements situated along the southwestern coastal lowlands. Grasslands predominate with few trees. Almost 15 percent of the island is covered by permanent glaciers and snowfields. Numerous lakes and rivers are located throughout the island.

Iceland may have been the legendary ULTIMA THULE visited by Greek scholar PYTHEAS in about 325 B.C. The earliest people known certainly to have reached Iceland were Irish. During the Middle Ages, Irish monks carried out sea pilgrimages, seeking barren islands to find solitude and enlightenment or inhabited islands where they might missionize native peoples. In the course of such expeditions they founded settlements in the Orkney Islands, the Shetlands, and the Faeroes. It is not known at what point they reached Iceland. The legendary ST. BRENDAN'S ISLE, supposedly reached by monk SAINT BRENDAN in the sixth century A.D., may have been Iceland. In any case, Irish settlements existed there by 800.

The Vikings reached Iceland later in the ninth century. Traditional Norse literature holds that, in about 860, NADDOD was blown off course while traveling from Norway to the Faeroe Islands and reached the east coast of Iceland; he named it Snaeland for "Snowland." Another Norse saga holds that, about the same time, GARDAR SVARSSON circumnavigated Iceland, determining it was an island and naming it Gardarsholm, or "Gardar's Island," then building the first Viking house there, on the north coast. There is a possibility that both the accounts are derived from the same actual voyage. Floki Vilgerdarsson, another early traveler, built a house on the east coast. Ingólfur Arnarson, who established a farm at present-day Reykjavík on the southwest coast in about 874, is considered the first permanent settler of Iceland. By that time, the Irish had abandoned the island. During subsequent decades, other settlers flocked to the island from both the British Isles and Scandinavian countries. In 930, a general legislature called the Althing was established for all the colonies. Iceland became a home for Vikings as well as a stopover for voyages farther west. ERIC THE RED, who settled in Iceland, sailed from there to Greenland in about 982–85. LEIF ERICSSON, who reportedly reached North America, may have been born in Iceland.

In 1262, Iceland came under the rule of Norway. In 1380, Denmark assumed control. In 1918, Iceland became an independent kingdom in union with Denmark. Reykjavík is the capital. The people of Iceland are predominantly of Scandinavian and Celtic ancestry.

ice pack   See PACK ICE.

Indian Ocean, exploration of the

The Indian Ocean is the third-largest ocean in the world, after the Pacific Ocean and the Atlantic Ocean, covering more than 23 million square miles. It is bounded by the Malay Archipelago and Australia in the east, the continent of Asia in the north, Africa in the west, and Antarctica in the south.

In its southern regions, the Indian Ocean has counterclockwise currents similar to those of the Atlantic and Pacific. To the north, the currents are dominated by seasonal monsoon winds. In the winter, the winds north of the EQUATOR blow from the northeast, creating a current in the same direction; south of the equator they curl from the northwest. In the summer, the winds reverse general direction, blowing from the south and west.

Among other smaller rivers, the Indian Ocean is fed by the ZAMBEZI RIVER of Africa, the Tigris and Euphrates Rivers of the Middle East, and the INDUS RIVER and GANGES RIVER of the Indian subcontinent. The waters of the Indian Ocean are generally warm, except near Antarctica, where they contain PACK ICE and DRIFT ICE for most of the year.

The Indian Ocean contains several subdivisions, which are important bodies of water in their own right. The Arabian Sea (or Erythraean Sea as it was known in antiquity) in the northwest connects to the Persian Gulf and the RED SEA. The Bay of Bengal in the northeast is also named separately. These waters formed the basis of trade between Africa and Asia. The regularity of the monsoonal wind system, despite the great number of storms, has facilitated navigation over the centuries.

Ancient Travel

The various principalities along the shores of the Indian Ocean did not always know of one another, and their early history is uncertain. Ancient Egyptians were traveling down the Red Sea to the land of PUNT as early as 2450 B.C. (see EGYPTIAN EXPLORATION). By that early time, in the land of Ur in southern Mesopotamia, buildings were made of teak imported from the Malabar Coast in western India. To the east the history is even more unclear. It is likely that Indians brought goods from Sumatra and Java several thousand years before Christ, but because of the destruction of the Indus River civilizations in about 1500 B.C. by Aryans from the north, knowledge of this time is limited. Buddhist texts from 1000 to 500 B.C. mention lands to the east of great wealth. A trade connection with the SPICE ISLANDS (the Moluccas) at that time has not been proven.

There is some speculation that Arabs were venturing past Africa's CAPE OF GOOD HOPE by the eighth century B.C. to trade with the peoples of East Africa. Moreover, the question of the source of cinnamon among civilizations in the MEDITERRANEAN SEA at this time is interesting, since the spice probably originated in CEYLON (present-day Sri Lanka), indicating extensive early East-West contacts.

There survives an account of Phoenicians making a journey from the Red Sea, through the Indian Ocean, and around Africa through the Strait of Gibraltar (see GIBRALTAR, STRAIT OF) in about 600 B.C. (see PHOENICIAN EXPLORATION). The story, as told by fifth-century B.C. Greek historian HERODOTUS, though impossible to confirm, has details that give it credibility.

ALEXANDER THE GREAT, who began his military conquest of the east from Macedonia in 334 B.C., arrived in the land that is now Pakistan in 325 B.C. On the Indus River, Alexander's army constructed 150 boats. NEARCHUS, one of his generals, was given command of an expedition to explore the coast of the Erythraean Sea on a return trip to the western end of the Persian Gulf. It was Alexander's intention to unite the lands he had conquered, with trade routes by both land and sea. The report of this journey survives through Greek historian Arrian, who wrote of it in his work *Indica* in the second century A.D. The empire that Alexander created fragmented with his death, as did the hoped-for trade routes.

In about 45 B.C., Greek merchant HIPPALUS, seeking a faster route to India and hoping to avoid the pirates along the coasts of Arabia and Persia (present-day Iran), sailed across the Indian Ocean to the Malabar Coast, finding favorable winds. His route became well traveled by traders bringing back exotic goods for the wealthy Romans (see GREEK EXPLORATION; ROMAN EXPLORATION). Meanwhile, the Indians also extended their influence, colonizing the Malayan Peninsula and other lands of Southeast Asia, which came to be known as "Greater India." India's central location gave it its role as the middleman of Indian Ocean traffic. It was at this time that a connection was made with the Spice Islands at the eastern extent of the Indian Ocean.

The Middle Ages

With the breakup of the Roman Empire in the fifth century A.D., Europe again became isolated from India. This was exacerbated with the founding of Islam in the seventh century. Persia came into ascendancy and traded energetically with India as the West languished. The Chinese also made efforts to obtain goods from their southern neighbors. They sent their own ships to Malaysia and India, but were also serviced by the merchants of these countries. The Chinese preferred to have as much control over their balance of payments as possible, which made them inconsistent in their trade policy and often isolationist. In A.D. 758, Arabs ransacked the port of Canton in southeastern China, which led to the city being closed to outsiders for 50 years. Muslims were also sailing farther down the coast of East Africa, settling on the island of Madagascar by the ninth century. Madagascar became an important center of trade with Africa, for ivory, agricultural products, and slaves. It also had a vital seafaring culture.

During much of the Middle Ages, trade was at a minimum between Europe and Asia. What little contact there was grew out of the port city of Venice, which came to dominate the Mediterranean Sea and eventually trade with the East. Venetian trader MARCO POLO traveled through Asia and into China with his father, NICCOLÒ POLO, and uncle, MAFFEO POLO, in 1271–75. In 1292, he made a journey by ship from the South China Sea through the Strait of Malacca into the Indian Ocean. After several stopovers in India, he continued westward to Ormuz, a center of trade at the mouth of the Persian Gulf. He arrived back in Venice in 1295. The published account of his travels opened up a whole new world to Europeans. Arab traveler ABU ABD ALLAH MUHAMMAD IBN BATTUTAH visited much of the civilized world during his lifetime, including Europe, and the stories of his journeys became known there. In 1349–54, he sailed the Arabian Sea, the open waters of the Indian Ocean, and the Bay of Bengal (see MUSLIM EXPLORATION).

Two other figures are important in the history of the Indian Ocean before the route from Europe around Africa was discovered by the Portuguese. The first was Italian adventurer NICCOLÒ DEI CONTI, who sailed from the Persian Gulf to India, Sumatra, Burma, and Vietnam. His travels, from 1414 to 1437, formed the basis of a book by Poggio Bracciolini dealing with the conflict between Christianity and Islam. It also proved a rich source of information on the culture and geography of the east. The second great traveler at this time was Chinese admiral CHENG HO. Between 1405 and 1434, he mounted seven expeditions to the south under the sponsorship of the Ming dynasty. These voyages were on a grand scale, with 62 main ships and 27,000 soldiers. Cheng Ho's efforts took him as far as the Persian Gulf. He exacted tribute from many different peoples and brought back many luxuries to his homeland (see CHINESE EXPLORATION).

Around Africa

When HENRY THE NAVIGATOR, prince of Portugal, conquered the Muslim port of Ceuta in North Africa at the Strait of Gibraltar in 1415, a new chapter in European exploration was begun, sometimes referred to as the EUROPEAN AGE OF EXPLORATION. Inspired by the richness and vigor of the Islamic culture, and knowing of the profits that could be made by circumventing their hold on the SPICE TRADE, Henry began a concerted effort to sail around Africa to the source of these goods. The ambition was not realized in his lifetime but was pursued by his fellow countrymen. King John II of Portugal sent BARTOLOMEU DIAS on the first European voyage to round the southern tip of Africa into the Indian Ocean, which he accomplished in 1487–88. VASCO DA GAMA embarked on a journey intending to reach India in 1497. On April 14, 1498, he reached Malindi on the coast of East Africa where Kenya is today, and secured the services of an Arab pilot to take his fleet to India. The uneventful trip was made in 23 days. The Hindu leader he met at Calicut was not overly friendly. The Muslim traders, who were well entrenched, were even more antagonistic, realizing that their way of life was severely threatened. After attacking the city, da Gama sailed southward to Cochin, where he managed to form an alliance with the Hindus. A second Portuguese journey in 1500, led by PEDRO ÁLVARS CABRAL, was even more successful, and the time of European ships sailing the Indian Ocean was well under way. With the first CIRCUMNAVIGATION OF THE WORLD by FERDINAND MAGELLAN's Spanish expedition in 1519–22, Europeans first entered the Indian Ocean from the east. A century later, European ships would also sail Indian Ocean waters along Australia's west coast.

Southern Waters

The northern Indian Ocean continued to be a primary route of transportation between four of the world's seven continents—Africa, Asia, Europe, and Australia—over the next centuries. Yet its southern latitudes remained uncharted until the late 18th century. In 1772, Frenchman YVES-JOSEPH DE KERGUÉLEN-TRÉMAREC led an expedition to southern waters in search of the fabled GREAT SOUTHERN CONTINENT, or Terra Australis, during which he located the Kerguelen Islands in the southern Indian Ocean, close to the parallel of latitude referred to as the ANTARCTIC CIRCLE. At about the same time, in 1772–75, Englishman JAMES COOK circumnavigated Antarctica, proving that the fabled land did not exist in southern waters. While encircling Antarctica, he navigated the Pacific, Atlantic, and Indian Oceans and crossed the Antarctic Circle three times. The Antarctic coast was not sighted until the 19th century—the Indian Ocean side later than the others—and was not thoroughly charted until the 20th century.

❖

The Indian Ocean holds a special place in the history of exploration as the ancient maritime link between three continents, Europe, Africa, and Asia. The arrival of the Portuguese along the route around Africa renewed its significance as a highway of cross-cultural contact and commerce.

Indus River

The Indus River runs some 1,800 miles from its source, glacial streams in the high HIMALAYAS, to the Arabian Sea. It flows northwestward from western Tibet into India, passing between the far western edge of the Himalayas and the northern extent of the Hindu Kush mountain range. Made navigable by a junction with the Kabul River flowing out from Afghanistan, the Indus, after flowing through the Pakistani province of Sind, finally branches into an infertile delta of some 3,000 square miles. Other major tributaries are the Sutlej, Ravi, and Chenab.

Harrapa Civilization

The Indus Valley was the location of one of the oldest civilizations on record. The Harrapa culture flourished there by about 2500 B.C.—at the same time as the highly developed civilizations of Mesopotamia, Egypt, and Crete—and came to encompass one of the largest geographic areas covered by a single Bronze Age culture. Harrapa people built cities reaching a population of 40,000, dug complex irrigation channels, and even had indoor plumbing. There is evidence that they traded with civilizations as far east as Arabia. By 1500 B.C., however, the Indus Valley civilization had disappeared, to be rediscovered by archaeologists in the 20th century.

In about 2340 B.C., SARGON of Akkad consolidated his power over all of Mesopotamia and began looking outward. He sent out expeditions in all directions for conquest and trade. It is known that Sargon established trade contacts with the Harrapa civilization, and the boundaries of the Akkadian Empire perhaps extended as far as the Indus Valley. After only 40 years, the Akkadian Empire contracted under political pressure and finally collapsed.

The Harrapa civilization collapsed about the time Aryan tribes established themselves in the Indus Valley as well as farther east in Persia (present-day Iran). Several empires flourished in the east until about 550 B.C., when Persians from the southern region of the Iranian plateau, led by Cyrus the Great, gained control of the former Assyrian Empire, which had stretched over much of Anatolia and Mesopotamia. Before long, the Persians also invaded the Indus River Valley.

Greek Travels and Writings

The Greeks had an early knowledge of the Indus (see GREEK EXPLORATION). Greek geographer HECATAEUS OF MILETUS traveled in the eastern Mediterranean between 520 and 494 B.C. He used his observations and information from merchants and mariners to write the first systematic geographic account of the world. With knowledge gleaned from the Persians, Hecataeus described the newly conquered Indus River Valley and first introduced the terms *Indus* and *India* into a European language.

In 510 B.C., Darius I, the successor to Cyrus of Persia, sent Greek mariner SCYLAX to investigate the course of the Indus River in the hope of improving trade and communication with that part of the Persian Empire, as well as providing tactical military information. Scylax traveled overland throughout the Near East, then is thought to have entered the Kabul River, sailing into the Indus and descending it to the Arabian Sea. CTESIAS OF CNIDUS, another Greek, served as court physician to Darius II and traveled throughout the Persian Empire and India on his behalf in the late fifth century B.C. He wrote two accounts of his journeys, *Indicus* and *Persicus,* attempting to discredit the accounts of his contemporary, Greek historian HERODOTUS, who recounted Scylax's expedition down the Indus.

In 331 B.C., Macedonian ALEXANDER THE GREAT, after consolidation of his rule of the Greek city-states and military victories against the Persians in Asia Minor and the Egyptians in North Africa, he marched across into what is now Afghanistan. Informed by the accounts of Herodotus and Ctesias, he descended into India in 327 B.C. After crossing the Indus River and defeating Indians at the Jhelum River, Alexander's army refused to proceed farther east. In 325 B.C., Alexander and his army sailed from the Jhelum to the Indus, following it to the Arabian Sea.

Alexander's empire collapsed into smaller kingdoms shortly after his death in 323 B.C. In about 300–290 B.C. MEGASTHENES, a Greek, and a servant to the king of Syria, one of these kingdoms, traveled as a diplomat making observations of India. With Megasthenes's account, which exists only in fragments, the story of Western travel into the East and through the Indus River Valley, ended for a time.

Chinese Voyages

With the rise of the kingdom of China farther east in the early centuries A.D., the Indus River Valley again became important (see CHINESE EXPLORATION). Due to the imposing central band of the Himalayan mountain range separating the Indian subcontinent from the rest of central Asia, travelers from the east seeking to enter India, or seeking to leave it, were best served by traveling through the less-imposing Hindu Kush range farther west and following the Indus River Valley southward into India.

One such traveler was FA-HSIEN, a Buddhist monk and scholar from east-central China. In A.D. 399, he set out to India with three other monks in order to locate Sanskrit originals of Buddhist texts, which he planned to translate. Fa-hsien crossed into present-day Afghanistan after a long journey through the deserts of central Asia. He followed the Kabul River and entered the Indus Valley. He returned to China by boat after three years in India. Another Buddhist monk, HSÜAN-TSANG, made a similar journey in 629 A.D., crossing into India through the KHYBER PASS from Afghanistan. After years of study and pilgrimage through India, Hsüan-tsang returned but this time followed the Indus River into Afghanistan, returning to China in an overland trade caravan.

❖

In ancient times, the Indus River Valley served as the cradle of the Harrapa civilization. Afterward it was a line of demarcation between the near east lands hellenized by Alexander the Great's conquest and the rest of the Indian subcontinent. For centuries, it remained an important route for travel from central Asia, but as Europeans developed and exploited routes to India over the Arabian Sea, its importance waned. It now serves as an artery of local traffic and also provides irrigation for surrounding lands.

See also ASIA, EXPLORATION OF; EGYPTIAN EXPLORATION.

International Date Line

The International Date Line is an imaginary line extending between the NORTH POLE and the SOUTH POLE, which marks off one calendar day from the next, with a time difference of 24 hours on each side. Situated on the opposite side of Earth from the PRIME MERIDIAN, which is designated as zero degrees longitude, the International Date Line as defined on a map, chart, or GLOBE corresponds most of its length to the 180-degree meridian of longitude, bending eastward around the eastern tip of SIBERIA, westward around the Aleutian Islands and eastward again around various island groups in OCEANIA, thereby avoiding a time change in populated areas.

Throughout history, most localities set their time by the rising and setting of the Sun. By the late 1800s, with increased long-distance communication and travel, a standard time system was needed. By international agreement, Earth's 360 degrees were divided into 24 zones, each measuring about 15 degrees in width, based on Earth's rotation of 15 degrees of longitude per hour. Clocks within a given time zone are set to the same time, with local noon corre-

sponding approximately to the time at which the Sun crosses the central longitude of that zone. Each of the 24 zones is generally one hour later than the zone to its west. A hypothetical eastward traveler from the prime meridian would set a clock ahead one hour for each 15 degrees of longitude, the clock thus gaining 12 hours; a westward traveler from the prime meridian would set a clock back one hour for each 15 degrees, the clock losing 12 hours. The two clocks would therefore differ by 24 hours, or one calendar day, which necessitates a date change.

See also GEOGRAPHY AND CARTOGRAPHY; LATITUDE AND LONGITUDE; MAPS AND CHARTS.

International Geophysical Year (IGY)

Geophysics is the study of the structure, composition, and dynamic changes of Earth and its cosmic environment, involving a variety of scientific disciplines. The International Geophysical Year (IGY) was an 18-month period, from July 1957 to December 1958, designated for cooperative study of Earth's geophysics. The time frame was selected because it was a period of intense solar activity. Scientists of 66 nations participated. Studies were conducted on solar activity, cosmic rays, auroras, the ionosphere, the upper atmosphere, geomagnetism, gravity, meteorology, glaciers, oceanography, and LATITUDE AND LONGITUDE. Some of the endeavors relate to the history of exploration.

Among the many accomplishments during IGY were the launching into space of *Sputnik 1*, the first artificial SATELLITE by the Union of Soviet Socialist Republics (USSR; Soviet Union) on October 4, 1957. The Soviet Union launched the much larger *Sputnik 2* on November 3, 1957, which carried a dog, Laika. The first U.S. satellite, *Explorer 1*, launched on January 31, 1958, discovered the Van Allen belts, a zone of trapped radiation surrounding Earth; subsequent satellites performed additional tests. In the field of oceanography, soundings were made of the floor of both the Pacific and Atlantic Oceans. The surveys led to the discovery of seismically active rifts in submarine mountains and furthered knowledge of plate tectonics. More than 300 observation stations were set up in Arctic regions. Knowledge of Antarctic geography was furthered in the Commonwealth Trans-Antarctic Expedition of 1957–58, headed by Englishman SIR VIVIAN ERNEST FUCHS and New Zealander SIR EDMUND PERCIVAL HILLARY. (The U.S. Navy's Operation Deep Freeze to Antarctica, involving aviator RICHARD EVELYN BYRD, was carried out in 1956 in preparation for IGY.) The spirit of cooperation generated around IGY led to the Antarctic Treaty, declaring the continent a nonmilitary area to be used only for scientific study and used to govern Antarctica since 1961.

IGY was followed in 1964–65 by the International Years of the Quiet Sun (IQSY) to obtain data for comparison of a time of minimum solar activity with that of the earlier studies. IGY has led to continuing research and monitoring of geophysics, partly because of a growing sense of urgency among scientists regarding the effects of human activities on Earth, such as increasing levels of carbon dioxide in the atmosphere resulting from the burning of fossil fuels, the so-called greenhouse effect.

See also NATURAL SCIENCE AND EXPLORATION; OCEANOGRAPHY AND EXPLORATION; SPACE EXPLORATION).

J

junk

The junk, a type of ship designed by the Chinese, has several unique features. Among them are a broad and square bow and a raised poopdeck—a partial deck at the rear of the boat above the main deck—on which is mounted a center long rudder for steerage. The rudder can be lowered in deep water to act as a centerboard, or raised in shallow water where necessary; it is controlled by a long tiller, which enables it to be moved quickly for fast maneuverability. This rudder design was achieved centuries before Europeans also adapted it. The bottom of the boat is flat, sometimes with a small keel. The junk has two or more masts with battened four-cornered sails, known as lugsails. The battens, or bamboo rods dividing the sail into sections, make the sail stiffer than single-section sails and more efficient in using wind. Moreover, the sections can be raised or lowered depending on condition. The junks of today use cotton sails, but in the past they were made with various types of fiber matting. The Chinese compare this type of sail to an ear, which "listens for the wind."

Chinese have used junks for millennia. The earliest known reference to the boat is from the time of emperor Fu Hsi, in about 2800 B.C. They were used for fishing, transportation, trading, and warfare. Junks would sail the oceans, traveling southward from China to the Malay Peninsula, India, CEYLON (present-day Sri Lanka), and even to the east coast of Africa. The recovery of ancient Chinese coins is evidence of these journeys. In writings by Muslims are found descriptions of junks on the Euphrates River in the seventh century A.D.

The great age of the seafaring junks lasted from the 12th to the 15th century. At this time the Chinese were active in trade with the merchants in the EAST INDIES and India. One of the first known Europeans to see a fleet of junks was Italian MARCO POLO in the 13th century. He described them in some detail, with their watertight compartments, helping to prevent sinking in case of a puncture (and able to carry liquid cargoes), iron nails to secure its planks, and dovetailed joints for strength. He was in awe of their size and related how a junk might have 50 to 60 cabins, each one occupied by a trader and his goods, and supporting him in comfort. By the 15th century, junks had become colossal in size, some of them 400 feet long and 160 feet wide. CHENG HO, a Chinese admiral and explorer of that century, commanded a vast fleet of large junks.

The ease of control and dependability in poor conditions have made the junk useful in the modern coastal waters and in the rivers of the Far East—especially in China, Japan, and Indonesia—for fishing and commerce. Some seen in seaports are 70 feet long, displacing some 100 tons. Some families live on their junks.

See also CHINESE EXPLORATION; MUSLIM EXPLORATION; SHIPBUILDING AND EXPLORATION.

Shown here, in a photograph from the early 20th century, is a Chinese junk in the harbor of Hong Kong. *(North Bennington, Vt.: H.C. White Co., c1907; Library of Congress [LC-USZ62-118818])*

K

---

keelboat

The term *keelboat* refers to a long, slender, shallow boat with a keel and a covering to protect cargo and crew. It was principally powered by poles or oars, although some keelboats had hand-cranked paddle wheels or sails to take advantage of useful winds. The design of the keelboat made it suitable for use on rivers, especially the moving of freight. A large keelboat could carry 80 tons of goods. But they were also used as early passenger vessels, especially on the MISSISSIPPI RIVER and MISSOURI RIVER. Early U.S. expeditions up the Missouri, such as those under MERIWETHER LEWIS and WILLIAM CLARK in 1804 and ZEBULON MONTGOMERY PIKE in 1805, made use of the keelboat. It was also an essential craft in the Missouri River FUR TRADE of the early 1800s.

When steamships came into use (the first one on the Mississippi in 1811), they generally replaced the keelboat (although, in 1825, Colonel HENRY ATKINSON used keelboats for a second military expedition along the Missouri and Yellowstone Rivers after steamships broke down on the first). Two-way traffic on the river, with and against the current, was accomplished more efficiently by steam power. In modern usage, the term *keelboat* refers to a sailing vessel with a ballasted keel giving stability in ocean racing.

See also SHIPBUILDING AND EXPLORATION.

Khyber Pass

The Khyber Pass is the most important mountain pass in western Asia. Connecting modern-day Afghanistan and Pakistan, it runs just more than 30 miles through the Safed Koh mountain range, extending to the south from the Hindu Kush mountain range. Of the five passes that connect Afghanistan to Pakistan through these mountains, the Khyber Pass is favored because it is the shortest route. Winding through the mountains, it varies in width from 450 to 15 feet. Before modern improvements, travelers could touch both walls with outstretched hands while passing the narrowest region of the pass. Near Kabul, Afghanistan, the altitude of the pass is about 1,404 feet; on its opposite end near Peshawar, Pakistan, it reaches a maximum elevation of 3,517 feet. Two streams run through the pass, and on either side rise sheer shale and limestone cliffs between 600 and 1,000 feet high.

Because of the many mountain ranges surrounding the Indian subcontinent, the Khyber Pass, before air travel, provided the best route from central Asia into India, and played an important part in trade along the SILK ROAD, linking the major route between China and the MEDITERRANEAN SEA with India. It also provided easy access to the INDUS RIVER, which merchants could use to sail into the Arabian Sea. Many travelers to India followed the trade routes through the Hindu Kush, including the first Chinese explorers of India. The Khyber Pass was also a convenient route for invasion, and Darius I of Persia (present-day Iran), part of Macedonian ALEXANDER THE GREAT's army, and people of the Islamic Mughal (Mogul) Empire all traversed it, attempting to invade India.

In the 19th century, as Britain and Russia vied for superiority in central Asia, Afghanistan and the Khyber Pass became a contested area. In the course of shoring up their defense of its Indian possessions and later during the Anglo-Afghan wars, there were many skirmishes between the British and Afghan natives. In January 1842, some 16,000 British and Indian soldiers were killed fighting in the pass. The British made modifications to the pass, constructing a road in 1879, and expanding that road in the 1920s as well as building a railroad.

The importance of the Khyber Pass was greatly diminished with the advent of air travel, but it is still used today. During the Afghan civil war of the 1980s, 3 million refugees fled through the pass into Pakistan.

Kilimanjaro, Mount

Mount Kilimanjaro, part of Africa's Eastern Highlands, is a mountain located in northeastern Tanzania, near its border with Kenya. The highest mountain on the continent, it actually consists of two peaks, seven miles apart and connected by a ridge. Kibo is the higher peak at 19,341 feet above sea level; Mawensi is 16,893 feet.

Greek merchant DIOGENES perhaps viewed Mount Kilimanjaro in the first century A.D. Hellenized Egyptian PTOLEMY produced a map the next century showing the MOUNTAINS OF THE MOON, most often associated with the Ruwenzori Mountains, but possibly representing Mount Kilimanjaro and the second-highest peak in Africa, Mount Kenya, at 17,057 feet. German missionaries JOHANN REBMANN and JOHANN LUDWIG KRAPF are known to have seen Kilimanjaro in 1848. Krapf also sighted Mount Kenya.

Kibo was first scaled in 1889 by German geographer HANS MEYER and Austrian mountain climber Ludwig Purtscheller. Meyer had made two earlier unsuccessful attempts, in 1887 and 1888. On his 1889 expedition, Meyer explored the ice-covered crater at the top and determined that the mountain is a dormant volcano. Since that time, numerous other expeditions have reached the summit of both peaks. Tourism related to MOUNTAIN CLIMBING, as well as farming along the mountain's lower southern slopes, provide income for inhabitants in the region.

King Solomon's mines   See OPHIR.

L

land bridge

A land bridge is a stretch of land connecting two landmasses, such as islands or continents. In the history of exploration, the term is applied to the land bridge across the BERING STRAIT, once connecting Asia and North America. It is theorized that over it came the Paleo-Indians, Stone Age peoples from Asia, the real discoverers of the Americas.

Earth's most recent ice age, referred to as the Wisconsin glaciation with regard to North America and the Wurm glaciation with regard to Europe, lasted from about 90,000 or 75,000 to 8000 B.C. It is theorized that at various times during the Wisconsin glaciation, enough of the planet's water was locked up in ice to lower the oceans and expose what is now submerged land. The narrowest part of the Bering Strait, between Cape Dezhnyov in Russia and Cape Prince of Wales in Alaska, is 51 miles. During the ice age, along with more coastal lands revealed, there would have been a stretch of land, possibly as much as 1,000 miles wide, bridging the two continents. The Bering Strait land bridge, or Beringia, would have consisted of the treeless plains of the tundra; the islands of today in the region, such as the Diomede Islands, would have been mountains.

Based on archaeological evidence, it is known that Mongolian peoples of Asia hunted large mammals, such as big game, including woolly mammoths, mastodons, and saber-toothed tigers. The big game of the ice age could have migrated across the land bridge. And the human hunters and their families could have followed them. The time of the first such travelers is not known. The estimated time frequently cited by scholars has been before 11,200 years ago. More recent archaeological finds have led scholars to an estimated time of before 12,500 years ago. Other archaeological evidence in both North and South America, along with DNA and linguistic evidence, has resulted in an estimated time of before 33,000 years ago. Possibly other Paleo-Indians reached the Americas by boat. Descendants of all these ancient explorers spread throughout the Americas over subsequent generations. Later voyagers, in particular Inuit (Eskimo) and Aleut peoples of the Arctic region, were known to have traveled by boat from SIBERIA after the land bridge had been flooded again.

It is thought that Aborigines on the island of TASMANIA reached there by way of a land bridge before 35,000 years ago. When waters rose and the land was covered, they became isolated from Australia's Aborigines. The Isthmus of Panama in CENTRAL AMERICA is sometimes discussed as a current land bridge.

lateen rig

The term *lateen rig* refers to the triangular sails used by boats and ships that optimize speed and control in adverse winds, in contrast to square-rigged sails. A lateen-rigged ship had sails attached to a long yard and pivoted skyward on a relatively short mast. Although this arrangement was not as sturdy as square rigging in strong, favorable winds, it was

Shown here, in an early 20th-century engraving, is a sailboat with a lateen rig. *(Library of Congress, Prints and Photographs Division [LC-USZ62-105524])*

ideal for lighter, contrary winds, where sailing close to shore was desired. Lateen-rigged ships would often have two or three masts, and the sails could be turned to catch the best wind. This is also known as a fore-and-aft rig. Another advantage of the lateen-rigged ships was their ability to make the most efficient use of tacking when sailing windward. Large square-rigged vessels came to use a triangular sail on their mizzenmast (mast behind the main mast) for added maneuverability.

The lateen rig was imported from the Arab DHOW and employed by shipbuilders, who worked for 15th-century sponsor of expeditions HENRY THE NAVIGATOR, prince of Portugal, in the making of the CARAVEL. With a small but robust hull, stern-mounted rudder, and lateen rig, the caravel proved a major advance in ship design. It was used to

great advantage in navigating the difficult and unpredictable African coastal waters at the beginning of the EUROPEAN AGE OF EXPLORATION.

See also SHIPBUILDING AND EXPLORATION.

latitude and longitude

The term *latitude,* used geographically, is the angular distance of any point on the surface of Earth north or south of the EQUATOR. *Longitude* refers to the angular distance on Earth's surface measured along the equator east or west from its intersection with a designated north-south line known as the PRIME MERIDIAN. Latitude and longitude together provide a grid—a system of geometrical coordinates—which can be used in identifying any location on the Earth's surface.

Parallels of latitude, imaginary east-west parallel circles around Earth, enable one to locate a place north or south of the equator. The equator is the longest of the parallels, with the length of the others decreasing the farther north or south they are represented; they are measured in angles from zero degrees at the equator to 90 degrees at the NORTH POLE and the SOUTH POLE. Meridians of longitude, imaginary parallel half-circles running through the North Pole to the South Pole, enable one to locate a place east or west of the prime meridian; they all are the same length. They are measured in angles from zero degrees at the prime meridian to 180 degrees at the INTERNATIONAL DATE LINE. Each degree of latitude and longitude is divided into 60 minutes, and each minute, into 60 seconds, to allow for precise numerical designations.

In most current cartographic representations—either a GLOBE, map, or chart—parallels of latitude are indicated in multiples of five degrees. In addition, most representations show four fractional parallels, which have special meanings, based on the Sun's relation to Earth and climate: They are, north to south, the ARCTIC CIRCLE, TROPIC OF CANCER, TROPIC OF CAPRICORN, and ANTARCTIC CIRCLE. The equator, tropic of Cancer, and tropic of Capricorn were the first three reference lines on maps.

Greek Scholarship

The ancient Greeks determined these lines based on the Sun's movement. The tendency of Greek scholars was to focus more on the abstract and theoretical than on the empirical; they believed that the most important goal of philosophy was to discover the Ideal Forms, of which the forms we perceive with our senses are but imperfect imitations; the study of mathematics was the high road to such knowledge. Thus, it was natural for them to try to discover mathematical principles underlying everything in the universe, including the shape and size of Earth and its relationship with the heavenly bodies. The generally accepted idea about this was that Earth, a perfect sphere, lay in the exact center of a much larger sphere on the surface of which were fixed the heavenly bodies. As noted elsewhere, for the Greeks physical existence was nested, as it were, firmly within metaphysical existence, as the spherical Earth nested within the concentric celestial sphere, beyond which, so Plato believed, lay heaven itself, the abode of the gods.

The celestial sphere rotated around Earth on an axis running through the poles; thus the different heavenly bodies as they moved described imaginary lines around Earth's surface that were parallel to one another, the largest of these being the equator. The best way to define or fix the position of any locality on Earth lay in finding its relationship with the celestial sphere, which was eternal, perfect, and divine. This was done by determining, at any given locality, the angle between a line drawn from the observer through a point on the horizon and a line through the North Pole and South Pole, the axis of rotation of the celestial sphere. This angle would be exactly the same for all localities along a line parallel to that of the equator, running east and west, and perpendicular to the celestial axis. A system of parallel lines running around Earth, called *klimata*, which means inclination, began to be devised, sometime before third-century B.C. Greek astronomer and geographer ERATOSTHENES himself worked on these matters, adding other lines. A second-century B.C. Greek astronomer and mathematician, HIPPARCHUS, further developed the concept, making the east-west lines parallel and the north-south lines at right angles to them.

By the second century A.D., these lines were referred to as latitude and longitude. Hellenized Egyptian PTOLEMY made the system of coordinates more accurate by choosing lines so that the longest day of the year differed from one to the next by a quarter of an hour. In 1569, the publication of a map accurately depicting latitude and longitude—the technique created by Flemish cartographer GERARDUS MERCATOR known as the MERCATOR PROJECTION—revolutionized mapmaking.

Early Navigational Instruments

For the purposes of navigation, instruments were needed to determine latitude and longitude. Early devices, such as the ASTROLABE, CROSS-STAFF, and Davis QUADRANT, gave readings of latitude. For centuries, finding longitude depended on DEAD RECKONING—a system of collecting information involving the use of a magnetic COMPASS, an hourglass, a measuring line, and a TRAVERSE BOARD for recording the information, in order to estimate distance traveled east or west. The inaccuracy of this method is illustrated by Italian mariner CHRISTOPHER COLUMBUS's famous error in believing, when he made landfall in the Americas on behalf of Spain, after traveling only 66 degrees, that he had arrived in the islands of the China Sea, some 230 degrees from Spain. The solution of the "longitude problem" awaited the invention of an accurate way of keeping time since comparing the time of day at any location with that of the current time at one's point of departure will give the number of degrees traveled east or west from that point. (Since Earth revolves once in 24 hours and each horizontal circle of latitude measures 360 degrees, a difference in time of one hour between two points means they are 15 degrees apart.) This method, in principle, was first proposed in the 17th century by Italian scientist Galileo after he made his discovery of the moons of Jupiter. He realized that they could be used as an extraterrestrial clock by observing and noting the times at which each passed behind Jupiter and then reappeared; using a diary of the timing of their movements compiled at one's home port, observations made on board a ship would give the current time back home. However, it proved impractical to make accurate enough sightings of Jupiter's moons at sea.

The Longitude Problem

During the 18th century, the French and British governments were engaged in an equivalent of the 20th-century space race between the United States and Union of Soviet Socialist Republics (USSR; Soviet Union) as they strove to solve the longitude problem; on the accurate determination of location at sea depended supremacy in trade, naval warfare, and world dominance. For this reason, the two governments built observatories at Greenwich in England and in Paris, since it was assumed that longitude would be able to be determined by celestial observation as latitude was. Isaac Newton, a 17th- to 18th-century English physicist and mathematician, was the principal proponent of this theory; he insisted that no timepiece could be accurate enough to be relied upon. (Newton's strength as a theorist, able to comprehend universal laws of nature, perhaps tended to blind him to practicality.) The idea was to take Galileo's idea a step further and use the whole sky as a clock; if the Moon's movements among the stars were tracked and compared to the "sun time" for any locality, this information could be used to tell the time for that locality from anywhere on Earth. Astronomers of the time realized that current knowledge about star and Moon positions was insufficiently accurate for this purpose; thus the principal reason the British and French observatories were built was to gain more precise astronomical data. In this way the search for better navigational techniques contributed to the advancement of science in general.

However, the ultimate solution to the "longitude problem" turned out to be more humble—the invention of a very accurate timepiece, or CHRONOMETER. John Harrison, a carpenter in Yorkshire, England, became interested in clock design while serving as a bell ringer in his church and watching the pendulumlike swing of the bells. In 1714, the English Parliament in conjunction with the ROYAL SOCIETY had offered a prize of £20,000 to whomever succeeded in making the accurate determination of longitude possible. The Longitude Prize was a result of a naval disaster that took place in 1707, in which a large proportion of the nation's navy was wrecked, killing thousands of sailors, when the fleet crashed into a reef off the Scilly Islands because of uncertainty over their position. Realizing that an accurate timepiece might be the solution, Harrison engaged in extensive experimentation using different materials, beginning with woods, then different metals. He compared his clocks to star movements to assess their accuracy and to each other. In 1735, he completed his first model, which made use of different metals in the mechanism to adjust to temperature differences; it was tested at sea in 1736 on a particularly stormy voyage and proved to be accurate to within five to 10 seconds a day. Only after many years of work, in the 1760s, were his chronometer clocks accurate enough to win the Longitude Prize. Meanwhile, in the early 1730s, various inventors developed the SEXTANT, an improvement on earlier instruments used to measure the angular elevation of celestial bodies. English optician John Hadley built a version (based on Newton's notes), and American Thomas Godfrey constructed one in Philadelphia, both of which could determine latitude but not longitude. John Campbell designed a sextant that could measure longitude as well in 1757.

❖

The concept of latitude and longitude, in addition to its terrestrial application, is used in various celestial coordinate systems. One of these is the ecliptic coordinate system, based on an imaginary ecliptic, or great circle of the celestial sphere, with the imaginary plane with coordinates passing through the centers of both Earth and Sun.

See also GEOGRAPHY AND CARTOGRAPHY; GREEK EXPLORATION; MAPS AND CHARTS; NAVIGATION AND EXPLORATION.

legends and exploration

Mythology has helped inspire world exploration from ancient to modern times. Explorers have set out on numerous expeditions in search of wealthy lands, lost peoples, hoped-for routes, or cures. Geographic misconceptions have endured over the centuries, and exploration can be regarded as an empirical method to confirm or disprove myths. Some of these myths have endured to present times. And some unconfirmed exploratory journeys have also taken on legendary status.

Enduring Myths

An example of a geographic myth that still endures in some circles is the sunken island of ATLANTIS. First mention of Atlantis is found in the fourth-century B.C. writings of Greek philosopher Plato. He spoke of a Western Ocean, where the great civilization of Atlantis had thrived. The location has been identified with various locations in the MEDITERRANEAN SEA and the Atlantic Ocean, and new theories still crop up.

Another Greek myth, this one associated with the voyage of scholar PYTHEAS to the Arctic Sea in the fourth century B.C., is that of ULTIMA THULE, reputed to be the northernmost land, six days travel north of the British Isles. Since Pytheas's writings on the voyage have not survived, details are from later sources, one from Roman scholar PLINY THE ELDER of the first century A.D., who coined the name for the land. Varying theories hold that the northernmost land described by Pytheas was Norway, ICELAND, or Jan Mayen Island in the Arctic Ocean. The question surrounding this myth, unlike the story of Atlantis, is not whether such a place existed, but what the place attached to the myth really is.

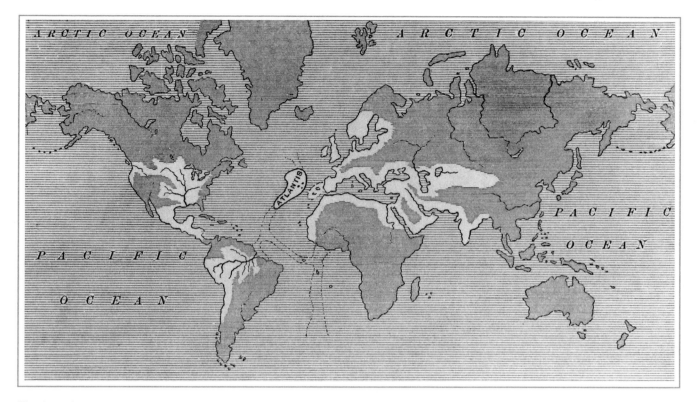

This hypothetical world map shows the empire of Atlantis; it appeared in Ignatius Donnelly's book *Atlantis: The Antediluvian World*, published in 1882. *(Library of Congress, Prints and Photographs Divisions [LC-USZ62-90566])*

Disproved Myths

An example of a geographic myth that has been disproved is that of the GREAT SOUTHERN CONTINENT, also known as Terra Australis or Terra Australis Incognito, a continent supposedly located in the Southern Hemisphere. This myth also originated among the ancient Greeks (see GREEK EXPLORATION), who, on determining that the Earth was a sphere, theorized that, based on a concept of balance and symmetry, the south must contain a similar ratio of land to sea as the north. The story lasted through the Middle Ages and RENAISSANCE, with ships of various nations searching for Terra Australis in the southern oceans. It came to be associated with another fabled land supposedly reached by Frenchman Binot Palmière de Gonneville in 1503, GONNEVILLE'S LAND. It was not until the late 18th century, when Englishman JAMES COOK journeyed far enough south to determine that Terra Australis did not exist. Other continents, not quite fitting the theories, were discovered, however—Australia and Antarctica.

Truth in Legends

Truth often blends with myth, as in the case of the supposed voyages of sixth-century Irish monk SAINT BRENDAN and an island known as ST. BRENDAN'S ISLE. Historical evidence indicates that, in the course of his sea pilgrimages, Brendan visited Wales on the British Isles, Brittany, in what is now northwestern France, and the Hebrides Islands west of Scotland. But, in some medieval literature, he is also purported to have visited an island somewhere in the Atlantic, hypothesized as Iceland, GREENLAND, the CANARY ISLANDS, the AZORES, the Madeira Islands, or the Bahama Islands. If Saint Brendan did in fact reach the Bahamas, he would have been the European discoverer of the Americas, even before the Vikings, a theory that, without any archaeological evidence, has to remain as myth as do theorized transatlantic voyages—by DRIFT VOYAGE—of other seagoing peoples of the Mediterranean region.

The writings describing Viking journeys at the turn of 11th century—the *Saga of Eric the Red* and the *Saga of the Greenlanders*—regarding the travels of ERIC THE RED, LEIF ERICSSON, and other Norsemen, were long considered largely myth until archaeological evidence in Newfoundland indicated a Viking presence in North America. Both Irish and Viking accounts, mythical or not, reportedly influenced later explorers to look for lands across the Atlantic. A map, supposedly from the mid-15th century and found in 1957—the so-called VINLAND MAP—which cartographically confirmed the Norse voyages to North America, turned out to be a forgery—in effect a legendary map—but, because of the archaeological evidence, did not do anything to detract from the truth of the Norse discovery of North America.

KUPE, a 10th-century Polynesian, as legend has it, pursued the Squid King in the South Pacific Ocean, leading to the discovery of NEW ZEALAND. It is known that the Polynesians did in fact migrate to New Zealand and became ancestral to the Maori, another case of truth blending with myth.

Venetian merchant MARCO POLO, who traveled extensively in the Far East in the late 13th century, described CIPANGU as an island containing palaces with roofs of gold and streets paved in marble, one of more than 7,000 islands in an archipelago in the Sea of China, off the Pacific coast of Asia. Two centuries later, both CHRISTOPHER COLUMBUS, an Italian sailing for Spain, and JOHN CABOT, an Italian sailing for England, sought this fabled island, thought to be a major source of spices, which has come to be associated most with Japan.

Another example of a legend with some truth is that of the Strait of Anian (see ANIAN, STRAIT OF), a mythical version of a NORTHWEST PASSAGE through North America from the Atlantic Ocean to the Pacific Ocean. Such a strait supposedly extended from the Atlantic coast somewhere north of Labrador to a more southerly latitude on the Pacific coast. Although a concept of the 15th century until late 18th century, its name was gleaned from the writings of Marco Polo, one of the texts that explorers studied in the hope of finding a practical water route from Europe to Asia. No such waterway fitting that description was located, although, in 1903–06, Norwegian ROALD ENGELBREGT GRAVNING AMUNDSEN did navigate a water route in the Arctic Ocean north of North America. Unlike the legendary Strait of Anian, supposedly a year-round route, the real Northwest Passage proved impractical because of annual freezing.

Legends out of History

Theories surrounding the LOST COLONY—part of the story of the first attempt at an English colony as sponsored by SIR WALTER RALEIGH in the late 16th century—demonstrate how legends evolve out of historical fact. The story of the colonists and how they struggled to survive along the coast of what is now northeastern North Carolina is known up to the point that their leader JOHN WHITE departed for England in 1587. When he returned to the region three years later, there was no trace of the colonists—who included his daughter, Eleanor White Dare, and his granddaughter, Virginia Dare—other than the word "CROATOAN" written on a stockade post. Since no evidence has been found to prove or disprove speculation regarding what happened to them, various myths endure, such as that they became ancestral to certain area tribes, some of whom have non-Indian blood. Reports of blue-eyed or bearded Native Americans passed down over the years often were associated with the Lost Colonists. Much folklore and literature surrounds Virginia Dare, the first English child born in the America, one of the most fantastic fables of which is that she was transformed into a white doe.

Wealthy Kingdoms

Among the most persistent myths are those involving wealthy lands. South America has the legends of the City of LOS CÉSARES and of EL DORADO, which set in motion numerous expeditions by various European nations in the 16th and 17th centuries. North America has the Seven Cities of CIBOLA and the related QUIVIRA, sought by FRANCISCO VÁSQUEZ DE CORONADO in the 16th century. Real encounters with native peoples—in particular the Aztec and Inca—who did possess quantities of gold, silver, and gemstones—helped further legends of such lands. The legend of the Seven Cities of Cibola has its origins in that of the Seven Cities of Antillia from centuries before, more evidence of the endurance of myths. Meanwhile, the French—JACQUES CARTIER in the 16th century and SAMUEL DE CHAMPLAIN in the 17th century—sought the legendary land of SAGUENAY in Quebec. FOOL'S GOLD, another name for iron pyrites, was mistakenly thought to be real gold by a number of explorers, including Jacques Cartier, as he searched for Saguenay.

The location of another wealthy land, OPHIR, referenced in the Bible in connection with the Hebrews—where King Solomon's mines are supposed to have been located—has been debated over the years: lands in Africa or Asia; or as far away in Asia as India, the Ural Mountains, or Japan; or on other continents altogether, in the Americas, Australia, or New Zealand.

Individuals and Myth

Some legends involve specific people. A "White King" was reported to rule a kingdom somewhere in South America, which was absorbed into the legends of Los Césares and El Dorado. Surrounding a real-life Welsh prince MADOC of the 12th century, there arose a legend that he had made a voyage in the Atlantic Ocean to a faraway land where there were human inhabitants and, after his return to Wales, set out on a colonizing expedition, never to be heard from again. It is not known whether geographer RICHARD HAKLUYT and others who promoted the idea in the late 16th century actually were convinced the story was true or were using it as propaganda on behalf of Queen Elizabeth I of England to make a claim for the discovery of North America more than three centuries before Italian Christopher Columbus's voyage for Spain. In any case, the legend persisted into the 19th century, when some travelers tried to establish a connection with the Mandan Indians of the upper Missouri and a lost Welsh people. The story resembles that of the 10 Lost Tribes of Israel, who supposedly, on being conquered by the Assyrians, were exiled from their

homeland in the eighth century B.C. Since the ultimate fate of these people is unknown, there has been speculation over the centuries regarding where they settled, leading to theories that they ended up in various places in Asia, Africa, Europe, or the Americas.

PRESTER JOHN is one of the most famous of all legendary individuals. Numerous texts and maps from the 12th to the 17th centuries refer to a Christian ruler and his wealthy kingdom in Asia or Africa. Numerous explorers, such as Italian Marco Polo, who traveled to Asia in the 13th century, and Portuguese PERO DA COVILHÃ, who visited East Africa in the 15th century, hoped to find such a person. The start of the legend, which became ever more fantastic over the centuries, may have been based in truth since a community of Nestorian Christians were thought to have migrated from Constantinople (present-day Istanbul) somewhere in Asia east of territory controlled by Muslims. (Nestorianism—the name taken from Nestorius, the fifth-century patriarch of Constantinople—was a theological position maintaining the human nature of Christ was independent from the divine nature.) One of the writers on Prester John is legendary himself. *Travels of Sir John Mandeville,* a work originally written in Norman French and published between 1357 and 1371, with some 300 total translations in English and most European languages, is thought to have been written by a citizen of Liège in present-day Belgium under the pseudonym of SIR JOHN MANDEVILLE. That the work is obviously a compilation of other medieval explorers' travels—such as Marco Polo and Italian missionary ODORIC OF PORDENONE of the 14th century—has led scholars to this interpretation of "Mandeville" as a pseudonym, although some maintain he was a real person who borrowed from other travel accounts.

The FOUNTAIN OF YOUTH, a water source that supposedly gave eternal life, was a concept associated with Prester John, who supposedly drank from it. It later became a primary motivation for JUAN PONCE DE LEÓN—who had heard about such a phenomenon while Spanish governor of Puerto Rico—in his explorations of the Bahamas and Florida in the early 16th century.

❖

The history of cartography demonstrates the evolution of myths and their debunking as voyages of exploration defined the world map. Some of those myths—such as sea or land monsters—although partly based on ignorance, were actually a kind of misinformation purposely passed to prevent other peoples from traveling the same routes.

Levant

The term *Levant,* in its historical usage, referred to the countries along the eastern MEDITERRANEAN SEA, especially in the Near East, but also Egypt, Turkey, and Greece. The name is derived from the Italian word *levante,* which means "rising," as with regard to the Sun—the French verb *lever* means to rise. It came to be applied to the concept of east and was originally applied to all of the Orient. People of the Levant have been referred to as Levantines by other Europeans. The Arabic equivalent of *Levant* is *Mashriq,* for "the country where the sun rises."

Italy was the dominant European power in the Mediterranean during the second half of the Middle Ages and into the RENAISSANCE, acting as the middleman for trade between the Levant and the rest of Europe. In 1581, the LEVANT COMPANY was chartered in England to develop trade with the region. In recent times, Syria and Lebanon have been called the Levant States.

See also ASIA, EXPLORATION OF.

Levant Company

The Levant Company—also known as the Turkey Company—was one of the first of the English-chartered trading companies. It formed a commercial bridge between East and West in a way that had not been previously developed.

In 1579, Queen Elizabeth I sent her ambassador William Harburn to Murad III, the sultan of Turkey, to request permission to trade on terms equal to those then existing between Turkey and other Europeans, such as the Venetians of northern Italy. The request was granted, and in 1581, Elizabeth chartered the Levant Company for a period of seven years, and with limited membership. To accommodate this new opportunity, larger, stronger ships were built (see MERCHANT SHIP). Soon the English were trading wool and tin, abundant in England, with the region of the LEVANT, flanking the eastern MEDITERRANEAN SEA, for dates, figs, hemp, coffee, and medicines. The Venetians, who had previously enjoyed a monopoly on this traffic, objected. The Spanish attacked English vessels, as did the pirates of the BARBARY COAST. The company agreed in short order to pay the tribute demanded by these pirates. Still, the price of Eastern goods decreased substantially in England, and the company was profitable.

In 1605, James I, Elizabeth's successor, revised the Levant Company's charter as a joint-stock venture. Any English person with £25 could buy a share in the concern. Along with those of the investor community, the interests of the government became increasingly entwined with that of the company, with customs duties and payments made for the continuation of its privileges. Profits continued to soar, however, and the Levant Company's rate of return was about 300 percent at this time.

The company's trade was relatively stable for much of the 17th century. In 1680, after an ongoing dispute with the BRITISH EAST INDIA COMPANY over the importation of raw silk, Parliament agreed to hear the Levantine's grievances. The Levant Company accused the British East India Company of sending weavers to India to teach them their skills, thus attempting to destroy the Lancashire industries. The British East India Company countered by accusing the Levant Company of exporting too much bullion. Without gaining satisfaction from Parliament, the Levant Company responded by sending ships on "the Cape Route" to India, that is around the CAPE OF GOOD HOPE of Africa. They eventually gained the right to trade in India as well.

With increased competition from home and abroad, the Levant Company experienced a steady decline throughout the 18th century. The French, who had established a Levant Company of their own, were more conveniently located and paid more attention to the Eastern market than did the British. They exported lighter and fancier cloth, which was better suited to the climate, and undercut the British company's profits. The Treaty of Paris in 1763 between France and England marked a turning point from which the company never recovered because of growing French competition. In 1780, Parliament earmarked £10,000 to keep the company afloat, a noteworthy change of circumstances. In 1825, the Levant Company closed its doors, as trade in the Mediterranean became increasingly deregulated.

See also COMMERCE AND EXPLORATION.

Lhasa

Lhasa is a city located near the Lhasa River, a tributary of the Brahmaputra, in the southeastern end of the Tibetan HIMALAYAS. Surrounded on three sides by mountains, Lhasa receives little rain and has sparse vegetation. Temperatures vary from 85 degrees Fahrenheit during the day to minus two degrees at night. The city is the capital of Tibet, part of present-day China, as well as the center of Tibetan Buddhism.

Lhasa enters recorded history in the seventh century A.D., when Songtsen Gampo, a Tibetan born about A.D. 608, united Tibet through conquest and made Lhasa his capital. After conquering Nepal in 640, Gampo married a Nepalese princess, and, the following year, in a display of his power, took the daughter of the Tang Emperor in China as his second wife. Under the influence of his two wives, Gampo converted to Buddhism, then established it as the state religion. Gampo built the first palace of Potala and the temple of Jokhang. In 836, the kingdom of Tibet collapsed as Lang Darma captured the throne through fratricide and outlawed Buddhism. With the dissolution of the kingdom, Lhasa dwindled in importance.

Gradually, Buddhism reasserted itself through the influence of missionaries from India and China. In the late 14th century, Tsung-Khapa established the Yellow-Hat sect of Buddhism, which dominated Tibetan Buddhism. The chief abbot or lama of the Yellow-Hat sect was revered by the Mongols, who called him Dalai for his great wisdom. It was during the reign of the fifth Dalai Lama, in 1641, that Lhasa again became the capital of a unified Tibet.

Early European Visitors

The first Europeans to arrive in Lhasa, in 1661, were two Jesuit missionaries, JOHANN GRUEBER of Germany and ALBERT D'ORVILLE of Flanders (although Italian missionary ODORIC OF PORDENONE may have reached it in the 14th century). Grueber and D'Orville remained in Lhasa for a month, reporting that the "common people" ate raw meat and never washed. They were most impressed, however, by the great Potala palace, which had originally been built by Songtsen Gampo. The currently standing Potala palace was built to replace the original palace between 1645 and 1693. The palace contains over a thousand rooms, stands 330 feet, or 13 stories, high, and stretches 1,310 feet east to west and 1,150 feet from north to south.

The next Westerners to visit Lhasa were an Italian Jesuit, IPPOLITO DESIDERI, and a Portuguese Jesuit, Emmanuel Freye. Desideri had spent several months in India studying the Persian language before he set out from Delhi, India, in September 1714. He continued north to Lahore, making his way with a native caravan through the mountains before setting foot in Lhasa in March 1716. Desideri remained in Lhasa for five years, studying the Tibetan language and preaching. He was recalled abruptly from Tibet by Rome, and the account of his travels remained unpublished for 200 years. After Desideri, Capuchin monks of the Franciscan order stayed and preached in Lhasa, the last leaving in 1745. By the end of the 18th century, Tibet had become closely allied with China, and, under Chinese influence, closed its borders to all foreigners with penalty of torture and death. Lhasa became known to Europeans as the "Forbidden City."

In 1811, THOMAS MANNING, a British scholar in the service of the BRITISH EAST INDIA COMPANY, attempted to reach Lhasa but was refused entrance. Manning, however, disguised himself heavily and rode up to the Potala palace. He was recognized as a European but was allowed a five-month stay and an audience with the seven-year-old Dalai Lama.

Two French-Canadian Lazarists, ÉVARISTE-RÉGIS HUC and Joseph Gabet, who had been serving as missionaries in China, joined a Tibetan caravan that was returning to Lhasa from Peking (Beijing). Huc and Gabet traveled 18 months with the caravan and reached Lhasa in January 1846. They remarked on the incredible commercial activity and noise in the streets of the city. After only two months, they were expelled at the urging of the lead Chinese official in Tibet.

Huc and Gabet were the last Europeans to enter Lhasa for more than 50 years.

The Pundits

Throughout the 19th century, the British trained and equipped native Indians to perform survey missions. These Indian surveyors, known as PUNDITS, ventured into the Himalayas and Tibet under disguise for the British and took instrument readings in secret. In this way, the British acquired knowledge of Lhasa and its environment. Meanwhile, a famous Russian explorer, NIKOLAY MIKHAILOVICH PRZHEVALSKY, as he explored central Asia, made four attempts to reach Lhasa. In 1879, Przhevalsky crossed Sinkiang, entering Tibet from the north. He was within 125 miles of Lhasa when Tibetans forced him to turn him back.

20th Century

In 1900, a young Russian student, GOMBOZHAB TSYBIKOV, entered Lhasa disguised as a Buddhist. He remained there two years and visited a number of monasteries. He was soon followed by another Russian, Agran Dorjien. Dorjien became the Dalai Lama's teacher and his political adviser. This worried the British, who, at the time, were vying with Russia for economic control of central Asia; in 1904, they sent SIR FRANCIS EDWARD YOUNGHUSBAND with 1,000 troops into Tibet. Younghusband advanced on Lhasa until the Tibetans relented and agreed to sign the Treaty of Lhasa, which forced them to pay an indemnity to the British and opened up trade between India and Tibet. The British, who had established influence over China, convinced the Chinese to take control of Tibet. In 1910, Chinese troops occupied Lhasa. After the Chinese revolution of 1911–12, Tibet again became independent.

The last famous Western visit to Lhasa was that of the Frenchwoman ALEXANDRA DAVID-NÉEL. A student of Eastern philosophy and frequent traveler in India and China, she learned Sanskrit and Tibetan. In 1912, she moved to Sikkim, a province of India very near to Tibet. David-Néel made several trips into Tibet, never reaching Lhasa. In Japan, she met Ekai Kawaguchi, a Japanese philosopher and monk who had managed to spend 18 months in Lhasa disguised as a Chinese Buddhist monk. In 1924, after more than three years traveling through China and Mongolia, David-Néel, disguised as a beggar at Kawaguchi's side, finally reached Lhasa. She remained two months in Lhasa, visiting all the holy sites.

In 1951, Tibet again lost its independence with the invasion by Communist China. Many temples and Buddhist holy sites were destroyed to make way for a modern city in Lhasa, in order to house the new Chinese officials. The Dalai Lama fled and continues to live in exile. In the early 1980s, China again allowed pilgrims to visit holy sites. The Potala is presently a state museum.

See also ASIA, EXPLORATION OF; MONGOL EXPLORATION.

London Company   See VIRGINIA COMPANY.

longitude   See LATITUDE AND LONGITUDE.

longship

The longship was a type of GALLEY ship used by the Vikings (see VIKING EXPLORATION) in the fjords of their homeland in Scandinavia and for their travels to other parts of Europe and North America from about A.D. 800 to 1100. Two types of Viking ships have come to be called by that name: the *drakkar* for "dragon ship," or *langskip* for "longship"; and the *knörr,* or *hafskip* for "half-ship," also called a *kautskip* for "merchant ship." The drakkar, or longship proper, was long and sleek, as its name would indicate, and had a shallow keel, with pointed ends, curving upward in the shape of a serpent. The knörr, shorter and broader and with a much higher freeboard (height of a ship's sides that ride above water) and wider keel, was deeper in draught; it two had a pointed bow and stern but without the dragon symbol. It also was sometimes decked at bow and stern, offering some shelter. The longship was the warship of the Vikings; the knörr was the ship used for long voyages and carrying cargo. Both types of Viking ships had a single bank of oars, the primary source of propulsion, although a single square sail, made of *wadmal,* a coarse woolen cloth, was also employed. The knörr sails could be close-hauled so they could beat to windward.

The drakkar were typically about 70 feet in length, but it is believed some reached a length of 100 feet. The knörr was about 50 feet. Withies (lashings) of a variety of materials, such as hide or baleen (the horny substance from the mouths of baleen whales used in feeding), and small iron plates and iron nails were used to secure the rib-style oak frameworks of Viking ships. They were clinker-built, meaning the planks, typically of pine, overlapped, providing multiple places for caulking by twisted animal hair soaked in tar. Such construction, with ribs that were not directly attached to the keel, allowed the ship the flexibility to twist in the waves without leaking. Keels were also typically made of oak. Steering was accomplished with a rudder mounted to the right side of the stern, the steerboard (which gave its name to the term *starboard* for the right side of a boat). A generally three-foot right-angled tiller enabled good control in poor conditions. Riggings and anchor cable were typically made of walrus hide.

The drakkar, long and low with fearsome serpentine heads on the prow and stern, was built for speed and

Shown here, in an 1893 photograph, is a replica of a Viking drakkar, or dragon ship. *(Library of Congress, Prints and Photographs Division [LC-D4-21183])*

maneuverability in war although its flexibility made it durable in relatively rough seas. With its shallow draught, it could negotiate coastal regions and rivers. Its light weight made it easy to drag upstream and even overland when necessary. It is estimated that it was capable of speeds of 10 or 11 knots and more in short bursts. The drakkar carried crews of 25 to 60 men who were all also free warriors, in contrast to the galley slaves of the Romans; thus, they were able to forgo carrying extra provisions for nonfighters. They sat on benches in the open and hung their shields along the side for extra defense when fighting. An awning in the front offered a measure of shelter, but the drakkar was basically an open shell. Most often it was used for a day trip and beached on shore at night. When a voyage lasted longer without land in sight, the sailors would sleep in leather sleeping bags wherever they could find room. The Vikings used the drakkar in their raids on European coastal settlements and inland wa-

terways. Sea battles between fleets of opposing peoples were rare; the method of fighting in these cases was for ships to rope themselves together and send a barrage of arrows and other missiles against the enemy. After this, individual ships would come together, and each war band attempted to board and take the other's ship; the aim was not to destroy the enemy's ship but to take the precious commodity.

The even more seaworthy knörr was used to carry people and cargo over long distances. Such ships could carry three or four dozen men, livestock, and the timber for building a new farmstead. With its robust construction, some have speculated that it was the knörr that Vikings such as NADDOD, ERIC THE RED, and LEIF ERICSSON used to cross open waters of the Atlantic and colonize the Faeroe Islands, ICELAND, GREENLAND, and North America.

The Vikings' personal attachment to their ships was more than a little mystical. The ship was often highly decorated on the sides, the prow, and especially the sail. Women participated in the decorating. Vikings saw their ships as the means to their worldly achievements, as well as their reward in the afterlife. Young men would be given command of a longship to establish their manhood and prove their viability as leaders. These ships would be well cared for and given lyrical names like "Snake of the Sea." The stories of these vessels—both drakkars and knörrs—being carried overland by their crews from river to river inside Russia also gives testimony to the value they placed on them. Much is known about the Viking ships, since they were often buried with their captains. Many have been excavated and reconstructed for exhibition in museums around the world.

Both the drakkar and the knörr design elements were incorporated in other European ships, such as the ROUNDSHIP, which evolved during the latter part of the Middle Ages and the RENAISSANCE and facilitated the EUROPEAN AGE OF EXPLORATION.

See also SHIPBUILDING AND EXPLORATION.

Los Césares (City of the Caesars, City of los Césares, Ciudad de los Césares)

Los Césares, or the City of los Césares, also appearing as Ciudad de los Césares and City of the Caesars, was one of the early legends concerning kingdoms in South America wealthy in precious metals and jewels. The name was taken from Francisco Cesar, who explored for Italian SEBASTIAN CABOT in his Spanish expedition of 1526–30 to Río de la Plata and other inland waterways of present-day Brazil, Uruguay, Paraguay, and Argentina, and who probably reached the edge of the ANDES MOUNTAINS. Los Césares eventually was thought to be in the Andes in the present-day Arauco province of Chile.

The discovery and appropriation of Inca Indian gold in the 1530s under FRANCISCO PIZARRO helped create a fervor around the idea of other such civilizations and riches. Any rumors of such places heard from native peoples, or perhaps created by nonnative explorers themselves to justify expeditions, led to new expeditions. Reports of the adventures of ALEJO GARCÍA, a shipwrecked sailor of the 1515–16 expedition of JUAN DÍAZ DE SOLÍS, and of a "White King" who ruled over mountains of silver also spurred on Cabot and his men. Reports of a kingdom to the north that came to be known as EL DORADO led to a similar legend.

The legend of Los Césares endured for decades. It was at least part of the incentive for the 1535–37 expedition of DIEGO DE ALMAGRO and the 1540–41 expedition of PEDRO DE VALDIVIA from Peru southward into Chile, as well as the 1580 expedition of JUAN DE GARAY south from present-day Buenos Aires, Argentina.

See also LEGENDS AND EXPLORATION; TREASURE AND EXPLORATION.

Lost Colony (Roanoke Island)

Lost Colony is the name applied to the first English colony in the Americas in what is now northeastern North Carolina. The people who disappeared are called the "Lost Colonists."

First Expedition

In July 1584, an English exploratory expedition under captains Philip Amadas and Arthur Barlowe, sponsored by SIR WALTER RALEIGH and with the support of Queen Elizabeth I, reached the Outer Banks, or Barrier Islands, and explored Roanoke Island as well as parts of the neighboring mainland. Amadas and Barlowe and their men had friendly contacts with native peoples. It was decided that two Native Americans would return to England with the expedition— Manteo, a Hatteras Indian of the village of Croatoan on the Outer Banks, and Wanchese, a Roanoke Indian, cousin to the brothers and chiefs Granganimeo and Wingina. They departed the Americas in August, reaching England in mid-September.

First Roanoke Colony

In London, Manteo and Wanchese met Raleigh and Queen Elizabeth I. Their presence helped Raleigh raise funds for a permanent colony, granted as a part of the original Virginia patent. Roanoke Island, sheltered from the ocean by the Barrier Islands, seemed a favorable site to establish a presence in the Americas, from where PRIVATEERS could carry out raids on Spanish ships. In April 1585, Raleigh's fleet of seven ships, commanded by his cousin SIR RICHARD GRENVILLE, set forth with some 600 men, among them intended colonists. The ships reached Pamlico and Albemarle Sounds by June. The colonists under Governor Ralph Lane built Fort Raleigh on Roanoke Island and explored the region, having contact with many of the area's Algonquian-speaking tribes.

Scientist THOMAS HARRIOT studied the native peoples and catalogued the wildlife and resources. (His work was published on his return to England as *A Briefe and True Report of the New Found Land of Virginia*.) Also among the colonists was JOHN WHITE, who, in addition to serving as the cartographer, made watercolor drawings of peoples, animals, and plants, which were published in Europe. Meanwhile, the Algonquian showed the English methods of farming and fishing.

Relations between the English and area Native Americans deteriorated over a variety of issues. In one incident, in summer 1585, the English burned a village on the mainland because a Secotan Indian had stolen a silver cup. A subsequent series of events led to more hostilities. To assure the cooperation of the upriver tribes in offering supplies to his men during their search for gold and pearls, Lane had Skyco, son of the Chowanoc Indian sachem Menatonon, taken hostage in spring 1586. The deaths from European disease of Granganimeo and his father, Ensenore, who headed the pro-English faction of Roanoke Indians, further hurt relations. Wingina, taking a new name, Pemisapan, turned militant and attempted to starve out the English. Wanchese, his cousin, who had traveled to England, turned against the English as well. Manteo, the Hatteras, remained pro-English.

Using rumors of a planned Indian attack as his excuse and pretending to seek council with Wingina, Lane led an attack on a mainland coastal village of the Roanoke on June 1, 1586. Wingina was shot and beheaded. Less than three weeks later, the colonists, no longer receiving any help from local tribes in acquiring food, departed Roanoke Island with the visiting fleet of SIR FRANCIS DRAKE. Manteo again accompanied them, this time with an Indian by the name of Towaye.

Second Roanoke Colony

In May 1587, another fleet set sail from England for North America. The 150 colonists in Raleigh's second attempt at a colony, with John White as governor, included women and children. Manteo returned with them. (Towaye's fate is not known; he may have died in England.) Although the intended place of settlement was Chesapeake Bay to the north, Simon Fernandes, the pilot of the fleet, on reaching the Roanoke Island region in July, refused to take the colonists any farther. They were forced to rehabilitate the former settlement and reestablish tenuous relations with area tribes. An attack soon followed: Roanoke warriors, now led by Wanchese, killed a colonist while he was fishing away from the fort.

That August, White christened Manteo and made him Lord of Roanoke and Dasamonquepeuk, thus attempting to

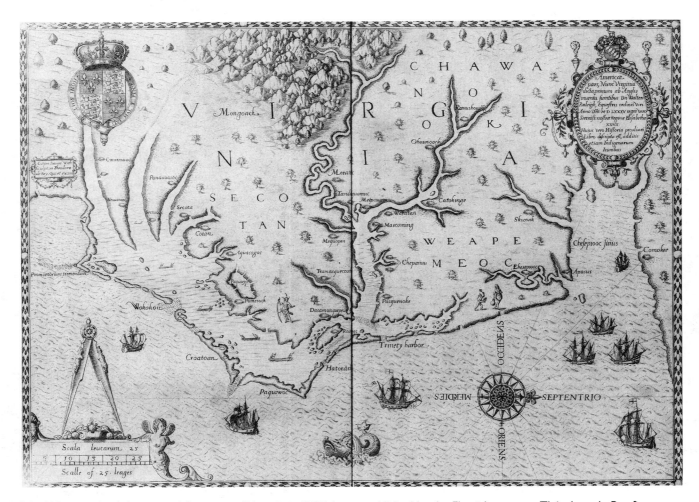

John White created this map of the coast of Virginia in 1585. It was published by the Flemish engraver Théodore de Bry five years later. *(Library of Congress, Prints and Photographs Division [LC-USZ62-54020])*

usurp Wanchese's power. Also that month, the first English child was born in the Americas—Virginia Dare—to John White's daughter Eleanor White Dare and son-in-law Ananias Dare.

At the end of August, with supplies dwindling and winter approaching, the colonists convinced White to return with Fernandes to Europe for supplies. In England, at White's request, Raleigh organized a relief expedition under Grenville for March 1588, but it was ordered not to sail because of warfare with Spain. White lined up two small ships for a crossing, but his ship was intercepted and looted by French pirates. The invasion of the British Isles by the Spanish Armada in July–August 1588 further delayed his return. When White finally reached Roanoke Island in August 1590, the colonists had dis-

appeared. The only clue White found was the word *CROATOAN* carved on the stockade post, probably indicating that at least some among the settlers had relocated to Manteo's village on the Outer Banks. Others may have built a boat in an attempt to reach Chesapeake Bay. It is possible all were killed in attacks by Roanoke, Powhatan, or other area tribes. Some may have intermarried with native peoples. Theories on the fate of the Lost Colonists have led to much speculation over the centuries and an entire literature.

Less than two decades later, in 1607, the English would found their first permanent settlement in the Americas at Jamestown to the north among the Powhatan Indians.

See also LEGENDS AND EXPLORATION.

M

Madoc

Madoc was a legendary Welsh prince of the 12th century, son of King Owain Gwynedd of North Wales. He reportedly had a love of the sea and some skills as a sailor. Legends indicate that, in order to escape family tensions, he sailed to the south of Ireland in 1170 and, after a long time traveling in the Atlantic Ocean, came upon a land with human inhabitants, from which he returned. Upon his return, he gathered up a group of companions to colonize the land and set out on a second journey, after which he and the emigrants were not heard from again.

In 1583, Sir George Peckham published a pamphlet, which made the case that England had a claim to the Americas because of Madoc's discoveries. In his *Historie of Cambria* of 1584, Dr. David Powell, drawing on earlier work of the geographer Humphrey Llwyd, made the claim that Madoc had reached either Mexico or Florida, giving to England rights over those regions rather than to Spain. In the same period, geographers RICHARD HAKLUYT and John Dee promoted the notion of the English discovery of North America more than three centuries before CHRISTOPHER COLUMBUS, sailing for Spain, had reached the WEST INDIES. Hakluyt divined that Madoc had landed somewhere in the Caribbean Sea. There were obvious nationalistic incentives for the English to expand the exploits of Madoc beyond any solid evidence. England was beginning to explore these regions, and any basis for sovereignty over new territories could have geopolitical consequences.

The legend was promoted in numerous ways, even to the point at which explorers returning from the North American continent would falsely claim to have encountered Welsh-speaking Indians. In 1795, a Welshman named John Evans accompanied a Spanish fur-trading expedition headed by Scotsman James Mackay up the MISSOURI RIVER to the villages of the Mandan Indians in search of evidence to verify the legend of Madoc. None was found. The legend endured, however, continuing to inspire literature and poetry over the centuries, including Robert Southey's poem "Madoc" from 1805. Frontier painter GEORGE CATLIN, who spent time among the Mandan Indians in the 1830s, theorized that the tribal name might be derived form *Madawgwys,* for "followers of Madoc." As late as 1953, the Daughters of the American Revolution placed a plaque at Mobile Bay in Alabama, where Madoc made a supposed landing.

Although it is thought that Prince Madoc was a real person, any claims to his accomplishments in the Americas, as vague as they are, were made by others on his behalf. The phenomenon of his legend is thus of more interest for its political content than as an expansion of geographic knowledge.

Magellan, Strait of (Estrecho de Magallanes)

The Strait of Magellan (or Estrecho de Magallanes in Spanish) is a narrow passage at the southern extremity of South America between the Atlantic Ocean and Pacific Ocean. About 350 miles long and two to 15 miles wide, this submerged valley follows a winding course between the mainland of South America to the north, and the Tierra del Fuego Archipelago to the south. The southernmost island in the archipelago contains CAPE HORN, beyond which is Drake Passage between South America and the South Shetland Islands off the Antarctic Peninsula of the continent of Antarctica. Dungeness Point on the north and Cape Espíritu Santo on the south mark the entrance of the Strait of Magellan on the Atlantic side; Cape Pilar at the northwestern end of Desolación Island marks the entrance on the Pacific side. Except for a few miles of the modern nation of Argentina on the Atlantic end, the strait passes through lands belonging to Chile. The Chilean city of Punta Arenas is located along the strait on Isla Grande de Tierra del Fuego.

The strait is named after Portuguese mariner FERDINAND MAGELLAN, the first European to navigate it over 38 days in October–November 1520 while sailing for Spain in the first CIRCUMNAVIGATION OF THE WORLD. He also named the large island to the south Tierra del Fuego, Spanish for "Land of fire"; the westernmost cape, Cape Deseado, for "Desired cape" (also known as Cape Pilar); and the Pacific Ocean itself for its apparent calmness. Over the next decades, the Strait of Magellan became the favored route for Spanish ships entering the Pacific. Although often foggy, it offered protection from the frequent ocean storms in Drake Passage.

In 1578, Englishman SIR FRANCIS DRAKE passed through the strait, the first English ship to do so. Blown off course, he ended up in the waters of Drake Passage before sailing west and north again. Along the coasts of Peru and Mexico, he successfully raided Spanish settlements and ships. The next year, Spanish mariner and scientist PEDRO SARMIENTO DE GAMBOA attempted to intercept Drake in the Strait of Magellan, his likely route back to the Atlantic and Europe. Drake sailed westward across the Pacific, however, and eventually completed the second voyage around the world in 1580. In the meantime, Sarmiento de Gamboa conducted a 16-month survey of the strait, returning to Spain in 1580.

With the construction of the Panama Canal in Central America in the early 20th century, the Strait of Magellan no longer served as the main passage between oceans. Yet it still serves as a sea lane for southern commerce.

See also CENTRAL AMERICA, EXPLORATION OF; SOUTH AMERICA, EXPLORATION OF.

magnetic poles
See NORTH MAGNETIC POLE; SOUTH MAGNETIC POLE.

Mandeville, Sir John
It is not known whether Sir John Mandeville was a real person or a made-up name, a pseudonym attached to a 14th-century book. The book attributed to him was originally written in Norman French and translated into Latin and other European languages in some 300 different volumes. Its English title appears as *The Voyages and Travels of Sir John Mandeville, Knight*; as *The Travels of Sir John Mandeville*; or simply as *Mandeville's Travels*. Published between 1357 and 1371, the work consists of a first-person narrative describing travels in Africa and Asia, including Egypt, Jerusalem, Persia (present-day Iran), India, and China, and lands in between. It is obvious from comparative studies of medieval texts that the work is a compilation of other people's travel accounts, including those of Italians MARCO POLO and ODORIC OF PORDENONE.

The author has been variously theorized as being Jean de Bourgogne (also Jean à la Barbe), a physician, or as Jean d'Outremeuse, a historian, both from Liège, in what is now Belgium. Some scholars maintain that Mandeville was in fact a real person from St. Albans in England, who spent much of his life in other parts of Europe, and who drew on other writers to create a travel guide for pilgrims to the Holy Land and beyond. Many of the descriptions in the work are fantastic. One section describes the kingdom of legendary figure PRESTER JOHN. Travel accounts written for entertainment were a popular genre in England. The work is said to have influenced subsequent English writers, such as Geoffrey Chaucer, William Shakespeare, and John Milton. Milton himself proclaimed that Mandeville influenced a generation of explorers, including Italian CHRISTOPHER COLUMBUS.

mappa mundi (mappemonde)
Mappa mundi (plural form, *mappae mundi*) is Latin for "cloth of the world," as the first world maps were drawn on pieces of cloth. Sometimes the word is written as one. The French version is *mappemonde*. A medieval term, it still appears in discussions of early cartography, referring to early world maps. Almost 600 *mappae mundi* are still in existence, having been produced in Europe from the years 300 to 1300. One map is known specifically by the name Mappa Mundi, or the Hereford map, dating from about 1290 and housed since that time in a cathedral at Hereford, England, and depicting Hereford on it.

Mappae mundi demonstrate the limited geographic knowledge of the Middle Ages. No attempt was made to represent true scale or LATITUDE AND LONGITUDE. They are now considered works of art and religious and philosophical statements as much as cartographic representations. Their most common shape is circular, with a *T* in the center, hence the descriptive name "T-O maps." Around the *O* is the world's ocean. Within the *O* are the three continents known at the time—Asia, Europe, and Africa. Since east is shown at the top, Asia is depicted above the *T*, with Europe and Africa flanking the base. The top of the *T* represents the NILE RIVER and the Don (Tanais) River. The bottom of the *T* is the MEDITERRANEAN SEA. The T-O design probably originated among the ancient Greeks and was also used by Arab cartographers. In maps drawn by Christian cartographers, Jerusalem typically appears at the center.

The Hereford map also reveals religious themes and is thought to have served as an altarpiece. Its English cartographer, Richard of Haldingham, reportedly based much of the content on the writings of Orosius, a religious scholar of the fifth century A.D. and a pupil of Saint Augustine. It is drawn within a circle 52 inches in diameter, on a 64-by-54-inch sheet of vellum supported by an oak frame. Most of its writing is black ink, with red and gold leaf used for emphasis, and blue or green for rivers and seas, except red for the RED SEA. Scalloped designs indicate mountain ranges, and walls and towers indicate towns. The map shows Jerusalem at its center, as well as routes there. Other religious images include angels, Jesus Christ, the Apostles, the Garden of Eden, the Tower of Babel, and Noah's Ark. Biblical inscriptions accompany the images. Non-Christian themes, such as a dragon, unicorn, and mermaid, also appear. An inscription cites Roman general JULIUS CAESAR of the first century B.C.: "The measurement of the world was begun by Julius Caesar. All the East was measured by Nicodoxus, the North and West by Theodoxus, the southern parts by Policlitus." Irish monk SAINT BRENDAN of the sixth century A.D. is also mentioned in association with six islands near the CANARY ISLANDS.

Two other types of maps came into use in the Middle Ages. The road map and the sailing chart served practical purposes and were less decorative.

See also GEOGRAPHY AND CARTOGRAPHY; GREEK EXPLORATION; MAPS AND CHARTS.

maps and charts

A map is any graphic representation of Earth's surface, or some part of it, according to some given scale or projection. The related term *chart* is sometimes used interchangeably with *map* but most often refers to a navigator's map, relating to the marine environment, or an aviator's map, for flying. A GLOBE is a spherical map, although the terms *map* and *chart,* with regard to exploration, are generally used for representations drawn on flat surfaces. Cartography is the art and science of making maps and charts. An atlas is a book containing a collection of maps or charts (after mythological Greek deity Atlas, who was often depicted supporting Earth on the title pages of early map collections).

Maps are used for a variety of purposes and show quantitative and qualitative facts, such as physical features, boundaries, sites, patterns, and distribution. The information communicated might relate to geography, geology, physiography, meteorology, politics, economics, or demography. Maps are typically aligned with north at the top and south at the bottom. Pictures as well as a conventionalized system of symbols are used along with words to convey natural and cultural features.

Among the symbols utilized are a circular compass rose indicating the four primary directions. True north and magnetic north are often both indicated (see NORTH POLE; SOUTH POLE; NORTH MAGNETIC POLE; SOUTH MAGNETIC POLE). Another common map element is a geographic grid for accurate determination of location, the most common being intersecting lines of LATITUDE AND LONGITUDE. A scale shows the ratio of the distance between two points on Earth's surface and the distance between the two corresponding points on a map. Drawings of physical features, contour lines, hachure marks, shading, and coloring are different ways to indicate relief, the varying elevations and depressions on Earth's surface. Dots are typically used to indicate towns and cities. Lines—continuous or broken—indicate boundaries. Specialized maps have an array of other symbols. A key or legend, often set off graphically in a box, gives their meaning.

One of the great challenges in mapmaking is the representation of Earth's curvature on a flat surface, known as projection. Different kinds of map projections have been devised, using geometry and mathematical analysis. An early technique, known as orthographic projection, was conceived by Greek HIPPARCHUS in the second century B.C. Earth is presented as seen from an observer high above it; the center is true to scale, but the scale contracts with greater distance from the center. In the MERCATOR PROJECTION, named after the 16th-century Flemish cartographer GERARDUS MERCATOR, Earth is represented as a rectangle on which lines of latitude and longitude appear as straight lines intersecting at right angles. Many modern maps use azimuthal projections of one kind or another, in which true direction from the center of the map is preserved.

There are many different kinds of maps. The two general categories are topographic maps and thematic maps. Topographic maps show both natural and cultural features, such as lakes, rivers, mountains, and various political entities, including nations, states, and municipalities, along with borders. A thematic map is any map used for special purposes, such as to show an explorer's route. Thematic maps might include some of the same information as topographic maps. A relief map is the three-dimensional model of the terrain of an area. Another type of thematic map is the navigator's chart, also called marine chart or hydrographic chart (see HYDROGRAPHY). Such charts are used for the navigation of ships and show features of bodies of water. Information includes coastlines and harbors (with landmarks, natural and human-made), channels, winds, tides, currents, undercurrents, depth, bottom features (sand, mud, rock), hazards (rocks, bars, reefs, shoals, shipwrecks), and signals (lighthouses, lightships, buoys, beacons). The PERIPLUS and PORTOLAN CHART were early navigation charts. Aeronautical charts, also called aviation charts, give similar information as topographic maps, along with elevations, flight paths, forbidden fly zones, radio-navigation stations and their areas of coverage, and radio communication channels.

Many different materials were used in early mapmaking, among them clay, papyrus, silk, calico, rawhide, ivory, and cane. Many maps were drawn by hand on paper. Early printed maps were made from woodcuts. Photoengraving, wax engraving, lithography, or modeling in clay, plaster of paris, or plastic are some modern processes.

See also GEOGRAPHY AND CARTOGRAPHY.

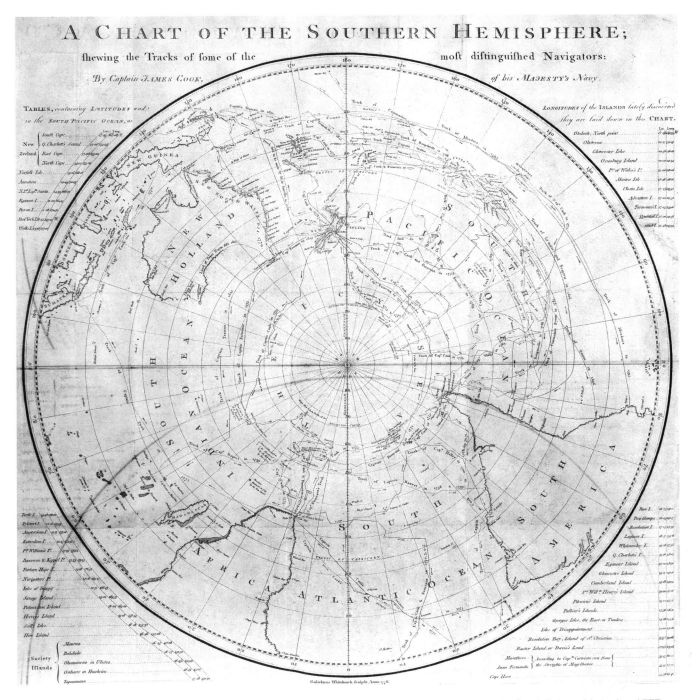

This chart of the Southern Hemisphere by James Cook appeared in his book *A Voyage towards the South Pole*, published in 1777. *(Library of Congress, Prints and Photographs Division [LC-USZ62-77400])*

Marianas Trench (Mariana Trench)

The Marianas Trench is a depression in the Pacific Ocean located east of the Mariana Islands, formed by the collision of two tectonic plates. It is also spelled as Mariana, without the *s*.

The arc-shaped trench or valley extends generally northeast to southwest for 1,580 miles at an average width of 40 miles. Near its southwesternmost point, about 210 miles southwest of Guam, the Marianas Trench has the deepest point in the oceans of the world, at a depth of 36,198 feet, known as the Challenger Deep, named after the ship of its discovery in 1948, the HMS *Challenger II.*

The Marianas Trench and the Challenger Deep were explored by Swiss scientist JACQUES ERNEST-JEAN PICCARD and U.S. Navy lieutenant Donald Walsh in 1960, using the BATHYSCAPH *Trieste.*

See also PACIFIC OCEAN, EXPLORATION OF THE.

McKinley, Mount (Bulshia, Denali, Doleyka, Dunsmore's Mountain, Gora, Tenada, Traleika)

Mount McKinley is a mountain in the Alaska Range of south-central Alaska. At 20,320 feet above sea level, it is the highest mountain in North America. Its twin peaks rise some 17,000 feet above the timber line. It also has one of the steepest vertical rises in the world. Year-round snowfields cover more than half the nonvolcanic mountain. Although it is not as high as some of the other mountains that challenge explorers around the world, Mount McKinley's harsh weather conditions and difficult terrain make its peaks especially dangerous to summit.

Mount McKinley was named after President William McKinley, the 25th president of the United States, in 1897. It has been known variously as Doleyka, Traleika, Bulshia, Gora, Tenada, and Dunsmore's Mountain. Its Native American name in local Athapascan dialects is Denali, which translates as "The High One" or "The Great One." There have been unsuccessful attempts over the years to make Denali the official name.

The first attempts at scaling Mount McKinley's summit began in 1903. FREDERICK ALBERT COOK claimed to have reached the summit of the north peak in 1906, although his claim (along with that of reaching the NORTH POLE in 1908) was later discredited. Peter Anderson and William Taylor, Alaskan gold prospectors, who, along with Charley McGonagall were known as the Sourdough Party, made the first successful climb of the north peak in 1910, which until that time was considered the higher peak. Anglo-American clergyman HUDSON STUCK, along with Harry Karstens, Robert Tatum, and Walter Harper, accomplished the ascent up the 850-foot taller north peak in 1913. Four years later, Harry Karstens became the first superintendent of Mount McKinley National Park, now known as Denali National Park and Preserve.

Climbers scale Mount McKinley, as shown in an early 20th-century photograph. *(Library of Congress, Prints and Photographs Division [LC-USZ62-62301])*

Mediterranean Sea

The Mediterranean Sea takes its name from the Latin for "in the middle of the land." Almost entirely landlocked, the Mediterranean is bordered by three continents—Europe, Asia, and Africa—and connected to the Atlantic Ocean by the Strait of Gibraltar (see GIBRALTAR, STRAIT OF). It occupies an area of 969,000 square miles, extending east-west about 2,400 miles and achieving a maximum width of about 990 miles. Due to a shallow coastal shelf stretching from

Spain to Morocco, the circulation through the Strait of Gibraltar is highly restricted. This makes for a small tidal range and, in concert with high rates of evaporation, makes the water saltier than that of the Atlantic. The Mediterranean is divided into smaller seas, including the Aegean and Ionian Seas off Greece, the Adriatic Sea between Italy and the Balkan Peninsula, and the Tyrrhenian Sea off the west coast of Italy. The Black Sea, connected to the Aegean by the Bosporus Strait, the Sea of Marmara, and the Dardanelles, is also an arm of the Mediterranean. Large islands in the Mediterranean include Malta, Sicily, Sardinia, Corsica, and Cyprus. The world's longest river, the NILE RIVER, drains into it from Africa.

The Mediterranean was formed about 30 million years ago, as tectonic activity, caused by the collision of the continental plates for Eurasia and Africa, shrunk the much larger Sea of Tethys. The Strait of Gibraltar, the only remaining connection to the Atlantic Ocean, at 40 miles long, with a width varying from eight to 24 miles, separates northeastern Africa from the southern tip of Spain. The eastern entrance to the Strait of Gibraltar is bordered by two rocks, called in ancient times Calpe (the modern-day Rock of Gibraltar) and Ceuta, also called the Pillars of Hercules.

The Mediterranean Sea was the barrier and ultimately the link of many ancient civilizations that rose to dominance along its various shores. It offered trade and military routes among them. The Minoans, Egyptians, Phoenicians, and Greeks were early seafaring peoples who explored parts of the Mediterranean, starting in eastern regions. As seafaring technology and knowledge increased, they were able to overcome the limitations of their natural resources, reaping the benefits of shipping and trade. The Phoenicians and Greeks eventually established colonies on islands and coasts throughout the Mediterranean region. Without the SEXTANT and other mechanical means for navigation, early mariners originally depended on the stars. It was thought that ancient mariners hugged the coasts, not crossing open waters for centuries. This conclusion disagreed with reports in ancient myths and legends and accounts by later ancient historians, which were written off as exaggeration. New archaeological evidence, however, is beginning to change scientists' opinions of ancient seafaring skill, and it is probable that the ancients were excellent navigators and had trade routes across open ocean.

Ancient Voyages

The earliest voyages of exploration and trade can be gleaned from myths, such as the voyage of Odysseus (Ulysses), an account of which, the *Odyssey*, is attributed to ca. ninth-century Greek poet Homer. Odysseus's legendary destinations have been equated to islands and coastal regions throughout the Mediterranean. The travels of Odysseus, the voyage of Jason and the Argonauts and other myths show a knowledge of the African coast, Sicily, smaller is-

lands, and even the Strait of Gibraltar and the Pillars of Hercules. By about 1400 B.C., the Mediterranean was fairly well charted by ancient mariners. By about 500 B.C., the Greeks had established colonies not only on the islands in the eastern Mediterranean but throughout southern Italy, while the Phoenician colonies including Carthage were prospering on the North African coast.

The quest for domination of Mediterranean trade sparked the Punic Wars between Republican Rome and Carthage. Carthage originated as a colony of Phoenicia, but grew into an empire controlling nearly all of North Africa from western Libya to the Strait of Gibraltar. Carthage also controlled much of southern Spain and the islands of Sardinia and Corsica. The Carthaginians came to dominate most Mediterranean trade, and some of their mariners, in particular HANNO and HIMILCO, even reached the Atlantic waters in the fifth century B.C. The first of three wars was started in the middle of the third century B.C. The Romans had extended their influence over southern Italy and fought the Carthaginians over control of the island of Sicily. With no decisive winner, Carthage maintained most of its control of Mediterranean trade. As Rome grew in power, however, two more wars were fought, the final war ending in 146 B.C. with the utter destruction of Carthage and Rome in total control of Mediterranean trade.

Muslim Use

After the fall of the Roman Empire, and the rise of the Islamic Arab empire, the Mediterranean became a place of curiosity again. The Arabs invented superior methods of seafaring, using the sextant for navigation. The Mediterranean was a desirable route for Muslims in the western part of the empire, including southern Spain, to aid them in traveling to Egypt then over the RED SEA to take part in the hajj, the required pilgrimage to the Islamic holy cities of Medina and Mecca in Arabia. Many pilgrims, such as ABU AL-HASAN MUHAMMAD IBN JUBAYR of Spain of the 12th century, recounted their voyages across the Mediterranean, including visits to Sicily and Malta, which were at the time Arab possessions.

❖

Even before the digging of the Suez Canal in the mid-19th century, the Mediterranean was the starting point for many expeditions of exploration, allowing explorers from Europe to reach Africa, the Middle East, and the far Eastern coast of the Black Sea from which they could continue their journeys to far-off destinations. Once the canal opened up a passage from the Mediterranean to the Red Sea, ships could sail directly from Europe to Arabia, the east coast of Africa, India, Southeast Asia, and Australia. The Mediterranean continues to provide an important path for global shipping, especially of oil from the Middle East. It is also a popular tourist destination, where tourists cruise through the islands immortalized in the myths and legends of the ancient Greeks.

See also ATLANTIC OCEAN, EXPLORATION OF THE; CARTHAGINIAN EXPLORATION; EGYPTIAN EXPLORATION; GREEK EXPLORATION; MINOAN EXPLORATION; MUSLIM EXPLORATION; PHOENICIAN EXPLORATION; ROMAN EXPLORATION.

Mercator projection

Mercator projection is a mapmaking technique named after 16th-century Flemish cartographer GERARDUS MERCATOR. Drawing on the work of other mapmakers of his day, he used Mercator projection to create a map of the world, the publication of which in 1569 revolutionized cartography and facilitated navigation.

A GLOBE is the most accurate means of depicting relationships of location, distance, and direction on Earth but is not as convenient as a map. Projection addresses the problem of creating a flat representation of a curved surface, and many different types of projections have been developed mathematically, resulting in varying types of distortion. A cylindrical projection is obtained by projecting the surface of Earth on a cylinder tangent along the EQUATOR and then rolling the cylinder out along the plane around the globe. Meridians of longitude, which on the globe converge at the NORTH POLE and SOUTH POLE, are thus represented as parallel to one another. In a Mercator projection, a variation of a cylindrical projection, parallels of latitude, although equidistant on a globe, are drawn with increasing separation as their distance from the equator increases. As a result, the equatorial regions appear normal, but the high latitudes appear distorted. GREENLAND, for example, is exaggerated in size and appears larger than even South America, which in reality is eight times Greenland's size.

Mercator projection maps are practical for purposes of navigation in that directions are represented accurately. Meridians of longitude and parallels of latitude appear as straight lines intersecting at right angles. Since any line intersecting two or more meridians at the same angle also appears as a straight line, it is possible to plot a course by drawing such a line (known as a rhumb line) between two points and determining its COMPASS direction from the map. Mercator's projection maps were favored by both cartographers and navigators for centuries.

See also GEOGRAPHY AND CARTOGRAPHY; LATITUDE AND LONGITUDE; MAPS AND CHARTS; NAVIGATION AND EXPLORATION.

merchant ship

The term *merchant ship* is used in two distinct ways. In the general usage, a merchant ship is any ship whose main purpose is to carry cargo for trading purposes. The ancient Egyptians, Greeks, and Romans all used various forms of the GALLEY as merchant ships. The trading ship used in the Far East was the JUNK; the Arabs had the DHOW. In Scandinavia around A.D. 1000, the knörr, a variety of the LONGSHIP, was the standard merchant ship, and the COG was the merchant ship of the north coast of Europe during the Middle Ages. For trading in the MEDITERRANEAN SEA, the galley continued to be used as the primary merchant ship by the Venetians through the RENAISSANCE. The giant East Indiamen, the large, armed cargo ships built by the East India companies in the 17th century—the BRITISH EAST INDIA COMPANY, DUTCH EAST INDIA COMPANY, and FRENCH EAST INDIA COMPANY—were a type of merchant ship.

A more specific use of the term is as a synonym for ROUNDSHIP, a tubby vessel awkward to maneuver, but economical for the quantity of freight it could hold. The roundship developed in northern Europe in the latter half of the Middle Ages.

Merchant ships are relevant to the history of exploration in that they are part of the history of international trade (see COMMERCE AND EXPLORATION). But they were also sometimes used specifically for exploration. Rarely was an individual ship built to an explorer's specifications. There are notable exceptions in Arctic exploration, but, for the most part, an explorer had to take the available craft of his day and, in many cases, it turned out to be what had previously functioned as a merchant ship. Moreover, the process of trial and error in the use of merchant ships helped lead to the development of more specialized craft, such as the CARAVEL.

See also EGYPTIAN EXPLORATION; GREEK EXPLORATION; ROMAN EXPLORATION; SHIPBUILDING AND EXPLORATION.

Mercury program (Project Mercury)

The Mercury program of 1961–63, named after the speedy messenger of Greek and Roman mythology, was the first manned space program carried out by the United States. One of a series of programs run by the NATIONAL AERONAUTICS AND SPACE ADMINISTRATION (NASA), it worked in conjunction with the APOLLO PROGRAM of 1961–72, the goal of which was to put the first human on the Moon, and was followed by the GEMINI PROGRAM of 1964–66. The goal of the Mercury program, in addition to putting humans into space and developing technologies for future SPACE EXPLORATION, was to investigate their ability to survive and work in space over a period of time.

On May 5, 1961, ALAN BARTLETT SHEPARD, JR., became the first American in space, when the Freedom 7 made a 15-minute suborbital flight. (YURI ALEKSEYEVICH GAGARIN had become the first human in space less than a month before on April 12, 1961, as part of the VOSTOK PROGRAM of the former Union of Soviet Socialist Republics). There were five other Mercury flights. On July 21, 1961, Virgil I. (Gus) Grissom also made a suborbital flight, only 15 seconds longer than the first Mercury flight. On February 20, 1962, JOHN HERSCHELL GLENN, JR., became the first of the U.S. ASTRONAUTS to orbit Earth, in a flight of three orbits. On May 24, 1962, Malcolm Scott Carpenter orbited Earth in a flight lasting almost five hours. On October 3, 1962, Walter (Wally) M. Schirra, Jr., orbited Earth six times on a flight of more than nine hours. On May 15, 1963, Leroy Gordon Cooper, Jr., circled Earth 22 times over a period of more than 34 hours.

The first two Mercury missions made use of one of the U.S. Army's Redstone ROCKETS to launch capsules beyond Earth's atmosphere in a suborbital flight. In subsequent missions the U.S. Air Force's more powerful Atlas rocket was used to put the capsules in orbit. A retro-rocket system was used to bring the capsules back to space. Parachutes slowed their descent into the ocean, where they were designed to float until they were recovered by a ship. Although the Mercury flights were controlled from the ground, experiments were carried out to develop the piloting of spacecraft.

meridian   See LATITUDE AND LONGITUDE; PRIME MERIDIAN.

migration and exploration

Migration is the movement of groups of people from one region to another, resulting in settlement in a new location. In earliest times, the migrations of peoples were tied in with the hunting and gathering of food. Migrating groups of peoples tracked herds of game or sought new hunting grounds or sought new land to farm. A catastrophic event in one's homeland—change of climate, drought, flood, earthquake, volcanic eruption, fire, soil depletion, invasion—and resulting

In this 1961 photograph, workmen assemble Mercury program space capsules for American astronauts at McDonell Aircraft Corporation, St. Louis, Missouri. *(Library of Congress, Prints and Photographs Division [LC-USZ62-121450])*

lack of water, food, shelter, or safety might have precipitated the move. Some people migrated as a way of life—nomads, who wandered with their herds of domesticated animals or who preyed on other peoples. In historical times there were other social causes of migration, such as overpopulation, defeat in war, and ethnic or religious persecution.

The drive toward looking beyond one's homeland plays a part in travel of all kinds, whether exploratory or migratory. Implicit in the notion of exploration as it has come to be studied is that information about the new lands explored is passed back to one's original home—through word of mouth, writings, or charts—which is not necessarily the case in migration. Yet migration in prehistory and early history can be said to be a form of exploration in that migrating people came to experience a new land. The concept of migration in modern times is distinct from exploration in that the lands where migrants traveled are well known.

However they are defined, studies on exploration encounter the theme of migration time and time again. In some cases, it can be said that exploration precedes migration and settlement; in some cases, exploration and migration are simultaneous. Conquest and commerce and searches for riches are often part of migration. Colonization results from and causes more migration. Spreading a religious doctrine and obtaining religious freedom—part of the history of exploration—are also related to both exploration and migration. Moreover, the subject of migration is part of the philosophical debate regarding exploration as in discussing what it means to "discover" a new land. For example, the use of the word *discovery* of North America by Europeans has been questioned since Paleo-Indians arrived to the continent millennia earlier. A subject related to both migration and exploration is geography. Certain geographic features—bodies of water, mountain ranges, deserts, ice formations—slowed exploration and impeded migration. Exploratory routes and migratory routes were often one and the same. The spread of culture is another theme central to both concepts as well: The movement of peoples over the ages, whether by migration, exploration, or conquest, inevitably has been accompanied by the movement of ideas and beliefs, such as agriculture. And since it is now known through archaeological and genetic studies that ancestral humans and early humans moved about considerably in their migrations, it has become apparent that exploration is deeply rooted in human ancestry.

See also COLONIZATION AND EXPLORATION; COMMERCE AND EXPLORATION; CONQUEST AND EXPLORATION; RELIGION AND EXPLORATION; TREASURE AND EXPLORATION.

Minoan exploration

The Minoans, so-named in modern times after the legendary king Minos, were an ancient people of the island of Crete, in the MEDITERRANEAN SEA, who flourished from about 3000 to 1000 B.C. They are associated with the Greek myth of the Minotaur, a creature with a bull's head, very likely derived from the Minoan sport of bull-leaping. Minoan origins are not known, although it has been theorized that they were related to peoples of what is now mainland Greece (Crete is a part of present-day Greece). Their culture, known as the Minoan civilization, was one of three known highly-developed Bronze Age cultures of pre-Hellenic Greece, the other two being the Mycenaean culture on the mainland and the Cycladic culture on the Cyclades island group. All three are treated as the Aegean civilization, distinct from the civilization of the Greeks.

Minoan civilization is organized into three phases: Early Minoan (ca. 3000 B.C.–2200 B.C.), Middle Minoan (ca. 2200 B.C.–1500 B.C.), and Late Minoan (ca. 1500 B.C.–1000 B.C.). The Minoans were at their most powerful in the Middle Minoan period. From Knossos, where a great palace was built, and other population centers on Crete, they became a maritime power on the Mediterranean Sea and, as such, were among the earliest explorers of the region.

By about 1580 B.C., Minoan civilization is known to have spread northward to neighboring islands in the Aegean Sea and to the mainland of Greece. The dispersion of artifacts, as determined archaeologically, indicates that the Minoans developed extensive trade contacts. They are thought to have traded for grain with farming peoples on the shores of the Black Sea. Minoan artifacts themselves have been found as far west as the Balearic Islands off the east coast of Spain. They traded at least as far south as Egypt and as far east as Mesopotamia.

Tin was central to Minoan trade. The island of Cyprus, east of Crete, became part of the trading network, with copper mined there and alloyed with imported tin to produce bronze. Isotopic analysis of the tin in some Mediterranean bronze objects from the period indicates that it came from as far away as Britain, although, without confirmation that the Minoans traveled there, the tin very likely passed through the hands of many different peoples on its way to the Mediterranean region. In any case, the Minoans crafted objects of bronze that they used to barter for other goods. In addition to bronze ax heads and other metalwork, they traded stone and ivory carvings, pottery and other objects for agricultural products, and raw materials, such as obsidian, copper, gold, and silver.

The Minoan culture is known for its hieroglyphic writing and a complex system of weights and measures, both of which enabled its efficient mercantile bureaucracy. With their wide-ranging travels, it can be assumed the Minoans were proficient mariners, having a mastery of navigational techniques necessary for Mediterranean travel. Images on stone reveal that they traveled in a type of GALLEY ship, with high sterns and forecastles.

It is not known what caused the decline and eventual disappearance of Minoan civilization. Archaeological evidence indicates that earthquakes damaged some of their buildings, as did fire. Another theory maintains that as iron tools became common in the region, the tin trade network ended, leading to a decline in the Minoan economy. The Mycenaeans flourished in the years after the Minoan decline, and it has been theorized that they attacked Minoan centers. The Minoans themselves were remarkable in that they apparently thrived in that time without developing a sizable military. During the Late Minoan phase, the Phoenicians replaced them as the greatest of maritime traders. Over the centuries, some writers have hypothesized that knowledge of Crete and Minoan civilization among later ancients led to the myth of the lost continent of ATLANTIS.

See also EGYPTIAN EXPLORATION; GREEK EXPLORATION; PHOENICIAN EXPLORATION.

missionaries   See RELIGION AND EXPLORATION.

Mississippi River ("Old Man River")

The Mississippi River is the second-longest river in the United States; only the MISSOURI RIVER, which feeds it, is longer. It travels 2,340 miles from Lake Itasca in northern Minnesota to the Gulf of Mexico; from the headwaters of the Missouri River to the Gulf of Mexico, the distance is 3,680 miles, making the combined rivers the fourth-largest river system in the world, after the NILE RIVER, AMAZON RIVER, and YANGTZE RIVER (Chang). The Mississippi has the largest drainage area in North America and the third-largest in the world. It drains some 1,247,300 square miles between the Great Divide of the APPALACHIAN MOUNTAINS and the Continental Divide of the ROCKY MOUNTAINS. It varies in depth from nine to 100 feet. Its name is Native American-derived, an Algonquian term meaning "big water." A prevalent nickname is "Old Man River."

From its source in Lake Itasca the Mississippi flows slightly northward before flowing eastward through a series of small lakes to Grand Rapids, Minnesota. From there, it travels southward. Along its route it is joined by the Minnesota and St. Croix Rivers. The Mississippi River forms the lower boundary between the states of Minnesota and Wisconsin. As it travels southward, it forms most of the eastern borders of Iowa, Missouri, Arkansas, and Louisiana, and western borders of Illinois, Kentucky, Tennessee, and Mississippi.

The Illinois River and the Missouri River next join the Mississippi. The muddy Missouri in turn makes the Mississippi River mud-colored. At its confluence with the Ohio River, the geographic point designated as separating the Mississippi into upper and lower sections, it doubles in volume; south of the juncture with the 975-mile-long Ohio River, its width extends up to 50 miles, and its valley becomes wide and fertile. Through this section the river loops back and forth and is joined along its route by the Red and Arkansas Rivers. In the loops, lakes—known as oxbow lakes—are formed. In Louisiana one quarter of the river follows the Atchafalaya River.

Near the Gulf of Mexico large deposits of sediment have formed the extensive Mississippi Delta—some 13,000 square miles. The river is divided into several channels known as distributaries, which enter the Gulf of Mexico, including Main Pass, South Pass, North Pass, and Southwest Pass, known locally as the Passes.

Spanish Exploration

In the 16th and 17th centuries, the river served as a route for French and Spanish explorers. Later in the 1800s the river became a major transportation and trade route for steamboats. It was already home to many Native American tribes along its course, including bands of Chippewa (Ojibway), Santee Sioux (Dakota), Winnebago (Ho-Chunk), Fox (Mesquaki), Sac, Illinois, Kickapoo, Missouria, Quapaw, Chickasaw, Choctaw, Tunica, Natchez, and Chitimacha.

The first Europeans known to have seen the Mississippi were the Spanish. In May 1539, HERNANDO DE SOTO and 600 men landed in Florida and headed northward along the Gulf of Mexico. During the four-year expedition, they covered some 350,000 square miles of what is now the southeastern United States. On May 8, 1541, they came upon the Mississippi River—probably south of present-day Memphis, Tennessee. They constructed barges in order to cross it and explored westward into present-day Arkansas and Oklahoma. The expedition eventually returned to the Mississippi. De Soto died there a year later, on May 21, 1542, at its confluence with the Red River. In order to keep secret the knowledge of their leader's death from the Indians of the region, the CONQUISTADORES weighted his body with rocks so that it would sink in the Mississippi. After traveling southwest into Texas in the hope of reaching Mexico by land, the new leader, LUIS DE MOSCOSO, led the survivors back to the Mississippi, where they spent the winter of 1542–43. The Spanish built seven barges and, when the river flooded on July 2, 1543, they embarked on them, reaching the Gulf of Mexico on July 18, from where they followed the coastline to Mexico, arriving at the settlement of Tampico the following September.

French Exploration

The Mississippi remained the domain of only Native Americans for more than a century. It was the French who next came to frequent it, using it as a highway from the region of the western Great Lakes. In 1654–56, French fur trader MÉDARD CHOUART DES GROSEILLIERS, while developing relations with the Indian tribes of the region, explored the rivers to the west of Lake Michigan, including the Fox and Wisconsin as well as a stretch of the Mississippi. In 1659–60, he returned to the region with his brother-in-law PIERRE-ESPRIT RADISSON and explored Lake Superior and the upper eastern Mississippi Valley.

Yet the extent of the great river was still not known to Europeans. The French hoped that the Mississippi flowed westward to the Western Sea—the Pacific Ocean—and would thus prove a good trade route to the Far East. In 1673, Governor General Comte de Frontenac of New France sent LOUIS JOLLIET, a fur trader, to trace its course. JACQUES MARQUETTE, a missionary who knew several languages, accompanied him. Jolliet, Marquette, and a party of five Miami Indians and VOYAGEURS traveled by CANOE from Green Bay on the west shore of Lake Michigan, along the Fox River to Lake Winnebago. They then crossed to the Wisconsin River and descended it to the mouth of the Mississippi, which they reached on June 17. The expedition then descended the Mississippi, passing the mouth of the Missouri River, to the junction of the Arkansas River. They soon concluded, however, that the Mississippi flowed southward and probably emptied into the Gulf of Mexico rather than westward to the Pacific. On the return trip they branched off into the Illinois River, which took them near the south shore of Lake Michigan.

Over the next decades, French fur traders continued to be active in the upper Mississippi region. In 1679, RENÉ-ROBERT CAVELIER DE LA SALLE and his lieutenant HENRI DE TONTI founded Fort Crèvecoeur on the Illinois River. In spring 1680, La Salle sent trader MICHEL ACO and Jesuit missionary LOUIS HENNEPIN on a mission northward to explore the Mississippi, Wisconsin, and Minnesota Rivers and perhaps determine the source of the Mississippi. They descended the Illinois to its mouth on the Mississippi, then proceeded northward. At some point, probably along the Mississippi, they were captured by a party of Sioux. In the course of his travels, perhaps while in captivity, Hennepin saw and named the Falls of St. Anthony near present-day St. Paul, Minnesota. They eventually were taken to a Sioux village in central Minnesota. In the meantime, in search of a route to the Western Sea, trader DANIEL GREYSOLON DU-LUTH, Tonti's cousin, followed the St. Croix River—the upper portion of the present boundary between Wisconsin and Minnesota; he reached its mouth on the Mississippi near present-day Prescott, Wisconsin. On learning of the capture of Aco and Hennepin, he returned north and negotiated their release.

In February 1682, La Salle and Tonti set out from the Illinois River on a journey down the Mississippi and completed the first known European journey from the river's northern regions to its mouth on the Gulf of Mexico on April 9. During this journey, he claimed the entire Missis-

sippi Valley for France, naming the region Louisiana in honor of the French king Louis XIV. On the return journey, he and Tonti founded another post on the Illinois—Fort St. Louis. Tonti was left in charge, while La Salle returned to Montreal. In France La Salle raised backing for a colonizing expedition to the Mississippi Delta in 1684. However, he misjudged the location and ended up at Matagorda Bay on the Texas coast, about 500 miles to the west. Starting in 1685, he led several attempts to reach the Mississippi from the Gulf Coast. During one in 1687, La Salle was killed by one of his own men in a quarrel. HENRI JOUTEL led the survivors to the lower Arkansas River, where they met with Tonti, who had traveled the length of the Mississippi in search of the colony the year before as well.

In 1698, Tonti led Jesuit missionary ALBERT DAVION to the lower Mississippi and helped him found a mission to the Tunica near the confluence of the Yazoo River. Tonti would later join the colonizing efforts along the lower Mississippi of PIERRE LE MOYNE, Sieur d'Iberville and JEAN-BAPTISTE LE MOYNE, Sieur de Bienville's colonizing expedition to the lower Mississippi in 1698–99. Over the next years, Sieur de Bienville founded a number of posts in the region, including Fort Rosalie among the Natchez Indians in 1716, which would become modern-day Natchez, Mississippi, and New Orleans in 1718. In 1700, trader PIERRE-CHARLES LE SUEUR, in the service of Sieur d'Iberville, ascended the Mississippi from the Gulf of Mexico all the way to the Minnesota River, where he established a post, Fort L'Huiller, among the Sioux.

Other important early settlements in the FUR TRADE were Cahokia, to the south of the mouth of the Missouri River, founded by missionaries in 1699, and Kaskaskia to the south near the mouth of the Kaskaskia River, founded in 1703, also by missionaries. Both were named after Illinois Indian subtribes. In 1720, French historian PIERRE-FRANÇOIS-XAVIER DE CHARLEVOIX traveled from the Illinois down the Mississippi to New Orleans, writing about his journey in the *History of New France,* published in 1744.

St. Louis, named after the French medieval king Louis IX, canonized as a saint, was founded in 1764 on the west bank in what is now Missouri, where the river makes a great bend to the east, a short distance downstream from the mouth of the Missouri River and opposite Cahokia, by French fur traders PIERRE LIGUESTE LACLEDE and RENÉ AUGUSTE CHOUTEAU. It further added to the commerce along the river.

U.S. Interests

France ceded its North American holdings to Great Britain and Spain at the end of the French and Indian War in 1763. The United States gained Great Britain's holdings, other than Canada, at the end of the American Revolution two decades later. France again gained control of the western

Mississippi Valley in 1800, but sold it to the United States in the Louisiana Purchase of 1803. The Mississippi became for the United States, as it had been for colonial powers, a primary transportation route. Early trade was by RAFT, flatboat, and KEELBOAT; the first steamboat on the Mississippi was the *New Orleans* in 1811. St. Louis served as a gateway to the West, with many exploratory, trade, and military expeditions organized and launched from there. WILLIAM CLARK, while recruiting the Corps of Discovery for his expedition with MERIWETHER LEWIS, set up camp opposite the settlement in winter 1803–04.

Despite all the activity along the Mississippi in the 17th and 18th centuries, its true source was not known. In 1805, General James Wilkinson of the U.S. Army chose ZEBULON MONTGOMERY PIKE to search for the Mississippi's headwaters. He followed the river northward until he found the Red Cedar Lake (Cass Lake) and Leech Lake in Minnesota. He wrongly believed these to be the headwaters of the Mississippi. In 1823, Italian GIACOMA COSTANTINO BELTRAMI, traveling with a U.S. military surveying expedition under STEPHEN HARRIMAN LONG, traveled up the Minnesota River and located what he mistakenly cited as the source, Lake Julia. In 1832, in an expedition sent out by Michigan territorial governor Lewis Cass, geologist and ethnologist HENRY ROWE SCHOOLCRAFT was led by a Chippewa Indian from Cass Lake to a lake known to the French as Lac la Biche (Elk Lake), which he determined to be the source. He renamed it Lake Itasca, from the Latin words *veritas,* "truth," and *caput,* "head."

❖

A major route of transportation, the Mississippi is presently navigable by ship for 1,800 miles from St. Paul, Minnesota, and the Falls of St. Anthony to the Gulf of Mexico. It is still a principal artery for commerce, with more freight transported on it than any other inland waterway in North America.

See also NORTH AMERICA, EXPLORATION OF.

Missouri Fur Company   See ST. LOUIS MISSOURI FUR COMPANY.

Missouri River

The Missouri River is the longest river in the United States. From its source at the confluence of the Gallatin, Jefferson, and Madison Rivers in the mountainous terrain of southwestern Montana, through the grasslands of the northern plains, to its mouth on the MISSISSIPPI RIVER, it extends some 2,540 miles. It first flows northward along the edge of the ROCKY MOUNTAINS, where it passes through the Gates of the Mountains, a gorge. It then turns northeast-

ward past the Great Falls before heading eastward across Montana. It flows first westward and then curves southeastward in North Dakota, continuing in that direction across South Dakota, forming a section of the border between South Dakota and Nebraska. It then flows southward and forms the border between Nebraska and Kansas on the west and Iowa and Missouri on the east, then heads eastward across Missouri. Its course follows what once was the edge of the ice sheets extending down from the north during the ice ages.

The Missouri can be divided into three sections: the upper where it is clear and swift-moving; the middle where it crosses the plains and begins to live up to its nickname of the "Big Muddy"; and the lower that is slower and muddier still than the midsection. Among its tributaries are the Marias, Musselshell, Milk, and Yellowstone Rivers in Montana; the Knife River in North Dakota; the Grand, Cheyenne, White, and James (Dakota) Rivers in South Dakota; the Niobrara and Platte Rivers in Nebraska; the Kansas River in Kansas; and the Osage River in Missouri. It in turn is the largest tributary of the Mississippi River, turning the Mississippi mud-colored. The river has a drainage basin of 529,000 square miles and drains areas of 10 states and two Canadian provinces.

Before Europeans began to explore the Missouri River, it was home to bands of a number of Indian tribes, including the Missouria (who gave their name, probably meaning "people with dugout canoes," to the river), Omaha, Ponca, Arikara, Mandan, Hidatsa, Nakota Sioux and Gros Ventre. Bands of other tribes, such as the Osage, Kaw (Kansa), Ioway, Otoe, Pawnee, Assiniboine, Lakota Sioux, Northern Cheyenne, Northern Arapaho, Crow, Shoshone, and Blackfeet, were centered on the Missouri's tributaries, yet frequented and camped along the Missouri itself.

French Exploration

French-Canadian explorers LOUIS JOLLIET and JACQUES MARQUETTE were the first known Europeans to reach the mouth of the Missouri River during their descent of the middle stretch of the Mississippi River in 1673. The lower Missouri became an important route for the FUR TRADE with Indians. The earliest traders in the region, such as Frenchman HENRI DE TONTI, a lieutenant of RENÉ-ROBERT CAVELIER DE LA SALLE, who together descended the Mississippi in 1682, passed the mouth of the Missouri numerous times on subsequent expeditions, but did not follow it on its course northwestward. French trader ÉTIENNE-VENIARD BOURGMONT is known to have explored much of the lower portion of the river in 1712–17, possibly exploring as far north as the mouth of the Platte River in eastern Nebraska. In 1738, French-Canadian trader PIERRE GAULTIER DE VARENNES DE LA VÉRENDRYE and his son LOUIS-JOSEPH GAULTIER DE LA VÉRENDRYE reached the Mandan villages, where the river makes its big bend westward in North Dakota, overland from their post, Fort Rouge, on the Red River of the North near the site of present-day Winnipeg, Manitoba. His sons, Louis-Joseph and François, headed southwestward across the Missouri onto the northern plains possibly into northeastern Wyoming, circling back by way of South Dakota and a stretch of the Missouri.

Out of St. Louis

The founding of St. Louis in 1764 on the Mississippi's west bank, a short distance downstream from the mouth of the Missouri River in what is now Missouri, by French traders PIERRE LIGUESTE LACLEDE and RENÉ AUGUSTE CHOUTEAU led to increased activity in the region. In 1792, a Frenchman named Jacques d'Église made the first known European journey upriver from the Missouri's mouth, reaching the Mandan villages. In 1793, St. Louis merchants formed the Company of Explorers of the Upper Missouri (the Missouri Trading Company). In 1794–95, French-Canadian JEAN-BAPTISTE TRUTEAU traveled up the Missouri River on its behalf as far as the Black Hills in what is now western South Dakota. In 1795, a Welshman named John Evans accompanied a Scottish fur trader, James Mackay—formerly of the NORTH WEST COMPANY, now in the employ of the Spanish—on an expedition up the Missouri River to the Mandan villages. Evans hoped to verify the legend of Welsh prince MADOC, who had supposedly colonized some foreign land, but found no evidence among native peoples. Soon afterward, in 1802, Frenchman FRANÇOIS MARIE PERRIN DU LAC, accompanying a fur trader, traveled up the Missouri as far as the mouth of the White River in south-central South Dakota.

Lewis and Clark

The Missouri River was included as part of the Louisiana Purchase from France by the United States in 1803. The following year, President Thomas Jefferson sent out an expedition under MERIWETHER LEWIS and WILLIAM CLARK to explore the newly acquired lands, and they chose the Missouri as their route westward, organizing their expedition at a camp opposite St. Louis. They hoped to find a manageable water route all the way to the Pacific—the NORTHWEST PASSAGE. The Corps of Discovery set out on May 14, 1804, by KEELBOAT and other small craft, over the stretch of river well known to traders, reaching Mandan country in present-day North Dakota on October 27, where they built a post, Fort Mandan, and wintered. On April 7, 1805, they proceeded to the upper Missouri, now accompanied by Shoshone Indian woman SACAJAWEA. On June 2, they reached the mouth of the Marias in present-day Montana and were unable to determine whether that river was the Missouri, but accurately chose the Missouri. On June 13, they reached the Great Falls, which the Mandan claimed marked the end

of the river. On July 27, however, they reached the true source of the river—the Three Forks of the Missouri, which Lewis named the Gallatin, Jefferson, and Madison. After crossing the Rockies and traveling along the Snake River and the COLUMBIA RIVER, the expedition reached the Pacific Ocean on November 15, 1805, where they built Fort Clatsop in present-day Oregon and spent the winter. In June 1806, on their return journey, the party split up: Clark explored the Yellowstone River, and Lewis, the Marias to the north. They met up at the mouth of the Yellowstone and returned to St. Louis by way of the Missouri, arriving September 23. Some of the men who were part of the Corps of Discovery remained active in the Missouri River region, such as JOHN COLTER.

Traders, Painters, and Writers

The Missouri River remained the primary route west for a number of years, especially for the continuing fur trade up the river and beyond in the Rockies. In 1808, JOHN JACOB ASTOR founded the AMERICAN FUR COMPANY, with various subsidiaries to follow. The next year, a group of traders in St. Louis founded the ST. LOUIS MISSOURI FUR COMPANY. Among the partners were JEAN PIERRE CHOUTEAU, his eldest son AUGUSTE PIERRE CHOUTEAU, MANUEL LISA, WILLIAM CLARK, ANTOINE PIERRE MENARD, and ANDREW HENRY. People and goods were transported by keelboat and later by steamboat, the first voyage by the *Independence* in 1819. That same year, the U.S. army established a presence on the river with the founding of Fort Atkinson by Colonel HENRY ATKINSON at Council Bluffs in northeastern Nebraska (where Lewis and Clark had met with Sioux tribal leaders in 1804). Another American entrepreneur, WILLIAM HENRY ASHLEY, became a powerful force in the fur trade with his ROCKY MOUNTAIN FUR COMPANY, founded by him and Andrew Henry in 1822. Many of the men who worked for and traded with him came to be known as the MOUNTAIN MEN. Among the most famous of them were THOMAS FITZPATRICK, JEDEDIAH STRONG SMITH, and WILLIAM LEWIS SUBLETTE.

Men of other callings used the river to explore westward. In 1811, for example, American writer HENRY MARIE BRACKENRIDGE and Scottish naturalist JOHN BRADBURY traveled up the Missouri River to the Mandan villages with a trading expedition headed by Manuel Lisa. In 1832, American frontier painter GEORGE CATLIN traveled from St. Louis to the mouth of the Yellowstone, seeking out Native American subjects along the way. In 1833–34, German naturalist ALEXANDER PHILIPP MAXIMILIAN and Swiss artist KARL BODMER also traveled upriver to the mouth of the Marias River. By this time, there were a number of army posts along the Missouri.

❖

With the advent of the railroads in 1858, the Missouri saw fewer travelers. Nowadays, for the most part, the lower river is used commercially for shipping, while the upper river is used for recreation. In 1844, with the Missouri River Basin Program, a series of locks, dams, and reservoirs were constructed for the sake of navigation, irrigation, flood control, and hydroelectric power.

See also NORTH AMERICA, EXPLORATION OF.

Moluccas   See SPICE ISLANDS.

Mongol exploration

The Mongols are a people of east-central Asia, distributed in the country of Mongolia as well as contiguous parts of Russia to the north and China to the south, east, and west. They originally consisted of nomadic tribes inhabiting steppe and desert country, with an economy based on herds of horses and sheep, and living in tents. The various tribes, who competed for territory, organized at times into loose alliances. In the early 13th century, a chieftain of the Yakka Mongols, GENGHIS KHAN, defeated his rivals and united the various tribes, founding a capital at Karakorum in the northern GOBI DESERT, establishing codes of law and creating a powerful army, masters of the use of cavalry for the swift attack; every adult Mongol male in fact was a mounted warrior.

Under Genghis's leadership and the leadership of subsequent khans—the most powerful after him being his sons Ogadai and Guyuk and his grandsons Mangu and Kublai—the Mongols invaded much of Asia and eastern parts of Europe, penetrating as far as present-day Hungary and Germany. Their armies came to include other peoples, such as Turkic peoples who became known collectively as the Tartars or Tatars (the name *Tartars* has been applied to the Mongols by Europeans as well, who did not distinguish between invading tribes from the East). And the Mongols came to adapt many of the customs of peoples they conquered, in particular the Chinese (see CHINESE EXPLORATION), whose capital Yen-King (present-day Beijing) Genghis occupied in 1215. Genghis's son Ogadai succeeded him as supreme khan, while Ogadai's brother Juchi was granted territory comprising much of present-day Russia. In 1235, Batu Khan, Juchi's son, along with his chief general Subutai, campaigned in the west. In 1238, Batu's warriors—referred to in Russia as the Golden Horde because of Batu's golden tent—captured Moscow (in present-day Russia) and, in 1240, Kiev (in present-day Ukraine). His razing of Kiev, at the time ruled by the Rus—a people of Viking and Slavic descent—led to the rise of Muscovite Russia.

The Mongols proceeded westward and, within two years, had also conquered present-day Hungary and Poland and made military incursions into Germany. Batu laid the groundwork for the founding of the Kipchak Khanate (also known as the Empire of the Golden Horde) between the Volga and Danube Rivers in 1243, with a capital first at Sarai Batu, near present-day Astrakhan, on the lower Volga and later at Sarai Berke also on the Volga, near present-day Volgograd. This had been territory of a Turkic people known as the Kipchak or Cuman. The death of Ogadai in 1241 led to Batu's recall to Karakorum in 1242, and the Mongols therefore did not proceed into western Europe.

By 1260, the Mongol Empire was subdivided into four khanates, that is, territories ruled by khans, descendants of the royal line founded by Genghis Khan. The subdivisions included the Great Khanate, comprising all of China and most of East Asia; the Jagatai Khanate in Turkistan; Il-Khanid Khanate in Persia (present-day Iran); and the Kipchak Khanate in western Russia.

The geographic extent of the Mongol Empire was the greatest ever known to human history, reaching for part of its existence from the Pacific Ocean west to the Adriatic Sea and from Mongolia to the Indian Ocean in the south. The Mongol age of expansion led to a new age of exploration within Asia and between Asia and Europe. The movement of the armies and subsequent occupation led to the passing of knowledge between cultures. Routes became secure, leading to increased travel. The khans maintained a system of mounted couriers for communication throughout the empire. The SILK ROAD, which had been controlled by the Muslims, now was open to other entrepreneurs. Moreover, the khans encouraged exploration for better understanding of peoples under their domain as well as for military reconnaissance. In 1221–22, for example, Genghis sent out an expedition under Chinese Taoist CH'ANG-CH'UN to explore central Asia, from China to Afghanistan.

With the Golden Horde in eastern Europe, Europeans became more aware of and concerned with Asian issues. Papal and political diplomatic missions were sent out, such as that of Italian GIOVANNI DA PIAN DEL CARPINI in 1245–47 and Flemish WILLIAM OF RUBROUCK in 1253–55. European traders followed. In 1271–75, Italian merchants MAFFEO POLO, NICCOLÒ POLO, and MARCO POLO traveled across central Asia to Cambaluc (present-day Beijing), the new Mongol capital founded by Genghis's successor Kublai Khan. Marco Polo, in 1275–92, explored on behalf of the khan, visiting other parts of China, Tibet, Southeast Asia, Indonesia, Mongolia, and possibly SIBERIA. His book, *The Travels of Marco Polo*, with descriptions of Mongol customs, was influential in Europe over the next two centuries and influenced CHRISTOPHER COLUMBUS in his 1492 attempt to reach the Orient by way of the Atlantic Ocean.

By the 14th century, however, the far-flung Mongol Empire had weakened due to internal conflicts as well as resistance from conquered peoples. By 1382, the Mongols were completely expelled from China back into their original homeland. The Mongols of today are still a pastoral people, maintaining sheep, horses, cattle, camels, and goats and living much as their ancestors did. In addition to shamanism, many of them practice Lamaism, a branch of Buddhism.

Mont Blanc See BLANC, MONT.

mountain climbing

Mountain climbing, or mountaineering, is the practice of climbing to Earth's most elevated points for exploration, scientific research, or sport. The three types of mountaineering are trail climbing (also called scrambles or walkups), which involves hiking on trails to the tops of some mountains; rock climbing, the scaling of steep mountain faces using technical climbing gear, like ropes and pitons; and ice

climbing, the ascent on snow and ice of the world's highest mountains, whose peaks soar above the timber line.

Trail climbing requires proper attire and food and water, but no special climbing equipment. For rock climbing, in which the hands are used as well as the feet, climbers use special footwear, ropes, hammers, and steel spikes, known as pitons, driven into the rock for support, or, in more recent times, hardware placed into cracks. In ice climbing (or ice and snow climbing), additional equipment includes ice axes and attachable boot spikes, known as crampons. Mountaineers sometimes carry bottles of oxygen for high-altitude climbing. Naturally, warm clothing, as well as tents and blankets or sleeping bags, are also needed for overnight survival on mountains.

The history of mountain climbing, in particular ice climbing, is closely tied to the history of world exploration. The high peaks were some of the last areas explored on the planet. The first recorded climb of a high-altitude mountain

Climbers ascend Mont Blanc in the Alps, as shown in this late 19th-century photograph. *(Library of Congress, Prints and Photographs Division [LC-USZ62-108854])*

was in A.D. 633, with the ascent of Mount Fuji (or Fujiyama), the highest peak in Japan at 12,387 feet above sea level.

Alpinism

Modern mountain climbing took its early shape in the European Alps. The ascent to the summit of France's Mont Blanc (see BLANC, MONT), the highest alpine peak, by Frenchman Michel Gabriel Paccard and guide JACQUES BALMAT in 1786 was the crowning moment of early mountaineering attempts. Their accomplishment, without rope or ice axes, but with alpenstocks—long wooden staffs with iron tips to poke for crevasses and cut steps in the ice—was widely publicized. As a result many Europeans, especially the British, began climbing other alpine summits, often with the help of local guides from Savoy (now part of France) and Switzerland. Mountaineering thus became for some climbers a calling and for others a hobby; still other climbers were geologists and topographers. The goal of being the first to "summit" various peaks spurred on many climbers, and the growing elite class of professional guides, like Jacques Balmat, took many of the firsts.

In 1858, the Alpine Club was founded in London; in 1863, the *Alpine Journal* began publication. The mid-1800s are sometimes referred to as the golden age of mountain climbing because of widespread interest in the activity and the number of alpine peaks conquered. The golden age is said to have ended with EDWARD WHYMPER's 1865 ascent of the Matterhorn in Switzerland, the last high alpine peak to be scaled.

During this period of great activity, an approach to mountain climbing known as alpinism (or alpine climbing) was developed. The techniques, equipment, and safety measures of alpinism are still in use today in both ice and rock climbing. In alpinism, climbers work in teams, of typically two to four climbers, who are attached by ropes and who carry all the equipment they need; in addition to ice axes and crampons, food, and water, they haul a camping stove and fuel, sleeping bags, sleeping mats, a tent or bivouac sacks, and first aid gear onto the mountain. If the climbers cannot reach the summit and return in a single day, they bivouac, or spend the night on a mountain ledge, before continuing. Slings and other specialized equipment are used for glacier routes, where crevasses—deep fissures in the ice—are a danger.

Mountain Topography

Much had been learned about mountain topography in other parts of the world by the mid-19th century. Italian poet Petrarch climbed Mont Ventoux in France in the 14th century, and Italian scientist Leonardo da Vinci climbed Monte Bo in Italy in the 15th century; both men passed on their experiences in writings. Some early explorers who

helped gather information about mountain ranges were seeking passes through these ranges; others, such as the MOUNTAIN MEN in North America's ROCKY MOUNTAINS, were working in the mountains, trapping for furs. Some early explorers climbed mountains simply to reach the top, as Spaniard DIEGO DE ORDAZ did in climbing Mexico's Popocatépetl in 1520, and American JOHN CHARLES FRÉMONT did in the climbing of Fremont Peak in Wyoming's Wind River Mountains in 1843. In the 18th and early 19th centuries, naturalists and geologists hiked up mountains and even climbed difficult peaks for purposes of scientific study. In 1740, for example, French naturalist CHARLES-MARIE DE LA CONDAMINE, and, in 1801, German naturalist ALEXANDER VON HUMBOLDT, accompanied by French botanist Aimé Bonpland, attempted to climb Mount Chimborazo in the ANDES MOUNTAINS of Ecuador in South America, but failed to reach the top. In the 1860s–70s, American naturalist JOHN MUIR and American geologist CLARENCE KING hiked and climbed much of the Sierra Nevada of California in North America. The Great Trigonometrical Survey of India of the 19th century, headed for a time by SIR GEORGE EVEREST and carried on by the PUNDITS (trained Indian emissaries), led to the mapping of the HIMALAYAS and a calculation of the heights of the main peaks. In 1854–57, German brothers ADOLF VON SCHLAGINTWEIT, HERMANN VON SCHLAGINTWEIT, and ROBERT VON SCHLAGINTWEIT explored and surveyed the Himalayas, the Karakoram Range, and Kunlun Mountains for the BRITISH EAST INDIA COMPANY.

The Challenge of the High Peaks

Mountain climbing as an end in itself continued to increase in popularity. By the end of the 19th century, many more climbing clubs besides the Alpine Club had been organized in Europe and North America, and many climbers were ascending peaks without guides. With no more firsts to be accomplished in the Alps, many climbers turned their attention to other ranges. In 1868, Englishman Douglas Freshfield and French guide François Devouassoud, along with two other team members, climbed two of the main peaks—Kasbek and Elbrus—of the Caucasus Mountains of Georgia, Armenia, Azerbaijan, and southwest Russia (the Caucasus is considered a boundary between Europe and Asia). Other expeditions followed, in particular from Great Britain, Germany, Italy, and, in the 20th century, the Union of Soviet Socialist Republics (USSR; Soviet Union).

The HIMALAYAS of central Asia, which boast many of the world's highest peaks, lured professional mountain climbers as did the Andes Mountains of South America and the Southern Alps of NEW ZEALAND. Italian guide MATTHIAS ZURBRIGGEN, who had developed his mountaineering skills in the European Alps, participated in expeditions in all three ranges. In 1897, he became the first person to climb ACONCAGUA, the highest peak in the Andes and the entire Western and Southern hemispheres. Tanzania's Mount Kilimanjaro (see KILIMANJARO, MOUNT), Africa's tallest peak, was first scaled in 1889 by German geographer HANS MEYER and Austrian mountain climber Ludwig Purtscheller. In 1899, Englishman Sir Harold Mackinder climbed Africa's second-highest peak, Mount Kenya, located in Kenya. Anglo-American clergyman HUDSON STUCK, along with Harry Karstens, Robert Tatum, and Walter Harper, climbed North America's highest mountain, Mount McKinley (see MCKINLEY, MOUNT), in 1913.

In the late 19th and early 20th centuries, Italian LUIGI AMEDEO DI SAVOIA D'ABRUZZI (duke of Abruzzi) was an active mountaineer. He made the first ascent of Mount Saint Elias in Alaska and of various peaks of the Ruwenzori Mountains in East Africa—associated with the MOUNTAINS OF THE MOON as described by second-century hellenized Egyptian geographer PTOLEMY. He also attempted the world's second-highest peak, K2 (formerly known as Mount Godwin-Austen after the explorer Henry Haversham Godwin-Austen), at 28,250 feet, in the Karakoram range of the western Himalayas. The duke of Abruzzi began the tradition of mountain climbers putting their skills to work in polar exploration. Also at the turn of the century, Americans FANNY BULLOCK WORKMAN in the Alps and Himalayas, and ANNIE PECK SMITH in the Alps and Andes, competed for altitude records and, in the process, helped develop a tradition of women mountain climbers.

The ascent of Mount Everest (see EVEREST, MOUNT) in the Himalayas, the world's highest peak at 29,035 feet above sea level, remained an elusive prize well into the 20th century. In the 1920s, the British, with assistance from Nepalese SHERPAS as guides and porters, made attempts to climb it. During an attempt in 1924, GEORGE HERBERT LEIGH MALLORY and Andrew "Sandy" Irvine lost their lives. Nepalese TENZING NORGAY and Englishman SIR EDMUND PERCIVAL HILLARY finally reached the summit on May 29, 1953. The next year, Italians Achille Compagnoni and Lino Lacedelli, part of Ardido Desio's expedition, summitted K2. Other Himalayan mountains were conquered in the 1950s–60s, including the third-highest peak in the world, Kangchenjunga (or "Kang" or "Kanch"), as well as Annapurna, Nanga Parbat, Cho Oyu, Makalu, Lhotse, Manaslu, Gasherbrum II, Broad Peak, Hidden Peak, Dhaulagiri, and Shisha Pangma (or Gosainthan). With the highest peaks conquered, the challenge of Himalayan mountaineering has evolved into a pursuit of specialized assaults—by especially difficult routes, in wintertime, without oxygen bottles, solo, or in a series of related climbs. For example, in 1978, Italian Reinhold Messner and Austrian Peter Habeler climbed Mount Everest for the first time without bottled oxygen. Two years later, Messner accomplished a solo climb of Everest. In the course of 17 years, ending in 1986, Messner completed his goal of climbing the 14 highest mountains in the world, located in Nepal, Pakistan, China, and Tibet. Climbs in other Asian mountain ranges—Tien Shan, Pamir, Kunlun, and Hindu Kush—as well as other ranges around the world have also been undertaken by climbers of many different nationalities. In 1985, American Dick Bass became the first to climb the "Seven Summits," the highest peak on each of the seven continents. Because of the difficulty of such assaults, mountain climbers continue to lose their lives in falls, storms, and avalanches.

Modern Climbing

In recent times, new technologies have helped refine mountain-climbing clothing for warmth, waterproofing, and evaporation of perspiration. Equipment has also been developed to allow for climbing vertical and overhanging rock faces. Such equipment includes chocks, cams, and nuts to wedge into rock crevices; carabiners to attach ropes to the chocks; and loops of nylon webbing used as ladders. Cellular telephones make communication while mountain climbing easier. Another recent development is a new environmental awareness. Some countries now require climbing permits and even environmental bonds to ensure the removal of waste from expeditions. The placement of pitons and other hardware is also regulated in some locations. Rock climbing, which started as a method of training for ascents of high mountains, has grown as a sport in its own right. Climbers today are able to train in indoor rock-climbing gyms and to compete in rock-climbing tournaments. Many climbing clubs and organizations have formed around the world for both rock and ice climbing.

❖

The history of mountain climbing is a rich saga unto itself, apart from other kinds of exploration. Each high peak has its story, and many other individuals not mentioned above have contributed to their conquest. Mountaineering, despite all the accomplishments from the past and the advancements in its technology, remains one modern-day activity offering the thrill of exploration in some of the most remote places on Earth. As such, mountain climbing represents a continuum of exploration from ancient times to the present.

mountain men

The mountain men were frontiersmen active in the FUR TRADE in the ROCKY MOUNTAINS and surrounding regions of the American West. The term is most often applied to fur hunters, trappers, and traders working the northern and central Rockies in U.S. territory, seeking especially beaver furs and active in the 1820s and 1830s, but is sometimes also used in reference to those active in the southern or

Canadian Rockies, and in other decades. Most mountain men operated at a time when there were no permanent posts in that region and lived off the land, adopting Native American customs, including the wearing of leather and deerskin clothing. Some lived among tribes and married Indian women.

Many of those who became known as mountain men began their careers in the fur trade in the employ of the ROCKY MOUNTAIN FUR COMPANY, founded by WILLIAM HENRY ASHLEY and ANDREW HENRY in 1822. The earlier ST. LOUIS MISSOURI FUR COMPANY, also involving Henry, had been active along the MISSOURI RIVER. The AMERICAN FUR COMPANY, founded by JOHN JACOB ASTOR, had been working the country west of the Rockies. The Canadian HUDSON'S BAY COMPANY, which merged with the NORTH WEST COMPANY in 1821, had built most of its posts in the northern forests. And the RUSSIAN-AMERICAN COMPANY had developed the fur trade in Alaska. But some of the more difficult mountainous terrain and the routes through them were still virgin territory to non-Indians, and the activities of the mountain men opened much of the West to non-Indians.

Early in his operations, Ashley instituted the "brigade system," in which trappers were sent out in numbers to defend against Indian attacks, especially by the Blackfeet Indians who were hostile to outsiders crossing their territory. Many of the mountain men developed friendships that would endure over the next decades. JAMES PIERSON BECKWOURTH, JAMES BRIDGER, ROBERT CAMPBELL, JAMES CLYMAN, HUGH GLASS, THOMAS FITZPATRICK, HENRY FRAEB, CALEB GREENWOOD, DAVID E. JACKSON, ÉTIENNE PROVOST, EDWARD ROSE, JEDEDIAH STRONG SMITH, WILLIAM LEWIS SUBLETTE, WILLIAM HENRY VANDERBURGH, LOUIS VASQUEZ, and JOHN WEBER all worked for Ashley. The annual rendezvous—the first, in July 1825, organized by Ashley at Henrys Fork of the Green River in what is now northern Utah—was an essential part of the fur-trading economy. There would be 15 more such gatherings. At these meeting places, the mountain men delivered their furs to their employers, received their year's wages, obtained new supplies, and socialized. Native Americans also brought their catch to barter for supplies.

In 1826, Ashley sold out his fur-trading interests to three of his former employees, David Jackson, Jedediah Smith, and William Sublette. They maintained a loose company over the next years, as did other mountain men. Some came to work for the American Fur Company, which also began working the Rockies. BENJAMIN LOUIS EULALIE DE BONNEVILLE, a U.S. military man on leave who led a number of fur-trading expeditions west of the Rockies in 1832–35, employed mountain men JOSEPH REDDEFORD WALKER, ZENAS LEONARD, and JOSEPH L. MEEK. Not all the mountain men were white. Edward Rose was part Cherokee and part African American. Jim Beckwourth was part African American. Another trapper from the same period who has been referred to as a mountain man is CHRISTOPHER HOUSTON CARSON (Kit Carson).

Following the change in fashion with the beaver hat going out of style in favor of the silk hat and the drop-off in the international demand for furs in the late 1830s, the mountain men put their wilderness skills to work as guides and interpreters, leading many of the early exploratory expeditions of the West, such as those under JOHN CHARLES FRÉMONT, as well as wagon trains, especially along the Oregon Trail and the branching California Trail, which mountain men had pioneered. Others became soldiers and scouts, proving effective against the native peoples from whom they had learned so much. After working as a trapper and a guide for Frémont, Kit Carson went on to become an Indian agent

Frederic Remington, known for his works on the American West, painted these mountain men, probably in 1904. *(Library of Congress, Prints and Photographs Division [LC-USZ62-107676])*

as well as brigadier general against tribes of the Southwest. Many former mountain men settled in California. A number wrote accounts of their exploits.

Mountains of the Moon

The concept of the Mountains of the Moon, as associated with Africa, originated with DIOGENES, a Greek merchant who, in about A.D. 50, traveled inland in East Africa and reportedly sighted a range of snowcapped mountains feeding two large bodies of water. The next century, PTOLEMY, a hellenized Egyptian living in the North African city of Alexandria and a renowned geographer, produced an early map of Africa on which a group of mountains south of the EQUATOR were identified as *Lunae Montes,* or "Mountains of the Moon," and wrote about them as the source of the NILE RIVER.

The source of the Nile was not determined for centuries. In 1613, PEDRO PÁEZ, a Spanish missionary sent out by Portugal, reported that the source of the Blue Nile, one of the two branches converging into the great river, was Lake Tana in the mountains of Ethiopia, a discovery corroborated by Scotsman JAMES BRUCE in 1770. Then, in 1858, Englishman JOHN HANNING SPEKE theorized that the source of the White Nile, the main branch, was Lake Victoria, confirmed by Anglo-American SIR HENRY MORTON STANLEY in 1875. A decade later, in 1889, Stanley and MEHMED EMIN PASHA explored the Ruwenzori Mountains on the border of present-day Uganda and the Democratic Republic of the Congo. It was determined that the Ruwenzori were at least part of the watershed feeding the Nile, some streams flowing southward through Lake Edward and Lake George to Lake Victoria and to the Nile, and others flowing northward to Lake Albert and to the Nile. The range thus came to be associated with the fabled Mountains of the Moon.

The Ruwenzori Range consists of six mountains, including Mount Stanley, named after the explorer, with Margherita Peak, at 16,762 feet above sea level, the third-highest summit in Africa. Mount Speke is named after John Hanning Speke; Mount Emin, after Mehmed Emin Pasha; Mount Baker, after SIR SAMUEL WHITE BAKER; and Mount Gessi, after Italian Romlo Gessi, who explored the Nile to Lake Albert in 1876. In 1906, LUIGI AMEDEO DI SAVOIA D'ABRUZZI completed the first ascent of Margherita Peak, naming it for Italy's queen mother; he climbed five of the six peaks in the range as well. Mount Luigi di Savoia is named after him.

There is no way to prove that the Ruwenzori were in fact Diogenes's and Ptolemy's mountains. It is possible that Mount Kilimanjaro (see KILIMANJARO, MOUNT), Africa's highest mountain, and Mount Kenya, the second-highest, both closer to the Indian Ocean, were the mountains viewed by Diogenes and represented on Ptolemy's map. Yet the name is widely used for the Ruwenzori.

Mount Everest   See EVEREST, MOUNT.

Mount Kilimanjaro   See KILIMANJARO, MOUNT.

Mount McKinley   See McKINLEY, MOUNT.

Muscovy Company (Company of Merchant Adventurers; Merchant Adventurers of England for the Discovery of Lands, Territories, Isles, Dominions and Seignories Unknown; Mystery and Company of Merchant Venturers for the Discovery of Regions, Dominions, Islands and Places Unknown; Russia Company)

The Muscovy Company, a joint-stock corporation, was created in England to discover a NORTHEAST PASSAGE eastward from Europe to Cathay (present-day China), and to profit from the exclusive trade along such a route. It was referred to at different times by a number of other names, such as the Russia Company; the Company of Merchant Adventurers; the Merchant Adventurers of England for the Discovery of Lands, Territories, Isles, Dominions and Seignories Unknown; and the Mystery and Company of Merchant Venturers for the Discovery of Regions, Dominions, Islands and Places Unknown.

English merchants became interested in alternative trade routes as they saw their fellow European nations grow rich from their arrangements. Robert Thorne, a Bristol merchant in the mid-16th century, was especially enthusiastic about finding a passage to China by sailing past the northern border of Scandinavia, along Russia's north coast, and around the northeastern edge of the Asian continent. The Company of Merchant Adventurers was founded on December 18, 1551, with Italian-born SEBASTIAN CABOT as first governor. The son of the even more renowned explorer JOHN CABOT, Sebastian Cabot had had an eminent career in his own right, including a search, in 1509, for an alternative NORTHWEST PASSAGE westward through the Americas. Although Cabot was elderly at the time of his appointment, with no plans to accompany an expedition, his knowledge and wisdom were considered vital to the company's mission.

The waters to the east of Scandinavia and north of Russia were well known to native peoples inhabiting northern European shores at the time. Many made their living by fishing and hunting. Russia had had regular conflicts with their northern native neighbors, but cooperation was poor. In addition, most of the seafarers plying these waters were illiterate, so reliable records of their knowledge was difficult to attain. Thus, the expeditions of the Muscovy Company took on a diplomatic element, as well as unifying the geographic understanding of the regions.

Trade Links

The first expedition outfitted by the company was to be headed by SIR HUGH WILLOUGHBY, an English soldier; RICHARD CHANCELLOR, an English mariner, was to serve as pilot general; and STEPHEN BOROUGH, another English mariner, was to captain one of the ships. Their task was to sail to China and establish trade links with the rulers of distant lands, and they carried letters from the king for this purpose. Setting out in May 1553, they rounded the northern border of Norway, where the ships were separated by a storm. Willoughby continued eastward, where he sighted Novaya Zemlya, although he was unable to land due to ice. He turned back, coming ashore on the Kola Peninsula, where he and his crew perished during the winter. Meanwhile, Borough had turned back prematurely because of icy conditions. Chancellor had proceeded southward and entered the White Sea. He dropped anchor at the mouth of the Dvina River, where the trading port of Archangel was located—later to become an important point of contact with England—and traveled overland. Learning of his presence, Czar Ivan IV (Ivan the Terrible) invited him to Moscow, where he and his party were well received. The following summer, Chancellor and his men returned to their ship and sailed back to England.

With friendly contact made between Russia and England, the newly christened Muscovy Company was granted a royal charter in 1555 and given a monopoly in trade between the two countries. Chancellor made a second journey that same year to clarify agreements with the Russian government, but lost his own life on the return trip.

Another voyage in search of the Northeast Passage sponsored by the company was made in 1556 by Stephen Borough, who had captained a ship in the Willoughby expedition. With a crew of only eight and a small vessel named the *Searchthrift,* they made their way along Norway's coast to the Barents Sea. Along the way, they discovered Vaigach Island, and then came upon Novaya Zemlya. Here they encountered the Samoyed (now know as the Nentsi), a nomadic people. Turned back by ice from entering the Kara Sea, his descriptions of the unfavorable conditions that lay ahead discouraged the English from further exploration for several decades.

The Muscovy Company then turned its attention to capitalizing on trade links, exchanging English textiles for Russian furs. In 1561, Englishman ANTHONY JENKINSON was given the task of pushing farther south to open up relations with Persia (present-day Iran). Passing through Russia, he took a boat down the Volga River to Astrakhan. From there, he managed to navigate the rough conditions on the Caspian Sea, eventually reaching the court of the shah in the capital of Kazvin. He was rebuffed, but did manage to reach an agreement with the ruler at Shirvan. On another British expedition in 1564, Thomas Alcock, the leader, was killed. Four more trips, taking place from 1565 to 1580, were unsuccessful.

New Attempt at a Northeast Passage

The next English expedition in search of the Northeast Passage sponsored by the company was headed by Arthur Pet and Charles Jackman. They set sail in separate ships in June 1580: a 40-ton vessel, *George,* was commanded by Pet, and the 20-ton ship, *William,* was under Jackman's command. These were small boats, but their captains had experience from earlier expeditions—Pet with Chancellor, and Jackman under SIR MARTIN FROBISHER in the western Arctic. They found the strait between Vaigach Island and the mainland (currently called the Yugor Strait) but were stopped by the ice on the Kara Sea, having penetrated only a few more miles than Borough's expedition.

In 1607, the Muscovy Company hired Englishman HENRY HUDSON to find the Northeast Passage. He sailed westward to GREENLAND, then returning east and north, he came upon Spitsbergen (present-day Svalbard), a collection of islands situated to the north of Norway, visited in 1696 by a Dutch expedition under WILLEM BARENTS. Hudson's progress farther eastward impeded by ice, he returned to England. His reports of whales in northern waters led to the development of the English whaling industry, with some participation of the Muscovy Company. On a second trip in 1608, he took the more conventional route used by his predecessors and explored Novaya Zemlya, but was again forced back by ice.

Enduring Legacy

Despite their failure to accomplish their original objective of a Northeast Passage to China, the Muscovy Company left an enduring legacy. They were the first major joint-stock trading company in England, paving the way for numerous monopoly ventures to follow. Their trade with Russia was lucrative and continued for centuries, being interrupted only from 1646 to 1660, when English merchants were banned from Russia. Their monopoly privileges were long a subject of controversy, but these they were able to maintain until 1698, when the political pressure became too strong for the English monarchy to resist. The company remained active over the next centuries, however, finally closing its books in 1917.

See also COMMERCE AND EXPLORATION.

Muslim exploration

The term *Muslim,* also written *Moslem,* is Arabic and translates as "one who submits," referring to a believer in the religion of Islam. Islam, the youngest of the three monotheistic world religions after Judaism and Christianity and evolving out of them, was founded by the Prophet Muhammad (or Mohammed) in the seventh century A.D. Muhammad was born in about 570, a native of Mecca in what is now western Saudi Arabia. After experiencing a vision at age 40, he began preaching his revelations about the one god, known as Allah in Arabic, to the polytheistic Meccans. He eventually recorded his beliefs in the Qur'an (Koran). In

This photograph from the 1880s shows Muslims gathered at a sacred shrine in Mecca during the hajj. *(Library of Congress, Prints and Photographs Division [LC-USZ62-99278])*

622, on alienating that city's political and religious rulers, he fled with his followers in a migration known as the hegira, the event from which the Islamic calendar is dated, and settled in Yathrib (later known as Medina) to the north. His influence and power grew as more and more Arab tribes declared their allegiance to him. In 630, he and his followers conquered Mecca.

At the time of Muhammad's death two years later, the new religion was spreading rapidly, largely through military conquest, as directed by the first three caliphs, Abu Bakr, Omar, and Othman. In 637, Jerusalem fell to Arab armies. Muslims also conquered Mesopotamia, Persia, and Syria. Under later rulers, Muslims came to control lands in central Asia to the edge of the Chinese Empire, all of North Africa, as well as territory in Spain, which they first invaded in 711 under Moorish leader Tariq. They were active traders even beyond these regions and came to dominate commerce along the SILK ROAD among other trade routes.

In later years, other Islamic peoples besides the Arabs came to dominate extensive regions. At the beginning of the 11th century, the Seljuk Turks under Togul began consolidating their power, conquering much of Asia Minor and surrounding areas. It was their ascendancy and harassment of Christian pilgrims to Jerusalem and their threatening Constantinople (present-day Istanbul, Turkey), the seat of the Eastern Roman Empire (Byzantine Empire) that helped prompt the CRUSADES, the military expeditions by European Christians to the Near East through the late 13th century. After proclaiming their independence from the Seljuks in 1290 under Osman I, the Ottoman Turks rose to power in the region and established the Ottoman Empire, which at the height of its power in the mid-16th century under Suleiman the Magnificent included much of southeastern Europe, western Asia, and northern Africa.

The Middle Ages, from the ninth to the 14th century, was a time of inquiry in the Muslim world, and comparisons can be made between this period of Muslim intellectual activity and the earlier Classical Age of the Greeks, and with the later RENAISSANCE in Europe (and the related EUROPEAN AGE OF EXPLORATION). There was a new mobility among its population. People traveled for religious purposes, with pilgrimages to Mecca, the holiest city of the Islamic faith as the birthplace of Muhammad (travel to which became regarded as an essential act of faith, known as the hajj). Religious research was part of devotion, and Islamic scholars journey throughout Muslim lands to research the *hādith,* oral teachings attributed to Muhammad and his followers. People also traveled for economic reasons, with Muslim merchants developing new markets. And people traveled for scientific reasons, even beyond the Muslim world, seeking knowledge of foreign lands. There resulted a wealth of Muslim literature: cosmographies, world geographies, regional geographies, geographies of particular routes, chronologies of nations, and astronomical studies. The Arabs designed the DHOW, a craft with a LATEEN RIG, which became a common sight in the MEDITERRANEAN SEA, RED SEA, Arabian Sea, Persian Gulf, and Indian Ocean. The Muslims became proficient in navigation in oceans. They used the sundial, QUADRANT, ASTROLABE, and magnetic COMPASS. As early as the 10th century, they recorded nautical data in texts known as *rahmānī,* similar to the peripli of the Greeks and Romans (see PERIPLUS).

Many of the Muslim travelers were Arab, but not all, some descended from other peoples and venturing forth from other homelands. In some instances their exact nationality is not known. One of the most renowned early travelers was Arab merchant SOLEYMAN, also known as Sulaimen el Tagir, who, in about 850–51, traveled from the Persian Gulf by sea to India and China, visiting en route the Maldive Islands and Laccadive Islands, CEYLON (present-day Sri Lanka), and the Andaman Islands. He wrote a book that came to be known as *Sequence of Historical Events,* with geographic as well as cultural information about the places he visited. In the early part of the 10th century, another Arab merchant, ABU ALI AHMAD IBN RUSTA, traveled throughout the lower Volga region of eastern Europe as well as to Malay in Asia. In his writings he describes both European and Asian peoples.

Two scholars traveled in the early 10th century as well, ABU AL-HASAN ALI AL-MASUDI, an Arab historian who reportedly visited every country in the Islamic world, and AHMAD IBN FADLAN, a non-Arab scholar who traveled from Baghdad into the Volga region of European Russia. Another individual who traveled throughout the Islamic world was merchant and scholar ABU AL-QASIM IBN ALI AL-NASIBI IBN HAWQAL. He also reportedly traveled across the SAHARA DESERT. His travels, beginning in 943, lasted about three decades. The next century, in about 1017, Arab scholar ABU AR-RAYHAN MUHAMMAD IBN AHMAD AL-BIRUNI traveled to India from Afghanistan; he later wrote a book on Indian customs and geography.

In 1145–54, after extensive travels in northwestern Europe, Arab ABU ABD ALLAH MUHAMMAD ASH-SHARIF AL-IDRISI, working for Roger II, the Norman king of Sicily, revolutionized cartography in *The Book of Roger,* which contains accurate geographic information based on his travels and the use of a grid system. In 1182–85, a son of a prominent Muslim family of Spain, ABU AL-HASAN MUHAMMAD IBN JUBAYR, explored the lands of the Mediterranean on pilgrimage from Spain to Arabia. His writings in a travel account known as a *Rihla* for "Journey" include a description of the holy places in Mecca. Another cartographer, SHIHAB AL-DIN ABU ABD ALLAH YAQUT AL-RUMI, was a Greek-born Muslim who traveled throughout the Middle East for a Baghdad merchant. In 1228–29, he published *Mu'jam al*

Buldan (Dictionary of Countries), a gazetteer-type geographic study.

The most famous of all the Muslim travelers was ABU ABD ALLAH MUHAMMAD IBN BATTUTAH, an Arab born in Tangier, Morocco. In 1325–50, as a pilgrim and scholar, he traveled throughout Egypt, Arabia, central Asia, Africa, and Spain. In Africa, he reached the city of TIMBUKTU in the kingdom of Mali, south of the Sahara. He, too, recorded his experiences in a *Rihla* travel account, published in 1357. At the time of his death in 1378, he was considered the most widely traveled person in history.

There are many other Muslim individuals who contributed to the growing body of knowledge of the medieval period and afterward and who are a part of the history of exploration.

The Muslim tradition of wide-ranging travel—both for religious purposes and for commerce—continued after the Middle Ages, and Islam continued to spread to new peoples, especially in Africa and Asia. Moreover, Muslim individuals continued to play a part in world exploration, even as part of other traditions, their religious affiliation not necessarily the motivation for travel. CHENG HO, who carried out seven maritime expeditions to the Indian Ocean on behalf of the Ming rulers of China in the early 15th century, was the son of Chinese Muslims. Muslims were hired for their expertise as navigators during the EUROPEAN AGE OF EXPLORATION of the 15th, 16th, and 17th centuries. It is widely believed that Italian mariner CHRISTOPHER COLUMBUS used Muslim navigators in crossing the Atlantic Ocean for Spain in 1492. At the very least, he made use of Arabic navigational techniques and charts. (Based on ancient documents which, for example, tell of Muslims of African origin sailing from Spain across an ocean of "darkness and fog" and returning with evidence of a "strange and curious land," it is theorized by some that Muslim mariners even reached the Americas before Columbus, as early as the ninth and 10th centuries.) ESTEVANICO, a slave out of North Africa who participated in Spanish explorations of the American Southeast and Southwest in the first half of the 16th century, is assumed to have been Islamic. Many other Muslims were taken to the Americas as slaves and contributed to European expansion into new territory. The fact that they were Islamic has rarely been documented. (One exception is Omar Ibn Sayyid, a West African slave in North Carolina, known to be Muslim from a letter he wrote in 1831.) There is also a legacy of a Muslim presence in Australia predating European settlement: It is thought fishermen and traders from the Indonesian archipelago reached Australia's north shore as early as the 16th century. Afghan Muslims are known to have traveled to Australia in the 19th century to help with the exploration of the interior as camel drivers. Yet Muslim exploration as a subject of study generally relates to the Middle Ages, which might be called the Age of Muslim Exploration (as well as the Golden Age of Muslim Travel Writing).

nao See CARRACK.

NASA See NATIONAL AERONAUTICS AND SPACE ADMINISTRATION.

National Aeronautics and Space Administration (NASA)

The National Aeronautics and Space Administration, better known as NASA, is an agency of the U.S. government, established by the National Aeronautics and Space Act of July 1958, for the purpose of SPACE EXPLORATION. In managing the U.S. space program, NASA conducts research in aviation and in ROCKET design, as well as related communications. It also directs scientific experiments in space. Moreover, it works in organizational aspects of space exploration, including the selection and training of ASTRONAUTS and the development of alliances between nations and partnerships between government and business or academia.

NASA was founded in response to the early success of the Union of Soviet Socialist Republics (USSR; Soviet Union) in its space program. In October 1957, the Soviets put the first artificial SATELLITE, *Sputnik 1,* into space, the start of the "space race." To coordinate all space-related activities in one agency, NASA replaced the National Advisory Committee for Aeronautics (NACA), which had been founded in 1915 and had been geared toward research, and

absorbed some of the responsibilities of other government agencies as well.

NASA is based in Washington, D.C., and is overseen by the U.S. president, who helps plan policy and determine budget. Moreover, the administrator of NASA, a civilian, is appointed by the president, with the advice and consent of the Senate; under him is a staff of thousands of scientists, engineers, and technicians. The five NASA branches are the Office of Aero-Space Technology; the Office of Earth Science; the Office of Space Flight; the Office of Life and Microgravity Sciences and Applications; and the Office of Space Science. Facilities include the John F. Kennedy Space Center at Merritt Island, Florida; the Lyndon B. Johnson Space Center in Houston, Texas; the Goddard Space Flight Center in Greenbelt, Maryland; the George C. Marshall Space Flight Center in Huntsville, Alabama; and the Jet Propulsion Laboratory, operated under contract by the California Institute of Technology, in Pasadena.

NASA directed the MERCURY PROGRAM of 1961–63 to launch the first Americans into space; the manned GEMINI PROGRAM of 1964–66 to help develop the necessary techniques for a lunar mission; the unmanned Surveyor Program of 1966–68 to probe the lunar surface; and the APOLLO PROGRAM of 1961–72 to land a human on the Moon. Other projects include the unmanned exploratory flights to Mars. Since 1981, NASA has been directing flights of the reusable space vehicle, the SPACE SHUTTLE. Although originally conceived as a civilian agency, NASA has been increasingly involved in aiding military research, carried out through space shuttle flights. NASA teamed up with the EUROPEAN SPACE AGENCY (ESA) to launch and maintain the *Hubble Space Telescope*. NASA has also been involved with the development of an international SPACE STATION.

native peoples and exploration

The history of exploration from ancient to modern times is not just about travel in uncharted lands, but also about contacts among peoples. The exploration of any continent, except Antarctica, cannot be discussed without relating the role of and impact on indigenous peoples. Since studies on exploration and explorers involve the stories and viewpoints of individuals who traveled from their homelands to foreign lands and helped diffuse knowledge, the related stories of indigenous peoples are sometimes neglected. The long-term use of the word *discover* as applied to already inhabited lands is an obvious example of how native peoples have been historically minimized in accounts on exploration. Moreover, there has been until recent years a tendency to glorify "discoveries" without offering a balancing account of the negative impact contacts with outsiders had on aboriginal populations—through disease, conquest, slavery, displacement from lands, and dispossession of culture. There also has been a minimizing of the role many indigenous individuals had in the success of specific expeditions as guides, interpreters, canoeists, and carriers, as well as the fact that some were explorers in their own right, opening up regions for their own people.

Conquest and Colonization

Some expeditions were launched with conquest and colonization of native peoples as the express purpose. The explorations of Macedonian ruler ALEXANDER THE GREAT in the fourth century B.C. in Africa and Asia, of Roman general GAIUS JULIUS CAESAR in the first century A.D. in Europe, and of Mongol leader GENGHIS KHAN in the 13th century A.D. in Asia involved the conquest and colonization of peoples. So did the early 16th-century Spanish expeditions of HERNÁN CORTÉS and FRANCISCO PIZARRO in the Americas. The very name applied to such Spanish explorers—CONQUISTADORES—implies conquest of indigenous peoples. Such military ventures had a direct impact on the history of peoples, and, in some cases, entire civilizations. The highly organized civilizations of the Aztec and Inca collapsed under the Spanish invasion.

Varying Contacts

Other expeditions were initiated having peaceful contacts with native peoples in mind. Italian mariner CHRISTOPHER COLUMBUS, exploring for Spain, hoped to find a new trade route to the Orient with the SPICE TRADE in mind when he set out westward across the Atlantic Ocean in the late 15th century. Russian fur traders journeyed to Alaska in the mid-18th century to develop the FUR TRADE with native peoples. The religious conversion of native peoples provided incentive for many voyages into the wilderness, such as those of Frenchman CLAUDE-JEAN ALLOUEZ in the western Great Lakes country of North America in the mid-17th century. Knowledge of native peoples, as well as knowledge of geography, was a motivating factor in other expeditions, such as the U.S. government-sponsored expedition headed by MERIWETHER LEWIS and WILLIAM CLARK to the Pacific Northwest of North America in the early 19th century.

Part of the story of these expeditions, however, like those undertaken in the name of conquest, is the negative impact on peoples. When Columbus failed to reach the wealthy civilizations of Asia, he sought to obtain enough gold from Native Americans of the WEST INDIES to satisfy his sponsors. When that endeavor failed, he turned to the SLAVE TRADE as a means of profit. Colonization of the region followed, as did the eventual extermination of local tribes. The exploitation of native labor became central to the operations of the early Russian fur traders, who took Aleut hostages to force the delivery of furs. Allouez's work among a reported 22 tribes—as that of other missionaries throughout the world—altered traditional ways of life. And the Lewis and Clark Expedition, despite peaceful contacts with more than 50 Native American tribes, can be seen as the start of the similar pattern for those tribes of nonnatives entering the native domain and beginning the process of destructive change.

The outcome of some expeditions involving native peoples as the primary motivation can be viewed in a positive light. For example, American GEORGE CATLIN, who traveled in North, South, and Central America in the mid-19th century, helped preserve knowledge of native peoples. In the early 20th century, American historian HIRAM BINGHAM helped preserve the Inca legacy in his studies of their ruins in Peru.

In the case of many other expeditions, the interaction with native peoples is incidental to the undertaking, but central to the story. Most accounts of expeditions to uncharted lands include mention of encounters with native peoples, both friendly and hostile. The explorations along the coast of Australia, such as those carried out by Englishman WILLIAM DAMPIER in the late 17th century, and in the interior by Scotsman SIR THOMAS LIVINGSTONE MITCHELL in the first half of the 19th century, resulted in engagements with Aborigines, some of them violent. In many instances, native peoples determined the outcome. Some of the most famous explorers were killed in confrontations, such as Spanish JUAN PONCE DE LÉON, who made the European discovery of Florida in North America in the early 16th

Jacques Le Moyne painted a watercolor of the French, led by René de Laudonnière, encountering Native Americans in 1562 at St. Johns River in Florida. It was published by the Flemish engraver Théodore de Bry in 1591. *(Library of Congress, Prints and Photographs Division [LC-USZ62-380])*

century, and Portuguese FERDINAND MAGELLAN in the course of the first CIRCUMNAVIGATION OF THE WORLD soon afterward.

Benefactors, Guides, Interpreters, and Porters

In other instances, native peoples were essential to the success of expeditions. In the Americas, Arawak (Taino) Indian chief GUANCANAGARI helped Columbus in the West Indies as a protector, guide, and interpreter. Aztec Indian woman MALINCHE helped Cortés in the same role. Huron (Wyandot) Indian DONNACONNA aided Frenchman JACQUES CARTIER in his 16th-century explorations along the Gulf of St. Lawrence and the St. Lawrence River in what is now northeastern Canada. Native American TURK and Ysopete served as guides, also in the 16th century, to Spanish FRANCISCO VÁSQUEZ DE CORONADO in the American Southwest. The PILGRIMS, who sought a new life in northeastern North America in the early 17th century, would not have survived without help from Native Americans—a course of events leading to the American holiday of Thanksgiving. The Wampanoag Indian SQUANTO was invaluable to them

as both a diplomat and interpreter, as well as a guide on their later coastal explorations. The Chipewyan MATONABBEE was central to the survival and success of Englishman SAMUEL HEARNE's 18th-century voyages west of HUDSON BAY in Canada. Shoshone Indian woman SACAJAWEA (Sacagawea) deserves as much credit for the success of the early 19th-century Lewis and Clark Expedition as anyone, as a guide and interpreter, as well as a diplomat since the presence of a Native American woman provided safe passage through tribal lands. Ioway Indian woman MARIE DORION played a similar role for the Astorians, who traveled to the Pacific Northwest under WILSON PRICE HUNT several years later. In the mid-19th century, Mojave Indian IRATEBA served as a guide for several U.S. military topographic expeditions. At about the same time on South Island in NEW ZEALAND, a Maori named Ekuhu proved essential as a guide in the explorations of Englishman THOMAS BRUNNER.

An example of an Asian native offering assistance is NIKOLAY DAURKIN of the Chukchi tribe of northeastern SIBERIA. He served as an interpreter under Russia's Northeastern Secret Geographical and Astronomical Expedition of the late 18th century, headed by Englishman JOSEPH BILLINGS.

The history of African exploration is also filled with the stories of native participants. HUGH CLAPPERTON and RICHARD LEMON LANDER, explorers of West Africa in the early 19th century, traveled with WILLIAM PASCOE, a Hausa tribesman and freed slave who acted as a servant and cook as well as a guide and interpreter. European explorers of Africa would not have been able to venture into the interior of Africa without the help of African porters—the *pagazi*—to carry their supplies. The porters' leader—the *kirangozi*—helped organize day-to-day life of an expedition. The Yao tribal member SIDI BOMBAY was critical to the success of a number of 19th-century British expeditions, including those of SIR RICHARD FRANCIS BURTON, JOHN HANNING SPEKE, SIR HENRY MORTON STANLEY, and VERNEY LOVETT CAMERON, as a caravan leader, guide, and interpreter.

In the 20th century, SHERPAS have been essential to the success of numerous MOUNTAIN CLIMBING expeditions in the HIMALAYAS as guides and porters. One of them, TENZING NORGAY, who accompanied Englishman SIR EDMUND PERCIVAL HILLARY in an assault on Mount Everest (see EVEREST, MOUNT) in 1953, became the first human to summit the world's highest mountain. There are numerous other native individuals known to have led foreigners through their lands and beyond. The names of many others, however, have been lost to history.

Native Explorers

Native peoples carried out their own travels to new lands. Most books about exploration do not discuss ancient migrations as exploratory expeditions, however. If the history of world exploration is perceived as the record of diffusion of geographic and cultural knowledge—with the mapping of the world, as a result of particular expeditions, at the heart of the saga—then ancient migrations determined through archaeological investigation are not part of the story. Yet, in the case of the Americas, so much is made as to their discovery, with 1492 as one of the best-known dates in history and Christopher Columbus as the most famous explorer, that it becomes necessary to discuss the migrations of Paleo-Indians across the LAND BRIDGE formed in the BERING STRAIT during the last ice age and attribute to them the true discovery of the Americas by humankind.

Accounts of some native explorers have been passed down orally. For example, the tradition of the Maori people holds that KUPE, a chieftain of the Polynesians, reached New Zealand in the mid-10th century. The legendary story contains some fantastic elements—such as the pursuit of a Squid King—yet the fact of a Polynesian migration to New Zealand is considered fact.

The PUNDITS, native peoples of India or neighboring countries working for the British in the 19th century, are central to the story of the mapping of the Himalayas. Men such as NAIN SINGH, KISHEN SINGH, and KINTUP were able to disguise themselves as Buddhist merchants and pilgrims to travel in Tibet, a land forbidden to Europeans.

Some explorers were part native, their ancestry playing a part in the success of their accomplishments. EDWARD ROSE, who worked as a guide for a number of fur-trading expeditions, as well as interpreter and negotiator among Native American tribes along the MISSOURI RIVER and to the west in the early 19th century, had Cherokee ancestry along with European and African. Another part-Cherokee, JESSE CHISHOLM, similarly worked as a guide and interpreter in the American West; in 1865, he blazed the Chisholm Trail from Texas to Kansas, which soon became a major cattle drive route. Anthropologist KNUD JOHAN VICTOR RASMUSSEN—who studied GREENLAND and its Inuit (Eskimo) peoples in the early 20th century—had an Inuit mother and a Danish father.

❖

One other point should be made regarding indigenous peoples and exploration. From the native point of view, some among them "discovered" lands foreign to them just as Europeans are said to have "discovered" other places. For example, when Squanto was taken to Europe as a slave in the early 17th century, then managed to return to North America, in relating his experiences to his people, he no doubt was perceived as an explorer who had lived a remarkable adventure. Omai, the Tahitian man who returned to Europe with TOBIAS FURNEAUX in 1774, and who, as a guest of SIR JOSEPH BANKS, made a splash in London society, can be said, as the first South Pacific native to visit England, to have "discovered" Europe for his people.

See also COLONIZATION AND EXPLORATION; COMMERCE AND EXPLORATION; CONQUEST AND EXPLORATION; DISEASE AND EXPLORATION; POLYNESIAN EXPLORATION; RELIGION AND EXPLORATION.

natural science and exploration

The precursor of a wide range of sciences—from the study of life-forms, such as biology, zoology, botany, paleontology, and anthropology, to the earth sciences, such as geology, geography, and oceanography—was the discipline of natural science. Also referred to as natural history, the discipline was practiced over the centuries by naturalists who studied "nature," the natural world both animate and inanimate. In ancient times, such studies related to other scientific studies as well: mathematics, physics, and astronomy. Even in the golden age of natural history, the 17th to 19th centuries, European naturalists as part of others' expeditions or on their own, would conduct studies in a wide range of subjects: animal and plant species, native peoples, rock formations,

Earth's magnetic fields, OCEAN CURRENTS, and so on. The scope of their study must be hard to imagine for scientists today who have become increasingly specialized.

Foundations of Natural Science

It is difficult to separate out natural history from a general quest for knowledge in ancient times. The ancient Egyptians, for example, sent out expeditions—such as that of Queen HATSHEPSUT in about 1492 B.C., to the land of PUNT to the south—in order to collect among other things exotic plants and animals (see EGYPTIAN EXPLORATION). Many different peoples around the world, such as the ancient Chinese and Native Americans, also developed a remarkable body of knowledge about herbs for healing (see CHINESE EXPLORATION).

It can be said, however, that the philosophical foundation of modern science, empiricism and the objective observation of phenomena without reference to the observer, was developed by the ancient Greeks (see GREEK EXPLORATION). Thales of Miletus, who was active in the seventh to sixth century B.C., established some of the earliest principles of natural science, in astronomy, geography, and hydrology. In 585 B.C., he accurately predicted an eclipse of the Sun. Aristotle of the fourth century B.C. considered him the father of Greek philosophy. The philosophers of the ancient world thought in terms of a metaphysical "first cause," which created the world and set it in motion toward an appointed end or "final cause," and tended to denigrate the material world perceivable to our senses in favor of abstract ideas and theories. The fifth- to fourth-century B.C. Greek philosopher Plato, for example, maintained that the forms we see are but shadows of ideal forms. Yet the ancient Greeks placed much more emphasis on empirical observation and experimentation than did philosophers of the Middle Ages, and the Greeks traveled the known world observing and describing what they had observed.

CTESIAS OF CNIDUS was drawn to the fantastic, however. A Greek physician who traveled in Persia and India from 420 to 400 B.C., he later wrote accounts of his experiences, which, he claimed, discredited earlier accounts by fifth-century B.C. Greek historian HERODOTUS. Yet most of his information was based on hearsay from Persian courtiers; he wrote down everything he was told, no matter how incredible. Ctesias serves as an example of the importance to the Greeks of factual reporting, for as soon as Macedonian ALEXANDER THE GREAT traveled the same regions in the fourth century B.C., Ctesias's work was superseded by eyewitness accounts, some of them by scientists and surveyors traveling with Alexander's army. His scientists even sent back specimens of wildlife to Greece. The difference in worldview of the ancient Greeks from that of medieval Europeans is clearly shown by the latter's credulous acceptance of everything Ctesias wrote. For example, his account of a race of men with a single huge foot, which may have originated from tales of Indian holy men who would spend hours meditating while standing on one foot, resulted in medieval depictions of big-footed men.

Ctesias's importance may derive more from the effect his writings had on others; his books were read by many educated Greeks including Aristotle, a fourth-century B.C. Greek philosopher, as well as Alexander, who studied under Aristotle. It is likely that, during his travels in Persia and India, Alexander sought confirmation of Ctesias's information. Moreover, Alexander sent back to Aristotle multitudes of natural specimens and reports on the natural phenomena. Aristotle was thus a naturalist-explorer by proxy; one of his assistants may actually have accompanied Alexander's army and worked to systematize their findings before sending them home. Aristotle differed from Plato by insisting that ideal form, the ultimate object of study for philosophers, was inherent in concrete individual things, resulting in his preoccupation with observable nature.

Natural Science during the Middle Ages

For all the profound influence Aristotle's writings had on European beliefs about the natural world, Plato's philosophy became the essential framework for medieval Christian theology and philosophy, with a belief in the dualism of matter versus spirit or soul and a profound mistrust of the physical. It is ironic that the basic beliefs of scholars of the Middle Ages led them to study Aristotle's works rather than studying nature for themselves as he had done.

Science in the Middle Ages combined the physical with the metaphysical; the precursor of chemistry was alchemy, that of astronomy was astrology. The aim was to discover evidence of a preconceived order in the world; thus, early maps showed landmasses arrayed in the perfect symmetry that God must have bestowed on them, with Jerusalem at the center of Earth (see GEOGRAPHY AND CARTOGRAPHY). Also, during the Middle Ages, animals were studied not by direct observation but as they appeared in bestiaries, books with depictions and descriptions that used animal lore to teach Christian values. The core material of most medieval bestiaries came from *Physiologus,* a text written by an anonymous author, possibly a contemporary of Saint Augustine, the bishop of Hippo in north Africa, who lived in the fourth to fifth centuries A.D. This writer took the assertions of earlier authors as undeniable fact without making any attempt at independent verification. Stories such as that of the mythical bird known as the phoenix, which burns itself to death and rises on the third day from the ashes, had symbolic value, this particular one representing Christ's resurrection.

Stirrings of a new way of regarding nature began to be discernable in the 13th century. Italian friar Saint Francis of Assisi deposed man from the dominion over all nature given him in the Bible; this dominion had long been reinforced by the belief that man with his soul and his reasoning mind was highest of all creatures on Earth in the hierarchy from matter to spirit. To Saint Francis, however, nature consisted of a harmonious democracy of all creatures.

Saint Francis's contemporary, Friederich I of Hohenstaufen, king of Germany and Holy Roman Emperor, an avid falconer, wrote *De Arte Venandi cum Avibus* (The art of hunting with birds), using his own careful observations, and displayed a different attitude toward textbook natural history than had predominated for so long. "No certainty comes by hearsay," he declared, and carefully tested as many of Aristotle's facts as he could, writing only about what he had observed himself; he refuted many of the tales of the bestiaries. German scholar Albertus Magnus, the patron saint of natural scientists, translated into German Aristotle's *Historia animalium,* making it more accessible for confirmation or refutation. During his travels, Venetian MARCO POLO, who traveled to the Far East in the latter part of the century, was able to refute many bestiary "facts," such as that of the rhinoceros, which he described were not very likely "to be taken by maidens" (a reference to scholars' confusion of the rhinoceros with the unicorn, which in legend could be captured only by a virgin). Italian monk Rufinus of Naples wrote a treatise on plants in 1287, which presented them as a subject worthy of study on their own, aside from any moral lessons they might tell and without reference to their medicinal uses.

Natural Science during the Renaissance

With the humanists of the Italian RENAISSANCE of the 16th century came a more widespread return of interest in the classical approach to science, instead of simple acceptance of the facts of the ancients. An example is English naturalist William Turner, who, in 1544, printed a small book devoted entirely to birds; he included the descriptions of Aristotle and Roman writer PLINY THE ELDER of the first century A.D., but added many accurate descriptions based on his own extensive studies.

Artists at this time of the great flowering of Italian Renaissance painting were as devoted to the ideal of close observation and exact depiction of nature as many naturalists; the science of perspective drawing allowed for a realism never seen before. Italian artist, architect, and poet Michelangelo risked criminal prosecution to dissect corpses in an effort to study the muscular structure of the body. Italian artist and architect Leonardo da Vinci, also a talented scientist and inventor, dissected cadavers as well and studied other aspects of natural history, such as the flight of birds. German painter Albrecht Dürer, who made woodcuts for Konrad Gesner's enormously influential encyclopedia, *Historia Animalium* (1551–58), brought scientific drawing to new heights of accuracy.

By the end of the century 16th century, the struggle between the old and new attitudes was in full swing. The latter found its major champion in Italian mathematician, astronomer, and physicist Galileo, an early practitioner of modern science. He, too, explored the physical aspects of the natural word to better understand the theoretical world.

A contemporary of Galileo's was Englishman THOMAS HARRIOT, a geographer, surveyor, and naturalist for the expedition of SIR WALTER RALEIGH to North America in 1585. Harriot helped locate the site for the Roanoke colony and designed its fort. He identified more than 86 species of birds and many trees and shrubs unknown to Europe; in 1588, he wrote the first critical study of the flora and fauna of North America. Harriot was also an astronomer and independently discovered some of the same sunspots as Galileo. He even preceded Galileo (by a few months) in making the first telescope-based drawing of the Moon in 1609; he made the first drawing of sunspots in 1610.

Naturalistic study of lands discovered in the first wave of exploration in the 16th century was mostly carried out by clerics, especially Jesuits such as JOSÉ DE ACOSTA, a Spaniard who traveled to Peru and Mexico in the 1570s–80s. Yet the Protestant Reformation caused the Catholic Church to retreat into an increasingly defensive posture on all fronts, especially intellectual. Heresy was suspected and found everywhere, and in this atmosphere of suspicion Galileo ran afoul of Church authority. His affair had a chilling affect on intellectual endeavor within the church, and, by the 18th century, it had become more common for lay naturalists to accompany exploratory expeditions.

From Descartes to Darwin

A modern approach to science fully came into play only in the 17th century, largely as a result of the work of French mathematician and philosopher René Descartes, who promoted the rigorous separation of the realm of the mind, *res cogitans,* from that of material phenomena, *res extensa.* In 1660, the ROYAL SOCIETY was founded in England by a number of intelligentsia. Its full title—Royal Society of London for Improving Natural Knowledge—indicates how natural science had become an impassioned cause.

In the 18th century—culturally defined in Europe as the Age of Enlightenment, when for many human reason displaced religion as the source of truth and the primary force for good in the world—the stream of discoveries of new species of plants and animals became a flood. Naturalists now were traveling to many areas of North and South America, Africa, Asia, and the Indian and Pacific Oceans, and the lands they found, vastly different from those of Europe, were profoundly changing Europeans' worldview, enlarging their sense of the scope and variety of the life-forms of Earth. There was a pressing need for a truly universal system of classification of species. Carl Linnaeus, a Swedish physician and botanist, was one of those in the forefront of carrying out and promoting expeditions of naturalistic study. In 1731, he mounted a solo botanical and ethnographic expedition to Lapland. He became a professor at the University of Upsalla in 1741; during his tenure there, he arranged for many of his students to accompany voyages of discovery. Perhaps his most famous student, fellow Swede DANIEL CARL SOLANDER, was assistant to British naturalist SIR JOSEPH BANKS on Captain JAMES COOK's CIRCUMNAVIGATION OF THE WORLD in 1768–71. The expedition, backed by the Royal Society, brought back the first plant collections from Australia and the South Pacific to Europe. Solander introduced the Linnaean system into Britain and was a pioneer in its use to classify new species. Banks and Solander recognized that the kangaroos, wallabies, and other marsupial mammals were fundamentally different from and more primitive than placental mammals. JOSEPH-PHILIBERT COMMERSON, a French physician, studied for many years with Linnaeus; he later accompanied LOUIS-ANTOINE DE BOUGAINVILLE on the first French circumnavigation of the world in 1766–69 and sent back to France more than 5,000 specimens of plants and animals, most of them hitherto unknown to science.

Early on, Linnaeus had seen the need for an improved system of classification and, in 1735, he had published the first slim volume of his *Systema Naturae,* which later would grow to many volumes. Paradoxically, since his system would ultimately facilitate 19th-century British naturalist CHARLES ROBERT DARWIN in his development of the theory of natural as opposed to divine selection, Linnaeus's basic conception of the study of nature was that it furnished a natural theology whereby one could learn about God's wisdom by studying His creations. But his system of classification was based not on moralistic judgments about species but on their physical characters; beginning with plants, he used the number and arrangement of their reproductive organs to classify them. In the end, this approach proved unworkable, and his lasting contribution was to group organisms not only as species sharing common characteristics, which Aristotle had done, then species into genera, but also into higher groupings: genera were grouped into orders, orders into classes, and classes into kingdoms. Formerly, species had been grouped as, for example, those which lived in water, or domesticated species; thus, fish and whales had been considered to occupy the same grouping. The use of common physical characteristics to organize species on all taxonomic levels shifted the focus to familial relationships and inheritance. Based on this concept, Darwin—in the mid-19th century, after his trip around the world on the *Beagle* captained by ROBERT FITZROY—would make his controversial identification of humans, apes, and monkeys as belonging to the same order, Primates, all sharing a single common ancestor. British naturalist ALFRED RUSSEL WAL-LACE, who had traveled to South America with fellow naturalist HENRY WALTER BATES and later to Southeast Asia, developed a theory of natural selection independently of Darwin. In the meantime, Darwin's cousin SIR FRANCIS GALTON traveled to Africa and carried out studies in a variety of fields relating to natural science.

An Expanding Field

A listing of some other early observations of phenomena that are now common knowledge—and some of the names of other naturalists involved in making them—gives an idea of the Europeans' enlargement of vision and the shift in sense of their place in the world.

During the same period in which Linnaeus created a new classification system, British naturalist MARK CATESBY studied wildlife in Virginia, the Carolinas, Bermuda, and Bahamas and wrote a two-volume study beginning the practice of interpretative ornithology, published serially in 1731–43. German physician and naturalist DANIEL GOTTLIEB MESSERSCHMIDT, on a 1719 expedition to SIBERIA, found a complete mammoth skeleton, evidence of an extinct species that challenged the creation story of Genesis, which told that all species had been created at one time; for a long time theologians had explained such finds as remnants of creatures destroyed during Noah's Flood. In the 1730s–40s, during Danish VITUS JONASSEN BERING's explorations of Siberia, the Kamchatka Peninsula, the Aleutians, and Alaska on behalf of Russia, Germans JOHANN GEORG GMELIN and GEORG WILHELM STELLER and Russian STEPAN PETROVICH KRASHENINNIKOV participated as naturalists and conducted organized studies of the wildlife and indigenous peoples of those regions for the first time. In 1735, French scientist and cartographer CHARLES-MARIE DE LA CONDAMINE went to South America as near to the EQUATOR as possible to make measurements that would help ascertain whether Earth was flattened there or at the NORTH POLE and SOUTH POLE, as adherents of 17th- to 18th-century British mathematician and physicist Sir Isaac Newton insisted; a simultaneous expedition to Lapland proved the latter. La Condamine also became one of the first Europeans to encounter the material now known as rubber. German naturalist JOHANN REINHOLD FORSTER, who accompanied James Cook on his second voyage to the Pacific in 1772–75, pioneered the study of comparative anthropology in studying South Pacific islanders. He also collected specimens of king and emperor penguins, a type of bird utterly unknown in Europe and worthy of inclusion in the medieval bestiaries for their strangeness, and carried out some of the earliest oceanographic studies, measuring differences in surface and subsurface temperatures (see OCEANOGRAPHY AND EXPLORATION).

In the 19th century, before Darwin's great accomplishments, German naturalist GEORG HEINRICH RITTER VON

LANGSDORFF, during a Russian expedition to the Pacific headed by ADAM IVAN RITTER VON KRUSENSTERN in 1803–08, discovered that ocean phosphorescence was caused by tiny microorganisms. German botanist CARL FRIEDRICH PHILLIPP VON MARTIUS was the first European to see the giant rain forest trees of the upper AMAZON RIVER in his South American expedition of 1817–20. French naturalist ALCIDE-CHARLES-VICTOR DESSALINES D'ORBIGNY's study of micro-fossils in South America in the 1820s–30s laid the foundations for stratigraphic paleontology. German naturalist and geographer ALEXANDER VON HUMBOLDT, active at the same time, was notable for going beyond simply collecting and observing natural phenomena, applying his knowledge of physical processes to interpret what he found. He was among the first to use isotherms, lines on a map connecting locations with the same temperature at a given time, comparable to lines on a topographic map, to get a larger picture of climate patterns and their relationship with altitude. He made important studies of ocean currents and of magnetic intensity in relation to proximity to the equator.

A number of painters contributed to natural history and exploration both (see PAINTING AND EXPLORATION). Some of them were part of expeditions, assigned the task of creating visual representations of native peoples, flora, and fauna; British painter JOHN WEBBER, for example, sailed with James Cook in 1776–80. Others, such as American GEORGE CATLIN, who painted Native Americans in North America and South America in the mid-19th century, traveled alone.

❖

With explorations of the most remote regions of Earth—such as the interior of the Antarctic continent starting in the early 20th century, and the ocean depths in the mid-20th century—new natural science studies were undertaken using ever more sophisticated instruments and techniques. Moreover, in the 20th century, natural science became a cooperative venture. During the INTERNATIONAL GEOPHYSICAL YEAR, for example, an 18-month period from July 1957 to December 1958, designated for cooperative study of Earth's geophysics, scientists from 66 nations participated. Part of the effort was in SPACE EXPLORATION, humankind's latest exploratory endeavor, which also combines physical and scientific exploration.

navigation and exploration

Navigation is the art, science, and technology of finding the position of a craft and charting a course for that craft from one point to the other. The term originally referred to directing the course of watercraft, but it has come to be applied to maneuvering aircraft as well. The history of navigation reflects the history of science and technology from ancient times to the age of SPACE EXPLORATION.

Early Navigational Techniques

Much of ancient navigation was in sight of land, that is, "coastal navigation." Ancient seafarers in oceans, seas, and lakes around the world used coastlines and their landmarks—mountain peaks, rocks, trees, or waterways—to determine location. They gave these landmarks colorful names to help remember them. Yet they used other methods as well. When out of sight of land, they could use the position of the Sun in the daytime and the stars at night to help steer a course, an early form of "celestial navigation." They measured the depth of water with sounding poles, perhaps the earliest navigational tool. They also used "adventitious aids," as they are called, based on knowledge passed from generation to generation of seafarers: knowledge of winds, water depth, tidal streams, currents, reefs, shoals, and the habits of birds, fish, and sea mammals. The kind of waves, long and rolling or short and sharp, could give them an idea of direction based on knowledge of how, for example, westerly or northerly winds in a given region affect the sea as a result of the water depth and the positions of surrounding landmasses. The color of water could indicate to them when they were in a current or particular sea channel or over a fishing bank.

Navigators of the Mediterranean

Peoples of varying civilizations became skillful navigators of the MEDITERRANEAN SEA and adjoining waterways, the NILE RIVER, the RED SEA, and the Black Sea. Some among them reached the Indian Ocean and Atlantic Ocean as well. The Minoans and Egyptians and later the Phoenicians, Greeks, and Romans all developed a seagoing tradition and made use of the type of oar-propelled boat known as the GALLEY (see EGYPTIAN EXPLORATION; MINOAN EXPLORATION). They followed coastlines when convenient but also came to venture into open waters. The Phoenicians and their offshoot, the Carthaginians, were the most wide-ranging of the ancient travelers and were even hired by other peoples for their services at sea (see CARTHAGINIAN EXPLORATION; PHOENICIAN EXPLORATION). They traveled into the Red Sea and may have even circumnavigated Africa. Historical record indicates that the Carthaginians passed through the Strait of Gibraltar (see GIBRALTAR, STRAIT OF) into the Atlantic Ocean. It is known that they navigated by the NORTH STAR, the most basic technique of celestial navigation. But there are references to constellations as aids to navigation in ancient writings. As early as about the ninth century B.C., according to Greek poet Homer, who may have lived then, in his epic poem the *Odyssey*, Odysseus was instructed by the gods to "keep the Great Bear on his left" when sailing from Calypso's Island.

The Greeks created the PERIPLUS as early as the sixth century B.C., and the Romans continued to use it (see GREEK EXPLORATION; ROMAN EXPLORATION). Peripli began as accounts of voyages, then evolved into sailing guides, describing landmarks, harbors, anchorages, watering places, winds, and currents of waterways. Through them, knowledge could be passed among mariners from generation to generation.

The Greeks are also credited with founding the science of geometry, the principles of which came to be applied to navigation, and inventing the ASTROLABE—a device for determining the angle of celestial bodies and latitude—possibly in the third or second century B.C. HIPPARCHUS of the second century B.C., who cataloged about 1,000 stars, may have been the inventor. It used a sighting arm to point toward a given celestial body and a plumb line to determine the horizon plane, which would be perpendicular to the plumb line. However, it was used more for theoretical studies and did not become widespread as a navigational tool for centuries, after being reinvented by the Arabs.

Navigation During the Irish Age of Saints

The earliest transoceanic voyages of exploration by Europeans were carried out by Irish monks beginning in the sixth century A.D. Written accounts of SAINT BRENDAN perhaps attribute to him collective sea experiences of a number of Irish mariners, and the actual location of SAINT BRENDAN'S ISLE is not known. There is more reliable information about the travels of Saint Columba, the founder of Iona, and the monks of the many monasteries he and his followers founded. Abbot Adamnan of Iona, writing in the next century, documents some of these journeys, including four ocean pilgrimages. One of these was led by a monk named Cormac, who was searching for a deserted island on which to settle; Cormac sailed in his CURRAGH for 14 days and nights straight out to sea with a south wind until, it seemed to him, he had traveled "beyond the limit of human wanderings." Another monk, Baitan, reportedly traveled a great distance in stormy seas. It may have been during such a voyage as these that the Faeroe Islands were reached, perhaps in the seventh century. The Faeroe Islands were the first overseas landmass unknown to the Greco-Roman world reached by Europeans. Irish monks eventually traveled even farther into the Atlantic and reached ICELAND, possibly as early as A.D. 795. Once these islands were colonized, traffic was carried on between them and the British Isles, which obviously required considerable navigational skills. The fact that the monks were out of sight of land for two weeks implies that they steered by Sun and stars. According to Faeroese tradition, the monks avoided sailing during the months with "luminous nights"—that is, during summer when at high latitudes the stars are invisible in the nightlong twilight.

According to some accounts, Irish seamen listened for the roar of breakers to tell them of land nearby or watched for land birds such as falcons; they may have guessed at the existence of Iceland by observing migratory land birds flying out to sea beyond the Faeroes. Certain peaks could serve as landmarks for the starting point of a voyage, with traditional sea lore to tell them what to expect when sailing in a given direction from that point.

Vikings

The techniques practiced by the Irish were also practiced by the Vikings, who began raiding the coasts of Europe toward the end of the eighth century in a type of galley ship known as the LONGSHIP (see VIKING EXPLORATION). In later centuries, they navigated westward, eventually reaching North America. It is possible that the Vikings learned much about the waters to the west from the Irish whom they displaced. Accounts of the earliest Viking voyages to the Faeroes and Iceland say nothing about their discovery, indicating that they were already known to mariners.

Vikings used the shorelines of Scandinavia as an approximate north-south reference for bearing, with east-west determined by sunrise and sunset. They referred to lands to the east as "Land-North" or "Land-South," corresponding to northeast and southeast; and seas to the west as "Out-North" and "Out-West," corresponding to northwest and southwest. They also used a type of sundial known as a Sun-measuring disk or shadow board, which floated in a tub of water to keep it level. It was marked with concentric circles and had an adjustable center pin—a GNOMON—which would be raised or lowered based on the height of the Sun at different times of the year. The shadows cast on the circles on which were marked the above directional points helped determine latitude.

Adventitious aids included patterns of fog in relation to landmasses. Moreover, a luminous white sky could indicate the presence of snow-covered land or DRIFT ICE below. Another phenomenon of Arctic regions that may have shown them lands far out to sea is the Arctic mirage, which occurs when an air mass rests on an ocean surface of colder temperature, causing the image of objects viewed through it to be displaced optically upward, so that distant lands or ships normally below the horizon can be seen. They also released ravens to determine distance. Whether a bird flew back in the direction of the starting point, or to the ship, or in the direction where they were heading helped determined distances to landmasses.

Polynesians

The Polynesians, inhabitants of the islands of Polynesia in the South Pacific, are thought to have originated in the Malay Peninsula of Southeast Asia. Sometime after the second century B.C., invasion of the peninsula by Malays drove the proto-Polynesians out to sea. Over a period of many centuries until about A.D. 1000, they settled on many Pacific islands, including the HAWAIIAN ISLANDS and NEW ZEALAND (see POLYNESIAN EXPLORATION).

Polynesians utilized celestial navigation and adventitious aids. Their techniques, which they referred to as "wayfinding," made use of the horizon, using the rising points of the stars and terrestrial markers, supplemented by observations of the Sun, Moon, and ocean swells. They had knowledge of the "houses of the stars" (some 220 known and named). Certain stars were "on-top" stars to them, in that they were directly above certain landmasses, such as Sirius over Tahiti or Arcturus over Hawaii. They had sidereal compasses, devices with a pointer that could be aligned to a particular star to set a course. They also judged direction by the Sun's rising and setting, using the color of the Sun's path on the water to gauge how long it was after sunrise—as the Sun rose its usefulness as a direction finder diminished. At sunrise the direction of waves would be noted and used to determine bearing after the Sun had risen too high. Even when it was too dark to see and clouds hid the stars, skilled navigators could tell the run of the seas by feeling the impact of waves on their vessels (a CANOE, or a canoe with a float or double canoe known as an OUTRIGGER). Like the Vikings, the Polynesians used a known point of departure with information about their subsequent course, which they had memorized. They stayed aware of their speed and took into account each change of course. The Polynesians also made charts from palm sticks tied together with coconut fiber, with shells threaded on the sticks to represent islands.

Arabs

During the Middle Ages, Arabs sailed the waters of the Mediterranean Sea, the Red Sea, and the Indian Ocean in a type of LATEEN RIG craft known as the DHOW (see MUSLIM EXPLORATION). They used the age-tested techniques of mariners before them. Yet they developed new methods of determining location, some of it for navigating desert regions. They gathered significant knowledge in the science of astronomy. In about A.D. 700, Arab Muslims reinvented the astrolabe to measure the angle of celestial bodies and thereby determine latitude. But since it had to be stabilized, they used it primarily on land.

At sea, Arabs were more likely to use a device they called the *al-kemal,* for "the consummation," also known as a "guiding line." A rectangular piece of horn was held at arm's length with its bottom lined up to the horizon. It was then moved toward the user until the North Star was aligned with the top. A cord from the center of the rectangle was then placed on the user's nose. The knots, which represented points of latitude, were then counted.

Chinese

Since ancient times, the Chinese also practiced coastal and celestial navigation in their boats of the JUNK design and came to know the waterways of Asia's coastlines, along both the Pacific and Indian Oceans (see CHINESE EXPLORATION). The Chinese are credited with inventing the magnetic COMPASS. Sometime before A.D. 1040, they discovered that an iron needle rubbed on a lodestone (a variety of magnetite with natural magnetism), if allowed to float freely on water on a piece of straw, would always point to the same direction (the Chinese aligned their compasses to the south). But the Chinese themselves did not use the compass for navigation but for feng shui, a practice which assigns spiritual properties to the four different directions; the compass was used to align buildings in the most propitious direction. It is thought that they first introduced the compass to Arabs, who in turn passed it to Europeans, who developed it in the 13th and 14th centuries.

Application of Mathematics to Navigation

The crucial and fundamental difference between the navigational methods of European explorers and those of their predecessors lies in the use of mathematics and, in particular, geometry to describe Earth and the movements of celestial bodies. The word *geometry* means the measurement of Earth; the study of geometry began with the ancient Greeks. The tendency of Greek philosophers and later European navigators trying to fix their position, rather than amassing large amounts of particular data on winds, currents, and landmarks of a given region, as the Irish, Viking, and Polynesian navigators had done, was to resort more to general principles. The concepts of geometry freed European navigators from the limitations experienced by early practitioners of celestial navigation, that is, of only being able to use the Sun's position at sunrise and sunset (since the angle in relation to the horizon that the Sun travels through on its daily cycle is different at each latitude and in each season). The principle that its course describes a circle parallel to that of the EQUATOR allowed Europeans to calculate their position in terms of latitude at any time of day. The concept of LATITUDE AND LONGITUDE, in effect, allowed navigators to view Earth from a vantage point above the celestial sphere and predict with precision the flight of Sun and stars as they revolved around Earth.

The European Age of Exploration

The RENAISSANCE—the cultural period beginning in the 14th century and marking the end of the Middle Ages—in Europe saw great advances in navigational methods and technology and helped inspire the EUROPEAN AGE OF EXPLORATION from the 15th century to 17th century. In the early 1400s, HENRY THE NAVIGATOR founded an observatory and a school of navigation at Sagres near Cape St. Vincent in southwestern Portugal, bringing together astronomers, mapmakers, and mariners. Among the projects was the development of the type of ship known as the CARAVEL—which combined elements of European and Arab ships—studying navigational equipment and making maps and charts, improvements on the PORTOLAN CHART first made in the Middle Ages. During the reign of Queen Elizabeth in England in the second half of the 16th century, navigation as practice became organized. New laws of navigation were established. Trinity House, a guild that had been created in 1514 for the piloting of ships and the regulation of English navigation, was given more powers. HYDROGRAPHY, the studies and charting of bodies of water, received governmental support. Mariners came to have a good understanding of TRADE WINDS and OCEAN CURRENTS.

Meanwhile, navigational instruments were making long-distance sea travel a possibility. The introduction of the compass enabled mariners to determine direction accurately. They used a method of navigation known as DEAD RECKONING, a system of collecting information involving the use of a compass, a sandglass, a measuring line (a chip log—a float with a knotted line attached to it), and a TRAVERSE BOARD (for recording the information), in order to estimate distance traveled east or west. Regarding celestial navigation,

the first instrument used to measure celestial bodies and to determine latitude according to Greek principles was the astrolabe, which was reinvented by Arabs and passed back to Europeans, who further developed it for use on ships. In the early 15th century, the CROSS-STAFF—a staff of wood with a sliding crossbar—was invented in Europe. In the late 16th century, English mariner JOHN DAVIS created a version known as the backstaff—with a reflector enabling the user to take readings of the Sun. He also developed the Davis QUADRANT, which incorporated elements of both the astrolabe and the cross-staff.

Developments in geography and cartography, with more and more accurate maps and charts being drafted, also facilitated transoceanic voyages. In the mid-16th century, Flemish cartographer GERARDUS MERCATOR used a new

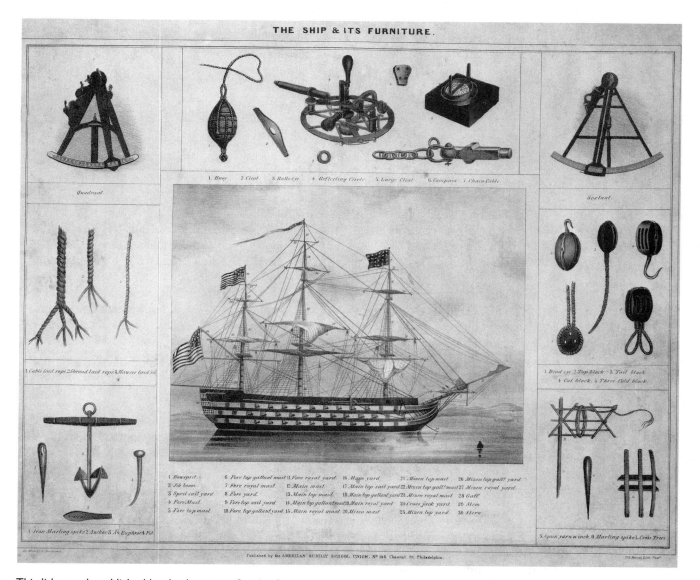

This lithograph, published by the American Sunday School Union in the mid-19th century, shows a ship and nautical equipment of that era. *(Library of Congress, Prints and Photographs Division [LC-USZC4-1942])*

cartographic technique to facilitate navigation—the MERCATOR PROJECTION—with directions represented accurately, with lines of latitude and longitude appearing as straight lines intersecting at right angles. By the end of the 16th century, charts showed compass variation and ocean currents.

18th and 19th Centuries

During the 18th century, sometimes defined as the Age of Enlightenment, a growing scientific approach to navigation developed. In the 1730s, the invention of the SEXTANT, a complex device with a mounted telescope and mirror system, made readings of latitude more precise. Its refinement, along with the invention of an accurate timepiece—the CHRONOMETER—also enabled mariners to take readings of longitude, solving the last great challenge of navigation. The 1767 publication of a *Nautical Almanac and Astronomical Ephemeris* (or the *Nautical Almanac*) by the British Royal Observatory at Greenwich, providing astronomical data to aid in navigation also aided mariners (see EPHEMERIS). Englishman JAMES COOK, who traveled in all the world's oceans in the second half of the 18th century, exemplifies the skilled navigator and hydrographer of the period. His expeditions were scientific as well as geographic endeavors, with scientists participating and conducting a variety of experiments.

In the 19th century, existing navigational methods and equipment became more and more refined. An example of a technological improvement was the patent log—a small rotor towed behind the ship's stern, the revolutions of which were counted—to replace the chip log. Also, in the 19th century, the discipline of oceanography, which, like techniques of navigation, had been developed over centuries, was coming into its own as a scientific and organized field of study (see OCEANOGRAPHY AND EXPLORATION).

Electronic Navigation

In the 20th century, new navigational systems were developed making use of electronic technologies. Radio direction finding—determining location by sending out radio beacons—was the first form of electronic navigation, for ships in 1911 and for airplanes in 1924. Another major breakthrough was radar (for *ra*dio *d*etecting *a*nd *r*anging), developed simultaneously in several countries in 1935–40. Radar detects the position, motion, and nature of a distant object by means of radio waves reflected from its surface. In addition to navigation, radar has been used in geographic, astronomical, and meteorological studies, as well as in military applications. Sonar (for *so*und *na*vigation *r*anging), a form of electronic depth sounding, is based on the reflection of underwater sound waves. Loran (for *lo*ng-*ra*nge *n*avigation) is a specific radio navigational system used to guide ships and aircraft to their destinations. It measures the time-of-arrival difference between two electronic pulses broadcast from two different ground stations. The system became widespread in the 1960s–1970s. The more recently developed inertial guidance systems allow navigation without contact with a ground station by means of an inertial navigator device consisting of a GYROCOMPASS (to measure direction), an accelerometer (to measure changes in speed and direction), and a computer. Such systems are often used in a SUBMARINE, aircraft, or spacecraft. Another development has been computerized electronic charts and electronic plotting tools.

SATELLITE technology has further revolutionized navigation. The U.S. Department of Defense initiated what was originally known as the Navstar Global Positioning System (GPS) in 1973 and still manages it. But GPS—and similar systems, such as GLONASS (the Global Orbiting Navigation Satellite System), developed by the former Union of Soviet Socialist Republics (USSR; Soviet Union)—has been used for many applications besides military and, in fact, has become the primary system of navigation. As 24 satellites orbit 10,000 miles overhead, their atomic clocks are monitored for almost perfect accuracy. With a GPS receiver, it is possible to determine one's exact position anywhere on Earth, at any time and in any weather. The ancient Greeks' metaphorical view of Earth from beyond the celestial sphere, which enabled them to devise their latitude and longitude system, has thus become a reality.

New Zealand

New Zealand is a country in the South Pacific Ocean to the southeast of Australia, part of the region referred to as OCEANIA. It is composed of two main islands—North Island and South Island—as well as numerous smaller islands in surrounding waters, including Great Barrier Island in the north and Stewart Island to the south. The total land area is 104,454 square miles. The Chatham Islands, 536 miles to the east, are also New Zealand territory. Both North Island and South Island are mountainous, with some active volcanoes and hot springs. The Southern Alps on South Island extend nearly the entire length of the island. Seventeen peaks in that range exceed 10,000 feet; Mount Cook is the highest at 12,316 feet above sea level. North Island contains New Zealand's largest lake, Lake Taupo, 234 square miles, from which flows the country's longest river, the Waikato. Much of New Zealand's coastline is irregular, especially that of North Island; South Island has deep fjords in the southwest, however. With its temperate climate, New Zealand is hospitable to a variety of plant and animal species, some of which are unique to the island due to prolonged isolation from other landmasses.

The Maori

The oldest human inhabitants of New Zealand are the Maori, a subgroup of the Polynesians (see POLYNESIAN EX-

PLORATION). They call their homeland Aotearoa. According to Maori legend, their original ancestors arrived by OUTRIGGER, a type of CANOE, in New Zealand in around A.D. 950, led by a mariner, KUPE. Legend also holds that, several generations later, Maori arrived in a fleet of outriggers and colonized Aotearoa. The legends are impossible to authenticate, but it has been proven archaeologically that Maori reached New Zealand by about 1200. The majority settled on the coasts and rivers of North Island, but spread to South Island as well. A second wave of migration, probably from Tahiti, occurred in the 1300s.

Early European Explorers

Dutchman ABEL TASMAN is credited with the European discovery of New Zealand, sighting the west shore of South Island on December 13, 1642. He named the land Staten Landt, believing he had reached the coast of South America explored by fellow Dutchman WILLEM CORNELIS SCHOUTEN several decades earlier. The Dutch were attacked by Maori tribesmen, who rammed their scouting boats with war canoes. Four crew members were killed. Unable to obtain fresh water, Tasman continued his journey, locating the Fiji Islands to the north.

The next European visitor to the islands was JAMES COOK. In October 1769, on his first expedition to the Pacific for England, he came upon North Island and spent some time exploring its coastline. Sailing from the east to the west shore, he conducted the first mapping of the island. In January, after entering what became known as Cook Strait, he realized that New Zealand was made up of two large islands, a fact unknown to Tasman. Cook then circumnavigated South Island, but came to some false conclusions of his own. He believed Banks Peninsula to be an island and Stewart Island to be a peninsula. The Maori were hostile to him as well, and expedition members spent little time on shore. Cook would make three more visits to the islands between 1769 and 1777.

The coastlines were charted by various British mariners in the early 19th century. Owen Folger Smith charted the Foveaux Strait, between South Island and Stewart Island, in an expedition of 1803–04. Then, in 1809, William Stewart charted Stewart Island's coasts. A Captain Chase of the *Pegasus* corrected Cook's error concerning Banks Peninsula on trying to sail around the supposed island.

As Australia came to be settled, interactions between that continent and New Zealand increased. The Maori recognized the advantages of European technology, trading food, water, and labor for guns and powder from whaling vessels, which would stop for repairs and provisions at the Bay of Islands on the northeast coast of North Island. Their relations with Europeans continued to be volatile, however. In 1809, a British ship named the *Boyd* arrived in Whangaroa Harbor to collect timber. A Maori boy reported to tribal members that he had been treated harshly while visiting the ship. In retaliation, the Maori lured the captain and crew of the vessel to their *pa* (a fortified village) to share in a harvest and attacked and killed 70 men in all. The crew of a British whaling ship exacted revenge, destroying the *pa* and killing all the villagers.

Other nations launched scientific expeditions to the Pacific, stopping at New Zealand, such as a Spanish expedition under ALESSANDRO MALASPINA in 1789–94. During his expedition of 1826–29, Frenchman JULES-SÉBASTIEN-CÉSAR DUMONT D'URVILLE made a study of New Zealand wildlife along Cook Strait, becoming the first known European to see the kiwi bird in its native habitat. D'Urville Island to the north of South Island is named for him. Frenchman ANTOINE-RAYMOND-JOSEPH DE BRUNI, chevalier d'Entrecasteaux, during his expedition of 1791–93, also sailed along New Zealand's west coast. A British expedition to southern waters in 1839–43 under SIR JAMES CLARK ROSS stopped over at the Bay of Islands, where naturalist SIR JOSEPH DALTON HOOKER collected more than 1,700 plant specimens.

Missionaries

The exploration of much of New Zealand's interior, especially on North Island, was undertaken by British missionaries. In December 1814, SAMUEL MARSDEN, the chaplain of New South Wales in Australia, arrived at the Bay of Islands with a handful of followers and two Maori chiefs. Marsden explored the interior of North Island on foot, traveling between Bay of Islands and Waitemata Harbor, covering some 400 miles and preaching to the Maori. Duties in Australia interrupted his mission work, but he had a great impact on the Maori with the force of his personality. He also inspired other missionaries, such as WILLIAM COLENSO, Thomas Chapman, and Henry Williams, who braved the rugged terrain and treacherous rivers to reach remote villages. WILLIAM WILLIAMS, the brother of Henry Williams, made the first south-to-north crossing of the North Island. On this journey, he located the hot springs near Lake Taupo.

Colonists

After a number of unsuccessful attempts to establish permanent colonies in New Zealand, a new effort was undertaken by Edward Gibbon Wakefield. He had founded the New Zealand Company in order to apply the principles of "scientific colonization," which had been useful in the settlement of southern Australia. Purchasing large tracts of land from the Maori in the southern part of North Island in 1840, he founded the town of Wellington on Cook Strait, which would prove to be New Zealand's first permanent settlement. Also in 1840, Wakefield signed the Treaty of Waitangi with 50 Maori chieftains, agreeing that they could keep possession of their lands if they acknowledged the colonial sovereignty of Great Britain. Wakefield was dedicated to exploration as well as profits and sponsored expeditions by Ernst Dieffenbach, a professional naturalist. Among Dieffenbach's achievements was the scaling of the 8,260-foot-high Mount Egmont (*Taranaki* to the Maori) on the western end of North Island, a feat he accomplished without Maori guides, who considered the peak sacred.

The search for the best farmlands had begun. Working for the New Zealand Company, Charles Kettle and Alfred Wills found an ideal expanse of grazing land around Lake Wairarapa northeast of Wellington in 1842. Colonists soon established large sheep ranges in the area. On South Island, that same year, the settlement of Nelson was founded. The best land was located along the Wairau River flowing into Cook Strait. As more and more British colonists arrived and violated Maori land rights, the Maori offered resistance. In 1843, after their protests were ignored, they attacked the colonists of South Island, killing 22 of them and suffering the loss of five of their own, beginning the First Maori War, which lasted until 1848. The Second Maori War took place in 1860–70.

Thomas Brunner

The best-known explorer of South Island was THOMAS BRUNNER, also in the employ of the New Zealand Company. In 1843, he carried out the first European explorations of the island's interior, heading southward from Tasman Bay to the Richmond Range. In 1845, Brunner, Charles Heaphy, and William Fox were sent to find arable land to the south of Cape Foulwind. With the help of Maori guide Ekuhu, they pushed through dense forest and negotiated steep mountains to reach Lake Rotoroa. Brunner began his most arduous trek in 1846. This time, with Ekuhu and another Maori and their wives, he set off to follow the Buller River to its mouth, to continue southward along the west coast of the island, and then to return by another route. The expedition began at a promising pace, but then, heavy rains, fog, and a paucity of game brought great hardship. After reaching the end of the Buller, Brunner explored the little-known coastline to the Grey River. He followed the Grey upstream, then crossed the Southern Alps. Brunner suffered a twisted ankle, blindness, and paralysis, causing the party to stop for rest on several occasions. The explorer rallied his forces, however, and returned to the west coast, where he continued southward to Tititira Head. The trip, which came to be known as "The Great Journey," took 550 days. Soon afterward, the region was colonized and became productive farm country.

Late 19th Century

In the latter part of the 19th century, sheep raising and gold mining provided income for most colonists. During the 1890s, after many of the farmlands had been settled, the most intimidating regions of South Island were explored by Charles Douglas. In the province of Westland, to the west of the Southern Alps, is an area of New Zealand's highest mountains and glaciers. Douglas, who had been born in Scotland, spent 40 years of his life exploring these mountains and sometimes doing surveying work for the government.

❖

New Zealand's colonial status was formally terminated in 1907. Like its neighbor, Australia, it is now a self-governing member of the Commonwealth of Nations. Its capital, Wellington, is located on the southern end of North Island. Auckland, also on North Island, is New Zealand's largest city. Christchurch is South Island's largest city. Most New Zealanders live in coastal cities.

Niger River

The Niger River is the great river of West Africa, 2,600 miles in length, the third-largest river in all of Africa. From a plateau in the Republic of Guinea, it flows northeastward into Mali, where it forms an inland delta of channels, lakes, and swamps. Just past the city of TIMBUKTU, the Niger bends to the east, and then to the southeast in the Republic of Niger. It meanders on its course through Nigeria, where it forms the largest coastal delta in Africa, spanning almost 120 miles, emptying into the Atlantic Ocean at the Gulf of Guinea. The Niger's drainage basin is about 808,000 square miles.

Due to its length and the nature of its course, the Niger held long-term mysteries for explorers of Africa. Not only was its source unknown, its direction and even its delta were obscure. Answering these questions involved many, largely English, expeditions, and the untangling of much misinformation. These expeditions were undertaken from the late 1700s to the mid-1800s. The exploration of the Niger was largely a matter of geographic curiosity, for trade had been carried out in the surrounding regions by other means for centuries.

Riddle of the Niger

The Niger was known to Europeans as early as the fifth century B.C. Relating the stories of travelers in North Africa who saw a river flowing to the east, Greek historian HERODOTUS speculated that this was the source of the NILE RIVER. The name Niger can be traced to the writings of PLINY THE ELDER, a Roman of the first century A.D., and hellenized Egyptian PTOLEMY of the second century, who called it the *Nigris,* Latin for "black river." During the Middle Ages, Arab geographers described the river as forming the southern border of the SAHARA DESERT. They, too, confused the Niger with the Nile. They also helped to create the confusion concerning its direction. ABU AL-QASIM IBN ALI

AL-NASIBI IBN-HAWQAL had correctly stated the general direction from west to east in the 10th century, but ABU ABD ALLAH MUHAMMAD ASH-SHARIF AL-IDRISI contradicted him several hundred years later. LEO AFRICANUS, who actually visited the Niger in the early 1500s, perpetuated the error in his book, *Description of Africa* (see MUSLIM EXPLORATION).

As information on the Niger filtered into Europe, so too did descriptions of the places surrounding the river. In 1352, Arab traveler ABU ABD ALLAH MUHAMMAD IBN BATTUTAH ventured from Fez in North Africa, across the Sahara, to visit the kingdom of Mali when it was at its peak. His writings included information on gold as well as educational systems. Leo Africanus, during his visit to the region, made a trip to Timbuktu and described in enthusiastic terms the variety of trade goods, the bustle of activity, and the high value placed on books in the city. Europeans had known of the gold trade, conducted by the camel caravans of the Sahara, but the origin of the gold was a carefully guarded secret. News from the Niger Basin focused attention on such riches. Still, Europe could not hope to challenge the entrenched Muslims of the western Sudan. If they were to take a share of the gold trade, another approach would be necessary. The Portuguese, who began exploring the West African coast in the 15th century, with expeditions sponsored by HENRY THE NAVIGATOR, prince of Portugal, did succeed in gaining access to gold through the Gambia and Senegal Rivers, and on the Gold and Ivory Coasts. Other countries, such as England, Spain, France, and the Netherlands would soon launch expeditions to the region.

18th Century

Geographic theories concerning the Niger abounded in England in the late 18th century during the Age of Enlightenment. English geographer James Rennell postulated that the river must empty into a large inland lake. Others continued to support the idea that it was the western tributary of the Nile, including the high-ranking British navy officer SIR JOHN BARROW. Another popular theory of the day, held by Scotsman MUNGO PARK among others, was that the Niger formed an estuary that emptied into the CONGO RIVER (Zaire River). Park theorized a series of lakes along the Niger's route, based on the massive quantity of water flowing in the Congo.

Active measures to solve the puzzle of the Niger began with the founding of the AFRICAN ASSOCIATION in London in 1788. The association's first expedition of significance was led by DANIEL HOUGHTON in 1790. He ascended the Gambia River, working westward through hostile territory. In 1791, he sent word of his progress back to England but was never heard from again. Subsequent investigations revealed he had reached a point 160 miles from the Niger, the farthest-known European journey into the interior of Africa at that time.

The first European to see the Niger and return to tell about it was Mungo Park. In another African Association expedition, carried out in 1795–97, he set out along the same route and encountered the same intertribal rivalries that Houghton had described. On July 21, 1796, Park came upon the Niger at Segou. Observing its flow from west to east, he settled the question of its course. After a lengthy journey home, during which he was given up for dead, he became an instant celebrity for his findings.

German FRIEDRICH CONRAD HORNEMANN developed a plan to approach the Niger from the Arab enclaves in North Africa and succeeded in also gaining the sponsorship of the African Association. Disguised as a Muslim, he arrived in Cairo in 1797, traveled westward to the oasis at Murzuk, and later southward to Lake Chad. He died of dysentery while on his way to the Niger, having underestimated the size of Africa's interior and misjudging the location of the river.

19th Century

In 1805, Mungo Park returned to Africa to test his theory that the Niger was connected to the Congo. With a group of soldiers, carpenters, and companions, he sailed up the Gambia and trekked overland to Mali. Disease proved devastating to the company, and by the time he had reached the Niger, most of his contingent had died. With the few survivors, he followed the flow of the river. It was later learned that, after much struggle with hostile tribes along the river, his remaining party was finally overwhelmed at the Bussa Rapids.

Because of the regular loss of life on their journeys, the African Association became discouraged and more conservative in backing expeditions. In 1815, the British government sent out two expeditions with the hope of tracing the Niger. The first, under the command of Captain James Kingston Tuckey, was to sail up the Congo, mapping the river and locating its confluence with the Niger. The second, directed by Major John Peddie, was to follow Park's route, taking the Niger to its end. Both expeditions were disasters, with many men dying and little information gathered.

One of the triumphs of this period of exploration was accomplished by RENÉ-AUGUSTE CAILLIÉ. He was a working-class Frenchman with a long-held fascination with Africa. He had traveled there previously with a British expedition in search of Mungo Park. In 1825, he heard that the Geographical Society of Paris was offering 10,000 francs to the person who visited Timbuktu, then returned to report on his findings. Determined to win the prize, Caillié set off eastward from Freetown in Sierra Leone on his quest in March 1827. Arriving at the Niger, he took a CANOE to a point near Timbuktu and reached the city. After spending two weeks there, he returned to France via a caravan heading northward and was awarded the prize.

There were still many unanswered questions about the Niger. In 1818, the British began a series of expeditions out of Tripoli. The first was led by JOSEPH RITCHIE and GEORGE FRANCIS LYON. After completing the first leg of the journey, from Tripoli to Murzuk, Ritchie died. Lyon gathered information from the area and learned falsely that the Niger emptied into Lake Chad before joining the Nile. The Bornu Mission of 1820–25 failed to accomplish its goal of tracing the Niger but did visit a large section of previously unexplored territory. In 1824, as part of the Bornu Mission, Englishman DIXON DENHAM debunked the notion that Lake Chad was connected to the Niger. In 1826, Scotsman ALEXANDER GORDON LAING reached Timbuktu but was murdered as he returned to the north.

Among the more renowned Englishmen to seek the Niger was HUGH CLAPPERTON. As part of the Bornu Mission, he had been among the first to make a north-south crossing of West Africa and to see Lake Chad. In 1825, he made a novel approach to the river from the Bight of Benin in the Gulf of Guinea. Traveling northward, he found the Niger at Bussa within two months. Continuing to Sokoto, to the northwest of Bussa, Clapperton had the intention of reaching Timbuktu and tracing the course of the Niger to its mouth. This plan was cut short when he died of dysentery in 1827. His cause was taken up by a member of his expedition. In 1830, RICHARD LEMON LANDER returned to the Niger at Bussa and, with his brother John Lander and Hausa guide WILLIAM PASCOE, followed its course southward. They discovered the Niger's major tributary from the east, the Benue, where they were held for a time by natives. On being released, they continued downriver, eventually reaching the Bight of Benin and solving the riddle of the mouth of the Niger.

There were to be many more British expeditions to and along the Niger, for scientific purposes, to promote commerce, and to discourage the SLAVE TRADE, among them one headed by Macgregor Laird in 1832, and one headed by Henry Dundas Trotter in 1841. Both teams traveled up the lower Niger by ship and both suffered a great number of casualties. In a British expedition in 1850–51, headed by JAMES RICHARDSON and ADOLF OVERWEG, only one man survived, HEINRICH BARTH. He explored along much of the Niger's course and studied the tribal societies in the region. In a journey in 1854 to find Barth, WILLIAM BALFOUR BAIKIE explored the Benue River 150 miles beyond the point charted by other explorers.

❖

Today, the Niger River offers a supply of fish and regional transportation to peoples of varying nations. Through irrigation projects, it also provides water for farmlands.

See also AFRICA, EXPLORATION OF.

Nile River

At 4,160 miles in length, the Nile River of northeastern Africa is the world's longest river. It has two main branches, the Blue Nile and the White Nile. The source of the Blue Nile, the shorter branch to the east, is Lake Tana in the mountains of Ethiopia. The White Nile, the longer branch, originates in Lake Victoria, which sits on the EQUATOR and is bordered by Kenya, Tanzania, and Uganda. The two Niles meet at the city of Khartoum in the center of the country of Sudan, some 1,857 miles from the sea. From there, the Nile winds its way into Egypt, where it forms Lake Nasser, with the help of the Aswan Dam. From the former rapids at Aswan, the river is navigable for 550 miles to the sea. The Nile's outlet to the MEDITERRANEAN SEA is a delta 100 miles long and more than 100 miles wide. This delta represents the majority of the cultivated land in Egypt, the location of one of Earth's oldest civilizations. Carvings dating to between 6000 and 5000 B.C. depict boats on the Nile River, but, until less than two centuries ago, the source of the Nile waters remained a mystery. The search for the source of the Nile is one of the most famous stories in the annals of exploration.

Riddle of the Nile

The Nile was the starting point for the first voyage of exploration in recorded history. In about 2450 B.C., HANNU traveled up the Nile on a trading mission for Egyptian pharaoh Sahure. Near where the Nile becomes impassable, he left the river and traveled overland, eventually coming to the land known as PUNT, where many of Egypt's luxury goods were produced. Trade between the nations was already well established, and Hannu was able to obtain gold, silver, ebony, and incense, and to have boats built to convey these goods back to Egypt via the RED SEA. It is believed the Egyptians used the Nile extensively for internal trade and communication and to learn the art of seamanship (see EGYPTIAN EXPLORATION).

The Greeks would have known of the Nile through their trade with the Egyptians (see GREEK EXPLORATION). When the Romans replaced the Greeks as the preeminent world power, they used Greek middlemen in their trade with the region (see ROMAN EXPLORATION). In 30 B.C., the Romans conquered Egypt and made it part of their empire and, before long, visited parts of the upper Nile in Ethiopia and Sudan while on military campaigns. Also in the first century A.D., Nero commissioned an expedition to find the source of the Nile. His party is believed to have reached the swamplands of the White Nile, the Sudd, where papyrus grows thick and decaying vegetation makes passage difficult.

Nero's men were the last known Europeans to visit the region until the 1800s. The accounts of both these expeditions and those of Greek merchant DIOGENES, who explored overland into East Africa from the Indian Ocean, are thought to have influenced hellenized Egyptian PTOLEMY. In the second century A.D., the astronomer and geographer described the source of the Nile as the MOUNTAINS OF THE MOON, possibly the Ruwenzori Mountains.

During the Middle Ages, the lands of Ethiopia contained a black Christian community which became isolated from the Arab Muslims to the north (see MUSLIM EXPLORATION). This isolation effectively obscured the origin of the Blue Nile. To the west, the White Nile went on for such a length and disappeared into the equatorial jungle that Arab traders had little inducement to track its source. The next mention of the Nile's sources comes from the 17th-century Portuguese. They came to establish friendly relations with Christians in Ethiopia, whom they associated with the legend of PRESTER JOHN. Spanish Jesuit PEDRO PÁEZ, who was working for the Portuguese, made the European discovery of Lake Tana in the mountains of Ethiopia in 1613. He correctly determined Lake Tana to be the source of the Blue Nile, although the Portuguese policy of secrecy meant his findings were not disclosed.

Growing Knowledge

For much of modern history, credit for the discovery of Lake Tana went to 18th-century explorer JAMES BRUCE, although even he had a hard time convincing skeptical Europeans. He began his search for the source of the Nile by first taking the river to Aswan, then crossing the desert to the east and sailing down the Red Sea to Ethiopia. He reached Gondar, the capital city, in February 1770. It took some time for Bruce to receive permission to travel farther, but, after helping to save the royal family from a smallpox epidemic, it was granted. In November 1770, he located the Springs of Geesh emanating from Lake Tana and named them the "Fountain of the Nile." The following year, he followed the Blue Nile to its convergence with the White Nile, then continued to Cairo. On his return to England, he published his adventures in a five-volume work, *Travels to Discover the Source of the Nile*, but not until after his death in 1794 were his achievements properly recognized.

The first half of the 19th century saw regular explorations along the Nile, but no great breakthroughs. The approach was always the same: Follow the river upstream. Such a strategy became a test of stamina, and the traders and missionaries who made these journeys either lost interest or ran out of supplies. The most successful expedition was conducted by Mehemet Ali, the viceroy of Egypt. Seeking to develop commercial interests in the southern Sudan, Mehemet

Ali led trips in 1839 and 1841, along the Nile, reaching as far as Gondokoro, the last navigable point between the river and its source.

Burton and Speke

The most famous names associated with the search for the Nile's source are SIR RICHARD FRANCIS BURTON and JOHN HANNING SPEKE, both British army officers. After collecting and studying the information from previous expeditions, Burton devised a unique plan to approach the source of the Nile from the east coast of Africa. He surmised that the large inland lakes (supposed to be located over the mountains from the coast of Tanzania), might hold the key to the age-old mystery of the source of the Nile. After recruiting porters and outfitting the expedition in Zanzibar, a small island off the coast of Tanzania, Burton and Speke began their journey in June 1857. SIDI BOMBAY accompanied them as guide and interpreter. Following slave-trading routes, they crossed the mountains and reached the commercial hub of Ujiji on the shores of Lake Tanganyika in February 1858. They were the first Europeans to visit that region. But both men had come down with malaria. Speke recovered sufficiently to explore the lake, but his results were inconclusive. They decided to return to the coast in the summer and agreed to rest in Tabora. Weary from his illness and fed up with Speke's company (the two never did get along), Burton agreed that Speke should search for the other great lake in the region. When Speke reached Lake Victoria in August 1858, he believed he had found the source of the Nile. Because of Lake Victoria's immense size, Speke decided to return to Burton rather than try to bolster his theory with geographic evidence. Speke and Burton reunited in Tabora and then continued on to the coast. According to Burton, Speke promised to keep his findings secret until they both returned to England; nonetheless, Speke, on reaching England several weeks before his leader, announced his theory.

In England, Speke had both champions and skeptics. In 1860, in an effort to resolve the issue of the source of the Nile once and for all, the ROYAL GEOGRAPHICAL SOCIETY sent Speke and JAMES AUGUSTUS GRANT to explore Lake Victoria. In 1860–63, the two men traveled along the western side of the lake to its outlet at Ripon Falls and into Lake Kyoga. From Lake Kyoga, they continued northward overland, crossing the Nile only once on their way to the cities of Juba and Gondokoro. His failure to keep the Nile in sight meant that once again, Speke did not come up with conclusive proof.

Burton and Speke were scheduled to debate the source of the Nile, but a day before their encounter was to take place, in September 1864, Speke was killed in a hunting accident. He left behind a legacy as a careless scientist, yet history proved him correct: Lake Victoria is the true source of the Nile.

Continuing Exploration

While on their own journey of exploration, SIR SAMUEL WHITE BAKER and his wife, FLORENCE BAKER, had come across Speke and Grant. Disappointed that others had already found Lake Victoria's outlet, the Bakers continued on their travels. In March 1864, they came upon Lake Albert and discovered it was fed by Lake Victoria, which in turn fed the Albert Nile section of the White Nile. Returning to England in 1866, Baker was given the ROYAL GEOGRAPHICAL SOCIETY's gold medal and was knighted by Queen Victoria.

Although the major discoveries of the source of the Nile had been made, there was still enough uncertainty to warrant further explorations. German GEORG AUGUST SCHWEINFURTH explored the separation of the Nile and CONGO RIVER (Zaire River) watersheds on his 1868–71 journeys. Scotsman DAVID LIVINGSTONE was convinced that the Lualaba River was part of the Nile River system, and was working on the problem when he died in 1873. (It was later discovered that the Lualaba is actually a tributary of the Congo River.) Anglo-American SIR HENRY MORTON STANLEY tied up many of the loose ends of the Nile watershed during the first half of his 1874–77 expedition. During this trip, he circumnavigated both Lake Tanganyika and Lake Victoria, discovered Lake Tanganyika joined the Congo, and confirmed Speke's assertion that Lake Victoria was the primary source of the Nile. On his mission to relieve the MEHMED EMIN PASHA in 1887–89, Stanley explored Lake Albert and corroborated the discoveries of the Bakers. He also explored the Ruwenzori Mountains, part of the Nile's watershed, which came to be associated with the Mountains of the Moon.

❖

With its great length, variety of terrain it traverses, and long history, the Nile has inspired the human imagination for millennia. As in the past, when seasonal flooding replenished the soil of its banks in Egypt, the Nile continues to sustain life. Today, irrigation systems increase the Nile's productive capacity, and hydroelectric dams generate power for African nations.

See also AFRICA, EXPLORATION OF.

Norsemen   See VIKING EXPLORATION.

North America, exploration of

North America is the world's third-largest continent. Situated entirely in the Western Hemisphere and Northern Hemisphere, it is linked to South America by a region referred to as Central America, which is defined by geographers as being part of North America. The Arctic Ocean and HUDSON BAY (which can be considered either an inlet of the Arctic Ocean or the Atlantic Ocean) lie to its north; the Atlantic Ocean (including the Gulf of St. Lawrence, Gulf of Mexico, and Caribbean Sea, arms of the Atlantic) to its east; and the Pacific Ocean (including its inlet, the Gulf of California) and Bering Sea to its west. The largest of the many offshore islands or island groupings are GREENLAND, the Canadian Arctic Archipelago, the Aleutian Islands, the Alexander Archipelago, Vancouver Island, Newfoundland, and the WEST INDIES. Three modern-day nations occupy North America: the United States, Canada, and Mexico. Mexico and Central America are sometimes discussed as Middle America with regard to their history, and sometimes the West Indies are grouped with them as well.

North America, extending from near the NORTH POLE to near the EQUATOR, embraces every climate zone. Much of the continent has temperate climates suited to human settlement and agriculture. Yet there are extreme desert regions as well, where mountain ranges block rain-bearing westerly winds, such as Death Valley in the western Great Basin in California, the lowest point in North America, at 262 feet below sea level. Mount McKinley (see MCKINLEY, MOUNT) in the Alaska Range of Alaska is the highest point, at 20,320 feet above sea level. The APPALACHIAN MOUNTAINS and Laurentian Highlands of eastern North America are old and eroded ranges; the ROCKY MOUNTAINS extending along much of the western part of the continent are younger and taller. Much of the central part of the continent is prairie country, with the Great Plains sloping up to the Rocky Mountains. Lake Superior is the largest lake in North America, part of the five Great Lakes, which include Lake Michigan, Lake Huron, Lake Erie, and Lake Ontario. The longest river is the MISSOURI RIVER; the MISSISSIPPI RIVER, which it feeds, is the third longest; their waters drain into the Gulf of Mexico. Other major North American rivers include the Rio Grande, which also drains into the Gulf of Mexico; the COLORADO RIVER, which drains into the Gulf of California; the COLUMBIA RIVER and Snake River, which drain into the Pacific Ocean; the Delaware River, Hudson River, and Susquehanna River, which drain into the Atlantic Ocean; the St. Lawrence River, which drains into the Gulf of St. Lawrence; the Mackenzie River—the second-longest river in North America, if the Slave, Peace, and Finlay Rivers are considered part of it—which drains into the Arctic Ocean; and the Yukon River, which drains into the Bering Sea. The wide variety of landscape and climate leads to a wide variety of flora, from tundra to rain forest, with evergreen trees growing on much of the continent, and a wide variety of fauna.

Native Peoples

As is the case with all the continents—except Antarctica, uninhabited until modern-day expeditions—both North America and South America were inhabited by indigenous peoples in ancient times long before 1492, when they became part of documented world exploration. The migrations of Mongolian peoples out of Asia across a LAND BRIDGE between Asia and Alaska at the BERING STRAIT during the last ice age are sometimes discussed as the first explorations of the Americas. Based on archaeological evidence, it is theorized that Mongolian peoples tracked big game across the land exposed because of lower oceans. The latest estimated time based on archaeological evidence in America, along with DNA and linguistic evidence, is between 15,000 and 18,000 years ago. Possibly other Asian peoples reached the Americas by boat. Descendants of all these travelers—Paleo-Indians—spread throughout the Americas over subsequent generations and became known to peoples of other continents as Indians, or Native Americans, and by their native names or adaptations of native names. Later voyagers, in particular Inuit (Eskimo) and Aleut peoples of the Arctic region, arrived in North America by boat after the land bridge had been flooded.

What is known about Native Americans before the arrival of Europeans in their homelands is based primarily on archaeological and linguistic evidence, with some information gleaned from legends passed down through oral traditions. Regarding population levels in pre-Columbian times, estimates vary considerably, from an approximation of 15 million for the entire continent of North America to as much as 60 million, with Middle America having the majority. The population for the region north of Mexico is estimated at a native population of one to 1.5 million to 10 to 12 million. Aboriginal populations were generally densest where agriculture was highly developed or along coastal areas with marine resources. And rivers and lakes also supported denser populations, in particular the St. Lawrence, the Great Lakes, the lower Mississippi, the upper Missouri, the upper Rio Grande, and the Little Colorado. Conversely, population densities were lowest in extreme environments, such as the Arctic, Subarctic, and Great Basin.

It is also impossible to determine the number of tribes, even for the early post-contact period. The fact that different social groupings are under discussion as "tribes" (i.e., tribe, band, village, city-state, confederacy, and culture) makes such a determination inexact to begin with. Moreover, some peoples perhaps died out before Europeans even reached them, since the first tribes having contact with Europeans may have carried European diseases to them—coastal tribes, for instance, trading with inland tribes (see DISEASE AND EXPLORATION). In any case, native peoples in thousands of different political groupings lived a variety of lifestyles, determined by environment. Subsistence patterns, dwellings, clothing, belief systems, rituals, and social organization all varied significantly. Each group had worked out stable adaptations to their local environments and available resources. Language varied significantly as well. It has been estimated that there were as many as 2,200 distinct native languages in all the Americas, with as many as 650 in North America, about 350 of those in Middle America.

Scholars have devised a system of culture areas to group the various peoples and tribes together for purposes of study. One such system speaks of the Northeast, Southeast, Southwest, Great Basin, California, Plateau, Northwest Coast, Subarctic, Arctic, Great Plains, Mesoamerica (Mexico), and Circum-Caribbean (West Indies and Central America).

Algonquian-speaking woodland peoples, many of whom were the first Indians to have contact with explorers along the coasts, and Iroquoian-speaking peoples, such as the tribes of the Iroquois (Haudenosaunee) League of Six Nations, lived in the Northeast. In the Southeast, Muskogean-speaking peoples—such as the Chickasaw, Choctaw, and Creek—made up the largest group; the Cherokee, an Iroquian-speaking people, as well as Siouan-speaking and Timucuan-speaking tribes, also lived in this region. Peoples of both these woodland regions were farmers as well as hunter-gatherers.

What is defined as the Southwest Culture had Athapascan-speaking nomads—the Apache and Navajo (Dineh)—as well as the village-dwelling and farming Pueblo Indians, who spoke a number of different languages. The Great Basin Indians, such as the Ute, Paiute, and Shoshone, were primarily Uto-Aztecan-speaking hunter-gatherers, eking out a living in the harsh, arid landscape.

The densely populated California, Northwest Coast, and, to a lesser degree, Plateau regions had tribes of many different language families and peoples; they were hunter-gatherers, many of who depended heavily on fishing. Northwest Coast peoples were also known for hunting sea mammals. Plateau Indian subsistence involved fishing salmon along the Columbia River.

In the sparsely populated Subarctic region were found Algonquians in the east—the Cree, for example—and Athapascans—the Chipewyan, for example—in the west. The Arctic culture area was the home of the Aleut on the Aleutian Islands, and the Inuit in Alaska, northern Canada, and Greenland; they spoke related languages grouped together as Eskimaleut.

The Great Plains culture area is different from the others in that the typical nomadic way of life of its tribes developed in the 18th and 19th centuries, long after Europeans had reached North America and brought horses with them. Peoples from other regions, speaking many different languages—such as the Siouan-speaking Sioux (Dakota, Lakota, Nakota); the Algonquian-speaking Blackfeet, Cheyenne, and Arapaho; and the Uto-Aztecan-speaking Comanche—took to the use of the horse and, living in portable hide tipis, tracked the buffalo herds. Some tribes classified as part of the Great Plains culture area were a semisedentary people, living in villages for much of the year, but leaving them to track buffalo; the Arikara, Hidatsa, and Mandan, for example, had villages along the Missouri River with permanent earth lodges as dwellings.

The most powerful people in the densely populated Mesoamerica culture area when Europeans first arrived were the Nahuatl-speaking Aztec. They had developed a complex civilization centered in the Valley of Mexico with cities, the largest being Tenochtitlán, the site of present-day Mexico City, and a class system supported by agriculture. Their extensive empire, which had begun to take shape in the 14th century and which followed the earlier Toltec Empire, included an elaborate trade network and tributary of peoples. The Mayan-speaking Maya, centered on the Yucatán Peninsula, also had developed a highly organized system of city-states supported by farming. They were also found in Central America. Most of the peoples in Central America had more in common with the Arawak (Taino) and Carib of the West Indies, with whom they are grouped in the Circum-Caribbean Culture Area. They lived in autonomous bands united politically and religiously under chieftains. For subsistence, they farmed as well as hunted and fished.

By the time Europeans reached the Americas, some highly organized societies had declined long before. In the Southwest, for example, the Anasazi civilization had fragmented, its peoples becoming ancestral to the Pueblo Indians. The Mound Builders of the east—peoples of the Adena, Hopewell, and Mississippian cultures located along the Ohio and Mississippi Valleys—had also dispersed. The Natchez living at the mouth of the Mississippi are thought to be direct descendants of Mississippian peoples, showing some of the cultural traits by the time Europeans settled among them.

In post-contact times, through all the stages of exploration of North America, Native Americans are part of the story not only with regard to the impact Europeans—and Euro-Americans in later generations—had on them, but also as guides and interpreters. (See NATIVE PEOPLES AND EXPLORATION.)

The Vikings

The Vikings are now credited with being the first Europeans to reach both Greenland and mainland North America (see VIKING EXPLORATION). The traditional Norse literature from the Middle Ages—the "sagas," as they are known—refer to the discovery and temporary settlement of a place west of Greenland known as VINLAND. Such accounts were treated as legend until 1960, when archaeological evidence at L'Anse aux Meadows in the north of Newfoundland verified a Viking presence. Because knowledge of this land was not passed to other Europeans, there would be still another "discovery" five centuries later.

BJARNI HERJULFSSON is considered the first European to see North America. On a trip from ICELAND to visit his father in Greenland, in about A.D. 985 or 986, he was blown off course, to the southwest. Although he reported spotting land, some of it wooded and some of it ice-covered—indicating any number of locations along northeastern North America—he did not claim to have made landings before returning to Greenland.

On a follow-up voyage of exploration, LEIF ERICSSON, the son of ERIC THE RED, the first Viking colonizer of Greenland—sailed westward from his new home in about 1001. He came upon and named three different regions: Helluland, after its extreme flatness; Markland, referring to a land of woods; and Vinland, the third, and most southerly. At Vinland, the Vikings built shelters and explored the area. The location might very well have been L'Anse aux Meadows in Newfoundland, or possibly a location in Labrador or Quebec. Ericsson also perhaps reached Nova Scotia, the St. Lawrence Seaway, or even other regions to the south, such as Cape Cod or Chesapeake Bay. In any case, he eventually returned to Greenland, where he lived out his life.

Some years later, in about 1005–07, Leif's brother, THORVALD ERICSSON, led a colonizing expedition to North America's east coast and perhaps settled at the same Vinland site. His time in North America was noted for the first contacts with indigenous peoples, whom the Vikings called Skraelingar or Skraelings. These may have been either Indians or Inuit depending on location. THORFINN KARLSEFNI, in about 1010, led still another colonizing expedition to North America's east coast; the colony lasted until about 1013. The next year, Leif's half sister, FREYDIS EIRÍKSDOTTIR, who had been part of Karlsefni's group, joined her husband, Thorvard, in another attempt at a colony, supposedly at the same Vinland site, taking over previously built houses, returning to Greenland the next year after fighting broke out among the colonists.

The various accounts of these voyages vary in different Norse sagas. Nor is there any way to determine the exact location of the various colonies, despite the known Viking site at L'Anse aux Meadows.

European Awareness of the Americas

It is not known if the Vikings had a sense of the vastness of the lands they reached. If they followed the North American coastline southward, they may have conceived of Vinland as even larger than Greenland. However, no such information survived in Europe, and, if it had, later mariners would very likely have believed that the Vikings had reached Asia. Italian mariner and map dealer CHRISTOPHER COLUMBUS was one of several Europeans to devise a plan to sail westward across the Atlantic Ocean to the Orient, and King Ferdinand II and Queen Isabella I of Spain were eventually convinced to sponsor him on such an expedition. In August 1492, Columbus set sail, reaching the West Indies in the Americas the following October 12. Between 1493 and

1502, Columbus led three more transatlantic expeditions, and he explored many of the region's islands and eventually reached the mainland of South America. Although he never saw or made landfall in North America and he insisted until his death in 1506 that he had reached Asia, he began the process that made Europeans aware of the landmasses in the Western Hemisphere and the size of Earth.

On June 24, 1497, another Italian, JOHN CABOT, sailing for England, became the first known European since the time of the Vikings to see North America. Cape Breton Island, the eastern part of present-day Nova Scotia, is thought to be the likely location of a landfall, although he may have landed first on the coast of Newfoundland or even Labrador. He explored parts of northeastern North America and may have navigated as far south as Maine. That same summer, Italian AMERIGO VESPUCCI may have explored along coastal North America from Mexico to Cape Hatteras in present-day North Carolina, but his claim is unsubstantiated. In 1501–02, Vespucci later traveled to South America. In his account of his travels, he was the first to suggest that the lands he had visited were a continent previously unknown to Europeans and applied the term "New World" to the great landmass for the first known time. In 1507, German cartographer MARTIN WALDSEEMÜLLER, using Vespucci's account as a source, applied the Latinized version of Vespucci's first name to the continent of South America.

A Rush of Nations

Soon after John Cabot reached northeastern North America for England, so did GASPAR CÔRTE-REAL for Portugal. He probably reached the west coast of Greenland in 1500. Then, the next year, he navigated as far as the coast of Newfoundland and Labrador. In 1509, John Cabot's son SEBASTIAN CABOT explored North America's east coast from Newfoundland to Long Island, in search of a water route to the Orient—the NORTHWEST PASSAGE.

The Spanish established colonies in the West Indies and fanned out from there, overrunning native lands and expanding their knowledge of both South and North America. In 1513, JUAN PONCE DE LÉON explored northward to Florida, exploring both its Atlantic and Gulf coasts. That same year, in Central America on the Isthmus of Panama, VASCO NÚÑEZ DE BALBOA became the first European to see the Pacific Ocean from the west coast of the Americas. In 1517, FRANCISCO FERNÁNDEZ DE CÓRDOBA explored the Yucatán, and JUAN DE GRIJALVA explored the east coast of present-day Mexico, which he called New Spain. In 1519–21, Spanish CONQUISTADORES under HERNÁN CORTÉS invaded the Valley of Mexico and conquered the Aztec Indians, establishing a permanent presence in their homeland. The extent of the Americas and the Pacific Ocean beyond became known to Europeans with the Spanish expedition under Portuguese mariner FERDINAND

MAGELLAN in 1519–22. After sailing southward along the coast of South America, he passed through the Strait of Magellan (see MAGELLAN, STRAIT OF) into the Pacific, then followed South America's west coast for a time before crossing the Pacific. After Magellan's death in the Philippines, one of his ships completed the first CIRCUMNAVIGATION OF THE WORLD. In 1528, PÁNFILO DE NÁRVAEZ led a colonizing expedition to Florida. Nárvaez was lost at sea in the Gulf of Mexico, but four survivors, including ÁLVAR NÚÑEZ CABEZA DE VACA and ESTEVANICO, a former slave from North Africa, landed in Texas and proceeded westward, eventually reaching Mexico in 1536, in what is considered the first extensive overland voyage by Europeans in what was to become the continental United States.

Other overland expeditions were soon organized. In 1539, ANTONIO DE MENDOZA, the viceroy of New Spain, sent out Franciscan missionary MARCOS DE NIZA, along with Estevanico, northward from Mexico. They reached as far as the Zuni Indian pueblos in present-day New Mexico, where Estevanico was killed by the Zuni. The Spanish hoped to locate wealth on a par with that of the Aztec as well as that of the Inca Indians of Peru, who had been conquered by FRANCISCO PIZARRO in the 1530s, and, based on Marcos de Niza's reports, believed that the Zuni pueblos were in fact the fabled Seven Cities of CIBOLA. In 1540, a much larger expedition under FRANCISCO VÁSQUEZ DE CORONADO entered the region. Various of his lieutenants explored throughout what was to become the American Southwest and made contact with various Indian peoples. Coronado himself led a contingent onto the southern plains as far as present-day Kansas, but failed to locate the hoped-for riches.

During the same period, starting in 1539, another Spanish expedition under HERNANDO DE SOTO, after landing on Florida's west coast, traveled throughout the American Southeast, crossing the Appalachians and reaching the Mississippi River. On de Soto's death, LUIS DE MOSCOSO assumed command and explored into present-day Texas. The survivors eventually built barges and descended the Mississippi to the Gulf of Mexico and the Spanish settlement of Tampuco in northern Mexico by 1543.

The Spanish also explored by sea northward along the Pacific coast. In 1539–40, FRANCISCO DE ULLOA, sent out by Hernán Cortés, explored the Gulf of California, the mouth of the Colorado River, and the Pacific coast of the Baja Peninsula. In 1540–41, HERNANDO DE ALARCÓN, the seaward portion of Coronado's expedition, organized by Antonio de Mendoza, also explored the Gulf of California and traveled a good distance up the Colorado. In 1542, JUAN RODRÍGUEZ CABRILLO headed a Spanish maritime expedition, sponsored by Antonio de Mendoza, along North America's west coast, reaching what is now northern California. On his death, BARTOLOMÉ FERRELO assumed command and is thought to have reached as far as the present-day Oregon-California border in 1543. SEBASTIÁN MELÉNDEZ RODRÍGUEZ CERMEÑO, in 1595, and SEBASTIÁN VISCAÍNO, in 1602–03, continued Spanish explorations along the California coast, exploring Monterey Bay and elsewhere.

The English explored the Pacific coasts of North and South America as well. In the course of the first English circumnavigation of world in 1577–80, SIR FRANCIS DRAKE reached as far north as Vancouver Island.

In the meantime, the French had also launched expeditions to the Americas. Once again, as was the case with Spain and England, it was an Italian mariner who carried out the first explorations in this part of the world for them. GIOVANNI DA VERRAZANO explored North America's east coast from present-day South Carolina to Newfoundland in 1524. Then, in the 1530s–40s, in the course of three expeditions, JACQUES CARTIER explored the St. Lawrence River system and surrounding areas in what is now eastern Canada. Both explorers, like other mariners before them, sought a Northwest Passage to the Orient.

The outlines of North America and parts of the interior were becoming known. European cartographers were recording information reported to them by various explorers. In 1585–94, Flemish cartographer GERARDUS MERCATOR published a comprehensive world atlas in which he applied the name *America* to both North and South America.

First Colonies

Although a number of permanent Spanish settlements were founded in the West Indies, Central America, and Mexico in the 16th century, a number of attempts to do so to the north failed. The French under JEAN-FRANÇOIS DE LA ROQUE DE ROBERVAL, in conjunction with Jacques Cartier's third expedition, founded a settlement on the St. Lawrence River in 1541. Because of hardship, the colonists returned to France the following year. In 1562, JEAN RIBAULT attempted to found a French Huguenot colony on Port Royal Sound in present-day South Carolina. When a relief expedition failed to arrive, the French abandoned the site. RENÉ GOULAINE DE LAUDONNIÈRE, in 1564, attempted to build a settlement on the St. Johns River in Florida. The next year, a Spanish military expedition under PEDRO MENÉNDEZ DE AVILÉS defeated the French, and that site was also abandoned. Artist JACQUES LE MOYNE DE MORGUES was one of the colonists who escaped along with de Laudonnière. His images of wildlife and Timucua Indians were the earliest known such images by a European in what is now the continental United States. On his expedition, Menéndez de Avilés founded St. Augustine 40 miles to the south of the French site, the first permanent European settlement in the continental United States.

Spanish expeditions out of Mexico eventually led to colonies in the American Southwest as well. In 1582–83,

ANTONIO ESTEVAN DE ESPEJO headed an expedition to western New Mexico and eastern Arizona, exploring the upper Rio Grande, upper Pecos River, and Little Colorado River. His reports helped lead to a subsequent colonizing expedition in 1598 under JUAN DE OÑATE, who founded a settlement, San Juan de los Caballeros, near an Indian pueblo and present-day Santa Fe, eventually moving to a new site, near another pueblo, San Gabriel de Yungue-Ouinge. From there, over the next years, he launched exploratory expeditions, leading some himself.

The English attempted a number of failed colonies along the Atlantic seaboard in the 1580s. In 1583, SIR HUMPHREY GILBERT led a colonizing expedition to Newfoundland, having been granted a commission by Queen Elizabeth I. Gilbert took formal possession of the island, although he decided to abandon the colony after only one month because of loss of life at sea, illness, and food shortages. Gilbert himself perished on the return journey. His half brother, SIR WALTER RALEIGH, received the commission to settle North America instead and, in 1584–87, sponsored three voyages to the Outer Banks region of present-day North Carolina. The second two were attempts at colonies. The first colony on Roanoke Island failed, in large part because of conflicts with Native Americans. The second colony, originally planned for Chesapeake Bay to the north, was headed by JOHN WHITE, who became known for his paintings of Native Americans. It, too, failed and, after White's return to England for supplies, the colonists were never seen again, resulting in the name the LOST COLONY.

Just to the north, in present-day Virginia, the English founded another colony. CHRISTOPHER NEWPORT commanded the fleet carrying colonists, and JOHN SMITH was military leader of a colony founded at Jamestown in 1607, the first permanent English settlement in the Americas. In 1620, the PILGRIMS, an English religious breakaway group, among them EDWARD WINSLOW, founded Plymouth Colony in present-day Massachusetts.

The French, after other failed attempts at colonies on the St. Croix River, the present border of Maine and New Brunswick, and at Port Royal in southeastern Nova Scotia, founded their first permanent French settlement in the Americas at Quebec City (the Huron Indian settlement of Stadacona) in 1608 under SAMUEL DE CHAMPLAIN. The Dutch, following the 1609 exploration by Englishman HENRY HUDSON of the Hudson River in present-day New York on their behalf and the follow-up expedition to the region under Dutchman ADRIAN BLOCK, founded the colony of New Amsterdam on the island of Manhattan in 1621.

The Swedish also maintained a colony in North America for a time, laying a claim in 1638 to some of the original Dutch holdings along the Delaware Bay. In 1655, with a stepped-up military effort, the Dutch ousted them and reclaimed the territory.

These various colonies served as launching points for exploratory and trading expeditions and led to further colonial development.

Early Explorations of Arctic North America

European maritime expeditions continued to seek the Northwest Passage—and a version of the same known as the Strait of Anian (see ANIAN, STRAIT OF), thought to exist along a more southerly route. In the 1570s–80s, Englishman SIR MARTIN FROBISHER headed a series of expeditions to the Arctic region, seeking an all-water northern route. The English especially were active in northern waters. In the first half of the 17th century, Henry Hudson, now sailing for his country of birth, and others, including SIR THOMAS BUTTON, WILLIAM BAFFIN, ROBERT BYLOT, LUKE FOXE, and THOMAS JAMES, explored Hudson Bay and surrounding waterways. English claims to the region were based on Hudson's 1610–11 journey. (See ARCTIC, EXPLORATION OF THE.)

Land, Furs, and Converts

With increasing numbers of settlers, new land was sought and new settlements were established in the 17th and 18th centuries during the colonial period. The French, located along the St. Lawrence River, developed their colonial economy around the FUR TRADE with Native Americans. They traveled along the Great Lakes and Mississippi River and onto the eastern plains to develop trading contacts. They eventually settled the mouth of the Mississippi as well. Many of the English traveled to North America as families and farmers, in the hopes of staking a claim and working a homestead. They settled along the Atlantic coast and, over time, pushed westward into and beyond the Appalachians. Soon after the founding of the HUDSON'S BAY COMPANY in 1670, the English built trading posts on Hudson Bay for the fur trade and began exploring westward in search of fresh supplies of furs. The Spanish also sought land for economic development, in particular mining, ranching, and farming, and pushed out of the Southwest west and east into California and Texas. The Dutch came to North America originally as traders under the auspices of the United New Netherland Company and the DUTCH WEST INDIA COMPANY but settled more and more farms along the Hudson Valley until losing their territorial claim to the English in 1664 (when the Dutch colony of New Netherland became New York). In the meantime, missionaries—especially of the Jesuit and Franciscan orders of the Catholic Church—traveling with traders or soldiers or on their own sought North American converts (see RELIGION AND EXPLORATION). All the activities of the various nationalities had impacts of one kind or another on native peoples—if not loss of life from disease or warfare, then displacement from lands and cultural dispossession.

Numerous explorers played a part in explorations of the colonial period, opening up new regions to subsequent settlement. In 1659–60, French fur traders MÉDARD CHOUART DES GROSEILLIERS and PIERRE-ESPRIT RADISSON explored Lake Superior and traveled to the headwaters of the Mississippi River. In 1668–69, they headed a maritime expedition to Hudson Bay, leading to the start of the fur trade in that region. In 1665–69, CLAUDE-JEAN ALLOUEZ served as a French missionary to peoples of the western Great Lakes and explored the south shore of Lake Superior and the Fox and Wisconsin Rivers. He is said to have preached to 22 tribes and to have baptized some 10,000 Indians. In 1673, French fur trader LOUIS JOLLIET and missionary JACQUES MARQUETTE explored from the western Great Lakes southward along the Mississippi River. In 1682, RENÉ-ROBERT CAVELIER DE LA SALLE and his associate, Italian HENRI DE TONTI, led a French expedition along the Mississippi River all the way to the Gulf of Mexico. During this journey, he claimed the entire Mississippi Valley for France. The next century, a number of French traders ventured onto the Great Plains. These included LOUIS-JOSEPH GAULTIER DE LA VÉRENDRYE and one of his brothers, François, who, in 1742–43, explored the northern plains as far west as the Black Hills of western South Dakota and eastern Wyoming (or possibly even the Bighorn Mountains in western Wyoming, part of the Rocky Mountain system); and PIERRE-ANTOINE MALLET and his brother, Paul Mallet, who, at about the same time, explored the central plains.

Early English colonial expeditions included that of German-born physician JOHN LEDERER in 1669–70; he explored the Piedmont and Blue Ridge of Virginia and North Carolina on behalf of the Virginia colony. His trip was soon followed, in 1671–73, by other explorations westward to the Appalachian frontier of Virginia and North Carolina, sponsored by ABRAHAM WOOD. In 1685, physician HENRY WOODWARD explored from Charleston, South Carolina, beyond the Savannah River into Georgia. In 1701–08, JOHN LAWSON explored the interior of the Carolinas northwestward from Charleston. In 1716, ALEXANDER SPOTSWOOD led an expedition to the Shenandoah Valley of western Virginia. By the mid-18th century, there was increasing activity in the Appalachian and trans-Appalachian regions. Among those involved, in 1750, another physician, THOMAS WALKER, explored and named the CUMBERLAND GAP through the Blue Ridge of the Appalachians, crossing it into what is now eastern Kentucky. DANIEL BOONE led hunting and colonizing expeditions through the mountain pass in the 1760s–70s.

Far to the north, Hudson's Bay Company employees began mapping lands to the west. In 1690–92, HENRY KELSEY explored the Assiniboine and Saskatchewan Rivers. In 1754–55, ANTHONY HENDAY explored the Canadian plains within 40 miles of the Rocky Mountains. In the

1760s–70s, SAMUEL HEARNE, with the help of Chipewyan Indian MATONABBEE, reached the Arctic Ocean and the Great Slave Lake. In 1772–75, MATTHEW COCKING explored what is now western Saskatchewan.

For the Spanish, in 1689, ALONSO DE LEÓN, born in Mexico, headed a Spanish military expedition from Coahuila, Mexico, across the Rio Grande to the Gulf Coast of Texas and founded a number of settlements in the Neches River region of eastern Texas. In 1748–50, JOSÉ DE ESCANDÓN led a colonizing expedition from Mexico to the lower Rio Grande in southeastern Texas. In 1698–1706, Italian Jesuit missionary EUSEBIO FRANCISCO KINO explored the Gila and Colorado Rivers in present-day Arizona, the latter of which he is credited with naming. He also explored the Gulf of California. The Spanish settled California after the 1769–70 expedition of GASPAR DE PORTOLÁ and Franciscan missionary JUNÍPERO SERRA. Serra stayed on to found a string of missions to the Indians, from present-day San Diego to San Francisco. The route between New Mexico and California was pioneered by colonial official JUAN BAUTISTA DE ANZA and Franciscan missionary FRANCISCO TOMÁS HERMENEGILDO GARCÉS in the 1774. Soon afterward, in 1776–77, Franciscan missionaries FRANCISCO ATANASIO DOMÍNGUEZ and FRANCISCO SILVESTRE VÉLEZ DE ESCALANTE, in an unsuccessful effort to create a route between the Spanish settlements of Santa Fe, New Mexico, and Monterey, California, explored parts of central Utah.

In the 18th century, Russia joined the other European nations in staking a claim in North America, based on the exploratory expedition of Danish mariner VITUS JONASSEN BERING in 1740–41 to the Aleutian Islands and Gulf of Alaska.

New Nations

The colonial phase of North American exploration can be said to have ended with the Declaration of Independence in 1776, or the Treaty of Paris of 1783—when Great Britain conceded defeat in the American Revolution—or the drafting of the first constitution of the United States of America in 1787. Yet there was still colonial activity. France, although it had ceded its North American holdings to Great Britain and Spain in an earlier Treaty of Paris at the end of the French and Indian War in 1763, for a brief period, from 1800 to 1803, controlled land in North America with the retrocession from Spain of the region stretching from the Mississippi River to the Rocky Mountains, known as the Louisiana Territory. The United States purchased these vast holdings in 1803 in what is known as the Louisiana Purchase. Canada remained under British control until the British North America Act of 1867 created the Dominion of Canada. Mexico achieved independence from Spain in 1821. Russia also maintained a North American presence until 1867 and its sale of Alaska to the United States. Present-day boundaries among the three North American nations—the United States, Canada, and Mexico—were not decided until well into the 19th century. Yet, with the birth of the United States, came a new stage of exploration and settlement, which came to be called "Westward Expansion."

In the decades after the American Revolution, much of the exploratory activity was in the Old Northwest, a region north of the Ohio River, west of the Appalachians, east of the Mississippi River, and south of Canada.

In 1776, British naval officer and accomplished navigator JAMES COOK explored the Pacific Northwest coast in search of the western opening of the Northwest Passage and reached as far north as Bering Strait. By the 1780s, British and American traders also regularly worked the Pacific coast, especially in Nootka Sound in present-day British Columbia. But they also extended their activity to Alaska in the north and in California in the south. A number of maritime expeditions increased geographic knowledge of the Pacific coast. American fur trader ROBERT GRAY, who had earlier commanded the first circumnavigation of the world in a U.S. vessel, explored the coast of the Pacific Northwest, including the mouth of the Columbia River in 1792. A British expedition under GEORGE VANCOUVER and WILLIAM BROUGHTON, which also circled the world in 1791–95, explored the same region.

Meanwhile, the Hudson's Bay Company and a rival out of Montreal, the NORTH WEST COMPANY, sent out expeditions to map the Canadian West and what would become part of the American West. Its representatives included American-born PETER POND and SIMON FRASER and Scotsman SIR ALEXANDER MACKENZIE.

The Lewis and Clark Expedition

In early 1803, while the Louisiana Purchase was being finalized between the United States and France, MERIWETHER LEWIS, an army captain and private secretary of President Thomas Jefferson, won the appointment to head a government-funded expedition to explore the region. Lewis requested a former army comrade, WILLIAM CLARK, to be his coleader. The Corps of Discovery of just under 50 men (not all would complete the journey and others would join later) departed St. Louis by boat in May 1804. After wintering among the Mandan Indians at the confluence of the Missouri and Knife Rivers, during which time Shoshone Indian woman SACAJAWEA was hired as a guide and interpreter, the Corps of Discovery continued upriver, crossed the Rockies and reached the Columbia River, which carried them to the Pacific. They spent the winter of 1805–06 at the mouth of the Columbia in present-day Oregon. On the return trip Lewis and Clark separated for a time: Lewis explored the Marias River, which branched off from the Missouri to the north; Clark and his contingent, including

Sacajawea, explored the Yellowstone River to the south, another branch. The Corps of Discovery returned triumphantly to St. Louis in September 1806.

The Lewis and Clark Expedition, the first government-sponsored expedition across the uncharted western portion of North America, covering some 8,000 miles, established an overland route to the Pacific Ocean. Its contact with more than 50 Indian tribes—all peaceful except for one incident with the Blackfeet—contributed to the knowledge of North America's indigenous peoples. The expedition also made studies of wildlife, as requested by Jefferson, and brought back a large number of botanical species. Its geographic determinations led to subsequent expeditions, some relating to the western fur trade and others, government-sponsored. Former members of the Corps of Discovery continued to play a part in western exploration.

Dunbar, Freeman, and Pike

President Thomas Jefferson sponsored other expeditions to explore the newly acquired Louisiana Territory, including one under Scottish surveyor SIR WILLIAM DUNBAR. The expedition intended to ascend the Mississippi to its confluence with the Red River and attempt to find the Red River's source. Because of the threat of Spanish action against them, they decided instead to explore the Ouachita River northward into present-day Arkansas. In 1806, an Irish-born surveyor named THOMAS FREEMAN again attempted to explore the Red River for Jefferson, making it as far west as present-day Texarkana, Texas, before being turned back by Spanish authorities.

Meanwhile, in 1805–06, when the Lewis and Clark Expedition was on its return trip, army officer ZEBULON MONTGOMERY PIKE led a military expedition with a contingent of soldiers up the Mississippi from St. Louis by boat and sled as far as Leech Lake in present-day Minnesota. In 1806–07, Lieutenant Pike led a contingent of soldiers by boat from the Missouri River to the Osage River, then overland by horseback across the plains to the Republican River and southward to the Arkansas River, exploring it westward into present-day Colorado. In the Rocky Mountains Pike attempted to climb Pikes Peak, which is named after him. On the return trip, the expedition crossed the Rio Grande into Spanish territory; Pike and his men were captured by the Spanish and held for a time in Santa Fe. Pike's subsequent report discouraged settlement on the arid southern plains but led St. Louis traders to develop commerce by way of the Santa Fe Trail.

Traders West

The city of St. Louis, on the Mississippi River near the mouth of the Missouri, served as gateway to the West. Most travel westward from there in the early 19th century related to the fur trade. In 1808, American businessman JOHN JACOB ASTOR founded the AMERICAN FUR COMPANY, and its subsidiaries soon afterward—the Pacific Fur Company and the Southwest Fur Company—with the plan of building a string of trading posts along the route Lewis and Clark pioneered. In order to create a western terminus, Astor sponsored a seaward expedition under ROBERT STUART, from New York City around South America, in 1810, to build Fort Astoria at the mouth of the Columbia River; the next year, he sent an overland expedition out of St. Louis—the Astorians—under WILSON PRICE HUNT.

In 1809, the ST. LOUIS MISSOURI FUR COMPANY was founded by William Clark, MANUEL LISA, JEAN PIERRE CHOUTEAU, AUGUSTE PIERRE CHOUTEAU, ANTOINE PIERRE MENARD, ANDREW HENRY, and others. The company eventually established a number of posts upriver.

With time, traders became familiar with the lands along the Missouri and its tributaries and in the Rocky Mountains as well. In 1822, another American entrepreneur, WILLIAM HENRY ASHLEY, along with Andrew Henry, founded the ROCKY MOUNTAIN FUR COMPANY. Many of the men who worked for and traded with Ashley came to be known as the MOUNTAIN MEN. They included legendary figures such as JAMES PIERSON BECKWOURTH, JAMES BRIDGER, JAMES CLYMAN, HUGH GLASS, THOMAS FITZPATRICK, EDWARD ROSE, JEDEDIAH STRONG SMITH, and WILLIAM LEWIS SUBLETTE. In the 1820s–1830s, they traveled the Native American trails and passes of the West and passed along geographic knowledge to others. Jed Smith, the "Knight of the Buckskin," as his peers called him, traveled more than 16,000 miles in his career and pioneered the westward route via SOUTH PASS across the Rockies and from the Great Basin into California.

The fur traders came from many different places and many different walks of life. In 1832–35, BENJAMIN LOUIS EULALIE DE BONNEVILLE, a French-born former U.S. army officer led a fur-trading expedition across the Rocky Mountains and into Oregon. Mountain men JOSEPH WALKER, ZENAS LEONARD, and JOSEPH L. MEEK worked for him and helped pioneer the California Trail.

Working out of Alaska, in the meantime, Russian interests, organized as the RUSSIAN-AMERICAN COMPANY in 1799, developed the fur trade southward under the leadership of ALEKSANDR ANDREYEVICH BARANOV. By 1812 company fur traders had established a post in northern California.

In 1821, the Hudson's Bay Company and the North West Company merged under the name of the Hudson's Bay Company. It would continue as formidable opposition to the American fur companies. Other merchants developed the trade in buffalo hides as well as providing goods along routes west. In 1833, CHARLES BENT, born in Virginia and raised in St. Louis, established Bent's Fort as a trade center on the Arkansas River in southeastern Colorado.

In the late 1830s, the international fur market went into decline, partly because the beaver hat went out of style in favor of the silk hat. The depletion of fur-bearing animals and the advance of farming settlements also contributed to a changing way of life in the West. Many of the mountain men stayed active as soldiers, scouts, and guides in the subsequent period of expanding settlement.

Continuing Government Expeditions

The U.S. government continued to sponsor westward explorations long after Lewis and Clark. In 1819, Colonel Henry Atkinson led the first Yellowstone Expedition up the Missouri River, reaching as far as Council Bluffs in present-day Nebraska, where he founded Fort Atkinson. Other expeditions embarked from there, including that of Major STEPHEN HARRIMAN LONG of the U.S. Army Corps of Topographical Engineers, which crossed the Great Plains and reached the Rockies. In his report on the expedition, Long referred to the Great Plains as the "Great American Desert," unsuitable for agriculture, which supported the earlier findings of Zebulon Pike. In 1825, Colonel Atkinson headed the second Yellowstone Expedition, which did in fact manage to navigate up the Yellowstone into present-day Montana, where he negotiated with Indian tribes.

The next decade, in 1834, General HENRY LEAVENWORTH, who for a time had been the commander at Fort Atkinson, and Colonel HENRY DODGE headed an expedition to the southern plains in order to negotiate treaties with tribes of the region—a region designated as the Indian Territory, where eastern tribes would be relocated—and explored the Arkansas and Red Rivers. The next year, Dodge explored from Oklahoma to the Rockies and explored the eastern portion of the Oregon Trail.

In the 1840s, as the army built more and more posts west of the Mississippi, the most active explorer for the federal government was JOHN CHARLES FRÉMONT. In 1838–39, after receiving a commission as second lieutenant in the Corps of Topographical Engineers, he joined Frenchman JOSEPH NICOLAS NICOLLET in a survey of the region between the upper Mississippi and Missouri Rivers. In 1841, Frémont led an expedition in a survey of the Des Moines River in Iowa. In 1842, Frémont headed his own expedition to the Oregon Territory, during which he mapped most of the Oregon Trail and determined the longitude of the South Pass. CHRISTOPHER HOUSTON CARSON (Kit Carson) served as guide for part of the expedition. In 1843–44, Frémont, again with Carson and with Thomas Fitzpatrick also as a guide, explored the Great Basin, more of the Rockies, and the eastern Cascade Range, and reached the mouth of the Columbia. Part of his mission was to complement the findings of the maritime expedition of Lieutenant CHARLES WILKES along the Pacific coast, part of the U.S. South Sea Surveying and Exploring Expedition. Frémont led his party

south and then east and crossed the Sierra Nevada in midwinter. Frémont's reports on the Great Plains—in particular the fertile regions of present-day Nebraska, Kansas, and Oklahoma—helped dispel the notion of a "Great American Desert."

Other expeditions explored westward onto lands previously known only to Native Americans. In 1845, Colonel STEPHEN WATTS KEARNY led an expedition from Fort Leavenworth in Kansas to the upper Platte and Arkansas Rivers; Thomas Fitzpatrick again found work as a guide. JAMES WILLIAM ABERT led a party, under Kearny's command, to western Oklahoma and the Texas Panhandle. Frémont led a party under Kearny in explorations of the Great Basin and Sierra Nevada, as well as northern California and southern Oregon; during and after this expedition, Frémont became involved in the Bear Flag Revolt of American settlers against the Mexicans in northern California and helped secure California for the United States in the U.S.-Mexican War of 1846–48. Kearny also participated in the war. Serving under him, Lieutenant WILLIAM HEMSLEY EMORY created the first scientific map of the Southwest, from the Gulf of Mexico to the Pacific Ocean.

In 1848–49, Frémont led a privately funded expedition from the plains into the mountains of northern New Mexico, in the hope of locating a practical central route for a proposed transcontinental railroad. He headed one last expedition in 1853, another privately funded one, exploring the Wasatch Mountains of northern Utah and the Sierra Nevada for another proposed railroad route.

Over the next decades, especially in the 1850s, the U.S. army conducted a number of topographic and surveying expeditions for wagon roads and railroads (see SURVEYING AND EXPLORATION). One of the last such exploratory and surveying expeditions was under the command of Lieutenant HENRY TUREMAN ALLEN to the Yukon, Koyok, and Copper Rivers of eastern Alaska in 1885.

Many Callings

In addition to the fur traders and military men, people of many callings helped increase awareness of the geography and natural science of North America in the 19th century and helped pioneer routes leading to non-Indian settlement. In the 1830s, a number of painters followed the fur traders and the military men on their expeditions: artist GEORGE CATLIN traveled on an American Fur Company ship up the Missouri, and later with General Henry Leavenworth and Colonel Henry Dodge to the southern plains; and Swiss artist KARL BODMER, along with German naturalist ALEXANDER PHILIPP MAXIMILIAN, also traveled on a fur company boat up the Missouri, in order to paint and study Native Americans. In the same period, another painter, JOHN JAMES AUDUBON, ventured from settled areas into the wilderness on his own—from Florida to Texas to

Labrador—to paint wildlife, becoming one of the foremost authorities of North American birds. Other frontier painters traveled to wilderness lands in the 1840s–50s: Canadian PAUL KANE, across Canada, from Toronto to Vancouver; and Swiss RUDOLPH FRIEDERICH KURZ, up the Missouri into the Dakotas.

Pioneers in the West also came from a variety of backgrounds. In 1841, Belgian missionary PIERRE-JEAN DE SMET led the first large-scale wagon train migration on the Oregon Trail, another journey for which former mountain man Thomas Fitzpatrick served as guide. That same year, JAMES SINCLAIR, a Métis working for the Hudson's Bay Company, pioneered a wagon route through the Canadian Rockies. In 1843, JESSE APPLEGATE, a Kentuckian who had worked as a surveyor in St. Louis, and Presbyterian missionary MARCUS WHITMAN from New York helped lead the "Great Migration of 1843," the largest wagon train of emigrants to date along the Oregon Trail. In 1847, BRIGHAM YOUNG, who was a prominent leader in the Church of Jesus Christ of Latter Day Saints—better known as the Mormons—after journeying from New York, led a party of Mormons from winter quarters on the Missouri River to the Great Salt Lake Valley in Utah, pioneering what became known as the Mormon Trail. In 1863, JOHN MERIN BOZEMAN, who had originally traveled to the West from Georgia as a gold prospector, pioneered the Bozeman Trail, a wagon route from Colorado to Montana along the east side of the Bighorn Mountains and through the Bozeman Pass of the Belt Mountains. In 1865, JESSE CHISHOLM, a trader of Cherokee ancestry, blazed the Chisholm Trail, which became a primary cattle route from Texas to railheads in Kansas.

A number of scientists helped open both the American and Canadian West. In 1832, HENRY ROWE SCHOOLCRAFT, a geologist, ethnologist, and Indian agent, led an expedition to find the source of the Mississippi, which he identified correctly as Lake Itasca in northern Minnesota. In 1857–60, Englishman JOHN PALLISER, originally a sportsman and hunter, led a scientific expedition to western Canada for the British government, which explored the 49th Parallel from Lake Superior to the Pacific Ocean as well as passes in the Canadian Rockies. Geologist HENRY YOULE HIND, also born in England, led a simultaneous government expedition exploring the river systems of Manitoba and Saskatchewan.

In the 1860s–1870s, self-taught naturalist JOHN MUIR conducted studies in the Yosemite Valley and the Sierra Nevada in California. In 1869, in a federally funded expedition, geologist and ethnologist JOHN WESLEY POWELL led the first successful navigation of the Colorado River. He went on to head the U.S. Geological Survey, succeeding its first director CLARENCE KING. Another geologist, FERDINAND VANDEVEER HAYDEN, worked for the government in the same period in studies of the Great Plains and Rocky Mountains.

West and North

The growing number of military forts and roads linking them enabled travel through and settlement in Native American ancestral lands. By the 1860s, the major routes linking east and west in the United States—the Santa Fe Trail, the Old Spanish Trail, the Oregon Trail, and its offshoots (the Central Overland Route, the California Trail, the Bozeman Trail, and the Mormon Trail)—were well established. The railroads would soon follow. By 1850, they connected the Atlantic coast with the Great Lakes; by 1853, with Chicago; and, by 1856, with the west side of the Mississippi. In the early 1860s, a transcontinental line was begun; by the end of the decade, in 1869, the Union Pacific and the Central Pacific met at Promontory Point, Utah. The 1880s saw another burst of railroad building. To the north, the transcontinental Canadian Pacific Railroad was completed in 1885.

A series of gold rushes affected the course of settlement in North America and accelerated the pace of westward expansion: the California gold rush of 1849; the Colorado (Pikes Peak) Gold Rush of 1858–59; gold rushes in Idaho and Montana in the 1860s; gold rushes in Arizona and Nevada in the 1870s; and the Klondike gold rush (to the Yukon Territory and Alaska) in 1896–98. In 1859, silver was discovered in Nevada, the Comstock Lode as it came to be known, and silver would soon be found in other western states as well.

To the north, Arctic exploration continued over the centuries, with a great number of expeditions—many of them British and many spurred on by the disappearance of Englishman SIR JOHN FRANKLIN in 1845. The first successful navigation of the Northwest Passage above the North American mainland was accomplished by Norwegian ROALD ENGELBREGT GRAVNING AMUNDSEN in 1903–06. In 1904–11, French Canadian JOSEPH ELZÉAR BERNIER charted northern islands in Arctic waters for Canada. To the south, in 1914, the opening of the Panama Canal across the Isthmus of Panama provided a practical passage between the Atlantic and Pacific Oceans and separated the continents of North America and South America by water.

❖

The political map of North America continued to take shape well into the 20th century, with the United States, Canada, and Mexico, as well as the countries of Central America and the West Indies, defining external and internal boundaries. The demographic map continues to evolve as in earlier centuries, with North America a melting pot of peoples from around the world. Growing environmental awareness in the latter part of the 20th century has led many people to rediscover and appreciate the land, with a sense of curiosity, adventure, and reverence inspired by both Native Americans and explorers from other continents.

Northeast Passage

The Northeast Passage is the sea route between the Atlantic Ocean and Pacific Ocean, from along the north coast of Norway to the eastern edge of SIBERIA at the BERING STRAIT. Many nations sought this passage to use as a trade route between Europe and China, and the quest to find it led to many geographic discoveries.

Europeans had knowledge of the seas to the north and east of Norway since at least A.D. 870, when a Viking by the name of Ottar sailed into the White Sea. Other Vikings later reached as far north and east as Novaya Zemlya. Also, the various peoples who lived in northern parts of much of Scandinavia, Russia, and Siberia over the centuries had extensive knowledge of these northern seas, due to their often nomadic lifestyles and their use of the sea for hunting and fishing. In the history of exploration, the search for the Northeast Passage was thus largely a European venture, motivated primarily by the desire for a predictable, commercially viable waterway between Europe and Asia.

The first attempts at a sea route westward from the Atlantic through the Americas to the Pacific—the NORTHWEST PASSAGE—were made in the late 1490s, following CHRISTOPHER COLUMBUS's first voyage of exploration for Spain in 1492. The interest in a Northeast Passage came later, European countries hoping to find a more direct route past Africa than the long southerly route around the CAPE OF GOOD HOPE.

Early English Expeditions

England was the first country to make a concerted effort at finding the Northeast Passage. Envious of the riches being acquired by the Portuguese and Spanish through commerce with the Orient during the 16th century, and frustrated by expensive and as yet unsuccessful attempts to find a Northwest Passage, the English augmented their search for new trade routes by looking east. They were encouraged in this endeavor by the 1549 publication of *Rerum Moscoviticarum Commentarii* (Notes on Muscovite Affairs). In this book, written by Sigismund von Herberstein, an ambassador from the Holy Roman Emperor to Russia, the author describes his journeys earlier that century and offers reports of regular sea voyages between the north coast of Russia and the west coast of Norway.

The first expedition in search of the Northeast Passage was sponsored by the MUSCOVY COMPANY. In 1553, under the directorship of SEBASTIAN CABOT, the company outfitted a fleet of three ships under SIR HUGH WILLOUGHBY, with RICHARD CHANCELLOR as second in command. During a storm off the north coast of Norway, their ships were separated. Willoughby continued to the east, where he sighted Novaya Zemlya, making the first known European sighting of this island group since the Vikings. Icy conditions kept him at a distance, however. Heading back westward, his ship became trapped in ice at the northern end of the Kola Peninsula, and he and his crew perished there during the winter. Chancellor, meanwhile, had managed to reach the port of Archangel at the mouth of the Dvina River, from where he traveled southward. He was invited to Moscow at the request of Czar Ivan IV (Ivan the Terrible). The prospect of trade with England appealed to the czar, and Chancellor returned to England with agreements in hand.

The Muscovy Company sponsored a follow-up expedition in 1556, giving STEPHEN BOROUGH, who had sailed with Chancellor, a small ship and crew. With help from Russian fishermen near the Kola Peninsula, Borough made his way to the north coast of Russia near the mouth of the Pechora River. From there, he continued eastward and eventually located a strait between Vaigach Island and Novaya Zemlya leading from the Barents Sea to the Kara Sea. As with Chancellor, icy conditions forced Borough's expedition to turn back prematurely. His report of the harsh conditions in that region dissuaded others from making further explorations there for 25 years.

In 1580, the Muscovy Company launched another expedition in search of the Northeast Passage: They sent two vessels, one captained by Arthur Pet and the other by Charles Jackman. Their instructions were to follow and then extend Borough's route. Pet succeeded in finding another channel to the Kara Sea, between Vaigach Island and the mainland (Yugor Strait), but ice and fog compelled him to make a swift return. Jackman's ship was lost with all hands.

Early Dutch Expeditions

In addition to the English, the Dutch were interested in a Northeast Passage for the purpose of trade. To compete with the English at Archangel, they founded the White Sea Trading Company in 1565. Their most visible agent was OLIVIER BRUNEL, who explored the region and made successful trading arrangements in Russia. He went farther east than the English had by traveling overland to the Ob River. In 1584, on a voyage of trade and exploration, Brunel fell short of the Kara Sea and drowned after making a landing in Pecora Bay.

Among the more renowned navigators to search for the passage was WILLEM BARENTS, also a Dutchman. In 1594, he reached the northern tip of Novaya Zemlya before ice blocked his fleet of three ships. Barents led a second expedition a year later, attempting to sail around the southern end of Novaya Zemlya. Near Vaigach Island, ice once again prevented progress eastward. Geographer JAN HUYGHEN VAN LINSCHOTEN was part of both expeditions.

The Dutch launched seven expeditions that year, none of which came closer to attaining the passage. With two ships, Barents conducted a third voyage in June 1596. Sailing to the north of Norway in order to investigate conditions in these untested waters, he charted Bear Island and reached the Spitsbergen group (both now part of Svalbard). The seas farther to the north proved inhospitable, and Barents sailed eastward to Novaya Zemlya and rounded its northern tip into the Kara Sea.

His second ship, headed by Jan Cornelizoon Rijp, returned to the west. With the change of seasons, Barents found his vessel trapped in the ice. He and his crew set up camp at the place he called Ice Haven on Novaya Zemlya, fashioning a shelter from driftwood. The group supplemented their dwindling rations by hunting foxes, but this was not enough to prevent the onset of SCURVY, from which Barents and several of his crew died. In July 1597, the surviving crew were aided by two Russian ships; they eventually reached the Kola Peninsula, where they found Rijp, who returned with them to the Netherlands in November 1597.

Henry Hudson

HENRY HUDSON, an Englishman, sailed for both the English and the Dutch in the early 17th century. In 1607, sponsored by the Muscovy Company, Hudson reached the east coast of GREENLAND and Spitsbergen, north of Norway. In 1608, again sailing for English interests, he reached the Barents Sea and Novaya Zemlya and was subsequently stopped by ice. In 1609, in the employ of the DUTCH EAST INDIA COMPANY, Hudson again attempted the Northeast Passage. He approached Novaya Zemlya once again, but, with icy seas beginning to trap his vessel and, under threat of mutiny, he headed westward across the Atlantic to the Americas and investigated the coast of Newfoundland and the Hudson River. As these expeditions seemed to prove the Kara Sea unnavigable, both the Dutch and the English turned their attention to the rich fishing and whaling grounds near Spitsbergen.

Russian Expeditions

The Russians initiated the next phase of exploration for a Northeast Passage. They had had knowledge of the north coast of their continent for centuries, through trade with and collecting taxes from indigenous peoples, but the desire to conduct wide-ranging commerce had been stifled by conflicts closer to home. In 1648, it is possible that SEMYON IVANOVICH DEZHNEV passed the eastern point of Siberia at East Cape (now known as Cape Dezhnev) while on a trading mission, but his account of that region's geography is somewhat confused. It was not understood at this time whether the Asian and North American continents were joined at this location. The lure of the unknown prompted Peter the Great, who became czar of Russia in 1682, to or-

ganize a number of voyages, known as the Great Northern Expeditions, to explore and map the Siberian coastline.

In one of them Danish explorer VITUS JONASSEN BERING set out overland in 1725 through Russia and Siberia to the Kamchatka Peninsula. In 1728, after building a boat, he and his men, including Russian naval officer ALEKSEY ILYICH CHIRIKOV, navigated through enough of the Bering Strait—which is named after Bering—to be satisfied that Asia and North America were separate landmasses. Bering returned to St. Petersburg in 1730, where authorities greeted his findings with skepticism. In 1733, Bering set out again, this time with a much larger expedition, which traced the Arctic coast from Archangel to the east, charting the region section by section, all the way to the mouth of the Kolyma River. In 1741, Bering again navigated the Bering Strait. It was on this voyage that he sighted the south coast of Alaska. After becoming stranded off the Kamchatka Peninsula, Bering and many of his men died of scurvy. Survivors managed to return to Russia, where they delivered a report of their findings. The survey of the Siberian coast was completed with the four-year journey of Baron Ferdinand Petrovich von Wrangel for Russia near the end of the 18th century.

James Cook

In 1776, the HUDSON'S BAY COMPANY backed an expedition to the Pacific headed by JAMES COOK in search of a water route across North America. In 1778, after passing through the Bering Strait and attempting to navigate eastward north of Alaska, it turned back westward because of PACK ICE and tried to locate the eastern outlet of the Northeast Passage, also finding that route blocked by ice.

Through the Northeast Passage

On a voyage in 1878–79, NILS ADOLF ERIK NORDENSKJÖLD, using the combination steamship–sailing ship *Vega*, finally navigated the Northeast Passage. Nordenskjöld, born in Finland of Swedish parents and trained as a chemist and mineralogist, was already a seasoned explorer by the time he attempted this expedition. With backing from the kings of Sweden and Norway and with coal and foodstuffs to last two years, he left Tromso, Norway, on July 21, 1878. Conditions were favorable in the Kara Sea, and he reached Port Dickson on August 6, thus beginning the exploratory phase of the journey. On August 19, he sailed past the northernmost point of the Asian continent at Cape Chelyuskin and, on September 27, he reached North Cape. The following day, the *Vega* became icebound, and captain and crew made preparations for the winter. Superior planning made their winter at sea relatively comfortable, and Nordenskjöld kept himself and the others busy with numerous scientific projects. With the melting of the ice, the *Vega* was freed. On July 18, 1879, the expedition entered the Bering Strait, having completed the passage. It later visited Japan and Sri Lanka before making use of the Suez Canal to return to Sweden on August 24, 1880. Nordenskjöld's two-volume account published the following year, *The Voyage of the Vega*, is a classic in the field of exploration as both an adventure story and as a scientific study, with detailed information on geography, climate, and native peoples.

❖

Although the Northeast Passage had been traversed, the prospect of provisioning for a two-season journey made its use commercially unattractive. The Russo-Japanese War of 1904–05, however, awakened the Russians to the benefits of such a route, and the Russian government soon commissioned the construction of a pair of icebreakers to undertake more detailed surveys of these waters. In 1909, the *Taymyr* and the *Vaygach* were put into service. Between 1909 and 1915, these ships conducted hydrographic studies (see HYDROGRAPHY) in the waters of the Bering Strait and completed the first east-to-west navigation of the passage. In 1932, under the direction of the Union of Soviet Socialist Republics (USSR; Soviet Union), OTTO Y. SCHMIDT made the first single-season passage. The Soviet Union established the Northern Sea Route Administration in that year for the development of Siberia's resources and for regular commercial shipping. Today, use of these northern sea-lanes has become practical and routine because of large fleets of icebreakers, ongoing aerial reconnaissance, and meteorological monitoring stations. The cargoes that pass through its waters are typically timber, ore, and other raw materials en route to processing factories in northern Asia.

North Magnetic Pole (Magnetic North Pole)

The Earth has a magnetic field, an area surrounding the planet in which objects experience an electromagnetic force. In other words, Earth acts as a giant magnet. The exact cause of terrestrial magnetism is unknown; theories relate to the matter and structure of Earth's core, one of which is the dynamo theory involving the interaction of motion and electrical currents in the liquid outer core. At one end of Earth, the northern end, the magnetic force is toward the ground; at the other end, the southern end, the magnetic force is away from the ground. (Earth's magnetic field reverses polarity on an irregular basis, from several thousand years to 35 million years, resulting in the opposite effect; the last such reversal was some 780,000 years ago.) The exact location of these points of magnetic polarity are referred to as the magnetic poles. The magnetic pole at the northern end is known as the North Magnetic Pole (written with or without capitalization). That at the southern end is known as the SOUTH MAGNETIC POLE. The terms also appear as magnetic north pole and magnetic south pole. The angle that Earth's magnetic field makes with the horizon is called the magnetic dip, leading to the alternative names dip poles or magnetic dip poles.

The North Magnetic Pole and the South Magnetic Pole do not correspond with the geographic poles of Earth's imaginary axis, known as the NORTH POLE and SOUTH POLE. Moreover, their location varies in the course of almost a century—as they do to a much less degree annually and even daily—a phenomenon known as polar wandering. The present location of the North Magnetic Pole is in the Queen Elizabeth Islands of northern Canada, about 800 miles from the North Pole.

For purposes of study, scientists have also defined Earth's magnetic field as a symmetrical magnetic field, averaging its direction and strength, and the hypothetical poles are known as geomagnetic poles, south and north. The North Geomagnetic Pole is situated near Thule, GREENLAND, about 780 miles from the geographic North Pole.

The effect of terrestrial magnetism had been evident for centuries through use of the magnetic COMPASS. William Gilbert, an English physician and scientist, carried out the first comprehensive study of Earth's magnetic field, publishing his findings in *De magnete* in 1600.

On May 31, 1831, British explorer SIR JAMES CLARK ROSS, as part of the 1829–33 expedition under SIR JOHN ROSS, located the North Magnetic Pole on the west coast of the Boothia Peninsula. During his expedition of 1903–06, in which he made the first successful crossing of the NORTHWEST PASSAGE, ROALD ENGELBREGT GRAVNING AMUNDSEN again measured the location of the North Magnetic Pole, finding it had moved from Ross's calculation. In 1948, Canadian scientists Paul Serson and Jack Clark confirmed that it had moved and determined that its location was 160 miles from Ross's calculation.

See also ARCTIC, EXPLORATION OF THE.

North Pole (North Geographic Pole, Geographic North Pole)

The North Pole, a cartographic point in the ice-covered Arctic Ocean, is considered the northernmost place on Earth, at a latitude of 90 degrees north and a longitude of 0 degrees, where all meridians of longitude converge. Its location is determined by the imaginary line, or axis, around which Earth rotates from west to east. The axis is perpendicular to the plane of the EQUATOR and passes through the center of Earth, terminating at geographic points referred to as the North Pole in the Northern Hemisphere and the SOUTH POLE in the Southern Hemisphere. From the North Pole, all directions on the surface of Earth are read as to the south. The North Pole is also referred to as the North Geographic Pole, to distinguish it from the NORTH MAGNETIC POLE, which is determined by Earth's magnetic field. Reaching the North Pole was one of the great goals of world exploration and is part of the larger story of human activity in the Arctic.

In ancient times, as put forth by Roman scholar PLINY THE ELDER in the first century A.D., based on information from the travels of Greek scholar PYTHEAS, who explored the Arctic Ocean in the fourth century B.C., the northernmost place on Earth was thought to be ULTIMA THULE. It can be assumed that the Vikings, familiar with northern waters in the Middle Ages, came to know the dangers of venturing too far north because of DRIFT ICE and the limits of navigable waters because of PACK ICE. Starting in the 16th century, the European search for a NORTHEAST PASSAGE—a water route from the Atlantic Ocean to the Pacific Ocean, eastward across northern Europe and Asia—and a NORTHWEST PASSAGE—a water route westward through the Americas—led mariners, especially among the British and Dutch, to explore Arctic waters and sail as far north as possible. Even with growing awareness of Earth's true geography, belief in an open polar sea that would provide a route to Earth's northernmost point persisted well into the 19th century despite repeated encounters with the pack ice of the Arctic Ocean.

Concerted efforts to reach the North Pole began in the late 18th century and continued through the 19th century, with northernmost records being broken. In 1773, a British naval expedition under CONSTANTINE JOHN PHIPPS attempted to reach the North Pole by water and came up against impassable ice east of GREENLAND. In 1818, a British expedition, with ships commanded by DAVID BUCHAN and SIR JOHN FRANKLIN, reached European Arctic waters north of Spitsbergen (present-day Svalbard) before being forced back by pack ice. In 1827, another British naval expedition under SIR WILLIAM EDWARD PARRY, along with SIR JAMES CLARK ROSS, made an attempt on the North Pole from Spitsbergen, setting a northernmost record.

Attempts accelerated in the latter part of the century. In 1860–61, American ISAAC ISRAEL HAYES hoped to locate an open polar sea north of Greenland and Ellesmere Island, Canada's northernmost point, but failed. In 1868, the First Swedish North Polar Expedition under NILS ADOLF ERIK NORDENSKJÖLD failed to reach the North Pole from Spitsbergen; he failed again in 1872–73 on the Second Swedish North Polar Expedition. Meanwhile, in 1871, American CHARLES FRANCIS HALL reached as far as the Lincoln Sea from northern Ellesmere Island, setting a new record. In 1875–76, SIR GEORGE STRONG NARES made an unsuccessful attempt, again from northern Ellesmere Island, breaking the record. In 1879–81, in the course of an American expedition headed by GEORGE WASHINGTON DE LONG, into the Arctic Ocean by way of the BERING STRAIT, the ship became trapped in ice north of Wrangel Island, resulting in the eventual death of De Long and 12 others on the Lena River of SIBERIA. In 1893–96, a Norwegian expedition under FRIDT-

JOF NANSEN attempted to approach the North Pole by purposely having his ship become icebound and drift northward from the New Siberian Islands, after which he and his men continued by kayak and sledge, eventually turning back because of ice conditions after setting a new northernmost record. In 1897, Swede SALOMON AUGUST ANDRÉE tried to reach the Pole from Spitsbergen by air, in a BALLOON, perishing in the attempt. At the turn of the century, in 1899–1900, LUIGI AMEDEO DI SAVOIA D'ABRUZZI led an Italian expedition which attempted to reach the Pole from Franz Josef Land, setting the new northernmost record.

American ROBERT EDWIN PEARY, who carried out four Arctic expeditions to Greenland between 1886 and 1900, resolved to reach the North Pole. In his first attempt in 1902, from Cape Hecla on northern Ellesmere Island, he set a northernmost record for the Western Hemisphere. In a subsequent attempt in 1905–06, by way of the Robeson Channel, the north section of the passage between Ellesmere Island and Greenland, he set the new northernmost record in both hemispheres. In July 1808, Peary departed from New York for a third attempt. From Cape Columbia on Ellesmere Island, Peary, his assistant, MATTHEW ALEXANDER HENSON, and four Inuit (Eskimo) set out on March 1, 1909, and, after a monthlong trek across the frozen sea with sledges and dogs, reached the North Pole on April 6 (although there is some evidence he missed the Pole by a couple of miles). In the meantime, another American, FREDERICK ALBERT COOK, claimed to have reached the North Pole by the Ellesmere Island route on April 21, 1908. The controversy on who actually had been first to the Pole lasted for some time. Peary, with more geographic data to support his claim, received official recognition from U.S. Congress in 1911.

American RICHARD EVELYN BYRD and Floyd Bennett are credited with making the first airplane flight over the North Pole on May 9, 1926, although there is also controversy as to whether they missed the mark, which would make Norwegian ROALD ENGELBREGT GRAVNING AMUNDSEN, American LINCOLN ELLSWORTH, and Italian UMBERTO NOBILE, who passed over it by AIRSHIP three days earlier on May 12, the first to do so. In 1931, Australian SIR GEORGE HUBERT WILKINS attempted unsuccessfully to reach the Pole from Spitsbergen by submarine; that feat was accomplished in 1958, when the U.S. atomic submarine *Nautilus* under Commander William R. Anderson passed beneath the polar ice. Another milestone in the history of exploration was the first flight over the North Pole by a woman, American LOUISE ARNER BOYD, in 1955. In 1977, the nuclear icebreaker *Arktika* of the then Union of Soviet Socialist Republics (USSR; Soviet Union) became the first surface ship to reach the Pole. In 1981, British explorers Sir Ranulph Fiennes and Charles Burton reached the North Pole, having traveled there from the South Pole, becoming the first men to circle the Earth Pole to Pole, having done so over a period of three years.

See also ARCTIC, EXPLORATION OF THE.

North Star (Pole Star, Polaris, Stella Maris)

The North Star—also called Pole Star or Polaris, or Stella Maris, for "star of the sea"—is the star located along the axis of the NORTH POLE. It is of value in navigation because its position remains relatively fixed throughout the year.

The North Star is a second magnitude star, meaning it is 1/30th as bright as the brightest star in the sky. For this reason it was not always obvious that it retained its position in the sky as the seasons changed. Located in the constellation Ursa Minor (the Little Dipper) at the end of the handle, the North Star is not presently along the exact polar axis, but rather about one degree off. This causes it to appear to wobble by two degrees throughout the course of a day.

The earliest information we have on the use of the North Star for navigation is from the Phoenicians. Using the North Star as their reference, they were able to sail at night, a competitive advantage for the trading nation. The Greeks learned how to navigate using the North Star from the Phoenicians, and they called it the "Phoenician Star." The Venetian traveler to the Far East, MARCO POLO, reported use of the North Star in the Indian Ocean in 1290.

Arab travelers used the North Star along with a tool called the *al-kemal,* Arabic for "the consummation," a rectangular plate made of horn or other material on which a string of knots was affixed to the center. The user placed the bottom of the rectangle on the horizon, and, by moving one's arm toward oneself or away from oneself, located the North Star at the top of the rectangle. The user would determine a distance from the rectangle to his or her nose by means of the string of knots, each knot representing a previously determined latitude. In this manner, the user determined location along the latitudinal but not the longitudinal scale.

Interestingly, the North Star has not been the same star throughout history, a phenomenon caused by Earth's rotation very slowly on its axis, like a spinning top pushed slightly off balance, causing the axis to point in a different direction over time. More than 4,000 years ago, the star indicating north would have been located in the constellation Draco. In about 10,000 years, the new North Star will be Vega of the constellation Lyra.

See also GREEK EXPLORATION; LATITUDE AND LONGITUDE; MUSLIM EXPLORATION; NAVIGATION AND EXPLORATION; PHOENICIAN EXPLORATION.

North West Company

The North West Company was one of two great Canadian fur-trading concerns that helped open the West, what is now Canada and northern parts of the United States. It coalesced in Montreal, Quebec, the center of commerce on the St. Lawrence River, in 1779, then reorganized in the 1780s and was active under that name until 1821, when it merged with its older rival, the HUDSON'S BAY COMPANY. The North West Company's founders and its traders, known as Nor'westers (or Northwesters), were mostly Scottish.

18th Century

Many Scots moved to Montreal after the British takeover of New France in 1763; other Scots, loyal to Great Britain, took refuge there during and after the American Revolution of 1775–83. With the city being a center of the FUR TRADE, Scottish merchants began investing in their own operations. Some allied themselves with French merchants, or hired French VOYAGEURS, traders who had worked for other firms, as well as the COUREURS DE BOIS, unlicensed traders, to take advantage of their expertise. In the field, however, the competition between traders often led to violence. In 1779, a number of Scots active in the fur trade—Simon McTavish, James McGill, and Isaac Todd—formed a company, which, after other merchants had joined, became organized as the North West Company in the winter of 1783–84. A rival firm, Gregory and McLeod, merged with the North West Company in 1787. It was decided that the various trading companies who invested in the North West Company, some of which had interests other than the fur trade, could maintain their separate identities, working in conjunction with other shareholders known as "wintering partners," who conducted the trade in the field with Native American tribes.

Much of the activity of the Nor'westers was in Prince Rupert's Land, or Rupert's Land, an area of northern and western Canada comprising the drainage basin of HUDSON BAY. The territory had been granted to the Hudson's Bay Company by King Charles II at the time of that company's founding in 1670, but much of the fur-rich region remained untapped. Grand Portage on western Lake Superior became the primary meeting place, where goods were exchanged. Traders, traveling by large CANOE, took European trade goods from Montreal to rendezvous with traders, generally in smaller canoes, carrying furs collected in the wilderness. The furs were then shipped to Montreal, then England.

In 1778–79, Connecticut-born PETER POND, who had gone into partnership with McTavish in 1777, led a fur-trading expedition from Cumberland House on the Saskatchewan River northwest to the Athabasca River as far as Lake Athabasca, where he traded with Chipewyan Indians. Pond also made the first map of the region. A decade later, in 1789, SIR ALEXANDER MACKENZIE, who migrated from Scotland to Canada via New York with his father, explored from the Great Slave Lake along the Mackenzie

River (named after him) to the Arctic Ocean. On a subsequent expedition, in 1792–93, in search of a water route to the Pacific Ocean, Mackenzie explored the Peace and Smoky Rivers, followed the Parsnip River into the ROCKY MOUNTAINS, located the Fraser River and descended Bella Coola River to the Pacific Ocean, completing the first overland journey across North America north of the Rio Grande.

19th Century

Among other Nor'westers who made a significant geographic contribution was Vermont-born SIMON FRASER. In 1805–08, exploring west of the Canadian Rockies, he followed the Fraser River (named after him), to its Pacific Ocean outlet in British Columbia. London-born DAVID THOMPSON of Welsh descent, who had started out as a Hudson's Bay Company trader, was in the North West Company's employ during two expeditions, in 1797–99, in which he explored and surveyed a vast region: from Lake Superior to Lake Winnipeg and Lake Winnipegosis; around the upper Red River, the Assiniboine River, and the upper MISSOURI RIVER; perhaps even the source of the MISSISSIPPI RIVER; and around Lesser Slave Lake and the Athabasca River. In 1800, he located the source of the Saskatchewan River in the Canadian Rockies. In 1804, Thompson became a partner in the company. In 1807–11, he carried out additional surveys, locating House Pass and Athabasca Pass in the Canadian Rockies and tracing the COLUMBIA RIVER from its source to the Pacific. Later settling in Montreal, he created the first accurately detailed map of the Canadian and American West, an area encompassing some 1.7 million square miles.

One of the founding partners in the North West Company was New Jersey–born ALEXANDER HENRY (the older). In 1791, his nephew ALEXANDER HENRY (the younger) acquired his shares in the company and began establishing and commanding trading posts along the Red River in present-day North Dakota. Over the next years, he founded a chain of posts for the company all the way to the Pacific Ocean. Similarly, in 1816–19, DONALD MACKENZIE, Alexander Mackenzie's Scottish-born cousin, after working for the Pacific Fur Company, a subsidiary of JOHN JACOB ASTOR's AMERICAN FUR COMPANY, founded a number of North West Company posts in the Pacific Northwest. From them, he sent out fur-trapping brigades in what is now Washington, Oregon, and Idaho. After 1803, Fort William (present-day Thunder Bay, Ontario) became the primary rendezvous depot, replacing Grand Portage, which by then was American territory.

Relations between the wintering partners and the eastern merchants were not always smooth, with the former feeling that Simon McTavish and other merchants ignored many of their recommendations and were taking more than a fair share of profits. In 1798, a group of dissatisfied traders broke away from the new North West Company and formed what became generally known as the XY Company because of the identifying marks on the fur bales. Alexander Mackenzie joined them in 1800. After the death of Simon McTavish in 1804, the breakaway group rejoined the North West Company.

The North West Company, meanwhile, with its wide-ranging traders, made significant headway in its competition with its rivals. In the north, it was active even in the region of Hudson Bay, formerly just the Hudson's Bay Company's domain. In the Pacific Northwest, it was active in Oregon Country, claimed by both the United States and England. During the War of 1812 between the United States and England, the North West Company eventually purchased Astoria from the American Fur Company. Astor's Southwest Fur Company, a subsidiary of the American Fur Company, established in 1811, involved some North West Company interests for a short time, until the war.

Meanwhile, in 1811, the Hudson's Bay Company granted one of their stockholders, Thomas Douglas, earl of Selkirk, a small part of Rupert's Land, along the Red River in present-day Manitoba, for an agricultural community. The first settlers, predominantly Scottish and some Irish peasants, arrived on the land patent in the summer of 1812. Their governor, Miles Macdonnell, fearing food shortages, gave notice to the Métis—the mixed-blood descendants of Cree and other Indians and French and Scots—that they were bound to sell their extra meat to his community rather than elsewhere. He also forbade the running of buffalo on horseback. The Métis ignored both edicts. The North West Company, aggravated by this sponsoring of farmers in fur country by their rival, supplied arms to the Métis and incited them to action. Violence broke out in 1816. Robert Semple, who had replaced Macdonnell as the colony's governor, and a number of militiamen were killed. Although the opposing factions agreed to the compromise outlined in the Selkirk Treaty of 1817, ill feelings and harassment lasted. The Selkirk incident and other conflicts led to involvement of the British government, which encouraged a merger of the two Canadian companies. It was realized in 1821, with licensing by the British government of additional territory extending to the Pacific Ocean on the west and the Arctic Ocean on the north. Although the North West Company was the more active of the two in the fur trade at that time, with more partners, the older Hudson's Bay Company controlled many of the favored westward routes, and the name of the latter company was retained.

❖

In 1987, the Hudson's Bay Company, then active in the retail business, sold off some of its department stores in northern Canada. The company that purchased them took the name of the North West Company and currently operates out of Winnipeg, Manitoba.

See also COMMERCE AND EXPLORATION.

North-West Company
See COMPANY OF MERCHANTS OF LONDON DISCOVERERS OF THE NORTH-WEST PASSAGE.

Northwest Passage

The Northwest Passage is the sea route linking the Atlantic Ocean and Pacific Ocean, located north of the North American continent. In the course of the search for a Northwest Passage—and a variation on the concept, the Strait of Anian (see ANIAN, STRAIT OF)—explorers came to define the boundaries of North America. The story of this search involves not only the stubborn desire of many individuals to find a profitable trade route but also their refusal to abandon an unproven idea in the face of difficult odds. From the time that Europeans found the Americas blocking their way to the Pacific until the time that the Northwest Passage was successfully navigated by ship, more than four centuries would elapse.

Europeans Reach the Americas

When Italian mariner CHRISTOPHER COLUMBUS, exploring for Spain, came upon islands of the WEST INDIES in the Caribbean Sea in December 1492, he believed that he had reached the SPICE ISLANDS (the Moluccas) of the EAST INDIES in the Pacific Ocean. Over the course of three voyages in 1493–1504, Columbus continued searching for confirmation of his whereabouts. These travels would ultimately take him south and west, to present-day Venezuela and Panama. Other Spanish voyages would begin to reveal the scope of the Americas.

The Portuguese expedition of PEDRO ÁLVARS CABRAL in 1500–01, which made the European discovery of present-day Brazil, also furthered knowledge of South American geography. In a bold attempt to find a passage westward, Portuguese mariner FERDINAND MAGELLAN, in service to Spain, sailed along South America's east coast, eventually passing CAPE HORN and entering the Pacific in 1520. Magellan proved a sea journey westward from Europe to Asia possible but not profitable: Most Europeans were deterred from using this route for trade because it was prohibitively time-consuming and expensive. The need for a passage to the north—a Northwest Passage—would soon take hold in the minds of European geographers, explorers, and businessmen.

First Attempts to Locate a Passage

Italian mariner JOHN CABOT was the first European to begin exploring the North American coast systematically. Sailing for England in 1497, he made the European discovery of the islands of Labrador and Newfoundland. His expedition had been financed with the hope of his reaching the Orient. On coming upon these islands, Cabot believed, like Columbus, that he was in Asia. His misconception would soon become apparent. Still, the discovery of the rich fishing grounds of the Grand Banks proved a boon to the English fishing industry, and the king rewarded Cabot for his accomplishment. The results of Cabot's follow-up expedition in 1498 also failed to find the hoped-for passage. In 1500 and 1509, Cabot's son, SEBASTIAN CABOT, also made voyages of exploration in that area. The younger Cabot sailed past the northern tip of Newfoundland and possibly some miles into HUDSON BAY as well.

The Portuguese also explored the northern coastal regions of North America in the late 15th century. GASPAR CÔRTE-REAL claimed to have made a 1499 voyage, in which he explored the seas to the west of GREENLAND and found an outlet to the fabled Strait of Anian—another name for a supposed passage, this one thought to angle southwestward and separate North America from Asia. Now in competition with England after John Cabot's voyages, King Manuel I authorized a continuation of his explorations. In 1500, Côrte-Real sailed along the west coast of Greenland, possibly crossing the ARCTIC CIRCLE, but was forced to turn back by PACK ICE. Like his predecessor Cabot, Côrte-Real mistakenly believed that he had reached the northern latitudes of Asia on this voyage. On a subsequent voyage in 1501, he and his crew were lost at sea. In 1502, MIGUEL CÔRTE-REAL mounted an expedition in search of his younger brother, and he too disappeared.

The French began their quest for a westward route to the Pacific in 1524 by sponsoring Italian mariner GIOVANNI DA VERRAZANO. He set off in January of that year for the North American continent and a passage west, expecting initially to find it to the south. Blown by uncooperative winds, Verrazano landed north of his destination along the coast of the Carolinas. Sighting Pamlico Sound near Cape Hatteras, he divined that he had found the Pacific. Continuing northward, he explored New York harbor and the mouth of the Hudson River. On the final leg of his journey, Verrazano sailed along the coast of present-day Maine and on to the southern regions of Newfoundland, making a claim for French possession of the lands he had seen.

France sponsored another search for the Northwest Passage 10 years later with an expedition headed by JACQUES CARTIER. In April 1534, Cartier took two ships to the then well-known fishing grounds of the Grand Banks and sailed around Newfoundland, which he was the first to describe correctly as an island. Entering the Gulf of St. Lawrence, he proceeded westward to the Gaspé Peninsula. There, he made friendly contact with the Huron (Wyandot) Indians, among them chief DONNACONNA, who offered two of his sons as guides. After exploring the shores of Quebec, Cartier returned to France. He was again instructed to find the Northwest Passage and lands of wealth. On a second journey to Canada in 1535, he explored up the St. Lawrence River to the site of present-day Montreal. He mounted a third trip to Canada in 1541, during which his progress up the St. Lawrence was blocked by the Lachine Rapids.

With more and more ships rounding South Africa into the Pacific and with knowledge of the Pacific Ocean growing, European nations began searching for the western outlet of the Northwest Passage, although the search in the west focused on the mythical Strait of Anian with a hoped-for outlet in a warm climate. The Spanish—who, by the first part of the 1520s, had established themselves in Mexico—sought a route by which they could carry Aztec gold and trade goods back to Europe. Hoping to help Spain dominate both sea and land in North America, HERNÁN CORTÉS solicited the cooperation of his king in the exploration and discovery of such a passage. While exploring California's coast in 1535, he mistook Baja California, a peninsula, for an island and assumed that the Gulf of California was the desired passage. In 1539, FRANCISCO DE ULLOA was sent to confirm the findings of Cortés and ventured northward in the Gulf of California. He found the mouth of the COLORADO RIVER instead. A 1542 expedition by JUAN RODRÍGUEZ CABRILLO explored the northwest coast nearly as far north as San Francisco. Cabrillo died the following year, and his pilot, BARTOLOMÉ FERRELO, made a trip farther north, reaching Cape Blanco on the Oregon coast. Failing to find better passage, the Spanish thus had to content themselves with the route around the tip of South America.

A New Round of Expeditions

After a hiatus of nearly 70 years, the English experienced a renewed interest in the discovery of the Northwest Passage and/or the Strait of Anian. Inspired by the geographic theories of SIR HUMPHREY GILBERT, SIR MARTIN FROBISHER organized an expedition. In June 1576, he sailed westward with a complement of three ships "in search of the passage to Cathay," as China was then known. He thought for a time he had discovered a passage, but it turned out to be a bay on the southern end of Baffin Island, now known as Frobisher Bay. He returned to England with a piece of ore that an assayist of questionable character claimed to contain gold. While Frobisher's two subsequent expeditions to that area were motivated chiefly by the desire for gold, the explorer did manage to penetrate several hundred miles into the Hudson Strait. Frobisher's quest for gold ultimately proved futile: The ore he discovered was nothing more than FOOL'S GOLD, the mineral pyrite.

English ambitions for the passage continued with the voyages of JOHN DAVIS. He was an excellent navigator and the inventor of the Davis QUADRANT, an improved version of earlier navigational tools. Davis's first voyage took place in 1585, during which he continued the English exploration of Baffin Island, including Cumberland Sound. He thought the sound to be the long-hoped-for passage, but pack ice prevented him from confirming this. A kidnapped Inuit (Eskimo) man aided Davis in his second expedition; he guided Davis and his crew northward along the west coast of Greenland. From there, Davis then continued his exploration of Baffin Island and explored Exeter Sound. He also revisited Cumberland Sound. On a third journey the following year, Davis set a new record for northernmost point achieved, nearly 73 degrees north latitude, but was once again turned away by ice. He continued to be confident, however, that the passage lay just beyond, waiting to be discovered when the weather proved satisfactory.

On the North American west coast, the English became a major nuisance to the Spanish treasure ships, largely in the person of SIR FRANCIS DRAKE. As he conducted raids on the Spanish in the Pacific, Drake also sought the western end of the Northwest Passage. A trip in 1579 took him as far as Vancouver Island near the present United States–Canada border without results. The 1602–03 voyage of the Spaniard SEBASTIÁN VISCAÍNO traced a similar portion of coastline, with equally disappointing results.

The 1609 voyage to the North Atlantic by HENRY HUDSON, an Englishman funded by the DUTCH EAST INDIA COMPANY, is notable in that he searched for both the NORTHEAST PASSAGE and the Northwest Passage. He first headed northward along the west coast of Norway. Encountering treacherous ice near Novaya Zemlya and receiving strong criticism from his crew, he turned back. Hudson was a willful captain, however, and asserting his prerogatives, he chose to head westward. On the east coast of North America he investigated both Chesapeake Bay, Delaware Bay, New York Bay, and the Hudson River (named for him) before returning to Europe. The following year, this time in the employ of English merchants, Hudson forged through the strait that now bears his name and came upon Hudson Bay (also named for him). Heading southward, he and his crew entered James Bay. The ship wintered at the southernmost point; the next summer, as they were heading back north, the crew mutinied and set Hudson, his son John, and seven loyal sailors adrift. They were never heard from again.

The western side of Hudson Bay was still unexplored, and, with the belief that it would reveal a passage to the east, a new company was formed in England. The COMPANY OF MERCHANTS OF LONDON DISCOVERERS OF THE NORTHWEST PASSAGE, with some of the same members as the MUSCOVY COMPANY, sent SIR THOMAS BUTTON to the bay on a scouting mission in 1612. He landed on Hudson Bay's west shore at the mouth of the Nelson River. The expedition wintered there; the following spring, Button sailed northward along the coast as far as Southampton Island. Once again, a promising body of water had yielded no route west. Nevertheless, Button had charted 600 miles of previously unknown coastline.

In 1615, WILLIAM BAFFIN, accompanied by ROBERT BYLOT (who had sailed with both Hudson and Button), again searched for an outlet along the west shore of Hudson Bay. In a second expedition the following year, Baffin and Bylot took a different route in search of the passage. Making for the extreme north along the coast of Greenland, they were determined to go beyond the haunts of the whalers of Davis Strait. Entering the region that came to be known as Baffin Bay, they set a new northernmost record at 78 degrees latitude. On the way home they discovered and named Lancaster Sound, which would later prove to be the opening to the actual Northwest Passage.

Another journey of note was conducted by Danish explorer JENS ERIKSEN MUNK. He embarked in May 1619, winding his way past Greenland to Frobisher Bay, then on to Hudson Strait and Hudson Bay. He and his crew wintered at Churchill River on the west shore of the bay and became severely ill with SCURVY and, perhaps, food poisoning. Only Munk and two others survived, managing to return to Denmark in September 1620.

The last search of this era occurred between two rival English expeditions. In May 1631, LUKE FOXE and THOMAS JAMES left England only two days apart, both bound for Hudson Bay. In August of that year, the two captains had dinner together at James Bay. Foxe returned to England, having been convinced by his observations that no outlet to the west existed in Hudson Bay, while James wintered on Charlton Island. James and his crew suffered horribly through the winter, the weather being severe and scurvy claiming some of his crew. When summer 1632 arrived, James investigated Foxe Channel before returning to England.

Hudson's Bay Company

Over the ensuing decades, the English and the French fought for decades for dominance of Hudson Bay and its lucrative FUR TRADE with the Indians. The HUDSON'S BAY COMPANY, chartered in 1670, was the sole legal representative of England in the area, while a number of French interests attempted to develop the region. Following the Treaty of Utrecht in 1713, which secured its outposts in the region, the Hudson's Bay Company began a new phase of exploration in the area. The newly appointed governor for the company was JAMES KNIGHT. In 1715, he sent William Stuart on a diplomatic mission to the Indians west of the post at Churchill. Stuart's travels lasted nearly a year. He returned with Chipewyan Indians, who told Knight of "Ships in the

Western Seas" and "a Yellow Mettle" to the northwest. Such tales proved irresistible to Knight, who sought support from his company for an expedition. He was close to 80 years old when he and his two ships sailed northward in 1719. It was late in the season, and they became trapped in the ice off Marble Island. In a particularly sad episode in the search for the passage, all members of the group perished. The remains of the ships were not found for another 50 years.

Political heat began to grow against the Hudson's Bay Company. Their royal charter granted the group a monopoly on trade in the region, yet they were lax in fulfilling their duty to explore the area and to expand the power of England, which was still in competition with France. A member of Parliament, Arthur Dobbs, enlisted the help of the Royal Navy and, in 1742, sent an expedition under CHRISTOPHER MIDDLETON to form a basis to challenge the company's monopoly. Middleton chose the warmest time of year for his expedition and achieved the northernmost point of the bay yet discovered. The European discovery of Wager Bay is credited to him, as is the discovery of Repulse Bay, where the narrow seas between Southampton Island and the continent were frozen. Dobbs insisted on a second expedition, which was captained by WILLIAM MOOR in 1746–47. He sailed into Chesterfield Inlet and farther into Wager Bay than Middleton had gone, once again to no avail.

SAMUEL HEARNE's overland expedition of 1770–72 for the Hudson's Bay Company helped dispel remaining myths. With the help of the Chipewyan MATONABBEE, he headed northwestward from Fort Churchill in the employ of the Hudson's Bay Company. At the Great Slave Lake, he turned to the north, eventually reaching the north shore of North America on the Arctic Ocean at the mouth of the Coppermine River. He was fully aware of his achievement on this journey, reporting back the absence of an inland waterway capable of accommodating oceangoing ships and making it apparent that the search for the Northwest Passage would have to concentrate on more northerly regions, counter to prevalent views of the Strait of Anian.

Pacific Northwest

In the 1770s, the Spanish stepped up their activities in the Pacific Northwest, including the search for a western outlet for a passage across North America. JUAN JOSEF PÉREZ HERNÁNDEZ was deployed in 1774 to explore the coast and to claim all the lands attractive for settlement as far north as 60 degrees north latitude. He made it as far north as Queen Charlotte Island, where he traded with the Haida Indians, a tribe that had been previously unknown to the Europeans. Unfavorable winds prevented him from proceeding farther, and he fell approximately 17 degrees short of completing his mission. The next year, two ships were sent north, one under the command of BRUNO HECETA and the other captained by JUAN FRANCISCO DE LA BODEGA Y QUADRA. Heceta reached as far north as Vancouver Island before turning back, the ship taking on water and the crew beset by scurvy. Bodega y Quadra's ship continued northward. After achieving 58 degrees 30 minutes north latitude, he was turned away by rough seas. The most dramatic results were accomplished by Bodega y Quadra and Ignacio de Arteaga in 1779, when they passed the coast of Canada and explored the islands and bays of the Gulf of Alaska. Arteaga took possession of Hinchinbrook Island in July and sailed westward, grazing the tip of Kodiak Island before returning southward. Arteaga had found no passage and thus confidently reported that there was no chance of the British finding it either. Such an assessment was premature, since Arteaga had not ventured beyond the Alaskan Peninsula, where the sea offers entry among the Aleutian Islands.

The expedition that did go beyond the Aleutians had occurred the previous year, under the direction of Englishman JAMES COOK. After Hearne's discovery of the north shore of the continent in 1771, hope had been renewed for finding the passage. Jacob Stählin published a map that showed a great strait to the north of "Alaschka." In spring 1778, Cook sailed along the shore of Alaska, not realizing how far west he would have to go. He had hopes raised and dashed several times as so many prior expeditions had experienced. He explored Prince William Sound and found it to be a dead end. Cook Inlet, which doubled back to the east for a substantial distance, also proved not to be the desired passage. By August, Cook had found the BERING STRAIT and sailed northward, tracing the coastline as he went. Setting a record for northernmost point in that part of the world on August 18, at 70 degrees 41 minutes, he was turned back by ice as high and solid as a wall.

Trading became more established along North America's northwest coast in the following years, and competition intensified between Spain, England, France, and the United States. The Strait of Juan de Fuca still had not been adequately described, and, from 1786 until the mid-1790s, all four of these nations sent expeditions to stake their claims. The most thorough of these expeditions was conducted by GEORGE VANCOUVER in 1792–94. Sailing for the British, he mapped the coastline, circumnavigated Vancouver Island, and determined that the coastline from California and Alaska offered no outlet.

Meanwhile, others continued to seek a Northwest Passage by exploring westward by land. American-born ROBERT ROGERS, who established his reputation in the French and Indian War of 1754–63, dreamed of locating a water route to the Pacific and dispatched fellow soldier JONATHAN CARVER to the western Great Lakes and beyond to the MISSISSIPPI RIVER. But, because of a lack of supplies, the expedition proceeded no farther, lands to the west remained uncharted, and the issue of a water route west remained unresolved.

19th Century

At the start of the 19th century, there was still a belief that there was a practical water connection through North America. Even American MERIWETHER LEWIS of the U.S. Lewis and Clark Expedition of 1804–06 thought he might determine such a passage as he headed up the MISSOURI RIVER with the Corps of Discovery, eventually coming up against the ROCKY MOUNTAINS. Later exploration for such a passage concentrated on Arctic waters.

As Great Britain entered the second decade of the 19th century, it had a large and powerful navy that was underoccupied in the wake of the Napoleonic Wars. The growth of an interest in natural science, and Russian activity in Alaska ever since the voyages of VITUS JONASSEN BERING in the 1720s–1740s, helped to renew talk of exploration in the polar sea. The event that began this next phase came in 1817, when WILLIAM SCORESBY, JR., returned from a whaling expedition to the North Atlantic with the report of unusually clear seas north of the Arctic Circle. The news reached SIR JOSEPH BANKS who passed it to SIR JOHN BARROW, the head of the Admiralty, who immediately began preparations. An 1818 expedition led by SIR JOHN ROSS, with SIR WILLIAM EDWARD PARRY commanding a second ship, set out to explore east of Baffin Island. The first portion of their journey took them north along Greenland's west coast into Smith Sound. Finding it impassable, they looped to the south along the east coast of Ellesmere Island, where they came upon Jones Sound. This, too, was blocked by ice, and they proceeded southward to Lancaster Sound. Ross believed he sighted a chain of mountains blocking the end of the sound, which he named the "Croker Mountains." No one else had seen them, including Parry, who was greatly dismayed at having to turn back for England. Ross was criticized for this incident for some time to come.

The British navy wasted no time in planning another expedition to the Canadian Arctic for 1819. The navy decided to mount a two-pronged strategy, with a naval component headed by Parry and an overland caravan to the mouth of the Coppermine River led by SIR JOHN FRANKLIN. Parry entered Lancaster Sound, whereupon he soon debunked Ross's mountains as a mirage (and seeming to take some pleasure as he described in his journal the good conditions his ship encountered). After investigating Prince Regent Inlet, he headed westward, passing the NORTH MAGNETIC POLE as he skirted the permanent pack ice to the north. In August 1820, Parry was halted by ice at the northern end of Bank Island and headed back to England. Franklin's expedition traveled eastward, where they mapped more than 500 miles of coastline. They soon ran short of food, however, and the situation quickly deteriorated; murder and cannibalism infected the group. Franklin and a small group of survivors managed to return to Hudson Bay in 1822. Meanwhile, in 1821, Parry made another voyage from Hudson Strait to Foxe Basin, entering Fury and Hecla Straits on the northern end of Melville Peninsula.

Franklin mounted a second expedition in 1825, this time traveling down the Mackenzie River to its outlet in the Beauford Sea. Here, his party split: Franklin and GEORGE BACK traveled westward, and SIR JOHN RICHARDSON, also part of the original party, eastward. Franklin had hoped to meet with Captain FREDERICK WILLIAM BEECHEY, coming from the west via Alaska, but Beechey had been stopped by ice buildup. Franklin returned to the east after finding and naming Prudoe Bay.

More than 10 years after the "Croker Mountains" incident, Captain John Ross was given a chance to redeem himself by the philanthropist Felix Booth, who, in 1829, financed Ross's next expedition to map the passage. Returning to the region through Lancaster Sound, Ross and his nephew, SIR JAMES CLARK ROSS, sailed southward along the Boothia Peninsula, conducting land excursions as well. The expedition proved to be a long one. In May 1832, with their ship trapped in ice, captain and crew headed northward on foot. After about 300 miles, they came upon the wreck of the *Fury,* a ship Parry had used. They set up camp for the winter, living off the provisions on the abandoned ship. In spring, they made for Lancaster Sound and were rescued in August 1833. Ross was knighted the following year; he was also awarded a prize of £5,000 by Parliament, which he shared with his men.

As of 1837, the mapping of the Northwest Passage remained incomplete. On an expedition for the Hudson's Bay Company in 1837–38, PETER WARREN DEASE and SIR THOMAS SIMPSON sketched in the northern edge of the continent between the Return Islands and Point Barrow. On a second expedition, from 1838 to 1839, they mapped the coast from Coronation Gulf to Rae Strait. Here they just missed solving the riddle of the passage because the strait, which Ross had navigated just a few years earlier, was frozen.

The most publicized story in the search for the Northwest Passage was the final voyage of Sir John Franklin. Leaving England in May 1845 with two ships, the *Erebus* and the *Terror,* he passed through Lancaster Sound, continuing northward past Devon Island into Wellington Channel. After circling Cornwallis Island and navigating Barrow Strait, he headed southward through Peel Strait and into Franklin Strait. In September 1846, pack ice began to form, and off the coast of King William Island in Victoria Strait the Franklin expedition was trapped. In June the following year Franklin died. Some of his men managed to make it south to the Boothia Peninsula, where they perished in 1848. The lack of news from the expedition was slow to generate a response. No rescue missions went out immediately to find Franklin and his crew, since it was known that they had supplies enough for three years. When it became ap-

parent that Franklin was missing, however, there ensued a great outpouring of effort: Between 1847 and 1878, some 50 expeditions set out to find Franklin and to garner information of his expedition's fate (see SEARCHES FOR MISSING EXPLORERS).

Through the Northwest Passage

ROALD ENGELBREGT GRAVNING AMUNDSEN headed the expedition that finally succeeded in traveling the whole length of the Northwest Passage in 1903–06. In making this journey, Amundsen used a small Norwegian fishing boat named the *Gjoa,* which proved easy to handle and quite sturdy. Amundsen was a meticulous planner and had provisions on board to last five years; furthermore, he was careful to take measures to provide safety and comfort for the crew of six. In order to avoid having his ship impounded by creditors, Amundsen left Norway in June 1903, under cover of night and in pouring rain. His expedition succeeded in its mission by sailing beyond Greenland into Baffin Bay and Lancaster Sound, then down Peel Strait into Franklin Strait. Along with the completion of the Northwest Passage, it was Amundsen's objective to locate the North Magnetic Pole. Amundsen wintered at a bay on the south coast of King William Island, and he and his crew made measurements in the area until August 1905. In making the passage, he then proceeded through Rae Strait, staying close to the shore in Queen Maud Gulf, through Dease Strait and Coronation Gulf, into what came to be known as Amundsen Gulf. On September 2, the group became trapped in ice near King Point. While waiting for the thaw, Amundsen made an overland trek through the Yukon. In July 1906, when the ship was finally freed from the ice, he continued along the northern Canadian border, around Alaska, through the Bering Strait, and on to California. Amundsen had been preparing a navigation of the Northwest Passage for years. When he finally accomplished the elusive goal, he made it seem simple.

❖

By the time it had been fully mapped and explored, the Northwest Passage was no longer considered to be the "holy grail" of trade routes. The Panama Canal, completed in Central America in 1914, created a practical water route through the Americas. Activity continued in Arctic waterways, for both trade and military purposes, but not as a passage between oceans. For a time it was thought that the route might be used west to east for carrying oil from the North Slope of Alaska to the eastern United States, but the building of the Alaska pipeline made that notion obsolete. The history of the Northwest Passage and the four-century-long search for it thus has more relevance in the geographic knowledge gained than in pioneering a new water route.

O

ocean currents

Earth's oceans have patterns of movement known as ocean currents. There are several major factors that contribute to the direction of ocean currents: Earth's rotation; wind friction at the surface of the water; variations in water density resulting from differences in temperature and salinity; and the effect of landmasses.

Surface currents flow in several basic circulatory patterns known as gyres. There are numerous regional exceptions, with many branch and feeder currents helping circulate waters. Surface currents are classified by intensity as "streams," the fastest at two to four miles per hour; the slower "drifts"; or the barely perceptible "creeps." Tidal currents, a type of surface current, are shaped by tide, the alternate rise and fall of waters caused by the gravitational effect of the Moon, Sun, and, to a lesser extent, other celestial bodies. There are also flow patterns in the deep ocean, including immense underwater cascades, or cataracts, that develop when cold water near the ocean floor spills over the edge of one ocean basin into another.

The TRADE WINDS are the basic wind systems in the Atlantic, the Pacific, and the Indian Oceans in both the Northern Hemisphere and Southern Hemisphere. In the Northern Hemisphere, they circulate in a clockwise direction, while in the Southern Hemisphere they move counterclockwise. They contribute significantly to the circular motion of the oceans. Another significant factor is the Coriolis effect (or, Coriolis force or Coriolis acceleration), named for its dis-

coverer Gaspar Coriolis, a 19th-century French civil engineer. This is an apparent force on winds, cloud, and aircraft caused by the rotation of Earth under them, such that their motion is deflected clockwise in the Northern Hemisphere and counterclockwise in the Southern Hemisphere, although speed is unaffected. The Coriolis effect arises from the fact that, because of the higher pressures at higher altitudes of the warm air masses near the EQUATOR relative to those at the same altitudes to the north, an airflow toward the NORTH POLE and the SOUTH POLE occurs. In the Northern Hemisphere this flow is deflected by friction to the right or eastward as Earth's surface rotates from west to east beneath it. The effect is zero at the equator and increases with increasing latitude; it is responsible for the prevailing westerly winds over North America. When winds and the Coriolis effect interact with the continents, the major circular current systems of the ocean, or gyres, are created. It is useful to remember that meteorologists name winds for the direction from which they come, and oceanographers cite the direction in which currents go.

The surface waters of the Atlantic have two large gyres, one in the North Atlantic and one in the South Atlantic. The currents of the North Atlantic, including the North Equatorial Current, the Canaries Current, and the GULF STREAM, flow in a clockwise direction, again caused by heating at the equator, which causes ocean water to move northward at the same time as it is being carried eastward by Earth's rotation. The Gulf Stream is thought to have been slowed in the past by warming of North Atlantic waters, perhaps contributing to the ice ages. The currents of the South Atlantic, including the South Equatorial Current, Brazil Current, and Benguela Current, flow in a counterclockwise direction.

The North Pacific has a clockwise current system divided into four main sections. In the north is the North Pacific Current. This feeds the California Current, which becomes the North Equatorial Current, and then the Japan (Kuroshio) Current. The South Pacific has currents rotating in a counterclockwise direction, from the Antarctic Drift, to the Peru Current, and the South Equatorial Current, which is split into three parts by Australia and New Guinea.

In its southern regions, the Indian Ocean has counterclockwise currents similar to those of the Atlantic and Pacific. These include the South Equatorial Current, the Mozambique Current, and the West Australian Current. In the north, the currents are dominated by the seasonal monsoon winds.

In the higher latitudes of the Northern and Southern Hemispheres are counter-rotating gyres, one rotating counterclockwise in Arctic regions and one rotating clockwise in Antarctic regions. The Antarctic Circumpolar Current (West Wind Drift) encircles the globe, merging the waters of the Atlantic, Pacific, and Indian Oceans without interference of land.

Just to the north of the equator, in all three oceans, there runs an eastward-flowing equatorial countercurrent. When the two westward-flowing currents from each hemisphere meet land near the equator, water pressure builds up. Some of the water flows north and some flows south. A third current is formed in the middle, encouraged by the band of upwelling air in the region known as the DOLDRUMS. The doldrums are relatively calm and, combined with the slow-moving equatorial countercurrents, have been feared by sailors for centuries.

Once a current system was understood, it could be used to great advantage by the skilled navigator. By taking a route in harmony with a strong current, the sailor can add several knots to the speed of his ship. One of Italian mariner CHRISTOPHER COLUMBUS's accomplishments on his first transatlantic journey was using the Gulf Stream to return to Europe in 1493. The first charts to show ocean currents were drafted in about 1665.

Oceania

The term *Oceania* refers to a vast expanse of islands in the tropical and the subtropical regions of the Pacific Ocean. The islands of Oceania are divided into three main groups—Melanesia, Micronesia, and Polynesia. They are differentiated by the physical characteristics of the islands, as well as by the inhabitants on them. Of the physical characteristics, the islands of Oceania are of two basic types—volcanic and coral. The volcanic islands are almost always the larger, and the only ones with mountains. They are primarily composed of basalt, a black volcanic rock. The coral islands, also called atolls, have a limestone base formed from the skeletons of the coral animal. These are small, low-lying, and have limited resources, although some are large enough to sustain human populations. The formation of atolls is not completely understood geologically, but it is believed that they, too, have a volcanic origin, their underwater formations offering corals a place to grow. When the volcanic substrate was eroded, or otherwise retreated to the ocean floor, the coral would continue to expand upon its base. In all, the islands of Oceania number some 25,000, only a few thousand of which are named.

In the west, Oceania begins where the Moluccas (SPICE ISLANDS) end. One of the largest of its islands, New Guinea, marks the western extent of Melanesia. The name *Melanesia*—based on the Greek roots for "black islands"—refers to their volcanic origin. Extending east and south, Melanesia includes the Bismarck Archipelago, the Solomon Islands, the Santa Cruz Islands, the New Hebrides, New Caledonia, and the Fiji Island group. To the north of Melanesia, yet forming an arc to the southeast, are the islands of Micronesia. The name *Micronesia* is from the Greek for "small islands." Micronesia contains the Mariana Islands in the northwest, the Caroline Islands to the south, the Marshall Islands to the east and the Gilbert and Ellice groups. The name *Polynesia* means "many islands." Polynesia is the most widely scattered group and also the most diverse morphologically. Polynesia forms a triangle to the east of Melanesia and Micronesia. The HAWAIIAN ISLANDS are at its apex to the north; NEW ZEALAND occupies the southwest corner; and Easter Island is situated in the southeast corner. Island groups and islands in the middle of the triangle include American Samoa, Cook Islands, French Polynesia (Society Islands, Marquesas Islands, Tubuai Islands, Tuamotu Islands, and Gambier Islands), Niue, Pitcairn Islands, Samoa (formerly Western Samoa), Tokelau, Tonga, Tuvalu, and the Wallis and Futuna Islands.

First Inhabitants

The process by which the islands of Oceania were settled is the subject of ongoing study. The best information comes from research on those peoples who are alive today—their physical characteristics, their technologies, religions, and arts. This is not a simple task, for there has been much mixing among the various ethnic groups that migrated to the islands. It is widely accepted that Melanesia was the first section of Oceania to be settled. Between 20,000 and 11,000 years ago, as the last ice age was ending, these islands became isolated from one another and the rest of Southeast Asia. It is believed that the first residents of the area at the time were a group having Negroid characteristics. The stone-age tribes who continue to inhabit the mountains of New Guinea are the best living representatives of these people. As they diffused through the islands, they were met by another strain of aboriginal people, the Negritos, who were shorter of stature and came from the Andaman Islands, the Philippines, and Malaya. These may have been the peoples who also migrated to Africa and became the Mubuti. A third group also figures into the ancient settlement of Melanesia, and these are called the Ainoids; they possess Caucasian features, with lighter skin and hairier bodies. The Ainu people of Northern Japan are a modern incarnation of this stock. There were two or three great waves of migration of these peoples more than 10,000 years ago to the islands of Melanesia, which resulted in the mixing of blood and the creation of a new group. Melanesians of ancient ancestry have dark skin, curly hair, and a strong build. These people were hunter-gatherers and fishermen. They were joined by yet another group, a Proto-Malay people, between 4,000 and 5,000 years ago, who had light brown skin, straighter hair, and broad cheekbones. The Proto-Malays introduced the cultivation of plants and raising animals. They also made more advanced tools from stone.

The settlement of Micronesia was more recent than that of Melanesia, since many of the atolls of the region had yet to be formed when Melanesia was becoming populated. Micronesia was probably settled around 5,000 years ago, as the Proto-Malays swept into Melanesia. As the former Melanesians came upon these smaller, less fertile islands, they adapted their lifestyles to the resources available. They were no longer able to make pottery, and agriculture was more limited, so they became more practiced in the arts of the sea. Boat-building, seafaring, and navigation became the center of the culture in Micronesia.

The islands of Polynesia were populated last, probably starting with the Marquesas. It is generally held that the Polynesians originated in Southeast Asia, although some scholars believe they migrated to the region from the Americas. They show characteristics of a mixture of ethnic groups, with Asian and Caucasian features most apparent.

Arrival of Europeans

The European discovery of Oceania occurred in the early 16th century. The arrival of Europeans to the South Pacific was inspired by the SPICE TRADE, which had been monopolized by Arab merchants. The Portuguese were the first Europeans to arrive in the region, and it may have been Antonio d'Abreu who first saw Oceania when he made the European discovery of New Guinea in 1511. Commercial interests were paramount, however, and, after setting up operations in the Spice Islands, the Portuguese carried out few explorations of islands to the east. The Spanish, who had been excluded from the Portuguese route around Africa, es-

tablished the westward route to the Pacific in 1520, when FERDINAND MAGELLAN rounded South America. He made the European discovery of the Marianas Islands the next year.

In later years, growing commercial competition between Portugal and Spain led to growing knowledge of the South Pacific Islands. The Spanish took the lead. In 1528, ÁLVARO DE SAAVEDRA CERÓN found parts of the Caroline and the Marshall groups. In hopes of finding the GREAT SOUTHERN CONTINENT (Terra Australis), ÁLVARO DE MENDAÑA, also working for Spain, came upon the Solomon Islands in 1567. On a later expedition in 1595, he found the Marquesas and the Santa Cruz Islands. De Mendaña died on this journey, and command was assumed by his pilot, PEDRO FERNÁNDEZ DE QUIRÓS, who proved to be one of Oceania's more successful explorers, and, on his voyage of 1605–06, he made the European discovery of islands in the Samoa group, the Cook group, and the New Hebrides.

Other European nations began exploring the region for new markets. The Dutch began to challenge the Portuguese in the Spice Islands and started to reap great profits. WILLEM CORNELIS SCHOUTEN, who sailed for the DUTCH EAST INDIA COMPANY, discovered the Bismarck Archipelago in 1616. ABEL JANSZOON TASMAN, another Dutchman working for the same company, made the European discovery of New Zealand, parts of the Friendly Islands, and the Fiji group on his expedition of 1642–43. The other great Dutch explorer to navigate the waters of Oceania was JAKOB ROGGEVEEN, who located Easter Island and islands in the Samoan chain in 1722.

Growing Knowledge

Though they were late in arriving, the British made important contributions to the exploration of Oceania. Improved navigational technology helped fix the position of islands that had been discovered and rediscovered, names were sorted out, and more accurate maps were made. In his expedition of 1764–66, JOHN BYRON explored previously uncharted islands in the Marshalls and Marianas. SAMUEL WALLIS and PHILIP CARTERET were commissioned by the British Admiralty to journey to the Pacific in 1766; Wallis went on to make the European discovery of Tahiti, part of the Society Island group; Carteret made the European discovery of Pitcairn Island. Their findings were followed up by the most tireless and successful of all the explorers of Oceania and the Pacific, JAMES COOK. Cook visited the Society Islands and New Zealand on his first Pacific voyage of 1768–71. On his second Pacific voyage, in 1772–75, he returned to those islands again and visited New Caledonia and the New Hebrides. Cook's greatest accomplishments were made on his third Pacific voyage of 1776 to 1780. It was then that he made the European discovery of the Hawaiian Islands and charted the Cook and the Friendly Islands.

Modern Oceania

Because of their wide range, and the minute size of some of the islands, the complete cataloging of Oceania did not take place until the advent of SATELLITE technology. Their populations are still in flux, as atolls become depleted of resources, and political boundaries are shifted. Colonization has had a profound effect on the native peoples, because of foreign diseases, slavery, new religions, and other cultural practices. The human population of 1.2 million is still largely indigenous, with only 20 percent Asian and 7 percent European stock. Oceania has exported agricultural products such as copra (from the coconut), fruits, and timber. It has also given up her mineral deposits to the west, including phosphates. Today, tourism presents the best hope for a sustainable economy on many of the islands of Oceania.

See also PACIFIC OCEAN, EXPLORATION OF THE; POLYNESIAN EXPLORATION.

oceanography and exploration

Oceanography is the study of the world's oceans and makes use of all the scientific disciplines in studying them and studying their interactions with land and atmosphere. As HYDROGRAPHY—the surveying, charting, and sounding of water bodies—oceanography is a branch of geography.

It is often said that we know less about the world's oceans than we do about space. To deep-sea explorers, the water pressure in ocean depths presents technical challenges that rival those of walking on the Moon. Underwater exploration is also a resource-intense activity, involving significant risks and uncertain reward. In recent decades deep-sea risks to both life and equipment have been reduced but by no means eliminated. For these reasons, the active environment of the undersea world has yet to be comprehensively explored, and there are still many species of plants and animals yet to be discovered.

Four Oceanographic Specialties

In order to allow for precise study of the world's oceans, oceanography has been divided into four principal specialties. One is physical oceanography, which is concerned with the motion of water in the oceans, from fast-moving OCEAN CURRENTS to the slower mixing processes that take place. The study of winds and temperatures are central to this specialty. Another division of oceanography is chemical oceanography. This field examines the chemical composition of seawater and its local variations, as well as all chemical reactions that occur in the ocean (and between the ocean and the ocean floor). As salinity (salt content) varies with temperature, the disciplines of chemical and physical oceanography intersect frequently. The third type of study, geological oceanography, looks at the changing topography of the ocean floor, in the past and present. The bottom of the ocean is an active place and at least as varied in morphology as surface land. Finally, biological oceanography is the study of the flora and fauna living in the ocean. Water temperature, nutrients in the water, and conditions on the ocean's floor all influence which species thrive in which seas. For example, in the process of upwelling, winds generate surface currents that draw cool, nutrient-rich water from the ocean's bottom, creating favorable conditions for the development of plankton, which plays a critical part in the food chain for all other ocean life. Perhaps even more than in terrestrial systems, ocean subspecies are interconnected: The study and understanding of a single species is extremely difficult in isolation.

The Foundations of Oceanography

Humankind's study of the oceans began for practical reasons. The ancients traveled on the seas for a variety of purposes, including migration, trade, warfare, fishing, and tourism. To make these activities safer, travelers sought to understand the oceans' weather conditions and hazards. The MEDITERRANEAN SEA, a relatively hospitable body of water, served as an ideal laboratory for ancient peoples, such as the Minoans, Egyptians, Phoenicians, and Greeks, to practice their sea craft and to learn about the oceans, starting with the mariners, but also pursued by scholars, especially among the Greeks. The type of ancient text known as a PERIPLUS (plural form, *peripli*), associated especially with the Greeks and Romans, served as sailing and harbor guides, describing landmarks, harbors, anchorages, watering places, and winds and currents of familiar regions.

In the fifth century B.C., Greek philosopher Parmenides hypothesized that the Earth was round. At that time, there was much speculation concerning what lay at the edges of the world, such as unbearably frigid zones and whirlpools. As it developed, Greek geography became more accurate and detailed. ERATOSTHENES, a mathematician, astronomer, and geographer, calculated the circumference of Earth with good precision in about 250 B.C. The ratio of land to ocean and the geography and geology of coastlines were of interest to later Greek scholars such as STRABO, who, in about A.D. 18, theorized that one could circumnavigate the globe (see CIRCUMNAVIGATION OF THE WORLD) and wrote the work known as *Geographia*. The Greeks also began to classify living things into groups and subgroups and recognized the difference between oceanic mammals, such as whales, dolphins, and fish.

One aspect of oceanic exploration that has always depended more on the courage and fortitude of the individual than on the precepts of science and technology is the art of free diving. Archaeological evidence from Mesopotamia (in the form of shells that could only have been collected from the ocean floor) demonstrates that man has been free diving since at least 4500 B.C. Decorative objects made from mother-of-pearl were popular in Egypt starting about 3200 B.C., which indicates that harvesting the oysters from which these decorative objects were made was an industry in its own right. Collecting sponges from the ocean bottom for various practical uses has been an activity of many ancient peoples. The Greeks are perhaps the most famous for their sponge diving, an endeavor that continues to this day.

Superstitions of the Middle Ages slowed the advancement of all the sciences, including oceanography. When HENRY THE NAVIGATOR, prince of Portugal, developed the CARAVEL to navigate the waters along the west coast of Africa in the 15th century, oceanography underwent a resurgence, again for practical reasons. Trade with the East was the goal, and maritime transportation, the means. Inclement weather and dangerous coastlines were merely obstacles to overcome. Europeans learned of the monsoon winds of the Indian Ocean from the Arab Muslims, who had been trading in the East for centuries. Ocean currents, which sailors always sought to take advantage of, became more important in navigation. In the late 15th century, Italian CHRISTOPHER COLUMBUS, who was innovative in many areas of seamanship, used the GULF STREAM to return to Spain, the sponsoring country of his expeditions. In the 17th century, on the way around Africa to the SPICE ISLANDS (the Moluccas), the Dutch discovered the "roaring forties," winds which send a sailing ship speedily on its way eastward.

Pioneers of Oceanography

As trade routes were established, and the hydrography of ports and dangerous waters were mapped, ocean science began to be developed more independently. Englishman JAMES COOK, an excellent hydrographer in his day, is often credited with helping to legitimize study of ocean geography as a scientific inquiry in its own right. In 1759–60, working for his homeland of England, he mapped the lower portion of the St. Lawrence River and its outlets in northeastern North America. He returned to the region in 1763 and spent three years mapping the coast of Newfoundland. Cook is most famous, however, for his three expeditions to the Pacific Ocean, between 1768 and 1780. These voyages included explorations to the northern Arctic and the southern Antarctic regions. A staff of scientists traveled with him to make observations of the physical condition of the seas and to collect specimens of living creatures. JOHANN REINHOLD FORSTER, a German naturalist, made some of the earliest oceanographic studies, discovering differences in ocean temperature at different depths, the key to understanding the genesis of ocean currents and ultimately worldwide weather patterns. Cook was greatly aided in the accurate recording of his data by the use of the CHRONOMETER, which had recently been invented. Using the chronometer, Cook was able to compute longitude accurately, which then enabled him to map more precisely the location of land, islands, currents, and weather patterns.

Another pioneer in oceanography was Frenchman LOUIS-FERDINAND MARSIGLI. In 1706–08, while living in southern France, he surveyed and studied the Mediterranean's coastline and floor, including the ocean's waves, tides, and currents. He also collected wildlife specimens, especially corals, and examined them under a microscope.

German naturalist and traveler ALEXANDER VON HUMBOLDT had a keen sense of the physical world, and his scientific inquiries led to the development of many of the basic concepts in geography and meteorology. During his extensive travels in South America at the turn of the 19th century, he observed the cool, humid climate of Peru and rightly made the connection between Peru's climate and a low-temperature current generated by the southern winds.

In 1770, Benjamin Franklin published a map of the Gulf Stream, using information he had obtained from whalers. For this he is credited with having originated oceanography in America. His pioneering study of detailed records—that is, ships' logs as an aid to oceanography—yielded the practical benefit of decreasing shipping times for merchant vessels. Another American innovator, MATTHEW FONTAINE MAURY, working for the U.S. Navy, studied the interaction between the weather and currents in the Atlantic Ocean. In 1842, the navy employed him as chart-keeper, which provided him with a wealth of material to study. The routes he designed made sea travel much more efficient. His 1855 book, *The Physical Geography of the Sea,* dealing with currents and depth soundings, is considered the first textbook of modern oceanography.

Englishman EDWARD FORBES took a multidisciplinary approach to the study of the sea. Trained in geology, biology, and paleontology, Forbes described the different layers of ocean and the life that inhabited them. In 1850, he postulated that beyond 1,800 feet below sea level, in what he labeled the Azoic zone, no life could exist. From a sample dredged on the ocean floor and preserved in alcohol, he came to believe in a primordial ooze that gave rise to life as we know it. It was later realized that his gelatinous ooze was a precipitate of calcium sulfate, caused by a reaction between the alcohol and seawater. Despite some of his wrong conclusions, Forbes has been referred to as the "father of marine biology" because of his focus on marine life and his methodology.

The *Challenger* Expedition

Several factors led the British government, in cooperation with the ROYAL SOCIETY, to sponsor the voyage of the *Challenger* in 1872–76. Though scientists had made oceanographic trips before it, the *Challenger* expedition is considered the beginning of serious ocean exploration. The controversy that Forbes had generated with his theories and

Britain's desire to maintain a lead in ocean science helped bring about the journey's funding. The leader of the expedition was SIR CHARLES WYVILLE THOMSON, a Scottish naturalist who had previous experience in ocean exploration, including dredging the North Atlantic. Among the scientific staff was Scottish chemist John Young Buchanan and Canadian John Murray, who would later play the key role of analyzing data from the voyage.

The *Challenger,* captained by SIR GEORGE STRONG NARES, departed Portsmouth on December 21, 1872. She had equipment on board to make meteorological, hydrographic, and magnetic measurements, as well as to conduct dredging operations. After taking readings in the North Atlantic, the ship proceeded to the South Atlantic and then on to the Pacific. The journey lasted three and a half years, covering 68,890 nautical miles. On its way, the expedition made 492 depth soundings, including one of 26,850 feet off the coast of Guam, a record that surpassed any previously imagined. The crew recorded temperatures at both the ocean's surface and in deep water, and took detailed measurements at 362 points concerning currents, water composition, and marine life. More than 4,700 new species of plants and animals were collected as well. From the dredging operations, Forbes's theory that life did not exist on the ocean floor was debunked. By the journey's end, on May 24, 1876, at Spithead, the ship had circumnavigated the world, but the bulk of the work remained to be done. Twenty-three years later, when the final report was compiled, it contained 29,500 pages bound in 50 volumes. The expedition, for all the knowledge gained, revealed how little humankind actually knew about the world's oceans.

National Expeditions

The *Challenger* expedition inspired other countries to explore the ocean as well. In 1874–76, the German ship *Gazelle* circumnavigated the world for oceanographic studies. The Russian ship *Vitiaz* also sailed around the world in 1886–89. Between 1890 and 1898, the Austrian ship *Pola* did important work on shorter trips in the Mediterranean Sea and RED SEA. One of the leaders in oceanography during this time was Alexander Agassiz, a Swiss-American businessman who used his fortune to pursue an interest in ocean topography. His travels, from 1877 to 1905, took him over 100,000 miles through the Caribbean Sea and the Pacific, mapping the ocean floor. During this time Agassiz developed new techniques in sounding and dredging. Another wealthy patron of oceanography was Albert I, prince of Monaco, active from 1848 to 1922. He was a naturalist and oceanographer who studied currents and topography and gave money to support research in many countries. Norwegian explorer FRIDTJOF NANSEN pioneered navigation in the Arctic Ocean on his expedition between 1893 and 1896. With his design of the *Fram,* with which he intended to drift across the NORTH POLE, he demonstrated that a ship could survive being frozen in ice as it moves. Other nations that launched oceanographic studies at this time were the Netherlands, France, Japan, and the United States.

Expanding Technologies

Oceanography entered a new era in 1925 with the German ship *Meteor.* This craft was the first to use new electronic technology to take continuous soundings of the ocean floor while in motion. For two years, *Meteor* crossed and recrossed the Atlantic, mapping the bottom. Its studies gave oceanographers a much clearer picture of the varied terrain that exists there. The results of these expeditions also gave Germany an advantage in SUBMARINE warfare during World War II. Other technological developments expanded the scope of oceanography. In the 1930s, Americans CHARLES WILLIAM BEEBE and Otis Barton invented the BATHYSPHERE, a type of SUBMERSIBLE, making the DIVING BELL, nonpressurized and with an attached oxygen supply, obsolete. In the 1940s–1950s, Swiss AUGUSTE PICCARD improved on its design with the BATHYSCAPH. His son JACQUES ERNEST-JEAN PICCARD continued work on the bathyscaph, and, in 1960, he reached the bottom of the MARIANAS TRENCH in the Pacific, the deepest point on Earth. Remotely operated vehicles (ROVs) of varying designs have also become essential equipment in oceanographic studies. Moreover, the evolution of the DIVING SUIT has given divers greater freedom underwater. Developments in oceanography and technology have helped make possible recent advancements in underwater archaeology (see ARCHAEOLOGY AND EXPLORATION).

Oceanographic Institutions

A number of oceanographic institutions have been founded over the years. Among the first was the marine biological station at Naples, Italy, established in 1872. The Scripps Institution of Oceanography at La Jolla, California, was founded in 1901 and later became part of the University of California. The Oceanographic Museum of Monaco was established in 1910, and the Oceanographic Institution of Woods Hole in Massachusetts was founded in 1930.

International Cooperation

In the mid-20th century, a cooperative spirit grew around oceanographic research, with international institutions realizing that the ocean ties mankind to a common fate. Nowhere was this more apparent than in conducting the INTERNATIONAL GEOPHYSICAL YEAR (IGY) in 1957–58. For this project, 37 nations contributed the use of 80 ships to study the world's oceans. Scientists observed currents, tracked ice floes, collected meteorological data, and conducted magnetic surveys. Further, teams tested new oceanographic equipment and performed extensive mapping. The

Jacques Cousteau peers out of a two-person underwater observation chamber on the deck of the *Calypso,* as it docks in New York City for the 1969 International Oceanographic Congress. *(Library of Congress, Prints and Photographs Division [LC-USZ62-119520])*

IGY accomplished the most thorough investigation of the Indian Ocean done until that time. Members of the project also discovered that water at the bottom of the sea near Antarctica was as old as 2,000 years. French oceanographer and inventor JACQUES-YVES COUSTEAU, who founded the Cousteau Society in 1973, increased awareness of the world's oceans through his writings, documentaries, and television show.

❖

As oceanography enters the 21st century, the main practical questions involve the effects of pollution and the sustainability of fishing stocks. With ever-larger oil tankers plying the world's oceans, the safety of these ships and the long-term damage to the oceans from the regular spills that occur, are debated. With the world's human population increasing, and the technology available to harvest large quan-

tities of marine life, the issue of fish population maintenance has become more important. Regions where cod and whales, for example, were once abundant are now regulated by severe restrictions or bans on harvest due to overfishing. The balanced use of the ocean has led to another field of study, marine policy, which seeks to integrate the acquired knowledge of the past and present to draft sensible international treaties.

See also ATLANTIC OCEAN, EXPLORATION OF THE; GEOGRAPHY AND CARTOGRAPHY; INDIAN OCEAN, EXPLORATION OF THE; PACIFIC OCEAN, EXPLORATION OF THE.

octant   See QUADRANT; SEXTANT.

Ophir (King Solomon's mines)

Ophir is a city or region or mine mentioned in the Bible's Old Testament, the location of which is not known. It is the place of "King Solomon's mines," the source of great quantities of gold. Solomon, king of the ancient Hebrews from about 972 to 932 B.C., reportedly entered into a contract with Hiram II, the king of Tyre, a city of the Phoenicians in present-day Lebanon, to build and navigate ships for an expedition. From the port city of Ezion-geber on the Gulf of Aqaba, the northeastern arm of the RED SEA, the fleet sailed to the land of Ophir. The expedition is said to have lasted three years and returned with gold as well as silver, gemstones, sandalwood, ivory, apes, and peacocks.

The story of Ophir, as well as Tarshish, another land mentioned in the Bible relating to King Solomon's mines, proved an inspiration to explorers throughout history. MARCO POLO associated it with Japan; CHRISTOPHER COLUMBUS thought he might find it in the Caribbean Sea; ÁLVARO DE MENDAÑA named the Solomon Islands in the West Pacific Ocean after Solomon because of his belief he had found Ophir and Tarshish.

Ophir's location has also been theorized as present-day Yemen on the south coast of the Arabian Peninsula; various locations in Africa, such as West Africa (the Gold Coast), Ethiopia, or Zimbabwe; the Indian subcontinent; the Ural Mountains in Asia; and even Australia or NEW ZEALAND. A recent theory holds that the site of Ophir is present-day Saudi Arabia, in the mountainous area, inland from the RED SEA, between Mecca and Medina, known as Mahd adh Dhahab ("cradle of gold"). Geological studies have revealed a large-scale ancient mining operation there with traces of gold remaining. Moreover, the region is along a 4,000-year-old trade route running south from the Gulf of Aqaba.

See also LEGENDS AND EXPLORATION; PHOENICIAN EXPLORATION.

Orinoco River

The Orinoco River, one of South America's longest rivers, flows some 1,500 miles from the Serra Parima highlands in southern Venezuela, westward then northward, forming part of the Colombia-Venezuela border with its branch, the Guaviare. It then arcs northeastward to Venezuela's Atlantic coast. (If the Guaviare branch is included, the Orinoco stretches 1,700 miles.) The chief tributary of the Orinoco is the Apure River, which, like the Guaviare, is part of the watershed of the ANDES MOUNTAINS. The Orinoco's waters are also augmented by the Ventuari, Arauca, Meta, Mawaca, Caura, and Caroni Rivers. The Casiquiare, a unique river in that it does not have a reversible current but flows over marshland, forms a natural canal between the Orinoco and the Río Negro, a branch of the larger AMAZON RIVER. The Orinoco begins as a thin stream in the mountains, gradually expanding with runoff from rainwater and its many tributaries. It cascades over rocks, down a steep-sided valley, through rain forests and across the Llanos—the plains—of central Venezuela. The river ends in a wide marshy delta of about 7,800 square miles, bounded by streams, the Corosimi and the Vagre, with the Corosimi considered the main stream of the river. Natural canals cut across the delta, which is made of giant sandbars with islands of fertile soil. The total drainage area of the Orinoco system is some 450,000 square miles. The Orinoco, four miles wide on average, is navigable for ships about 260 miles, and for smaller boats about 1,000 miles.

First Approaches

On his third voyage in 1498, after discovering the island of Trinidad, Italian mariner CHRISTOPHER COLUMBUS, backed by Spanish interests, reached the mainland coast of South America at the Gulf of Paria, near the Orinoco delta. Columbus stopped to explore the coast of present-day Venezuela westward before sailing back to the island of Hispaniola (present-day Haiti and Dominican Republic). The next year, Spaniard ALONSO DE OJEDA, who had commanded one of Columbus's ships during his second expedition to the WEST INDIES, was given permission to explore the mainland coast Columbus had explored. While Spaniard AMERIGO VESPUCCI, part of Ojeda's expedition, explored south and east from their landing point five degrees north of the EQUATOR, Ojeda followed Columbus's track, exploring north and west. He gave the name Venezuela, or "Little Venice" to the coastal region on seeing a Native American settlement built in the water on piers. Ojeda made several attempts to colonize Venezuela, all of which were unsuccessful.

The later colonization attempts by Spanish conquistador DIEGO DE ORDAZ, beginning in 1530, led to a greater European understanding of the Orinoco. Ordaz sailed with Spanish expeditions to the West Indies in his early 20s. He served with Alonso de Ojeda in his conquest of parts of present-day Colombia and Panama in 1509 and with DIEGO DE VELÁSQUEZ in 1511 in his conquest of Cuba. He also served as an officer under HERNÁN CORTÉS in 1519–21, during the Spanish conquest of Mexico. After returning to Spain to report to King Charles I (Holy Roman Emperor Charles V), Ordaz was himself commissioned by the monarch to explore, conquer, and colonize the area of the coast of South America, called Venezuela, from the mouth of the Amazon River to Cape Vela. Ordaz sailed from Spain with three ships and 500 men. While he was able to locate the mouth of the Amazon River, he did not find a suitable landing place and sailed westward, into the Gulf of Paria. Native peoples told him of another great river, the Orinoco and, by June 1531, he had located its delta. Ordaz entered the Orinoco's main outlet and explored upriver about 800 miles to its junction with the Meta River. He lost many men in the thick jungles, to disease, to the poison-tipped darts of the native peoples, and to the treacherous terrain.

El Dorado and the Orinoco

The native peoples told tales of a land of immense wealth in gold peopled by a white race like the Europeans that the natives called "Guiana," somewhere in the highlands around the Orinoco. Ordaz searched vainly for this city of gold before returning to the coast. The stories convinced many of the existence of an empire to rival that of the Aztec Indians of Mexico and the Inca Indians of Peru, which supposedly had a capital city, Manoa, paved with gold and which glittered with jewels. This was one of the many tales that came to be associated with the mythical land of EL DORADO, which inspired numerous journeys on the Orinoco, with Spanish and other Europeans penetrating the dense jungles of the interior.

In the 1530s, several Germans who had been sent by Charles I of Spain to colonize Venezuela—AMBROSIUS ALFINGER, GEORG HOHERMUTH VON SPEYER, AND NIKOLAUS FEDERMANN—explored the inland plains and highlands and the Orinoco River system. Spaniard GONZALO JIMÉNEZ DE QUESADA searched around the Magdalena River in Colombia in 1536. In 1541, Jiménez de Quesada's brother, Hernán Perez de Quesada, traveled along the plains of the Orinoco. Later, from 1569–72, Jiménez de Quesada himself led a second expedition in search of El Dorado in eastern Colombia as far as the confluence of the Orinoco with the Guaviare River. To the south, in 1560, LOPE DE AGUIRRE, a Spanish conquistador, joined an expedition to search for El Dorado led by PEDRO DE URSÚA in the Amazon Basin. After a dangerous crossing of the Andes and following the Huallaga and Marañón Rivers, Aguirre incited a mutiny and murdered de Ursúa. The mutineers sailed down the Amazon, then crossed at some point somehow to the Orinoco. Aguirre led the mutineers down the Orinoco to the Caribbean coast before he was captured and beheaded.

In 1584, another Spaniard, ANTONIO DE BERRÍO, married to the daughter of the Spanish colonial governor of what is now eastern Colombia, embarked on his own search for El Dorado and ended up searching the Orinoco region for 10 years. In 1595, he was taken prisoner on the island of Trinidad by SIR WALTER RALEIGH, an Englishman who had been granted permission from Queen Elizabeth I to find the riches of Guiana for the English. Based on Berrío's intelligence, Raleigh embarked from Trinidad to explore the Orinoco. He took 100 men in small boats up the different branches of the river until its confluence with the Caroni, one of the rivers bounding the Orinoco's delta, about 100 miles from the sea. Raleigh and his men also explored other tributaries and Lake Parime. Shortage of supplies and tropical fever led him to abandon his search, and he crossed the Cano Macareo, one of many natural canals across the delta, and sailed back to England. In 1596, Raleigh published his account of his voyage through the Orinoco called *The Discoverie of the Beautiful Empire of Guiana, with a Relation of the Great and Golden City of Manoa . . . in the Year 1595.*

After James I ascended the throne, Raleigh was implicated in a plot against the king and sentenced to death in the Tower of London. He was released in 1616, after convincing King James to allow him to mount another expedition in search of El Dorado. In Trinidad in 1617, he was stricken with a fever. His son Walter and Lawrence Kemys continued up the Orinoco. Before very long, however, they entered Spanish territory and attacked the settlement of San Thomé. Raleigh's son was killed, and Kemys committed suicide. Raleigh himself returned to England, without having found Indian riches and having disobeyed the king's order not to attack the Spanish. In 1618, he was beheaded.

Colonial Boundaries

Raleigh's last expedition was the last great search for El Dorado, but the Orinoco continued to be explored for more mundane reasons. Of constant difficulty to the European nations was the determination of the boundaries of colonial territories, a source of strife among them. The Spanish established the Boundary Line Commission of Yturriaga and Solano, which surveyed the inland areas of Venezuela and other parts of the Spanish possessions in South America from 1757 to 1763, during which José Solano and Díaz de la Fuente made careful surveys of the Orinoco, especially its upper waters. The investigation confirmed the existence of the naturally formed Casiquiare canal.

In the Name of Science

German naturalist ALEXANDER VON HUMBOLDT and French botanist Aimé Bonpland had planned to travel to Egypt in 1798, but Napoléon's conquest changed their plans. After the pair made a survey of Spain's central plateau, Spanish king Charles IV gave Humboldt and Bonpland permission to explore Spanish possessions in the Americas. In November 1799, the pair left Caracas in Venezuela to study the Orinoco. Humboldt studied the fauna of the Orinoco, including the capybara, the largest rodent in the world, as well as the egg-laying habits of turtles along one of the Orinoco's tributaries. He charted the course of the upper Orinoco and the Río Negro, making a CANOE voyage through the Casiquiare canal.

In 1849, British naturalist ALFRED RUSSEL WALLACE carried out ornithological research along the Río Negro and into the Orinoco by way of the Casiquiare. Still another explorer of the Orinoco was Francisco Michelena y Rojas, a Venezuelan diplomat and journalist. He traveled across the world, through America, Europe, Asia, and Africa from 1822 to 1842. He was commissioned in 1856 to explore the Río Negro. In the course of his expedition, he crossed the Casiquiare canal into the Orinoco and ascended the river 170 miles upstream, and a few miles up the Mawaca, one of its tributaries.

❖

The Orinoco was of lesser importance for trade and transport than the Amazon, and today remains sparsely traveled. An important port city on the river is Ciudad Bolívar—formerly known as Angostura for "narrow," because it is situated 373 miles from its mouth where the river narrows—founded in 1764 in northeastern Venezuela. Many of the river's tributaries remained unexplored into the 20th century. In 1944, aerial exploration located the river's main source in the Guiana highlands, and later explorations discovered small rivulets considered the river's headwaters.

See also SOUTH AMERICA, EXPLORATION OF.

outrigger

An outrigger is a type of boat with a float attached parallel to the main hull by poles. The term *outrigger* can also refer to the float itself. The attached float or floats gives the craft greater stability. Outriggers are made in a variety of configurations. They may be sail-powered, oar-powered, or both. The double-hulled CANOE relates to the concept of the outrigger. The double outrigger has floats extending from both sides for maximum safety. The outrigger can be built to quite large dimensions, more than 100 feet long. Some used in Sri Lanka carry as much as 30 tons of cargo.

Outriggers were unique to the Pacific Ocean and Indian Ocean until their concepts were incorporated into modern boats. The Polynesians and other peoples used them to travel among the islands, and they no doubt played a central role in migrations to NEW ZEALAND, HAWAIIAN ISLANDS, Tahiti, and countless other islands. With the proper skill, an outrigger was next to impossible to sink, a trait that would have encouraged the adventurous to explore. The vessel could also be quite fast, with a speed of 20 knots not uncommon.

See also SHIPBUILDING AND EXPLORATION.

Shown here, in a photograph from about 1922, are outrigger canoes in Hawaii. *(Library of Congress, Prints and Photographs Division [LC-USZ62-105953])*

P

Pacific Ocean, exploration of the

The Pacific Ocean is the largest ocean on the planet, covering nearly a third of Earth's surface, 70 million square miles if adjoining seas are included. It is also the deepest ocean, with an average depth of about 14,000 feet, and contains the deepest point in all the oceans, the Challenger Deep of the MARIANAS TRENCH, at 36,198 feet. The Pacific is bounded by North America and South America in the east; Asia, Indonesia, and Australia in the west; and Antarctica in the south. (Antarctic waters are sometimes referred to as the Southern Ocean.) The BERING STRAIT separates the Pacific from the Arctic Ocean in the north. On rounding South America from the Atlantic Ocean, Portuguese mariner FERDINAND MAGELLAN, sailing for Spain in 1520, gave the waters the name *Pacific,* meaning "peaceful."

The portion north of the EQUATOR, or North Pacific, generally has a clockwise system of OCEAN CURRENTS, such as the Japan (or Kuroshio) Current. The portion south of the equator, the South Pacific, has currents rotating in a counterclockwise pattern.

The Pacific Ocean has more than 25,000 islands of volcanic and coral origin. Many are too small to support human populations, but of those that can, most were settled before the arrival of Europeans. OCEANIA refers to the region where the majority of Pacific islands are found. It is further classified into three groups according to geology and inhabitants: Melanesia, Micronesia, and Polynesia.

The Ancients and the Pacific

There is remarkably little ancient history of Pacific exploration. The Chinese, who bordered the ocean in the west, had large seaworthy ships by about 2800 B.C., which they used to sail into the Indian Ocean for trade with Malaysia, Indonesia, and India, but they were not inclined to venture eastward into the unknown (see CHINESE EXPLORATION). The Romans, who had contact with the Chinese by sea, starting in the first century B.C., had little concept of the vast ocean that lay beyond the Asian shoreline (see ROMAN EXPLORATION). Arab Muslims of the Middle Ages were not known to venture beyond the SPICE ISLANDS (the Moluccas), where the southwestern Pacific Ocean and northeastern Indian Ocean meet (see MUSLIM EXPLORATION). While the Indian Ocean was active with commerce, the Pacific remained largely untested. Even the voyages of CHENG HO for the Ming Dynasty in China in the early 15th century traveled south along Asia's coast to the familiar territory of the Indian Ocean rather than into the open Pacific. The Polynesians became early masters of the Pacific, using a tradition known as "wayfinding" for island-hopping expeditions over great expanses of Polynesia, but they did not document voyages (see NAVIGATION AND EXPLORATION; POLYNESIAN EXPLORATION).

Venetian merchant MARCO POLO, who traveled throughout China in the 13th century, was an early European to bring back word of the Pacific to Europe. He did not see the ocean himself but heard of it from his Chinese hosts. Europeans did not know that continents lay between Europe and Asia until the late 15th century. Even after reaching the Americas in 1492, CHRISTOPHER COLUMBUS, an Italian mariner sailing for Spain, did not let go of the notion that he had in fact crossed the Atlantic Ocean to Asia.

Early European Sightings

Spaniard VASCO NÚÑEZ DE BALBOA made the first definitive European contact with the Pacific. While exploring present-day Panama in Central America with a small army, he saw the ocean on September 25, 1513. He claimed it for Spain, with no way of knowing its extent, and called it the Great South Sea. In 1516, he retraced his footsteps to the Pacific and explored along the Panamanian coast with boats he had built. At this time, Spain was in a heated rivalry with Portugal. The Portuguese had found the route around Africa to the Indian Ocean with the journey of BARTOLOMEU DIAS in 1487, and consequently they claimed exclusive right to trade with India and the Spice Islands. In order to challenge this monopoly, the Spanish needed to find an alternative route. This was the impetus for sponsoring Christopher Columbus on his 1492 expedition. As Spain was exploring the lands in the western Atlantic, they also hired Ferdinand Magellan away from Portugal to find a route around South America to the lucrative SPICE TRADE. They had little idea of the size of the Pacific at this point.

The epic journey of Ferdinand Magellan, from 1519 to 1521, is one of the most well known in the history of exploration. Departing from Spain on September 20, 1519, he made stops in Madeira and the CANARY ISLANDS before exploring the South American coast for a passage to the Pacific. On October 21, 1520, he finally found what would be named the Strait of Magellan (see MAGELLAN, STRAIT OF). In an incredible feat of seamanship, he managed to navigate the strait and entered the Pacific on November 28, 1520. After sailing northward along the South American coast, he found winds that carried his ships westward. The crossing took more than three months, and many of the crew died of SCURVY, caused by malnutrition. In March 1521, the expedition acquired fresh food and water in the Marianas Islands of Micronesia. Magellan was later killed in the Philippines, and command of the expedition eventually fell to JUAN SEBASTIÁN DEL CANO, who reached the Spice Islands. Continuing westward into the Indian Ocean and around Africa into the Atlantic Ocean, he completed the first CIRCUMNAVIGATION OF THE WORLD.

Continuing Spanish Exploration

After several conflicts with Portugal in the EAST INDIES, Spain negotiated for peace, signing the Treaty of Saragossa in 1529, in which Spain acknowledged Portuguese control of the Spice Islands in exchange for a large sum of money. Spain did have possession of the Philippines, however, and it became important to them to find dependable routes between Spanish ter-

ritories in the Pacific and the Americas. This was done with great difficulty and much loss of life. One such expedition, in 1564–65, under MIGUEL LÓPEZ DE LEGAZPI, westward from Mexico, led to the colonization of the Philippines. Alonso de Arellano, who captained one of the ships under Lopez de Legazpi's command, was separated from the fleet and managed to return to the Americas by way of the northeastward-flowing Japan Current. ANDRÉS DE URDANETA, a geographer and priest who had accompanied Lopez de Legazpi, was navigator on a return trip to the Americas in 1565, following the same route. By the 1580s, an annual commercial fleet known as the Manila Galleon made the eastward crossing, carrying trade goods from the Orient to the Americas, from where they were shipped to Spain.

The Portuguese and Spanish both are known to have reached Japan in the 1540s. FERNÃO MENDES PINTO, who worked as a diplomat for the Chinese, and FRANCIS XAVIER, a Spanish missionary, both reached the islands of Japan.

The Spanish had by this time navigated Pacific waters northward from Mexico along the North American coast. In 1542–43, JUAN RODRÍGUEZ CABRILLO and BARTOLOMÉ FERRELO reached the approximate latitude of the present-day Oregon-California border. The Spanish also turned their attention to the South Pacific, with Peru as a launching point. In 1567–69, ÁLVARO DE MENDAÑA and PEDRO SARMIENTO DE GAMBOA led an expedition in search of the GREAT SOUTHERN CONTINENT (Terra Australis)—a continent theorized by the ancients to exist in the Southern Hemisphere balancing out landmasses of the Northern Hemisphere—in the course of which they made the European discovery of the Solomon Islands and Marshall Islands. In a 1595 voyage in search of more lands to colonize, Mendaña, on this expedition accompanied by PEDRO FERNÁNDEZ DE QUIROS, made the European discovery of the Marquesas Islands and Santa Cruz Islands.

Early English Exploration

In the meantime, the English had begun exploring the Pacific. SIR FRANCIS DRAKE headed an expedition in 1577–80, in search of the Great Southern Continent, as well as the western outlet of the Strait of Anian (see ANIAN, STRAIT OF), a fabled NORTHWEST PASSAGE from the Atlantic to the Pacific. He became the first European to navigate Drake's Passage, as the waters between the Atlantic and Pacific came to be known, and explored the west coast of North America as far north as Vancouver Island before continuing westward to the Spice Islands and into the Indian Ocean and back to the Atlantic, completing the first English circumnavigation of the world—and the second altogether.

Dutch Exploration

After declaring independence from Spain in 1581, the Dutch began looking to the Far East for trading opportunities. In 1602, they formed the DUTCH EAST INDIA COMPANY to reap profits from both the Indian Ocean and Pacific lands. In a 1605 expedition for the company, WILLEM JANSZ, while exploring the seas around New Guinea, made the European discovery of Australia, although not realizing they had observed two separate landmasses. (Several months later, LUIS VÁEZ DE TORRES, sailing for Spain, charted the strait, now known as Torres Strait, separating New Guinea from Australia.) In 1611, a Dutch captain named Brouwer used the westerly winds in the high southern latitudes to find a faster route to the East Indies. In 1616, Dirk Hartog made the European discovery of Dirk Hartog's Island and explored Australia's west coast. In 1615–16, JAKOB LE MAIRE and WILLEM SCHOUTEN, sailing for a rival Dutch company, sailed through Drake's Passage around the southern tip of South America, naming it CAPE HORN; they later made the European discovery of the Juan Fernández Islands off the coast of present-day Chile and determined the eastern extent of New Guinea. In 1642, ABEL JANSZOON TASMAN, searching for Terra Australis for the Dutch East India Company, made the European discovery of an island south of Australia, naming it Van Diemen's Land (present-day TASMANIA), as well as NEW ZEALAND, Fiji, and other islands. JAKOB ROGGEVEEN, also in the employ of the Dutch East India Company, made the European discovery of Easter Island and Samoa Island in 1722.

Continuing English Exploration

After Drake's earlier exploits, the next English pioneer in the Pacific was WILLIAM DAMPIER, who had completed a circumnavigation of the world over the years 1670 to 1691. He was chosen to command an ambitious scientific expedition to the Pacific. In 1699–1701, he explored Australia's west and northwest coast (although he had hoped to reach the east coast) and located Dampier Archipelago, then explored New Guinea's east coast and located Dampier Strait between New Guinea and the island of New Britain. His voyage set the precedent for other scientific journeys to the Pacific—one purpose of which was still discovering the Great Southern Continent—including those of JOHN BYRON in 1664–66 and SAMUEL WALLIS and PHILIP CARTERET in 1766–68. Byron explored previously uncharted islands in the Marshall and Mariana island groups. In the course of the Wallis-Carteret expedition, Wallis made the European discovery of Tahiti, and Carteret, of Pitcairn Island.

In the subsequent years, from 1768 to 1780, Englishman JAMES COOK headed three Pacific expeditions, which led to a new understanding of the world's largest ocean. He traveled to both the South Pacific and the North Pacific. Among his accomplishments were charting the coasts of New Zealand, proving that there were in fact two main islands; charting the east coast of Australia; crossing the ANTARCTIC CIRCLE; circumnavigating Earth in southern latitudes and proving that the Great Southern Continent did not exist; charting islands of Oceania not visited since the earlier explorations of other nations in previous centuries, making the European discovery of New Caledonia; making the European discovery of the HAWAIIAN ISLANDS; charting the coastlines of northwestern North America as far north as the Aleutian Islands; and crossing the Bering Strait. A number of renowned scientists traveled with Cook, among them SIR JOSEPH BANKS on Cook's first Pacific expedition. (Banks went on to become president of the ROYAL SOCIETY and helped found the AFRICAN ASSOCIATION.)

French Exploration

In the late 17th century under the auspices of the FRENCH EAST INDIA COMPANY, the French began trading in the Indian Ocean and all the way to China by way of the Pacific. By 1695, they were making trips to the Spanish ports in Chile and Peru. French scientists sometimes traveled on board French trading ships and recorded information. French interest in the Pacific leaned toward the scientific, with commercial and colonial ambitions secondary, since the British navy was superior to theirs. In 1766–69, the same period Wallis and Carteret were on their journey, LOUIS-ANTOINE DE BOUGAINVILLE commanded the first French expedition around the world. The purpose of the government-sponsored scientific expedition was to locate the Great Southern Continent as well as to chart islands in the Pacific. In the western Pacific de Bougainville explored the Solomons and other island groups. Later French scientific expeditions were carried out by JEAN-FRANÇOIS DE GALAUP, comte de La Pérouse, in 1785–88 in the North and South Pacific, and by ANTOINE-RAYMOND-JOSEPH DE BRUNI, chevalier d'Entrecasteaux, in 1791–95 in the South Pacific.

Russian Exploration

Early Russian expeditions, in the meantime, approached from the west overland through SIBERIA, many of them related to the FUR TRADE. By 1639, Russians were known to have reached the Sea of Okhotsk. The earliest recorded sighting of the Bering Strait was by a party of Cossacks under SEMYON IVANOVICH DEZHNEV in 1648. The next century, in 1725–30, Danish VITUS JONASSEN BERING, in service to the Russian navy, led the First Kamchatka Expedition to Siberia's Pacific coast. In 1740–41, Bering headed Russian naval exploration of the Bering Strait, the Gulf of Alaska, Kodiak Island, the Aleutian Islands, and the Commander Islands. In 1785–93, Englishman JOSEPH BILLINGS headed the Russian naval Northern Secret Geographical and Astronomical Expedition in search of the NORTHEAST PASSAGE from Siberia's northeast coast into Bering Strait and further explored the Aleutians and the Gulf of Alaska. In 1803–06, ADAM IVAN RITTER VON KRUSENSTERN headed the first Russian circumnavigation of the world, during which he searched for outlets of both the Northeast Passage and Northwest Passage in the North Pacific.

Antarctica

The last Pacific region to be charted thoroughly was that of Antarctica. James Cook had failed to sight the mainland in his voyage of the late 18th century. The earliest confirmed sightings of the Antarctic mainland in 1820 were made by British naval officer EDWARD BRANSFIELD and American sealer NATHANIEL BROWN PALMER, where Pacific and Atlantic waters meet near the Antarctic Peninsula. German-born Russian naval officer FABIAN GOTTLIEB BENJAMIN VON BELLINGSHAUSEN made the earliest extensive exploration of the high latitudes near the coast in the course of his expedition of 1819–21 (and some claim made the first sighting of the Antarctic mainland). In the ensuing decades, explorers of varying nationalities approached Antarctica along different routes from the Pacific, Atlantic, and Indian Oceans. SIR JAMES CLARK ROSS led the first British scientific expedition to the region since Cook, reaching previously uncharted regions along the Pacific coast, while unsuccessfully searching for the SOUTH MAGNETIC POLE. The South Magnetic Pole was located on the Pacific coast in 1909 by Australian scientist SIR DOUGLAS MAWSON. The Pacific coast of Antarctica proved to be the launching point for the successful attempt to reach the SOUTH POLE by Norwegian ROALD ENGLEBREGT GRAVNING AMUNDSEN in 1910–12.

Oceanography

By the mid-19th century, oceanography—the study of the world's oceans, a branch of geography—had become more scientific in its approach. The English voyage of the *Challenger* under SIR GEORGE STRONG NARES and SIR CHARLES WYVILLE THOMSON in 1872–76 was a breakthrough in knowledge gained. In 1948, during the voyage of the *Challenger II,* the deepest point in the oceans of the world—Challenger Deep in the Marianas Trench—was discovered. In 1960, Swiss scientist JACQUES ERNEST-JEAN PICCARD and U.S. Navy lieutenant Donald Walsh, using the BATHYSCAPH *Trieste,* explored the trench. During the INTERNATIONAL GEOPHYSICAL YEAR (IGY) of 1957–58, 37 nations contributed the use of 80 ships to study the world's oceans (see OCEANOGRAPHY AND EXPLORATION).

❖

In addition to being a link between continents on exploratory expeditions, the Pacific Ocean, with its some 25,000 islands, became a place of exploration unto itself through much of history. It has also proven a challenge to mariners over the centuries—from the ancient Polynesians, to the first circumnavigators, to early scientific explorers such as James Cook, all the way to modern times and explorers of the deepest places on earth.

pack ice (ice pack, pack, pack-ice)

The term *pack ice,* also written *pack-ice,* or the *ice pack,* or simply the *pack,* is one of many terms relating to sea ice in both Arctic and Antarctic waters, much of which freezes over in wintertime, then thaws and breaks up to varying degrees in summertime. The term is sometimes used to denote the general ice field, that is, any extensive area of frozen water, such as that which covers much of the Arctic year-round. (One also sees the term *ice sheet* applied to an ice field of frozen water, but it more often is used to denote a permanent ice field on land.) But, more specifically, the term *pack ice* refers to the mixture of ice created by the annual freezing and thawing of water, along with various types of drifting ice, or DRIFT ICE, from the winter or winters before. The various formations of drift ice are squeezed together as the sea freezes over, often creating jagged shapes in the pack ice.

The term *ice island* refers to stretches of pack ice at least 10 times thicker than most of the ice surrounding it, formed from chunks of ice that once adhered to the shore. The term *ice shelf* is applied to a permanently frozen ice field extending from the Antarctic continent, such as the Ross Ice Shelf, Filchner Ice Shelf, Larson Ice Shelf, and Shackleton Ice Shelf.

At the edge of pack ice, where water is whipped up by sea swells, thick fog often forms. When set in motion by a storm, pack ice grinds together, creating noise. The vast winter pack ice extends hundreds of miles from the year-round frozen waters of the Arctic and from the ice-covered Antarctic continent, beyond the North and South Frigid Zones, invading the North and South Temperate Zones.

In the history of exploration, pack ice has played a role in setting the limits of regions explored or in the destruction of ships. A tragic example in the Arctic is the 1845–47 British expedition of SIR JOHN FRANKLIN, whose ships—the *Erebus* and the *Terror*—became icebound, and the crews eventually perished. Another British expedition, in 1914–17, headed by SIR ERNEST HENRY SHACKLETON, lost its ship—the *Endurance*—to the pack ice off Antarctica, although Shackleton managed to lead his men to safety.

Some explorers, such as Norwegian FRIDTJOF NANSEN in 1893–96, attempted to use pack ice to get closer to a goal—in this case an unsuccessful attempt on the NORTH POLE—having a specially designed ship, with a saucer-shaped hull to withstand the pressure of the ice and ride on top of it—the *Fram* (Forward)—purposely become icebound so that it would drift northward.

Icebreakers, ships with specialized hull designs and reinforced bows, first effectively used in the latter part of the 19th century, have become ever more efficient in pushing through pack ice.

In 1915, Sir Ernest Henry Shackleton's ship the *Endurance* was trapped in Antarctic pack ice. This photograph was probably taken by expedition member Frank Hurley. *(Library of Congress, Prints and Photographs Division [LC-USZ62-104242])*

See also ANTARCTIC, EXPLORATION OF THE; ARCTIC, EXPLORATION OF THE.

padrão

Padrão is the Portuguese word for "pillar." Starting in the late 15th century, Portuguese maritime expeditions carried limestone pillars surmounted by a cross—typically with Portuguese, Latin, and Arabic inscriptions—on voyages of exploration in order to proclaim sovereignty over territory.

DIOGO CÃO was the first to carry *padrãos* in his expedition of 1482–84 along the east coast of Africa. He placed a 13-foot pillar with Portuguese, Latin, and Arabic inscriptions at the mouth of the CONGO RIVER (Zaire River). For a time, the great river was known to Europeans as the Rio de Padrao, or "Pillar River." Cão left a second marker about 500 miles to the south at Cape St. Mary. During a second voyage in 1485–86, he placed a pillar at Cabo Negro in present-day Angola and at Cape Cross in present-day Namibia. In 1487, BARTOLOMEU DIAS passed Cão's pillar and placed one several hundred miles to the south; the next year, he erected one at the CAPE OF GOOD HOPE. In the course of his expedition of 1497–99, VASCO DA GAMA placed a marker at Mossel Bay in present-day South Africa; a second one in present-day Mozambique; and a third one at Calicut in present-day India. On the return trip, he placed a fourth at Malindi in present-day Kenya, and a fifth one at another location in Mozambique.

Some *padrãos* have survived to modern times. One erected by Diogo Cão is housed at the museum of the Sociedade de Geografia in Lisbon; a second, at the Museum für Deutsche Geschichte in Berlin.

painting and exploration

Among artists, especially representational painters, there is a tradition of travel to seek out new subject matter. Before photography, painting, the application of shapes and colors on a surface, and the related drawing, the use of lines to create images, were the only means of documenting scenes. Artists willing to travel to remote places, sometimes referred to as "frontier artists" or "frontier painters," made a special contribution to the chronicles of exploration by making pictorial records of past ages. Some traveled on their own. Some were hired as official artists and drafts people on expeditions for pictorial documentation of places, peoples, and wildlife. Without the work of such artists, we would have no visual reference point of the pre-photographic age. Moreover, they further contributed to awareness of geography, anthropology, and natural history through their journals, letters, and travel accounts.

Early North American Scenes

The first known European artist to paint scenes in what is now the United States is Frenchman JACQUES LE MOYNE DE MORGUES, one of the colonists in the short-lived French Huguenot colony on St. Johns River in present-day Florida, led by RENÉ GOULAINE DE LAUDONNIÈRE in 1564–65. He created watercolors of animals, plants, and Timucua Indians. Similarly, in 1584–87, Englishman JOHN WHITE created a pictorial record of the Outer Banks region of present-day North Carolina as part of SIR WALTER RALEIGH's attempted colonies (one of them the LOST COLONY).

Frontier Painters

American GEORGE CATLIN traveled on his own throughout North America in the 1830s–60s, with a trip to South America as well in the 1850s. He especially sought out images of Native Americans. Other such frontier artists specializing in Native American and western themes were American ALFRED JACOB MILLER, who painted landscapes

This engraving by G. Cook from a painting that Frederick William Beechey completed sometime before 1856 shows an exaggerated attack by walruses in a British expedition to Arctic waters in 1818 headed by David Buchan and John Franklin. Beechey was part of the expedition. *(Library of Congress, Prints and Photographs Division [LC-USZ62-20109])*

and native peoples along the Oregon Trail in the 1830s; Canadian painter PAUL KANE, active in western Canada in the 1840s; and Swiss RUDOLPH FRIEDERICH KURZ, who sought subjects for his work on the MISSOURI RIVER and western plains in the 1840s–50s. Swiss artist KARL BODMER, traveled up the MISSOURI RIVER with German naturalist ALEXANDER PHILIPP MAXIMILIAN in the 1830s, in a productive collaboration. One individual who is famous as both an artist and naturalist, becoming one of the foremost authorities on North American birds, was American JOHN JAMES AUDUBON, active in the early to mid-1800s.

Military Expeditions

Some artists active in North America in the mid-1800s were part of military land expeditions. For example, in the 1840s,

lieutenant and artist HENRY JAMES WARRE traveled with lieutenant MERVIN VAVASOUR in a British military reconnaissance of the Pacific Northwest. His sketches of Oregon country were later made into engravings and published. American brothers, trained in art and drafting, BENJAMIN JORDAN KERN, EDWARD MEYER KERN, and RICHARD HOVENDON KERN served as naturalists and topographers for JOHN CHARLES FRÉMONT, who headed an expedition for the U.S. Army's Corps of Topographical Engineers in the ROCKY MOUNTAINS in the 1840s.

Maritime Expedition Artists

Many maritime exploratory expeditions had official artists, who often doubled as or worked closely with naturalists. Englishman JOHN WEBBER was part of a British expedition to the Pacific Ocean in search of the NORTHWEST PASSAGE in 1776–80, headed by JAMES COOK. Austrian FERDINAND LUCAS BAUER and Englishman WILLIAM WESTALL served under MATTHEW FLINDERS in the British expedition to Australia of 1801–03. German LOUIS CHORIS was part of OTTO VON KOTZEBUE's Russian naval expedition to the Pacific in search of outlets of NORTHEAST PASSAGE or Northwest Passage in 1815–18. Frenchman JACQUES ARAGO was the official artist and writer under LOUIS-CLAUDE DE SAULCES DE FREYCINET in the French naval CIRCUMNAVIGATION OF THE WORLD in 1817–20. Englishman FREDERICK WILLIAM BEECHEY, who went on to become a naval officer, painted scenes while on Arctic expeditions under SIR JOHN FRANKLIN and SIR WILLIAM PARRY in 1818–20.

Travelers and Painters

THOMAS BAINES, an English painter, participated in land expeditions in both Australia and Africa in the mid-19th century. In Africa, he was part of Scottish missionary DAVID LIVINGSTONE's Zambezi expedition. In Asia, also in the mid-19th century, Englishman THOMAS WITTLAM ATKINSON, traveling with his wife, writer LUCY ATKINSON, visited SIBERIA, Mongolia, and central Asia and produced hundreds of paintings. Renowned Russian painter NICHOLAS CONSTANTINOVICH ROERICH, traveled with his wife, writer Elena Blavatsky Roerich, to central Asia in the 1920s, and also produced an enormous body of work.

A more recent example of an artist continuing the tradition of artist/traveler is MARGARET URSULA MEE, a British botanical painter who worked in the Brazilian rain forest of South America from the 1950s to 1980s.

❖

The above are just a small sampling of artists who, throughout the ages, have explored little known parts of the world and re-created what they saw on paper and canvas.

See also PHOTOGRAPHY AND EXPLORATION.

papyrus boat   See CANOE.

periplus

The term *periplus* (plural form, *peripli*) is the Latin transcription of the Greek *periplous* (plural form *periploi*) for "a sailing around" or "circumnavigation." In its usage, as associated with the explorations of the ancient Greeks and Romans, it came to refer to maritime voyages in general, along stretches of coasts as well as around entire bodies of water or islands. It also came to be used for written accounts of such voyages, sometimes as a report of newly explored lands and sometimes as sailing guides, describing landmarks, harbors, anchorages, watering places, and winds and currents of familiar regions. Or it was a combination of both. Many of the peripli from ancient times have not survived, or survive only in fragments as quoted in the works of later historians.

Peripli—some existing in whole or in part, or mentioned in other accounts—offer geographic information of the MEDITERRANEAN SEA, Black Sea, RED SEA, Persian Gulf, Arabian Sea, Indian Ocean, and their coastal regions; as well as the Atlantic coast of parts of Africa and Europe, including the British Isles. An early periplus that is not extant but receives mention in later accounts indicates Greek activity along the Atlantic coast of Europe in the sixth century by a Greek sailor from Massilia (present-day Marseille, France). The reported Greek translation, entitled *Periplous,* of HANNO's account of his journey along the Atlantic coast of Africa in about 470 B.C., as well as the Roman poem relating HIMILCO's voyages along the Atlantic coast of Africa in about 450 B.C., indicate how the Carthaginians ventured from the Mediterranean Sea to unknown regions for the purpose of exploration and not commerce or colonization. An extant periplus dating from about 350 B.C. and bearing the name Scylax (although certainly not the Greek SCYLAX from the sixth century B.C. who sailed for the Persians) contains information on the Mediterranean Sea, the Black Sea, and a stretch of the African coast. Greek historian Arrian, in his famous work *Indica* of the second century A.D., draws on the periplus of the Greek NEARCHUS about his expedition from the coast of India to the head of the Persian Gulf on behalf of ALEXANDER THE GREAT in 325–324 B.C. Greek STRABO and Roman PLINY THE ELDER, in their writings in the first century A.D., take information from Greek PYTHEAS's account of his Atlantic journey to northern parts of Europe in about 325 B.C.

A frequently cited periplus, because it provides such a wealth of information about early East Africa, including commercial activities among peoples of Egypt, East Africa, and the Indian subcontinent, as well as about navigation in the Indian Ocean, is the *Periplus of the Erythraean Sea* (also spelled *Erythrean*). It was written in about A.D. 100 by an anonymous Greek merchant who lived in Alexandria, Egypt.

The Italians continued the tradition of the periplus with similar pilot books known as *portolano* (plural form, *portolani*), which evolved into a graphic representation known as a PORTOLAN CHART.

See also CARTHAGINIAN EXPLORATION; GEOGRAPHY AND CARTOGRAPHY; GREEK EXPLORATION; MAPS AND CHARTS; NAVIGATION AND EXPLORATION; ROMAN EXPLORATION.

Phoenician exploration

The ancient people known as the Phoenicians lived along the east coast of the MEDITERRANEAN SEA, starting in the third millennium B.C. About 200 miles long and five to 15 miles wide, Phoenicia extended eastward along the coast roughly to the Lebanon Mountains in present-day Lebanon; northward to the Eleutherus River (now known as the Kebir River); and southward to Mount Carmel. The Phoenicians came to be influential as traders throughout the Mediterranean Sea region. In the Bible they are referred to as Sidonians, related to the Canaanites. The Greeks first referred to them as Phoenicians, from the word for "purple," because of a dye they traded.

The Phoenicians lived in allied city-states. Byblos, a site near present-day Beirut, Lebanon, inhabited since about 5000 B.C., came to be an important Phoenician center by about 2800 B.C. Early in their history, the Phoenicians were under the influence of Mesopotamian peoples, the Sumerians and the Akkadians. The Egyptians, out of northern Africa, occupied their territory from about 1800 to 1400 B.C. The conflict between the Egyptians and Hittites of present-day Syria, starting in about 1400 B.C., led to eventual Phoenician independence and the rise of many city-states. The port cities of Sidon (Sayda) and Tyre (Sour; Sur), 22 miles to the south, came to alternate as the primary seat of Phoenician political power. By the mid-13th century B.C., the Phoenicians had become known in the region as accomplished shipbuilders and mariners and as reliable traders. In later centuries, they established colonies in the western Mediterranean as well, such as Utica and Carthage in North Africa. Each Phoenician city-state had its special deity, referred to as Baal for a god and Baalat for a goddess; temples were centers of political and civic activities.

The Phoenicians are known as the first people to develop an exclusively alphabetic system of writing, that is, creating a standardized system of symbols representing sounds, instead of the hieroglyphics and cuneiform of the other cultures in the region; the Greeks eventually adopted and altered their alphabet. The Phoenicians also devised a standardized system of weights and measures and were known as skillful architects. Their manufactured goods—textiles and dyes, colored glass, metalwork, and ivory carvings—were highly valued as well. They also traded wood from the cedar trees of their homeland.

In later centuries, the Phoenician city-states had to resist peoples from the east, in particular the Assyrians, Chaldeans, and Persians. Although some city-states fell to invaders, the Phoenicians continued to operate as navigators, traders, and artisans, sometimes in the servitude or employ of other peoples. The Greeks came to take over much much of the region's trade. With the Greeks evolving into a naval power, the Phoenician traders lost their monopoly. Phoenician culture of the eastern Mediterranean came to be absorbed into Hellenistic culture. In 332 B.C., Tyre fell to Greco-Macedonian forces under ALEXANDER THE GREAT during his push into Asia. The Carthaginians, the predominantly Phoenician inhabitants of Carthage, remained a powerful presence in the western Mediterranean until defeated by the Romans in the second century B.C. In A.D. 64, Phoenicia became part of the Roman province of Syria, and the name *Phoenician* was no longer used.

As wide-ranging seafarers, the Phoenicians are important to the history of exploration in establishing contacts between peoples and gaining and spreading geographic knowledge. They explored the entire Mediterranean, from the Dardanelles to the Iberian Peninsula, in their large boats, GALLEY ships propelled mostly by oarsmen with some wind power, the pilots using stars and landmarks for navigation. It is thought that they established coastal colonies on the southeastern Iberian Peninsula by about 1100 B.C. Among these were Gadir (later Gades, or modern Cádiz, Spain) beyond the Strait of Gibraltar (see GIBRALTAR, STRAIT OF), which perhaps served as a stopover point for expeditions into the Atlantic Ocean.

An early expedition in which the Phoenicians participated, as recorded in the Bible, was to OPHIR in the 10th century B.C. Under a contract between King Solomon of Israel and Hiram II, the king of Tyre, Phoenicians served as shipwrights and navigators for the three-year expedition. The location of Ophir, which is known as the location of "King Solomon's mines," the source of gold, is not known, but it may have been in Arabia, which would indicate the Phoenician exploration of the RED SEA. The writings of fifth-century B.C. Greek historian HERODOTUS indicate that, sailing for the pharaoh NECHO II in about 600–597 B.C., Phoenician seafarers navigated the Red Sea southward from the Gulf of Aqaba to the Indian Ocean and possibly carried out the first circumnavigation of Africa, returning to the Mediterranean by way of the Atlantic and the Strait of Gibraltar. It is also possible that the Phoenicians ventured westward through the Strait of Gibraltar long before the historical record indicates. It is in fact recorded by Greek and Roman writers that Carthaginians—HANNO and HIMILCO of Phoenician descent—reached the Atlantic in the fifth century B.C.

See also CARTHAGINIAN EXPLORATION; EGYPTIAN EXPLORATION; GREEK EXPLORATION; ROMAN EXPLORATION.

photography and exploration

Photography, or "writing with light" as the Greek root words translate, revolutionized exploration starting in the 19th century, much as other technological advancements did in earlier ages. With the means of obtaining permanent images through chemical reaction on light-sensitive materials, explorers could bring back an objective visual record from their journeys and not have to rely on the artist's eye (see PAINTING AND EXPLORATION).

Origins of Photography

No one individual is credited with inventing photography. The camera obscura of the 16th century was the antecedent of the camera. The optical apparatus consisted of a box into which light passed through a tiny hole or lens and projected an image onto a glass screen; artists use the device to recreate the perspective of three-dimensional space on a flat surface through tracing. An important breakthrough in chemistry was that of the German anatomy professor Johann Heinrich Schulze, who, in 1727, discovered that silver nitrate darkened upon exposure to light. By the early 1800s, British chemists Thomas Wedgwood and Sir Humphry Davy succeeded in producing images of objects on leather treated with silver salts and exposing them to sunlight (now called "photograms"). However, they were unable to halt the darkening and disappearance of the images.

Drawing on other progress in optics (the science of the laws of light) as well as in chemistry, a number of different individuals invented photography in the first half of the 19th century. In 1816, French physicist Joseph Nicéphore Niépce created the first negative, on paper, and, in 1827, the first known photograph, on metal. In 1839, his colleague, French painter Louis Jacques Mandé Daguerre, invented a method of making a direct positive image on a silver plate, which came to be known as the daguerreotype. In the meantime, in 1839, British scientist Sir John Frederick William Herschel had discovered a chemical solution—hyposulfite of soda or "hypo"—which acted as a fixing agent on photosensitive paper, and, by 1841, fellow English scientist William Henry Fox Talbot had refined the calotype, a process in which a paper negative was developed outside the camera and bathed in a chemical solution, enabling an infinite number of paper positives. (His *The Pencil of Nature,* published in 1844, with 24 original prints, was the first book ever to contain photographs.) In 1851, another Englishman, Frederick Scott Archer, invented the collodion negative process or "wet plate" technique, in which a glass plate was coated with silver iodide and exposed while still wet, a process which came to displace the others. The collodion

William Henry Jackson took this photograph of a Manchu shaman in Russia in 1895. It was published in *Harper's Weekly* two years later. *(Library of Congress, Prints and Photographs Division [LC-USZ62-78790])*

process was used for the ambrotype, a glass negative backed with black material, creating the effect of a positive image, and the tintype, which substituted an iron plate for glass.

The Beginnings of Photojournalism

The daguerreotype, the first photographic process to gain popularity, was especially used for portraits. But early photographers also used it to capture less contrived images of historic events, such as the California gold rush of 1849. French photographer Maxime DuCamp traveled to Egypt in 1849–50 and made calotypes of temples and pyramids. British photographer Roger Fenton's work in the Crimean War of 1853–56 is considered the first work of a photojournalist. Another early photojournalist, American Mathew Brady, who had first taken daguerreotypes, created a photographic corps to document the American Civil War of 1861–65, using equipment for the collodion process, including large cameras, tripods, and portable darkrooms.

Photography and Government Surveys

Photography became an official tool of exploration in the United States after the Civil War. Timothy O'Sullivan, who originally worked under Brady, traveled with CLARENCE KING and GEORGE MONTAGUE WHEELER in U.S. governmental surveys of the American West in the 1860s–1870s; John K. Hillers explored the Grand Canyon with JOHN WESLEY POWELL in the 1870s; and William Henry Jackson accompanied FERDINAND VANDEVEER HAYDEN to the Yellowstone River and ROCKY MOUNTAINS, also in the 1870s.

Images from the Frontier

Other photographers traveled to other continents, such as British Samuel Bourne in India and Scotsman John Thomson in China. Books with photographs of foreign lands, containing the first such views seen by many, became bestsellers for publishers. Starting in 1900, American Edward

Curtis began documenting Native Americans with photographs, much as GEORGE CATLIN had done with painting.

Photography in Arctic and Antarctic Exploration

Photography played an important part in early 20th-century exploration of the Arctic and the Antarctic. Australian photographer and later aviator SIR GEORGE HUBERT WILKINS was official photographer of the Canadian Arctic Expedition of 1913–18 under VILHJALMUR STEFANSSON. Another Australian, James Francis ("Frank") Hurley, was official photographer for the Imperial Trans-Antarctic Expedition of 1914–17 under SIR ERNEST HENRY SHACKLETON.

An Evolving Technology

With continuing improvements, photography became more and more practical in the 20th century. By 1925, the 35-mm camera had been designed in Germany by Oskar Barnack of the Ernst Leitz company. Black-and-white film became faster, freeing the photographer from such great dependency on the artificial light of the flash. Ten years later, color film for transparencies, or slides, was introduced, and, in 1942, color negative film. Advancements in photography were carried over into motion pictures, which Thomas Alva Edison and his employee William K. L. Dickson helped develop in the United States in the 1880s–90s, and the brothers Auguste and Louis Lumière introduced to the world in France in 1895. Digital photography, the process of recording still images electronically rather than photochemically, and video recording, doing so with moving images, are now widespread technologies.

Modern Uses

Photography has played a part in modern surveying and cartography; the term *photogrammetry* refers to the use of photography in surveying and in making MAPS AND CHARTS (see SURVEYING AND EXPLORATION). AERIAL PHOTOGRAPHY has been used for photogrammetry and, in conjunction with advancements in aviation, has revolutionized exploration; early aviators in the Arctic and Antarctic, such as American RICHARD EVELYN BYRD, first demonstrated the value of taking photographs from the air (see AVIATION AND EXPLORATION). Aerial photography has also given us a visual record of other celestial bodies in SPACE EXPLORATION.

Pilgrims

A pilgrim is a person who travels to foreign lands, generally for religious purposes, such as visiting a sacred place or seeking religious freedom. These journeys are known as pilgrimages. When capitalized, *Pilgrim* refers to any of the group of early English settlers who founded the Plymouth colony in present-day Massachusetts. Established in 1620, theirs was the first permanent English settlement in the Northeast,

founded 13 years after the Jamestown settlement in Virginia. The Pilgrims have also been referred to as the "Forefathers" or "Founders."

The group originally came together at Scrooby, a village in Nottinghamshire, England. By the early 17th century, they had formed a separatist Protestant church opposed to the rites and the monolithic control of the Church of England; they were part of the general religious movement known as Puritanism. Early leaders included John Robinson and William Brewster. In 1607–08, most of the Separatists (as they became known) emigrated from England to the Netherlands, where the religious laws were more liberal, and settled in Leyden. In their new homeland they worked mostly as artisans and laborers.

Hoping for a better life in the Americas, some members of the group voted to emigrate there. In 1619, William Brewster and William Bradford received backing from the Virginia Company of London, one of two English companies chartered to colonize North America (see VIRGINIA COMPANY). About half the church members—some among those who had moved to the Netherlands and some among those still in England—planned to go. The initial intent was that the Netherlands Pilgrims would sail the *Speedwell* to England and join their English brethren. The *Speedwell* would then cross the Atlantic together with a second ship bearing other émigrés. But the *Speedwell* proved unseaworthy, and 102 men, women, and children crammed onto the *Mayflower,* a ship of 180 tons burden formerly used to carry wine. The vessel sailed under Captain Christopher Jones. The Leyden group of Separatists, who referred to themselves as "Saints," were only 35 in number; they called the other passengers "strangers." The *Mayflower* left Plymouth, England, on September 16, 1620. A storm drove it north of its intended landing site, and, on November 21, it reached Provincetown, Cape Cod, in present-day Massachusetts. For a month, the Pilgrims explored along the coast; on

This bank note vignette on American history from the 1870s–80s shows the Pilgrims. *(Library of Congress, Prints and Photographs Division [LC-USZ62-96003])*

December 21, they entered Plymouth Harbor, territory granted to the Virginia Company of Plymouth.

While still on board ship, the leaders drew up the Mayflower Compact, which was signed by every adult male, Separatists and Strangers alike. The document formed a government based on the principle of rule by the will of majority and promising allegiance to the English king. John Carver was selected as governor of the Plymouth colony (he was succeeded in 1621 by William Bradford). EDWARD WINSLOW was elected to the ruling council. The Pilgrims later obtained patents from the Council for New England that legalized the chosen settlement site at present-day Plymouth, Massachusetts.

The winter of 1620–21 proved difficult for the colonists, and many of them died. The following spring, the Pilgrims were helped greatly by Native Americans of the Wampanoag Confederacy. Under the leadership of the grand sachem Massasoit, and with SQUANTO, who had earlier traveled to Europe, interpreting, the Wampanoag taught the newcomers planting and fishing methods. That fall, the Pilgrims and the Wampanoag shared a bountiful harvest; out of this event there developed the American tradition of an annual Thanksgiving.

Over the next years, the Pilgrims explored the surrounding region. Trade was conducted up and down the coast. In 1622, Squanto led an expedition by ship to Narragansett Bay in present-day Rhode Island. Miles Standish, who had been a professional soldier in Europe, became the Pilgrims' military leader and led a number of expeditions against Native American and rival colonists in neighboring regions. In 1632, Edward Winslow undertook one of the earliest European explorations of present-day Connecticut.

The Plymouth colony was absorbed by the Massachusetts colony in 1691. William Bradford wrote the *History of Plimoth Plantation,* published in 1656. He is credited with the first use of the term *Pilgrims* for the founders of the colony.

See also RELIGION AND EXPLORATION.

Pillars of Hercules   See GIBRALTAR, STRAIT OF.

pinnace

The term *pinnace* refers to a small ship used for auxiliary duties connected with a larger vessel. It is taken from the Latin root word for "pine," a wood used in shipbuilding. Among the Romans, a pinnace was propelled by oarsmen and camouflaged for reconnaissance missions. During the EUROPEAN AGE OF EXPLORATION of the 15th, 16th, and 17th centuries and afterward, it was more often a sailing ship. A pinnace would usually be transported on the deck of the flagship vessel during a voyage. Sometimes they sailed alongside the fleet, but their small size made them vulnerable to loss in the open

ocean. They were used as tenders for the larger ships, that is, for transporting people and supplies to and from shore. They are also associated with the exploration of coasts, inlets, and rivers.

See also ROMAN EXPLORATION; SHIPBUILDING AND EXPLORATION.

piracy

An act of piracy is a crime on the high seas outside the normal jurisdiction of any nation and without the granted authority of a nation. A pirate—a word from the Greek *peirateia* and Latin *piratia,* the same root of "peril"—refers to a person who commits an act of piracy. They can be thought of as the "highwaymen" or "brigands" of the sea. Piracy is an ongoing story throughout maritime history and, as a result, is associated with world exploration.

Some among the Phoenicians, who, by the mid-13th century B.C., had become the dominant seafaring people of the MEDITERRANEAN SEA, were known to commit acts of piracy, raiding ships without official sanction. They and early mariners among the Greeks were also the victims of piracy. The Romans, who became a naval power in the Mediterranean and into the Atlantic Ocean from the third century B.C. to the fifth century A.D., helped counter piracy. In the Middle Ages, the Vikings raided ships as well as coastal settlements throughout western Europe. Private vessels operated by Arab Muslims raided ships in the Mediterranean. Pirates also preyed on merchant ships in the North Sea and Baltic Sea; one of the purposes of the HANSEATIC LEAGUE, an association of German merchants and communities founded in the 13th century, was to counter this constant threat.

Starting in the 16th century, the tradition of piracy continued with ships based along the BARBARY COAST of North Africa (a region named for the Turkish pirate Khayr ad-Din Barbarossa), following the final Christian defeat of the Muslims in Spain in 1492 and their dispersion there. Barbary pirates came to be known as "corsairs," a French word for a ship from the Latin root word for "course." Some of them were in effect PRIVATEERS, independent mariners (and their ships) having been granted the right by a nation to participate in a naval military action against an enemy. Some of them preyed as far north as the English Channel. The corsairs were active into the early 19th century.

Meanwhile, English privateers, such as SIR FRANCIS DRAKE and SIR JOHN HAWKINS of the 16th century, preyed on Spanish trade in both the Atlantic and Pacific Oceans, following the European discovery of the Americas and Spanish plunder of Native American civilizations (see TREASURE AND EXPLORATION). Pirates and privateers of the 17th century—mostly English, Dutch, and French who operated out of the Caribbean Sea against Spanish interests—became known as "buccaneers," from the French word *boucan,* a type of grill used to cook meat plundered from Spanish cattle plantations (see SPANISH MAIN). Another term for pirates is *freebooters,* from the Dutch *vrijbuiter* for "free booty."

The growth of national navies in the 17th, 18th, and 19th centuries helped decrease piracy, as did the development of new maritime technologies—the steam engine in the 19th century and diesel engines in the 20th century. Yet one still hears of acts of modern piracy.

See also GREEK EXPLORATION; MUSLIM EXPLORATION; PHOENICIAN EXPLORATION; ROMAN EXPLORATION.

pirogue (piragua)

A pirogue (also *piragua*) is a type of dugout CANOE, built with a variety of features and in a range of sizes. The pirogue could be shaped by carving and by burning out the center of a log. Often, sections within the boat were separated by bulkheads, to form a place to store cargo and to give the vessel strength. Most commonly the pirogue was propelled by oarsmen, but some used the supplementary power of a sail. Although heavier than other varieties of river craft, and, as a result, less convenient for portaging over land, the pirogue was sturdy and dependable in strong currents.

Dugout canoes have been made and used all over the world where trees grow to a sufficient size. In America, the pirogue was developed for navigating river systems and carrying goods, especially furs. When North America was being explored by Europeans and Euro-Americans, there was an abundance of large trees along the rivers, some six feet in diameter with trunks running 40 feet before the first limbs. Subsequently, the builder was not limited in the size of his craft by the available timber. An average-sized pirogue was eight feet long and two to three feet wide. Cedar, cottonwood, and walnut were the preferred woods for making a pirogue.

The typical crew of a larger pirogue was three—a rower in the front, one amidships, and a steersman at the stern. To construct a raft, two pirogues would be bound together at a distance of eight to 10 feet and planks would be placed on the intervening space to create a deck for the crew and goods.

In addition to the KEELBOAT, early expeditions along the MISSISSIPPI RIVER and MISSOURI RIVER—such as that under MERIWETHER LEWIS and WILLIAM CLARK in 1804—made use of the pirogue.

See also SHIPBUILDING AND EXPLORATION.

planisphere

Planisphere refers to the representation of the circles of a sphere on a plane, that is, a two-dimensional representation of a three-dimensional space. It is a word that was used commonly in antiquity with regard to cartography.

The term has fallen out of use as the variety and sophistication of mapmaking techniques have developed. Modern maps are labeled according to the method used to generate them, such as a MERCATOR PROJECTION, or Lambert Equal-Area Projection.

Today, the term *planisphere* is most often used to refer to a projection of the celestial sphere and the stars on a plane, sometimes with adjustable circles for showing the varying position of the stars.

See also GEOGRAPHY AND CARTOGRAPHY.

Plymouth Company   See VIRGINIA COMPANY.

Polaris   See NORTH STAR.

Pole Star   See NORTH STAR.

Polynesian exploration

Polynesians are the peoples of Polynesia, islands in a vast triangular-shaped area of the Pacific Ocean, which along with Melanesia and Micronesia make up the South Pacific Islands, or OCEANIA. In the north, the HAWAIIAN ISLANDS form the top point of Polynesia's triangle; to the southeast, Easter Island occupies the right-hand corner; to the southwest NEW ZEALAND bounds the left-hand corner. Polynesia consists of American Samoa, Cook Islands, Easter Island, French Polynesia (Society Islands, Marquesas Islands, Tubuai Islands, Tuamotu Islands, and Gambier Islands), Hawaiian Islands, New Zealand, Niue, Pitcairn Islands, Samoa, Tokelau, Tonga, Tuvalu, and the Wallis and Futuna Islands. Fittingly, the term *Polynesia* is derived from a Greek word for "many islands."

There are many characteristics, both physical and cultural, which make the Polynesians a group unto themselves. There are also variations within the group, which point to a complex ancestry. The questions of where they originated and where they migrated and how they managed to travel great distances by water are still being debated.

Physically, Polynesians are tall, well-proportioned, and strong. They have lighter skin than their neighbors to the west in Melanesia and to the northwest in Micronesia, and their hair is straight or wavy. There is, however, a range of features among these peoples, with very light skin found, people with red hair, and men with beards. In short, they show characteristics of a mixture of ethnic groups, with Asian and Caucasian features most apparent.

The strongest indication of Polynesian common identity is shared language. All speak the same language with different dialects. They have other cultural characteristics in common as well. They typically worship some form of sun god, produce similar-looking statues and artwork, and before the arrival of Europeans, had no concept of money and did not weave or make pottery.

That a group of people could maintain such changeable features of their culture while spread out over such a wide area suggests a fairly recent migration over a relatively short period of time. On this topic, the questions are far from settled. The earliest estimate for the start of the migrations is about 1000 B.C. Many scholars now agree, based on linguistic and agricultural traits, that Polynesians originated from Southeast Asia. They possibly reached the Marquesas Islands and radiated outward in about A.D. 300. The Marquesas manifest some of the earliest evidence of human habitation in Polynesia (120 B.C.), and are centrally located. Others have suggested that Polynesians came from the shores of North America, South America, or both. The wind and current systems of the Pacific are more favorable for a westward migration than eastward travels from Asia. Norwegian anthropologist THOR HEYERDAHL has supported the view that Polynesians migrated from the Americas, and he conducted his famous voyage of the *Kon-Tiki* in 1947 to prove the possibility.

Whatever the time frame, or place of origin, the feats of seamanship accomplished by the Polynesians were admirable. There are several factors that made transoceanic voyages possible. One was the double CANOE. Arising from the OUTRIGGER, a craft unique to the Pacific Ocean, the double canoe could carry people and cargo in significant quantity and was fairly stable in the open ocean. Another was knowledge of techniques of navigation. Polynesians practiced a rudimentary form of stellar navigation by identifying certain islands with the stars that were found directly above them; for example, Sirius marks the location of Tahiti. By sailing in the direction of a particular star, one could reach their destination. Polynesians also made maps with sticks bound together by coconut fiber, with shells added to represent islands. (See NAVIGATION AND EXPLORATION.)

An ancient Polynesian mariner whose name has endured in the legends of the Maori, New Zealand's native peoples, is KUPE. According to Maori tradition, he traveled across much of Polynesia in the 10th century and reached New Zealand.

portolan chart

The Italian term *portolano* or *portulano* (plural forms, *portolani* or *portulani*) refers to early written descriptions about landmarks, winds, and currents used by pilots in navigating waters, similar to the Greek manual known as a PERIPLUS. With time, the portolani evolved into charts, graphic representations of bodies of water and coastlines, probably first created to be used in conjunction with pilot books for purposes of navigation. The growing use of the magnetic COM-

PASS, or mariner's compass, for multiple readings of a coastline, enabled the making of more accurate charts and resulted in their orientation north-south, not east-west. Although lines showed the bearings between important ports, portolan charts did not depict LATITUDE AND LONGITUDE as devised by ancient Greek cartographers, such as PTOLEMY.

The earliest reports of such charts date from the late Middle Ages. MARCO POLO, an Italian explorer of the Far East in the latter part of the 13th century, mentions a chart of the coast of CEYLON (present-day Sri Lanka). But it is assumed there had been earlier graphic representations. The oldest existing portolan chart—the Pisan Chart by Italian cartographer Petrus Vesconte—represents coastlines and ports of the MEDITERRANEAN SEA and dates from about 1300. Its high degree of accuracy, with distances drawn to scale, indicates that its makers drew on the work of earlier cartographers. Early portolan charts were published individually on single sheets of parchment. In time, they began to appear in atlases. The Laurentian Portolano, for example, published in 1351, includes eight charts and covers territory from the British Isles to India, including parts of Africa.

A French-derived word for a nautical chart is "rutter."

See also GEOGRAPHY AND CARTOGRAPHY; MAPS AND CHARTS; NAVIGATION AND EXPLORATION.

Prester John

Prester John was a legendary monarch and priest, whose kingdom was believed to exist in Asia and Africa. The myth began in the Middle Ages but endured into the RENAISSANCE and provided incentive for numerous voyages of exploration. *Prester* is an early version of "priest" or "presbyter," an elder in the early Christian church.

The earliest known reference to the mythic figure of Prester John is found in the writings of Otto von Freisingen, bishop of Freising (Otto of Freising). In his *Historia de Duabus Civitatibus,* published in 1158, he described how, in about 1145, Hugh, the bishop of Jabala in what is now Syria, in a meeting with Pope Eugenius in Rome, reported that a priest-king named John ruled a Nestorian Christian kingdom beyond lands controlled by Muslims. (The Nestorians were a sect of Eastern Christians who followed the teachings of Nestorius, patriarch of Constantinople, condemned as a heretic by the Council of Ephesus in A.D. 431 for believing in two distinct natures, God as a divine being and Jesus as a man.) According to Hugh, the Christian ruler had defeated an army of infidels and would likely help with further support of the CRUSADES. (The time frame fits a real battle occurring in September 1141 near Samarkand in present-day Uzbekistan in which Yeliutashi, ruler of the empire of Kara-Khitai, defeated Sultan Sanjar, the Seljuk Turk ruler of Persia; rumors soon reached Europe that Yeliutashi was a Christian, and it has been theorized that his people, the Kara-Khitai, were confused with the Kerait tribe, a Nestorian Christian people of central Asia.)

The second known mention of Prester John is in a letter from about 1165 from Prester John himself—presumably forged by a European—addressed to Emanuel I, the Byzantine emperor of Rome, describing a huge peaceful and wealthy Christian kingdom in India, but one besieged by infidels. Some of the later hundreds of published versions of similar letters are addressed otherwise, such as to the pope or the king of France. In 1177, Pope Alexander III sent out his physician, Magister Philippos, with a reply for Prester John, but there is no record what became of him.

The belief in Prester John's Asian kingdom persisted into the 13th and 14th centuries. Early European travelers to Asia, such as GIOVANNI DA PIAN DEL CARPINI, WILLIAM OF RUBROUCK, MAFFEO POLO, NICCOLÒ POLO, MARCO POLO, JOHN OF MONTECORVINO, ODORIC OF PORDENONE, and GIOVANNI DE MARIGNOLLI, hoped to make contact. Marco Polo heard of a Christian ruler of the Kerait people, who had been slain by the forces of GENGHIS KHAN of the Mongols in the early 1200s and thought perhaps he had been Prester John.

Without any confirmation of the legend in Asia, attention shifted to Africa in the 14th century. Letters appeared as early as 1340, describing Abyssinia (as Ethiopia was then called) as the location of Prester John's illusive kingdom. Because geography of the period was so vague, with eastern lands—from East Africa to India—lumped together in the minds of many Europeans, what now seems such a shift of attention appears less arbitrary. *The Travels of Sir John Mandeville* by SIR JOHN MANDEVILLE (perhaps a made-up traveler), published between 1357 and 1371, was one of the various works describing Prester John's fantastic kingdom.

The hope of finding Prester John was reported as one motivation for the 15th-century voyages along the coast of West Africa, sponsored by HENRY THE NAVIGATOR, prince of Portugal. Prester John was increasingly reported as a "white" Christian king, and his land was becoming ever more exotic in descriptions—a gold-laden kingdom through which a mighty river flowed whose banks were sprinkled with precious stones and where there was a FOUNTAIN OF YOUTH from which he drank. He also supposedly had an army of thousands of warriors who could help in a Christian holy war against Islam. In 1487, King John II of Portugal dispatched PERO DA COVILHÃ to Abyssinia to confirm reports of a Christian emperor there. Covilhã reached the region and became an adviser to the monarch, known as the Negus, but did not return to Europe. In 1520, a Portuguese priest, FRANCISCO ÁLVARES, also spent time with the Negus. He wrote an account of his African experiences, entitled *The Prester John of the Indies,* published in 1540.

Some of the earliest printed maps show Prester John's realm in Africa, and cartographic references lasted into the 17th century. But with more and more European travelers reaching the region, the association of Prester John with East Africa gradually faded as did the legend in general.

See also LEGENDS AND EXPLORATION; MONGOL EXPLORATION; MUSLIM EXPLORATION.

prime meridian (Greenwich meridian)

The term *meridian,* also known as a line of longitude, is the name applied to any imaginary line on Earth's surface, running north-south and passing through the NORTH POLE and the SOUTH POLE, and at a right angle to the EQUATOR. *Prime meridian* refers to the meridian designated as zero degree longitude, from which all other points of longitude are measured.

With regard to a line of latitude, the equator, at Earth's widest point of circumference and equidistant from the North and South Poles, is a natural choice for being considered prime, that is, zero latitude. But no one meridian can be so determined, and countries established varying systems for setting the time of day. As a result, early world maps lacked a standardized grid of LATITUDE AND LONGITUDE. In 1884, the Washington Meridian Conference was held to determine an international standard and established that the prime meridian passed through the original site of the Royal Observatory in Greenwich, England. As a result, the prime meridian is also known as the Greenwich meridian. A number of terms have been applied to the standard of time based on the prime meridian: Greenwich Meridian Time, Greenwich Mean Time, Greenwich Civil Time, and Greenwich Time.

See also GEOGRAPHY AND CARTOGRAPHY; MAPS AND CHARTS.

privateers

A privateer is a private ship, or the commander or one of the crew of that ship, commissioned by a sovereign nation to take action against an enemy. The commission, known as letters of marque and reprisal (or, more commonly, letters of marque), enabled private individuals to fit out an armed vessel and attack and seize ships, crews, and merchandise. The practice started in the Middle Ages, when European nations hired private merchant vessels to create a navy or help fill out an existing navy. Privateers, in their wide-ranging voyages for military and commercial purposes, played a part in world exploration.

The term *pirate* refers to a person who commits a crime on the high seas, or an act of PIRACY. Some of the men who worked as privateers and whose vessels also became known by that term, began as pirates on pirate ships. (The terms *corsair, buccaneer,* and *freebooter* are also applied to pirates, some of whom were in effect acting as privateers.) But other men were private businessmen and mariners who received authorization from their governments to commit what would otherwise be considered acts of piracy and to keep much of the profits for themselves.

An explorer who may have participated in at least one privateering expedition in his early career was Italian CHRISTOPHER COLUMBUS, who later had the sponsorship of the Spanish government in his expeditions across the Atlantic Ocean in the late 15th and early 16th centuries. In 1522, Italian GIOVANNI DA VERRAZANO, sailing as a privateer on a French ship, successfully raided two of HERNÁN CORTÉS's ships, returning from Mexico with Aztec Indian gold. This led to his commission for a French voyage to the Americas.

Englishman SIR JOHN HAWKINS developed the SLAVE TRADE in the 1560s, between England, Africa, and the Americas, considered at that time a violation of international law, which led to his arrest by the Spanish. He eventually went on to serve in the Royal Navy and helped secure English victory against the Spanish Armada in 1588. His younger cousin, SIR FRANCIS DRAKE, who sailed with him on several occasions against Spanish interests, carried out the first English CIRCUMNAVIGATION OF THE WORLD in 1577–80 as a privateer. SIR JAMES LANCASTER, who was part of the expedition, went on to sponsor and organize expeditions in search of the NORTHWEST PASSAGE. CHRISTOPHER NEWPORT, who also accompanied Drake on raids, carried the first English colonist to Virginia in 1607. SIR MARTIN FROBISHER, another Englishman, also sailed as a privateer in the 1560s, later becoming an Arctic explorer. Englishman SIR ANTHONY SHERLEY, who later became a diplomat, led a privateering expedition in 1596. GEORGE POPHAM, who founded a short-lived colony in Maine in 1607–08, was a part of privateering raids in the WEST INDIES. Englishman WILLIAM DAMPIER, in the late 17th century, served in both pirating and privateering raids in the South Pacific Ocean and Caribbean Sea. With an interest in the natural sciences, he was later commissioned an officer in the Royal Navy and placed in command of the first English government-sponsored expedition to the Pacific, carried out in 1699–1701. In 1703, he embarked on another privateering expedition to the Pacific coast of South America. A Scottish crew member, ALEXANDER SELKIRK, was marooned in the Juan Fernandez Islands. After his rescue in 1709, his story became the inspiration for the 1719 novel *Robinson Crusoe* by Daniel Defoe. It is interesting to note how many of the above were knighted in the course of their careers.

Privateering was practiced on a large scale in the American Revolution in 1775–83 and the War of 1812. In the former, the Patriot navy consisted of almost 1,700 re-outfitted private merchant ships as opposed to 64 official Continental Navy ships. The practice of privateering was abolished by the Declaration of Paris of 1856, of which the United States, Spain, Mexico, and Venezuela were not signatories. In the American Civil War of 1861–65, only the Confederacy made use of privateers. The United States officially renounced the practice during the Spanish-American War of 1898. At the Hague Conference of 1922–23, the international ban on privateering was extended to aircraft.

pundits

The word *pundit* is a variation of *pandit,* a Hindi term for a "learned expert," applied especially to scholars, teachers, officials, and clerks. It is derived from the Sanskrit *pandita* of the same meaning. It also came to be applied by the British to native Indian explorers of the 19th century, hired to work on the Great Trigonometrical Survey of India.

The British survey of the Indian subcontinent had begun in the early 19th century, first under the direction of the BRITISH EAST INDIA COMPANY, then under the British government. SIR GEORGE EVEREST participated from 1819 to 1843. During that time most of India was mapped. The British, concerned about the intentions of both Russia and China in the region, wanted geographic knowledge of border countries as well, in particular Tibet to the north in the HIMALAYAS, which had been closed to Europeans since 1792.

In the 1860s, Thomas George Montgomerie, a captain in the Bengal Engineers who had headed surveys in Kashmir, devised a plan to accomplish this task. The British would hire native Indians or inhabitants of neighboring countries, train them as surveyors, and have them travel the countries disguised as Buddhist merchants or pilgrims. Since the surveyors were to enter countries illegally, they were in effect spies and would possibly be executed if captured. The recruits were trained in geography, astronomy, and memorization. They also received medical training. They practiced walking with a consistent stride for purposes of measurement. Each was provided with special instruments, crafted in British India: what seemed like traditional Buddhist prayer beads, but with 100 beads instead of the normal 108 and with every 10th bead larger than the rest, for keeping track of paces; a prayer wheel holding a COMPASS and slips of paper for taking notes; a hollowed-out book concealing plane tables for mapping; a hollow walking stick holding a thermometer for measuring the temperature at which water boils, a way to measure altitude; and a false-bottomed travel chest to carry a SEXTANT for determining latitude.

Each surveyor was given a code name. Some of their names are now famous in the history of exploration, although, for years, even into the 20th century, they were given little recognition. NAIN SINGH, the first native surveyor in the field, was called "the Pundit." Eventually, all the native surveyors came to be known as such. In 1864–66, Nain Singh crossed the eastern Himalayas into Tibet and visited the city of LHASA and explored the upper Brahmaputra River. In 1867, he explored the western Himalayas and the upper INDUS RIVER. In 1873, Nain Singh traveled with his cousin, KISHEN SINGH, from northern India to Chinese Turkestan, reaching the Takla Makan desert. In 1878–82, Kishen Singh journeyed as far north as Mongolia's GOBI DESERT. Pundit KINTUP explored Tibet in 1879–84 and determined that Tibet's Tsangpo River is the same as India's Brahmaputra. Another pundit, Hari Ram, explored the region around the world's tallest mountain, MOUNT EVEREST, in 1871–72; later in his career, he crossed northern Nepal from west to east.

Not all the pundits succeeded in their missions, and some were executed or sent back to India. Yet, over the decades, the pundits managed to map many of the lands north of India.

Punt (Pwnt)

Punt, an ancient land, was a source of luxury goods for the ancient Egyptians. The name *Punt,* or *Pwnt,* means "the sacred." The exact location of Punt, and its cities or villages, is unknown, but much can be extrapolated concerning it from historical descriptions. It was a fertile land, with a variety of plant and animal species, requiring some days to reach from the head of the NILE RIVER by way of the RED SEA. The most likely locations for Punt are the Horn of Africa, either along the north coast along the Gulf of Aden, or the south coast in the Indian Ocean where Somalia is today. But Punt may have included lands in what is now eastern Sudan, Eritrea, and Ethiopia in Africa, or Yemen on the Arabian Peninsula. Or the name may have referred to all the southern parts of Africa and Arabia, of which the Egyptians were aware.

The first record of Punt is from HANNU's trade expedition for Egypt in about 2450 B.C. Hannu carried back precious minerals and spices to Egypt during the reign of Sahure. In about 1492 B.C., Queen HATSHEPSUT of Egypt organized a mission to Punt to obtain spices, exotic trees, precious metals, ivory, leopard skins, and monkeys. Records of these journey survive as carved reliefs, narrated with hieroglyphics, adorning the walls of her temple of Deir el-Bahari. Some of the inscriptions relate that the people of Punt believed the visitors from the north were supernatural beings who had descended from the sky.

See also EGYPTIAN EXPLORATION.

Q

quadrant

A quadrant is an instrument used to measure the angular elevation of a celestial body and thereby determine geographic location for purposes of navigation. The name derives from the graduated arc displaying the reading, which spans 90 degrees, one fourth of a circle. The term *quadrant* is sometimes used interchangeably with other measuring devices based on the same principles. The octant, based on an arc of 45 degrees, and the SEXTANT, based on an arc of 60 degrees, were invented at about the same time in the 18th century. Hadley's Quadrant, invented by Englishman John Hadley in the early 1730s, was actually the first octant. The sextant became the tool of choice in celestial navigation. (The term *sextant* is now the most widely used term and is sometimes applied to all such measuring devices.)

The first quadrant, actually a version of the ancient ASTROLABE, was a simple wooden triangle with a wooden plumb bob on a thread, used to give a reading of the celestial body's altitude in relation to the horizon, which could be compared to tables of figures from earlier readings (see EPHEMERIS). From the computations, the user could determine approximate latitude. Later quadrants were made from brass. The CROSS-STAFF was a T-shaped device, which gave a more accurate reading. In the late 1500s, English mariner JOHN DAVIS added a reflector to the cross-staff so the Sun could be observed without damage to the eyes; that device became known as the backstaff.

Davis went on to invent what is known as the Davis Quadrant, probably during his Arctic voyages of the 1580s–90s; the device was first described in 1595. The Davis Quadrant consisted of two triangles instead of one. The smaller triangle had a mounted lens, which projected an image of the celestial body to a sighting slot aimed at the horizon. The larger triangle had two handles, a big arc with a scale, and an arm that slid along the arc to give measurements.

See also LATITUDE AND LONGITUDE; NAVIGATION AND EXPLORATION.

quintent   See SEXTANT.

Quivira (Aguivira, Cuivira, La Gran Quivira, Quebira)

The legend of Quivira, also spelled Cuivira, Quebira, and Aguivira, is part of the story of the legend of CIBOLA, supposedly the location of seven cities, also known as the Seven Cities of Antillia, founded by seven Portuguese bishops, with wealth on a par with that of the Aztec and Inca civilizations. Such legends spurred on European exploration of the Americas, in particular among the Spanish. A 1540 expedition sent out from Mexico by ANTONIO DE MENDOZA, the viceroy of New Spain, and led by FRANCISCO VÁSQUEZ DE CORONADO, sought to determine if the Zuni Indian pueblos in what is now western New Mexico were the kingdom of gold and jewels. Finding no great wealth here, the Spanish were primed for rumors of another location. A Plains Indian, probably of the Pawnee tribe, the TURK, who had been held captive among the Towa Indians of Cicuye Pueblo (Pecos Pueblo) on the Pecos River, described a wealthy civilization to the northeast on the southern plains to HERNANDO DE ALVARADO, one of Coronado's lieutenants.

In spring 1541, Coronado, Alvarado, and Franciscan friar JUAN DE PADILLA, who was driven by the hope of locating the cities founded by the seven bishops, set out with a large expedition from New Mexico, across the Texas Panhandle, and then north through present-day Oklahoma and into Kansas. The Spanish came into contact with Plains Indians, probably in what is now central Kansas near the great bend of the Arkansas River (although some writers have assigned the location of contact with Plains Indians to be the Canadian River area of the northeast Texas Panhandle), but found no wealthy cities. It is thought that the villages were of the Wichita Indians. The Spanish also encountered a party of Pawnee Indians. Coronado eventually had the Turk executed, because of his deception as well as an attempt to incite the Pawnee against the Spanish. Another Plains Indian by the name of Ysopete then became the chief guide. The mythic land was never found, but the Spanish returned to Mexico with new geographic knowledge.

It has been theorized that the Turk sincerely believed that the powerful medicine of the Pawnee represented riches. It is more likely that the Pueblo Indians promoted the idea of wealth to be found elsewhere to rid themselves of the Spanish, and that the Turk, as part of the scheme, hoped to be taken back to his homeland.

In the early 1600s, the Spanish colonizer of New Mexico, JUAN DE OÑATE, searched for both Cibola and Quivira in the lands surrounding his settlement near present-day Santa Fe.

The legend of Cibola and Quivira persisted. Quivira became known as La Gran Quivira and, depending on rumors, its believed location shifted, the name appearing on early maps of the southern plains, Southwest, and even California. One of the ruins at the Salinas Missions National Monument, south of present-day Albuquerque, New Mexico, where the Piro Indians once lived, is known as Gran Quivira. Quivira has also endured as a place name in Kansas.

See also LEGENDS AND EXPLORATION.

R

raft

A raft is a floating structure, made from a variety of materials attached together, such as logs or bundled reeds. In some instances, certain materials, such as airtight animal bladders, are added to provide greater buoyancy. Rafts have been used from prehistoric times and can be considered the earliest watercraft. With time, ancient peoples devised ways to hollow out a single log or shape materials so that they moved through water with less resistance, making a type of craft generally known as the CANOE.

The balsa raft, or simply the balsa, consists of five or six logs of buoyant balsa wood bound together with cordage or hardwood pins. Propelled by oars or poles in shallow water, it might also have a sail, typically triangular. Some balsa rafts have a tent on deck for shelter and supplies, enabling them to stay at sea for weeks. Drag anchors make them safer than other types of small craft which can be sunk by waves. Some also have centerboards, making them less prone to drift.

In the legends of South American peoples, there is knowledge of the abundant islands of the South Pacific Ocean. Balsa rafts were made by the Inca Indians, who may have used them to colonize Polynesia (see POLYNESIAN EXPLORATION). Norwegian explorer and anthropologist THOR HEYERDAHL set out to prove the possibility of this migration by making a balsa raft and sailing it from Peru. After three months at sea, he landed on the Tuamotu Archipelago in Polynesia. The journey is chronicled in his book *Kon-Tiki* (1948).

According to legend, in the 15th century, Inca ruler Tupac Yupanqui led a fleet of 400 balsa rafts in an exploration of the Pacific, a trip that lasted about a year. In the 16th century, Spanish conquistador FRANCISCO PIZARRO observed Native Americans using balsa rafts to conduct trade along Ecuador's coast. The raft would not have been practical for overseas trade, however, due to the lack of space for cargo. The balsa raft is still in use today in Brazil where it is called a *jangada*.

A type of raft common to Native Americans in present-day California, made from bundled tule reeds, is also sometimes referred to as a balsa.

See also SHIPBUILDING AND EXPLORATION.

Red Sea

The Red Sea is an inland sea separating northeastern Africa from the Arabian Peninsula of Asia. Its name results from the color at times cast by dying algae. It stretches 1,200 miles from Suez, Egypt, to the strait of Bab el Mandeb and obtains a maximum depth of 9,970 feet and a maximum width of 220 miles. The northern end of the sea is divided into the gulfs of Suez and Aqaba by the Sinai Peninsula. The Gulf of Suez is connected to the MEDITERRANEAN SEA by the Suez Canal, dug in the 19th century. At its southern end, the strait of Bab el Mandeb, about 20 miles long, connects the Red Sea to the Gulf of Aden, part of the Arabian Sea. The dangers of navigating the strait of Bab el Mandeb led to its name, meaning "gate of tears" in Arabic. The Red

Shown here, in a late 19th- or early 20th-century photograph, is a raft of inflated pigskins in India. *(Library of Congress, Prints and Photographs Division [LC-USZ62-35117])*

Sea formed some 20 million years ago as tectonic activity along what is called the Great Rift Valley separating the Arabian Peninsula from Africa.

Ancient Trade and Exploration

The Red Sea is first encountered in recorded history with the rise of the Egyptian civilization. As trade with other parts of the world developed, Egyptians developed a taste for spices, incense, and other products from Asia and Africa, which were carried to Egypt by camel caravan arriving from the Arabian Peninsula. The first recorded explorer, HANNU, was sent by pharaoh Sahure in about 2450 B.C. to search for the sources of the riches. He is thought to have traveled to what the Egyptians referred to as the land of PUNT—a land to the south either in Africa or on the Arabian Peninsula—by way of the NILE RIVER and returned by way of the Red Sea. The Egyptians launched other such large expeditions southward over the centuries (see EGYPTIAN EXPLORATION). Hieroglyphics indicate that in about 1492 B.C., HATSHEPSUT sent five ships

to Punt by way of the Red Sea route, which successfully obtained and returned with valuable goods—spices, woods, minerals, and animals. As early as the 13th century B.C., Egyptian rulers had a canal dug from the Red Sea to the Nile River delta and thus a water route to the Mediterranean.

The Phoenicians and Greeks, known as mariners, mastered the waterways of the region (see GREEK EXPLORATION; PHOENICIAN EXPLORATION). The writings of fifth-century B.C. Greek historian HERODOTUS indicate that, sailing for the pharaoh NECHO II in about 600–597 B.C., Phoenician seafarers followed a Red Sea route southward from the Gulf of Aqaba to the Indian Ocean and possibly carried out the first circumnavigation of Africa, returning to the Mediterranean by way of the Atlantic Ocean and Strait of Gibraltar (see GIBRALTAR, STRAIT OF). The first Greek credited with navigating the Red Sea was SCYLAX, a mariner sent by Darius I, emperor of Persia, in 510 B.C., to explore the course of the INDUS RIVER to the east. It is reported that Scylax traveled that river to the Arabian Sea, then around the tip of Arabia into the Red Sea, on which he reached the Gulf of Suez, from where he returned to Persia.

The importance of the spice and incense trade to the Mediterranean region was immeasurable. Before his death in 323 B.C., ALEXANDER THE GREAT planned an expedition to the southern tip of Arabia to set up a sea route for the trade, but with the dissolution of his empire, it was never undertaken. The Romans gained control of Egypt with the defeat of Antony and Cleopatra. In about 25 B.C., a Roman prefect of newly annexed Egypt, GAIUS AELIUS GALLUS, left the port of Cleopatris in present-day Suez with a large expedition in order to wrest control of the spice and incense trade from the kingdom of Saba. Gallus sailed along the Arabian coast of the Red Sea, then headed inland near the northern border of present-day Yemen. He was, however, unable to overcome the Sabaeans in their principal city of Marib, and he returned unsuccessful to Egypt.

Overland travel was very expensive, and spices, silks, and incense, all at a high demand in Egypt and throughout the Roman Empire, were brought by trade caravans coming to the Romans from the East over Persia or from the south over the Arabian Peninsula (see ROMAN EXPLORATION). To further complicate Roman travel access, Arabs withheld their knowledge of the Arabian Sea. Roman sailors gradually learned to navigate the Arabian Sea and Indian Ocean, using monsoon winds. By the first century A.D., the Romans had established a direct sea route from Egypt to India, sailing through the middle of the Red Sea to avoid the pirates centered on the Arabian coast (see PIRACY).

When the Muslims conquered Egypt in the seventh century A.D., Red Sea traffic became mainly that of transporting Islamic pilgrims to Mecca from western lands, including present-day Morocco and Spain (see MUSLIM EXPLORATION).

Sea Routes

Toward the end of the Middle Ages, as contact and trade between West and East increased, so did interest in sea routes. The Portuguese, who were sending expeditions to try to discover a sea route from the Atlantic Ocean to India by rounding the southern tip of Africa, sent an expedition in 1487 to explore the southeast coast of Africa. PERO DA COVILHĀ, a Portuguese bodyguard to King John II of Portugal, sailed with Afonso de Paiva to Alexandria. The two disguised themselves as Arab traders and sailed with an Arab trading vessel in the Red Sea to the Arabian port of Aden in present-day Yemen. Covilhā continued across the Arabian Sea to India, then along the east coast of Africa.

The Portuguese continued their quest to dominate sea routes to Asia. In 1497–99, VASCO DA GAMA reached India by rounding Africa. Several years later, in 1506, the Portuguese attempted to gain complete control of the trade routes between Egypt and India when AFONSO DE ALBU-QUERQUE conquered the island of Socotra in the Gulf of Aden. The Portuguese, however, failed to conquer Aden.

By the eighth century A.D., the ancient Egyptian canal between the Nile and the Red Sea was atrophied with misuse. It was not until 1858 that a Frenchman, Vicomte Ferdinand Marie de Lesseps, having obtained the blessings of the Egyptian ruler Said Pasha, formed a company that endeavored to build a canal to connect the Red Sea with the Mediterranean via Suez. The canal, 121 miles long, was completed in 1869.

The British purchased Egypt's share of the canal in 1875, mostly in order to facilitate transport to its colonial possessions in the East and exercise dominance over trade. In 1882, Britain occupied the Sinai Peninsula and the rest of Egypt. In response, the French set up trade agreements and finally established a colony, French Somaliland, on the African coast, at the strategic entrance to the Red Sea.

❖

Today, the Red Sea continues to be an important link between East and West. The Suez Canal was nationalized by the Egyptians in 1956. The canal and the Red Sea serve as an essential route for oil tankers bringing oil from Africa and Arabia to Europe and the United States. There are continued archaeological discoveries in the Red Sea, including ships and their cargoes from prior centuries, bringing to life the richness of ancient trade and travel in the region.

See also INDIAN OCEAN, EXPLORATION OF THE.

reed-bundle canoe   See CANOE.

religion and exploration

The movement of peoples, which has occurred throughout history, whether by migration, conquest, or exploration, inevitably has been accompanied by the movement of ideas and beliefs. In some instances, the beliefs themselves have spurred on travel to foreign lands, as in the case of missionaries, purposely sent to propagate religion. Since many of the missionaries followed an academic tradition, many of them were well equipped to record information of their experiences abroad.

The Ancient World

The development of organized "religions" as opposed to tribal cults was completely intertwined with the development of kingship. The first chiefdoms, kingdoms, and cities emerged when agricultural practices improved enough to generate food surpluses. In order to have chiefs and priests who do not themselves produce any food, it is obviously necessary to have surplus food. Though archaeologists disagree as to which came first, food surpluses or chiefs demanding them, at some point the cycle was set in motion; rulers demanding ever greater production leading to greater concentration of power in a few hands in order to coordinate still greater food production. Rulers—the chief or king—were presented as deities who could influence the supernatural world and ensure rain and a good harvest.

However, the conquests of the ancient world were not accompanied by missionary zeal as we think of it today. Religion in the ancient world was relativistic rather than absolute. The gods of one culture could be adapted to those of another—thus Jupiter and Minerva of the Romans (see ROMAN EXPLORATION) were easily identified with the Zeus and Athena of the Greeks (see GREEK EXPLORATION); Mercury fused with Hermes and also with Lugus of the Celts. When the Hyksos—a Semitic people from Syria—ruled Egypt, their Storm God became one with Seth of the Egyptians (see EGYPTIAN EXPLORATION). Based as they were upon the forces of nature, the essential identity of these gods was clear. Assyrians adopted most of their gods from their rivals the Babylonians even as the two empires competed and warred against each other. Peoples from all over the Near East, including Elamites, Medes, Persians, and Jews, lived in the city of Babylon; yet apparently there were no ethnic or religious conflicts. Most outsiders worshiped both their own gods and those of Babylon. The unification of Upper and Lower Egypt in about 3000 B.C., which might have occasioned the imposition of one region's gods upon another, instead brought about a revision of religious belief in which all gods, both local and regional, were unified into a single scheme or hierarchy. The Greek city-states of the Hellenic world often fought bitter wars with one another, yet they shared belief in the Olympian gods. For the Olympic Games, held every four years, a sacred truce was declared and erstwhile rivals in war, such as Spartans and Athenians, competed on the athletic field.

Conquest typically followed the pattern of initial military subjugation, taking of prisoners, slaves, and booty; imposition of control, tribute, and taxes; decrees to make sacrifices to the conquerors' gods—but then settlement and mutual cultural influence. This was particularly true when the conquerors were nomads. In some instances, nomadic conquest would be preceded by a period of contact between nomads and a civilization during which the former would be strongly influenced by the latter—thus the Goths and Vandals, whose invasions helped cause the breakup of the Roman Empire, were already half-Romanized and, within a century, began rebuilding Rome in a semblance of its old image and constructing elaborate Christian churches.

The Missionary Impulse

In their travels, humans obviously carry culture, technology, and spiritual beliefs with them. The missionary impulse largely appeared first during the period from the fifth century B.C. to the seventh century A.D., during which Buddhism, Christianity, and Islam were born. Other major world religions—Hinduism, Confucianism, Judaism, Taoism (Daoism), and Shinto—have shown few missionary tendencies. Confucianism, in part blended Taoism and Buddhism, with its ethics of humaneness and tolerance, did not foster missionary aspirations except within China as its scholars traveled to different cities to converse with their rulers (see CHINESE EXPLORATION). Part of the tenets of Shinto, a religion of and for Japan alone, is the acceptance of the validity of other religions.

Perhaps the earliest expression of the missionary impulse came from the prophet Zarathustra (Zoroaster) in Persia probably in the sixth century B.C. His first convert, Prince Vishtapa of Bactria, was so zealous as to fight several holy wars in defense of his new faith. Missionaries carried word of Zarathustra's doctrine, which because known as Zoroastrianism, throughout the Persian Empire.

The Spread of Buddhism

Although Buddha (Siddhārtha Gautauma) lived in the sixth century B.C., significant Buddhist missionary activity only began about 200 years after his death. As a result of the third of four "Major Councils," which explored and codified Buddha's message over a period of several centuries, in the third century B.C., Ashoka, ruler of the Mauryan Empire, sent missionaries to southern and northwestern India and even as far as the MEDITERRANEAN SEA. Between the second century B.C. and the first century A.D., Mahayana Buddhists developed the doctrine of the triple nature of Buddha; one of these was the "body of transformation," in which form the Buddha nature appears on Earth to convert mankind. Buddhism spread to central Asia and from thence to China around the first century A.D. Its missionaries arrived in Korea in the fourth century A.D., in Japan in the sixth century, and came to Tibet by the seventh century. Though not explorers in the European sense, Buddhist missionaries traveled to lands utterly foreign to them, their motivation being the conviction of the rightfulness of Buddha's teachings. Later on in the seventh century A.D., religious fervor led Chinese Buddhist monk HSÜAN-TSANG to travel back to India in search of Buddhist texts, braving a Chinese imperial ban on leaving the country. In the end he traveled more than 40,000 miles through central Asia, bringing back to China a wealth of religious, cultural, and geographic knowledge.

A central characteristic of Buddhism has always been its promotion of freedom of thought. Buddha himself did not seek to impose his ideas on others but instead invited people to investigate them and decide for themselves. One can freely follow Buddha's teachings without abandoning one's own traditions and culture. For example, the Tantric form of Buddhism followed by Tibetans incorporates the many gods and demons of traditional Tibetan belief.

The Spread of Islam

At the time of Muhammad's birth in about 570, central Arabia was the only part of Arabia free of Sassanian Persian domination. Mecca was the principal city-state in this central region; the Meccans were important traders and caravan leaders and had permission from surrounding empires—Persia, Byzantium, and Abyssinia—to conduct trading expeditions through their territories. The culture of the Arabian peninsula had long been characterized by a contradictory mix of rural backwardness and urban sophistication, the large desert interior inhabited by nomads and the periphery having urban centers whose existence depended upon the SPICE TRADE. Rather like barbarian Europe during the same period, Arabia was profoundly influenced by the civilizations of Mesopotamia and later of the Mediterranean without itself developing a cohesive civilization until the rise of Islam, as Europe was to do under the influence of Christianity. Arabian peoples had been trading with southern Mesopotamia since the sixth millennium B.C. The spice trade became important by 1200 B.C.; myrrh and frankincense were traded to Egypt as well as Mesopotamia. Arabia was for millennia a crossroads of the ancient world. Mecca was situated close to a spice route along the Red Sea to Gaza. By the seventh century, as beneficiary of self-destructive wars between the Bedouin of the interior and the Byzantine and Sassanian Persian urban cultures of the periphery, Mecca had inherited from the Roman and Byzantine cities of Petra and Palmyra centrality in the spice trade. Mecca was spared as a result of its unique status as possessing the shrine of the Ka'ba, which attracted pilgrims from all over Arabia. It was in a mountain cave near Mecca that Muhammad, a wealthy merchant, reportedly received revelations from the angel Gabriel in a long series of visitations beginning in A.D. 610.

Though the spiritual primacy of Mecca gave Muhammad his opportunity to gather followers, the presence in the Ka'ba of the shrines of many gods and cults also ensured that there would be many bitter rivals to this new faith whose god aimed to displace all others. The persecution Muhammad and his first followers experienced, so severe that they were driven out of Mecca to Medina in 622, together with their victorious war to recapture Mecca in 630, may have set off the first explosive wave of conquests. By the 640s, the Muslims had overrun most of Syria, Iraq, Persia, and Egypt.

Islam focused the competing energies of the Arabian tribes through a novel type of political consolidation wrought by an elite of sedentary tribesmen from Mecca and Medina, heirs to Muhammad's legacy, a combination of spiritual, political, and commercial influence. The means of consolidation ranged from the ideological to the materialistic. The latter included the granting of gifts and promises of booty and land from conquered territories.

Missionary fervor seems to have been directed more or less exclusively toward Arabs, however. What early Muslims wanted from their new subjects was peaceful acceptance of their rule, one of their main aims being to secure new territories within which to pursue trade.

In many instances, the Arab conquerors encountered sophisticated civilizations far in advance of their own tribal culture. They swept through lands ruled by the Byzantine and Persian Sassanian empires. The Arabs left the apparatus of government and of educational institutions in place, allowing their bureaucracies to continue their activities unimpeded, only reserving the top positions for themselves. Over time, non-Arabs in the conquered lands, wishing to take part in the Arabs' success, began converting to Islam, the only way to rise in government. Only Muslims could serve in the army and this, too, attracted converts who wanted to share in the booty won by the always victorious Arab armies. Arabs thus were missionaries by example; the fantastic success of their enterprise seemed to prove the superiority of their religion. By the eighth century, non-Arab converts were exerting considerable influence on affairs throughout the Arab empire.

Muhammad and his new religion benefited from his connection through his wife, a wealthy spice merchant, with the spice trade. Her status facilitated acceptance of Islam in Arabia and the spice routes acted as conduits for its doctrine to travel. Here, too, conversion was often based on the elevated status accorded Muslims with regard to trading opportunities. Later in the ninth and 10th centuries, the spice networks would be the vehicle for the spread of Islam to southeast Asia, central Asia, and China and sub-Saharan Africa. Later still, when Portuguese explorers arrived in southeast Asia in search of black pepper, Islam became a rallying cry for resistance against the newcomers.

The Islamic requirement to make a pilgrimage to Mecca led some Muslims living in one corner of the Islamic world to continue their travels beyond Mecca. ABU ALI AHMAD IBN RUSTA, for example, in the 10th century, traveled to Europe's lower Volga region and on to Malaya and Indonesia. ABU AL-HASAN MUHAMMAD IBN JUBAYR, in the 12th century, traveled from his native Spain to Mecca, then on to Egypt and Iraq, visiting Sicily on his return journey.

As Christian missionaries were to do, Muslim travelers contributed greatly to the intellectual and scientific aspects of exploration. The tolerance of Islamic culture toward other cultures made it the heir of the intellectual traditions of the Greeks and Romans, rejected by the Christian world as pagan; many Latin and Greek texts were translated into Arabic. This resulted in a flowering of philosophic, literary, and scientific endeavor by Muslims, such as 12th-century Arab author and cartographer ABU ABD ALLAH MUHAMMAD ASH-SHARIF AL-IDRISI, who drafted what were considered the finest world maps of his time.

Early Christian Travels

During Christianity's first centuries, missionary work was largely confined to the Greco-Roman world. With the conversion of fourth-century Roman emperor Constantine, Christianity became the official religion of the Roman Empire, and conversion beyond the inner circle of true believers who had formed the early Catholic Church was at first a largely pro forma affair, as with non-Arab converts to Islam, undertaken for political and economic advancement. The Greco-Roman world was largely an urban culture, and concern for pagans and barbarians in rural areas and beyond Roman control was minimal.

Aside from St. Martin of Tours in the fourth century, who worked in Roman Gaul, the first missionary to venture beyond the periphery of the Roman world was St. Patrick, a Roman Briton who converted the Irish in the first part of the fifth century. His missionary zeal was carried on by Irish monks in succeeding centuries, though at first their urge to wander arose from an extreme asceticism as a substitute for actual martyrdom, a withdrawal from secular society first into hermits' cells and monasteries in the most isolated places and storm-racked islands they could find in Ireland, then out of Ireland altogether. In general in the Middle Ages, religious zeal led people to want to abandon normal life, to loosen the bonds of the ordinary in search of the eternal. Many entered monasteries; many more went on pilgrimages.

The movement out of Ireland, which would lead to Irish missionary work in Scotland, England, on the Continent, and beyond, was led by Saints Columba and Columbanus in the latter half of the sixth century, Columba to the island of Iona off Scotland and Columbanus to Gaul; both founded important monasteries. The half-legendary SAINT BRENDAN, who may have explored the Atlantic Ocean in a CURRAGH, was said to have been ordained a priest in A.D. 512, only some 50 years after Saint Patrick's death. He may have been an early precursor of Columba and Columbanus and in his later years seems to have lived on Iona.

For centuries after the fall of the Roman Empire, European society was focused mainly inward, as the tribal peoples who had overrun the empire struggled to cohere into stable regimes and as the feudal system developed. The main impetus for travel abroad remained religious, and many made pilgrimages to the Holy Land. One of these was ARCULF, a Frankish cleric who traveled to Palestine, Alexandria, and Constantinople (present-day Istanbul) in the 680s. His was the only journey of the time to be documented in writing, because he landed on Iona and described his experiences to the abbot, Saint Adamnan, who wrote a book about them; at this period of widespread illiteracy the Irish monasteries were the center of learning in Europe.

The Crusades

The CRUSADES, a series of military expeditions undertaken by European Christian powers to recover the Holy Land in the Near East from the Muslims, lasting from the late 11th century through the late 13th century, were religious in inspiration and marked the first attempt at expansionism and colonialism by Christian nations beyond Europe. Alexius I Comnenus, the emperor of the Eastern Roman (Byzantine) Empire, appealed to European nations for help against Islamic invaders. Soon afterward, in 1095, Pope Urban II gave a speech at the Council of Clermont in France encouraging aid to Byzantium against the threat. Peter the Hermit (Peter of Amiens) and other wandering preachers helped spread the message of a "holy war." Over the next year, Europeans from all walks of life joined in the effort, with economic and territorial implications as well as religious. There were nine officially sanctioned Crusades as well as other endeavors to assert Christian rule and worship in the Near East and North Africa.

Christian Envoys to the Far East

During the Crusades, Italy had become the primary launching point for travel from Europe to the Near East and North Africa. As a result, Italian cities prospered, and Italian merchants replaced Byzantines and Muslims as the dominant traders in the Mediterranean. Italian port cities remained the commercial center of activity in the Mediterranean—and the link between East and West—for years to come. Yet significant European expansion to the east in this period was blocked not only by the Islamic empire but also by the rising power of the Mongols. Under GENGHIS KHAN in the early 13th century, the Mongols conquered China, then pushed westward to Russia, eventually reaching eastern Europe. The Mongols allowed local populations to practice their own religions and even adopted Buddhism to a degree. Yet, concerned with their intentions and hoping to develop a political and economic relationship, Christian rulers sent envoys to Mongol-held territory (see MONGOL EXPLORATION.)

In 1245, GIOVANNI DA PIAN DEL CARPINI, a Franciscan friar, traveled as an envoy of the Catholic Church to the current khan of the Mongol Empire, Ogadei. Leaving Lyons, France, he traveled some 3,000 miles across eastern Europe and central Asia to the Mongol imperial encampment in Karakorum. Though his peace overtures were rebuffed by the khan, he was able to assess the Mongols' strength and the danger they posed to the disunified European powers. Del Carpini's mission paved the way for other papal envoys to the khans, such as WILLIAM OF RUBROUCK, a Flemish Franciscan who, in 1253, sailed from Constantinople over the Black Sea and by way of the Volga and Ural Rivers to the Caspian Sea, making the observation that it was not connected with the northern ocean as had been thought in Europe. In his account of his journey, he made the earliest known speculation that silk originated in a land east of Mongolia called Cathay. Less than 10 years later, two Venetian merchants, MAFFEO POLO and NICCOLÒ POLO, traveled to the court of Kublai Khan at Cambaluc (present-day Beijing, China). Thus were the links forged that would enable the diplomatic career of MARCO POLO, who in 1275–92 traveled throughout the Far East on behalf of Kublai Khan.

Meanwhile, the papacy continued in its diplomatic and missionary efforts in China. Kublai Khan was more welcoming to Westerners than his predecessors had been, and he permitted the establishment of a cathedral and church school in Peking (Beijing) by Italian Franciscan friar JOHN OF MONTECORVINO in the 1290s. In 1307, John was named the first archbishop of Peking, though his successor, appointed in 1333, never arrived there. In 1318, ODORIC OF PORDENONE, another Italian Franciscan, perhaps inspired by John's success in converting thousands of Chinese, began an epic 12-year journey through Asia, visiting John but traveling also to CEYLON (Sri Lanka), Borneo, and Java, observing the spice trade there, through Southeast Asia, and later into Tibet, to the city of LHASA and along the northern slopes of the HIMALAYAS. Also in the late 13th century, in the opposite direction, a Nestorian Christian monk born in China, RABBAN BAR SAUMA, during the course of a pilgrimage to Jerusalem, became involved in diplomatic efforts to the West on behalf of the Mongols. Though he never arrived in Jerusalem, he did travel to Constantinople, Rome, and even Paris.

The Black Death, the bubonic plague, which reached Europe in the mid-14th century, slowed down European expansionism for several decades (see DISEASE AND EXPLORATION). When European society finally emerged from this difficult period, it was energized. And the Catholic Church, the authority of which was questioned because of its powerlessness in the face of the epidemic, became opportunistic once again.

Catholicism and Conversion

VASCO DA GAMA, a Portuguese explorer who pioneered the sea route to Asia around the CAPE OF GOOD HOPE in 1497–99, when asked in India what he sought coming so far, replied, "Christians and spices." Spanish and Portuguese expansion received its initial impetus from the Reconquista, or reconquest, of the Iberian Peninsula from the Moors, the Muslims who had originally invaded the region in 711. Over the next centuries, there was close cooperation between the Vatican and the Portuguese crown. During the 15th century, the papacy issued a bull, *Romanus Pontifex,* which constituted a formal charter for Portuguese expansion. Portuguese explorers were instructed to "subdue, enslave or conquer any Pagan or Muslim" they encountered. In 1493, five papal bulls granted to King Ferdinand II and Queen Isabella I of Spain spiritual and material sovereignty over a region vaguely defined as "such islands and lands . . . as you have discovered or are about to discover." The European explorers of the 15th and 16th centuries in Africa and the Americas believed that they were carrying a superior religion to heathens, and missionaries accompanied many voyages of exploration in order to convert any indigenous peoples they encountered. The very humanity of native peoples was questioned. In 1512, Pope Julius II issued a doctrine proclaiming that Indians of the Americas were after all descended from Adam and Eve.

Another institution that would play a major role in missionary efforts was the Spanish Inquisition, begun in 1483 at the command of monarchs Ferdinand and Isabella. An offshoot of the Reconquista, the Inquisition was fueled by the anxieties and spiritual instability caused by the long presence in Spain of non-Christians, principally Muslims and Jews who had settled in Spain protected by the cloak of Islamic religious tolerance. In its first 15 years, the Inquisition, conducted by the Dominican order, executed 2,000 Spaniards; in the 1540s, its efforts were directed against Protestants in Spain.

The Protestant Reformation

This movement to propagate Christianity abroad had no sooner begun than there arose at the Catholic Church's back in Germany a grave challenge to the supremacy of the universal Christian empire: the Protestant Reformation. In 1517, German monk Martin Luther published his Ninety-Five Theses. The Church had come to seem remote from the needs and sufferings of ordinary people, a perception that must have been strengthened by the trauma of the Black Death and the worsening climate, and Luther based his initial attack on the sale of indulgences to finance the building of St. Peter's Basilica in Rome, perhaps seen as particularly egregious in the midst of such hard times. One of the first results of Luther's work was the Peasants' War of 1524–26, whose proponents justified their actions by invoking (though mistakenly) his ideas. The Catholic Church's Counter-Reformation in response to Luther's movement further spurred the Catholic countries of Portugal, Spain, and France to win new territories for the one true Church.

Jesuits in Asia and Africa

If a large part of the impetus and justification for conquest of new lands derived originally from the Crusades and the struggle against the Moors, a primary mission of the religious order that would be in the forefront of missionary work, the Society of Jesus, known as the Jesuits, was to carry out the Counter-Reformation. The primary focus of its founder, Saint Ignatius Loyola, was conversion of Muslims; the name the order was given in the papal bull, which approved its founding in 1540, "Societas Jesu," had been borne a century before by a military order whose mission was to fight the Turks. Yet, although Ignatius may have known little about the schism in the Church taking place in Germany, soon after his order was founded its members were sent by the pope to southern and western Germany and Austria to win back their people to the fold.

At first the Portuguese were slower than the Spanish to mount a major missionary effort in newly claimed lands. In India, such work only began in earnest with the arrival in 1542 in Goa, a major port on the west coast of India, of FRANCIS XAVIER, one of the seven founding members of the Jesuit order. Xavier established missions and made many converts in India, the Malay Peninsula, and Japan. The Jesuits were soon deeply engaged in exploration of the Asian interior. BENTO DE GÓES, for example, in the early 17th century, journeyed from India to China, the first inland trip there by a European in 300 years. In 1624, ANTONIO DE ANDRADE became the first European to reach Tibet since Odoric of Pordenone three centuries before. Andrade established a mission at Tsarapang and discovered one of the sources of the GANGES RIVER.

The Portuguese conquest of Ceuta in North Africa led to attempts to extend their sphere of influence deeper into that continent. HENRY THE NAVIGATOR, prince of Portugal, perhaps in retaliation for the defeat and death of his brother Prince Fernando in an attempt to capture Tangier in 1437, became obsessed with the desire to find the kingdom of PRESTER JOHN and join forces with fellow Christians in conquering all of Africa. The church granted him spiritual jurisdiction over all lands to the south of Portuguese territories on the north coast. Later, in the late 16th century, PEDRO PÁEZ, a Spanish Jesuit, sought Prester John in Ethiopia, during his journeys discovering the source of the Blue Nile and converting the emperor of Ethiopia, Negus Susenyos, to Christianity.

Franciscans in the Americas

The Franciscan order, born out of a movement inspired by the life of Saint Francis of Assisi in the late 12th and early 13th century, also carried out extensive missionary work. In the early 16th century, as the Spanish engaged in the conquest of Mexico, beginning in 1519 with the expedition of HERNÁN CORTÉS, the Franciscans were convinced that the end of the world was near, which would usher in the final and third age of man, the age of the spirit. This age would be characterized by love, peace, and unity for all mankind. When word came of the presence in the Americas of the Aztec, Franciscans believed that they were one of the 12 Lost Tribes of Israel who were prophesied to appear at the Last Judgment. By 1524, Franciscan missionaries, led by a group called the "Twelve Apostles," were engaged in conversion of the native Mexicans. The fact that the Aztec had a religion very different from that of Jews and Christians led the Franciscans to conclude that they had been taken over by the devil; in their eyes the destruction that accompanied the Spanish conquest, the victories of Cortés, even the plague of smallpox, which killed many thousands of the native

Mexicans, were miracles that would clear the way for the reestablishment of Christ's kingdom. Their missionary work among the survivors, however, was relatively benign; they conducted mass baptisms and marriages during the first years of the conquest in the 1520s. They believed that in order to combat the devil in Mexico, they had to learn as much as they could about native culture. As a result, almost all surviving eyewitness accounts of Aztec culture were written by Franciscan monks. When priests of the Dominican order arrived in 1526 with their Inquisition, they were skeptical about the genuineness of these conversions, observing that the native peoples continued to carry on idolatrous practices. By the 1530s, the Inquisition was in full swing in the Americas, with interrogations, torture, and burnings at the stake.

The Spanish CONQUISTADORES were organized into a type of military/commercial expedition with roots both in the Reconquista and in maritime trading ventures; heavily armed troops were led by a "captain" who was very likely the main investor in the expedition; in return for paying most of their own expenses in arms and provisions, the troops could expect a share in whatever wealth the expedition realized. Often such expeditions included a missionary and chaplain, such as JUAN DE PADILLA, a Franciscan who was with Cortés in Mexico in 1528 and later was attached to the expedition of FRANCISCO VÁSQUEZ DE CORONADO, which traveled north to present-day Arizona and New Mexico and onto the southern plains in 1540–42. With a detachment from this expedition, Padilla visited seven villages of the Hopi and also heard about a great river to the west later to be named the COLORADO RIVER. Another participant in this expedition was Franciscan MARCOS DE NIZA, whose report of mistakenly seeing what he took to be one of the legendary Seven Cities of CIBOLA, during an earlier expedition, helped prompt the expedition.

The pattern of a missionary traveling with a military man continued over the centuries in Spanish exploration. In 1768, for example, Franciscan missionary JUNÍPERO SERRA traveled with army officer GASPAR DE PORTOLÁ to California, where, over the next decade and a half, Serra founded a string of missions between San Diego and San Francisco. This was the start of the creation of the so-called Mission Indians, California Indians who were forced to live at or near the missions and became identified by the name of the mission.

Jesuits in the Americas

The Jesuits were in the forefront of missionary exploration in the Americas as elsewhere. JOSÉ DE ACOSTA, for example, ministered to the Inca in Peru and also to the Aztec for 15 years from 1571. Beneficiary of the high academic standards of his Jesuit education, Acosta was a naturalist and engaged in detailed study of the flora and fauna of South

America and also of the languages and customs of the native peoples. On his return to Europe he produced one of the earliest accounts of the natural history of the Western Hemisphere, which included descriptions of the use of the coca leaf and of the experience of altitude sickness in the ANDES MOUNTAINS. CRISTÓBAL DE ACUÑA, a Spanish Jesuit who traveled on the AMAZON RIVER in the mid-17th century, published the earliest known account of that region. This pattern of activity was to be followed many times by missionary explorers all over the world, who often were the most highly educated members of expeditions and wrote detailed accounts of new geographic features, rivers, lakes, seas, and mountains, and of new plants and animals that would have been ignored by their lay companions more interested in discoveries that could make them rich.

In New France to the north and beyond, French Jesuits such as JACQUES MARQUETTE and other missionaries continued to play a leading role in exploration and scientific study of the peoples, flora, and fauna of the new land, and also in consolidation of France's hold on its new territories. The impetus for the establishment of a French presence in Canada came from the burgeoning FUR TRADE, the result of new methods of processing the fur into felt for hats, highly fashionable in Europe. In the 40 years after the founding of New France by SAMUEL DE CHAMPLAIN in 1608, a dozen Jesuit mission posts were built in Huron (Wyandot) Indian territory. FRANÇOIS DOLLIER DE CASSON, a Sepulcian priest, in the 1670s helped to develop Montreal into a major city, laying out plans for streets, public buildings, and churches. He went with several expeditions throughout the Great Lakes region, including to Lake Erie, where he erected a cross to claim the territory for Louis XIV.

The continuing existence of New France soon began to be threatened by incursions by the Iroquois (Haudenosaunee) Indians who, having decimated the beaver populations in their native Mohawk Valley in trading with the Dutch of Fort Orange, the precursor of Albany, New York, had become determined to seize control of the Huron trapping grounds. In 1648, the Iroquois gained a decisive victory over the Huron, destroying the Christian mission posts and killing missionaries. GABRIEL LALEMANT and JEAN DE BRÉBEUF were two Jesuits killed in this war; they were later canonized by the Church as martyrs of North America. For decades after this the Iroquois continued to fight a kind of guerrilla war with the French; in the latter 17th century, Jesuit SIMON LE MOYNE joined with an Iroquois of the Onondaga nation and a Christian convert, Daniel Garakontie, to work for peace. The two organized prisoner exchanges, which helped defuse tensions; Le Moyne established ties with tribal leaders of the Iroquois and obtained permission to send Jesuit missionaries to the region. One of these, JACQUES BRUYAS, lived for several years with the Mohawk and other tribes and subsequently produced a dictionary of the Mohawk language. In 1665–69, CLAUDE-JEAN ALLOUEZ served as a French missionary to peoples of the western Great Lakes and explored the south shore of Lake Superior and the Fox and Wisconsin Rivers. He is said to have preached to 22 tribes and to have baptized some 10,000 individuals.

Jesuits continued missionary activity among Native Americans well into the 19th century, moving on to new tribes as exploration and emigration shifted west. PIERRE-JEAN DE SMET, a Belgian, studied to become a Jesuit at a seminary near St. Louis, Missouri, in the 1820s. After spending 10 years in Europe raising funds for missions, he returned to St. Louis and traveled up the MISSOURI RIVER to found a mission among the Potawatomi. Over the next decades, he worked and traveled among tribes of the northern plains, including the Sioux (Dakota, Lakota, Nakota), Flathead, Blackfeet, and Nez Perce.

Protestant Missionaries

Protestant denominations also became active around the world. The PILGRIMS, a breakaway group, part of the Puritan movement out of England, founded the second permanent English settlement in North America in 1620. In the ensuing decades, Puritans and ministers of other Protestant denominations ventured onto Native American lands. One of these was John Eliot, a nonconformist influenced by the Congregationalists. He established a number of religious communities in Massachusetts, backed by the Society for the Propagation of the Gospel Among the Indians, created in 1649 by the English Parliament. He became known as the "Apostle to the Indians" and set an example of effectiveness for later Protestant missionaries.

In the early 19th century, JOHN CAMPBELL, a Scot, worked in the interior of South Africa having been sent there by the London Missionary Society, founded in 1795 during the evangelical revival taking place in England. Intended as a nondenominational body, it also had its roots in the Congregationalist movement in England and the United States. ROBERT MOFFAT and MARY MOFFAT, Methodists who worked in South Africa and explored the Kalahari Desert, were affiliated with the London Society, which also sent missionaries to China, where they would become important agents of change. GEORGE GRENFELL, an English Baptist, worked in the Congo region of central Africa in the late 19th century.

Social Activism

Although missionaries helped to bring about European expansion into new lands, in many cases they worked to mitigate the hardships faced by native peoples being displaced by European settlers. Bartolomé de las Casas, a Catholic missionary to the Arawak (Taino) Indians of the WEST INDIES, exemplified a socially active missionary concerned with the rights of indigenous peoples. English minister JAMES RICHARDSON was an antislavery activist in Africa in the mid-19th century. Part of the impetus for Scottish missionary DAVID LIVINGSTONE's extraordinary efforts to discover the source of the NILE RIVER and his exploration of other important waterways in Africa was to foster the development of a commerce to replace the African SLAVE TRADE. He hoped that water routes would facilitate trade among the many tribes skilled in crafts and farming who inhabited central Africa. SAMUEL MARSDEN worked to reform the penal colony in New South Wales in Australia in the early 19th century and negotiated a peace treaty with the Maori of NEW ZEALAND.

❖

Religion, the means by which humans have tried to come to grips with or comprehend a reality beyond reach of our senses, has always been intertwined with the material, from the first chiefs and kings who, in return for their supposed intercession with the gods, assured the fertility of the land, to the Muslims, whose military prowess and commercial success helped propagate Islam, and to Christian missionaries who aided in European expansion. The role religion should play in worldly affairs has been problematic. The Franciscan order, for example, grew out of a movement advocating a life of poverty and simplicity, modeled on the life of Saint Francis, whose inspiration was Jesus himself. Yet very quickly challenges to this ideal arose among Franciscans, which split into two groups, one adhering to the ideal of poverty and the other modifying this to allow monks to hold property in common. During the Middle Ages, popes wielded great political power and even waged wars. While missionaries aiding in exploration and conquest seems paradoxical, missionary efforts exemplified the best and the worst aspects of expansion.

Renaissance

The term *Renaissance,* French for "rebirth," is applied to a cultural movement and a time period in Europe in the 14th, 15th, and 16th centuries, and carrying over into the 17th century. It is considered the transitional phase between the Middle Ages and modern times. The concept of rebirth is associated with the Renaissance because of a revival of pre-medieval classical influences, in particular from the civilizations of the ancient Greeks and Romans. Such cultural classifications are of course too pat. It is an oversimplification to regard the Middle Ages as the stagnant Dark Ages. Scholarship and the arts are a continuum, and individuals grew even as societies and institutions stagnated. Moreover, other peoples, such as the Arab Muslims and the Chinese, were breaking new intellectual ground during the medieval period, and some of their learning in geography and other fields reached Europeans as well. The CRUSADES of the 11th through 13th centuries, in which Christian European armies invaded the Near East, led to increasing cultural contacts. Yet there were events and developments—many of them surrounding individuals—during the centuries associated with the Renaissance that can be regarded as culturally transforming, making the concept of such a period a helpful one in historical studies.

Culture and Transformation

During the 14th century, scholars and writers, especially in Italy, read the classics with a new focus on the power of reason and the worth of the individual. The movement associated with this fresh interpretation has come to be known as humanism, as heralded by 14th-century Italian poet and scholar Petrarch (Francesco Petrarca). The fall of Constantinople (present-day Istanbul) to the Ottoman Turks in 1453—in effect, the end of the Eastern Roman Empire (or Byzantine Empire), which had been centered there—drove Byzantine scholars to western Europe, giving new impetus to classical and Muslim studies and their relevance in contemporary life. Moreover, Spanish victories over the occupying Moors out of North Africa—the final victory in 1492—and the capture of various universities, led to greater access to Muslim scholarship, as well as to Greek scholarship from texts that had been in Muslim hands. The development of the movable type printing press by German goldsmith and printer Johannes Gutenberg, in the mid-15th century, made texts available to a wider audience. A new freedom of expression in painting, sculpture, architecture, and music, as well as in philosophy and writing, emphasizing the contribution of the individual as opposed to the anonymity of many of the artists of the Middle Ages, resulted. In the sciences, intellectual curiosity, a willingness to experiment, and an adherence to reason and objectivity led to new discoveries, such as the telescope early in the 17th century. A 15th–16th-century Italian artist, architect, and scientist, Leonardo da Vinci, is representative of this new approach to intellectual and creative pursuits in the Renaissance. Dutch scholar Desiderius Erasmus, his contemporary, made the case that the study of Christian theology should be open to all, not just the clergy. Such views played a part in the Reformation, led by Martin Luther, another contemporary, whose activities in Germany resulted in the founding of Protestantism. Political and social institutions were also reexamined during these centuries, with a new sense of optimism regarding the lot of humankind and a new emphasis on education.

Age of Exploration

The other great theme running through the Renaissance—and that which relates directly to the history of exploration—is the expanding worldview resulting from geographic

This frontispiece from a 1496 text shows Ptolemy and his Renaissance translator, Joannes Regiomontanus, beneath a sphere representing the heavens. *(Library of Congress, Prints and Photographs Division [LC-USZ62-95164])*

discoveries. HENRY THE NAVIGATOR, prince of Portugal, who had the vision to sponsor voyages of exploration from Portugal along the coast of Africa in the 15th century, is an important Renaissance figure. Certain expeditions—that of Italian CHRISTOPHER COLUMBUS for Spain across the Atlantic Ocean to the Americas in 1492, of Portuguese VASCO DA GAMA for Portugal around Africa to India in 1497–98, and of Portuguese FERDINAND MAGELLAN for Spain in the first CIRCUMNAVIGATION OF THE WORLD in 1519–21, along with others of the period—were momentous in that they changed cartographic awareness and set in motion the colonizing and commercial endeavors of the great international powers. Portugal, Spain, the Netherlands, France, and England became active around the world over the next centuries. Developments in shipbuilding and in navigation contributed to expanding frontiers (see also SHIPBUILDING AND EXPLORATION; NAVIGATION AND EXPLORATION). The latter part of the Renaissance, starting in the 15th century into the 17th century, when Europeans came to get a closer-to-accurate sense of the extent of the Earth, has been referred to as the EUROPEAN AGE OF EXPLORATION.

rocket

As wind power was to the EUROPEAN AGE OF EXPLORATION, so is rocketry to 20th- and 21st-century SPACE EXPLORATION. A rocket is a conveyance powered by a self-contained supply of fuel and an agent of combustion, usually oxygen. The force of the resulting exhaust gases of the rocket engine propel the rocket, a cylindrical tube, in the opposite direction. The term *rocket* is applied to primitive black-powder devices as well as to giant space launch vehicles.

Jet engines are different from rocket engines in that they are not self-contained, drawing an oxidizer from the surrounding atmosphere; they are also called air-breathing engines. Rocket engines provide the most powerful thrust for their weight. And since they provide their own oxygen, they can operate above Earth's atmosphere. In addition to the launching and maneuvering of a spacecraft carrying people or of an artificial SATELLITE or SPACE PROBE for exploratory and scientific aeronautics, rockets are used for a number of purposes: as projectiles and missiles in warfare; as emergency signaling devices (signal rockets); to carry scientific equipment into the upper atmosphere for collecting data (sounding rockets); to assist in the takeoff of airplanes with heavy loads; and to boost pilots from jet planes in distress. Rockets have also been used for centuries as fireworks. Model rockets are another form of entertainment.

It is believed that the CHINESE (see CHINESE EXPLORATION) invented the rocket, originally paper or cloth tubes filled with gunpowder (an explosive mixture of potassium nitrate, sulphur, and carbon) and attached to long sticks for stabilization, creating "arrows of flying fire." They are men-

tioned in accounts of 13th-century battles involving Chinese, Mongols (see MONGOL EXPLORATION), and Arab Muslims (see MUSLIM EXPLORATION). Europeans tended to use early rockets as signaling devices or as fireworks. Firearms, which were more accurate, became the preferred weapon. In India rockets—iron tubes attached to bamboo sticks—were used in warfare against British forces in the early 1800s. A British inventor by the name of William Congreve developed a rocket capable of traveling two miles and conceived the idea of attaching explosive devices to rockets, the first warheads. England used Congreve rockets against the United States in the War of 1812, leading to "the rockets red glare" in *The Star-Spangled Banner,* the U.S. national anthem. In the mid-1800s, another British inventor, William Hale, invented a stickless rocket that was spin-stabilized, thus improving accuracy. Similar barrage rockets, acting as incendiary devices, were used in other wars of the 19th century, such as the Civil War.

Scientist Robert H. Goddard poses with an early rocket in this photograph, thought to have been taken in 1925. *(Library of Congress, Prints and Photographs Division [LC-USZ62-127240])*

In the late 1800s, Austrian physicist Ernst Mach theorized the use of rockets to obtain supersonic speeds and German inventor Hermann Ganswindt reached the conclusion that a self-contained rocket would be the only engine able to function in the vacuum of space. In the early 20th century, Russian inventor Konstantin Eduardovich Tsiolkovsky, American physicist Robert Hutchings Goddard, and Rumanian-born mathematics teacher Hermann Oberth, who worked in Germany, independently promoted the use of rocketry in spaceflight, developing ideas of liquid fuel and multistage booster rockets as launch vehicles.

In the 1920s and 1930s, rocket engineers of many different nationalities developed rocket technology. A number of successful liquid-propellant launches were carried out in Germany, the United States, and the Union of Soviet Socialist Republics (USSR; Soviet Union). Germany also began a secret rocket program for military purposes in the 1930s. In 1942, during World War II, the Germans under Wernher von Braun conducted the first successful launch of the A-4 (later called the V-2) rocket, a long-range guided missile (about 200 miles) propelled by liquid fuel. A total of 1,027 V-2s were launched against Allied targets. The Germans also worked on solid-fuel rockets.

After World War II, the United States and the Soviet Union intensified their lagging rocket research, competing over German research and technology. Wernher von Braun, in fact, began working for the Americans. The cold war between the two nations, as well as the "space race," led to the development of intercontinental ballistic missiles, which travel in the outer atmosphere, and multistage launch vehicles, capable of carrying payloads beyond Earth's atmosphere. Other rocket technology was applied to thrusters, small rockets used to steer or change the speed of spacecrafts or satellites, for changing their orbit or sending them back to Earth (retrorockets).

U.S. rockets have included the Viking, Vanguard, Redstone, Jupiter, Atlas, Titan, Agena, Centaur, Saturn, Athena, Taurus, and Delta. A Saturn-type three-stage rocket, the *Saturn V,* the largest rocket ever built, was used in the APOLLO PROGRAM to launch spacecraft to the Moon. The U.S. SPACE SHUTTLE is a reusable rocket and spacecraft in one. The Soyuz rocket, developed as part of the SOYUZ PROGRAM, has been central to both the Soviet Union's and Russia's space program, replacing the earlier Vostok rocket used in the VOSTOK PROGRAM and the VOSKHOD PROGRAM. A more recent Russian rocket is the Proton, with K and M models. Rockets of other nations include the EUROPEAN SPACE AGENCY's *Ariane 4* and *5;* the Chinese *Long March 2C* and *2E;* the Japanese *H-2;* the Indian *PSLV* (Polar Satellite Launch Vehicle); the Israeli *Shavit 2;* and the multinational, privately owned *Sea Launch Zenit-3SL,* which is launched from a converted oil platform in the Pacific Ocean southeast of Hawaii.

Rocket design has to take into consideration a number of factors: type of propellant; size and shape of exit (exhaust) nozzle; the number of stages required to lift an intended payload; and navigation equipment, such as internal gyroscopes (a device with a spinning disk mounted in a stationery base) to track orientation. Chemical rocket engines are powered by either liquid propellants (typically hydrogen as fuel and oxygen as oxidant) or solid propellants (typically nitroglycerine) burned in a combustion chamber, the gas of which is expelled at supersonic velocities. Rockets with nuclear engines, which heat fuel by radiation from reactor cores, and ion engines, which use thermoelectric power to expel ions rather than gases, have also been built and used experimentally.

Rocky Mountain Fur Company

The Rocky Mountain Fur Company was one of several fur-trading companies established to pursue the North American FUR TRADE, at its peak in the 1820s–1830s. In February 1822, WILLIAM HENRY ASHLEY, a Virginian, and ANDREW HENRY, a Pennsylvanian, formed the company and organized the first expedition up the MISSOURI RIVER to its headwaters in the northern ROCKY MOUNTAINS in present-day Montana. Henry, who been involved with the earlier ST. LOUIS MISSOURI FUR COMPANY, was active in the field the first years of operation, but, on returning to St. Louis with a load of furs in summer 1824, gave up the fur trade to develop lead-mining interests in Missouri.

The Rocky Mountain Fur Company employed many of the men who would become known as MOUNTAIN MEN: JAMES PIERSON BECKWOURTH, JAMES BRIDGER, ROBERT CAMPBELL, JAMES CLYMAN, HUGH GLASS, THOMAS FITZPATRICK, HENRY FRAEB, CALEB GREENWOOD, DAVID E. JACKSON, EDWARD ROSE, JEDEDIAH STRONG SMITH, WILLIAM LEWIS SUBLETTE, WILLIAM HENRY VANDERBURGH, LOUIS VASQUEZ, and JOHN WEBER. In July 1825, at Henrys Fork of the Green River in what is now northern Utah, Ashley sponsored the first annual rendezvous of trappers and Indians, where goods were exchanged.

At the rendezvous the following year, Ashley sold his interests to David Jackson, Jedediah Smith, and William Sublette, who reorganized again in 1830. James Bridger, Robert Campbell, and CHRISTOPHER HOUSTON CARSON (Kit Carson) trapped for the Rocky Mountain Fur Company. Thomas Fitzpatrick eventually became a principal in the company. The company was dissolved in 1834, although the principals remained active in the western trade for some years.

See also COMMERCE AND EXPLORATION.

Rocky Mountains

The Rocky Mountains (also called the Rockies) are the largest mountain system in North America. Although estimates vary, they extend at least 2,000 miles from central Mexico through Canada to the Arctic. Their borders are not clearly defined; some consider the Yukon, Mackenzie, and Alaskan Ranges in Canada and Alaska as part of the Rocky Mountain system, and the Sierra Madre Occidental in Mexico as well. Geographers do agree the system includes at least 100 distinct ranges. The Rocky Mountains are bordered on the east by the Great Plains, and on the west by the Interior Plateau and Coast Mountains (in Canada) and by the Rocky Mountain Trench (a valley that runs from northwestern Montana to northern British Columbia), the Columbia Plateau, and the Great Basin (in the United States). In Mexico, a central plateau separates the southern continuation of the Rockies. The characteristic jagged peaks and flat-topped elevations of the relatively young Rockies were formed by crustal uplifts reshaped by glaciers.

The Rocky Mountain system is divided into four sections: the southern, central, northern, and Canadian Rockies. The southern Rockies (located in New Mexico, Colorado, and southern Wyoming) include the Sangre de Cristo, Laramie, San Juan, Sawatch, and Park Ranges. The Colorado Plateau of the Four Corners region (northeastern Arizona, southeastern Utah, southwestern Colorado, and northwestern New Mexico) is sometimes discussed as part of the southern Rockies. The central Rockies, or middle Rockies (located in northeastern Utah, western Wyoming, eastern Idaho, and southern Montana) include the Bighorn, Beartooth, Asaroka, Wind River, Salt River, Teton, Snake River, Wasatch, and Uinta Mountains. The Uinta Mountains are the only range in the Rockies running east-to-west, instead of north-to-south. The northern Rockies (located in northern Idaho, western Montana, and northeastern Washington) include the Sawtooth, Cabinet, Salmon River, Clearwater Mountains, and Bitterroot Range. The Canadian Rockies are located in southwestern Alberta and eastern British Columbia. (To the north the Yukon Territory and Alaska are part of the same mountain system; and the Sierra Madre Oriental in Mexico can be considered a southern extension of the chain.)

Shown, in a 1941 photograph, is a vista of the Rocky Mountains in Glacier National Park, Montana. *(Library of Congress, Prints and Photographs Division [LC-USF34-058094-D])*

The various subdivisions differ geologically (that is, by origin, ages, and types of rocks) and physiographically (that is, by landforms, drainage, and soils), yet they all have high elevations and great local relief (that is, the vertical difference between the base and the summit of ranges). The highest peak in the Rocky Mountain system is Mount Elbert in Colorado, at 14,433 feet above sea level. More than 100 named peaks measure at least 10,000 feet; these include Pikes Peak (14,110 feet) and Longs Peak (14,255 feet) in the Southern Rockies; Gannett Peak (13,804 feet), Grand Teton (13,771 feet), and Fremont Peak (13,730 feet) in the central Rockies; and Granite Peak (12,799 feet) and Borah Peak (12,662 feet) in the northern Rockies. The highest peak in Canada is Mount Robson, at 12,972 feet.

North America's Continental (or Great) Divide, the highest points of land separating the waters flowing west and south from the waters flowing east and north, runs along the Rocky Mountain ranges. (Early travelers along the Oregon Trail called it "Uncle Sam's Backbone.") Among the largest rivers that are part of this watershed is the longest river in the United States, the MISSOURI RIVER, which originates in the northern Rockies and flows generally east and south to join up with the MISSISSIPPI RIVER near St. Louis, Missouri; the Mississippi feeds the Gulf of Mexico, an arm of the Atlantic Ocean. The Arkansas River begins in the central Rockies and flows south and east to the Mississippi River in Arkansas. The Rio Grande flows from the southern Rockies south and east to the Gulf of Mexico. The COLORADO RIVER flows from the central Rockies south and west to the Gulf of California, part of the Pacific Ocean. The COLUMBIA RIVER flows from the Canadian Rockies south and west to the Pacific Ocean. The Snake River, out of the central Rockies, flows generally west to the Columbia. The Fraser River flows out of the Canadian Rockies first northwest, then south to the Pacific. The Saskatchewan River flows out of the Canadian Rockies generally east into Lake Winnipeg, which is drained by the Nelson River, flowing to HUDSON BAY, an arm of both the Atlantic and Arctic Oceans. The Pace River flows out of the Canadian Rockies generally east and north to the Great Slave Lake, which has an outlet to the Mackenzie, which flows to the Arctic Ocean. And the Liard River, farther north, flows out of the Canadian Rockies generally east and north, also to the Mackenzie River.

Grasslands cover much of the Rockies' lower elevations. Higher up are found extensive forests, mostly of conifers. The forests give way to grasses and scattered shrubs. The peaks have little vegetation up high. Some of the tallest have year-round snow and ice caps.

First Reports

The high peaks, rough terrain, and early winters of the Rockies proved a significant barrier to western movement, and the Rockies were one of the last regions of North America to be thoroughly explored by nonnative peoples. The earliest European explorers to see the Rockies were Spaniards, and the first sightings were from the south. In 1540, an expedition under FRANCISCO VÁSQUEZ DE CORONADO entered present-day New Mexico and explored some of the country north of present-day Albuquerque, the southern limits of the Sangre de Cristo Mountains. In 1582–83, Spanish merchant and prospector ANTONIO ESTEVAN DE ESPEJO, who traveled north out of Mexico, ventured farther northward in the Sangre de Cristo Mountains. Starting in 1598, JUAN DE OÑATE founded a number of Spanish settlements near the upper Rio Grande, but, over the next decades, the occupants were not known to venture northward into the Rocky Mountain system, instead venturing eastward onto the Great Plains, or westward toward California.

Early Traders

Nearly a century and a half later, in 1742–43, a French Canadian fur trader, LOUIS-JOSEPH GAULTIER DE LA VÉRENDRYE, led an expedition across the Missouri River and northern plains—probably as far west as the Black Hills of western South Dakota and eastern Wyoming. Yet the mountains they later described may have been the Bighorn Mountains in western Wyoming. The next decade, in 1754–55, ANTHONY HENDAY, a British fur trader for the HUDSON'S COMPANY, explored the Canadian plains to territory known to be within 40 miles of the Rockies, although he made no mention of sighting peaks in his journals. In 1776–77, Franciscan missionaries FRANCISCO ATANASIO DOMÍNGUEZ and FRANCISCO SILVESTRE DE ESCALANTE, in an unsuccessful effort to create a route between Santa Fe, New Mexico, and Monterey, California, headed northward and traveled through Rocky Mountain country, including the San Juan Mountains in Colorado and the Wasatch Mountains in central Utah.

In 1793, SIR ALEXANDER MACKENZIE, a Scottish-born fur trader in the employ of the NORTH WEST COMPANY, traveled into the Canadian Rockies of British Columbia and crossed the Continental Divide, eventually descending the Blackwater River westward, then crossing over to the Bella Coola River and descending it to the Pacific, thus completing the first overland journey across North America north of the Rio Grande.

In the ensuing years, other fur traders worked the Canadian and northern Rockies, establishing numerous posts, among them British-born DAVID THOMPSON, who worked for the Hudson's Bay Company and the North West Company in the course of his career and mapped much of the Pacific Northwest. In 1798–1800, he explored the Athabasca and North Saskatchewan Rivers of Alberta. In 1807, he established a route through the Canadian Rockies of British

Columbia by way of Howse Pass and, in 1810, to the north, by way of the Athabasca Pass. Thompson then descended the Columbia all the way to its mouth, reaching it on July 14. Another explorer for the North West Company, American-born SIMON FRASER, thoroughly explored the watershed of the river named after him, the Fraser.

Lewis, Clark, and Pike

The U.S. government had launched the Lewis and Clark Expedition several years prior. After departing from St. Louis in spring 1804 and wintering in the Mandan Indian villages in North Dakota, where the river bends westward, MERIWETHER LEWIS and WILLIAM CLARK and the Corps of Discovery, including their Shoshone Indian guide SACAJAWEA (Sacagawea), set out on April 7, 1805, reaching the Great Falls of the Missouri on June 2. From that point they could have headed directly west and reached the Rockies in four days (as they were later told by Indians) but followed the Missouri to its source—the Three Forks of the Missouri, arriving on July 27. Two weeks later, on August 12, Lewis climbed up to the Continental Divide. He had hoped to look down upon a plain to the west, with a large river that would carry them to the Pacific, but saw only more mountains.

The Corps of Discovery crossed Lemhi Pass on the present-day border between Montana and Idaho. The expedition came upon a Shoshone village and Sacajawea's brother Cameahwait. The Shoshone provided them with horses, which the Corps of Discovery used to cross the rugged Bitterroot Range by way of Lolo Pass into present-day Idaho. The expedition eventually reached the Clearwater River Valley. Nez Perce Indians instructed them in the making of the dugout CANOE that they used to descend the Clearwater out of the mountains. They eventually reached the Snake River, then the Columbia, following it to the Pacific, where they spent the winter before returning eastward. On the return trip, in the eastern Rockies, Lewis took the more direct northern route from Lolo Pass through Lewis and Clark Pass to the Great Falls of the Missouri, while Clark followed the original loop to the south. They met up at the mouth of the Yellowstone and together rode the Missouri back to St. Louis, arriving on September 23.

In 1806, U.S. Army officer and explorer ZEBULON MONTGOMERY PIKE was commissioned to explore the headwaters of the Arkansas and Red Rivers. He followed the Arkansas River to the tablelands in the southern Rockies of present-day Colorado. While there, he attempted to climb Pikes Peak, which was later named for him.

Later Traders

Much of the subsequent 19th-century exploration of the Rockies was motivated by an interest in the FUR TRADE. In 1808, American businessman JOHN JACOB ASTOR founded the AMERICAN FUR COMPANY, planning to establish a string of trading posts east and west of the northern Rockies. Astor sponsored a seaward expedition under Scotsman ROBERT STUART, from New York City around South America, in 1810, to build Fort Astoria at the mouth of the Columbia River as the westernmost post. The next year, he sent out an overland expedition from St. Louis—the Astorians—under WILSON PRICE HUNT that crossed the southern reaches of the Bighorn Mountains and the Wind River Mountains, then through Teton Pass into the Snake River Valley. In 1812–13, Robert Stuart, still working for Astor, traveled from Astoria in Oregon eastward through the SOUTH PASS through the Wind River Range in Wyoming, then descended the Platte and Missouri Rivers to St. Louis.

In 1809, a number of traders centered in St. Louis founded the ST. LOUIS MISSOURI FUR COMPANY. Among them were William Clark, MANUEL LISA, JEAN PIERRE CHOUTEAU, AUGUSTE PIERRE CHOUTEAU, ANTOINE PIERRE MENARD, and ANDREW HENRY. With time, traders pushed farther and farther into the Rocky Mountains.

In 1822, WILLIAM HENRY ASHLEY, along with Andrew Henry, founded the ROCKY MOUNTAIN FUR COMPANY. Many of the men who worked as trappers and traders for Ashley came to be known as the MOUNTAIN MEN after the Rockies, including THOMAS FITZPATRICK and JEDEDIAH STRONG SMITH. The mountain men traveled the trails, passes, and rivers of the Rockies, especially the northern and central ranges. In 1824, Jed Smith rediscovered the South Pass and spread word of it to other trappers.

Meanwhile, Canadians remained active in the region. In 1816–19, DONALD MACKENZIE, Alexander Mackenzie's cousin, also sent out fur-trapping brigades for the North West Company throughout the Pacific Northwest and the northern Rockies. In the 1820s–30s, JOHN MCLOUGHLIN, based on the Columbia River, also directed operations in the region for the Hudson's Bay Company. PETER SKENE OGDEN worked a wide area for him, including the northern Rockies.

A number of traders established posts to the south, convenient to work the southern Rockies. ANTOINE ROBIDOUX, an American born in St. Louis of French Canadian ancestry, was perhaps the earliest non-Spanish trader working out of Taos, New Mexico. In 1828, he founded Fort Uncompahgre on the Gunnison River in southwestern Colorado; in 1837, he also founded Fort Uinta, or Robidoux Rendezvous, in northeastern Utah. From 1832 to 1844, he and his five brothers dominated the trade between that region and southern Arizona, providing north-south supply routes along the Rockies' eastern and western slopes. In 1833, brothers CHARLES BENT and WILLIAM BENT, whose parents from Virginia had raised them in St. Louis, along with CÉRAN DE HAULT DE LASSUS DE ST. VRAIN, born in

St. Louis of French ancestry, founded Bent's Fort on the Arkansas River in southeastern Colorado and developed their fur trade in that region. That same year, LOUIS VASQUEZ, another St. Louis native who had worked for Ashley, established a post, Fort Vasquez, on the South Platte River near present-day Colorado and, in the late 1830s, blazed a trail to Bent's Fort. Kentucky-born CHRISTOPHER HOUSTON CARSON (Kit Carson), who had trapped in the Rockies in the 1830s, worked as a hunter and guide out of Bent's Fort in 1840–42.

Another fur trader, BENJAMIN LOUIS EULALIE DE BONNEVILLE, born in France but raised in the United States and a former U.S. army officer, led a fur-trading expedition across the Rocky Mountains by way of South Pass to Utah in the early 1830s.

Across the Great Divide

Crossing the Rockies along the Oregon Trail, which included South Pass, became an accepted part of travel west. In 1841, Belgian missionary PIERRE-JEAN DE SMET led the first organized wagon train migration on the Oregon Trail, with Thomas Fitzpatrick serving as guide. That same year, to the north, Métis JAMES SINCLAIR pioneered a wagon route through the Canadian Rockies by way of White Man's Pass in British Columbia for the Hudson's Bay Company.

Mapping the Rockies

Over the years, the U.S. government sponsored expeditions to the eastern Rockies, among them those under Major STEPHEN HARRIMAN LONG in 1820 and Colonel HENRY DODGE in 1835. During the 1840s–50s, JOHN CHARLES FRÉMONT, appointed a lieutenant in the army's Corps of Topographical Corps of Engineers, led a number of expeditions into the Rockies, with Kit Carson as guide for some of them. Frémont crossed the range by way of South Pass twice, climbed Frémont Peak in the Wind River Range, explored the Wasatch, Uinta Ranges, Sangre de Cristo, and San Juan Ranges. Frémont produced accurate surveys including elevations, distances, and LATITUDE AND LONGITUDE that were a boon to pioneers and explorers. In 1845, STEPHEN WATTS KEARNY, again with Thomas Fitzpatrick as guide, explored the Rockies, including South Pass. In the 1860s–80s, the U.S. government sponsored various scientific surveys of the Rockies and other parts of the West under geologists FERDINAND VANDEVEER HAYDEN, CLARENCE KING, and JOHN WESLEY POWELL. In 1857–59, JOHN PALLISER led a British scientific expedition to western Canada, during which he surveyed the passes of the Canadian Rockies.

❖

Nowadays, the Rockies are developed for mining, lumbering, livestock, and recreation.

See also NORTH AMERICA, EXPLORATION OF.

Roman exploration (ancient Roman exploration)

According to legend, ancient Rome was founded in 753 B.C. on Palatine Hill, a hill on the east bank of the Tiber River in what is now west-central Italy, just inland from the MEDITERRANEAN SEA. The settlement eventually expanded into a city on six other hills. The native inhabitants of the region known as Latium (now part of Lazio) spoke Latin, although, with time, the city became a melting pot of many different peoples and cultures.

In its early stages, the Etruscans, living in the northwest in what is now the region of Tuscany, exerted political influence on the native inhabitants, and Rome was ruled by kings. By 509 B.C., the Romans had rid themselves of outside rule and developed a republican government. In subsequent centuries they gradually expanded their domain into other parts of Italy and neighboring lands. Victory in the Punic Wars against the Carthaginians in 264–146 B.C., and in the Macedonian Wars against the Macedonians and Greeks in 215–168 B.C., as well as other military actions, led to increasing Roman power. Rome assumed control of Egypt in 30 B.C., wresting power from the Greeks. In 27 B.C., the republic collapsed, and Rome was ruled by emperors, the first being Augustus (formerly Gaius Octavius). The Roman Empire reached its greatest extent by A.D. 117, including territory in northern Africa, northern Europe, and the Middle East. Emperor Constantine I (Constantine the Great) recognized Christianity as the official religion and established a new capital, Constantinople (present-day Istanbul, Turkey) in A.D. 330. In 395, the empire was divided into the Western Roman Empire and the Eastern Roman Empire. The Western Roman Empire gradually broke up by the fifth century because of economic decline, internal political unrest, and invasions by Germanic peoples from the north. The Eastern Roman Empire, also known as the Byzantine Empire, endured for another millennium until 1453, when Constantinople was captured by the Ottoman Turks.

Although the Romans took over some of the trading activities of the Greeks, they did not develop a trading culture on a level with other Mediterranean peoples, such as the Minoans, Phoenicians, Egyptians, and Greeks. Much of their trade, especially into Asia for exotic products, such as spices and silk, was carried out by foreigners. As was the case with the great military trek into Asia by Macedonian ALEXANDER THE GREAT, most of the Roman expeditions into unknown lands were for the purpose of conquest. The subsequent building projects of the Romans, including roads and bridges and even entire towns, served to unite lands that had previously been isolated from one another. A great dissemination of ideas resulted as the Roman Empire absorbed other cultures, and eventually there was also a consolidation of geographic knowledge, as recorded by scholars.

Rome's greatest contribution to the history of exploration is the opening of contact between Mediterranean peoples and peoples of northern Europe, including the British Isles. An early expedition by Greek PYTHEAS in about 325 B.C. through the Strait of Gibraltar (see GIBRALTAR, STRAIT OF) along the coast of Spain, France, and Britain as far as the Baltic Sea, brought back some knowledge of northern regions, but it was the Roman military machine and its actions against northern tribes that united Europe. In 58 B.C., general GAIUS JULIUS CAESAR led a military expedition to Gaul (present-day France), and, in 55–54 B.C., he reached Britain. The Roman subjugation of Britain was not completed until the following century. In A.D. 59–61, forces under general SUETONIUS PAULINUS, appointed military governor of Britain, suppressed a Druid revolt. General GNAEUS JULIUS AGRICOLA, also military governor, further explored the British Isles in A.D. 77–84, possibly sailing around them. He also led a military exploration into Scotland in A.D. 80.

The Romans also furthered geographic knowledge of Asia and Africa. In 19 B.C., Cornelius Balbus, a Roman governor of Tunisia, crossed Africa's Libyan Desert in actions against desert tribes. In about 25 B.C., army officer GAIUS AELIUS GALLUS led a military expedition to the Arabian Peninsula. Before his service as military governor of Britain, in A.D. 42, Suetonius Paulinus led a military expedition from the coast of North Africa southward across the Atlas Mountains to the northern edge of the SAHARA DESERT. Eight years later, army officer JULIUS MATERNUS led a military expedition from Africa's north coast across the Sahara, possibly reaching Lake Chad. In A.D. 45, HIPPALUS, a Greek mariner in service of Egypt, then under Roman domination, navigated a direct sea route across the Arabian Sea from Africa to India, furthering earlier knowledge gained by another Greek, EUDOXUS, who had explored the water route between Africa and India in two expeditions between 120 and 115 B.C. Other military expeditions, as the Roman Empire expanded, brought back new geographic information to Rome. By A.D. 29, a Roman military expedition had reached Africa's upper NILE RIVER in Ethiopia and Sudan. The emperor Nero, who ruled in A.D. 54–68, sent out an advance party with an exploratory purpose—to locate the source of the Nile—prior to a planned military campaign. Based on descriptions, the party is thought to have reached the marshes of the White Nile, known as the Sudd.

Many of the discoveries of Roman military expeditions were published in about A.D. 18 by STRABO, a Greek scholar working in Rome. PLINY THE ELDER , who had served as a Roman cavalry officer in both Europe and Africa, also was active as a geographer in the first century A.D. The only one of his works to survive, *Historia Naturalis,* published in A.D. 77, offered a comprehensive study of the known world at that time. PTOLEMY, a hellenized Egyptian living in Alexandria while it was under Roman rule, published a description of world geography in A.D. 127–147.

See also CARTHAGINIAN EXPLORATION; EGYPTIAN EXPLORATION; GREEK EXPLORATION; MINOAN EXPLORATION; PHOENICIAN EXPLORATION.

roundship

The roundship was the vessel typical of northern European countries during the second half of the Middle Ages. Its most direct ancestor was the LONGSHIP of the Vikings. It shared some of the design features of the COG. In the course of evolving from the longship, the roundship took on its own characteristics and was used in warfare as well as commerce.

The first roundships were clinker-built, that is, having overlapping planks. This had been advantageous for the longships due to the integrity of the seams and flexibility in rough seas. With the invention of the saw in Europe, shipbuilders could fashion square planks, which could be laid edge to edge, or carvel-built, thus creating a smoother surface that could pass more easily through water. The shape of the roundship also evolved. The roundship was stouter than the longship, sitting deeper in the water and with more room for cargo. A deck was added on top of the ship's shell, giving the crew more room to work and sleep, while the hull could be filled with supplies and trade goods.

The roundship became a multipurpose vessel, used for both trading and for war. Being the workhorse of its day, it also was referred to as the MERCHANT SHIP. For warfare, additional platforms—castles—were built on the front and back of the vessel allowing better observation and offering additional shelter underneath. As roundships became too heavy to propel by oars, sails were added for propulsion, initially a single square sail, then several larger sails for larger hulls. Eventually smaller sails were added to the bow and stern castles. The masts on which these sails were attached would later be built on the main deck. A spar was sometimes added to the bow to hold a spritsail.

Another innovation the roundship incorporated was the stern rudder. A rudder mounted to the side was adequate for the longship, but to navigate the larger and tubbier roundship, the center-mounted stern rudder proved much more efficient and reliable.

As the design of the roundship became well understood, its length grew beyond the 100-foot mark. The smooth, round hull was stable in the ocean, and made the ship dependable, if not elegant. The roundship predated the EUROPEAN AGE OF EXPLORATION, but many of its features were incorporated into the CARAVEL and the CARRACK, which would carry European explorers throughout the world's oceans.

See also SHIPBUILDING AND EXPLORATION.

Royal Geographical Society (RGS)

The Royal Geographical Society (RGS), founded in England in 1830, is an organization dedicated to advancing the science and public knowledge of geography. Now affiliated with the Institute of British Geographers (IBG), RGS-IBG is the largest geographic society in Europe with a membership of almost 15,000, among them academics and professionals in the field of geography and related disciplines as well as lay people. At its central offices in London, a library, picture library, and map room have extensive collections. There are eight regional branches on the British Isles and one overseas in Hong Kong. RGS-IBG holds more than 150 lectures and conferences each year and directs three overseas field research programs. Its Expedition Advisory Centre helps train youth for careers in geography-related occupations. RGS-IBG currently publishes three scholarly journals, a research bulletin, a newsletter, and a popular magazine. It also bestows awards to people around the world for accomplishments in geography and exploration.

The Royal Geographical Society can trace its origins to the founding of the Raleigh Dining Club—named after 16th–17th-century Englishman SIR WALTER RALEIGH—in 1827. Members divided the world into cartographic divisions and became responsible for studying and passing on knowledge of a particular area. SIR JOHN BARROW, second secretary of the Admiralty, and other members eventually decided to establish a more organized institution and, under the patronage of King William IV, the RGS came into being in 1830. The next year, it merged with the AFRICAN ASSOCIATION, which had been founded by SIR JOSEPH BANKS in 1788 for the promotion of British voyages of exploration to Africa. Barrow was the organization's first vice president, then, following the terms of Viscount Goderich, earl of Ripon, and Sir George Murray, served as president in 1835–37.

In the 19th century and early 20th century, the Royal Geographical Society, often working in conjunction with the British government, was active in the sponsoring of expeditions in addition to furthering knowledge of geography. In the 1830s, it offered financial and other support in the explorations of German-born naturalist SIR ROBERT HERMANN SCHOMBURGK to British Guiana in South America. THOMAS SIMPSON, who explored the Arctic regions of Canada, received a medal the first year of the society's existence. Schomburgk received one in 1840. Queen Victoria, who began her reign in 1837, eventually granted the society a Royal Charter for "the advancement of geographical science" and "the improvement and diffusion of geographical knowledge."

Not all investments in exploratory expeditions paid off, however, and, by the late 1840s, the Royal Geographical Society's activities were limited. Sir Roderick Murchison, who served as president of the society from 1851 to 1870, helped bring the society to international prominence by sponsoring expeditions, especially to Africa. Among the explorers who received at least partial backing were SIR RICHARD FRANCIS BURTON, JOHN HANNING SPEKE, JAMES AUGUSTUS GRANT, SIR SAMUEL WHITE BAKER, and DAVID LIVINGSTONE.

Many notable explorers were members of, were sponsored by, or received awards from the Royal Geographical Society. To name a few, scientist SIR FRANCIS GALTON received an award in 1853. Pundit NAIN SINGH, who helped survey India, received a medal in 1877. World traveler ISABELLA LUCY BIRD BISHOP became the first woman member of the Royal Geographical Society in 1892, and GERTRUDE MARGARET LOWTHIAN BELL, who explored the Middle East, was the first woman to receive a medal in 1919. During the presidency of Sir Clements Markham in 1893–1905, the Royal Geographical Society made a mark in polar exploration, sponsoring the British Antarctic Expedition under ROBERT FALCON SCOTT among other expeditions. Asian explorer SIR FRANCIS YOUNGHUSBAND served as president late in his career in 1919–22. The society also helped back a British Mount Everest Expedition of 1953, in which SIR EDMUND HILLARY and Sherpa TENZING NORGAY reached the summit of Mount Everest (see EVEREST, MOUNT) in the HIMALAYAS. Hillary received a medal in 1958. French oceanographer JACQUES-YVES COUSTEAU and Norwegian anthropologist THOR HEYERDAHL were awarded medals in the 1960s.

Some of the work of the Royal Geographical Society has been carried out in conjunction with the much older ROYAL SOCIETY (of London for Improving Natural Knowledge), founded in 1660.

Royal Society (Royal Society of London for Improving Natural Knowledge)

The Royal Society is the oldest scientific organization in Britain, and among the oldest in Europe. Founded in 1660 by a group of upper-class and well-educated men in London, it was incorporated in 1662 with the full title, Royal Society of London for Improving Natural Knowledge.

At the time of its founding, European culture was in a period of transition from the RENAISSANCE to the Enlightenment. While the Renaissance had occurred in response to the superstition of the Middle Ages, and placed an emphasis on creative expression and secularism, the Enlightenment sought to foster the gains made in rational thought. With inventions, such as the telescope in the early 17th century, and the beginnings of the scientific method pioneered by philosophers such as Francis Bacon, the European mind began to form a mechanistic view of the universe, with the aim of gaining control over the destiny of human society. The founders of the Royal Society were interested in encouraging the exchange of ideas of natural science, especially the physical sciences. Physicist Sir Isaac Newton served as its president from 1703 until his death in 1727.

With the prestige and political connections of its membership, the Royal Society has worked closely with the British government to plan and outfit a number of notable voyages of exploration. Among the most well-known was JAMES COOK's first expedition to the South Pacific Ocean in 1768, in order to time the transit of Venus across the Sun. Accompanying Cook on this journey was wealthy naturalist SIR JOSEPH BANKS, future president of the Royal Society and founder of the AFRICAN ASSOCIATION. The society has shown particular interest in polar exploration, aiding in many expeditions, including the 1818 expedition by DAVID BUCHAN to the Arctic Ocean, SIR JAMES CLARK ROSS's search for the SOUTH MAGNETIC POLE in 1840, and ROBERT FALCON SCOTT's first voyage to Antarctica in 1901. In some instances it has cosponsored expeditions with the ROYAL GEOGRAPHICAL SOCIETY, founded in 1830.

The Royal Society continues to operate to this day and continues to have many important scientists on its rolls. Since the society acts as advisers to the British government, members receive annual stipends for their efforts. Among the society's regular contributions to scientific debate is publication of its *Proceedings* and *The Philosophical Transactions*.

Rub' al-Khali   See EMPTY QUARTER.

Russian-American Company

The Russian-American Company was a colonial trading company, established to develop the North American FUR TRADE for Russian interests. The brainchild of merchant GRIGORY IVANOVICH SHELIKOV and directed in its most productive years by ALEKSANDR ANDREYEVICH BARANOV, it existed from 1799 to 1867.

Promyshlenniki

Soon after VITUS JONASSEN BERING's and ALEKSEY ILYICH CHIRIKOV's voyage of exploration to Alaska on behalf of Russia in 1741, the *promyshlenniki*—Russian fur traders and hunters—who had been active in SIBERIA, reached the Aleutian Islands and eventually the Alaskan mainland, where they found a bountiful supply of furs, especially sea otter, seal, and fox. In the early years, the traders formed ad hoc companies to work the region with no rules governing their operations or their exploitative treatment of the Aleut, the native peoples on the Aleutians, and the Inuit (Eskimo), on the mainland. The royal court in St. Petersburg was primarily concerned with the *yasak*, the 10 percent tax on furs. Nor did the *promyshlenniki* have competition from other colonial powers.

Shelikov's Vision

By the 1780s, however, British and American traders also worked the region. To protect their territorial claims and economic interest, the Russians, under the impetus of Shelikov, and his employer Ivana L. Golikiv, who had set up a base at Okhotsk on the Pacific coast of Siberia, began establishing permanent colonies in North America, the first at Three Saints on Kodiak Island in 1784. The efforts of Shelikov and Baranov, in his employ, led to profitable returns. By the 1790s, they had eliminated much of the competition, and the 40 or so ad hoc companies formed each year had become only three and then finally one, the United American Company. During the next several years, while Baranov ran the field operation, Shelikov lobbied for a royal charter in St. Petersburg. Czar Paul I granted the charter in 1799, four years after Shelikov's death, to his widow, Natalia Aleksievna, and son-in-law, Nikolay Petrovich Rezanov, authorizing the formation of the Russian-American Company. The charter granted the company monopoly trading privileges in all Russian territory in North America, including the Aleutians, Alaska, and territory as far south as 55 degrees latitude north. The czar was to receive a third of the profits.

Under Baranov

Baranov served as director of the company from 1800 to 1818. In 1799, he established a settlement at New Archangel (present-day Sitka) on what became known as Baranof Island in the Alexander Archipelago. It was destroyed by Tlingit Indians in 1802, but was rebuilt two years later, becoming the headquarters of expanding fur-trading operations. In 1812, Baranov also founded a southern settlement, Selenie Ross (later known as Fort Ross), near Bodega Bay in northern California. Because of reported involvement with foreign traders as well as complaints by Russian traders regarding abusive treatment of native peoples, the directors of the company retired Baranov in 1818. The new royal charter of 1821, which expanded operations to 51 degrees north latitude, also stipulated that the managers (or governors as they came to be known) of the Russian-American Company had to be naval officers.

Later Years

The Russian-American Company, despite its success in harvesting millions of furs, never established a large colonial population of Russians, partly because of the czar's refusal to allow the presence of serfs in North America. The harshness of conditions and the shortages of supplies also kept the colony small. Other trading companies—the HUDSON'S BAY COMPANY (which had merged with the NORTH WEST COMPANY in 1821) and the AMERICAN FUR COMPANY—offered growing competition. Moreover, the naval officers in charge were more concerned with territorial encroachments than the fur business. The continuing resistance of the Tlingit, known to the Russians as the *Kolush,* also limited operations. With declining profits in the 1840s, the czarist government took over operations from the merchants.

The Crimean War in 1853–56, in which Russia was defeated by an alliance of nations, including Great Britain, France, the Kingdom of Sardinia (now parts of Italy and France), and the Ottoman Empire (now Turkey), drained resources from other international endeavors. In 1867, Russia sold Alaska to the United States, at which time the Russian-American Company was dissolved.

Trade and Exploration

Considerable exploration was carried out in conjunction with the fur trade as well as under the direct auspices of the Russian-American Company. In the 1780s, Shelikov himself initiated exploratory expeditions along the Gulf of Alaska. DMITRY IVANOVICH BOCHAROV, who explored the Aleutians and coastal Alaska in the 1780s and who, in 1791, located a passage through the eastern end of Alaska Peninsula, connecting Bristol Bay and Gulf of Alaska, worked for Shelikov. GERASIM ALEKSEYEVICH IZMAILOV sailed with Bocharov on some of these expeditions and, in 1791, explored the Kenai Peninsula on the Gulf of Alaska in command of his own ship. GAVRILOV LOGINOVICH PRIBYLOV, who located the Pribilof Islands in the Bering Sea in 1786, was a fur trader.

Baranov explored the Gulf of Alaska and various inlets, such as Cook Inlet, Prince William Sound, and Yakutat Bay in the 1790s, and explored southward along the coast from the Gulf of Alaska to San Francisco Bay in present-day California in 1804–05. GAVRIIL IVANOVICH DAVYDOV of the Russian navy worked for the Russian-American Company for part of his career in the early 1800s. ANDREY GLAZUNOV was in the employ of the Russian-American Company when he explored the Yukon and Kuskokwim Rivers of western Alaska in 1834–35. LAVRENTY ALEKSEYEVICH ZAGOSKIN commanded company ships in exploratory expeditions of the Yukon, Kuskokwim, and other rivers of the Alaskan interior in 1842–44.

Other expeditions related to the fur trade in that maps and charts were sought to develop commercial interests. In 1768–70, PYOTR KUZMICH KRENITSYN led a maritime expedition charting the Aleutian Islands and the western end of Alaska Peninsula. Other explorations of coastal Alaska were carried out by VASILY MIKHAILOVICH GOLOVNIN in the course of his voyage of 1807–11; by Swedish-Finnish ARVID ADOLF ETHOLEN sailing for Russia in 1821; and by ALEKSANDR FILIPPOVICH KASHEVAROV in 1832–42.

Still other Russian voyages of exploration sought to establish a water route between Russian America and European Russia to further develop commercial interests in conjunction with the Russian-American Company. Englishman JOSEPH BILLINGS, along with ANTON BATAKOV and GAVRIIL ANDREYEVICH SARYCHEV, led the Russian naval Northern Secret Geographical and Astronomical Expedition of 1785–93 in search of a passage from Siberia's northeast coast into the BERING STRAIT and also explored the Aleutians and the Gulf of Alaska. In 1803–06, the first Russian CIRCUMNAVIGATION OF THE WORLD under ADAM IVAN RITTER VON KRUSENSTERN and YURY FYODOROVICH LISIANSKY sought to find a water route to avoid transport across Siberia. In 1815–18, a Russian naval expedition under OTTO VON KOTZEBUE searched for outlets of the NORTHEAST PASSAGE or NORTHWEST PASSAGE in the North Pacific. Other Russian circumnavigations of the world were carried out by MIKHAIL PETROVICH LAZAREV, in 1822–25, and FYODOR PETROVICH LITKE, in 1826–29.

Through some of these and other expeditions, much geographic and navigational knowledge of North America was accumulated. Mikhail Dmitrievich Tebenkov, governor of the Russian-America Company, compiled it in *Atlas of the Northwest Coasts of America: From Bering Strait to Cape Corrientes and the Aleutian Islands,* published in 1852.

See also COMMERCE AND EXPLORATION.

S

Saguenay

The legend of a fabled land known as Saguenay originated with the Huron (Wyandot) Indians. Frenchman JACQUES CARTIER, who explored along the St. Lawrence River in his second expedition to Canada in 1535–36, visiting the Huron villages of Stadacona (present-day Quebec City, Quebec) and Hochelaga (present-day Montreal, Quebec), was informed by Chief DONNACONNA of a land rich in jewels and precious metals, with white-skinned inhabitants. Supposedly, it could be reached from a branch of the St. Lawrence River.

Cartier took the Huron chief to Europe with him in order to gain backing for a subsequent expedition. Donnaconna, who met King Francis I of France and other members of the royal court, never returned to his homeland, succumbing to disease. Yet Cartier received the backing he desired and returned to North America in 1541.

Cartier and his expedition entered a branch of the St. Lawrence located to the north of Stadacona—now known as the Saguenay—and followed it westward, eventually reaching a region where he found what he thought was gold and precious stones. The French took samples and returned to France with them in 1542. When tested, the minerals turned out to be pyrite (FOOL'S GOLD) and quartz. In 1543, JEAN-FRANÇOIS DE LA ROQUE DE ROBERVAL, who had provided financing for Cartier, also searched for Saguenay along the St. Lawrence and Saguenay Rivers.

Frenchman SAMUEL DE CHAMPLAIN retraced Cartier's route along the St. Lawrence and into the Saguenay years later, in 1603. He also explored along the Ottawa River in 1613, still hoping to find the fabled land.

See also LEGENDS AND EXPLORATION.

Sahara Desert

The Sahara of North Africa is the world's largest desert at some 3.5 million square miles. East to west, it extends more than 3,000 miles from the Atlantic Ocean to the RED SEA, and, north to south, about 1,200 miles from on or near the MEDITERRANEAN SEA to the valley of the NIGER RIVER and the steppes of the Sudan to the south. In western stretches of the north, the Atlas Mountains and steppes lie between it and the sea; and, in western stretches of the south, the Sahel, a semiarid region of sparse grasses and shrubs, lies between arid desert lands and wetter tropical areas. The Sahara's boundaries are ever shifting, with parts of the Sahel, for example, turning to desert in recent years because of drought. The Sahara Desert includes most of Mauritania, Western Sahara, Algeria, Niger, Libya, and Egypt; southern portions of Morocco and Tunisia; and northern portions of Senegal, Mali, Chad, and the Republic of Sudan. The western Sahara is sometimes referred to as the Sahara proper. The eastern Sahara is discussed as three regions: the Libyan Desert, west of the valley of the NILE RIVER in eastern Libya, central and western Egypt, and northwestern Sudan; the Arabian Desert, or Eastern Desert, between the Nile Valley and the Red Sea; and the Nubian Desert in the northeastern Sudan. The name *Sahara* is Arabic for "desert."

The vast Sahara region is not uniform. Terrain varies from regions of sandy wastes and dunes (making up about 15 percent of the Sahara, much of it in the Libyan Desert), to rocky and gravelly plains and plateaus (about 70 percent), to mountains, oases, and transition zones (about 15 percent). The Sahara as a whole is a tableland with an average elevation from about 1,300 to 1,600 feet; some areas in the north, such as the Qattara Depression in Egypt, are below sea level. Mountains include the Ahagger (Hoggar) in southern Algeria, rising to more than 9,000 feet; the Tibesti in northern Chad, rising to more than 11,000 feet; and the Aïr (Azbine, Asben) in northern Niger, rising to more than 6,000 feet. With an average annual total of less than five inches of rainfall during the winter months, with some torrential downpours in the summer, vegetation is sparse and shrubby, with none at all in sand dune country; in the oases can be found some trees, in particular date palm, doum palm, tamarisk, and acacia. There are no permanent rivers in the Sahara; the bordering Nile and Niger Rivers are fed by rains outside the desert. With the rains come wadis, intermittent streams descending from highlands. A number of chotts, or lakes, and boggy salt marshes can be found. Scattered oases are formed by the water table reaching the surface. Winds can be fierce; names for the dust-laden, damaging winds include *harmattan, khamsin, simoom,* and *sirocco.* Wildlife includes gazelle, antelope, hyena, jackal, fox, badger, hare, hedgehog, chameleon, cobra, and migratory birds.

Inhabitants of the Sahara's interior include the Tuareg, one of the non-Arab Berber tribes, centered in mountainous regions of the central Sahara; the Tibbu (Tébu), another Berber people, in the Tibesti Mountains; and mixed Berber and Arab peoples in western lands.

Ancient Reports

The Sahara has always been a formidable barrier, separating Mediterranean peoples from those to the south. The ancient Egyptians controlled oases in desert regions east and west of the Nile, providing routes of commerce (see EGYPTIAN EXPLORATION). The Carthaginians also traded with peoples to the south. In about 480 B.C., Carthaginian admiral HANNO led an expedition from Carthage through the Strait of Gibraltar (see GIBRALTAR, STRAIT OF) to the open waters of the Atlantic, then southward, exploring Africa's coastal lands to the south, some of them the western extent of the Sahara (see CARTHAGINIAN EXPLORATION). Greek historian HERODOTUS, in his writings later that century, described an expedition of five Berber princes across the Sahara to a great southern river, perhaps the Niger (see GREEK EXPLORATION). The Romans carried out a number of military expeditions to the south between 19 B.C. and A.D. 86, among them those headed by SUETONIUS PAULINUS across the Atlas Mountains to the desert's northern edge in A.D. 42, and by JULIUS MATERNUS, who possibly commanded the first Eu-

ropean crossing of the desert north-to-south as far as Lake Chad in A.D. 50 (see ROMAN EXPLORATION). Earlier that century, Greek geographer STRABO had written of the Sahara in his *Geography,* published in about A.D. 18. Roman geographer PLINY THE ELDER wrote about it in *Historia Naturalis,* published in A.D. 77. Hellenized Egyptian PTOLEMY of the second century A.D. also described desert lands of North Africa.

Berbers and the Arabs

It is thought that the camel was introduced into North Africa in the first century A.D., enabling a greater range of activity for nomadic peoples, first the Berbers, centered in the highlands, then the Arabs. Trans-Saharan trade was developed during the Middle Ages, involving salt from the desert, gold, and slaves from West Africa and cloth, jewelry, and other products from Mediterranean cities. Control of the oases was interdependent with control of commerce. A number of Muslims wrote about the Sahara, including 10th-century merchant ABU AL-QASIM IBN ALI AL-NASIBI IBN HAWQAL, 12th-century scholar ABU ABD ALLAH MUHAMMAD ASH-SHARIF AL-IDRISI, and 14th-century scholar ABU ABD ALLAH MUHAMMAD IBN BATTUTAH. Spanish cartographer ABRAHAM CRESQUES, in his *Catalan Atlas* of about 1375, indicated camel caravan routes across the Sahara, based on information from Jewish traders.

European Interest

In the ensuing centuries, European nations showed increasing interest in the Saharan trade, in particular Italy and Portugal. Mariners sailing along Africa's west coast for HENRY THE NAVIGATOR, prince of Portugal, in the 15th century, such as Italian ALVISE DA CADAMOSTA and Portuguese DIOGO GOMES, sought information about inland trade. Gomes reported of the city of TIMBUKTU on the Niger, part of the great trading network. Meanwhile, Berbers and Arabs continued to control the overland routes. In the 16th century, Arab LEO AFRICANUS, as a diplomat for the sultan of Morocco, crossed the Sahara to Timbuktu.

The extent and limits of the Sahara were not understood by Europeans until the end of 19th century. Much of what was learned resulted from British expeditions seeking to define the course of the Niger and reach Timbuktu. German FRIEDRICH CONRAD HORNEMANN, who entered the Sahara from the northeast out from Cairo in Egypt, is credited as the first modern European to travel there in 1798–1801, soon to be followed by Scotsman MUNGO PARK in 1805–06, who approached from the southwest and the Gambia River. Later expeditions included those of JOSEPH RITCHIE and GEORGE LYON in 1818–19, and WALTER OUDNEY, HUGH CLAPPERTON, and DIXON DENHAM in 1821–25, both British expeditions heading southward from Libya. In 1827–28, Frenchman RENÉ-AUGUSTE CAILLIÉ crossed the Sahara from

This photograph from the late 19th or early 20th century shows merchants in the Sahara Desert. *(Library of Congress, Prints and Photographs Division [LC-USZ62-93064])*

south to north. Later expeditions to explore and chart the Sahara were headed by Frenchman HENRI DUVEYRIER in the 1850s–60s, German FRIEDRICH GERHARD ROHLFS in the 1860s–70s, German GUSTAV NACHTIGAL in the 1860s–70s, and Frenchman PAUL-XAVIER FLATTERS in the 1880s. In the 20th century, scientific expeditions and surveys from the air were carried out as well.

❖

The Sahara remains a sparsely inhabited region, with few maintained roads. The nomadic way of life continues, with desert inhabitants traveling by camels and maintaining herds of sheep and goats; some peoples still transport salt over the old trade routes. New oases have been created through drilling. The Sahara is rich in metallic minerals such as iron, copper, manganese, tin, nickel, chromium, zinc, lead, cobalt, silver, and gold, resulting in mining activity. Deposits of oil and natural gas are also found.

See also AFRICA, EXPLORATION OF.

St. Brendan's Isle

St. Brendan's Isle was a land in the Atlantic Ocean purported to be visited by sixth-century Irish monk SAINT BRENDAN. It has been identified as various actual places by a number of different scholars, but the truth of the past has been mingled with myth to the point where final conclusions are impossible. Accounts of Saint Brendan's voyage demonstrate real knowledge of the waters of the Atlantic, however, and, as a result, are considered worthy of study as possible history and not just legend.

Brendan was born in county Kerry in the Irish town of Tralee, or nearby, in about A.D. 484. Having been ordained in 512, he showed great zeal in propagating the Catholic faith, founding a monastery in Ardfert to the north of Tralee and one at Clonfert in Galway. Reliable evidence credits him with embarking on a number of voyages: to Wales on the British Isles; to Brittany in what is now northwestern France; and to the Hebrides Islands west of Scotland. Whatever the true extent of his travels, he seems to have been energetic and restless and to have departed his homeland for extended periods of time. Perhaps it was due to these absences that he became the center of tales incorporating the experiences of a number of different missionaries. Known also as Saint Brendan the Navigator, he has continued to be a popular figure and is the patron saint of Kerry. Place names commemorating Brendan throughout the islands and coasts of western Ireland and Scotland attest to his significance; there is even a Brendansvik or Brendan's Bay in the Faeroe Islands, more than 350 miles north of Scotland.

An activity that was performed around the time of Brendan was the sea pilgrimage. This practice, analogous to Christ's time in the desert, entailed an Irish monk traveling out to sea in a CURRAGH, a type of small craft, to search for a barren island where he might obtain solitude and wisdom. Some of these journeys took on a missionary aspect if the lands were inhabited. Monks sometimes led a group of pilgrims on these journeys. In the course of such expeditions, Irish travelers founded settlements in the Orkney Islands, the Shetlands, and the Faeroes. There were also Irish colonies in ICELAND by the ninth century.

After three centuries, Irish colonial activity drew to a close, and many great romantic tales came to be written about the sea pilgrimages. The literature surrounding the travels of the Irish monks, including Brendan, came into popularity about the same time that the English were fascinated with the Arthurian legends. In this way, the Irish came to understand and contend with the politics and morality of their time and to take pride in their heritage. Brendan became the hero in several of these works. One of the earliest surviving accounts is *The Book of Lismore* from the early 10th century. In this work, Brendan hears the voice of God, who tells him that he has been chosen to find a resting place. He collects a number of monks and three curraghs and sets out among the islands of the North Atlantic. As a sign from God, a whale visits them every Easter at sea, on whose back they celebrate Mass. The search for land proves futile, however, and, after five years, they return to Ireland.

In the *Navigatio Sancti Brendani* (The Voyage of St. Brendan), written sometime between 900 and 920, the tales become even more fanciful. Hearing of an Eden from a monk, Barinthus, Brendan decides to search for it. For this trip, he builds a large curragh and sets out westward with other monks. After visiting several islands, the geography of which correspond to real places, he and his followers proceed westward. On the way, they encounter a number of fantastic creatures—a race of small people, pygmies, giant sheep, and sea-cats. Fifteen days sailing from an island of strong men, they spot a bird of exotic plumage carrying a cluster of grapes the size of apples. After seven more days, they reach the island from where the grapes had come. They interpreted this as the way station to their paradise, for next

they proceeded through a fog bank and came upon a vast land of sweet-smelling flowers and mild weather. After hiking for weeks, they reached a river, where an angel informed them that this land—the "Land Promised to the Saints"—was reserved for others to Christianize in the future and that it was time to return to their vessel.

The *Navigatio,* despite its embellishments, contains the most cohesive narrative of these early tales, without the large gaps between places visited that other writings have. It also demonstrates a real knowledge of winds and currents that gives the modern reader reason to believe that at least some of the book has a basis in fact.

St. Brendan's Isle has been identified as any number of places. In one of the stories, Brendan observes an island where volcanic activity is taking place. This could only have been Iceland. Other island groups are identified, some of which had Irish outposts. Since GREENLAND is visible from the mountains of Iceland and would probably be found in the course of a circumnavigation of Iceland, it is likely that the Irish knew of it before the Vikings. Some of the legends describe icebergs encountered by the travelers, which also fits the idea of the legendary isle being situated in the North Atlantic.

Other theories associate Saint Brendan's voyages with island groups off southern Europe and northern Africa. The CANARY ISLANDS, the AZORES, and the Madeira Islands all have been put forth as a possible landing place. On his 1492 globe of the world, German MARTIN BEHAIM placed a "Saint Brendan's Island" west of the Canaries. It has also been theorized that Brendan crossed the Atlantic to the Bahama Islands off North America. The description in the *Navigatio* of an extensive land with a friendly climate would apply to the east coast of North America, but whether this had its roots in actual experience or in the wishful thinking of those making a case for the Irish discovery of the Americas even before the Vikings in about 1000 will probably never be known for certain.

See also LEGENDS AND EXPLORATION.

St. Louis Missouri Fur Company

The St. Louis Missouri Fur Company, which came to be known as the Missouri Company, was one of the early North American companies established to develop the FUR TRADE up the MISSOURI RIVER to its headwaters in the northern ROCKY MOUNTAINS and beyond. It was founded in St. Louis in February 1809, 10 months after JOHN JACOB ASTOR chartered the AMERICAN FUR COMPANY. Both sought to compete with the HUDSON'S BAY COMPANY and the NORTH WEST COMPANY, Canadian enterprises.

The founding partners of the St. Louis Missouri Fur Company were JEAN PIERRE CHOUTEAU and one of his sons, AUGUSTE PIERRE CHOUTEAU; MANUEL LISA, who had conducted trade with the Osage Indians in the Missouri region; WILLIAM CLARK of the Lewis and Clark Expedition; Reuben Lewis, MERIWETHER LEWIS's brother; ANTOINE PIERRE MENARD; ANDREW HENRY; Benjamin Wilkinson; Sylvestre Labadie; William Morrison; and Dennis Fitzhugh. Articles of Association and Copartnership were signed in front of Meriwether Lewis.

The first expedition, including all the partners and 172 men, departed St. Louis in spring 1808, traveling up the Missouri with nine barges loaded with trade goods. The company's main outposts were Ft. Mandan at the confluence of the Missouri and Knife Rivers in present-day North Dakota, built during that expedition, and Ft. Manuel (also known as Ft. Raymond) at the confluence of the Yellowstone and Bighorn Rivers in present-day Montana, established by Lisa two years before.

The company was successful in its first few years. Yet, with shrinking profits, it gave up its activity in the northern Rockies, abandoning Ft. Manuel in 1811 and Ft. Mandan in 1812, concentrating its trade along the Missouri. The War of 1812 also interfered with some of its activity. JOSHUA PILCHER became a partner in 1819, then became president the next year after Lisa's death. CHARLES BENT also became involved with the company in its final years. One of the company's fur brigades was wiped out by Arikara Indians in 1823, leading to a punitive military campaign under Colonel HENRY LEAVENWORTH. Meanwhile, Astor's American Fur Company was thriving. By 1825, the partners in the Missouri Fur Company had given up their shared endeavor.

See also COMMERCE AND EXPLORATION.

Sandwich Islands   See HAWAIIAN ISLANDS.

satellite (artificial satellite)

The term *satellite* refers to any natural or human-made object moving in orbit around Earth or around another celestial body. The Moon is thus a "satellite" of Earth. In popular usage, the term has come to be applied primarily to artificial objects. The earliest SPACE EXPLORATION was carried out by artificial satellites before humans were launched into space, by the former Union of Soviet Socialist Republics (USSR; Soviet Union) and the United States.

Both nations began developing their satellite programs in the 1950s, as advances in ROCKET technology made launches possible. The INTERNATIONAL GEOPHYSICAL YEAR (IGY), from July 1, 1957, to December 31, 1958, was the target time for launches by both nations. Project Vanguard of the U.S. Navy was selected as the first official U.S. program. (The U.S. Army meanwhile had a rival plan, Project Orbiter.)

The first artificial satellite, the Soviet Union's *Sputnik 1* (the full name: *Iskustvennyi Sputnik Zemli* for "fellow world traveler of the earth"), almost 23 inches in diameter and about 183 pounds, was launched on October 4, 1957, an event that is considered the start of the "space race" between the Soviet Union and the United States. On November 3, 1957, the much larger *Sputnik 2,* at about 1,120 pounds was launched, carrying the first animal (a dog named Laika) into space.

The rocket that was to carry the first Vanguard into space exploded the following December 6. The first U.S. satellite, *Explorer 1,* was launched on January 31, 1958, with help from the Army Ballistic Missile Agency engineers. It made a significant discovery, the first indications of the Van Allen belts, a zone of trapped radiation surrounding Earth. *Explorer 3,* launched on March 26 of that year, performed tests that proved their existence. In the meantime, *Vanguard 1* was successfully launched on March 17, 1958. The following July, the United States founded the NATIONAL AERONAUTICS AND SPACE ADMINISTRATION (NASA).

Satellite technology was soon applied to specific needs on Earth. Since April 1, 1960, and the launching of *Tiros 1,* the first weather (meteorological) satellite, thousands of artificial satellites have been launched into orbit around Earth—by many different nations and of varying sizes and serving a variety of purposes. In addition to weather satellites, there are application satellites, which test ways of improving satellite technology itself; communications satellites, for television and other systems; navigation satellites, for navigation systems on Earth; reconnaissance satellites, to survey Earth's landforms and resources as well as human activity (some of them specifically "spy satellites" or "military satellites"); and research satellites, which are also called exploratory satellites, for scientific studies of space (the Hubble Space Telescope, launched by the United States in April 1990, is a research satellite). A SPACE STATION is also a type of artificial satellite, although in popular usage it is rarely referred to as such. A SPACE PROBE is not considered a satellite since it leaves the orbit of Earth (yet may become a satellite of another planet or a moon).

Artificial satellites have been placed into orbit mainly through the use of rocket technology. Since 1984, the United States has also used the SPACE SHUTTLE to launch, service, and retrieve satellites. The systems of the satellites are powered in a number of ways: by solar cells; by batteries (in some cases charged by solar cells); by nuclear reactors; and by generators (which produce electricity from the decay of radioisotopes). Satellites, which are computerized, contain control, tracking, receiving, transmitting, information collecting, and storing equipment.

Satellite technology has made possible the Global Positioning System (GPS), which has become the primary system of navigation (see NAVIGATION AND EXPLORATION).

scurvy

Scurvy is a deficiency disease caused by a lack of vitamin C. Failure to satisfy the body's need of the vitamin causes the weakening of capillaries. Hemorrhaging eventually occurs, and a multitude of symptoms may result. These include swollen gums, loosened teeth, internal bleeding, lethargy, difficulty in thinking, and various forms of bodily disfigurement. If left untreated, scurvy results in death.

Scurvy was described in an Egyptian papyrus of 1550 B.C., but its causes remained unknown for centuries. It probably caused more loss of life during the EUROPEAN AGE OF EXPLORATION than shipwrecks. It was a particularly difficult condition to diagnose because the early symptoms resembled those of many other diseases. Once it had taken hold of a crew, the effects would be devastating.

The voyage of Portuguese VASCO DA GAMA around the CAPE OF GOOD HOPE in 1497–99, in which half the crew were lost to scurvy, demonstrated the dangers of long trips without fresh provisions. Among other famous examples of the blight of scurvy occurred on the first CIRCUMNAVIGATION OF THE WORLD, headed by FERDINAND MAGELLAN for Spain in 1519–21. On the first leg of his journey, before reaching the islands of the South Pacific Ocean, he lost a large percentage of his crew to the disease. After his death on the island of Mactan in 1521, his crew straggled home. Of an original complement of 250 men, only 18 remained to complete the voyage, the majority of the dead victims of scurvy. The 1595–97 voyage of Dutchman CORNELIUS HOUTMAN to the island of Java resulted in the loss of two-thirds of his crew to scurvy and fever. Perhaps the largest loss of life occurred on the circumnavigation carried out by Englishman GEORGE ANSON in 1740–44, where he lost more than 1,000 men to scurvy. This extreme number of casualties led the Royal Navy to increasing its efforts to cure the problem.

The problem of scurvy was not limited to long, open-sea voyages. Since the science of the disease was not well understood, scurvy occurred on trips along coastlines and also on dry land. The 1774 Spanish exploration of the Oregon coast by BRUNO HECETA is an example of one such journey cut short by scurvy. Frenchman RENÉ-AUGUSTE CAILLIÉ suffered from scurvy while exploring the upper water of Africa's NIGER RIVER in 1827.

Knowledge of a cure for scurvy was slow to materialize. In winter 1535–36, the French expedition under JACQUES CARTIER to northeastern North America suffered an outbreak of scurvy. The Huron (Wyandot) Indians demonstrated how to make a tea made from evergreen trees, which, because it contained vitamin C, saved many Frenchmen without their recognizing the cure. Among the first Europeans to propose a remedy was Sir Richard Hawkins, who, in 1593, wrote that citrus fruit seemed to help cure the problem. James Lind, a Scottish naval doctor who had suc-

cessfully treated sailors with oranges and lemons, publicized a cure in *A Treatise on Scurvy* years later, in 1753. Understanding was still incomplete, however, and his solution was met with skepticism among experienced seamen, for fruit juices did not retain their vitamin C indefinitely. Attempted antidotes for the disease are many and varied throughout the annals of exploration. They include coconut milk, beans, fresh turtle meat, berries, spruce beer, wild celery, purslane, fresh fish, hops, and watercress.

The man who is given credit for getting the problem of scurvy under control was Englishman JAMES COOK. On his voyage to the South Pacific in 1768–71, he used a variety of foodstuffs to ensure the health of his crew. The biggest breakthrough was in the use of sauerkraut, a preserved food high in vitamin C. He did not lose a single man to scurvy on the voyage. The replacement of sailing vessels with the steamship in the mid-1800s finally solved the centuries-long problem of scurvy at sea. The speed of these new ships allowed for food to retain its vitamin content before going bad. Yet explorers still had to deal with the disease. Examples abound of Arctic and Antarctic expeditions caught short of supplies and suffering outbreaks of scurvy, for example that of Englishmen SIR JOHN FRANKLIN in the 19th century and ROBERT FALCON SCOTT in the 20th century. Scurvy was the first disease to be understood as being caused by a vitamin deficiency. Advances in food preservation such as canning and refrigeration have helped eliminate it as a general problem. The isolation and production of vitamin C has also contributed to reduced risk of scurvy. Today, scurvy may be treated with tablets or syrup and is seen only in the most critical of circumstances.

See also DISEASE AND EXPLORATION.

searches for missing explorers

A recurring theme in the history of exploration is the search for missing explorers, with a number of expeditions prompted, at least in part, by the disappearance of earlier expeditions. In the course of many of these searches, new geographic discoveries were made.

The Lost Colony

The mysteries and failures in the history of exploration have captured the public's imagination as much as the successes. A case in point is the story of the LOST COLONY in North America—the failed attempt of the 1587 English colony sponsored by SIR WALTER RALEIGH in what is now northeastern North Carolina—which still fosters speculation. Part of the power of the story is that the colony's governor, JOHN WHITE, returned to England for supplies, leaving his daughter and newly born granddaughter there, but was unable to return for three years because of the Spanish Armada's invasion of England. White found only a single word of the colonists' whereabouts—"CROATOAN"—the name of an Indian village. With a storm approaching, the relief ship was unable to investigate further, and White was never able to mount another relief operation. The search still continues, with archaeologists still hoping to turn up some definitive trace.

The La Pérouse Expedition

Well-publicized official French searches for a missing expedition occurred in the late 18th century and early 19th century. The two ships of the expedition under renowned French naval officer and navigator JEAN-FRANÇOIS DE GALAUP, comte de La Pérouse—the *Astrolabe* under his command and the *Boussole* under PAUL-ANTOINE-MARIE FLEURIOT DE LANGLÉ—went missing in 1788. The comte de La Pérouse expedition had departed France on August 1, 1785. After sailing around CAPE HORN and exploring in the Pacific Ocean, including coastal regions of North America and Asia, the expedition had sailed to Botany Bay, the location of present-day Sydney, on the east coast of New Holland (Australia). On March 10, 1788, the Frenchmen had departed Botany Bay with the intention of exploring the continent's north coast around the Gulf of Carpenteria and had vanished. (Some of the expedition's geographic findings survived, however, because interpreter JEAN-BAPTISTE-BARTHÉLEMY DE LESSEPS, as planned, had traveled overland from the Kamchatka Peninsula on the Bering Sea by way of SIBERIA to Paris with records taken through the fall of 1787.)

In 1791, rear admiral ANTOINE-RAYMOND-JOSEPH DE BRUNI, chevalier d'Entrecasteaux, was given the assignment of finding La Pérouse. The expedition, consisting of two ships, the *Recherche* and the *Espérance,* had other purposes as well. It was to survey the coasts of Australia, Van Diemen's Land (TASMANIA), and New Caledonia (see OCEANIA). Departing France in September 1791, it accomplished many of its goals, including various coastal surveys. It also located new islands west of the Solomons, known as the D'Entrecasteaux Islands. Yet d'Entrecasteaux found no evidence indicating the fate of the La Pérouse expedition, not even in the Admiralty Islands, where rumors placed the lost Frenchmen. Off the east coast of New Guinea, d'Entrecasteaux explored Vanikoro Island, one of the Santa Cruz group north of the New Hebrides. Soon afterward, d'Entrecasteaux died at sea from SCURVY and dysentery.

Another French expedition, this one headed by naval officer JULES-SÉBASTIEN-CÉSAR DUMONT D'URVILLE, set out to the South Pacific in April 1826 to map and study the natural history and native languages of the same region that d'Entrecasteaux had explored; it had the additional assignment of searching for La Pérouse. While the Dumont d'Urville expedition was underway, Peter Dillon, the captain of a British vessel, had seen relics from a shipwreck among the natives of Tikopia Island, also in the Santa Cruz group.

As with all mariners of the day, he was well aware of the missing French expedition. From the locals as well as Europeans living among them from earlier voyages, Dillon learned that a European ship had been stranded on a reef and that the crew had built a small boat from the wreckage and eventually had headed westward. Some accounts told of a second ship destroyed on the reef, the few survivors of which had been attacked and killed by natives. Two castaways from one ship or the other had supposedly lived for a time on Vanikoro Island—one now dead and the other having departed with a group of native peoples. Dillon managed to recover a number of objects from a shipwreck in the region, including a bronze ship's bell, and eventually took them to Paris. In the meantime, Dumont d'Urville, who had named his ship the *Astrolabe* in honor of La Pérouse's vessel, traveled to Vanikoro Island and retrieved other objects. He also erected a monument there to the memory of the lost Frenchmen. In France, Baron de Lesseps, who had left the La Pérouse expedition in Kamchatka in 1787, confirmed that the found relics were indeed from the original *Astrolabe.* In 1964, a search expedition located the remains of the second ship, the *Boussole,* off Vanikoro Island, confirming the native peoples' stories.

The Franklin Expedition

The most famous of missing expeditions—and certainly the one that helped spur on the most subsequent voyages of exploration—was that of SIR JOHN FRANKLIN. Franklin had built a successful career as a British naval officer by charting much of the Arctic coast of the Canadian mainland in expeditions in 1819–22 and 1825–27, of which he had written in two well-received books. In 1828, he received a knighthood. Later that same year, he married Jane Griffin, who became Lady JANE FRANKLIN. In 1836–43, he served as governor of Van Diemen's Land. In 1844, after his return to England, Franklin received a commission from the British Admiralty to lead another expedition to the Canadian Arctic with the goal of navigating east to west through the long-sought NORTHWEST PASSAGE.

The *Erebus* under Franklin's command, along with the *Terror* under Lieutenant FRANCIS RAWDON MOIRA CROZIER, sailed from England on May 29, 1845. The ships were last seen by a Scottish whaling vessel on July 26, 1845, in upper Baffin Bay, west of GREENLAND, near the approach to Lancaster Sound. By 1847, without any word from or of the expedition, concern began to mount. Franklin's disappearance became international news. Over the next decades, some 50 expeditions, involving approximately 2,000 men, were launched to solve the mystery of what happened to the *Erebus* and the *Terror* and, during them, much was learned of the Arctic regions of the Western Hemisphere.

In 1847–49, SIR JOHN RICHARDSON, along with JOHN RAE of the HUDSON'S BAY COMPANY, led a British land-based expedition which reached Canada's Arctic coastline by way of the Mackenzie River, then proceeded eastward to Dolphin and Union Strait. In 1849–50, Rae continued the search on his own, reaching Victoria Island. In 1848–49, SIR JAMES CLARK ROSS led a British naval expedition, which traveled through Lancaster Sound as far as Barrow Strait and southward from Somerset Island into Peel Strait. In 1850–51, James Clark Ross's uncle, SIR JOHN ROSS, wintered in Barrow Strait on the schooner *Felix,* sponsored privately by Sir Felix Booth, in the hope of finding some trace of Franklin, but to no avail.

The British Admiralty sponsored a number of expeditions in the 1850s to the Canadian Arctic, part of the motivation of which was to determine the outcome of the Franklin expedition. In 1850–54, SIR ROBERT JOHN LE MESURIER McCLURE, who had sailed on the earlier expedition with James Clark Ross, led an expedition that entered Arctic waters from the west by way of the BERING STRAIT. While proceeding eastward, he located Prince of Wales Strait between Banks Island and Victoria Island; he also reached a point far enough west—Mellville Island, which had previously been reached from the east—to prove that a Northwest Passage did in fact exist. At about the same time, in 1850–55, SIR RICHARD COLLINSON, also approaching from the west, explored the Arctic coasts of Alaska and Canada as far east as Victoria Island. Spending the winter of 1852–53 there, he retrieved some pieces of iron from Inuit (Eskimo) that had probably come from one of Franklin's ships. Also during this period, in 1852–54, SIR EDWARD BELCHER headed an expedition from the east that navigated west of Lancaster Sound. SIR FRANCIS LEOPOLD McCLINTOCK, part of this expedition as well as the earlier James Clark Ross's expedition, located Eglington Island and Prince Patrick Island at the edge of the Beaufort Sea.

In the meantime, Lady Franklin, distraught over the disappearance of her husband, had been using her resources and prestige to promote continuing searches. In 1848, she offered a reward for the rescue of her husband or for information as to his fate. She later gained the support of American shipping magnate Henry Grinnell, who, in 1850–51, sent out an expedition under EDWIN JESSE DE HAVEN, a U.S. naval officer. While trapped in the PACK ICE north of Baffin Island and Lancaster Sound and drifting with it for some 1,000 miles, he located Grinnell Land on northern Devon Island. Lady Franklin paid for a number of expeditions from her own funds as well. In 1853–55, ELISHA KENT KANE, another U.S. naval officer, led the Second U.S. Grinnell Expedition in search of John Franklin. On this voyage, expedition members explored Greenland's Humboldt Glacier and Ellesmere Island.

The expedition that located the first irrefutable proof of the missing Franklin expedition was headed by John Rae, who had explored earlier with Richardson. In his expedition of 1853–54, during which he explored the Boothia Peninsula and located a strait (Rae Strait), thus proving that King William Island was not connected to the Canadian mainland, he interviewed an Inuit who told him of a story of Europeans marching southward from King William Island toward the estuary of the Back River and eventually perishing. Rae also managed to retrieve relics of the Franklin expedition. Yet Rae also reported that expedition members perhaps had resorted to cannibalism in their final days.

Lady Franklin, upset at these reports and determined to find more evidence, hired experienced Arctic explorer Francis McClintock to mount still another expedition in 1857. While in Arctic waters, he erected a monument on Beechey Island commemorating Franklin's Arctic exploits. He also circumnavigated King William Island, confirming that it was an island. On King William Island, a party headed by McClintock found a sledge and several skeletons. Another party led by Lieutenant W. R. Hopson crossed Simpson Strait to the Boothia Peninsula on the Canadian mainland and found letters written by Franklin's men, indicating that Franklin and other expedition members had died while the ship had been icebound and that the survivors under Lieutenant Crozier had perished in an abortive attempt to reach the Hudson's Bay Company's post, Fort Resolution, on the Back River. The expedition returned to England in 1859.

Although the fate of the Franklin expedition had been determined, other expeditions continued to search for clues as to the exact course of events. Two American expeditions found additional remains, skeletons as well as artifacts: One, in 1864–69, again backed by Grinnell and headed by American journalist CHARLES FRANCIS HALL, traveled by ship to King William Island and Boothia Peninsula; another, in 1878–80, sponsored by the AMERICAN GEOGRAPHICAL SOCIETY and a whaling company, and headed by physician and lawyer FREDERICK SCHWATKA, traveled overland by sledge from Hudson Bay to King William Island. Schwatka's expedition covered more than 3,000 miles, the longest sledge journey on record until that time.

Norwegian ROALD ENGELBREGT GRAVNING AMUNDSEN, during the first crossing of the Northwest Passage in 1903–06, located two skeletons of expedition members on King William Island.

Dr. Livingstone

Another famous search that fascinated the general public took place in Africa. After establishing his reputation on earlier expeditions to Africa and receiving acclaim in England, Scottish missionary DAVID LIVINGSTONE had returned to Africa in 1866 to investigate the continent's central watershed and locate the source of the NILE RIVER. After departing from Mikindani on the coast of present-day Tanzania in

East Africa, he lost touch with the outside world. Three years passed without any word. James Gordon Bennett, Jr., publisher of the *New York Herald,* sponsored British-born SIR HENRY MORTON STANLEY to undertake a search for Livingstone. Bennett instructed Stanley to cover other stories first, however, so that he stood a better chance of determining the fate of the missing explorer rather than just report that he was still missing. Eighteen months later, in January 1871, Stanley arrived in Zanzibar, an island off Tanzania, and, with funds provided by the newspaper, he hired *pagazi* (porters), guides, hunters, and armed escorts, along with pack animals. He departed Bagamoyo on the mainland on March 21, 1871, and, based on reports from slave traders, headed for Ujiji on the east shore of Lake Tanganyika, reaching it on November 10. There, he found the missionary and greeted him with probably the most famous words in the history of exploration, "Dr. Livingstone, I presume."

Livingstone was short on supplies and weakened by disease but did not consider himself lost or missing. He convinced Stanley to explore the northern end of Lake Tanganyika with him but refused in turn to accompany Stanley back to Europe, continuing with his explorations of the great lakes of Africa and their relation to the great rivers. Livingston succumbed to dysentery in a native village near Tabora on May 1, 1873. Native people working for him transported his body to the coast, from where it was shipped to England. He received a state funeral in London's Westminster Abbey on April 18, 1874.

In the meantime, Stanley had returned to England and published *How I Found Livingstone* in 1872, which became a best-seller. He also received a gold medal from the ROYAL GEOGRAPHICAL SOCIETY. Stanley's experiences on his search for Livingstone inspired him to embark on his own African explorations, and he would make a number of important geographic findings through 1889.

Australian Expeditions

A missing expedition in Australia's interior has remained a mystery. In 1848, German FRIEDRICH WILHELM LUDWIG LEICHHARDT, who had led a number of other successful expeditions, set out from McPherson Station west of Brisbane on the Darling Downs in present-day Queensland with seven others in an attempt to cross Australia from east to west, but was never heard from again.

Over the next 90 years, various expeditions—nine major ones and numerous small ones—searched for Leichhardt's party. All subsequent explorers of Australia's interior hoped to solve the mystery. The fact that Leichhardt had set out with plans to cross the continent meant that the search could not be narrowed down. Englishman SIR AUGUSTUS CHARLES GREGORY received sponsorship from the British government as well as the Royal Geographical Society for an 1855 expedition in search of lands suitable for livestock in what is now the Northern Territory as well as traces of the missing expedition. From the Joseph Bonaparte Gulf, Gregory traveled generally eastward and, on reaching the Pacific at Bustard Head in Queensland, had located thousands of square miles of lands suitable for grazing and had completed the first west-to-east crossing of northern Australia. But he had found nothing of Leichhardt.

Skeletal remains turned up by Aborigines prompted a search from the west in 1869 by Australian-born JOHN FORREST. He set out from the west coast, from Perth in Western Australia. The bones turned out to be those of stray horses from an 1854 expedition. Forrest continued eastward, however, as far as Mount Weld on the western edge of the GREAT VICTORIA DESERT, and he charted much new territory suitable for livestock.

Other expeditions turned up objects—bones, a coin, and a tomahawk—but nothing that could be linked directly to Leichhardt's party. Various theories have been put forth. One holds that some among Leichhardt's party mutinied and killed their leader, only to be killed by Aborigines. Rumors persisted that one among them—Adolf Classen—lived among the Aborigines for years. It has also been theorized that the men were caught in one of the frequent flash floods of Queensland, or that they died in bushfires, or simply of thirst in desert lands.

The 1860–61 Australian expedition of Irishman ROBERT O'HARA BURKE and Englishman WILLIAM JOHN WILLS—an attempt to cross the continent south to north, from Melbourne to the Gulf of Carpentaria—cost them their lives. A total of four rescue expeditions were sent out. Camel driver John King was found alive; the remains of Burke, Wills, and expedition member Charles Gray were also eventually found. It was determined that, during the doomed expedition, an advance party of four had separated from a larger party. Of the smaller group, Burke, Wills, and Gray had perished from starvation and exposure. John King had managed to survive on food provided by Aborigines. The relief expeditions furthered geographic knowledge of the region.

20th-Century Searches

In the 20th century, in the Arctic and Antarctic regions as well as in MOUNTAIN CLIMBING around the world, search and rescue operations have searched for the missing. After the British expedition under ROBERT FALCON SCOTT had reached the SOUTH POLE in January 1912, his team was trapped in a nine-day blizzard on the return journey and perished at the end of March. It took another eight months for a search party to locate their remains and records of the expedition, at a point only 11 miles from a depot with food and fuel.

In the Arctic, one famous explorer lost his life while searching for another famous explorer. In 1928, after Italian

UMBERTO NOBILE's AIRSHIP passed over the NORTH POLE, it was forced to make a crash landing after icing over and in dense fog on its way back to Spitsbergen (present-day Svalbard). Some 1,500 men—from Italy, Norway, Sweden, and the Union of Soviet Socialist Republics (USSR; Soviet Union)—and 16 ships and 21 airplanes took part in search and rescue efforts. One of them was Norwegian ROALD ENGELBREGT GRAVNING AMUNDSEN, who had beaten Scott to the South Pole by a month and who had also flown with Nobile over the North Pole in an earlier airship expedition in 1926. Despite having publicly feuded with Nobile over the use of airships in polar exploration, Amundsen set out by airplane to Spitsbergen, but perished in a crash in northern waters. Nobile was later rescued, but eight men died in his expedition, and he was officially condemned for the disastrous outcome.

In 1924, on Mount Everest (see EVEREST, MOUNT) in the HIMALAYAS, Englishmen GEORGE HERBERT LEIGH MALLORY and Andrew "Sandy" Irvine disappeared when nearing the summit. Despite searches over the years, Mallory's body was not found until 1999.

Seven Cities of Cibola   See CIBOLA.

sextant

A sextant is a highly accurate instrument used to measure the angular elevation of celestial bodies and thereby determine geographic location. The name derives from the graduated arc displaying the reading, which spans 60 degrees, or a sixth of a circle. In modern terminology, the word *sextant* is used to refer to a number of instruments based on the same principals, such as the QUADRANT, quintant, and octant. But, in more accurate usage, the quadrant is based on an arc of 90 degrees; the quintant is based on an arc of 72 degrees; and the octant (also called Hadley's Quadrant) is based on an arc of 45 degrees.

The sextant is operated by aligning three reference points: an object in the heavens, the horizon, and the location of the observer. The reading is based on the principle that a reflected ray of light leaves the surface of a plane at the same angle at which a direct ray strikes the surface. The device's frame is triangular in shape, the bottom side being an arc of 60 degrees with a scale written on it (the vernier). An arm—known as the index or image arm—fixed at the top point of the triangle swings along the arc. A small index mirror is mounted perpendicular to the frame near the top. A telescope is attached just below. In front of the telescope is a horizon glass, half transparent and half mirror. The index mirror is used to reflect the celestial body (Sun, Moon, star, or planet) into the mirror half of the horizon glass, then into the telescope. The index arm is then slid along the arc so that the horizon can be seen through the transparent half of the horizon glass and the reflected image of the Sun lined up with it. The position of the index arm on the arc indicates the altitude of the celestial body. The time of day or night is noted simultaneously by the position of the index arm on the arc. The reading along with navigational tables (see EPHEMERIS) enables a navigator to determine LATITUDE AND LONGITUDE. Multiple readings are often taken to ensure accuracy.

On land, the irregularity of the terrain makes the use of the sextant impractical but not impossible. An artificial horizon can be utilized, consisting of a pool of mercury or another horizontal reflecting surface; by observing both the celestial body itself and its reflection in the mercury, a reading can be obtained.

The sextant, which revolutionized celestial navigation, was developed over the course of several centuries and replaced the ASTROLABE and CROSS-STAFF. Its earliest ancestor was the Davis Quadrant, a variation on the cross-staff, invented by English mariner JOHN DAVIS in the late 16th century. The 17th–18th-century English physicist Sir Isaac Newton articulated the optical principles by which the instrument could operate and even drew a sketch of it, but never made a working model. The sextant was invented independently in England and America in the early 1730s in response to a challenge by England's ROYAL SOCIETY and the English parliament to solve the problem of how to measure longitude accurately.

The proper use of a sextant requires practice and skill. For this reason, its usefulness has always depended on the navigator operating it. The instrument itself has also become more accurate over the years. One variation is the bubble sextant (and bubble octant) used in stormy weather at sea and in aerial navigation. The image of the celestial body under observation is lined up with the edge of the bubble (much like the bubble of a carpenter's level) instead of the edge of the horizon, allowing the observer to find a horizontal plane for the field of view.

See also NAVIGATION AND EXPLORATION.

Sherpas

Sherpas are a people of the HIMALAYAS living on the mountains' southern slopes mostly in Nepal, as well as some in Sikkim, a northern state of India. They are Tibeto-Nepalese, their ancestors having entered the region from Tibet to the north. (Other Nepalese, known as Indo-Nepalese, entered the region from the south.) The Sherpas for the most part practice Buddhism. They are known for their MOUNTAIN CLIMBING skills. In fact, the term, which is derived from the Tibetan *Sharpa,* for "inhabitant of an eastern country," is also used specifically for Himalayan mountain guides and porters.

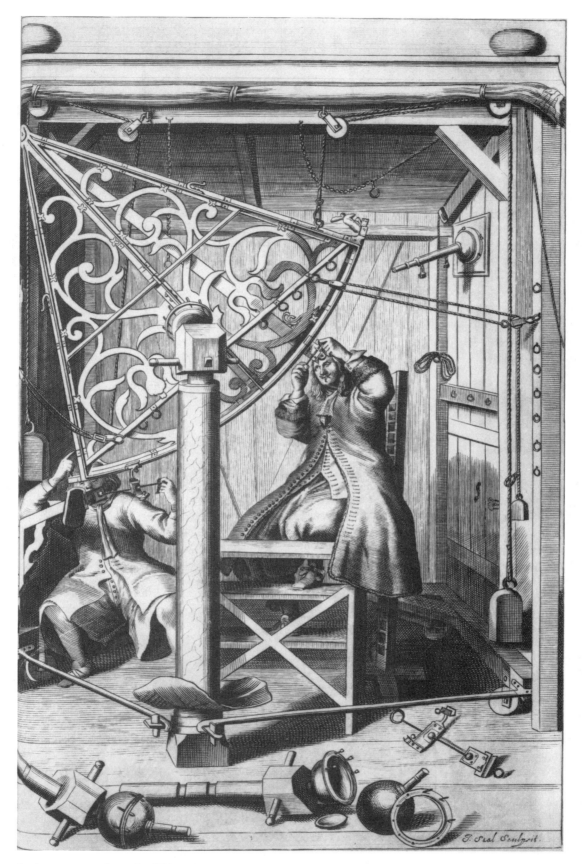

In this engraving from the 17th century, a six-feet-long sextant is being used to measure angular distances between pairs of stars. *(Library of Congress, Prints and Photographs Division [LC-USZ62-95177])*

European climbers, especially the British teams who made attempts on climbing Mount Everest (see EVEREST, MOUNT) in the 1920s, recognized the Sherpas as invaluable for their geographic knowledge, physical prowess, and survival skills. The Sherpas participated in many of the 20th-century expeditions in the Himalayas and the Karakoram Range; expedition leaders often teamed the best Sherpa climbers with the best of the Europeans. The partition of the subcontinent into India and Pakistan in 1947 limited some of the activities of the Sherpas, however, because they could no longer travel unimpeded to the Karakoram and other western Himalayan ranges.

TENZING NORGAY, the most famous of all Sherpa climbers, was teamed with Englishman SIR EDMUND PERCIVAL HILLARY in an assault on Mount Everest in 1953, and became the first human to reach the summit. He also became the Sirdar (chief) of a professional association of Sherpa climbers. Other Sherpas became legendary as well: Ang Dawa, Gyalzan, Niyima, Pa Norbu, Pasang, and Pemba, among many others. Many have passed on the tradition of mountaineering to their offspring, who continue to earn their living as guides for modern-day expeditions.

shipbuilding and exploration

People have used waterways for transportation since ancient times and crafted vessels of many different materials, shapes, and sizes to do so. Design was determined by the types of waterways to be navigated, as well as materials available for construction. The evolution of watercraft is also related to the organization of humankind into larger and larger societies, where larger vessels made trade more efficient. Simultaneously, the need to defend a nation's shores or a nation's ships from PIRACY or from naval actions of other nations became important. Ships thus became specialized for both commercial purposes and military purposes.

Myriad Watercraft

The earliest craft—any floating structure used to carry people or possessions—can be grouped together under the category RAFT. With time, humans began making them more practical out of which came the first true boats. Prehistoric drawings illustrate the use of animal skins sewn together around wooden frames in Europe, and archaeological evidence indicates the use of skin coverings and reindeer antler frames as early as 9000 B.C.

The dugout CANOE—the basic design, a hollowed-out log—was one of the earliest forms of watercraft, found in places where trees grew large enough to make them. They were propelled by a paddle or paddles. Other peoples made use of bark for their canoes—especially birch bark—or animal skin as a covering over a wood frame. Reed-bundle canoes were made in other places, such as the NILE RIVER region in Africa (the papyrus boat) and in the ANDES MOUNTAINS of South America (the bulrush boat). The round CORACLE of northern Europe used skins.

From the simplest designs, more sophisticated and specialized boats evolved. The Inuit (Eskimo) of Arctic regions shaped the double-paddled kayak out of the skin of sea mammals and wood or bone frames. Native Americans of the Pacific Northwest used large cedar trees to make dugouts as long as 100 feet. Some eastern Native Americans began using the light birch bark as a covering over wooden frames to make their canoes practical for inland portages. The Polynesians devised the OUTRIGGER—a type of canoe with attached floats or double-hulled to keep it from flipping over in travel among ocean islands (see POLYNESIAN EXPLORATION). A type of seaworthy skin boat known as the CURRAGH evolved in the British Isles out of the coracle. The PIROGUE, which came to be used on the MISSISSIPPI RIVER and MISSOURI RIVER in North America in the 19th century, evolved from the canoe.

The Ancient Tools of Shipbuilding

The earliest shipbuilding tools were stone and bone. The invention of the metal-casting process dates to the inception of the Bronze Age, in about 3500 B.C., in the Middle East. This was followed by the Iron Age, which began in the second millennium B.C. The adz was perhaps the most basic tool necessary, used for hollowing out logs and shaping wood. Others include the modern equivalent of the ax, chisels, and hammer. Drills were made with a bit, handle, and leather straps for turning the apparatus back and forth. Saws were also made, both small and larger ones operated by two to cut planks. Much of what we know of the early shipwright's tools comes from the recovery of wrecks.

Early Mediterranean Ships

The best representations of early craft come from relief carvings of the ancient Egyptians (see EGYPTIAN EXPLORATION). As their society along the Nile River became more unified in the third millennium B.C., the Egyptians expanded their trading and military activities into the RED SEA and MEDITERRANEAN SEA. They received aid in building their ships from the Phoenicians. The vessel that dominated the region was the GALLEY, a vessel of shallow draft, propelled by oars. The Minoans also used early galleys (see MINOAN EXPLORATION).

The Phoenicians became known as professional shipbuilders and mariners (see PHOENICIAN EXPLORATION). Much of their economy was based on their advantageous position between the East and the West; they could trade for products arriving in the region by land from lands to the east, and transport them by ship to the west. In their homeland in present-day Lebanon, the Phoenicians also had access to cedar trees, which were well suited to produce large vessels. They eventually imported metals to fashion fittings for their ships. They also produced the finest sailors, who were hired by other area powers, to mount expeditions.

The next great shipbuilders in the Mediterranean region, supplanting the Phoenicians, were the Greeks, who also crafted galleys (see GREEK EXPLORATION). Greece was developed into a maritime power, not only because of her abundance of raw materials, but also because of the great length of her coastline, with hospitable bays and inlets, and the large number of islands off the mainland. Like the Egyptians, Greeks also learned a great deal concerning shipbuilding, navigation, and commerce from the Phoenicians.

Galleys were built as warships as well as cargo ships, leading to design differentiation, with some vessels favoring speed and maneuverability while others sought to maximize cargo capacity. Larger and larger galleys came to be built, with, it is reported, as many as six levels of rowers. As such extravagant ships were ordered, placement of the rowers became a major challenge to the designers.

The Romans, who also utilized galleys, came to control the Mediterranean as their empire grew, and they needed grain and other supplies from their provinces. The Etruscans of the Po River valley in northern Italy were skillful shipbuilders. They also had the most experience in navigation and trade.

Designs of the East
During the third millennium B.C., by about 2800, while the galley was being developed in the West, independently, in China, the JUNK was created, a seaworthy craft that uses battened sails. The Chinese used junks to sail from the East Pacific into the Indian Ocean (see CHINESE EXPLORATION).

The Chinese had an incentive to develop their own ocean-going fleets during the Roman era to bypass the overland SILK ROAD and the monopoly that the Persians had in the silk trade. Reports of direct contact between Rome and China date from 100 B.C. Water routes had been developed by the dawn of the Christian era.

Probably in the first century B.C., Arab boatmakers shaped the first DHOW, a boat high in the stern with a pointed bow and a LATEEN RIG triangular sail. They became common in the Indian Ocean and the Mediterranean and helped the Muslims gain dominance in the Middle East starting in the seventh century A.D. (see MUSLIM EXPLORATION).

The designs of both the junk and the dhow have endured to this day.

Ancient Harborworks
Over the course of its lifetime, a ship would need to use a variety of facilities for repair and storage, in addition to the standard docks for loading and unloading of cargo. These harborworks were more permanent than the ships them-

selves, and their excavation has revealed that large ships were in regular use a long time ago, and that much of our knowledge of them has been lost. The earliest known artificial enclosure for ships was discovered in Lothal, India, on the Arabian Sea. It has an entrance and exit for ships, a sluice gate to control the water level, and was constructed with kiln-fired brick. It dates from the third millennium B.C. In the sixth century B.C., the Greeks built numerous breakwaters to shield their harbors from the abuse of waves. Such investments point to a thriving industry. Today the Mediterranean continues to reveal harborworks of varied design, which were built before the time of Christ.

Viking Longships
The Vikings of Scandinavia also built a type of galley, generally known as the LONGSHIP. The longship proper was actually the Viking warship; they crafted shorter versions with a deeper draught as cargo ships. They made use of sails as well as oars. Their seaworthy ships provided them with a mobility unmatched in the history of Europe, during their years of extensive exploration and colonization, from about 800 to 1100 (see VIKING EXPLORATION). Of major importance was the fact that the Viking ships were clinker- or clincher-built—that is, the planks were fastened to one another instead of to a rigid skeleton of ribs. This gave them a great deal of flexibility—they could flex and give when hit by a heavy sea. As a result, they could withstand a great deal of battering while at the same time being light in weight.

Southern and Northern Europe in the Middle Ages
After the fall of Rome in the fifth century A.D., there was a lull in the construction of large ships in the West. This situation changed later in the Middle Ages—notably in the Mediterranean and the Baltic Sea. In the Mediterranean, the Italian city of Amalfi built trading vessels and became the most important commercial center of its time. It was soon eclipsed, however, by Venice, which displayed great energy and was able to produce more ships. After the Fourth Crusade in the early 13th century (see CRUSADES), Venice obtained a trading monopoly with Constantinople (present-day Istanbul, Turkey), partially as a result of supplying transportation to the invaders. The fleets of Venetian galleys continued to grow, making Venice fabulously wealthy. The city began to decline only with the coming of the RENAISSANCE, when the distribution of resources became more widespread.

On the north coast of Europe, a different type of trade was taking place, and, to withstand the rigorous conditions of the sea, a different type of ship was being built. The Baltic, Germanic, and Scandinavian countries of the region were located near rich fishing grounds and had timber forests. For transport they built sturdy, rounded vessels—the ROUNDSHIP and the COG. The HANSEATIC LEAGUE, which arose in this area, consolidated its power with a treaty in 1241. It became highly profitable, in no small measure due to its shipbuilding. The center of the shipbuilding industry was Gdańsk (formerly also known as Danzig).

The city of Bruges in the Netherlands rose to prominence in the 13th century as the western edge of the Hanseatic League territories. Its location provided a convenient stopover for ships on their way to the Mediterranean. Its strategic position was not lost on the Dutch, who used their profits to develop their own industries, including shipbuilding. They also improved their waterways by deepening rivers and building canals. Dutch vigor was soon to be eclipsed by the Portuguese, however.

The European Age of Exploration

Much credit for the EUROPEAN AGE OF EXPLORATION, starting in the 15th century and lasting into the 17th century, goes to HENRY THE NAVIGATOR, prince of Portugal. After conquering the port of Ceuta in North Africa in 1415, and being impressed by the cosmopolitan nature of the city, he established a naval college at Sagres the following year and gathered experts in navigation and shipbuilding. His shipbuilders developed the CARAVEL, a ship of moderate size and rounded shape with a LATEEN RIG, a hybrid between ships of northern design with Arab-style lateen rigging. The resulting craft was easy to maneuver and relatively sturdy. The exploration of the African coast was accomplished with caravels, and gave Portugal a head start in shipbuilding. Profits from the trade route to the East around the CAPE OF GOOD HOPE provided resources for further expansion, and the city of Lisbon, at the north of the Tagus River—the Iberian Peninsula's longest river—became Europe's center of ship construction. Lisbon was better suited than Bruges or Venice for this activity, not only for the quality of its harbors, but also because the expansive forests along the Tagus River were easily harvested and logs could be floated down the river to the sea. Lisbon dominated European shipbuilding from the 15th century well into the 16th century. Much of the Spanish Armada was built in its yards.

The wealth that Portugal and Spain gathered from across the seas eventually corrupted their economies through inflation and waste. This allowed England, the Netherlands, France, and the other countries of Europe to increase in importance. Building ships was a key part of their efforts. King Henry VII of England commissioned the *Great Harry*, a CARRACK of large proportions, which was completed in 1515, the first ship of the English navy.

While England focused on warships, the Dutch were more concerned with trading vessels. The "Dutch Merchantman" became a workhorse of world trade. The Dutch were also aggressive in exploiting fisheries in the Baltic and North Atlantic Seas, at one point having more than 3,000 ships in use. The busiest ship-building city came to be Zaandam, surpassing Lisbon in the 1600s.

The Colonial Age

In the struggle to dominate the seas, the Dutch and the English emerged triumphant in the 17th century. In France, economic reforms by King Henry IV and Cardinal Richelieu made shipbuilding a national priority in the late 16th and early 17th centuries. Two war fleets and a merchant marine were built. In Sweden, Gustavus Adolphus, who ruled as king in 1611–33, made special efforts to expand his navy. Peter the Great, czar of Russia from 1689 to 1725, was alarmed that Russia was being left behind by western European nations, and he personally studied the art of shipbuilding. His efforts at bringing his country up to date were highly successful.

With the creation of the East India companies in the 17th century—the BRITISH EAST INDIA COMPANY, DUTCH EAST INDIA COMPANY, and FRENCH EAST INDIA COMPANY—shipbuilders of the various nations built a type of large MERCHANT SHIP known as the East Indiamen, three-masted, armed with cannons, and displacing some 800 tons.

Throughout the history of exploration, countries built ships in their colonies, first to replace those that were no longer seaworthy, and later as an industry unto itself. Mexican shipyards built ships of the GALLEON type for Spain and for trade with the Philippines and the Americas in the 16th century. The French also built ships in North America.

The English colonies in America found abundant timber to build their own vessels. In 1641, Massachusetts took an active role in its destiny by beginning to build its own merchant fleet. The colony had become frustrated by the unfavorable terms that English merchants imposed on it due to its lack of hard currency. With their own ships, they could market their goods independently. They even built metal works to custom-make the fittings for their ships from the raw iron, which they imported. Shipyards sprang up all along the coast of North America, but the Massachusetts industry retained the lead. In 1722, there were 15 yards in Boston alone. In the 1770s, before the Revolutionary War, the colonies produced more than 2,000 ships for domestic use and for lease or sale to other countries.

Ships became more and more varied and specialized. Speed became a primary concern in certain types of commerce, in order to prevent PIRACY and to outrun warships, such as in the Atlantic SLAVE TRADE. The quest for speed led to the development of clipper ships by the 1830s, with streamlined hulls, sharp bows, an overhanging stern to reduce contact with the water, and three tall masts with as many as five sails each.

Working Conditions

As the size of ships grew larger, their construction became more hazardous. Injury and death of workers resulted from two primary causes—falling timber during the plank-cutting process, and falling off the scaffolding during a ship's assembly. The degree to which voluntary labor was used by an employer varied according to time and place; for example, in colonial America, indentured servitude was a common way for the builder to increase profits. Slavery was used in other parts of the world more extensively. In Europe, however, shipyard workers had above-average status and were paid accordingly.

With Exploration in Mind

The usual situation of the explorer with regard to the ships he could use was dependence on what was available. The stories are many of explorers being promised one thing and being given far less. Also, a ship could deteriorate rapidly from consumption by shipworms and the battering of the sea. Italian CHRISTOPHER COLUMBUS needed to make re-

A descendant of the Inca navigates his bulrush boat with sail on Lake Titicaca in Peru in 1924. *(Library of Congress, Prints and Photographs Division [LC-USZ62-106341])*

pairs to his ships in the AZORES before crossing the Atlantic in 1492.

Englishman JAMES COOK's *Endeavour,* with which he made his first Pacific voyage in 1768–71, was originally built to carry coal along the English coast but was refitted for a long voyage.

The PACK ICE encountered by polar explorers inspired innovations in design, notably the *Fram,* designed by Colin Archer, a Scot, under the guidance of Norwegian FRIDTJOF NANSEN, for an Arctic expedition of 1893. The *Fram,* with a saucer-shaped hull, was made to sit on top of the ice as it froze, rather than being crushed, and was highly successful in fulfilling its mission.

Much exploration was carried out by PINNACE, an auxiliary boat carried aboard the main vessel—either a rowboat or sailboat—used to navigate coastal inlets and rivers. Other boats played a part in the history of exploration in that they were a primary means of transportation during certain periods of history, such as the KEELBOAT, used in the FUR TRADE on the MISSOURI RIVER in the early 19th century, as well as by MERIWETHER LEWIS and WILLIAM CLARK when they journeyed upriver in 1804.

Into Modern Times

In 1769, Scottish engineer James Watt patented the steam engine, ushering in a new age in water transport. Change was not immediate, with sailing ships being built, and many of the early steamships having both sails and engines. Early steamships had paddle wheels for propulsion. In 1838, regular passage across the Atlantic Ocean was offered by steamship. The introduction, in 1840, of the screw propeller, with submerged rotating blades to propel boats, further revolutionized shipbuilding. With time, ships came to be built of iron and steel. Steam engines also evolved, from coal-fired to oil-fired by the late 19th century. In 1897, a diesel engine—running on petroleum-based liquid fuel—was introduced. These improvements made year-round navigation in the Arctic and Antarctic more feasible, with icebreakers able to break through pack ice. The diesel-powered SUBMARINE was developed by a number of different nations in the early 20th century. Some submarines came to be nuclear-powered. In 1958, the first nuclear submarine succeeded in making an undersea transit of the North Pole.

See also NAVIGATION AND EXPLORATION.

Siberia

Siberia is a vast area of land stretching over 5,207,900 square miles from the Ural Mountains in the west to the Pacific Ocean in the east, and from the Arctic Ocean in the north to Kazakhstan, Mongolia, and China in the south. Most of it lies in the present-day nation of Russia, with a small part in northern Kazakhstan. Siberia is divided into three geographic regions: The West Siberian Plain, a swampy and forested area is situated between the Urals and the Yenisey River; from there, the Central Siberian Plateau, at a height between 1,000 and 4,000 feet extends to the Lena River; and, from there, to the Pacific Ocean, often called Far East Russia, lie mountain ranges and uplands.

Three large rivers cross Siberia, all flowing north and draining into the Arctic Ocean: the Lena, the Ob, and the Yenisey. Another major river, the Amur, flows east to the Sea of Okhotsk, which opens to the Pacific. Just southeast of the central Asian Plateau is Lake Baikal. With a maximum depth of 5,371 feet, Lake Baikal is the deepest lake in the world and is estimated to hold one-fifth of Earth's freshwater. Siberia has several mountain ranges, including the Yablonovy and Stanovoy Mountains, which run from the border of Mongolia northeast, to the Sea of Okhotsk. The Altai Mountains, with peaks generally between 10,000 and 13,000 feet, stretch along the bottom of the West Siberian Plain, while the Sayan mountains lie just south of the Central Siberian Plateau. To the northeast, along the Kamchatka Peninsula, which extends into the Bering Sea, is a chain of volcanic peaks, including some active volcanoes, and Siberia's highest peak, Klyuchevskaya Sopka, at 15,584 feet.

Siberia for the most part has long, cold winters and short, moderate summers and is divided into three zones of vegetation. Directly south of the Arctic Ocean is the tundra, a marshy, treeless plain about 270 miles wide covered with permafrost, bearing moss, lichens, and flowers, as well as small shrubs in the summer. South of the tundra is the taiga, a belt of primarily coniferous forests, followed by more deciduous forests. And finally the steppe, a large grassland, stretches to Siberia's southern limits.

Early Reports

There is evidence that nomadic peoples roamed across Siberia 50,000 years ago, but the first settled communities date from the 11th century B.C. These communities, along southern Siberia, had intercourse with the SILK ROAD, a principal route of trade between the East and the West. The southern steppe of Siberia was the road for the Scythians as they advanced into Europe ca. 700 B.C., the Sarmartians in the third century B.C., and the Hsiung-Nu (Huns) in the fourth century A.D. Conquered by the Mongols in the 13th century A.D., southwestern Siberia became an independent Mongolian kingdom called Siber, with the dissolution of the Mongolian Empire in the 15th century (see MONGOL EXPLORATION). The term Siber, from which Siberia is derived, is Mongolian for "sleeping land."

It is thought that in the ninth century A.D. people to the west of Siberia began to form states. One of the most prosperous of these was located at Novgorod, subsisting on hunting and trading furs. The earliest recorded voyage into Siberia by a Novgorodian was Uleb in 1032, who reported his voyage to the land called "the Iron Gates," which is probably the region around the Pechora River. Other voyagers visited what they called the "land of Yugra," or the Ural

This photograph demonstrates one method of transportation in Siberia in the late 19th century. *(Library of Congress, Prints and Photographs Division [LC-USZ62-128127])*

Mountains; "the country beyond the portage"; and the "land of midnight," which probably referred to the area around the lower Ob River. In 1363, a large expedition of Novgorodians explored the lower Ob.

Looking Eastward

Another principality arose around this time along the Volga River, called Moscow. Moscow extended its power and fought with people living further east, the Voguls. The Muscovites chased the Voguls into Siberia, in the region of the Irtysh River, a tributary of the Ob. In 1478, Moscow conquered Novgorod, and, by the middle of the 15th century, was receiving tribute from the Tatar rulers of Siberia. A powerful merchant family of Moscow, the Stroganovs, were given title to a large stretch of land up to the Ural Mountains. With their lands harassed by Vogul raiders from over the mountains in Siberia, the Stroganovs sent YERMAK and a band of Cossacks to subdue them. Yermak conquered the Mongolian khanate of Sibir', as it was known, claiming all of Siberia for the Russian leader or czar, Ivan IV Vasilyevich, or Ivan the Terrible. He was, however, killed in 1584 or 1585, trying to maintain command of the region. The Muscovites moved into Sibir' and took control, establishing forts along the Ob. The route from Moscow to Siber was long and dangerous because of the warlike Voguls, and Muscovites continued to search for better routes. In 1597, Artemy Babinov discovered a land route to the Tura River, which cut 700 miles from the journey and which remained the principal land route to Siberia for almost 200 years.

By the beginning of the 17th century, the Russians had explored and occupied most of the Ob River Valley. Russian merchants then moved on to explore the Yenisey Basin, sailing down the Yenisey River, and building forts. Fur hunters ventured eastward and reached the Lena River. There, they encountered the Yakuts, a Siberian people with a highly advanced culture who lived in houses, wore Russian-like clothing, and kept horses. The fine quality of furs returned from the eastern reaches of Siberia inspired more expeditions there. In 1639, a small band, broken off from a group exploring the rivers in the east, crossed a pass in the Dzhugdzhur Range and sailed down the Ulya River to the Sea of Okhotsk. The Russians had reached the North Pacific Ocean. Other expeditions soon followed. In the 1640s–50s, MIKHAIL STADUKHIN explored the Arctic coast of Siberia around the Kolyma River and on the Gulf of Anadyr. The earliest recorded sighting of the BERING STRAIT was by a party of Cossacks under SEMYON IVANOVICH DEZHNEV in 1648.

Russian exploration continued in Siberia into the Amur River Valley, much of it also carried out by Cossacks and much of it for the FUR TRADE (see COSSACK EXPLORATION). Cossacks PYOTR BEKETOV and VASILY DANILOVICH POYARKO in the 1630s–40s spread Russian influence eastward.

The Russian fur trader YEROFEY PAVLOVICH KHABOROV established the first Russian settlements along the Amur in the 1650s. Cossacks also soon reached the Kamchatka Peninsula. LUKA MOROZKO and VLADIMIR VASILYEVICH ATLASOV explored Kamchatka in 1695–96. In time, the native Kamchadals had been conquered, and the Russians had founded posts along the length of the peninsula.

Peter the Great

At that time, in 1696, Peter the Great became czar of Russia. Interested in the West, and hoping to assemble a coalition against the Ottoman Empire of the Turks, Peter traveled with a great embassy to Europe. He brought back with him hundreds of skilled Europeans to work and train Russians and tried to learn as much as possible about European navigation. This exposure to the West, combined with the expanding power of what was becoming a Russian empire, under the hand of Peter, spurred the scientific exploration of Siberia in the 18th century. Peter was most interested in the possibility of a water route from the Arctic Ocean to China and India, due to the difficulties and expense of reaching those countries over land.

In 1719, Peter sent an expedition of two topographers, Ivan Yevreinov and Fyodor Luzhin, to explore the Kuril Islands off the southern end of the Kamchatka Peninsula. Later, in January 1725, Peter sent Dutch seaman VITUS JONASSEN BERING to head an expedition to determine once and for all if Asia and America were connected. It was not until 1728, after the czar's death, that Bering and his expedition were able to set out. Bering was unable to determine conclusively, but surmised that there existed a strait of passage from the Pacific to the Arctic Ocean. A later British expedition under FREDERICK WILLIAM BEECHEY thoroughly explored the Bering Strait in 1828.

DANIEL GOTTLIEB MESSERSCHMIDT, a German scientist, was another European who Peter brought to Russia in 1716. Messerschmidt, trained in medicine, was also acquainted with natural history, geography, and archaeology. From 1720 to 1727, he traveled throughout Siberia, exploring many rivers and steppes, discovering many mineral resources, and collecting specimens. He even discovered the skeleton of a mammoth.

Great Northern Expedition

Meanwhile, Bering's expedition had failed to satisfy the Russian Admiralty, and a second, much larger expedition was ordered in 1733. Often called the "Great Northern Expedition" for its scope and investigations of the Arctic, it consisted of an unprecedented 977 members. The expedition was divided into parts, reminiscent of the steps in Russia's eastward expansion over Siberia: surveying the Arctic Ocean from Arkhangelsk to the mouth of the Ob River; from the Ob to the Yenisey; from the Yenisey to the Lena;

and from the mouth of the Lena to the Kamchatka Peninsula. In concert with these divisions, Bering again led an exploration of the strait bearing his name. The expedition included many Western European-trained scientists, who made notes of ethnography, botany, geology, geography, and history.

Later Expeditions

Other Russians continued to explore the coast of Siberia and the Arctic Ocean through the latter half of the 18th century and the first part of the 19th century. Many of them, such as GRIGORY IVANOVICH SHELIKOV and ALEKSANDR ANDREYEVICH BARANOV, were fur traders. Others, such as ANTON BATAKOV and GAVRIIL ANDREYEVICH SARYCHEV were mariners (Batakov worked under JOSEPH BILLINGS, an Englishman hired by the Russian government to head the Northeastern Secret Geographical and Astronomical Expedition).

❖

In the 20th century, during the years the territory was part of the Union of Soviet Socialist Republics (USSR; Soviet Union), Siberia became known to the West as a place of exile for criminals and political prisoners, as it had been in earlier centuries. With vast stands of timber and huge deposits of oil, gas, and minerals, Siberia now plays an important role in the Russian economy. Industrialization that started under the Soviet Union has created a serious pollution problem, however.

See also ARCTIC, EXPLORATION OF THE; ASIA, EXPLORATION OF.

Silk Road

The Silk Road was not a constructed road but rather the name applied to a collection of overland routes crossing nearly 4,000 miles of Asia and used for about 1,500 years for trade between the East and the West. It was named for silk, the most precious and desired commodity that passed over it, an exceptionally soft fabric made by hand in the East from the cocoons of the silkworm, which was originally native to China and lived on the mulberry tree.

Even before the establishment of the Silk Road in the second century B.C., Chinese goods like silk, jade, and bronzes reached the Near East and ultimately the West on small camel caravans as early as 1000 B.C., ancient traders braving harsh terrain and dangerous brigands on the road. But these caravans were dangerous and few. Silk was worn by Persian nobility and coveted by ALEXANDER THE GREAT, the Macedonian leader of the fourth century B.C., becoming a sign of wealth in ancient Greece and Rome. The Asian goods were bartered for European goods, such as glass, amber, coral, pearls, woolens, and linens.

But the Silk Road was not established because of increasing demand of what were and remained expensive luxury items. Instead, it was the result of a diplomatic mission intending to secure an alliance to defend the nascent Han Empire of China from Mongolian nomads called the Huns (Hsiung-nu, or Xiongnu) who threatened settlements of the Chinese.

Founding of the Silk Road

In 128 B.C., the Han emperor, Wu Ti, sent diplomat CHANG CH'IEN to gain an alliance with people the Chinese called Yue-chi in central Asia (and known in the West as the Scythians). In about 118 B.C., after having been captured and then escaping from the Huns, Chang Ch'ien continued westward, reaching Bactria in northern Afghanistan. He returned to China from there, but received reports of peoples farther to the west, including the Persians, Greeks, and Romans. Chang Ch'ien failed to gain any alliances, but his stories of Western civilizations encouraged a desire to trade. Embarking on a second mission in 115 B.C., he sent envoys to Persia and the eastern Roman provinces, laden with silks and gold. The route that Chang Ch'ien had taken developed into the Silk Road, kept stable and passable by the power of the Chinese Empire and the Parthian Empire of Persia as well as the flourishing Roman Republic (see CHINESE EXPLORATION; ROMAN EXPLORATION).

Roman geographer PLINY THE ELDER of the first century A.D. wrote about the Silk Road in *Historia Naturalis* of A.D. 77. Twenty years later, in A.D. 97, Chinese diplomat KAN YING was sent on a mission to Rome during the Han dynasty in the hope of forming an alliance to secure the Silk Road in the face of central Asian rivals. He failed to reach Rome but did reestablish contacts with peoples in China's western provinces. In about A.D. 120, a Greek merchant by the name of Maës Titanius sent out representatives along the Silk Road; they reached Kashgar. Their reports reportedly were used by hellenized Egyptian PTOLEMY in his writings about the silk trade in his *Geographia,* produced in A.D. 127–147 (see GREEK EXPLORATION).

Traveling the Silk Road

Goods from China were carried by caravan from city to city and oasis to oasis—where water and food, as well as fresh camel and horses, could be obtained. Few caravans or merchants traveled the entire Silk Road. Goods were bartered all along the Silk Road. Moreover, a new caravan might be organized to transport the cargo to the next trade center. Most of the traders were peoples of central Asia or Persians, since for much of China's history, Chinese travel outside its territorial holdings was forbidden. Local residents of the many different ethnic groups along the way served as translators among peoples from many lands. In addition to merchants, other travelers used the routes developed by them, such as diplomats and missionaries, as well as emigrants seeking out new opportunities. Many travelers from China, such as religious scholars FA-HSIEN in the fourth–fifth century A.D. and HSÜAN-TSANG in the seventh century A.D., used parts of the route to reach India. But travel was dangerous—because of climatic extremes as well as bandits—and corpses and bones reportedly littered the Silk Road.

The caravans would leave first from Chang'an in northern China, heading west along a narrow corridor between the GOBI DESERT and the Nan Shan mountains, before splitting into two routes, one skirting the northern and another the southern edge of the forbidding Takla Makan desert, 360,000 square miles of shifting sand dunes squeezed between the Kunlun range to the south and the Tian Shan range to the north. These two paths rejoined in the foothills of the Pamir range. Other routes crossed the steppes of Mongolia before continuing into Europe, or merged at the forks of the main road, which had split in the Pamirs, part of which headed through the Tian Shan range for Samarkand, part headed for Bactria and Kabul in present-day Afghanistan (where a route connected the road to India through the KHYBER PASS). Routes varied somewhat due to climate, openings and closings of mountain passes, and the drying up of oases, as well as political situations, the rise and fall of empires, and the fortunes of nomadic brigands who preyed on the caravans.

Later Use

Trade was reduced by the fall of the Han Empire in China in the third century A.D., and reignited by the rise of the T'ang (Tang) in the seventh century. Trade declined again, with the fall of the T'ang dynasty in the 10th century, only to be renewed by the vast conquests of the Mongols under GENGHIS KHAN in the 13th century (see MONGOL EXPLORATION). Westerners now ventured over the caravan routes to China, most important was the Polo family of Venetian merchants—MAFFEO POLO, NICCOLÒ POLO, and MARCO POLO—who, upon their return to Europe, brought back stories of Chinese wealth, which fanned the flames of European imagination and the desire for Oriental goods. After the dissolution of the Mongol empire into smaller states, and increased warfare among them, travel and trade became dangerous. The rise of the Islamic Turks who, in 1453, conquered Constantinople (present-day Istanbul), the capital city of Byzantium that sat on one of the most important arms of the Silk Road as it passed into Europe, effectively cut off much of the trade. But because of growing demand and the increasing power of nations in Europe, such as Spain, Portugal, and England, sea routes to the East were sought.

By Sea

With the discovery of routes from the Atlantic Ocean around the CAPE OF GOOD HOPE of Africa into the Indian Ocean by the Portuguese, and other sea routes to the East, and because sea travel was faster and safer and could transport more cargo quickly, the Silk Road dwindled in importance in the 15th and 16th centuries before falling entirely out of use, while its oases became deserts.

❖

The Silk Road no longer exists as a trade route. But following what once constituted it offers a fascinating view into the past. Modern cities of Bukhara, Kashgar, Khiva, Samarkand, Tashkent, and Turfan are full of history. In 1906–08, Anglo-Hungarian archaeologist SIR MARC AUREL STEIN followed a stretch of the ancient Silk Road into western China and discovered the Caves of the Thousand Buddhas, a series of temples built into caves, at Tunhuang.

See also COMMERCE AND EXPLORATION.

slave trade

Slavery, a practice in which humans are considered property for labor or other services, has occurred in all parts of the world and in all types of societies—from primitive hunting-gathering groups to complex agriculturally based civilizations. It has endured from ancient to modern times, sanctioned by many nations through much of the 19th century. And the slave trade, like other areas of commerce, has played a part in world exploration by providing incentive to reach distant lands and opening up routes of travel.

Slavery in Ancient Times

The Egyptians, Greeks, Romans, and Chinese, known for their explorations, as well as most other ancient peoples around the world, utilized slavery to maintain a labor force. Many slaves were acquired as prisoners of war; others in raids specifically for the purpose of slaving; and others in trade. Those captured or traded might end up as workers on roads or buildings or farms; as concubines and prostitutes; as domestic servants and, in some instances, when educated, as tutors; and as soldiers. Another common use of slaves in the ancient world was as oarsmen on GALLEY ships. The Romans also used slaves in gladiatorial combats. In many societies, the number of slaves and their country of origin were considered matters of prestige. (See CHINESE EXPLORATION; EGYPTIAN EXPLORATION; GREEK EXPLORATION; ROMAN EXPLORATION.)

Slavery in the Middle Ages

Slavery persisted through the Middle Ages. The early forms of Christianity and of Islam did not condemn the practice. Arab and Berber Muslims had developed trade routes across Africa's SAHARA DESERT and the RED SEA for markets in the Middle East in pre-Islamic times and continued using them; other peoples, seafaring Muslims from Arabia and Persia, came to use the Indian Ocean as a trade route to East Africa for markets in Asia, especially Arabia, Persia (present-day Iran), and India (see MUSLIM EXPLORATION). During the same period, the Vikings out of the north raided coastal areas and also took slaves, but mainly for personal use, not in trade for profit (see VIKING EXPLORATION). Meanwhile,

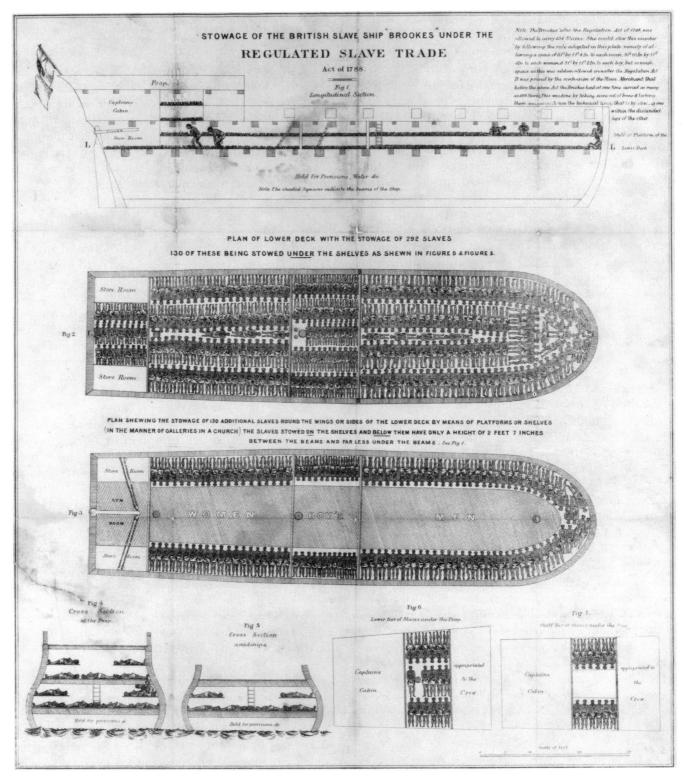

This etching shows deck plans and cross sections of a late 18th-century British slave ship. *(Library of Congress, Prints and Photographs Division [LC-USZ62-44000])*

in the Americas, pre-Columbian civilizations, such as the Maya, Aztec, and Inca, made use of slave labor in building, agriculture, and warfare on a large scale. Other peoples kept captives among them as slaves.

Slavery in most societies was regulated by custom or law. Various social systems were practiced in which laborers were not considered property themselves, although they were legally bound to their work. Serfdom, involving agricultural laborers in medieval Europe, was one such system. Some societies made provisions for the earning of freedom by slaves.

Early Portuguese Slave Trade

The 1440s are cited as the start of the institutionalized European slave trade. In 1441, an expedition sponsored by HENRY THE NAVIGATOR, prince of Portugal, under NUÑO TRISTÃO and Anton Gonçalves, sailed in the Atlantic Ocean along Africa's west coast. Tristão reached Cape Blanco; Gonçalves landed at the Rio de Oro and captured a number of natives, whom he took back to Portugal and presented to Prince Henry. Three years later, Tristão reached Arguin Island, part of present-day Mauritania. In 1448, he established a fort there, which became the first Portuguese slaving station. With subsequent expeditions along the coast, the Portuguese extended their influence and built more posts.

A thriving and systematized trade developed, with Europeans exchanging trade goods—textiles, beads, tools, alcoholic beverages, and eventually guns—to Africans for African captives. Farther south, Portuguese merchants also came to travel the Senegal and Gambia Rivers into the interior. Meanwhile, Muslim slavers continued to use the trans-Saharan routes as far south as what became known as the Slave Coast—the coasts of present-day Nigeria, Benin, and Togo along the Bight of Benin. The Portuguese reached this region by the 1470s. By the 1480s, they were also slaving as far south as the CONGO RIVER (Zaire River) beyond the Muslim trading territory. At the end of the 15th century, with the voyage of VASCO DA GAMA, the Portuguese had sailed all the way around Africa and reached India by water. Soon afterward, along Africa's east coast, they were raiding Muslim trading centers and establishing their own posts. At the various slave ports would be found slave camps, where slaves were interred after forced marches and before being shipped to markets.

Other Nations Enter the African Slave Trade

Portugal had a head start on other European countries in the large-scale slave trade, but, starting in the latter half of the 16th century, England entered the field. SIR JOHN HAWKINS completed the first successful English transatlantic slave-trading expedition in 1562–63, sailing to present-day Sierra Leone, where he obtained a cargo of slaves from Portuguese traders, then to the Caribbean island of Hispaniola (present-day Haiti and the Dominican Republic), where he ex-

changed the slaves to Spanish colonists for sugar and hides, then back to England. France, the Netherlands, Denmark, Sweden, and Prussia soon entered the trade as well.

Native American Slaves

In the meantime, early European visitors to the Americas—CHRISTOPHER COLUMBUS, an Italian exploring for Spain at the end of the 15th century, being one of them—took Native Americans as slaves, and the enslavement of Native Americans would persist for centuries in a variety of forms, some of them limited slavery or indentured servitude, that is, forced tribute or labor resembling European serfdom. Yet it never reached the scale of the African slave trade, partly because the system surrounding the acquisition of new slaves was already in place in Africa. Another factor limiting the use of Native Americans in the slave trade was that it was in the new colonies themselves where slave labor was desired, and peoples near their homelands were more likely to attempt escape or revolt. Native Americans also proved more susceptible to European diseases (see DISEASE AND EXPLORATION).

Triangular Trade

The colonization of the Americas created new markets for slaves, and the slave trade between Europe, Africa, and the Americas became known as the "triangular trade." That is to say, the commerce surrounding the Atlantic slave trade moved in a triangle. European ships transported manufactured goods to Africa's west coast, where they would be bartered for slaves. The slaves were then transported to the colonies in North and South America, where they would be exchanged for mostly agricultural goods, especially cotton, tobacco, sugar, and molasses, as well as rum. These products would then be carried back to Europe.

The development of the plantation system—self-contained estates dedicated to farming particular crops on a large scale, especially tobacco and cotton—in the Caribbean and in North America's southern colonies in the latter half of the 17th century led to a growing demand for slaves. Business interests of various American colonies also entered the slave trade, providing their own vessels for shipping. An estimated 12 million slaves were taken from Africa to the Americas in the transatlantic slave trade, with as many as two million perishing from malnutrition and disease on the ocean journeys. The majority of the surviving 10 million ended up in the WEST INDIES, Central America, and South America, with lesser numbers to North America. (It is estimated that some 42 percent of the African slaves were sold to the sugar plantations of the Caribbean; 38 percent to Brazilian sugar plantations and mines; 15 percent to plantations and mines in other parts of Latin America; and 5 percent to North American colonies.) The African Diaspora, as it is known—the dispersion of African peoples resulting from the slave trade—led to the collapse of West African civilizations. Starting in the 17th century, European traders

Possibly engraved in the late 1700s or early 1800s, this slave auction house was in New York City. *(Library of Congress, Prints and Photographs Division)*

also operated in the Indian Ocean, acquiring slaves to work on Indian Ocean island colonies, such as the Mascarene Islands. Some slaves out of East Africa were also transported westward around the CAPE OF GOOD HOPE to the Americas.

Abolitionism

Throughout history, there has been a dedicated opposition balancing and modifying the practice of slavery. Some of the earliest voices speaking out against it were missionaries (see RELIGION AND EXPLORATION). SAMUEL FRITZ, a Jesuit missionary from Bohemia (part of the present-day Czech Republic) who explored the AMAZON RIVER and its tributaries in South America in the late 1600s and early 1700s, attempted to protect Indians from Portuguese slavers. The humanistic precepts of 18th-century French philosopher Jean-Jacques Rousseau and of other individuals associated with the Age of Enlightenment, along with growing democratic ideals in Europe, helped create a climate antithetical to slavery. German naturalist and geographer ALEXANDER VON HUMBOLDT, who also explored northern parts of South America at the turn of the 19th century, was outspoken in denouncing the practice.

The antislavery movement became organized and effective in the 19th century. JAMES RICHARDSON, who participated in a British expedition to West Africa in the 1850s with HEINRICH BARTH and ADOLF OVERWEG, was a leading member of the English Anti-Slavery Society. DAVID LIVINGSTONE, a Scottish missionary who traveled widely in Africa in the 1850s–1870s, hoped to abolish the slave trade by establishing Christian missionary stations and alternative commerce. Before his explorations in Africa in the 1870s–1880s, VERNEY LOVETT CAMERON served as a naval officer in a British campaign against Ethiopia to end the East African slave trade.

The slave trade was abolished before slavery itself, with Denmark banning it in 1792, and Great Britain in 1807, and other European nations soon afterward. The United States prohibited the foreign slave trade in 1808. By the end of the 19th century, institutionalized slavery itself was abolished in most nations, although various forms of slavery are still practiced on a small scale in some parts of the world.

See also COMMERCE AND EXPLORATION.

South America, exploration of

With an area of about 6.8 million square miles, South America is the fourth-largest continent on the globe. It is bordered by the Pacific Ocean to the west, the Atlantic Ocean to the east, and the Caribbean Sea, an arm of the Atlantic, to the north. South America, from the Caribbean Sea in the north to its tip in the south, where the Atlantic and Pacific meet, stretches 4,600 miles, and from east to west, at its widest point, is 3,210 miles wide. The continent is joined to Central America (see CENTRAL AMERICA, EXPLORATION OF), considered the southern extent of North America, by the narrow isthmus of Panama.

Modern-day South America is divided into 12 nations, including Argentina, Bolivia, Brazil, Chile, Colombia, Ecuador, Guyana, Paraguay, Peru, Suriname, Uruguay, and Venezuela. The Galápagos Islands, noted for their unique species of animals, lie 650 miles into the Pacific from the South American coast. The Juan Fernández Islands and Easter Island also lie in the Pacific, while the Fernando de Noronha Archipelago and the Falkland Islands lie in the Atlantic. In the north lie Trinidad and Tobago, the Netherland Antilles, and other islands of the WEST INDIES. The Tierra del Fuego Archipelago sits at the southern end of South America, separated from it by the Strait of Magellan (see MAGELLAN, STRAIT OF), four to 20 miles wide and 200 miles long. CAPE HORN on Horn Island is the continent's southernmost point of land.

The continent is divided into high mountains and plateaus, thick rain forest and jungle, and shallow valleys and long flat plains. The ANDES MOUNTAINS, the second-highest mountain range in the world, rise on the western side of the continent. Its peaks include ACONCAGUA, which is the highest in the Western Hemisphere at 22,834 feet above sea level, as well as Mercedario, Tupungato, Illampu, and Illimani, all more than 20,000 feet. The Andes also includes active volcanoes, especially in Chile, such as Cotopaxi and Tunguragua. In the Andes, between southeastern Peru and western Bolivia, is Lake Titicaca, 12,545 feet above sea level, with an area of about 5,000 square miles, and a maximum depth of 700 feet that never freezes over, making it the highest navigable lake in the world. Other, shorter highlands lie to the east. One is usually called the Guiana Highlands, a plateau, forest covered on the main, but also with flat grassy plains, which lies in southern Venezuela, Guiana, and northern Brazil. Other South American highlands include the Brazilian and Patagonian Highlands.

South America has three principal lowlands, the largest being the basin of the AMAZON RIVER, followed by the basin of the ORINOCO RIVER to the north, and the Paraguay-Paraná basin to the south, which merges with the valleys and plains of the Pampas and the Gran Chaco of Argentina and Brazil. The three rivers drain an area of about 3.7 million square miles. The Amazon River is the second-longest in the world, at 4,000 miles, but is the largest in terms of volume, discharging a fifth of all the freshwater that drains into the oceans. It flows roughly west to east, rising in the Andes, and drains into the Atlantic Ocean just below the EQUATOR. The Orinoco, at about 1,500 miles (1,700 if a particular branch is considered), flows in an arc through Venezuela, originating in the Guiana Highlands and draining into the Caribbean. The Paraguay-Paraná basin supports the Paraguay and Uruguay Rivers, which enter the Atlantic through the La Plata estuary in Argentina.

The climate of South America is mainly determined by distance from the equator. The area around the equator is hot, with long, wet summers and short, dry winters. The farther away from the equator, the shorter the summer and longer the winter, with the risk of drought. Much of the area around the equator is filled with dense rain forest, supported by the heat and summer rains. The west coast of South America is dryer, and with the high elevations of the Andes, cooler. Past the TROPIC OF CANCER, the winters are cold and the summers cool with higher precipitation to the south.

Animal life displays great isolation and singularity, having many different species from those found on North America. The rain forest in particular has a myriad of species. Large South American mammals include the tapir, jaguar, peccary, coati, giant anteater, spectacled bear, and monkeys, as well as alpacas, llamas, and vicuñas (members of the camel family). Among the larger birds are the condor, flamingo, and rhea. Large reptiles include anacondas, boas, caimans, crocodiles, and iguanas.

Native Peoples

It is estimated that as many as 30 million Native Americans lived in South America when Europeans first arrived. Some of them had developed complex civilizations, many of them centered in the Andes. The various peoples speaking as many as 1,550 distinct languages are sometimes grouped into the following culture areas for purposes of study: the central and southern Andes and adjacent Pacific coastal regions, where complex farming civilizations, such as that of the Inca, developed; northern South America, where the peoples lived a way of life similar to lower Central America and Caribbean peoples, with small villages and some farming; the tropical forests of eastern South America, which offered a wealth of resources to the hunting-and-gathering peoples also living in scattered villages, many of them along the Amazon River; and the colder regions in the south, to the east and south of the Andes, consisting of nomadic hunter-gatherers.

The Quechua-speaking Inca became the most dominant people on the continent. It is thought that some groups were consolidated as early as A.D. 1000 in what is known as the pre-Inca period; they had evolved out of and had been influenced by earlier dominant cultures of the region, such as Tiahuanacan, Chavin, Chimu, Nazca, Moche (Mochica), and Paracas. Inca legend has it that the Inca lived first around Lake Titicaca in the Andes of southeast Peru and northwest Bolivia, and later moved, in about 1200 A.D., northward into the more fertile valley of Cuzco, where they conquered the inhabitants and established their capital. The name *Inca* is derived from *Ynca* for the prince of the ruling family.

The early Inca period is given as A.D. 1200 to 1440. From 1440 to 1500, the Inca expanded their territory, conquering the Chibcha Indians of present-day Colombia, the Aymara Indians of present-day Bolivia, and the Araucanian Indians of present-day Chile. At its height, the empire of tributary tribes covered about 350,000 square miles centered in the Andes, but stretching to the Pacific coast, and into the Amazon Basin—from what is now northern Ecuador to central Chile. Two emperors, Pachacuti Inca Yupanqui and his son, Topa Inca Yupanqui, developed a state religion and set up a complicated system of administration to govern their lands. The empire was divided into quarters, each governed by a blood relative of the emperor. Each quarter was divided further with an elaborate collection of officials, which at its base had an official to oversee every group of 10 peasants. Peasants throughout the empire were required to provide as a tax a certain amount of labor every year for public works. This facilitated the creation of a system of 10,000 miles worth of stone roads and rope bridges across gorges.

The Inca also built great cities, such as Cuzco and Machu Picchu, with stone palaces, temples, and fortresses, often covered with precious metals. They developed elaborate art forms, especially in metalwork and textiles, as well as writing, calendar, and counting systems.

Inca emperor Topa Inca Yupanqui died in 1493, just as Europeans were arriving in South America, and was succeeded by Huayna Capac. In 1525, both Huayna Capac and his successor died, setting off a civil war between Huayna Capac's remaining sons, Huáscar and Atahualpa, in which Atahualpa triumphed. It was Atahualpa who would face off against the Europeans.

First European Sighting

Italian mariner CHRISTOPHER COLUMBUS, sailing for Spain, was the first European to see South America. The Portuguese had been developing a route to the markets of the Orient south and east around Africa into the Indian Ocean, a program that began under the auspices of HENRY THE NAVIGATOR, prince of Portugal. Columbus proposed to sail west over unexplored ocean, thinking he would circle the globe and reach the east coast of Asia in less than 3,000 miles. King John II of Portugal rejected his plan in 1484, and, again in 1488, after Portuguese BARTOLOMEU DIAS reported reaching the CAPE OF GOOD HOPE, which signaled success in the Indian Ocean route. In 1492, however, Queen Isabella I of a newly united Spain agreed to the small initial bankroll, advised that the cost was slight and the potential for payoff great. Columbus sailed westward from Spain with three ships on August 3, 1492.

With the crew of one ship on the verge of mutiny after over a month sailing in open ocean, land was spied on October 12. The first land is thought to have been a small island of the Bahamas that Columbus named San Salvador. Columbus later found a larger island he called Española—later Hispaniola (present-day Haiti and the Dominican Republic)—and eventually returned to Spain with gold, parrots, and native peoples. He made a second, larger expedition of 17 ships in 1493, with soldiers, colonists, livestock, tools, and seeds. Columbus passed and named many islands in the Caribbean, also exploring along the coasts of Cuba and Jamaica. Still thinking he had reached the outlying islands of Asia—thus the eventual name of WEST INDIES for the islands of the region—he returned to Europe in 1496.

Columbus embarked on his third voyage in 1498. He sent half his fleet of six ships directly to Hispaniola and sailed with others to the Cape Verde Islands off Africa, then followed a more southerly route across the Atlantic. On July 31, 1498, he sighted and named the island of Trinidad. Continuing southward, he entered the Gulf of Paria off present-day Venezuela. He met native peoples there and traded with them for pearls. Although he only sighted islands, he noted the abundance of freshwater flowing into the gulf and surmised he had found a great mainland. He never sighted the delta of the Orinoco River, but sailed westward, examining the coast before returning to Hispaniola.

Coastal Explorations

ALONSO DE OJEDA commanded one of Columbus's ships on his second voyage in 1493 and remained to help establish the settlement of Isabella on Hispaniola, exploring the interior of the island and warring with native peoples. In 1497, he returned to Spain, seeking authority and supplies to mount his own voyage of exploration. Ojeda was granted permission in 1499 to explore the mainland territory that Columbus had discovered the previous year. He set sail with a small fleet in May 1499, accompanied by JUAN DE LA COSA, a cartographer who had been Columbus's pilot, and AMERIGO VESPUCCI, a Florentine who represented Italian banking interests that had partly financed the voyage. Ojeda's ship reached South America off the coast of present-day French Guiana, five degrees north of the equator. Ojeda sailed northwestward, stopping at Trinidad and Margarita Island. On August 9, along a coastal inlet on the mainland, he spied a native settlement of houses supported in the water by piers. Reminded of Venice, Ojeda gave the name *Venezuela* to the place, which came to be used for the entire area.

Vespucci's ship reportedly arrived on the coast of Brazil, near Cape São Roque, about five degrees south of the equator. He sailed northwestward and may have explored the Brazilian coast as far as the mouth of the Amazon River, which he explored a short distance upstream. After meeting up with the rest of the expedition in Santo Domingo, Vespucci returned to Spain, arriving in September 1500. By that time, Portuguese admiral PEDRO ÁLVARS CABRAL had reached Brazil and taken formal possession for the Portuguese. Cabral, who had close ties to the Portuguese court but little experience as a navigator, was selected in 1499 to lead a trading mission to India, after Portuguese mariner VASCO DA GAMA reported success in rounding Africa's Cape of Good Hope.

Cabral commanded 13 ships, carrying more than 1,200 men, including merchants, soldiers, missionaries, and some convicts. While earlier voyages had kept close to the coastline of Africa, Cabral followed the advice of Vasco da Gama and sailed due south from the Cape Verde Islands, far into the open ocean to avoid unfavorable winds. Cabral intended to utilize strong westerly winds south and west of Africa to carry his fleet past the Cape of Good Hope and into the Indian Ocean. On April 22, 1500, after sailing southwest into uncharted waters, he sighted the coast of Brazil, at about 17 degrees south of the equator. The fleet anchored there, within sight of Mount Pascoal. Cabral went ashore four days later, taking formal possession of Brazil for Portugal, calling it Terra da Vera Cruz (land of the true cross). He did not know, however, if he had discovered an island or a continent.

A Spaniard had landed earlier that year in northeastern Brazil. The navigator, VICENTE YÁÑEZ PINZÓN, was one of a group of brothers who had served with Columbus on his voyages to the Americas. In 1495, he was given permission by the Spanish crown to lead his own expedition to the Indies. Pinzón did not sail until November 1499, with a fleet of four ships. After reaching the Cape Verde Islands, he sailed southwestward, crossing the equator. On January 20, 1500, he sighted South America, naming the cape Santa María de la Consolación. From that point, Pinzón sailed northwestward and explored the mouth of the Amazon River, which he named La Mar Dulce (the sweet water sea) because of its abundance of freshwater, which was fit to drink a distance out to sea. He explored the Amazon for about 50 miles, before sailing farther northwest along the coast of the Guianas and Venezuela. In the Gulf of Paria, he sighted the island of Tobago, Trinidad's smaller companion, which he called the Isla de Mayo. Pinzón returned to Spain in September 1500, carrying a cargo of tropical wood, 20 native slaves, and a South American opossum, the first marsupial seen in Europe.

At this time, Amerigo Vespucci, who had just returned from his voyage with Alonso de Ojeda, was taken into service by Portuguese king Manual I to explore the land of eastern Brazil. After sailing from Lisbon, he landed again at Cape São Roque in August 1501. Vespucci headed southward from that point, hoping to determine the extent of the mainland. He reached a harbor on New Year's Day, 1502, which he named Rio de Janeiro. Continuing southward, he reached the mouth of the Río de la Plata. He followed the Patagonian coast southward and, according to his account, reached a point 50 degrees south of the equator. He returned to Portugal in September 1502.

Vespucci's accounts were published in 1507 by German cartographer MARTIN WALDSEEMÜLLER, along with updated maps of the world based on the most recent explorations. While Columbus continued to imagine he had encountered islands off the Japanese archipelago or off the coast of China, Vespucci referred to the lands using the phrase *New World.* Waldseemüller agreed that the lands were new, and called them "America," using the Latinized version of Vespucci's name. (Later, in 1585–94, when Flemish cartographer GERARDUS MERCATOR published his world atlas, he gave the name to the northern continent as well, and, from that time, the two continents have been called North and South America.)

The Spanish still hoped to find a southwest passage, by which they could sail past the South American continent and reach the Orient. King Ferdinand of Spain commissioned JUAN DÍAZ DE SOLÍS, a Spaniard who had become an accomplished navigator sailing with the Portuguese around the Cape of Good Hope, to search the South American coast for the passage in 1508. Díaz de Solís had sailed with Vicente Yáñez Pinzón in 1506 throughout the Caribbean, and, in June 1508, he sailed with two ships from Spain, joined as commander by Pinzón. They had abandoned their search for a strait in the Caribbean, and sailed southward, as Vespucci had done. But they continued to follow the coast to 41 degrees south, discovering the mouth of the Río Negro. Pinzón and Díaz de Solís disagreed over how to continue the journey, and the expedition returned to Spain and to rebuke from the crown.

Early European Settlements

Years before, in January 1502, Alonso de Ojeda himself embarked on another voyage to South America, in order to es-
tablish a colony in Venezuela. Ojeda established a settlement in Venezuela he called Santa Cruz. It was constantly besieged by native peoples, and when supplies dwindled after nine months, his men mutinied. Ojeda was arrested, and brought in chains to Hispaniola and the Spanish authorities. Spain had established a council, called the Council of the Indies, to direct exploration and settlement in the new territories. Its president, Bishop Fonseca, interceded and obtained Ojeda's release.

In 1505, Ojeda attempted yet again to colonize the Venezuelan coast and was again unsuccessful. Then, in 1508, Ojeda sent Juan de la Cosa to Spain in order to obtain a royal commission to colonize Venezuela. The Spanish crown named Ojeda governor of the area from Cape Vela to the Gulf of Darien, roughly the coast of present-day Colombia all the way to Panama. On Hispaniola, among others Ojeda recruited was FRANCISCO PIZARRO, a Spaniard who was to play the greatest and perhaps most infamous part in the exploration and conquest of South America. Pizarro made his first voyage to the West Indies in 1502, after running away from home as a young man, sailing with the fleet of Nicolás de Ovando, who had been appointed governor of Hispaniola to replace Christopher Columbus's short tenured successor, Francisco de Bobadilla.

From Hispaniola, Pizarro sailed with Ojeda in November 1509. Ojeda's first landfall was at present-day Cartagena, Colombia, but he suffered a disastrous attack by native peoples. Rescued by the forces of another colonizing expedition led by Diego de Nicuesa, Ojeda moved his colony to the west, founding San Sebastián on the east shore of Panama's Gulf of Uraba. Supplies were running dangerously low, however, and Ojeda set sail for Hispaniola, leaving Pizarro in charge. After 50 days, Ojeda had not returned, since his ship had been wrecked off the coast of Cuba. Pizarro was forced to kill the horses for food, and then, with the remaining men, he abandoned the settlement. He encountered Martín Fernández de Enciso, who had financed Ojeda's expedition, and was sailing for San Sebastián with relief supplies. Together they changed course and sailed to the coast of Panama not far from Colombia, where they endeavored to create a new colony.

En route, Fernández de Enciso discovered a stowaway on his ship, VASCO NÚÑEZ DE BALBOA. At this time in his early thirties, he had sailed to the Americas with Rodrigo de Bastidas in 1501, but, by 1510, his career as a conquistador had not been successful, and he found himself in debt, with few possessions other than his sword and his dog, Leoncico. Enciso let Núñez de Balboa, who had experience on the coast of Panama, remain aboard his ship reluctantly. Núñez de Balboa helped Enciso and Pizarro choose a site for the new settlement, which was called Santa María de la Antigua.

In 1511, Enciso incited a mutiny among his men by forbidding them to trade with the native peoples for gold.

Núñez de Balboa took command of the colony. The Spanish crown commissioned him interim governor and captain-general of Panama, known then as Darién, in Central America. Pizarro became Núñez de Balboa's chief lieutenant. In 1513, Núñez de Balboa led an expedition across the Isthmus of Panama. He and his dog ascended the hill, becoming the first European to sight the Pacific Ocean on September 25. Four days later, he and his men reached the coast.

After Núñez de Balboa's sighting of the Pacific, the search for a passage across the continent gained urgency. Juan Díaz de Solís, who had been imprisoned for ending his search for a passage in 1509, was released two years later, and, in 1512, named Spain's Pilot Major, succeeding Amerigo Vespucci in that post. In November 1514, Díaz de Solís was commissioned to again search for a southwest passage to the Pacific, which Núñez de Balboa had named the South Sea. In October 1515, Díaz de Solís sailed from Spain in command of three ships. After reaching Rio de Janeiro on the South American coast, he headed southward and took possession of the lands that now make up much of Uruguay. Díaz de Solís came across an estuary, which he imagined at first to be the opening of a southwest passage.

Díaz de Solís sailed up one of the main tributaries of what he called the Río Solís, which is today the Uruguay River. Near present-day Buenos Aires, he took a landing party ashore to capture Native Americans to bring back to Spain during which he was killed. The expedition was taken over by Francisco de Torres, Díaz de Solís's brother-in-law. Before returning to Spain, he collected a cargo of Brazil wood, which served as a textile dye and was highly prized. As they returned, one ship was wrecked on the Island of Santa Catarina. Eleven men survived the wreck and befriended the native peoples.

Around the Continent

Those who returned to Spain on the second ship of Francisco de Torres reported that the coast of South America appeared to curve southwestward. This gave hope to Portuguese navigator Fernão de Magalhães, who, in 1517, after a falling out with the King of Portugal crossed into Spain, renounced his citizenship, and was called by the Spanish name FERDINAND MAGELLAN. Magellan had sailed with the Portuguese in the EAST INDIES, and it is likely he sailed with his friend FRANCISCO SERRANO to the SPICE ISLANDS (the Moluccas), one of the principal goals of European explorers. He surmised, based on MARTIN BEHAIM's 1492 globe, and data provided by the astronomer and cosmographer Ruy Faleiro, that the Spice Islands really fell within the portion of the world granted to Spain by the Treaty of Tordesillas. Furthermore, the evidence of Díaz de Solís's men combined with secret Portuguese navigational charts he had most likely seen convinced him there was a strait separating South America from the GREAT SOUTHERN CONTINENT that was believed to exist in the southern latitudes, which would allow him to sail westward and reach the East Indies.

In September 1519, after gaining approval of Spanish king Charles I (Holy Roman Emperor Charles V), Magellan sailed from Spain with five ships and about 250 men. He sailed along the coast of Africa as far as Sierra Leone before crossing the Atlantic. He explored inlets on the Brazilian coast including the Bay of Guanabara and the estuary of the Río de la Plata, which Díaz de Solís had also imagined to be the opening of a southwest passage. Along the southwest coast of present-day Argentina, he entered the bay of San Julián, to wait out the Southern Hemisphere's winter months. He called the area Patagonia, or "Land of Big Feet," after the native peoples he observed who wore large footgear. He quelled a mutiny among his Spanish crew, who resented a Portuguese commander, and, after one ship wrecked on the Patagonia coast, Magellan set out before the end of winter to continue to search for the passageway.

The ships passed 50 degrees south of the equator, and after a few days sighted a strait beyond a cape, named Cape Vírgenes. The passage was narrow in places, and winding. One night, a ship mutinied and returned to Spain. The three remaining ships continued to traverse the passage. The southern side of the strait was a rocky land, scattered with strange fires, the camps of native peoples. Magellan called it Tierra del Fuego, or Land of Fire. After 38 days sailing through icy waters, the ships passed into a great tranquil ocean, which Magellan named the Pacific. The 360-mile-long strait was later named the Strait of Magellan. Eventually, the expedition, after Magellan's death in the Philippines, completed the first CIRCUMNAVIGATION OF THE WORLD.

Conquest of the Inca

The east and north coasts of South America had been well charted by this time, but the interior remained relatively untouched, and the west coast a complete mystery. One of the men of Díaz de Solís's expedition left behind on the Island of Santa Catarina, Portuguese sailor ALEJO GARCÍA, married a Native American woman, and together they had a child. With the aid of the native peoples, García explored thoroughly the area of the Paraguay-Paraná basin. Probably in 1524, he ascended the Paraguay River nearly to its source. The next year, García accompanied a band of Native Americans into the Andes. He heard tales of a great civilization located in the mountain range, with great wealth in gold and silver. He obtained several bars of silver himself, and was perhaps the first European man to come to the attention of the Inca.

In 1522, Basque-born Spaniard PASCUAL DE ANDAGOYA, sailing from Panama, began to survey the west coast of South America, after the Spanish conquest of the Aztec in

Mexico. He sailed as far south as Cape Corrientes on the Pacific shore of Colombia and returned to Panama with reports of a highly advanced and wealthy native kingdom called "Biru." These were the Inca.

In Panama, Francisco Pizarro heard of Andagoya's report, which bolstered rumors he had heard from native peoples, and decided he would conquer the people of "Biru" and gain their wealth. The next year, Pizarro entered into partnership with DIEGO DE ALMAGRO, a Spanish conquistador of whose life little is known before he arrived in Panama in 1514. In 1524, the two set out to explore the Pacific coast of present-day Colombia. Exploring the Gulf of Buenaventura, Pizarro lost two-thirds of his 80 men to attacks from native peoples and to disease. The Spanish authorities prohibited any further exploration, but Pizarro and Almagro ignored them and, in 1526, reached as far south as the Gulf of Guayaquil on the coast of what is now southern Ecuador. The expedition landed at the Inca town of Tumbes, where the Spanish found evidence of the highly advanced civilization of the Inca and of their riches. Pizarro's chief mariner, Bartolomeo Ruíz, after sailing farther down the coast, reported the existence of greater Inca cities.

Pizarro sailed for Spain in 1528 in order to seek support from the crown for a large-scale conquest of the Inca. He brought back, among other things, gold and jewels from Peru, captured native peoples, and a llama to show to King Charles I. At about the same time, HERNÁN CORTÉS had returned to Spain with reports of his successful conquest of the Aztec. Pizarro's expedition received enthusiastic support. He returned to Panama with his half brothers GONZALO PIZARRO, HERNANDO PIZARRO, Juan Pizarro, and Martín Pizarro.

In January 1531, the expedition left Panama with 180 men and 27 horses. Francisco Pizarro landed at San Mateo Bay and occupied the Inca town of Tumbes without opposition. The current Inca emperor, Atahualpa, decided to allow the Spaniards to penetrate deep into the realm, where they would be trapped and easily destroyed.

Pizarro was joined by HERNANDO DE SOTO, who had arrived in Panama in 1514, and took part in exploration and conquest of parts of Central America. De Soto took men and horses from Panama and Nicaragua to the island of Puna off the coast of Peru at his own expense. He was also joined by SEBASTIÁN DE BENALCÁZAR, who had accompanied Columbus in 1498, and later established himself as a military and colonial leader in Central America. Pizarro led the combined forces over the Royal Inca Road, eastward through the Andes and the Piura valley, entirely without Inca resistance. Finally, on November 15, 1532, the Spanish arrived in the deserted city of Cajamarca, where just out of town Inca emperor Atahualpa encamped, with reportedly 50,000 men.

Pizarro sent his half brother Hernando as an emissary to the emperor. Hernando presented Atahualpa with a Bible, which he said would teach him about Christ. When the Bible did not speak to him, Atahualpa cast it to the ground. The Spaniards took it as an insult to their faith and as a good excuse to attack. They charged the Inca with horses, which the native peoples had never seen, and fired upon them with their cannon. The Spanish killed thousands of Inca, and took Atahualpa prisoner, suffering few casualties.

Atahualpa offered the Spanish a roomful of gold for his release. Pizarro agreed, and the Inca began to bring gold from across their empire. During the months of his captivity, Atahualpa learned Spanish and writing, and spent time playing chess with Pizarro. The room was filled with artistic and religious works, which the Spaniards melted down. All told, the Inca brought 1,325 pounds of gold. This did not satisfy Pizarro. The emperor, while in captivity, had ordered his half brother Huáscar killed, lest he make an alliance with the Spanish. Pizarro tried and convicted Atahualpa for conspiracy, and sentenced him to be burned. In deference to Atahualpa's partial embrace of Christianity, Pizarro baptized him, and had him publicly strangled in July 1533.

While destroying Inca resistance in the surrounding areas, Pizarro and his men learned of another Inca kingdom in Ecuador to the north, based around the provincial Inca capital of Quito. In 1534, Sebastián de Benalcázar set off to capture Quito. Benalcázar gained the support of local Canari native peoples as he traveled northward. He was met by the forces of Inca chief Ruminahui beneath Ecuador's highest peak, Chimborazo, and he defeated them. He occupied Quito and, in 1535, he established the port city of Guayaquil.

Pizarro marched through Peru on the roads created by the Inca, capturing the Inca capital at Cuzco, enslaving many of its inhabitants and seizing its gold. Diego de Almagro, Pizarro's erstwhile partner, quarreled with him over their respective positions and power. The conflict was averted in December 1534, when the Spanish authorities appointed Almagro the governor of a new Peruvian province called New Toledo and allowed him to lead an expedition of conquest to the south. Pizarro founded a new capitol called the City of Kings, which he adorned with his riches, at the mouth of the Rimac River. This became Lima, Peru.

Almagro left Cuzco in July 1535 with 750 Spaniards and thousands of native allies. He embarked in the middle of winter, and his men suffered in the severe cold of the high Andes. After traveling through the central Andes, Almagro turned westward and reached the coastal Copiapó Valley, then followed the coastal plain of modern Chile into the Central Valley. Repeatedly attacked by native peoples, and unable to find another civilization like the Inca, Almagro turned back, dissatisfied.

Pizarro had established Manco Capac II, one of Huayna Capac's sons, as ruler in Cuzco for a time, in an effort to maintain the illusion of a continuity of Inca rule. In 1536, during the turmoil that accompanied the rift between Pizarro and Almagro, the Inca ruler escaped from Cuzco and led a revolt against Spanish rule. Pizarro defeated assaults on Lima by four Inca armies. The Inca loss of life from European diseases also helped in the Spanish conquest (see DISEASE AND EXPLORATION).

Almagro's men, on their return journey to the north, crossed the Atacama Desert along the north coast of Chile; many died of thirst. In 1537, after crossing the Andes again, they finally reached Cuzco, which, at the time, was besieged by Manco Capac. Almagro succeeded in breaking the siege, but he was soon embroiled in another conflict with Francisco Pizarro, as both claimed Cuzco as part of their dominion. Hernando Pizarro's forces captured Almagro in Cuzco in April 1538, and, with the tacit approval of Francisco, Almagro was publicly executed.

Legendary Kingdoms

Spanish conquests of the Aztec in Mexico, then later the Inca, had fueled the excitement generated by tantalizing hints of another advanced civilization with great wealth.

In 1525, Venetian mariner SEBASTIAN CABOT was commissioned to lead a large Spanish expedition to the EAST INDIES, after report of Magellan's voyage proved the feasibility of an all-water route to the Orient around South America. Cabot was charged with visiting the Spice Islands and to make a geographic survey of the South American coast. Cabot left Spain with four ships and 200 soldiers and colonists in April 1526. He sailed southwestward from the Cape Verde Islands and, the following September, reached the port of Recife, Brazil.

Sailing south along the coast, Cabot sighted and named the island of Santa Catarina. Entering the estuary of the river the expedition of Juan Díaz de Solís had explored 10 years earlier, Cabot discovered and rescued the shipwrecked survivors. The survivors told him of legends of riches in the South American interior, and they gave him the Inca silver that Alejo García had obtained. Cabot named the river Río de la Plata, or the River of Silver, and he abandoned his plans of traveling to the Far East. Instead, Cabot explored the inland waterways of the Paraguay and Barmejo Rivers in present-day Argentina, Uruguay, Paraguay, and Brazil, as well as the Paraná River. Cabot found little gold, however, and returned to Spain in 1530.

Spaniard DIEGO DE ORDAZ, like Pizarro, served with Alonso de Ojeda in 1509, in his efforts to colonize present-day Colombia and Venezuela. Returning to Spain after serving in the conquest of Mexico, Ordaz was given his own commission to explore, conquer, and colonize Venezuela. He sailed with 500 men from Spain, reaching the mouth of the Amazon, but chose to sail on to the mouth of another great river of which the native peoples had informed him, the Orinoco. He explored upriver about 800 miles and heard tell of a land somewhere in the Guiana highlands around the source of the river ruled by a group of white people like the Europeans, and in possession of wealth in gold and jewels. This was similar to stories Sebastian Cabot had heard from native peoples and survivors of Díaz de Solís's expedition, but with a more definite location to the mythical empire.

Sebastián de Benalcázar in Quito heard tales from a captured Native American in 1535 of a kingdom to the east, toward the Guiana highlands, ruled by a monarch speckled with gold dust, whom Benalcázar called EL DORADO, the gilded one. Benalcázar headed northward into the interior of modern-day Colombia, where he established the settlements Popayán and Cali, then he turned east to search for the city of gold. The same decade, the region was being explored from the east in search for the Guiana empire by Germans involved in a colonizing expedition in Venezuela that had been sponsored by the king of Spain, Charles I (Holy Roman Emperor Charles V). AMBROSIUS ALFINGER, GEORG HOHERMUTH VON SPEYER, and NIKOLAUS FEDERMANN traveled inland in Venezuela and Colombia.

Another mission, led by GONZALO JIMÉNEZ DE QUESADA, was sent from Santa Marta on the Caribbean coast of Colombia to explore the Magdalena River, to search for El Dorado and to locate a passable route to the Spanish in Peru. Jiménez de Quesada heard reports that an advanced civilization existed to his west, on the slopes of the Andes, and took his expedition away from the river. He entered the lands of the Chibcha and, in March 1537, began his conquest. He claimed "New Granada" and founded the city of Santa Fe de Bogotá as its capital. He acquired a fortune in gold and precious stones from the native peoples and finished his conquest in 1539. Around this time, two European expeditions appeared in the area, one led by German explorer Nikolaus Federmann, and the other that of Sebastián de Benalcázar. The three disagreed over who had rights to the territory, and all three sailed in late 1539 or 1540 for Spain to have their dispute arbitrated.

European Inroads

By this time, Francisco Pizarro had appointed his half brother Gonzalo governor of Quito. He, too, had heard stories from the native peoples about riches to the east, including a land that was supposed to contain forests of cinnamon, a very valuable spice, and again of the land of El Dorado, where the bottom of a lake was lined with gold and jewels. Francisco authorized Gonzalo to search for La Canela, the Land of Cinnamon, and for El Dorado. Pizarro took with him 300 Spaniards, about 4,000 native slaves from Quito, as well as a large herd of pigs for food, llamas as pack animals, and hunting dogs. FRANCISCO DE ORELLANA, lieutenant governor of Guayaquil, joined Pizarro's expedition, which after seven months reached the upper Coca River. He located some cinnamon there, but not nearly as much as he had been led to believe existed. With the men facing starvation, he sent Orellana downriver to locate food.

In late 1541, Orellana and his men improvised a boat, and, along with Native Americans traveling by CANOE, sailed down the Coca, with promises to return within 12 days. After being swept into the Napo River, Orellana discovered a village with plenty of food. He decided then to construct a larger boat and continue sailing downriver into what the Spanish called the Marañón, or tangle of rivers. The Spanish passed into the Río Negro, one of the tributaries of the Amazon, and, on their way, they were attacked by a group of native peoples in which the women fought alongside the men and were likened to the Amazons of Greek legend, thus possibly resulting in the name of the river; the name of the river is more likely probably derived from the native word *amassona* for "boat destroyer." Orellana and his men entered the Atlantic Ocean on August 26, 1542, the first Europeans to sail the length of the Amazon.

At about the same time, Spaniard DOMINGO MARTÍNEZ DE IRALA was exploring the upper Paraguay River in South America's southernmost river basin. Martínez de Irala had first sailed to South America with PEDRO DE MENDOZA in 1535. Mendoza had been appointed the first governor of the territory that had been claimed by Juan Díaz de Solís for Spain, had been explored by Sebastian Cabot, and had had its southernmost extremity fixed by Ferdinand Magellan's passage through the Strait of Magellan. Mendoza's expedition, departing in August 1535, had consisted of 14 ships carrying more than 2,000 colonists to the Río de la Plata, where he had established the city Santa María del Buen Aire (of the fair winds), which later became Buenos Aires.

Mendoza, in addition to colonizing, had been charged with exploring the area, especially the river system, in an effort to find a route to Peru and the riches of which Cabot had reported. He sent two of his deputies, JUAN DE AYOLAS and Martínez de Irala. The two had explored the Río de la Plata up to the Paraná and Paraguay Rivers. Mendoza had died at sea, and Martínez de Irala had succeeded him as governor, serving until 1540, when ÁLVAR NÚÑEZ CABEZA DE VACA, who had explored the Southeast and Southwest of North America between 1528 and 1536, took his place. It was Cabeza de Vaca who had sent Martínez de Irala to explore the Paraguay River in 1542. Martínez de Irala followed the river 250 miles above the settlement Asunción. On his return there, Cabeza de Vaca was deposed by the settlers, and Martínez de Irala regained his place. In 1546, he embarked on another expedition into the interior, reaching the eastern slopes of the Andes.

Gonzalo Pizarro had returned from his failed expedition to search for El Dorado in 1542 to discover his half brother Francisco murdered by followers of the late Diego de Almagro's half-Indian son and heir, Don Diego Almagro, and a Spanish viceroy set in his place. Gonzalo, who had been intended as his half brother's successor, began a rebellion against the viceroy. In 1547, Spaniard PEDRO DE VALDIVIA, who had been an officer under Francisco Pizarro, returned from his explorations in present-day Chile to assist in putting down Gonzalo Pizarro's revolt. He was rewarded with support against Gonzalo for an expedition to colonize Chile to the south of Peru. Valdivia followed the Inca road along the Pacific coast, crossing the Atacama Desert as Almagro had done before. On February 12, 1541, he founded Santiago, Chile, the first permanent Spanish settlement there. He encouraged agricultural settlements in Chile, because it did not possess the mineral resources Peru did. He explored across the Andes into the plains of western Argentina, and, in 1544, reestablished the seaport at Valparaíso.

That same year, the Spanish viceroy of Peru commissioned Spanish adventurer PEDRO DE URSÚA to lead an expedition to search for the legendary wealth of El Dorado and the native peoples of Omagua. Ursúa had set out for Peru in 1552 after spending a handful of successful years as governor of Bogotá (a post he occupied at age 20) and later as the mayor of the coastal town Santa Marta. He left Lima, Peru, in February 1559 with 300 Spaniards as well as native peoples and slaves, and began to cross the Andes. After many delays due to inadequate financing, Ursúa led his men down the Huallaga River, into the Marañón, finally entering the main course of the Amazon in December 1560. On January 1, 1561, one of his men, LOPÉ DE AGUIRRE, murdered Ursúa and his deputy and incited a mutiny. Aguirre hoped to take the mutineers to Panama to rebel against the Spanish authorities. He and his men sailed down the Amazon, crossing into the Orinoco, likely by way of the Río Negro, and they followed it to the Caribbean, laying waste to several native villages along the way. Aguirre and his men attacked and captured the island of Margarita, before they were besieged in the mainland town of Barquisimeto. The Spanish beheaded Aguirre and quartered his body as a warning to rebels.

In 1562, cartographer DIEGO GUTIÉRREZ incorporated the reports of many of these explorations into the interior of South America into a map of the continent. Gutiérrez was employed by Spain's House of Trade for the Indies, an arm of the Spanish government, which licensed sailors and maintained maps of the world. By this time, lusting after gold and other riches, Spanish CONQUISTADORES had visited much of South America's interior, in comparison to North America, the interior of which would not be so well known until the early 19th century.

With much of South America under their sway, the Spanish continued their colonization and exploitation. Spain's other main competitor, Portugal, also had laid claim to a large part of South America. After Christopher Columbus landed in the Americas in 1492, Spain petitioned Pope Alexander VI for a monopoly on trade in the western Atlantic, which resulted in a line of demarcation to the west of which Spain was given trading rights, and to the east of which rights were granted to Portugal. After the 1494 Treaty of Tordesillas, this longitudinal line was fixed at 370 leagues west of the AZORES. The landing of Pedro Álvars Cabral in Brazil in 1500, in territory allowed to the Portuguese, gave them rights to colonize Brazil.

Despite Spain and Portugal's claims to the territory, other European powers attempted to make inroads into the continent as well. In 1598, Dutch sailor OLIVER VAN NOORT was commissioned by a collection of Dutch merchants to embark on an expedition to the Spice Islands and the Far East, through the Strait of Magellan. The expedition sailed from Rotterdam in September 1598, heading for Rio de Janeiro on the South American coast. The ships, driven back by storms, sought shelter on the Brazilian coast, where crew members were lost to attacks from the native peoples. After wintering on the uninhabited island of Santa Clara, the expedition followed the coast of Patagonia and entered the Strait of Magellan in November 1599. Crew members frequented the north shore of the strait, suffering more native attacks and loss of life. They explored three uncharted bays. In early February 1600, the expedition and its ships entered the Pacific and followed the coast of Chile northward, attacking Spanish ships and Spanish settlements. The viceroy of Peru sent a fleet to capture them, but the Dutch escaped, sailing westward into the Pacific.

The English, too, had a capable navy, and it was not long before the stories of El Dorado attracted their attention. In 1595, Queen Elizabeth I approved the plans of English adventurer and explorer SIR WALTER RALEIGH to search for the city of Manoa and the empire of Guiana and its supposed riches. Raleigh sailed with five ships in February, and, after a stormy crossing landed in Trinidad, where he attacked Spanish settlements. Capturing ANTONIO DE BERRÍO, a Spanish official, he heard more reports of El Dorado. He centered his exploration on the Orinoco River, which he explored upstream in small boats. Lacking supplies and afflicted with fevers, Raleigh and his men abandoned their search and returned to England.

In 1610, Englishman SIR THOMAS ROE sailed on a voyage to find gold on the northeast coast of South America. With approval from King James I and the financial backing of Raleigh, Roe left Plymouth with two vessels on February 24. He landed on the coast of the Guianas highlands, and after locating the mouth of the Amazon, he sailed 200 miles upriver. From there, he explored another 100 miles farther using small boats. Afterward, Roe explored the coastline as far as the delta of the Orinoco before returning empty-handed to England in 1611.

In 1617, Raleigh undertook one more expedition to search for El Dorado. He had been sentenced to death after being implicated in a plot against King James I, but convinced the monarch to let him search for the City of Gold one last time. His ships reached Trinidad, where Raleigh became sick with fever. Raleigh's son, Walter, and Lawrence Kemys entered the Orinoco but soon entered Spanish territory, and fought with Spanish settlers at San Thomé, in violation of orders from the king. Walter was killed, and Kemys committed suicide shortly thereafter. Raleigh also returned empty-handed to England, and, under his original sentence, he was beheaded in 1618.

In 1616, Dutch merchant JAKOB LE MAIRE organized an expedition with navigator WILLEM CORNELIS SCHOUTEN, which departed Holland in June 1615. Early the next year, after passing through what became known as Le Maire Strait, they found South America's southernmost point of land, part of the Tierra del Fuego Archipelago, south of the Strait of Magellan. They named it Cape Horn, not because the area resembled a horn, but after their home port of Hoorn in the Netherlands.

While the Portuguese claimed the area of Brazil east of the line of demarcation set by the Treaty of Tordesillas, French, Dutch, and English trading settlements arose in the territory around the Amazon Basin. In the early 17th century, the Portuguese began to take heightened military action against foreign encroachment. Throughout the 1620s, Portuguese soldier PEDRO DE TEIXEIRA took part in many raids to evict foreign settlers throughout the region, around the Amazon's Xingu tributary and the northern delta near the Guianas highlands. Afterward, the only real threat to the Portuguese hold on its Amazonian territory came from the Spanish, who were slowly pushing eastward from Peru and modern-day Ecuador. In 1637, the Portuguese were spurred into action when two Spanish Franciscans arrived in Portuguese territory after a journey down the Amazon from Ecuador. Teixeira was ordered by the local Portuguese colonial governor to map the length of the Amazon and claim territory for Portugal. He assembled a large expedition, which embarked upstream by canoe in October. In July 1638, Teixeira made the European discovery of the Río Negro and arrived on foot in Quito, Ecuador, in the late summer, to the great astonishment of the Spanish. The alarmed authorities sent Teixeira and his expedition back down the Amazon, with a group of Spanish observers led by Jesuit priest CRISTÓBAL DE ACUÑA. On the return trip, Teixeira marked a point on the Aguarico River, the point at which the river crossed the boundary line, which according to treaty separated Spanish from Portuguese territory in the New World.

With the Spanish and Portuguese militarily asserting their control of the northern part of the continent, the French turned their attention to the continent's southern portion, which had not yet been settled by Europeans. In 1665, the French sent priest CHARLES-EDOUARD DE LA NOUÉ to explore the territory, which, while nominally belonging to the Spanish since the explorations of Magellan, France hoped to colonize. Traveling in the region of Patagonia and Tierra del Fuego for several years, Noué was captured by native peoples. He learned their language and customs, adapted their form of dress, and was eventually accepted as an equal. After a time, Noué was allowed to escape on a passing ship. In 1675, he published an account of his travels, describing the region's rugged terrain and inhospitable climate and hostile native peoples, which discouraged further French attempts to colonize the area.

In 1675, the Dutch sent another mission to the southern tip of South America, not for purposes of colonization, but, as before, to explore and improve the route to the Pacific, around Cape Horn. The expedition, led by German sailor SIGISMUND NIEBUHR, first sailed to Rio de Janeiro, before heading southward, and entered the Le Maire Strait, off the south coast of Tierra del Fuego. He mapped out navigational hazards and made depth soundings along the strait. Returning to Holland, he published an account and a navigational chart of the Le Maire Strait, which showed it to be a more practical alternative to the Strait of Magellan for a journey around South America.

Scientific Exploration

The first exploration of South America in the enlightenment tradition, entirely without political, pecuniary, or religious motive, was made by French scientist and mathematician CHARLES-MARIE DE LA CONDAMINE in the first half of the 18th century. La Condamine was hampered in his efforts by the Spanish authorities, who continued to suspect the presence of foreigners.

In 1735, after being elected to the French Academy of Science, La Condamine set out for South America as leader of part of an expedition to measure the arc of a meridian of longitude at the equator and near the Poles in order to determine whether English physicist and mathematician Sir Isaac Newton, who had died eight years earlier, had been correct in believing the Earth to bulge out at the equator. The team began their work outside of Quito on the Plain of Yarqui, but due to interference from local authorities, La Condamine was forced to make an eight-month-long journey to Peru. By his return, the results had come in from Labrador, where the other half of the study was being conducted. The results validated Newton.

La Condamine remained in the area around Quito, making inquiries in natural science until 1743, when he decided to journey down the length of the Amazon River before sailing back to France. Before he embarked, he obtained copies of the only map of the entire length of the Amazon, made by SAMUEL FRITZ, a Jesuit missionary from Bohemia who had lived among the native peoples of the Amazon River in the late 17th and early 18th centuries.

In his trip down the Amazon, La Condamine studied the life of the native peoples and made navigational observations. He determined that the Río Negro flowed into the Amazon from the northwest and not the north. But most important, he put his geographic and mathematical skills to use, and finally determined the coordinates of the line of demarcation established by the Treaty of Tordesillas, ending at last the dispute between the Portuguese and Spanish.

A later naturalist, Spaniard FÉLIX DE AZARA, had traveled to South America in 1781 as commissioner of a Spanish government survey. He stayed on in South America until 1801, during which time he studied the natural history of the Paraná and Paraguay Rivers.

German naturalist ALEXANDER VON HUMBOLDT carried out some of the most important natural science studies of South America. Along with French botanist Aimé Bonpland, Humboldt was granted permission to perform scientific surveys throughout the Spanish possessions in the Americas. Humboldt had had a keen interest in natural sciences from an early age, and, in his studies, he gained an extensive knowledge of languages, biology, astronomy, and geology. With his family connections, he was able to obtain the backing of Charles IV of Spain for a plan to explore the Americas. Humboldt and Bonpland sailed from La Coruna in northern Spain and arrived on the Venezuelan coast in July 1799. Over the next year, they pursued various scientific inquiries around the Orinoco River basin. Humboldt made many astronomical observations to clear up discrepancies in maps of South America. He also studied animals, including the capybara, the world's largest rodent; electric eels; and the Arrau turtles who laid their eggs by the millions on the bank of one of the Orinoco's tributaries. Later, Humboldt and Bonpland started from Cartagena and, ascending the Magdalena River, headed toward the eastern slopes of the Andes. Humboldt made observations of the effect of high altitude on the boiling point of water. In Ecuador, the pair attempted to climb Mount Chimborazo, reaching a record 19,000 feet, before lack of oxygen forced them to turn back. Humboldt also plotted the magnetic equator and proved that Earth's magnetic field decreases as one approaches the equator. He studied the climate along the coast of Peru. In his travels, he crossed the Andes five times. He and Bonpland went on to explore Mexico.

The flora and fauna of South America and its islands, the most distinctive after those of Australia and highly varied, drew many European naturalists in the 19th century. One of these was Frenchman ALCIDE-CHARLES-VICTOR DESSALINES D'ORBIGNY, who collected plant and animal specimens there in the 1820s–30s.

Studies in South America led to one of the most important biological theories ever formulated. In 1831, a young theology student at Cambridge University, who had recently abandoned a medical career, was appointed the official naturalist for a British scientific expedition to the coast of South America after his skills as a naturalist had come to the attention of John S. Henslow, a Cambridge professor of geology and botany. CHARLES ROBERT DARWIN sailed from Devonport in December 1831, aboard the HMS *Beagle*, commanded by ROBERT FITZROY.

The *Beagle* sailed to Bahia, Brazil, where Darwin explored inland, collecting specimens from the Brazilian rain forest. He collected more specimens by traveling with an Irish planter to his coffee plantation 100 miles north of Rio de Janeiro. Later, Darwin explored up the Río de la Plata, discovering fossilized bones in Uruguay. In Patagonia, he followed the Santa Cruz River to within sight of the Andes. He studied the native peoples of Tierra del Fuego, then, after rounding Cape Horn, he made explorations into the interior of Chile. In Chile, Darwin experienced a heavy earthquake and witnessed the eruption of Osorno. Before heading westward, the *Beagle* stopped at the Galapagos Islands, where Darwin noticed similar species on different islands adapted differently to local conditions. The expedition circled the Earth and returned to England in 1836.

Over the following years, Darwin formulated a theory of evolution by natural selection as an explanation for the origin of species, but he was reluctant to publish it until 1858, when he received a paper from ALFRED RUSSEL WALLACE, another British naturalist who had formulated a similar theory. Wallace and fellow self-taught naturalist HENRY WALTER BATES had read Humboldt's accounts of South America, as well as Darwin's own report of the voyage of the *Beagle*, and, in 1848, the two had sailed to the mouth of the Amazon to make their own exploration. They had explored and collected specimens in the Amazon Basin. Wallace had explored the Orinoco River before returning to England in 1852. Wallace next traveled to Southeast Asia, and it was there he wrote the paper that would come into the hands of Darwin in 1858. The two agreed to publish jointly, and, in 1859, with Wallace's supporting text, Darwin came out with his landmark volume, relying on his observations in South America, *On the Origin of Species*. Bates meanwhile had continued his studies in South America, returning to England in 1858.

Darwin and Wallace got together again, along with British botanist WILLIAM HOOKER, to secure a pension for RICHARD SPRUCE. Spruce was a self-educated botanist who, after spending some time in the Pyrenees in France, em-

barked on an expedition to the Amazon Basin in 1849. Primarily an expert in mosses, Spruce was also charged by the British to collect seeds of the cinchona tree to be grown outside of the Amazon and Andes for its bark. In the 17th century, a monk in Peru had observed the native peoples using the tree's ground-up bark to treat fevers. The use spread to Europe, where it was found effective against malaria. The drug isolated from the bark is called quinine and is known to kill some stages of the malaria parasite. Spruce spent a total of 17 years in the Amazon and Andes, during which time he discovered many new plant species. He also investigated the religious use of plant-based hallucinogens by native tribes. (See NATURAL SCIENCE AND EXPLORATION.)

Explorers in the 20th Century

Even after extensive European settlement, parts of South America remained unexplored and a challenge to explorers. One such adventurous traveler was American HARRIET CHALMERS ADAMS, who traveled more than 40,000 miles on the continent and made four crossings of the Andes in 1903–06, writing about the lands she visited for *National Geographic* and other magazines. Another American, historian HIRAM BINGHAM, explored Inca sites in the Andes, also in the early 20th century.

It was not until the advent of airplanes that the most remote places became known, and some tributaries of main rivers remained mysterious and uncharted well into the 20th century. In 1924–25, American ALEXANDER HAMILTON RICE made the first use of aircraft to explore South America. (See AVIATION AND EXPLORATION.)

❖

The Amazon rain forest continues to be a source for medicines and a haven for an amazing diversity of animal and plant life. Outside of the Inca Empire, which methodically expanded through the Andes and even into the rain forest, much of South America was crisscrossed by small bands of native tribes leaving scarce traces. With the coming of the Europeans, first the coastlines were mapped, then conquistadors plunged into the interior, usually with one goal in mind—riches. On a whole, the native peoples were treated ruthlessly, and the lands and forests were pillaged of resources, which included brazil wood, rubber, silver, gold, and diamonds. There were rare exceptions to the rapacity among the European conquerors, mostly rewarded by mutiny, as in the case of Fernandez de Enciso, who refused to allow his Spaniards to engage in predatory trading with the native peoples. Rare, too, was any encouragement to develop sustainable settlements, as Pedro de Valdivia was forced to do in Chile because of a lack of mineral wealth and resources. Much of South America has remained impoverished, its wealth flowing back to Europe, and its own manufacturing and educational institutions left undeveloped.

Today, eagerness to exploit South America's resources combined with the legacy of colonial neglect threatens to destroy much of the continent's natural wealth and native ways of life, which attracted so many biologists, botanists, and anthropologists in the 19th century, and still does today.

South Magnetic Pole (Magnetic South Pole)

Earth has a magnetic field, an area surrounding it in which objects experience an electromagnetic force. In other words, Earth acts as a giant magnet. The exact cause of terrestrial magnetism is unknown; theories relate to the matter and structure of Earth's core, one of which is the dynamo theory involving the interaction of motion and electrical currents in the liquid outer core. At one end of Earth, the northern end, the magnetic force is toward the ground; at the other end, the southern end, the magnetic force is away from the ground. (Earth's magnetic field reverses polarity on an irregular basis, from several thousand years to 35 million years, resulting in the opposite effect; the last such reversal was some 780,000 years ago.) The exact location of these points of magnetic polarity are referred to as the magnetic poles. The magnetic pole at the southern end is known as the South Magnetic Pole (written with or without capitalization). That at the northern end is known as the NORTH MAGNETIC POLE. The terms also appear as magnetic south pole and magnetic north pole. The angle that Earth's magnetic field makes with the horizon is called the magnetic dip, leading to the alternative names dip poles or magnetic dip poles.

The South Magnetic Pole and the North Magnetic Pole do not correspond with the geographic poles of Earth's imaginary axis, known as the SOUTH POLE and NORTH POLE. Moreover, their location varies in the course of almost a century—as they do to a much less degree annually and even daily—a phenomenon known as polar wandering. The present location of the South Magnetic Pole is off the Adélie Coast of eastern Antarctica, 1,600 miles from the geographic South Pole.

For purposes of study, scientists have also defined Earth's magnetic field as a symmetrical magnetic field, averaging its direction and strength, and the hypothetical poles are known as geomagnetic poles, south and north. The South Geomagnetic Pole is situated near Vostok, Antarctica, about 780 miles from the geographic South Pole.

The effect of terrestrial magnetism had been evident for centuries through use of the magnetic COMPASS. William Gilbert, an English physician and scientist, carried out the first comprehensive study of Earth's magnetic field, publishing his findings in *De Magnete* in 1600.

In his Antarctic expedition of 1839–43, Englishman SIR JAMES CLARK ROSS, having located the North Magnetic Pole in an earlier expedition, tried vainly to pinpoint the South Magnetic Pole. On January 16, 1909, Australian scientist SIR DOUGLAS MAWSON, British geologist T. W. Edgeworth David, and physician Alistair F. Mackay, part of the 1907–09 British Antarctic Expedition under SIR ERNEST HENRY SHACKLETON, reached a point 190 miles inland from the west shore of the Ross Sea, where they determined by their compass readings that they had reached the South Magnetic Pole. Confirmation of the magnetic poles shifting resulted from a 1948 study of the North Magnetic Pole by Canadian scientists, Paul Serson and Jack Clark.

See also ANTARCTIC, EXPLORATION OF THE.

South Pass

The ROCKY MOUNTAINS once presented a formidable obstacle for anyone heading westward. During the 19th century, most western-bound travelers made their way across the Continental Divide via the South Pass. Located in southwestern Wyoming at the southern end of the Wind River Range, the South Pass has an elevation of 7,550 feet. It is not a narrow gorge flanked by rock faces, however, but a 25-mile-wide plateau covered with grass and shrubs. Peaks can be seen in the distance. Originally a Native American trail, the South Pass became known as the easiest way across the Rocky Mountains, with wagon travel possible, and was incorporated into three pioneer routes across Wyoming, the Oregon, Mormon, and California Trails, thus becoming a gateway to the Far West. The climb was so gradual up and over the pass that travelers did not realize they had crossed the Great Divide until they noticed streams flowing the other direction. A number of explorers are associated with it.

Scotsman ROBERT STUART, in the employ of JOHN JACOB ASTOR and his Pacific Fur Company, a subsidiary of the AMERICAN FUR COMPANY, is credited with making the non-Indian discovery of the South Pass. He had traveled by ship to the trading post Astoria at the mouth of the COLUMBIA RIVER in 1810–11. In June 1812, he set out with six companions eastward overland for St. Louis, following the Columbia and Snake Rivers (although one man, John Day, reportedly went insane and had to be sent back to Astoria). Fearing an attack by Crow Indians, Stuart and his party detoured to the north to the valley known as Jackson Hole. They then followed an Indian trail through Hoback Canyon along the western edge of the Wind River Range. On October 23, ascending into the mountain, they located an opening, which would come to be known as the South Pass.

After descending the Sweetwater River, the North Platte River, the Platte River, and finally the MISSOURI RIVER, they reached St. Louis, where Stuart reported the pass through the Rockies to Astor. Both men and the others who traveled with Stuart kept knowledge of it to themselves, apparently for the transportation advantages it gave them in the FUR TRADE.

In 1823, because the Missouri River route through present-day Montana to the Rockies was cut off by resistance from Arikara Indians, JEDEDIAH STRONG SMITH and a party of MOUNTAIN MEN, including JAMES CLYMAN, THOMAS FITZPATRICK, and WILLIAM LEWIS SUBLETTE, headed southeastward into present-day Wyoming. They crossed the Bighorn Range by way of the Granite Pass to the Bighorn River, but were prevented from proceeding westward to the Union Pass by heavy snows. From Crow Indians, Smith learned of another pass to the south. The party headed for it and, by following the Wind River, then the Sweetwater River, they located the South Pass in February 1824 and crossed over to the Green River near the present Wyoming-Utah border, which would become the location of the first annual fur traders' rendezvous.

From that time on, the South Pass was known to fur traders. The earliest known successful crossing with loaded wagons through the pass was carried out by an expedition under BENJAMIN LOUIS EULALIE DE BONNEVILLE in 1832, heading for a summer rendezvous. In 1836, missionaries MARCUS WHITMAN and HENRY HARMON SPALDING traveled with an American Fur Company caravan from St. Louis, guided by Thomas Fitzpatrick. They became the first non-Indian travelers along route not involved in the fur trade, and their wives became the first known non-Indian women to cross the Continental Divide. In 1841, Belgian missionary PIERRE-JEAN DE SMET led the first organized wagon train migration on the Oregon Trail, with Thomas Fitzpatrick serving as guide. Other emigrants came to use the pass as well, and it became part of what became known as the Oregon Trail, from Independence in western Missouri across central Nebraska following the Platte and North Platte Rivers and southern Wyoming through the South Pass, then following the Snake River across Idaho to the Columbia River and Oregon. In 1843, JESSE APPLEGATE, Marcus Whitman, and others organized the "Great Migration of 1843," a wagon caravan of some 1,000 emigrants to the Oregon Country.

The year before, JOHN CHARLES FRÉMONT led a U.S. government expedition to the region, one purpose of which was to chart the South Pass. Frontiersman CHRISTOPHER HOUSTON CARSON (Kit Carson) served as a guide. In 1843–44, Frémont headed another exploratory expedition, during which he again traveled the South Pass with Carson. In 1845, STEPHEN WATTS KEARNY led a U.S. military expedition that crossed through the South Pass. More and more emigrants continued to use the pass. In 1847, BRIGHAM YOUNG, who was a prominent leader in the Church of Jesus Christ of Latter-Day Saints—better known as the Mormons—led a party of Mormons along a trail, which for some stretches paralleled and which

made use of the South Pass, then headed southwest into Utah.

With the California Gold Rush of 1849, the South Pass saw even more traffic west. What became known as the California Trail branched off from the Oregon Trail at Soda Springs, Idaho, then traversed desert country of Nevada to eastern California. The trail followed the Donner Pass through the Sierra Nevada. Between 1841 and 1866, approximately 350,000 migrants traveled through the South Pass. In 1858, the Lander Road, the first road to be surveyed and built in the Rockies, provided a shortcut from the South Pass to Fort Hall on the Snake River. In 1860–61, the Pony Express made use of the South Pass in carrying mail westward from St. Joseph, Missouri. In 1862, stagecoaches began using Central Overland Trail that branched off from the Oregon Trail at the junction of the North Platte and South Platte Rivers, then ran south of the Oregon Trail in southern Wyoming and bypassed the South Pass.

When gold was discovered on the southeastern end of the Wind River Range in 1867, South Pass City was founded along the pass. The completion of the transcontinental railway two years later limited travel along the South Pass since it followed the Overland Trail through the Rockies.

South Pole (South Geographic Pole, Geographic South Pole)

The South Pole, a cartographic point on the Antarctic continent, is considered the southernmost place on Earth, at a latitude of 90 degrees south and at a longitude of 0 degrees, where all meridians of longitude converge. Its location is determined by the imaginary line, or axis, around which Earth rotates from west to east. The axis is perpendicular to the plane of the EQUATOR and passes through the center of Earth, terminating at geographic points referred to as the South Pole in the Southern Hemisphere and the NORTH POLE in the Northern Hemisphere. From the South Pole, all directions on the surface of Earth are read as to the north. The South Pole is also referred to as the South Geographic Pole or Geographic South Pole, to distinguish it from the SOUTH MAGNETIC POLE, which is determined by Earth's magnetic field. A marker of the precise location of the South Pole has to be set every year because a glacier caps the pole and drifts slightly more than one inch a day. (The Ceremonial South Pole, marked by international flags of nations that signed the Antarctic Treaty of 1961, is allowed to drift with the ice.) The South Pole, like the North Pole, took on great symbolic significance for explorers, and the quest to reach it is part of the larger story of human activity on the Antarctic continent.

The British Antarctic Expedition of 1907–09, led by SIR ERNEST HENRY SHACKLETON, after locating the Beardmore

Glacier and crossing the Polar Plateau, missed reaching the South Pole by only 97 miles. ROBERT FALCON SCOTT led another British attempt on the Pole, with a plan to set out from McMurdo Sound and follow the route across the Beardmore Glacier and Polar Plateau pioneered by Shackleton. In the meantime, a Norwegian expedition under ROALD ENGELBREGT GRAVNING AMUNDSEN planned an approach from the Bay of Whales on the edge of the Ross Ice Shelf and across the Axel Heiberg Glacier. Amundsen's party of five set out on October 19, 1911, and reached the South Pole on December 14. Scott's party set out on November 1, 1911, and reached the Pole on January 17, 1912, whereupon they learned that they had failed in their attempt to be first. On the return journey, Scott's team of five all perished on being trapped in a nine-day blizzard. Another milestone in the history of Antarctic exploration was accomplished by American RICHARD EVELYN BYRD, who, on November 29, 1929, during the First Byrd Antarctic Expedition, became the first man to fly over the South Pole.

The United States maintains a base at the South Pole, known as the Amundsen-Scott South Pole Research Station, for the purposes of scientific study, including earth sciences, meteorology, glaciology, geophysics, upper-atmosphere physics, astrophysics, and biomedicine. The first permanent station there was established in 1957 as part of the INTERNATIONAL GEOPHYSICAL YEAR, and it functioned until 1975, when the present station was occupied.

See also ANTARCTIC, EXPLORATION OF THE.

Soyuz program

The Soyuz program is a program of SPACE EXPLORATION of the former Union of Soviet Socialist Republics (USSR; Soviet Union) and now Russia, the name of the program referring to spaceflights using the Soyuz type of piloted spacecraft as well as the Soyuz type ROCKET. The program began in 1967, subsequent to the VOSTOK PROGRAM and the VOSKHOD PROGRAM, having been proposed five years earlier as part of the Soviet Union's push to put the first human on the Moon. When the United States succeeded in doing so in 1969 in its APOLLO PROGRAM, the Soyuz spacecrafts were redesigned to carry people and supplies to SPACE STATIONs, which included the Salyut stations, *Mir,* and currently the *International Space Station.*

The first piloted Soyuz missions, after several unmanned test flights of the new spacecraft, put the cosmonaut (*cosmonauts* is the Russian term for ASTRONAUTS) Vladimir M. Komarov into orbit on April 23, 1967. He became the first person to die in a spaceflight when the parachute on his descent module malfunctioned. During a dual flight, *Soyuz 2* and *Soyuz 3* failed in an attempt to rendezvous and dock in space in October 1968; *Soyuz 4* and *Soyuz 5* succeeded in doing so in January 1969. The suc-

cessful U.S. Moon landing the following July led to the redirection of the Soyuz program. The Soviet Union placed three spacecraft in simultaneous orbit in October 1969, with *Soyuz 6, Soyuz 7,* and *Soyuz 8.* Launched in June 1970, *Soyuz 9* set a record at the time for humans in space, 17 days. In April 1971, *Soyuz 10,* the first space station mission, failed to dock with *Salyut 1.* But *Soyuz 11* successfully accomplished the task the following June. In July 1975, *Soyuz 19,* with ALEXEI ARKHIPOVICH LEONOV as commander, in the first such joint mission, rendezvoused and docked in space with an American Apollo spacecraft. There have been some 80 Soyuz flights.

The Soyuz rocket uses liquid fuel, kerosene, and liquid oxygen to launch the Soyuz spacecraft. Soyuz spacecrafts have three modules: the front orbital module is oval in shape; the middle descent module, for entry, is bell-shaped; and the rear service module, containing rocket engines and solar panels to supply electricity, is cylindrical.

space exploration

Humans have always looked to the Sun, Moon, and stars and have devised systems of thoughts to explain them and have dreamed of ways to reach them. In recent time, space exploration has become a remarkable reality.

The Science of Astronomy

Space exploration can be said to begin with the early astronomers, who utilized the scientific method to explain celestial phenomena. HIPPARCHUS of Greece and PTOLEMY of Alexandria of the second century B.C. were among those laying the foundations of the science of astronomy, although they theorized an Earth-centered solar system, a concept that endured well into the RENAISSANCE. In 1543, astronomer Nicolaus Copernicus of Poland published *De revolutionibus orbium coelestium,* in which he described the Sun as the center of a solar system, with the planets in orbit around it. In 1609, Johannes Kepler, a German, established that the orbits of planets are elliptical, not circular. The next year, Italian scientist Galileo constructed the first complete astronomical telescope and began viewing features on the Moon and eventually the moons of Jupiter. His studies determined a more accurate scale of distance in space. English physicist Sir Isaac Newton, active in the late 17th and early 18th centuries, helped further the understanding of the solar system with his studies of the laws of motion and laws of gravitation.

Rocketry and Aviation

In the meantime, ROCKET technology was being developed. Probably the Chinese, in the 13th century, were the first to conceive the notion of placing gunpowder within a tube to propel a device as gases rushed out (see CHINESE

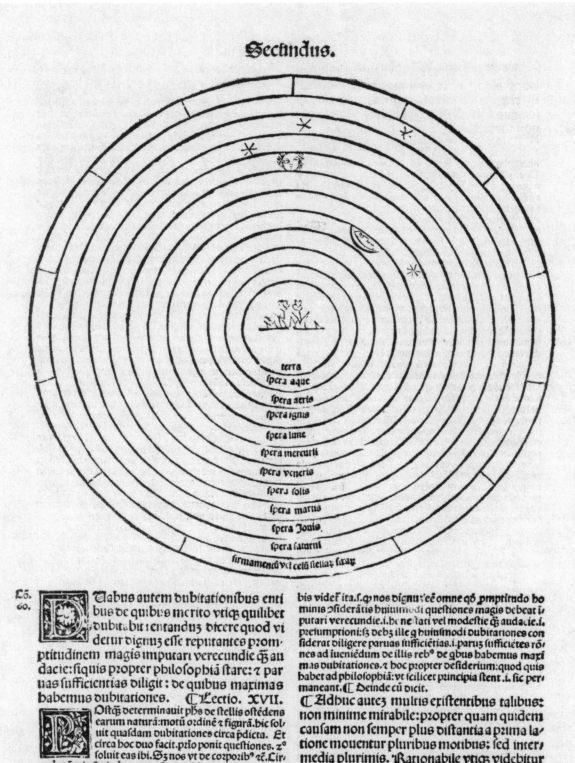

terra
spera aque
spera aeris
spera ignis
spera lune
spera mercuri
spera veneris
spera solis
spera martis
spera Jouis.
spera saturni
firmamentū vel celū stellaꝶ fixaꝶ

Lō.
60.

Uabus autem dubitationibus enti
bus de quibus merito vtiꝗ quilibet
dubitabit : entanduꝲ dicere quod vi
detur dignuꝲ esse reputantes prom
ptitudinem magis imputari verecundie ꝗ̄ au
dacie: siquis propter philosophiā stare: ꝛ par
uas sufficientias diligit: de quibus maximas
babemus dubitationes.   ◖Lectio. XVII.

Ostꝗ̄ determinauit phs de stellis ostēdens
earum naturā:motū ordinē ꝛ figurā. bic sol
uit quasdam dubitationes circa pdicta. Et
circa boc duo facit.prio ponit questiones. z°
soluit eas ibi.Sꝫ nos vt de corporibꝰ ꝛc.Lir
ca pmū tria facit.pmo excusat se a psumptione ptractan
di bas difficiles questiones. z° mouet eas ibi.Adbuc aut
ꝛc.z.° ostēdit questionū difficultatē ibi.De bis gdē ꝛc. Di
cit ergo pmo,cuꝲ circa stellas sint dubitationes:id gд no

bis vider ita.s.ꝗ nos dignuꝛꝰeē omne gд prmptitudo bo
minis psiderātis bniusmodi questiones magis debeat i
putari verecundie.i.bc nestati vel modestie ꝗ̄ audacie.i.
presumptioni:sꝫ debꝫ ille ꝗ buiusmodi dubitationes con
siderat diligere paruas sufficiētias.i.paruꝲ sufficiētes rō
nes ad iueniēdum de illis rebꝰ de gbus babemus maxi
mas dubitationes.ꝛ boc propter desiderium:quod quis
babet ad philosophiā:vt scilicet principia stent.i.sic per
maneant.◖ Deinde cū dicit.

◖ Adbuc autez multis existentibus talibus:
non minime mirabile:propter quam quidem
causam non semper plus distantia a prima la
tione mouentur pluribus motibus; sed inter
media plurimis. Rationabile vticꝗ videbitur
esse primo corpore vna latio latione propings
simum in minus moueri motibus: puta duo
bus: babitu autem tribus aut aliquo alio tali

f 4

This 1495 print shows one interpretation of an Earth-centered universe; the orbits of the Moon and planets are represented in concentric circles. *(Library of Congress, Prints and Photographs Division [LC-USZ62-95317])*

EXPLORATION); such methods of propulsion were refined over the centuries, typically for purposes of warfare until the 20th century, when three scientists—Russian inventor Konstantin Eduardovich Tsiolkovsky, American physicist Robert Hutchings Goddard, and Romanian-born mathematics teacher Hermann Oberth—began theorizing rocket use in spaceflight.

While rocketry progressed, so did techniques of aviation (see AVIATION AND EXPLORATION). The first ascents in a hot-air BALLOON were conducted in the late 18th century, and the first ascents in an AIRSHIP, in the mid-19th century, all in France. And, in 1903, American brothers Orville and Wilbur Wright accomplished the first airplane flight.

Rocket technology progressed rapidly in the 1930s and 1940s, World War II providing impetus to develop it as weaponry. Advances were applied by the United States and the former Union of Soviet Socialist Republics (USSR; Soviet Union) to space exploration in the 1950s, during the cold war between the two nations.

Science Fiction as Inspiration

While science and technology were making spaceflight a possibility, writers were providing inspiration. In A.D. 160, Lucian of Samos, a Greek, wrote a story of flight to the Moon on artificial wings. Centuries later, a number of writers captured the public's imagination with their science fiction novels, in particular Frenchman Jules Verne's *De la Terre à la Lune (From the Earth to the Moon)*, published in 1865, and Englishman H. G. Wells's *The First Men on the Moon,* published in 1900. Science fiction, as a literary genre, and later a film and television genre, continued to presage developments in space exploration throughout the 20th century.

Satellites in Space

The first triumph of space exploration was the launching of the artificial SATELLITE *Sputnik 1* by the Soviet Union on October 4, 1957. On November 3, *Sputnik 2* carried the first living creature into space, a dog. The United States launched its own satellite on January 1, 1958, and reorganized its space program under the NATIONAL AERONAUTICS AND SPACE ADMINISTRATION, better known as NASA.

Humans in Space

The Soviet Union, with the VOSTOK PROGRAM, also achieved another first, placing the first human in space—cosmonaut YURI ALEKSEYEVICH GAGARIN—on April 12, 1961. He was also the first human to orbit space. Three weeks later, on May 5, the United States placed its first human in space—ALAN BARTLETT SHEPARD, JR.—on a suborbital flight. On July 21, 1961, American Virgil I. (Gus) Grissom completed a second suborbital flight. JOHN HER-SCHELL GLENN, JR., became the first American to orbit Earth on February 20, 1962. These early U.S. flights were part of the MERCURY PROGRAM. On June 16, 1963, the Soviets put the first woman in space—VALENTINA VLADIMIROVNA TERESHKOVA—aboard *Vostok 6.* An American woman, SALLY KRISTEN RIDE, first reached space 20 years later, on June 18, 1983. Still another Soviet first was part of the VOSKHOD PROGRAM: On March 1965, ALEKSEI ARKHIPOVICH LEONOV performed the first extravehicular activity (EVA), or "space walk." The following June, EDWARD HIGGINS WHITE, II, carried out the first American EVA, as part of the GEMINI PROGRAM.

Space Probes

In addition to Earth-orbiting satellites and piloted spacecraft, various nations have made use of the SPACE PROBE for exploration, unmanned space vehicles carrying scientific equipment launched beyond Earth's gravitational field and directed to the Moon, another planet, or another planet's moon or moons. The United States launched the first probe, *Pioneer,* on October 11, 1958, but it failed to escape Earth's pull. *Luna 1,* a Soviet probe, launched in January 1959, became the first human-made object to escape Earth's orbit. In September of that year, *Luna 2* became the first artificial object to hit the Moon. And that October, *Luna 3* sent back the first photographs of the dark side of the Moon.

Humans on the Moon

The Soviet Luna and Zond probes and the U.S. Ranger, Surveyor, and Lunar Orbiter probes were launched with the goal in mind of sending humans to the Moon. The United States achieved this significant first in space exploration with its APOLLO PROGRAM; on July 20, 1969, with the *Apollo 11* mission, NEIL ALDEN ARMSTRONG and Edwin "Buzz" Aldin, Jr., became the first humans to land on the lunar surface. Five subsequent Apollo missions carried humans to the Moon.

Space Stations

With the U.S. success on manned lunar missions, the Soviets shifted their SOYUZ PROGRAM to developing a SPACE STATION and studying the effects of long-term spaceflight on humans. Between 1971 and 1984, they launched seven Salyut space stations. The United States built its own space station, *Skylab,* which was occupied by three sets of crews in 1973. The first module of the *Mir* space station was launched in 1986, with other components added over the next 10 years (with Russia taking over control of it in 1991, after the breakup of the Soviet Union). Starting in 1995, Russia and the United States participated in joint *Mir* missions, with both cosmonauts and ASTRONAUTS spending extended periods of time in space. In 1995, Russian Valeriy

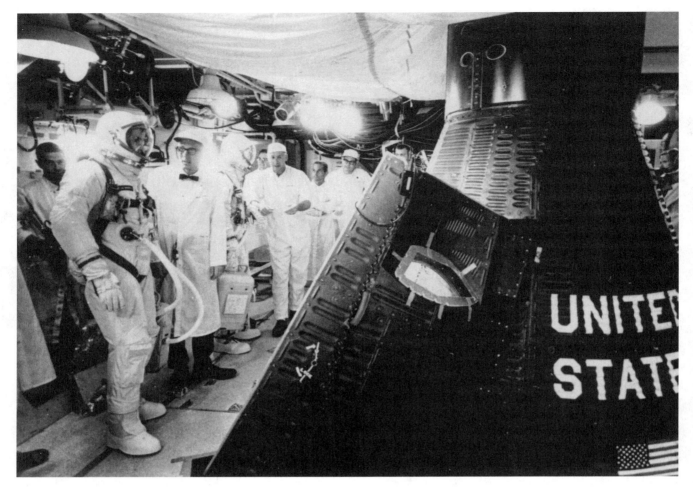

In this 1965 photograph, astronauts prepare for a simulated Gemini test at Cape Kennedy in Florida. *(Library of Congress, Prints and Photographs Division [LC-USZ62-121458])*

Polyakov completed a record 14 months aboard *Mir;* the next year, astronaut Shannon Lucid set an American spaceflight endurance record of 188 days.

International cooperation in space programs has continued to the present. Many different nations are involved in the building of an *International Space Station* to be finished by 2006. The first module was launched in 1998. Eleven of the participating nations are members of the EUROPEAN SPACE AGENCY, an organization of presently 15 nations founded in 1975; Brazil, Canada, and Japan are also involved in the project.

Space Shuttle

In the 1980s, the United States began using the Space Transportation System (STS), popularly known as the SPACE SHUTTLE. It is a reusable spacecraft, launched by rockets but with gliding capabilities for landings. It has become the primary vehicle for building and taking supplies to the *International Space Station* and for the launching, servicing, and repairing of artificial satellites. It has also the ability to conduct numerous scientific experiments. The *Columbia* disaster in 2003 (following the earlier *Challenger* disaster of 1986) has led to a reexamination of space shuttle safety issues, however.

❖

Humans have thus traveled as explorers into Earth orbit time and again; they have even reached the Moon. Interplanetary travel might someday become a reality. Exploration to the Sun and other planets has been carried out by space probes, with humans participating from Earth, since the 1960s; the Sun, Mars, Venus, Mercury, Jupiter, Saturn, Uranus, Neptune, and some of their moons have been visited or approached. There have even been rendezvous with asteroids and Halley's Comet. Many more such missions are planned.

Space has been referred to as the final frontier. Its highly organized missions, depending to such a degree on technology and such a large support team, seem to have little in common with the expeditions of ancient and even more recent explorers on land and sea. Yet the impulse to visit, examine, and understand unknown places is consistent with motivation for exploration through the ages.

space probe

Humans have traveled in orbit around the Earth time and again. They have also journeyed to the Moon. But for travel to other parts of the solar system, they have been dependent on space probes, which have instrumentation, including cameras, to collect scientific data and radio transmitters to send the data back to Earth. Unlike an artificial SATELLITE that is placed in orbit around Earth, a space probe is launched by a powerful enough ROCKET so that it escapes Earth's gravitational field and can navigate among other celestial bodies. Some probes are directed to orbit the Moon, another planet, or another planet's moons (becoming satellites, in effect), or to fly by one or more planets; others are directed to soft-land scientific equipment on lunar or planetary surfaces.

The first space probe, *Pioneer 1,* was launched by the United States, under the direction of the NATIONAL AERONAUTICS AND SPACE ADMINISTRATION (NASA), on October 11, 1958, one year after the first satellite, *Sputnik 1,* was launched by the Union of Soviet Socialist Republics (USSR; Soviet Union) and almost nine months after the first U.S. satellite, *Explorer 1,* was launched. *Pioneer* did not accomplish its attempted goal of orbiting the Moon, but it reached an altitude of some 72,800 miles in outer space, gathering data on meteors, temperature, radiation, and magnetic fields, before falling back toward Earth and disintegrating in the atmosphere.

The Soviet Union achieved the greatest early success in lunar exploration with the Luna series. *Luna 1,* launched in January 1959, became the first human-made object to escape Earth's orbit, but missed striking the Moon. The following September, *Luna 2* became the first artificial object to do so. That October, *Luna 3* sent back the first photographs of the far side of the Moon.

The United States, after a number of failures, achieved some success, and gained experience for its APOLLO PROGRAM and the goal of placing humans on the Moon, with its Ranger, Surveyor, and Lunar Orbiter probes of the 1960s, which sent back photographs, performed soft-landings, and mapped the Moon. In 1968, the Soviet Union sent the first Zond probes in preparation for their own piloted missions. On July 20, 1969, with the *Apollo 11* mission, NEIL ALDEN ARMSTRONG and Edwin "Buzz" Aldrin, Jr., became the first humans on the Moon's surface. In 1970, with *Luna 17,* the Soviet Union succeeded in placing the first wheeled vehicle on the Moon, *Lunakhod 1,* a re-

mote-controlled rover. The final Luna mission, *Luna 24,* took place in 1976. The United States put the probe Clementine in Moon orbit in 1994, using a laser to study topography, and the Lunar Prospector in orbit in 1999, to study surface composition as well as gravitational and magnetic fields.

There have been numerous space probes into interstellar space beyond the Moon. The United States has launched many probes, exploring to the end of the solar system and beyond from the 1960s to the present. The Mariner series explored Mars, Venus, and Mercury in the 1960s–70s. *Pioneer 10* passed through the asteroid belt and became the first artificial object to escape the solar system in 1973; *Pioneer 11* studied Jupiter and Saturn. Because of the great distances involved, some of these missions last decades; *Pioneer 11,* for example, launched in 1973, continued to send data back to Earth until 1994. The Viking series of the 1970s studied Mars, *Viking 2* of 1975–76 being one of the early success stories, with transmission of photographs and chemical analyses. Yet it found no trace of life on the Red Planet. The Voyager series launched in the 1970s passed by and made studies of Jupiter, Saturn, Uranus, Neptune, and their moons. In 1980, *Voyager 1* exited the solar system, followed by *Voyager 2* in 1989; in 1998, *Voyager 1* passed *Pioneer 10* to become the most distant human-made object in space. The *Magellan* probe, launched in 1989, orbited Venus. The *Ulysses* probe (shared by the EUROPEAN SPACE AGENCY) of the 1990s conducted studies of the Sun. The *Galileo* probe of the 1990s studied Venus, the Moon, the asteroids, Jupiter, and Jupiter's moons. The Mars *Pathfinder* and Mars *Global Surveyor* of the 1990s continued studies of Mars: *Pathfinder* returned many images from the surface and carried out 15 chemical analyses; *Global Surveyor,* in orbit, mapped the planet and took photographs of features to suggest the presence of water on or below the surface. The NEAR (Near Earth Asteroid Rendezvous)-Shoemaker studied the asteroid Mathilde and landed on the asteroid Eros. Launched in 2001, *Odyssey* is a successful orbiter around Mars, sending back numerous images into 2004.

Meanwhile, other nations have launched probes. The Soviet *Mars* probes of 1971–74 studied Mars. The Soviet Venera series of the 1960s–80s studied Venus. The Soviet Union's *Vega 1* and *2* probes, Japan's *Sakigake* and *Suisei* probes, and the European Space Agency's *Giotto* probe rendezvoused with Halley's Comet in 1986. The Japanese *Nozomi* probe of the late 1990s studied Mars.

Those mentioned are the success stories. Some probes, like the Soviet Union's *Phobos 1* and *2* to Mars in the late 1980s, and the U.S. *Mars Climate Orbiter, Mars Polar Lander,* and twin probes referred to as *Deep Space 2* in the late 1990s, failed in their missions. In fact, two-thirds of all probes to Mars have failed.

Many more space probes are planned, some of them already launched for later rendezvous with their targets. The joint U.S.-European *Cassini* probe, for example, launched in 1997, is intended to explore Saturn, its rings, and some of its moons on arrival in 2004. With the planet Mars closer to Earth in 2003–04 than it has been in 7,300 years, numerous nations have sent space probes to study it.

space shuttle

Space shuttle is the popular name of the Space Transportation System (STS), a reusable spacecraft of the United States. It was developed by the NATIONAL AERONAUTICS AND SPACE ADMINISTRATION (NASA) in the 1970s and first used in the 1980s as a reusable launch, orbital, and landing vehicle, which can transport humans and cargo to and from Earth. Despite setbacks over the years, it has proven a practical means of SPACE EXPLORATION. It has been used for the launching, servicing, and repairing of a variety of types of artificial SATELLITE; to retrieve previously deployed spacecraft; for the building and carrying of supplies to a SPACE STATION; and to conduct scientific experiments. For many of these tasks, extravehicular activities, popularly known as space walks, are required.

The space shuttle is launched vertically, two solid rocket boosters propelling the spacecraft for about two minutes to an altitude of about 28 miles before separating and falling into the ocean, where they are retrieved and later refurbished for reuse. The orbiter has three main liquid-propellant engines, the first reusable ROCKET engines, which fire for about eight minutes until reaching the desired altitude for orbit. An external fuel tank, the only part of the shuttle that is not recycled, is jettisoned, breaking up in the upper atmosphere and falling in pieces into the ocean. Other smaller engines are used for maneuvers when in orbit. The spacecraft's hull is protected from the friction and heat of reentry into the atmosphere by some 24,000 silicate fiber tiles. Directed by the crew, the winged orbiter glides to Earth and makes a horizontal landing on a runway.

The space shuttle crew consists of the commander and pilot, trained ASTRONAUTS, as well as up to five more people, some of them nonastronauts, including a mission specialist and payload specialists. The crew compartment is the front of the craft with a cargo bay (60 by 15 feet) behind it. The orbiter's crew compartment has three levels: the flight deck, from where the commander and pilot control the craft; the mid-deck, where the galley, toilet, sleep stations, along with storage and experiment lockers are located; and the utility area, with air and water tanks. In the mid-deck are also a hatch for entrance and egress before and after landing, and an airlock hatch into the cargo bay. The cargo bay doubles as a workstation; its doors give access to space.

The first space shuttle, *Columbia,* was launched on April 12, 1981. The space shuttle program completed numerous successful launches over the course of five years until January 28, 1986, with the *Challenger* disaster. A failure of a rubber sealant ring between two segments of one of the solid rocket boosters, made brittle by cold weather, led to the escape of burning fuel and an explosion 73 seconds after launch. The entire seven-member crew perished, among them Christa McAuliffe, a high school teacher from New Hampshire, who would have been the first teacher in space. The space shuttle program was suspended for design modifications until September 28, 1988, with the flight of the shuttle *Discovery.*

Three other space shuttles have been used in addition to the *Columbia* and *Challenger:* the *Discovery,* since 1983; the *Atlantis,* since 1985; and the *Endeavour,* since 1991. (The *Enterprise,* named after the vehicle in the fictional television series *Star Trek,* a prototype space shuttle, was launched from a 747 airplane in 1977 to test design features.) The vehicles' frames have remained the same, with the technology evolving and the craft being refitted over the years.

Successful missions since the *Challenger* disaster have included the launching of several exploratory spacecraft: *Magellan* in May 1989, a probe to the planet Venus; *Galileo* in October 1989, a probe to Jupiter; *Ulysses* in October 1990, a probe to the Sun; and the *Hubble Space Telescope* in April 1990, the placement in orbit of a telescope for astronomical studies, and a follow-up mission in December 1993, for repair of the telescope. In July 1995, the shuttle *Atlantis* rendezvoused and docked with the Russian space station *Mir,* the first in a series of nine linkups. The shuttle is also central to the building of the *International Space Station,* the first module of which was launched in 1998.

On February 1, 2003, the space shuttle program suffered another disaster when the *Columbia,* the first shuttle ever to fly a mission, broke up over Texas on reentry—because of damage to protective paneling on the left wing when a piece of foam insulation from the external fuel tank came loose and struck it during launch. This was the first accident during landing for NASA in 42 years of spaceflight. All seven crew members died, among them the first Israeli astronaut, Ilan Ramon.

The Union of Soviet Socialist Republics (USSR; Soviet Union) began its own space shuttle program in 1988, designing the Buran spacecraft; on the breakup of the Soviet Union in 1991, Russia inherited the program but halted it two years later. The United States plans to retire the space shuttle in 2012 and is designing a new generation of shuttle vehicles.

space station (space platforms)

The term *space station* refers to a facility in space, where humans live for extended periods of time. They are a type of artificial SATELLITE, in permanent orbit around Earth, unlike spacecraft, which stay in orbit relatively short periods of time. They relate to SPACE EXPLORATION as service centers for spacecraft and as laboratories for scientific experiments. In the future, they may serve as spaceports for travel to other parts of the solar system. They are self-contained systems, with their own oxygen, water, and food, yet need maintenance and restocking from Earth. They also have been referred to as space platforms.

A Russian inventor and ROCKET designer, Konstantin Eduardovich Tsiolkovsky, is credited with conceptualizing orbiting space stations for the purpose of interplanetary travel, in the early 20th century, long before the first spaceflight. The former Union of Soviet Socialist Republics (USSR; Soviet Union) launched the first space station, *Salyut 1*, in April 1971, 14 years after it launched the first artificial satellite, *Sputnik 1*. The *Soyuz 10* crew, part of the SOYUZ PROGRAM, docked with the space station four days later but could not enter it. The *Soyuz 11* crew, cosmonauts Georgi Dobrovolski, Viktor Patsayev, and Vladislav Volkov, made a successful docking on June 7, 1971, and lived on the station for three weeks. The Salyut series of space stations, a total of nine, were relatively small structures launched fully assembled and designed for up to three people. New docking and space assembling technologies were developed in the course of the program. The first Salyut stations had open-loop life support systems, designed to discard all waste matter into space. But closed-loop life-support systems were developed—the recovery of oxygen from carbon dioxide and the recycling of water—to decrease dependency on supplies carried from Earth.

The United States launched its first space station, *Skylab,* on May 14, 1973, its crew of three ASTRONAUTS—Pete Conrad, Joe Kerwin, and Paul Weitz—following on May 25 after a delayed launch. The NATIONAL AERONAUTICS AND SPACE ADMINISTRATION (NASA) provided rockets and spacecraft for *Skylab* missions from the APOLLO PROGRAM. Like the first Salyut stations, *Skylab* was fully assembled on Earth and had open-loop systems. With a telescope mount, it was the first manned solar observatory in space. Two other sets of crews lived on *Skylab* that year. It remained unoccupied until July 1979, when it reentered the atmosphere and disintegrated from the heat of friction, its pieces brought down in the Indian Ocean, with some mistakenly hitting isolated parts of Australia.

The Soviet Union followed its Salyut program with the *Mir* space station, the first permanently manned space station. The first core module was launched on February 19, 1986; six other modules were added through 1996. Soviet spacecraft of the Soyuz program originally ferried crews and supplies to *Mir*, but later the United States helped with the SPACE SHUTTLE. Crews of the *Mir* over the years consisted of people of many different nationalities, more passengers

than all previous space stations combined. After numerous repairs and growing technical problems, *Mir* was directed back to Earth, falling into the Pacific Ocean in March 2001.

The United States began a program to launch its own permanent space station, *Freedom,* in 1984. Ten years later, after the breakup of the Soviet Union, the program was combined with Russia's *Mir 2* project, with the goal of building an *International Space Station (ISS).* Eleven nations in the EUROPEAN SPACE AGENCY, along with Brazil, Canada, and Japan, are involved in the project. The first component, a Russian-built core module, was launched in 1998. The first crew, two Russians and one American, arrived in 2000. Construction is planned through 2006; *ISS* will eventually support a crew of seven.

Spanish Main

The phrase *Spanish Main* was first generally applied to the "mainland" of Spanish America, especially the territory along the north coast, from the mouth of the ORINOCO RIVER westward to the isthmus of Panama, and comprising most of present-day coastal Venezuela, all of Colombia, and part of Panama. The phrase also came to be used in reference to waters off the mainland, that is, the southern portion of the Caribbean Sea, along with Spanish-held islands. Sometimes it was applied to the entire Caribbean basin.

The earliest use of the phrase is not known. Early mariners used the term *the main* to refer to any mainland. Non-Spanish people active in the Caribbean were most likely to cite the Spanish Main as distinct from territory controlled by other European nations. Starting in the late 16th century, along with the Spanish colonization of the region and its use as a transatlantic shipping center—especially to transport gold, silver, and gemstones plundered from indigenous peoples or forcibly mined by them—came PIRACY, some of it carried out by PRIVATEERS sanctioned by the English government, such as SIR FRANCIS DRAKE (see TREASURE AND EXPLORATION). Pirates were active in the Caribbean into the 19th century, and the phrase *Spanish Main* is most often associated with their activities.

speleology

Speleology is the scientific study of caves and cave systems. A cave is a natural underground cavity large enough for people to enter (sometimes the term *cavern* is used for a large cave). *Cave system* refers to a number of interconnected caves. Speleology includes classifying caves geologically, measuring and mapping them, analyzing their water systems, and reporting on flora and fauna found in them. In its infancy as a discipline in the late 19th century, speleology was regarded as a branch of geography since much of the activity associated with it was finding caves. Now it is perceived as a subdivision of geology. It also draws on the disciplines of chemistry, hydrology, climatology, and biology. Speologists also employ surveying techniques (see SURVEYING AND EXPLORATION). And since caves have long served as shelters for humans, speleology and archaeology sometimes go hand-in-hand (see ARCHAEOLOGY AND EXPLORATION). One now-common application of speleology is the tracing of underground waters to monitor and prevent pollution.

The term *speleology* is derived from the Greek words for "cave" and the "study of." In Middle English, *spelunk,* from the Latin *spelunca,* a derivation from Greek, was another name for a cave or grotto. *Speluncar* endured into modern English as an adjective form, meaning "pertaining to caves," but fell out of usage by the mid-19th century. In 1895, Frenchman Edouard-Alfred Martel founded La Société de Spéléologie, the bulletin of which was called *Spelunca.* The term *spelunker* for someone who explores caves and *spelunking* for the act itself came into usage in the United States in the late 1930s and early 1940s. *Spelunking* remains a common term for the exploration of caves, along with *spelunker,* the term for those people who do the exploring. Yet most nonscientists skilled in spelunking techniques and equipment—such as special shoes, helmets, ladders, cables, and lamps—prefer the terms *caving* and *caver.* The term *cave diving* refers to exploring caves underwater.

Speologists and geologists have classified caves into primary caves and secondary caves. Primary caves were formed at the same time as the surrounding rocks, with the space of the cave remaining empty. Secondary caves were formed sometime after the formation of the surrounding rocks. Most caves are secondary caves, and the most common type of secondary cave is a karst cave, formed in limestone, gypsum, or other soluble rocks by dissolution.

The exploration of caves has grown in popularity in recent decades. The National Speleology Society, a U.S. organization, founded over 60 years ago and located in Huntsville, Alabama, now has more than 10,000 members. The National Caves Association, founded in 1965 and centered in Park City, Kentucky, is a nonprofit organization of publicly and privately owned caves and caverns developed for public visitation. There are many other such organizations in countries around the world. The Union Internationale de Spéléologie (UIS), founded in 1965 with its central office in the Czech Republic, is the international body for speleology and caving.

spelunking   See SPELEOLOGY.

Spice Islands (Moluccas, Maluka)

Spice Islands is a former name for the Moluccas, a collection of islands between Celebes and New Guinea in the Malay Archipelago, situated where the South Pacific Ocean and Indian Ocean meet. They encompass some 32,307 square miles, 90 percent of which is ocean. The Moluccas (or Maluka) are currently a province in the eastern portion of the Republic of Indonesia. The largest island is Halmahera, and the province's capital is the city of Ambon on the island of Ambon. Other significant islands in the group are Ternate, Ceram, Buru, and Tidore. Because they were formed by volcanic activity, the Moluccas are mountainous. The climate is humid, and the soil fertile. The cloves, nutmeg, mace, and pepper produced by the islanders, and their central role in the SPICE TRADE, gave rise to the name Spice Islands.

For centuries before the arrival of Europeans, the Spice Islands were visited by Chinese from the east and Arab Muslims from the west; traveling by ship, both peoples were attracted by the islands' agricultural goods (see CHINESE EXPLORATION; MUSLIM EXPLORATION). To protect their profits, the Arab traders who sold these commodities to Europe kept secret their location. The desire of European merchants to circumvent these Arab traders was a major motivating factor in what became the EUROPEAN AGE OF EXPLORATION, beginning in the 15th century.

The probable first European visitor to the Moluccas was Italian LUDOVICO DI VARTHEMA in 1505. The Portuguese, who had already begun trading in India with VASCO DA GAMA's voyage of 1497–99, were anxious to get to the source of these precious spices. In 1511, Portuguese mariner and trader FRANCISCO SERRANO, after accompanying AFONSO DE ALBUQUERQUE in the conquest of the Malayan port of Malacca on the west coast of the Malay Peninsula, investigated the Spice Islands. After being appointed viceroy of Ternate, he established a Portuguese trading post there in 1513. A Spanish expedition originally headed by Portuguese mariner FERDINAND MAGELLAN reached the Spice Islands across the Pacific from the east in 1521 during the first CIRCUMNAVIGATION OF THE WORLD. Portuguese domination of the Spice Islands was henceforth challenged by the Spanish, who asserted that the islands were located in their half of the world according to Alexander VI's papal bull of 1493. The dispute was resolved with the Treaty of Saragossa of 1529, in which the Spanish emperor, more interested in developing Spain's possessions in the Americas, agreed to drop the claim in exchange for a cash payment from Portugal.

For most of the 16th century, Portugal held a tight monopoly on exports from the Spice Islands to Europe. In October 1579, SIR FRANCIS DRAKE made the first English voyage to the region and reached a trade agreement with the sultan of Ternate, beginning an intermittent English presence in the region. In 1595, CORNELIUS HOUTMAN was recruited by a group of Dutch merchants to open trade with the Spice Islands. Although not profitable, the expedition was successful in its defiance of the Portuguese. In April

1602, the newly chartered DUTCH EAST INDIA COMPANY sent its first fleet of ships to the islands. By the mid-1600s, through naval actions and privateering, the Dutch had gained control of the island group. Conflict with England was resolved by an agreement between the two countries to divide up their interests. England expanded its trading activities in India, and the Dutch maintained their presence in the Spice Islands.

The population of the Moluccas is ethnically diverse, including Malay, Papuan, and Javanese peoples. The native population has intermarried with Europeans over the centuries, especially the Portuguese and Dutch. About 60 percent of the people are Muslim; the rest, mostly Christian. Agriculture is still central to the economy; food crops include cassava, taro, yams, and sweet potatoes. The sago palm provides starch as a dietary staple as well as wood for building. Spices are no longer the main export products, but rather coconut, coffee, and wood products.

See also ASIA, EXPLORATION OF.

Spice Route

The SPICE TRADE, that is, the trade of spices and incense from the East to the West has followed many routes over its long history from Asia to the Near East, Africa, and Europe. The main overland route stretched over thousands of miles of forbidding landscape through central Asia and is commonly called the SILK ROAD, because it carried in addition to spices and incense, silks and other luxury items from China and India. The caravans traveling this route often consisted of thousands of camels. The goods might be sold to lands along the eastern and southern MEDITERRANEAN SEA, or distributed by sea by Phoenicians, Greeks, or other mariners to more distant lands (see GREEK EXPLORATION; PHOENICIAN EXPLORATION).

Yet overland travel was more expensive, dangerous, and slower than travel by sea, and so, even before the establishment of the Silk Road, in the second to first century B.C., spices and incense were brought by ship from India, across the Indian Ocean, through the Arabian Sea to the south coast of the Arabian Peninsula. Traders would hug close to the land, sailing through the Indian Ocean, to the coast of present-day Yemen. From there, where several wealthy kingdoms flourished in the centuries B.C., the goods would travel by boat through the RED SEA, which was dangerously infested with pirates, or by caravan to Mediterranean coastal regions, such as Alexandria in North Africa, another center of the spice trade.

The southern area of Arabia, occupied by modern-day Yemen, was called Arabia Felix (Happy Arabia) by the Romans for its great wealth as an important intermediary in the spice trade, as well as the source of frankincense and myrrh, gathered from trees growing just south of the Rub' al-Khali,

the desert region also known as the EMPTY QUARTER. The wealth supported the development of great kingdoms and many wealthy cities. The most noted kingdom was that of the Sabaeans, which flourished from the 10th century B.C. until about 115 B.C.; Marib was the capital city. This area was possibly that referred to as PUNT by the ancient Egyptians, who sent several seafaring expeditions through the Red Sea, including that of HANNU in about 2450 B.C., which returned to Egypt with spices and incense (see EGYPTIAN EXPLORATION). The Red Sea and the Arabian Sea were dangerous routes to take because of the pirates who habitually sallied out from the Arabian and African shores. The Sabaeans controlled the overland trade routes to Palestine and to Egypt, which cross deserts and mountains, passing through the part of Arabia called Arabia Petrea (Stone Arabia) by the Romans.

In about A.D. 45, a Greek merchant by the name of HIPPALUS endeavored to avoid the coasts altogether, sailing down the center of the Red Sea and through the Arabian Sea to India, and his route became commonplace, reducing the length and dangers of the journey East, as well as the dependence on the Arabs. Traders, at great risk to their ships and cargoes, began catching the yearly monsoon winds to sail across the Arabian Sea and back.

The Red Sea/Arabian Sea route remained a standard route for hundreds of years. Ships could travel between the Red Sea and the NILE RIVER by an ancient Egyptian canal, and from the Nile to the Mediterranean Sea. The growth of the Roman Empire resulted in the eradication of PIRACY in the Mediterranean Sea and Red Sea (see ROMAN EXPLORATION). Even after the breakup of the Roman Empire in the fifth century, Arab traders continued to do a brisk business, and the wealth fueled the expansion of the Islamic empire after the founding of Islam in the seventh century.

The main artery for the overland spice trade was Constantinople (present-day Istanbul, Turkey), the capital of the Eastern Roman Empire (or Byzantine Empire). After the CRUSADES of the late 11th to the late 13th centuries, the merchants in the Italian port city of Venice became responsible for most of the spices entering Europe, bringing them through the Mediterranean from ports on the coast of the Near East, a region known as the LEVANT.

With the Venetians holding a monopoly on Mediterranean trade with the Middle East, and with the rise to power of the Turks in Asia Minor, trade through Constantinople slowed to a trickle. European nations began sending out ambitious oceangoing expeditions to locate new trade routes with the East. The 1497–99 Portuguese voyage of VASCO DA GAMA southward in the Atlantic along the west coast of Africa, around the CAPE OF GOOD HOPE, then northward in the Indian Ocean along Africa's east coast, and across the Indian Ocean to India, created a viable route. A Spanish expedition headed by Portuguese mariner

FERDINAND MAGELLAN in 1619–22, which crossed the Atlantic, rounded South America, and crossed the Pacific, eventually completing the first CIRCUMNAVIGATION OF THE WORLD, proved that the EAST INDIES could be reached from the west. The English and the Dutch continued searching for water routes to the Orient, both a NORTHWEST PASSAGE through the Americas and a NORTHEAST PASSAGE to the north of Europe and Asia. These passages were not accomplished for centuries, however, because of ice conditions in the Arctic Ocean.

In the 19th century, even after the importance of the spice trade had dwindled, the establishment of European colonies in the East created a demand for other commodities. A quick route was therefore needed, which led to the digging of the Suez Canal, completed in 1869.

See also COMMERCE AND EXPLORATION.

spice trade

The common seasonings used to flavor foods today, including pepper, nutmeg, cinnamon, and cloves, were, for much of history, precious luxuries. As late as the 16th century in Europe, one small ship full of spices could make a fortune for the investors on an expedition of several ships and make its crew rich as well. Spices played an important role in flavoring foods and preserving their freshness, and incense was used in religious ceremonies by all the early peoples of the Near East and North Africa. Spices and herbs also served as the primary ingredients in many medicines. These spices, for the most part, along with fragrant resins and gums, such as frankincense, myrrh, and other incense, came from the East, over land and by sea. The importance of the spice trade endured from ancient times throughout the Middle Ages and RENAISSANCE and led to the establishment of various land and sea routes between Europe, Africa, and Asia and spurred on the search for oceanic routes as well (see SPICE ROUTE).

The Ancient Trade

The quest for spices and incense inspired what some consider the first voyage of exploration. An Egyptian, HANNU, set out to the RED SEA coast with 3,000 men at the orders of the Egyptian pharaoh Sahure in around 2450 B.C. and built ships which he sailed to the land the Egyptians called PUNT. It is not known what Hannu brought back, but later, in about 1492 B.C., Egyptian Queen HATSHEPSUT sent another expedition to Punt. It returned with incense, including frankincense, myrrh, and, of special importance, myrrh seedlings, which were planted in Egypt (see EGYPTIAN EXPLORATION). The conquests of ALEXANDER THE GREAT in the fourth century B.C. brought more contact between Mediterranean peoples and those in the East. At this time, Arab traders still had a monopoly on the spices traveling by

sea, and told fabulous stories of how they were obtained, in order to preserve the secret of their origin and to discourage any attempt to break their lucrative monopoly.

By about the time the Romans became interested in gaining hold of the spice trade, demand for spices was so great that Eastern traders were taking advantage of powerful monsoon winds to sail from India to Arabia, at great risk to life and cargo. The returns were great enough, though, to justify any risk. The spice trade passed through Alexandria, making it one of the most important centers for commerce in the ancient world. In about 25 B.C., after the Romans had annexed Egypt, under the reign of Augustus, officer GAIUS AELIUS GALLUS set out on an expedition to Arabia in order to conquer the Sabaeans, who occupied a kingdom on the southern end of the Arabian Peninsula, from where much of the trade passing through Alexandria originated. The Romans called this southern tip of the Arabian Peninsula, in modern-day Yemen, Arabia Felix, or Happy Arabia, because of the wealth it derived from trade in spices and resins. Gallus failed to subjugate the Sabaeans and to conquer their principal city of Marib, and returned to Egypt with only new geographic knowledge for the Romans (see ROMAN EXPLORATION).

The Spice Trade in the Middle Ages

The Arabs maintained control of much of the spice trade for centuries, and their control solidified with the rise of Islam. The Prophet Muhammad, who launched the religion, was married to a woman made wealthy by the spice trade. The Muslims carried Islam throughout Arabia, uniting the entire peninsula by the time of his death in A.D. 632 (see MUSLIM EXPLORATION).

By the eighth century, the Islamic empire had spread from North Africa in the West to Persia in the East. Trade continued between the East and West, if somewhat abrogated, until the conquest of the Arabs by Turks from the Anatolian Peninsula in the mid-11th century. The Turks, converting to Islam as they conquered, were more hardened against the Christians in the West than their Arab predecessors. The Turks threatened Constantinople (present-day Istanbul, Turkey), the seat of the Eastern Roman Empire (Byzantine Empire), and cut off Christian pilgrimages to the Holy Land. This sparked the CRUSADES, the military actions by European Christians against the Muslims of the Near East from the late 11th century to the late 13th century. Crusaders returning to Europe from the East had a greater desire for Eastern goods, among them spices.

Venice, a city in northern Italy, was the primary port for trade between East and West at this time. It was from Venice that Venetian merchant MARCO POLO set out for the East in 1271 with his father, NICCOLÒ POLO, and uncle MAFFEO POLO, and wound up traveling throughout China and the vast empire of the Mongols. Returning by sea, after 24 years, Marco Polo's account brought back detailed reports of the source of the spices craved by Europeans.

The Enduring Spice Trade

Just as early mariners attempted new routes to profit from the spice trade, so did mariners during the RENAISSANCE, helping prompt what has become known as the EUROPEAN AGE OF EXPLORATION. The Portuguese established a route around Africa. The Spanish ended up reaching the Americas and navigating the Pacific Ocean.

HENRY THE NAVIGATOR, prince of Portugal, developed a plan to reach India and the SPICE ISLANDS (the Moluccas) by rounding the tip of Africa. BARTOLOMEU DIAS rounded the CAPE OF GOOD HOPE in 1488, and VASCO DA GAMA, in 1497–99, crossed the Indian Ocean to India and returned to Portugal with a load of pepper. Meanwhile, Italian mariner CHRISTOPHER COLUMBUS was proposing a plan to sail westward across the uncharted waters of the Atlantic Ocean to reach the Spice Islands in the east. In 1492, sailing for Spain, he reached the WEST INDIES, so named because he thought them the outlying islands of the EAST INDIES, and began to search for gold and spices. In 1497, another Italian, JOHN CABOT, who had experience sailing for Venice in the spice trade, sailed under English sponsorship in 1497, reaching North America.

Portuguese mariner FERDINAND MAGELLAN, after a rift with the king of Portugal, moved to Spain and proposed a southwest passage through or around South America, in order to reach the Spice Islands. Five ships were provided. Magellan managed to sail from the Atlantic through South America's Strait of Magellan (see MAGELLAN, STRAIT OF) to the Pacific Ocean, then cross it to the Philippines, where he died in 1521, wounded by native arrows. Two of his ships reached the Spice Islands, and one ship, the *Victoria,* under JUAN SEBASTIÁN DEL CANO, managed to return to Spain in 1522, completing the first CIRCUMNAVIGATION OF THE WORLD. The load of cloves more than paid for the entire expedition and made the surviving sailors rich.

With ocean routes established, in the 17th century, European merchants founded companies, typically with royal charters and stockholders, to develop the Eastern trade, among them the BRITISH EAST INDIA COMPANY, the DUTCH EAST INDIA COMPANY, and the FRENCH EAST INDIA COMPANY. As the reach of European mariners expanded and as colonial empires grew, spices became a more affordable commodity. Spices were farmed on plantations and transplanted around the globe, and, in the 17th and 18th centuries, other commodities grew in importance, and other motives for exploration superseded the demand for spices. Yet many of the spices at the center of the centuries-long spice trade are still widely used throughout the world.

See also COMMERCE AND EXPLORATION.

sponsors of exploration

Not all individuals important to the history of exploration traveled to uncharted lands. Some among them changed the course of history by sponsoring expeditions. Some were sponsors and explorers both, who spent part of the time in the field. Sponsorship was provided for a variety of purposes; included among those backing expeditions were government leaders, merchants, scholars, mapmakers, publishers, and wives.

Henry the Navigator

Perhaps the most famous visionary and sponsor who made a huge impact on how the world was perceived was Portuguese nobleman Prince Henry. Although he never traveled beyond the region of the MEDITERRANEAN SEA, he became known to history—because of an 1868 biography by British writer Richard Henry Major—as HENRY THE NAVIGATOR. He also has been referred to as "the explorer who stayed home." In 1416, Henry decided to live at Sagres near Cape St. Vincent, the southwesternmost point in Portugal, and there founded a naval depot and, soon afterward, an observatory and a school of navigation, where he brought together astronomers, mapmakers, and mariners. Over the next years, he sponsored numerous expeditions to the AZORES and along the coast of West Africa. Just after his death in 1460, his mariners reached as far as Cape Palmas, where the African coast turns eastward. Henry's contribution to exploration as a sponsor is often cited as the start of the EUROPEAN AGE OF EXPLORATION.

Kings, Queens, Presidents, and Other Officials

Many of those sponsors cited with regard to continuing the European Age of Exploration are kings and queens. In Portugal, after Prince Henry's death, various Portuguese kings sent out expeditions. King John II, who ruled from 1481–95, sponsored a new round of expeditions southward along the coast of Africa, including those of DIOGO CÃO in 1482–84, which reached the CONGO RIVER (Zaire River), and BARTOLOMEU DIAS in 1487–88, which sailed around the tip of the continent, locating the CAPE OF GOOD HOPE. Manuel I, who ruled Portugal from 1495 to 1521, dispatched VASCO DA GAMA on a voyage in 1497, in which he rounded Africa, reached India, then returned to Portugal in 1499.

The joint rulers of Aragon and Castile in Spain in 1479–1504—Ferdinand II and Isabella I—are famous for having sponsored CHRISTOPHER COLUMBUS's voyage across the Atlantic Ocean in 1492, as well as his subsequent expeditions in the Americas. Their grandson, Charles I, king of Spain from 1516 to 1556 (and as Charles V, Holy Roman Emperor from 1519 to 1556) sponsored the first CIRCUMNAVIGATION OF THE WORLD under FERDINAND MAGELLAN in 1519–22, as well as many expeditions in the

Americas for purposes of colonization, such as that of FRAN-CISCO PIZARRO in Peru in 1531–33.

Many of the Spanish CONQUISTADORES in turn became sponsors. For example, Pizarro sent out his half brother GONZALO PIZARRO and FRANCISCO DE ORELLANO to the AMAZON RIVER in 1541–42. Another Spaniard, DIEGO VELÁSQUEZ, who became governor of Cuba in 1514, sent out numerous expeditions in the Caribbean region, including that of HERNÁN CORTÉS, who explored Mexico in 1519–21 (although Cortés later tried to bypass Velásquez by seeking the endorsement of King Charles directly). Cortés later sent out FRANCISCO DE ULLOA, who explored northward to the Gulf of California and Baja California in 1539–40, as well as other expeditions. Another Spanish official known as a sponsor of explorations is ANTONIO DE MENDOZA, viceroy of New Spain in 1535–49, who sent out expeditions to the American Southwest, such as that of FRANCISCO VÁSQUEZ DE CORONADO in 1540–41.

An English courtier, soldier, and man of letters—SIR WALTER RALEIGH—although he headed two expeditions to the ORINOCO RIVER in northern South America, in 1595 and 1617, is best known regarding the history of exploration as a sponsor for failed colonies in 1584–87 along the coast of what is now northeastern North Carolina. The colonists of the second attempt vanished, leading to the mystery of the LOST COLONY.

Elizabeth I, who ruled England and Ireland from 1558 to 1603, was known as a sponsor of explorations in her own right. In 1577–80, for example, with her backing and that of English merchants, SIR FRANCIS DRAKE completed the first English circumnavigation of the world.

Nearly a century later, from Fort Henry, just to the north in what is now southeastern Virginia, colonial military leader ABRAHAM WOOD sent out exploratory expeditions westward. The men whom he sponsored—THOMAS BATTS, ROBERT FALLAM, GABRIEL ARTHUR, and JAMES NEEDHAM —were the first known Englishmen to explore the APPALACHIAN MOUNTAINS and beyond.

The third president of the United States, Thomas Jefferson, who served from 1801 to 1809, had long contemplated an overland expedition across the North American continent and recommended his private secretary MERIWETHER LEWIS to the Congress as leader of the Corps of Discovery. Lewis enlisted former soldier WILLIAM CLARK as his coleader. In 1804–06, the Lewis and Clark Expedition traveled from St. Louis in present-day Missouri to the Pacific Ocean at the mouth of the COLUMBIA RIVER and back.

Trading Companies and Geographical Societies

Many expeditions received backing in the name of commerce. Various trading companies—the HANSEATIC LEAGUE, LEVANT COMPANY, MUSCOVY COMPANY, CATHAY COMPANY, COMPANY OF MERCHANTS OF LONDON DISCOVERERS OF THE NORTHWEST PASSAGE, VIRGINIA COMPANY, BRITISH EAST INDIA COMPANY, FRENCH EAST INDIA COMPANY, DUTCH EAST INDIA COMPANY, and DUTCH WEST INDIA COMPANY—all played a part in world exploration (see COMMERCE AND EXPLORATION).

Various fur-trading companies—the HUDSON'S BAY COMPANY, NORTH WEST COMPANY, AMERICAN FUR COMPANY, ST. LOUIS MISSOURI FUR COMPANY, ROCKY MOUNTAIN FUR COMPANY, and RUSSIAN-AMERICAN FUR COMPANY—had much to do with the opening of North America to non-Indian settlement. Some of the owners or directors of these firms, such as JOHN JACOB ASTOR of the American Fur Company, were businessmen who sent representatives into the wilderness. Others, such as ALEKSANDR ANDREEVICH BARANOV of the Russian-American Company and WILLIAM HENRY ASHLEY of the Rocky Mountain Fur Company, traveled to remote areas themselves. Ashley was also known as the trader who employed many of the MOUNTAIN MEN early in their careers (see FUR TRADE).

Other organizations sponsored expeditions for the purpose of knowledge. Among these were the ROYAL SOCIETY and ROYAL GEOGRAPHICAL SOCIETY of England and the AMERICAN GEOGRAPHICAL SOCIETY of the United States, all three still in existence today, although now acting as disseminators of information and not as sponsors of expeditions. Another company, the AFRICAN ASSOCIATION, important in sponsoring early British expeditions to Africa, merged with the Royal Geographical Society. SIR JOSEPH BANKS, founder of the African Association, was a naturalist. SIR JOHN BARROW, founder of the Royal Geographical Society, had studied mathematics and geography before becoming second secretary of the Admiralty.

A Wife and a Newspaper Publisher

One sponsor of a number of expeditions—Englishwoman JANE FRANKLIN—did so out of loss. Her husband, SIR JOHN FRANKLIN, had departed for the Canadian Arctic in 1845. By 1848, with no word of him, she began raising support for privately funded expeditions. American shipping magnate Henry Grinnell became involved as a sponsor as well, backing a number of expeditions: under EDWIN JESSE DE HAVEN in 1850–51; ELISHA KENT KANE in 1853–55; and CHARLES FRANCIS HALL in 1860–62 and in 1864–69. An expedition Lady Franklin financed herself under SIR FRANCIS LEOPOLD McCLINTOCK in 1857–59 helped determine that her husband's ship had become icebound and that he and the entire crew had perished (see SEARCHES FOR MISSING EXPLORERS).

James Gordon Bennett, Jr., publisher of the American newspaper *New York Herald,* decided to back an expedition for the sake of a story when, in 1871, he sent out journalist

SIR HENRY MORTON STANLEY to search for missing Scottish missionary DAVID LIVINGSTONE. He sponsored subsequent explorations as well, such as that to the Arctic under GEORGE WASHINGTON DE LONG in 1879–81.

❖

It should be kept in mind that, although some voyages of exploration were conceived of and paid for by the travelers themselves, most of those affecting world history had sponsors. Gaining the sponsorship and raising the funds to mount expeditions were sagas in themselves. Italian Christopher Columbus, for example, had conceived of his expedition westward across the Atlantic years before he made the journey and had presented his plan to King John II of Portugal—and had sent his brother Bartholomew to do so to King Charles VII of France and King Henry VII of England—and had invested a great deal of time and resources before gaining the eventual support of Ferdinand and Isabella of Spain.

Sri Lanka   See CEYLON.

Strait of Anian   See ANIAN, STRAIT OF.

Strait of Gibraltar   See GIBRALTAR, STRAIT OF.

Strait of Magellan   See MAGELLAN, STRAIT OF.

submarine

A submarine is a water craft designed to spend substantial periods of time underwater. Unlike a SUBMERSIBLE, which is usually intended to make deep dives and collect a variety of scientific information, a submarine is more like a surface boat in its mobility. The development and use of the submarine has been closely tied to military objectives, although it did play a role in exploring the Arctic.

The earliest record of a submarine-type vessel comes from the writings of Olaf Magnus, a Swedish historian. He mentioned the capture of two underwater boats that the residents of GREENLAND had made in the early 16th century to attack European trading ships because of unfair practices. The underwater craft were enclosed with sealskin and had oars on either side for locomotion. Dutchman Cornelius van Drebbel built a similar vessel in 1620. He lived in England, where he built a submarine covered with leather, with six oars on each side, capable of diving to about 12 feet. His second submarine became well known as it traveled the Thames. King James I took a ride in it.

During the American Revolution of 1775–83, a submarine was invented by David Bushnell to sink British ships in New York Harbor. The *Turtle* was a single-person, egg-shaped craft moved by a propeller turned by the operator. On its first mission in 1776, Sergeant Ezra Lee could not affix an explosive device to the British flagship, the *Eagle,* because of a layer of copper used to protect the vessel from shipworms. Although it was spotted, the *Turtle* managed to escape British capture. It was then taken ashore and dismantled, remaining a secret until after the war. The first successful sinking of a ship by submarine occurred during the U.S. Civil War when the Confederate craft *Hunley,* using an explosive charge attached to a long pole, managed to sink the *Housatonic* on February 17, 1864. The explosion that sunk the *Housatonic* also took the *Hunley* and all her crew.

There were many attempts at building submarines in the 19th century. American Robert Fulton, inventor of the steamship, designed a vessel and won a contract with the French government to produce it. His 21-foot-long craft, the *Nautilus,* was built at Rouen, France. Fulton used water for ballast and compressed air for surfacing. The craft was operated successfully in 1800 and 1801, remaining submerged for six hours while fresh air was supplied by a tube from above, but it did not excite the French enough to continue the project. Englishman Reverend George William Garrett built the first steam-powered submarine in 1878. The ship given credit for being the first modern submarine was the *Gymnote,* built in France in 1886. It was cigar shaped, 60 feet long and 6 feet wide, and electrically powered. It could travel at five knots underwater to a distance of 100 miles. This vessel spurred England, Germany, and the United States to increase their efforts at submarine development.

The U.S. Navy contracted John Philip Holland in 1895 to build a state-of-the-art submarine. The first model he and his partner, Simon Lake, made did not fulfill the navy's expectations. Holland then produced a craft independently, which proved more useful. It was 54 feet long, had a crew of six, and used a dual-propulsion system—a gasoline engine for surface cruising and a battery-powered electric motor for underwater travel. In 1900, the U.S. Navy purchased it from Holland, naming it the *Holland.*

By World War I (1914–18), the United States, the United Kingdom, Germany, and Russia had all developed diesel-powered submarines, which operated on electrical batteries while underwater and could range across entire oceans. For a time, German U-boats (*Uterseeboot*) had the advantage until the Allied powers developed depth charges to counter them. Diesel-electric submarines, with improved torpedo designs, continued to play a significant role in naval battles of World War II (1939–45).

The idea of exploring the sea under the NORTH POLE by submarine is thought to have been first conceived by

French writer Jules Verne in his novel *20,000 Leagues Under the Sea,* published in 1870. This prospect fascinated SIR GEORGE HUBERT WILKINS, an Australian explorer who had been to the Arctic with VILHJALMUR STEFANSSON, and in the Antarctic with SIR ERNEST HENRY SHACKLETON. In 1930, Wilkins began modifications on the U.S. Navy submarine O-12 with Simon Lake and Commander Danenhower. The retrofitting included vertical drills for making holes in the ice. The rechristened *Nautilus* (the name taken from Verne's novel) sailed in June 1931. After accidents and mechanical problems, she arrived at the PACK ICE near Spitsbergen (present-day Svalbard), where the decision was made to proceed despite the mysterious disappearance of part of the diving apparatus. Wilkins and the *Nautilus* did not succeed in reaching the North Pole, for his craft was not powerful enough to penetrate the ice along its journey, but he did set a new record for farthest north, at 82 degrees.

Reaching the North Pole by submarine and breaking through the ice was more difficult and dangerous than had been imagined. The underwater surface of the pack ice varied greatly in thickness and terrain. Several technological advances came together to make it possible. One was the GYROCOMPASS, which minimized the effects of the submarine's steel hull on directional readings. Another was sonar (*sound na*vigation *r*anging), which could detect obstacles without visual information. A third advance was the invention of the nuclear submarine, championed by Admiral Hyman G. Rickover. The nuclear submarine could remain submerged for much longer periods than conventional craft, since nuclear reactors could move the large vessels quietly and efficiently and maintain the crew in relative comfort. In August 1958, another submarine named the *Nautilus,* the first nuclear submarine (built by the Electric Boat Company, which had been founded by John Philip Holland), succeeded in making the first undersea transit of the North Pole, cruising under the polar ice from Point Barrow, Alaska, to a point between Spitsbergen, Norway, and Greenland. On March 17, 1959, at the North Pole, another U.S. craft, the *Skate,* succeeded in breaking through a fairly thin layer of ice to the surface. There, the crew scattered the ashes of Hubert Wilkins, who had died the previous December.

Nuclear submarines have been used for other scientific missions. In the 1990s, for example, the U.S. Navy and

The *Nautilus,* the U.S. Navy's first atomic-powered submarine, is shown here on its initial sea trials in 1955. *(Library of Congress, Prints and Photographs Division [LC-USZ62-103120])*

civilian scientists conducted SCICEX (Scientific Ice Expeditions) under the polar ice, during which the Arctic Ocean floor was mapped, ice was measured, and water samples were analyzed.

See also OCEANOGRAPHY AND EXPLORATION; SHIPBUILDING AND EXPLORATION.

submersible

A submersible, or research submersible, is a specialized vehicle or station used to explore the ocean bottom. Many are designed for specific projects, and so they are often unique in their features and capabilities. Many are also designed to withstand extreme water pressure, which exists at great depths. A submersible differs from a SUBMARINE in having greater diving range but less mobility.

The development of submersibles relied on the construction of an apparatus that could resist water pressure while a person or persons made observations in an undersea environment. Americans CHARLES WILLIAM BEEBE, a biologist, and Otis Barton, an engineer, developed the BATHYSPHERE in 1926. They established various records for depth on several occasions, including a dive in 1934, when they came to the end of their cable at 3,028 feet. The BATHYSCAPH *Trieste II,* designed by Swiss physicist AUGUSTE PICCARD, was another important invention in the evolution of the submersible. In January 1960, it reached the greatest depth in the ocean at 35,800 feet in the MARIANAS TRENCH.

With the success of the *Trieste II,* the ultimate challenge of the ocean had been met, but it was not necessary for all craft to explore the greatest depths. Auguste Piccard and his son, JACQUES ERNEST-JEAN PICCARD, also designed a mesoscaphe for diving to 6,000 feet. The mesoscaphe used propellers like a helicopter to maintain its depth. In 1959, JACQUES-YVES COUSTEAU designed and built a two-man diving saucer. His vehicle was limited to a depth of 1,000 feet but was well suited to exploring the continental shelf due to its excellent maneuverability.

The *Aluminaut* was one of the largest mobile submersibles ever produced. Designed to operate to 15,000 feet, the 51-foot vehicle incorporated durable construction with a buoyancy system similar to that of a submarine. It was built by the General Dynamics Corporation for the Reynolds Aluminum Company and carried a crew of six. Perhaps the most well-known submersible is the R.V. *Alvin.* Based at the Woods Hole Oceanographic Institute, *Alvin* has proven to be a flexible and effective research tool with a long life. In 1966, both the *Aluminaut* and *Alvin* participated in the successful recovery of a hydrogen bomb, which the U.S. military had lost off the coast of Spain. In 1974, *Alvin,* along with two French submersibles, the *Archimede* and the *Cyana,* conducted Project FAMOUS (French-American

Mid-Ocean Undersea Study). This project explored the Mid-Atlantic Ridge, diving as deep as 9,000 feet. It was the most extensive study of a region of the ocean floor to date, finding evidence of recent volcanic activity and support for theories of seafloor spreading.

Along with moving underwater craft, submersibles may be stationary structures from which saturation diving may occur. These are also known as research habitats or habitat projects. Not all of them are designed for great depths either; in fact, most function at less than 60 feet. The pioneering work in this field has been carried out by the U.S. Department of the Interior with the Tektite project. Tektite I was conducted in 1969 off St. John in the Virgin Islands and experimented with an artificial atmosphere and its physiological effects on divers over the course of several weeks. Later, the Sealab missions were also in this category, with Sealab III operating at more than 500 feet.

The 1960s were the heyday for submersibles, with many projects developed. In the 1970s, many of the tools that had been developed for scientific purposes were bought by commercial interests and the military. Today, submersibles are mainly used for oil exploration, defense, and underwater archaeology, including the study and recovery of sunken ships. The cost of operating a submersible is high since most vehicles require that ballast be replaced after each dive and that a support ship and crew accompany them. The trend has been toward smaller, unmanned probes operated by remote control—remotely operated vehicles (ROVs).

See also ARCHAEOLOGY AND EXPLORATION; OCEANOGRAPHY AND EXPLORATION.

surveying and exploration

Surveying is the accurate measurement of Earth's surface or just beneath it. A branch of applied mathematics, it determines position, dimension, and contour of land areas through linear or angular measurements based on principles of geometry and trigonometry. The results of a survey are typically represented on a chart, map, GLOBE, or plans (see MAPS AND CHARTS). Many explorers were trained in surveying methods, and many exploratory expeditions had the primary or secondary purpose of surveying.

Techniques of Surveying

There are two basic types of surveying: land and hydrographic. Land surveying is further subdivided into plane surveying and geodetic surveying. In plane surveying, a small portion of Earth's surface, in which Earth's curvature is negligible, is treated as a horizontal plane. Plane surveys are usually calculated on a rectangular grid, aligned north-south and east-west. Two methods of measurement are utilized, depending on the type of terrain to be surveyed: In a traverse survey, the directions (bearings) and distances of successive lines are calculated; in triangulation, an area is divided into hypothetical triangles from a known baseline, that is, the position of a third point is determined by the angle it makes with each end of the baseline. Geodetic surveying, or geodesy, is used for larger areas where the curved shape of Earth, the geoid, must be taken into consideration. Two points, or stations, many miles apart are selected, and the LATITUDE AND LONGITUDE of each is determined astronomically, creating a baseline from where triangulation can be applied. Hydrographic surveying deals with bodies of water—seas, rivers, harbors, and lakes—and coastlines. Soundings from control points are carried out by hand, sonar soundings, or radar. The findings—bottom contours, channels, shoals, and buoys—are recorded on charts for purposes of navigation.

Other subgroups of surveying are classified according to purpose or methods. As for purpose, topographic surveying determines the contour of the land—or relief—through both horizontal and vertical measurements (three-dimensional traversing). Cartographic surveying is used for the specific purpose of making maps. Engineering surveying, construction surveying, route surveying, and mine surveying are other applied types of surveying. Terms such as *transit surveying, plane-table surveying,* and *photogrammetic surveying* (using photography) refer to methods of surveying.

Surveying equipment ranges from simple measuring tools to electronic devices. Instruments used for direct linear measurements include the COMPASS, Gunter's chain (or surveyor's chain), the tape, the rod, the plumb bob, the level, and the telescope. The compass enables a surveyor to determine directions. A chain is the standard unit of length or measuring band used in surveying, equivalent to 66 feet. Gunter's chain, named after its inventor, Edmund Gunter, a 16th–17th-century English mathematician, is divided into 100 links, as is the alternative engineer's chain. The calibrated tape has largely replaced the chain. The rod, with marked gradations, allows for a sighting from a specially designed telescope. The plumb bob—a weight on a line—enables the determination of a vertical line. The level enables the determination of a horizontal line; early levels used a bubble of water centered in a glass tube. The plane table is an early measuring device, consisting of a drawing board mounted on a tripod, with a ruler for pointing at objects, allowing for the plotting of lines directly from observations. The first telescope designed specifically for surveying was known as a theodolite and consisted of a telescope that could swing vertically. A variation, the transit theodolite—also known as the transit compass or simply the transit—can be transited (rotated) about both horizontal and vertical axes. Transits are tripod-mounted and have leveling devices, such as the spirit-level bubble, and magnetic compasses on them. Various electronic instruments are now also utilized to determine distances in surveying, such as the geodimeter,

which uses light waves, and the tellurometer, which uses microwaves. Photography is also used in surveying, especially AERIAL PHOTOGRAPHY.

History of Surveying

Surveying dates from ancient times and has played a part in marking boundaries in many societies. It was highly developed among the ancient Egyptians (see EGYPTIAN EXPLORATION). In the fourth century B.C., bematists, or surveyors, traveled with ALEXANDER THE GREAT's army into Asia, measuring their progress. During their occupation of Egypt starting in 30 B.C., the Romans acquired Egyptian surveying instruments, knowledge of which passed to other peoples (see ROMAN EXPLORATION). Many explorers were trained surveyors, and many surveyors went on to other professions as well. The first and the third presidents of the United States, George Washington and Thomas Jefferson, for example, both worked as surveyors as young men.

Many maritime expeditions included men trained as surveyors who charted coastlines. Some surveying expeditions were sent out as follow-ups to other expeditions: In his expedition of 1579–80, PEDRO SARMIENTO DE GAMBOA, a Spanish mariner also trained as a scientist, surveyed the Strait of Magellan (see MAGELLAN, STRAIT OF), which had been reached by a Spanish expedition earlier that century under FERDINAND MAGELLAN. Surveying is central to the story of other maritime expeditions. English mariner JOHN KNIGHT, during a 1601 expedition in search of the NORTHWEST PASSAGE for the BRITISH EAST INDIA COMPANY, disappeared after going ashore with a surveying party on the Atlantic coast of Labrador. The first official U.S. government CIRCUMNAVIGATION OF THE WORLD in 1838–42 under CHARLES WILKES and GEORGE FOSTER EMMONS was known as the United States South Sea Surveying and Exploring Expedition.

As for the exploration of land areas, many official surveys were carried out in the 19th century. Many of the most famous explorers of Australia's interior were surveyors. Both JOHN JOSEPH WILLIAM MOLESWORTH OXLEY and SIR THOMAS LIVINGSTONE MITCHELL served as surveyor general of New South Wales. Brothers SIR AUGUSTUS CHARLES GREGORY and FRANCIS THOMAS GREGORY were surveyors, as were JOHN MCDOUALL STUART and JOHN FORREST. In India, first the British East India Company, then the British government, sponsored the Great Trigonometrical Survey, headed for a time by SIR GEORGE EVEREST. After India had been surveyed and mapped, the PUNDITS, locally born emissaries, surveyed parts of Tibet and other lands to the north.

In the United States, a number of official expeditions were sent out starting in the 1830s. JOHN CHARLES FRÉMONT and JOSEPH NICOLAS NICOLLET headed such early expeditions. Subsequent surveys, from the late 1840s to the

This photograph by William Henry Jackson shows expedition members of the U.S. Geological and Geographical Survey of the Territories in the 1870s. Ferdinand V. Hayden sits at the far end of the table. *(National Archives, Photographs [NWDNS-57-HS-282])*

late 1870s, especially to establish wagon routes and railroads, were carried out by the U.S. Army Corps of Topographical Engineers and other branches of the military under a number of officers, including RANDOLPH BARNES MARCY, JAMES HERVEY SIMPSON, HOWARD STANSBURY, LORENZO SITGREAVES, JOHN WILLIAM GUNNISON, AMIEL WEEKS WHIPPLE, EDWARD GRIFFIN BECKWITH, JOHN GRUBB PARKE, JOHN B. POPE, HENRY LARCOM ABBOTT, JOSEPH CHRISTMAS IVES, EDWARD FITZGERALD BEALE, JOHN N. MACOMB, WILLIAM FRANKLIN RAYNOLDS, GEORGE MONTAGUE WHEELER, and DAVID SLOAN STANLEY. (Mojave Indian chief IRATEBA served as a guide for Sitgreaves, Whipple, and Ives.) The U.S. government also sponsored geological surveying

under FERDINAND VANDEVEER HAYDEN, CLARENCE KING, and JOHN WESLEY POWELL.

Some of the later African explorations that gained new geographic knowledge were sent out as surveys, such as in the SAHARA DESERT by Frenchmen PAUL-XAVIER FLATTERS in 1880–81 and FERNAND FOUREAU in 1900–01.

Also in the 20th century, much of the Arctic and Antarctic came to be surveyed, especially through the use of aerial photography. RICHARD EVELYN BYRD, LINCOLN ELLSWORTH, and SIR GEORGE HUBERT WILKINS were aviators who conducted aerial surveys of these regions.

See also GEOGRAPHY AND CARTOGRAPHY; NAVIGATION AND EXPLORATION.

T

Tasmania

Tasmania lies 150 miles off the southeast coast of Australia. Bass Strait separates the two landmasses. To the west and south is the Indian Ocean; to the east is the Tasman Sea, an arm of the Pacific Ocean. An island of 26,383 square miles, Tasmania is associated with a number of smaller islands, most important is the Furneaux Group, situated to the northeast. The terrain of Tasmania is mountainous, its highlands a geological continuation of Australia's GREAT DIVIDING RANGE. Mount Ossa, rising 5,305 feet from a central plateau, is Tasmania's highest peak. Coastal plains are found in the northwest and northeast. Southern and western regions are especially exposed to ocean winds and heavy rain. The Tasmanian devil and the Tasmanian wolf (also called Tasmanian tiger), both marsupials (pouched mammals), are found on the island.

Dutchman ABEL TASMAN made the European discovery of Tasmania. While searching for the GREAT SOUTHERN CONTINENT (Terra Australis), under the sponsorship of the DUTCH EAST INDIA COMPANY, he sighted land on November 24, 1642. Difficult seas prevented him from landing, but he managed to send the ship's carpenter ashore to perform the rites of possession. Tasman named the territory Van Diemen's Land after the governor-general of the EAST INDIES. (It was renamed Tasmania in 1853.)

The island was not visited again by Europeans until 1773, when Englishman TOBIAS FURNEAUX explored part of its coastline as captain of the *Adventure* on JAMES COOK's second British expedition to the Pacific in 1772–74. Separated from Cook aboard the *Resolution,* Furneaux made the European discovery of Adventure Bay on the south coast, one of the finest anchorages in the world. Furneaux incorrectly concluded that Tasmania was part of mainland Australia. In 1798, MATTHEW FLINDERS and GEORGE BASS, also sailing for England, circumnavigated the island. Flinders named the waterway between the island and Australia Bass Strait. In 1791–94, a French expedition under ANTOINE-RAYMOND-JOSEPH DE BRUNI, chevalier d'Entrecasteaux surveyed the south coast. PHILIP PARKER KING conducted surveys of coastal Australia and Tasmania in his British expedition of 1817–22.

Great Britain, which had claimed the island in 1788, sent an 18-year-old lieutenant by the name of John Bowen there to establish a penal colony in 1803. Tasmania became known as the "jail of the Empire." The European population of the island grew, and, by 1825, the city of Hobart at the mouth of the Derwent River had become as large as Sydney, Australia. The island also became a way station for the colonization of New South Wales, the southeastern region of Australia. The Van Diemen's Land Company sponsored the exploration of the interior of Tasmania. Among those working for it was Danish mariner JORGEN JORGENSON in the 1820s–30s. In 1840–42, Polish geologist SIR PAUL EDMUND DE STRZELECKI engaged in explorations of the interior, some of them sponsored by SIR JOHN FRANKLIN, then governor of the colony. Another scientist who explored

Tasmania was British naturalist SIR JOSEPH DALTON HOOKER who, as part of SIR JAMES CLARK ROSS's expedition to southern waters in 1839–43, made an inventory of the island's plant life.

Tasmania's Aborigines are thought to have crossed to the island by way of a LAND BRIDGE more than 35,000 years ago. They numbered about 5,000 when Europeans arrived. A tribal people, probably of Melanesian stock, they had a remarkable relationship with their environment, which bordered on the magical when viewed through the eyes of the European observer. CHARLES ROBERT DARWIN commented on their powers of camouflage when he visited the island in 1836, during his travels on the *Beagle*. With increasing European settlement, they were driven from ancestral lands and systematically persecuted. The Aborigines retaliated against the settlers on a number of occasions, and, in 1830, the British began an offensive to isolate them once and for all. They were removed to Flinders Island, part of the Furneaux Group, where the population languished. Later, some were allowed to return, but, in 1876, the last of the Tasmanian Aborigines died.

In 1901, with Australian independence from Great Britain, Tasmania was federated as a state of the Australian Commonwealth. Its capital is Hobart.

See also AUSTRALIA, EXPLORATION OF.

Terra Australis See GREAT SOUTHERN CONTINENT.

Thule See ULTIMA THULE.

Timbuktu (Timbuctoo, Tombouctou, Tombuto)

The city of Timbuktu is in the West African country of Mali. It sits on the southern edge of the SAHARA DESERT, just to the north of the great bend of the NIGER RIVER. In the latter half of the Middle Ages, Timbuktu was at its peak as a center of trade. Guarded to the north by Muslims and insulated to the west and south by thick jungle and African tribes, Timbuktu was inaccessible to Europeans. Still, information of the city made it to Europe, with exaggerated descriptions of wealth. Such stories made Timbuktu a destination for explorers, long after its glory had faded. The name of the city has been variously spelled as Tombouctou, Timbuctoo, and Tombuto.

Timbuktu was founded in the 11th century by the Tuareg, a nomadic Berber people of the Sahara who practiced Islam, yet retained vestiges of their earlier tribal religion. As a place to meet and trade on the Saharan camel caravan routes, the city grew and was eventually incorporated into the Mali Empire in the 14th century. During this period it prospered, as salt was brought from the north and ex-changed for gold from the west. The earliest mention of the lands that would become Mali come from Greek historian HERODOTUS in the fifth century B.C. He mentions the "Silent Trade," a curious practice that endured through the 15th century, when it was described by Italian navigator ALVISE DA CADAMOSTO. He related how the Moors brought salt across the Sahara from the north to the middlemen of Mali. From Mali, the salt traveled to the fringes of the gold-mining regions, where the blocks of salt were left in a known location while the traders of Mali retreated and built a fire. The smoke from the fire alerted the Wangara, who mined the gold, and a quantity of the metal was placed on each salt block. After the Wangara had disappeared, the Malinese returned, and if the payment was deemed acceptable, the gold was taken and the salt left. If not, the gold and salt were left for the bargaining to continue.

Food, copper, textiles, and slaves were traded as well. Later, as part of the Songhai Empire in the 15th and 16th centuries, Timbuktu reached its height of prosperity with a population of as many as 1 million. It also became a center of Muslim education. The first of various raids and plunder by neighboring peoples occurred in 1591, beginning the city's economic and cultural decline.

Arab traveler ABU ABD ALLAH MUHAMMAD IBN BATTUTAH's reports of Timbuktu from a visit in 1352 are among the earliest to have survived. Over a century later, in 1458, DIOGO GOMES was exploring the Gambia River for Portugal and brought back news of the city from his contact with native peoples. Based on his travels of 1512–14, Arab LEO AFRICANUS wrote a vivid description of the busy city. He told of large quantities of gold possessed by the king; a cavalry of 3,000; an educated class of doctors, priests, and judges; artisans who sold their handiwork; and slaves taken as tribute from surrounding lands.

The European expeditions in search of Timbuktu began with Englishman DANIEL HOUGHTON in 1790. Traveling for the AFRICAN ASSOCIATION, he began his journey from the Gambia River and made it inland 400 miles before being robbed and left to die by an Arab caravan. Scotsman MUNGO PARK came closer on a trip in 1795, most likely sighting the city as he sailed down the Niger in 1806. But he did not live to tell about it. In 1825, Scotsman ALEXANDER GORDON LAING led an expedition from the north across the Sahara, which reached Timbuktu in August 1826. He was the first European confirmed to have seen the city. He also died on the return journey, however.

RENÉ-AUGUSTE CAILLIÉ was the first person from Europe to reach Timbuktu and return to describe it. The son of a baker in France, Caillié became fascinated with Africa while young. In 1816, at age 17, he found work on a ship bound for Africa, and deserted his post once he got there to join an expedition in search of Mungo Park. In 1825, the Geographical Society of Paris offered a prize of 10,000 francs for the first person to visit Timbuktu and report on the city. Caillié, who was in Sierra Leone at the time, was determined to win the prize. In 1827, after preparing himself by learning Arabic, he departed Freetown on the west coast and proceeded eastward. On April 20, 1828, he reached Timbuktu. In Paris, where he claimed the prize, he described Timbuktu as mud houses surrounded by yellow sand and no longer a political or economic power.

Another explorer of note who sought Timbuktu was Scotsman HUGH CLAPPERTON, who, in 1825, investigated the Niger to the west with the hope of reaching the city. He died of dysentery in the city of Sokoto before he could fulfill his ambition. In 1853, German scholar HEINRICH BARTH reached Timbuktu while on an extensive tour of Africa and spent nine months studying the peoples. Another German, OSKAR LENZ, also was a visitor to Timbuktu, which he reached on his 1879–80 expedition. A colonial French army occupied Timbuktu in 1893–94.

Timbuktu, as it has been for centuries, is a regional trade center, with salt a principal commodity.

See also AFRICA, EXPLORATION OF; MUSLIM EXPLORATION.

trade winds

The trade winds are the basic wind systems in the Atlantic, the Pacific, and the Indian Oceans in both the Northern Hemisphere and Southern Hemisphere. In the Northern Hemisphere, they circulate in a clockwise direction, while in the Southern Hemisphere they move counterclockwise. Trade winds form in the subtropical regions known as the horse latitudes (between 25 and 30 degrees) to the north and south of the EQUATOR, regions of high pressure. Their direction is determined by the Coriolis effect (or Coriolis force or Coriolis acceleration, an apparent force on winds, clouds, and aircraft because of the rotation of the Earth under them, such that their motion is deflected clockwise in the Northern Hemisphere and counterclockwise in the Southern Hemisphere, although speed is unaffected). This gives the winds an angular component of approximately 20 degrees.

Among the most positive aspects of the trade winds, as far as sailors were concerned, is their predictability. Their direction remains fairly constant throughout the seasons, with only a slight shift to the north during summer in the Northern Hemisphere. Their constancy gives them the primary influence they have on ocean currents.

Winds are named for the direction from which they originate, and so, off the coast of the Iberian Peninsula are the northeast trades. These were the winds Italian mariner CHRISTOPHER COLUMBUS, sailing for Spain in the 1490s, used to convey his ships to the Caribbean Sea.

A major exception to the trade winds system occurs seasonally in the Indian Ocean. There, with the Indian subcontinent heated during the summer, the moist air from the Tropics is drawn to the land. The trade winds are supplanted by the monsoon winds, and the direction of the wind is reversed. This phenomenon was observed in ancient times, and used to advantage by Arab sailors, who would time their travels accordingly. When Portuguese VASCO DA GAMA made the first European journey to India in 1497–99, he hired a pilot in Africa who insisted on waiting for the monsoon winds before proceeding eastward.

traverse board

In the 15th to 17th centuries, the word *traverse* was a nautical term meaning to tack or to change the direction of a vessel when heading close into the wind (or beating to windward), thus making a zigzag course because sailing directly into the wind is impossible. The traverse board became an important device in early navigation because it enabled a navigator to keep track of the direction and speed a vessel sails. It consists of a small wooden board in the shape of a COMPASS with directions marked on it and eight holes for each half hour of the watch. At its rectangular base are other holes laid out in horizontal lines.

It was the responsibility of the officer of the watch to stick a peg into the compass holes every half hour (or sometimes every hour) to record each of the courses sailed, and stick a peg into the other holes to record the estimated speed during each course based on the process of DEAD RECKONING. The courses and calculated distances were then recorded on a chart.

An accomplished English navigator, JOHN DAVIS of the late 16th century, who also invented the Davis QUADRANT, designed a traverse book, or deck log, which served the same purpose as the traverse board. It is in the form of a ship's log or journal with a column for time spent on each course, a column for calculated distance of each watch, a column for observations of the Sun, and a column for additional comments. One also sees the term *traverse table* in texts describing early navigational tools, including Davis's traverse book. It is also used in a general sense to describe a table giving the difference of latitude and departure that corresponds to any given course and distance.

See also LATITUDE AND LONGITUDE; NAVIGATION AND EXPLORATION.

treasure and exploration

The quest for treasure is a recurring theme in the saga of world exploration. Discovering precious metals and stones in foreign lands, raiding shipping routes established by other nations, and reaching newly discovered goldfields have all been an incentive for numerous expeditions.

Ancient Treasure-Hunting

Gold, silver, and gemstones have been a standard of wealth from ancient times. The ancient Egyptians sought riches in distant lands, as indicated by Egyptian queen HATSHEPSUT's expedition down the RED SEA to the land of PUNT in the 15th century B.C. (see EGYPTIAN EXPLORATION). Her envoys returned with gold and silver among other desired items, such as spices, incenses, and exotic animals (another form of treasure in ancient times). The Egyptians developed mining as central to their economy to the point that they had a papyrus map—dated to about 1300 B.C.—showing the location of all the gold mines in their empire. The Bible's Old Testament tells of OPHIR, the location of "King Solomon's mines."

Conquest and plunder go hand in hand, and civilizations preyed on one another for treasure. ALEXANDER THE GREAT led his armies from Macedon and Greece to North Africa and Asia in the fourth century B.C. and plundered the riches of many different peoples. Numerous expeditions of the Romans, such as those against the Carthaginians in North Africa in the third and second centuries B.C., or those led by GAIUS JULIUS CAESAR into northern Europe in the first century B.C., brought booty from conquered peoples and helped pay for new expeditions (see ROMAN EXPLORATION). The first confirmed historical reference to diamonds occurs in first-century A.D. Roman literature, and it assumed they came from the mines of Golconda in India, the only source of the stones at the time.

Spain's Plunder of the Americas

Discovering treasure provided justification for military and exploratory expeditions. In the course of his late 15th-century voyage to the Americas, the acquisition of gold became an early focus for CHRISTOPHER COLUMBUS, an Italian mariner sailing for Spain, after he failed to reach the Orient. By trading gold to Columbus's men, the Arawak (Taino) tribe, led by GUANCANAGARI, raised the first expectations of finding gold in those lands newly visited by Europeans.

Columbus failed to make a fortune in his explorations, but the Spanish soon did so in other parts of the Americas. The Spanish conquest of the Aztec and Inca Indians under HERNÁN CORTÉS and FRANCISCO PIZARRO respectively in the first half of the 16th century led to a redistribution of great wealth between continents. By that time, the Aztec and Inca had accumulated vast amounts of gold and silver through mining or by exacting tribute from peoples they themselves had conquered and had shaped the precious metals into exquisite objects. BERNAZ DÍAZ DEL CASTILLO, a firsthand witness, described the Aztec wealth and the Spanish plunder of it in his history of the conquest of New Spain, published in 1632, long after his death. The Aztec and Inca also used gemstones in their ornamental objects and jewelry, including jade, obsidian glass, crystal, turquoise, and emeralds.

The Spanish CONQUISTADORES appropriated the precious metals and gemstones. They melted down most of the gold and silver artwork into ingots for shipping back to Europe, where it was given to King Charles I of Spain (Holy Roman Emperor Charles V). The Spanish also took control of the mines in the lands they had conquered, using Native American labor. Other mines were sought and developed. For example, in 1545, silver was discovered in the ANDES MOUNTAINS of southern Bolivia. The next year, the town of Potosí in what is now Bolivia was founded and eventually became the world's leading silver center, with a population of some 150,000. The flow of precious metals from the Americas to Europe shaped world economy for years to come, with Spain becoming the richest and most powerful nation and building its overseas empire (see COMMERCE AND EXPLORATION). The wealth helped pay for continuing explorations and continuing exploitation of colonies (see COLONIZATION AND EXPLORATION).

Treasure Fleets

The transport of treasure also shaped maritime history. A complicated trading route was developed by Spain's Indies Bureau of Trade, a government office founded in 1503. The route was maintained for more than two centuries, from 1530 to 1792. A royal fleet of ships—of the GALLEON-type vessel, designed to carry heavy cargoes or armaments—sailed from Spain every year with European items. In the Americas, it separated into three smaller fleets and spread out, delivering its goods at various ports. One group eventually reached Portobello in present-day Panama and picked up silver from Peru (shipped there by way of the Pacific Ocean, then carried by mule to the Atlantic coast). Its next stop was Cartagena in present-day Colombia to collect emeralds from Colombia, gold from Ecuador, and pearls from Venezuela. A second group sailed to Veracruz, where it picked up gold and silver from Mexico, and spices, silks, and porcelain from China (shipped to Acapulco in Mexico via the Philippines on the Manila Galleon—an annual fleet established in the 1580s—then transported overland to the Atlantic coast). A third, smaller group traveled to Trujillo in present-day Dominican Republic to receive indigo dye. The fleet met up in Havana in present-day Cuba, the departure point back to Spain.

Sailing in numbers helped protect shipping against PIRACY. Some of the raids on treasure ships were carried out by PRIVATEERS, sanctioned by governments. English privateers, including SIR FRANCIS DRAKE in the 16th century and WILLIAM DAMPIER in the 17th century, raided Spanish ships in both the Atlantic and Pacific. Pirates based in the Caribbean as well as on the BARBARY COAST of North Africa were active well into the 19th century.

Legendary Lands

The Spanish sponsored many more expeditions throughout much of the Americas, hoping to locate treasure on a par with that of the Aztec and Inca. Various expeditions fanned out from Spanish holdings in Aztec and Inca territory, eventually to North America as well. In the early 1540s, HERNANDO DE SOTO led the first extensive expedition in the American Southeast, seeking treasure. At the same time, FRANCISCO VÁSQUEZ DE CORONADO explored much of the American Southwest and the southern plains. Legends of wealthy cities and lands—that of EL DORADO in South America and the Seven Cities of CIBOLA and QUIVIRA in North America—spurred on these explorers as well as those of other nations. Such legends typically involved treasure (see LEGENDS AND EXPLORATION). A pattern emerged in which Native American tribes described rich tribal lands elsewhere as a tactic to rid themselves of the outsiders.

A comparable legend surrounding the mythical PRESTER JOHN took shape in the 12th century as that of a Christian ruler of a kingdom in Asia who might offer help to European nations against Muslims. But it expanded by the 14th century into that of a ruler of an extravagantly wealthy kingdom in Africa, where gold and gemstones were bounteous.

The French sought a land known as SAGUENAY in what is now Canada in the early 16th century. Their dreams of Native American treasure led to JACQUES CARTIER's mistakenly believing that iron pyrites were gold, leading to the alternate name for the mineral, FOOL'S GOLD. Later in the century, Englishman SIR MARTIN FROBISHER, exploring for England, brought a sample of fool's gold back from Baffin Island in northern Canada, believing it to be gold, leading to the organization of the CATHAY COMPANY and expeditions to mine the valueless ore.

Gold Rushes

Another phenomenon related to treasure and exploration is that of gold rushes, the travel to areas where gold has been discovered. New routes were explored and established to remote places. The California Gold Rush of 1849, the Colorado (Pikes Peak) Gold Rush of 1858–59, and the

THE WAY THEY GO TO CALIFORNIA.

This cartoon satirizes the frenzy in obtaining passage to California during the gold rush of 1849. (Library of Congress, Prints and Photographs Division [LC-USZ62-104557])

This photograph shows miners heading for the Klondike gold fields by way of Chilcoot Pass, Alaska, in 1898. *(Library of Congress, Prints and Photographs Division [LC-USZ62-057312])*

Klondike Gold Rush to the Yukon Territory and Alaska of 1896–98 helped lead to the opening of parts of North America. Similarly, the discovery of gold on other continents—in wilderness areas north of Rio de Janeiro in Brazil in the late 17th century, in New South Wales and Victoria in Australia in 1851, in Western Australia in the 1880s, and in Witwatersrand in South Africa in 1884—has also led to migrations of peoples and a redrawing of the world map. And the discovery of other precious minerals or stones—such as diamonds in Brazil in 1726 and South Africa in 1866—led to movements of peoples and the opening of new regions.

tropic of Cancer

The tropic of Cancer is a parallel of latitude, a cartographic feature based on natural phenomena, 23°27' north of the EQUATOR. On a representation of the world, it delineates the farthest point north at which the Sun can be seen directly overhead at noon, the Sun's rays striking the Earth vertically. This event happens one day a year: the summer solstice in the Northern Hemisphere, on or about June 22.

The tropic of Cancer marks the northern boundary of the tropical, or torrid, zone, as separate from the north temperate zone. The imaginary line crosses the SAHARA DESERT in Africa, central India, southern China, the Pacific Ocean north of Hawaii, Mexico, and the Caribbean Sea.

The name *Cancer,* from the Latin word for "crab," was originally applied to one of 12 astrological constellations. In the second century B.C., Greek astronomer HIPPARCHUS observed that, on the summer solstice in the Northern Hemisphere, the Sun appeared to be within the boundaries of the Cancer sector of the zodiac. The first European expedition to reach the tropic of Cancer was under Portuguese AFONSO GONÇALVES BALDAYA in 1436.

See also GEOGRAPHY AND CARTOGRAPHY; LATITUDE AND LONGITUDE; MAPS AND CHARTS.

tropic of Capricorn

The tropic of Capricorn is a parallel of latitude, a cartographic feature based on natural phenomena, 23°27' south of the EQUATOR. On a representation of the world, it delineates the farthest point south at which the Sun can be seen directly overhead at noon, the Sun's rays striking the Earth vertically. This event happens one day a year: the summer solstice in the Southern Hemisphere, on or about December 22.

The tropic of Capricorn marks the southern boundary of the tropical (or torrid) climatic zone, as separate from the south temperate zone. The imaginary line crosses southern Africa, the island of Madagascar, the Indian Ocean, central Australia, the Pacific Ocean south of Tonga, and south-central South America.

The name *Capricorn,* from the Latin words *caper,* for "goat," and *cornu,* for "horn," was originally applied to one of 12 astrological constellations. In the second century B.C., Greek astronomer HIPPARCHUS observed that, on the winter solstice in the Northern Hemisphere (that is, the summer solstice in the Southern Hemisphere), the Sun appeared to be within the boundaries of the Capricorn sector of the zodiac.

See also GEOGRAPHY AND CARTOGRAPHY; LATITUDE AND LONGITUDE; MAPS AND CHARTS.

Turkey Company   See LEVANT COMPANY.

U

Ultima Thule

Ultima Thule is a phrase coined by Roman scholar PLINY THE ELDER in the first century A.D. to describe the northernmost land that could be reached by humankind. His information was based on the travels of Greek scholar PYTHEAS, who reportedly explored Arctic waters in the fourth century B.C.

Pytheas was a remarkable figure, not only for being perhaps the first Arctic explorer, but also for his scientific accomplishments. His first endeavors were in astronomy and geography, including the calculation of the latitude of his city to an accuracy of half a percent. Yet his geographic findings were met with skepticism for centuries after his death. His most vigorous detractor was Greek geographer STRABO of the first and second centuries A.D., who accused him of spreading untruths. History has been much kinder to Pytheas than Strabo was. Much of what Pytheas observed has been verified. Unfortunately, Pytheas's account of his journey, *On the Ocean,* has not survived. The sources that have come down are quotes and paraphrases from those ancients who had access to his work, many of them his critics.

The voyage that Pytheas made, in about 325 B.C., was probably financed by the merchants of Massilia (present-day Marseilles), a bustling trading town on what is now France's south coast. His mission was to find the source of tin and amber in the north, which had previously been carried overland, or on the ships of Carthaginians, who made handsome profits through their control of the sea-lanes (see CARTHA-GINIAN EXPLORATION). Pytheas managed to navigate past the Strait of Gibraltar (see GIBRALTAR, STRAIT OF) into the Atlantic Ocean and head northward in his GALLEY or galleys, eventually reaching the British Isles. The people of England had experience in mining tin and gathering amber. They regularly traded with foreigners, and Pytheas was given a friendly reception.

In the course of his commercial transactions, Pytheas was told of the northern land of Thule. The etymology of the word remains the subject of great debate and numerous theories. Among them is the Old Saxon word *Thyle,* meaning "boundary" or "limit" as the root word. The Gothic word *Tiule* has a similar meaning. There are even words of Nordic origin, which mean "sun" or "darkness," which could have given rise to the name *Thule.*

The time for travel to Thule was said to be six days from the north of Britain. Considering such a journey feasible, Pytheas set off to find it. There are few details of the land itself, but the observations he made confirm that he approached or even crossed the ARCTIC CIRCLE. First, he mentions visiting a place where the Sun never sets, indicating northern latitudes. He also describes an ocean where the elements mix into a thick substance he calls "sea lung." This was the source of much ridicule by Strabo. Yet such a description is consistent with the PACK ICE, frothy water agitated by the wind and dense fog of northern waters. It was the ice that stopped Pytheas, forcing a return southward.

The actual location of Thule continues to be argued, and with little hope of resolution. There are three major theories. The 19th–20th-century Norwegian explorer FRIDTJOF NANSEN supported the idea that Thule was Norway. In his scholarly work *In Northern Mists,* he uses a process of elimination to persuade the reader of this point of view. A second theory, that Thule was ICELAND, has the largest number of supporters. Although this is the most southern location of the three, the distance of six days sail from England is consistent with its location, and the pack ice would certainly have presented problems for the ancient explorer. The third theory names Jan Mayen Island as Thule's location. The location of this island is certainly far enough to the north, but the conditions of the ocean would most likely have been too severe for the ships of Pytheas's expedition. Others name the Shetland Islands off the coast of Scotland, but this is a less likely choice because of its more southerly location.

Today, there exists a town of Thule on the northwest coast of GREENLAND. The Danish-Inuit (Eskimo) explorer KNUD JOHAN VICTOR RASMUSSEN established a scientific observatory there that has evolved into the most important military base of the United States on Greenland. The mystery of Ultima Thule receded over the centuries as humankind pushed to the NORTH POLE.

See also LEGENDS AND EXPLORATION.

V

Van Diemen's Land   See TASMANIA.

Viking exploration

The people known as Vikings were actually a number of different Scandinavian peoples of northern Europe—ancient Danes, Norwegians, and Swedes related in their Germanic language and culture—who have come to be identified as one for a period of their history. During the Middle Ages, from about 800 to 1100, they traveled widely as traders, raiders, and settlers. They became known by other names in other parts of Europe, including Norsemen (from North-men), and were feared as warriors. *Viking* in fact means "warrior." Much of what is known about the Vikings comes from medieval literature of other European peoples, as well as from their own literature—the Norse sagas—accounts of historical events celebrating their heroic past, including exploratory sea voyages—which the Scandinavians began writing after adopting Christianity and writing in the Roman alphabet in addition to their traditional runic writing. These sagas, once thought to be legends, have proven to be accounts of real events, based on archaeological evidence.

Scandinavian peoples lived in small, scattered villages, and practiced farming, fishing, and hunting. With extensive coastlines in their homelands containing numerous fjords, they used the sea for fishing and trade and for raiding to capture slaves. They developed the LONGSHIP, a type of GALLEY, propelled primarily by oars but with a single sail used in some winds. The *drakkar* (or *lanskip,* for "longship") was the warship, and the *knörr* (or *hafskip* for "halfship"), shorter and much deeper in draught, the voyaging and cargo ship. The knörr especially was sturdy and enabled the Vikings to travel in open seas (see SHIPBUILDING AND EXPLORATION). During what is referred to as the Viking age, Scandinavian mariners were the most skilled navigators and traveled farther than any other people (see NAVIGATION AND EXPLORATION).

Living in the extreme north of Europe, Scandinavians had not been conquered by the Romans, nor, during the Viking age, had they yet come under Christian influence. Rather, they practiced their traditional pagan religion, similar to that of other Germanic peoples. Their gods included Odin, the god of war; Thor, the god of thunder; and Balder, the god of light. In their mythology, Loki and other evil giants did battle with the Norse gods.

The Scandinavians had a political organization in which warfare played a central role. A warrior elite gained status through success in raiding by which they obtained booty to distribute to their retainers. The spoils of war were desired as much or more as proofs of warrior prowess and bravery as for material gain. Moreover, Viking warriors believed that if they died heroically in battle, they would join Odin in Valhalla, a palace in the realm of the gods.

By the beginning of the ninth century, parts of Scandinavia had begun to consolidate into kingdoms. This growing centralization may have played a part in Viking expansion in that some chieftains or warriors, used to an independent status, sought to earn prestige and carve out their own power base or even establish a new homeland. A growing population also strained local resources. Knowledge of the wealth of certain peoples to their south no doubt provided incentive.

The earliest Viking raids were quick forays against coastal settlements by small groups of warriors. In the late eighth and early ninth centuries, single or several ships typically carried out solo raiding ventures. The Vikings sometimes camped in foreign lands for the winter. By about 850, the expeditions grew in size, and participants chose to settle some of the conquered lands. The Danes and Norwegians tended to engage in raiding and colonization more than the Swedes, who focused on trading. The Swedes generally went east and south; the Danes and Norwegians generally west and south.

Swedes settled the east coast of the Baltic Sea and traded with and sometimes raided inland peoples. There is evidence that the Vikings traveled inland into present-day eastern Europe as early as the eighth century. Some groups followed the Neva River, which took them to Lake Ladoga. Viking travel into eastern Europe often involved dragging their ships against the current of the predominantly north-flowing streams and portaging them over stretches of land.

To Slavic peoples of eastern Europe, the Scandinavians were generally known as Varangians. Some of the Viking raiders united under the leader Rurik in 862 at Novgorod, a center of trade on the Volkhov River in present-day Russia, which feeds Lake Ladoga, and became known as Rus, or Ruser.

The Scandinavians eventually reached the south-flowing Dnieper River, establishing a base at Smolensk in present-day Russia. By way of the Dnieper, they had access to the Black Sea and the city of Constantinople (present-day Istanbul, Turkey), which they had first raided in 860 and where they came to trade regularly. From there, they also sailed by way of the Dardanelles (a strait), the Sea of Marmara, and the Bosporus Strait into the MEDITERRANEAN SEA. The Vikings also traveled the south-flowing Volga River, which took them to the Caspian Sea. The Swedish Vikings are also thought to have reached even Baghdad and Jerusalem. Among the settlements they reestablished was Kiev on the Dnieper in present-day Ukraine, which under Prince Oleg, from about 882 to 912, was capital of a Rus principality.

In the course of their travels, the Vikings met with Finnic, Slavic, and Turkic peoples. At Bulgar, a trade center at the bend of the Volga River, they also probably encountered caravans of Chinese as well as Arab Muslims. A traveler AHMAD IBN FADLAN, a non-Arab Muslim who was at Bulgar in summer 922, later described Scandinavians in his work *Kitah* (Book).

The Viking presence in England began at least by about 790, when Lindisfarne (Holly Island) in the north was attacked. The Viking presence in Ireland, according to medieval records, began five years later with an attack on an unidentified island called Rechru. Scandinavian kingdoms eventually arose at Dublin, Limerick, and Waterford. The Viking king of Dublin was able to launch his own raids in England.

The Vikings in the British Isles came mostly from what is now Denmark and were generally referred to as Danes by the local peoples among whom they settled. In addition to coastal settlements, they also came to control surrounding islands, such as the Hebrides, Orkneys, and Shetlands. Norwegian Vikings settled the Faeroe Islands, far out to sea in the North Atlantic.

In the early ninth century, Vikings also gained control of parts of coastal France and traveled up rivers for other raids. In 845, the Vikings navigated the Seine River to attack Paris. Those Vikings who settled in Normandy (French for "land of the Northmen"), which was officially ceded to them by the king of France, Charles III, in 911, became known as Normans.

From their new staging areas or homes on the British Isles or on the coastal mainland—typically at the mouths of rivers—the Vikings launched expeditions farther to the south. In about 858, Bjorn Ironside, the son of a Danish king, and his lieutenant Hastein led a fleet of 62 longships in raids from the mouth of the Loire River in France along the Iberian Peninsula through the Strait of Gibraltar (see GIBRALTAR, STRAIT OF) and into the Mediterranean Sea, where they reached coastal North Africa, the Balearic Islands off Spain, and coastal southern France. A fleet of Moorish ships eventually drove them back to the Atlantic, and they returned to France four years after departure. Normans came to expand their holdings; in the second half of the 11th century, William the Conqueror invaded England, and Roger I, Sicily.

The Vikings reached ICELAND in the North Atlantic in the second half of the ninth century. The Irish had already settled the island by 800 and possibly a lot earlier (see SAINT BRENDAN'S ISLE). According to one saga, in about 860, NADDOD, a Norwegian Viking, was blown off course while traveling from Norway to the Faeroe Islands and reached the east coast of Iceland. Another Norse saga holds that, about the same time, GARDAR SVARSSON, a Swedish Viking, circumnavigated Iceland and built the first Viking house there on the north coast. Floki Vilgerdarsson, another Norwegian, is said to have built a house on the east coast. The first permanent settler is said to have been Ingólfur Arnarson, who established a farm at present-day Reykjavík on the southwest coast in about 874.

From Iceland, the Vikings ventured even farther to the west. Norwegian Viking ERIC THE RED is considered the European discoverer of GREENLAND in about A.D. 982, although it may have been earlier sighted by Bjarni Gunnbjörn. Eric the Red established a settlement at present-day Julianehaab. From Greenland, the Vikings traveled farther westward. Norwegian BJARNI HERJULFSSON, in about 985 or 986, was blown off course and spotted land, three distinct coastlines, he later reported to those in Greenland. In about 1000, Eric the Red's son, LEIF ERICSSON, also reportedly blown off course, came to a land that came to be known as VINLAND, somewhere in northeastern North America, very likely Newfoundland, Labrador, or Quebec. (The VINLAND MAP, supposedly found in 1957, showing the location of Vinland, turned out to be a forgery.) Other Vikings would later attempt to colonize Vinland, among them Leif's brother THORVALD ERICSSON in about 1005, THORFINN KARLSEFNI in about 1010, and his half sister FREYDIS EIRÍKSDOTTER in about 1014. Those colonies failed. The Norse settlement in Greenland endured until the early 15th century, when the outbreak of the bubonic plague cut off communication with Scandinavia. Yet their settlements in Europe endured and the Vikings became part of the ethnic mix of many European nations.

What is defined as the Viking age ended by the 12th century. By that time, European kingdoms were able to defend themselves against their raids; three great Scandinavian kingdoms had emerged that became Denmark, Norway, and Sweden; and Christianity had been introduced into Scandinavia.

Vinland

Vinland is the name given to a place in North America visited by the Vikings in the beginning of the 11th century. It represents the location of the first known European visit to the Americas (see VIKING EXPLORATION).

The earliest surviving reference to Vinland is from *Adami Gesta Hammaburgensis ecclesiae pontificum* (translated as *History of the Archbishops of Hamburg-Bremen*) written by Adam of Bremen in about 1075. He was a German who had obtained his information from Danish king Sweyn Estrithson. In this work, Adam of Bremen mentions a land with grapes, which make superior wine, as well as self-sown wheat. He also mentions an ice buildup to the north, which makes sailing impossible. Scholarly research has shown that Adam's writings were not always accurate, and it is likely that his mention of grapes and wine came from the interpretation of the word *Vinland.* In German this would refer to a land of wine, but in the Old Norse the prefix *vin* means a grassy field. In any case, the work of Adam of Bremen led to the repetition of this characteristic of Vinland in the sagas written more than a century later.

The chief sources of information on Vinland come from two Norse sagas, *Groenlendinga* (or the *Saga of the Greenlanders*) and *Eiríks saga* (or the *Saga of Eric the Red*). These stories had been passed down by word of mouth for centuries before being written. The first to be recorded, the *Saga of the Greenlanders,* written in ICELAND in about 1200, has proven to be the more reliable of the two.

The story of the temporary settlement of Vinland begins with Viking BJARNI HERJULFSSON in about 985 or 986. On a trip from Iceland to visit his father in GREENLAND in a LONGSHIP, he was blown off course, to the southwest. Although he spotted land—three distinct coastlines, he reported—he did not make a landing. Eventually, he made his way to Greenland, where he related his findings.

According to the sagas, on a voyage of exploration to find the land that Herjulfsson had seen, LEIF ERICSSON embarked with a crew of 35 from Greenland in about 1001. He came upon three different regions: The first he named Helluland, after its extreme flatness; the second he named Markland, referring to a land of woods; the third, and most southern, he called Vinland. At Vinland, he built houses and probably stayed for a year. He then returned to Greenland.

The next reported visit to Vinland involves Leif's brother THORVALD ERICSSON in about 1005. He took up residence in the houses Leif had built and was the first to see the native inhabitants of the land, whom he called Skraelingar or Skraelings, a derogatory term meaning a "wretched and ugly creature." It is significant because it is the first account of European and Native American contact. In a confrontation with the Skraelings, Thorvald was killed. After two years in Vinland, the remaining members of the party decided to return to Greenland.

Despite earlier troubles encountered, the following expedition was a journey of colonization. Gudrid, the widow of Thorstein—Leif and Thorvald's brother—convinced her new husband, THORFINN KARLSEFNI, to organize a group to settle Vinland in about 1010. With four ships, as many as 160 people, livestock, and supplies, they landed on its shores. Conditions in their settlement were poor, and, after trading and fighting with the native peoples, Karlsefni and his company returned to Greenland.

FREYDIS EIRÍKSDOTTER, the half sister of Leif, looms large in the sagas' account of a follow-up effort in about 1014. Freydis sailed to Vinland with her husband, Thorvard, in a small longship with two Norse brothers, Helgi and Finnbogi, who owned a larger boat. In Vinland, she reportedly took over the houses her brother had built. Later, desiring the boat owned by Helgi and Finnbogi, she fomented a murderous rampage in which the brothers and their allies were killed. On their return to Greenland, the story of the murders came out, but Freydis's punishment was mitigated because of her relationship to Leif.

Although different sagas give different details about these various voyages and colonies, the fact of Norse settlements in Iceland and Greenland is not in dispute. It seems likely that from Greenland the enterprising Vikings would reach the North American continent a short distance away. The actual location of Vinland is another matter. Academic speculation has yielded more than 500 hypothetical sites, from Labrador to Florida. To support their theories, scholars have not only used the latitudes where grapes are found, but also astronomical observations in the sagas, which relate to the seasons and the length of days. The one thing lacking in the theories was physical evidence.

In 1960, Norwegian explorer and writer Helge Ingstad and his wife, archaeologist Anne Stine Ingstad, began an excavation at the town of L'Anse aux Meadows in the north of Newfoundland. They discovered the remnants of eight houses of Norse design, similar to those excavated in Iceland and Greenland, with walls and roofs, which had been sod, laid over a supporting frame. In the middle of the floor were long narrow firepits used for heating, lighting, and cooking. Recovered artifacts also resembled those from other Viking sites: a stone oil lamp; a soapstone spindle whorl, used as the flywheel of a handheld spindle; a whetstone for sharpening tools; a bronze, ring-headed pin, used to fasten cloaks; the fragment of a bone needle, probably used in knitting; a small decorated brass fragment that once had been gilded; and iron nails or rivets used in boat-making. A great deal of slag from smelting and working of iron was also present. Some of these implements confirm the presence of women in the settlement.

Their findings did not preclude all other locations for Vinland, but established archaeological proof that the Viking discovery of North America predated that of CHRISTOPHER COLUMBUS for Spain by nearly 500 years. The site of the excavation is now a National Historic Site of Canada as well a World Heritage Site.

A map known as the VINLAND MAP, reportedly found in 1957, showing the location of Vinland in North America, turned out to be a forgery.

Vinland Map

The Vinland Map is a world map that shows an island to the southwest of GREENLAND called Vinland. There are two inlets on the island, which could easily correspond to Hudson Strait, with HUDSON BAY at its end, and the Gulf of St. Lawrence leading to the St. Lawrence River. If authentic, the Vinland Map would be the earliest map to represent North America, confirming the Norse sagas and the discovery of the Americas by the Vikings.

In 1957, the Vinland Map was reportedly found in a manuscript relating the mid-13th-century travels of Friar GIOVANNI DA PIAN DEL CARPINI to the lands of the Mongols. The best estimate of the time of its creation was in about 1440, since it contained close similarities to a map published in 1436 by Venetian B. Andrea Bianco.

Donated to Yale University in 1965, the Vinland Map was revealed to the public that same year by R. A. Seton, Thomas E. Marston, and George D. Painter in their book *The Vinland Map and the Tartar Relation.* Upon its publication, the Vinland Map generated much excitement, scrutiny, and skepticism. The skepticism proved well founded, for, in 1974, Yale announced that the map was a forgery. The ink used to make it contained a titanium oxide compound, which had not been invented until the 1920s. Although it was revealed as a fraud, experts on early Scandinavian exploration pointed out that the Vinland Map in no way detracted from what was known of Viking travels to North America.

See also VIKING EXPLORATION.

Virginia Company

Virginia Company refers to two English commercial joint-stock corporations, chartered by King James I at the same time in 1606, for the purpose of reasserting sovereignty over North America and colonizing it. One was the Virginia Company of London, which also came to be known as the London Virginia Company, or the London Company. The second was the Virginia Company of Plymouth, also known as the Plymouth Company and later the Council of New England. The name *Virginia,* honoring the Virgin Queen, Elizabeth I, James's predecessor, was used broadly to describe the Atlantic coast of North America. The new colonizing attempts were the first since the failed attempts of the 1580s on Roanoke Island in present-day North Carolina, sponsored by SIR WALTER RALEIGH for Queen Elizabeth.

The Virginia Company of London received a patent to develop a colony in a 100-square-mile region on the Atlantic Ocean between latitude 34 and 41 degrees north; the Virginia Company of Plymouth received a patent to do so between 38 and 45 degrees north. The overlapping territory could be settled by either company, although any settlement by one had to be at least 100 miles away from the other. Each company had the power to appoint a local council, which was under the authority of a council in England, acting on behalf of the king, as well as a governor and other officials. The companies also had the responsibility to provide settlers, ships, and supplies for the colonization attempts.

In December 1606, the Virginia Company of London dispatched a fleet of three ships under CHRISTOPHER NEWPORT, with military leader JOHN SMITH. The colonists landed in Chesapeake Bay near the mouth of the James River in May 1607, where they erected James Fort. The colony became known as Jamestown, the first permanent English settlement in America. Because of the mortality rate from disease and conflicts with the Powhatan Indians, as well as the lack of profits, the charter for the Virginia Company of London was revoked in 1624, and Virginia became a Crown colony.

The ships of the Virginia Company of Plymouth's first colonizing expedition were captured by the Spanish. A second attempt led by GEORGE POPHAM departed from Plymouth in May 1607 and settled on the west bank of the Kennebec River, near present-day Popham Beach, Maine, the following August. After a severe winter, during which Popham died, the colonists finally abandoned the site, returning to England in October 1608. By 1609, the Virginia Company of Plymouth had become inactive, and the Virginia Company of London received an individual charter.

In 1620, the Virginia Company of Plymouth received a new charter from James I as the Council for New England, with rights to develop territory between 40 and 48 degrees north, from sea to sea. That same year, the PILGRIMS, among them EDWARD WINSLOW, had secured a patent to settle in territory of the Virginia Company of London to the south. They sailed from Plymouth, England, on the *Mayflower,* and landed at present-day Plymouth, Massachusetts, in December 1620, to the north of the agreed-on territory. At that time, they drew up the Mayflower Compact, pledging allegiance to the English king, later obtaining patents from the Council for New England, legalizing their settlement site. The Pilgrims, through the FUR TRADE with Native Americans, eventually liquidated their debts to the merchants of the Council for New England. The Virginia Company of Plymouth was disbanded in 1635.

Voskhod program

The Voskhod program of the former Union of Soviet Socialist Republics (USSR; Soviet Union) consisted of SPACE EXPLORATION using the Voskhod type of spacecraft, accommodating two or three people with more functions controlled by the crew than in the smaller but similar spacecraft of the earlier VOSTOK PROGRAM. The name *Voskhod* means "dawn" in Russian. The Voskhod program competed with the GEMINI PROGRAM of the United States.

The first mission of the Voskhod program, *Kosmos 47,* launched on October 6, 1964, was to test modifications of the Vostok capsule. Six days later, three cosmonauts (see ASTRONAUTS), Vladimir Komarov, Konstantin Feoktistov, and Boris Yegorov were launched on *Voskhod 1.* They completed 15 orbits of Earth, the first three-person spaceflight in history. Moreover, Feoktistov, who had helped design the spacecraft, became the first engineer in space, and Yegerov became the first physician in space. Another flight, *Kosmos 57,* was launched on February 22, 1965, to test the airlock design. Despite its malfunctioning, on March 18, 1965, Pavel Belyayev and ALEKSEI ARKHIPOVICH LEONOV were launched on *Voshkod 2.* During the mission of 17 orbits, Leonov carried out the first extravehicular activity, or "space walk."

Vostok program

The Vostok program of the Union of Soviet Socialist Republics (USSR; Soviet Union) accomplished several firsts in SPACE EXPLORATION. On April 12, 1961, in *Vostok 1,* YURI ALEKSEYEVICH GAGARIN became the first human to be in space and to orbit Earth. On June 16, 1963, in *Vostok 6,* VALENTINA VLADIMIROVNA TERESHKOVA became the first woman in space.

The Vostok program (*vostok* means "east" in Russian) competed with the MERCURY PROGRAM of the United States, which put the first American in space, ALAN BARTLETT SHEPARD, JR., on May 5, 1961. The "space race" between the two nations had begun in 1957, with the launch of the first SATELLITE, *Sputnik 1,* by the Soviet Union. The design of the Vostok spacecraft evolved from that of Kosmos spy satellites; early models were tested under the name Kurabl-Sputnik, with dogs aboard. They consisted of two basic parts, the capsule and the equipment module. The next generation were designed to carry a single cosmonaut (see ASTRONAUTS).

A total of six Vostok spacecraft were launched carrying cosmonauts. After Gagarin's pioneering mission, Gherman Titov became the first human to eat and sleep while in space during the *Vostok 2* mission of August 1961. *Vostok 3* and *4,* in August 1962, were in orbit at the same time, another first. Over the course of five days in June 1963, cosmonaut Valeri Bykovskii orbited Earth 81 times on *Vostok 5,* establishing a record for the longest solo space mission. Tereshkova, the first woman in space, flew the last Vostok mission. A seventh launch was planned, but the Soviet Union decided to concentrate on the VOSKHOD PROGRAM, developing spacecraft able to carry two or three people.

The cosmonauts in Vostok flights controlled few of the spacecraft functions. In emergencies they could, however, override an automatic orientation system with a code provided in an envelope attached to the capsule wall. A retrorocket directed the craft out of orbit and back to Earth. A heat shield protected the capsule from incineration during reentry into the atmosphere. The equipment module, which separated from the capsule, burned up as it plunged toward Earth. The capsule's descent was slowed by parachute and it was eventually retrieved. At about two miles above Earth, the cosmonaut ejected from the capsule in an ejection seat, then separated from the seat and also landed by parachute.

The Vostok program proved that humans could survive the rigors of spaceflight: launching under the force of ROCKET propulsion; weightlessness over an extended period of time; reentry into Earth's atmosphere; and landing.

voyageurs

The term *voyageur* is French for "traveler." It came to be applied to a man who traveled into wilderness areas, typically by CANOE, to conduct the FUR TRADE. The profession began in New France (present-day eastern Canada) under SAMUEL DE CHAMPLAIN, who sent out expeditions by way of Native American waterways—first along the Ottawa and French Rivers, then in the Great Lakes. The first voyageurs were therefore French, and the term originally applied to them alone.

The term came to be used for any wilderness participants in the fur trade, such as trappers—something akin to the MOUNTAIN MEN of the American West. In later years, the term came to be applied to paddlers transporting goods and people for the licensed companies, such as the HUDSON'S BAY COMPANY and NORTH WEST COMPANY, as distinct from the COUREURS DE BOIS, the "runners of the woods," unlicensed fur traders. Early official expeditions, such as that of LOUIS JOLLIET and JACQUES MARQUETTE in 1673, which traced the course of the MISSISSIPPI RIVER, made use of voyageurs. Many later explorers of Canada, such as PETER POND and SIR ALEXANDER MACKENZIE, active in the late 18th century, also traveled with voyageurs. Regular trades routes were eventually established into the Canadian West and Northwest, as well as northern parts of present-day United States, and men of other European ancestry, especially the Scottish, took up the profession as well, as did the Métis, people of mixed ancestry, many of them descended from French voyageurs and their Native American mates.

The voyageurs adapted many Native American customs. They copied canoe designs, using birch bark as a covering, which made the boats light enough to portage over land between rivers, streams, lakes, and ponds. They also traveled by dogsleds and snowshoes. Buckskin was the favored material for clothing. Pemmican—a food made from dried meat, melted fat, and berries—served as a practical trail food.

West Indies

The West Indies is an archipelago lying between southeastern North America and northern South America. The arc formed by the thousands of islands stretches about 2,500 miles from off the coast of Florida to the coast of Venezuela, and separates the Atlantic Ocean from the Gulf of Mexico and Caribbean Sea. The West Indies, also called the Antilles, include the Bahamas in the north; the Greater Antilles (Cuba, Jamaica, Puerto Rico, as well as a single island, formerly known as Hispaniola, with two nations, Haiti and the Dominican Republic) in the center; and the Lesser Antilles (Virgin Islands, Leeward Islands, Windward Islands, Barbados, Netherland Antilles, Trinidad, Tobago, Aruba, and other islands off Venezuela) in the south.

Italian mariner CHRISTOPHER COLUMBUS first applied the name "Indies" when he explored the region for Spain in 1492, believing he had reached islands off the coast of India, associating them with the EAST INDIES. The name *Antilles* also came to be used in Spain and in France; Antillia was the supposed name of a mythical land supposedly existing in the Atlantic (the antecedent of the legend of the Seven Cities of CIBOLA).

Many of the West Indies are mountainous, formed by a partly submerged mountain range, and some islands have active volcanoes; other islands are flat, formed from coral and limestone. All the islands, except the northern Bahamas, have a tropical climate, moderated by the cooling effect of the Atlantic Ocean and the TRADE WINDS, which blow from the northeast (enabling passage in sailing ships from Europe). Hurricanes occur frequently in summer and fall. Some of the islands were originally heavily forested with altitude and latitude determining tree types, from pine to palm. Animal life includes the hutia and agouti—types of rodents—the iguana, and a wide variety of turtles, birds, and fish. Native peoples practiced some farming along with hunting, fishing, and gathering. The Ciboney Indians, their origin unknown, lived in small areas of western Hispaniola and western Cuba. They were eventually pushed westward by the Arawak Indians, or Taino, out of South America. Another people, the Carib Indians, displaced the Arawak from the Lesser Antilles before the islands were visited by Europeans.

Spanish Arrivals

A saga of exploration and colonialism is of course attached to each one of the many islands in the West Indies. Spanish arrival among them is also the beginning of the story of the European exploration of all the Americas (apart from the Vikings in northeastern North America centuries before), with explorers and colonizers venturing south, west, and north from the islands. The region was the first colonized by Europeans and the last to remain as colonies. The West Indies became a cultural crossroads, with many different European nations active among them. The transatlantic SLAVE TRADE led to an African presence there as well.

Christopher Columbus landed first on a small island of the Bahamas that he named San Salvador, probably Watling

Island (although some scholars have theorized that he first landed on Samana Cay, 65 miles to the southeast), on October 12, 1492, at two o'clock in the morning. His expedition later reached Cuba, which he believed the Asian mainland, and Hispaniola, which he believed to be Japan. On Hispaniola, he made contact with the Arawak Indian GUANCANAGARI. Columbus returned with gold, parrots, and native people to Spain in March 1493, but not the hoped-for riches. That same year, he headed a second, larger expedition of 17 ships back to the West Indies, still believing they were part of Asia. This time, he took with him soldiers, colonists, livestock, tools, and seeds. He navigated a more southerly route, and, before returning to Hispaniola again, he passed and named many of the Lesser Antilles and sighted the Virgin Islands and Puerto Rico. Later on, he further explored the coast of Cuba and reached Jamaica. Columbus had attempted to found settlements at two different sites on Hispaniola during his first expedition. On the second voyage, he gave orders to found Santo Domingo on the south shore of Hispaniola in the present-day Dominican Republic. The oldest permanent settlement in the Americas, it became the seat of Spanish rule in the West Indies and, as a base of expansion, the "mother of settlement" of Latin America. Columbus returned to Europe in 1496. He later led two more expeditions to the Americas—in 1498–1500 and 1502–04. On his third voyage, he reached the South American mainland—the so-called SPANISH MAIN—and the island of Trinidad. On his fourth voyage, he explored the coast of Central America.

The transatlantic crossing became commonplace for Spanish ships. Before long, they had conquered the tribes of Jamaica, Hispaniola, and Cuba. DIEGO VELÁSQUEZ, who had sailed with Columbus in 1493, along with his lieutenant PÁNFILO DE NÁRVAEZ, were central to these military operations. Velásquez, who declared himself governor-general of Cuba, founded Havana in 1519, which became another launching point for Spanish exploratory expeditions. San Juan, founded in 1511 on an island in a bay off Puerto Rico, became still another center of activity.

Staging Posts

Other Spaniards famous for explorations elsewhere—many of whom became known as CONQUISTADORES—spent part of their careers in the West Indies. JUAN PONCE DE LEÓN, who explored Florida in 1519, had previously served as governor of Puerto Rico. LUCAS VÁSQUEZ DE AYLLÓN, who organized an expedition to the coast of present-day South Carolina in 1520, was a colonial official at Santo Domingo. HERNÁN CORTÉS, who conquered the Aztec of Mexico in 1521, had served under Velásquez in Cuba. FRANCISCO PIZARRO, who conquered the Inca of Peru in 1533, had served under Nicolás de Ovanda, governor of Hispaniola. In 1535, GONZALO FERNÁNDEZ DE OVIEDO Y VALDEZ, who was a colonial official in the West Indies and the official historian of the Americas, published the first volumes of *Historia general y natural de las Indias Occidentales* (General and Natural History of the West Indies).

The ports of West Indies eventually served as staging posts for Spanish ships carrying cargo to other settlements and plundered riches from the Aztec and Inca back to Spain (see TREASURE AND EXPLORATION). In the second half of the 16th century, other nations began to show interest in the region. SIR JOHN HAWKINS completed the first successful English transatlantic slave-trading expedition in 1562–63, exchanging African slaves to Spanish colonists for sugar and hides, which he transported back to England. With ongoing conflict between England and Spain, English PRIVATEERS, such as SIR FRANCIS DRAKE, commissioned by Queen Elizabeth I, began raiding Spanish shipping in the 1560s.

Colonial West Indies

By the end of the 16th century, the native population of the West Indies had been decimated—from the spread of European diseases, warfare, and forced labor—with only a few pockets remaining. By the mid-17th century, England, France, and the Netherlands had established settlements in the West Indies. By that time also, sugar plantations had been introduced to the region. During the colonial period, most islands were deforested.

Colonial conflicts would continue over the next centuries, with colonial influence enduring to modern times. In the late 19th century, the United States also became active in the region politically and economically. With the Spanish-American War of 1898, Spain lost its last possessions in the West Indies. Great Britain granted independence to most of its colonies in the 1960s. Some of the West Indies islands are still British, French, Dutch, and American dependent territories, however. The island of Margarita is part of Venezuela.

See also CENTRAL AMERICA, EXPLORATION OF.

whaling and sealing

The hunting of sea mammals took mariners to waters of high latitudes and played a part in the history of exploration. Whaling and sealing as a means of subsistence have been a traditional activity of native peoples of Arctic regions for millennia. Yet, in more recent centuries, whaling to obtain oil, meat, bone, and other by-products, and sealing, especially for furs, became an organized business.

Whaling and Exploration

Whaling of many of at least 75 species of whales as a commercial enterprise dates back to the ninth century, early such activity carried out by the Basques of northern Spain and southwestern France in the Bay of Biscay of the Atlantic

Ocean. By the mid-16th century, when those waters became depleted, whalers ventured as far as Newfoundland off northeastern North America. After a Dutch expedition under WILLEM BARENTS in search of the NORTHEAST PASSAGE reached Spitsbergen (present-day Svalbard) in the Arctic Ocean north of Norway in 1596, and an English expedition under HENRY HUDSON for the MUSCOVY COMPANY in 1607 reported whales in the archipelago's vicinity, Spitsbergen became a center of whaling for the Dutch and the English. Basques were often hired for their crews. By the mid-17th century, when whale herds had been reduced in those waters, whalers hunted around GREENLAND. During whaling expeditions in 1806–17, especially in Arctic waters east of Greenland, an English whaler and his son, WILLIAM SCORESBY, SR., and WILLIAM SCORESBY, JR., made studies of natural science and navigation, reporting to England's ROYAL SOCIETY. The Davis Strait to the west of Greenland also was a rich hunting ground for a time.

America also became involved in the whaling business, starting in the mid-17th century, early hunters setting out from such places as Sag Harbor on Long Island in New York, and Provincetown on Cape Cod in Massachusetts, and the Island of Nantucket also in Massachusetts. In 1791, an American ship first rounded South America's CAPE HORN for hunting in the Pacific Ocean. By 1830, New Bedford on coastal Massachusetts had become the most important whaling center. New London, Connecticut, and San Francisco, California, also became important whaling ports. Norway, Japan, and Russia also became active in whaling.

Early hunters launched their rowboats from shore, in order to kill whales with handheld lances and hand-thrown harpoons. They later began launching their rowboats from ships. Whaling ships became larger over the centuries, from sloops of 30 to 40 tons, to schooners and brigs of 100 to 150 tons, and, by the 19th century, to ships and barks of twice that weight. By the late 19th century, large steamships were also used, some of them factory ships, on which whales could be processed after being killed. By the 19th century, voyages commonly lasted three or four years. The invention, in about 1856, of a harpoon containing an explosive head by the Norwegian Sven Foyn revolutionized whaling. The last rich hunting grounds were found in the waters off Antarctica. In 1904, a whaling station was founded on the island of South Georgia in the South Atlantic (where SIR ERNEST HENRY SHACKLETON sought help in his aborted Antarctic expedition of 1914–16). Modern whaling is heavily regulated, with many of the species endangered, such as the sperm whale, whose oil was once valued above that of all others.

Seal Hunting and Exploration

Seal hunting for food, oil, and hides, like whale hunting, has been a traditional part of subsistence for a number of northern peoples, in particular the Inuit (Eskimo) of the North American Arctic. The term *seal* is applied broadly to a number of pinnipeds, or fin-footed mammals: the eared seals, which include the fur seal, the species most hunted for furs, and the sea lion; and the earless seals—the true seals—some of which are also valued for their furs, especially the harp seal, whose pups have fluffy white coats, and the ringed seal. The commercial hunting of seals dates back to 1515, when a cargo of fur seal skins arrived from Uruguay to the markets in Seville, Spain. During the next centuries, sealing was carried out on a small scale. In the 18th century, various nations became active in the seal fur business. In 1786, during the period that the Russians were expanding their fur-trading activities into Alaska, GAVRILO LOGINOVICH PRIBILOV (also known as Gerasim Pribilof) made the European discovery of the Pribilof Islands in the Bering Sea, which serve as an annual mating place for a large portion of the fur seal population. The Pribilof Islands are also known as the Fur Seal Islands.

At about the same time, sealers began hunting in southern waters and on southern islands, such as the Falklands. American EDMUND FANNING, who participated in and sponsored many expeditions to the South Pacific, participated in the sealskin trade. He was one of the sponsors of NATHANIEL BROWN PALMER's sealing expedition to waters south of CAPE HORN in 1829, which led to one of the earliest sightings of the Antarctic Peninsula. A Scottish sealer, JAMES WEDDELL, sailing for Great Britain in 1822–23, explored the South Orkney Islands and reached a southernmost point in the Atlantic's Weddell Sea not surpassed until the next century. Englishman JOHN BISCOE, also a sealer, circumnavigated Antarctica in 1831–32. Macquarie Island, south of TASMANIA in the South Pacific, as well as the Crozet Islands and Kerguelen Islands in the southern Indian Ocean, also became places for sealing.

It has been estimated that more than 25 million fur seals have been slaughtered for their skins from 775 to 1900. In the late 19th and early 20th centuries, nations came to agree on regulations to protect diminishing herds and endangered species. The controversy has continued to modern times because of the threat to the survival of certain species and the cruelty involved in clubbing seals to death, including pups, in order not to damage their coats.

women explorers

In historical studies of exploration, one encounters the names of many more men than women. Yet women played a significant role as wives of explorers, sponsors of expeditions, as well as explorers in their own right. Like men, they explored for a variety of reasons: to break free of society's constraints; to earn a living; out of religious conviction; as inspiration for their writing; to find subjects for painting; for scientific studies; or, simply, in order to rise to the challenge of being a woman explorer.

Since the beginning of time, those with wanderlust have found a way and means to travel. While the opportunity to explore traditionally has come to men in many ways, it has not been readily granted to women. Women typically had to overcome societal obstacles before even facing the obstacles of the journeys themselves.

Some of those who managed to voyage beyond their homeland were women of privilege; others came from poverty and repression. Traveling as a companion to a husband or lover enabled travel for some women. Some women traveled as guides to expeditions, or as captives. Others dressed in the clothes of a man in order to travel.

Sponsors

In some instances, the role of sponsor—that is, the person having vision, incentive, wherewithal, and dedication to launch an expedition—was as critical as actions in the field (see SPONSORS OF EXPLORATION). In the case of HATSHEPSUT, the first woman pharaoh, who, in about 1492 B.C., sent a maritime trading expedition southward via the RED SEA to the land of PUNT in the region of the Gulf of Aden—one of the first known exploratory expeditions—her name has survived as the most significant with regard to the journey.

Ferdinand II and Isabella I, the joint rulers of Aragón and Castile in Spain in 1479–1504 sponsored Italian mariner CHRISTOPHER COLUMBUS's voyage across the Atlantic Ocean in 1492, leading to European awareness of the Americas. It is thought that it was indeed Isabella, called la Católica (the Catholic), an energetic and involved leader, who first believed such an undertaking was worth the investment, having been so advised by the finance minister Luis de Santangel. One of her motivations was the finding of new converts to Christianity.

Elizabeth I, who ruled England and Ireland from 1558 to 1603, also recognized the economic possibilities of exploration and colonization—in large part because of competition with Spain—and supported the ventures of such men as SIR FRANCIS DRAKE, SIR HUMPHREY GILBERT, and SIR WALTER RALEIGH.

In the mid-19th century, Lady JANE FRANKLIN, widow of SIR JOHN FRANKLIN, lost in the Canadian Arctic after departure from England, persistently raised funds for private expeditions to find him, when she was not satisfied with the results of government-backed endeavors.

For Better or for Worse

A number of wives played important roles in the lives of explorer husbands—and not only in offering moral support and maintaining their interests at home, but also as companions in foreign lands.

One wife, through happenstance, became known as an explorer in her own right. Ecuadorean woman ISABELA GODIN DES ODANAIS was wife of Frenchman Jean Godin des Odanais, part of a French scientific team. In 1769, after waiting for almost two decades, she set out on a journey down the AMAZON RIVER out of central Peru to be reunited with him. When everyone in her party perished, she had to wander in the rain forest alone for nine days before being rescued by Indians and rejoining her husband in Cayenne in French Guiana. She is the first known woman to descend the entire Amazon.

Protestant missionaries were very often a husband and wife team. Englishwoman MARY MOFFAT traveled to southern Africa to marry and be with missionary ROBERT MOFFET and helped him found a mission at Kuruman on the edge of the Kalahari Desert. She remained in Africa until 1870. Their eldest daughter Mary married Scottish missionary DAVID LIVINGSTONE in 1845 and traveled with him on a number of his subsequent African expeditions, dying on the ZAMBEZI RIVER in 1862.

In 1872, Englishwoman ELIZABETH SARAH MAZUCHELLI and her husband, Anglican clergyman Francis Mazuchelli, traversed the Singalila Mountains of eastern Nepal during a two-month, 600-mile trek from Darjeeling into the HIMALAYAS of northern Sikkim. She wrote about her Himalayan journey in the book *The Indian Alps and How We Crossed Them,* published in 1876.

The wives of two American missionaries to the American West—Narcissa Whitman, wife of MARCUS WHITMAN, and Eliza Spalding, wife of HENRY HARMON SPALDING—became the first known non-Indian women to cross the ROCKY MOUNTAINS while traveling with their husbands in 1836.

In the 20th century, two different wives, DELIA JULIA DENNING AKELEY and MARY LEONORE JOBE AKELEY, both American-born, worked and traveled with their husband, American naturalist CARL ETHAN AKELEY, in Africa. They were known as explorers in their own right, Delia in East Africa after her divorce, and Mary in the Canadian northwest before her marriage and in the Belgian Congo after her husband's death. Both wrote about their travel experiences.

Wives and Guides

Another woman who traveled with her husband—and actually proved much more critical to the success of the expedition than he—was Shoshone Indian SACAJAWEA. When her husband, French Canadian fur trapper TOUSSAINT CHARBONNEAU was hired by MERIWETHER LEWIS and WILLIAM CLARK at the Mandan Indian villages on the MISSOURI RIVER in early 1805, he had to convince them to allow his wife (whom he reportedly had won in a gambling game with Hidatsa Indians) to accompany them. Her giving birth to a baby (JEAN-BAPTISTE CHARBONNEAU) that February did not help his case. Yet, on the journey to the Pacific Ocean and back with the Corps of Discovery, she proved invaluable as a guide and interpreter. She even managed to procure horses from her brother Cameahwait, chief of a Shoshone band, in the course of the trip. Her participation through the return to the Mandan villages helped the expedition maintain mostly peaceful relations with the many other tribes encountered. In his writings about the journey, William Clark praised Sacajawea for her resourcefulness and criticized her husband for general incompetence.

Several years later, in 1811–12, another Native American woman, MARIE DORION of the Ioway tribe, played a similar role for the Astorians under WILSON PRICE HUNT for fur trader JOHN JACOB ASTOR, serving as a guide beside her husband PIERRE DORION, JR.

Earlier in history, in 1519–21, Aztec woman MALINCHE served as HERNÁN CORTÉS's interpreter during the Spanish conquest of the Aztec Indians in present-day Mexico. Although they had a son together, Cortés eventually presented her as a gift to one of his military colleagues.

One Hand on the Pen

Many women are known as explorers through their writings. One of the earliest to record her experiences away from home was Chinese woman WEN-CHI, who, in about A.D. 190, at age 12, was abducted by the Hsiung-Wu, also known as the Huns. She later wrote about her experiences living as a nomad on the Mongolian steppes in a series of

In this early 20th-century photograph, Harriet Chalmers Adams is shown on an expedition to the Gobi Desert. *(Library of Congress, Prints and Photographs Division [LC-USZ62-97426])*

poems, known as *Eighteen Songs of a Nomad Flute.* A woman who helped begin the tradition of travel writing was Englishwoman CELIA FIENNES, who, in the late 17th and early 18th centuries, traveled throughout the British Isles on horseback. Her journals were published as *Through England on a Side-Saddle* in 1888.

IDA REYER PFEIFFER, an Austrian woman, circumnavigated the world twice, from west to east and east to west. She wrote about it in *A Woman's Journey Round the World,* published in 1852, and *A Woman's Second Journey Round the World,* published in 1856. ISABELLA BIRD BISHOP, the first woman member of the ROYAL GEOGRAPHICAL SOCIETY, earned this honor by also traveling much of the globe. She was initially instructed to travel by her doctor. She wrote about her travels in *The English Woman in America,* published in 1856, among many other works.

Many women continued this tradition of travel writing in the late 19th and early 20th centuries. ISABELLE EBERHARDT, a Russian-German woman born in Switzerland, converted to Islam, began dressing as a man, and traveled through North Africa in the late 19th century, chronicling her expeditions in many books and French newspapers. MAY FRENCH SHELDON, an American publisher and author in central Africa, was one of the first European women to visit many villages in present-day Kenya and Tanzania. She wrote an account of her experiences in East and central Africa, including her attempt to scale MOUNT KILIMANJARO, in *Sultan to Sultan,* published in 1892. British author MARY HENRIETTA KINGSLEY recorded her two-year journey through West and central Africa in three books, including *Travels in West Africa,* published in 1897.

American HARRIET CHALMERS ADAMS wrote about crossing the ANDES MOUNTAINS of South America and of other travels, including to the GOBI DESERT of central Asia, in the early 20th century, for *National Geographic* and other magazines. She was elected to the Royal Geographical Society and became the first president of the Society of Women Geographers. British archaeologist GERTRUDE MARGARET LOWTHIAN BELL traveled widely in the Middle East in the late 19th and early 20th centuries; she wrote extensively about her experiences, including *Amurath to Amurath,* published in 1911.

Frenchwoman ALEXANDRA DAVID-NÉEL became known as a journalist after she became the first European woman to obtain an audience with the Dalai Lama in exile in India, in 1911. She later became the first European woman to reach the Tibetan city of LHASA, which she described in *My Journey to Lhasa,* published in 1927. British travel writer and archaeologist FREYA MADELINE STARK had many maladies in her life, among them heart attacks, malaria, and dengue fever. None of them detoured her from her travels in the Hadramawt region of southern Arabia and central Asia, which she wrote about in a number of works, including *The Valley of the Assassins,* published in 1934.

Natural Science

Some women traveled for the sake of science. In the 1860s–70s, German naturalist KONCORDIE AMALIE NELLE DIETRICH spent 10 years collecting the single largest assemblage of natural flora and fauna in Australia. British painter MARGARET URSULA MEE traveled throughout the Amazon Basin over a period of 32 years in the mid-20th century, making a visual record of plant life.

Disguised as Men

Ancient Egyptian queen Hatshepsut was known for wearing men's clothing to further her position of power. Writer Isabelle Eberhardt, mentioned above, also donned men's clothing to facilitate travels. Spanish woman CATALINA DE ERAUSO is also among those successful at traveling as a man. In the early 17th century, in disguise, she fought as a soldier and worked in mining camps in Argentina and Chile. In the 1760s, Frenchwoman JEANNE BARET, disguised as a male crewmember, participated in LOUIS-ANTOINE DE BOUGAINVILLE's official French expedition to the South Pacific, and she may have been the first woman to circumnavigate the world. In the early 19th century, Englishwoman HESTER LUCY STANHOPE adopted male dress in order to travel freely in Israel, Lebanon, and Syria. During her travels, she lived among the Bedouin in the Syrian Desert.

In the Name of Exploration

As has been the case with men, some women considered exploration a calling. Dutch woman ALEXANDRINE PETRONELLA FRANCINA TINNÉ and American LOUISE ARNER BOYD pursued careers as explorers. In the 1860s, Tinné explored portions of the NILE RIVER and SAHARA DESERT, eventually losing her life there to Tuareg tribesmen. Boyd, who came from a wealthy family, organized and led a number of expeditions to the Arctic in the mid-20th century. Both women supported the efforts of scientists, who were with them on some of their travels. In 1955, Boyd became the first woman to fly over the NORTH POLE.

Mountain Climbing

Two early woman mountaineers were ANNIE SMITH PECK and FANNY BULLOCK WORKMAN, both American and both active in the late 19th and early 20th centuries. After climbing in the Alps, Peck turned her attention to South and Central American peaks. Workman traveled throughout Europe, North Africa, the Far East, and central Asia. Among the mountains she climbed were the Himalayas.

The first woman to climb Mount Everest (see EVEREST, MOUNT) was Japanese Junko Taibei on May 16, 1975. Eleven days later, on May 27, Phantog, a Tibetan woman,

Fanny Workman sits next to climbing equipment on one of her expedition in the late 19th or early 20th century.
(Library of Congress, Prints and Photographs Division [LC-USZ62-70538])

also made the ascent. The first American woman to reach the summit of the tallest mountain in the world was Stacey Allison in 1988.

Women in Space

With the arrival of the space race, certain women—in particular VALENTINA VLADIMIROVNA TERESHKOVA of the Union of Soviet Socialist Republics (USSR; Soviet Union) and SALLY KRISTEN RIDE of the United States—had a chance to make space history. In 1963, the VOSTOK PROGRAM mission made Valentina Tereshkova the first woman launched into space. She spent 70 hours in orbit. Twenty years later, Sally Ride became the first American woman in space. She orbited Earth for six days aboard the SPACE SHUTTLE.

❖

The above are but a few of the women whose travels are relevant to the history of exploration. They journeyed for varied reasons, but all can be said to be adventurers and pioneers. They endured hardships and demonstrated resourcefulness that many considered beyond the capabilities of women, helping change stereotypical views even as they contributed to knowledge of the regions they visited. In modern times, it has become commonplace for women to travel widely and help explore the remote places of Earth and beyond.

writing and exploration

A rich literature is attached to world exploration. Writings by explorers or about them is filled with challenge, adventure, drama, and description. It is writing and documentation that defines history, and the history of exploration and the gaining of geographic knowledge provides a fascinating view of the saga of humankind. Yet writing is not just the means of telling and preserving the story; it is part of the story. Accounts about travels spurred on other travels. The success of books regarding one expedition helped justify and pay for others. Moreover, travel writing developed as a calling unto itself.

Writing and the Ancients

Tracing the careers of early explorers helps give a sense of the importance of writing in both preserving and shaping the chronicle of exploration. Four Greeks of the sixth and fifth centuries B.C., HECATAEUS OF MILETUS, HERODOTUS, CTESIAS OF CNIDUS, and XENOPHON, who traveled beyond their homeland—Hecataeus and Herodotus up the NILE RIVER, Ctesias to Persia (Iran) and India, and Xenophon from Persia to Greece—are sources for much of what we know about the period (see GREEK EXPLORATION). But they also sparked interest about foreign lands among their contemporaries and subsequent generations. While ostensibly a historical account of the wars between the Greeks and Persians, Herodotus's *History* consists of a mixture of observation and myths, which sometimes veer wildly from the truth, similar to earlier Greek poetry, and with literary themes examining the consequences of the meetings of different peoples, and contrasting the values of democracy and tyranny. They helped inspire ALEXANDER THE GREAT in his campaign against Persia in the fourth century B.C., which resulted in the hellenization of much of the Middle East and a dissemination of Greek culture and literature. The Romans took up this tradition as they expanded their domination over the Mediterranean world in the early centuries B.C., spreading Roman culture and the Latin language (see ROMAN EXPLORATION).

Cartographers, who are also part of the story of writing and publishing, drew on their accounts and those of other early travelers. Those who recorded and passed on the evolving view of the world from their own travels and/or the travels of others include Greeks ERATOSTHENES of the third and second centuries B.C. and STRABO of the first century A.D., Roman PLINY THE ELDER of the first century A.D., and hellenized Egyptian Ptolemy of the second century A.D. (see GEOGRAPHY AND CARTOGRAPHY).

Writings of the East

Writers and cartographers of the East, as in China, also disseminated knowledge gained through exploration (see CHINESE EXPLORATION). In about A.D. 220, the Han dynasty collapsed, which had united China in an empire for about 400 years. In subsequent years, Buddhism, a religion that had developed on the GANGES RIVER in India, was passed into China. But the Chinese Buddhists had learned from translated texts and word of mouth, leading to doctrinal disagreements. In A.D. 399, a Buddhist monk in China, FA-HSIEN, embarked on a voyage to India in order to make copies of original Buddhist texts in Sanskrit, translate them, and resolve these questions. Fa-hsien's journey lasted 15 years, and took him over the Takla Makan desert and through the HIMALAYAS to the INDUS RIVER and then across northern India, but he eventually returned to China with a wealth of Buddhist texts.

Fa-hsien was followed two centuries later, in A.D. 629, by another Chinese Buddhist monk, HSÜAN-TSANG, for the same purpose. After a long journey through central Asia and India, he too returned with Buddhist scriptures. Another scholar, I-CHING, set out for India in 671 in search of Sanskrit texts and traveled in Indonesia as well. Chinese cartographers, such as CHU SSU-PEN of the 14th century, defined the known world at the time based on others' accounts.

Many of the most famous Arab Muslims who played a part of the history of world exploration were geographers as well as writers (see MUSLIM EXPLORATION). ABU AL-HASAN

THE

LAKE REGIONS OF CENTRAL AFRICA,

A PICTURE OF EXPLORATION.

BY

RICHARD F. BURTON,

Capt. H. M. I. Army; Fellow and Gold Medalist of the Royal Geographical Society.

" Some to discover islands far away."—Shakspeare.

NEW YORK:

HARPER & BROTHERS, PUBLISHERS,

FRANKLIN SQUARE.

1860.

This title page is from an 1860 book on Africa by Sir Richard Burton. *(Library of Congress, Prints and Photographs Division [LC-USZ62-108547])*

ALI AL-MASUDI traveled to Islamic lands in the 10th century; ABU ABD ALLAH MUHAMMAD ASH-SHARIF AL-IDRISI did so in the 12th century; and ABU ABD ALLAH MUHAMMAD IBN BATTUTAH did so in the 14th century. Ibn Battutah also voyaged southward into Africa beyond the world known to his peers.

Renaissance Writings

Among Europeans, early explorers such as German PETHAHIA OF REGENSBURG of the 12th century, Italian MARCO POLO of the 13th century, and Italian ODORIC OF PORDENONE of the 14th century shaped the European worldview during and after their lives with their tales of foreign lands (all three men had the help of writers in recording their travel accounts). In 1375, ABRAHAM CRESQUES published a world atlas based largely on their accounts. This work was a milestone of the early RENAISSANCE, the name applied to a cultural phase in Europe from the 14th century into the 17th century, a time of new accomplishments in scholarship and the arts and a new awareness of the world (see EUROPEAN AGE OF EXPLORATION).

The development of the movable type printing press by German goldsmith and printer Johannes Gutenberg in the mid-15th century, part of the phenomenon of the Renaissance, made books accessible to a wider audience, and some of the most successful early books capturing the public's imagination involved accounts of distant lands. For example, Italian FRANCESCO ANTONIO PIGAFETTA, who served as Portuguese FERDINAND MAGELLAN's private secretary in the first CIRCUMNAVIGATION OF THE WORLD in 1519–20, kept a daily record of the voyage, which was published in Paris in 1540 and reached a large readership. BERNAL DÍAZ DEL CASTILLO's account of the Spanish conquest of the Aztec Indians of the 1520s in Mexico, in which he participated, was not published until the 17th century, but became the primary source for that event.

Various Approaches to Writing

Many different approaches to writing have furthered knowledge of exploration and geography. An 18th-century French historian PIERRE-FRANÇOIS-XAVIER DE CHARLEVOIX traveled in North America for the purpose of research, which was later incorporated in his six-volume *History of New France.* Other scholars who traveled for their work—such as German naturalist ALEXANDER VON HUMBOLDT in the late 18th century and 19th century, and British archaeologist JAMES THEODORE BENT in the late 19th century—recorded their findings in writing, which were passed on to the public through publishing (see NATURAL SCIENCE AND EXPLORATION and ARCHAEOLOGY AND EXPLORATION). The journals of MERIWETHER LEWIS and WILLIAM CLARK about their 1803–06 expedition have been published time and again. The role of the less renowned MOUNTAIN MEN in the FUR TRADE in the 1820s–30s, such as WARREN ANGUS FERRIS, might not be known if not for their own accounts of their careers, or as told to others who wrote about them. In some instances, professional writers became known in other capacities. For example, British-American journalist SIR HENRY MORTON STANLEY, who was in Africa in much of the 1870s–80s, became known as an explorer and colonizer first and as a writer second.

Travel Writing

In its modern incarnation of travel writing, the purpose of the trip is writing about the trip. Yet, with regard to earlier ages, the phrase is applied to any account involving travels.

Cloud from avalanche descending between two granite peaks on Bilaphond glacier.

Frontispiece.

TWO SUMMERS IN THE ICE-WILDS OF EASTERN KARAKORAM

THE EXPLORATION *of* NINETEEN HUNDRED SQUARE MILES OF MOUNTAIN AND GLACIER

By FANNY BULLOCK WORKMAN *and* WILLIAM HUNTER WORKMAN

WITH THREE MAPS AND ONE HUNDRED AND FORTY-ONE ILLUSTRATIONS BY THE AUTHORS

E. P. DUTTON & COMPANY
681 FIFTH AVENUE, NEW YORK

This frontispiece and title page were included in a 1917 book by Fanny Workman and her husband. *(Library of Congress, Prints and Photographs Division [LC-USZ62-108069])*

WEN-CHI, a Chinese woman who was abducted by the Hsiung-nu (Huns) and who lived as a nomad on the Mongolian steppes in the second century A.D., wrote about her experiences in *Eighteen Songs of a Nomad Flute.* This might also be called a captivity narrative. In the 16th century, Portuguese FERNÃO MENDES PINTO wrote about his travels in the Far East on returning to Portugal and earned the sobriquet "Prince of Lies" because many of his adventures seemed too fantastic to be believed.

An early traveler whose writings became an intrinsic part of her wanderings was CELIA FIENNES. In the late 17th and early 18th century, she journeyed throughout England, keeping a journal of her experiences. Travel writing became a tradition for the British in the 19th century, especially for women. LUCY ATKINSON, ISABELLA LUCY BISHOP, ANNE ISABELLA BLUNT, MARY HENRIETTA KINGSLEY, and ELIZABETH SARAH MAZUCHELLI all can be said to have engaged in travel writing. This tradition carried over into the 20th century with ALEXANDRA DAVID-NÉEL and FREYA MADELINE STARK.

Austrian IDA REYER PFEIFFER, active in the 19th century, and Swiss ISABELLE EBERHARDT, active at the turn of the 20th century, might also be called travel writers. Americans who engaged in travel writing in the 19th century are HENRY MARIE BRACKENRIDGE, JOHN TREAT IRVING, and MAY FRENCH SHELDON; and, in the 20th century, HARRIET CHALMERS ADAMS and PAUL BELLONI DU CHAILLU.

Exploration and Literature

Once, when in old age, the British author and explorer CHARLES MONTAGU DOUGHTY had been asked why he had made his journey through the deserts of the Arabian Peninsula in the 1870s, he replied that he had made his voyage "to redeem the English language." The only way for Doughty to capture his experience, far from the orderly landscape of England, was to abandon the built-up literary conventions, and to adopt a mode of expression from his environment, the Arabian desert. Doughty wrote his account of his explorations, *Travels in Arabia Deserta,* published in 1888, a work of more than 600,000 words, in a style that hearkened back to an earlier period of English literature, to Edmund Spenser and the King James Bible, but he injected in it something new too, unique to the desert, for he took the inspiration for his style from the looser grammar and foreign rhythms of Arabic. His account was read by a generation of 20th-century writers including D. H. Lawrence, T. S. Eliot, and James Joyce, and inspired THOMAS EDWARD LAWRENCE (Lawrence of Arabia) in his Arabian travels and in writing his own account of his experiences in the Middle East, *Seven Pillars of Wisdom,* published in 1935. Whether or not Doughty had truly made his journey for the sake of language, his comment illustrates his understanding of the potential impact of exploration on the world's literature.

Beyond firsthand accounts of explorers, traders, and adventurers such as Doughty's account, are the works that take up exploration as a conceit around which main themes are built. These stories are older than written records, going back to the third millennium B.C., to the epic story of *Gilgamesh,* a legendary king of ancient Sumeria who embarks on a mythical journey in search of the secret of everlasting life. This could represent a journey through the Near East, up to the Black Sea. The myth wrestles with the questions of an individual's life and death and his place in the universe, while he makes a long voyage, much like the ones that were made by Sumerian and later Akkadian rulers (such as SARGON) in Mesopotamia to secure trading rights and maintain hold of the kingdom. Another early work of literature that uses a voyage through unknown lands as its central theme is the *Odyssey*—a Greek epic attributed to a circa ninth-century Greek poet Homer—recounting the 10-year voyage of Odysseus (the Roman Ulysses) home, from Troy. While grappling with fate and the gods, Odysseus encounters lands throughout the MEDITERRANEAN SEA, an area explored by early Greek traders. The work relates observations of the strange peoples and lands visited by Odysseus and his ship similar to those made by later Greek historians, such as Herodotus and Xenophon, whose writings reflect growing contacts among foreign cultures.

The effects of the travels of Chinese scholars had a profound influence on Chinese culture and literature. The influences can be seen in a 16th-century Chinese novel *Hsi Yu Chi* (known in the West as *Monkey* because one of the supernatural characters is a monkey spirit), by Wu Ch'eng-en, written during the Ming dynasty in China, when the Chinese were undergoing a reappraisal of their past after being freed from the rule of the Mongols. The work's Chinese title literally means a "Journey to the West," and, in it, Hsüan-tsang is fictionalized alongside a motley group of fantastic characters who embark on a journey to India. The book mixes both Confucian and Buddhist philosophy and religious images, reflecting the mixing of Chinese culture under influence from Indian thought in the West, and the many fabulous happenings along the way represent the issues raised by the interaction of foreign cultures.

The European explorers of South America wrote accounts no less fabulous than those of Herodotus. Missionaries told stories of giants with oversized feet, of cities of gold and forests of cinnamon, and of women who fought like men. European seafarers spread throughout the seas, and Europeans established settlements. In 1609, nine ships under English sea captain CHRISTOPHER NEWPORT set out from England with 500 colonists on board, heading for John Smith's Virginia colony, and one ship, the *Sea Adventure,* (also listed as *Seaventure*) was wrecked in a storm off the coast of Bermuda. The island was a miraculous haven, and after nine months, the colonists were rescued. The accounts of survivors, by SILVESTER JOURDAIN and William Strachey, are generally regarded to have been the inspiration for Shakespeare's purportedly last and one of his most popular plays, *The Tempest.* Set on an island ruled by a European castaway, Prospero, and his daughter, Miranda, and populated by an indigenous native, Caliban, whom Prospero enslaves, a frightful storm strands a group of Europeans on the island. Among the themes dealt with are the implications of colonizing inhabited lands, and the dubious but compelling prospect of founding a utopian kingdom in new worlds.

A shipwreck inspired another work of literature, which is in great part a meditation on European exploration and colonization. ALEXANDER SELKIRK, a Scottish seaman on a privateering expedition along the Pacific coast of South America, was marooned on the island of Mas Tierra, one of the Juan Fernández Islands, in 1704. He survived four years on the island, building himself a shelter and hunting wild goats, before being rescued by other PRIVATEERS. This story came to the attention of Daniel Defoe, who then wrote his first novel based upon it, *Robinson Crusoe,* published in 1719. The novel was instantly popular, dealing with the novelties and excitement of exploration, as well as touching on the fundamental human problem of isolation. *Robinson Crusoe* has remained popular up until the present day, spawning many versions and imitations.

Irish satirist Jonathan Swift embarked on his own exploration of human nature, in a more pointed and fantastic way than Defoe had done. In a direct literary line from Homer's *Odyssey,* but, drawing on the abundant travel narratives of his day, he told the story, in *Gulliver's Travels,* published in 1726, of Lemuel Gulliver, a country doctor who enlists himself as a ship's doctor and embarks on a sea voyage during which he visits strange lands. In Swift's book, however, the discoveries of the inhabitants of these strange lands tell the reader more about the inhabitants of England than anything else.

The genre of science fiction—although wide-ranging in themes, some of them beyond the range of human possibility—draws from the spirit of exploration. One of the earliest writers associated with the genre, Frenchman Jules Verne, wrote a number of books which presaged real events, *De la Terre à la Lune* (*From the Earth to the Moon*), published in 1865, and *Vingt Mille Lieues sous les mers* (*20,000 Leagues Under the Sea*), published in 1870. These works, along with other works such as *Voyage au centre de la Terre* (*Journey to the Center of the Earth*), published in 1864, create fictional characters very much in keeping with real-life explorers.

❖

Exploration challenges humankind's view of the world and has led to the dissemination of knowledge as well as a body of literature. Moreover, the literature itself has inspired further voyages. The above-mentioned writers and their works help give a sense of the intrinsic relationship of writing and exploration, but it should be kept in mind they are just a sampling. Many explorers wrote accounts of their expeditions. And many writers and historians not known as explorers have added to the literature of exploration.

Y

Yangtze River (Chang, Changjiang)

The Yangtze River, also known as the Chang, is the longest river in China and the third-longest in the world, after the NILE RIVER and the AMAZON RIVER. It extends for 3,900 miles, originating in the snows of the Kunlun mountain range at the eastern end of the Tibetan Plateau, and flows through central China into the East China Sea, a small arm of the Pacific Ocean. The Yangtze and its tributaries have a drainage area of some 650,000 square miles, taking the bulk of its waters from a number of tributaries: the Han, Yalong, Jialing, Min, and Tuo He, on the north and the Wu, on the south. As it discharges about 770,000 cubic feet of water into the sea, the Yangtze deposits 6 billion cubic feet of sediment annually, creating fertile soil, ideal for the growing of rice.

From its delta, the Yangtze rises gradually by only about 130 feet in its first 1,000 miles, making an excellent channel for ship traffic, except for the steep Yangtze gorges the river passes through at a distance of about 200 miles. Farther upriver, navigation becomes difficult due to shifting sandbars and becomes unnavigable at Pingshan at a height of about 1,000 feet above sea level. The river quickly rises in Upper Tibet to an altitude of 16,000 feet. While the river is commonly called the Yangtze, the name applies in China only to its last 300 to 400 miles of its extent, Changjiang (long river) being its official name. Local names apply to other parts of the river, such as Jinsha (golden sand) in its upper reaches.

Communication and Trade

The Yangtze has served as the principal route of communication and trade in China, from ancient times until the present (see CHINESE EXPLORATION). The first European on record to have seen the river is MARCO POLO, a Venetian merchant who traveled through China for almost 20 years in the 13th century. In his account, he recorded his impressions of the vast magnitude of ships on the Yangtze, saying that in one place they dwarfed all the traffic on every European waterway, put together. The first systematic exploration of the river from the West took place in the middle of the 19th century. The French, who had begun to colonize Indochina, sent expeditions to explore the Mekong River, which runs parallel to the Yangtze, though farther south and separated by a high ridge. Frenchman MARIE-JOSEPH-FRANÇOIS GARNIER accompanied an expedition, which followed the Mekong River before heading northward into China. When ERNEST-MARC-LOUIS DE GONZAGUE DOUDART DE LAGRÉE, the leader of the expedition, died, Garnier took control and under his command the expedition followed the upper Yangtze to the port city of Shanghai.

Once China was opened to Western travel, the port of Shanghai became an important entry point. Christian missionaries, such as Englishwoman ANNIE ROYLE TAYLOR, who, in 1892, attempted to enter LHASA, the Forbidden City of Tibet, traveled from there, as did other Westerners hoping to penetrate the interior of China. Another Frenchman, CHARLES BONIN, spent seven years exploring China

Shown here, in a photograph from about 1918, are Chinese junks on the Yangtze River. *(Library of Congress [LC-USZ62-102719])*

at the end of the 19th century and made the first scientific survey of the river, charting its course. At the turn of the 20th century, the Yangtze and its tributaries carried nearly half of China's maritime commerce.

Canal and Dam

The river is still an immensely important waterway, and is joined by a canal called the "Great Canal," more than 1,100 miles long, to China's other important river, the YELLOW RIVER (or Huanghe). This canal has been of importance to transportation since it was first dug during the Wu Dynasty in about 486 B.C. It has been extended over time and redone for the last time over six years during the Sui dynasty from A.D. 605 to 610. In addition, the Chinese government has been building a dam since 1994—the Three Gorges complex—near Yichang, in order to control the annual flooding of the river caused by snowmelt in the mountains. It will also generate electricity. The lake formed by the dam will displace some 1 million people and will flood many historical sites.

See also ASIA, EXPLORATION OF.

Yellow River (Huang, Huanghe, Hwang Ho)

At 3,395 miles, the Yellow River, or Huanghe (also spelled in English Hwang Ho), is China's second-longest river after the

taries, the Wei and Fen Rivers. Thereafter, the river emerges onto the broad North China Plain where it meanders for a little more than 100 miles through one of China's principal agricultural regions before emptying into the Gulf of Bo Hai, an arm of the Yellow Sea.

Civilization and Sorrow

The Yellow River is known as the "Cradle of Chinese Civilization" because the earliest evidence of Chinese civilization is found in its valley, and Chinese tradition traces its history, and indeed all Chinese ancestry, back to Huang Ti (Huangdi), the Yellow Emperor. Huang Ti, legend has it, was a marauder making his living plundering throughout the North China Plain but moved up into the plateaus of yellow loess soil. The settlement he founded supposedly prospered and gave birth to Chinese civilization. It is known that the Yellow River Valley was populated by scattered groups of neolithic peoples from about 9,000 to 6,000 years ago, and by 4,000 years ago, settled populations and technological and agricultural developments are found in the loess regions. Not yet highly eroded, the elevated fertile plains provided a perfect location for development.

The Yellow River is also called "China's Sorrow" because of the catastrophic flooding to which it is prone. As farming spread through the North China Plain, farmers built dikes to protect their crops from periodic flooding. These dikes caused the river to deposit more silt as sediment on the riverbed, raising the river, and necessitating yet higher dikes. Now, in places, the river is as high as 30 feet above the surrounding ground level and far more susceptible to flooding. There is always danger of the many dikes or levees breaking. Historically, the river has flooded thousands of times, most devastatingly in 1931, when flooding covered 34,000 square miles of the densely populated North China Plain, leaving 80 million people homeless and 1 million people dead.

East and West

Chinese civilization developed in the Yellow River Valley and in the Yangtze River Valley in relative isolation, due to surrounding mountains and deserts and to the marauding tribes, which threatened trade caravans. Technological innovations such as the wheel made their way from the West, but it was not until the second century B.C. that communication with peoples living to the west became regular (see CHINESE EXPLORATION). The Han dynasty flourished in China but was threatened by the activities of the Hsiung-nu (Xiongnu, or Huns) in central Asia. CHANG-CH'IEN, a Chinese diplomat, was sent west in 138 B.C. to make a military alliance with the Yue-chi (known in the West as the Scythians). His expedition failed and he was held in captivity by the Huns for many years, but he eventually brought back reports of the West, including of the Roman Empire. A second

YANGTZE RIVER (Chang), and the sixth-longest in the world. The Chinese call the river Yellow on account of the silt it carries in exceptionally high concentration. The river originates in the Kunlun Mountains of western China, fed by springs and high lakes, flowing turbulently eastward through deep gorges before turning northeast into the Ordos Desert, a part of the GOBI DESERT. This part of the river, called the "great northern bend," ends after the river flows several hundred miles due east and turns to the south. Here, between the Shaanxi and Shanxi provinces, the river flows through a valley of especially fertile soil, known as loess. The river picks up the majority of its silt in this region where sudden heavy rains erode the soil, and where it is joined by its main tribu-

expedition revealed a trade route from the headwaters of the Yellow River, which skirted hostile tribes, and led to the establishment of the SILK ROAD, which developed into a main pathway for East-West trade.

The Yellow River, aside from its signal agricultural importance, was an important river for travel and trade. Its traffic—mostly of a type of boat known as the JUNK—amazed one of the first Western visitors to China, Italian merchant MARCO POLO. At that time, in the 13th century, the Yellow River emptied directly into the Yellow Sea. It has changed its course in the eastern portion of the river several times in its history.

Starting in 1893, CHARLES BONIN spent seven years exploring China, during which he made the first modern scientific surveys of the Yangtze and Yellow Rivers, charting their courses.

See also ASIA, EXPLORATION OF.

Z

Zaire River See CONGO RIVER.

Zambezi River (Zambesi River)

The Zambezi River (also spelled Zambesi), the fourth-largest river of Africa, follows a double S-shaped course as it flows 1,700 miles across much of southern Africa. It begins in northwestern Zambia, about 5,000 feet above sea level, and flows south through eastern Angola and western Zambia, to the border of northeastern Botswana, then flows east between Zambia and Zimbabwe, finally crossing central Mozambique and emptying into the Indian Ocean through many outlets. The Zambezi's many tributaries were once confused with the river systems of the CONGO RIVER (Zaire River) and the NILE RIVER to the north. Much early African exploration was carried out for the purpose of understanding the various sources and tributaries.

Portuguese Exploration

The Portuguese were the first to explore and make use of the Zambezi River. In 1505–14, a convict named Antonio Fernandes explored the region on a quest for gold. Although he found no gold, he determined that the Zambezi was navigable for 300 miles from its mouth upriver and concluded that it presented the best route for inland trade. In 1531, the Portuguese founded the outpost of Sena, and, in 1560, Tete farther upriver, both in present-day Mozambique. The Sena settlement became the first point of contact between Europeans and the Bantu people. The Bantu claimed that the Zambezi was a river so great that no one knew its source. Portuguese traders eventually traveled some 800 miles inland.

In 1798, in the hope of joining Portuguese possessions on Africa's east and west coast, FRANCISCO DE LACERDA ascended the Zambezi from Tete and managed to make it past the Quebrabasa Rapids. He then entered the Luangwe River, one of the Zambezi's major tributaries. He died of fever near Lake Mweru, and his men returned to Tete via the Zambezi, failing to accomplish the east-to-west crossing of the continent.

The Livingstones

The Zambezi later captured the imagination of one of Africa's greatest explorers, Scottish missionary DAVID LIVINGSTONE. In 1851, after traveling northward through the Kalahari Desert with his wife, MARY MOFFAT LIVINGSTONE, and children, he stumbled upon a section of the upper Zambezi not yet seen by Europeans. Realizing the danger of the tropical climate, he sent his family back to England and resumed explorations in the region in 1853. Traveling from Capetown with oxcarts and native porters, he came to Linyanti, the capital of the Makololo people. After a month-long fever, he hired more men and proceeded up the river by CANOE to the north. He succeeded in exploring a large portion of the upper Zambezi before heading west to the coast, reaching Luanda in present-day Angola. On his way back

This photograph shows a vista of the Zambezi River in the mid-20th century. *(Library of Congress, Prints and Photographs Division [LC-USZ62-98036])*

from Luanda, he once again traveled the river. In 1855, he became the first European to witness the 420-foot Victoria Falls, which he named after Queen Victoria (local native peoples called it Mosiottatunya for the "smoke that thunders"). Continuing by river and overland, he reached the east coast at Quelimane in 1856. In so doing, he completed the first known voyage across the southern section of the continent.

Livingstone returned to England after his continental crossing and found himself a national hero. He had witnessed the misery of the SLAVE TRADE in Africa and had made it his goal to replace it with "Christianity and commerce," believing that, if Africans could produce their own commodities for export, there would be less slaving. The Zambezi was a key part of his vision. For his next series of expeditions beginning in 1858, he obtained a paddle-wheel steamship to explore up the Zambezi from the east coast and establish trade contacts. His wife accompanied him. His expedition was soon frustrated by the rapids at Quebrabasa. When Livingstone had made his extensive studies of the Zambezi, he had heard of the Quebrabasa Gorge, but had not seen it. The description he was given, of "a few rocks in the river," gave him hope that river would be navigable for

some distance. When this proved impossible, he steamed northward up the Shire River, and reached Lake Nyasa (Lake Malawi). While traveling on the Zambezi in 1862, his wife died of tropical fever. This sent Dr. Livingstone into a deep depression and may have been the reason that he quit his activities on the Zambezi. For the next two decades, he continued to explore Africa, but in other locations, pursuing other mysteries.

Livingstone had outlined the course of the Zambezi and described its independence from the Congo and Nile systems. More work would remain to be done concerning its minor tributaries. During his 1873–75 expedition, Englishman VERNEY LOVETT CAMERON studied various of the region's smaller rivers, traveling the watershed between the Congo and Zambezi. In 1890, Scotsman JOSEPH THOMSON made additional explorations of the upper Zambezi.

❖

Today, many of the lands that surround the Zambezi are fertile and populated, and long sections are used for local traffic. A number of hydroelectric plants along the river generate power for the peoples of Africa.

See also AFRICA, EXPLORATION OF.

Appendix
MAPS

I. REGIONAL

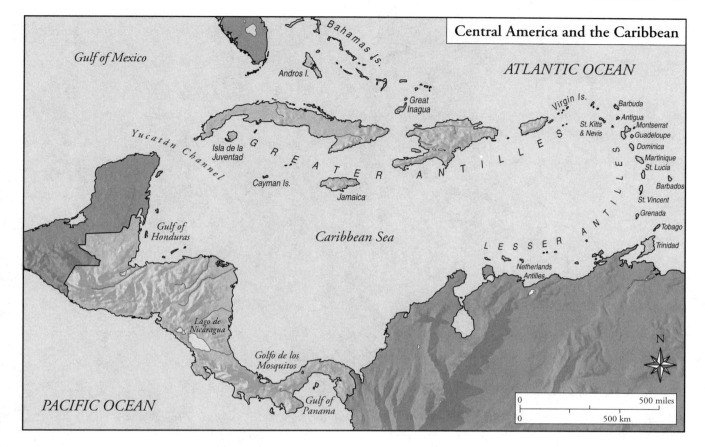

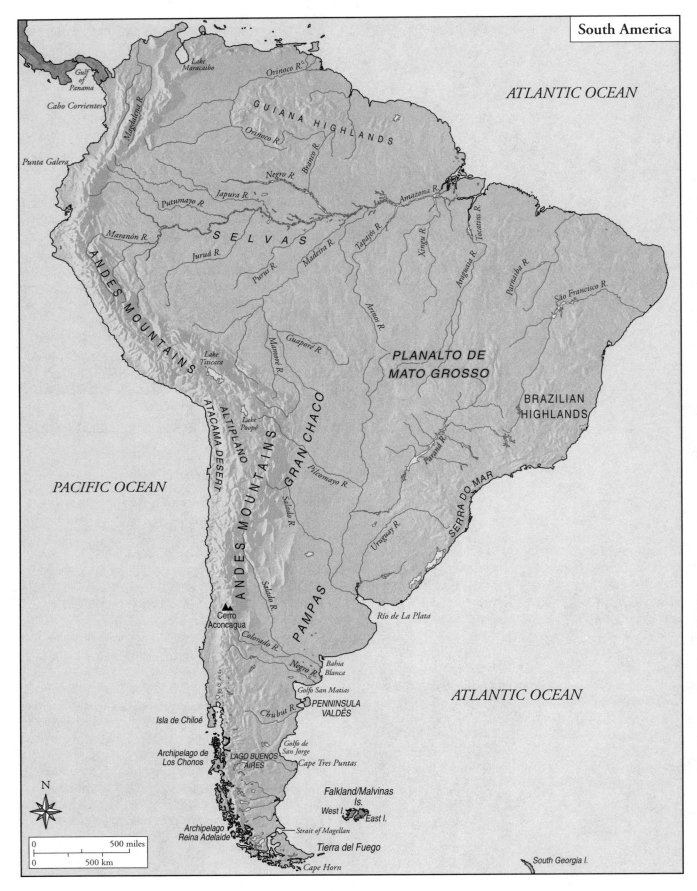

South America

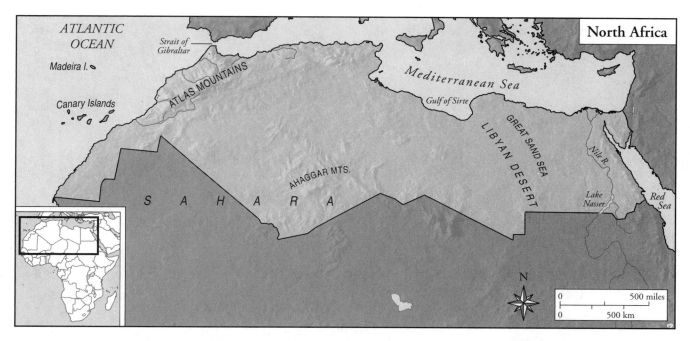

North Africa

ATLANTIC
OCEAN

Madeira I.

Canary Islands

Strait of
Gibraltar

ATLAS MOUNTAINS

Mediterranean Sea

Gulf of Sirte

GREAT SAND SEA

LIBYAN DESERT

Nile R.

AHAGGAR MTS.

S A H A R A

Lake
Nasser

Red
Sea

N

0   500 miles
0   500 km

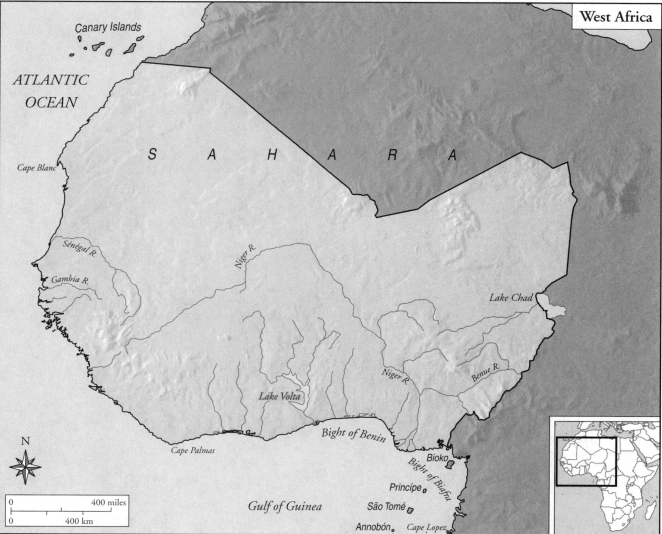

West Africa

Canary Islands

ATLANTIC
OCEAN

Cape Blanc

S A H A R A

Sénégal R.

Niger R.

Gambia R.

Lake Chad

Niger R.

Benue R.

Láke Volta

Bight of Benin

Cape Palmas

Bioko

Bight of Biafra

Príncipe

N

São Tomé

0   400 miles
0   400 km

Gulf of Guinea

Annobón   Cape Lopez

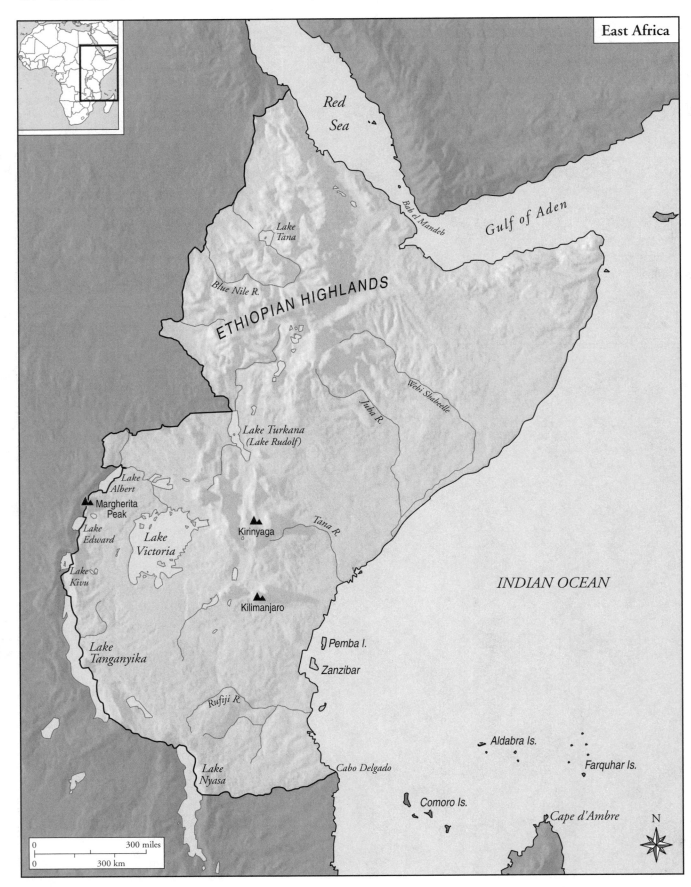

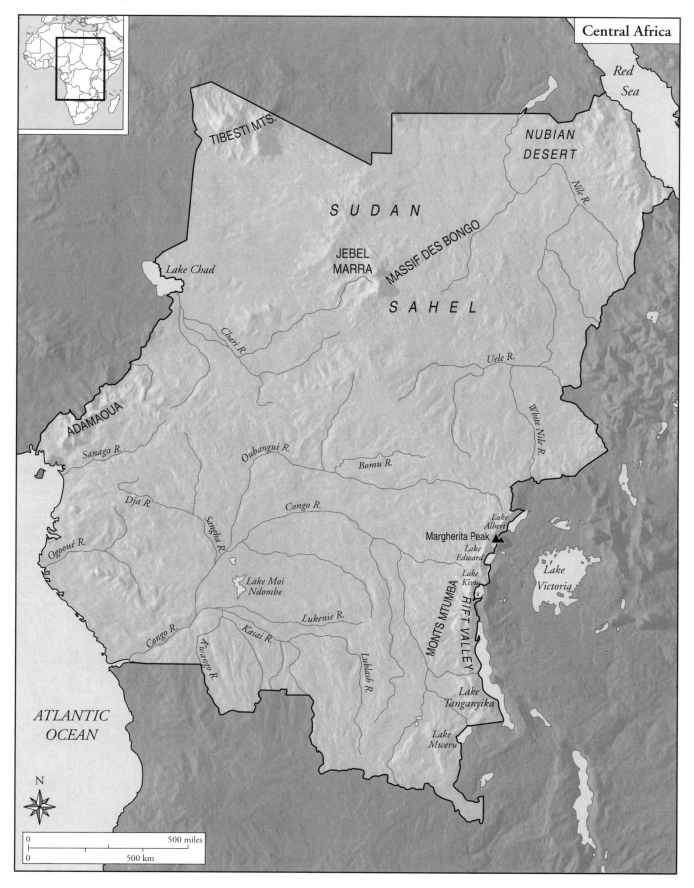

Central Africa

Red
Sea

TIBESTI MTS.

NUBIAN
DESERT

S U D A N

Nile R.

Lake Chad

JEBEL
MARRA

MASSIF DES BONGO

S A H E L

Chari R.

Uele R.

ADAMAOUA

Sanaga R.

Oubangui R.

Bomu R.

White Nile R.

Dja R.

Congo R.

Lake
Albert

Margherita Peak ▲

Sangha R.

Ogooué R.

Lake Moi
Ndombe

Lukenie R.

Lake
Edward

Lake
Kivu

Lake
Victoria

Congo R.

Kwango R.

Kasai R.

Lubilash R.

MONTS MTUMBA

RIFT VALLEY

ATLANTIC
OCEAN

Lake
Tanganyika

N

Lake
Mweru

0   500 miles

0   500 km

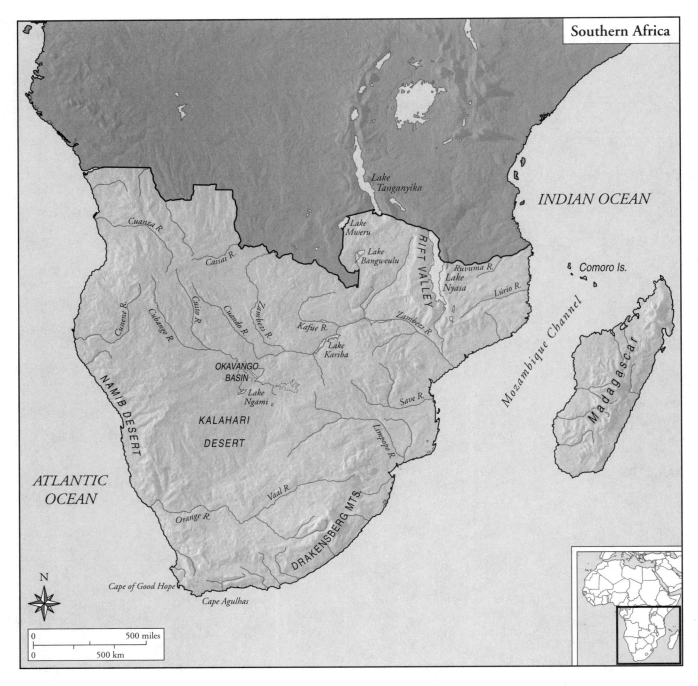

Southern Africa

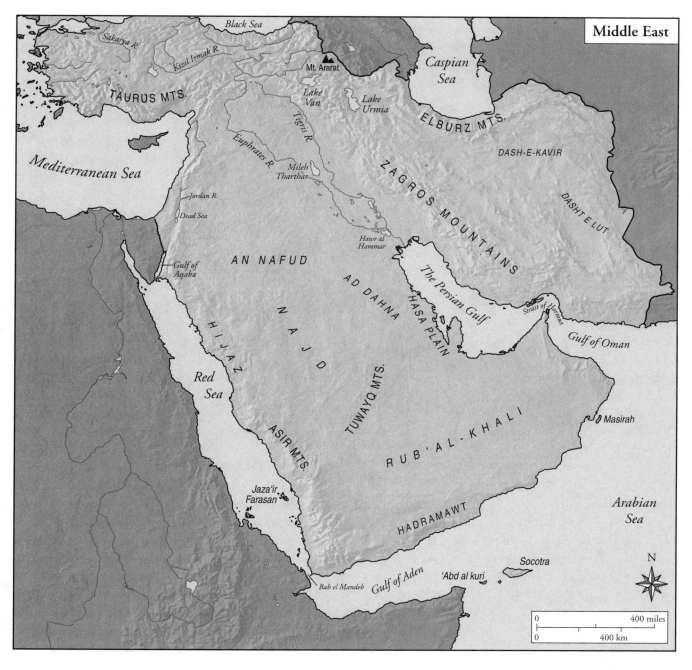

Middle East

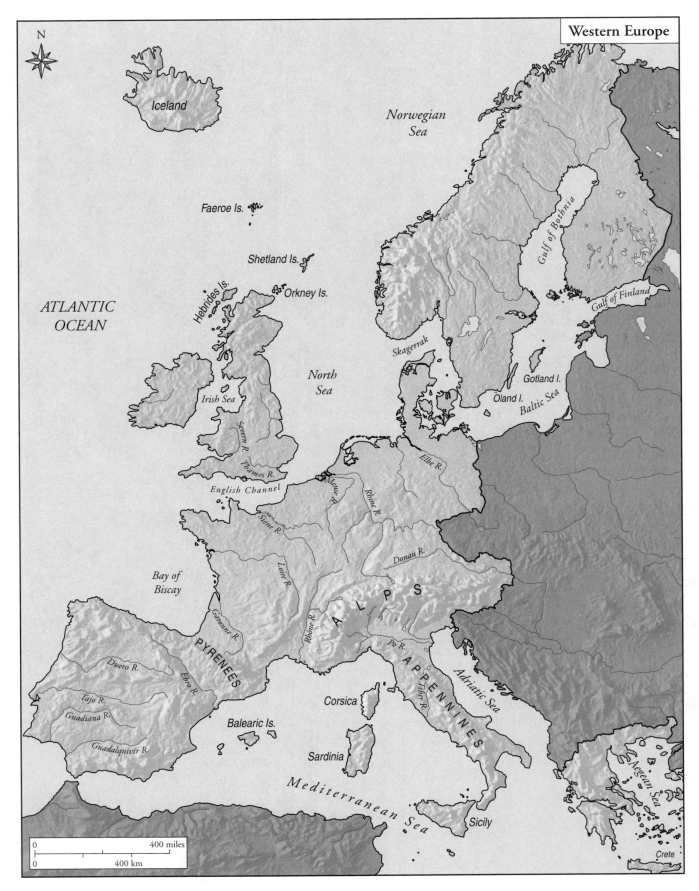

Eastern Europe

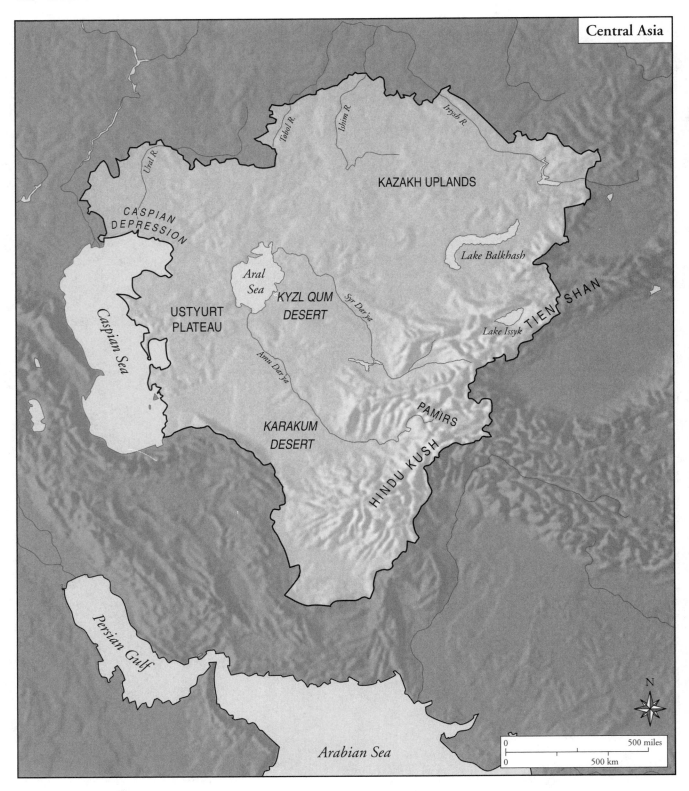

Central Asia

Tobol R.

Ishim R.

Irtysh R.

Ural R.

KAZAKH UPLANDS

CASPIAN
DEPRESSION

Lake Balkhash

Aral
Sea

KYZL QUM
DESERT

Syr Dar'ya

USTYURT
PLATEAU

TIEN SHAN

Caspian Sea

Lake Issyk

Amu Dar'ya

KARAKUM
DESERT

PAMIRS

HINDU KUSH

Persian Gulf

N

0   500 miles

0   500 km

Arabian Sea

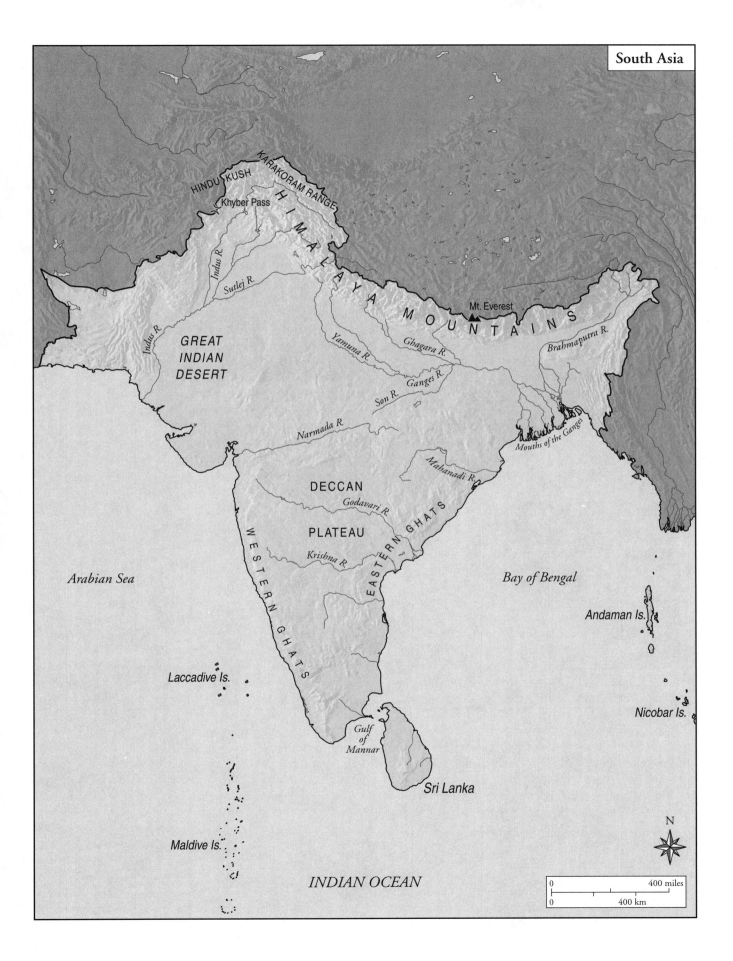

South Asia

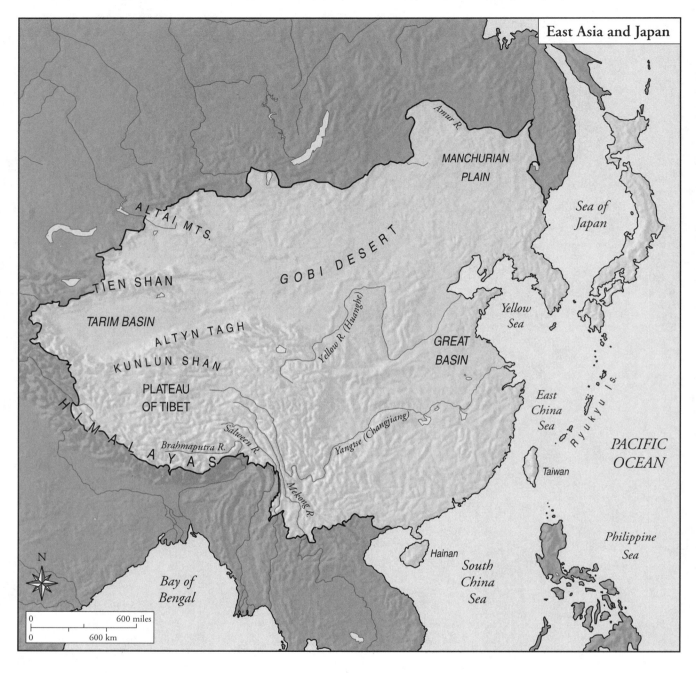

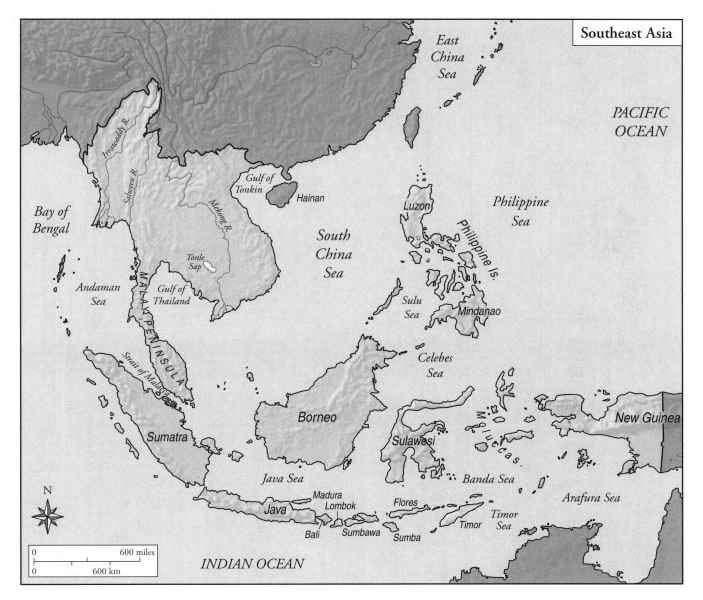

Southeast Asia

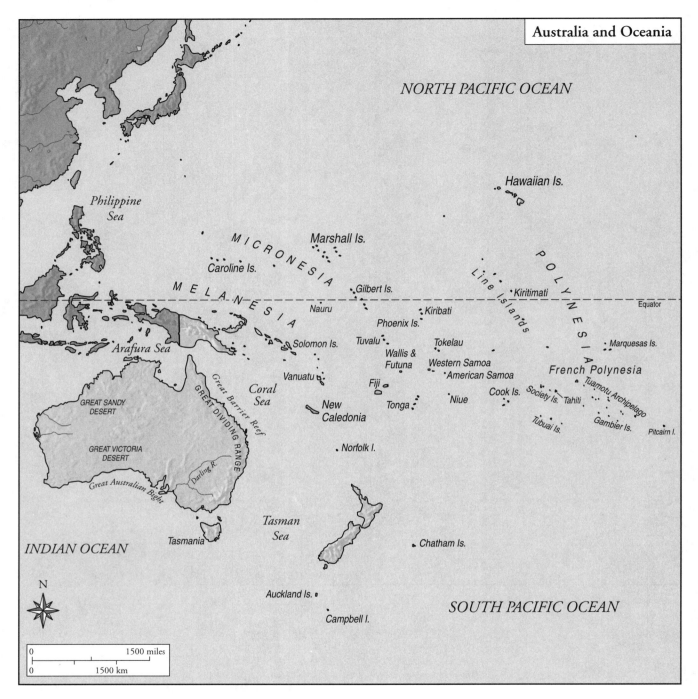

Australia and Oceania

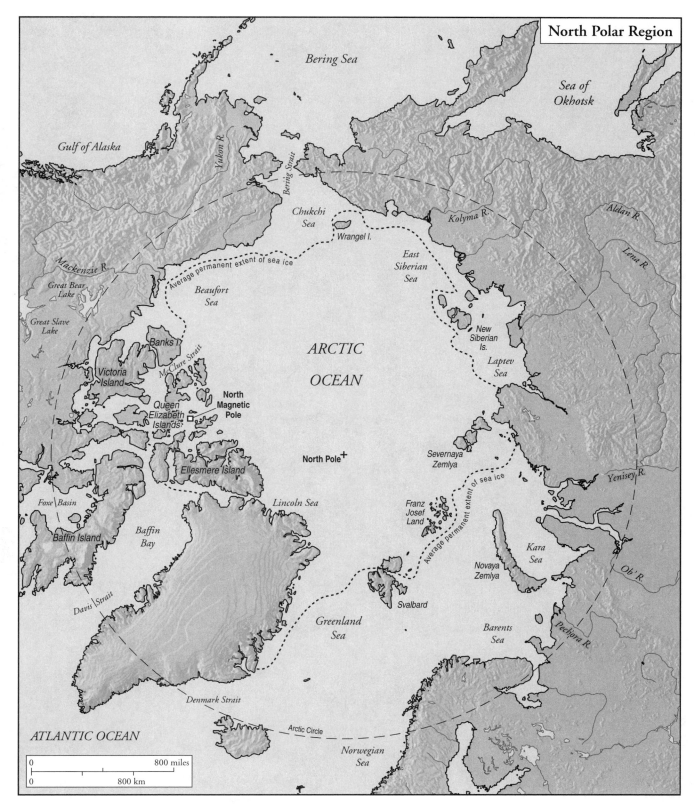

North Polar Region

Bering Sea

Sea of Okhotsk

Gulf of Alaska

Yukon R.

Bering Strait

Chukchi Sea

Kolyma R.

Aldan R.

Wrangel I.

East Siberian Sea

Lena R.

Mackenzie R.

Average permanent extent of sea ice

Beaufort Sea

Great Bear Lake

New Siberian Is.

Great Slave Lake

Banks I.

McClure Strait

Victoria Island

ARCTIC OCEAN

Laptev Sea

Queen Elizabeth Islands

North Magnetic Pole

North Pole +

Severnaya Zemlya

Yenisey R.

Ellesmere Island

Franz Josef Land

Lincoln Sea

Foxe Basin

Kara Sea

Baffin Island

Baffin Bay

Novaya Zemlya

Ob' R.

Davis Strait

Svalbard

Average permanent extent of sea ice

Pechora R.

Greenland Sea

Barents Sea

Denmark Strait

Arctic Circle

ATLANTIC OCEAN

Norwegian Sea

0		800 miles
0		800 km

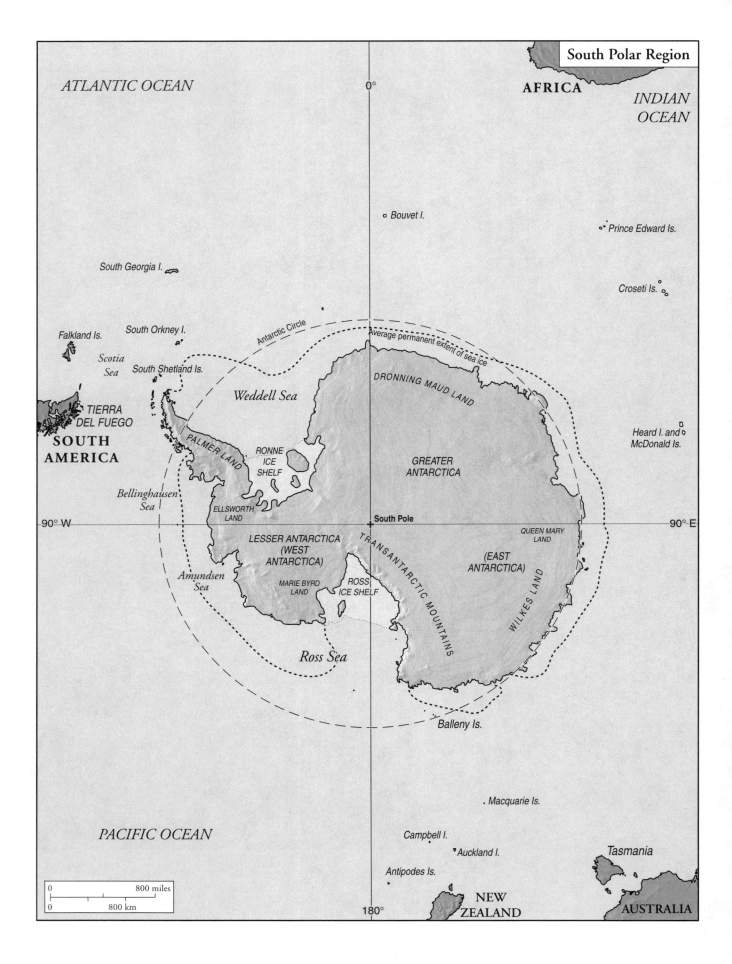

South Polar Region

ATLANTIC OCEAN

0°

AFRICA

INDIAN OCEAN

Bouvet I.

Prince Edward Is.

South Georgia I.

Croseti Is.

Falkland Is.

South Orkney I.

Antarctic Circle

Average permanent extent of sea ice

Heard I. and McDonald Is.

Scotia Sea

South Shetland Is.

DRONNING MAUD LAND

Weddell Sea

PALMER LAND

RONNE ICE SHELF

GREATER ANTARCTICA

TIERRA DEL FUEGO

SOUTH AMERICA

Bellinghausen Sea

ELLSWORTH LAND

South Pole

90° W

QUEEN MARY LAND

90° E

LESSER ANTARCTICA (WEST ANTARCTICA)

TRANSANTARCTIC MOUNTAINS

(EAST ANTARCTICA)

Amundsen Sea

MARIE BYRD LAND

ROSS ICE SHELF

WILKES LAND

Ross Sea

Balleny Is.

Macquarie Is.

PACIFIC OCEAN

Campbell I.

Auckland I.

Tasmania

Antipodes Is.

0   800 miles

0   800 km

180°

NEW ZEALAND

AUSTRALIA

II. ANCIENT ROUTES: THE MEDITERRANEAN REGION, EUROPE, AND ASIA

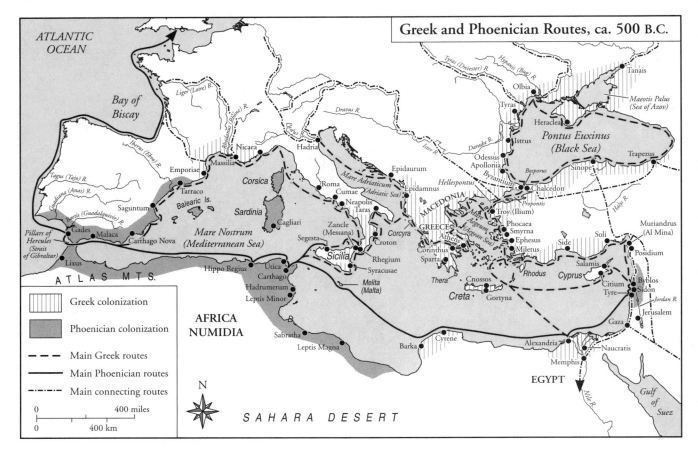

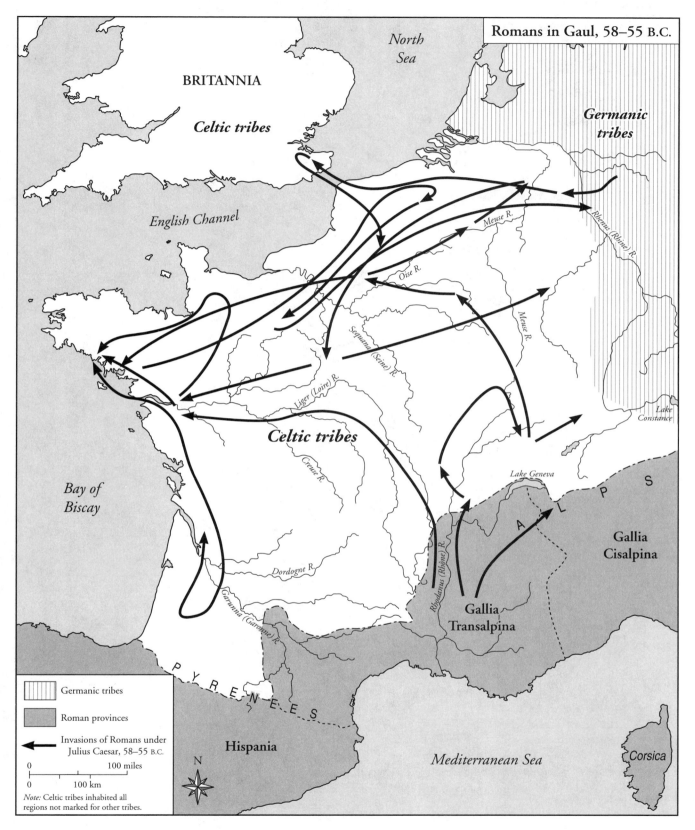

Romans in Gaul, 58–55 B.C.

North Sea

BRITANNIA

Celtic tribes

Germanic tribes

English Channel

Rhenus (Rhine) R.

Meuse R.

Oise R.

Sequana (Seine) R.

Meuse R.

Bay of Biscay

Liger (Loire) R.

Celtic tribes

Lake Constance

Creuse R.

Lake Geneva

A L P S

Gallia Cisalpina

Dordogne R.

Rhodanus (Rhône) R.

Gallia Transalpina

Garumna (Garonne) R.

P Y R E N E E S

Germanic tribes

Roman provinces

Invasions of Romans under Julius Caesar, 58–55 B.C.

0   100 miles

0   100 km

N

Note: Celtic tribes inhabited all regions not marked for other tribes.

Hispania

Mediterranean Sea

Corsica

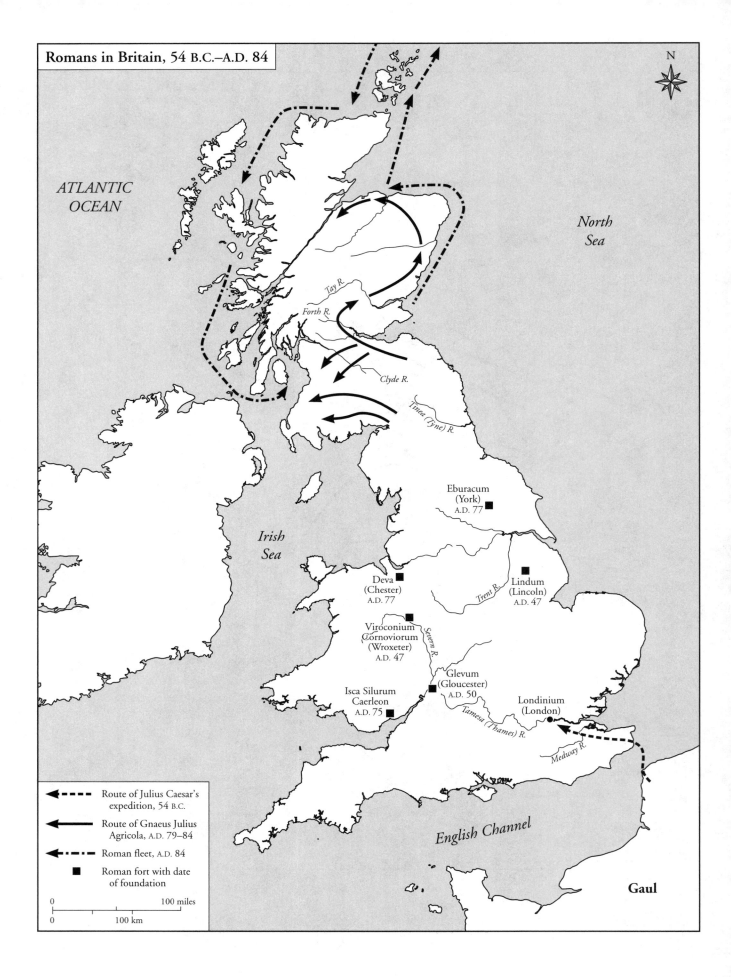

Romans in Britain, 54 B.C.–A.D. 84

N

ATLANTIC
OCEAN

North
Sea

Tay R.

Forth R.

Clyde R.

Tinea (Tyne) R.

Irish
Sea

Eburacum
(York)
A.D. 77

Deva
(Chester)
A.D. 77

Lindum
(Lincoln)
A.D. 47

Trent R.

Viroconium
Cornoviorum
(Wroxeter)
A.D. 47

Severn R.

Glevum
(Gloucester)
A.D. 50

Isca Silurum
Caerleon
A.D. 75

Londinium
(London)

Tamesa (Thames) R.

Medway R.

English Channel

Gaul

Route of Julius Caesar's
expedition, 54 B.C.

Route of Gnaeus Julius
Agricola, A.D. 79–84

Roman fleet, A.D. 84

Roman fort with date
of foundation

0   100 miles

0   100 km

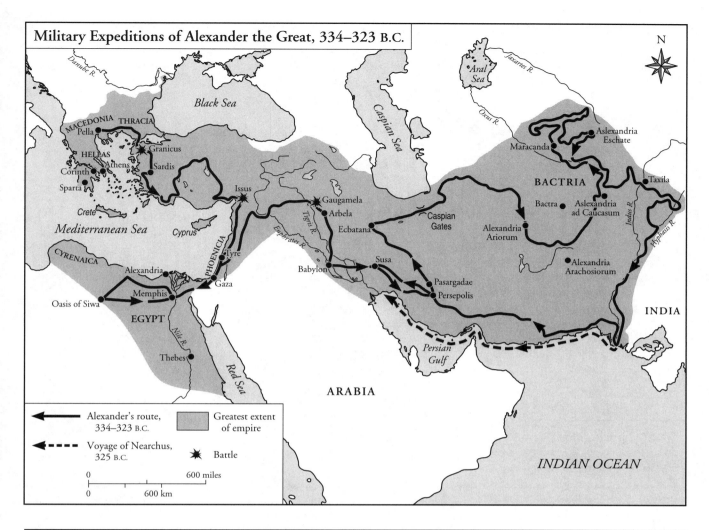

Military Expeditions of Alexander the Great, 334–323 B.C.

N

Danube R.

Black Sea

Aral Sea

Jaxartes R.

MACEDONIA
THRACIA
Pella
HELLAS
Granicus
Athens
Corinth
Sardis
Sparta
Crete

Mediterranean Sea

Cyprus

Issus

Oxus R.

Maracanda

Aslexandria Eschate

BACTRIA

Taxila

Gaugamela
Arbela
Tigris R.
Ecbatana

Caspian Gates

Bactra
Aslexandria ad Caucasum

Indus R.

Hyphasis R.

CYRENAICA

Alexandria
PHOENICIA
Tyre
Memphis
Gaza

Babylon
Susa

Alexandria Ariorum

Pasargadae
Persepolis

Alexandria Arachosiorum

INDIA

Oasis of Siwa

EGYPT

Nile R.

Thebes

Red Sea

Persian Gulf

ARABIA

Caspian Sea

Euphrates R.

Alexander's route, 334–323 B.C.

Voyage of Nearchus, 325 B.C.

Greatest extent of empire

✴ Battle

0   600 miles
0   600 km

INDIAN OCEAN

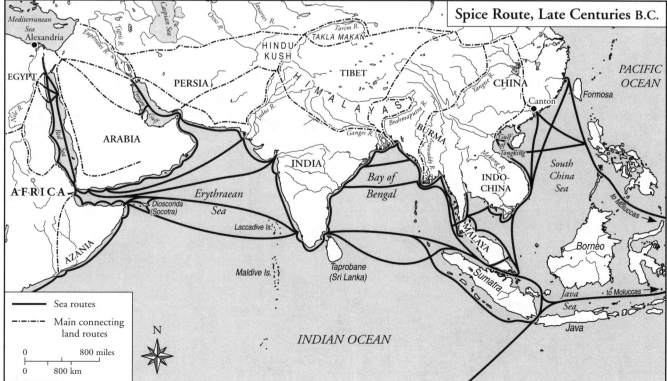

Spice Route, Late Centuries B.C.

Mediterranean Sea
Alexandria

Caspian Sea

Euphrates R.
Tigris R.
Oxus R.
Jaxartes R.

Tarim R.
TAKLA MAKAN

HINDU KUSH

TIBET

CHINA
Yangtse R.

PACIFIC OCEAN

EGYPT
Nile R.

PERSIA

Indus R.

H I M A L A Y A S

Brahmaputra R.

Canton

Formosa

ARABIA

Red Sea

Persian Gulf

INDIA

Ganges R.

BURMA

Irrawaddy R.
Mekong R.

Gulf of Tongking

South China Sea

AFRICA

Dioscorida (Socotra)

Erythraean Sea

Laccadive Is.

Bay of Bengal

INDO-CHINA

to Moluccas

AZANIA

Maldive Is.

Taprobane (Sri Lanka)

MALAYA

Borneo

Sumatra

Java Sea

Java

to Moluccas

Sea routes

Main connecting land routes

N

0   800 miles
0   800 km

INDIAN OCEAN

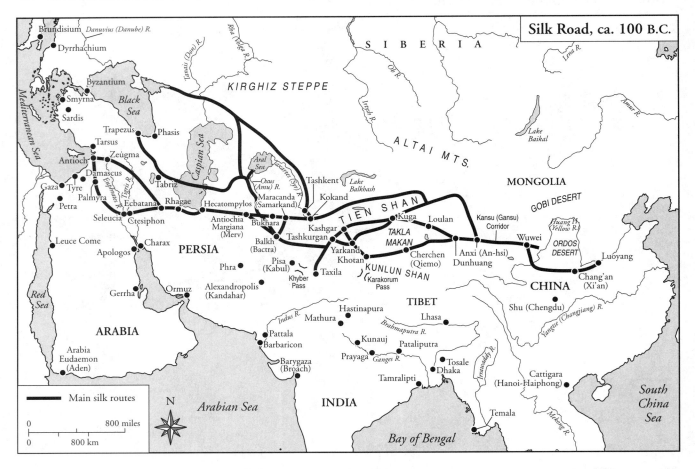

III. NEW WATER ROUTES AROUND THE WORLD

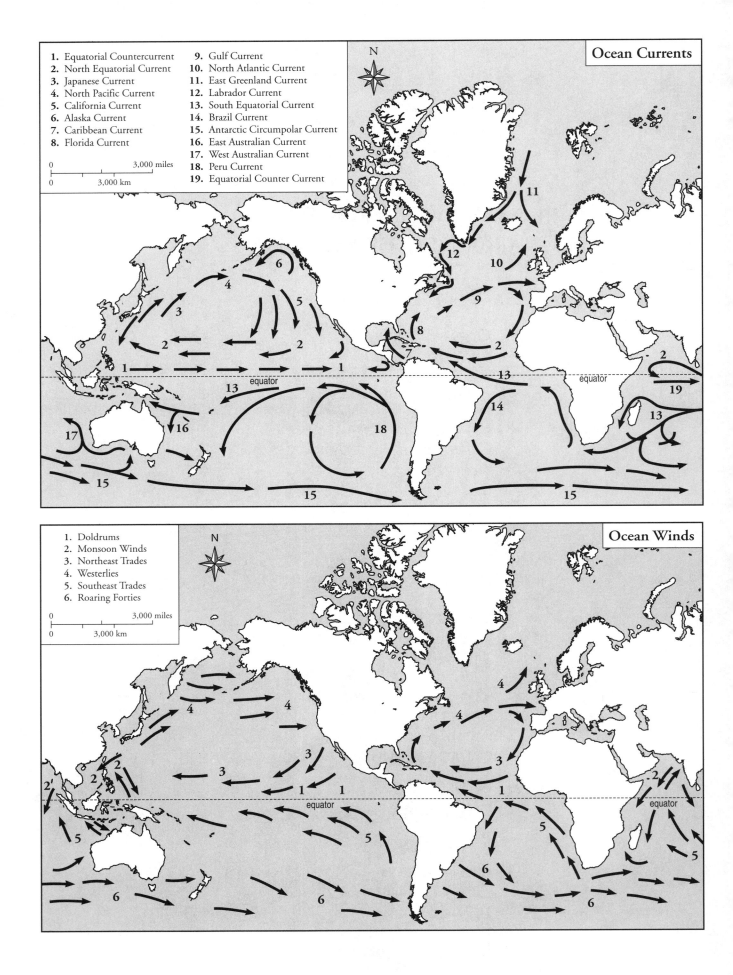

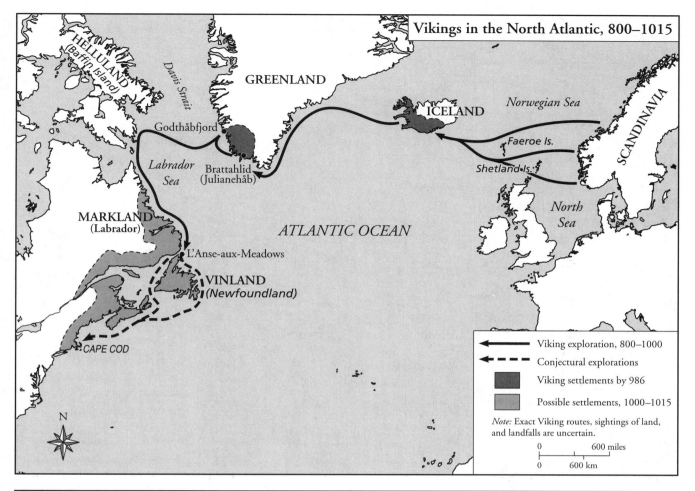

Vikings in the North Atlantic, 800–1015

HELLULAND (Baffin Island)

GREENLAND

Davis Strait

ICELAND

Norwegian Sea

Faeroe Is.

Shetland Is.

SCANDINAVIA

Godthåbfjord

Labrador Sea

Brattahlid (Julianehåb)

MARKLAND (Labrador)

North Sea

ATLANTIC OCEAN

L'Anse-aux-Meadows

VINLAND (Newfoundland)

CAPE COD

N

⟵	Viking exploration, 800–1000
◀╌╌	Conjectural explorations
▓	Viking settlements by 986
░	Possible settlements, 1000–1015

Note: Exact Viking routes, sightings of land, and landfalls are uncertain.

0 — 600 miles

0 — 600 km

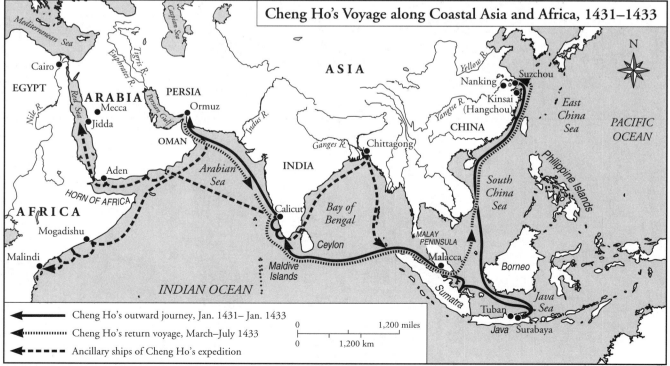

Cheng Ho's Voyage along Coastal Asia and Africa, 1431–1433

Mediterranean Sea

Cairo

EGYPT

Caspian Sea

Nile R.

ARABIA

Mecca

Jidda

Euphrates R.

Tigris R.

PERSIA

Ormuz

OMAN

Aden

HORN OF AFRICA

AFRICA

Mogadishu

Malindi

Persian Gulf

Arabian Sea

Indus R.

INDIA

Ganges R.

Calicut

Ceylon

Maldive Islands

ASIA

Yellow R.

Suzhou

Nanking

Kinsai (Hangchou)

CHINA

Yangtse R.

Chittagong

Bay of Bengal

MALAY PENINSULA

Malacca

East China Sea

South China Sea

Philippine Islands

PACIFIC OCEAN

Borneo

Sumatra

INDIAN OCEAN

Java Sea

Tuban

Java Surabaya

N

⟵	Cheng Ho's outward journey, Jan. 1431– Jan. 1433
◀··········	Cheng Ho's return voyage, March–July 1433
◀╌╌╌	Ancillary ships of Cheng Ho's expedition

0 — 1,200 miles

0 — 1,200 km

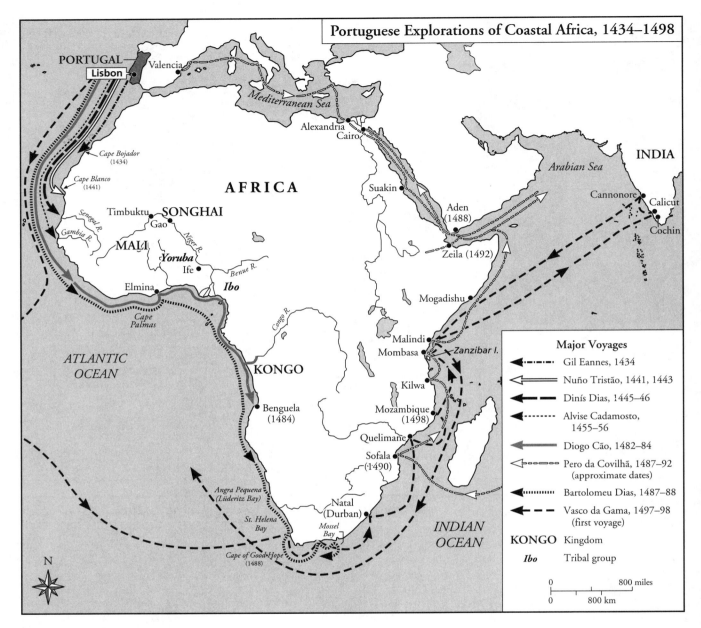

Portuguese Explorations of Coastal Africa, 1434–1498

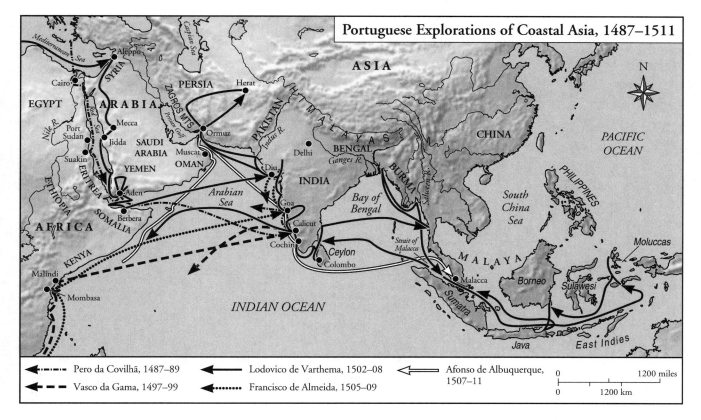

Portuguese Explorations of Coastal Asia, 1487–1511

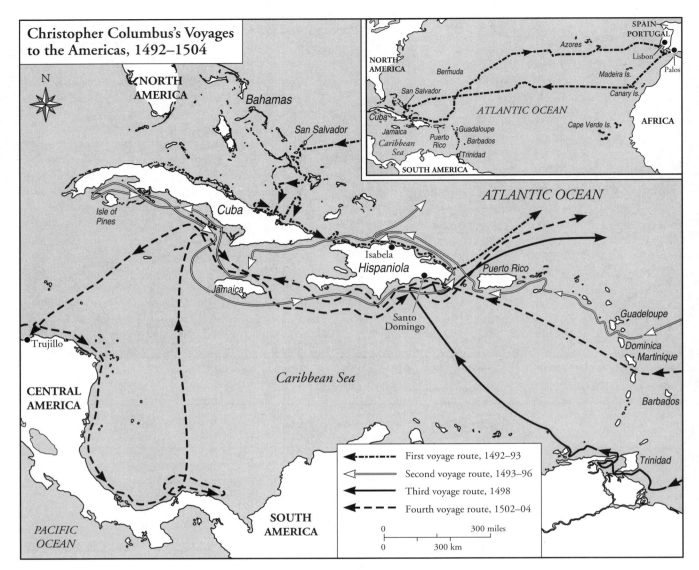

Christopher Columbus's Voyages to the Americas, 1492–1504

First voyage route, 1492–93
Second voyage route, 1493–96
Third voyage route, 1498
Fourth voyage route, 1502–04

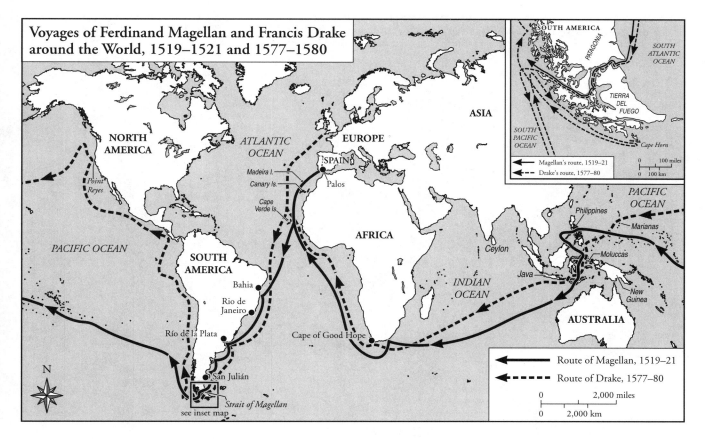

Voyages of Ferdinand Magellan and Francis Drake around the World, 1519–1521 and 1577–1580

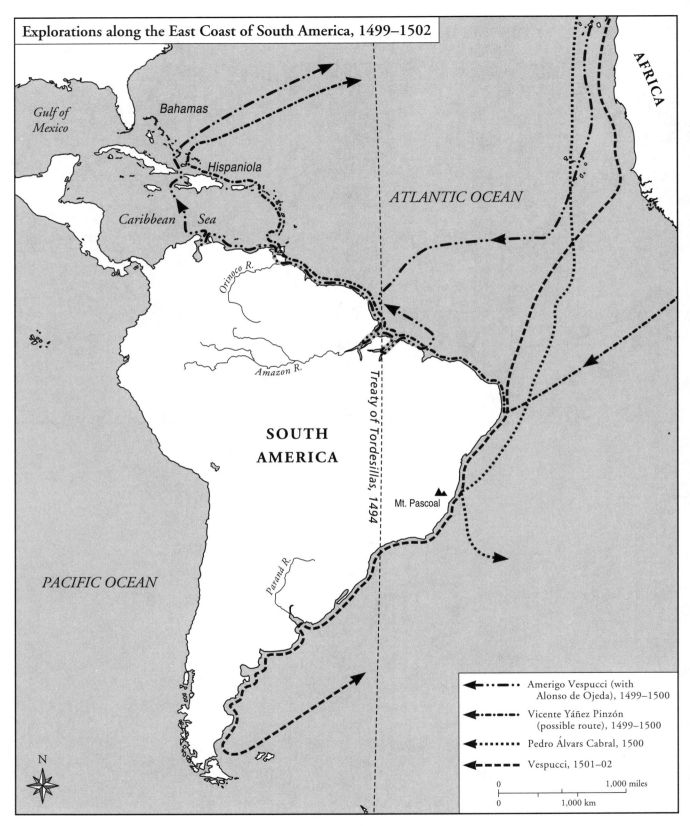

Explorations along the East Coast of South America, 1499–1502

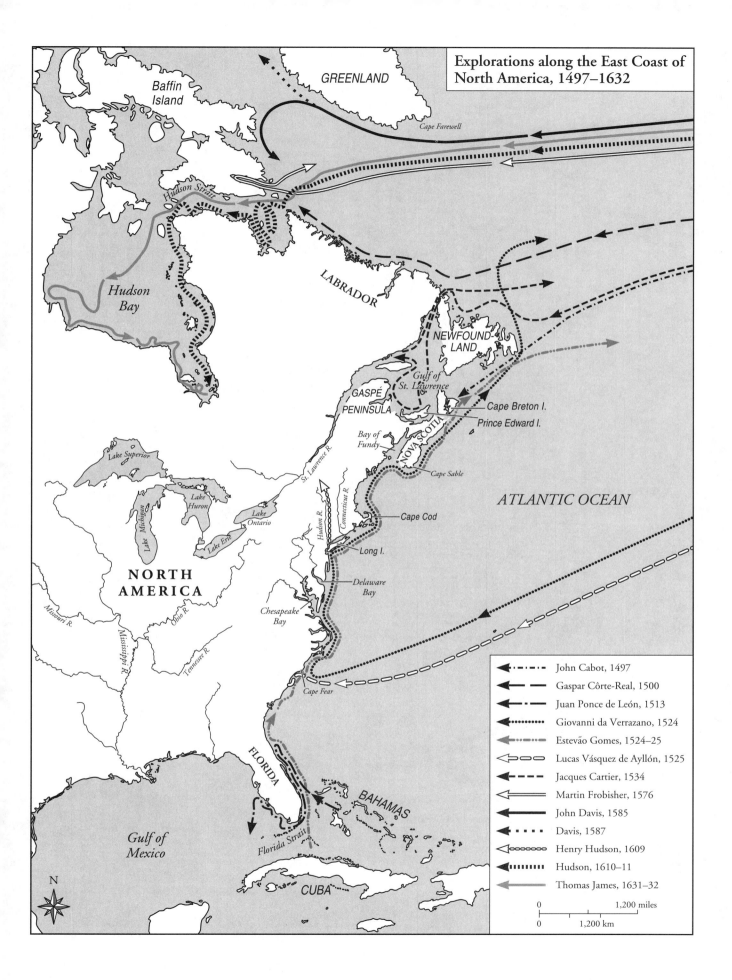

Explorations along the East Coast of North America, 1497–1632

GREENLAND

Baffin Island

Cape Farewell

Hudson Strait

LABRADOR

Hudson Bay

NEWFOUND-LAND

GASPÉ PENINSULA

Gulf of St. Lawrence

Cape Breton I.

Prince Edward I.

Bay of Fundy

NOVA SCOTIA

Cape Sable

Lake Superior

Lake Michigan

Lake Huron

Lake Ontario

Lake Erie

St. Lawrence R.

Hudson R.

Connecticut R.

ATLANTIC OCEAN

Cape Cod

Long I.

NORTH AMERICA

Delaware Bay

Chesapeake Bay

Missouri R.

Mississippi R.

Ohio R.

Tennessee R.

Cape Fear

FLORIDA

BAHAMAS

Gulf of Mexico

Florida Strait

CUBA

N

◄━·━·━	John Cabot, 1497
◄━ ━ ━	Gaspar Côrte-Real, 1500
◄━·━·━	Juan Ponce de León, 1513
◄·······	Giovanni da Verrazano, 1524
◄┅┅┅	Estevão Gomes, 1524–25
◁□□□	Lucas Vásquez de Ayllón, 1525
◄─ ─ ─	Jacques Cartier, 1534
◁────	Martin Frobisher, 1576
◄─────	John Davis, 1585
◄·······	Davis, 1587
◁○○○○	Henry Hudson, 1609
◄▪▪▪▪▪	Hudson, 1610–11
◄─────	Thomas James, 1631–32

0	1,200 miles
0	1,200 km

IV. ASIA

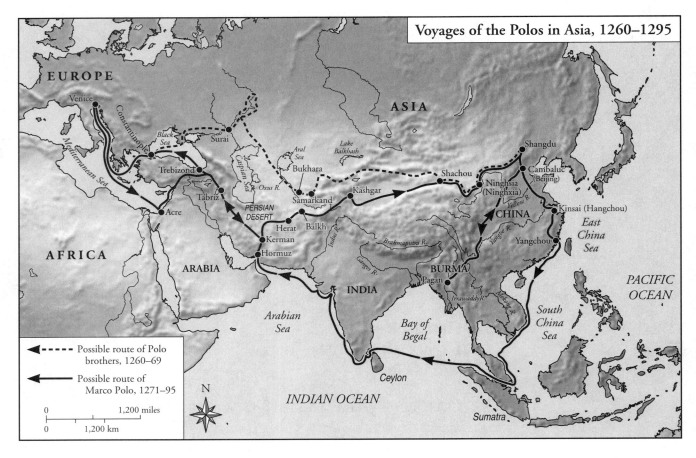

Voyages of the Polos in Asia, 1260–1295

Legend:
- - - - ◄ Possible route of Polo brothers, 1260–69
- ──── ◄ Possible route of Marco Polo, 1271–95

0 _____ 1,200 miles
0 _____ 1,200 km

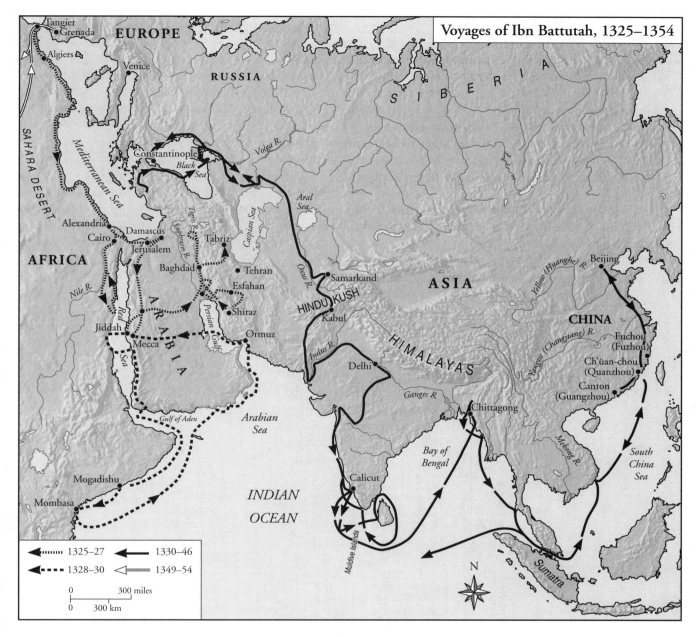

Voyages of Ibn Battutah, 1325–1354

Tangier
Grenada
EUROPE
Algiers
Venice
RUSSIA
SIBERIA
Constantinople
Black Sea
Volga R.
SAHARA DESERT
Mediterranean Sea
Aral Sea
Alexandria
Damascus
Tabriz
Caspian Sea
AFRICA
Cairo
Jerusalem
Tigris R.
Euphrates R.
Oxus R.
Samarkand
ASIA
Yellow (Huanghe) R.
Beijing
Baghdad
Tehran
HINDU KUSH
Nile R.
Esfahan
Kabul
CHINA
Red Sea
ARABIA
Shiraz
Persian Gulf
Indus R.
HIMALAYAS
Yangtse (Changjiang) R.
Fuchou (Fuzhou)
Jiddah
Mecca
Ormuz
Delhi
Ch'üan-chou (Quanzhou)
Gulf of Aden
Arabian Sea
Ganges R.
Chittagong
Canton (Guangzhou)
Mogadishu
Bay of Bengal
Mekong R.
South China Sea
Mombasa
INDIAN OCEAN
Calicut
Maldive Islands
N
Sumatra

1325–27   1330–46
1328–30   1349–54

0   300 miles
0   300 km

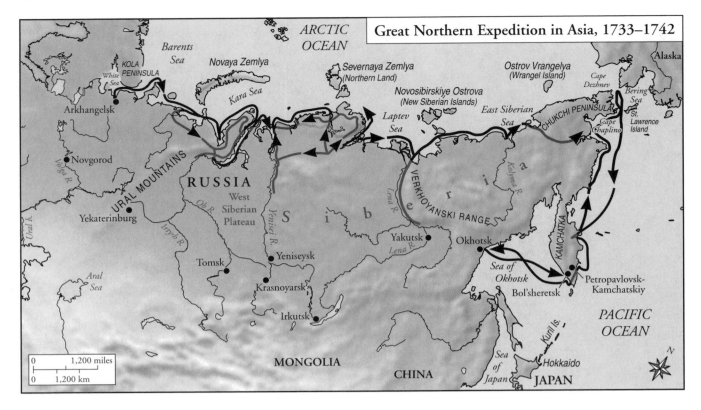

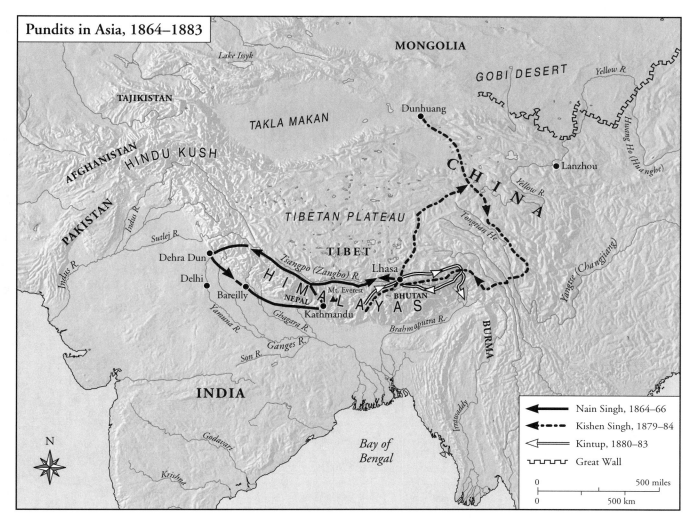

Pundits in Asia, 1864–1883

MONGOLIA

GOBI DESERT

Lake Issyk

TAJIKISTAN

TAKLA MAKAN

Dunhuang

AFGHANISTAN

HINDU KUSH

CHINA

Lanzhou

Yellow R.

Huang Ho (Huanghe)

PAKISTAN

Indus R.

Sutlej R.

TIBETAN PLATEAU

Yellow R.

Tongtian He

Indus R.

Dehra Dun

Delhi

TIBET

Tsangpo (Zangbo) R.

Lhasa

H I M A L A Y A S

Yangtse (Changjiang)

Bareilly

NEPAL

Mt. Everest

Kathmandu

BHUTAN

Yamuna R.

Ghagara R.

Son R.

Ganges R.

Brahmaputra R.

BURMA

INDIA

Godavari

Irrawaddy

Krishna

Bay of Bengal

N

Nain Singh, 1864–66

Kishen Singh, 1879–84

Kintup, 1880–83

Great Wall

0   500 miles

0   500 km

V. THE AMERICAS

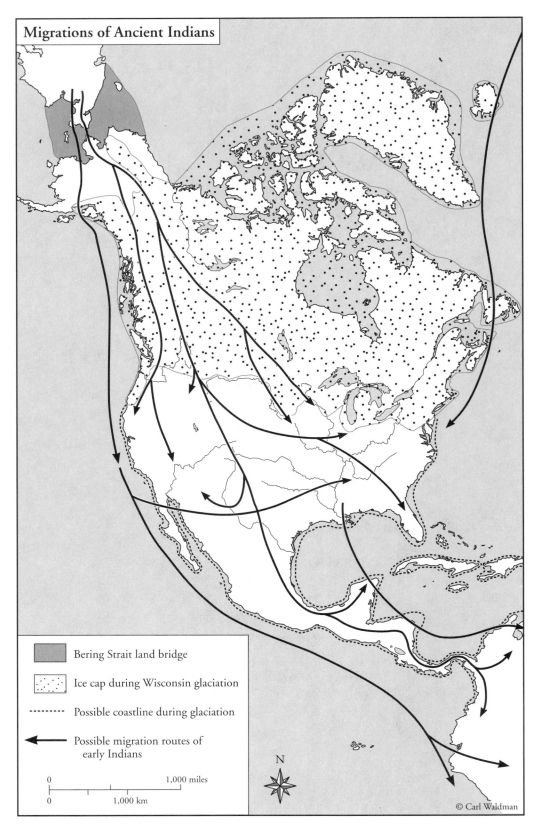

Migrations of Ancient Indians

Bering Strait land bridge

Ice cap during Wisconsin glaciation

Possible coastline during glaciation

Possible migration routes of early Indians

0   1,000 miles
0   1,000 km

N

© Carl Waldman

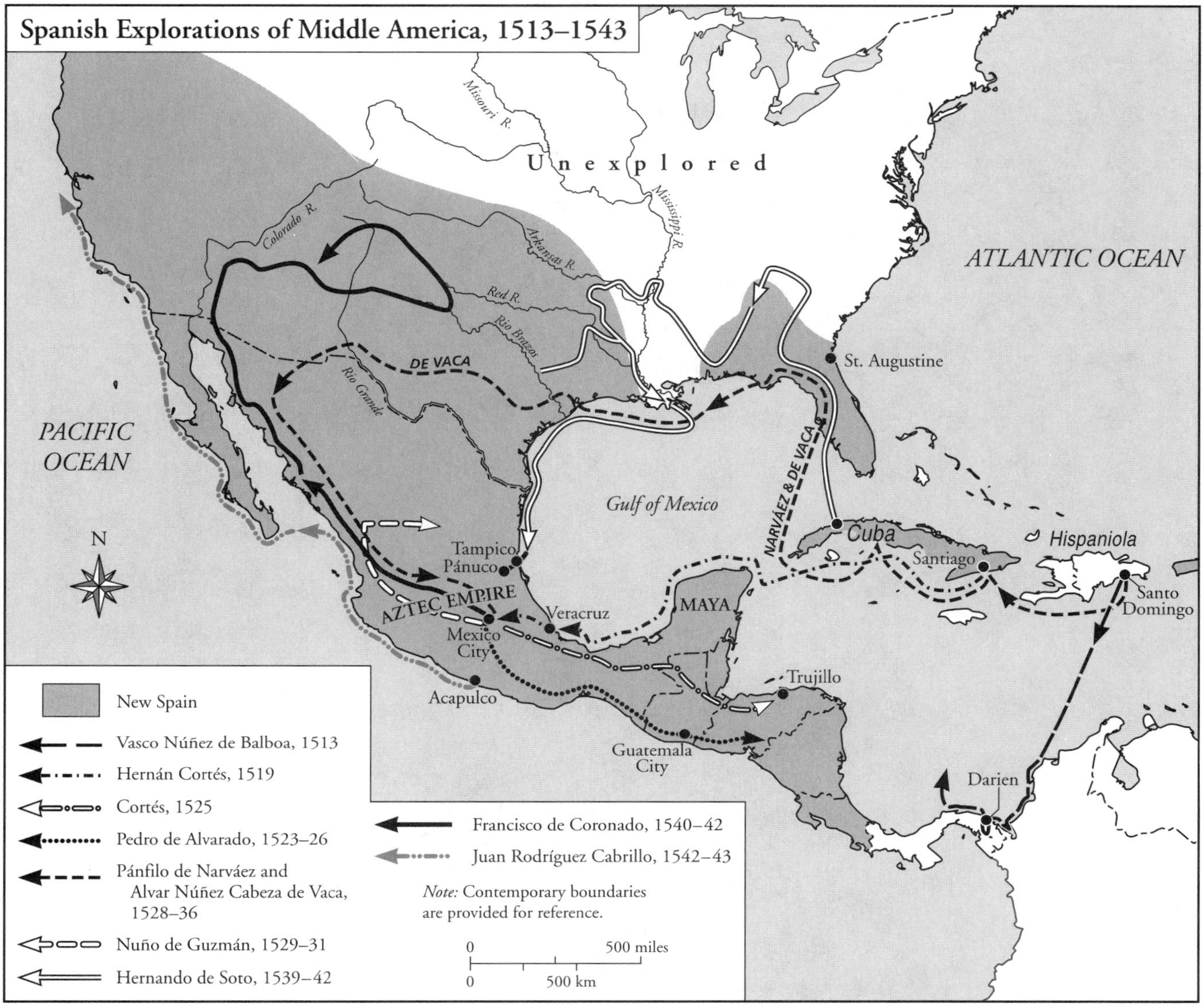
Spanish Explorations of Middle America, 1513–1543
Unexplored
Missouri R.
Mississippi R.
Colorado R.
Arkansas R.
Red R.
Rio Brazos
Rio Grande
DE VACA
ATLANTIC OCEAN
PACIFIC OCEAN
St. Augustine
Gulf of Mexico
NARVÁEZ & DE VACA
Cuba
Hispaniola
Santiago
Santo Domingo
N
Tampico
Pánuco
AZTEC EMPIRE
Veracruz
MAYA
Mexico City
Trujillo
Acapulco
Guatemala City
Darien
New Spain
Vasco Núñez de Balboa, 1513
Hernán Cortés, 1519
Cortés, 1525
Pedro de Alvarado, 1523–26
Pánfilo de Narváez and Alvar Núñez Cabeza de Vaca, 1528–36
Nuño de Guzmán, 1529–31
Hernando de Soto, 1539–42
Francisco de Coronado, 1540–42
Juan Rodríguez Cabrillo, 1542–43
Note: Contemporary boundaries are provided for reference.
0 500 miles
0 500 km

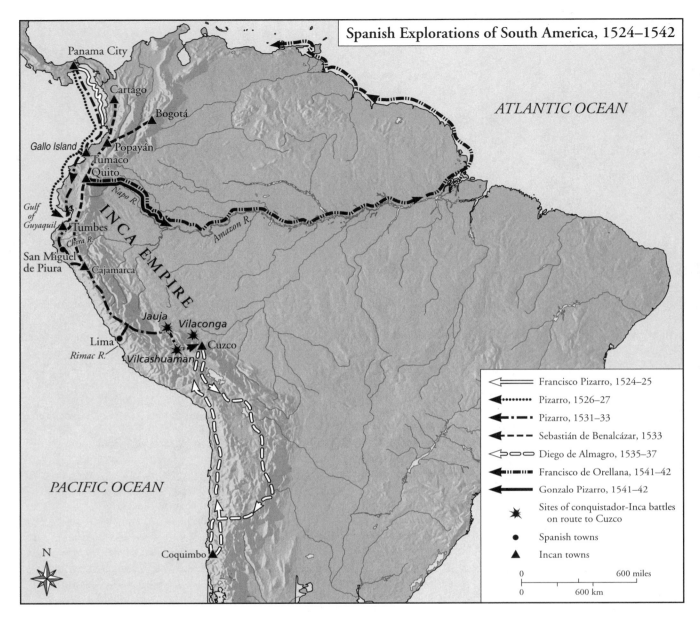

Spanish Explorations of South America, 1524–1542

ATLANTIC OCEAN

Panama City
Cartago
Bogotá
Gallo Island
Popayán
Tumaco
Quito
Napo R.
Gulf of Guyaquil
Tumbes
Chira R.
Amazon R.
San Miguel de Piura
Cajamarca
INCA EMPIRE
Jauja
Vilaconga
Lima
Cuzco
Rimac R.
Vilcashuaman

PACIFIC OCEAN

Coquimbo

N

→ Francisco Pizarro, 1524–25
•••• Pizarro, 1526–27
–·–· Pizarro, 1531–33
– – – Sebastián de Benalcázar, 1533
⇦□□□ Diego de Almagro, 1535–37
◄▮▮▮ Francisco de Orellana, 1541–42
← Gonzalo Pizarro, 1541–42
✳ Sites of conquistador-Inca battles on route to Cuzco
● Spanish towns
▲ Incan towns

0   600 miles
0   600 km

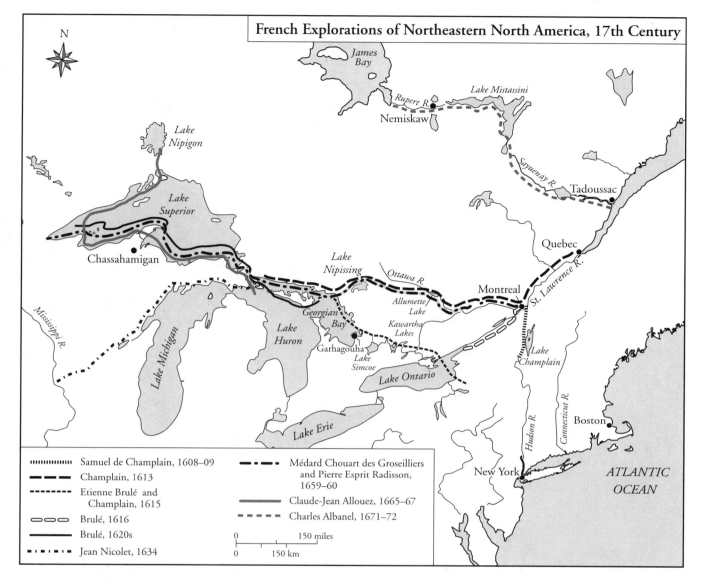

French Explorations of Northeastern North America, 17th Century

N

James Bay

Lake Mistassini

Rupert R.

Nemiskaw

Saguenay R.

Tadoussac

Lake Nipigon

Lake Superior

Chassahamigan

Lake Nipissing

Ottawa R.

Quebec

Montreal

St. Lawrence R.

Allumette Lake

Kawartha Lakes

Lake Champlain

Lake Michigan

Mississippi R.

Lake Huron

Georgian Bay

Garhagouha

Lake Simcoe

Lake Ontario

Lake Erie

Hudson R.

Connecticut R.

Boston

New York

ATLANTIC OCEAN

Legend	
▪▪▪▪▪▪▪ Samuel de Champlain, 1608–09	▪-▪-▪- Médard Chouart des Groseilliers and Pierre Esprit Radisson, 1659–60
▬ ▬ ▬ Champlain, 1613	
---- Etienne Brulé and Champlain, 1615	▬▬▬ Claude-Jean Allouez, 1665–67
◦◦◦ Brulé, 1616	▪▪▪▪ Charles Albanel, 1671–72
▬▬ Brulé, 1620s	
▪-▪-▪ Jean Nicolet, 1634	

0   150 miles

0   150 km

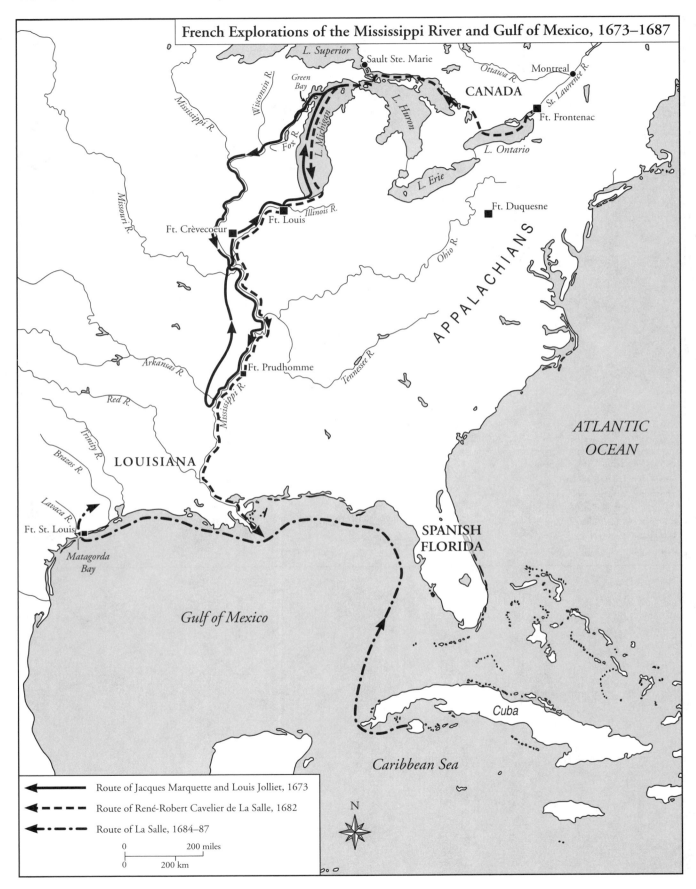

French Explorations of the Mississippi River and Gulf of Mexico, 1673–1687

Route of Jacques Marquette and Louis Jolliet, 1673

Route of René-Robert Cavelier de La Salle, 1682

Route of La Salle, 1684–87

0   200 miles

0   200 km

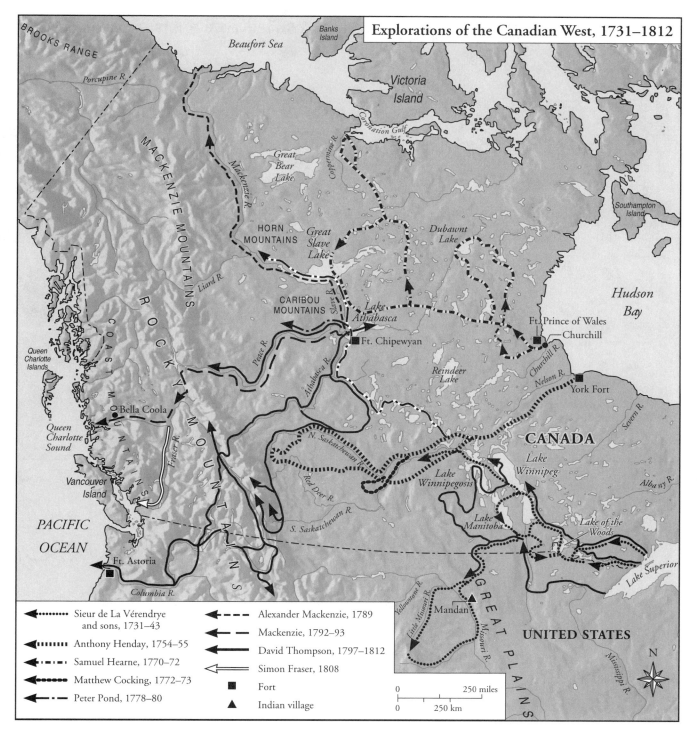

Explorations of the Canadian West, 1731–1812

BROOKS RANGE · Porcupine R. · Beaufort Sea · Banks Island · Victoria Island · Coronation Gulf · Coppermine R. · MACKENZIE MOUNTAINS · Mackenzie R. · Great Bear Lake · Dubawnt Lake · Southampton Island · Liard R. · HORN MOUNTAINS · Great Slave Lake · Hudson Bay · ROCKY MOUNTAINS · COAST MOUNTAINS · CARIBOU MOUNTAINS · Slave R. · Lake Athabasca · Ft. Prince of Wales · Churchill · Queen Charlotte Islands · Peace R. · Athabasca R. · Ft. Chipewyan · Reindeer Lake · Churchill R. · Nelson R. · York Fort · Queen Charlotte Sound · Bella Coola · Fraser R. · N. Saskatchewan R. · CANADA · Lake Winnipeg · Severn R. · Albany R. · Vancouver Island · Red Deer R. · Lake Winnipegosis · Lake Manitoba · Lake of the Woods · PACIFIC OCEAN · S. Saskatchewan R. · Lake Superior · Ft. Astoria · Columbia R. · MOUNTAINS · Yellowstone R. · Little Missouri R. · Mandan · GREAT PLAINS · Missouri R. · UNITED STATES · Mississippi R. · N

Legend	
•••••• Sieur de La Vérendrye and sons, 1731–43	– – – Alexander Mackenzie, 1789
ⅠⅠⅠⅠⅠ Anthony Henday, 1754–55	— — Mackenzie, 1792–93
–·–·– Samuel Hearne, 1770–72	—— David Thompson, 1797–1812
●●●●● Matthew Cocking, 1772–73	⇦ Simon Fraser, 1808
—·—· Peter Pond, 1778–80	■ Fort
	▲ Indian village

0   250 miles
0   250 km

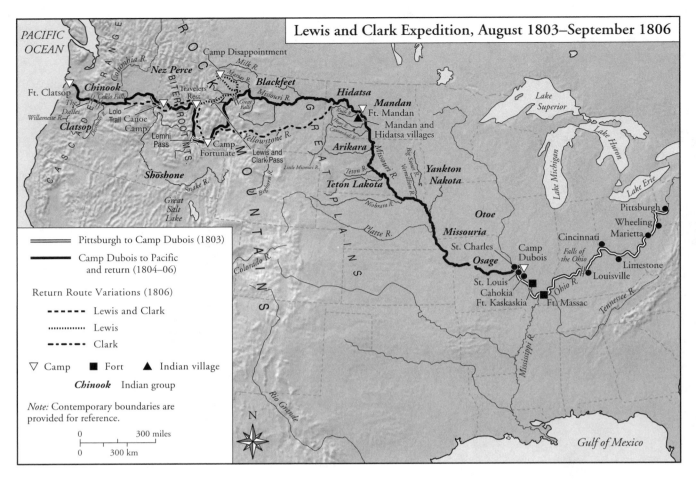

Explorations of the American West, 1804–1846

Meriwether Lewis and
William Clark, 1804–06

Zebulon Pike, 1806–07

Astorians, 1811–12

Stephen H. Long, 1817–20

Jedediah Smith, 1826–29

John C. Frémont, 1842–44

Frémont, 1845–46

Note: Contemporary boundaries are provided for reference.

0   400 miles
0   400 km

CANADA

Great Falls

Yellowstone R.

Mandan

Missouri R.

Mississippi R.

ROCKY

BITTERROOT RANGE

Columbia

Astoria

Columbia R.

Clearwater R.

Snake R.

Great
Salt
Lake

Sacramento

San Francisco

SIERRA NEVADA

San Gabriel

Los Angeles

PACIFIC
OCEAN

Colorado R.

Rio Grande

Chihuahua

MEXICO

N

MOUNTAINS

GREAT
AMERICAN
DESERT

N. Platte R.

S. Platte R.

Pikes Peak

SANGRE DE CRISTO RANGE

Taos

Santa Fe

Canadian R.

Arkansas R.

Council
Bluffs

Kansas
City

St. Louis

Mississippi R.

Nacogdoches

Natchitoches

New Orleans

Gulf of Mexico

Gulf of California

VI. THE PACIFIC OCEAN AND AUSTRALIA

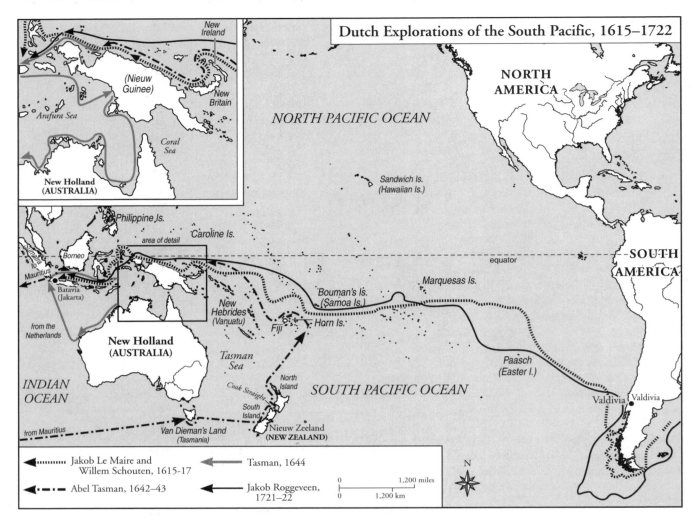

Dutch Explorations of the South Pacific, 1615–1722

NORTH AMERICA

NORTH PACIFIC OCEAN

Sandwich Is.
(Hawaiian Is.)

equator

SOUTH AMERICA

New Ireland

(Nieuw Guinee)

New Britain

Arafura Sea

Coral Sea

New Holland (AUSTRALIA)

Philippine Is.

Caroline Is.

area of detail

Borneo

Sumatra to Mauritius

Batavia (Jakarta)

from the Netherlands

New Holland (AUSTRALIA)

New Hebrides (Vanuatu)

Fiji

Bouman's Is. (Samoa Is.)

Horn Is.

Marquesas Is.

Paasch (Easter I.)

Valdivia   Valdivia

INDIAN OCEAN

Tasman Sea

Cook Straight

North Island

South Island

Nieuw Zeeland (NEW ZEALAND)

SOUTH PACIFIC OCEAN

from Mauritius

Van Dieman's Land (Tasmania)

Jakob Le Maire and
Willem Schouten, 1615-17

Abel Tasman, 1642–43

Tasman, 1644

Jakob Roggeveen,
1721–22

0   1,200 miles
0   1,200 km

N

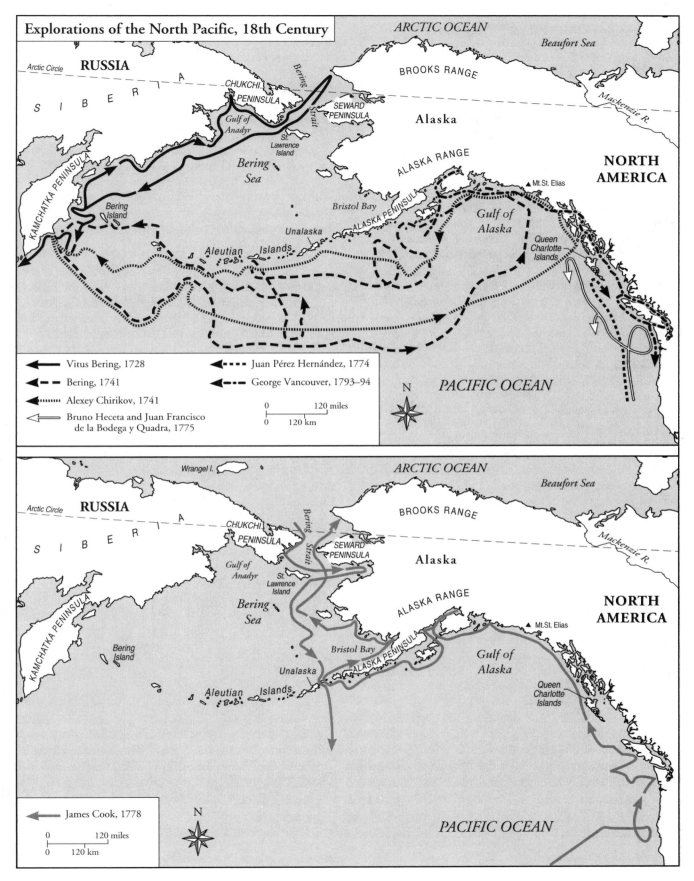

Explorations of the North Pacific, 18th Century

RUSSIA

Arctic Circle

S I B E R I A

ARCTIC OCEAN

Beaufort Sea

BROOKS RANGE

CHUKCHI PENINSULA

Bering Strait

SEWARD PENINSULA

Alaska

Mackenzie R.

Gulf of Anadyr

St. Lawrence Island

KAMCHATKA PENINSULA

Bering Island

Bering Sea

ALASKA RANGE

▲ Mt. St. Elias

NORTH AMERICA

Bristol Bay

Unalaska

ALASKA PENINSULA

Gulf of Alaska

Aleutian Islands

Queen Charlotte Islands

← Vitus Bering, 1728	◄- - - Juan Pérez Hernández, 1774
◄- - Bering, 1741	◄-·-·- George Vancouver, 1793–94
◄····· Alexey Chirikov, 1741	
⇐ Bruno Heceta and Juan Francisco de la Bodega y Quadra, 1775	

0 ——— 120 miles
0 ——— 120 km

N

PACIFIC OCEAN

Wrangel I.

ARCTIC OCEAN

Beaufort Sea

RUSSIA

Arctic Circle

S I B E R I A

BROOKS RANGE

CHUKCHI PENINSULA

Bering Strait

SEWARD PENINSULA

Alaska

Mackenzie R.

Gulf of Anadyr

St. Lawrence Island

KAMCHATKA PENINSULA

Bering Island

Bering Sea

ALASKA RANGE

▲ Mt. St. Elias

NORTH AMERICA

Bristol Bay

Unalaska

ALASKA PENINSULA

Gulf of Alaska

Aleutian Islands

Queen Charlotte Islands

← James Cook, 1778

0 ——— 120 miles
0 ——— 120 km

N

PACIFIC OCEAN

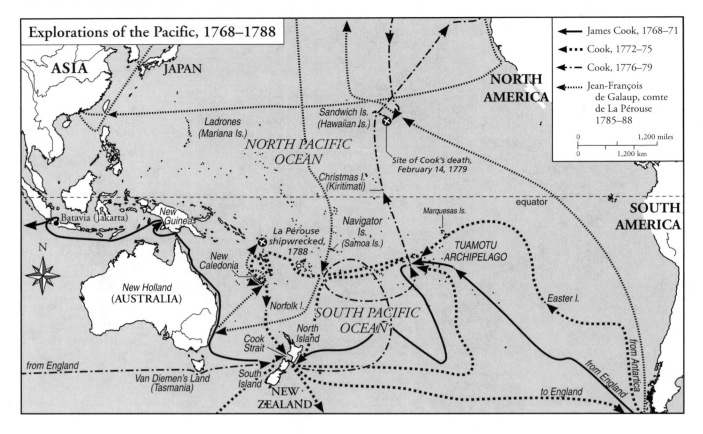

Explorations of the Pacific, 1768–1788

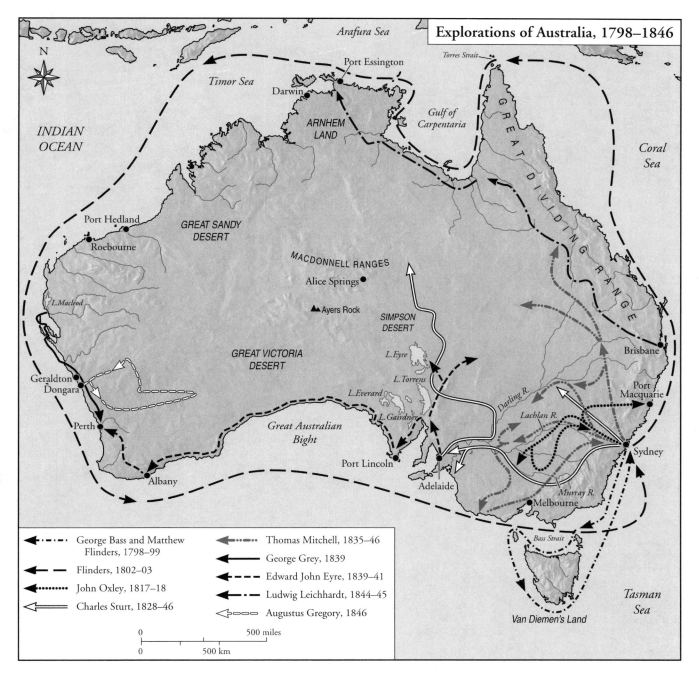

Explorations of Australia, 1798–1846

George Bass and Matthew Flinders, 1798–99
Flinders, 1802–03
John Oxley, 1817–18
Charles Sturt, 1828–46
Thomas Mitchell, 1835–46
George Grey, 1839
Edward John Eyre, 1839–41
Ludwig Leichhardt, 1844–45
Augustus Gregory, 1846

0   500 miles
0   500 km

VII. AFRICA

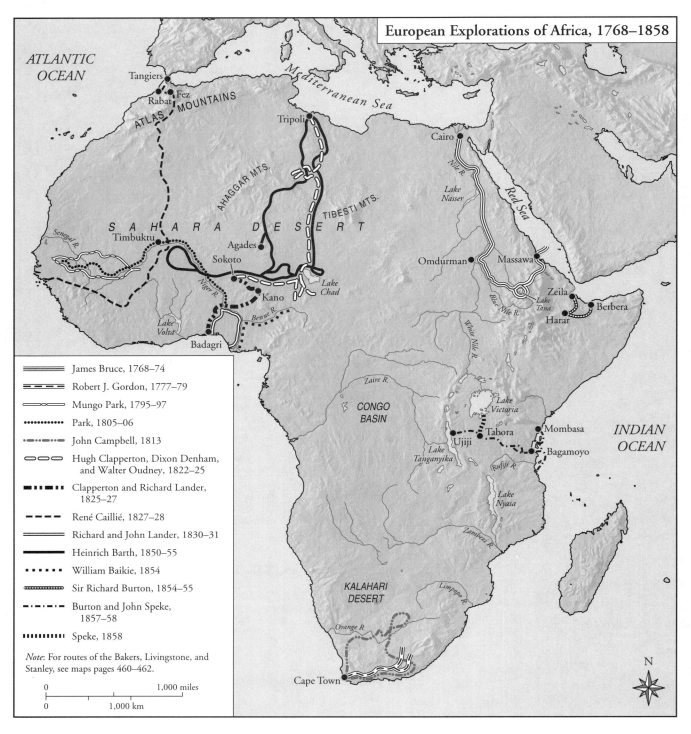

European Explorations of Africa, 1768–1858

ATLANTIC OCEAN

Mediterranean Sea

Tangiers
Rabat Fez
ATLAS MOUNTAINS

Tripoli

Cairo

Nile R.

Lake Nasser

Red Sea

AHAGGAR MTS.

SAHARA DESERT

TIBESTI MTS.

Senegal R.

Timbuktu

Agades
Sokoto

Niger R.

Kano

Benue R.

Lake Chad

Omdurman

Massawa

Blue Nile R.

Lake Tana

Zeila
Harar
Berbera

Lake Volta

Badagri

Zaire R.

CONGO BASIN

White Nile R.

Lake Victoria

Tabora
Ujiji

Lake Tanganyika

Rufiji R.

Mombasa

Bagamoyo

INDIAN OCEAN

Lake Nyasa

Zambezi R.

KALAHARI DESERT

Limpopo R.

Orange R.

Cape Town

N

Legend:
- James Bruce, 1768–74
- Robert J. Gordon, 1777–79
- Mungo Park, 1795–97
- Park, 1805–06
- John Campbell, 1813
- Hugh Clapperton, Dixon Denham, and Walter Oudney, 1822–25
- Clapperton and Richard Lander, 1825–27
- René Caillié, 1827–28
- Richard and John Lander, 1830–31
- Heinrich Barth, 1850–55
- William Baikie, 1854
- Sir Richard Burton, 1854–55
- Burton and John Speke, 1857–58
- Speke, 1858

Note: For routes of the Bakers, Livingstone, and Stanley, see maps pages 460–462.

0 ——— 1,000 miles
0 ——— 1,000 km

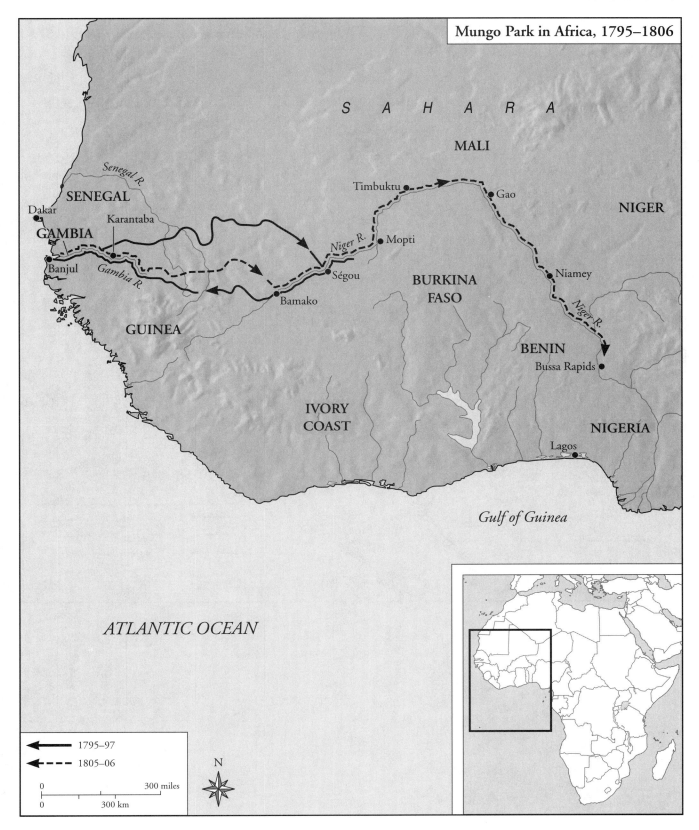

Mungo Park in Africa, 1795–1806

SAHARA

MALI

Timbuktu ● ➤ Gao ●

NIGER

Senegal R.

SENEGAL

Dakar ●

Karantaba ●

GAMBIA

Banjul ●

Gambia R.

Niger R. ● Mopti

Ségou ●

Bamako ●

GUINEA

BURKINA FASO

Niamey ●

Niger R.

BENIN

Bussa Rapids ●

IVORY COAST

NIGERIA

Lagos ●

Gulf of Guinea

ATLANTIC OCEAN

← ——— 1795–97

← - - - 1805–06

N

0   300 miles

0   300 km

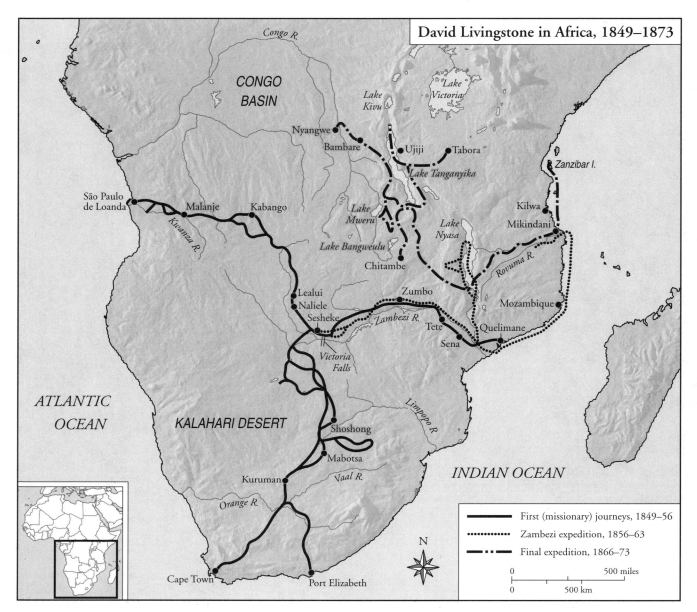

David Livingstone in Africa, 1849–1873

Congo R.

CONGO BASIN

Lake Kivu

Lake Victoria

Nyangwe

Bambare

Ujiji

Tabora

Zanzibar I.

Lake Tanganyika

São Paulo de Loanda

Malanje

Kabango

Kwanza R.

Lake Mweru

Lake Nyasa

Kilwa

Mikindani

Lake Bangweulu

Chitambe

Rovuma R.

Mozambique

Lealui

Naliele

Sesheke

Zumbo

Zambezi R.

Tete

Quelimane

Victoria Falls

Sena

ATLANTIC OCEAN

KALAHARI DESERT

Limpopo R.

Shoshong

Mabotsa

INDIAN OCEAN

Kuruman

Vaal R.

Orange R.

N

Cape Town

Port Elizabeth

First (missionary) journeys, 1849–56

Zambezi expedition, 1856–63

Final expedition, 1866–73

0   500 miles

0   500 km

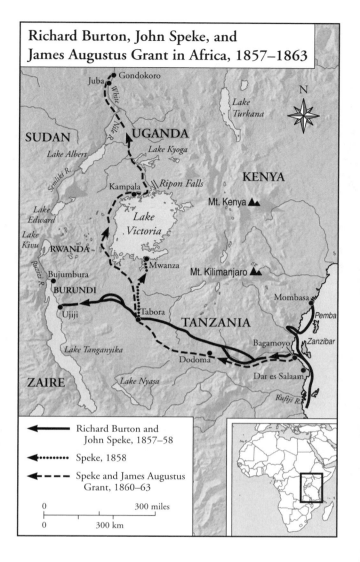

Richard Burton, John Speke, and James Augustus Grant in Africa, 1857–1863

Richard Burton and John Speke, 1857–58

Speke, 1858

Speke and James Augustus Grant, 1860–63

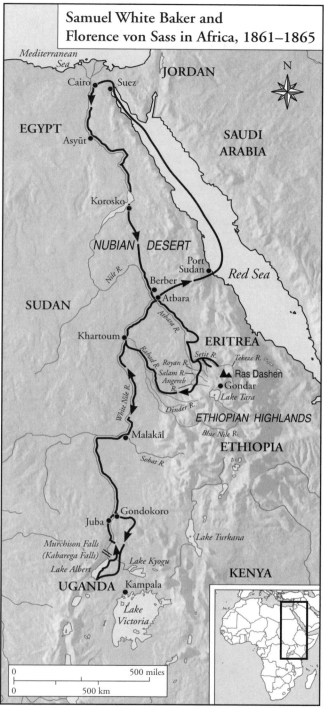

Samuel White Baker and Florence von Sass in Africa, 1861–1865

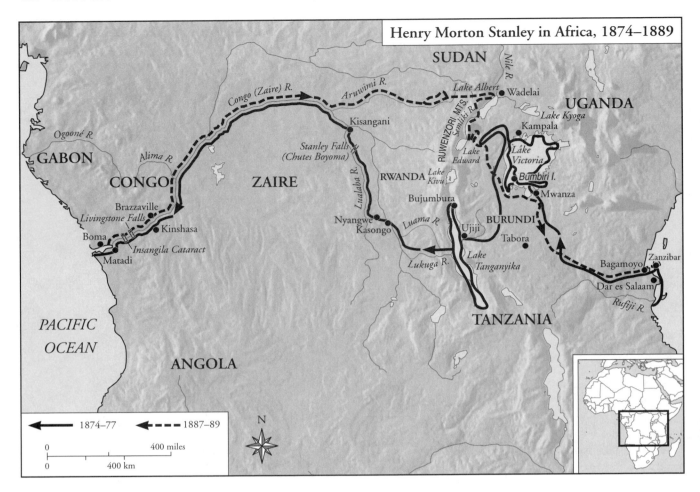

Henry Morton Stanley in Africa, 1874–1889

VIII. THE ARCTIC

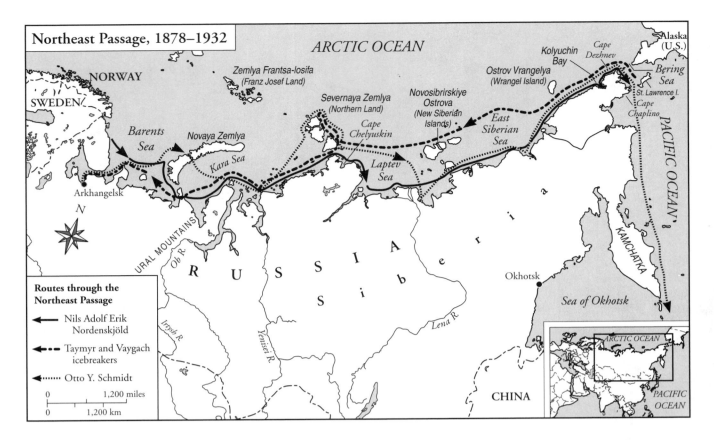

Northeast Passage, 1878–1932

ARCTIC OCEAN

NORWAY

SWEDEN

Alaska (U.S.)

Kolyuchin Bay

Cape Dezhnev

Ostrov Vrangelya (Wrangel Island)

Zemlya Frantsa-Iosifa (Franz Josef Land)

Bering Sea

Severnaya Zemlya (Northern Land)

Novosibrirskiye Ostrova (New Siberian Islands)

St. Lawrence I.

Cape Chaplino

Barents Sea

Novaya Zemlya

Cape Chelyuskin

East Siberian Sea

Kara Sea

Laptev Sea

Arkhangelsk

N

URAL MOUNTAINS

Ob R.

Irtysh R.

Yenisei R.

Lena R.

R U S S I A

S i b e r i a

Okhotsk

KAMCHATKA

Sea of Okhotsk

PACIFIC OCEAN

Routes through the Northeast Passage

→ Nils Adolf Erik Nordenskjöld

–·→ Taymyr and Vaygach icebreakers

····→ Otto Y. Schmidt

0   1,200 miles
0   1,200 km

ARCTIC OCEAN

PACIFIC OCEAN

CHINA

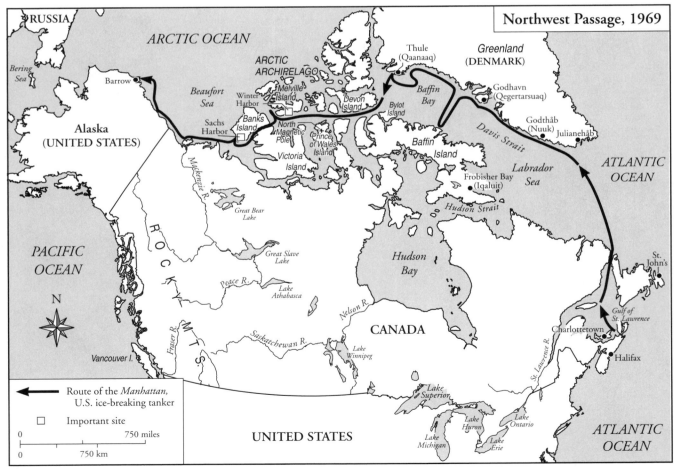

Northwest Passage, 1969

RUSSIA

ARCTIC OCEAN

Bering Sea

Barrow

Beaufort Sea

ARCTIC ARCHIPELAGO

Melville Island

Winter Harbor

Thule (Qaanaaq)

Greenland (DENMARK)

Baffin Bay

Godhavn (Qegertarsuaq)

Alaska (UNITED STATES)

Sachs Harbor

Banks Island

North Magnetic Pole

Devon Island

Bylot Island

Godthåb (Nuuk)

Julianehåb

Victoria Island

Prince of Wales Island

Baffin Island

Davis Strait

Mackenzie R.

Great Bear Lake

PACIFIC OCEAN

N

ROCKY

Great Slave Lake

Peace R.

Lake Athabasca

Fraser R.

MTS.

Saskatchewan R.

Nelson R.

Frobisher Bay (Iqaluit)

Labrador Sea

ATLANTIC OCEAN

Hudson Strait

Hudson Bay

CANADA

St. John's

Gulf of St. Lawrence

St. Lawrence R.

Charlottetown

Halifax

Vancouver I.

Lake Winnipeg

Lake Superior

Lake Huron

Lake Michigan

Lake Ontario

Lake Erie

UNITED STATES

ATLANTIC OCEAN

→ Route of the *Manhattan*, U.S. ice-breaking tanker

☐ Important site

0   750 miles
0   750 km

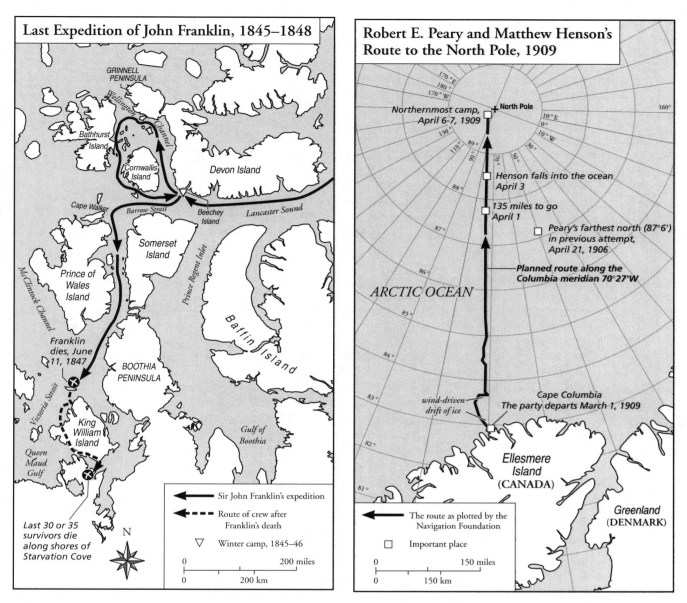

Last Expedition of John Franklin, 1845–1848

GRINNELL PENINSULA

Wellington Channel

Bathurst Island

Cornwallis Island

Devon Island

Cape Walker

Barrow Strait

Beechey Island

Lancaster Sound

Somerset Island

Prince Regent Inlet

Prince of Wales Island

McClintock Channel

Baffin Island

Franklin dies, June 11, 1847

BOOTHIA PENINSULA

Victoria Strait

King William Island

Queen Maud Gulf

Gulf of Boothia

Last 30 or 35 survivors die along shores of Starvation Cove

N

→ Sir John Franklin's expedition

▪▪▪→ Route of crew after Franklin's death

▽ Winter camp, 1845–46

0   200 miles

0   200 km

Robert E. Peary and Matthew Henson's Route to the North Pole, 1909

North Pole

Northernmost camp, April 6-7, 1909

Henson falls into the ocean April 3

135 miles to go April 1

Peary's farthest north (87°6') in previous attempt, April 21, 1906

Planned route along the Columbia meridian 70°27'W

ARCTIC OCEAN

wind-driven drift of ice

Cape Columbia The party departs March 1, 1909

Ellesmere Island (CANADA)

Greenland (DENMARK)

→ The route as plotted by the Navigation Foundation

▫ Important place

0   150 miles

0   150 km

IX. THE ANTARCTIC

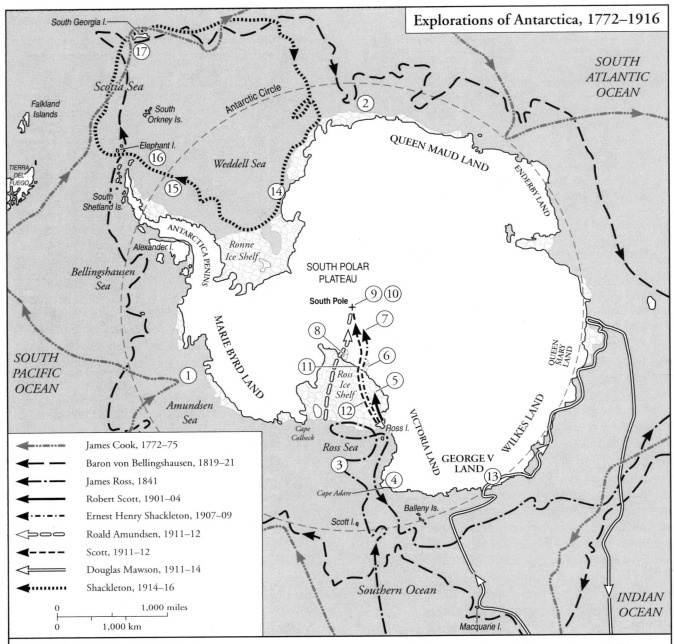

Explorations of Antarctica, 1772–1916

Legend:

- James Cook, 1772–75
- Baron von Bellingshausen, 1819–21
- James Ross, 1841
- Robert Scott, 1901–04
- Ernest Henry Shackleton, 1907–09
- Roald Amundsen, 1911–12
- Scott, 1911–12
- Douglas Mawson, 1911–14
- Shackleton, 1914–16

0 — 1,000 miles
0 — 1,000 km

1. January 30, 1774: James Cook's farthest south—71°10'S, 106°54'W; dense ice prevents him from continuing.

2. January 28, 1820: Fabian Gottlieb von Bellingshausen makes the first sighting of the Antarctic continent.

3. January 1841: James Ross becomes the first to force a passage through the Antarctic pack ice; he discovers the Ross Sea, Victoria Land, and the Ross Ice Shelf.

4. 1899: Carsten Egeberg Borchgrevink becomes the first to winter on Antarctica.

5. December 30, 1902: Robert Scott's farthest south—82°17'S.

6. December 1908: Ernest Henry Shackleton discovers the huge Beardmore Glacier and climbs it to reach the 10,000-foot-high Antarctic Plateau.

7. January 9, 1909: Shackleton's farthest south—88°07'S; 97 miles from the Pole.

8. November 17, 1911: Roald Amundsen discovers the Axel Heiberg Glacier.

9. December 14, 1911: Amundsen is the first to reach the South Pole.

10. January 17, 1912: Scott reaches the South Pole.

11. February 17, 1912: Death of Edgar Evans, the first of Scott's party to die.

12. March 21, 1912: Scott's last camp; Scott, Wilson, and Bowers die here; Oates dies nearby on March 17; the camp is just 11 miles from a large food depot, about 79°39'S.

13. 1913: Douglas Mawson reaches George V Land

14. January 18, 1915: Shakleton's ship *Endurance* becomes icebound.

15. November 21, 1915: *Endurance* sinks.

16. April 15, 1916: Shackleton's party reaches Elephant Island; Shackleton leaves by boat for South Georgia Island on April 24.

17. May 9, 1916: Shackleton reaches South Georgia Island and returns to Elephant Island to rescue his men on August 30.

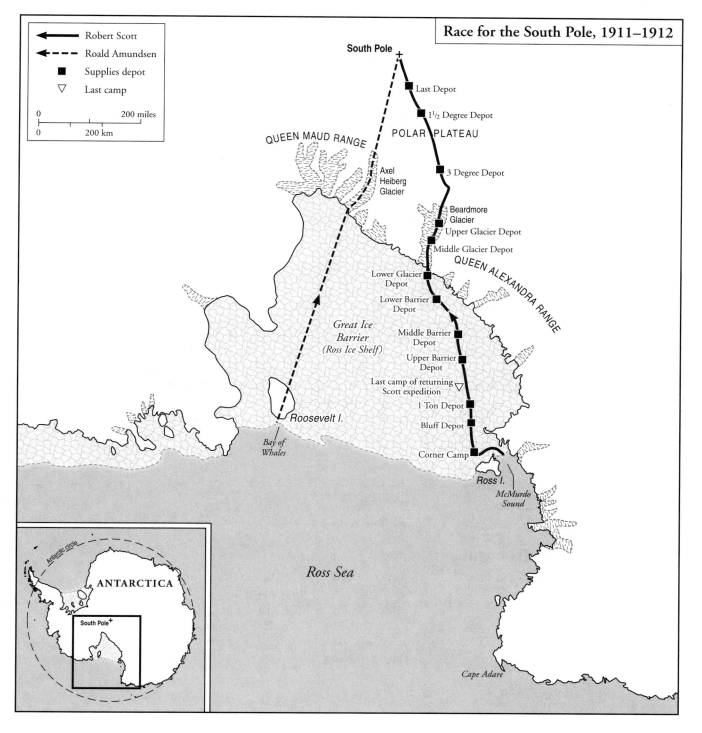

Race for the South Pole, 1911–1912

Legend:
- Robert Scott
- Roald Amundsen
- ■ Supplies depot
- ▽ Last camp

0 — 200 miles
0 — 200 km

South Pole

Last Depot

1½ Degree Depot

POLAR PLATEAU

QUEEN MAUD RANGE

3 Degree Depot

Axel
Heiberg
Glacier

Beardmore
Glacier

Upper Glacier Depot

Middle Glacier Depot

QUEEN ALEXANDRA RANGE

Lower Glacier
Depot

Lower Barrier
Depot

Great Ice
Barrier
(Ross Ice Shelf)

Middle Barrier
Depot

Upper Barrier
Depot

Last camp of returning
Scott expedition

1 Ton Depot

Bluff Depot

Roosevelt I.

Corner Camp

Bay of
Whales

Ross I.

McMurdo
Sound

Ross Sea

Cape Adare

Antarctic circle

ANTARCTICA

South Pole +

Chronology of Exploration

The following chronology of world exploration includes events relating directly to exploration, giving at least one date for the individuals listed in Volume I and other important dates from Volume II. Many general historical events, such as migrations of peoples and the establishment of nations, although important as a frame of reference to the subject matter, are not provided. To the left of certain entries is indicated the general geographic regions of exploration. The parenthetical place-names refer to modern-day nations, states, and provinces are further used to describe locations.

❖

ca. 2450 B.C.

AFRICA/ASIA
- Egyptian HANNU sails into the RED SEA along the African coastline and Arabian Peninsula.

ca. 2340–2305

ASIA/EUROPE
- SARGON, the ruler of Akkad in Mesopotamia, establishes trade contacts with peoples of the Indus Valley, Arabian Peninsula, and eastern MEDITERRANEAN SEA. He launches naval campaigns in the Persian Gulf and possibly in the Mediterranean.

ca. 2270

AFRICA
- Egyptian provincial governor HERKHUF heads a trading expedition from the upper NILE RIVER southward to the interior of central East Africa.

ca. 1492

AFRICA
- Egyptian queen HATSHEPSUT sends a maritime trading expedition into the RED SEA to territory south of the Gulf of Aden in East Africa.

ca. 600

- Greek philosopher Thales of Miletus establishes natural science principles. On 585 B.C., he accurately predicts an eclipse of the Sun.

ca. 600–597

AFRICA

- Egyptian king NECHO II commissions a Phoenician maritime expedition into the RED SEA and Indian Ocean, which perhaps circumnavigates Africa.

ca. 575

- Greek philosopher Anaximander drafts the first known map to represent a concept of the world.

ca. 520–494

ASIA/AFRICA

- Greek historian HECATAEUS OF MILETUS travels in Asia Minor and Egypt and ascends the NILE RIVER.

510–507

ASIA

- Greek mariner SCYLAX descends the Indus River for Persian emperor Darius I and sails from the Arabian Sea to the RED SEA.

ca. 475

- Greek philosopher Parmenides hypothesizes that Earth is round.

ca. 470

AFRICA

- HANNO heads a Carthaginian maritime expedition from the MEDITERRANEAN SEA through the Strait of Gibraltar (see GIBRALTAR, STRAIT OF) along Africa's Atlantic coast.

ca. 457–443

ASIA/AFRICA/EUROPE

- Greek historian HERODOTUS travels in the Mediterranean region and ascends the NILE RIVER.

ca. 450

EUROPE

- HIMILCO heads a Carthaginian maritime expedition from the MEDITERRANEAN SEA through the Strait of Gibraltar (see GIBRALTAR, STRAIT OF) along Europe's Atlantic coast.

ca. 420–400

ASIA

- Greek physician CTESIAS OF CNIDUS travels in Persia (Iran) and India.

401

ASIA

- Greek soldier XENOPHON leads mercenaries from Persia (Iran) through Iraq, Turkey, Armenia, and Georgia to Greece.

350

- Greek philosopher Plato writes of the lost continent of ATLANTIS in his dialogues *Timaeus* and *Critias*.

334–323

ASIA

- Macedonian leader ALEXANDER THE GREAT conquers territory from the eastern Mediterranean to the Indus Valley of Pakistan and India.

ca. 325

- Greek philosopher Aristotle determines scientific principles relating to navigation, among them that, in traveling from north to south, new constellations become visible while others disappear.

EUROPE

- Greek scholar PYTHEAS heads a maritime expedition along the coasts of Spain, France, and Britain, exploring the North Sea and Baltic Sea.

325–324

ASIA

- Greek soldier NEARCHUS, under ALEXANDER THE GREAT, explores the coasts of Pakistan and Iran from the INDUS RIVER delta to the head of the Persian Gulf.

300–290

ASIA

- Greek diplomat MEGASTHENES travels from Syria to northern India, reaching the GANGES RIVER.

240–195

- Greek scholar ERATOSTHENES heads a library at Alexandria and writes the first systematic treatise of geography.

ca. 170–120

- Greek scholar HIPPARCHUS makes astronomical and geographic observations.

ca. 150

- Greek geographer Crates of Mallus constructs the first known GLOBE.

ca. 138–109

ASIA

- CH'ANG-CH'IEN heads two Chinese diplomatic missions to western lands, during which he explores the Altai Mountains of central Asia and Afghanistan and visits Sinkiang in western China. The route he travels develops into the SILK ROAD, a trade route between East and West.

120–115

INDIA/AFRICA

- Greek navigator EUDOXUS, in service to Egypt, makes two trips across the Arabian Sea to India. On the second, he lands on East Africa's coast and later unsuccessfully attempts to circumnavigate Africa.

58

EUROPE

- GAIUS JULIUS CAESAR commands a Roman military expedition to Gaul (France).

55–54

EUROPE

- GAIUS JULIUS CAESAR commands a Roman military expedition to Britain.

ca. 25 B.C.

ASIA

- GAIUS AELIUS GALLUS commands a Roman military expedition to the Arabian Peninsula.

ca. A.D. 18

- Greek geographer STRABO publishes *Geography* in Rome.

42

AFRICA

- SUETONIUS PAULINUS commands a Roman military expedition from North Africa's coast southward across the Atlas Mountains to the northern edge of the SAHARA DESERT.

45

ASIA

- Greek HIPPALUS, in service to Egypt, navigates a direct sea route across the Arabian Sea between Africa and India.

ca. 50

AFRICA

- JULIUS MATERNUS commands a Roman military expedition from Africa's north coast across the SAHARA DESERT and possibly reaches Lake Chad.

50

AFRICA

- Greek merchant DIOGENES explores inland in East Africa, possibly as far as Lake Victoria and Lake Albert.

59–61

EUROPE
- SUETONIUS PAULINUS heads a Roman military expedition in Britain.

77

- Roman PLINY THE ELDER publishes *Historia Naturalis* with geographic accounts of Europe, Asia, and Africa. He coins the name ULTIMA THULE for the northernmost land, based on the fourth-century B.C. travels of the Greek PYTHEAS.

77–84

EUROPE
- GNAEUS JULIUS AGRICOLA commands a Roman naval exploration of the Orkney Islands and possibly circumnavigates Britain; he explores Scotland.

97

ASIA
- Chinese diplomat KAN YING travels to central Asia and the Middle East.

100

- The *Periplus of the Erythraean Sea,* a surviving PERIPLUS, provides information about East Africa, including commercial activities in the region.

127–147

- Greek-Egyptian geographer PTOLEMY publishes *Geographia.*

ca. 190

ASIA
- A Chinese woman, WEN-CHI, is abducted by the Hsiung-nu (Huns) and lives as a nomad on Mongolian steppes. She later writes *Eighteen Songs of a Nomad Flute* about her experiences.

399–414

ASIA
- Chinese Buddhist monk FA-HSIEN travels west and south across China. He crosses the Takla Makan desert, Pamirs, and HIMALAYAS into Afghanistan and northern India, then sails to CEYLON (Sri Lanka).

ca. 548

- Egyptian merchant COSMAS INDICOPLEUSTES publishes *Topographia Christiana,* a Christian interpretation of geography.

ca. 566–573

ATLANTIC OCEAN
- According to legend, Irish monk SAINT BRENDAN sails westward from Ireland into open wa-

ters of the Atlantic and reaches SAINT BREN-DAN'S ISLE.

629–645

ASIA

- Chinese Buddhist monk HSÜAN-TSANG travels across the GOBI DESERT into western China and the Kirghiz region of central Asia, then crosses the Hindu Kush mountain range into Afghanistan. He explores Pakistan and India and returns to eastern China by way of the Takla Makan desert and the Tarim River.

671–695

ASIA

- Chinese Buddhist monk I-CHING travels to Indonesia and India.

ca. 680

ASIA

- Frankish pilgrim ARCULF travels to the Middle East.

ca. 700

- The Arabs reinvent the ASTROLABE (first used by ancient Greeks in the third or second century B.C.), a navigational tool.

776

- Spanish cartographer BEATUS OF VALCAVADO produces a map focusing on Jerusalem.

ca. 850–851

ASIA

- Arab merchant SOLEYMAN travels from the Persian Gulf by sea to India and China, visiting the Maldive Islands, Laccadive Islands, CEYLON (Sri Lanka), and the Andaman Islands.

ca. 860

ICELAND

- Viking NADDOD, blown off course on the way from Norway to the Faeroe Islands, reaches ICE-LAND.

ca. 860–861

ICELAND

- Viking GARDAR SVARSSON circumnavigates ICE-LAND.

ca. 900–925

EUROPE/ASIA

- Muslim merchant ABU ALI AHMAD IBN RUSTA travels throughout the lower Volga region of eastern Europe and to Malay in Asia.

ca. 914–934

ASIA/AFRICA/EUROPE
- Arab historian ABU AL-HASAN ALI AL-MASUDI visits every country in the Islamic world.

921–922

EUROPE
- Muslim scholar AHMAD IBN FADLAN travels from Baghdad into the Volga region of European Russia.

943–973

AFRICA/EUROPE/ASIA
- Arab merchant and scholar ABU AL-QASIM IBN ALI AL-NASIBI IBN HAWQAL visits Islamic lands of the Middle East, Europe, and North Africa, then travels across the SAHARA DESERT.

ca. 950

PACIFIC OCEAN
- Polynesian chieftain KUPE reaches NEW ZEALAND.

ca. 982–986

GREENLAND
- Viking ERIC THE RED sails westward from ICELAND, reaching GREENLAND; he explores the west coast as far as Disko Island. In about 986, he founds a settlement on the southwest coast.

ca. 985–986

NORTH AMERICA
- Viking BJARNI HERJULFSSON possibly sights North America's northeast coast.

ca. 1001–02

NORTH AMERICA
- Viking LEIF ERICSSON heads a maritime expedition to VINLAND, probably at L'Anse aux Meadows in Newfoundland, or in Labrador or Quebec.

ca. 1005–07

NORTH AMERICA
- Viking THORVALD ERICSSON heads a colonizing expedition to North America's east coast.

ca. 1010–13

NORTH AMERICA
- Viking THORFINN KARLSEFNI heads a colonizing expedition to North America's east coast.

ca. 1014–15

NORTH AMERICA
- Viking woman FREYDIS EIRÍKSDOTTIR heads a colonizing expedition to North America's east coast.

ca. 1017

ASIA
- Arab scholar ABU AR-RAYHAN MUHAMMAD IBN AHMAD AL-BIRUNI travels to India from Afghan-

istan and writes a book, *India,* on Indian customs and geography.

1095

ASIA

- Pope Urban II calls for the liberation of the Holy Land (Palestine); in 1096–99, the First Crusade is undertaken, culminating in the capture of Jerusalem from the Seljuk Turks; other CRUSADES follow, the last in 1228–29.

1145–54

- Arab author and cartographer ABU ABD ALLAH MUHAMMAD ASH-SHARIF AL-IDRISI revolutionizes mapmaking in *The Book of Roger,* with accurate geographic information based on travels and use of the grid system.

ca. 1150–1200

- The HANSEATIC LEAGUE, a commercial union of German cities and towns and their merchants, becomes active.

1158

- Otto von Freisingen, bishop of Freising (Otto of Freising), publishes *Historia de Duabus Civitatibus,* in which is found the earliest known reference to the legendary Christian ruler PRESTER JOHN.

1159–73

ASIA

- Spanish rabbi BENJAMIN OF TUDELA travels from Spain to the Middle East and central Asia, possibly as far as China, and visits India and CEYLON (Sri Lanka).

ca. 1180–87

EUROPE/ASIA

- German PETHAHIA OF REGENSBURG travels in eastern Europe and the Middle East.

1182–85

ASIA/AFRICA/EUROPE

- Muslim official and scholar ABU AL-HASAN MUHAMMAD IBN JUBAYR journeys from Spain to Arabia, exploring the lands of the Mediterranean region.

1215–27

ASIA

- Mongol emperor GENGHIS KHAN leads armies westward from China to the Caspian Sea.

1221–22

ASIA

- Chinese sage CH'ANG-CH'UN travels from China through central Asia and reports to GENGHIS KHAN in Afghanistan.

1228–29

- Greek-born Muslim SHIHAB AL-DIN ABU ABD ALLAH YAQUT AL-RUMI publishes *Mu'jam al Buldan* (Dictionary of countries), a gazetteer-type geographic study.

1230

- English mathematician JOHN HOLYWOOD publishes *Treatise on the Sphere,* presenting the idea that Earth might be spherical.

1245–47

ASIA

- Italian GIOVANNI DA PIAN DEL CARPINI heads a papal mission to the court of the Great Khan of the Mongol Empire, traveling from Lyon in France, across eastern Europe and central Asia, to northern Mongolia and lands east of the Volga River.

1253–55

ASIA

- Flemish missionary WILLIAM OF RUBROUCK travels from Constantinople (Istanbul) across central Asia to Mongolia. He visits the Mongol capital at Karakorum.

1260–69

ASIA

- Italian merchants MAFFEO POLO and NICCOLÒ POLO travel the SILK ROAD across central Asia to the court of Kublai Khan in China.

1271–75

ASIA

- Italian merchants MAFFEO POLO, NICCOLÒ POLO, and MARCO POLO travel across central Asia to the court of Kublai Khan in China.

1275–92

ASIA

- Italian merchant MARCO POLO, in service to Kublai Khan, travels widely throughout the Mongol Empire, exploring China, Tibet, Southeast Asia, Indonesia, Mongolia, and possibly SIBERIA. The account of his experiences, *The Travels of Marco Polo,* inspires later explorers to locate CIPANGU, the Strait of Anian (ANIAN, STRAIT OF), and other places he references.

1280–1313

ASIA/EUROPE

- Turkish monk RABBAN BAR SAUMA travels from China to the Middle East and Europe.

ca. 1290

- The Hereford map, an early *MAPPA MUNDI,* is drafted in England.

1291

ATLANTIC OCEAN
- Italian mariner UGOLINO VIVALDI attempts to reach India across the Atlantic but fails.

1291–94

ASIA
- Italian missionary JOHN OF MONTECORVINO travels to India and China.

1292–95

ASIA
- Italian merchants MAFFEO POLO, NICCOLÒ POLO, and MARCO POLO sail from China to Persia by way of the Strait of Malacca and the Indian Ocean and return to Italy by way of the Black Sea and Constantinople (Istanbul).

ca. 1300

- The mariner's COMPASS is developed in Amalfi, Italy.
- The Italian cartographer Petrus Vesconte drafts the Pisan Chart, the oldest existing PORTOLAN CHART, representing coastlines and ports of the MEDITERRANEAN SEA.

1311–20

- Chinese cartographer CHU SSU-PEN produces a world map with accurate information about Africa.

ca. 1318–22

ASIA
- Italian missionary ODORIC OF PORDENONE travels throughout much of Asia, including Persia (Iran), India, China, and Tibet.

1325–52

ASIA/AFRICA/EUROPE
- Arab scholar ABU ABD ALLAH MUHAMMAD IBN BATTUTAH travels throughout Egypt, Arabia, central Asia, Spain, and Africa. He explores the SAHARA DESERT.

1339–53

ASIA
- Italian missionary GIOVANNI DE MARIGNOLLI travels to China, India, and Indonesia.

ca. 1365

- An account of travel in Africa and Asia known as *Mandeville's Travels,* supposedly written by SIR JOHN MANDEVILLE, probably a pseudonymous name, is published in England.

ca. 1375

- Spanish cartographer ABRAHAM CRESQUES produces the *Catalan Atlas,* a world map based on geographic information obtained from travelers such as MARCO POLO.

ca. 1400

- The CROSS-STAFF, a navigational tool, is developed in the Low Countries.

1403–06

ASIA

- RUY GONZÁLEZ DE CLAVIJO heads a Spanish diplomatic mission to Samarkand in central Asia.

1405–34

INDIAN OCEAN

- CHENG HO heads seven Chinese maritime expeditions, sailing from China to the Indian Ocean, reaching East Africa.

1416

- Portuguese prince HENRY THE NAVIGATOR establishes a base for explorations and eventually a naval depot, a school of navigation, and an observatory at Sagres in Spain, where his shipmakers develop the CARAVEL.

1418–60

AFRICA

- Portuguese prince HENRY THE NAVIGATOR sponsors voyages of exploration along Africa's west coast.

1419–44

ASIA

- Italian NICCOLÒ DI CONTI travels from Venice to Damascus in Syria, then across India to Burma (Myanmar) and Indonesia, returning to Europe by way of Southeast Asia, CEYLON (Sri Lanka), India's Malabar Coast, Arabia, and Egypt.

1432–34

ATLANTIC OCEAN

- GONÇALO VELHO CABRAL heads a Portuguese maritime expedition to the AZORES.

1433–35

AFRICA

- GIL EANNES heads three Portuguese maritime expeditions to Cape Bojador and beyond.

1436

AFRICA

- AFONSO GONÇALVES BALDAYA heads a Portuguese maritime expedition along Africa's west coast as far south as the TROPIC OF CANCER.

1441–43

AFRICA
- NUÑO TRISTÃO heads three Portuguese maritime expeditions along Africa's west coast, exploring Cape Blanco, Arguin Island, and the Senegal River delta. A fort he establishes on Arguin Island in 1848 becomes a center of the early African SLAVE TRADE.

1444–45

AFRICA
- DINÍS DIAS heads a Portuguese maritime expedition along Africa's west coast, reaching Cape Verde, Africa's westernmost point.

1445–47

AFRICA
- ÁLVARO FERNANDES heads two Portuguese maritime expeditions along Africa's west coast, south of Cape Verde. He explores the Gambia River and reaches just north of Sierra Leone.

ca. 1450

- German inventor Johannes Gutenberg develops printing with movable type, helping make texts available to a wider audience.

1455–56

AFRICA
- ALVISE DA CADAMOSTO heads two Portuguese maritime expeditions along Africa's west coast, exploring the lower Senegal and Gambia Rivers and the Cape Verde Islands.

1458–62

AFRICA
- DIOGO GOMES heads two Portuguese maritime expeditions along Africa's west coast, exploring Cape Palmas and the Gambia River and reaching the Cape Verde Islands.

1469–75

AFRICA
- Portuguese merchant FERNÃO GOMES trades along Africa's west coast as far as the Gulf of Guinea and the island of Fernando Po.

1482–86

AFRICA
- DIOGO CÃO heads two Portuguese maritime expeditions along Africa's west coast, exploring the lower CONGO RIVER (Zaire River). He travels as far south as Namibia, almost reaching the TROPIC OF CAPRICORN.

1487–88

AFRICA
- Portuguese BARTOLOMEU DIAS heads a Portuguese maritime expedition around Africa's southern tip, reaching the CAPE OF GOOD HOPE.

1487–93

AFRICA/ASIA
- Portuguese diplomat PERO DA COVILHÃ heads a mission to India and North Africa, reaching as far south as Sofala, opposite the island of Madagascar. He remains in Ethiopia.

1488

AFRICA
- DUARTE PACHECO heads a Portuguese maritime expedition to Africa's southwest coast. He is shipwrecked on Principe Island in the Gulf of Guinea.

1492

- German cartographer MARTIN BEHAIM develops a GLOBE of the world depicting a large island west of the AZORES, perhaps indicating European knowledge of South America before subsequent voyages.

1492–93

CARIBBEAN
- Italian CHRISTOPHER COLUMBUS heads a Spanish maritime expedition seeking a westward route across the Atlantic. He reaches the Bahamas, Cuba, and Hispaniola (Haiti and Dominican Republic) of the WEST INDIES; Arawak (Taino) Indian GUANCANAGARI provides help.

1493–96

CARIBBEAN
- Italian CHRISTOPHER COLUMBUS heads a Spanish maritime expedition to the WEST INDIES. He explores coasts of the Lesser Antilles, Puerto Rico, Cuba, and Jamaica.

1497

NORTH AMERICA
- Italian AMERIGO VESPUCCI heads a Spanish maritime expedition to the WEST INDIES and possibly North America's east coast as far north as Cape Hatteras, North Carolina.

1497–98

NORTH AMERICA
- Italian JOHN CABOT heads two English maritime expeditions to North America. He reaches Newfoundland and the east coast of Labrador and travels southward along the Atlantic coast, possibly to Chesapeake Bay.

1497–99

AFRICA/ASIA
- VASCO DA GAMA heads a Portuguese maritime expedition from Europe around Africa to India.

1498–1500

SOUTH AMERICA
- Italian CHRISTOPHER COLUMBUS heads a maritime expedition from the Cape Verde Islands to the southern Caribbean Sea. He reaches Trinidad and the mainland of South America, then explores the Gulf of Pará, the coast of Venezuela, and the Orinoco Delta.

1499–1500

SOUTH AMERICA
- VICENTE YÁÑEZ PINZÓN, FRANCISCO MARTÍN PINZÓN, and ARIAS MARTÍN PINZÓN head a Spanish maritime expedition to South America's east coast. They reach the mouth of the AMAZON RIVER.

SOUTH AMERICA
- ALONSO DE OJEDA heads a Spanish maritime expedition along the coast of Venezuela.

ca. 1500

- Leonardo da Vinci researches human and avian flight.

1500

ARCTIC/GREENLAND
- GASPAR CÔRTE-REAL heads a Portuguese maritime expedition to North America, reaching GREENLAND's west coast and possibly the ARCTIC CIRCLE.

GREENLAND
- JOÃO FERNANDES heads a Portuguese maritime expedition to North America, reaching at least as far as GREENLAND.

1500–01

SOUTH AMERICA/ASIA
- PEDRO ÁLVARS CABRAL heads a Portuguese maritime expedition to India by way of the CAPE OF GOOD HOPE. Driven westward by unfavorable winds, he claims Brazil for Portugal.

1501

NORTH AMERICA
- GASPAR CÔRTE-REAL and MIGUEL CÔRTE-REAL head a Portuguese maritime expedition to Labrador and Newfoundland.

SOUTH AMERICA/ MIDDLE AMERICA
- RODRIGO DE BASTIDAS heads a Spanish maritime expedition to South America's northeast coast. He explores the Caribbean coast of Venezuela, Colombia, and Panama, exploring the Magdalena River, Cartagena Bay, and the Gulf of Darien.

1501–02

SOUTH AMERICA

- Italian AMERIGO VESPUCCI heads a Portuguese maritime expedition to the coast of Brazil. He explores the harbor at Rio de Janeiro, then sails southward along South America's coast, possibly as far as South Georgia Island.

1502–04

MIDDLE AMERICA

- Italian CHRISTOPHER COLUMBUS heads a Spanish maritime expedition to Central America, from Honduras southward to Panama.

1502–08

AFRICA/ASIA

- Italian LUDOVICO DI VARTHEMA travels in Egypt, the Middle East, India, and Southeast Asia, returning to Europe by sailing around Africa. It is thought he was the first European to reach the SPICE ISLANDS (the Moluccas) in the EAST INDIES.

1503

- The Indies Bureau of Trade, a government office, is founded in Spain to regulate Spanish commerce in the Americas.

1503–05

AFRICA/ASIA

- FRANCISCO DE ALMEIDA heads two Portuguese naval expeditions around Africa's CAPE OF GOOD HOPE to India. His son, LOURENÇO DE ALMEIDA, serves under him.

1504

SOUTH AMERICA

- JUAN DE LA COSA heads a Spanish maritime expedition to the Gulf of Uraba in Colombia.
- French mariner Binot Palmière de Gonneville claims to have visited a paradise across the Atlantic Ocean; GONNEVILLE'S LAND becomes associated with the GREAT SOUTHERN CONTINENT.

1506–07

AFRICA/ASIA

- Portuguese AFONSO DE ALBUQUERQUE commands a naval expedition to the Indian Ocean. He explores Africa's east coast and establishes a Portuguese outpost in Asia at Hormuz in the Persian Gulf.

CARIBBEAN

- VICENTE YÁÑEZ PINZÓN and JUAN DÍAZ DE SOLÍS head a Spanish maritime expedition to the Caribbean Sea. They circumnavigate Cuba and reach the Yucatán Peninsula and Bay of Campeche.

1507

- German cartographer MARTIN WALDSEEMÜLLER publishes the first world map depicting South America as a distinct continent, calling it "America," taken from AMERIGO VESPUCCI's name.

1507–18

AFRICA/ASIA

- Moroccan diplomat LEO AFRICANUS travels in North Africa, the Middle East, and central Asia.

1508–09

SOUTH AMERICA

- VICENTE YÁÑEZ PINZÓN and JUAN DÍAZ DE SOLÍS head a Spanish maritime expedition along the east coast of South America, reaching as far south as the mouth of Río Negro in Argentina.

CARIBBEAN

- JUAN PONCE DE LEÓN heads a Spanish maritime expedition to Puerto Rico.

ASIA

- DIEGO LÓPEZ DE SEQUIRA heads a Portuguese maritime expedition to Malacca on the Malay Peninsula and circumnavigates Sumatra.

1509

NORTH AMERICA/ ARCTIC

- Italian SEBASTIAN CABOT heads an English maritime expedition to North America's east coast, seeking the NORTHWEST PASSAGE. He sights Newfoundland, Nova Scotia, and Long Island.

1509–11

MIDDLE AMERICA

- DIEGO DE NICUESA heads a Spanish colonizing expedition to Panama.

1511–13

ASIA

- Portuguese FRANCISCO SERRANO heads a Portuguese maritime expedition to the SPICE ISLANDS (the Moluccas) in the EAST INDIES and explores northern Java.

1511–14

CARIBBEAN

- DIEGO VELÁSQUEZ commands the Spanish conquest of Cuba.

1513

NORTH AMERICA

- JUAN PONCE DE LEÓN heads a Spanish maritime expedition from Puerto Rico to Florida. He explores from St. Augustine on Florida's Atlantic coast to Pensacola Bay on the Gulf of Mexico, in search of the FOUNTAIN OF YOUTH.

MIDDLE AMERICA

- VASCO NUÑEZ DE BALBOA heads a Spanish expedition across the Isthmus of Panama, reaching the Pacific Ocean.

1515–16

SOUTH AMERICA
- JUAN DÍAZ DE SOLÍS heads a Spanish maritime expedition along South America's east coast. He reaches Río de la Plata south of Uruguay.

1517

MIDDLE AMERICA
- FRANCISCO FERNÁNDEZ DE CÓRDOBA heads a Spanish maritime expedition to the Bahamas. When blown off course to Mexico's Yucatán Peninsula, he explores westward to the Bay of Campeche.

ASIA
- Portuguese envoy TOMÉ PIRES travels by ship from India to China.

1518

MIDDLE AMERICA
- JUAN DE GRIJALVA heads a Spanish maritime expedition from Cuba to the Yucatán Peninsula, from the Bay of Campeche and the Panuco River.

1518–19

NORTH AMERICA
- ALONSO ÁLVAREZ DE PINEDA heads a Spanish maritime expedition in the Gulf of Mexico, from Florida to Tampico.

1519

MIDDLE AMERICA
- PEDRO ARIAS DE ÁVILA founds Panama City for the Spanish.

1519–21

MIDDLE AMERICA
- HERNÁN CORTÉS commands a Spanish expedition from Cuba to Mexico and conquers the Aztec; BERNAL DÍAZ DEL CASTILLO serves under Cortés and later writes a history of the conquest. MALINCHE, an Aztec woman, serves as Cortés's interpreter.

1519–22

WORLD
- Portuguese FERDINAND MAGELLAN heads a Spanish maritime expedition seeking a westward route to the Far East; he reaches the Strait of Magellan (see MAGELLAN, STRAIT OF) at the tip of South America and crosses the Pacific to the Mariana Islands and the Philippines. On Magellan's death in the Philippines in 1521, JUAN SEBASTIÁN DEL CANO assumes command and completes the first CIRCUMNAVIGATION OF THE WORLD. FRANCESCO ANTONIO PIGAFETTA, as Magellan's private secretary, keeps a journal, which is later published as *Primo Viaggio Intorno al Mondo* (First journey around the terrestrial globe).

1520

NORTH AMERICA
- LUCAS VÁSQUEZ DE AYLLÓN heads a Spanish maritime expedition from Santo Domingo on the island of Hispaniola (Haiti and Dominican Republic) to the coast of South Carolina.

1520–27

AFRICA
- Portuguese FRANCISCO ÁLVARES travels in Ethiopia. In 1540, he publishes an account of his experiences, *The Prester John of the Indies.*

1522

SOUTH AMERICA
- PASCUAL DE ANDAGOYA heads a Spanish maritime expedition to South America's west coast below Panama as far south as Colombia.

MIDDLE AMERICA
- ANDRÉS NIÑO heads a Spanish maritime expedition along the Pacific coast of Panama, Costa Rica, Nicaragua, and Honduras as far north as Mexico. He explores the interior of Nicaragua and reaches Lake Nicaragua.

1522–24

MIDDLE AMERICA
- FRANCISCO FERNÁNDEZ DE CÓRDOBA heads a Spanish expedition from Panama into Nicaragua, exploring and colonizing the region around Lake Managua and Lake Nicaragua.

1522–26

SOUTH AMERICA
- Portuguese castaway ALEJO GARCÍA explores inland from the Brazilian coast to the ANDES MOUNTAINS in Bolivia seeking Indian riches. Reports of his travels contribute to the legend of the wealthy kingdom of LOS CÉSARES.

1523–26

MIDDLE AMERICA
- PEDRO DE ALVARADO heads a Spanish expedition from Mexico to Guatemala and El Salvador.

1524

NORTH AMERICA
- GIOVANNI DA VERRAZANO heads a French maritime expedition to North America's east coast from South Carolina to Newfoundland.

1524–25

NORTH AMERICA
- ESTEVÃO GOMES heads a Spanish maritime expedition along North America's east coast, seeking the NORTHWEST PASSAGE.

1524–28

SOUTH AMERICA
- FRANCISCO PIZARRO heads a Spanish maritime expedition southward from Panama along the Pa-

cific coast of Colombia, Ecuador, and northern Peru.

1525

MIDDLE AMERICA

- HERNÁN CORTÉS heads a Spanish expedition of CONQUISTADORES from Mexico to Honduras.

1526

MIDDLE AMERICA

- PEDRO ARIAS DE ÁVILA commands a Spanish military expedition in the conquest of Indian tribes of Nicaragua.

1526–27

NORTH AMERICA

- LUCAS VÁSQUEZ DE AYLLÓN heads a Spanish colonizing expedition from Santo Domingo on the island of Hispaniola (Haiti and Dominican Republic) to the Santee River in South Carolina. He explores southward to the Savannah River in Georgia.

1526–30

SOUTH AMERICA

- Italian SEBASTIAN CABOT heads an English maritime expedition to the Río de la Plata and explores inland waterways of Brazil, Uruguay, Paraguay, and Argentina.

1527

NORTH AMERICA

- JOHN RUT heads an English maritime expedition to Newfoundland.

1527–29

PACIFIC OCEAN

- ÁLVARO DE SAAVEDRA CÉRON heads a Spanish maritime expedition from South America to Guam, the Philippines, and the SPICE ISLANDS (Moluccas). In an unsuccessful eastward return passage, he reaches Ponape Island in the Carolines and Eniwetok Island in the Marshalls.

1528–35

MIDDLE AMERICA

- FRANCISCO DE MONTEJO commands a Spanish military expedition against the Maya of the Yucatán Peninsula. His son, FRANCISCO DE MONTEJO Y LÉON, campaigns in 1537–46.

1528–36

NORTH AMERICA

- PÁNFILO DE NÁRVAEZ heads an Spanish expedition to Florida; after the disappearance of Nárvaez at sea, four survivors, including ÁLVAR NÚÑEZ CABEZA DE VACA and former slave ESTEVANICO, wander from the coast of Texas into the American Southwest and northern Mexico as far west as the Gulf of California.

1529–33

MIDDLE AMERICA
- NUÑO BELTRÁN DE GUZMÁN commands the Spanish conquest of Indian tribes in western Mexico.

1530–31

SOUTH AMERICA
- Diego de Ordaz heads a Spanish maritime expedition to the mouth of the AMAZON RIVER, exploring the Orinoco and Meta Rivers.

1530–36

SOUTH AMERICA
- German NIKOLAUS FEDERMANN heads two expeditions to the interior of Venezuela, seeking the fabled land of EL DORADO. On the second, he explores the plains of eastern Colombia and makes the first east-to-west crossing of the ANDES MOUNTAINS.

1531

- Italian physicist Guglielmo de Lorena constructs a large barrel used to walk along the bottom of a body of water, a primitive DIVING BELL.

1531–33

SOUTH AMERICA
- FRANCISCO PIZARRO commands the Spanish conquest of the Inca in Ecuador and Peru. His half brothers, GONZALO PIZARRO and HERNANDO PIZARRO, serve under him.

SOUTH AMERICA
- German AMBROSIUS ALFINGER explores the interior of Venezuela, seeking the fabled land of EL DORADO, and reaches Rio Magdalena.

1534

NORTH AMERICA
- JACQUES CARTIER heads a French maritime expedition to northeastern Canada; he explores Newfoundland, the Gaspé Peninsula, Labrador's south coast, the Gulf of St. Lawrence and islands in the Bay of Fundy. Huron Indian DONNACONNA provides help. Cartier searches for the legendary land of SAGUENAY.

1534–35

SOUTH AMERICA
- SEBASTIÁN DE BENALCÁZAR commands the Spanish conquest of Ecuador.

1535

NORTH AMERICA
- HERNÁN CORTÉS heads a Spanish maritime expedition from Mexico to the Gulf of California.
- GONZALO FERNÁNDEZ DE OVIEDO Y VALDEZ publishes the first volume of *Historia general y*

natural de las Indias Occidentales (General and natural history of the West Indies), a history of Spanish activity in the WEST INDIES.

1535–36

NORTH AMERICA
- JACQUES CARTIER heads a French maritime expedition to northeastern Canada. He explores the St. Lawrence River as far as Montreal and determines that Newfoundland is an island.

1535–37

SOUTH AMERICA
- DIEGO DE ALMAGRO heads a Spanish expedition south from Cuzco, Peru, through the ANDES MOUNTAINS of Bolivia and Argentina, into Chile as far south as Concepción, and back across the Atacama Desert.

SOUTH AMERICA
- PEDRO DE MENDOZA heads a Spanish colonizing expedition to the lower Río de la Plata region of Argentina and founds a settlement on the site of Buenos Aires.

SOUTH AMERICA
- JUAN DE AYOLAS heads a Spanish expedition from Buenos Aires, Argentina, along the Río de la Plata, to the Paraná and Paraguay Rivers.

1535–38

SOUTH AMERICA
- German GEORG HOHERMUTH VON SPEYER explores Río Meta and its tributaries and Río Ariari in Colombia, seeking the fabled land of EL DORADO.

1536–39

SOUTH AMERICA
- GONZALO JIMÉNEZ DE QUESADA heads a Spanish expedition to the upper Magdalena River in Colombia, seeking the fabled land of EL DORADO.

SOUTH AMERICA
- SEBASTÍAN DE BENALCÁZAR heads a Spanish expedition to the interior of Colombia, seeking the fabled land of EL DORADO.

1539

NORTH AMERICA
- MARCOS DE NIZA and ESTEVANICO head a Spanish expedition from Mexico to the American Southeast, organized by ANTONIO DE MENDOZA. They explore Arizona and New Mexico as far north as the Zuni Indian pueblos.

1539–40

NORTH AMERICA
- FRANCISCO DE ULLOA heads a Spanish maritime expedition, which explores the Gulf of California, the mouth of the COLORADO RIVER, and the Pacific coast of Baja California.

1539–43

NORTH AMERICA

- HERNANDO DE SOTO heads a Spanish expedition through the American Southeast. After landing on Florida's west coast, he explores the northern panhandle. He heads northward into Georgia and the Carolinas, westward across the APPALACHIAN MOUNTAINS, southward into Alabama, then westward into Mississippi, locating the MISSISSIPPI RIVER. He crosses the Mississippi into Arkansas and eastern Oklahoma. De Soto dies in 1542 on the Mississippi River, and LUIS DE MOSCOSO takes command. Moscoso explores Texas as far as the Trinity River before descending the Mississippi to the Gulf of Mexico.

1540–41

SOUTH AMERICA

- PEDRO DE VALDIVIA heads a Spanish expedition from Peru into Chile, crossing the Atacama Desert, and founds Santiago.

1540–42

NORTH AMERICA

- FRANCISCO VÁSQUEZ DE CORONADO heads a Spanish expedition from Mexico into the American Southwest in search of the seven cities of CIBOLA, as organized by ANTONIO DE MENDOZA. He explores Arizona and New Mexico. He also explores the southern plains of the Texas Panhandle, Oklahoma, and Kansas in search of the legendary kingdom of QUIVIRA, as guided by the TURK, a Plains Indian. HERNANDO DE ALVARADO, under Coronado, explores the upper Rio Grande, the Canadian River, and the Pecos River. PEDRO DE TOVAR and JUAN DE PADILLA explore northeastern Arizona. GARCÍA LOPEZ DE CÁRDENAS explores northern Arizona as far as the Grand Canyon. MELCHOR DÍAZ explores southern Arizona and northern Baja California. In 1540–41, HERNANDO DE ALARCÓN heads a Spanish maritime expedition to the Gulf of California and the lower COLORADO RIVER, the seaward portion of Coronado's expedition, as organized by Mendoza.

1541–42

NORTH AMERICA

- JACQUES CARTIER heads a French maritime expedition to northeastern Canada. He explores the St. Lawrence River and the Saguenay River.

SOUTH AMERICA

- ÁLVAR NÚÑEZ CABEZA DE VACA explores the Río de la Plata as well as the Paraná, Iguaçú, and Paraguay Rivers of Argentina and Paraguay for Spain.

| SOUTH AMERICA | ▪ FRANCISCO DE ORELLANA heads a Spanish expedition down the AMAZON RIVER, from the Napo River to the Atlantic coast. |
| ASIA | ▪ Portuguese FERNÁO MENDES PINTO travels from China to the Mekong Delta in Vietnam and Japan. |

1541–46

| SOUTH AMERICA | ▪ German PHILIP VON HUTTEN explores Río Meta and its tributaries plus Río Ariari in Colombia. |

1541–51

| ASIA | ▪ Spanish missionary FRANCIS XAVIER travels to India, Indonesia, and Japan. |

1542–43

NORTH AMERICA	▪ JEAN-FRANÇOIS DE LA ROQUE DE ROBERVAL heads a French colonizing expedition, which establishes a short-lived settlement on the St. Lawrence River near Quebec City.
NORTH AMERICA	▪ JUAN RODRÍGUEZ CABRILLO and BARTOLOMÉ FERRELO command a Spanish maritime expedition along North America's west coast, as organized by ANTONIO DE MENDOZA, from Mexico to the Oregon-California border.
SOUTH AMERICA	▪ ÁLVAR NÚÑEZ CABEZA DE VACA heads a Spanish expedition to the Paraguay River north of Asunción in Paraguay.

1542–46

| SOUTH AMERICA | ▪ DOMINGO MARTINEZ DE IRALA heads two Spanish expeditions to the upper Paraguay River. In the second, he reaches the eastern slopes of the ANDES MOUNTAINS. |

1543

| | ▪ Polish astronomer Nicolaus Copernicus publishes *De revolutionibus orbium coelestium,* describing the Sun as the center of a solar system, with the planets in orbit around it. |

1551

| | ▪ The MUSCOVY COMPANY, a joint-stock trading company, is founded in England to locate a NORTHEAST PASSAGE. |

1553–54

| EUROPE/ARCTIC | ▪ HUGH WILLOUGHBY, RICHARD CHANCELLOR, and STEPHEN BOROUGH head an English maritime expedition to northern Russia, seeking the NORTH- |

EAST PASSAGE. They sight Novaya Zemlya before Willoughby perishes; Chancellor and Borough travel overland to Moscow.

1554–62

NORTH AMERICA
- FRANCISCO DE IBARRA heads a Spanish expedition to north-central Mexico as far north as the Sonora Valley.

1556–57

EUROPE/ARCTIC
- Englishman STEPHEN BOROUGH heads an English maritime expedition seeking the NORTHEAST PASSAGE. He sails as far east as Novaya Zemlya, reaching the entrance to the Kara Sea. He explores the Arctic coast of European Russia.

1557–64

EUROPE/ASIA
- English trader ANTHONY JENKINSON undertakes two expeditions to Russia and central Asia. He becomes the first Englishman to visit Bukhara in Uzbekistan.

1559–61

SOUTH AMERICA
- PEDRO DE URSÚA heads a Spanish expedition from Lima, Peru, across the ANDES MOUNTAINS, and into the Amazon Basin. LOPE DE AGUIRRE mutinies and takes over the expedition, following the ORINOCO RIVER to its mouth in Venezuela.

1562

NORTH AMERICA
- JEAN RIBAULT heads a French colonizing expedition to Florida and South Carolina. He founds a short-lived Huguenot colony at Port Royal Sound in South Carolina.
- Spanish cartographer DIEGO GUTIÉRREZ produces the first map of South America detailing the inland river systems.

1562–69

AFRICA/ CARIBBEAN
- Englishman JOHN HAWKINS establishes the transatlantic SLAVE TRADE between England, Africa, and the Americas.

1564–65

NORTH AMERICA
- Frenchman RENÉ GOULAINE DE LAUDONNIÈRE founds a short-lived Huguenot colony on the St. Johns River in Florida. Artist JACQUES LE MOYNE DE MORGUES is one of the colonists.

PACIFIC OCEAN
- MIGUEL LÓPEZ DE LEGAZPI heads a Spanish maritime expedition from Mexico to the western Pa-

cific. He explores the Mariana Islands and the Marshall Islands and founds the first permanent Spanish settlement in the Philippines.

1565

PACIFIC OCEAN

- ANDRÉS DE URDANETA heads a Spanish maritime expediton eastward across the Pacific from the Philippines to Mexico, via the Japan Current.

1565–67

NORTH AMERICA

- PEDRO MENÉNDEZ DE AVILÉS heads a Spanish colonizing expedition to coastal regions of the American Southeast. He founds St. Augustine, Florida, the first permanent European settlement on the North American mainland north of Mexico, and sends expeditions inland.

1567–69

PACIFIC OCEAN

- ÁLVARO DE MENDAÑA and PEDRO SARMIENTO DE GAMBOA head a Spanish maritime expedition from Peru westward, seeking the fabled GREAT SOUTHERN CONTINENT, and reach the Solomon Islands and Marshall Islands. Mendaña names the Solomon Islands after King Solomon from the Bible, believing he has reached the legendary land of OPHIR and King Solomon's mines.

1569

- Flemish cartographer GERARDUS MERCATOR produces a MERCATOR PROJECTION world map.

1569–72

SOUTH AMERICA

- GONZALO JIMÉNEZ DE QUESADA heads a Spanish expedition to eastern Colombia, from Bogotá to the confluence of the ORINOCO RIVER and the Guaviare River.

1570–98

- Flemish cartographer ABRAHAM ORTELIUS produces an annual world atlas.

1576

- English geographer HUMPHREY GILBERT publishes *A Discourse of a Discoverie for a Passage to Cataia*, furthering the idea of a NORTHWEST PASSAGE through North America to Cathay (China).

1576–78

ARCTIC

- MARTIN FROBISHER heads three English maritime expeditions to the Canadian Arctic, seeking the

NORTHWEST PASSAGE, the second two backed by the CATHAY COMPANY. He reaches Frobisher Bay on southeastern Baffin Island.

1577–80

WORLD

- FRANCIS DRAKE heads the first English CIRCUMNAVIGATION OF THE WORLD. He navigates Drake Passage south of CAPE HORN in South America and explores North America's west coast as far north as Vancouver Island.

1579

ASIA

- English missionary THOMAS STEVENS travels to India on a Portuguese ship, becoming the first known Englishman in India.

1579–80

SOUTH AMERICA

- PEDRO SARMIENTO DE GAMBOA heads a Spanish expedition surveying the Strait of Magellan (see MAGELLAN, STRAIT OF).

1580

SOUTH AMERICA

- JUAN DE GARAY reestablishes the Spanish settlement of Buenos Aires, Argentina, formerly occupied in 1536–41.

1581

- The LEVANT COMPANY, a company to develop trade with the LEVANT, is founded in London.

1581–82

ASIA

- Russian Cossack YERMAK commands a military campaign across the Ural Mountains, initiating Russian expansion into SIBERIA.

1582–83

NORTH AMERICA

- ANTONIO ESTEVAN DE ESPEJO heads a Spanish expedition to western New Mexico and eastern Arizona, exploring the upper Rio Grande, the Sangre de Cristo Mountains, the Little Colorado River, and the upper Pecos River.

1582–89

- English geographer RICHARD HAKLUYT publishes three influential books on exploration and geography: *Diverse Voyages Touching the Discovery of America and the Islands Adjacent; A Discourse Concerning Western Planting;* and *The Principal Navigations, Voyages, and Discoveries of the English Nation.*

1583

NORTH AMERICA
- English geographer HUMPHREY GILBERT heads a colonizing expedition to Newfoundland.

1583–84

- Pamphlets are published making the claim that England had a prior claim to the Americas based on the supposed travels of MADOC, a legendary 12th-century Welsh prince.

1583–85

ASIA
- Merchant JOHN NEWBERRY escorts an English trade and diplomatic mission to India.

1583–91

ASIA
- English merchant RALPH FITCH heads a trading expedition to India by way of Syria; he visits Burma (Myanmar) and Southeast Asia.

1584–85

EUROPE/ARCTIC
- OLIVIER BRUNEL heads two Dutch expeditions seeking the NORTHEAST PASSAGE, reaching Novaya Zemlya.

SOUTH AMERICA
- ANTONIO DE BERRÍO heads a Spanish expedition to the ORINOCO RIVER and the Guiana region, seeking the fabled land of EL DORADO.

1584–87

NORTH AMERICA
- Englishman WALTER RALEIGH sponsors three Roanoke voyages to the Outer Banks region of North Carolina that explore the Carolina coast. RICHARD GRENVILLE commands the fleet transporting colonists in the second voyage and a failed attempt at a colony, with THOMAS HARRIOT serving as naturalist and JOHN WHITE as artist. A second colonizing attempt under John White also fails, becoming known as the LOST COLONY.

1585–87

ARCTIC
- JOHN DAVIS heads three English maritime expeditions to the Canadian Arctic, seeking the NORTHWEST PASSAGE. He reaches as far north as 73 degrees north latitude in the Davis Strait and explores the eastern entrance of the Hudson Strait.

1585–94

- Flemish cartographer GERARDUS MERCATOR produces a comprehensive world atlas.

1590

- Spanish missionary JOSÉ DE ACOSTA, after serving in Peru and Mexico, publishes an account of the natural science of the Americas, *The Natural and Moral History of the Indies.*

1592

NORTH AMERICA

- Greek mariner JUAN DE FUCA reportedly explores the Pacific coast of California, Oregon, and Washington.

1594–95

- Geographer JAN HUYGHEN VAN LINSCHOTEN heads two Dutch expeditions in search of the NORTHEAST PASSAGE, reaching Novaya Zemlya.

ca. 1595

- The English mariner JOHN DAVIS invents the Davis QUADRANT, a navigational tool.

1595

SOUTH AMERICA

- WALTER RALEIGH heads an English expedition to the ORINOCO RIVER, seeking the fabled land of EL DORADO.

PACIFIC OCEAN

- ÁLVARO DE MENDAÑA heads a Spanish colonizing expedition to the South Pacific; he reaches the Marquesas Islands and Santa Cruz Islands.

NORTH AMERICA

- SEBASTIÁN MELÉNDEZ RODRÍGUEZ CERMENHO heads a Spanish maritime expedition to the California coast, reaching Monterey Bay.

1595–97

ASIA

- CORNELIUS HOUTMAN heads a Dutch maritime expedition to the EAST INDIES.

1596–97

ARCTIC

- WILLEM BARENTS heads a Dutch maritime expedition seeking the NORTHEAST PASSAGE, reaching Bear Island and Spitsbergen (Svalbard).

1598

NORTH AMERICA

- JUAN DE OÑATE heads the first Spanish colonizing expedition into New Mexico. In subsequent years, he explores much of the American Southwest.
- MARTIN LLEWELLYN publishes the first English atlas showing the sea routes to the Far East.

1598–1600

ASIA

- Englishman ANTHONY SHERLEY travels to Persia. He heads diplomatic missions to Moscow,

Prague, and Rome on behalf of the Persian shah.

1598–1601

WORLD

- OLIVER VAN NOORT heads the first Dutch CIR-CUMNAVIGATION OF THE WORLD. He explores coastal South America.

1599–1600

ASIA

- Englishman WILLIAM ADAMS serves as the pilot for a Dutch trade fleet, which reaches Japan by way of the Strait of Magellan (see MAGELLAN, STRAIT OF) and Chile.

1600

- The British East India Company, a joint-stock trading company, is founded in London.

1601–03

ASIA

- JAMES LANCASTER heads the first maritime trading voyage of the BRITISH EAST INDIA COMPANY to the EAST INDIES.

1601–07

ASIA

- Italian missionary MATTEO RICCI travels in China from a mission in Peking (Beijing).

1602

NORTH AMERICA

- BARTHOLOMEW GOSNOLD heads an English maritime expedition to New England. He explores Cape Cod, Martha's Vineyard, Buzzards Bay, and Naragansett Bay.
- The DUTCH EAST INDIA COMPANY, a joint-stock trading company, is founded in the Netherlands.

1602–03

NORTH AMERICA

- SEBASTIÁN VISCAÍNO heads a Spanish maritime expedition along the California coast. He explores Monterey Bay and surveys beyond Cape Mendocino as far north as southern Oregon.

1603

NORTH AMERICA

- SAMUEL DE CHAMPLAIN heads a French fur-trading expedition to eastern Canada. He explores the Gulf of St. Lawrence, the Saguenay River, and the St. Lawrence River as far as the Lachine Rapids.

NORTH AMERICA

- MARTIN PRING heads an English trading expedition along the New England coast, from Maine to the Long Island Sound.

1603–07

ASIA
- Portuguese missionary BENTO DE GÓES travels from India through Afghanistan and makes an eastward crossing of China as far as Suchow.

1603–20

SOUTH AMERICA
- Spanish woman CATALINA DE ERAUSO, disguised as a man, fights as a soldier and works in mining camps in Argentina and Chile.

1604–05

NORTH AMERICA
- SAMUEL DE CHAMPLAIN heads a French colonizing expedition to eastern Canada; he explores the Bay of Fundy and establishes Acadia on the St. Croix River, eventually moving the colony to Port Royal in southeastern Nova Scotia.

1604–08

SOUTH AMERICA
- HERNANDO ARIAS DE SAAVEDRA heads Spanish expeditions inland from Buenos Aires, Argentina.

1605

NORTH AMERICA
- GEORGE WEYMOUTH heads an English maritime expedition along the coast of Maine to establish trade contacts with Native Americans.

AUSTRALIA
- WILLEM JANSZ heads a Dutch maritime exploration of the south coast of New Guinea. He sights the Australian mainland.

1605–06

PACIFIC OCEAN
- Portuguese PEDRO FERNÁNDEZ DE QUIRÓS heads a Portuguese maritime expedition from Peru to the southwestern Pacific, seeking the fabled GREAT SOUTHERN CONTINENT. He explores island groups, including parts of Samoa, the Cook Islands, and New Hebrides. LUIS VÁEZ DE TORRES explores New Guinea's eastern end and reaches Louisade Archipelago and the Torres Strait.

ARCTIC/GREENLAND
- Englishman JAMES HALL heads two Dutch maritime expeditions to GREENLAND's west coast.

1605–07

NORTH AMERICA
- SAMUEL DE CHAMPLAIN heads a French maritime expedition to coastal regions of northeastern North America, including Cape Breton Island, New Brunswick, Maine, and Massachusetts.

1606

NORTH AMERICA
- JOHN KNIGHT heads an English maritime expedition to the north coast of Labrador, seeking the

NORTHWEST PASSAGE. He disappears with a surveying party.

- The Virginia Company of London and the Virginia Company of Plymouth are founded to reassert English sovereignty over North America and colonize it; they both are referred to as the VIRGINIA COMPANY.

1607–08

ARCTIC/GREENLAND
- HENRY HUDSON heads two English maritime expeditions seeking the NORTHEAST PASSAGE. He explores GREENLAND's east coast and the European Arctic coast.

NORTH AMERICA
- GEORGE POPHAM founds Fort St. George, a short-lived English settlement on Monhegan Island off Maine.

1607–09

NORTH AMERICA
- CHRISTOPHER NEWPORT and JOHN SMITH found the first permanent English settlement in the Americas at Jamestown, Virginia. Newport explores inland beyond the falls of James River in Virginia and possibly reaches the mouth of the Rivanna River. Smith explores the Chesapeake Bay and the Potomac, Rappahannock, and Chickahominy Rivers.

1608

NORTH AMERICA
- SAMUEL DE CHAMPLAIN founds the first permanent French settlement in the Americas at Quebec City.

1608–17

ASIA
- English trader JOHN JOURDAIN travels to India, Sumatra, Java, and the EAST INDIES.

1609

NORTH AMERICA
- SAMUEL DE CHAMPLAIN heads a French expedition southward from the St. Lawrence River along the Richelieu River, reaching Lake Champlain.

NORTH AMERICA
- Englishman HENRY HUDSON heads a Dutch maritime exploration of New York Bay and the Hudson River, seeking the NORTHWEST PASSAGE.

ATLANTIC OCEAN
- SILVESTER JOURDAIN's shipwreck leads to an English claim on Bermuda.
- German astronomer Johannes Kepler establishes that the orbits of planets are elliptical, not circular.

1610

- Italian scientist Galileo constructs the first complete astronomical telescope and begins viewing features on the Moon and eventually the moons of Jupiter.

1610–11

NORTH AMERICA	▪ HENRY HUDSON heads an English maritime expedition to the Hudson Strait, HUDSON BAY, and James Bay, seeking the NORTHWEST PASSAGE.
SOUTH AMERICA	▪ THOMAS ROE heads an English maritime expedition to coastal South America; he explores from the mouth of the AMAZON RIVER to the ORINOCO RIVER delta.

1611–12

NORTH AMERICA	▪ ÉTIENNE BRÛLÉ, under SAMUEL DE CHAMPLAIN, heads a French expedition to Lake Huron and Lake Ontario.

1612

▪ The COMPANY OF MERCHANTS OF LONDON DISCOVERERS OF THE NORTHWEST PASSAGE is chartered in England.

1612–13

ARCTIC	▪ THOMAS BUTTON heads an English maritime expedition to HUDSON BAY, seeking the NORTHWEST PASSAGE. He explores the mouth of the Nelson River and the coast of the Southampton Island.

1613

NORTH AMERICA	▪ SAMUEL DE CHAMPLAIN heads a French expedition to the Ottawa River as far as Allumette Island.
AFRICA	▪ Spanish missionary PEDRO PÁEZ explores Lake Tana and the nearby Springs of Geesh, determining them as the principal source of the Blue Nile.

1613–14

ASIA	▪ JOHN SARIS heads an English maritime expedition to Japan.

1614

NORTH AMERICA	▪ JOHN SMITH heads an English maritime expedition from Cape Cod to Penobscot Bay. He names the region New England.
NORTH AMERICA	▪ ADRIAEN BLOCK heads a Dutch maritime expedition to the East River, in modern-day New York. He enters Long Island Sound from the west through the narrow channel known as Hell Gate. He explores the New England coastline, reaching the Housatonic and Connecticut Rivers as well as Block Island.

1615

ARCTIC
- Englishmen WILLIAM BAFFIN and ROBERT BYLOT head an English maritime expedition to HUDSON BAY's northwest coast and the Foxe Basin, determining that Hudson Bay provides no navigable outlet westward to the Pacific.

1615–16

NORTH AMERICA
- SAMUEL DE CHAMPLAIN and ÉTIENNE BRÛLÉ head a French expedition from Montreal along the Ottawa River and Lake Nipissing to the French River and the Georgian Bay on the northeast shore of Lake Huron. They proceed southward along the eastern end of Lake Ontario to upstate New York. Étienne Brûlé explores the Susquehanna River from New York to Chesapeake Bay in Maryland.

ATLANTIC OCEAN/ PACIFIC OCEAN
- JAKOB LE MAIRE and WILLEM CORNELIS SCHOUTEN head a Dutch maritime expedition around South America's CAPE HORN; they locate the Juan Fernandez Islands and determine the eastern extent of New Guinea.

1615–19

ASIA
- THOMAS ROE heads an English diplomatic mission to the Mogul (Mughal) Empire in northern India.

1616

ARCTIC/GREENLAND
- WILLIAM BAFFIN and ROBERT BYLOT head an English maritime expedition to the west coast of GREENLAND, as well as Baffin Bay, Baffin Island, and Lancaster Sound.

AUSTRALIA
- DIRK HARTOG heads a Dutch maritime expedition to the EAST INDIES. He reaches Dirk Hartogs Island and explores Australia's west coast.

1619

AUSTRALIA
- FREDERIK HOUTMAN heads a Dutch maritime expedition to the EAST INDIES. He sights Australia's west coast.

1619–20

NORTH AMERICA
- JENS ERIKSEN MUNK heads a Danish maritime expedition to HUDSON BAY, seeking the NORTHWEST PASSAGE. He explores the Churchill River region.

1620

NORTH AMERICA
- Englishman EDWARD WINSLOW sails with the PILGRIMS to Massachusetts and helps found Plymouth colony.

1621

NORTH AMERICA
- ÉTIENNE BRÛLÉ heads a French expedition to the western Great Lakes, reaching Lake Superior.
- The DUTCH WEST INDIA COMPANY, a joint-stock trading company, is founded in the Netherlands.

1621–22

NORTH AMERICA
- Wampanoag Indian SQUANTO aids the PILGRIMS in the exploration of coastal Massachusetts.

1622–30

NORTH AMERICA
- Spaniard ALONZO DE BENAVIDES serves as missionary to the American Indians of the Gila River Valley, Rio Grande, and the Pecos River Valley.

1624–25

ASIA
- Portuguese (or possibly Spanish) missionary ANTONIO DE ANDRADE travels from northern India across the HIMALAYAS, where he reaches a source of the GANGES RIVER, and continues into Tibet.

1626

ASIA
- Portuguese missionaries JOÃO CABRAL and ESTEVÃO CACELLA travel from India to Tibet.

1627

AUSTRALIA
- FRANÇOIS THYSSEN heads a Dutch maritime expedition eastward across the southern Indian Ocean to southwestern Australia and explores the Great Australian Bight.

1627–29

ASIA
- English writer THOMAS HERBERT explores Persia (Iran).

1628

AFRICA
- Portuguese missionary JERONIMO LOBO explores the Lake Tana region in Ethiopia. He reaches the source of the Blue Nile River and Tisisat Falls.

1631

NORTH AMERICA/ ARCTIC
- LUKE FOXE heads an English maritime expedition to western and northern HUDSON BAY, seeking the NORTHWEST PASSAGE.

1631–32

NORTH AMERICA/ ARCTIC
- THOMAS JAMES heads an English maritime expedition to HUDSON BAY and James Bay, seeking the NORTHWEST PASSAGE.

1631–33

ASIA

- Russian Cossack PYOTR BEKETOV expands the Russian dominion to the Yenisey, Lena, and Aldan Rivers of central SIBERIA.

1631–35

ASIA

- Portuguese (or Spanish) missionary FRANCISCO DE AZEVADO crosses the HIMALAYAS from India into Tibet.

1634

NORTH AMERICA

- French missionary JEAN NICOLET explores Lake Michigan and Green Bay.
- Dutch cartographer WILLEM JANZOON BLAEU publishes a comprehensive atlas detailing recent explorations.

1637–38

SOUTH AMERICA

- Portuguese PEDRO DE TEIXEIRA heads an expedition up the AMAZON RIVER. He reaches Río Negro and Quito by way of the Napo River and the ANDES MOUNTAINS. On the return journey in 1639, he is accompanied by Jesuit missionary CRISTÓBAL DE ACUÑA.

1640–49

NORTH AMERICA

- French missionary JEAN DE BRÉBEUF explores the eastern Great Lakes. He is joined by GABRIEL LALEMENT at Georgian Bay in 1648.

1640–80

EUROPE/ASIA/AFRICA

- Turkish writer ÇELEBI EVLIYA travels in eastern Europe, the Balkans, the Middle East, and North Africa.

1641

NORTH AMERICA

- French missionary ISAAC JOGUES explores Lake Superior and Lake Michigan.

1641–44

ASIA

- Russian Cossack MIKHAIL STADUKHIN explores the Arctic coast of SIBERIA, reaching the Kolyma River.

1642–43

PACIFIC OCEAN

- ABEL JANSZOON TASMAN heads a Dutch maritime expedition from Indonesia, seeking the fabled GREAT SOUTHERN CONTINENT. He explores TASMANIA, NEW ZEALAND, and the Fiji Islands.

1643–46

ASIA

- Russian Cossack VASILY DANILOVICH POYARKOV commands a Russian military expedition down the Amur River to the Sakhalin Gulf and the Sea of Okhotsk.

1644

AUSTRALIA

- ABEL JANSZOON TASMAN heads a Dutch maritime expedition from Indonesia to the South Pacific. He explores New Guinea's south coast and Australia's north and west coasts.

1644–48

NORTH AMERICA

- Italian missionary FRANCESCO-GIOSEPPE BRESSANI explores the eastern Lake Huron region of Ontario.

1646

NORTH AMERICA

- French missionary ISAAC JOGUES explores Lake George in New York and Vermont.

1648

ASIA

- Russian Cossack SEMYON IVANOVICH DEZHNEV heads an expedition from the mouth of Kolyma River eastward along the Arctic coast of SIBERIA. He rounds Cape Dezhnev and sights the BERING STRAIT.

1649–52

ASIA

- YEROFEY PAVLOVICH KHABAROV heads two Russian expeditions to the Amur River region in southeastern SIBERIA.

1652–60

ASIA

- Russian Cossack PYOTR BEKETOV expands Russian dominion to the Amur River of eastern SIBERIA.

1654

NORTH AMERICA

- French missionary SIMON LE MOYNE explores Onondaga Lake in New York.

1654–56

NORTH AMERICA

- French fur trader MÉDARD CHOUART DES GROSEILLIERS, one of the COUREURS DE BOIS, explores Illinois, Michigan, and Wisconsin, including the Fox and Wisconsin Rivers. He also explores the upper reaches of the MISSISSIPPI RIVER in Minnesota.

1659–60

NORTH AMERICA
- French COUREURS DE BOIS MÉDARD CHOUART DES GROSEILLIERS and PIERRE-ESPRIT RADISSON explore from Lake Superior to Chequamegon Bay.

NORTH AMERICA
- French missionary RENÉ MÉNARD founds a mission at Keweenaw Bay on Lake Superior.

1660

- The ROYAL SOCIETY (Royal Society of London for Improving Natural Knowledge) is founded in London.

1661–62

ASIA
- Jesuit missionaries JOHANN GRUEBER and ALBERT D'ORVILLE travel from Peking (Beijing) across western China to Tibet, becoming the first Europeans to visit LHASA. They cross the HIMALAYAS into India.

1664

- The FRENCH EAST INDIA COMPANY, a joint-stock trading company, is founded in France.

1665

SOUTH AMERICA
- CHARLES-EDOUARD DE LA NOUÉ heads a French expedition to Tierra del Fuego and Patagonia.

1665–69

NORTH AMERICA
- French missionary CLAUDE-JEAN ALLOUEZ explores the south shore of Lake Superior and the Fox and Wisconsin Rivers.

1666–67

SOUTH AMERICA
- AGOSTINHO VIALE heads a Portuguese expedition from São Paolo, Brazil, to the Mato Grosso region south of the AMAZON RIVER.

1667

NORTH AMERICA
- French missionary JACQUES BRUYAS travels from Quebec to upstate New York.

1667–71

NORTH AMERICA
- French fur trader NICOLAS PERROT explores the western Great Lakes.

1668–69

NORTH AMERICA
- Frenchman MÉDARD CHOUART DES GROSEILLIERS, backed by a British group of merchants, carries out a fur-trading expedition by sea from

England to HUDSON BAY. PIERRE-ESPRIT RADISSON, in a separate ship, is forced to turn back.

1669–70

NORTH AMERICA
- German physician JOHN LEDERER explores the Piedmont and Blue Ridge of Virginia and North Carolina for the British colony of Virginia.

NORTH AMERICA
- French missionaries RENÉ DE BRÉHANT DE GALINÉE and FRANÇOIS DOLLIER DE CASSON explore Niagara River, Lake Erie, and Lake Huron.

1670

- The HUDSON'S BAY COMPANY is founded in London to develop the FUR TRADE in North America. PIERRE-ESPRIT RADISSON reaches HUDSON BAY.

1671–72

NORTH AMERICA
- French missionary CHARLES ALBANEL travels from the St. Lawrence River to HUDSON BAY.

1671–73

NORTH AMERICA
- Englishman ABRAHAM WOOD sponsors Virginia colonial expeditions to the Appalachian frontier of Virginia and North Carolina. THOMAS BATTS and ROBERT FALLAM cross the Blue Ridge into West Virginia. GABRIEL ARTHUR and JAMES NEEDHAM reach Tennessee.

1673

NORTH AMERICA
- French fur trader and missionary LOUIS JOLLIET and JACQUES MARQUETTE explore the Fox River, the Wisconsin River, and the MISSISSIPPI RIVER to the mouth of the Arkansas River. On the return journey, they explore the Illinois River.

1675–77

SOUTH AMERICA
- German SIGISMUND NIEBUHR heads a Dutch maritime expedition to the southern tip of South America; he explores Le Maire Strait, CAPE HORN, and Tierra del Fuego.

1679

- The first EPHEMERIS, *Connaissance de Temps,* a table of astronomical data for purposes of navigation, is published in France.

1679–80

NORTH AMERICA
- French fur trader DANIEL GREYSOLON DULUTH explores the headwaters of the MISSISSIPPI RIVER in Wisconsin and Minnesota.

| NORTH AMERICA | • HENRI DE TONTI heads a French expedition to the north shore of Lake Erie and the south shore of Lake Michigan. |

1680

| NORTH AMERICA | • LOUIS HENNEPIN and MICHEL ACO head a French expedition to the Minnesota River and the Falls of St. Anthony. |

1682

| NORTH AMERICA | • RENÉ-ROBERT CAVELIER DE LA SALLE heads a French expedition along the MISSISSIPPI RIVER to the Gulf of Mexico. |

1683–92

| ASIA | • German ENGELBRECHT KAEMPFER travels on behalf of Sweden to Persia, Sri Lanka (CEYLON), Java, Thailand, and Japan. |

1685

| NORTH AMERICA | • Dutchman JOSEPH DE LA PENHA explores the interior of Labrador. |
| NORTH AMERICA | • English physician HENRY WOODWARD explores from Charleston, South Carolina, to beyond the Savannah River into Georgia. |

1685–1717

| EUROPE | • Englishwoman CELIA FIENNES begins traveling throughout England, writing a journal, later published as *Through England on a Side-Saddle*. |

1686–1713

| SOUTH AMERICA | • Bohemian missionary SAMUEL FRITZ explores the AMAZON RIVER and its tributaries in Ecuador, Peru, and Brazil. |

1687–88

| NORTH AMERICA | • Frenchman HENRI JOUTEL, an aide to RENÉ-ROBERT CAVELIER DE LA SALLE, explores eastern Texas and western Arkansas. |

1688–89

| NORTH AMERICA | • French soldier Baron LOUIS-ARMAND DE LOM D'ARCE DE LAHONTAN explores Lake Michigan and perhaps reaches the MISSISSIPPI RIVER. |

1689

| NORTH AMERICA | • ALONSO DE LEÓN heads a Spanish expedition from Coahuila in Mexico across the Rio Grande to the Gulf Coast of Texas. |

- French physicist Denis Papin designs a DIVING BELL with fresh air from the surface pumped through a tube.

1690–92

NORTH AMERICA
- English fur trader HENRY KELSEY explores the Assiniboine and Saskatchewan Rivers for the HUDSON'S BAY COMPANY, reaching the Canadian prairies.

1696–1700

ASIA
- Russian Cossacks VLADIMIR VASILYEVICH ATLASOV and LUKA MOROZKO command the exploration and conquest of Kamchatka Peninsula.

1698–99

NORTH AMERICA
- JEAN-BAPTISTE LE MOYNE and PIERRE LE MOYNE head a French colonizing expedition to the mouth of the MISSISSIPPI RIVER and about 100 miles upriver.

NORTH AMERICA
- French missionary ALBERT DAVION explores the lower MISSISSIPPI RIVER and the Yazoo River in Mississippi.

1698–1706

NORTH AMERICA
- Italian missionary EUSEBIO FRANCISCO KINO explores the Gila River and the COLORADO RIVER in Arizona. He reaches the Gulf of California.

1699–1701

PACIFIC OCEAN/ AUSTRALIA
- WILLIAM DAMPIER heads an English scientific expedition to the Pacific and explores Australia's west coast, reaching the Dampier Archipelago. He explores New Guinea and New Britain Island.

1700–01

NORTH AMERICA
- French trader PIERRE-CHARLES LE SUEUR ascends the MISSISSIPPI RIVER, from the Gulf of Mexico to the Minnesota River.

1701

NORTH AMERICA
- ANTOINE LAUMET DE LA MOTHE founds the French post of Detroit on the Detroit River.

1701–08

NORTH AMERICA
- Englishman JOHN LAWSON explores the interior of the Carolinas northwestward from Charleston.

1704–09

PACIFIC OCEAN
- Scottish mariner ALEXANDER SELKIRK is marooned in the Juan Fernández Islands. His story is adapted by Daniel Defoe in the 1719 novel *Robinson Crusoe.*

1706–08

MEDITERRANEAN
- Italian count LUIGI FERDINANDO MARSILI engages in the first underwater exploration, investigating the MEDITERRANEAN SEA.

1712–17

NORTH AMERICA
- Frenchman ÉTIENNE-VENIARD DE BOURGMONT explores the central MISSOURI RIVER region, possibly as far north as the mouth of the Platte River in eastern Nebraska.

1712–26

NORTH AMERICA
- English naturalist MARK CATESBY studies wildlife in Virginia, the Carolinas, Bermuda, and the Bahamas.

1713–14

NORTH AMERICA
- French-Canadian LOUIS JUCHEREAU DE ST. DENIS establishes a trading post at Natchitoches on the Red River. He crosses Texas to San Juan Bautista on the Rio Grande.

ASIA
- Russian Cossack fur trader SEMYON ANABARA explores eastern SIBERIA, from Yakutz on the Lena River to the southeast shore of the Sea of Okhotsk. He reaches the Shantar Islands.

1714–16

ASIA
- Italian missionary IPPOLITO DESIDERI travels from Delhi in India northward through Kashmir and the HIMALAYAS to LHASA in Tibet.

1715–16

ASIA
- Russian IVAN DMITRYEVICH BUKHGOLTS commands a military expedition southward from Tobolsk, descending the Irtysh River to the Om River.

1715–17

ASIA
- Russian navigator and military leader ALEKSANDR BEKOVICH-CHERKASSKY explores the rivers feeding the Caspian Sea.

1716

NORTH AMERICA
- British colonial governor ALEXANDER SPOTS-WOOD heads an expedition into Virginia's Shenandoah Valley and Blue Ridge.

1719

NORTH AMERICA
- Frenchman JEAN-BAPTISTE BÉNARD DE LA HARPE heads a trading expedition from Louisiana through Texas to Santa Fe, New Mexico.

1719–21

NORTH AMERICA/
ARCTIC
- British fur trader JAMES KNIGHT explores northwestern HUDSON BAY for the HUDSON'S BAY COMPANY. After being shipwrecked on Marble Island, the entire crew perishes.

NORTH AMERICA/
ARCTIC
- British fur trader HENRY KELSEY explores the Marble Island region of HUDSON BAY for the HUDSON'S BAY COMPANY.

1719–27

ASIA
- DANIEL GOTTLIEB MESSERSCHMIDT heads a Russian scientific expedition to central SIBERIA, from the Lena and Yenisey Rivers in the north to Lake Baikal and the Amur River in the south.

1720

NORTH AMERICA
- French historian PIERRE-FRANÇOIS-XAVIER DE CHARLEVOIX explores the Great Lakes, the Illinois River, and the MISSISSIPPI RIVER.

1721

ARCTIC/GREENLAND
- Norwegian HANS EGEDE founds the first permanent settlement in GREENLAND.

1721–22

PACIFIC OCEAN
- JAKOB ROGGEVEEN heads a Dutch maritime expedition seeking the fabled GREAT SOUTHERN CONTINENT; he explores South America's west coast and explores Easter Island and the Samoa Islands in the South Pacific.

1724

NORTH AMERICA
- ÉTIENNE-VENIARD DE BOURGMONT heads a French expedition into western Kansas, the deepest French penetration to date into the territory west of the MISSISSIPPI RIVER.

1724–28

NORTH AMERICA
- PEDRO DE RIVERA Y VILLALÓN heads a Spanish expedition inspecting and mapping northern New

Spain, including parts of Mexico, New Mexico, and Texas.

1725–30

ASIA

- VITUS JONASSEN BERING and ALEKSEY ILYICH CHIRIKOV command First Kamchatka Expedition for the Russian navy to SIBERIA's Pacific coast.

1726–33

ASIA

- Russian Cossack EMELYAN BASOV heads expeditions along SIBERIA's Lena River, seeking a seaward route to the Pacific.

1731–37

NORTH AMERICA

- CONRAD WEISER, a colonial American interpreter to the Indians, explores western Pennsylvania.

1731–43

NORTH AMERICA

- French fur trader PIERRE GAULTIER DE VARENNES DE LA VÉRENDRYE explores the northern plains as far west as the Bighorn Mountains in Wyoming. His sons, including LOUIS-JOSEPH GAULTIER DE LA VÉRENDRYE, work with him.

1733–40

ASIA/ARCTIC

- VITUS JONASSEN BERING and ALEKSEY ILYICH CHIRIKOV command the Great Northern Expedition (including the Second Kamchatka Expedition) for the Russian navy to the Arctic and Pacific coasts of SIBERIA, Kuril Islands, and inland areas of eastern Siberia. JOHANN GEORG GMELIN, STEPAN PETROVICH KRASHENINNIKOV, and GEORG WILHELM STELLER serve as naturalists.

1735

- French cartographer JEAN-BAPTISTE BOURGUIGNON D'ANVILLE produces the first accurate map of China.
- English carpenter John Harrison designs a practical CHRONOMETER to help measure longitude for purposes of navigation.

1738–39

ATLANTIC OCEAN

- Frenchman JEAN-BAPTISTE-CHARLES BOUVET DE LOZIER locates Bouvet Island in the South Atlantic near the ANTARCTIC CIRCLE.

1739–40

NORTH AMERICA

- French-Canadian fur traders PIERRE-ANTOINE MALLET and younger brother Paul Mallet explore the central plains, including the Niobrara, Platte, Republican, Smoky Hill, Arkansas, and Canadian Rivers.

1740–41

NORTH AMERICA
- VITUS JONASSEN BERING and ALEKSEY ILYICH CHIRIKOV head a Russian maritime expedition to BERING STRAIT, the Gulf of Alaska, Kodiak Island, the Aleutian Islands, and the Commander Islands.

1740–44

WORLD
- GEORGE ANSON commands a British military fleet in warfare with Spain. In the course of a CIRCUM-NAVIGATION OF THE WORLD, he explores islands off Chile.

1740–75

NORTH AMERICA
- British trader JAMES ADAIR explores the South Carolina frontier.

1741

NORTH AMERICA/ ARCTIC
- CHRISTOPHER MIDDLETON heads a British maritime expedition to HUDSON BAY, seeking the NORTHWEST PASSAGE. He reaches Wager Bay and Repulse Bay.

1742–43

ARCTIC
- SIMEON CHELYUSKIN heads a Russian maritime expedition to the Arctic coast of Russia from the White Sea to the Leptev Sea. He rounds Cape Chelyuskin.

1743

SOUTH AMERICA
- Frenchman CHARLES-MARIE DE LA CONDA-MINE heads a scientific expedition down the AMAZON RIVER, from northern Peru to the coast of Brazil.

1746–47

NORTH AMERICA/ ARCTIC
- WILLIAM MOOR heads a British maritime expedition to HUDSON BAY, seeking the NORTHWEST PASSAGE. He explores Chesterfield Inlet and Wager Bay.

1748–50

NORTH AMERICA
- JOSÉ DE ESCANDÓN heads a Spanish colonizing expedition from Mexico to the lower Rio Grande in southeastern Texas.

1750

NORTH AMERICA	▪ Colonial American THOMAS WALKER crosses through the CUMBERLAND GAP of Virginia's Blue Ridge into eastern Kentucky.

1750–51

NORTH AMERICA	▪ Colonial American traders CHRISTOPHER GIST and GEORGE CROGHAN explore trans-Appalachian regions of western Pennsylvania, southern Ohio, eastern Kentucky, and West Virginia.

1752

NORTH AMERICA	▪ Irish-American trader JOHN FINLEY visits the bluegrass country of Kentucky.
AFRICA	▪ Dutch pioneer AUGUST BEUTLER leads colonists eastward from Cape Town along Africa's south coast into the Transkei region.

ca. 1753

NORTH AMERICA	▪ Colonial American trader THOMAS CRESAP and Lenni Lenape (Delaware) Indian Nemacolen explore the Redstone and Monongahela Rivers in western Pennsylvania.

1753

	▪ Scottish naval doctor James Lind successfully publicizes a cure for SCURVY, citrus fruit, in *A Treatise On Scurvy*.

1753–58

NORTH AMERICA	▪ Russian fur trader PYOTR BASHMAKOV explores the Aleutian Islands.

1754–55

NORTH AMERICA	▪ British fur trader ANTHONY HENDAY explores the Canadian plains for HUDSON'S BAY COMPANY, within 40 miles of the ROCKY MOUNTAINS.

1756

	▪ Frenchman CHARLES DE BROSSES publishes *Histoire de la navigation aux terres australes* (*History of Navigation to Southern Lands*) furthering the idea of a large landmass in southern latitudes, a GREAT SOUTHERN CONTINENT.

1760

ASIA	▪ Russian NIKOLAY DAURKIN heads an expedition north and east of the Anadyr River into the Chukchi Peninsula.

1760–62

ARCTIC/ASIA
- IVAN BAKHOV heads a Russian maritime expedition to the Arctic coast of northern SIBERIA, from the Lena River eastward to the mouth of the Kolyma River.

1761–63

ASIA
- German CARSTEN NIEBUHR heads a Danish expedition to the southwestern Arabian Peninsula.

1763

ARCTIC/ASIA
- STEPAN ANDREYEV heads a Russian military expedition from Fort Anadyr on the Bering Sea to the Arctic coast of SIBERIA. From the Bear Islands, he sights New Siberia Island.

1763–64

NORTH AMERICA
- French fur traders PIERRE LIGUESTE LACLEDE and RENÉ AUGUSTE CHOUTEAU found St. Louis on the MISSISSIPPI RIVER.

1764–66

WORLD
- JOHN BYRON heads a British CIRCUMNAVIGATION OF THE WORLD. He claims Falkland Islands in the South Atlantic for Great Britain and explores South Pacific island groups.

1765

ATLANTIC OCEAN/ PACIFIC OCEAN
- PIERRE-NICOLAS DUCLOS-GUYOT heads a French naval expedition from the Falkland Islands to South America's Pacific coast. He reaches South Georgia Island in the South Atlantic.

1765–66

NORTH AMERICA
- Colonial American naturalists JOHN BARTRAM and WILLIAM BARTRAM explore eastern Florida and Georgia.

1766

NORTH AMERICA
- Colonial American frontiersman JAMES SMITH explores west of the CUMBERLAND GAP into eastern Kentucky.

1766–68

NORTH AMERICA
- ROBERT ROGERS and JONATHAN CARVER head a British expedition to Wisconsin and Minnesota, seeking the NORTHWEST PASSAGE.

WORLD
- SAMUEL WALLIS and PHILIP CARTERET command a British naval expedition to the South Pacific.

Wallis reaches Tahiti and Wallis Archipelago. Carteret explores Pitcairn Island and the Admiralty, Santa Cruz, and Solomon Islands.

1766–69

WORLD

- LOUIS-ANTOINE DE BOUGAINVILLE heads the first French CIRCUMNAVIGATION OF THE WORLD; he explores the western Pacific and charts the Solomons and other island groups. On the trip JOSEPH-PHILIBERT COMMERSON serves as naturalist and JEANNE BARET becomes the first woman known to sail around the world.

1767

- The British Royal Observatory at Greenwich begins publishing the *Nautical Almanac and Astronomical Ephemeris* (or the *Nautical Almanac*), an early EPHEMERIS.

1768–70

NORTH AMERICA

- PYOTR KUZMICH KRENITSYN heads a Russian maritime expedition charting the Aleutian Islands and the western end of the Alaska Peninsula.

1768–71

PACIFIC OCEAN

- JAMES COOK heads a British naval expedition to the South Pacific. He explores Tahiti and the Society Islands and charts the coasts of NEW ZEALAND and eastern Australia. JOSEPH BANKS and DANIEL CARL SOLANDER serve as naturalists.

1768–74

AFRICA

- Scotsman JAMES BRUCE seeks the source of the NILE RIVER, traveling from Alexandria, Egypt, to Gondar, Ethiopia, by way of the RED SEA and Arabia. He visits Lake Tana and Tisisat Falls and mistakenly describes the Blue Nile as the main branch of the Nile rather than the White Nile.

1768–80

NORTH AMERICA

- French-Canadian missionary PIERRE GIBAULT works among Native Americans in French settlements in Illinois and Indiana.

1769

- Scottish engineer James Watt patents the steam engine.

1769–70

NORTH AMERICA
- GASPAR DE PORTOLÁ and JUNÍPERO SERRA head a Spanish colonizing and missionary expedition to the coast of California, including San Diego Bay, Monterey Bay, and San Francisco Bay.

SOUTH AMERICA
- Ecuadoran ISABELA GODIN DES ODANAIS becomes the first known woman to descend the entire AMAZON RIVER, from central Peru to French Guiana.

1769–71

NORTH AMERICA
- Frontier hunter DANIEL BOONE explores the CUMBERLAND GAP of southwestern Virginia and Warriors' Trace into Kentucky, reaching the Falls of the Ohio.

1770–72

NORTH AMERICA
- SAMUEL HEARNE and Chipewyan Indian MATONABBEE head an expedition for the HUDSON'S BAY COMPANY from HUDSON BAY overland to the Arctic Ocean, seeking the NORTHWEST PASSAGE. They reach the Great Slave Lake.

1771–73

NORTH AMERICA
- Colonial American SIMON KENTON explores the upper Ohio River region in Kentucky.

1772

PACIFIC OCEAN
- YVES-JOSEPH DE KERGUÉLEN-TRÉMAREC heads two French maritime expeditions seeking the fabled GREAT SOUTHERN CONTINENT; he reaches the Kerguelen Islands.

1772–75

PACIFIC OCEAN/ ATLANTIC OCEAN
- JAMES COOK heads a British naval expedition to the South Pacific, during which he visits the Polynesian and Melanesian islands. He undertakes the first recorded crossing of the ANTARCTIC CIRCLE and circumnavigates the Antarctic continent, and he explores South Georgia Island and the South Sandwich Islands in the South Atlantic. During the expedition, TOBIAS FURNEAUX reaches Adventure Bay in TASMANIA. JAMES BURNEY serves as lieutenant and JOHANN GEORG ADAM FORSTER, JOHANN REINHOLD FORSTER, and ANDERS SPARRMAN serve as naturalists.

NORTH AMERICA
- British trader MATTHEW COCKING explores from southern HUDSON BAY to western Saskatchewan for the HUDSON'S BAY COMPANY.

AFRICA
- Swedish naturalist CARL PETER THUNBERG, in service to the Dutch, carries out three botanical expeditions north of Cape Town.

1773

ARCTIC
- CONSTANTINE JOHN PHIPPS heads a British naval expedition in an attempt to reach the NORTH POLE by water; passage is blocked by ice east of GREENLAND.

1774

NORTH AMERICA
- JUAN JOSEF PÉREZ HERNÁNDEZ heads a Spanish naval expedition to the Queen Charlotte Islands and Nootka Sound. He sites Mount Olympus.

NORTH AMERICA
- JUAN BAUTISTA DE ANZA heads a Spanish expedition from Tubac, Arizona, to San Gabriel Arcangel, California.

ASIA
- GEORGE BOGLE heads a British diplomatic expedition from Calcutta, India, across the HIMALAYAS into Tibet.

1775

NORTH AMERICA
- BRUNO HECETA heads a Spanish naval expedition along the northwest coast, seeking the outlet of the NORTHWEST PASSAGE; he reaches Grays Harbor in coastal Washington.

1775–76

NORTH AMERICA
- Spanish missionary FRANCISCO TOMÁS HERMENEGILDO GARCÉS explores the COLORADO RIVER and the Grand Canyon.

NORTH AMERICA
- Colonial American fur trader ALEXANDER HENRY (the elder) explores northwestern Saskatchewan.

1776–77

NORTH AMERICA
- Spanish missionaries FRANCISCO SILVESTRE VÉLEZ DE ESCALANTE and FRANCISCO ATANASIO DOMÍNGUEZ explore central Utah.

1776–80

PACIFIC OCEAN
- JAMES COOK heads a British naval expedition seeking the NORTHWEST PASSAGE, during which he visits the HAWAIIAN ISLANDS. He explores North America's west coast from Oregon to the Gulf of Alaska and Unalaska Island in the Aleutians, and he reaches northeastern SIBERIA's Chukchi Peninsula. After Cook's death in the HAWAIIAN ISLANDS in 1779, CHARLES CLERKE assumes command. On Clerke's death that same year, JOHN GORE assumes command. JAMES BURNEY and JAMES KING serve as lieutenants, JOHN LEDYARD serves as a marine, and JOHN WEBBER serves as artist.

1777–79

AFRICA
- Scotsman ROBERT GORDON explores South Africa's interior.

1778–82

NORTH AMERICA
- American trader PETER POND explores and charts northwestern Canada, from the Saskatchewan River to Lake Athabasca.

1779

- The NORTH WEST COMPANY is founded in Montreal to develop the FUR TRADE in North America.

1779–80

NORTH AMERICA
- American frontiersman JAMES ROBERTSON heads an expedition of settlers into Tennessee's Cumberland River region.

1781–1801

SOUTH AMERICA
- Spanish official FÉLIX DE AZARA explores and surveys the Río de la Plata and the Paraná and Paraguay Rivers of South America.

ASIA
- British diplomat SAMUEL TURNER heads a mission from India to Tibet.

1783

- French brothers Jacques Étienne Montgolfier and Joseph Michel Montgolfier launch the first BALLOON.

1783–86

NORTH AMERICA
- Russian trader GRIGORY IVANOVICH SHELIKOV directs the explorations of the Gulf of Alaska.

1783–92

SOUTH AMERICA
- Brazilian naturalist ALEXANDRE RODRIGUES FERREIRA conducts studies along the AMAZON RIVER and its tributaries.

1784

NORTH AMERICA
- Haitian French fur trader JEAN BAPTIST POINT SABLE settles on the site of present-day Chicago.

1785–88

PACIFIC OCEAN
- JEAN-FRANÇOIS DE GALAUP, comte de La Pérouse, heads a French maritime expedition to the Pacific; he explores the Gulf of Alaska and the coast of

Asia. PAUL-ANTOINE-MARIE FLEURIOT DE LANGLÉ commands the expedition's second ship. JEAN-BAPTISTE-BARTHÉLEMY DE LESSEPS serves as interpreter. Both ships disappear.

NORTH AMERICA
- French-Canadian trader JULIEN DUBUQUE explores the region west of Prairie du Chien on the upper MISSISSIPPI RIVER.

1785–93

ARCTIC
- JOSEPH BILLINGS, ANTON BATAKOV, and GAVRIIL ANDREYEVICH SARYCHEV command the Russian naval Northeastern Secret Geographical and Astronomical Expedition, seeking the NORTHEAST PASSAGE, from SIBERIA's northeast coast into BERING STRAIT. They explore the Aleutian Islands and the Gulf of Alaska.

1786

ASIA
- Russian fur trader GAVRILO LOGINOVICH PRIBYLOV explores the Pribilof Islands in the Bering Sea.

EUROPE
- Frenchmen JACQUES BALMAT and Michel Paccard make the first ascent of MONT BLANC (see BLANC, MONT) in the Alps.

1786–87

NORTH AMERICA
- Frenchman PEDRO VIAL pioneers a route for the Spanish from San Antonio, Texas, to Santa Fe, New Mexico.

1787–89

PACIFIC OCEAN
- WILLIAM BLIGH heads a British naval expedition to Tahiti, which ends in mutiny. With 18 others, he sails in a small, open boat 4,000 miles across the western Pacific to Timor in Indonesia.

1787–90

WORLD
- American captain and trader ROBERT GRAY sails from Boston to British Columbia, then to China and back to Boston, in the first CIRCUMNAVIGATION OF THE WORLD by a U.S. flagship.

1788

AFRICA
- JOSEPH BANKS founds the AFRICAN ASSOCIATION, a society to encourage the exploration of Africa, in England.

AUSTRALIA
- ARTHUR PHILLIP founds a British penal colony at present-day Sydney, the first permanent European settlement in Australia.

1789

NORTH AMERICA

- Scottish fur trader ALEXANDER MACKENZIE explores from the Great Slave Lake along the Mackenzie River to the Arctic Ocean for the NORTH WEST COMPANY.

1789–94

WORLD

- ALESSANDRO MALASPINA heads a Spanish naval scientific CIRCUMNAVIGATION OF THE WORLD, during which he explores the east and west coasts of South America. He charts North America's west coast and searches for an outlet of the NORTHWEST PASSAGE in southeastern Alaska; and he visits Australia and NEW ZEALAND.

1789–97

NORTH AMERICA

- Russian navigator GERASIM ALEKSEYEVICH IZMAILOV explores the coastal regions of southern Alaska.

1790–91

AFRICA

- Englishman DANIEL HOUGHTON explores up the Gambia River in West Africa, seeking the NIGER RIVER.

1791

NORTH AMERICA

- Russian fur trader DMITRY IVANOVICH BOCHAROV locates a passage through the eastern end of the Alaska Peninsula, connecting Bristol Bay and the Gulf of Alaska.

1791–93

NORTH AMERICA

- Russian fur trader ALEKSANDR ANDREYEVICH BARANOV explores Alaska's Kodiak Island, Cook Inlet, and Prince William Sound.

1791–94

PACIFIC OCEAN

- ANTOINE-RAYMOND-JOSEPH DE BRUNI, chevalier d'Entrecasteaux, heads a French naval expedition in search of JEAN-FRANÇOIS DE GALAUP, comte de La Pérouse. He explores the south coast of TASMANIA and the Great Australian Bight and reaches the Solomon Islands. JEAN-MICHEL HUON DE KERMADEC reaches Esperance Bay in western Australia. On the death of d'Entrecasteaux in 1793, ALEXANDRE HESMIVY D'AURIBEAU assumes command. ELISABETH-PAUL-EDOUARD DE ROSSEL is one of the naval officers. CHARLES-FRANÇOIS BEAUTEMPS-BEAUPRÉ serves as cartographer, and

JACQUES-JULIEN HOUTOU DE LA BILLARDIÈRE and CLAUDE-ANTOINE-GASPARD RICHE serve as naturalists.

1791–95

WORLD

- GEORGE VANCOUVER and WILLIAM ROBERT BROUGHTON head a British naval CIRCUMNAVIGATION OF THE WORLD. They sail around the CAPE OF GOOD HOPE to Australia, NEW ZEALAND, and the HAWAIIAN ISLANDS, and survey North America's Pacific coast, from the Gulf of Alaska to southern California. Vancouver and Broughton explore the Strait of Juan de Fuca and Puget Sound. In 1792, Broughton explores the mouth of the COLUMBIA RIVER.

1791–1814

NORTH AMERICA

- American fur trader ALEXANDER HENRY (the younger) establishes and manages NORTH WEST COMPANY posts from Lake Superior to the Oregon coast.

1792

NORTH AMERICA

- American captain and trader ROBERT GRAY explores the Northwest Coast, including the mouth of the COLUMBIA RIVER and Grays Harbor.

1792–93

NORTH AMERICA

- Scottish-Canadian fur trader ALEXANDER MACKENZIE, exploring for the NORTH WEST COMPANY, travels the Peace and Smoky Rivers. He follows the Parsnip River into the ROCKY MOUNTAINS. After reaching the Fraser River, he descends the Bella Coola River to the Pacific, completing the first overland journey across North America north of Rio Grande.

NORTH AMERICA

- JUAN FRANCISCO DE LA BODEGA Y QUADRA heads a Spanish naval expedition to the coasts of British Columbia and southeastern Alaska, seeking an outlet of the NORTHWEST PASSAGE.

1793–1811

NORTH AMERICA

- British fur trader DAVID THOMPSON maps the Canadian West and northern parts of the American West for the HUDSON'S BAY COMPANY, then for the NORTH WEST COMPANY.

1794–95

NORTH AMERICA

- French-Canadian fur trader JEAN-BAPTISTE TRUTEAU travels up the MISSOURI RIVER, from St. Louis to the Dakotas and Black Hills.

1795

NORTH AMERICA
- Russian fur trader ALEKSANDR ANDREYEVICH BARANOV explores the Gulf of Alaska around Sitka and Yakutat Bay.

1795–96

AUSTRALIA
- Englishmen GEORGE BASS and MATTHEW FLINDERS explore Australia's Botany Bay, Georges River, and the east coast south of Sidney.

1795–97

AFRICA
- Scottish surgeon MUNGO PARK reaches the NIGER RIVER in West Africa.

1798

PACIFIC OCEAN
- American sea captain EDMUND FANNING explores Fanning's Islands in the South Pacific.

AFRICA
- Portuguese colonial official FRANCISCO DE LACERDA attempts to cross Central Africa, exploring the ZAMBEZI RIVER and Luangwe River.

1798–99

AUSTRALIA
- Englishmen GEORGE BASS and MATTHEW FLINDERS circumnavigate TASMANIA.

1798–1801

AFRICA
- German FRIEDRICH CONRAD HORNEMANN heads a British scientific expedition across the SAHARA DESERT, seeking the source of the NIGER RIVER.

1799

- The RUSSIAN-AMERICAN COMPANY is founded to promote the Russian FUR TRADE in North America.

1799–1800

SOUTH AMERICA
- German naturalist and geographer ALEXANDER VON HUMBOLDT explores the upper ORINOCO RIVER in Venezuela and determines it is connected to the AMAZON RIVER by the Casiquiare River.

1800–04

AUSTRALIA
- THOMAS-NICOLAS BAUDIN heads a French scientific expedition to the coast of TASMANIA and Australia; FRANÇOIS PÉRON and CHARLES-ALEXANDRE LESUEUR serve as naturalists.

1801

SOUTH AMERICA
- German naturalist and geographer ALEXANDER VON HUMBOLDT explores the ANDES MOUNTAINS in Ecuador and Peru.

1801–03

AUSTRALIA
- MATTHEW FLINDERS heads a British maritime expedition to Australia's south, east, and west coasts. He reaches the Spencer Gulf, Kangaroo Island, and Gulf St. Vincent and circumnavigates Australia. FERDINAND LUCAS BAUER, ROBERT BROWN, and WILLIAM WESTALL serve as artists and naturalists.

1802

NORTH AMERICA
- FRANÇOIS-MARIE PERRIN DU LAC heads a French expedition up the MISSOURI RIVER, from St. Louis to the White River in South Dakota.

1802–11

AFRICA
- Portuguese PEDRO JOÃO BAPTISTA heads an expedition from Angola to Mozambique and back, the first known crossing of the African continent.

1803–06

WORLD
- ADAM IVAN RITTER VON KRUSENSTERN and YURY FYODOROVICH LISIANSKY head the first Russian CIRCUMNAVIGATION OF THE WORLD. They explore uncharted islands and reefs of the HAWAIIAN ISLANDS.

1804

- The BRITISH EAST INDIA COMPANY organizes the Great Trigonometrical Survey of the Indian subcontinent. The British government later directs it and, starting in the 1860s, hires native surveyors, known as PUNDITS.

NORTH AMERICA
- Scottish surveyor WILLIAM DUNBAR heads a U.S. government exploration to southern Louisiana Territory.

1804–05

NORTH AMERICA
- Russian fur trader ALEKSANDR ANDREYEVICH BARANOV explores North America's west coast, from the Gulf of Alaska to San Francisco Bay.

1804–06

NORTH AMERICA
- MERIWETHER LEWIS and WILLIAM CLARK head a U.S. expedition from St. Louis up the MISSOURI RIVER, across the ROCKY MOUNTAINS, to the mouth of the COLUMBIA RIVER on the Pacific and back. Shoshone Indian woman SACAJAWEA and her husband TOUSSAINT CHARBONNEAU and infant son JEAN-BAPTISTE CHARBONNEAU partici-

pate, as do JOHN COLTER, GEORGE DROUILLARD, PIERRE DORION, SR., PIERRE DORION, JR., and RENÉ JUSSEAUME.

1805–06

AFRICA
- Scotsman MUNGO PARK heads a British expedition from the Gambia River to the NIGER RIVER, possibly reaching Bussa in northern Nigeria. He identifies the southern limit of the SAHARA DESERT.

NORTH AMERICA
- GAVRIIL IVANOVICH DAVYDOV heads a Russian naval expedition to Alaska and Sitka.

1805–07

NORTH AMERICA
- ZEBULON MONTGOMERY PIKE heads two U.S. military expeditions to the upper MISSISSIPPI RIVER and the eastern ROCKY MOUNTAINS.

1805–08

NORTH AMERICA
- American fur trader SIMON FRASER explores west of the Canadian ROCKY MOUNTAINS for the NORTH WEST COMPANY; he follows the Fraser River to its Pacific outlet in British Columbia.

1806

NORTH AMERICA
- THOMAS FREEMAN heads a U.S. expedition along the Red River, from southwestern Mississippi to Texas.

1806–22

ARCTIC/GREENLAND
- British whaler WILLIAM SCORESBY, SR., and his scientist son WILLIAM SCORESBY, JR., explore the Arctic regions of GREENLAND, pioneering Arctic navigation and scientific studies.

1807

NORTH AMERICA
- American fur trader JOHN COLTER explores the Wind River and Teton Mountains in Wyoming.

1807–11

WORLD
- VASILY MIKHAILOVICH GOLOVNIN heads a Russian naval expedition from Europe, rounding Africa rather than the intended South America. He explores coastal Alaska, then reaches the Kamchatka Peninsula of Asia. He also explores the Kuril Islands of Japan.

ASIA
- British diplomat HARFORD JONES BRYDGES heads an expedition from Bombay in India to Persia (Iran). He visits Baluchistan on the Arabia Sea, Afghanistan, and the Caucasus Mountains.

1808

NORTH AMERICA
- American JOHN JACOB ASTOR founds the AMERICAN FUR COMPANY to develop the western FUR TRADE.
- The AMERICAN GEOGRAPHICAL SOCIETY is founded in New York City.

1809

NORTH AMERICA
- American fur traders MANUEL LISA, ANDREW HENRY, ANTOINE PIERRE MENARD, WILLIAM CLARK, and brothers AUGUSTE PIERRE CHOUTEAU, JEAN PIERRE CHOUTEAU, PIERRE CHOUTEAU, and RENÉ AUGUSTE CHOUTEAU found the ST. LOUIS MISSOURI FUR COMPANY to develop the western fur trade.

1810–11

NORTH AMERICA
- American JOHN JACOB ASTOR sponsors a maritime trading expedition from New York to the Oregon coast under ROBERT STUART and GABRIEL FRANCHÈRE. They found the post of Astoria on the COLUMBIA RIVER.

1810–12

ASIA
- Englishmen CHARLES CHRISTIE and HENRY POTTINGER command an expedition to the interior of Pakistan into Afghanistan, and to the Persian Gulf.

1810–13

ASIA
- Englishwoman Lady HESTER LUCY STANHOPE travels in Israel, Lebanon, and Syria. She lives among the Bedouin in the Syrian Desert.

1810–15

AFRICA
- British naturalist WILLIAM JOHN BURCHELL explores the interior of South Africa west and north of Cape Town.

1811

NORTH AMERICA
- American writer HENRY MARIE BRACKENRIDGE and Scottish naturalist JOHN BRADBURY travel up the MISSOURI RIVER with fur traders.

1811–12

NORTH AMERICA
- American fur trader JOHN JACOB ASTOR sponsors the Astorians under WILSON PRICE HUNT in an overland journey from St. Louis to Astoria on the Oregon coast. Ioway Indian woman MARIE DORION and her husband PIERRE DORION, JR., serve as guides.

ASIA
- Englishman THOMAS MANNING travels from Calcutta, India, through Bhutan to LHASA in Tibet.

1812

ASIA
- HYDER JUNG HEARSEY and WILLIAM MOORCROFT head a British expedition from India across the HIMALAYAS to Tibet.

1812–13

NORTH AMERICA
- Scottish fur trader ROBERT STUART, working for JOHN JACOB ASTOR, travels from Astoria in Oregon eastward through the SOUTH PASS of the ROCKY MOUNTAINS. He descends the Platte River and MISSOURI RIVER to St. Louis.

1812–14

AFRICA
- Englishman JOHN CAMPBELL explores the interior of South Africa, from Algoa Bay northward to the southern edge of Kalahari Desert, reaching the Vaael River. He returns to the Atlantic coast by way of the Orange River.

1812–15

AFRICA
- JOHANN LUDWIG BURCKHARDT heads a British expedition to the NIGER RIVER from North Africa. Although failing to reach the Niger, Burckhardt explores parts of Egypt, Sudan, and Arabia.

1813

AUSTRALIA
- Australian colonists GREGORY BLAXLAND and WILLIAM CHARLES WENTWORTH cross the BLUE MOUNTAINS west of Sydney and view the Bathurst Plains.

1814

NEW ZEALAND
- Englishman SAMUEL MARSDEN establishes an Anglican mission at the Bay of Islands on North Island, New Zealand.

1815–18

WORLD
- Otto von Kotzebue heads a Russian naval expedition searching for outlets of the NORTHEAST PASSAGE or the NORTHWEST PASSAGE in the North Pacific. He names Kotzebue Sound and explores island groups in the South Pacific, including the Marshalls and Gilberts. LOUIS-CHARLES-ADÉLAÏDE CHAMISSO DE BONCOURT and JOHANN FRIEDRICH ESCHSCHOLTZ serve as naturalists. LOUIS CHORIS serves as draftsman.

1816–19

NORTH AMERICA
- Scottish-Canadian fur trader DONALD MACKEN-ZIE sends out fur-trapping brigades throughout the Pacific Northwest and the northern ROCKY MOUNTAINS for the NORTH WEST COMPANY.

1817–18

AUSTRALIA
- British-born surveyor general JOHN JOSEPH WILLIAM MOLESWORTH OXLEY heads two Australian expeditions to the Lachlan River and the Macquarie River. He reaches the Arbuthnot Range and Liverpool Plains.

1817–20

WORLD
- LOUIS-CLAUDE DE SAULCES DE FREYCINET heads a French naval CIRCUMNAVIGATION OF THE WORLD. He explores western Australia, Timor, the Moluccas (SPICE ISLANDS), Samoa, and the HAWAIIAN ISLANDS. CHARLES GAUDICHARD-BEAUPRÉ, JEAN-RENÉ-CONSTANT QUOY, and JOSEPH-PAUL GAIMARD serve as naturalists. JACQUES ARAGO serves as artist and writer.

SOUTH AMERICA
- German botanist CARL FRIEDRICH PHILLIPP VON MARTIUS explores eastern Brazil and the upper Amazon Basin.

1817–22

AUSTRALIA
- PHILIP PARKER KING heads a British coastal survey of northern Australia and TASMANIA.

1818

ARCTIC
- DAVID BUCHAN heads a British naval expedition attempting a seaward passage across the Arctic Ocean to the Pacific, passing as close as possible to the NORTH POLE.

ARCTIC
- JOHN ROSS heads a British naval expedition to Baffin Bay in the Canadian Arctic, seeking the NORTHWEST PASSAGE. He explores Lancaster Sound.

1818–19

MIDDLE EAST
- JOSEPH RITCHIE and GEORGE FRANCIS LYON command a British expedition southward across the SAHARA DESERT, from Tripoli to the NIGER RIVER region of West Africa.

1818–20

NORTH AMERICA
- British naturalist THOMAS NUTTALL explores the Arkansas River and Red River in Louisiana, Arkansas, and Oklahoma.

1819

NORTH AMERICA	• HENRY ATKINSON heads the U.S. military's first Yellowstone Expedition up the MISSOURI RIVER into Nebraska.
ASIA	• British diplomat GEORGE FOSTER SADLIER becomes the first European to cross the Arabian Peninsula, from Quatif on the Persian Gulf to Yenbo on the RED SEA.
AUSTRALIA	• JOHN JOSEPH WILLIAM MOLESWORTH OXLEY and HAMILTON HUME head an Australian maritime expedition to Jervis Bay.
	• German inventor Augustus Siebe develops the first efficient DIVING SUIT, consisting of a copper helmet attached to a watertight canvas and leather jacket with weights attached around the chest.

1819–21

ANTARCTIC	• Baron FABIAN GOTTLIEB BENJAMIN VON BELLINGSHAUSEN heads a Russian naval expedition, which makes an early sighting of Antarctica. He explores the Fiji Islands and Tuamotu Archipelago in the South Pacific. On returning to Antarctica, he sights Peter I and Alexander I Islands.
AFRICA	• Englishman JOHN CAMPBELL reaches the source of the Limpopo River in South Africa.

1819–22

NORTH AMERICA/ ARCTIC	• JOHN FRANKLIN heads a British naval overland expedition eastward along the Arctic coast of Canada, from the mouth of the Coppermine River, along the Coronation Gulf, to the Kent Peninsula. ROBERT HOOD and GEORGE BACK serve as midshipmen. JOHN RICHARDSON serves as naturalist.

1819–25

ARCTIC	• WILLIAM EDWARD PARRY heads three British naval expeditions to the Canadian Arctic, seeking the NORTHWEST PASSAGE. He reaches Barrow Strait and as far west as Melville Island. He explores HUDSON BAY, Foxe Basin, and Fury and Hecla Straits as well as Prince Regent Inlet and the Gulf of Boothia.

1819–26

ASIA	• GRIGORY GAVRILOVICH BASARGIN heads a Russian naval expedition to the Caspian Sea.

1820

NORTH AMERICA	• STEPHEN HARRIMAN LONG heads a U.S. military expedition to the central plains and eastern ROCKY MOUNTAINS.

| **ANTARCTIC** | - British naval officer EDWARD BRANSFIELD charts the South Shetland Islands and sights the Antarctic Peninsula. |

1820–21

| **ANTARCTIC** | - American sealer NATHANIEL BROWN PALMER reaches the Palmer Archipelago and South Orkney Islands and sights the Antarctic Peninsula. |

1821

| | - The HUDSON'S BAY COMPANY and the NORTH WEST COMPANY merge under the name of the former. |
| **NORTH AMERICA** | - Swedish-Finnish naval officer ARVID ADOLF ETHOLÉN conducts a Russian maritime exploration of the coast of Alaska north of the Alaskan Peninsula as far as the Kuskokwim River. |

1821–22

| **NORTH AMERICA** | - American traders JACOB FOWLER and Hugh Glenn pioneer a route known as the Old Taos Trail through the Sangre de Cristo Mountains of southern Colorado into New Mexico. |

1821–23

| **ATLANTIC OCEAN** | - Scottish sealer JAMES WEDDELL explores the South Orkney Islands in the South Atlantic. He reaches the Weddell Sea east of the Antarctic Peninsula. |

1821–25

| **AFRICA** | - WALTER OUDNEY, HUGH CLAPPERTON, and DIXON DENHAM lead the British-backed Bornu Mission from Libya across the SAHARA DESERT into West Africa. They reach Lake Chad and the Chari River and seek the NIGER RIVER. |
| **AFRICA** | - British missionaries ROBERT MOFFAT and MARY MOFFAT found missions near the Kalahari Desert in South Africa; they explore the region in years to come. |

1822

| **NORTH AMERICA** | - American trader WILLIAM BECKNELL pioneers a wagon route from Missouri via the Cimarron Cutoff of the Santa Fe Trail. |

1822–25

| **WORLD** | - LOUIS-ISADORE DUPERREY heads a French naval CIRCUMNAVIGATION OF THE WORLD. He explores coastal South America and visits island |

groups in the Pacific. RENÉ-PRIMEVÈRE LESSON serves as zoologist.

WORLD
- MIKHAIL PETROVICH LAZAREV heads a Russian naval CIRCUMNAVIGATION OF THE WORLD.

1822–26

NORTH AMERICA
- Americans WILLIAM HENRY ASHLEY and ANDREW HENRY found the ROCKY MOUNTAIN FUR COMPANY in 1822. Over the next years, Ashley sponsors trading expeditions to the northern ROCKY MOUNTAINS and the Great Basin. MOUNTAIN MEN working for Ashley include JAMES PIERSON BECKWOURTH, JAMES BRIDGER, ROBERT CAMPBELL, JAMES CLYMAN, THOMAS FITZPATRICK, HENRY FRAEB, HUGH GLASS, CALEB GREENWOOD, DAVID E. JACKSON, ÉTIENNE PROVOST EDWARD ROSE, JEDEDIAH STRONG SMITH, WILLIAM LEWIS SUBLETTE, WILLIAM HENRY VANDERBURGH, LOUIS VASQUEZ, and JOHN H. WEBER, many of whom continue trapping, trading, and guiding in the subsequent years. Ashley and others undertake the first known successful navigation of the Uinta River and explore the Green River and the Great Salt Lake region of Utah.

1823

AUSTRALIA
- British-born surveyor general JOHN JOSEPH WILLIAM MOLESWORTH OXLEY heads an Australian expedition to Moreton Bay. He reaches the Brisbane River.

AUSTRALIA
- British naturalist ALLAN CUNNINGHAM explores a route from Bathurst through Pandora's Pass to the Liverpool Plains north of Sydney.

NORTH AMERICA
- Italian GIACOMO COSTANTINO BELTRAMI explores the MISSISSIPPI RIVER and Minnesota River.

1823–26

PACIFIC OCEAN
- OTTO VON KOTZEBUE heads a Russian naval expedition to the South Pacific, exploring the Tuamotu, Society, and Marshall island groups.

1823–43

ASIA
- GEORGE EVEREST heads Britain's Great Trigonometrical Survey of India.

1824

NORTH AMERICA
- Scottish-Canadian fur trader ALEXANDER ROSS explores the Snake River, from Montana to the mouth of the Boise River in Idaho, for the HUDSON'S BAY COMPANY.

AUSTRALIA
- Englishmen WILLIAM HILTON HOVELL and HAMILTON HUME explore southeastern Australia, from Lake George to Geelong, reaching the Australian Alps.

1824–26

WORLD
- HYACINTHE-YVES-PHILLIPE POTENTIEN DE BOUGAINVILLE heads a French CIRCUMNAVIGATION OF THE WORLD.

1824–30

NORTH AMERICA
- Canadian fur trader PETER SKENE OGDEN explores the Pacific Northwest and the Great Basin for JOHN MCLOUGHLIN and the HUDSON'S BAY COMPANY.

1825

NORTH AMERICA
- HENRY ATKINSON heads the U.S. military's second Yellowstone Expedition to eastern Montana.

1825–26

AFRICA
- ALEXANDER GORDON LAING heads a British expedition seeking the source of the NIGER RIVER. He reaches the city of TIMBUKTU in Mali.

1825–27

NORTH AMERICA
- JOHN FRANKLIN heads a British expedition westward from the mouth of the Mackenzie River to Prudhoe Bay on Alaska's North Slope.

1825–28

AFRICA
- HUGH CLAPPERTON and RICHARD LEMON LANDER head a British expedition into the interior of Nigeria. They reach the NIGER RIVER, where Clapperton dies. WILLIAM PASCOE of the Hausa tribe serves as guide.

PACIFIC OCEAN
- FREDERICK WILLIAM BEECHEY heads a British naval expedition to the Pacific, exploring South America's west coast, the Gambier Islands in central Polynesia, the BERING STRAIT and Alaska's west coast, and the islands off southern Japan.

1825–29

SOUTH AMERICA
- GEORG HEINRICH RITTER VON LANGSDORFF heads a Russian scientific expedition to the Amazon Basin.

1825–32

AUSTRALIA
- Danish mariner JÖRGEN JÖRGENSON explores TASMANIA.

1826–27

NORTH AMERICA	▪ American fur trader EWING YOUNG heads a trapping expedition from Taos in New Mexico into southern Arizona.
NORTH AMERICA	▪ American fur trader JAMES OHIO PATTIE establishes an overland route from New Mexico to California.

1826–29

PACIFIC OCEAN	▪ JULES-SÉBASTIEN-CÉSAR DUMONT D'URVILLE heads a French maritime expedition to coastal Australia and NEW ZEALAND and the islands of the western Pacific. He finds relics of the JEAN-FRANÇOIS DE GALAUP, comte de La Pérouse, expedition.
WORLD	▪ FYODOR PETROVICH LITKE heads a Russian naval CIRCUMNAVIGATION OF THE WORLD. He explores the Carolines in the South Pacific. He charts islands in the Bering Sea and explores SIBERIA's Kamchatka and Chukchi Peninsulas. KARL HEINRICH MERTENS serves as naturalist.
NORTH AMERICA	▪ American fur trader JEDEDIAH STRONG SMITH leads expeditions from the Great Salt Lake to California. He makes the first eastward crossing of the Sierra Nevada and Great Salt Lake and explores northern California and Oregon.

1826–34

SOUTH AMERICA	▪ French naturalist ALCIDE-CHARLES-VICTOR DESSALINES D'ORBIGNY conducts studies throughout South America.

1827

ARCTIC	▪ WILLIAM EDWARD PARRY heads a British naval attempt on the NORTH POLE from Spitsbergen (Svalbard), setting the northernmost record at the time.
	▪ French physicist Joseph Nicéphore Niépce creates the first known photograph.

1827–28

AFRICA	▪ Frenchman RENÉ-AUGUSTE CAILLIÉ crosses Guinea to the upper NIGER RIVER and descends it to TIMBUKTU, then crosses the SAHARA DESERT from south to north.
AUSTRALIA	▪ British naturalist ALLAN CUNNINGHAM develops a route from Darling Downs through the GREAT DIVIDING RANGE to the Pacific coast.
NORTH AMERICA	▪ French naturalist JEAN-LOUIS BERLANDIER explores the interior of Texas.

1827–30

NORTH AMERICA
- American fur trader JOSHUA PILCHER heads an expedition from St. Louis, along the Platte River and through the ROCKY MOUNTAINS, to the COLUMBIA RIVER.

1828

NORTH AMERICA
- Scottish official GEORGE SIMPSON of the HUDSON'S BAY COMPANY travels across Canada to British Columbia via the Thompson and Fraser Rivers.

NORTH AMERICA
- French-Canadian ANTOINE ROBIDOUX extends the fur trade to Taos in New Mexico and northward into Colorado.

1828–29

AUSTRALIA
- Englishman CHARLES STURT explores the Macquerie and Darling Rivers in southeastern Australia.

1829–33

ARCTIC
- Englishmen JOHN ROSS and his nephew JAMES CLARK ROSS explore the Canadian Arctic, including the Boothia Peninsula. They travel from Prince Regent Inlet to Lancaster Sound. In 1831, James Clark Ross reaches the NORTH MAGNETIC POLE.

NORTH AMERICA
- Scottish-Canadian fur trader KENNETH MCKENZIE sends out expeditions to the northern ROCKY MOUNTAINS and northern plains for the AMERICAN FUR COMPANY.

1829–35

NORTH AMERICA
- American fur trader WARREN ANGUS FERRIS explores the upper MISSOURI RIVER and the northern ROCKY MOUNTAINS.

ca. 1830

- The SEXTANT is invented independently in England and America in response to a challenge by the ROYAL SOCIETY and the British parliament to solve the problem of how to measure longitude accurately.

1830

- JOHN BARROW founds Great Britain's ROYAL GEOGRAPHICAL SOCIETY.

NORTH AMERICA
- Irish fur trader JOHN WORK explores in the Snake River region of eastern Washington, western Idaho, northern Nevada, and central Oregon for the HUDSON'S BAY COMPANY.

1830–31

AFRICA
- RICHARD LEMON LANDER heads a British expedition, which traces the course of the NIGER RIVER to the Gulf of Guinea.

NORTH AMERICA
- American fur traders WILLIAM WOLFSKILL and GEORGE CONCEPCION YOUNT pioneer the Old Spanish Trail from Taos, New Mexico, through Utah and Arizona, to Los Angeles, California, as a trade route.

1830–36

NORTH AMERICA
- American GEORGE CATLIN paints Native Americans in the American West and Southeast.

1830–39

NORTH AMERICA
- American LUCIEN FONTENELLE develops the fur trade in Nebraska.

1831

- The ROYAL GEOGRAPHICAL SOCIETY and AFRICAN ASSOCIATION merge under the name of the former.

1831–32

ANTARCTIC
- JOHN BISCOE heads a British seal-hunting expedition, which circumnavigates Antarctica. He reaches Enderby Land and Biscoe Island.

1831–36

SOUTH AMERICA/ PACIFIC OCEAN
- ROBERT FITZROY and CHARLES ROBERT DARWIN conduct a British naval scientific expedition to coastal South America and the Galapagos Islands aboard the *Beagle*.

AUSTRALIA
- Scottish surveyor THOMAS LIVINGSTONE MITCHELL heads three expeditions west of Sydney to chart the continent's river system. He explores the Darling and Murray Rivers and their tributaries.

1831–39

NORTH AMERICA
- American artist and naturalist JOHN JAMES AUDUBON paints North American wildlife.

1831–44

SOUTH AMERICA
- German naturalist ROBERT HERMANN SCHOMBURGK heads a British expedition to the rivers of Guyana.

1832

NORTH AMERICA
- American geologist and ethnologist HENRY ROWE SCHOOLCRAFT determines that Lake

Itasca in Minnesota is the source of the MISSIS-SIPPI RIVER.

1832–33

NORTH AMERICA
- Spanish-born fur trader MANUEL ÁLVAREZ explores the region of Yellowstone National Park in northeastern Wyoming.

1832–35

NORTH AMERICA
- Former U.S. army officer BENJAMIN LOUIS EULALIE DE BONNEVILLE heads a fur-trading expedition across the ROCKY MOUNTAINS, including SOUTH PASS, to Utah and later explores Oregon. In 1833, he dispatches MOUNTAIN MEN JOSEPH REDDEFORD WALKER, ZENAS LEONARD, and JOSEPH L. MEEK across the Great Basin and Sierra Nevada to California, where they explore Yosemite Valley. Their route becomes the California Trail.

ASIA
- ALEXANDER BURNES heads a British military expedition across central Asia from Peshawar, Pakistan, through Afghanistan, to the Caspian Sea, Tehran, and the Persian Gulf.

1832–36

NORTH AMERICA
- American fur trader NATHANIEL JARVIS WYETH heads two expeditions to the Pacific Northwest. Fellow fur trader OSBORNE RUSSELL accompanies him in 1834.

1832–42

NORTH AMERICA
- American trapper and guide CHRISTOPHER HOUSTON CARSON (Kit Carson) explores the ROCKY MOUNTAINS.

NORTH AMERICA
- Russian-Aleut ALEKSANDR FILIPPOVICH KASHEVAROV heads a Russian expedition to Alaska's west coast, from Norton Sound to Point Barrow.

1833

NORTH AMERICA
- American fur traders CHARLES BENT, WILLIAM BENT, and CÉRAN DE HAULT DE LASSUS DE ST. VRAIN found Bent's Fort, a trading post on the Arkansas River in southeastern Colorado.

NORTH AMERICA
- American writer JOHN TREAT IRVING explores the plains of Kansas and Nebraska.

1833–34

NORTH AMERICA
- German naturalist Prince ALEXANDER PHILIPP MAXIMILIAN and Swiss artist KARL BODMER travel up the MISSOURI RIVER, from St. Louis to central

Montana. Bodmer paints the Mandan and other Native Americans.

1833–35

NORTH AMERICA

- GEORGE BACK heads a British naval overland expedition north and east of the Great Slave Lake, reaching the Great Fish (Back) River.

1834

NORTH AMERICA

- HENRY LEAVENWORTH and HENRY DODGE command a U.S. military expedition to the southern plains. They explore the Arkansas and Red Rivers. BLACK BEAVER and JESSE CHISHOLM serve as guides.

1834–35

NORTH AMERICA

- Russian fur trader ANDREY GLAZUNOV explores the Yukon and Kuskokwim Rivers of western Alaska.

1834–36

ASIA

- JAMES WELLSTED heads a British expedition surveying the south coast of the Arabian Peninsula. He explores Oman and sights the Rub' al-Khali desert (EMPTY QUARTER).

1835

NORTH AMERICA

- HENRY DODGE heads a U.S. military expedition from Oklahoma to the ROCKY MOUNTAINS and the Oregon Trail, returning along the Santa Fe Trail.

1836

NORTH AMERICA

- American missionaries MARCUS WHITMAN and HENRY HARMON SPALDING pioneer the Oregon Trail west of Fort Hall, Idaho, as a wagon route.

1836–37

ASIA

- WILLIAM C. MCLEOD heads a British military expedition to northern Burma (Myanmar).

1836–39

WORLD

- ABEL-AUBERT DUPETIT-THOUARS heads a French naval CIRCUMNAVIGATION OF THE WORLD. He explores South America's west coast and the South Pacific.

1837

NORTH AMERICA

- American ALFRED JACOB MILLER paints landscapes and Native Americans along the Oregon Trail.

1837–39

ARCTIC/ NORTH AMERICA
- Scotsman THOMAS SIMPSON and Canadian PETER WARREN DEASE explore the Arctic coastline of Alaska and Canada for the HUDSON'S BAY COMPANY.

AUSTRALIA
- GEORGE GREY heads a British expedition to western Australia. He reaches the Gascoyne River and the upper Swan River.

1837–40

ANTARCTIC
- JULES-SÉBASTIEN-CÉSAR DUMONT D'URVILLE heads a French naval expedition south of the ANTARCTIC CIRCLE. He reaches Adélie Land and the approximate position of the SOUTH MAGNETIC POLE. CHARLES-HECTOR JACQUINOT commands the second ship.

1837–42

NORTH AMERICA
- EDWARD BELCHER heads a British naval expedition to the Pacific coast of the Americas.

1838–39

NORTH AMERICA
- JOSEPH NICOLAS NICOLLET heads two U.S. surveying expeditions to the lands between the upper MISSISSIPPI RIVER and the MISSOURI RIVER.

1838–40

NORTH AMERICA
- American fur trader RICHENS LACY WOOTTON travels throughout the American West out of Bent's Fort, Colorado.

1838–42

PACIFIC OCEAN/ NORTH AMERICA
- CHARLES WILKES and GEORGE FOSTER EMMONS head the U.S. South Sea Surveying and Exploring Expedition, which completes the first U.S. government CIRCUMNAVIGATION OF THE WORLD. They explore South America, Antarctica, and Pacific island groups. They direct extensive inland penetration of Oregon and northern California. JAMES DWIGHT DANA serves as naturalist.

1838–52

SOUTH AMERICA
- Swiss naturalist JOHANN JAKOB VON TSCHUDI travels throughout the Peruvian Andes.

1839

NEW ZEALAND
- Englishman WILLIAM WILLIAMS makes a south-to-north crossing of North Island, NEW ZEALAND.

1839–41

AUSTRALIA
- British sheep farmer EDWARD JOHN EYRE explores the Flinders Range north of Adelaide and Lake Torrens. He travels across Eyre Peninsula to Streaky Bay. He explores north and west of Adelaide and sights Lake Eyre. He heads westward from Fowlers Bay along the coast of the Great Australian Bight to Albany and back to Fremantle, completing the first east-to-west crossing of Australia.

NORTH AMERICA
- American fur trader ROBERT NEWELL drives the first wagons along the entire length of the Oregon Trail.

1839–43

ANTARCTIC
- JAMES CLARK ROSS heads a British naval expedition to Antarctica. He reaches the Ross Sea, Victoria Land, Prince Albert Range, McMurdo Sound, and the Ross Ice Shelf. He explores Graham Land on the Antarctic Peninsula. JOSEPH DALTON HOOKER serves as botanist.

AUSTRALIA
- Polish geologist PAUL EDMUND DE STRZELECKI explores southeastern Australia and TASMANIA.

1840

NORTH AMERICA
- Scottish trader ROBERT CAMPBELL reaches the source of the Pelly River in the Yukon Territory for the HUDSON'S BAY COMPANY.

1841

NORTH AMERICA
- Belgian missionary PIERRE-JEAN DE SMET heads the first large-scale wagon train migration on the Oregon Trail. THOMAS FITZPATRICK serves as guide.

NORTH AMERICA
- JAMES SINCLAIR, a Métis, pioneers a wagon route through the Canadian ROCKY MOUNTAINS for the HUDSON'S BAY COMPANY.

1841–42

MEDITERRANEAN
- Scottish naturalist EDWARD FORBES studies a deep seabed in the MEDITERRANEAN SEA.

1841–47

NEW ZEALAND
- Englishman WILLIAM COLENSO carries out three expeditions to NEW ZEALAND's North Island.

1841–59

NORTH AMERICA
- American fur trader JAMES BAKER traps in northern Utah and southern Wyoming.

1842

NORTH AMERICA

- JOHN CHARLES FRÉMONT heads a U.S. military expedition to the Great Plains, exploring the Platte River and SOUTH PASS through the ROCKY MOUNTAINS.

1842–44

NORTH AMERICA

- Russian naval officer LAVRENTY ALEKSEYEVICH ZAGOSKIN explores the Yukon and Kuskokwim plus other rivers of Alaska's interior.

1842–45

NORTH AMERICA

- American fur traders WILLIAM SHERLEY WILLIAMS and WILLIAM THOMAS HAMILTON explore the Green River and the North Platte River in southern Wyoming and northern Utah.

1843

NORTH AMERICA

- Canadian-born fur trader NORMAN WOLFRED KITTSON promotes JOHN JACOB ASTOR's AMERICAN FUR COMPANY in the Red River of the North region of Minnesota and North Dakota.

1843–44

NORTH AMERICA

- JOHN CHARLES FRÉMONT heads a U.S. military expedition to the ROCKY MOUNTAINS, the Great Basin, Great Salt Lake, the eastern Cascade Mountains, and California.

1843–47

SOUTH AMERICA

- FRANÇOIS DE LA PORTE, comte de Castelnau, heads two French expeditions to the AMAZON RIVER. He explores the watershed between the Río de la Plata and the Amazon River and reaches the source of the Paraguay River. He completes the west-to-east crossing of the continent by way of Peru and Brazil.

1843–48

NEW ZEALAND

- Englishman THOMAS BRUNNER explores the interior of NEW ZEALAND's South Island, from Tasman Bay to Mount Cook. He travels around Lake Rotoroa and descends the Buller River to the Tasman Sea. He explores the Grey River and the Southern Alps, reaching Lake Brunner.

1844–45

AUSTRALIA

- German FRIEDRICH WILHELM LUDWIG LEICHHARDT makes the first successful crossing of northeastern Australia, from Moreton Bay to the

Gulf of Carpentaria, then through Arnhem Land to Port Essington.

1845

NORTH AMERICA

- STEPHEN WATTS KEARNY heads a U.S. military expedition to the Platte and Arkansas Rivers and the eastern ROCKY MOUNTAINS, including the SOUTH PASS. JAMES WILLIAM ABERT leads a party to western Oklahoma and western Texas.
- French chemist and physicist, Henri-Victor Regnault, develops a practical HYPSOMETER.

1845–46

AUSTRALIA

- Scottish-born surveyor general THOMAS LIVINGSTONE MITCHELL attempts a northwestward crossing of the continent from Darling Downs to the north coast. He explores the central region of Queensland.

NORTH AMERICA

- MERVIN VAVASOUR and HENRY JAMES WARRE carry out British military reconnaissance in Oregon.

ASIA

- French missionary ÉVARISTE-RÉGIS HUC travels from Mongolia across the Ordos Desert to LHASA in Tibet.

1845–47

NORTH AMERICA

- JOHN CHARLES FRÉMONT heads a U.S. military expedition to the Great Basin, the Sierra Nevada, northern California, and southern Oregon.

1845–48

NORTH AMERICA

- JOHN FRANKLIN commands a British naval expedition to the Canadian Arctic in an attempt to navigate the NORTHWEST PASSAGE. The ship is icebound in the Victoria Strait. On Franklin's death in 1847, FRANCIS RAWDON MOIRA CROZIER assumes command. All expedition members eventually perish.

1846

NORTH AMERICA

- WILLIAM HEMSLEY EMORY heads a U.S. military topographic expedition to the American Southwest and creates the first scientific map of the region.

NORTH AMERICA

- American HENRI CHATILLON leads historian Francis Parkman's expedition onto the Great Plains.
- The HAKLUYT SOCIETY, a charity furthering knowledge of exploration, is founded in London.

1846–47

ARCTIC

- Scottish physician JOHN RAE explores the northern extent of the Boothia Peninsula in the

Canadian Arctic for the HUDSON'S BAY COMPANY.

NORTH AMERICA
- American pioneer JESSE APPLEGATE explores the Humboldt River and the Black Rock Desert of northern Nevada. He establishes the Applegate Trail as a new and shorter southern route from Fort Hall, Idaho, to the Willamette Valley in Oregon. He explores the Umpqua Valley of west-central Oregon.

1846–48

NORTH AMERICA
- Canadian painter PAUL KANE explores western Canada, from Toronto to Vancouver.

1847

NORTH AMERICA
- American BRIGHAM YOUNG leads the Mormons from Winter Quarters on the MISSOURI RIVER to the Great Salt Lake Valley, establishing the Mormon Trail.

AUSTRALIA
- Australian EDMUND KENNEDY explores the interior of Queensland and the Barcoo River.

1847–49

ARCTIC
- JOHN RICHARDSON and JOHN RAE head a British expedition in search of JOHN FRANKLIN; they explore Canada's Arctic coastline eastward from the Mackenzie River to Dolphin and Union Strait. In 1849–50, Rae continues the search on his own, reaching Victoria Island.

1847–52

NORTH AMERICA
- Swiss painter RUDOLPH FRIEDERICH KURZ explores the MISSOURI RIVER and western plains.

1847–55

WORLD
- Austrian woman IDA REYER PFEIFFER travels twice around the world, west to east and east to west, and writes books, *A Woman's Journey Round the World* and *A Woman's Second Journey Round the World*.

1848

AFRICA
- German missionary JOHANN REBMANN explores the interior of East Africa from Mombasa and reaches MOUNT KILIMANJARO.

1848–49

NORTH AMERICA
- American JOHN CHARLES FRÉMONT seeks a route from the Great Plains to upper Rio Grande through Sangre de Cristo and the San Juan Mountains of northern New Mexico. Brothers BEN-

	JAMIN JORDAN KERN, EDWARD MEYER KERN, and RICHARD HOVENDON KERN serve as naturalists, topographers, and artists.
ARCTIC	▪ JAMES CLARK ROSS heads a British naval expedition to the Canadian Arctic in search of JOHN FRANKLIN. He travels through Lancaster Sound as far as Barrow Strait and southward from Somerset Island into Peel Strait.

1848–52

SOUTH AMERICA	▪ British naturalists HENRY WALTER BATES and ALFRED RUSSEL WALLACE explore the Amazon Basin. Bates continues his explorations until 1859.

1848–53

ASIA	▪ British couple THOMAS WITTLAM ATKINSON and LUCY ATKINSON travel in SIBERIA, Mongolia, and central Asia.

1849

NORTH AMERICA	▪ RANDOLPH BARNES MARCY and JAMES HERVEY SIMPSON head a U.S. military topographic survey of a wagon route between Fort Smith, Arkansas, and Santa Fe, New Mexico. Simpson locates Native American ruins at Chaco Canyon in New Mexico and Canyon de Chelly in Arizona.
AFRICA	▪ German missionary JOHANN LUDWIG KRAPF explores the interior of East Africa westward from Mombasa and sights Mount Kenya.

1849–50

NORTH AMERICA	▪ HOWARD STANSBURY heads a U.S. military topographic expedition to Utah. He surveys Great Salt Lake's west shore, Utah Lake, and River Jordan.

1849–55

ASIA	▪ GENNADY IVANOVICH NEVELSKOY heads two Russian naval expeditions to the Amur River and Tatar Strait. He determines that Sakhalin is an island, not a peninsula.

1849–63

AFRICA	▪ Scottish missionary DAVID LIVINGSTONE carries out three expeditions in central Africa, two of them accompanied by his wife MARY MOFFAT LIVINGSTONE. He crosses the Kalahari Desert and reaches Lake Ngami. He explores the ZAMBEZI RIVER and the Ruvuma River. He also reaches Victoria Falls on the Zambezi and Lake Nyasa (Lake Malawi). Artist THOMAS BAINES accompanies him on the Zambezi expedition.

1849–64

SOUTH AMERICA
- British botanist RICHARD SPRUCE conducts research along the AMAZON RIVER and Río Negro and other rivers in northern South America.

1850–51

ARCTIC
- EDWIN JESSE DE HAVEN heads a maritime expedition to the Canadian Arctic backed by shipping magnate Henry Grinnell in search of JOHN FRANKLIN. He is trapped in ice north of the Baffin Island and the Lancaster Sound; he reaches Grinnell Land on Devon Island.

ARCTIC
- JOHN ROSS heads a British maritime expedition in search of JOHN FRANKLIN; he winters in Barrow Strait.

1850–52

AFRICA
- British scientist FRANCIS GALTON conducts research in Damaraland and Ovamboland in southwestern Africa.

1850–54

ARCTIC
- ROBERT JOHN LE MESURIER McCLURE heads a British naval expedition to the Canadian Arctic in search of JOHN FRANKLIN. He reaches Prince of Wales Strait between Banks Island and Victoria Island. He completes the first transcontinental crossing of North America above the ARCTIC CIRCLE.

1850–55

AFRICA
- HEINRICH BARTH, ADOLF OVERWEG, and JAMES RICHARDSON head a British expedition into West Africa; they cross the SAHARA DESERT from north to south and explore the Lake Chad region. Barth explores the Benue River, the upper NIGER RIVER, and TIMBUKTU.

ARCTIC
- RICHARD COLLINSON heads a British naval expedition in search of JOHN FRANKLIN; he explores the Arctic coasts of Alaska and Canada as far east as Victoria Island.

1851

NORTH AMERICA
- LORENZO SITGREAVES heads a U.S. military topographic expedition from Santa Fe, New Mexico, to the Zuni and Little Colorado Rivers in Arizona. Mojave Indian IRATEBA serves as guide.
- The AMERICAN GEOGRAPHICAL SOCIETY is founded in New York City.

1852

NORTH AMERICA
- RANDOLPH BARNES MARCY heads a U.S. military topographic expedition, which reaches the source of the Red River near present-day Amarillo, Texas.
- French engineer Henri Gifford makes the first successful AIRSHIP flight.
- French physicist Jean-Bernard-Léon Foucault develops the modern version of the GYROSCOPE.
- The U.S. Naval Observatory begins publishing the *American Ephemeris and Nautical Almanac,* an early EPHEMERIS.

1852–54

ARCTIC
- EDWARD BELCHER heads a British naval expedition in search of JOHN FRANKLIN; he explores the Canadian Arctic west of Lancaster Sound. FRANCIS LEOPOLD McCLINTOCK, part of the expedition, reaches Eglington Island and Prince Patrick Island on the edge of the Beaufort Sea.

1853

NORTH AMERICA
- American JOHN CHARLES FRÉMONT explores the Wasatch Mountains and Sierra Nevada for a proposed railroad through Utah.

NORTH AMERICA
- JOHN WILLIAMS GUNNISON heads a U.S. military topographic expedition from Kansas across the plains and the Wasatch Mountains to northwestern Utah.

1853–54

ARCTIC
- JOHN RAE heads a British expedition in search of JOHN FRANKLIN. On the Boothia Peninsula, he recovers relics of the Franklin expedition. He reaches Rae Strait, establishing that King William Island is not connected to the mainland.

AFRICA
- Portuguese trader ANTONIO FRANCISCO DA SILVA PORTO explores the upper ZAMBEZI RIVER; he makes a west-to-east crossing of central Africa.

1853–55

ARCTIC/GREENLAND
- American ELISHA KENT KANE heads a second expedition backed by shipping magnate Henry Grinnell in search of JOHN FRANKLIN. Some expedition members explore GREENLAND's Humboldt Glacier; others explore Ellesmere Island.

1853–56

NORTH AMERICA
- AMIEL WEEKS WHIPPLE heads a U.S. military topographic expedition from Albuquerque, New Mexico, to San Bernardino, California. Mojave Indian IRATEBA serves as guide.

1854

AFRICA	▪ WILLIAM BALFOUR BAIKIE heads a British maritime expedition to West Africa in search of HEINRICH BARTH, exploring the NIGER RIVER and Benue River.
NORTH AMERICA	▪ EDWARD GRIFFIN BECKWITH heads a U.S. military topographic expedition from Fort Bridger, Wyoming, to Sacramento Valley, California, locating passes in the Sierra Nevada.
NORTH AMERICA	▪ JOHN GRUBB PARKE heads a U.S. military railroad surveying expedition to the Gila River in Arizona and the Rio Grande in Texas.

1854–55

NORTH AMERICA	▪ JOHN B. POPE heads a U.S. military railroad surveying expedition in Texas, from the Rio Grande to the Red River.

1854–57

ASIA	▪ German brothers ROBERT VON SCHLAGINTWEIT, ADOLF VON SCHLAGINTWEIT, and HERMANN VON SCHLAGINTWEIT explore India, Tibet, and China's Sinkiang Province.

1854–99

NORTH AMERICA/ PACIFIC OCEAN/ ASIA	▪ British woman ISABELLA BIRD BISHOP travels in North America, the Pacific islands, and Asia, writing about her experiences.

1855

NORTH AMERICA	▪ HENRY LARCOM ABBOTT heads a U.S. military railroad surveying expedition in California, Oregon, and Washington, exploring the Cascade Mountains. ▪ German AUGUST HEINRICH PETERMANN publishes the first edition of a geographic journal, *Petermann's Geographische Mitteilungen*. ▪ American naval officer MATTHEW FONTAINE MAURY publishes *The Physical Geography of the Sea*, the first textbook on oceanography.

1855–58

AUSTRALIA	▪ British surveyor AUGUSTUS CHARLES GREGORY undertakes two expeditions of Australia's interior. He completes a west-to-east crossing and a northeast-to-south crossing.

1855–59

AFRICA	▪ French-American PAUL BELLONI DU CHAILLU explores the Gabon and Okowe Rivers of west-central Africa.

1857–58

AFRICA
- RICHARD FRANCIS BURTON and JOHN HANNING SPEKE command a British expedition seeking the source of the NILE RIVER. They explore the interior of East Africa and reach Lake Tanganyika. Speke reaches Lake Victoria. SIDI BOMBAY of the Yao tribe serves as guide.

ASIA
- Russian scientist PYOTR PETROVICH SEMYONOV makes the first European crossing of the Tien Shan mountains between Russia and China. He explores the Dzungaria region and the Altai Mountains of China.

NORTH AMERICA
- JOSEPH CHRISTMAS IVES heads a U.S. military topographic expedition along the COLORADO RIVER. Mojave Indian IRATEBA serves as guide, and JOHN STRONG NEWBERRY serves as geologist.

NORTH AMERICA
- EDWARD FITZGERALD BEALE heads a U.S. wagon road-building project from Camp Verde in western Texas to Fort Tejon, California, using camels as draft animals.

1857–59

AFRICA
- WILLIAM BALFOUR BAIKIE heads a British expedition up West Africa's NIGER RIVER by steamboat, establishing a trading settlement at Lokoja at the confluence of the Niger and Benue Rivers.

ARCTIC
- British naval officer FRANCIS LEOPOLD McCLINTOCK heads an expedition in search of JOHN FRANKLIN in the Canadian Arctic, commissioned by JANE FRANKLIN. He explores southward from the Lancaster Sound. He circumnavigates King William Island. He recovers relics of the Franklin expedition.

NORTH AMERICA
- JOHN PALLISER heads a British scientific expedition to western Canada. He surveys the 49th Parallel from Lake Superior to the Pacific. He explores passes in the Canadian ROCKY MOUNTAINS. Meanwhile, in 1857–58, Englishman HENRY YOULE HIND explores the river systems of Manitoba and Saskatchewan.

1857–61

AFRICA
- Frenchman HENRI DUVEYRIER explores the SAHARA DESERT.

AUSTRALIA
- British surveyor FRANCIS THOMAS GREGORY charts the river systems of western Australia.

1858

- The Alpine Club, a society to promote MOUNTAIN-CLIMBING, is founded in London.

1858–61

ASIA
- French naturalist HENRI MOUHOT explores Southeast Asia; he reaches the ruins at Angkor in Cambodia.

1859

NORTH AMERICA
- JOHN N. MACOMB commands a U.S. military topographic expedition from Santa Fe, New Mexico, to southern Utah and southern Colorado. He locates Anasazi ruins at Mesa Verde and explores the upper COLORADO RIVER. JOHN STRONG NEWBERRY serves as geologist.

1859–60

NORTH AMERICA
- WILLIAM FRANKLIN RAYNOLDS heads a U.S. topographic expedition from Fort Pierre, South Dakota, to Wyoming and Montana.

1860–61

AUSTRALIA
- Irishman ROBERT O'HARA BURKE and Englishman WILLIAM JOHN WILLS attempt to cross Australia south to north, from Melbourne nearly to the Gulf of Carpentaria. Both die of starvation.

ARCTIC/GREENLAND
- American physician ISAAC ISRAEL HAYES explores the GREENLAND ice cap and Ellesmere Island. He fails to reach the NORTH POLE.

NORTH AMERICA
- American fur traders HENRY A. BOLLER and CHARLES LARPENTEUR work the Yellowstone River region.

1860–62

ARCTIC
- American journalist CHARLES FRANCIS HALL explores Frobisher Bay in the Canadian Arctic.

1860–63

AFRICA
- JOHN HANNING SPEKE and JAMES AUGUSTUS GRANT command a British expedition to Lake Victoria. He reaches Ripon Falls and follows the NILE RIVER from Uganda into Sudan.

1861–62

AUSTRALIA
- Scottish surveyor JOHN MCDOUALL STUART completes the first south-to-north crossing of Australia, from Adelaide to Van Diemen Gulf.

AUSTRALIA
- Scotsman WILLIAM LANDSBOROUGH completes a north-to-south crossing of Australia, from the Gulf of Carpentaria to Melbourne.

1861–64

ASIA
- Hungarian linguist ARMIN VAMBÉRY travels in Armenia, Persia (Iran), and Turkestan. He visits the cities of Bukhara and Samarkand.

1861–65

AFRICA
- Englishman SAMUEL WHITE BAKER and his Hungarian-born wife, FLORENCE BAKER, seek the source of the NILE RIVER in southern Sudan and Uganda, reaching Lake Albert and Murchison Falls.

1862

AFRICA
- Dutch woman ALEXANDRINE PETRONELLA FRANCINA TINNÉ sails up the NILE RIVER as far as Gondokoro in southern Sudan. She travels into the Mongalla Mountains and the upper White Nile River region of northeastern Zaire.

1862–63

ASIA
- British missionary WILLIAM GIFFORD PALGRAVE makes the first known west-to-east crossing of the Arabian Peninsula, from Ma'an in southern Jordan to Quatif on the Persian Gulf.

NORTH AMERICA
- Englishmen WALTER BUTLER CHEADLE and WILLIAM-WENTWORTH FITZWILLIAM MILTON cross the Canadian ROCKY MOUNTAINS through Yellowhead Pass and reach the Pacific by way of the North Thompson and Fraser Rivers.

1863

NORTH AMERICA
- American pioneer JOHN MERIN BOZEMAN establishes the Bozeman Trail, a wagon route from Colorado to Montana, along the east side of the Bighorn Mountains and through the Bozeman Pass of the Belt Mountains.

1863–73

AUSTRALIA
- German woman naturalist KONCORDIE AMALIE NELLE DIETRICH collects specimens in Queensland.

1864–66

ASIA
- Indian NAIN SINGH crosses the eastern HIMALAYAS to Tibet. He explores the upper Brahmaputra River for Great Britain's Great Trigonometrical Survey.

1864–69

ARCTIC	▪ American journalist CHARLES FRANCIS HALL explores King William Island and Boothia Peninsula. He finds evidence of the JOHN FRANKLIN expedition.

1865

AFRICA	▪ German FRIEDRICH GERHARD ROHLFS, a soldier in the French Foreign Legion, crosses West Africa from Tripoli through the SAHARA DESERT by way of Lake Chad and the Benue River and NIGER RIVER to the Gulf of Guinea.
NORTH AMERICA	▪ Cherokee Indian trader JESSE CHISHOLM blazes the Chisholm Trail from Texas to Wichita.
EUROPE	▪ Englishman EDWARD WHYMPER climbs the Matterhorn in the Alps.

1866–68

ASIA	▪ ERNEST-MARC-LOUIS DE GONZAGUE DOUDART DE LAGRÉE and MARIE-JOSEPH-FRANÇOIS GARNIER head the French naval Mekong Expedition along the Mekong River, from the coast of Vietnam to southeastern China.

1866–69

AFRICA	▪ Scottish missionary DAVID LIVINGSTONE carries out three expeditions in central Africa. He searches for the source of the NILE RIVER. He reaches Lake Mweru and the Lualaba River.
SOUTH AMERICA	▪ Englishman HENRY ALEXANDER WICKHAM explores the ORINOCO RIVER and its tributaries, the Atabapo River and Río Negro. He establishes a rubber plantation on the AMAZON RIVER near Santarem, Brazil.

1868

ARCTIC	▪ NILS ADOLF ERIK NORDENSKJÖLD heads the First Swedish North Polar Expedition, failing to reach the NORTH POLE.
ASIA	▪ Englishman THOMAS THORNVILLE COOPER travels westward from Shanghai across China.

1868–70

ARCTIC/GREENLAND	▪ KARL CHRISTIAN KOLDEWEY heads two German maritime expeditions to Spitsbergen (Svalbard) and GREENLAND's east coast.

1868–71

AFRICA	▪ German naturalist GEORG AUGUST SCHWEINFURTH explores the watershed between the White

ASIA

Nile River and the upper CONGO RIVER (Zaire River). He reaches the Uele River.
- Russians ALEKSEY PAVLOVICH FEDCHENKO and OLGA FEDCHENKO command a scientific expedition into the Pamir region of south-central Asia. They reach the Trans-Alai Mountains.

1868–72

ASIA
- German geologist FERDINAND PAUL WILHELM VON RICHTHOFEN explores China.

1868–74

AFRICA
- German physician GUSTAV NACHTIGAL travels southward across the SAHARA DESERT from Tripoli to Bornu in Nigeria. He explores Lake Chad and the Chari River. He makes a southeastward crossing of the Sahara to the White Nile River.

NORTH AMERICA
- American naturalist JOHN MUIR explores Yosemite Valley and the Sierra Nevada in California.

1869

NORTH AMERICA
- American geologist and ethnologist JOHN WESLEY POWELL explores the COLORADO RIVER and the Grand Canyon.

1869–70

SOUTH AMERICA
- Englishman GEORGE CHAWORTH MUSTERS makes a south-to-north crossing of Patagonia, from the Strait of Magellan (see MAGELLAN, STRAIT OF) to Río Negro in central Argentina.

1869–76

NORTH AMERICA
- FERDINAND VANDEVEER HAYDEN heads a U.S. geological and geographic study of the Great Plains and the ROCKY MOUNTAINS.

1870

NORTH AMERICA
- NATHANIEL PITT LANGFORD heads a U.S. expedition to the Yellowstone Park region of Idaho, Montana, and Wyoming.

1870–85

ASIA
- Russian NIKOLAY MIKHAILOVICH PRZHEVALKSY makes four scientific expeditions to central Asia, reporting on geography and wildlife.

1871

AFRICA
- British-American journalist HENRY MORTON STANLEY journeys from Zanzibar to Ujiji on Lake

Tanganyika and locates Scottish missionary DAVID LIVINGSTONE. Stanley also explores the lake's northern end.

1871–73

ASIA
- French trader JEAN DUPUIS explores the Red River, seeking a navigable water route between China's Yunnan Province and the coast of Southeast Asia.

ARCTIC
- CHARLES FRANCIS HALL heads a U.S. expedition, which attempts to reach the NORTH POLE from northeastern Ellesmere Island. He reaches the Lincoln Sea.

EUROPE/ASIA
- Russian geographer PETER KROPOTKIN undertakes scientific expeditions to northern Finland, SIBERIA, and Manchuria.

1871–74

ARCTIC
- JULIUS VON PAYER and KARL WEYPRECHT head the Austro-Hungarian Arctic expedition, reaching Franz Josef Land.

1871–79

NORTH AMERICA
- GEORGE MONTAGUE WHEELER heads U.S. military surveys of the American West.

1872

ASIA
- Englishwoman ELIZABETH SARAH MAZUCHELLI travels 600 miles through the eastern HIMALAYAS.

1872–73

ARCTIC
- NILS ADOLF ERIK NORDENSKJÖLD heads the Second Swedish North Polar Expedition. He explores Spitsbergen (Svalbard).

ASIA
- Englishman NEY ELIAS travels from China across the GOBI DESERT, the Altai Mountains, SIBERIA, and the Ural Mountains to Europe.

1872–76

ATLANTIC OCEAN/
PACIFIC OCEAN
- GEORGE STRONG NARES and CHARLES WYVILLE THOMSON head a British oceanographic research expedition aboard the *Challenger*.

1873

NORTH AMERICA
- DAVID SLOAN STANLEY heads a U.S. military Yellowstone Expedition from the Dakotas into Montana and Wyoming.

AUSTRALIA
- Englishman PETER EGERTON WARBURTON completes the first east-to-west crossing of western Australia, from Alice Springs to Roebourne on the Indian Ocean.

| AUSTRALIA | ■ Australian WILLIAM CHRISTIE GOSSE heads an unsuccessful attempt at an east-to-west crossing of the continent. He reaches Ayers Rock. |
| ANTARCTIC | ■ EDUARD DALLMAN heads a German whaling expedition to the Antarctic Peninsula. |

1873–75

| AFRICA | ■ VERNEY LOVETT CAMERON heads a British expedition to relieve DAVID LIVINGSTONE. He explores Lake Tanganyika and the Lukuga River. He travels from the Lualaba River to Angola's Atlantic coast. |

1874

| AUSTRALIA | ■ The brothers JOHN FORREST and ALEXANDER FORREST head an Australian surveying expedition and complete the first west-to-east crossing of western Australia. |

1874–75

| AFRICA | ■ American CHARLES CHAILLÉ-LONG, in service to Egypt, explores the upper White Nile in Uganda. He reaches the Kioga River in East Africa. He heads a military expedition from southern Sudan west into the great divide between the NILE RIVER and CONGO RIVER (Zaire River); he explores the Giuba River in Somalia. |

1874–77

| AFRICA | ■ British-American journalist HENRY MORTON STANLEY circumnavigates Lake Victoria and Lake Tanganyika. He reaches Lake Edward. He descends the Lualaba River and the CONGO RIVER (Zaire River) to the Atlantic, completing an east-to-west crossing of central Africa. |

1875–76

| AUSTRALIA | ■ Englishman ERNEST GILES heads a commercial expedition through the GREAT VICTORIA DESERT; he completes the first successful inland crossing of Australia, then returns through the Gibson Desert. |
| ARCTIC | ■ GEORGE STRONG NARES heads the British Arctic Expedition, which explores northern Ellesmere Island and makes an unsuccessful attempt on the NORTH POLE. |

1876–77

| SOUTH AMERICA | ■ Argentine naturalist FRANCISCO MORENO explores the southern region of the ANDES MOUNTAINS; he reaches Lake San Martin. |

1876–78

ASIA
- Englishman CHARLES MONTAGU DOUGHTY travels southward from Syria across Arabia; he visits the Najd Desert.

1876–79

SOUTH AMERICA
- Frenchman JULES-NICOLAS CREVAUX explores the northern tributaries of the AMAZON RIVER and crosses the Tumuc-Humuc Mountains in French Guiana.

1876–83

AFRICA
- German WILHELM JOHANN JUNKER explores the upper tributaries of the CONGO RIVER (Zaire River) and the NILE RIVER in North and East Africa.

1878–79

ARCTIC
- Swedish geologist NILS ADOLF ERIK NORDENSKJÖLD heads the Vega Expedition, making the first successful navigation of the NORTHEAST PASSAGE from Norway along Asia's Arctic coast to the BERING STRAIT. In 1880, he returns to Europe by way of the Suez Canal, completing the first circumnavigation of Europe and Asia.

ASIA
- British couple WILFRED SCAWEN BLUNT and Lady ANNE ISABELLA BLUNT explore the Arabian Peninsula and Iraq.

1878–80

ARCTIC
- American FREDERICK SCHWATKA heads a private expedition in search of JOHN FRANKLIN. He explores from northwestern HUDSON BAY to King William Island, exploring the Hayes River.

1878–82

ASIA
- KISHEN SINGH of India travels from northeastern India into western China as far as the GOBI DESERT for Great Britain's Great Trigonometrical Survey.

1878–83

AFRICA
- German physician MEHMED EMIN PASHA, as an Anglo-Egyptian governor, explores the watershed between the NILE RIVER and CONGO RIVER (Zaire River) in Sudan and in East Africa.

1879

AUSTRALIA
- Australian ALEXANDER FORREST explores northwestern Australia, including Dampier Land, Fitzroy River, and Daly River.

| AFRICA | ▪ JOSEPH THOMSON heads a British expedition from East Africa's coast to northern Lake Nyasa (Lake Malawi). He explores Lake Rukwa, southern Lake Tanganyika, and the Lukuga River. |

1879–81

| ARCTIC | ▪ GEORGE WASHINGTON DE LONG heads a U.S. expedition into the Arctic Ocean by way of the BERING STRAIT. He fails to reach the NORTH POLE when the ship is trapped in the ice north of Wrangel Island, then drifts westward. Expedition members set out for the Siberian mainland over the frozen sea, visiting some of the New Siberian Islands. Some of them perish in the Lena River delta. |
| NORTH AMERICA | ▪ American geologist CLARENCE KING organizes the U.S. Geological Survey. |

1879–82

| AFRICA | ▪ Italian PIERRE-PAUL-FRANÇOIS-CAMILLE SAVORGNAN DE BRAZZA explores and develops the CONGO RIVER (Zaire River) region for France in West Africa. |

1879–84

| AFRICA | ▪ British-American journalist HENRY MORTON STANLEY ascends the CONGO RIVER (Zaire River) on behalf of Belgium. He explores the interior of Zaire and reaches Lake Tumba and Lake Leopold II. |
| ASIA | ▪ KINTUP of India explores Tibet for Great Britain's Great Trigonometrical Survey. He determines that Tibet's Tsangpo River is the same as India's Brahmaputra River. |

1880

| SOUTH AMERICA | ▪ Englishman EDWARD WHYMPER climbs Chimborazo in the ANDES MOUNTAINS. |

1880–81

| AFRICA | ▪ PAUL-XAVIER FLATTERS heads two French surveying expeditions from the Mediterranean coast of Algeria into the SAHARA DESERT, reaching the Ahaggar region. |

1881–84

| ARCTIC/GREENLAND | ▪ ADOLPHUS WASHINGTON GREELY heads a U.S. military expedition to Ellesmere Island. Expedition member OCTAVE PAVY explores northern Ellesmere Island. Other expedition members explore GREENLAND's northwest coast. |

1883–84

AFRICA

- JOSEPH THOMSON heads a British expedition from Mombasa on the Indian Ocean across central Kenya's Masailand and along the Great Rift Valley to Lake Victoria. He reaches Lake Baringo and the Abedare Range.

1883–85

AFRICA

- German HERMANN VON WISSMANN, in service to Belgium, explores the Kasai River system in Zaire, reaching the Sankuru tributary.

1884

AFRICA

- HARRY HAMILTON JOHNSTON heads the British Kilimanjaro Expedition, exploring the region around Mount Kilimanjaro (see KILIMANJARO, MOUNT), Africa's highest peak.
- The Washington Meridian Conference establishes Greenwich, England, as the location of the PRIME MERIDIAN.

1884–87

AFRICA

- British missionary GEORGE GRENFELL surveys the CONGO RIVER (Zaire River).

1885

NORTH AMERICA

- HENRY TUREMAN ALLEN heads a U.S. military expedition to the Yukon, Koyukuk, and Copper Rivers in eastern Alaska.

1885–87

AFRICA

- German geologist OSKAR LENZ ascends the CONGO RIVER (Zaire River). He crosses Africa by way of the Lualaba River, Lake Tanganyika, and Lake Nyasa (Lake Malawi).

1886

- The *Gymnote,* this first modern SUBMARINE, is built in France.

1886–87

ASIA

- British army officer FRANCIS EDWARD YOUNG-HUSBAND travels east to west across China from Manchuria, through the GOBI DESERT, to Kashgar and Yarkand. He reaches the Mustagh Pass in the Karakoram Mountains.

1886–89

AFRICA

- Hungarians LUDWIG VON HOEHNEL and SAMUEL TELEKI explore Lake Rudolf, the Omo River, and

Lake Stefanie in northern Kenya and southern Ethiopia.

1886–1900

ARCTIC/GREENLAND
- American ROBERT EDWIN PEARY carries out five expeditions to the Arctic regions of GREENLAND and Ellesmere Island.

1887–89

AFRICA
- British-American journalist HENRY MORTON STANLEY travels up the CONGO RIVER (Zaire River) and across central Africa to relieve MEHMED EMIN PASHA. He reaches the Semliki River and Ruwenzori Mountains. He completes a west-to-east crossing of central Africa.

AFRICA
- LOUIS-GUSTAVE BINGER heads a French expedition into West Africa from Senegal. He explores the NIGER RIVER, the Volta River, and the Comoe River.

1888

ARCTIC/GREENLAND
- Norwegian FRIDTJOF NANSEN explores GREENLAND's interior.

1888–1911

EUROPE/ SOUTH AMERICA
- American woman ANNIE SMITH PECK climbs in the Alps and the ANDES MOUNTAINS.

1888–1912

ASIA/AFRICA
- American woman FANNY BULLOCK WORKMAN travels throughout Europe, North Africa, and the Far East. She climbs in the HIMALAYAS and other mountain ranges in central Asia.

1889

AFRICA
- HANS MEYER climbs Mount Kilimanjaro (see KILIMANJARO, MOUNT) in East Africa.

1891

AFRICA
- American woman publisher MAY FRENCH SHELDON travels from Mombasa on Africa's east coast to Mount Kilimanjaro (see KILIMANJARO, MOUNT). She explores Lake Chala.
- German engineer Otto Lilienthal makes the first successful glider flight.

1891–95

ASIA
- AUGUSTE-JEAN-MARIE PAVIE conducts the Pavie Mission surveys of Southeast Asia.

1892–93

AFRICA	▪ OSKAR BAUMANN heads a German expedition to Lake Victoria and the Kagera River, its principal source.
ASIA	▪ British missionary ANNIE ROYLE TAYLOR visits China.

1892–94

ARCTIC	▪ EDUARD VON TOLL heads a Russian expedition to the Siberian Arctic by way of Cape Chelyuskin; he explores the deltas of the Yana, Indigirka, and Kolyma Rivers.

1893–95

AFRICA	▪ British woman author MARY HENRIETTA KINGSLEY travels in West and central Africa.

1893–96

ARCTIC	▪ Norwegian FRIDTJOF NANSEN attempts to approach the NORTH POLE by having an ice-bound ship drift northward from the New Siberian Islands. The crew leaves the ship, continuing on kayaks and sledges, reaching Franz Josef Land.

1893–97

ASIA	▪ Swede SVEN ANDERS HEDIN heads two scientific expeditions to the Tarim Basin, the Takla Makan desert, and Lop Nor Lake in western China. He explores the Tibetan Plateau and maps the HIMALAYAS.
ASIA	▪ British archaeologist JAMES THEODORE BENT explores the Arabian Peninsula.

1893–98

ASIA	▪ British surveyor and diplomat PERCY MOLESWORTH SYKES explores Persia (Iran).

1893–1900

ASIA	▪ Frenchman CHARLES BONIN travels in Southeast and central Asia and charts the YANGTZE RIVER (Chang) and the YELLOW RIVER (Huanghe).

1894–95

ANTARCTIC	▪ CARSTEN EGEBERG BORCHGREVINK heads a Norwegian whaling expedition and makes the first known landing on the Antarctic continent.

1894–97

ARCTIC
- FREDERICK GEORGE JACKSON heads the British Jackson-Harmsworth Arctic Expedition to Franz Josef Land.

1897

ARCTIC
- Swedish SALOMON AUGUST ANDRÉE attempts to reach the NORTH POLE by BALLOON. He is forced down and eventually perishes on White Island.

NORTH AMERICA
- Italian LUIGI AMEDEO DI SAVOIA D'ABRUZZI makes the first successful ascent of Alaska's Mount Saint Elias.

SOUTH AMERICA
- Italian MATTHIAS ZURBRIGGEN makes the first successful ascent of Anaconda in the ANDES MOUNTAINS.

1897–99

ANTARCTIC
- ADRIEN-VICTOR-JOSEPH DE GERLACHE DE GOMERY heads a Belgian expedition to Antarctica; icebound, he winters off the Antarctic Peninsula.

1897–1904

AFRICA
- Swiss-born Russian-German woman writer ISABELLE EBERHARDT travels throughout North Africa.

1898–99

AFRICA
- JEAN-BAPTISTE MARCHAND heads a French military expedition from the mouth of the CONGO RIVER (Zaire River) to the upper White Nile region of southern Sudan.

1898–1902

ARCTIC
- OTTO NEUMANN SVERDRUP heads a Norwegian expedition to the Canadian Arctic. He explores the west coast of Ellesmere Island and the Sverdrup Islands.

1899–1900

ARCTIC
- LUIGI AMEDEO DI SAVOIA D'ABRUZZI heads an Italian expedition in an attempt to reach the NORTH POLE from Franz Josef Land, setting the northernmost record at the time.

ANTARCTIC
- CARSTEN EGEBERG BORCHGREVINK heads a Norwegian expedition and winters in Antarctica, exploring parts of the interior.

1900–02

ASIA
- Russian scholar GOMBOZHAB TSYBIKOV heads a political mission to Tibet for Russia.

1900–10

ASIA
- British archaeologist GERTRUDE MARGARET LOW-THIAN BELL travels throughout the Middle East.

1901–03

ANTARCTIC
- ERICH DAGOBERT VON DRYGALSKI heads a German Antarctic Expedition to the Antarctic coast in the Indian Ocean. He reaches and names Kaiser Wilhelm II Land and Mount Gauss.

ANTARCTIC
- NILS OTTO GUSTAF NORDENSKJÖLD heads a Swedish expedition to Antarctica. He explores the South Shetland Islands, Graham Land, and Mount Haddington on the Weddell Sea.

1901–04

ANTARCTIC
- ROBERT FALCON SCOTT heads the British National Antarctic Expedition. He explores Victoria Land and the Ross Ice Shelf and reaches Edward VII Land, setting the southernmost record at the time. ERNEST HENRY SHACKLETON and EDWARD ADRIAN WILSON are part of his team.

1902

ARCTIC
- American ROBERT EDWIN PEARY attempts unsuccessfully to reach the NORTH POLE from Cape Hecla on the northern Ellesmere Island, but he sets the northernmost record at the time.

1902–04

ANTARCTIC
- WILLIAM SPIERS BRUCE heads the Scottish National Antarctic Expedition. He explores the Weddell Sea and charts Coats Land.

ARCTIC/GREENLAND
- LUDWIG MYLIUS-ERICHSEN heads the Danish Greenland Expedition to Melville Bay. He reaches as far north as Cape York.

1903

- American brothers Orville Wright and Wilbur Wright make the first successful airplane flights.

1903–05

ANTARCTIC
- JEAN-BAPTISTE-ÉTIENNE-AUGUSTE CHARCOT heads a French expedition, which maps the Antarctic Peninsula, the Loubet Coast, and Adelaide Land.

1903–06

ARCTIC
- ROALD ENGELBREGT GRAVNING AMUNDSEN heads a Norwegian expedition, which locates the NORTH MAGNETIC POLE and makes the

first successful navigation of the NORTHWEST PASSAGE.

SOUTH AMERICA
- American woman HARRIET CHALMERS ADAMS tours South America, crossing the ANDES MOUNTAINS four times.

1904–11

ARCTIC
- JOSEPH ELZÉAR BERNIER heads a series of Canadian expeditions, claiming and charting islands in the Arctic Ocean north of the Canadian mainland.

1905–06

ARCTIC
- American ROBERT EDWIN PEARY attempts unsuccessfully to reach the NORTH POLE by way of the Robeson Channel, but he sets the northernmost record at the time.

1905–08

ASIA
- Swede SVEN ANDERS HEDIN reaches the sources of the INDUS RIVER, Brahmaputra River, and Sutlej River in the Transhimalaya Mountains of Tibet.

1905–11

AFRICA
- Americans CARL ETHAN AKELEY and DELIA JULIA DENNING AKELEY head two expeditions to East and central Africa for the Field Museum in Chicago and the Museum of Natural History in New York.

1906

AFRICA
- Italian LUIGI AMEDEO DI SAVOIA D'ABRUZZI makes the first ascent of peaks in East Africa's Ruwenzori Mountains.

1906–07

ARCTIC/GREENLAND
- LUDWIG MYLIUS-ERICHSEN heads a Danish expedition to northeastern GREENLAND, reaching the Northeast Foreland.

1906–08

ASIA
- Hungarian archaeologist MARC AUREL STEIN follows the ancient SILK ROAD into western China. He locates the Caves of the Thousand Buddhas at Tunhuang.

1906–12

ARCTIC/GREENLAND
- Danish-Inuit ethnologist KNUD JOHAN VICTOR RASMUSSEN explores northern GREENLAND. He determines that Peary Land is part of Greenland.

1906–14

SOUTH AMERICA
- British surveyor PERCY HARRISON FAWCETT explores the Amazon Basin and the central ANDES MOUNTAINS.

1907–09

ANTARCTIC
- ERNEST HENRY SHACKLETON heads a British Antarctic expedition, which reaches the Beardmore Glacier and the Polar Plateau within 97 miles of the SOUTH POLE. In 1909, expedition members including DOUGLAS MAWSON ascend Mount Erebus and reach the SOUTH MAGNETIC POLE.

1907–25

SOUTH AMERICA
- American ALEXANDER HAMILTON RICE surveys the rivers draining into the northwestern Amazon Basin. In 1924–25, he makes the first use of an aircraft to explore South America.

1908

ARCTIC
- American FREDERICK ALBERT COOK possibly reaches the NORTH POLE from northern GREENLAND and the Ellesmere Island, but his claim is disputed.

ARCTIC
- Russian mariner and fur trader NIKIFOR ALEKSEYEVICH BEGICHEV determines that Bolshoy Begichev is an island and not part of a peninsula on the Arctic coast of central SIBERIA.

1908–10

ANTARCTIC
- JEAN-BAPTISTE-ÉTIENNE-AUGUSTE CHARCOT heads a French expedition and surveys Palmer Archipelago. He reaches the Fallières Coast.

1909

ARCTIC
- Americans ROBERT EDWIN PEARY and MATTHEW ALEXANDER HENSON successfully reach the NORTH POLE by sledge from Cape Columbia on the north coast of Ellesmere Island.

ASIA
- Italian LUIGI AMEDEO DI SAVOIA D'ABRUZZI attempts the ascent of K2 in the HIMALAYAS, setting the altitude record at the time.

1910–12

ANTARCTIC
- ROALD ENGELBREGT GRAVNING AMUNDSEN heads a Norwegian expedition, which completes the first successful expedition to the SOUTH POLE, from the Bay of Whales by way of the Axel Heiberg Glacier (Antarctic).

ANTARCTIC
- ROBERT FALCON SCOTT heads a British expedition, which reaches the SOUTH POLE from McMurdo Sound by way of the Beardmore Glacier. All the expedition members, including the physician and zoologist EDWARD ADRIAN WILSON, perish on the return trip.

ANTARCTIC
- WILHELM FILCHNER heads the Second German Antarctic Expedition. He reaches the Filchner Ice Shelf on the Weddell Sea and Luitpold Land.

1911

SOUTH AMERICA
- American historian HIRAM BINGHAM reaches the Inca ruins at Machu Picchu.

1911–14

ANTARCTIC
- DOUGLAS MAWSON heads an Australian expedition to Antarctica, exploring George V Land.

1912

ANTARCTIC
- NOBU SHIRASE heads a Japanese expedition to Antarctica. He explores the Ross Ice Shelf and King Edward VII Land.

1912–15

AFRICA
- American military attaché CHARLES DENTON YOUNG charts the interior of Liberia.

1913

NORTH AMERICA
- Anglo-American HUDSON STUCK makes the first ascent of Mount McKinley (see MCKINLEY, MOUNT) in Alaska.

1913–18

ARCTIC
- VILHJALMUR STEFANSSON heads a Canadian Arctic expedition to the Beaufort Sea; he reaches uncharted islands in the Canadian Arctic Archipelago north of Prince Patrick Island.

1914–16

ANTARCTIC
- ERNEST HENRY SHACKLETON heads a British Imperial Trans-Antarctic expedition and attempts to cross the Antarctic continent from the Weddell Sea to the Ross Sea. After his ship sinks in the Weddell Sea, the crew takes refuge on Elephant Island. Shackleton and five others make the open boat voyage to South Georgia Island and cross the island overland to the inhabited side. Shackleton mounts a successful rescue of the crew still on Elephant Island.

1916–18

ASIA

- Englishman THOMAS EDWARD LAWRENCE (Lawrence of Arabia) explores the Hejaz region of the Arabian Peninsula while leading an Arab revolt against Turkey.

1917

ASIA

- Englishman HARRY ST. JOHN BRIDGER PHILBY makes an east-to-west crossing of the Arabian Peninsula from Qatar to Jidda.

1921–24

ARCTIC

- Danish-Inuit KNUD JOHAN VICTOR RASMUSSEN travels from western GREENLAND across the Canadian Arctic to the BERING STRAIT.

1923–24

ASIA

- Frenchwoman ALEXANDRA DAVID-NÉEL travels from China through the Dokar Pass of the Kha Karpo Mountains to LHASA in Tibet.

1924

ASIA

- Englishman GEORGE HERBERT LEIGH MALLORY and Andrew "Sandy" Irvine die while climbing Mount Everest (see EVEREST, MOUNT) in the HIMALAYAS.

1924–25

ARCTIC/GREENLAND

- American RICHARD EVELYN BYRD makes the first flights over the GREENLAND ice cap by airplane.

1924–28

ASIA

- Russian painter NIKOLAY KONSTANTINOVICH ROERICH explores in the HIMALAYAS and central Asia.

1926

ARCTIC

- American RICHARD EVELYN BYRD makes the first flight over the NORTH POLE by airplane.

ARCTIC

- ROALD ENGELBREGT GRAVNING AMUNDSEN, LINCOLN ELLSWORTH, and UMBERTO NOBILE fly over the NORTH POLE by AIRSHIP, completing the first flight from Europe to North America.

AFRICA

- Americans CARL ETHAN AKELEY and MARY LEONORE JOBE AKELEY collect specimens in the Belgian Congo for the American Museum of Natural History.

1927

- American aviator Charles Lindberg makes the first successful nonstop solo flight across the Atlantic Ocean.

1928

ARCTIC
- UMBERTO NOBILE heads an Italian expedition over the NORTH POLE by AIRSHIP.

ARCTIC
- Australian GEORGE HUBERT WILKINS makes an airplane flight over the Arctic from North America to Europe.
- American aviator Amelia Earhart becomes the first woman to fly solo across the Atlantic Ocean.

1928–33

ARCTIC/GREENLAND
- American woman LOUISE ARNER BOYD heads three scientific expeditions to the Arctic region of eastern GREENLAND.

1929–30

ANTARCTIC
- RICHARD EVELYN BYRD heads the First Byrd Antarctic Expedition; he makes the first flight over the SOUTH POLE.

ARCTIC/GREENLAND
- German ALFRED LOTHAR WEGENER heads the Greenland Expedition, which establishes the first permanent weather stations on the GREENLAND ice cap.

1929–31

ANTARCTIC
- DOUGLAS MAWSON heads Australian, NEW ZEALAND, and British aerial surveys of Antarctica. He explores the MacRobertson Coast and Enderby Land.

1930–31

ASIA
- Englishman BERTRAM SYDNEY THOMAS crosses the southeastern Arabian Peninsula's Rub' al-Khali desert (EMPTY QUARTER).

1930–32

ARCTIC/GREENLAND
- HENRY GEORGE WATKINS heads the British Arctic Air Route Expedition to GREENLAND. He explores the Greenland ice cap and surveys the southeast and southwest coasts. Expedition member AUGUSTINE COURTAULD spends the 1930–31 winter alone on the ice cap.

1931

- Belgian/Swiss physicist AUGUSTE PICCARD penetrates the stratosphere in a high-altitude BALLOON.

ARCTIC

- Australian GEORGE HUBERT WILKINS attempts to reach the NORTH POLE from Spitsbergen (Svalbard) by SUBMARINE.

1932

ARCTIC

- OTTO Y. SCHMIDT commands a USSR icebreaker completing the first crossing of the NORTHEAST PASSAGE in a single season.

1933–35

ANTARCTIC

- RICHARD EVELYN BYRD heads the Second Byrd Antarctic Expedition. He winters alone about 1,000 miles inland. He charts Marie Byrd Land and the Edsel Ford Mountains.

1934

- American CHARLES WILLIAM BEEBE sets the record for an ocean dive in the BATHYSPHERE with Otis Barton.

1935

ANTARCTIC

- American LINCOLN ELLSWORTH completes the first flight across the Antarctic continent.

ASIA

- Englishwoman FREYA MADELINE STARK visits the Hadramawt region of the southern Arabian Peninsula.

1937

ARCTIC

- OTTO Y. SCHMIDT establishes a manned scientific post on the frozen Arctic Ocean near the NORTH POLE for the USSR.
- The *Hindenburg,* a German-built AIRSHIP, crashes in New Jersey, killing 36 people.
- American aviator Amelia Earhart disappears as she attempts to become the first woman to fly an airplane around the world.

1937–38

ARCTIC

- American woman LOUISE ARNER BOYD heads two scientific expeditions to the Arctic Ocean northeast of Norway, between Bear Island and Jan Mayen Island.

1939–41

ANTARCTIC

- RICHARD EVELYN BYRD heads the U.S. Antarctic Service Expedition, establishing new bases.

1941

ARCTIC

- American woman LOUISE ARNER BOYD heads a U.S. scientific expedition studying the Arctic magnetic phenomenon.

1942

SPACE
- During World War II, German engineer Wernher von Braun conducts the first successful launch of the A-4 (later called the V-2) ROCKET, a long-range guided missile propelled by liquid fuel. In 1945, he moves to the United States and participates in American SPACE EXPLORATION.

1943

- Frenchman JACQUES-YVES COUSTEAU helps develop the Aqua Lung.

1946–48

ASIA
- Englishman WILFRED PATRICK THESIGER undertakes two journeys into the southeastern Arabian Peninsula's Rub' al-Khali (the EMPTY QUARTER).

1947

PACIFIC OCEAN
- Norwegian THOR HEYERDAHL travels from South America to Polynesia in the balsa RAFT *Kon-Tiki* to prove the theory of eastward transoceanic migrations of native peoples.

1947–48

ANTARCTIC
- RICHARD EVELYN BYRD heads U.S. Operation High Jump, an aerial reconnaissance of Antarctica.

1953

ASIA
- EDMUND PERCIVAL HILLARY and TENZING NORGAY head the British Mount Everest Expedition, reaching the top of Mount Everest (see EVEREST, MOUNT) in the HIMALAYAS.

1955

ARCTIC
- American LOUISE ARNER BOYD makes the first flight over the NORTH POLE by a woman.

1956–88

SOUTH AMERICA
- British botanical painter MARGARET URSULA MEE travels in the Brazilian rain forest.

1957

SPACE
- The USSR launches the first artificial SATELLITE, *Sputnik 1.*

SPACE
- The USSR launches the first animal into space, the dog Laika, aboard the SATELLITE *Sputnik 2.*

1957–58

ANTARCTIC
- Englishman VIVIAN ERNEST FUCHS and New Zealander EDMUND PERCIVAL HILLARY head the Commonwealth Trans-Antarctic Expedition, which completes the first crossing of the Antarctic continent.
- Thirty-seven nations participate in the INTERNATIONAL GEOPHYSICAL YEAR, a period of cooperative study of Earth's geophysics.

1958

SPACE
- The United States launches its first artificial SATELLITE, *Explorer 1,* and its first SPACE PROBE, *Pioneer.*

SPACE
- The U.S. government establishes the NATIONAL AERONAUTICS AND SPACE ADMINISTRATION (NASA). In 1959, it selects its first ASTRONAUTS.

ARCTIC
- The *Nautilus,* the first nuclear SUBMARINE, makes an undersea transit of the NORTH POLE.

1959

SPACE
- The USSR launches *Luna 1,* a SPACE PROBE; it becomes the first human-made object to escape Earth's orbit. *Luna 2* becomes the first artificial object to hit the Moon. *Luna 3* sends back the first photographs of the dark side of the Moon.

1960

PACIFIC OCEAN
- JACQUES ERNEST-JEAN PICCARD heads a U.S. Navy BATHYSCAPH dive to the bottom of the Challenger Deep in the Pacific's MARIANAS TRENCH, the deepest point on Earth.

1961

SPACE
- YURI ALEKSEYEVICH GAGARIN, in a USSR Vostok mission, becomes the first human in space and to orbit Earth.

SPACE
- ALAN BARTLETT SHEPARD, JR., in a U.S. Mercury mission, becomes the first American in space.

SPACE
- The Apollo program is organized by the United States to launch a person to the Moon.

1962

SPACE
- JOHN HERSCHELL GLENN, JR., in a U.S. Mercury mission, becomes the first American to orbit Earth.

1963

SPACE	▪ VALENTINA VLADIMIROVNA TERESHKOVA becomes the first woman in space in a USSR Vostok mission.
SPACE	▪ ALEXEI ARKHIPOVICH LEONOV, in a USSR Voskhod mission, becomes the first human to walk in space.
SPACE	▪ EDWARD HIGGINS WHITE II, in a U.S. Gemini mission, becomes the first American to walk in space.

1964

WORLD	▪ American aviator Geraldine Mock becomes the first woman to fly solo around the world.

1965

	▪ The Union Internationale de Spéléologie, the international body for SPELEOLOGY and caving, is founded with a central office in the Czech Republic.

1967

WORLD	▪ British yachtsman Sir Francis Charles Chichester completes the first solo maritime journey around the world.

1969

SPACE	▪ NEIL ALDEN ARMSTRONG, in an Apollo mission, becomes the first human to walk on the Moon. Edwin "Buzz" Aldrin also explores the lunar surface. Michael Collins, the third member of the expedition, orbits the Moon.

1970

ATLANTIC OCEAN	▪ Norwegian THOR HEYERDAHL travels from North Africa to South America in the papyrus boat *Ra* to prove that ancients could have made the journey.

1971

SPACE	▪ The USSR launches the first SPACE STATION, *Salyut 1.*

1973

SPACE	▪ The United States launches its first SPACE STATION, *Skylab.*
SPACE	▪ GPS, formally known as the Navstar Global Positioning System, a SATELLITE system, is initiated to aid in navigation.
SPACE	▪ The U.S. *Pioneer 10* SPACE PROBE passes through the asteroid belt and becomes the first artificial object to escape the solar system.

1975

ASIA
- The European Space Agency is founded, with headquarters in Paris.
- Junko Tabei of Japan becomes the first woman to summit MOUNT EVEREST.

1975–76

SPACE
- U.S. *Viking 2* SPACE PROBE lands on Mars and successfully transmits data.

1977

ARCTIC
- The USSR icebreaker *Arktika* reaches the NORTH POLE.

1981

SPACE
- The United States launches the first SPACE SHUTTLE, the *Columbia.*

ARCTIC/ANTARCTIC
- British explorers Sir Ranulph Fiennes and Charles Burton reach the NORTH POLE, having traveled there from the SOUTH POLE, becoming the first men to circle Earth Pole to Pole.

1983

SPACE
- SALLY KRISTEN RIDE, in a U.S. SPACE SHUTTLE mission, becomes the first American woman in space.

1986

SPACE
- The *Challenger* SPACE SHUTTLE breaks up during liftoff, killing all seven crew members.

SPACE
- The USSR launches the first permanently manned space station, *Mir;* six other modules are added through 1996.

1990

SPACE
- The United States launches the Hubble Space Telescope, a research SATELLITE.

1997

SPACE
- The U.S. SPACE PROBE *Pathfinder* returns images from the surface of Mars and carries out 15 chemical analyses.

SPACE
- The *Global Surveyor,* a U.S. SPACE PROBE in orbit around Mars, photographs and maps the planet.

1998

SPACE
- The first module of the International Space Station is launched.

| SPACE | ■ The U.S. SPACE PROBE *Voyager 1* passes *Pioneer 10* to become the most distant human-made object in space. |

1999

| WORLD | ■ Bertrand Piccard, AUGUSTE PICCARD's grandson, and Brian Jones, a British pilot, complete the first nonstop circumnavigation of Earth by BALLOON. |

2000

| SPACE | ■ The first crew, two Russians and one American, arrive on the International Space Station. |

2003

| SPACE | ■ The *Columbia* SPACE SHUTTLE breaks up on reentry, killing all seven crew members. |
| SPACE | ■ With the planet Mars closer to Earth than it has been in 7,300 years, numerous nations send SPACE PROBE missions to study it. |

2004

| SPACE | ■ The United States, in two SPACE PROBE missions, retrieves data from two Mars exploration rovers: Mars Rover-A, or *Spirit*, and Mars Rover-B, or *Opportunity*. *Opportunity* finds evidence of water having formerly existed on Mars. |

Further Reading for the Set

Many explorers wrote firsthand accounts of their expeditions, some of which are mentioned in the entries. The following are mainly secondary sources.

GENERAL INFORMATION

Albion, Robert Greenhalgh. *Exploration and Discovery.* New York: Macmillan, 1965.

Armstrong, Richard. *The Discoverers.* New York: Praeger, 1968.

———. *Themselves Alone: The Story of Men in Empty Places.* London: E. Benn, 1972.

Baker, John Norman Leonard. *A History of Geographical Discovery and Exploration.* New York: Houghton Mifflin, 1931.

Barker, Felix. *The First Explorers.* London: Aldus, 1971.

Bellec, François. *Unknown Lands: The Logbooks of the Great Explorers.* New York: Overlook, 2002.

Bettex, Albert Warner. *The Discovery of the World.* New York: Simon & Schuster, 1960.

Birkett, Dea. *Spinsters Abroad: Victorian Lady Explorers.* New York: Blackwell, 1989.

Bitterli, Urs. *Cultures in Conflict: Encounters between European and Non-European Cultures, 1492–1800.* Stanford, Calif.: Stanford University Press, 1989.

Bolton, Sarah (Knowles). *Famous Voyagers and Explorers.* New York: T. Y. Crowell, 1893.

Bonington, Chris. *Quest for Adventure: Ultimate Feats of Modern Exploration.* Washington, D.C.: National Geographic Society, 2000.

Boorstin, Daniel Joseph. *The Discoverers.* New York: Random House, 1983.

Brendon, John Adam. *Great Navigators & Discoverers.* London: G. G. Harrap, 1929.

Brosse, Jacques. *Great Voyages of Discovery: Circumnavigators & Scientists.* New York: Facts On File, 1985.

Castlereagh, Duncan. *The Great Age of Exploration.* London: Aldus, 1971.

Clark, Ronald William. *Explorers of the World.* London: Aldus, 1964.

Collinson, Clifford Whitely. *Explorers All!* London: Hutchinson, 1964.

Cook, John Lennox. *Six Great Travellers: Smith, Anson, Stanhope, Stanley, Fawcett, Hedin.* London: H. Hamilton, 1960.

Crone, Gerald Roe. *Man the Explorer.* London: Priory, 1973.

———, ed. *The Explorers: An Anthology of Discovery.* London: Cassell, 1962.

Delpar, Helen, ed. *The Discoverers: An Encyclopedia of Explorers and Exploration.* New York: McGraw-Hill, 1980.

Debenham, Frank. *Discovery and Exploration.* New York: Crescent Books, 1960.

De Vorsey, Louis. *Keys to the Encounter: A Library of Congress Resource Guide for the Study of the Age of Discovery.* Washington, D.C.: Library of Congress, 1992.

Dmytrysh, Basil. *Russia's Conquest of Siberia; Russian Penetration of the North Pacific; Russian America Colonies.* 3 vols. Portland, Oreg.: Western Imprints, 1990.

Farrington, Karen. *Historical Atlas of Expeditions.* New York: Facts On File, 2000.

Fernandez-Armesto, Felipe, ed. *The Times Atlas of World Exploration: 3,000 Years of Exploring, Explorers, and Mapmaking.* New York: HarperCollins, 1991.

Galvao, Antonio. *The Discoveries of the World.* New York: Franklin, 1971.

Goetzmann, William H., and Glyndwr Williams. *The Atlas of North American Exploration: From the Norse Voyages to the Race to the Pole.* Norman: University of Oklahoma Press, 1998.

Gosse, Phillip. *The History of Piracy.* Santa Fe, N.M.: Rio Grande, 1988.

Grafton, Anthony. *New World, Ancient Texts: The Power of Tradition and the Shock of Discovery.* Cambridge, Mass.: Belknap, 1995.

Grant, Neil. *The Great Atlas of Discovery.* Toronto, Canada: McClelland & Stewart, 1992.

Greely, Adolphus Washington. *Explorers and Travellers.* New York: C. Scribner's Sons, 1894.

Greenblatt, Stephen. *Marvelous Possessions: The Wonder of the New World.* Chicago: University of Chicago Press, 1992.

Grosseck, Joyce C., and Elizabeth Atwood. *Great Explorers.* Grand Rapids, Mich.: Fideler, 1962.

Hale, John Rigby. *Age of Exploration.* New York: Time, Inc., 1966.

Hampden, John. *New Worlds Ahead.* New York: Farrar, Strauss & Giroux, 1968.

Hebert, John R., ed. *1492: An Ongoing Voyage.* Washington, D.C.: Library of Congress, 1992.

Hemming, John (foreword). *Oxford Atlas of Exploration.* New York: Oxford University Press, 1997.

Hermann, Paul. *The Great Age of Discovery.* New York: Harper, 1958.

Humble, Richard. *The Explorers.* Alexandria, Va.: Time-Life, 1978.

Johnson, William Henry. *The World's Discoverers.* New York: Little, Brown, 1900.

Konstam, Angus. *Historical Atlas of Exploration: 1492–1600.* New York: Facts On File, 2000.

Langnas, Isaac Abram. *Dictionary of Discoveries.* New York: Philosophical Library, 1959.

Lansing, Marion Florence. *Great Moments in Exploration.* Garden City, N.Y.: Doubleday, Doran, 1928.

Ley, Charles D., ed. *Portuguese Voyages, 1498–1663: Tales from the Great Age of Discovery.* London: Phoenix, 2000.

Lucas, Mary Seymour. *Vast Horizons: A Story of True Adventure and Discovery.* London: G. G. Harrap, 1948.

Lunenfeld, Marvin, ed. *1492: Discovery, Invasion, Encounter; Sources and Interpretations.* Lexington, Mass.: D.C. Heath, 1991.

Markham, Sir Clements Robert. *The Sea Fathers: A Series of Lives of Great Navigators of Former Times.* London: Cassell, 1884.

Mason, Herbert Molloy. *Famous Firsts in Exploration.* New York: Putnam, 1967.

Matar, Nabil. *Turks, Moors, and Englishmen in the Age of Discovery.* New York: Columbia University Press, 2000.

McSpadden, Joseph Walker. *To the Ends of the World and Back.* New York: Thomas Y. Crowell, 1931.

Mitchell, James Leslie. *Earth Conquerors: The Lives and Achievements of the Great Explorers.* New York: Simon & Schuster, 1934.

Newby, Eric. *The Rand McNally World Atlas of Exploration.* New York: Rand McNally, 1975.

Newton, Arthur P. *The Great Age of Discovery.* Freeport, N.Y.: Books for Libraries, 1969.

Odle, Francis. *Picture Story of World Exploration.* London: World Distributors, 1966.

Olds, Elizabeth Fagg. *Women of the Four Winds.* Boston: Houghton Mifflin, 1985.

Outhwaite, Leonard. *Unrolling the Map.* New York: Reynal and Hitchcock, 1935.

Pagden, Anthony. *European Encounters with the New World: From Renaissance to Romanticism.* New Haven, Conn.: Yale University Press, 1994.

Parker, John. *Discovery: Developing Views of the Earth from Ancient Times to the Voyages of Captain Cook.* New York: Scribner, 1972.

Parry, John Horace. *The Age of Reconnaissance: Discovery, Exploration and Settlement, 1450 to 1650.* New York: Praeger, 1969.

———. *Trade and Dominion: The European Overseas Empires in the 18th Century.* New York: Praeger, 1971.

Penrose, Boies. *Travel & Discovery in the Renaissance.* Cambridge, Mass.: Harvard University Press, 1963.

Perkins, John. *To the Ends of the Earth: Four Expeditions to the Arctic, the Congo, the Gobi, and Siberia.* New York: Pantheon, 1981.

Polk, Milbry, and Mary Tiegreen. *Women of Discovery: A Celebration of Intrepid Women Who Explored the World.* New York: Clarkson Potter, 2001.

Reef, Catherine. *Black Explorers.* New York: Facts On File, 1996.

Reid, Alan. *Discovery and Exploration.* London: Gentry, 1980.

Roberts, David, ed. *Points Unknown: A Century of Great Exploration.* New York: W. W. Norton, 2000.

Rugoff, Milton Allan. *The Great Travelers: A Collection of Firsthand Narratives of Wayfarers, Wanderers, and Explorers in all Parts of the World from 450 B.C. to the Present.* New York: Simon & Schuster, 1960.

St. John, James Augustus. *The Lives of Celebrated Travellers.* 3 vols. New York: Harper and Bros., 1835–37.

Sawyer, Peter, ed. *The Oxford Illustrated History of the Vikings.* Oxford, U.K.: Oxford University Press, 1997.

Scammell, G. V. *The World Encompassed.* Berkeley: University of California Press, 1981.

Silverberg, Robert. *The Longest Voyage: Circumnavigators in the Age of Discovery.* Indianapolis, Ind.: Bobbs-Merrill, 1972.

Sparks, Edwin Erle. *Famous Explorers.* Boston: Hall and Locke, 1902.

Stefansson, Vilhjalmur. *Great Adventures and Explorations from the Earliest Times to the Present.* New York: Dial, 1947.

Stuster, Jack. *Bold Endeavors: Lessons from Polar and Space Exploration.* Annapolis, Md.: Naval Institute Press, 1996.

Sykes, Sir Percy. *A History of Exploration from the Earliest Times to the Present Day.* London: George Routledge & Sons, 1934.

Thesiger, Wilfred, and John Keay, ed. *The Mammoth Book of Explorers.* Berkeley, Calif.: Avalon, 2002.

Thomas, Lowell Jackson. *The Untold Story of Exploration.* London: G. G. Harrap, 1936.

Tinling, Marion. *Women into the Unknown: A Sourcebook on Women Explorers and Travelers.* New York: Greenwood, 1989.

Van Orman, Richard A. *The Explorers: Nineteenth Century Expeditions in Africa and the Americas.* Albuquerque: University of New Mexico Press, 1984.

Verne, Jules. *The Exploration of the World: The Great Navigators of the 18th Century* (originally published in 1881). Honolulu, Hawaii: University Press of the Pacific, 2001.

Vogel, Theodor. *A Century of Discovery.* London: Seeley, Jackson, and Halliday, 1877.

Wilcox, Desmond. *Explorers.* London: British Broadcasting Corporation, 1975.

Williams, Neville. *The Sea Dogs: Privateers, Plunder and Piracy in the Elizabethan Age.* London: Weidenfeld and Nicolson, 1975.

Wilson, Derek A. *The Circumnavigators.* London: Constable, 1989.

Wood, Herbert John. *Exploration and Discovery.* London, New York: Hutchinson's Univ. Library, 1951.

Wright, Helen. *The Great Explorers.* New York: Seeley, 1957.

SPECIFIC REGIONS

Europe, Iceland, and Eastern Atlantic Islands

Berry, Lloyd E., and Robert O. Crummey, eds. *Rude & Barbarous Kingdom: Russia in the Accounts of Sixteenth-Century English Voyagers.* Madison: University of Wisconsin Press, 1968.

Cassidy, Vincent H. *The Sea Around Them: The Atlantic Ocean A.D. 1250.* Baton Rouge: Louisiana State University Press, 1968.

Davidson, Hilda Roderick Ellis. *The Viking Road to Byzantium.* London: George Allen and Unwin, 1976.

Davies, Norman. *Europe: A History.* New York: Oxford University Press, 1996.

Fitzhugh, William W., and Elisabeth I. Ward. *Vikings: The North Atlantic Saga.* Washington, D.C.: Smithsonian Institution, 2000.

Halecki, Oscar. *Borderlands of Western Civilization: A History of East Central Europe.* New York: Ronald, 1952.

Hayword, John. *The Penguin Historical Atlas of the Vikings.* New York: Penguin, 1995.

Jesch, Judith. *Women in the Viking Age.* Woodbridge, U.K.: Boydell, 1991.

Jones, Gwyn. *A History of the Vikings.* London: Oxford University Press, 1968.

———. *The Norse Atlantic Saga.* Oxford, U.K.: Oxford University Press, 1986.

Jones, Prudence, and Nigel Pennick. *A History of Pagan Europe.* London: Routledge, 1995.

Lewis, Bernard. *The Muslim Discovery of Europe.* New York: W. W. Norton, 2001.

Logan, F. Donald. *The Vikings in History.* New York: Routledge. 1991.

Marcus, Geoffrey Jules. *The Conquest of the North Atlantic.* New York: Oxford University Press, 1981.

Pagden, Anthony. *Peoples and Empires: A History of European Migration, Exploration, and Conquest from Ancient Greece to the Present.* New York: Random House, 2001.

Roberts, David, and Jon Krakauer. *Iceland: Land of the Sagas.* New York: Harry N. Abrams, 1990.

Roberts, J. M. *A History of Europe.* New York: Penguin Putnam, 1996.

Whittle, Alasdair. *Europe in the Neolithic: The Creation of New Worlds.* Cambridge, U.K.: Cambridge University Press, 1996.

Wilson, David M. *The Northern World: The History and Heritage of Northern Europe AD 400–1100.* New York: Harry N. Abrams, 1980.

Woodhead, A. G. *The Greeks in the West.* New York: Praeger, 1962.

Mediterranean Sea

Aubet, Marie Eugenia. *The Phoenicians in the West: Politics, Colonies and Trade.* Cambridge, U.K.: Cambridge University Press, 2002.

Benjamin, Sandra. *The World of Benjamin of Tudela: A Medieval Mediterranean Travelogue.* London: Associated University Presses, 1995.

Casson, Lionel. *The Ancient Mariners: Seafarers and Seafighters of the Mediterranean in Ancient Times.* New York: Macmillan, 1959.

Grant, Michael. *The Ancient Historians.* New York: Scribner, 1970.

———. *The Ancient Mediterranean.* New York: Scribner, 1969.

Pryor, John H. *Geography, Technology, and War: Studies in the Maritime History of the Mediterranean, 649–1571.* Cambridge, U.K.: Cambridge University Press, 1992.

Warmington, Brian Herbert. *Carthage.* New York: Praeger, 1969.

North Africa and Coastal Africa

Axelson, Eric. *Congo to Cape: Early Portuguese Explorers.* New York: Barnes and Noble, 1973.

Crone, Gerald Roe, ed. *The Voyages of Cadamosto and other Documents on Western Africa in the Second Half of the Fifteenth Century.* London: Hakluyt Society, 1937.

Duyvendak, J. J. L. *China's Discovery of Africa.* London: A. Probsthain, 1949.

Hallet, Robin. *The Penetration of Africa: European Exploration in North and West Africa to 1815.* New York: Praeger, 1965.

Hart, Henry Hersch. *Sea Road to the Indies: An Account of the Voyages and Exploits of the Portuguese Navigators, to-*

gether with the Life and Times of Dom Vasco da Gama. Westport, Conn.: Greenwood, 1971.

Jayne, Kingsley Garland. *Vasco da Gama and His Successors, 1460–1580.* New York: Barnes & Noble, 1970.

Landstrom, Bjorn. *The Quest for India: A History of Discovery and Exploration from the Expedition to the Land of Punt in 1493 B.C. to the Discovery of the Cape of Good Hope in 1488 A.D., in Words and Pictures.* Garden City, N.Y.: Doubleday, 1964.

Porter, Philip Wiley. *Benin to Bahia: A Chronicle of Portuguese Empire in the South Atlantic in the Fifteenth and Sixteenth Centuries.* St. Paul, Minn.: North Central, 1959.

Prestage, Edgar. *The Portuguese Pioneers.* London: Adam & Charles Black, 1933.

Teague, Michael. *In the Wake of the Portuguese Navigators: A Photographic Essay.* Manchester, England: Carcanet, 1988.

Sub-Saharan Africa

Bennett, Norman R. *Africa and Europe: From Roman Times to the Present.* New York: Africana, 1975.

Blake, John W. *European Beginnings in West Africa 1454–1578.* Westport, Conn.: Greenwood, 1937.

Bovill, E. W. *The Niger Explored.* London: Oxford University Press, 1968.

Brent, Peter Ludwig. *Black Nile: Mungo Park and the Search for the Niger.* London: Gordon and Cremonesi, 1977.

Buel, James William. *Heroes of the Dark Continent: A Complete History of All the Great Explorations and Discoveries in Africa, from the Earliest Ages to the Present Time.* Freeport, N.Y.: Books for Libraries, 1971.

Craig, Hugh. *Great African Travelers: from Mungo Park (1795) to the Rescuing of Emin Pasha by Henry M. Stanley (1889).* New York: G. Routledge, 1890.

Gardner, Brian. *The Quest for Timbuktoo.* New York: Harcourt, Brace, 1968.

Hall, Richard Seymour. *Explorers in Africa.* London: Usborne, 1975.

Howard, Cecil. *West African Explorers.* London: Oxford University Press, 1951.

Hugon, Anne. *Exploration of Africa From Cairo to the Cape.* London: Thames and Hudson, 1993.

Ibazebo, Isimeme. *Exploration into Africa.* London: Belitha, 1994.

Johnston, Sir Harry H. *The Nile Quest.* New York: Frederick A. Stokes, 1903.

———. *The Opening Up of Africa.* New York: Henry Holt, 1911.

Jones, Charles H. *Africa: The History of Exploration and Adventure as Given in the Leading Authorities from Herodotus to Livingstone.* Westport, Conn.: Negro Universities, 1970.

Lloyd, Christopher. *The Search for the Niger.* London: Collins, 1973.

McLynn, Frank. *Hearts of Darkness: The European Exploration of Africa.* London: Vintage/Ebury, 1993.

Moorehead, Alan. *The Blue Nile.* London: Harper & Row, 1962.

———. *The White Nile.* London: H. Hamilton, 1960.

Oliver, Caroline. *Western Women in Colonial Africa.* Westport, Conn.: Greenwood, 1982.

Pakenham, Thomas. *The Scramble for Africa: Conquest of the Dark Continent from 1876 to 1912.* New York: Random House, 1991.

Perham, Margery, and Jack Simmons, eds. *African Discovery: An Anthology of Exploration.* London: Faber and Faber, 1942.

Rotberg, Robert, ed. *Africa and Its Explorers: Motives, Methods, and Impact.* Cambridge, Mass.: Harvard University Press, 1970.

Severin, Timothy. *The African Adventure: Four Hundred Years of Exploration in the "Dangerous Continent."* New York: Dutton, 1973.

Silverberg Robert. *The Realm of Prester John.* Garden City, N.Y.: Doubleday, 1972.

Simpson, Donald Herbert. *Dark Companions: The African Contribution to the European Exploration of East Africa.* New York: Barnes and Noble, 1976.

Welch, Galbraith. *The Unveiling of Timbuctoo: The Astounding Adventures of Caillie.* London: V. Gollantz, 1938.

Worth, Richard. *Stanley and Livingstone and the Exploration of Africa in World History.* Berkeley Heights, N.J.: Enslow, 2000.

Middle East

Donner, Frederick. *The Early Islamic Conquests.* Princeton, N.J.: Princeton University Press, 1981.

Farah, Caesar E. *Islam.* Hauppauge, N.Y.: Barron's, 2000.

Freeth, Zahra Dickson. *Explorers of Arabia: from the Renaissance to the End of the Victorian Era.* New York: Holmes & Meier, 1978.

Hogarth, David. *The Penetration of Arabia: A Record of the Development of Western Knowledge Concerning the Arabian Peninsula.* New York: Hyperion, 1981.

Kiernann, Reginald Hall. *The Unveiling of Arabia: The Story of Arabian Travel and Discovery.* London: G. G. Harrap, 1937.

Madden, Thomas F., ed. *The Crusades: Essential Readings.* New York: Blackwell, 2002.

Saunders, J. J. *The History of Medieval Islam.* New York: Barnes and Noble, 1965.

Smith, Ronald Bishop. *The First Age of the Portuguese Embassies, Navigations and Peregrinations in Persia (1507–1524).* Bethesda, Md.: Decatur, 1970.

Tidrick, Kathryn. *Heart-Beguiling Araby.* Cambridge, U.K.: Cambridge University Press, 1981.

Wolfe, Michael, ed. *One Thousand Roads to Mecca: Ten Centuries of Travelers Writing About the Muslim Pilgrimage.* New York: Grove, 1999.

Central Asia and the Indian Subcontinent

Bell, Christopher. *Portugal and the Quest for the Indies.* London: Constable, 1974.

Boxer, C. R. *Portuguese Conquest and Commerce in Southern Asia, 1500–1750.* London: Variorum Reprints, 1985.

Byron, Robert. *From Lisbon to Goa, 1500–1750.* London: Variorum Reprints, 1984.

Crone, Gerald Roe. *The Discovery of the East.* London: Hamilton, 1972.

Dulles, Foster Rhea. *Eastward Ho! The First English Adventurers to the Orient.* New York: Houghton Mifflin, 1931.

Edwardes, Michael. *East-West Passage: The Travel of Ideas, Arts, and Inventions between Asia and the Western World.* New York: Taplinger, 1971.

Grousset, René. *In the Footsteps of the Buddha.* London: G. Routledge and Sons, 1932.

Hart, Henry H. *Sea Road to the Indies.* New York: Macmillan, 1950.

Hopkirk, Peter. *Foreign Devils on the Silk Road: The Search for the Lost Cities and Treasures of Chinese Central Asia.* London: John Murray, 1980.

Keay, John. *The Gilgit Game: The Explorers of the Western Himalayas.* London: J. Murray, 1979.

Komroff, Manuel. *Contemporaries of Marco Polo.* New York: Boni & Liveright, 1928.

Lantzeff, George V., and Richard A. Pierce. *Eastward to Empire: Exploration and Conquest on the Russian Open Frontier, to 1750.* Montreal and London: McGill-Queens University Press, 1973.

Lattimore, Owen. *The Desert Road to Turkestan.* London: Methuen, 1928.

Lattimore, Owen, and Eleanor Lattimore, eds. *Silks, Spices and Empire: Asia Seen Through the Eyes of Its Discoverers.* New York: Delacorte, 1968.

Miller, Lurie. *On Top of the World: Five Women Explorers in Tibet.* New York: Paddington, 1974.

Mirsky, Jeannette, ed. *The Great Chinese Travelers.* New York: Pantheon, 1964.

Newton, Arthur Percival, ed. *Travel and Travellers of the Middle Ages.* New York: Alfred A. Knopf, 1926.

Prasad, R. C. *Early English Travellers in India.* New Delhi: Motilal Banarsi Dass, 1965.

Rawat, Indra Singh. *Indian Explorers of the 19th Century: Account of Explorations in the Himalayas, Tibet, Mongolia, and Central Asia.* New Delhi: Ministry of Information and Broadcasting, Government of India, 1973.

Severin, Timothy. *The Oriental Adventure: Explorers of the East.* Boston: Little Brown and Company, 1976.

Sutherland, Lucy S. *The East India Company in Eighteenth-Century Politics.* London: Oxford University Press, 1962.

Sykes, Sir Percy Molesworth. *Explorers All: Famous Journeys in Asia.* London: G. Newness, 1939.

Waller, Derek J. *Pundits: British Exploration of Tibet and Central Asia.* Lexington: University Press of Kentucky, 1990.

Warner, Langdon. *The Long Old Road to China.* New York: Doubleday, Page, 1926.

Wessels, Cornelius, S. J. *Early Jesuit Travellers in Central Asia, 1603–1721.* The Hague: M. Nijhoff, 1924.

The Far East and Eastern Siberia

Byron, Robert. *Portuguese Merchants and Missionaries in Feudal Japan, 1543–1640.* London: Variorum Reprints, 1986.

Coxe, William. *Account of the Russian Discoveries between Asia and America to which are added the Conquest of Siberia and the History of the Transactions and Commerce between Russia and China.* New York: A. M. Kelley, 1970.

Dawson, Christopher, ed. *The Mongol Mission: Narratives and Letters of the Franciscan Missionaries in Mongolia and China in the Thirteenth and Fourteenth Centuries, tr. by a nun of the Stanbrook Abbey.* New York: Sheed and Ward, 1955.

Forsyth, James. *A History of the Peoples of Siberia, Russia's North Asian Colony 1581–1990.* Cambridge, U.K.: Cambridge University Press, 1994.

Golder, Frank Alfred. *Russian Expansion on the Pacific, 1641–1850.* New York: Paragon, 1971.

Krasheninnikov, Stepan P. *Explorations of Kamchatka: North Pacific Scimitar.* Portland: Oregon Historical Society, 1972.

Levathes, Louise. *When China Ruled the Seas: The Treasure Fleet of the Dragon Throne, 1405–1433.* Oxford, U.K.: Oxford University Press, 1996.

Osborne, Milton. *River Road to China: The Mekong River Expedition, 1866–73.* New York: Liveright, 1975.

Saunders, J. J. *The History of the Mongol Conquests.* Philadelphia: University of Pennsylvania Press, 2001.

Stephan, John J. *The Russian Far East, A History.* Stanford, Calif.: Stanford University Press, 1996.

The West Indies, Central America, and Mexico

Hulme, Peter, and Neil L. Whitehead, eds. *Wild Majesty: Encounters with Caribs from Columbus to the Present Day.* Oxford, U.K.: Oxford University Press, 1992.

Kadir, Djelal. *Columbus and the Ends of the Earth: Europe's Prophetic Rhetoric As Conquering Ideology.* Berkeley: University of California Press, 1992.

Kirkpatrick, F. A. *The Spanish Conquistadores.* London: A. & C. Black, 1934.

Klein, Herbert S. *African Slavery in Latin America and the Caribbean.* New York: Oxford University Press, 1986.

Leon Portilla, Miguel, ed. *The Broken Spears: The Aztec Account of the Conquest of Mexico.* Boston: Beacon, 1962.

Todoroff, Tzvetan. *The Conquest of America.* Norman: University of Oklahoma, 1999.

Weddle, Robert S. *Spanish Sea: The Gulf of Mexico in North American Discovery, 1500–1685.* College Station: Texas A&M University Press, 1985.

Whitmore, Thomas M. *Disease and Death in Early Colonial Mexico: Simulating Amerindian Depopulation.* Boulder, Colo.: Westview, 1992.

South America, the South Atlantic, and the East Pacific

Burkholder, Mark A., and Lyman L. Johnson. *Colonial Latin America.* New York: Oxford University Press, 1990.

Cieza de León, Pedro de. *The Discovery and Conquest of Peru.* Durham, N.C.: Duke University Press, 1999.

Davis, Wade. *Exploration and Discoveries in the Amazon Rain Forest.* New York: Simon & Schuster, 1997.

Hanson, Earl Parker. *South from the Spanish Main: South America Seen through the Eyes of its Discoverers.* New York: Delacorte, 1967.

Hemming, John. *The Conquest of the Incas.* New York: Macmillan, 1970.

Herndon, William Lewis. *Exploration of the Valley of the Amazon, 1851–1852.* New York: Grove, 2000.

Medina, Jose T., ed. *The Discovery of the Amazon.* New York: Dover Publications, 2nd ed., 1988.

Morison, Samuel Eliot. *The European Discovery of America: The Southern Voyages, 1492–1616.* New York: Oxford University Press, 1974.

Richardson, James B., III. *People of the Andes.* Washington, D.C.: Smithsonian Books, 1994.

Smith, Anthony. *Explorers of the Amazon.* New York: Viking Penguin, 1990.

Vellinho, Moyses. *Brazil South: Its Conquest & Settlement.* New York: Alfred A. Knopf, 1968.

Wood, Michael. *Conquistadors.* Berkeley: University of California Press, 2001.

Worcester, Donald E. *Brazil: From Colony to World Power.* New York: Charles Scribner's Sons, 1973.

North America

EAST OF MISSISSIPPI RIVER

Arbman, Holger. *The Vikings.* New York: Praeger, 1961.

Axtell, James L. *The European and the Indian.* New York: Oxford University Press, 1981.

Bakeless, John. *The Eyes of Discovery: The Pageant of North America as Seen by the First Explorers.* Philadelphia, Pa.: Lippincott, 1950.

Brebner, John Bartlett. *The Explorers of North America, 1492–1806.* London: A. & C. Black, 1933.

Briceland, Alan Vance. *Westward from Virginia: The Exploration of the Virginia-Carolina Frontier, 1650–1710.* Charlottesville: University of Virginia Press, 1987.

Burpee, Lawrence J. *The Discovery of Canada.* Ottawa: Graphic, 1929.

Crouse, Nellis M. *In Quest of the Western Ocean.* New York: W. Morrow, 1928.

Deacon, Richard. *Madoc and the Discovery of America.* New York: Braziller, 1967.

Eccles, William John. *The French in North America, 1500–1783.* East Lansing: Michigan State University Press, 1978.

Fagan, Brian. *The Great Journey: The Peopling of Ancient America.* New York: Thames & Hudson, 1987.

Fiske, John. *The Discovery of America.* Boston: Houghton Mifflin, 1892.

Gathorne-Hardy, G. M. *The Norse Discoverers of America.* Oxford, U.K.: Clarendon, 1921.

Gonzalez, Ray. *Without Discovery: A Native Response to Columbus.* Seattle, Wash.: Broken Moon, 1992.

Hodge, Frederick W., and Theodore Lewis, eds. *Spanish Explorers in the Southern United States, 1528–1543.* New York: Charles Scribner's Sons, 1907.

Houston, Lebame, and Barbara Hird, eds. *Roanoke Revisited: The Story of the First English Settlements in the New World and the Fabled Lost Colony of Roanoke Island.* Manteo, N.C.: Penny, 1997.

Ingstad, Helge. *Westward to Vinland.* London and New York: Cape, 1969.

Ingstad, Helge, and Anne Stine Ingstad. *The Viking Discovery of America: The Excavation of a Norse Settlement in L'Anse aux Meadows, Newfoundland.* New York: Facts On File, 2001.

Johnston, Charles Haven Ladd. *Famous Discoverers and Explorers of America.* Freeport, N.Y.: Books for Libraries, 1917.

Magnusson, Magnus, and Hermann Palsson, trs. *The Vinland Sagas: The Norse Discovery of America.* New York: Penguin, 1965.

Morison, Samuel Eliot. *The European Discovery of America: The Northern Voyages, A.D. 500–1600.* New York: Oxford, 1971.

Norman, Charles. *Discoverers of America.* New York: T. Y. Crowell, 1968.

Parkman, Francis. *The Jesuits in North America in the Seventeenth Century.* Boston: Little Brown, 1899.

———. *La Salle and the Discovery of the Great West (Part III of France and England in North America).* Boston: Little Brown, 1894.

———. *Pioneers of France in the New World (Part I of France and England in North America).* Boston: Little Brown, 1878.

Pohl, Frederick J. *The Viking Explorers: Their Lives, Customs, and Daring Voyages.* New York: T. Y. Crowell, 1966.

Randolph, F. Ralph. *British Travelers Among the Southern Indians.* Norman: University of Oklahoma Press, 1973.

Severin, Timothy. *Explorers of the Mississippi.* New York: Alfred A. Knopf, 1968.

WEST OF MISSISSIPPI RIVER

Albright, George Leslie. *Official Explorations for Pacific Railroads, 1853–55*. Berkeley: University of California Press, 1921.

Bancroft, Hubert Howe. *History of Alaska, 1730–1885*. San Francisco: A. L. Bancroft, 1886.

———. *History of California, 1542–1890*. San Francisco: The History Company, 1886–90.

———. *History of Oregon, 1848–1888*. San Francisco: The History Company, 1888.

———. *History of Utah, 1540–1886*. San Francisco: The History Company, 1889.

Billington, R. A. *The Far Western Frontier, 1830–1860*. New York: Harper, 1956.

———. *Westward Expansion*. New York: Macmillan, 1949.

Briggs, Harold E. *Frontiers of the North-west: A History of the Upper Missouri Valley*. New York and London: Appleton-Century, 1940.

Burpee, Lawrence J. *The Search for the Western Sea: The Story of the Exploration of North-western America*. London: Alston Rivers, 1908.

Butruille, Susan G., and Kathleen Petersen. *Women's Voices from the Oregon Trail: The Times That Tried Women's Souls and a Guide to Women's History Along the Oregon Trail*. Boise, Idaho: Tamarack Books, 1994.

Carter, Hodding. *Doomed Road of Empire: The Spanish Trail of Conquest*. New York: McGraw-Hill, 1963.

Cook, Warren L. *Flood Tide of Empire: Spain and the Pacific Northwest, 1543–1819*. New Haven, Conn.: Yale University Press, 1973.

Cutter, Donald C. *Malaspina & Galiano: Spanish Voyages to the Northwest Coast, 1791 and 1792*. Vancouver, B.C.: Douglas & McIntyre, 1991.

Dale, Harrison C. *The Ashley-Smith Explorations and the Discovery of a Central Route to the Pacific, 1822–1829*. Glendale, Calif.: Arthur H. Clark, 1941.

De Voto, Bernard A. *Across the Wide Missouri*. Boston: Houghton Mifflin, 1947.

———. *The Course of Empire*. Boston: Houghton Mifflin, 1952.

Ferris, Robert G., ed. *Explorers and Settlers*. Washington, D.C.: U.S. National Park Service, 1968

Fowler, Harlan D. *Camels to California*. Stanford, Calif.: Stanford University Press, 1950.

Gibson, James R. *Imperial Russia in Frontier America*. New York: Oxford University Press, 1976.

Gilbert, Edmund William. *The Exploration of Western America, 1800–1850: An Historical Geography*. Cambridge, U.K.: Cambridge University Press, 1933.

Goetzmann, William H. *Army Exploration in the American West, 1803–63*. New Haven, Conn.: Yale University Press, 1959.

———. *Exploration and Empire: The Explorer and the Scientist in the Winning of the American West*. New York: Alfred A. Knopf, 1966.

———. *New Lands, New Men*. New York: Viking, 1986.

Hasse, Adelaide R. *Reports of Explorations Printed in the Documents of the United States*. Washington, D.C.: U.S. Government Printing Office, 1899.

Howay, Frederic W. *Voyages of the "Columbia" to the Northwest Coast, 1787–1790 and 1790–1793*. Portland: Oregon Historical Society, 1990.

Jackson, Donald Dean, ed. *Letters of the Lewis and Clark Expedition, with related documents, 1783–1854*. Urbana: University of Illinois Press, 1978.

Jackson, W. Turrentine. *Wagon Roads West*. New Haven, Conn.: Yale University Press, 1964.

Kendrick, John S. *The Men With Wooden Feet: The Spanish Exploration of the Pacific Northwest*. Toronto: NC Press, 1985.

McDermott, John F. *Travelers on the Western Frontier*. Ann Arbor, Mich.: University Microfilms International, 1970.

McFarling, Lloyd, ed. *Exploring the Northern Plains, 1804–76*. Caldwell, Idaho: Caxton, 1955.

Mirsky, Jeannette. *The Westward Crossings: Balboa, Mackenzie, Lewis and Clark*. London: A. Wingate, 1951.

Parkman, Francis, and Anthony Brandt. *The Oregon Trail*. Washington, D.C.: National Geographic, 2002.

Preston, Douglas. *Cities of Gold: A Journey across the American Southwest in Coronado's Footsteps*. Albuquerque: University of New Mexico Press, 1999.

Roberts, David. *A Newer World: Kit Carson, John C. Frémont, and the Claiming of the American West*. New York: Simon & Schuster, 2001.

Ronda, James P. *Finding the West: Explorations with Lewis and Clark*. Albuquerque: University of New Mexico Press, 2001.

Sauer, Carl O. *Sixteenth Century North America: The Land and the People as Seen by the Europeans*. Berkeley: University of California Press, 1971.

Selby, John. *The Conquest of the American West*. Totawa, N.J.: Rowman and Littlefield, 1976.

Van Every, Dale. *The Final Challenge: The American Frontier, 1804–1845*. New York: Morrow, 1964.

Vaughn, Thomas. *Voyages of Enlightenment: Malaspina on the Northwest Coast, 1791–1792*. Portland: Oregon Historical Society, 1977.

Wagner, Henry R. *Spanish Voyages to the Northwest Coast of America in the Sixteenth Century*. San Francisco: California Historical Society, 1929.

The South and West Pacific Islands and Coastal Australia

Allen, Oliver E. *The Pacific Navigators*. Alexandria, Va.: Time-Life, 1980.

Arnold, Carolyn. *Easter Island: Giant Stone Statues Tell of a Rich and Tragic Past*. New York: Clarion, 2000.

Barthel, Thomas S. *The Eighth Land: The Polynesian Discovery and Settlement of Easter Island*. Honolulu: University of Hawaii Press, 1978.

Calder, Alex. *Voyages and Beaches: Pacific Encounters, 1769–1840*. Honolulu: University of Hawaii Press, 1999.

Cushner, Nicholas P. *The Isles of the West: Early Spanish Voyages to the Philippines, 1521–1564.* Quezon City: Ateneo de Manila University Press, 1966.

Dodge, Ernest Stanley. *Beyond the Capes: Pacific Exploration from Captain Cook to the "Challenger," 1776–1877.* London: Gollanz, 1971.

Dunmore, John. *French Explorers in the Pacific.* Oxford, U.K.: Clarendon, 1965–69.

Finney, Ben. *Voyage of Rediscovery: A Cultural Odyssey Through Polynesia.* Berkeley: University of California Press, 1994.

Henry, Teuira, et al. *Voyaging Chiefs of Havai'i.* Honolulu: Kalamaku, 1995.

Lewis, David. *The Voyaging Stars: Secrets of the Pacific Island Navigators.* New York: W. W. Norton, 1978.

———. *We, the Navigators: The Ancient Art of Landfinding in the Pacific.* Honolulu: University of Hawaii Press, 1994.

Schilder, Gunter. *Australia Unveiled: The Share of the Dutch Navigators in the Discovery of Australia.* Amsterdam: Theatrum Orbis Terrarum, 1976.

Taylor, Nancy M. *Exploration of the Pacific.* Wellington, New Zealand: School Publications Branch, Dept. of Education, 1967.

Triebel, Louis Augustus. *French Exploration of Australia.* Sydney, Australia: Les Editions du Courrier Australian, 1943.

Ward, Ralph Gerard, ed. *American Activities in the Central Pacific, 1790–1870.* Ridgewood, N.J.: Gregg, 1966–67.

Continental Australia and New Zealand

Binks, C. J. *Explorers of Western Tasmania.* Launceston, Tasmania: Mary Fisher Bookshop, 1980.

Colwell, Max. *The Journey of Burke and Wills.* Sydney, Australia: P. Hamlyn, 1971.

Cumpston, J. H. L. *The Inland Sea and the Great River: The Story of Australian Exploration.* Sydney, Australia: Angus and Robertson, 1964.

Favenc, Ernest. *The Explorers of Australia and Their Life Work.* Christchurch, N.Z.: Whitcomb and Tombs, 1908.

Feeken, Erwin Herman Joseph, and Gerda E. E. Feeken. *The Discovery and Exploration of Australia.* Melbourne, Australia: Thomas, Nelson, 1970.

Flannery, Tim F. *The Explorers: Stories of Discovery and Adventure from the Australian Frontier.* New York: Grove, 2000.

Kerr, Colin Gregory, and Margaret Kerr. *Australian Explorers.* Adelaide, Australia: Rigby, 1978.

McClymont, W. G. *The Exploration of New Zealand.* London: Oxford University Press, 1959.

Murgatroyd, Sarah P. *The Dig Tree: The Story of Bravery/Insanity/the Race to Discover Australia's Wild Frontier.* New York: Broadway, 2002.

Steele, John Gladstone. *The Explorers of the Moreton Bay District.* Brisbane, Australia: University of Queensland Press, 1983.

Taylor, Nancy M. *Early Travellers in New Zealand.* Oxford, U.K.: Clarendon, 1959.

The Canadian, European, and Siberian Arctic, Greenland, and the North Pole

Berton, Pierre. *Arctic Grail: The Quest for the North West Passage and the North Pole, 1818–1909.* Guilford, Conn.: Lyons, 2000.

Bryce, Robert. *Cook & Peary: The Polar Controversy, Resolved.* Mechanicsburg, Pa.: Stackpole, 1997.

Burkhanov, Vasillii Fedotovich. *Achievements of Soviet Geographical Exploration and Research in the Arctic.* Ottawa: Directorate of Scientific Information Service, 1957.

Burney, James. *Chronological History of Northeastern Voyages of Discovery.* New York: Da Capo, 1969.

Caswell, John Edwards. *Arctic Frontiers: United States Explorations in the Far North.* Norman: University of Oklahoma Press, 1956.

Cooke, Alan, and Clive Holland. *The Exploration of Northern Canada, 500 to 1920.* Toronto: Arctic Historical Press, 1978.

Cookman, Scott. *Ice Blink: The Tragic Fate of Sir John Franklin's Lost Polar Expedition.* New York: Wiley, 2001.

Cross, Wilbur. *Disaster at the Pole: The Tragedy of the Airship* Italia *and the 1928 Nobile Expedition to the North Pole.* Guilford, Conn.: Lyons, 2002.

Delgado, James P. *Across the Top of the World: The Quest for the Northwest Passage.* New York: Facts On File, 1999.

Grierson, John. *Sir Hubert Wilkins: Enigma of Exploration.* London: R. Hale, 1960.

Guttridge, Leonard F. *Icebound: The Jeannette Expedition's Quest for the North Pole.* New York: Berkeley, 2001.

Herbert, Wally. *The Noose of Laurels: Robert E. Peary and the Race to the North Pole.* New York: Atheneum, 1989.

Hunt, William R. *To Stand at the Pole: The Dr. Cook–Admiral Peary North Pole Controversy.* New York: Stein and Day, 1981.

Jones, Lawrence F., and George Lonn. *Pathfinders of the North.* Toronto: Pitt, 1970.

Mirksy, Jeannette. *To the North! The Story of Arctic Exploration from Earliest Times to the Present.* New York: Viking, 1934.

Mowat, Farley. *The Polar Passion.* Boston: Little Brown, 1967.

Neatby, Leslie H. *Discovery in Russian and Siberian Waters.* Athens: Ohio University Press, 1973.

Oswalt, Wendell H. *Eskimos and Explorers.* Novato, Calif.: Chandler and Sharp, 1979.

Owen, Roderic. *The Fate of Franklin.* London: Hutchinson, 1978.

Rasky, Frank. *The North Pole or Bust.* New York: McGraw-Hill Ryerson, 1977.

———. *The Polar Voyagers.* New York: McGraw-Hill Ryerson, 1976.

Seaver, Kirsten A. *Frozen Echo: Greenland and the Exploration of North America, c. A.D. 1000–1500.* Stanford, Calif.: Stanford University Press, 1996.

Weems, John Edward. *Race for the Pole.* New York: Holt, 1960.

Williams, Glyndwr. *The British Search for the Northwest Passage in the Eighteenth Century.* London: Longmans, 1962.

Wright, Theon. *The Big Nail: The Story of the Cook-Peary Feud.* New York: John Day, 1970.

The Antarctic and the South Pole

Debenham, Frank. *Antarctica: History of a Continent.* London: H. Jenkins, 1959.

———. *In the Antarctic.* London: Murray, 1964.

Hatherton, Trevor. *Antarctica.* New York: Praeger, 1965.

Herbert, Wally. *A World of Men: Exploration in Antarctica.* London: Eyre & Spottiswoode, 1968.

Huntford, Roland, and Jon Krakauer, eds. *The Last Place on Earth: Scott and Amundsen's Race to the South Pole.* New York: Random House, 1999.

Land, Barbara. *The New Explorers: Women in Antarctica.* New York: Dodd, Mead, 1981.

Mitterling, Philip I. *America in the Antarctic in 1840.* Urbana: University of Illinois Press, 1959.

Ronne, Finn. *Antarctic Conquest.* New York: G. P. Putnam's Sons, 1949.

SPECIFIC TOPICS

Cartographers, Geographers, and Sponsors

Beazley, C. Raymond. *The Dawn of Modern Geography.* 3 vols. London: J. Murray, 1897–1905.

Brown, Lloyd A. *The Story of Maps.* Boston: Little Brown, 1949.

Bunbury, Edward H. *A History of Ancient Geography.* 2 vols. London: John Murray, 1879.

Crone, Gerald R. *Maps and Their Makers: An Introduction to the History of Cartography.* London, New York: Hutchinson's University Library, 1966.

Dickinson, Robert Eric, and O. J. R. Howarth. *The Making of Geography.* Oxford, U.K.: Oxford University Press, 1933.

Duvoisin, Roger Antoine. *They Put Out to Sea: The Story of the Map.* New York: Alfred A. Knopf, 1943.

Goss, John. *The Mapmaker's Art: An Illustrated History of Cartography.* London: Rand McNally, 1993.

Greenhood, David. *Mapping.* Chicago and London: University of Chicago Press, 1964.

Karrow, Robert W., Jr. *Mapmakers of the Sixteenth Century and Their Maps.* Chicago: Speculum Orbis for the Newberry Library, 1993.

Skelton, Raleigh Ashlin. *Explorers' Maps: Chapters in the Cartographic Record of Geographical Discovery.* Feltham, N.Y: Spring Books, 1958.

Thomson, J. Oliver. *History of Ancient Geography.* Cambridge, U.K.: Cambridge University Press, 1948.

Thrower, Norman J. W. *Maps and Man: An Examination of Cartography in Relation to Culture and Civilization.* Englewood Cliffs, N.J.: Prentice-Hall, 1972.

Tooley, Ronald Vere. *Maps and Map-Makers.* New York: Bonanza, 1961.

Warmington, Eric Herbert. *Greek Geography.* New York: E. P. Dutton, 1934.

Commerce

Catton, Ted, and Marcia Montgomery. *Special History: The Environment and the Fur Trade Experience in Voyageurs National Park, 1730–1870.* Missoula, Mont.: Historical Research Associates, 2000.

Cawston, George. *The Early Chartered Companies.* New York: Burt Franklin, 1968.

Chaudhuri, K. N. *The English East India Company.* New York: Augustus M. Kelley, 1965.

Chittendon, Hiram Martin. *The American Fur Trade of the Far West.* 2 vols. New York: Press of the Pioneers, 1935.

Foster, Sir William. *England's Quest for Eastern Trade.* London: A. and C. Black, 1933.

Franck, Irene M., and David Brownstone. *To The Ends of the Earth: The Great Travel and Trade Routes of Human History.* New York: Facts On File, 1984.

Hafen, Le Roy Reuben. *Fur Traders, Trappers, and Mountain Men of the Upper Missouri.* Lincoln: University of Nebraska Press, 1995.

———, ed. *French Fur Traders and Voyageurs in the American West.* Lincoln: University of Nebraska Press, 1997.

Jeudwine, John Wynne. *Studies in Empire and Trade.* London: Longmans, Green, 1923.

Jones, Robert F., ed. *Annals of Astoria: The Headquarters Log of the Pacific Fur Company on the Columbia River, 1811–1813.* New York: Fordham University Press, 1999.

Major, John. *The Silk Route: 7,000 Miles of History.* New York: HarperCollins, 1995.

Malloy, Mary. *Boston Men on the Northwest Coast: The American Fur Trade, 1788–1844.* Fairbanks: University of Alaska Press, 1998.

Newman, Peter. *Empire of the Bay: The Company of Adventurers That Seized a Continent.* New York: Penguin, 2000.

Skinner, Constance. *Adventures of Oregon: A Chronicle of the Fur Trade.* Temecula, Calif.: Reprint Services Corporation, 1991.

Steensgaard, Niels. *Carracks, Caravans and Companies: The Structural Crisis in the European-Asian Trade in the Early 17th Century.* Copenhagen: Studentlitteratur, 1973.

Tracy, James D., ed. *The Political Economy of Merchant Empires.* New York: Cambridge University Press, 1991.

———, ed. *The Rise of Merchant Empires.* New York: Cambridge University Press, 1990.

Webster, William Clarence. *A General History of Commerce.* Boston: Ginn, 1903.

Mountain Climbing
Bernstein, Jeremy. *Ascent: Of the Invention of Mountain Climbing and Its Practice.* Lincoln: University of Nebraska Press, 1979.

Frison-Roche, Roger, and Sylvain Jouty. *A History of Mountain Climbing.* New York: Flammarion, 1996.

Quinn, James W. *Men to Climb My Mountains: The Early Explorers.* Newbury, Oreg.: BookPartners, 1997.

Rebuffat, Gaston, and Jon Krakauer, eds. *Starlight and Storm: The Conquest for the Great North Faces of the Alps.* New York: Random House, 1999.

Sale, Richard, and John Cleare. *Climbing the World's 14 Highest Mountains: The History of the 8,000-Meter Peaks.* Seattle, Wash.: Mountaineers Books, 2000.

Natural Science
Adams, Alexander B. *Eternal Quest: The Story of the Great Naturalists.* New York: G. P. Putnam's Sons, 1969.

Barber, Richard, and Anne Riches. *A Dictionary of Fabulous Beasts.* London: Macmillan London, 1971.

Bates, Marston. *The Nature of Natural History.* Princeton, N.J.: Princeton University Press, 1990.

Beebe, William, ed. *The Book of Naturalists.* Princeton, N.J.: Princeton University Press, 1988.

Burroughs, Raymond Darwin, ed. *The Natural History of the Lewis and Clark Expedition.* East Lansing: Michigan State University Press, 1995.

Clair, Colin. *Unnatural History: An Illustrated Bestiary.* New York: Abelard-Schumann, 1967.

Evans, Howard Ensign. *The Natural History of the Long Expedition to the Rocky Mountains, 1819–1820.* Oxford, U.K.: Oxford University Press, 1997.

Hays, Hoffman Reynolds. *Birds, Beasts, and Men: A Humanist History of Zoology.* Baltimore, Md.: Penguin, 1973.

Koerner, Lisbet. *Linnaeus: Nature and Nation.* Cambridge, Mass.: Harvard University Press, 1999.

Maslow, Jonathan Evan. *Footsteps in the Jungle: Adventures in the Scientific Exploration of the American Tropics.* Chicago: Ivan R. Dee, 1996.

Stefoff, Rebecca. *Scientific Explorers.* New York: Oxford University Press, 1992.

Oceanography
Earle, Sylvia A. *Atlas of the Ocean: The Deep Frontier.* Washington, D.C.: National Geographic Society, 2001.

Marx, Robert F. *The History of Underwater Exploration.* New York: Dover, 1990.

Piccard, Jacques, and Robert S. Dietz. *Seven Miles Down: The Story of the Bathyscaph* Trieste. New York: G. P. Putnam's Sons, 1961.

Pirie, R. Gordon, ed. *Oceanography.* London: Oxford University Press, 1973.

Polking, Kirk. *Oceanographers and Explorers of the Sea.* Berkeley Heights, N.J.: Enslow, 1999.

Ross, David A. *Introduction to Oceanography.* Englewood Cliffs, N.J.: Prentice-Hall, 1977.

Trevor, Norton. *Stars Beneath the Sea: The Pioneers of Diving.* New York: Carroll & Graf, 1999.

Weisberg, Joseph, and Howard Parish. *Introductory Oceanography.* New York: McGraw-Hill, 1974.

Shipbuilding and Navigation
Bass, George F., ed. *A History of Seafaring Based on Underwater Archaeology.* New York: Walker and Company, 1972.

Casson, Lionel. *Ships and Seamanship in the Ancient World.* Baltimore, Md.: Johns Hopkins University Press, 1997.

Chatterton, Edward Keble. *Sailing the Seas: A Survey of Seafaring through the Ages.* London: Chapman & Hall, 1931.

Culver, Henry B. *The Book of Old Ships.* New York: Dover Publications, 1869.

Dunlap, G. D., and H. H. Shufeldt. *Dutton's Navigation and Piloting.* Annapolis, Md.: Naval Institute Press, 1972.

Gardiner, Robert, and Arne Emil Christensen. *The Earliest Ships: The Evolution of Boats into Ships.* Annapolis, Md.: Naval Institute Press, 1996.

Goldberg, Joseph A. *Shipbuilding in Colonial America.* Charlottesville: University Press of Virginia, 1976.

Hourani, George Fadlo, and John Carswell. *Arab Seafaring.* Princeton, N.J.: Princeton University Press, 1995.

Ifland, Peter. *Taking the Stars: Celestial Navigation from Argonauts to Astronauts.* Newport News, Va.: Mariners Museum, 1998.

Kemp, Peter. *The Oxford Companion to Ships and the Sea.* Oxford, U.K.: Oxford University Press, 1994.

Landstrom, Bjorn. *The Ship.* New York: Doubleday, 1961.

Lewis, David, and Derek Oulton, ed. *We, the Navigators: The Ancient Art of Landfinding in the Pacific.* Honolulu: University of Hawaii Press, 1994.

Lindsey, W. S. *History of Merchant Shipping and Ancient Commerce.* New York: AMS, 1965.

Lobley, Douglas. *Ships through the Ages.* London: Octopus Books, 1972.

Samhaber, Ernst. *Merchants Make History.* London: G. G. Harrap, 1963.

Taylor, Eva Germaine Rimington. *The Haven-Finding Art: A History of Navigation from Odysseus to Captain Cook.* New York: American Elsevier, 1971.

Torr, Cecil. *Ancient Ships.* Chicago: Argonaut, 1964.

Tunis, Edwin. *Oars, Sails and Steam.* Cleveland and New York: World, 1952.

Unger, Richard W., and Robert Gardiner, eds. *Cogs, Caravels and Galleons: The Sailing Ship, 1000–1650.* London: Conway Maritime, 1994.

Villiers, Alan John. *Men, Ships and the Sea.* Washington, D.C.: National Geographic Society, 1973.

Wachsmann, Shelley. *Seagoing Ships and Seamanship in the Bronze Age Levant.* College Station: Texas A&M University Press, 1997.

Space Exploration and Aviation

Angelo, Joseph A., Jr. *A Dictionary of Space Technology.* New York: Facts On File, 1999.

———. *Encyclopedia of Space Exploration.* New York: Facts On File, 2000.

Baker, David. *Flight and Flying: A Chronology.* New York: Facts On File, 1994.

———. *Spaceflight and Rocketry: A Chronology.* New York: Facts On File, 1996.

Burrows, William E. *A History of the First Space Age.* New York: Random House, 1998.

Cole, Michael D. *NASA Space Vehicles: Capsules, Shuttles, and Space Stations.* Berkeley Heights, N.J.: Enslow, 2000.

Harland, David M. *Exploring the Moon: The Apollo Expeditions.* London: Springer Verlag, 1999.

Harland, David M., and John E. Catchpole. *Creating the International Space Station.* London: Springer Verlag, 2002.

Johnson, Nicholas L. *Handbook of Soviet Lunar and Planetary Exploration.* Springfield, Va.: American Astronautical Society, 1980.

Kluger, Jeffrey. *Journey Beyond Selene: Remarkable Expeditions Past Our Moon and to the Ends of the Solar System.* New York: Simon & Schuster, 1999.

———. *Moon Hunters: NASA's Remarkable Expeditions to the Ends of the Solar System.* New York: Simon & Schuster, 2001.

Kraemer, Robert S. *Beyond the Moon: A Golden Age of Planetary Exploration, 1971–1978.* Washington, D.C.: Smithsonian Institution, 2000.

Lee, Wayne. *To Rise from Earth: An Easy-to-Understand Guide to Spaceflight.* New York: Facts On File, 2000.

Madders, Kevin. *New Force at a New Frontier: Europe's Development in the Space Field in the Light of Its Main Actors, Policies, Law and Activities from Its Beginning up to the Present.* Cambridge, U.K.: Cambridge University Press, 1997.

Miller, Ron. *The History of Rockets.* Danbury, Conn.: Franklin Watts, 1999.

Zimmerman, Robert. *Chronological Encyclopedia of Discoveries in Space.* Westport, Conn.: Greenwood, 2000.

———. *Genesis: The Story of Apollo 8: The First Manned Flight to Another World.* New York: Four Walls Eight Windows, 1998.

Individual Biography

Adams-Ray, Edward, tr. *Andree's Story: The Complete Record of His Polar Flight, 1897.* New York: Viking, 1930.

Adorno, Rolena, and Patrick Charles Pautz. *Alvar Núñez Cabeza de Vaca: His Account, His Life, and the Expedition of Pánfilo de Narváez.* Lincoln: University of Nebraska Press, 1999.

Albornoz, Miguel. *Hernando de Soto, Knight of the Americas.* New York: Franklin Watts, 1986.

Alexander, Caroline, and Frank Hurley. *The Endurance: Shackleton's Legendary Antarctic Expedition.* New York: Alfred A. Knopf, 1998.

Allan, Mea. *Palgrave of Arabia: The Life of William Gifford Palgrave, 1826–1888.* London: Macmillan, 1972.

Alter, J. Cecil. *James Bridger: Trapper, Frontiersman, Scout and Guide.* Salt Lake City, Utah: Shepard, 1925.

Anderson, Charles L. G. *Life and Letters of Vasco Núñez de Balboa.* New York: Fleming H. Revill, 1941.

Anderson, Jean. *Henry the Navigator, Prince of Portugal.* Philadelphia, Pa.: Westminster, 1969.

Anema, Durlynn. *Louise Arner Boyd: Arctic Explorer (Notable Americans).* Greensboro, N.C.: Morgan Reynolds, 2000.

Arciniegas, German. *Amerigo and the New World.* New York: Octagon, 1978.

Armstrong, Joe C. W. *Champlain.* Toronto: Macmillan of Canada, 1987.

Ashe, Geoffrey. *Land to the West: St. Brendan's Voyage to America.* London and New York: Viking, 1962.

Bakeless, John. *Daniel Boone, Master of the Wilderness.* New York: W. Morrow, 1939.

Beaglehole, John C. *Captain Cook and Captain Bligh.* Victoria: University of Wellington Press, 1967.

———. *The Death of Captain Cook.* Wellington, Australia: Alexander Turnbull, 1979.

———. *Exploration of the Pacific.* Stanford, Calif.: Stanford University Press, 1966.

———. *The Life of Captain James Cook.* Stanford, Calif.: Stanford University Press, 1974.

Beale, Edgar. *Sturt, the Chipped Idol: A Study of Charles Sturt, Explorer.* Sydney, Australia: Sydney University Press, 1979.

Beazley, C. Raymond. *Prince Henry the Navigator: The Hero of Portugal and of Modern Discovery, 1394–1460 A.D.* New York: G. P. Putnam's Sons, 1911.

Bedini, Silvio A., ed. *The Christopher Columbus Encyclopedia.* 2 vols. New York: Simon & Schuster, 1992.

Benson, Edward Frederic. *Ferdinand Magellan.* London: John Lane, 1929.

Berry, Andrew, ed. *Infinite Tropics: An Alfred Russel Wallace Anthology.* New York: Verso, 2002.

Bierman, John. *Dark Safari: The Life Behind the Legend of Henry Morton Stanley.* New York: Alfred A. Knopf, 1990.

Bishop, Morris. *Champlain: The Life of Fortitude.* New York: Alfred A. Knopf, 1948.

———. *The Odyssey of Cabeza de Vaca.* New York: Century, 1933.

Boissonnault, Real. *Jacques Cartier: Explorer and Navigator.* Ottawa: Environment Canada, Parks, 1987.

Bolton, Herbert E. *Coronado on the Turquoise Trail: Knight of the Pueblos and Plains.* Albuquerque: University of New Mexico Press, 1949.

————. *Rim of Christendom: A Biography of Eusebio Francisco Kino, Pacific Coast Pioneer.* New York: MacMillan, 1936.

Bonsal, Stephen. *Edward Fitzgerald Beale: A Pioneer in the Path of Empire, 1822–1903.* New York: G. P. Putnam's Sons, 1912.

Bray, Martha Coleman. *Joseph Nicollet and His Map.* Philadelphia, Pa.: American Philosophical Society, 1980.

Brodie, Fawn M. *The Devil Drives: A Life of Sir Richard Burton.* New York: Norton, 1967.

Brosnan, Cornelius J. *Jason Lee. Prophet of New Oregon.* New York: Macmillan, 1948.

Brown, Don. *Uncommon Traveler: Mary Kingsley in Africa.* New York: Houghton-Mifflin, 2000.

Browne, Janet. *Charles Darwin: Voyaging.* Princeton, N.J.: Princeton University Press, 1996.

Burne, Glenn S. *Richard F. Burton.* Boston: Twayne, 1985.

Cameron, Ian. *Magellan: And the First Circumnavigation of the World.* London: Weidenfield and Nicolson, 1974.

Chaffin, Tom. *Pathfinder: John Charles Frémont and the Course of American Empire.* New York: Hill and Wang, 2002.

Chevigny, Hector. *Lord of Alaska: Baranov and the Russian Venture.* New York: Viking, 1942.

Chidsey, Donald Barr. *Sir Walter Raleigh: That Damned Upstart.* New York: John Day, 1931.

Collingridge, Vanessa. *Captain Cook: A Legacy Under Fire.* Guilford, Conn.: Lyons, 2002.

Collis, John Stewart. *Christopher Columbus.* New York: Viking Penguin, 1989.

Collis, Maurice. *Cortes and Montezuma.* London: Faber and Faber, 1954.

Connell, Gordon. *The Mystery of Ludwig Leichhardt.* Carlton, Australia: Melbourne University Press, 1980.

Conner, Daniel, and Lorraine Miller. *Master Mariner: Captain James Cook and the Peoples of the Pacific.* Vancouver: Douglas & McIntyre, 1999.

Cutter, Donald C. *Malaspina in California.* San Francisco: J. Howell, 1960.

Day, Arthur Grove. *Coronado's Quest.* Berkeley: University of California Press, 1940.

De Nevi, Donald P. *Junipero Serra: The Illustrated Story of the Franciscan Founder of California's Missions.* San Francisco: Harper and Row, 1985.

Dionne, Narcisse Eutrope. *Champlain.* Toronto: University of Toronto Press, 1963.

Diubaldo, Richard J. *Stefansson and the Canadian Arctic.* Montreal: McGill-Queen's University Press, 1978.

Dolan, Edward F. *Matthew Henson: Explorer.* New York: Dodd, Mead, 1979.

Drury, Clifford Merrill. *Marcus Whitman, M.D., Pioneer and Martyr.* Caldwell, Idaho: Caxton, 1937.

Dugard, Mark. *Farther than Any Man: The Rise and Fall of Captain James Cook.* Seattle, Wash.: Pocket, 2001.

Dunmore, John. *Pacific Explorer: The Life of Jean-François de La Pérouse, 1741–1788.* Annapolis, Md.: Naval Institute, 1985.

Dunn, Ross E. *Adventures of Ibn Battuta: A Muslim Traveller of the 14th Century.* Berkeley: University of California Press, 1988.

Dutton, Geoffrey. *In Search of Edward John Eyre.* New York: Macmillan, 1982.

Egan, Ferol. *Frémont, Explorer for a Restless Nation.* Reno: University of Nevada Press, 1985.

Ericksen, Ray. *Ernest Giles: Explorer and Traveller, 1835––1897.* Melbourne: Heinemann Australia, 1978.

Filippi, Filippo de. *Karakoram and Western Himalaya, 1909: An Account of the Expedition of H.R.H. Prince Luigi Amedeo of Savoy, Duke of the Abruzzi.* London: Constable, 1912.

Findlay, Elisabeth. *Arcadian Quest: William Westall's Australian Sketches.* Canberra, Australia: National Library of Australia, 1999.

Fisher, Raymond Henry. *The Voyage of Semen Dezhnev in 1648.* London: Hakluyt Society, 1981.

Fisher, Robin, and Hugh Johnston, eds. *Captain James Cook and His Times.* Seattle: University of Washington Press, 1979.

————, eds. *The Pacific World of George Vancouver.* Vancouver: University of British Columbia, 1995.

Ford, Corey. *Where the Sea Breaks Its Back: The Epic Story of Early Naturalist Georg Steller and the Russian Exploration of Alaska.* Anchorage: Alaska Northwest Books, 1992.

Foster, William C. *Sir Thomas Livingstone Mitchell and His World, 1792–1855: Surveyor General of New South Wales 1828–1855.* Sydney, Australia: Institution of Surveyors N.S.W., 1985.

Frank, Katherine. *A Voyager Out: The Life of Mary Kingsley.* Boston: Houghton Mifflin, 1986.

Giardini, Cesare. *The Life and Times of Columbus.* Philadelphia, Pa.: Curtis, 1967.

Gilbert, George D. *Captain Cook's Final Voyage.* Honolulu: University of Hawaii Press, 1982.

Gilham, Nicholas Wright. *A Life of Sir Francis Galton: From African Exploration to the Birth of Eugenics.* Oxford, U.K.: Oxford University Press, 2001.

Gilman, Michael. *Matthew Henson.* New York: Chelsea House, 1988.

Golder, Frank A. *Bering's Voyages: An Account of the Efforts of the Russians to Determine the Relation of Asia and America.* 2 vols. New York: American Geographical Society, 1922–25.

Gray, Edward F. *Leif Eriksson, Discoverer of America A. D. 1003.* London: Oxford University Press, 1930.

Greenlee, William B. *The Voyage of Pedro Alvares Cabral to Brazil and India.* London: Hakluyt Society, 1938.

Guillemard, Francis Henry Hill. *The Life of Ferdinand Magellan and the First Circumnavigation of the Globe.* New York: AMS, 1971.

Hall, Richard Seymour. *Lovers on the Nile: The Incredible African Journeys of Sam and Florence Baker.* London: Collins, 1980.

Hallenbeck, Cleve. *Alvar Núñez Cabeza de Vaca: The Journey and Route of the First European to Cross the Continent of North America.* Port Washington, N.Y.: Kennikat, 1970.

———. *The Journey of Fray Marcos de Niza.* Dallas: Southern Methodist University Press, 1987.

Haney, David. *Captain James Cook and the Explorers of the Pacific.* New York: Chelsea House, 1992.

Hart, Henry H. *Marco Polo: Venetian Adventurer.* Norman: University of Oklahoma Press, 1967.

Hebard, Grace Raymond. *Sacajawea.* Glendale, Calif.: Arthur H. Clark, 1933.

Hine, Robert V. *In the Shadow of Frémont: Edward Kern and the Art of American Exploration, 1845–1860.* Norman: University of Oklahoma Press, 1982.

Holman, F. V. *John McLoughlin: The Father of Oregon.* Cleveland: Arthur H. Clark, 1907.

Hoobler, Dorothy. *The Voyages of Captain Cook.* New York: Putnam, 1983.

Howard, Harold. *Sacajawea.* Norman: University of Oklahoma Press, 1971.

Hoyt, Edwin P. *The Last Explorer: The Adventures of Admiral Byrd.* New York: John Day, 1968.

Hunt, William R. *Stef: A Biography of Vilhjalmur Stefansson, Canadian Arctic Explorer.* Vancouver: University of British Columbia Press, 1986.

Huntford, Roland. *Nansen: Explorer as Hero.* New York: Barnes & Noble, 1998.

———. *Shackleton.* New York: Atheneum, 1985.

Hurley, Frank. *South with Endurance: Shackleton's Antarctic Expedition, 1914–1917.* New York: Simon & Schuster, 2001.

Huxley, Elspeth Joscelin Grant. *Scott of the Antarctic.* New York: Atheneum, 1977.

Ingleton, Geoffrey Chapman. *Matthew Flinders: Navigator and Chartmaker.* Guildford, Surrey, U.K.: Genesis, 1986.

Jackson, Donald, and Mary Lee Spence, eds. *The Expeditions of John Charles Frémont from 1838 to 1844.* Urbana: University of Illinois Press, 1970.

Johnson, Robert Eugene. *Sir John Richardson: Arctic Explorer, Natural Historian, Naval Surgeon.* London: Taylor and Francis, 1976.

Jones, Helen Hinckley. *Columbus, Explorer for Christ.* Independence, Mo.: Herald, 1977.

Kelly, John Eoghan. *Pedro de Alvarado, Conquistador.* Princeton, N.J.: Princeton University Press, 1941.

Kelsey, Harry. *Juan Rodriguez Cabrillo.* San Marino, Calif: Huntington Library, 1986.

Kiernann, Reginald Hall. *Lawrence of Arabia.* London: G. G. Harrap, 1942.

Kirk-Green, Anthony H. M., ed. *Barth's Travels in Nigeria.* London: Oxford University Press, 1962.

Kish, George. *To the Heart of Asia: The Life of Sven Hedin.* Ann Arbor: University of Michigan Press, 1984.

Knight, David. *Vasco da Gama.* Mahwah, N.J.: Troll, 1979.

Kushnarev, Eugenii. *Bering's Search for the Strait: The First Kamchatka Expedition 1725–1730.* Portland, Oreg.: Oregon Historical Society, 1990.

Lansing, Alfred. *Endurance: Shackleton's Incredible Voyage.* New York: McGraw-Hill, 1959.

Leacock, Stephen. *The Mariner of St. Malo: A Chronicle of the Voyages of Jacques Cartier.* Toronto: Brook, 1914.

Lupton, Kenneth. *Mungo Park: The African Traveler.* Oxford, U.K.: Oxford University Press, 1979.

Lyte, Charles. *Sir Joseph Banks: 18th Century Explorer, Botanist, and Entrepreneur.* North Pomfret, Vt.: David and Charles. 1980.

Maalouf, Amin. *Leo Africanus.* Chicago: Ivan. R. Dee, 1992.

Macdonald, Fiona, and Mark Bergin. *Marco Polo: A Journey through China.* Danbury, Conn.: Franklin Watts, 1998.

Major, Richard Henry. *The Life of Prince Henry of Portugal Surnamed The Navigator and Its Results from Authentic Contemporary Documents.* Reprint. London: Thomas Nelson, 1967.

Markham, Sir Clements Robert. *The Voyages of William Baffin, 1612–1622.* London: Hakluyt Society, 1881.

———. *A Life of John Davis, the Navigator, 1550–1605, Discoverer of Davis Straits.* London: Hakluyt Society, 1889.

Maynard, Charles. *John Muir: Naturalist and Explorer.* New York: Rosen, 2003.

McKee, Alexander. *The Queen's Corsair: Drake's Journey of Circumnavigation, 1577–1580.* London: Souvenir, 1978.

McLynn, Frank J. *Stanley: The Making of an African Explorer.* London: Constable, 1989.

McMinn, Winston Gregory. *Allan Cunningham, Botanist and Explorer.* Melbourne, Australia: Melbourne University Press, 1970.

Mirsky, Jeannette. *Balboa: Discoverer of the Pacific.* New York: Harper and Row, 1964.

———. *Elisha Kent Kane and the Seafaring Frontier.* Westport, Conn.: Greenwood, 1971.

———. *Sir Aurel Stein: Archaeological Explorer.* Chicago: University of Chicago Press, 1998.

Monroe, Elizabeth. *Philby of Arabia.* London: Faber & Faber, 1973.

Morgado, Martin J. *Junípero Serra's Legacy.* Pacific Grove, Calif.: Mount Carmel, 1987.

Morgan, Dale L. *The West of William H. Ashley.* Denver, Colo.: Old West, 1964.

Morison, Samuel Eliot. *Admiral of the Ocean Sea: A Life of Christopher Columbus.* 2 vols. Boston: Little Brown, 1942.

———. *Samuel de Champlain: Father of New France.* Boston: Little Brown, 1972.

Myer, Valerie Grosvenor. *A Victorian Lady in Africa: The Story of Mary Kingsley.* Southampton, U.K.: Ashford, 1989.

Nichols, Roger L., and Patrick Halley. *Stephen Long and American Frontier Exploration.* Newark: University of Delaware Press, 1980.

Norall, Frank. *Bourgmont: Explorer of the Missouri, 1698–1725.* Lincoln: University of Nebraska Press, 1988.

Ober, Frederick Albion. *Sir Walter Raleigh.* New York: Harper and Bros., 1909.

O'Brian, Patrick. *Joseph Banks: A Life.* Chicago: University of Chicago Press, 1997.

Parr, Charles McKew. *Ferdinand Magellan, Circumnavigator.* New York: Thomas Y. Crowell, 1964.

Partridge, Bellamy. *Amundsen, the Splendid Norseman.* New York: A. Stokes, 1929.

Phillips, William D., Jr., and Carla Rahn Phillips. *The Worlds of Christopher Columbus.* Cambridge, U.K.: Cambridge University Press, 1992.

Raby, Peter. *Alfred Russel Wallace: A Life.* Princeton, N.J.: Princeton University Press, 2001.

Ransford, Oliver. *David Livingstone, the Dark Interior.* London: Murray, 1978.

Ratchnevsky, Paul. *Genghis Khan: His Life and Legacy.* New York: Blackwell, 1993.

Reid, J. M. *Traveller Extraordinary: The Life Of James Bruce of Kinnaird.* New York: Norton, 1968.

Rice, Edward. *Captain Sir Richard Francis Burton: The Secret Agent who Made the Pilgrimage to Mecca, Discovered the Kama Sutra, and Brought the Arabian Nights to the West.* New York: Da Capo, 1990.

Robinson, Henry Morton. *Stout Cortez. A Biography of the Spanish Conquest.* New York and London: Century, 1931.

Romoli, Kathleen. *Balboa of Darién: Discoverer of the Pacific.* Garden City, N.Y.: Doubleday, 1953.

Rose, Lisle Abbott. *Assault on Eternity: Richard E. Byrd and the Exploration of Antarctica, 1946–47.* Annapolis, Md.: Naval Institute, 1980.

Ross, Michael. *Bougainville.* London and New York: Scribner, 1978.

Rubin, Nancy. *Isabella of Castile: The First Renaissance Queen.* New York: St. Martin's, 1991.

Rugoff, Milton Allan. *Marco Polo's Adventures in China.* New York: American Heritage, 1964.

Russell, Peter. *Prince Henry 'the Navigator': A Life.* New Haven, Conn.: Yale University Press, 2000.

Sanceau, Elaine. *Henry the Navigator.* London: Hutchinson, 1947.

Shay, Frank. *Incredible Pizarro: Conqueror of Peru.* New York: Mohawk, 1932.

Shirley, John W. *Thomas Harriot: A Biography.* Oxford, U.K.: Clarendon, 1983.

Sim, Katherine. *Desert Traveller: The Life of Jean Louis Burkhardt.* London: Gollancz, 1969.

Sinclair, Andrew. *Sir Walter Raleigh and the Age of Discovery.* New York: Penguin, 1984.

Smith, G. Hubert. *The Explorations of the La Verendryes in the Northern Plains, 1738–43.* Lincoln: University of Nebraska Press, 1980.

Solomon, Susan. *The Coldest March: Scott's Fatal Antarctic Expedition.* New Haven, Conn.: Yale University Press, 2001.

Stamp, Tom, and Cordelia Stamp. *William Scoresby, Arctic Scientist.* Whitby, U.K.: Caedmon, 1976.

Stefansson, Vilhjalmur. *The Three Voyages of Martin Frobisher in Search of a Passage to Cathay and India by the North-West.* London: Argonaut, 1938.

Strawn, Arthur. *The Golden Adventures of Balboa.* London: John Lane, 1929.

Subrahmanyam, Sanjay. *The Career and Legend of Vasco da Gama.* New York: Cambridge University Press, 1997.

Sugden, John. *Sir Francis Drake.* London: Barris and Jenkins, 1990.

Sullivan, Marion F. *Westward the Bells: A Biography of Junipero Serra.* Boston: St. Paul Books and Media, 1988.

Tarn, William Woodthorpe. *Alexander the Great.* 2 vols. Cambridge, U.K.: Cambridge University Press, 1948.

Thompson, Gerald. *Edward F. Beale and the America West.* Albuquerque: University of New Mexico Press, 1983.

Thomson, George Malcolm. *Sir Francis Drake.* London: Deutsch, 1988.

Ure, John. *Prince Henry The Navigator.* London: Constable, 1977.

Veer, Gerrit de. *The Three Voyages of William Barents to the Arctic Regions,* ed. Lt. Koolemans Beynen. London: Hakluyt Society, 1876.

Villiers, Alan. *Captain James Cook.* New York: Charles Scribner's Sons, 1967.

Wallace, Colin. *The Lost Australia of François Péron.* London: Nottingham Court, 1983.

Weber, David, J. *Richard H. Kern: Expeditionary Artist in the far Southwest, 1848–1853.* Albuquerque: University of New Mexico Press, 1970.

Welch, Galbraith. *The Unveiling of Timbuctoo: The Astounding Adventures of Caillié.* New York: Carroll & Graf, 1991.

Williams, Trevor. *James Cook: Scientist and Explorer.* London: Prior, 1974.

Winship, George Parker, ed. *The Journey of Coronado.* Golden, Colo.: Fulcrum, 1990.

Wollaston, Nicholas. *The Man on the Ice Cap: The Life of August Courtauld.* London: Constable, 1980.

Entries by Subject

GENERAL EXPLORATION

airship
animals and exploration
archaeology and exploration
aviation and exploration
balloon
circumnavigation of the world
colonization and exploration
commerce and exploration
    (see also subhead commerce
    and exploration)
conquest and exploration
conquistadores
Crusades
disease and exploration
European age of exploration
geography and cartography
    (see also subhead geography
    and cartography)
International Geophysical Year
legends and exploration
    (see also subhead legends and
    exploration)
migration and exploration
mountain climbing
    (see also subhead mountain
    climbing)
native peoples and exploration
natural science and exploration
navigation and exploration
    (see also subhead navigation)
oceanography and exploration
    (see also subhead oceanogra-
    phy and exploration)
painting and exploration

photography and exploration
Pilgrims
piracy
privateers
pundits
religion and exploration
Renaissance
searches for missing explorers
shipbuilding and exploration
    (see also subhead shipbuilding
    and exploration)
space exploration
    (see also subhead space
    exploration)
speleology
sponsors of exploration
surveying and exploration
treasure and exploration
whaling and sealing
women explorers
writing and exploration

ANCIENT PEOPLES

Carthaginian exploration
Chinese exploration
Cossack exploration
Egyptian exploration
Greek exploration
Minoan exploration
Mongol exploration
Muslim exploration
Phoenician exploration
Polynesian exploration
Roman exploration
Viking exploration

COMMERCE AND EXPLORATION

(see also ORGANIZATIONS)

commerce and exploration
coureurs de bois
fur trade
mountain men
Silk Road
slave trade
Spice Islands
Spice Route
spice trade
voyageurs

GEOGRAPHY AND CARTOGRAPHY

aerial photography
Antarctic Circle
Arctic Circle
equator
geography and cartography
globe
hypsometer
International Date Line
latitude and longitude
Mercator projection
maps and charts
mappa mundi
Northeast Passage
North Magnetic Pole
North Pole
Northwest Passage
padrão
periplus
planisphere

portolan chart
prime meridian
South Magnetic Pole
South Pole
tropic of Cancer
tropic of Capricorn
Vinland Map

LEGENDS AND EXPLORATION

Anian, Strait of
Atlantis
Cibola
Cipangu
El Dorado
fool's gold
Fountain of Youth
Gonneville's Land
Great Southern Continent
legends and exploration
Los Césares
Lost Colony
Madoc
Mandeville, Sir John
Mountains of the Moon
Ophir
Prester John
Quivira
Saguenay
St. Brendan's Isle
Ultima Thule
Vinland

MOUNTAIN CLIMBING

(see also individual mountains
under PLACES)
mountain climbing
Sherpas

NATURAL PHENOMENA

doldrums
drift ice
Gulf Stream
North Star
ocean currents
land bridge
pack ice
scurvy
trade winds

NAVIGATION

alidade
astrolabe

chronometer
compass
cross-staff
dead reckoning
drift voyage
ephemeris
gnomon
gyrocompass
navigation and exploration
quadrant
sextant
traverse board

OCEANOGRAPHY AND EXPLORATION

bathyscaph
bathysphere
diving bell
diving suit
hydrography
oceanography and exploration
submarine
submersible

ORGANIZATIONS

African Association
American Fur Company
American Geographical Society
British East India Company
Cathay Company
Company of Merchants of
    London Discoverers of the
    Northwest Passage
Dutch East India Company
Dutch West India Company
European Space Agency
French East India Company
Hakluyt Society
Hanseatic League
Hudson's Bay Company
Levant Company
Muscovy Company
National Aeronautics and Space
    Administration
North West Company
Rocky Mountain Fur Company
Royal Geographical Society
Royal Society
Russian-American Company
St. Louis Missouri Fur
    Company
Virginia Company

PLACES

Africa, exploration of
    Barbary Coast
    Canary Islands
    Cape of Good Hope
    Congo River
    Kilimanjaro, Mount
    Niger River
    Nile River
    Punt
    Sahara Desert
    Timbuktu
    Zambezi River
Antarctic, exploration of the
Arctic, exploration of the
    Greenland
Asia, exploration of
    Ceylon
    East Indies
    Empty Quarter
    Everest, Mount
    Ganges River
    Gobi Desert
    Himalayas
    Indus River
    Khyber Pass
    Lhasa
    Siberia
    Yangtze River
    Yellow River
Atlantic Ocean, exploration of
    the Azores
    Hudson Bay
    Iceland
    West Indies
Australia, exploration of
    Blue Mountains
    Great Dividing Range
    Great Victoria Desert
    Tasmania
Central America, exploration of
Europe, exploration of
    Blanc, Mont
Indian Ocean, exploration of the
    Red Sea
    Mediterranean Sea
    Gibraltar, Strait of
North America, exploration of
    Appalachian Mountains
    Colorado River
    Columbia River
    Cumberland Gap

McKinley, Mount
Mississippi River
Missouri River
Rocky Mountains
South Pass
Pacific Ocean, exploration of the
  Bering Strait
  Hawaiian Islands
  Marianas Trench
  New Zealand
  Oceania
South America, exploration of
  Aconcagua
  Amazon River
  Andes Mountains
  Cape Horn
  Magellan, Strait of
  Orinoco River
  Spanish Main

SHIPBUILDING AND EXPLORATION

canoe
caravel
carrack
cog
coracle
dhow
galleon
galley
junk
keelboat
lateen rig
longship
merchant ship
outrigger
pinnace
pirogue
raft
roundship
shipbuilding and exploration

SPACE EXPLORATION

(see also ORGANIZATIONS**)**
Apollo program
astronauts
Gemini program
Mercury program
rocket
satellite
Soyuz program
space probe
space shuttle
space station
Voskhod program
Vostok program

Contributors

The authors would like to thank all the writers, researchers, and editors who helped with Volume II of the *Encyclopedia of Exploration.* The areas of their invaluable contributions are listed parenthetically below.

Mary Ashwood, a teacher and freelance writer, has written for children's publications. She also writes a regular column for *The Freeman's Journal* in Cooperstown, New York. She holds a B.S. from the State University of New York at Oneonta and an M.A.T. from SUNY-Albany. (North American geography.)

Breath-Alicen Valentine Hand, née Cox, is a freelance writer, editor, researcher, and grant writer as well as Vice President of Hand & Hand Multimedia. (Photo research, women explorers, general research and editing.)

Benjamin Harnett, since graduating from Hamilton College, has studied the classics at the University of Pennsylvania and Columbia University. (Near East and the Mediterranean, central Asia, Far East, South America, commerce, literature of exploration.)

Catherine Mason, a freelance writer, has written about a wide range of subjects, including the history and natural science of upstate New York. A graduate of Lebanon Valley College, she currently works in development at the New York State Historical Association. (Religion, natural science and disease, navigation, European history.)

Elizabeth Smith is a writer and freelance editor who holds a B.A. in English and American literature from Harvard and an M.A. in literature from the University of Sydney, Australia. (General research and editing.)

Kathleen Taylor is host and producer of the nationally syndicated public radio program *Word for the Wise.* She holds an M.A. in communication and a B.A. in English and political science from the State University of New York at Albany. Her writings on language have appeared in a number of publications. (Africa, Australia, navigation, general research and editing.)

Chloe Shannon Waldman, a graduate of the State University of New York at Buffalo, is a freelance writer/researcher. (General research and editing.)

Cumulative Index for the Set

Roman numerals in **boldface** indicate the volume. Page numbers in **boldface** indicate main entries. Page numbers in *italics* indicate photographs. Page numbers followed by *c* indicate chronology entries. Page numbers followed by *m* indicate maps.